ON THE RELIABILITY
OF THE OLD TESTAMENT

ON THE RELIABILITY
OF THE OLD TESTAMENT

K. A. Kitchen

WILLIAM B. EERDMANS PUBLISHING COMPANY
GRAND RAPIDS, MICHIGAN / CAMBRIDGE, U.K.

© 2003 Wm. B. Eerdmans Publishing Co.

All rights reserved

Wm. B. Eerdmans Publishing Co.
255 Jefferson Ave. S.E., Grand Rapids, Michigan 49503 /
P.O. Box 163, Cambridge CB3 9PU U.K.

Printed in the United States of America

08 07 06 05 04 03   7 6 5 4 3 2 1

Library of Congress Cataloging-in-Publication Data

Kitchen, K. A. (Kenneth Anderson)
On the reliability of the Old Testament / K. A. Kitchen.
p.   cm.
Includes bibliographical references and index.
ISBN 0-8028-4960-1 (alk. paper)
1. Bible. O.T. — Evidences, authority, etc.
2. Bible. O.T. — History of Biblical events.   I. Title.

BS1180.K56   2003
221.1 — dc21

2003040764

www.eerdmans.com

CONTENTS

TABLES

FIGURES

The figures listed below appear in a section between pages 603 and 642.

1. The Ancient Near East and Biblical World: General Map

2. "Happy Families," Signed and Sealed. Hebrew Seals, 8th-6th Centuries BC

3. Calendars and Regnal Years in the Biblical World

4. The Assyrian Evidence for Non-Accession Years in 9th-Century Israel

5. Shoshenq I (Shishak): Megiddo Stela and Geography of His List

6. Segments of Shoshenq's Route in Palestine, from His List

7. The Campaign of Shoshenq I in Palestine, King and Other Troops

8. Contemporaries of Israel, 9th-8th centuries BC:
   A. Jezebel
   B. Hazael
   C. Osorkon IV

9. Sennacherib of Assyria vs. Judah and Allies, 701 BC

10. Sixth-Century Babylon and Jehoiachin:
    A. View of Babylon
    B. Plan of Babylon

PREFACE

The genesis of this little book goes back many years to a pleasant and wide-ranging conversation with a fellow Aberdonian (he, by academic post; I, by birth), namely, my long-standing friend, Professor I. Howard Marshall. And this was long before the present-day, rather frenetic conflict over the biblical writings and their authenticity (or otherwise) by so-called minimalists and maximalists, often high on rhetoric and counterclaims, if too often on precious little else.

During that conversation long ago, we had mused on the valuable role played by the late Prof. F. F. Bruce's redoubtable but graciously written little volume entitled *Are the New Testament Documents Reliable?* which gave an eminently judicious assessment of its theme and has deservedly passed through many editions and reprintings. Out of which musings, Howard asked me, why doesn't someone do a like service in assessing the Old Testament, and in particular why not the undersigned? Ah, I protested, but the task in each case is massively different. New Testament scholars need stray little beyond a single century (the first century A.D.), had only four main languages to deal with (Greek and Latin from Europe; Hebrew and Aramaic in Palestine), and but two basic cultures: Greco-Roman and Jewish. Doing equal justice to the Old Testament meant a minimum span of two thousand years overall (three thousand for full background), ability to draw upon documents in vast quantity and variety in some ten ancient Near Eastern languages, and a whole patchwork quilt of cultures. Be reasonable! But, I murmured, let's see what might be done eventually, if it seems at all possible. With which equivocation on my part, we parted; but still as good friends!

Thereafter I opened a file in which to put notes toward any such project, and a few dusty sheets found their way into it. But after that the sheer pressure of university teaching, supervisions, and other duties, and more immediate academic and publishing obligations, allowed little more than dust to accumulate on that file. Until now.

In the last few years increasingly extreme views about the Old Testament writings have been trumpeted loudly and proclaimed ever more widely and stridently; in the service of these views, all manner of gross misinterpretations of original, firsthand documentary data from the ancient Near East itself are now being shot forth in turn, to prop up these extreme stances on the Old Testament, regardless of the real facts of the case. Ideological claptrap has also interfered with the present-day situation. It has been said that "political correctness" has decreed a priori that the Old Testament writings are historically unreliable and of negligible value. Even if this judgment were proved correct, it is no business whatsoever of the politically correct to say so, merely as ideology. Such matters can *only* be assessed by expert examination of the available facts, and not by the ignorant pronouncements of some species of neo-Nazi "thought police." It has also been rumored that, in turn, such things as hard facts, objective fact, and (above all) absolute truth have been discarded by resort to the dictates of "postmodernism." Absolute truth in any deep philosophical sense is not the concern of this book, and thus will not be discussed. But individual absolute truths in the shape of objective fact, "hard facts" that exist independently of what any human being may choose or wish to think — these abound around us in their hundreds of thousands in everyday life, and (quite simply) cannot be gainsaid or wished away. Thus, outside of spaceships, etc., anyone letting go of this book in normal conditions will find that it will inevitably drop downward, to the table, floor, or whatever is below. If engineers do not properly allow for the innate strengths and properties of the materials they use, buildings and bridges collapse; planes may not fly, and boats turn turtle. If archaeologists dig into sites with clear strata laid in succession one upon another, that will be their proper historical sequence. At this stage in knowledge, no doubt can persist that it is possible to learn and to translate from ancient languages into modern ones — from Egyptian hieroglyphs, or Babylonian cuneiform, or West Semitic inscriptions into plain English, French, German, or whatever. And so on, ad infinitum. How the ancients left things is how things are. The Great Pyramid stands firm at Giza in Egypt (as it has done for at least 4,500 years), totally regardless of whether I know about this, or approve of this, or disapprove of this. The facts are wholly independent of me, my prejudices, or my knowledge, and of everyone else's. This itself is an absolute fact of life, along with countless others. And so, we must firmly say to philosophical cranks (politically correct, postmodernist, or whatever else) — "Your fantasy agendas are irrelevant in and to the real world, both of today and of all preceding time back into remotest antiquity. Get real or (alas!) get lost!"

The title of this book *(On the Reliability of the Old Testament)* yields the acronym *OROT;* my critics are free to repunctuate this as *O! ROT!* — if they so please! So, we now proceed peacefully and rationally to deal with the real world, both ancient and modern.

Before doing so, my warmest thanks go to my stalwart colleague, Professor Alan R. Millard, for taking time to read critically through the text of this book (all remaining errors, of course, remain mine) — and to my patient publishers for accepting this work, to share it with a wider public.

Woolton, September 2001   K. A. KITCHEN

ABBREVIATIONS

AB	Anchor Bible
ABD	D. N. Freedman et al., eds., *The Anchor Bible Dictionary* I-VI (New York: Doubleday, 1992)
ABY	*Archäologische Berichte aus dem Yemen*
AcOr	*Acta orientalia*
AfO (and Beihefte)	*Archiv für Orientforschung* (and supplements)
Aharoni, *LB*	Y. Aharoni, *The Land of the Bible: A Historical Geography,* 2nd revised edition, ed. by A. F. Rainey (London: Burns & Oates, 1979)
AHK	*See* Edel, *AHK*
AJA	*American Journal of Archaeology*
AJSL	*American Journal of Semitic Languages and Literatures*
ALB I, II	See Mazar, *ALB* I, and Stern, *ALB* II
ANET	J. B. Pritchard, ed., *Ancient Near Eastern Texts Relating to the Old Testament* (Princeton: Princeton University Press, 1950; 2nd ed., 1955, 3rd ed., 1969)
ANRW	*Aufstieg und Niedergang der römischen Welt*
AnSt	*Anatolian Studies*
AOAT	Alter Orient und Altes Testament
AOS	American Oriental Society
AOSTS	American Oriental Society Translation Series
ARE	J. H. Breasted, *Ancient Records of Egypt* I-V (Chicago: University of Chicago Press, 1906-7)
ARI	See Grayson, *ARI*
ARM(T)	*Archives Royales de Mari, Textes (Traductions)* (Paris: Imprimerie Nationale, I-XXI, 1950-83; Éditions Recherche sur les Civilisations, XXII-XXVIII, 1983-98 [continuing])
AS	Assyriological Studies, Oriental Institute, Chicago; continuing

ASAE	*Annales du Service des Antiquités de l'Égypte*
ASOR	American Schools of Oriental Research
AusBR	*Australian Biblical Review*
Avigad and Sass, *CWSS*	N. Avigad and B. Sass, *Corpus of West Semitic Stamp Seals* (Jerusalem: Israel Academy, Israel Exploration Society, and Institute of Archaeology, Hebrew University, 1997)
BA	*Biblical Archaeologist.* Continuation is now *NEA*
BACE	*Bulletin of the Australian Centre of Egyptology,* Sydney
BAR	*Biblical Archaeology Review*
BASOR	*Bulletin of the American Schools of Oriental Research*
BAT 1985, 1990	A. Biran et al, eds., *Biblical Archaeology Today* (1985), 1990 (and supplement 1990) (Jerusalem: IES, 1985, 1993, 1993)
BBB	Bonner biblische Beiträge
Bib	*Biblica*
BibOr	Biblica et orientalia
BiOr	*Bibliotheca Orientalis*
BR	*Bible Review*
Breasted, *ARE*	*See* ARE
BSac	*Bibliotheca Sacra*
BSAg	*Bulletin on Sumerian Agriculture*
BSFÉ	*Bulletin de la Société Française d'Égyptologie*
CAD	I. J. Gelb, et al. (and successors), *The Assyrian Dictionary* 1-26, A-Z (Chicago and Glückstadt: Oriental Institute, University of Chicago, and (formerly) Augustin Verlag, 1956-)
CAH	Various editors, *The Cambridge Ancient History* I/1–IV, 2nd ed. (Cambridge: Cambridge University Press, 1970-88)
CBQ	*Catholic Biblical Quarterly*
CdÉ	*Chronique d'Égypte*
CGC (+ number)	*Catalogue générale du Musée du Caire,* series
CHLI I-II	J. D. Hawkins, *Corpus of Hieroglyphic Luwian Inscriptions* I (Berlin: de Gruyter, 2000), and H. Çambel, II (1999)
CoS	W. W. Hallo and K. L. Younger, eds., *The Context of Scripture* I-III (Leiden: Brill, 1997, 2000, 2002)
cr	coregency
CRAIBL (+ date)	*Comptes-rendus de l'Académie des Inscriptions et Belles-lettres*
CRIPEL	*Cahier(s) de Recherches de l'Institut de Papyrologie et d'Égyptologie de Lille*
ctp	(a) contempory of/with . . .
CTU	A. Herdner, ed., *Corpus des tablettes en cuneiforms alphabétiques découvertesa à Ras Shamra-Ugarit de 1929 à 1939,* 2 vols. (Paris: Imprimerie Nationale and P. Geuthner, 1963)
CWSS	See Avigad and Sass, *CWSS*

DAA I-II	K. A. Kitchen, *Documentation for Ancient Arabia* I-II (Liverpool: University Press, 1994, 2000)
DANE	P. Bienkowski and A. R. Millard, eds., *Dictionary of the Ancient Near East* (London: British Museum Press, 2000)
DDD	K. van der Toorn, B. Becking, and P. W. van der Horst, eds., *Dictionary of Deities and Demons in the Bible* (Leiden: Brill, 1995)
Dever, *RADBR*	W. G. Dever, *Recent Archaeological Discoveries and Biblical Research* (Seattle: University of Washington Press, 1990)
Dever, *What . . . When . . . ?*	W. G. Dever, *What Did the Biblical Writers Know and When Did They Know It?* (Grand Rapids: Eerdmans, 2001)
EA (+ number)	El-Amarna letters, by number
EB	Early Bronze Age
Ebib	Etudes bibliques
Edel, *AHK* I-II	E. Edel, *Die ägyptisch-hethitische Korrespondenz aus Boghazköi in babylonischer und hethitischer Sprache* I-II (Opladen: West-deutscher Verlag, 1994)
EEF, EES	Egypt Exploration Society (formerly Egypt Exploration Fund), London
EI	*Eretz Israel*
EQ	*Evangelical Quarterly*
ERC	Éditions Recherche sur les Civilisations, Paris
FÉRÉ	Fondation Égyptologique Reine Élisabeth, Brussels
FM	*Florilegium Marianum,* Iff. (Mémoires de N.A.B.U. Paris: SEPOA, 1992ff., continuing)
FTH	A. R. Millard, J. K. Hoffmeier, and D. W. Baker, eds., *Faith, Tradition, and History* (Winona Lake, Ind.: Eisenbrauns, 1994)
GM	*Göttinger Miszellen*
Grayson, *ARI*	A. K. Grayson, *Ancient Records of Assyria* 1-2 (Wiesbaden: Harrassowitz, 1972, 1976)
Grayson, *RIMA* 1-3	*See under RIMA*
Hess et al., *Oath*	R. S. Hess, P. E. Satterthwaite, and G. J. Wenham, eds., *He Swore an Oath: Biblical Themes from Genesis 12–50* (Cambridge: Tyndale House, 1993; Carlisle: Paternoster; and Grand Rapids: Baker, 1994)
Hoch, *SWET*	J. E. Hoch, *Semitic Words in Egyptian Texts of the New Kingdom and Third Intermediate Period* (Princeton: Princeton University Press, 1994)
HTR	*Harvard Theological Review*
HUCA	*Hebrew Union College Annual*
IEJ	*Israel Exploration Journal*
IES	Israel Exploration Society, Jerusalem
IFAO	Institut Français d'Archéologie Orientale du Caire, Cairo
IOS	*Israel Oriental Studies*

ISIF	R. S. Hess and D. T. Tsumura, eds., *I Studied Inscriptions from before the Flood, Ancient Near Eastern, Literary, and Linguistic Approaches to Genesis 1–11* (Winona Lake, Ind.: Eisenbrauns, 1994)
JANES	*Journal of the Ancient Near Eastern Society,* Columbia University
JAOS	*Journal of the American Oriental Society*
JARCE	*Journal of the American Research Center in Egypt*
JBL	*Journal of Biblical Literature*
JCS	*Journal of Cuneiform Studies*
JEA	*Journal of Egyptian Archaeology*
JNES	*Journal of Near Eastern Studies*
JSOT	*Journal for the Study of the Old Testament*
JSOTSup	Journal for the Study of the Old Testament — Supplement Series
JSS	*Journal of Semitic Studies*
JSSEA	*Journal of the Society for the Study of Egyptian Antiquities,* Toronto
JTS	*Journal of Theological Studies*
JTVI	*Journal of the Transactions of the Victoria Institute* (later: *Faith & Thought*)
Kitchen, *DAA* I-II	See under *DAA* I-II
Kitchen, *RITA*	K. A. Kitchen, *Ramesside Inscriptions, Translated and Annotated, Translations,* I-IV (Oxford: Blackwell Publishers), 1993-2003, and continuing
Kitchen, *RITANC*	K. A. Kitchen, *Ramesside Inscriptions, Translated and Annotated, Notes and Comments,* I-III (Oxford: Blackwell Publishers), 1993-2003, and continuing
Kitchen, *Third Int. Pd.*	K. A. Kitchen, *The Third Intermediate Period in Egypt (1100-650 BC)* (Warminster: Aris & Phillips, 1973; 2nd ed., 1986; rev. 2nd ed., 1996)
KRI	K. A. Kitchen, *Ramesside Inscriptions* I-VIII (Oxford: Blackwell's, 1969-90)
KTU	M. Dietrich, O. Loretz, and J. Sanmartín, eds., *The Cuneiform Alphabetic Texts from Ugarit, Ras Ibn Hani and Other Places* (*KTU,* 2nd enlarged edition), ALASP 8 (Münster: Ugarit-Verlag, 1995)
KUB	*Keilschrifturkunden aus Boghaz-köi,* I-LX (Berlin: Staatliche Museen zu Berlin, then Akademie Verlag, 1921-1990)
LAPO	Litteratures anciennes du proche-orient (Paris: Les éditions du Cerf, 1967ff.), continuing
LB	See under Aharoni, *LB*
LB	Late Bronze Age
LCL	Loeb Classical Library

LdA	W. Helck, E. Otto, and W. Westendorf, eds., *Lexikon der Ägyptologie* I-VII (Wiesbaden: Harrassowitz, 1972-92)
Luckenbill, *ARAB*	D. D. Luckenbill, *Ancient Records of Assyria and Babylonia* I-II (Chicago: University of Chicago Press, 1926-27)
MARI	*Mari, Annales de Recherches Interdisciplinaires*
Mazar, *ALB* I	A. Mazar, *Archaeology of the Land of the Bible, 10,000-586* B.C.E. (New York: Doubleday, 1990). Cf. Stern, *ALB* II
MB	Middle Bronze Age
MDOG	*Mitteilungen der Deutschen Orient-Gesellschaft*
MIO	*Mitteilungen des Instituts für Orientforschung*
MMA	Metropolitan Museum of Art, New York
Muchiki, *Egyptian PN*	Y. Muchiki, *Egyptian Proper Names and Loanwords in North-West Semitic*, SBLDS 173 (Atlanta: Society of Biblical Literature, 1999)
NBD	D. R. W. Wood et al., eds., *New Bible Dictionary*, 3rd ed. (Leicester and Downers Grove, Ill.: Inter-Varsity Press, 1996)
NEA	*Near Eastern Archaeology*, continues *BA*
NEAHL 1-4	E. Stern et al., eds., *The New Encyclopedia of Archaeological Excavations in the Holy Land* 1-4 (Jerusalem: IES; New York: Simon & Schuster, 1993)
NEASB	*Near East Archaeological Society Bulletin*
NPN	I. J. Gelb, P. M. Purves, and A. A. Macrae, *Nuzi Personal Names* (Chicago: University of Chicago Press, 1943)
OBO	Orbis Biblicus et Orientalis
ODM	Ostracon Deir el-Medina (and number)
OLZ	*Orientalistische Literaturzeitung*
OMRO	*Oudheidkundige Mededelingen uit het Rijksmuseum van Oudheden te Leiden*
Or	*Orientalia*
OrAnt	*Oriens Antiquus*, Rome
OTS	*Oudtestamentische Studiën*
OUP	Oxford University Press (London, Oxford, and New York)
PC	political correctness — a current crank fad
PEF	Palestine Exploration Fund, London
PEQ	*Palestine Exploration Quarterly*
PM, I-VIII	B. Porter, R. L. B. Moss, E. Burney, J. Malek, eds., *Topographical Bibliography of Ancient Egyptian Hieroglyphic Texts, Reliefs & Paintings, Etc.*, I-VIII (Oxford: Clarendon, then Griffith Institute), 1st edition, 1927-1951, and 2nd, 1960-2002, in progress
PRU	J. Nougayrol and C. Virolleaud, eds., *Le Palais Royal d'Ugarit* II-VI (Paris: Imprimerie Nationale/Klincksieck, 1955-70)
PSAS	*Proceedings of the Seminar for Arabian Studies*
RA	*Revue Archéologique*

RAAO	*Revue d'assyriologie et d'archéologie orientale*
Ranke, *KMAV*	H. Ranke, *Keilschriftliches Material zur altägyptischen Vokalisation,* Aus dem Anhang zu den Abhandlungen der Königl. Preuss. Akademie der Wissenschaften vom Jahre 1910 (Berlin: Verlag der Königl. Akademie der Wissenschaften, 1910)
RB	*Revue Biblique*
RdÉ	*Revue d'Égyptologie*
REg	*Revue d'égyptologique*
Renz/Röllig I-III	J. Renz and W. Röllig, *Handbuch der althebräischen Epigraphik* I, II/1, III (Darmstadt: Wissenschaftliche Buchgesellschaft, 1995)
RGTC	*Répertoire Géographique des Textes Cunéiformes,* Beihefte zum Tübinger Atlas des Vorderen Orients, Reihe B (Geschichte) (Wiesbaden: L. Reichert)
RHR	*Revue de l'Histoire des Religions*
RIMA 1-3	A. K. Grayson, *Royal Inscriptions of Mesopotamia, Assyrian Periods: 1: Assyrian Rulers of the Third and Second Millennia* BC *(to 1115* BC*)* (1987); 2: *Assyrian Rulers of the Early First Millennium* BC, *I (1114-859* BC*)* (1991); 3: *Assyrian Rulers of the Early First Millennium* BC, *II (858-745* BC*)* (1996). All published in Toronto by University Press
RIMB 2	G. Frame, *Royal Inscriptions of Mesopotamia, Babylonian Periods: 2: Rulers of Babylonia from the Second Dynasty of Isin to the End of Assyrian Domination (1157-612* BC*)* (Toronto: University Press, 1995)
RIME 1-4	D. R. Frayne, *Royal Inscriptions of Mesopotamia, Early Periods: 1: Pre-Sargonic Period (2700-2350* BC*)* (2001); 2: *Sargonic and Gutian Periods (2334-2113* BC*)* (1993); 3/1: *Gudea and His Dynasty* (by D. O. Edzard) (1997); 3/2: *Ur III Period (2112-2004* BC*)* (1997); 4: *Old Babylonian Period (2003-1595* BC*)* (1990). Toronto: University Press
RLA	E. Ebeling and B. Meissner, followed by others, now D. O. Edzard, eds., *Reallexikon der Assyriologie* I-IX (and continuing) (Berlin: de Gruyter, 1930-1999/2000-)
Roth, *Law Collections*	M. T. Roth, *Law Collections from Mesopotamia and Asia Minor* (Atlanta: Scholars Press, 1995)
RSO XII	D. Pardee, *Ras Shamra-Ougarit* XII/1-2, *Les Textes Rituelles* (Paris: ERC, 2000)
SAA	State Archives of Assyria (series)
SAAS	State Archives of Assyria, Studies, series
SAK	*Studien zur Altägyptischen Kultur*
SAOC	Studies in Ancient Oriental Civilization
SBL	*Society of Biblical Literature*
SBLDS	SBL Dissertation Series

SDB	*Supplément au Dictionnaire du Bible* I- (in progress) (Paris, 1928 to present)
SEL	*Studi Epigraphi e Linguistici, sul Vicino Oriente Antico*
Sem	*Semitica*
SHAJ	*Studies on the History and Archaeology of Jordan*
SJOT	*Scandinavian Journal of the Old Testament*
SOAS	School of Oriental and African Studies, London
StBoT	Studien zu den Bogazköy-Texten (series)
Stern, *ALB* II	E. Stern, *Archaeology of the Land of the Bible*, II, *The Assyrian, Babylonian, and Persian Periods, 732-332 BCE* (New York: Doubleday, 2001). Cf. Mazar, *ALB* I
TA	*Tel Aviv*
Tadmor, *TP III*	H. Tadmor, *The Inscriptions of Tiglath-pileser III King of Assyria* (Jerusalem: Israel Academy of Sciences and Humanities, 1994)
ThIP	See above, Kitchen, *Third Int. PD.*
tp	temp.; i.e., in the time of . . .
TQ	*Theologische Quartalschrift*
TSSI 1-3	J. C. L. Gibson, *Textbook of Syrian Semitic Inscriptions* 1-3 (Oxford: OUP, 1971, 1975, 1982)
TUAT	O. Kaiser, et al., eds., *Texte aus der Umwelt des Alten Testaments*, I-III and Ergänzungslieferung (Gütersloh: Gütersloher Verlagshaus, 1982-2001)
TynB	*Tyndale Bulletin*
UFo	*Ugarit-Forschungen*
UP	University Press
UT	C. H. Gordon, *Ugaritic Textbook* I-III (Rome: Pontifical Biblical Institute, 1965)
VT	*Vetus Testamentum*
VTSup	Vetus Testamentum, Supplements
WTJ	*Westminster Theological Journal*
ZA	*Zeitschrift für Assyriologie*
ZAH	*Zeitschrift für Althebräistik*
ZÄS	*Zeitschrift für Aegyptische Sprache und Altertumskunde*
ZAW	*Zeitschrift für die Alttestamentliche Wissenschaft*
ZDMG	*Zeitschrift der Deutschen Morgenländischen Gesellschaft*
ZDPV	*Zeitschrift des Deutschen Palästina-Vereins*

First Things First — What's in Question?

Heat without light in biblical matters is less help than light without heat. "On the reliability of the Old Testament." The two terms of this title deserve to be defined for the purpose of our inquest. For practical purposes the second element, the Old Testament, is readily defined as the particular group of books written in Hebrew (with a few Aramaic passages) that form at one and the same time the basic canon of the Hebrew Bible, or "Tanak" of the Jewish community (*Torah, Nebi'im, Kethubim,* "Law, Prophets, Writings"), and the basic "Old Testament" (or "former covenant") of most Christian groups, who add to it (to form their fuller Bible) the briefer group of writings of the Greek New Testament (or "new covenant"), not studied in this book.

Anyone who opens and reads the books of the Hebrew Bible, the Old Testament, will find the essence of a fairly continuous story, from the world's beginnings and earliest humanity down briefly to a man, Abra(ha)m, founding "patriarch," from whose descendants there came a family, then a group of clans under the name Israel. He had moved from Mesopotamia (now Iraq) via north Syria into Palestine or Canaan, we are told; and his grandson and family came down to Egypt, staying there for generations, until (under a pharaoh's oppression) they escaped to Sinai, had a covenant and laws with their deity as their ruler, and moved on via what is now Transjordan back into Canaan. A checkered phase of settlement culminated in a local monarchy; David and Solomon are reputed to have subdued their neighbors, holding a brief "empire" (tenth century B.C.), until this was lost and the realm split into two rival petty kingdoms of Israel (in the north) and Judah (in the south). These lasted until Assyria destroyed Israel by 722 and Neo-Babylon destroyed Judah by 586, with much of their populations exiled into Mesopotamia. When Persia took over Babylon, then some of the captive Judeans (henceforth termed "Jews") were allowed back to Palestine to renew their small community there during the fifth century, while others stayed on in both Babylonia and Egypt. The library of writings that contains this narrative thread also includes versions of the laws and covenant reputedly enacted at Mount Sinai, and renewals in Moab and Canaan. To which must be added the writings in the names of various spokesmen or "prophets" who sought to call their people back to loyalty to their own god YHWH; the Psalms, or Hebrew hymns and prayers; and various forms of "wisdom writing," whether instructional or discussive.

That sums up baldly the basic narrative that runs through the Hebrew Bible, and other features included with it. Broadly, from Abram the patriarch down to such as Ezra and Nehemiah who guided the Jerusalem community in the fifth century, as given, the entire history (if such it be) does not precede circa 2000 B.C., running down to circa 400 B.C. Those who most decidedly dismiss this whole story point to the date of our earliest discovered MSS of its texts, namely, the Dead Sea Scrolls of the second century B.C. onward. They would take the most minimal view, that the biblical books were originally composed just before the time of the Dead Sea Scrolls, i.e., in the fourth/third centuries B.C. (end of Persian, into Hellenistic, times). With that late date they would couple an ultralow view of the reality of that history, dismissing virtually the whole of it as pure fiction, as an attempt by the puny Jewish community in Palestine to write themselves an imaginary past large, as a form of national propaganda. After all, others were doing this then. In the third century B.C. the Egyptian priest Manetho produced his *Aegyptiaka,* or history of Egypt, probably under Ptolemy II,[1] and by then so also did Berossus, priest of Marduk at Babylon, his *Chaldaika,* for his master, the Seleucid king Antiochus I.[2] Comparison with firsthand sources shows that these two writers could draw upon authentic local records and traditions in each case. So it is in principle possible to suggest that a group of early Hellenistic Jews tried to perform a similar service for their community by composing the books we now know as the Old Testament or Hebrew Bible.[3]

The difference is, however, twofold. Factually, the Old Testament books were written in Hebrew — for their own community — right from the start, and were only translated into Greek (the Septuagint) afterward, and again primarily for their own community more than for Greek kings. Also, while Manetho and Berossus drew upon authentic history and sources, this activity is denied to the Jewish writers of the Old Testament. So, two questions here arise. (1) Were the Old Testament books all composed within circa 400-200 B.C.? And (2) are they virtually pure fiction of that time, with few or no roots in the real history of the Near East during circa 2000-400 B.C.?

So our study on reliability of the Old Testament writings will deal with them in this light. Have they any claim whatsoever to present to us genuine information from within 2000-400? And were they originated (as we have them) entirely within, say, 400-200? In this little book we are dealing with matters of history, literature, culture, *not* with theology, doctrine, or dogma. My readers must go elsewhere if that is their sole interest. So "reliability" here is a quest into finding out what may be authentic (or otherwise) in the content and formats of the books of the Hebrew Bible. Are they purely fiction, containing nothing of historical value, or of major historical content and value, or a fictional matrix with a few historical nuggets embedded?

Merely sitting back in a comfy armchair just wondering or speculating about the matter will achieve us nothing. Merely proclaiming one's personal convictions for any of the three options just mentioned (all, nothing, or something historical) simply out of personal belief or agenda, and not from firm evidence on the question, is also a total waste of time. So, what kind of test or touchstone may we apply to indicate clearly the reliability or otherwise of Old Testament writers? The answer is in principle very simple, but in practice clumsy and cumbrous. We need to *go back* to antiquity itself, to *go back* to 400 B.C., to fly back through the long centuries, "the corridors of time" — to 500 B.C., 700 B.C., 1000 B.C., 1300 B.C., 1800 B.C., 2000 B.C., 3000 B.C., or even beyond — as far as it takes, to seek out what evidence may aid our quest.

All very fine, but we have no H. G. Wells "time machine" as imagined over a century ago. *We* cannot move lazily across from our armchair into the plush, cushioned seat of the Victorian visionary equivalent of a "flying bedstead," set the dial to 500 B.C. or 1000 B.C. or 1800 B.C., and just pull a lever and go flying back in time!

No. Today we have other means, much clumsier and more laborious, but quite effective so far as they go. In the last two hundred years, and with ever more refined techniques in the last fifty years, people have learned to dig systematically in the long-abandoned ruins and mounds that litter the modern Near East, and (digging downward) to reach back ever deeper into past time.[4] A Turkish fort (temp. Elisabeth I) might reuse a Byzantine church on the ruins of a Roman temple, its foundations dug into the successive levels of (say) Syrian temples of the Iron Age (with an Assyrian stela?), then back to Bronze Age shrines (with Egyptian New Kingdom monuments?), on through the early second (Middle Bronze cuneiform tablets?) and third millennia B.C., and back to full prehistory at the bottom of an ever-more-limited pit. And there would be parallel levels and finds in the surrounding mound, for local ancient palace, houses, and workplaces. But why be content with a theoretical example? In Syria, Mari yielded 20,000 tablets of the eighteenth century B.C., which are still in the course of publication; Ebla, Ugarit, and Emar have yielded more besides. To the north, the Hittite archives as published so far fill over one hundred volumes of cuneiform copies.[5] From Mesopotamia, rank upon rank of Sumerian, Babylonian, and Assyrian tablets fill the shelves of the world's major museums. Egypt offers acres of tomb and temple walls, and a myriad of objects inscribed in her hieroglyphic script. And West Semitic inscriptions continue to turn up in the whole of the Levant. These we know about; but a myriad other untouched mounds still conceal these and other material sources of data totally unknown to us, and wholly unpredictable in detail. Much has been destroyed beyond recall across the centuries; this we shall never recover, and never learn of its significance. So, much labor is involved in recovering as reliably as possible (including technological procedures) original documents and other remains accessible to us, so far as we have power and resources to investigate a fraction of them. But these are *authentic* sources, real touchstones which (once dug up) *cannot* be reversed or hidden away again. The one caveat is that they be rightly understood and interpreted; which is not impossible, most of the time.

Therefore, in the following chapters we will go back both to the writings of the Old Testament and to the very varied data that have so far been recovered from the world in which those writings were born, whether early or late. Then the two groups of sources can be confronted with one another, to see what may be found.

In doing this, it is important to note that two kinds of evidence will play their part: explicit/direct and implicit/indirect. Both are valid, a fact not yet sufficiently recognized outside the various and highly specialized Near Eastern disciplines of Egyptology, Nubiology, Assyriology/Sumerology, Hittitology, Syro-Palestinian archaeology, early Iranology, Old Arabian epigraphy and archaeology, and the rest. Explicit or direct evidence is the obvious sort that everyone likes to have. A mention of King Hezekiah of Judah in the annals of King Sennacherib of Assyria, or a state seal-impression ("bulla") of King Hezekiah or Ahaz or J(eh)otham — these are plain and obvious indications of date, historical role, etc. But implicit or indirect evidence can be equally powerful when used aright. Thus in two thousand years ancient Near Eastern treaties passed through six different time phases, each with its own format of treaty or covenant; there can be no confusion (e.g.) of a treaty from the first phase with one of the third phase, or of either with one from the fifth or sixth phases, or these with each other. Based on over ninety documents, the sequence is consistent, reliable, and securely dated. Within this fixed sequence biblical covenants and treaties equally find their proper places, just like all the others; anomalous exceptions cannot be allowed. And so on.

For the purpose of our inquest, the basic Old Testament "story" can be divided conveniently into seven segments, representing its traditional sequence, without prejudice as to its historicity or otherwise.

Table 1. The Seven Segments of Traditional Biblical "History"

1	2	3	4	5	6	7
Primeval Proto-History	The Patriarchs	Egyptian Sojourn and Exodus	Settlement in Canaan	United Monarchy	Divided Monarchy	Exile and Return

But we shall *not* follow this sequence in numerical order. Instead we shall go to the two most recent "periods" (6 and 7), first to 6, the divided monarchy, which is the period during which the Old Testament accounts are the most exposed, so to speak, to the maximum glare of publicity from external, non-biblical sources, during a period (ca. 930-580 B.C.) of the maximum availability of such evidence to set against the Old Testament data. Then, after tidying up the "tail end," period 7, we can go back through those long corridors of time (5 back to 1) to consider the case for ever more remote periods in the record, both ancient Near Eastern and biblical, and eventually sum up the inquest.

CHAPTER 2

"In Medias Res" — the Era
of the Hebrew Kingdoms

In 1 and 2 Kings and 2 Chronicles we find what is offered as concise annals of the two Hebrew kingdoms, Israel and Judah, that crystallized out of the kingdom of Solomon after his death. In those books we have mention of twenty kings of Israel and twenty kings and a queen regnant in Judah, and also of foreign rulers given as their contemporaries — all in a given sequence. It will be convenient to set out all these people in list form in Table 2 on page 8.

A few notes on this table. Regnal years serve to distinguish between reigns of average length (ca. sixteen years) or over and reigns brief or only fleeting. A string of three asterisks indicates a break between "dynasties" in Israel. "AramD" stands for (the kingdom of) Aram of Damascus. Also, names in **bold** are for kings involved in external, nonbiblical sources, while "LR" stands for "local (i.e., Hebrew) record" and "possible local record," as will become clear below.

We shall next proceed by the following steps:

1. To review the foreign kings mentioned in Kings, Chronicles, and allied sources, in terms of their mention in external records.
2. To review, conversely, mentions of Israelite and Judean kings in such external, foreign sources.
3. To review the "local records" (LR) in Hebrew, from Palestine itself, so far as they go.
4. To review concisely the sequences of rulers as given in both the external and biblical sources, and the range of the complex chronology of this period, in the Hebrew Bible and external sources.

Table 2. Hebrew Kings and Contemporaries
Given by the Biblical Sources

Israel		Judah	
Jeroboam I 22 years	Shishak of Egypt 1 Kings 11:40	Rehoboam 17 years	Shishak of Egypt 1 Kings 14:25
Nadab 2 years		Abijam 3 years	
	* * *		
Baasha 24 years		Asa 41 years	Benhadad (I) of AramD 1 Kings 15:18
Elah 2 years			(Zerah the Kushite 2 Chron. 14:9ff.)
	* * *		
Zimri 7 days	* * *		
Omri 12 years	(including rival Tibni first 6 years)		
Ahab 22 years	Ethbaal of Sidon 1 Kings 16:31 Benhadad (I/II), AramD 1 Kings 20	Jehoshaphat 25 years	Mesha of Moab 2 Kings 3
Ahaziah I 2 years		Jehoram I 8 years	
J(eh)oram II 12 years	Mesha of Moab 2 Kings 3 Hazael, AramD 2 Kings 8:3	**Ahaziah II** 1 year	Hazael, AramD 2 Kings 8:28
	* * *		
Jehu 28 years	Mesha of Moab 2 Kings 3 Hazael, AramD 2 Kings 10:32	Joash 40 years	Hazael, AramD 2 Kings 12:17-18 (including Queen Athaliah, first 6 years)
Jehoahaz 17 years	Hazael, AramD 2 Kings 13:22		
Jehoash 16 years	Benhadad (II/III), AramD 2 Kings 13:24-25	Amaziah 29 years	
Jeroboam II 41 years	(LR)	**Azariah/Uzziah** 52 years	(LR)
Zechariah 6 months	* * *	**Jotham** 16 years	Rezin, AramD 2 Kings 15:37 (LR)
Shallum 1 month	(LR) * * *		
Menahem 10 years	Pul/Tiglath-pileser (III) of Assyria 2 Kings 15:19; 1 Chron. 5:6, 26	**Ahaz** 16 years	Rezin, AramD 2 Kings 16:5 (LR) Tiglath-pileser (III), Assyria 2 Kings 16:7, 10
Pekahiah 2 years			

8

Israel		Judah	
	* * *		
Pekah 20 years	Tiglath-pileser (III), Assyria 2 Kings 15:29		
	* * *		
Hoshea 9 years	Shalmaneser (V) Assyria 2 Kings 17	**Hezekiah** 29 years	Shalmaneser (V) 2 Kings 18:9
	So of Egypt 2 Kings 17:4 (LR)		(Sargon [II] Isa. 20; after Ahaz)
	Fall of Samaria		Sennacherib, Assyria 2 Kings 18:13ff.
			Taharqa, Egypt 2 Kings 19:9
			Merodach-Baladan, Babylon 2 Kings 20:12
			(*x* yrs later: Esarhaddon, Assyria 2 Kings 19:37)
		Manasseh 55 years	(Assyrian king took him to Babylon 2 Chron. 33:11)
		Amon 2 years	
		Josiah 31 years	Necho II, Egypt 2 Kings 23:29 (LR)
		Jehoahaz 3 months	Necho II, Egypt 2 Kings 23:33ff.
		Jehoiakim 11 years	Necho II, Egypt 2 Kings 23:33ff. (LR)
			Nebuchadrezzar II, Babylon 2 Kings 24:1
		Jehoiachin 3 months	Nebuchadrezzar II, Babylon 2 Kings 24:1
			later Evil-Merodach, Babylon 2 Kings 25:27
		Zedekiah 11 years	Hophra of Egypt Jer. 44:30
			Nebuchadrezzar II, Babylon, 2 Kings 24:10-17; 25 (LR)
			Baalis king of Ammon (Jer. 40:14)
			Fall of Jerusalem

5. To review concisely the interlock of historical events, etc., that are attested in both the biblical and external sources.
6. To consider briefly the nature of the actual records we have to draw upon, both in the Bible and the nonbiblical sources.

1. ATTESTATION OF FOREIGN KINGS MENTIONED IN THE BIBLICAL RECORD

A. UNTIL THE ASSYRIANS CAME . . . EGYPT AND THE LEVANT

(i) Shishak of Egypt

In Hebrew *Shishaq* or *Shushaq* (marginal spelling) occurs as the name of a king of Egypt who harbored Jeroboam (rebel against Solomon) and invaded Canaan in the fifth year of Rehoboam king of Judah (1 Kings 11:40; 14:25).[1] This word corresponds very precisely with the name spelled in Egyptian inscriptions as *Sh-sh-n-q* or *Sh-sh-q*. This Libyan personal name is best rendered as *Shoshe(n)q* in English transcript; it belonged to at least six kings of Egypt within the Twenty-Second/Twenty-Third Dynasties that ruled that land within (at most) the 950-700 time period.[2]

Of all these kings, Shoshenq II-VI have no known link whatsoever with affairs in Palestine. In striking contrast, Shoshenq I, the founder of the Twenty-Second Dynasty, has left us explicit records of a campaign into Palestine (triumph scenes; a long list of Palestinian place-names from the Negev to Galilee; stelae), including a stela at Megiddo. Beyond rational doubt, these Egyptian data give us direct evidence that links up with the event mentioned under Rehoboam in Kings and Chronicles (history and chronology, cf. below, 4, 5), and Rehoboam's *Shushaq* is Shoshe(n)q I, a very solidly attested ruler.

(ii) Two Shy Characters — Zerah the Kushite and Benhadad I/II of Aram-Damascus

In 2 Chron. 14:9ff. we are told that one Zerah the Kushite (no rank given) came with "a myriad army" and 300 chariots (Kushites [= Nubians] and Lubim [= Libyans], 2 Chron. 16:8) against the Judeans under King Asa.[3] Zerah's name is neither Hebrew, Egyptian, nor (seemingly) Libyan, and may therefore be Nubian, as would befit a Kushite. Of him we possess no other record at present; not himself a king, he could have been a king's general. The combination of Libyan and Nubian troops suggests that his unstated starting point had been Egypt; the chronology (cf. 4. below) would set any such escapade late in the reign of Osorkon I. No pharaoh ever celebrates a defeat! So, if Osorkon had ever sent out a Zerah, with resulting defeat, *no* Egyptian source would ever report on such an incident, particularly publicly. The lack (to date) of external corroboration in such a case is itself worth nothing, in terms of judging historicity.

According to 1 Kings 15:18, the same Judean king Asa sought to buy an alliance with a Benhadad king of Aram in Damascus, while a Benhadad of Aram-Damascus was an opponent of Ahab king of Israel (1 Kings 20).[4] From the division of the Hebrew kingdom, on figures given in Kings, Asa's reign was for some forty years, from twenty years after the split, while Ahab's began nearly sixty years after that event, lasting almost twenty years beyond Asa's time. Thus, either one or two Benhadads may have reigned in Damascus, contemporary with Asa and Ahab; opinion has always been divided over this point. At present we have no clear external evidence for this king(s) (be it one or two kings, respectively).

This is hardly surprising for two very simple reasons. First, modern Damascus entirely overlies the site of the ancient city, with many rebuildings and much development through twenty-seven centuries since the demise of its Aramean kingdom. *Virtually nothing,* consequently, has so far been recovered at Damascus from those times. The only external evidence for kings of Aram-Damascus comes *exclusively from elsewhere.* (See on Hazael and Benhadad III below.) Second, before 853 there are *no* Assyrian war records that name any rulers from Damascus being in the Levant — simply because the mighty Assyrian war machine had not reached so far before 853! Thus we *cannot* expect any Assyrian mentions of any Levantine rulers (biblical *or* otherwise!) before 853 if the Assyrians had had no wars or other dealings with them.

The Hebrew *Benhadad* is simply the Hebrew equivalent of Aramaic *Bir-* or *Bar-hadad,* each meaning "son of (the god) Hadad." Bar-hadad is a genuine Aramean royal name, including at Damascus (see below on Benhadad III). From 853 to 845 the war records of Shalmaneser III of Assyria do report on a King Hadad-idri at Damascus. This, it is commonly conceded, is simply an alternative name for Bar-hadad (Benhadad), or else it represents a king who ruled between the Benhadad of King Ahab's time (ca. 860) and a possible short-lived Benhadad reigning from about 844 until ousted by Hazael by 841, as the Assyrian texts show.

Thus the total poverty in documents from Damascus and the lack of Assyrian penetration (with consequent mentions of kings) into Syria and south-ward are the basic reasons for lack of attestations of these local kings. Nonexistence of the rulers themselves cannot be alleged without tangible reasons (of which there are none). This is because of another example. If Assyrian mentions are the sine qua non (the absolute criterion) for a king's existence, then Egypt and her kings could not have existed before the specific naming of (U)shilkanni, Shapataka, and Ta(ha)rqa in 716-679! But of course, as in the case of Shishaq (above), we have a relative abundance of monuments from many sites in the large land of Egypt attesting her existence and kings for millennia before the Neo-Assyrian kings ever got there! The on-the-ground situation is radically different from that in Syria-Palestine, particularly in drastically over-built sites such as Damascus and Jerusalem.

There is one piece of supposed evidence for Benhadad I/II of Aram-Damascus that needs to be plainly eliminated — the so-called Melqart Stela of a King Bar-hadad, found just north of Aleppo.[5] With great boldness Albright had read the damaged text as belonging to a "Bar-hadad, son of [Tabrimmon, son of Hezion], king of Aram," to be identified with the Benhadad and ances-tors of 1 Kings 15:18. Thus he assumed that Aram-Damascus was intended as this king's realm.

But the square-bracketed part of the text (in the second of five lines) is so heavily damaged as to be virtually illegible, and thus there are now almost as many different readings for this Bar-hadad's ancestor(s) as there are scholars who attempt it! And "Aram" on its own can stand for other Aramean kingdoms besides Damascus — e.g., Zoba or Arpad also. If, as has been more recently sug-gested, Bar-hadad's father was an 'Atar-humki or 'Atar-sumki, then we may here have a Bar-hadad king of Arpad, to be set (if 'Atar-sumki be read) between his father 'Atar-sumki and his possible younger brother Mati-el. This would at one stroke settle this Bar-hadad's historical role and identity, and eliminate him from the line in Aram-Damascus, and from our immediate inquiries.

(iii) Ethbaal/Ittobaal I of Tyre and Sidon — Not Forgetting Jezebel!

According to 1 Kings 16:31, King Ahab of Israel took Jezebel to be his queen, that colorful lady being daughter of "Ethbaal, king of the Sidonians." Again, just like Damascus, Aleppo, or Jerusalem, the towns of Tyre and Sidon have been repeat-edly turned over and rebuilt across many centuries, with older stone records being recycled and defaced, to our permanent loss. So it is little surprise that we so far have not a single inscription from the sites of these two cities from the sixth century B.C. and earlier — virtually only from sarcophagi, preserved by having been buried in tombs from that very late date onward.

However, outside the Bible there is one other written source of some value for the Phoenician kings. This is the annotated Tyrian king list by Menander of Ephesus, cited and summarized by Josephus in his *Against Apion* 1.116-26.[6] This gives a series of eight kings, from Abibaal (father of Hiram I, named as contemporary of Solomon) down to one Phelles, inclusive. Then comes an Ittobaal (I), or Ithobalos in Greek, and a Balezoros, originally succeeded by (and then confused with) a second Baal-ma(n)zer,[7] named also in texts of Shalmaneser III, a contemporary of Ahab of Israel. This would make Ithobalos (Ittobaal I) an older contemporary of Ahab, and thus most likely the Ethbaal whose daughter Jezebel was married off to Ahab. Thus on this limited but valuable evidence, Ethbaal is no phantom.

And Jezebel? A Phoenician-style seal, well known, bears just the name *Yzbl*, "Jezebel," below Egyptian-style devices (recumbent winged sphinx, winged disc with uraeus-serpents, falcon of Horus — all royal symbols in Egypt), and is datable on its general style to the overall period of the late ninth to early eighth centuries.[8] (See fig. 8A.)

This need not necessarily have belonged to the infamous Jezebel, Ahab's wife, but it certainly attests the name (in a non-Israelite spelling) in a Phoenician-style context at her general period. And not too many women had their own seals in the ancient Levant. Thus there is no proof at all that this little seal stone has strayed from (say) the Iron Age palace ruins of Samaria; but attribution to the infamous Jezebel is by no means impossible either.

(iv) Mesha, the "Sheep Master" King of Moab

Here we briefly turn to what was a sensational find back in 1868. Second Kings 3 purports to give an account of conflict between Omri and Ahab's dynasty in Israel and one Mesha, king of Moab, whose principal wealth was in sheep. In 1868 a basalt stela was found at Dhiban (Dibon) in Transjordan, which bears a victory and building inscription and also mentions conflicts with the dynasty of Omri of Israel.[9] Thus there can be no doubt as to the reality of Mesha king of Moab, or of the state of conflict between the two countries involved.

B. DATA FROM ASSYRIA, THE LEVANT, AND EGYPT

(i) The Dynasty of Omri and Jehu, and the Arameans

(a) Hazael

Enemy of Israel (cf. 2 Kings 8:3, 28; 10:32; 12:17-18; 13:22), this ruler is known from ivory fragments found at Arslan Tash (ancient Hadatu; fig. 8B) in north Syria, and another found at Nimrud (ancient Calah) in Assyria proper, and from two bronze horse blinkers found at Eretria and Samos in faraway Greece.[10] Inscriptions on these all name Hazael, as the dedicator's "lord" (Aram. *mari*). Under Adad-nirari III, Hazael may be the king known by his epithet *Mari*, "Lord," given him by his subjects, but this may in fact be Benhadad III (cf. below). Hazael recurs as father of Bar-hadad (III) on the stela of Zakkur, king of Hamath and Hatarikka, his immediate neighbor to the north. He was, in fact, one of the most formidable of the Aramean kings of Damascus, and later Assyrian kings such as Tiglath-pileser III even called that kingdom *Bit-Hazail*, "House of Hazael," alongside *Bit-Khumri*, "House of Omri," for Israel.[11]

(b) Benhadad (III) Son of Hazael

He was supposedly a less successful king, cited in 2 Kings 13:24-25. He is attested externally on the stela of Zakkur of Hamath just mentioned. He may well be the king of Aram-Damascus cited by the epithet *Mari*, "Lord" (given him by his subjects). He was defeated by Adad-nirari III, if Hazael is not thus intended.[12]

(c) Rezin/Rakhianu of Damascus

In 2 Kings 15:37 and 16:5, it is said that Rezin king of Damascus and Pekah of Israel warred against Judah. Rezin was the last Aramean ruler at Damascus, suppressed by Tiglath-pileser III in 732 (2 Kings 16:9); in cuneiform (for phonetic reasons) he appears as Rakhianu.[13]

(ii) Transjordanian Kings

Two seals attest Baalis king of Ammon, mentioned in Jer. 40:14.[14]

14

(iii) The Assyrian Wolves and Their Babylonian Neighbors and Heirs

All the following are, of course, well known, but their presence is a necessary part of the total picture, and the nature of their presence will be of some importance later.[15]

Tiglath-pileser III, alias Pul (745-727), is the earliest Assyrian king named in Kings and Chronicles, and the third ruler of his name; also was known as Pul for short in one cuneiform record as in the biblical ones. Records of his reign are extensive, if sometimes fragmentary.[16]

Shalmaneser V (727-722) is the Shalmaneser of 2 Kings 18:9, linked with the fall of Samaria. His quite short reign is attested in the cuneiform record.[17]

Sargon II (722-705) is the king intended in Isa. 20 (as later than Ahaz of Judah), mentioning his officer, the *turtan* (a rank well attested in Assyrian records). Of Sargon II we have extensive texts and monuments.[18]

The records of Sennacherib (705-681) in cuneiform include the account of his Year 3 campaign to Palestine, which links up with his dealings with Hezekiah of Judah (2 Kings 18–19).[19]

Esarhaddon (681-669) is well known from Assyrian sources, besides 2 Kings 19:37.[20]

Merodach-Baladan II (721-710, 703) was an opportunist king in Babylon, well known from Assyrian records and in other documents, besides being mentioned with Hezekiah in 2 Kings 20:12ff.[21]

Nebuchadrezzar II of Babylon (605-562) was the greatest king of the Neo-Babylonian dynasty, who redeveloped Babylon, leaving many inscriptions (especially about buildings).[22]

Evil-Merodach/Awel-Marduk of Babylon (562-560) is mentioned in 2 Kings 25:27-28, regarding Jehoiachin of Judah in exile; he is known from minor inscriptions of his own.[23]

(iv) Last Links with Egypt

The name of King So is recorded only in 2 Kings 17:4.[24] It is not acceptable to try emending this clearly personal name into the place-name Sais, a town in the depths of the West Delta that played no role whatsoever in Near Eastern or biblical affairs. All Saite kings reigned from Memphis and used East Delta Tanis (Zoan) as their outlet to western Asia. Per dating (cf. 4. below), So falls into the time of the East Delta kings Iuput II and Osorkon IV. As the last certain king of the Twenty-Second Dynasty, the latter reigned in Tanis and Bubastis, the closest Egyptian sovereign to Palestine to whom Hoshea could have sent. (See fig. 8C.)

So is a perfectly feasible abbreviation for (O)so(rkon). Other royal names were thus abbreviated; cf. Shosh for Shoshenq, and the omission of the initial *Wa* from Wahibre in the Hebrew and Greek forms Hophra and Apries. Osorkon's own name was abbreviated both by occasional omission of the final *n* and (in Assyrian) by loss of initial vowel (<U>shilkanni). There is no valid excuse for taking So as anything other than Osorkon IV, in terms of our present knowledge.

Tirhaqah/Taharqa is a very well known pharaoh of the Nubian (Kushite) Twenty-Fifth Dynasty, reigning from 690 to 664. His presence in 2 Kings 19:9 and Isa. 37:9 was as lieutenant for the reigning Egypto-Nubian ruler Shebitku (Assyr. Shapataka), who ruled from either 706 or 702 to 690. In his biblical occurrences Taharqa is accorded the title king simply because that title had been his and was universally used for ten years already by 681, when the texts of 2 Kings and Isaiah took their present shape (death of Sennacherib, 2 Kings 19:37; Isa. 37:38).[25] It is the same as saying today (in 2003) that "Queen Elizabeth (II) was born in 1926"; she was, but only as Princess Elizabeth — which title would not immediately identify her to most people today. This kind of usage is universal (even used by Taharqa himself!), and cannot be dismissed.

Necho II of Egypt (610-595) is the well-known second king of the Twenty-Sixth Dynasty.[26]

Hophra/Apries/Wahibre of Egypt (589-570) is the known fourth king of the Twenty-Sixth Dynasty.[27] Both the Hebrew and Greek forms of his name show abbreviation (as with So!) by omission of the first syllable, *Wa*.

2. ATTESTATION OF HEBREW KINGS IN FOREIGN RECORDS

A. KINGS OF ISRAEL

(i) Omri

In 1 Kings 16:21ff. Omri features as founder of a dynasty, being followed by his son Ahab, and the latter by two sons, Ahaziah I and J(eh)oram II. For Omri the external sources are twofold: the mention of him and "his son" (= Ahab) by Mesha king of Moab on the latter's stela mentioned above,[28] and his role as dynastic founder in the term used to denote Israel by the Assyrian kings

16

Shalmaneser III and Tiglath-pileser III, namely, *Bit-Khumri*, or "House of Omri."[29] It became fashionable in the first millennium B.C. to name kingdoms after prominent dynastic founders, and the Assyrian royal inscriptions are full of such names: Bit-Ammana, Bit-Agusi, Bit-Adini, Bit-Bakhiani, Bit-Yakhiru, Bit-Haluppi, and half a dozen more. So Omri's reality as a ruler *and* as a dynastic founder is settled by these mentions.

(ii) Ahab

Ahab was the unnamed son of Omri in Mesha's inscription, mentioned just above. He is named by Shalmaneser III in 853 as a contemporary opponent and "Israelite king,"[30] which term implies his rule over all Israel, not simply the town of Samaria. For his Phoenician father-in-law and wife, see above, 1.A.iii. The notorious stela from Tell Dan in northernmost ancient Israel can be shown quite clearly to have been a victory stela by an Aramean king, celebrating the defeat and decease of both a king of Israel and a king of Judah, the latter termed the "House of David" (Bayt-Dawid; cf. the *Bit* names mentioned above).[31] Its sentences VI-VII read:

VI: "[. . .]ram, son of [xxxx], king of Israel;
VII: and [. . .] killed [xxxx]iah, son of [xxxxxx, . . .]g of the House of David."

These two lines (in context) can only reasonably be restored to read:

VI: "[I killed/defeated Jeho]ram, son of [Ahab], king of Israel;
VII: and [I] killed [Ahaz]iah, son of [Joram, kin]g of the House of David."

The preserved traces of royal names and text-breaks only fit the historical circumstances of 2 Kings 9:14-29, with the murder of two kings at once, of Israel (Jehoram son of Ahab) and of Judah (Ahaziah II son of Joram). The king of Aram would have to have been Hazael in this case, who arrogated Jehu's regicides to his own initiative and glory. This is no unusual thing in ancient Near Eastern royal rhetoric.

(iii) Succeeding Kings

J(eh)oram II is the "[. . .]ram, son of [Ahab], king of Israel" on the Tell Dan stela (just above), slain at the same time as "[Ahaz]iah, son of [Joram, kin]g" of

Judah on that stela, as in Kings. He may be included in the offspring of Omri in line 8 ("son" = Ahab; or "sons" = Ahab plus Ahaziah I and Jehoram) of the stela of Mesha.

Jehu is securely named and attested as paying tribute to Shalmaneser III in the latter's eighteenth year, in 841, on the Black Obelisk and in an annalistic fragment.[32]

J(eh)oash is mentioned by Adad-nirari III of Assyria, in relation to a campaign by the latter into Syria, probably in 796 (the Mansuate campaign to the environs of Damascus).[33]

Menahem is mentioned by Tiglath-pileser III (ca. 738) as Menahem of Samaria, twice.[34] Pekah is likewise so mentioned in two further records of Tiglath-pileser III, circa 733.[35] Hoshea is also mentioned by Tiglath-pileser III (claiming to have officially installed him, ca. 732), again in two documents.[36]

B. KINGS OF JUDAH

J(eh)oram II is mentioned (in a break) on the Tell Dan stela, as father of Ahaziah of Judah. Ahaziah II is mentioned (as defeated/killed) on the Tell Dan stela.[37]

Azariah/Uzziah may just possibly be the King Azriau of the fragmentary annals of Tiglath-pileser III for about 738;[38] the fragment that contains the land-name Yaudi (a good cuneiform equivalent of "Judah") is now commonly assigned (with a joining fragment) to Sennacherib, though not with total certainty. Hence we cannot certainly assert that this Azriau (without a named territory!) is Azariah of Judah; the matter remains open and undecided for the present and probably unlikely.

Ahaz appears with the fuller name-form Jeho-ahaz (I) in the annals of Tiglath-pileser III of Assyria, circa 734.[39] Hezekiah occurs in 701 in the well-known annals of the third campaign of Sennacherib, and other inscriptions of that king.[40] Manasseh is credited with a long reign, and thus fittingly crops up in the inscriptions of two successive kings of Assyria, namely, Esarhaddon (ca. 674) and Assurbanipal.[41]

Jehoiachin was the unnamed king of the Babylonian Chronicle who was deported from Jerusalem by Nebuchadrezzar II in 597, and (later) with his family is explicitly named in ration tablets found in the palace at Babylon for the years 594-570.[42] Zedekiah was clearly the successor king appointed in Jerusalem in 597 by Nebuchadrezzar II, when he deported Jehoiachin to Babylon (Babylonian Chronicle).[43]

3. KINGS OF ISRAEL AND JUDAH
IN LOCAL RECORDS (LR)

A. KINGS OF ISRAEL

The famous seal of "Shema servant [= minister of state] of Jeroboam" is almost universally recognized to belong to the reign of Jeroboam II of Israel (cf. fig. 2); attempts to date it to Jeroboam I are unconvincing. The Samaria ostraca (main lot) belong also to this period, and maybe to this particular reign.[44] To Shallum (I) (or much less likely, his Judean namesake, Jehoahaz III/Shallum II) may just possibly be attributed an eighth-century cylindrical seal stone of royal style (kingly figure, winged discs, etc.).[45] As for Hoshea, to his reign belongs the seal of one "Abdi, servant of Hoshea" (fig. 2).[46]

B. KINGS OF JUDAH

(i) Azariah/Uzziah, Jotham, Ahaz

To the reign of Azariah/Uzziah belong two seals, of the state ministers ("servants") Shebaniah *(Shebanyau)* and Abiah *(Abiyau)*.[47] Jotham is attested as Jehotham and father of Ahaz on a recently discovered seal impression ("bulla") that bears the text "Belonging to Ahaz (son of) Jehotham [= long form of Jotham], King of Judah."[48] A seal of this reign is known, of Ushna servant of Ahaz (for these, cf. fig. 2).[49] For Ahaz as father of Hezekiah, see under Hezekiah.

(ii) Hezekiah (Fig. 2)

His name is mentioned on another recently discovered bulla, which reads: "Belonging to Hezekiah (son of) Ahaz, King of Judah," and with it can now be matched a damaged bulla that bore the same text.[50] To these royal stamps can be added no less than three bullae of "servants" of Hezekiah: of Jehozarah son of Hilkiah, of Azariah son of Jeho'abi, and of one on which the name has been lost.[51]

Among inscriptions without the royal name but belonging to this time should certainly belong the famous Siloam tunnel inscription (cf. 2 Kings 20:20; 2 Chron. 32:30), and likewise the tomb inscription of the royal steward ("he who is over the house"), [. . .]iah, highly likely to have been [Shebna]iah —

and the same as Shebna (abbreviated form of this name), the royal steward of Hezekiah's day, condemned by the prophet Isaiah (Isa. 22:15-25).[52]

(iii) Manasseh

As a young prince he may have had his own personal seal for official purposes. Such a seal may be seen in a known seal inscribed "belonging to Manasseh, son of the king" (fig. 2), the latter being Hezekiah.[53]

(iv) Josiah

Several items may well belong to this reign, although they are without certainty and do not rank as firm evidence. But they can be conveniently set out here as a good example of items that (in almost every case) clearly belong to the later seventh (to early sixth) century in Judah. In this short period the choice of reigns is sometimes limited by year dates, too high to be anyone but either Manasseh or Josiah in practice.

These are:

(a) Ostracon Mousaieff 1, which required payment of three shekels of silver to "the House [= temple] of the LORD [YHWH]" in the name of 'Ashiah/'Oshiah the king, via a man [Z]echariah. The script is either eighth (so, Cross) or seventh century (so, Yardeni). In the former case, 'Ashiah/'Oshiah is a variant of Joash, king of Judah; in the latter case, of Josiah, which is the latest date possible. In Josiah's time a Levite named Zechariah was concerned with repairs to the Jerusalem temple (cf. 2 Chron. 34:12), so the later dating might well allow of our two Zechariahs being the same man.[54]

(b) Seal stones and impressions. These include both fiscal and personal seals. One fiscal seal is dated to a royal "Year 26" in late seventh-/early sixth-century script. Therefore its editors date it to Josiah, the only king who reigned that long, then. (However, it should be said that as Manasseh supposedly reigned fifty-five years, he cannot be ruled out absolutely.) Exactly similar fiscal stamps include dates in Years 13, 14, and 20 (another in a Year 3 is different).[55]

The personal seals include (fig. 2): one of a king's son Jeho-ahaz, probably Josiah's eventual successor; one of Azaliah son of Meshullam (father of Shaphan) (cf. 2 Kings 22:3); one of Ahikam son of Shaphan, this reign or Jehoiakim's (cf. 2 Kings 22:12-14; Jer. 26:24); a seal stone in ring, of Hanan son of Hilkiah, (high) priest in Jerusalem (cf. 2 Kings 22:8, 10).[56]

(v) Jehoiakim and Jehoiachin

Attributable to Jehoiakim's reign (fig. 2) may be the seal of the king's son Jerahmeel and a bulla from a second seal of the same man. Such a man was son of King Jehoiakim and involved with the prophet Jeremiah (Jer. 36:26). An impression or bulla of "Gemariah son of Shaphan" recalls the man of this name and filiation under Jehoiakim in Jer. 36:10-11.[57] For the seal of Gemariah's brother Ahikam, see above under Josiah. For Baruch in this reign and the next two, see under Zedekiah, below.

We have also the seal of the king's son Pedaiah, readily identifiable as one of the sons of Jehoiachin, named in 1 Chron. 3:16-18.[58] Cf. fig. 2.

(vi) Zedekiah

Here a series of personal seals belong to people who bear the names of characters active in this reign. Most famous are two bullae from seals of "Berechiah [= Baruch], son of Neriah the scribe," well known as the prophet Jeremiah's faithful secretary (Jer. 32:12; 36; 43:1-7; 45). Cf. Fig. 2.

Malkijah the king's son (Jer. 38:6) may be the same man as the owner of *CWSS*, 55, no. 15. Seraiah son of Neriah appears to be Baruch's brother; Azariah son of Hilkiah would be brother of Hanan (cf. under Josiah); cf. 1 Chron. 6:13; 9:11. Gedaliah "who is over the house" may have been the Gedaliah who briefly governed Judah after the Babylonian conquest in 586 (cf. 2 Kings 25:22-25). One or another of four seal owners Jaazaniah, one being "servant of the king," may again have been the army officer active in 586 (2 Kings 25:23). A king's son, Elishama, had descendants active at the fall of Jerusalem (2 Kings 25:25; Jer. 41:1); his probable seal would then date anytime from Josiah onward.[59]

A major inscriptional source at this time is the collection of ostraca found in the ruins of Lachish, known as the "Lachish Letters." Archaeologically they date from the last days of Lachish before it was destroyed by Nebuchadrezzar's troops.[60]

For the historical role of the foregoing documents, cf. further section 5 below.

4. THE SEQUENCES OF RULERS AND OVERALL CHRONOLOGY, CIRCA 930-580

A. THE BASIC SEQUENCES OF RULERS IN EXTERNAL AND BIBLICAL SOURCES

Now, after listing the rulers of Israel and Judah from the biblical record (tab. 2, pp. 8-9 above), then checking the foreign rulers there mentioned against the original foreign sources, and the witness of those external sources to Hebrew rulers, and finally the indigenous Hebrew sources so far as they go, we must set out first the basic results for the sequences of rulers in both external and biblical sources and compare notes. Then we may look at the chronology more closely, to establish practical limits during circa 950-580, so that we may gain a working framework within which to examine (in 5, below) the interlock of historical events in the two lots of sources.

The framework of ancient Near Eastern history in this epoch is provided by the two major hearths of complex civilization of that day, namely, Mesopotamia (Assyria and Babylonia) on the east and Egypt to the southwest. Before Alexander the Great (336-323) we have the Persian Empire, which ended the independence of Babylon in 539 (by Cyrus) and (for a time) of Egypt in 525 (by Cambyses). All these dates are firm and universally accepted. In Mesopotamia the Neo-Babylonian kings ruled Babylonia from 626 to 539. Overlapping at the end and preceding them, the kings of Assyria are dated to the year from 912 down to 648 (eponym lists, 911/910ff., plus king lists), and to the final end of Assyria in 609.

Before 912 Assyrian dates are closely correct back to 1180, before which a dispute over three or thirteen years for Ninurta-apil-ekur gives a maximum ten-year variation back to 1432/1422 for the accession of Enlil-nasir II. Thus from 1180 (and quite closely from the late fifteenth century) Assyrian dates provide a firm backbone of dating other, less securely fixed regions in the Near East.[61]

On the other side of the area, Egypt also makes a valuable contribution, essentially independent of Mesopotamia. Thus, before the Persian conquest in 525, the Twenty-Sixth (Saite) Dynasty reigned to the year during 664 to 525. The reign of Tanutamun was contemporary with the Twenty-Sixth Dynasty, and the Twenty-Third and Twenty-Fourth Dynasties were wholly contemporary with the Twenty-Second and with each other; so none of these affect the flow of successive dates. Before the Twenty-Sixth Dynasty, Taharqa of the Twenty-Fifth (Kushite/Nubian) Dynasty reigned from 690 to 664. Before this date, it is now clear that Shebitku reigned from at least 702 (and perhaps 706), and his predecessor Shabaka for fourteen years, thirteen over Egypt, maximally 719/minimally 715 to 702. Before him in Egypt, but not ending before 716 (Osorkon IV = Shilkanni of an Assyrian text in 716), the Twenty-Second (Libyan) Dynasty reigned an absolute minimum of close to 230 years, beginning with Shoshenq I ("Shishak") from 945 (or extremely close to it). *Note that this Egyptian chronology stands independently of both the Assyrian and Hebrew data.*

Before 945, the Twenty-First Dynasty goes back to 1070 within a year or so. Earlier still, the Ramesside Nineteenth and Twentieth Dynasties (New Kingdom) go back to firm dates of 1279-1213 (not 1212!) for Ramesses II, and for the preceding Eighteenth Dynasty and start of the New Kingdom to either 1550 or 1540 (again, varying because of a king [Tuthmosis II] who reigned either three or thirteen years).[62]

It is within this very close framework that the dates for the kingdoms of Israel and Judah have to be set. So, first, how do the sequences of rulers fit in these conditions? And then, how about possibly more precise dates?

(i) Mesopotamia: Reality and Sequence

The Hebrew record names the following kings of Assyria (A) and Babylon (B) in this order:

Tiglath-pileser (III)/Pul — A	(745-727)
Shalmaneser (V) — A	(727-722)
Sargon (II) — A	(722-705)
Sennacherib — A	(705-681)
Merodach-Baladan (II) — B	(722-710, 703)
Esarhaddon — A	(681-669)
Nebuchadrezzar (II) — B	(605-562)
Evil-Merodach — B	(562-560)

As the added Mesopotamian dates show, the Hebrew writers in Kings, etc., have their Assyrian and Babylonian monarchs impeccably in the right order, and (for Assyria) in close succession, corresponding to the frequent Assyrian interventions in the Levant. And the basic forms of names given are also known to be closely accurate, contrasted with what is found in writings of the fourth to first centuries B.C.[63] Thus the writers of Kings, Chronicles, and Isaiah and Jeremiah come out well here in terms of accuracy and reliability.

They also know their own royal sequence correctly. The Mesopotamian sources confirm directly the order of Israelite and Judean kings as found in Kings and Chronicles:

Shalmaneser III names:	853	Ahab of Israel	
	841	Jehu of Bit-Khumri (= Israel)	
Adad-nirari III names:	796	Jehoash of Samaria	
Tiglath-pileser III names:	738	Menahem of Samaria	
	(738	Azriau, probably *not* Azariah)	
	733	Pekah of Bit-Khumri (= Israel)	
	734		Ahaz of Judah
	732	Hoshea of Bit-Khumri (= Israel)	
Sargon II claims:	722	Fall of Samaria	
Sennacherib names:	701		Hezekiah of Judah
Esarhaddon names:	676		Manasseh of Judah
Assurbanipal names:	ca. 666		Manasseh of Judah
Nebuchadrezzar II	597		(Jehoiachin) sent to Babylon (Zedekiah) in Jerusalem
names:	594-570		Jehoiachin of Judah, captive in Babylon

These records also give us very definite dates for the floruit of the Hebrew kings mentioned. Thus the sequence of Hebrew kings in Kings, etc., is also straight and reliable, as are the biblical reports on Mesopotamian kings.

(ii) Egypt and the Levant

There is less material to notice here. Shoshenq I celebrated his campaign in Palestine by beginning huge temple-building projects from Year 21 (ca. 925; his stela at Gebel Silsila), his campaign tableau being part of the one at Karnak.

Osorkon I reigned after him, immediately spending vast wealth on Egypt's temple cults (Years 1-4, ca. 924-921; Bubastis text); Osorkon IV reigned circa 732/730–716. Thereafter Taharqa reigned from 690 to 664, Necho II from 610 to 595, and Hophra from 589 to 570, all in sequence alongside their Hebrew contemporaries. We may again tabulate:

Shoshenq I, war in Palestine, Yr 20	ca. 926/25	(Rehoboam, Yr 5)
Osorkon I, spending wealth	ca. 924–890/889	(tp Reh, Asa & Zerah)
Osorkon IV = So	ca. 732/730–716	ctp Hoshea of Israel
Taharqa: prince vs. Sennacherib	701	ctp Hezekiah of Judah
: king	690-664	
Necho II	610-595	ctp Josiah of Judah, 609
Hophra	589-570	ctp Zedekiah, 588/587

Again, the sequences and dating tally well, and the names are accurately transmitted.

We then turn to the Levant. Using combined sources for Aram, Phoenicia, and Jordan, we have:

9th cent. B.C.	Ittobaal I (Ethbaal)	Phoenicia	Ahab of Israel
(9th cent.)	(Mesha	Moab	Ahab & successors)
9th cent.	Hazael	Aram-D	Jehu & Jehoahaz of Israel
start 8th cent.	Benhadad "III,"	Aram-D	Joash of Israel;
	son of Hazael		Zakkur of Hamath
740s-732	Rezin/Rakhianu	Aram-D	Pekah of Israel; T-P III
			of Assyria
ca. 586	Baalis	Ammon	Fall of Judah, ca. 586; seal

And again, the sequences and general dates fit perfectly well. (Mesha is in parentheses because he is not securely dated except by the OT record and vaguely by paleography.) The names in Hebrew and the other northwest Semitic languages correspond closely.

(iii) Local Records

Finally, we examine the modest contribution of "local records." From the Samaria ostraca we have respectably long reign(s) of from nine to ten and/or fifteen years with organized administration in a palace in the first half of the eighth century B.C.; a minister's seal belongs to the time of a Jeroboam, certainly II. We might have the seal of the ephemeral Shallum, and certainly a private seal naming Hoshea. In Judah seals name the kings Uzziah, Jotham, Ahaz, Hezekiah, and most likely Manasseh as prince. Two royal bullae underline the lineage and succession of Jotham, Ahaz, and Hezekiah. Two well-known stone inscriptions (Siloam tunnel, tomb) make sense if attributed to Hezekiah's reign.

Then in the later seventh/early sixth century we have a good series of seals and bullae that belonged to or named a whole clutch of characters familiar specifically in this period in 2 Kings, 2 Chronicles, and Jeremiah. Their overall dating is clinched by those specimens that derive from such digs as that of the "City of David," with its "house of seals," belonging to the eve of the fall of Jerusalem in 586. The seals and bullae found outside such closed archaeological contexts are so close in nature to these provenanced specimens as to be guaranteed the same general date.[64]

The Lachish ostraca belong to that same political context. In other words, these local items do bear out the reality of kings and their subordinates in both kingdoms, the sequence of some, and the existence of proper governmental royal centers in Samaria (eighth century) and Jerusalem (seventh/early sixth centuries). All of this is consistent with the external evidence from other Near Eastern sources reviewed above.

B. THE DETAILED CHRONOLOGY OF THE DIVIDED MONARCHY PERIOD — CONCISELY!

This topic is complex in several ways. We must stick to essentials. The first thing to realize is that the chronological data in Kings in particular — regnal years, synchronisms, etc. — follow normal *Near Eastern* usage.[65] They cannot be understood by just totting up figures as if this were some modern, "Western" composition. That way lies confusion, as many have found to their cost. Ancient regnal years were calculated in one or another of two main ways, simply because kings never normally died conveniently at midnight on the last day of the last month of the year, so making their regnal years identical with the ordinary calendar year. So, as in Mesopotamia, one might use accession-year dating. When the throne changed hands during the civil year, that whole year was (in effect) credited to the king who had died, the new man treating it simply as his "accession year" (a year zero), and counting his Year 1 from the next New Year's Day. On this system, if a list says a king reigned eight years, then eight years should be credited to him.

But in Egypt the classical system was the opposite: i.e., nonaccession-year dating. In this case, when one king died and another ascended the throne, the whole year was credited to the new man (as Year 1, straightaway), and none of it to his recently deceased predecessor. In such cases a king who is known to have reached his eighth year can only be credited with seven full years. (Unless, under the New Kingdom system, his full years run independently of the calendar year, when a final six months or more = one full year. But this purely Egyptian problem will not concern us here.) These phenomena *do* affect the calculation of regnal years in Israel and Judah. A simple theoretical example may show this (see p. 27).

On the Egyptian method a king reaches his seventh year ("seven years"), but it is credited to his successor; so we subtract one, giving him a true reign of only six years. On the Mesopotamian method a king reaches his sixth year ("six years"), which is credited to him (merely = accession for next man), so he has a true reign of six years, nothing to subtract. These usages apply as much to Hebrew kings as to their neighbors, and cannot be ignored. This can be seen in a very special context, as long ago pointed out by Thiele. In the history of Israel,

26

Egypt	B.C.	Mesopotamia
King A — Year 12	980	*King A* — Year 12
King A — Year 13; dies	979	*King A* — Year 13; dies
Year becomes		counted to *King A*
King B — Year 1		King B — accession yr only
King B — Year 2	978	King B — Year 1
King B — Year 3	977	King B — Year 2
King B — Year 4	976	King B — Year 3
King B — Year 5	975	King B — Year 4
King B — Year 6	974	King B — Year 5
King B — Year 7; dies	973	King B — Year 6; dies
Year becomes		counted to King B
King C — Year 1		*King C* — accession year only
King C — Year 2	972	*King C* — Year 1
King C — Year 3 and so on	971	*King C* — Year 2 and so on

Ahab sent troops to the Battle of Qarqar in 853, as his opponent Shalmaneser III tells us. So Ahab at least lived into 853. But twelve years later, in 841, Jehu of Israel paid tribute, as Shalmaneser III also tells us. Yet within that span our data in Kings give two reigns in Israel, Ahaziah at two years and J(eh)oram at twelve years, which makes fourteen years to our Western minds. On the Mesopotamian accession-year system, this would also be true. But the founder of Israel, Jeroboam I, came not from Mesopotamia *but from Egypt* to found his kingdom (1 Kings 11:40; 12:2), and so he may well have brought the Egyptian usage with him. Because, on the nonaccession-year usage, Ahaziah would have only one full year and J(eh)oram eleven full years — total, twelve years, fitting neatly into the twelve years from 853 to 841. Then Ahab and his predecessors would also have used this mode. So six kings with eighty-four stated years had actually one full year each less, giving us eighty-four years - six years = seventy-eight years, back to 931/930, for the accession of Jeroboam I, and by inference that of his rival, Rehoboam of Judah. See diagrams, figs. 3 and 4.

There is one other control over this period in Hebrew history. Jehu gained his throne by murdering both his predecessor J(eh)oram II in Israel and Ahaziah II of Judah (2 Kings 9:14-29), an event now apparently vouched for by the Tell Dan stela independently of Kings, on which Hazael claims the credit for himself (perhaps viewing Jehu as his henchman). Thus the period from 931/930 down to 841 covers all the kings of Israel prior to Jehu and all the Judean kings down to Ahaziah II inclusive, who was killed by Jehu by or in 841 = eighty-nine or ninety years. The total for Judah, also six kings in that time, is ninety-five years, five or six years in excess of eighty-nine/ninety years on six kings. In theory Judah too could be using nonaccession years = eighty-nine real years, almost identical with Israel. If on the accession-year mode, then these five/six years may represent an error in the figure for either one or more reigns or for one or more coregencies.

Before looking at the period 931-841 more closely, it will be helpful to note the following underlying facts.

(i) Calendars

We have in practice to deal with three distinct calendars: (1) the ancient and Hebrew spring-to-spring calendar (months Nisan to next Nisan), (2) the ancient and Hebrew autumn-to-autumn ("fall") calendar (months Tishri to next Tishri), and (3) our modern winter-to-winter calendar (months January to December, next January), which we have to overlay upon the old calendars to "translate" them into our current usage. Any attempt to work out the two lines of Hebrew kings, assuming that they both used the same ancient calendar (whether spring/ Nisan or autumn/Tishri), soon falls apart, as neither the regnal years nor the synchronisms given between the two kingdoms make sense on this procedure. It is clear that the two kingdoms of Israel and Judah used different calendars, one Nisan to Nisan, the other Tishri to Tishri. But which used which? The two best and most recent scholars on the whole subject, Thiele and Galil, differ on this point. Thiele assigned the Tishri calendar to Judah and the Nisan one to Israel, while Galil did the opposite. Thiele had respectable reasons in the Hebrew text for his choice (Solomon's count of years, building the temple; Josiah's enactment of cult reforms; Nehemiah's [1:1; 2:1] datings), but they are not needfully decisive. Galil produced no clearly independent evidence for his opposite view (his adduction of Jer. 36:22, pp. 9f., proves nothing). Thiele's choice of calendars leads to consistently one-year-too-high and one-year-too-low figures being given respectively for Israelite years for accession of Judean kings and for Judean years for accession of Israelite kings. He explained this as due to each kingdom citing the other's years by its *own* count, not the years the other kingdom actually used. This is possible, but is considered by others complex, if consistent.

On Galil's choice of calendar, the synchronisms fit, without any other adjustment, which may speak in favor of attributing (with him) a Nisan-based calendar to Judah and a Tishri-based calendar to Israel. But careful examination of the total regnal data (at least for 931-841) shows that Thiele's treatment of coregencies is to be preferred to Galil's failure to account for a good number of regnal and synchronistic data. Coregencies tend to reflect political events or threats of such.

From Manasseh (in mid–seventh century) to the end of the Judean monarchy, dates are largely agreed. Between 841 and Hezekiah's reign, improvements on both Thiele and Galil can be made (cf. below), such that nearly all our data in Kings appear to be reasonably consistent.

(ii) Regnal Years

Again, any attempt to impose the same type of regnal year-count (accession or nonaccession) on both kingdoms overall is doomed to failure, and has to be discarded. Each used either form of year-count under particular circumstances.

But on this both Thiele and Galil are in close agreement; namely, that Israel used nonaccession dating in the tenth and ninth centuries but changed to accession-year dating in the eighth, and that, broadly, Judah held to accession-year dating throughout; here Thiele would attribute a brief use of nonaccession-year dating under just three kings, which appears justifiable on political grounds (Jehoram, Ahaziah II, Joash under Israelite influence). Thus we assemble a practical dating for these kings in table 3, on the following pages.[66] This table incorporates the fixed dates from external references (Egypt, Assyria, Babylon), here printed in bold figures. It also incorporates the entire corpus of years of reign and of synchronisms from 1-2 Kings (paralleled by Chronicles), nearly all of which fit well together, once the well-established Near Eastern usages are applied. Thiele's "pattern twelve-thirteen" kind of anomaly and Galil's dismissals of perfectly good data can now both be discarded. Only very minor miscopying need be assumed in (at most!) barely three instances out of scores of figures, and these may simply be correct figures not yet properly understood.

Coregencies usually have political significance, e.g., to affirm the succession under threats (real or potential) from within or without. And a new king might continue his old year-numbering at his accession to sole power, or choose to make a complete break to affirm that a different regime was now in power. A good example of the latter is Hezekiah starting a new year-numbering after the death of Ahaz, with whose pro-Assyrian policies he clearly disagreed.

Thus we find in Kings a very remarkably preserved royal chronology, mainly very accurate in fine detail, that agrees very closely with the dates given by Mesopotamian and other sources. Such a legacy would, most logically, derive from then-existing archives (such as the "book(s) of the annals of the kings of Judah" and "of Israel" mentioned in Kings), besides archives of administrative, legal, or other documents. It cannot well be the free creation of some much

Table 3. Kings of Israel and Judah, 931-586 B.C.: Basic Dates

B.C.	Judah	B.C.	Israel
931/930– 915/914	*Rehoboam,* 17 full yrs; **926/925** 1 Kings 14:21	931/930– 911/910	*Jeroboam I,* 21 full yrs (to 22nd); 1 Kings 14:20
915/914– 912/911	*Abijam,* 3 full yrs; acc. Yr 18 Jeroboam I 1 Kings 15:1f.	911/910– 910/909	*Nadab,* 1 full yr (>2nd); acc. Yr 2 Asa 1 Kings 15:25
912/911– 871/870	*Asa,* 41 full yrs; 1 Kings 15:9-10; acc. Yr 20 Jeroboam I	910/909– 887/886	*Baasha,* 23 full yrs (>24th); acc. Yr 3 Asa; 1 Kings 15:28, 33
871/870– 849/848 (cr: 873ff.)	*Jehoshaphat,* 25 full yrs; 1 Kings 22:41; acc. Yr 4 Ahab	887/886– 886/885	*Elah,* 1 full yr (>2nd); 1 Kings 16:8; acc. Yr 26 Asa
		886/885	*Zimri,* 7 days; 1 Kings 16:10, 15 *Tibni,* 5 full yrs (>6th); 1 Kings 16:21f. (rival to Omri)
		886/885– 875/874	*Omri,* 11 full yrs (>12th); (sole) acc. Yr 31 Asa (881/880); 1 Kings 16:23
		875/874–853	*Ahab,* 21 full yrs (>22nd); **853** acc. Yr 38 Asa; 1 Kings 16:29
849/848– 842	*J(eh)oram II,* 7 full yrs (>8th); 2 Kings 8:16; acc. Yr 5 Joram I	853-852	*Ahaziah I,* 1 full yr (>2nd); acc. Yr 17 Jehoshaphat; 1 Kings 22:51
842-841	*Ahaziah II,* 1 full yr (>2nd); acc. Yr 11/12 Joram I; 2 Kings 9:29; 8:25-26	852-841	*J(eh)oram I,* 11 full yrs (<12th); acc. Yr 18 Jehoshaphat/2 Joram II; 2 Kings 3:1; 1:17
----------------	------------------	--------------	
841-835	*Queen Athaliah,* 6 yrs; 2 Kings 11:34	841–814/813	*Jehu,* 27 (28?) full yrs (>28/29?); (no acc. link); 2 Kings 10:36; **841**

841/835–   *Joash I,* 39 full yrs
796/795   (>40) acc. (sole) 7th yr
            Jehu; 2 Kings 12:1

796/795–   *Amaziah,* 29 full yrs;   814/813–   *Jehoahaz I,* 16 full yrs
776/775   2 Kings 14:1-2; acc. Yr   806/805   (>17); acc. Yr 23
(cr: 805/804ff.) 2 Jehoash II   (cr: 822/21) Joash I; 2 Kings 13:1

776/775–   *Uzziah (Azariah),* 52   806/805–   *Joash II,* 15 full yrs
736/735   full yrs (not active   791/790   (>16); **796**; acc. Yr 37
(cr: 787ff.) 750ff.) 2 Kings 15:1-2;   Joash I; 2 Kings 13:10
             acc. as cr, Yr "27" (17?)
             Jeroboam II

                                              791/790–   *Jeroboam II,* 41 full
                                              750/749   yrs; acc. (sole) Yr 15
                                              cr: *804/803 Amaziah; 2 Kings
                                                          14:23

750–735/730 *Jotham,* 16/20 full yrs;   750/749   *Zachariah,* 6 mos;
             acc. "Yr 2" Pekah;   2 Kings 15:8; acc. Yr 38
             2 Kings 15:32-33, cf. 30   Uzziah

                                              749   *Shallum,* 1 mo;
                                                          2 Kings 15:13; acc. Yr
                                                          39 Uzziah

                                              749/748–   *Menahem,* 10 full yrs;
                                              739/738   2 Kings 15:17; acc. Yr
                                                          39 Uzziah **738**

                                              739/738–   *Pekahiah,* 2 full yrs;
                                              737/736   2 Kings 15:23; acc. Yr
                                                          50, Uzziah

735/734 or   *Ahaz,* 16/(20) yrs;   737/736–   *Pekah,* 5 yrs ("20"
731/730–715 2 Kings 16:1-2; acc.   732/731   back-dated); real acc.
             "Yr 17" Pekah; **734**   ("751/750"ff.) Yr 52 Uzziah; **733**
                                                          2 Kings 15:27

715–687/686 *Hezekiah,* 29 full yrs;   732/731–722 *Hoshea,* 9 full yrs; **732**
(cr: 728ff.) **701** 2 Kings 18:1-2;   acc. Yr 20 Jotham/Yr
             acc. Yr 3 Hoshea   12 Ahaz; 2 Kings 15:30/
                                                          17:1

                                                          Fall of Samaria, **722**

687/686–642 *Manasseh,* 55 full
(cr: 697/696ff.) yrs; 2 Kings 21:1;
             676; ca. **666**

642-640   *Amon,* 2 full yrs;
             2 Kings 21:19

640-609	*Josiah*, 31 full yrs; 2 Kings 22:1	
609	*Jehoahaz II*, 3 mos; 2 Kings 23:31	
609-598	*Jehoiakim*, 11 full yrs; 2 Kings 23:36	
598-597	*Jehoiachin*, 3 mos; 2 Kings 24:8	(597)
597-586	*Zedekiah*, 11 full yrs; 2 Kings 24:18	(597)
586	*Fall of Jerusalem*	

later writer's imagination that just happens (miraculously!) to coincide almost throughout with the data then preserved only in documents buried inaccessibly in the ruin mounds of Assyrian cities long since abandoned and largely lost to view.

5. HISTORY OF THE DIVIDED MONARCHY IN BIBLICAL AND EXTERNAL SOURCES

Here we look compactly at those episodes in ancient Near Eastern history that are common to both sets of sources — the biblical writings and the nonbiblical or external sources — and compare notes to see how far they match up with each other, if at all.

A. SHISHAK/SHOSHENQ I OF EGYPT INVADES PALESTINE

We have met this character already (p. 10, above). In 1 Kings 14:25-26 and in 2 Chron. 12:2-9, we have the succinct report (Kings) that "Shishaq" (better variant, "Shushaq") king of Egypt came up to Jerusalem in the fifth year of Rehoboam king of Judah, taking off as booty the wealth of the temple and palace there.[67]

Other details (Chronicles) list Shishak's considerable forces as including Libyans, Sukkiyim, and Nubians (Kushites); Jerusalem was not taken by force, but in effect its wealth was handed over as tribute, with vassal status ("service to earthly kingdoms," 2 Chron. 12:8). So, by these accounts, the Egyptian ruler went home enriched, and may have imposed tribute-paying vassal status upon Judah. As both Kings and Chronicles stem from Judean writers, they have nothing more to say about the neighboring kingdom of Israel, subsequent to Jeroboam's exit from Egypt, where he had enjoyed Shishak's patronage as a dissident (1 Kings 11:40; 12:2).

The Hebrew narratives do not stand alone. There is no reason whatever to doubt the identity of the Hebrew "Shushaq" with the very well known pharaoh Shoshenq I, founder of the Twenty-Second Dynasty, of Libyan origin, whose reign is closely datable to circa 945-924. Pharaohs from of old placed their "throne names" (adopted at accession) and personal names in royal ovals or cartouches. Those of Shoshenq I are, respectively, *Hedj-kheper-re Setepenre* and *Shoshenq Beloved-of-Amun,* Amun being Egypt's great imperial god, with a vast temple at Karnak in Thebes. These cartouches are *exclusive* to Shoshenq I; no other Shoshenq, of numbers II-VI(II), used that combination.

To this first Shoshenq belongs a series of monuments that link him explicitly with Palestine and war there. Conversely, *no other Shoshenq* has (so far) any known connection with Palestine or events there. And the dates of Shoshenq I (ca. 945-924) fit the dates for Rehoboam (ca. 931-914). Even more closely, Shoshenq I's unfinished works in celebration of his victory date to his Year 21 onward (Silsila stela, that year; ca. 925), setting his campaign in Years 19 or 20 (927f. or 926f.), while the fifth year of Rehoboam is about 926/925 also. The Egyptian and Hebrew dates series are independent of each other (pp. 24, 30 above) but match very well.

The Egyptian data for the campaign follow strictly Egyptian usage. The geographical point of proof is the top corner of a stela bearing the distinctive cartouches of Shoshenq I (and nobody else!) in the rubble of ancient Megiddo itself — his "visiting card" (fig. 5A).[68] Setting up such a monument indicates an Egyptian presence and (in this Egyptian historical context) a conquest. Such stelae were often set up or rock-carved in regions that the pharaohs then claimed as vassal states, as did Sethos I at Beth-Shan (north Canaan; two) and Tell Shihab (east of Lake Galilee), and Ramesses II at Beth-Shan, Byblos, Tyre, Adhlun, and Nahr el-Kalb (Lebanon; three) and Sheikh Said (east of Lake Galilee). This interpretation would agree with the remark at the end of 2 Chron. 12:8.

The place-name list in his huge triumph scene at Karnak is extensive, but damaged (names are lost in rows IV and XI). Like all such major lists, a rhetorical text runs above it, of very original stamp, mentioning the king's buildings as well as his valor. And exactly like almost all other such major lists, the rows of place-names (each in an oval) do *not* run in a continuous sequence (like an entire journey), but are made up of *segments* or extracts from routes; no capital cities are picked out, no defeated foreign ruler is ever mentioned, and (in Canaan and Syria) no nation or state is named, merely the townships encountered.[69] Cf. figs. 5B, 6, and 7.

So, this great list does not mention either a Rehoboam or a Jeroboam, or the "state names" of Judah or Israel; that was never done in such long town lists. What we *do* have is several series of names of places known in both Judah and Israel, from which Shoshenq's course of campaign can be discerned.[70] This is valuable, in that it shows that Shoshenq I chose not only to cow and loot Rehoboam of Judah, but also to bring his former protégé Jeroboam of Israel to heel. It may well be (a touch of speculation, for a moment!) that Shoshenq's price tag for helping Jeroboam into power in 931 was that Jeroboam should thereafter pay him tribute as a vassal. It would only need Jeroboam to default on his payment to bring the redoubtable pharaoh down upon him, and to lay hands on Judah's rumored wealth for good measure.

A Karnak stela of Shoshenq I (though fragmentary) clearly mentions conflict with "Asiatics" on the Sinai border of the East Delta — for a ruler bent on conquest, such an incident (however flimsy) would serve as a sufficient excuse to sweep across north Sinai into Judah, then up into Israel. So the Egyptian data add complementary details to our biblical information. The latter in turn hint at the mixed composition of Shoshenq's force: Libyans (as one would expect of a Libyan ruler); Nubians (from the many resident in Egypt, or recruited from Nubia); and — most interesting — some Sukkiyim, or scouts, Libyan auxiliaries known in Egyptian texts from the thirteenth/twelfth centuries onward, an intimate detail that we owe exclusively to the Chronicler and his (nonbiblical) sources.[71] Thus, overall, the very differently composed Egyptian and Hebrew sources usefully complement one another, to produce a fuller picture of a particular historical occasion.

B. MESHA KING OF MOAB VERSUS OMRI'S DYNASTY

In 2 Kings 3:4-27 we have an account of conflict between Israel and Moab. Under Ahab (and perhaps before), Mesha king of Moab had had to pay annual tribute to Israel, but he rebelled after Ahab's death. So Ahab's successor, Joram, engaged Jehoshaphat king of Judah and the king of Edom in a joint attack on Moab to bring Mesha back into subjection. After the allies achieved military success against Moab, the king of Moab resorted to grisly sacrifice, and the allies had to retreat. The reason is not stated, but it is assuming very little to infer that their king's drastic act spurred the Moabites into a frenzied counterattack that drove their opponents from the field. Nobody in antiquity liked to admit defeat, but writers would disguise or minimize it in one way or another (cf. 2 Kings 3:27b).

With the discovery at Dibon of a stela of Mesha himself (1868), we have a comparable account from the Moabite side. Mesha had succeeded his father after the latter's thirty years of rule. During that period and into his own reign, Omri king of Israel and his son (i.e., Ahab) oppressed Moab "many years" (ll. 5-6); under Omri and his sons (= descendants, e.g., Ahab, Joram), "40 years" (ll. 7-8). Then Mesha threw off Israel's yoke and proceeded to take (back) Madeba, Ataroth, Nebo, and Jahaz. In the south the "House of [Da]vid" (l. 31; fig. 13B) had held Horonen, so Mesha took that also. His stela celebrates his successes and his consequent building works.[72]

Here then there is overlap with the Hebrew account, but also additional information (just as in Shoshenq's case). Both accounts agree in portraying the basic situation; namely, that the Omride Dynasty in Israel had succeeded in imposing its overlordship upon Moab, turning the Moabite kingdom into a tribute-paying vassal, and that for a clear span of years, not just the odd year or two. That situation began under Omri and continued under Ahab until his death. But under Joram, the Moabite king rejected vassal status and rebelled. From this point each side goes on to stress its successes and to minimize its reverses. Initially the allies overran Moabite territory, defeating and killing the foe, and destroying all they could, until suffering a final reverse such that they withdrew; this is all passed over in silence by Mesha on his stela.

But the withdrawal from Moab by the allies gave Mesha the opportunity to consolidate his position, reoccupy places formerly held by his foes, and rebuild his towns and utilities, which are the aspects that he stresses on his monument — the capture of Madeba, Ataroth, Nebo, Jahaz, and Horonen; the building (*re*building?) of Baal-meon, Qiryaten, Qeriho, Aroer, Beth-Bamoth, and Bezer (both "destroyed" and "in ruins," l. 27); the making of cisterns (ll. 9, 23, etc.) — or in fact, their reclearing? In thanksgiving to his deity Kemosh, Mesha then also built temples in Diblaten, Baal-Meon, and possibly [Made]ba (ll. 29-30).

This process of renewal might have taken anywhere from a couple of years to five or ten years at most; there is no justification whatsoever for dating the contents or carving of the stela any later than that, after the clash with the allies, or for any more elaborate theory of the course of events than that just given. This monument was certainly not a postmortem memorial. With Jehoram's accession about 852, Mesha's successful rebellion would hardly be later than circa 850. Thus his subsequent consolidation would have been achieved within circa 850/840 at most. About 840/835 is therefore, historically, about the latest credible date (even too late) for the creation of this stela.

Thus, again, and as one would expect on the basis of innumerable other examples of this kind where distinct accounts are available from different sources, a fuller account emerges from careful comparison of the total evidence.

C. HAZAEL OF ARAM-DAMASCUS AND THE TEL DAN STELA

In 2 Kings 9:1-29 we are given an account of how Jehu, an Israelite army commander, proceeded to kill off both his own master Joram (I) king of Israel and the latter's ally Ahaziah (II) king of Judah during a lull in their war with Hazael, king of Aram of Damascus. This is the only occasion on which two monarchs of Israel and Judah met their deaths at virtually the same moment in time.

In recent years excavations at Tel Dan, ancient Dan, yielded two stone fragments (one broken) from a stela bearing the remains of at least thirteen lines of inscription in Old Aramaic.[73] Lines 3 to 9 are the clearest and best-preserved part. These read largely as follows:

> (3) And my father lay down, and he went to his [(fore)fathers]. And the king of I(4)[s]rael had come up earlier into my father's land. [But] Hadad made m[e] king, (5) (even) me.

> And Hadad went before me, (. . . *obscure* . . .) (6) my kings(?) And I killed [?might]y ki[ngs?] who harnessed two(?) th[ousand ch](7)ariots and two(?) thousand horsemen.[74]

> [And I killed? xxx]ram, son of [xxxx], (8) king of Israel.[75]

> And [I] killed [xxx]iah son of [xxxx.xx](9) ? the House of David (fig. 13A).

> And I set [destruction in their cities, etc.?/tribute on their people, etc.?] (10) their land [. . .].

The author of this text was clearly a king; his text is in Aramaic, and the god Hadad was his patron; the power that was Israel's next-door neighbor to her north was the kingdom of Aram ruled from Damascus. Thus the originator of this text was a king of Aram-Damascus beyond any serious doubt. In this text he did something (presumably nasty) to "[. . .]ram son of [xxxx], king of Israel," and slew a person "[xxx]iah son of [X]" related to the House of David, i.e., Judah. In the whole series of the kings of Israel, there is one *and only one* king whose name ends in *-ram,* and that is J(eh)oram, son of Ahab, circa 852-841. Therefore it seems at the present time inevitable that we should restore here "[J(eh)o]ram son of [Ahab], king of Israel."

In strict parallel with the sentence about [Jeho]ram of Israel, we have another that our Aramean king killed "[xxx]iah son of [X]," plus mention of the House of David = Judah. This person from Judah must have been of comparable importance to [Jeho]ram of Israel to be worth listing with him in the same breath as being slain. So he should be a king (or nearest deputy), and he has to be a contemporary of Joram of Israel. This dating immediately excludes such Judean kings as Amaziah, Uzziah, Hezekiah, and Zedekiah, who are all much too late to be with Joram in or before 841. The only other known suitable person is Ahaziah (II) king of Judah — who in fact is the very man killed off at the same time as Joram of Israel in the narrative of 2 Kings 9. This identification places the Aramean king's two victims on the same footing: king of Israel and king of Judah. Therefore it is extremely likely that we should further restore "[Ahaz]iah son of [Joram, . . .]*k* the House of David." Most scholars concede the further restoration [*m l*] *k,* "[kin]g," hence reading "A. son of J., king of the House of David," which makes good sense. Thus there is very good reason indeed to allow that the actions narrated here belong to the year 841, when both Ahaziah and Joram perished at the hand of Jehu. The author of the stela would then, inevitably, have been Hazael, king in Damascus, who was warring with these kings before their decease, and long survived them.[76]

His claim to have dispatched the two Hebrew monarchs at first contrasts with the attribution of this deed to Jehu in 2 Kings 9. But it is commonplace for Near Eastern rulers to claim credit for actions by others.[77] Hazael may have chosen to regard the usurper Jehu as a likely vassal in his own plans — but Jehu thought otherwise, and may (as a vulnerable new king of Israel) have appealed for support to Shalmaneser III of Assyria, hence his immediate offering of tribute in 841, recorded by that king. This was exactly what Ahaz of Judah did at a later date, appealing to Tiglath-pileser III when threatened by Rezin of Aram and Pekah of Israel (2 Kings 16:5-9). Hazael's father may have been a high army commander of his predecessor, or a younger son of his predecessor not entitled to the throne. But even as a usurper, he could use the term "father" of a predecessor, a well-known usage.[78]

Thus the Tell Dan stela is virtually certainly an additional witness to a particular set of events in 841 that are also featured in 2 Kings 9, particularly as [Jo]ram king of Israel is to be read.

D. TIGLATH-PILESER III AND THE HEBREW KINGDOMS

One of the most active Assyrian warrior-emperors, Tiglath-pileser III (alias Pul) first appears in the reign of Menahem, who paid him a massive tribute, 1,000 talents of silver, to gain the Assyrian's support as king in Israel (2 Kings 15:19-20). This payment may have been made circa 740 or earlier; his tribute in 738 may have been the regular kind. As Tadmor has pointed out, 1,000 talents of silver was the going rate of payment that "TP" commonly exacted from usurpers and local kings on wobbly thrones.[79] Tiglath-pileser's own annals cite Hoshea of Israel later paying 10 talents of gold and (1,000[?]) talents of silver; Hulli of Tabal (in southeast Anatolia), 10 talents of gold and 1,000 talents of silver; and Metenna king of Tyre, (1)50 talents of gold and 2,000 talents of silver. In fact, as those figures show, Menahem got off rather lighter than the others (no gold to pay!). Nevertheless, he had to raise his thousand (we are told) by levying fifty shekels on every wealthy man in his little kingdom. That general rate (fifty-sixty shekels), again, is attested in external records from Assyria itself.

In Judah, King Ahaz also sought to get the Arameans off his back by calling in the Assyrian colossus and paying up front with silver and gold (2 Kings 16:7-9). Tiglath-pileser's texts in turn record that Jeho-ahaz (longer form of Ahaz's name) was among tribute-paying rulers by about 734 — probably soon after his "bribe" following his takeover of power in Judah in 735.[80]

In 2 Kings 15:29, during the reign of Pekah (with echoes in 1 Chron. 5:6 and 26), Tiglath-pileser III is said to have taken over Gilead east of the Jordan and Galilee west of it, cities (like Hazor) being listed, and to have deported the inhabitants to Assyria. Tiglath-pileser did indeed invade Gilead and Galilee, as his own rather damaged records show. For 733-732 we read of the dethronement and exile of King Pekah of Israel, and (in damaged context) carrying off "all its people" from part of Bit-Khumri (= Israel).[81] Annals fragments (18/24) mention the towns Hannathon ("Hinatuna"), Jotbata ("Yatbite"), and probably Marom ("Marum"), all in Galilee. A relief scene celebrates the capture of the town of Astartu, the Ashteroth-(Qarnaim) just north of Gilead.[82]

From excavations and surveys it is clear that occupation of settlements in Galilee was drastically reduced in the late eighth century (our period), as shown by the occupation history of such sites as Tel Mador, Tel Gath Hepher, Khirbet Rosh Zayit ("Cabul"), and others.[83] At Hazor (end of level V), the ferocious destruction wrought by Assyrian troops left a layer of black ash a meter thick, which told its own grim tale. Only a few poor squatters hovered there afterward a while (level IV). Then nobody cared until a Babylonian watch post was set there about 150 years later (level III), followed by a rural Persian-age settlement (level II).[84]

Finally, the reign of Hoshea. In 2 Kings 15:30 we are told that Hoshea slew

Pekah to gain the throne for himself. The other side of the coin is to be seen, again, in the inscriptions of Tiglath-pileser III, where the change of king can still be seen in the fragmentary texts.[85]

E. SHALMANESER V, SARGON II, AND THE FALLS OF SAMARIA AND ASHDOD

(i) Samaria

In 2 Kings 17:3-6 we read of the final end of the kingdom of Israel. We are told that Hoshea ceased to pay tribute to Assyria, intrigued with King So of Egypt, and that Shalmaneser of Assyria in consequence seized Hoshea, besieging Samaria for three years until its fall. "The king of Assyria" then deported the people to Assyria. This episode features also in the cuneiform sources. The very prosaic, factual Babylonian Chronicle (no. 1, i:28) preserves a general entry on Shalmaneser V's reign, stating that he ravaged Samaria, after which it reports his death in his fifth year (= 722).[86] This would be consistent with the siege and capture of Samaria being a major event of his short (five-year) reign, and in effect its last event.

Regrettably, the equally prosaic, dry record in the eponym list is badly damaged in its "events" entries at this time. The year for 727 has the remains of Shalmaneser V's accession; 726 is "in [somewhere; any other event lost]"; 725-724-723 all have the tantalizing entry "to [somewhere, lost]." This has often been restored as "to [Samaria]" — which is possible, but entirely beyond proof unless fresh manuscript evidence (better-preserved tablet copies) turns up. Other restorations would be equally possible. The following entries (722-720) have nothing at all preserved, save for the names of the eponym officials themselves that marked off each year.[87]

However, following Shalmaneser's very brief reign, which ended before any account of his last year could be monumentalized, Sargon II replaced him in a coup d'etat, and subsequently claimed the capture of Samaria for himself, much later on in his reign. This was certainly a propaganda exercise, to cover the gap in military successes that would otherwise disfigure the accounts of his reign. The mere three months of his "accession year" were not adequate to run a campaign, nor the season suitable; and internal strife occupied his first year of reign. So the later annalists had to cover this over by attributing Shalmaneser's capture of Samaria to Sargon. To the biblical writers, it was of no importance which Assyrian king reduced Samaria — only the event and its significance for them (seen as a judgment) actually mattered.

But in Assyria, Sargon II was tantamount to a usurper, and had to justify himself then, and to later generations. Thus, despite a great deal of discussion, there is (as various Assyriologists have pointed out) no reason to doubt the basic events as indicated in both Kings and the other sources rightly understood. Namely, that Shalmaneser V's forces besieged Samaria for three years (725/724, 724/723, 723/722) to its fall in 722; Hoshea himself may have fallen into Assyrian hands before the final fall, but this is a moot point.

It fell to Sargon II to complete the deportation of the Israelite captives to Assyria, and to settle other people in Samaria in their place. In 720, any local revolt in the land (fomented by remaining locals?) was quickly crushed. Thus the biblical picture of events and Mesopotamian *factual* data agree well, and other speculations are largely profitless.[88]

(ii) Ashdod

Ashdod is a simpler matter. Its troubles with Assyria gave rise to the Bible's only mention of Sargon II of Assyria. In Isa. 20:1 a brief oracle is dated as given "in the year when the *turtan* ('commander') sent by Sargon of Assyria reached Ashdod, attacked it and took it." That event can be dated to either 712 or 711, by reference to the inscriptions of Sargon II, 712 being the preferable date.[89]

The Assyrian texts confirm that Sargon sent his commander; he was busy building a new capital city, Dur-Sharrukin, "Sargonstown" or "Sargonburg/Sargonville." The eponym list confirms that in 712 the king was "in the (home)land" and not warring abroad, hence his general would go to Palestine in his name.[90]

The conquest of Ashdod and Assyrian rule there is borne out by the discovery at Ashdod itself of fragments of a victory stela of the type Sargon II set up at home in Dur-Sharrukin.[91] The city had been badly damaged, as destruction of stratum VIII shows, and needed a rebuild (stratum VII). Thus our external resources (in texts and archaeology alike) provide a fuller context for the fleeting date line in Isa. 20:1.

F. SENNACHERIB VERSUS HEZEKIAH AND FRIENDS — TILL DEATH DID THEM PART

(i) 701 B.C.

In 2 Kings 18:13 to 19:37, closely similar to Isa. 36–37 (plus 2 Chron. 32:1-22), we find an account of Sennacherib's invasion of Judah. Jerusalem was not captured, but Hezekiah had to return to vassal status; the Assyrian king besieged and took Judean towns including Lachish, then went against Libnah. With this, one may compare the inscriptions from Sennacherib's scribes, which set the clash in a wider context.[92] From these, the sequence of events is perfectly clear in essence. The death in battle of Sargon II (705) and the need for Sennacherib to get control of his inheritance led to disquiet and revolt in his wide empire. He had first to secure the position in Babylonia (whence in 703 Merodach-Baladan II raised intrigue, perhaps then also with Hezekiah; cf. 2 Kings 20:12-19 and Isa. 39:1-8; 2 Chron. 32:31). Only thereafter in 701 could Sennacherib move westward. The Assyrian first secured most of Phoenicia — only Tyre on its off-shore rock proved impregnable. But with the rest of Phoenicia at his feet, Sennacherib held a *durbar* or rally of loyal vassals, who dutifully brought or sent their tribute, including arrears. Missing were Hezekiah of Judah (rebel), Padi of Ekron (in Hezekiah's custody), and Gaza (perhaps occupied by Egypto-Nubian forces). Sennacherib moved south, toward Philistia. Joppa fell, but at Eltekeh the allies opposed Sennacherib, although without success. The Assyrian could then recapture Ekron, and thus feel free to invade Judah, taking its towns as he went. Lachish put up stiff resistance to the Assyrian emperor (cf. here 2 Kings 18:14; 19:8). Hezekiah could smell potential disaster, so he sent word down to Lachish, offering to pay tribute once more (cf. 18:14-15). That encouraged Sennacherib to send high dignitaries up to Jerusalem with an intimidating army force, to demand full surrender (cf. 18:17 to 19:8). Sennacherib, meanwhile, moved on to Libnah, after overcoming Lachish.

Meantime also, the allies who had recoiled south toward base camp at Gaza saw their chance: to strike stealthily at Sennacherib from behind while his forces were split between Libnah and Jerusalem. So the regrouped allies came quietly back north, this time (unlike at Eltekeh) nominally led by Tirhakah of Egypt and Kush (and doubtless a clutch of generals); cf. 2 Kings 19:9. But the Assyrian intelligence (spies, no doubt) detected them, and so Sennacherib brought his forces together, down from Jerusalem and round from Libnah, to strike back at the allies. They got wind of this danger and quietly melted back south — in the case of Tirhakah and his force, conveniently to the safety of distant Egypt. See maps, fig. 9A-B.

At this point something happened to Sennacherib's troops, because (even though rid of the Egypto-Nubians, with only puny Gaza against him) he did not reengage against either Gaza or Judah, but set off home instead. Here 2 Kings 19:35-36 speaks of a visitation that brought sudden death to a large part of the Assyrian force. What this was in practice, we do not know — food poisoning or whatever? Sennacherib did not even wait for Hezekiah's tribute before quitting the noxious little province; he himself states that Hezekiah's tribute followed him to Assyria, doubtless the tribute that we see Hezekiah gathering up in 18:15-16. Viewed thus, with careful observance of the features of both the Assyrian and Hebrew texts, a coherent picture of the whole episode emerges. The verses in 18:15-16 simply round off in advance the source of Hezekiah's tribute, almost as a "footnote" to the king's offer and the Assyrian's fixing the rate, early on in the proceedings.[93]

A few other details are worth note in passing. Hezekiah is said to have had to produce 30 talents of gold and 300 talents of silver in the Hebrew account (2 Kings 18:14), but an identical 30 talents of gold and heavier 800 talents of silver in Sennacherib's account; if graphic or transmission errors be not responsible, it may be that Sennacherib at some point demanded more than his first "price" (perhaps in return for not pressing an assault on Jerusalem?). The siege and capture of Lachish (cf. 2 Kings 18:14, 17; 19:8) is not mentioned in Sennacherib's annals — curiously! — but it is the centerpiece to a splendid set of scenes showing the Assyrian forces attacking, then actively pressing their siege to break into Lachish, capture the town, and lead out captives to Sennacherib seated in triumph on his high throne. The mound of Tell ed-Duweir shrouds the remains of ancient Lachish, where excavations have revealed the battered bulk of the Assyrian siege ramp (as shown on the reliefs) up to the walls, plus a Hebrew counterramp within the walls. This city, destroyed by the Assyrians, is Lachish level III archaeologically. Later rebuilt, it became the diggers' Lachish level II, which — again — crashed in flames at the onset of the Babylonians barely 120 years later (cf. sec. H, below).[94]

(ii) The Death of Sennacherib

However, our biblical narratives about this king do *not* stop with the end of his war in the Levant in 701. In 2 Kings 19:37 (and Isa. 37:38) we read that the luckless Sennacherib was murdered by two of his sons, and was succeeded by another, namely, Esarhaddon. This is so; the Assyrian sources (including from Esarhaddon himself) and the Babylonian Chronicle plus later sources confirm the putsch. They mention murder by a son (Babylonian Chronicle) and by sons in the plural (Esarhaddon, Nineveh records); the biblical Adrammelek is a form of Arda-mulissi (the name of Sennacherib's murderous eldest son in contemporary documents), and is the Adramelos of Berossus and Ardamuzan of others; "Shar-ezer" is an abbreviation of the name type (Deity)-shar-usur. So, in one form or another, this sad affair became all too well known in various streams of tradition.[95]

G. JOSIAH'S FATAL MISSION AND THE FALL OF ASSYRIA

At the end of the seventh century the long-hated power of Assyria was at last showing signs of breaking down. Under a new Chaldean dynasty, founded by Nabopolassar, Babylon secured its independence and, with Median allies, could begin to push back Assyria into defending itself instead of dominating others. This led to the fall of Assyria's great cities, of ancient and ancestral Ashur in 614 and of mighty Nineveh itself in 612.

The last Assyrian king, Assur-uballit II, retreated westward to set up government in the venerable city of Harran, to make his nation's last stand. Under its vigorous new Twenty-Sixth Dynasty, Egypt had ceased to be an Assyrian vassal but stood by her as ally. By 610 the new Pharaoh Necho II was marching to his ally's aid; but he and Assur-uballit II retreated west of the Euphrates rather than take on the Medes and Babylonians full face. But the latter seized Harran. So in 609 came the final fling. Necho II marched just once more to his ally's support. But at this point a "bit player" came in. As 2 Kings 23:29-30 records, Josiah of Judah sought to obstruct Necho II, to stop him from reaching Assur-uballit in time to back him up against Babylon and the Medes. But Necho crushed the Judean force, killing Josiah, and swept on up to Carchemish, to rejoin Assur-uballit. However, the Babylonians held Harran and won the day, Assur-uballit fled (perhaps to the mountains of Urartu), and Assyria was no more. So the summer of 609 saw the death both of Judah's brave if reckless king and of the Assyrian empire that he had obviously hated.[96]

Thus the context from the Babylonian Chronicles and the brief entry in the book of Kings combine to give us a fuller picture. And also a more correct one. Before those chronicles were discovered and published, 2 Kings 23:29 was translated so that Pharaoh Necho went up *against* Assyria; but recovery of these documents showed that the rendering "against" was a mistranslation, and "to" (i.e., "to help") was what had been intended.

H. THE NEO-BABYLONIANS TAKE OVER

From 608 to 586 the little Judean kingdom survived, as the Neo-Babylonian Empire replaced that of Assyria. The years 608 to 594 are covered by the Babylonian Chronicle tablets;[97] we still lack the next thirty-seven years in tablets not yet recovered. In the Hebrew record Necho II dismissed Jeho-ahaz in favor of Jehoiakim (who became Babylon's vassal, then rebelled), he being succeeded by his own son Jehoiachin until the new prince was removed by the Babylonians (and exiled to Babylon) in favor of Zedekiah. Zedekiah in turn was a vassal, then rebelled, bringing down Nebuchadrezzar's wrath upon the land, ending the kingdom with the fall and substantial destruction of Jerusalem (in 587/586).

Our principal external source for this brief period is the Babylonian Chronicle until 594, as already noted. Its condensed narrative and datings (via the regnal years of Nebuchadrezzar II) dovetail with the biblical data already mentioned. Thus in 605 Nebuchadrezzar (on his father Nabopolassar's behalf) defeated Necho II of Egypt, taking on the overlordship of the Levant — but had to speed home to Babylon· to assume his crown and throne at Nabopolassar's death. So in 604 he could then return to reinforce his control in the Levant — which was when Jehoiakim of Judah became his full vassal, remaining so for three years (2 Kings 24:1), i.e., during 604/603, 603/602, and 602/601.

Then, about 601, the Judean king changed his mind and rebelled against Babylon (2 Kings 24:1-2). Why? Because in that year, on Egypt's borders, the armies of Egypt and Babylon "inflicted great havoc on each other" (as the Babylonian Chronicle puts it), such that Nebuchadrezzar's forces went back to Babylon so badly mauled that the year 600 was needed for a refit, and even in 599 they could only tackle the Syrian Arabs for a "trial spin." This discomfiture of Babylon lulled the foolish Jehoiakim into thinking that Babylon's day was done, and that he could defy them (and perhaps rely on Egypt for protection).

But finally, in his seventh year (598/597), Nebuchadrezzar could march west for a time of reckoning. Jehoiakim slipped his net, by dying, leaving his son Jehoiachin to face the music. The Babylonian Chronicle notes that Nebuchadrezzar II "besieged the city of Judah [i.e., its capital, Jerusalem], and on 2nd of Adar [15/16 March 597] he took the city and seized the king. A king of his own choosing he appointed (instead), received its massive tribute and sent them to Babylon." The siege is that of 2 Kings 24:10-11.

And on surrendering, Jehoiachin was indeed taken prisoner (24:12). As for massive tribute, 24:13 records that the Babylonians stripped out the temple and palace treasuries in Jerusalem of gold and the rest. Nebuchadrezzar chose his new king of Judah, specified as Zedekiah in 2 Kings. Thus we have available good, mutually complementary, and parallel records.

Of the time of Jehoiakim to Zedekiah, we read in Kings, Chronicles, and Jeremiah of various individuals of whom personal seals and seal impressions ("bullae") are known, and not only from such items recovered through modern trade but also in a firm archaeological context from the destruction of Jerusalem in 586. Of that destruction there is clear evidence both in the northwest quadrant of ancient Jerusalem and in the "City of David" area south of the Temple Mount.

In the former, Avigad found both a massive inner wall and (lower down) an outer wall, with part of a gateway, and of a turret farther west (all belonging to Iron II period). Burnt matter, including also arrowheads both Israelite and foreign by their types, testified to a fierce siege, and (in context) to the final fall of Iron II Jerusalem, as in 586. In the City of David area, analogous destruction of buildings is well attested. The "house of bullae" yielded a series of thus closely dated seal impressions, which confirm the date of those that have come through trade. For such people common to the seals and the mentions in 2 Kings, 2 Chronicles, and Jeremiah, see already above, section 3 (pp. 19-21).[98]

The fall of the kingdom of Judah during 597-586 is illustrated by the archaeology of other sites besides Jerusalem. Most famous is Lachish. Stratum II was destroyed by Nebuchdrezzar's forces along with Azekah (Jer. 34:6-7), after a siege. In a burnt room at the city gate was found a group of ostraca, the "Lachish Letters," which reflect the tense situation before the Babylonian attack; "we cannot see the (fire)-signals of Azekah," writes one correspondent, using the term employed also in Jer. 6:1.

Between 597 and 586 other towns too met their fate, such as Ekron, Timnah, Gezer, Beth-Shemesh, etc.[99] The combined data of texts, seals, and archaeological contexts suffice to indicate the realities behind the Hebrew accounts of the last decade of the kingdom of Judah.

6. THE NATURE OF THE SOURCES: BIBLICAL AND NONBIBLICAL

A. TEXTS: NONBIBLICAL

In the foregoing survey, the two books of Kings have been our principal source in the Hebrew Bible. From Rehoboam and Jeroboam onward, each reign is introduced and concluded in formal fashion; for more information the reader is referred to the writer's sources, namely, the book of the annals (lit. "daily affairs") of the kings of Judah, or of Israel, as the case may be. (Chronicles does much the same.) In other words, our present books of 1 and 2 Kings are not themselves the annals of the twin kingdoms, but are a separate work that drew upon such annals or chronicles; 1-2 Kings are not simply the "bare" history, but an interpretation of it.

But are there comparable writings (whether annals/chronicles or interpretative works) in the rest of the biblical world? In large measure, yes; the so-called Babylonian Chronicle we have heard from already. In fact, Egypt, Mesopotamia, the Hittites, and others offer us important material on this subject.

(i) Mesopotamia, Egypt, and the Hittites

The most famed are the historiographic writings from Sumer, Babylon, and Assyria.[100] The Babylonian Chronicle exists in a series of successive cuneiform tablets for the period from Nabonassar down to Seleucus III, 747-224, but with considerable gaps once filled by tablets now lost to us. It proceeds year by year (with omissions), each annual section ruled off by a line from the next, and beginning with the year date of the reigning king, king by king. This series is noteworthy for its high level of detached objectivity. It records Babylonian defeats and disasters, not just successes; it never invokes deity as "efficient cause" of the events narrated, which gives its entries a "modern" appearance. As Grayson has pointed out, this series is not itself the ultimate chronographic source in Babylonia (any more than was Kings in Judah/Israel), but drew upon a more extensive series of running reports, possibly such as astronomical diaries, that included all manner of information month by month (cf. the Kings mention of more extensive "annals" or daybooks of their kings). He cited the existence of common matter (and expressions) as between the Babylonian Chronicle no. 1 and an Esarhaddon Chronicle and the "Akitu Chronicle," and of additional matter not present in the Babylonian Chronicle but either unique to the Esarhaddon Chronicle or to it and the Akitu one.[101] Such data must have been drawn independently of Babylonian Chronicle no. 1, from a more extensive third source. That situation is amply replicated in the data preserved in the biblical 1-2 Chronicles but is not present in 1-2 Kings, especially details (like the Sukkiyim of 2 Chron. 12:3) known to be authentic from other sources. In such cases the Chronicler clearly drew upon other original sources (or passages in them) not used in Kings.

There are other types of chronicles in Mesopotamia, such as the Esarhaddon Chronicle showing this Assyrian king in a more favorable light than the Babylonian Chronicle does, by omitting episodes unfavorable to Esarhaddon so as to highlight his better side. But themes shared in common are often word-for-word identical; occasional changes appear. This is similar to biblical Chronicles highlighting David's positive achievements, for didactic purposes, but omitting his lapses (except over a census, 1 Chron. 21).

The oldest way of counting the years of kings in Mesopotamia was to name each year after a significant event (a battle, building a temple, etc.), and then to compile lists of year names for back reference. Such lists for successive kings of a dynasty could be summarized into king lists by totaling the number of years for each monarch and listing just their names, reign lengths, and a final total of rulers and years overall. Lists of year names, in principle, formed a rudimentary chronicle, and such compilations may have been the precursors of the later chronicles based on running records of all events deemed noteworthy.[102]

For Egypt we can go back to the beginnings almost directly. As in Mesopotamia, years were first named after events (again, after battles, buildings, festivals, etc.). Lists were evidently kept, and from these a year-by-year chronicle could be kept for administrative purposes. Eventually such a chronicle or annals of Egypt's first five dynasties — from the beginning of the pharaonic monarchy to the height of the Pyramid Age (ca. 3000-2500) — were transferred onto stone monuments, of which fragments have survived, the most famous being the Palermo Stone.[103] Such daybooks were maintained through the centuries (on papyrus), from which annals, etc., could be excerpted and carved on stone. From the Middle Kingdom, under Amenemhat II (ca. 1900), we have just two such stones, fragments of the record of two years in his reign (year numbers are not preserved). These, again, record endowments for temples, tribute from Nubia, army campaigns into the Levant, etc. And, as with the Palermo Stone annals of the Pyramid Age, here too all is expressed in a dry, laconic manner. Precisely as in Mesopotamian running chronicles, deity is never invoked as an active factor.[104]

We come now to the Hittites and Phoenicians. While not strictly annalistic, the Bilingual Edict of Hattusil I (seventeenth/sixteenth century) deals with family history, seeking to secure the succession; it, too, makes no invocation of deity, but merely insists that the proper offerings be maintained.[105] Daybooks and running accounts were evidently kept for commercial purposes by the Phoenician kings; witness Zakir-baal of Byblos taking out his scrolls to look up the past daybooks, to check prices paid by earlier Egyptian envoys for his timbers, in the story of Wenamun.[106]

(ii) Deities Intervene Everywhere!

However, ancient kings had to justify their deeds on high. They were deemed by the ancient peoples to be the go-betweens between the people and those invisible higher powers who seemed inscrutably to rule their world, manifested in the wonders and terrors of nature. The kings had, it seemed, to keep two constituencies happy: their subjects and the gods. Thus the personal annals of specific kings readily gave credit to, or claimed justification by, the role played by invisible powers. In Egypt the Karnak annals of Tuthmosis III give a vivid, straightforward account of his famous Battle of Megiddo, and briefer acounts of his later campaigns up to Phoenicia, Qadesh, and the river Euphrates. But at various points in his otherwise mundane narrative the king mentions (at scattered intervals) going forth at the god Amun's command, or Amun going before him and nerving his arm (while Re encouraged the army), or Amun guarding him in the heat of battle, or the defeated chiefs overawed by Amun. Of the general historicity of the narrative there can be no doubt; these scattered phrases are simply expressions of the king's faith in the justness of his cause, viewed as endorsed by his deity.[107] The same applies to Ramesses II at his notorious Battle of Qadesh. The accounts of Qadesh make no appeal to deity whatever, except for the king's urgent prayer to Amun in his moment of crisis (if we leave aside mere similes).[108]

The Hittite royal annals show a similar situation. For example, the Ten-Year Annals of Mursil II (turn of fourteenth to thirteenth century) give a straight, concise first-person narrative of the king's successive campaigns in his first ten years. At the beginning he invokes the sun goddess of Arinna as his patron; for each year (so far as preserved), Mursil claims in almost stereotyped fashion that he was victorious because the sun goddess, storm god, Mezulla, and the gods went before him. This apart, the gods play almost no direct part in his narrative; just once a lightning bolt struck Ephesus, then a city in Arzawa, which Mursil attributed to divine intervention (middle of Year 3).[109]

In Mesopotamia again, the Assyrian annals of successive kings give itineraries of their campaigns to many places and targets that can be found on our maps. Battles are fought but not always won, as the Assyrians would have us believe (e.g., Qarqar in 853, when the Levantine coalition stopped Shalmaneser III in his tracks). Alongside many conventional descriptions (and statistics that can vary), these campaign reports contain a large amount of good firsthand information. Yet at intervals the Assyrian kings also attribute this or that success to the overwhelming splendor of their god Assur, or of his terrible weapon. In his campaign against Hezekiah of Judah and allies in 701, Sennacherib did just this, "trusting in Assur my lord." That he did so has no bearing whatsoever on the historicity of his main account, successively conquering Phoenicia (except Tyre island), then Joppa and Ekron, and Lachish.[110]

B. TEXTS: BIBLICAL

We return to 1-2 Kings and related texts. Several important points become clear. First, it was common custom for ancient kingdoms (from the third millennium onward) to keep a series of running records for hardheaded, administrative purposes, on a daily, monthly, and annual basis. Naming of years after significant events, and compiling lists of these years with their events, perhaps formed rudimentary chronicles that recorded actual facts and happenings of all kinds. Daybooks became customary, whether called such or not, in the guise of running records as in first-millennium Babylonia, or annotated lists of annual eponym officers in Assyria. From these detailed running series of "annals" a variety of writers could draw, in order to compose their own works on historical matters. Such efforts could vary from such as the Babylonian Chronicle, which gave a compact, objective digest of mainly political events (military campaigns by successive kings, etc.), to more partisan texts as in the Synchronous History (Grayson, no. 21, probably derived from a stela) asserting Assyrian military and moral ascendancy over Babylonia. Or we find "special interest" chronicles, such as the Akitu Chronicle (no. 16), whose author noted years in which the Akitu feast of Marduk was not celebrated in Babylon, along with contemporary events, and the "Religious Chronicle" (no. 17), whose author noted celebration or otherwise of temple feasts and was obsessed with wild animals straying into Babylon (and there killed), among other phenomena.[111]

So too with biblical Kings and Chronicles. These works are not the official annals of Israel and Judah, but they explicitly refer their readers to the official annals or daybooks (Heb. "daily affairs") of the kings of Israel and of Judah. From Wenamun, it is clear that the kings of Byblos in the early eleventh century kept daybooks, incorporating records of past sales of timber to foreign kingdoms such as Egypt. At two removes, the king list of Tyre cited by Josephus after Menander of Ephesus (from the latter's history of Tyre and neighbors) clearly draws upon quite accurate tradition when compared with other evidence. Neo-Hittite kingdoms such as Carchemish, Malatya, and Gurgum maintained their royal traditions, as is implied by their known hieroglyphic texts.[112] Thus there is good reason to credit Israel and Judah with the same practices as everyone else in their world, namely, keeping running records upon which others (such as the authors of Kings and Chronicles) could draw for data in writing their own "special interest" works. To dismiss the references to these "annals" of Israel and Judah is wholly unjustified in this cultural context.

In terms of special interest, 1-2 Kings present a summary of their national history in terms of the loyalty or otherwise of successive rulers to the national covenant with their god, YHWH. It is often called the "Deuteronomic History," which is much too narrow a term, because the same basic covenant is visible in Exodus-Leviticus (set in Sinai) as well as more coherently in Deuteronomy, summarized extremely briefly in the renewal in Josh. 24, and treated as the basis of their recall of the Hebrews to their deity by the "preaching" prophets, symbolized at their peak by such as Isaiah and Jeremiah.[113] And it is too narrow a term because much in the so-called Deuteronomic religious concept is long known in neighboring religions and cultures, going back into the second millennium or beyond. As in the Near Eastern chronicles, the writers of Kings (and Chronicles) had no need to *invent* history; they merely *interpreted* it in terms of the beliefs they sought to express.

Ascriptions of help to deity's intervention in the historical narratives in

Kings and elsewhere in the Old Testament have been too easily dismissed by Old Testament scholars as nothing more than late embellishments added to the text (or invented wholesale) by subsequent theologically minded editors or rewriters. The account of Sennacherib versus Hezekiah is just such a case. The introductory verses of 2 Kings 18:13-16 have purely human actors, very concise. But the longer narrative in 18:17–19:37 includes Hezekiah's appeal to the prophet Isaiah, who delivers an oracle of deliverance from YHWH; Hezekiah taking the Assyrian response to YHWH's temple with prayer; and Isaiah giving an oracle with YHWH's reply of full deliverance. Then, as sequel, "the angel of YHWH" smote the Assyrian army. A discomfited Sennacherib returned to Nineveh. The divine element has been condemned as essentially religious fiction by some. Why, then, do such critics not also condemn the narratives by the scribes of Sennacherib? Have they not been embellished decades later, too? Of the Judean campaign, they write in Sennacherib's name: "In my 3rd campaign, I marched against Palestine ('Hattu'). The fearful radiance of my lordly splendour overwhelmed Luli King of Sidon, and he fled overseas. . . . The utter dread of the weapon of my Lord (god) Ashur . . . overwhelmed his strong cities." Later "in the plain of Eltekeh, (the hostile allies) drew up their ranks against me. . . . Trusting in the god Ashur my Lord, I fought with them and defeated them." This is every bit as theological as the role of YHWH in 2 Kings 18–19 — but it was *not* written up twenty years later, as is charged against the Hebrew text. Its first edition dates to 700, within a twelvemonth of the battles of 701! What is sauce for the goose is sauce for the gander. If Assyrian theological interpretation can be part of their *original* account, then *exactly the same* should apply to the Hebrew text. The point that, in its present form, the Hebrew account carries a brief codicil of twenty years later (2 Kings 19:37), recording the violent death of Sennacherib (in 681), is irrelevant, and has no bearing whatever on the main narrative originating in events of 701. We possess not only Sennacherib's theologically conditioned "first edition" of this campaign from 700, but also his "latest" (known) editions from 691 and 689, a dozen years later. They show no change whatever in their theological slant on this campaign.[114] Thus 2 Kings 18:17–19:36 may be every bit as authentic and early as 2 Kings 18:13-16. The author of the whole held his theological beliefs long before, during, and long after he wrote up that account — just as his Assyrian opposite numbers held theirs before, while, and after composing *their* accounts. The Old Testament scholars got it wrong, through not knowing the actual usage of the epoch; and their view of theological fiction writing, alas, distorts the facts. From Mesopotamia we also have both "secular" and "theologically tainted" reports on the same campaign from separate records. Thus the seventh campaign of Sennacherib was waged against Elam and its new king Kudur-nahhunte, who died shortly afterward. The Babylonian Chronicle no. 1 states the facts in this brief, nontheological form (as I have just done). But Sennacherib in his annals gets theological: "In my 7th campaign, (the god) Ashur my Lord supported me . . . against Elam. . . . At that time, at the command of Ashur my Lord, Kudur-nahhunte, King of Elam, did not (even) survive three months (more), but died suddenly."[115] Ashur did for Kudur-nahhunte, just as YHWH's angel did for Sennacherib's troops, in the eyes of the Assyrian and Hebrew annalists respectively. The chronicle proves that Sennacherib's seventh campaign is no fiction. Thus the ancient writer's theological beliefs in each case have nothing to do with the reality of the events — only with the imputed cause behind the events. So we can no more dismiss 2 Kings 18–19 (even if we believe in neither YHWH nor his angel of death) than the annals of Sennacherib (even though nobody today believes in Ashur!), backed up as they are by the nontheological précis in the Babylonian Chronicle.

In short, the Hebrew narratives in Kings and Chronicles should be treated as impartially and fairly as most properly knowledgeable Assyriologists, Hittitologists, and Egyptologists normally treat the firsthand and fully comparable ancient documents in their domain. Hypercriticism of the Hebrew data is wrong in attitude, methods, and results alike.[116]

C. ARCHAEOLOGY: A PROFILE

Texts are not the only sources, not the only evidence, although they remain the most explicit. The ancient town mounds of Palestine contain their own physical narrative — of layer upon layer of successive human occupations through decades and centuries (even millennia). Each epoch had its own fashions in artifacts (pottery, tools, weapons), architecture, art, burial usages, and the rest. In the last century or more, much skilled work has gone into establishing sequences that can be dated either approximately or closely (depending on circumstances). Alongside the Israel and Judah of the Assyrian and Neo-Babylonian texts (and, therefore, of the Hebrew 1-2 Kings also), it has been possible to establish a profile of material society, and of successive phases of human life (materially, occupation levels, strata) during the entire period. We shall sketch this only briefly, to etch out the more significant "pegs" upon which a profile can be outlined.[117]

(i) Individual Site Profiles, 0-900+ B.C.

Here we shall outline the ups and downs of actual occupation histories of various sites where there are good sequences and one can correlate these "histories" with external, nonbiblical, dated, written records. Biblical references will be omitted except where "outside" written data impose themselves, so to speak. In each case we will go back through time (just as archaeologists dig!) from a fixed baseline. Then the "profile" can be summarized.

(a) Jerusalem

Roman, Herodian, Hasmonean (Maccabean), and Seleucid/Ptolemaic (Hellenistic) Jerusalem back to the conquest of the Persian Empire by Alexander the Great (332-323) is all well attested (artifacts, buildings, tombs; all the classical sources), needing no comment here. Before 330 we have the two hundred or so years of the Persian Empire, when Judah (centered on Jerusalem) was but a province (Yehud) in the satrapy of Ebir-nari ("Trans-Euphrates"), for which traces of buildings, etc., are known, including in the old "City of David" (stratum 9); cf. chapter 3 for this period.[118] Before that time (539) Jerusalem was a heap of ruins, and destruction layers graphically mark the end of its Iron IIB existence (including City of David, stratum 10A) as from the final Neo-Babylonian conquest in 587/586. In level 10A, thus sealed in by destruction debris, finds included seal impressions of characters known from this period (ca. 610-585) in 2 Kings, Jeremiah, etc. (Gemariah son of Shaphan, Berechiah [Baruch] aide to Jeremiah, and others).[119] Strata 12 to 10B run through the eighth-seventh centuries and show (from the late eighth century) a sudden expansion of the city to cover not only the long, narrow City of David but also the hills west of that ancient nucleus, a "maxi-Jerusalem" that lasted some 120 to 140 years to the crash in 586. Clearly an additional population had crowded into the Jerusalem zone. Significantly the kingdom of Israel/Bit-Khumri/Samaria was ended by the Assyrians in 722, with considerable deportations (as they make clear). Seemingly some survivors went south to attach themselves to the Judean capital. Level 13 before all this goes back into the ninth century, and level 14 to the tenth, the reputed date of the united monarchy (cf. chap. 4 below).

(b) Lachish

This site runs parallel to Jerusalem. Its stratum I covers (modestly) the Hellenistic period back into Persian times. In the Persian period a Syro-Persian residency, temple, and new walls and gate were built, replacing the ruins of the Neo-Babylonian conquest of 586. That event brought the final, fiery destruction of city level II; from the gatehouse ruins come the Lachish ostraca, with their remarks about "fire-signals" (as in Jer. 6:1) and princes "weakening the hand" (i.e., morale) of others (as was said of Jeremiah, 38:4). After an interval, level II had been a rebuild of the level III city — the Lachish of Hezekiah and his foe Sennacherib of Assyria. Sennacherib commemorated his storming of Lachish in a famous palace relief. Hezekiah (named by the Assyrians in 701) had fortified and provisioned his cities, and many scores of storage jars exist from this end-of-eighth-century time, bearing the royal stamp *l-mlk,* "Of the King" (cf. our "OHMS"). Before level III and the eighth century, levels IV and V go back through the ninth and possibly the tenth centuries, but dating them any more precisely is currently mere conjecture.[120]

(c) Hazor

We go north into Galilee to a site with a dense, continuous series of occupations. Hazor level I belongs to the Hellenistic period, mentioned under the Maccabees (Hasmonean kings). Level II is of the Persian period, marked by artifacts and tombs. Prior to that, level III was a foreign military outpost, replacing local squatters (level IV) on the ruins of Hazor's last true city, level V. This Hazor perished in fiery destruction (as the remains show) when Tiglath-pileser III devastated Galilee in 733. Further back in the eighth century the prosperous Hazor level VI had been destroyed by an earthquake — precisely what the prophet Amos used to date his book, "two years before the earthquake, when Uzziah was king of Judah and Jeroboam (II) son of Jehoash was king of Israel" (Amos 1:1). These kings overlapped (on our dates) during 776-750, which would fit very well with the dating of the end of Hazor VI (and rebuild in V) at some interval before Hazor V ended in 733. Before Hazor VI (and the eighth century), we have alternating periods of high and low life in Hazor. Jeroboam II's well-appointed level VI had refurbished a seedier level VII. This, in turn, had followed on a splendid level VIII Hazor, whose main building had a royally fine entrance with massive Proto-Ionic capitalled pillars. Back now in the ninth century, this would fit such known builder kings as Omri and Ahab. Before their fresh enterprise there existed a seedier level IX, but it existed in two phases, which pushes us back to the beginning of the ninth century at least. The two-phased level X before it (a new, fortified city in its time) would then have to belong to at least the later tenth century, reputedly the united monarchy period (cf. chap. 4 below).[121]

(d) Dan

Farther north still, Dan complements Hazor. Dan existed in Hellenistic times (from the third century B.C.), being a mere village in Roman times. And back in the Persian period, almost nothing is known (yet). Tell Dan (Iron Age II) level I was the time of Assyrian provincial rule (after Tiglath-pileser III's conquest in 733/732), and this city lasted through the seventh century until nearer 600, when it may have suffered at the hands of the Babylonians. Before all this Dan level II flourished in the main part of the eighth century until 733/732, when its gateway was destroyed in the Assyrian onslaught on Galilee. (Possible earthquake traces would agree with a date under Jeroboam II; cf. Hazor VI, above.) Earlier still, in the ninth to early eighth centuries, level III had been a period of much building, of walls and gates and rebuilding of the supposed *bamah*-sanctuary (Omride Dynasty again?). Level IVA before it (later tenth into ninth century) had the first building of the *bamah*-sanctuary, a complex destroyed by fire, with "wanton destruction" (Biran), such that the rebuild (level III) was needed thereafter. On the dating as required by pottery types, and sequence of dated levels III-II, etc., level IVA and its first religious complex (end of tenth century) would have been the sanctuary established by Jeroboam I, while its destruction was probably the work of Benhadad I of Aram-Damascus, called in by Asa of Judah against Jeroboam I (1 Kings 15:20). Other building works at Dan in the preceding level IVB would take us back reputedly to the united monarchy (chap. 4, below).[122]

(e) Cabul and Its Land

Surveys in Lower Galilee and excavations at selected sites indicate a tenth-to-ninth century occupation with certain types of pottery (Gal 1988/89, nos. 3 and 9), plus the "hippo" jars in the late tenth/early ninth centuries (Alexandre), followed by occupation that used in the eighth century other types (Gal, nos. 6, 10). Gal could establish that of some thirty-six sites flourishing from the tenth into the middle of the ninth century, just over half were destroyed, while the rest continued in use until the late eighth century — nothing much survived into the seventh. Intervention by the Aramean kings of Damascus against Israel (as under Ahab, within 875-853) might well have caused destruction of Galilean settlements (cf. 1 Kings 20; 22). One destroyed permanently then was Khirbet Rosh Zayit (the Cabul of Solomon and Hiram). But the late-eighth-century destruction would, again, be that attested for Tiglath-pileser III in 733/732.[123]

(f) Dor

Here we return south and to the seaside, south from Mount Carmel. Dor, too, had a long history, Phoenicians being its main population from the mid–eleventh century. Again, down to Hellenistic times via the Ptolemies of Egypt and Seleucids of Syria, to be taken by Alexander Janneaus of Judea. Before this, "in the Persian period, Dor continued as the principal port of the Carmel coast" (Stern), of which extensive remains survive. Before this Dor served the Neo-Babylonian conquerors, before whom (605 and following) it may have had relations with Josiah of Judah (Judean weight, area B). In 733/732 our constant companion Tiglath-pileser III had sacked Dor (with others), but it arose again as a port and a local Assyrian governorate until Josiah and the Babylonians. During the ninth and eighth centuries Dor was seemingly under Israelite control, or served as port; traces of structures of this period resemble the work of Omri/Ahab elsewhere. This new phase appears to have followed the destruction (late tenth century, by Egypt's Shoshenq I?) of the previous city, which would (again) in principle bring us back to the united monarchy period.[124]

(g) Gezer

Farther south but inland is the notable strong point of Gezer. Like others, Gezer (strata III-II) is attested in the Hellenistic/Hasmonean period, when it was a walled, defended city. Before that, under the Persians, Gezer level IV is poorly attested (some walls, rich tombs). The place lay desolate after the Babylonian destruction (probably 586) of Gezer level V, which was a modest successor (under the Assyrians and maybe Josiah) to level VI, the city destroyed by (who else!) Tiglath-pileser III, 733/732. This was preceded by level VII (ninth century; new gate and residency), built after the fiery destruction of level VIII — supposedly by Shoshenq I of Egypt, making VIII Solomonic, in the wake of the destruction of a modest level IX (by Siamun of Egypt?) still earlier (but see chap. 4 on these matters). Gezer was not intensively occupied in any of these periods, or since the Philistine period (stratum XII, ending twelfth/eleventh centuries).[125]

(h) Samaria

This site had a limited history in Old Testament times. Herod rebuilt it as Sebaste in honor of Caesar Augustus, before which the Hasmonean king John Hyrcanus had destroyed the essentially Greek settlement of Alexander the

Great. Previously Samaria was the center of the Persian province of that name, just north of Judah (see chap. 3 below). Of Babylonian rule, little is so far known, and not too much under the Assyrians who ended the kingdom of Israel in 722 (Assyrianizing pottery; part of a stela [of Sargon II]). The Babylonian chronicle has that event under Shalmaneser V (like 2 Kings 17), while Sargon II claims credit for finishing the job. The site that the Assyrians stormed is marked by a series of palace buildings in an enclosure. The archaeology has proved difficult, technically. We do have three broad phases. (1) Preroyal, before 880, modest (private) occupation (pottery phases 1 [eleventh-tenth centuries] and 2 [ca. 1000-880]). (2) Royal palace buildings, 880-722 (pottery phases 3-6; building phases I-V). (3) Postroyal, after 722 (pottery phases 7-8; building phases VI-VII, 722-600; VIII, 600-587). A critical review of the disputed inner dating of (2) would suggest dating pottery phase 3 to 875-800 (buildings I-II, Omri/Ahab; buildings III[?], Jehu, Jehoahaz); then pottery phases 4-6 to circa 815-722 (buildings IV[+a], Joash, Jeroboam II; V, down to Hoshea).[126]

(i) Tirzah

Tirzah was the capital of Israel before Samaria, with a longer history in the Old Testament period. Before stray finds of Greco-Roman date, Tirzah (Tell el-Far'ah North) period VIIe (former stratum 1) followed the Assyrian conquest of 722, and was an Assyrian garrison-outpost (using Assyrian-style pottery) during the seventh century. In the sixth, the place declined into a modest affair of local squatters (VIIe1). The phase VIId (former stratum 2) had been a well-appointed town, with the building of an entirely new palace (VIIc), and fine houses, of the ninth/eighth centuries down to the Assyrian destruction of 722 (Shalmaneser V/Sargon II). This dating suggests a revival of Tirzah under Jeroboam II. Before this, early ninth century, VIIc had seen a new start (after destruction of VIIb), with the beginning of a palace, maybe unfinished. The phase VIIb (former stratum III) has been assigned to the tenth/early ninth centuries. It marked a period of renewal and refurbishment but was destroyed. Such a dating suggests that VIIb is the capital of Jeroboam I and successors; its destruction may reflect the rebel Zimri's fiery end (1 Kings 16:18), after which (when Tibni was done with) Omri began a palace at Tirzah before choosing Samaria. Before all this, phase VIIa (former stratum IV) had been a township of the twelfth/eleventh centuries.[127]

(j) Timnah

We now go back southwest, close to Philistia. Tel Batash has been plausibly identified as ancient Timna. It ended (level I) with scanty traces of the Persian period, and possibly of squatters during the Neo-Babylonian domination, after the destruction of the last true "city" of Timna (level II) that had lasted about a century (from ca. 700) until the Babylonians destroyed it probably within circa 605-600. Timnah level III had been a walled city from at any rate the eighth century; it was provisioned with supplies in *l-mlk* ("OHMS") jars before 701, as part of Hezekiah's resistance movement against Sennacherib reported by the latter. In his campaign in 701, Sennacherib boasts of capturing Timnah. He destroyed it only in part: the inner gate, a public building, and the *l-mlk* jar stores. But Timnah survived to live into the seventh century (as level II for us). Level III had two phases (B and A), marked by repairs and/or refurbishment; the famous earthquake of the mid–eighth century (under Uzziah/Jeroboam II) may have been the cause.[128]

(ii) The Resultant Overall Archaeological Profile and Its OT Counterpart

The time has come to bring together the sample of ten individual site "profiles" (only space forbids doing some more!) into an overall picture, and then to compare this archaeological "basic" profile or portrait with the history that was checked against external written sources above.

Table 4 (on p. 58) presents a graphic chart (ca. 1000 to the beginning of the Persian period) of the ten sample sites whose archaeological history was sketched above. In this table, the following abbreviations and symbols are used. UM = reputed united monarchy (specifically David and Solomon's reigns); Reh = Rehoboam; KhRZ = Khirbet Rosh Zayit; Om/Ahab = reigns of Omri and Ahab, and work of their day; Jer II = Jeroboam II's reign, and works of that time; Uzz = Uzziah, similarly; Phoen = time of Phoenician rule; a zigzag line across the columns for Dan, Hazor, Lachish, and Timnah = probable/possible earthquake traces, chronologically linkable with that mentioned in Amos 1:1, within circa 770-760; Assyr = Assyrian rule and/or settlement; Neo-Bb (and/or destr.) = Neo-Babylonian rule (and/or destruction interval); P. Pers. = Persian period. Close, horizontal double lines mark a destruction, and particularly those wrought by enemy forces. Wider sections of columns reflect periods of greater occupation and (usually) prosperity; narrower segments reflect less occupation, and often "poorer" periods. Dotted marginal lines indicate times of abandonment ("gap") or minimal occupation.

Table 4. Individual Site Profiles, ca. 1000-500 B.C.

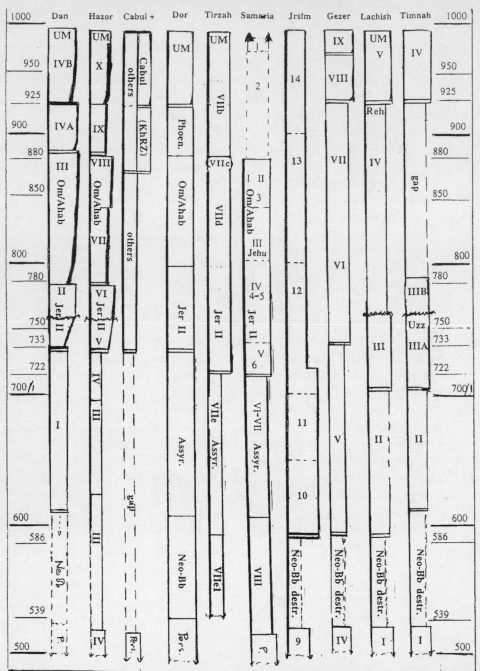

Bearing in mind the actual finds at the sites (in the excavation reports, and official summaries such as appear in *NEAHL* 1-4), which our summaries and chart can only "skeletonize," we begin to see an overall profile. At the end of our sequence, the identity of the Persian-period occupation of sites (539 and following) and earlier of the impact of Neo-Babylonian destruction at various places (and ongoing rule in some) are in both cases established beyond any reasonable doubt. The Babylonian impact was felt during 605 (when they first invaded) down to 586 (end of the Judean kingdom).

Before that period, we have to go back to the late eighth century (733, 722, 701) for explicitly datable archaeological links with external documentary history and chronology. First, in 701 Sennacherib claimed to have destroyed a number of Judean towns, and (in the famous British Museum scene) Lachish in particular. It is clear archaeologically that Lachish city II followed III at an interval, and was the one that Nebuchadrezzar II's forces destroyed, while 115 years earlier it was Lachish III that fell to a massive Assyrian onslaught in 701 (their siege ramp is there "unto this day," as the ancient phrase would run). Lachish III was founded well before that event, at a date not yet established.

Second, in 722 the siege and capture of Samaria (and end of the Israelite kingdom) was achieved in the last year of Shalmaneser V, whose throne and victory were alike usurped by Sargon II (coup d'etat), who brought away a good number of captives and crushed final dissent by 720. Thus the palace-building era at Samaria ended by then. Of those buildings (as currently understood), there were in effect four phases: buildings I/II (and pottery phase 3), the original major works; then III (also pots phase 3); then further work, buildings IV (pottery phases 4-5); and a final, lesser phase V (pots phase 6) by Samaria's fall. This fourfold sequence would correspond to that of (i) Omri and Ahab and dynasty, as founders and main builders; then (ii) to the poorer time of Jehu (afflicted by Arameans and Assyrians); then (iii) to the better times of Jeroboam II and his line; then finally (iv) to the unstable, last kings ending with Hoshea. In the external records, as we have already seen, the sequence Omri, Ahab, Joram, Jehu, Joash (father of Jeroboam II), Menahem, Pekah, and Hoshea is well attested and dated; so the overall sequence at Samaria is thus broadly dated (outside of fine tuning on technical details) during circa 870-720. This has wider impact (see below). But in 722, the end of the northern Hebrew kingdom led to some of its remnant migrating into the surviving southern kingdom (Judah) and to the environs of Jerusalem. It is no accident that Jerusalem suddenly and dramatically expanded in area (onto the western hill) by 700, and stayed large until the Babylonian onslaughts. Here we have a "refugee" reflex of the fall of Israel in 722.

Third, in 733/732 Tiglath-pileser III was actively subjugating and destroying places in Galilee and around. For that time, this activity shows up in a series of destructions in the archaeological record. Dan II perished, and Hazor V was left feet deep in ashes. The surviving series of settlements in Lower Galilee came to a virtually final end, until Persian times. Dor felt the Assyrian impact, but (as a valuable port facility) was able to continue under Assyrian rule, as it did under both earlier and later regimes. The cities that came to an end in 733 had been part of a period of some prosperity before that time — a period (C) which in turn (at times after a lesser interval) had been preceded by another epoch of prosperity (B). (Much earlier was another, "A".) The last such period ("C") fits well that of the line of Jeroboam II; so at Dan II, Hazor VI-V, Dor, Tirzah VIId (latter half), and correspondingly Uzziah's time as at Timnah IIIB/A. In just this period (about mid–eighth century), traces of damage have been noticed in the town ruins of Dan II, dividing between Hazor VI and V, and Timnah IIIB/A (perhaps = end of Lachish IV, start of Lachish III?). Such an earthquake is reported as a casual date line under precisely Jeroboam II and Uzziah in Amos 1:1. This agrees well with the general archaeological dating and possible traces.

Before our prosperity-period C, we have (sometimes) a lesser interval preceded by a prosperity-period B. This earlier period embraces the buildings I/II opening phase at Samaria, of Omri and Ahab. Along with it go the parallel periods of major buildings, etc., at Dan (III), at Hazor (VIII), contemporary Dor, and Tirzah VII"c" (abandoned for Samaria?), etc. In between we have Samaria III and Hazor VII, which probably reflect the less happy times of Jehu.

Finally, before the Omri-Ahab horizon, we are again confronted by two phases of prior occupation history: a "founding" or prosperous one ("A") and an intermediate one after it. Destructions by Shoshenq I of Egypt in some cases divide between the two. This is visible at Dan, IVB then IVA; at Hazor, XA/B then IXA/B; throughout in Lower Galilee (first long phase, including Cabul/Khirbet Rosh Zayit); Gezer VIII, then lesser VII; Timnah IV (prosperous phase, then long gap); and probably Lachish V, then IV (a Rehoboam fort).

As Omri-Ahab begin about 880 (buildingwise, at least), these sometimes multiple phases go through a mere twenty years, well back through the tenth century, toward the pre–Rehoboam/Jeroboam I beginnings of the Hebrew monarchy. This is the general date when the so-called united monarchy of David and Solomon must have ruled, if it existed in any meaningful form. But that belongs to chapter 4. Our case here is merely to exhibit the archaeological sequence of Iron II(B/C) Canaan alongside the external references to that land, and also to the established sequence of rulers in 1-2 Kings that those external sources have validated. See now table 5 on page 61.

Table 5. Outline Correlation of Archaeological Data,
External Written Sources, and Biblical Data

	Archaeological Data	Near Eastern Texts	OT Data
10th cent.: Prosperity and founding Period 'A'	(Dan IVB; Hazor XA/B; Cabul 1st phase 1; Dor; Tirzah VIIb; Gezer VIII; Lachish V; Timnah IV)	(Assyria, not yet in southwest Levant; no foreign sources in Egypt, since Siamun; no Aramean sources yet)	(Reputedly, united monarchy of David & Solomon, see chap. 4; start of twin kingdoms, Israel/Judah)
10th/early 9th cents.	An *intermed. phase A*, starts after a destruction (Shoshenq I?). (Dan IVA; Hazor IXA/B; Cabul 1st phase 2; Dor; Tirzah VII b [cont.]; Rehoboam, Lachish IV?)	Shoshenq I, invasion of Canaan, ca. 926/925. (Assyria not yet in southwest Levant; no Aramean sources yet)	Shishak's (Shoshenq I's) invasion from Egypt. Twin kingdoms bickering; involved with Aram-Damascus
9th cent.: Prosperity phase B	Dan III; Hazor VIII; Dor; Samaria bldgs I/II. *Intermed. phase B*. Samaria III; Hazor VII; others, cont.	*(i)* Omri, Ahab, in texts of Shalmaneser III; Mesha *(ii)* Jehu in texts, cf. Tell Dan and of Shalmaneser III. Texts of Hazael of Aram	Israel under Omri Dynasty; and Mesha of Moab. Jehu removes kings of Israel and Judah; Arameans trouble him, e.g., Hazael
8th cent.: Prosperity phase C	Dan II; Hazor VI-V; Dor; Tirzah VIId; Samaria IV; Timnah IIIB/A; Jerusalem 12. Earthquake, mid–eighth cent.	Adad-nirari III mentions Joash (father of Jeroboam II); Benhadad III on Zakkur stela (Mari of Assyria). Samaria ostraca; seal of Jeroboam II	Period of prosperity, line of Jeroboam II of Israel, and with Uzziah in Judah
Assyrian impact	*733:* end of Dan II, Hazor V, Cabul-area; ctp Dor; Gezer VI *722:* end, Samaria V, Tirza VIId *701:* end, Lachish III; Timnah IIIA	Tiglath-pileser III on Galilee, etc., and re. Menahem, Pekah, Hoshea (and Ahaz in Judah). Fall of Samaria Shalm. V/Sargon II. Sennacherib vs. Hezekiah, and fall of Lachish scene. Bullae of Jotham, Ahaz, Hezekiah	OT reports on Tig.-pil. III in Galilee, Gilead, etc., and on Menahem, Pekah, Hoshea; and Ahaz in Judah. Fall of Samaria. OT reports on Hezekiah vs. Sennacherib
Judah/ Babylon to end	Lachish II; Gezer V; Jerusalem 11-10; Timnah II	Esarhaddon texts; Babylonian Chronicle, to 594; Hebrew seals; Lachish ostr.	OT, to end of Assyria; takeover and conquest by Babylon, 597 and, finally, 586

ON THE RELIABILITY OF THE OLD TESTAMENT

7. THE BALANCE SHEET SO FAR

Now we must step back from all the detail and look at the whole picture so far. For close to 350 years (ca. 930-586) we have taken the series of Hebrew and foreign rulers, as found in 1-2 Kings (and paralleled in 1-2 Chronicles), and examined them and their histories from several angles. With what result? We may enumerate as follows.

a. *Foreign Rulers in the Hebrew Record.* Out of twenty foreign rulers (and a general), all but two (or three?) duly turned up in the external records available to date, usually on their home patch (Assyrians in Assyrian records, etc.). This is a highly satisfactory standard. Of the missing men, the general (Zerah), probably from Egypt, belongs to a period in which knowledge of the Egyptian military is currently close to zero (certainly for foreigners so employed). And Benhadad I (and/or II) came from before 853, when Assyrian records begin for Aram-Damascus, and before we have any local Aramaic historical records whatsoever, so far. Whatever is still in the ground is just not available to us (as was the case with the Tell Dan stela until less than ten years ago).

b. *Hebrew Kings in External Records.* Here the evidence began with Omri and Ahab, coming up to the mid–ninth century. Before that time no Neo-Assyrian king is known to have penetrated the southwest Levant, to gain (or record) knowledge of any local king there. And it was not Egyptian custom to name foreign rulers unless they had some positive relationship with them (e.g., a treaty). Foes were treated with (nameless) contempt. Therefore, under present conditions, we *cannot* expect to find any such mentions (Assyrian or Egyptian) of *any* southwest Levant kings, biblical or otherwise, unless or until an Egyptian treaty were found with one of them or the Assyrians were found to have had some detailed contact as yet unknown, and so unavailable to us currently. Under these conditions a negative knowledge is meaningless.

But from 853 onward we do have some data. Some nine out of fourteen Israelite kings are named in external sources. Of the five missing men, three were ephemeral (Zechariah, Shallum, Pekahiah) and two reigned (Jehoahaz, Jeroboam II) when Assyria was not active in the southwest Levant. And one of these (Jeroboam II) is in any case known from a subject's seal stone. Judah was farther away than Israel, so the head count is smaller: from Jehoram I to Zedekiah we have currently mention of eight kings out of fifteen. Of the seven absentees, Uzziah is not certainly mentioned in Assyrian records, but he is known from his subjects' seals. Amaziah reigned during Assyrian absence from the southwest Levant; Jotham came before Ahaz invited the Assyrians back, but is known from a bulla of Ahaz. Amon and Jeho-ahaz were ephemeral, while Josiah reigned during the Assyrian decline, without documentation by them of

Levantine kings. But seal impressions and possibly an ostracon come from his time.

c. *Local Records, Hebrew, etc.* Some have been cited already; kings Joram I (and II), Ahaziah II, Uzziah, Jeroboam II, Hoshea, Jotham, Ahaz, Hezekiah, are all known from seals and bullae, etc.

d. *Sequences of Rulers; Chronology.* The time-line order of foreign rulers in 1-2 Kings, etc., is impeccably accurate, as is the order of the Hebrew rulers, as attested by the external sources. As for chronology (dates B.C.), the elaborate date lines in 1-2 Kings show a very high degree of consistency and reliability (tying in with external dates) when they are given proper study in terms of their own, ancient Near Eastern world and are treated in accordance with the well-established norms and usages of that world; remaining problems are very few, and can be left to future research.

e. *The Course of History, in External and Biblical Sources.* Here were examined some ten different episodes that are attested both in the Hebrew text and in the contemporary external sources, on the basis of all the available data. In each case, when the total data had been collated, and careful distinction made between genuine overlaps from both sides and the complementary and additional data contributed by each lot of sources (biblical and external), a clear result emerged whereby repeatedly we gained a fuller, richer picture of the whole episode. There were no glaring errors, but certainly propaganda in some cases (more on the Near Eastern side).

f. *The Nature of the Sources.* The sources themselves show clear affinities in the kind of records used. Ancient kingdoms (large and small) *did* maintain running records (daybooks, etc.), exactly as were the annals (or daybooks) of Israel and Judah that are regularly cited as references by Kings and Chronicles. Scholars who would cavalierly dismiss such references are out of touch with the usage of three millennia (from the Palermo Stone to the Seleucid Babylonian chronicles), and thus go badly astray in their assessments of the origin and nature of the contents of Kings and Chronicles. Those two works are not themselves the annals of Israel and Judah, but are "special interest" works based on the original annals/daybooks, now lost to us exactly as in Egypt, Mesopotamia, and everywhere else. What *has* survived in the rest of the ancient Near East, as in Kings and Chronicles, is a series of special interest works that have drawn upon the running records. Those works include, e.g., the monumentalization in stone of parts of the Egyptian annals in the Old and Middle Kingdoms (Palermo Stone; annals extract of Amenemhat II), and of data from Tuthmosis III's Levant campaign daybooks in the New Kingdom, and the existing variety of chronicles from Mesopotamia, etc. By and large, the ancients did not *invent* spurious history, but normally were content to *interpret* real history, in accord with their views. This is true right across the board, as in the full range of Egyptian, Hittite, and Mesopotamian war reports, etc., and in West Semitic inscriptions. Once detected, the viewpoint can be "peeled back" if need be and the basic history made clear, especially when we have multiple sources, from more than one vantage point. Thus, reading Kings and Chronicles is (or should be) no different from reading the Battle of Qadesh of Ramesses II, the Hittite treaty prologues and royal annals, or Assyrian war and building inscriptions. From the Moabite Stone we (as neutral historians, the only legitimate variety!) can set aside the credits given to Kemosh by Mesha, but we ignore his positive statements on wars and buildings at our peril. We may not believe in Amen-Re of Egypt or the storm god of Hatti, or in the effulgence of Ashur, but the military or other acts of a Tuthmosis, Mursil, or Shalmaneser must be assessed in their own right. Again, if one lays aside (as a secular historian) the credits given to YHWH in Kings and Chronicles, one may still read off the basic facts about wars, buildings, and the rest precisely as in the rest of the Near East, where these compositions are concerned. Overall, "Deuteronomists" and Chronicler(s) interpreted their people's history, they did *not* need to make it up — the available data were ample for their purpose without need of such subterfuge.

g. *So what?* Therefore at this stage, and without prejudice as to what may yet be seen elsewhere, the basic presentation of almost 350 years of the story of the Hebrew twin kingdoms comes out under *factual* examination as a highly reliable one, with mention of own and foreign rulers who were real, in the right order, at the right date, and sharing a common history that usually dovetails together well, when both Hebrew and external sources are available. Therefore we have no valid reason to cast gratuitous doubt on other episodes where comparable external data are currently lacking, either because the records are long since destroyed or are still buried in the ground. All such episodes should be taken seriously, assessed objectively as to their nature, and compared with analogous material before passing judgment. They are likely to contain valuable information that we cannot afford to throw away but need to be able to use in writing wider history.

CHAPTER 3

Home and Away — Exile and Return

Already, in the last 150 years of the divided and Judean monarchies, we have seen through Assyrian eyes (besides biblical ones) the imposition of exile — removal from their homeland — of people(s) rebellious against their would-be overlords. Tiglath-pileser III removed people from Galilee and environs in the 730s; Shalmaneser V and Sargon II between them sent away many Israelites to eastern lands in 722-720; and Sennacherib did this to Judah in 701. Tiglath-pileser III took 13,520 people (totaled from lesser amounts — 226, 400 + x, 656, and [lost]).[1] Then Sargon II boasts of having removed 27,290 (var. 27,280) people from Samaria.[2] And in 701 Sennacherib claimed to have reduced forty-six of Hezekiah's walled towns and to have taken 200,150 people from them.[3] Such measures did not necessarily depopulate a given region entirely, and some Assyrian kings brought in new populations from elsewhere (Sargon II and 2 Kings 17; contrast Tiglath-pileser III). But the "Assyrian exile" of both Israelites and Judeans was considerable — and in the former case, permanent. As we shall see (cf. chap. 6), neither the concept nor the practice of "exile" even began with these later Assyrian kings. It was already a millennially old tradition, into which the Babylonian exile of the Judeans merely fits as one more such episode in a very long series, taking the long-term historical perspective.[4] The difference is the close-up impact that the Judean exile to Babylon makes upon the modern reader, particularly in 2 Kings and Jeremiah.

1. THE PERIOD OF THE EXILE

A. EN ROUTE TO BABYLON

(i) The Biblical Accounts

These are 2 Kings, 2 Chronicles, Jeremiah, and allusions in Ezekiel and Daniel. They have Nebuchadrezzar (II) of Babylon taking over the Levant, ousting the king of Egypt (cf. 2 Kings 24:1, 7), having Jehoiakim of Judah as a vassal (cf. 2 Chron. 36:6-7, a threat of exile, not fulfilled), and taking away selected personnel and goods (cf. Dan. 1:1-7) in 605/604. Then, three years later (by 601), Jehoiakim rebelled against Babylon (2 Kings 24:1). He did not live to witness Babylonian retribution. That fell upon his youthful son and successor, Jehoiachin, whom Nebuchadrezzar carried off to Babylon (597) with his family, his courtiers and officials, and 10,000 other ranks that included 7,000 soldiers and 1,000 craftsmen and artisans (and much loot), leaving only the rural population behind (2 Kings 24:10-16; 2 Chron. 36:10; Jer. 24:1; 52:28, citing 3,023 people). His uncle Zedekiah learned nothing from all this, but in turn rebelled (in conjunction with Hophra of Egypt, Jer. 44:30; cf. 37:5), only to bring down the wrathful Babylonian king again upon Jerusalem, who seized and destroyed that city (in 587/586), carrying away the remnant of its inhabitants, 832 people; cf. 2 Kings 25:1-21; 2 Chron. 36:17-20; Jer. 39:1–40:6; 52:1-27, 29. Finally Nebuchadrezzar's appointee governor, Gedaliah, was murdered by a dissident party (2 Kings 25:22-26), which led to further punishment and 745 more exiles, four years after Jerusalem's fall (Jer. 52:30), in 582. Ezekiel dated various of his visions by years-of-exile of Jehoiachin (Ezek. 1:2 and passim). Finally, thirty-seven years after the young king was carried into captivity in 562, Nebuchadrezzar II's successor, Awel-Marduk ("Evil-Merodach"), released Jehoiachin from arrest and gave him a palace food allowance (2 Kings 25:27-30). So far, the biblical data.

(ii) External Background

The series of Babylonian invasions of the Levant from 605 down to 594 (after which date, the records are lost) is well attested, if in brief form, in the Babylonian Chronicles.[5] The chronicle recounts the Babylonian victory at Carchemish (in 605; British Museum 21946 = Chronicle 5) that enabled Nebuchadrezzar to oust Egypt from the Levant, chasing Egypt's forces to the region of Hamath and beyond and taking over "the whole area of the Hattu-land" (= Syria-Palestine).

The death of Nabopolassar compelled Nebuchadrezzar to race back to Babylon to secure his throne, before returning to Syria-Palestine to enforce his rule and "take the massive booty" back to Babylon (as in Dan. 1:1ff.). Then in his first to third years (604-602), Nebuchadrezzar returned each year to levy tribute and (in Year 2, 603) to besiege a city (name lost). But in Year 4 (601) Egypt and Babylon clashed in battle with such severe losses to both sides that the Babylonian army had to stay at home for a full refit the next year (600), with light skirmishes the next year (599). Thus, as 2 Kings 24:1 states, after three years as vassal to Babylon, Jehoiakim of Judah rebelled — evidently after the clash of 601. Hence, of course, Nebuchadrezzar's determined reaction in his seventh year (598/597), when he "marched to the Hattu-land [Levant], besieged the city of Judah [Jerusalem], and captured the king" (by now, Jehoiachin, Jehoiakim having died). The young man was exiled to Babylon, as the chronicle reports that instead Nebuchadrezzar "appointed a(nother) king of his own choice" (= Zedekiah) and "received its (Judah's) heavy tribute, and sent (it) to Babylon," in agreement with the report in 2 Kings 24:13. The chronicle reports further visits to the Levant by Nebuchadrezzar in his eighth, tenth, and eleventh years (597 to 594), levying tribute regularly.

For the numbers of Judeans exiled by Nebuchadrezzar II (especially in 597 and 586), we have no Babylonian statistics so far — only the Hebrew figures in 2 Kings 24:14, 16 and Jer. 52:28-30. But these (7,000, 1,000, 3,023, 832, 745 people) are entirely consistent in scale with the range of figures for deportations from Israel practiced earlier by the Assyrian kings (cf. just above). Two facts here are worthy of comment: the relative modesty of almost all these figures compared to what the total populations of Israel/Samaria and Judah/Jerusalem would have been; and the status of the people taken away, and those left behind. The idea that the Babylonians carried *everybody* from both Jerusalem and Judah off to Babylon is true neither archaeologically nor to the biblical text itself. In the Hebrew accounts, we read that "the poorest people of the land were left (behind)" for 597 (2 Kings 24:14), and that "the commander [i.e., Nebuzaradan] left behind some of the poorest people of the land, to work the vineyards and fields" (2 Kings 25:12; Jer. 52:16). In other words, the land of Judah became in effect an imperial estate, to be cultivated for the profit of its conquerors by the local food-producing community (farmers and pastoralists). Precisely such procedures had been followed by Egypt's New Kingdom pharaohs nearly a millennium before this, and in turn by the Assyrians. Empires were not run just to give ancient kings militarily glorious ego trips, but to yield revenue! See further below. Nebuzaradan (also in Jer. 39:11-13) is known from the Babylonian "court list" as Nabu-zer-iddin, a high officer of Nebuchadrezzar's administration.[6]

The status of the people taken away to Babylon (royalty and the court, army personnel, artisans; cf. 2 Kings 24:14, 16) is significant, and very readily paralleled from the external sources. Exiled were: (a) the rebel king and his governing circle, as prisoners/hostages to be kept out of mischief, when not summarily executed (as in 2 Kings 25:18-21 = Jer. 52:24-27); (b) military personnel, to be conscripted into the imperial army; and (c) "useful" people, artisans and craftsmen, musicians, cultivators, etc., to be redeployed in the conqueror's service.

Regarding exiled rulers, 2 Kings (25:27-30) ends with Jehoiachin in Babylon being released by Awel-Marduk at his accession (562) into the court circle in Babylon, and being given his own regular allowance. This happened not for the first time, and he is not the only such person, as original Babylonian sources make clear. From a vaulted building closely adjoining the royal palace proper came a series of cuneiform tablets dated to the tenth to thirty-fifth years of Nebuchadrezzar II (595-570), being "ration tablets" for people kept or employed in Babylon and its palace. Among the beneficiaries in receipt of oil were "Jehoiachin king of Judah" (just once, "king's son of Judah") and "the 5 sons of the king of Judah in the care of (their guardian?) Qenaiah" (cf. fig. 10C). Thus the exiled young king and his infant children were already on a regular allowance in Nebuchadrezzar's time (one tablet is of Year 13, 592), but under the palace equivalent of house arrest. They were not the only royalties there at that time; oil was issued to "2 sons of Aga, king of Ascalon."[7]

As for the second category of exiles, redeployed military personnel, we go back briefly to Assyrian precedent. Tiglath-pileser III may have taken Israelite troops into service by 732; Sargon II conscripted Israelite chariots from fallen Samaria very explicitly, as from other defeated small states. This precedent was followed thereafter by other Mesopotamian rulers (e.g., Assurbanipal), hence too by Babylon.[8]

For the redeployed craftsmen, etc., we return to the Babylonian ration tablets cited for Jehoiachin. Here we meet a series of men of different origins and occupations. With Jehoiachin and family were Shelemiah a gardener and others untitled. From Philistine Ascalon came 3 sailors, 8 leaders, and an unknown number of chiefs of musicians. From Phoenicia, 126 Tyrians and $x \times 100 + 90$ Tyrian sailors; 8 carpenters hailed from Byblos and 3 from Arvad. From the east a leader, refugee, and 713 other men had come from Elam, plus 1 Mede and 4 Persians. From the far northwest in Anatolia, more sailors and carpenters were deployed to the boathouse or shipyard; from the far southwest, a large group of Egyptians included sailors, leaders, guards, and a keeper of monkeys! All on Nebuchadrezzar's payroll.[9] This is typical of the motley variety of people who were sucked into the central service and economy of the Assyrian and Neo-Babylonian empires alike. Being exiled to Nineveh or Babylon was not a purely Hebrew hazard!

On the greatness of Babylon as redeveloped by Nebuchadrezzar II (cf. Dan. 4:30) we can be brief. It had become a large city (by ancient standards), straddling the river Euphrates, its two parts linked by a bridge. The maximum width of both parts was about 3.5 kilometers (just over 2 miles) wide (west to east), and the north-south extent (omitting suburbs) about 2.5 kilometers (some 1½ miles), all surrounded by massive defense walls, pierced by named gates. The western part was the "new city." The heart of the city extended along the east bank of the Euphrates, from the "North Palace," museum, and royal gardens (origin of the "hanging gardens") to the main or "South Palace" adjoining the splendid Ishtar Gate, brilliant in deep blue tiles with alternating figures of dull yellow bulls and white and dull yellow lions and dragons. From there the long Processional Way ran straight as a die near to the south end of the city, separating off the palaces, the "tower of Babel," and main temple of the god Marduk from the main bulk of the old city, with its houses, bazaars, squares, many streets, a canal, and various temples. Compared with the towns of Palestine, it would have seemed a vast metropolis to anyone coming in from the Levant.[10] Cf. fig. 10A-B.

B. A REMNANT IN JUDEA

While the main groups of exiled Judeans were finding new employ in Babylon and still very sore about it (cf. Ps. 137), the rural population in Neo-Babylonian Judea had to become productive taxpayers for the new administration. For this purpose Nebuchadrezzar had appointed as local governor Gedaliah son of Ahikam, son of Shaphan (Jer. 40:5-6), with headquarters at Mizpah, now generally conceded to have been the modern Tell en-Nasbeh (in Benjamin) about eight miles north of Jerusalem.[11]

Among the clutch of late Judean seals and bullae of owners attested under kings Jehoiakim to Zedekiah (cf. p. 21 above), we have two men Gedaliah, either of whom may well have been our Gedaliah. One was "Servant of the King," the other was a high steward "who is over the house/estate." Most scholars prefer identification of the biblical Gedaliah with the high steward; this is not certain, but certainly possible.[12] As for Mizpah/Tell en-Nasbeh, restudy of the site-reports and records suggests that the Iron II town was internally redeveloped to become the Neo-Babylonian administrative center for Judea, as a Neo-Babylonian and Persian level can now be distinguished. The old outer gate was kept, but a stretch of old wall and inner gate were done away with, and large new buildings constructed.[13] This may well have been done by Gedaliah with Babylonian support during his brief four-year regime. That ended in his murder by jealous rivals (Jer. 40:7–41:15), egged on by Baalis, king of Ammon, for whom we also have a seal impression and the seal of one of his subjects.[14] So this dossier gives us some background for Judah becoming an economic unit early in the "exilic" period.[15]

C. IN EGYPT

Finally, some of the Judeans fled to Egypt, to escape Babylonian domination, and feared revenge in the wake of the murder of Gedaliah (Jer. 41:16–43:7), taking an unwilling Jeremiah with them. Their stopping point at Tahpanhes (Jer. 43:7ff.) had brought them to a fort of Psammetichus I, established for a garrison of Greek mercenaries, known to Herodotus as Daphnai. This name appears in modern Arabic Tell Defenneh. Tahpanhes is Egyptian: *Ta-ha(t)-pa-nehesi,* "The mansion of the Nubian/Panehsi," not yet known in Egyptian inscriptions, but it is attested in Phoenician (spelled as in Hebrew) from a sixth century B.C. papyrus found in Egypt. This document is a letter that invokes "Baal-Zephon and the gods of Tahpanhes."[16] Jeremiah's prophecy (44:30) of Pharaoh Hophra's coming untimely end was fulfilled when he was supplanted by Amasis II in 570, losing his life in consequence.[17] His further threat (Jer. 43:8ff.) that Nebuchadrezzar would invade Egypt, even hold court at Tahpanhes, may possibly have been fulfilled in 568, to judge from a fragmentary text that alludes to the thirty-seventh year of Nebuchadrezzar II, marching against Egypt for battle, seemingly against "[King Ama]su," i.e., (Amas)is II.[18] The continuing presence of Jews in Egypt is attested under Persian rule, in the late sixth and the fifth/fourth centuries B.C., as we shall see. Thus the people of Judah ended up in three different locations by about 580 — the elite and "useful" people in Babylon; the ordinary working people still in Judea; and sundry fugitives in Egypt.

2. THE EPOCH OF THE RETURN

A. BIBLICAL DATA

(i) Sources, Biblical

The biblical data that reflect the fall of Babylon to Cyrus of Persia in 539 and the Persian dominion down through the late sixth into the fifth/fourth centuries are (in explicit terms) basically the books of Ezra (from which 2 Chronicles took its closing colophon), Esther, and Nehemiah. The transfer of power from Babylon (in the person of Belshazzar) to Cyrus is also mirrored in Daniel. (Belshazzar: Dan. 5; 7:1; followed by Darius the Mede [Year 1 only]: 5:31; 6:1ff.; 9:1, who is paralleled by Cyrus the Persian in 6:28; Cyrus: Year 3, in 10:1.) Some genealogies in 2 Chronicles come down into the Persian period.

In the first part of Ezra (1–6) we have an outline of events from the accession to power of Cyrus of Persia (539) down to completion of rebuilding the temple at Jerusalem in the sixth year of Darius I (516); within this section is an insert (4:6-23) on outside interference against the Jews' attempt to renew the walls of Jerusalem, not just work on the temple. This happened early in the reigns respectively of Xerxes and Artaxerxes (I). The second part of the book (7–10) records Ezra's mission (in the seventh year of Artaxerxes [I]) to regulate the life of the Judean community in accord with their traditional Law — of YHWH to them, and of "the God of Heaven" in "Persian-Kingspeak." The book includes summary registers of returnees both of Cyrus's time and of Ezra's visitation.

The book of Nehemiah follows on from all this. In Year 20 of Artaxerxes (I), Nehemiah got word of Jerusalem's problems, with vandalized gates and walls, and sought his sovereign's permission to sort matters out. The king granted his cupbearer full facilities and the governorship of the district of Judah. Thus, on completion of the wall, Nehemiah and the veteran Ezra held appropriate ceremonies, sought to build up the city's population by bringing in new residents from the other Judean settlements, and sought further to encourage the people to live by their traditional Law (on Sabbath observance, mixed marriages, etc.). During his building work, Nehemiah had three foes among his neighbors: Sanballat, governor of the Samaria district to his north; Tobiah, the Ammonite, from just east, across the Jordan; and Geshem (or Gashmu), the Arabian, to his south. The latest date in his book is most likely the mention (Neh. 12:22) of the time of a king "Darius the Persian," in relation to records of priestly and Levitical families under the high priests from Eliashib to Jaddua (cf. for these, Neh. 12:1, 10; Ezra 2:36; 3:2), running down to Darius II.

In between the time of Darius I (with the temple's completion) and that of Artaxerxes I (restoring city walls and rule of ancient law) comes the reign of Xerxes, the setting of the book of Esther. This is set entirely within the Persian court in the palace of Susa, in what had been northernmost Elam, east from Babylonia. Going back in time, the transplanted people in Syria and others in Judea (Ezra 4:2, 10) harked back to Esarhaddon and Assurbanipal of Assyria.

(ii) Places

Quite a few have turned up, in outlining the biblical sources. The returning Jews had set forth from Babylon in the east but had lived in other districts — Tel Melah, etc., Ezra 2:59; the series of "Tel" names may reflect settlement of Jewish captives on abandoned terrain. Ezekiel long before mentioned the river Chebar (Ezek. 1:1; etc.), the Kabaru of the Murashu archives. Esther became a queen in Susa to the east; her sovereign's empire of 127 provinces extended from India in the east to (Egypt and) Kush in the west. Her mentor was a Jewish palace official, Mordecai; we read of banquets, daybooks of the realm. The temple decree by Cyrus had to be tracked down to Ecbatana in Persia (Ezra 6:1-2). Back in Palestine, besides Jerusalem and Samaria, we have listings of places in Judea when the returnees settled: Anathoth, Bethel, Gibeon, Netopha, Jericho, etc. (Ezra 2:21-35 paralleled by Neh. 7:26-38; further listing, Neh. 11:25-35).

(iii) Usages

Cyrus is seen consciously reversing his Babylonian predecessors' policy, by restoring symbols of deity (and adherents) to their home sanctuaries, as in Ezra 1:1-4. Both he and Darius (latter, 6:2-12) are shown giving support to local temple and cult, as at Jerusalem. We are shown incessant communications via letters to and from the imperial court, and issue of appropriate royal decrees, in part cited in Aramaic (4:8–6:18; 7:12-26).

B. THE NEAR EASTERN SETTING

(i) Sources

For all its vastness, and its immense impact in ancient history, we possess only very uneven original and allied sources for the Persian Empire.[19] Most familiar to Western readers are the accounts given by Herodotus, in his famous *Histories* — of great value, but much of it necessarily at second hand.[20]

We still have the Babylonian Chronicles, laconic but invaluable so far as they go. The Persian kings themselves left a series of official royal inscriptions (particularly at Persepolis) written in Old Persian, in its special cuneiform syllabary; best known is the Behistun inscription on a towering cliff face. In Babylonia, a series of business records, etc., from everyday life preserves regnal dates and contemporary customs. At Persepolis, from the treasury and the northeast fortification wall have come large series of administrative tablets written in Elamite cuneiform, being part of the accounts of the palace complex there, during the reigns of Darius I to Artaxerxes I. And from the west in Egypt we have a long series of Aramaic papyri and ostraca, the greater part hailing from archives of the Jewish community based on Elephantiné Island (close by Aswan) below the First Cataract of the Nile. Other finds come from Hermopolis in Middle Egypt and from Saqqara (cemetery of Memphis) in the north, plus an unprovenanced postbag and its leather scrolls. From Palestine come the Wadi Daliyeh papyri of the fourth century and various ostraca.[21]

(ii) The Historical Framework

The major rulers of the later Babylonian and Persian empires that touch on the biblical record can be tabulated simply, as follows.

Table 6. Neo-Babylonian and Persian Rulers in OT and External Sources

Late Neo-Babylonian, OT	Late Neo-Babylonian, other	B.C.
Belshazzar	Nabonidus (plus son, Bel-shar-usur as deputy)	(556-539)

Persian Empire (OT)	Persian Empire, other	B.C.
Cyrus (+ Darius the Mede)	Cyrus (II)	(539-530)
—	Cambyses (II)	(530-522)
	(and brief usurpers	[522])
Darius I	Darius I	(522-486)
Xerxes ("Ahasuerus")	Xerxes	(486-465)
Artaxerxes I	Artaxerxes I	(465-424)
Darius (II) the Persian	Darius II	(424-405)
(No more rulers mentioned)	(Artaxerxes II — Darius III	[405-331])

Most of this is self-explanatory, and shows overall correspondence. In the late Babylonian empire Nabonidus was largely an absentee ruler, spending ten of his seventeen years far, far southwest of Babylon (about 450 miles) in and around Teima in northwest Arabia, and returning barely a year or so before Babylon's fall in 539. During that long span, circa 550-540, the effective ruler in Babylon was in fact his son Belshazzar, as local documents attest, wherein oaths are sworn in the names of both men. Without actually having the title of king in official usage, Belshazzar enjoyed the powers, for (as one cuneiform chronicle has it) his father had in practice "entrusted the kingship into his hand." Thus it is (as often remarked) understandable that (in Dan. 5:7, 29) Daniel was reputedly offered the third- and not the second-highest place in the kingdom by Belshazzar — who was himself but second. In that same passage Belshazzar is, with almost mock obsequiousness, called "son" of his "father" Nebuchadrezzar (if one translates literally) — but this is a left-handed compliment, contrasting the prince with his (and his own father's) far more illustrious predecessor. Usurpers or indirect successors (and Nabonidus was not a direct successor of Nebuchadrezzar) often liked to claim a greater predecessor as an ex officio "father." (In Egypt, Sethos II was flattered by a correspondent as having Ramesses II [his grandfather] as his "father.") Darius the Mede (as such) is an ephemeral figure (only in Year 1), and bracketed directly with Cyrus the Persian (Dan. 6:28); here the simplest and best analysis is that the two are the same.[22]

In the Persian series, the would-be usurpers (Gaumata and the like) do not appear in the biblical accounts, as they were only ephemeral figures, usually far from Palestine. Nor does Cambyses, whose short reign saw no particular incident affecting the Jews in Judea. The main series of the Old Testament's Persian kings corresponds clearly and directly with the well-known emperors of the firsthand records and of Herodotus. Ezra's visitation in Year 7 of Artaxerxes I would fall in 458, the twelve-year governorship of Nehemiah of Years 20-32 of the same king in 445-433, and his second visit in about 432 (no lower limit given). Alternative interpretations for these dates have often been suggested, but fail to account any better for the total evidence.[23]

Of the lesser rulers that opposed Nehemiah, some evidence is known, even well known. Sanballat the Horonite, governor of Samaria, is now known to have been Sanballat I (first of three governors of this name, the second being named in the Wadi Daliyeh papyri, and a probable third by Josephus). He occurs as governor of Samaria and father of two sons, and is appealed to for help by the Jews in Elephantiné in Year 17 of Darius II in 407.[24] Tobiah the Ammonite was an early member in a long line of Tobiads established in Transjordan, west from Rabbath-Ammon. In the third century B.C., burial caves were used at 'Iraq el-Amir, next to which the name Tobiah was engraved in large Aramaic lettering; the family had dealings with Zeno in Ptolemaic Egypt, and about 180 B.C. Hyrcanus of this family built the magnificent structure (Qasr el-'Abd; a palatial residence?) still to be seen at 'Iraq el-Amir.[25] Nehemiah's third foe, Geshem the Arabian, turns out to have been a king of Qedar in northwest Arabia. In a small pagan sanctuary in Wadi Tumilat, in Egypt's East Delta, were found some splendid silver bowls, one being inscribed in Aramaic: "What Qaynu son of Geshem, King of Qedar, brought in offering to (the goddess) Han-ilat." The script, along with the finding of Greek coins of the fifth to early fourth centuries B.C., indicates a date of about 400 for this bowl, and the time of Qaynu; so his father Geshem may well have reigned in the 440s/430s as a foe of Nehemiah. A Geshem (as "Jasm") of some importance occurs in the date line with one ʿAbd, governor of Dedan, in an inscription at Dedan (Al-ʿUla); this is perhaps also our man.[26] So each of Nehemiah's opponents is attested from documents close to him in time, or by descendants in Tobiah's case. See, e.g., figs. 11A, B, C.

(iii) Places

In the East, some places are well known while others are not. Susa, location of a Persian palace in Nehemiah (1:1) and Esther (1:2; etc.), has been the site of much excavation by French expeditions. There the once-splendid buildings include a palace built by Darius I and Xerxes, and another of Artaxerxes I. Brilliant glazed tiling showed warriors at the entrance and lions in the outer court. Three great courts lay between the pillared audience-hall to their north and the large suites of royal apartments to their south, including inner halls or courts. Surviving Persian metalwork in gold, silver, etc. hints at the sumptuous wealth once found there.[27] Ecbatana was originally the capital of Media, then of that land as a Persian province; it is largely undug, but a variety of finds have come from its mound amidst modern Hamadan.[28]

In the West, in Palestine, many places listed in Ezra and Nehemiah are either not securely identified with present-day sites or have not been dug (or cannot be) — through no fault of theirs! And conversely, we have numerous sites in Palestine that show attested Persian-period remains or occupation, many of which find no mention in our two authors or are unidentified either in the Bible or in other sources. However, quite a number in Ezra-Nehemiah are also attested for this period archaeologically.[29]

(iv) Usages

The books of Ezra, Nehemiah, and Esther show the Persian Empire "at work," and its early rulers vigilant in securing their authority by (positively) supporting a "local" cult such as that of YHWH in Jerusalem (Ezra 1:2-4; 6:1-12; 7:12-26), or by (negatively) restraining the building of city defense walls, if it presaged even a hint of rebellion (cf. 4:8-22). Letters of safe conduct, like passports, could be issued (Neh. 2:7). Communication was by letter through couriers (e.g., Esther 3:15; 8:10, 14), between all parts of the empire and the effective capitals at

Susa and Babylon, besides the great ritual center at Persepolis and the old Median capital at Ecbatana. The royal administration and all such letters were conducted in Aramaic, already the current language in Syria-Palestine and Mesopotamia; hence, its use in several citations from official correspondence in Ezra 4–7. Versions were put into local languages as needed; cf. Esther 3:12; 8:9.

All of this has long been attested from a variety of documents, both in the sixth to fourth centuries and even surviving long afterward. Religion was the background and "social cement" in all communities in the ancient Near East throughout its early history. Support for a community's cult(s) was a sure way to gain its loyalty, and the Persian emperors were quick off the mark to secure their rule over the vast domains they inherited from Babylon and Media by this means. Thus, as a matter of propaganda, Cyrus ostentatiously sent back the images of the gods that Nabonidus had gathered (for safety from Cyrus's attack!) into Babylon, to their home temples throughout Babylonia, and he and his son Cambyses took care to involve themselves in the cult of Marduk, god of Babylon, the very year they gained power there.[30]

Up in Asia Minor, we have two examples of imperial involvement in local religion and cults. First, down to Roman times, in Magnesia, the temple of Apollo preserved record of its rights confirmed by Darius I (522-486) to Gadata (probably the satrap there); the Greek text would be a translation from the Aramaic original.[31] Second, we have an original document from Xanthus in Lycia, of the first year of Artaxerxes III (358), whereby Pixodarus, the satrap of Caria and Lycia, regulates the introduction of the cult of a Carian deity into the temple of Leto at Xanthus, with appropriate provision for sacrificial offerings. What is noteworthy is that this inscription is *trilingual*. The decree from the satrap's bureau is in Aramaic; next to it, on opposite sides of the stone to each other, are versions of the original request in Greek (main area language) and in Lycian (the local tongue). The three texts show significant differences in detail, reflecting their originators' interests.[32] The whole setup illustrates the rather compressed formula in Esther (3:12; 8:9), that decrees and documents would be written in the script/language of each province, not only in Aramaic. In Babylon, Cyrus's administrative orders to the Babylonian officers to repatriate the other Babylonian images would have been issued in Aramaic; but his propaganda texts for the temples were in traditional Babylonian cuneiform. This can be seen in the "Cyrus Cylinder" for Babylon; and in his building texts for the Ur and Sippar temples.[33]

In Egypt, under Cambyses and especially Darius I, the Persian kings sought to patronize the local cults. For Cambyses the high dignitary Udja-Hor-resenet acted in the role of an Egyptian adviser, and enlisted his interest in the temple of the goddess Neith of Sais. Darius I in turn was served by this same dignitary, sanctioned building work on Egyptian temples, and caused to be built a whole new temple at Hibis in the Great Oasis (Kharga).[34]

Thus it cannot be so surprising to find (Ezra 1–2) Cyrus authorizing a restoration of what was (for him!) the local cult of "the God of heaven" (YHWH to his worshipers) at Jerusalem in Yehud (Judea) subprovince in Palestine, and therefore granting that the deity's cult vessels (there being no image) and a goodly body of adherents should also go back there. Politically, we should remember, Palestine was the springboard for Egypt; a loyal populace there was a prerequisite for a successful Persian conquest there. And the same applies (both religiously and politically) in the case of Darius I, who confirmed the temple-building project, with appropriate provision for the cult (Ezra 5; 6:1-12), precisely as we saw happen later at Xanthus and as is implied in what remains of the Magnesian rescript of Darius I. Likewise, in Egypt Cambyses had the temple of Neith restored and renewed its revenues and festival provision; the Hibis temple of Darius I would also have had to be granted endowments to maintain its cult.

Direct royal Persian interest in Jewish cultic affairs is not limited to Ezra's text. During Cambyses' invasion of Egypt (525), much violence and damage was done, including to temples there, as Udja-hor-resenet (discreetly) and one of the later Jewish Aramaic papyri (Cowley, no. 30:13-14) from Elephantiné both agree. The latter also records that the Jewish temple at Elephantiné was not attacked then but was respected by Cambyses. Much later on we find direct Persian interest in its cult.[35] One document from Elephantiné (Cowley, no. 21) is a direct command from the Persian king, Darius II, that the Jews in Elephantiné should celebrate the Passover and feast of unleavened bread. Typically, the edict went from the king to the satrap of Egypt, Arsames, and by him via a Jewish emissary Hananiah (Cowley, no. 38:7) to the Elephantiné Jewish community itself. As one would not expect Darius II to know personally the details of these feasts, it appears that Hananiah was dispatched on a mission there by Darius II, much as Ezra (chap. 7) was sent out to the Jews in Jerusalem by Artaxerxes I. There is no rational reason to doubt the authenticity of Ezra's commission any more than that of Hananiah under Darius II.[36] In turn, when the Jewish temple at Elephantiné was destroyed in 410, the Jews there made appeal to both the governor of Judea, Bigvai, and Johanan high priest in Jerusalem, and likewise to the sons of Sanballat I, governor in neighboring Samaria down to the seventeenth year of the king in 407. But unlike Zerubbabel governor of Judea and the priest Jeshua in Jerusalem, who asked for help for their temple via Tattenai (governor of "Beyond the River")[37] in 520 (Ezra 4:24; 5–6), the appeal from Elephantiné seemingly fell on deaf ears; it may have been refused by the satrap Arsames.

77

And so one might continue. In terms of Persian imperial involvement with local peoples and communities, what we find in Ezra-Nehemiah (and Esther) is in harmony with what we see in the contemporary firsthand sources that we do have. The Persian kings supported local cults as a focus of local loyalties to the center; and that the local groups should invoke their deities' blessings on their rule. Various minor details in the biblical sources find echoes in our external data. Thus Nehemiah (2:7) asked for letters of safe conduct for his journey to Judea. Just such a "passport," with requests (by the satrap Arsames for his adjutant Nahti-hur) to a series of officials for safe conduct (and provision) all the way from Babylonia to Damascus (en route to Egypt), has survived from only a few years after Nehemiah, preserved with other letters in a leather postbag such as couriers might have used on such journeys.[38] So we can see what Nehemiah might have expected from his king.

The terminology in the biblical copies of letters to and from the Persian court is directly comparable with what we find in the external, firsthand documents. Inferiors call themselves the "servant(s)" of superiors and kings; the idiom for issuing decrees *(sam t'e'em)* is the same; the body of the typical Official Aramaic letter begins with the phrase "Peace *(sh-l-m)* and much well-being I send you," which is what is presupposed in Ezra 4:17 (lit. "Peace, etc."), where the formula is abbreviated for brevity's sake.[39] And so on, we may also say, on this topic. The form or stage of language of Aramaic used in Ezra and Daniel is precisely that used in the Neo-Babylonian and Persian period (sixth to fourth centuries), and is currently termed Official Aramaic. In the Old Testament the sole difference is that the spelling has been consistently modernized, to bring it into line with the Aramaic otherwise in popular use among the Jews by the third century. This was because of sound-shifts in Aramaic from at least the fifth century. For example, the consonant *dh* had coalesced with plain *d*. Before this it had been written as a *z* in Old and Official Aramaic, as there was no separate letter in the (originally Phoenician) script for the sound *dh*. But to continue writing a *d* (as *dh* had become) with a *z*, when all other *d*s were written as *d*, could only lead to confusion. Already in the fifth century some scribes began to write the occasional *d* instead of *z* in such cases. So the change had to come. Thus with the fall of the Persian Empire, Aramaic largely ceased to be used except by those who spoke it (not just wrote it), and the change took place. But the change only dates itself, not the documents to which it was applied, as elsewhere in the ancient Near East. There is no good reason to deny the authenticity of the biblical Aramaic correspondence and other usages that we find in the biblical books relating to this period.[40]

3. BACK TO THE BALANCE SHEET

We may now cast a retrospective glance over this much briefer period, circa 600-400. For the period of the Babylonian conquest of Judah and the exiling of an important part of its population to Babylon(ia), the biblical and external sources match closely in terms of history and chronology. The numbers exiled to Babylonia are comparable with previous Assyrian usage. The elite and "useful" people (military; skilled folk) were the ones taken away (as always in such circumstances), and other folk were left to raise revenues from working the land, in accord with ancient imperial usage. In Babylon Jehoiachin's presence and life on allowance is clearly evidenced. Babylon as an early metropolis is very visible. Back in Judea we have background for Gedaliah's brief regime, Ammonite foe, and Mizpah as local administrative center. The flight of Jews to Egypt via Tahpanhes (a known location) had later consequences.

With the triumph of Persia, Cyrus appears as liberator in both the Babylonian and biblical view. Up to Babylon's fall, Belshazzar had been prime mover in Babylon under a largely absentee father (so a Daniel could only play third fiddle). The sequence and dates of sixth- and fifth-century imperial rulers are closely agreed in biblical and other sources. Among lesser lights, Nehemiah's three foes find good background (Sanballat and family in papyri; Tobiah through his descendants' works; Geshem in contemporary records). As for places, Susa was indeed a major capital, and Palestine knew a period of developing resettlement. Persian interest in its subjects' cults is well attested. Biblical Aramaic usage and cultural traits (even "passports") correspond closely with external usage and data. We are in a clearly defined historical and cultural period with good mutual correlations.

CHAPTER 4

The Empire Strikes Back —
Saul, David, and Solomon

After our voyage through the busy half-millennium from 930 down to almost 400 B.C., we now return to 930 and begin our long ascent back through time into the years, centuries, and aeons before 930, the probable date by which the Israelite community in Canaan found itself divided into two often rival kingdoms, Israel in the north (with most of the tribal groups) and Judah (plus Benjamin) in the south.

Out of what sort of community did the twin kingdoms of Jeroboam (north) and Rehoboam (south) emerge? In the existing Hebrew texts that profess to describe the pre-930s period (Samuel, Kings, Chronicles), we find narratives about Israel's tribes demanding from their informal leader Samuel that a king be appointed "like the surrounding kingdoms," resulting in the selection of Saul. After his embattled reign, and his son Ishbaal's rapid demise, the strong young chieftain David quickly took over. He is shown as reuniting Israel around a new central capital, the fortress of Jerusalem (which he captures), and extending his power over most neighbors (in Transjordan and central Syria) but making alliance with others (Phoenicia; Hamath, a subject ally). His son Solomon is shown inheriting this mini-empire and indulging in conspicuous state display (building projects), along with wider international links (Egypt, Sheba, etc.), before decline leads to revolt within and without, so that most non-Hebrew territory was lost before his death — out of which crisis the twin kingdoms were born. It will be helpful, first, to sketch the principal features of these reigns as given by the biblical accounts, before looking into what external data (if any) we may properly draw upon to compare with them.

1. THE BIBLICAL DATA IN OUTLINE

A. BASIC CHRONOLOGY

Looking back through time, we find that Solomon is assigned forty years' reign (1 Kings 11:42), being succeeded by his forty-one-year-old son Rehoboam, his son by an Ammonite lady, Na'amah (14:21). Thus Rehoboam was born a year or so before his father's accession, under the aged David. Solomon himself was only a relatively young man at his accession (poetically described in 3:7), being the son of David by a later wife, Bathsheba (2 Sam. 12:24), at the end of David's major wars, about the middle of his reign of 33 + 7 = 40 years (2 Sam. 5:4). Solomon may well have acceded at twenty-plus years old, dying at fifty-plus. Within his reign he spent three or four years consolidating his power, then seven years (Years 4-11) building the temple at Jerusalem, plus a further thirteen years building his palace and government complex (1 Kings 7:1), the temple-building and palace projects totaling twenty years (9:10) during Years 4 to 24 of Solomon. Which accounts for all but sixteen years of the reign. Solomon had other building projects (cf. 9:17-18), perhaps partly contemporary with the Jerusalem undertakings, but at least in part following after these, to utilize the workforces still in being then. One such was the "Millo" (terracing?) at Jerusalem, built after Solomon moved his Egyptian princess into his new palace (9:24; 11:27). These other works would need some years, thus guaranteeing all but a few of the remaining sixteen years of the reign. With Solomon being a young son/successor of his father, there is no problem in having two successive reigns of about forty years each. Threats to the succession in David's old age led to Solomon's public appointment to kingship while his father yet lived (cf. 1:1–2:1). So there may have been an overlap of several months' coregency to secure the succession. (A lesson well learned by later Hebrew kings, as is clear in chap. 2 above.)

David had seven years, six months in Hebron as local Judean chief and king before the rest of Israel came under his jurisdiction (2 Sam. 2:11; 5:4). In that time, following Saul's death, Israel to the north had been scattered and disorganized, many fleeing to Gilead, etc., with Philistine occupation of their normal territory (1 Sam. 31:7), at least for a time. Thus three or four years might have elapsed before the northern tribes could be rallied by their "strong man," Abner (Saul's former army commander), who installed Saul's younger son Ishbaal ("Ishbosheth") as puppet ruler in Gilead under his own tutelage (2 Sam. 2:8-9). Ishbaal lasted a miserable two years (2:10) before being murdered — perhaps roughly equivalent to Years 5 and 6 of David in Hebron. Then, after deliberations of a year or so, the Israelites finally came over to David.

Before David and Ishbaal we have Saul, for whose reign we have the manifestly incomplete figure of ". . . and two" years in 1 Sam. 13:1. As his younger son Ishbaal was forty at accession (2 Sam. 2:10), at latest about four years after Saul's death, he would have been not less than thirty-five by that event. Thus Jonathan, Abinadab, and Malki-shua (who died with Saul — 1 Sam. 31:2) might have been born in the four or five years before Ishbaal. If Saul married between fifteen and twenty years old and was still a personable young man when appointed king (cf. 1 Sam. 9–10), able to lead troops (2 Sam. 11:11), he would most likely have been twenty to thirty years old at accession, and likelier nearer the latter age. Thus, an Ishbaal born to Saul aged (say) twenty-five to twenty-seven would have been thirty-five to thirty-seven years old by Saul's death after a thirty-two-year reign, and himself king at forty-one soon after. We may summarize our results, thus, as an approximate framework:

Table 7. Kings and Suggested Dates, Israelite United Monarchy

Dates B.C.	King	Years
1042-1010	Saul	[3]2
(1006-1004	Ishbaal	2)
1010-970	David (UM from 1003)	40
971/970–931/930	Solomon	40

B. SAUL IN SUMMARY

In the middle of the eleventh century Israel was still a fragmented tribal confederation without any formal, centralized authority, civil or military. Between the settlements in Ephraim in the northern hill country and their Judean brothers lay alien Jerusalem and other such places all the way down to Gezer, Aijalon, and Timnah. Northward, Ephraim was likewise largely cut off from Galilean brethren by alien settlements in the vale of Jezreel, such as Megiddo and Beth-Shan, while the Jordan River divided them all (if modestly) from other Hebrews in Gilead and environs. Cf. map, fig. 12. At their heart had been the old wilderness tabernacle, sheltering the ark of the covenant at Shiloh down to Samuel's time (cf. 1 Sam. 1–4). But after the fatal Battle of Aphek, the Philistines had not only captured the ark in the battle but had pressed home their attack ruthlessly eastward to destroy the old tabernacle's successor shrine at Shiloh itself — an event so painful in Hebrew memory that nobody cared to allude to it for centuries thereafter, until Jeremiah did (Jer. 7:12-15) in his equally stark message against Jerusalem's temple. (Oh, and one psalmist, Ps. 78:60.) It is significant that when the Philistines sent back the ark after a few months, it did *not* go back to Shiloh, but to other location(s) — e.g., Kiriath-jearim for a long time (1 Sam. 7:2, one spell of twenty years), if not Nob, which was a priestly shrine with the ephod (21:9).

After all this, the people (we are told) demanded of Samuel that a central, effective ruler be appointed, like other people had. He bluntly told them of the practical cost to their way of life that this would entail (1 Sam. 8:10-18). But Saul was appointed, and had to repel Ammonite hostility immediately, as his first test (1 Sam. 9–12). For the rest of his reign Saul had to battle all too often with the Philistines as a constant threat (1 Sam. 13–14; 17; 19; 23–24; 28–29; 31), but not exclusively. To the south he worsted the Amalekites (14:48; 15); to the east, not only Ammon but also Moab and tented Edom had to be repulsed (14:47). And in the north, significantly, the kings of Zobah were repulsed — the first-attested Aramean attack on Hebrew terrain, virtually certainly against either Gilead or Galilee. But not the last, as David found out. Saul's end came with his body pinned to the walls of Beth-Shan (1 Sam. 31).

Saul had held court generally from Gibeah/Geba in Benjamin, it becoming known as "Gibeah of Saul" (1 Sam. 11:4; 15:34; and much later, Isa. 10:29), primitive precursor to a "city of David." There he had his residence and his bevy of young aides; David began as one, noted for musical skill (1 Sam. 16:18, 21-23; Psalms, passim), before later becoming a fugitive in southern Judah and the Negev (cf. 1 Sam. 24:1; 27:8-12; 30:9-27). As king, Saul held assembly close by, with up to six hundred people in attendance (14:2). He developed some kind of army, with a chief commander (eventually, Abner son of Ner, 26:5) over other commanders (14:38). Some kind of taxation was now levied from the citizenry (cf. 17:25). So a rudimentary state was already taking shape, under adverse conditions; and the Philistines at least could see its potential danger to their own hegemony in much of Canaan.

C. DAVID IN SUMMARY

After seven years as local ruler in Hebron, David was accepted as king by all Israel (2 Sam. 5:1-4). His first move was to unify his realm by conquering Jerusalem, seemingly by artifice (5:6-8). Once installed, he eventually built himself a palace with the technical help of Hiram of Tyre, and built inward from the "Millo" structure, which was probably terracing (5:9-11).

However, wars, not buildings, had to be David's major concern. Immediately the Philistines smelled trouble and had to be repulsed decisively (7:17-25; 8:1), or at least for a considerable period, with one last vain attempt by them to crush David in four battles (21:15-22). Down south Amalek had been sorted out in Saul's time, so peace reigned there. But on the east, across Jordan, David defeated and effectively cowed both Moab (8:2, 12) and Edom (8:12, 13-14; cf. 1 Kings 11:14-22). With Ammon there had been friendly relations, until a new king (Hanun) insulted David's envoys. This led to war with the Ammonites, who involved Hadadezer king of Aram-Zobah on their side, besides the lesser polities of Maacah and Tob close by Gilead; Joab defeated the joint force (2 Sam. 10).

But the magnitude of the Aramean threat needed David's personal intervention. Based in the Lebanon/Anti-Lebanon Biqa Valley, the king of Zobah ruled both south over Damascus as a vassal (cf. 8:5) and north to the great west bend of the Euphrates, from beyond whence he had power to call upon further armed forces (10:16). After the defeat near Rabbath-Ammon, the southern Aramean vassals made a gesture of submission to David (10:19). But Hadadezer faced, it seems, still greater problems north to the Euphrates, which gave David his chance to vanquish him from behind (cf. 8:3-4), and then to impose his overlordship upon the Arameans of Damascus by garrisons and tribute (8:5-6). Freed from the yoke of Zobah, Toi, king of Hamath, then became David's subject ally (cf. 8:9-10, 11), thus admitting Hebrew indirect rule to the banks of the Euphrates. Meantime the conflict with Ammon could be consummated (11:1; 12:26-31), and Hanun son of Nahash could be replaced by his brother Shobi, as vassal-ruler of Ammon under David under friendlier auspices (cf. 17:27).

The rest of David's reign was marked by public power and the alliance with Tyre abroad, but at home by domestic strife and attempted coups d'etat into old age, until Solomon's appointment.

D. SOLOMON IN SUMMARY

The biblical accounts of Solomon's reign occupy all of 1 Kings 1–11 and 2 Chron. 1–9. It will be simplest here to summarize by theme, not sequence; for chronology, see 1.A above.

(i) Foreign Relations

Early in his reign (Years 1-3) Solomon made a marriage alliance with a pharaoh of Egypt, who gave him Gezer as his daughter's dowry, after conquering it (1 Kings 3:1; 9:16, 24; cf. 7:8; 11:1). As no pharaoh would go to the expense of a military campaign merely to reduce one town and then give it and its terrain to a neighbor, a much larger action was clearly involved; between Gezer and Egypt lay Philistia, rival to Israel, and perhaps no ally of Egypt either at this time. And a marriage alliance was not entered into lightly in antiquity. Trade in horses occurred, we are told (see just below).

In Phoenicia Solomon inherited David's alliance with Hiram of Tyre, who sent due greetings on Solomon's accession; this led to Solomon ordering Lebanese timber through Hiram and Byblos ("Gebal"), 1 Kings 5. Hiram also sent a metalworking specialist for the bronze furnishings of the temple at Jerusalem (1 Kings 7). This led to financial arrangements (involving land exchange) between the two (1 Kings 9:10-14; 2 Chron. 8:1-2), and to joint expeditions down the Red Sea to Ophir and beyond to obtain further wealth (1 Kings 9:26-28; 10:11-12, 22).

Solomon's most exotic link was with the distant land of Sheba, the Saba of southwest Arabia; thence came its queen, ostensibly to compliment him, and with gifts (1 Kings 10), but more likely also for talks on trade, as Ophir was almost certainly within her land's sphere of interests.

Next are Que and Musri. Musri is simply Egypt; Que is known to be Cilicia in southeast Asia Minor. Here Solomon acted as a middleman trader in horses and chariots for his royal neighbors (1 Kings 10:28-29), as he controlled most of the land route between these north and south extremes.

"Tadmor in the desert" (2 Chron. 8:4) may represent Solomon securing what was later the desert route via Palmyra, given the context of activity in Hamath-Zobah (8:3). Some read it as Tamar, south of the Dead Sea (because nearer to Judah), on the west side of the Arabah.

(ii) Buildings

The temple and its furnishings, in Jerusalem, take pride of place in the narratives (1 Kings 5–6; 7:13-51; 8). The temple had a two-columned porch, vestibule/hall, and sanctuary or "holy of holies"; around the exterior were storerooms on three levels, linked by stairs. At 60 cubits long × 20 cubits wide (i.e., about 90 feet × 30 feet) it was of modest size; but the carved cedar paneling of walls and floor and the gold overlay of the interior made it opulent.

The palace complex in Jerusalem included a great columned hall, a judgment hall, a royal residence, and an abode for his Egyptian princess, all walled round, as was the temple (7:1-12). This complex, too, had appropriately rich furnishings: a throne of gilded ivory upon steps; gold and silver vessels; gold shields in the great columned hall (10:16-21), to which should be added similar shields taken by David from Hadadezer of Aram-Zobah (2 Sam. 8:7).

Other works at Jerusalem include closing a modest gap in the walls; and work on the Millo (1 Kings 11:27); building foreign cult shrines east of the city (11:7-8); building work (unspecified!) at Gezer, Hazor, and Megiddo (9:15, 17a), as well as at Upper and Lower Beth Horon, Baalath, and elsewhere (9:17-19; 2 Chron. 8:5-6).

(iii) Royal Administration

Here (1 Kings 4:1-19) we have first almost a dozen top people: an army commander; a chief over the twelve district governors (listed separately, with their regions, which exclude Judah); a superintendent over the palace; a director of the corvée; a "recorder" and two secretaries; three priests plus one also as king's confidant ("friend"). Next to this we have a note of the scale of daily palace provisions, based on the monthly quotas of the twelve district governors (4:22-23). To which are added chariots and horses (4:26; 10:26; cf. 2 Chron. 9:25). Some details of corvées levied are given, plus payments to Hiram of Tyre (1 Kings 5:10-16). Some revenues are stated, regular and a one-off from Sheba (10:10, 14).

(iv) Culture

The king coveted wisdom, and had fame in it; had an interest in flora and fauna; composed both "wisdom" (proverbs) and "songs" (1 Kings 4:29-34). He spoke a long prayer at the dedication of the temple; two psalms (Pss. 72; 127) are assigned him by superscription; and two "books" of instructional wisdom bear his name, as compiler, Prov. 1–24 (including two sets of "Sayings of the Wise") and a posthumous collection (Prov. 25–29).

(v) Sunset

All earthly empires eventually break up; Solomon's was no exception. From Egypt after David's death there came young Prince Hadad to reclaim Edom from Israelite rule (1 Kings 11:14-22); his impact initially was probably modest. Much farther north a young brave, Rezon, survived the wreck of Hadadezer's brief empire of Zobah, eventually to take control in Damascus (11:23-25). This was more serious, because an independent regime in Aram-Damascus (if it also recovered rule over Zobah in the Biqa) would break off all direct contact between Israel and Hamath, thus ending all Israelite control north of Dan. Thus, before his death, Solomon had most likely lost control over Aram completely (and Hamath with it), and probably of outlying Edom, threatening the Red Sea trade via the Gulf of Aqaba. He would be left with Judah/Israel (with Gilead) and probably Ammon and Moab as vassals — a much reduced realm. Finally, the works overseer Jeroboam fled to Egypt, to be welcomed by Shishak (Shoshenq I, ca. 945-924), and later used by him to shatter even the unity of the Hebrew monarchy itself, with the aim of imposing vassal status (cf. chap. 2 above). To be welcomed by Shoshenq I, Jeroboam's arrival in Egypt would not predate 945 on the optimum dating for that king; hence, not before Year 24 or 25 of Solomon (and entirely possibly later, of course).

2. THE NEAR EASTERN BACKGROUND DATA

A. INTRODUCTORY

During the two succeeding periods, the twin monarchies and the exile and return, we have benefited from a variety of external sources embodying direct mention of biblical people and events, showing full agreement in sequences of rulers and in their general dating, and some clear archaeological background. But before 853 things are different. People complain loudly, "Why no mentions of David or Solomon? Where is their power and splendor?" — but without having the gumption to inquire into the circumstances of the period or into the total evidence for before 853/930 that we do actually have. Let us therefore fill this serious gap in method and understanding by looking at the facts of the case.

(i) Mesopotamia

The main reason things are so "bright" from 853 onward is that the kings of Assyria commonly named their adversaries in their reports, and from 853 they came into contact with Israel. This was *not* the case earlier. The first four campaigns of Shalmaneser III did not reach beyond north Syria, only to Patinu (formerly read Hattina) and the Orontes River. Before him his father, Assurnasirpal II (884-859), had also reached Patinu, then over the Orontes and Lebanon Mountains to the Mediterranean Sea (within 877-867). There the Phoenician centers from Arvad to Tyre sent him tribute (a "one-off"!), but no rulers of theirs are named.[1] Before that none of his three predecessors, Assurdan II, Adad-nirari II, and Tukulti-Ninurta II (935-884), got anywhere west of the Balikh River and the Middle Euphrates; Syria and Canaan were beyond their reach. And therefore, they make no mention of kings or states there.[2] Before 935, back to the death of Tukulti-Ninurta I (1245-1208), whose power had reached the Euphrates just across from Carchemish, hardly any Assyrian king had reached Syria (let alone name any kings and lands there) for almost two hundred years. The main exception was Tiglath-pileser I (1115-1076), who just once reached Arvad and Simyra in Phoenicia, receiving tribute also from Byblos and Sidon (another "one-off"). Assur-bel-kala (1074-1056) may have fleetingly done the same. Neither king named any western rulers except for Ini-Tesub (II) of Carchemish and Allumari of Malatya, both in the far north, and a couple of kings of Patinu in north Syria.[3] So, from 1200 to 1050 no Assyrian source named anyone in Philistia, Transjordan, Judah/Israel, or even Phoenicia, as there was no contact with any of these except minimally with Phoenicia. Not even the Egyptian king who sent a crocodile is named.

After Assur-bel-kala, it all went downhill for Assyria for well over a century under obscure kings from Eriba-Adad II to Tiglath-pileser II (1056-935) — precisely the period of Saul, David, and Solomon in Israel. Aramean expansion in Upper Mesopotamia cut them off from Syria and the Levant beyond it. Their contemporary texts are rare. Thus any mention by them of a far-distant David or a Solomon (up to 700 marching miles away) would be inconceivable without some very special reason. (None is known.)[4] As for Babylon, her rulers (even the energetic Nebuchadrezzar I) were limited in wars, etc., to relations with nearby Assyria and Elam, never with the far-distant Levant. They would know nothing whatever of a David or a Solomon, unless some direct trade link occurred — for which development we lack all evidence currently.

(ii) Egypt

In Egypt, imperial campaigns in the Levant ceased with Ramesses III by circa 1175. There is currently no reason whatever to postulate any further Egyptian warlike activity there until the reign of Siamun, in the late Twenty-First Dynasty, within circa 970-960, on the basis of his unusual triumph scene, and thereafter only Shoshenq I, who left indubitable record of *his* expedition in Palestine.[5] But exactly like all his New Kingdom predecessors, Shoshenq I did not deign to name his adversaries, and long, detailed topographical lists like his and theirs almost never name states, just series of settlements. So no mention of the names Judah, Israel, Rehoboam, Jeroboam was ever to be expected in his normal-type list that we do possess in this instance. Most Delta remains are destroyed,[6] and Upper Egyptian coffins bear magic spells, not war reports!

(iii) The Levant

If the erstwhile "great powers" had no role in the south Levant, and thus offer no mention of its kings in the tenth century, there is even less prima facie hope that lesser kingdoms might do so. And we find this is precisely so. The series of Luvian hieroglyphic texts from Neo-Hittite kingdoms such as Carchemish, Malatya, Gurgum, Patinu, and even Hamath are almost entirely concerned with their own affairs and their own area (northernmost Syria/southeast Anatolia) — not with (e.g.) Phoenicia, still less with Canaan.[7] No monumental Aramean inscriptions that predate the ninth century have yet been found (only the Melqart and Tell Dan stelae from the ninth in the Levant, so far), and no Aramean administrative texts whatever. In Phoenicia almost nothing precedes the local royal epigraphs of kings of Byblos, which run (at present) from circa 1000 onward, mentioning only themselves.[8] Nothing survives (so far) from Tyre and Sidon until centuries later. In principle, future discoveries could change the picture radically at any time — like the Ekron inscription that has given us a five-generation line of the Ekronite royal house down to circa 690.[9] Naturally we cannot cite what is not yet found, but future possibilities must be allowed for. The Tel Dan stela suddenly produced what has to be conceded as the first nonbiblical mention of David as a dynastic founder in Judah (cf. [v] below); other such finds may still await the fortunate researcher.

(iv) Israel/Judah Itself

But it has been asked, "Why no inscriptions of David's and Solomon's time?" Here the answer is probably twofold, and entails certainly the question of survival of artifacts and possibly the policy of the state. The question of survival is much more serious than people realize, especially as "official" inscriptions by kings tend to be found on, in, or at temples, palaces, and other official edifices — not just everywhere. In Israel/Judah such texts may mainly have been expected in the capitals: Jerusalem (and later, Samaria). But since the tenth century Jerusalem has suffered repeated changes, destructions and rebuildings, often on the grand scale; and (even after 130 years) only a very small percentage of it has been (or can be) excavated. Outdated Solomonic stelae, for example, might have been reused in fresh masonry by later kings; the Babylonians thoroughly destroyed the temple and palace of the "City of David" area in 586; Zerubbabel's "second temple" rebuilding, and even more, the massive rebuilding under Herod would have removed the last traces of prior Iron Age structures. Then, in turn, the Romans thoroughly destroyed Jerusalem; and the temple of Jupiter in Aelia Capitolina would not help survival of older work on the Temple Mount. Byzantine rebuildings, a damaging Persian incursion, and Muslim, Crusader, and later destructions and rebuilds all have taken their toll of earlier remains. It would be a miracle if anything like individual slabs such as inscribed stelae were to survive such a history of devastation and reuse.[10]

Further, on *policy*, we do not know whether Jerusalem's early Hebrew kings actually did leave formal inscriptions on stone, even as servants of YHWH. Inscriptions as such were not forbidden; compare the unofficial Siloam tunnel inscription, the tomb inscription of [Shebna?]iah, and two other scraps at Jerusalem.[11] Long after David and Solomon, in a probably less strict religious environment, the excavations at Samaria produced no series of official stone inscriptions either. Only one small possible fragment has ever been found, bearing the single anodyne word *'asher,* "who/which"! So this may indicate that later Israelite kings did have such texts. But again, Samaria suffered hostile damage in 722/720; in Herodian and Roman times, it was much redeveloped. No other towns probably merited major inscriptions; such would have been recycled in later buildings in any case. The "alien" inscriptions at Dan (Aramean; discovered by chance!) and Ashdod and Samaria (Assyrian) have survived only as small fragments of texts mainly lost because they were smashed and reused as building rubble. So we could hardly expect to find a serious surviving corpus of Davidic/Solomonic official texts, had they once existed.

This can be seen from the state of minimal survival in other, comparable Levantine kingdoms. Aram-Damascus has left us almost nothing from over two hundred years of its kingdom. Damascus has been repeatedly rebuilt during millennia, yielding (so far) no Iron Age inscriptions whatsoever. For all his power, Hazael of Aram-Damascus has left us only bits from elsewhere: the shattered Tel Dan stela, his name on ivories carried off to Assyria, and a couple of stray horse-blinker pieces. Just one stela of a Benhadad survives that may represent Aleppo. From all Moab's kings, only Mesha's stela and one other fragment have so far turned up.[12] Sealings apart, only about three small pieces commemorate kings of Ammon, and none commemorate the kings of Edom. We have short epigraphs of about four of the earlier kings of Byblos, but none pre–sixth century from Tyre and Sidon. And so on. Thus, in such a context we can hardly grumble at the near-total failure so far of texts to surface mentioning or belonging to David and Solomon.

(v) But Not Quite Total!

However, there are probably as many as three traces for David, and an indirect one for his major foe Hadadezer of Aram-Zobah.

(a) First for David

The publication of fragments of an Old Aramaic stela from Tell Dan in 1993/1995 brought to light the first recognized nonbiblical mention of the tenth-century king David, in a text that reflected events of the year 841 and would have been set up at no great interval after that date.[13] On the simplest interpretation (cf. pp. 36-37 above, with the footnotes) of the surviving middle lines (3-9) of this text, we have here the killing or defeating of "[. . .]ram, son of [. . .], king of Israel," and in parallel, the killing of "[. . .]iah son of [. . .]," relating to *Byt-Dwd*, "the House of David" — a phrase which cannot seriously be interpreted in any other way, it being of a very well known type. It corresponds exactly to the Assyrian Bit-Khumri = *Byt-ʿmry*, "the House of Omri" (= Israel). In this way a kingdom could be named after a prominent founder of a dynasty. Directly contrary to what some OT scholars claim, such mentions *are* strictly personal in almost all cases: they imply that a real man David and a real man Omri founded dynasties in the kingdoms concerned (Judah, Israel). Just as a real man (A)gusi founded a dynasty, Bit-(A)gusi, in the kingdom of Arpad, and another individual, Adini, founded his line and kingdom, Bit Adini, at Til-Barsip, and so on; a dozen or more examples are known. So "House of (= dynasty founded by the man) David" (fig. 13A) is the only acceptable translation and understanding of the phrase *Byt-Dwd*. The date of this monument stems from the identity of the people mentioned, as already pointed out. The only known king of Israel whose name ends in *-ram*, and whose father had a four-letter name, was J(eh)oram, son of Ahab, slain in 841. The other matching person, "[. . .]iah son of [. . .]," relating to the House of David slain at that time, could hardly be other than Ahaziah the contemporary Judean king, both slain by Jehu's action, for which the Aramean ruler here takes credit. In such a context, the latter would have been Hazael, with near total certainty. So we thus gain a clear mention of David as dynastic founder of the kingdom of Judah about 150 years after his death.

(b) Second for David

As often happens, one discovery can lead to others. Equally convincingly, Lemaire was subsequently able to show that *bt-[d]wd* is to be read in line 31 of the famous stela of Mesha king of Moab, dating to about the same period. Cf. fig. 13B. This links the "House of David" (= Judah) with an occupation of part of southern Moab (around Horonen), corresponding to Israel's penetration in the north under Omri and his dynasty. So we have David mentioned twice in retrospect, some six generations after his death.[14]

(c) And a Third for David?

Nor is this all, it seems. After his victory over Rehoboam and Jeroboam in 926/925, Shoshenq I of Egypt had engraved at Karnak a long list of Palestinian place-names. Some of these are now destroyed, and thus lost to us; many can be readily identified with known places in Israel, Judah, the Negev, and a few in western Transjordan. But quite a few have remained obscure. Among these, in a group of names clearly located by association in the Negev/south Judah area, is "the heights of *Dwt*."[15] It could not really be Dothan — no final *n*, and in entirely the wrong context for a north Palestinian settlement. However, in an Ethiopic victory inscription of the early sixth century A.D. in southwest Arabia, the emperor of Axum cited explicitly passages (Pss. 65; 19) from the "Psalms of Dawit," exactly the consonants *Dwt* as found with Shoshenq. In Egyptian transcriptions of foreign names (both places and personal), a *t* could and sometimes did transcribe a Semitic *d*. This happens in the New Kingdom in such familiar place-names as Megiddo (Egyp. *Mkt*), Edreʿi (Egyp. *ʾitrʿ*), Adummim *(Egyp. itmm)*, Damascus (Egyp. *Tmsq*), Dothaim/n (Egyp. *Ttyn*). Back in the Middle Kingdom the Execration Texts have a prince of Magdali (Egyp. *Mktry*). And just then, we have this use in personal names also, including a "David" — "the Asiatic, chief carpenter, *Twti*" is for a Dawid or Dodi on a stela; another is a probable Dodi-(H)uatu, Egyptian *Tt-wʾt*, in a papyrus. Thus there is no reason to doubt a final *-d* becoming a voiceless *t* in both Egyptian and Ethiopic (both, Afro-Asiatic languages).[16] And no better alternative seems forthcoming. This would give us a place-name that commemorated David in the Negev barely fifty years after his death, within living memory of the man. The Negev was an area where David had been prominent in Saul's time (1 Sam. 24:1; 27; 30; p. 84 above). His name being in such a place-name is analogous with the "field of Abram," also in Shoshenq's list. So, historically, we would be within fifty years of David's own lifetime. Cf. fig. 13C.

(d) Hope for Hadadezer of Zobah?

As we have seen, the biblical record would indicate that Hadadezer of Aram-Zobah had enough authority and power — clout — to commandeer troops from across the Euphrates (2 Sam. 10:15-16). He thus had sufficient control of the crossings of that river, in the south part of its westernmost bend, for this to be possible. These wars of David in Ammon and with Aram-Zobah can be set at about the 990s, say, about Years 15-20-plus in his reign (cf. p. 85, above). In Assyria this period corresponds to the long but feeble reign of Assur-rabi II (1013-972), under whom later Assyrian documents record: "at the time of Assur-rabi (II), King of Assyria, the king of the land of Arumu took (two cities) by force (*scil.*, Pitru = Pethor, and Mutkinu). . . ."[17] Pitru is long known to be biblical Pethor (Num. 22:5; Deut. 23:4), near the Euphrates, south of Carchemish. Shalmaneser III places it on the river Sajur that runs into the Euphrates; Mutkinu was opposite, on the east bank of the Euphrates. Arumu in its context is hardly other than a variant of Aramu, "Aram," the two last vowels being harmonized. It would be entirely appropriate to identify this "king of Aram" within 1013-972 as our Hadadezer of Aram-Zobah, who drew upon this region (later Bit-Adini) for troops. Politically there are no known "rivals" for him then, in this capacity of controller of Pitru and Mutkinu. So we have a highly likely reference for David's most powerful foe, as well as one possible and two solid references for David himself.

B. IMPLICIT BACKGROUND: INTRODUCTORY AND SAUL

So we can now see clearly why it is not permissible just to sit back and moan, "We have no literal mentions of Saul/David/Solomon — so, they never were." The question *why* has to be asked, and it has now been answered; and the traces even of such explicit mentions have just begun to emerge. But we have not exhausted the available evidence; direct, explicit mentions of people and events are *not* the only kind available. We have yet to examine the matter of *implicit* evidence.

The content of the basic biblical data on Saul, David, and Solomon was set out above (sec. 1, pp. 82-88). These data might in principle be wholly factual, or wholly fictional, or something in between. Adduction of appropriate, external *background* data will not prove the ultimate historical truthfulness of these reports. But it will enable us to affirm or eliminate fantasy, and to affirm or eliminate correspondence with known realities in the world of the tenth or other centuries B.C. in these narratives. Enough data exist and are known to make some tests practical, which we must now proceed to apply. Given the almost rustic and very limited regime of Saul, we cannot expect too much for his reign. For David more should be possible; and for Solomon much more is given that is open to external comparison.

(ii) Saul

(a) Nature of Levantine Kingship

The changeover from the rule of largely local chiefs to a centralized authority having power over them was a momentous one. In 1 Sam. 8 the prophet Samuel outlined what the practical cost of the rule by monarchy would be. His somber picture has often been treated by Old Testament scholars as an artificial retrojection from the bad days of the subsequent monarchy, put into the prophet's mouth by a late antimonarchical propagandist. For this purely theoretical view there exists no external supporting evidence. Rather, the evidence we do have points in diametrically the opposite direction — that Samuel's sentiments were a realistic assessment of what traditional Levantine kingship meant in practice.[18]

Comparison with the data from the courts of such kingdoms shows clear similarities with Samuel's warnings. (1) The Hebrews would see their sons impressed into a standing army, serving in the chariotry and as commanders (by fifties and thousands) of companies and divisions of soldiers. With this has been compared the service of *maryannu*, chariot warriors at Alalakh and later in Ugarit. At Ugarit conscription of the male inhabitants of local villages for military service, particularly as archers, is well attested (as well as for marine service).[19] (2) With 1 Sam. 8:12b, royal conscription for work on the land, one may compare the situation in Ugarit, where citizens in their villages were conscripted for this and other work, including on the royal estate *(dimtu/gt)*.[20] (3) With 8:12c, on people having to make (or produce) weapons (including for chariots) and equipment, we again may compare usage at Ugarit. There the required delivery of bronze vessels and of lances is mentioned.[21] (4) 8:13 continues with such a king taking on people's daughters to be perfumers, cooks, and bakers — probably to be understood as for royal service in the palace. This compares with bakers, launderers, oil workers, and perfumers in the palace records at Ugarit, and (several centuries before) with women bakers and confectioners, etc., among 400 women in the palace at Mari.[22] (5) In 8:14 Samuel warns of royal confiscation of choice land, vineyards and olive groves, to distribute to the king's officers. In the Canaanite and Levantine world the king of-

95

ten had considerable rights of disposal over the terrain in his realm, and could freely transfer land and title to it, as the Ugarit archives clearly illustrate.[23] (6) Further, 8:15, 17a attributes to the king the levying of a tithe of crops (grain, vintage) to supply his officers, and of livestock. The exercise of the royal tithe (crops, vintage, cattle) is again well attested at Ugarit, both in practice and by mention of special exemptions.[24] (7) And (8:16) the king can take over servants and livestock, or (8:17b) impress citizens into service.[25]

In the light of these extensive and well-attested usages, at Mari, Alalakh, and especially Ugarit (which fell in approximately 1175, barely 130 years before Saul's time), there is no need whatever to defer these usages as attested in 1 Sam. 8 to any period after the eleventh century — they have ancient and enduring roots. During the twelfth and into the eleventh century various former "Canaanite" political entities survived the passing impact of the Sea Peoples down the Mediterranean coast into eventual Philistia, and of a growing Aramean presence within Syria, from a mere enclave in the fourteenth and thirteenth centuries into nascent kingdoms of Zobah and then Damascus in the eleventh and tenth centuries.[26] On the one hand, seaport kingdoms such as Byblos and Tyre with Sidon and Arvad came through the changes, while inland around Mount Lebanon a rump kingdom of Amurru remained into the twelfth and possibly the eleventh century.[27] These, and surviving Canaanite cities such as Gezer and Megiddo, would amply have sufficed to pass on inherited Late Bronze ideas, ideals, and usages of the Late Bronze Age kingship of the thirteenth century and before. Military ranks such as "commander of a thousand" (cf. 1 Sam. 8:12) are attested not only at Ugarit; among the people who owned inscribed bronze arrowheads in the late twelfth to eleventh centuries, we have such an "arrow of Banaya, commander of a thousand," for example.[28]

(b) Glimpses of Topography and History

(1) Shiloh

Shiloh is locatable at the rocky mound of Khirbet Seilun; two excavation projects have worked here — Danish and Israeli.[29] It is a frustrating site to work at, as much is (or was) denuded to bare rock. Only the northern segment is clear enough to dig for pre-Roman remains; the high center has been successively cleared/denuded for successive buildings down to medieval times; and the southern half of the site was extensively redeveloped and built over during Roman and Byzantine times, to the detriment of whatever preceded them. Thus the result of limited digging in the northern segment is valuable so far as it goes, but cannot guarantee a full picture when so much is hidden or already lost and destroyed.

However, it is clear that Shiloh flourished during much of Iron Age I, in the twelfth and eleventh centuries, ending in a violent destruction. For at least a century (ca. 1150-1050, on Finkelstein's dates; but 1150 may be slightly too low), storehouses occupied at least some part of the northwest area of the site. No trace was found of the tabernacle precinct by him or the Danes, as the possibly preferred high central area is too denuded to yield any really ancient traces of anything. It should be said that a site for the tabernacle/temple has been suggested on the flat area adjacent to the north side of the settlement.[30] Despite summary rejection of the idea by Yeivin and Finkelstein, this remains a possible alternative to the interior summit, so long as not enough extensive investigation has been done there. Either way, the violent destruction of Shiloh can be assigned to circa 1050, in good agreement with the historical record for the election of Saul in opposition to the Philistine, Ammonite, and other menaces to early Israel.

(2) Gibeah of Saul/of Benjamin

Saul's capital, once he had assumed his kingship, this place is now conceded to have been at Tell el-Ful, a few miles north of Jerusalem, on an isolated, defensible bluff overlooking the main road north and south of it.[31] Upon this strategic point was found an Iron I occupation replaced (at an interval) by a fortress ("I"), subsequently refurbished ("II"), and then later in disuse. The oldest level may reflect the Gibeah of Judg. 19–20. The excavations by Albright, checked by Lapp, would favor the view that it was Saul who built the first fortress, later repaired by him or David. The first fort (quadrangular) had at least one rectangular corner-tower at its southwest angle; it may have had others at the other corners, but no traces were detected. This would be the setting of Saul's activities at Gibeah in 1 Samuel. Not far north was Geba, with a confusingly similar name. There the Philistines sought to establish a central stranglehold in the heart of Saul's kingdom, hence the bold action of Jonathan (1 Sam. 14:1), before his exploit at nearby Michmash.

(3) Other Places of Interest

Saul's wars with the Philistines involved him, young David, and Israel. When the Philistines captured the ark of the covenant, they installed it first in Dagon's temple at Ashdod and then inland at Gath and at Ekron, before sending it back up to the Hebrews (1 Sam. 5). Ashdod is well attested archaeologically, by its strata XII-X, for the twelfth to tenth centuries as an important Philistine city.[32] With good reason, Gath is now identified with Tell es-Safi (Tel Zafit); it and Ekron lie little more than fifteen miles inland from Ashdod. The location of Gath here (close to the land of Judah) fits well with the Goliath incident (1 Sam. 17) and as a close-by refuge for David escaping Saul's hand (1 Sam. 21:10–22:1; 27–28); archaeological traces indicate that it flourished during the Iron Ages I and II.[33] A few miles north of Gath, Ekron is now clearly set at Tel Miqne by an inscription; it was a major new Philistine center during the twelfth-eleventh centuries (then it was destroyed), as extensive excavations show.[34] Ascalon and Gaza also shared in returning the ark (6:17); extensive work at Ascalon and traces from Gaza illustrate the Philistine period at these sites.[35] The archaeology of Early Iron Beth-Shan (on whose walls the Philistines hung the bodies of Saul and his sons) has now been clarified. The Egyptian-ruled settlement (stratum Lower VI) crashed in flames in the mid-to-late twelfth century. By about 1100 a new township (stratum Upper VI) was built by Canaanites (and possibly with some Sea People settlers), which lasted a century or so to the tenth century — this was the Beth-Shan of Saul's decease and display. This, too, was destroyed in turn, and replaced (in stratum Lower V) by a new set of buildings on a different plan (with a governor's residence?) and typically Israelite red-slipped, burnished pottery. These facts would indicate an Israelite takeover *after* Saul's time, logically under David/Solomon.[36]

C. IMPLICIT BACKGROUND: DAVID

(i) Among the Mini-Empires

A fact that is almost totally unknown to nearly all commentators on 2 Sam. 8 to 1 Kings 11 is that the scale and nature of the wider realm of David and Solomon are *not* unique and belong to a specific period of history, namely, ca. 1200-900 — neither earlier nor later. The evidence for this is strictly factual, mostly from sources hardly heard of by such commentators, but clear in its import. The limits are set by the demise of the great Egyptian and Hittite Late Bronze Age empires within 1200/1180, just before our period (introducing it), and by the rise and initial expansion of the Neo-Assyrian Empire within circa 870-850 and onward, just following our period. Not too long before its breakup under the impact of external attack, the Hittite Empire was already indulging in devolution. The kings of Carchemish in north Syria (cousins of the emperors) had become effective viceroys of Syria on the central power's behalf; and the kings of Tarhuntassa in southeast Asia Minor then in effect obtained the same status in their region. With the fall of the capital and central power of Hatti, circa 1180, these two viceroyalties became independent mini–great powers in their own right, in their regions in Asia Minor and north Syria. During the later twelfth century the Arameans began to expand notably in north and central Syria, creating power centers in Zobah and Damascus by the early tenth — when Israel in turn reputedly became their successful rival for a season. We now follow through quickly the history of these mini-empires, in chronological and geographical (north to south) succession.

(a) The Mini-Empire of Tarhuntassa/Tabal (Southeast Asia Minor to Northwest of the Carchemish Zone)

Among the successors of Kurunta (contemporary of the last kings of the Hittite Empire) is most likely to be reckoned a ruler and "Great King" named Hartapus, son (and doubtless successor) of a Mursilis, the latter bearing a name from his imperial forebears. And possibly the "Great King" Ir-Tesub, who left a stela at Karahöyük-Elbistan, on the borders of Tarhuntassa and the Carchemish Zone.[37] Their ultimate successors in this remote region, some centuries later, were the "Great Kings" of Tabal, ending with Wassurme, deposed by the Assyrians circa 730/729.[38] These great kings of Tabal ruled over a series of vassals (hence their title as "great"); in 837 Shalmaneser III boasts of receiving gifts from "24 kings of Tabal," who would be such vassals.[39] Cf. fig. 15.1.

(b) The Mini-Empire of Carchemish (Southeast Asia Minor, North Syria, and West Bend of the Euphrates)[40]

Here, in the viceregal city of Carchemish, Talmi-Tesup (contemporary of the last Hittite emperor, Suppiluliuma II) was succeeded by his own son Kuzi-Tesup (I); he, or a like-named successor, assumed the title "Great King." Carchemish took for its own the zone of its former rule, and in fact maybe more as well. In the east the future principalities of Bit-Adini and Gozan bore Carchemishian rule between the Euphrates and the Habur River. To the northeast Melid (Malatya) and Kummuh were vassals. To the northwest and west Gurgum, the eventual Sam'al, and Unqi (Patinu) came under Carchemish, with Arpad and the larger entity of Hamath to the south. In Melid a junior branch of the Carchemish royal family held sway, from a grandson of Kuzi-Tesup (I or II).[41] By 1100 Tiglath-pileser I distinguished clearly between a king of Hatti (and so, of Carchemish), Ini-Tesup (II), and one Allumari, king in Malatya. So, by 1100 Melid was in effect the ally but maybe no longer the vassal of the Carchemishian "Great King." Then, in the tenth century, the ascendancy of Carchemish fell apart. By perhaps 985 the Aramean Adin founded the realm of Bit-Adini at Til Barsip in the western bend of the Euphrates, probably as a subject ally of Hadadezer of Zobah. One Bakhian set up his kingdom at Gozan (it becoming Bit-Bakhiani). Thus Carchemish lost its eastern possessions. Westward, Gurgum (at Mar'ash) broke away under its own line of nine kings, from Astuwatimais (ca. 990?) down to Halparuntas III, while in Sam'al any local Luvian rule was replaced by an Aramean regime from Gabbar onward (ca. 920 and following). Finally, to the south, Hamath was probably detached from the rule of Carchemish by Hadadezer of Aram-Zobah about 1000, only to be replaced as suzerain-ally by David of Israel, circa 990. Thus, within circa 1000 to 980 (Sam'al later?), Carchemish lost virtually all of its vassal territories, becoming simply a large city-state.[42] Circumstances having changed irrevocably, the last Great King, Ura-Tarhuns, had as a successor Suhis I, who kept only the simple title "King," no longer Great King. After almost 200 years, this (mini)-empire was over. Cf. fig. 15.2.

(c) The Mini-Empire of Aram-Zobah (Euphrates Western Bend, over Hamath and to the South of Damascus)

This ephemeral power is known to us from 2 Sam. 8, 10 and hinted at by an Assyrian reference (cf. above, p. 94). From Aram itself (either Damascus or Zobah) we do not possess even *one* narrative inscription; only the fragmentary Tell Dan stela found in Israelite territory, and rare mentions of rulers by the Assyrians (ninth century and following). So, apart from a few fragments, we are thrown back on the Old Testament narratives for Aram, precisely as for Israel. But if we patiently analyze these, something can be gained. Hadadezer's realm, of (Aram-)Zobah (cf. 2 Sam. 8:3, 5, 12; 10:8), was also known as Beth-Rehob (10:6; both terms conjoined), or "House of Rehob," just like Bayt-Dawid, "House of David," and many more examples.[43] Hadadezer is called "son of Rehob" (8:3, 12), which may well have been true if Rehob had been his father and immediate predecessor. But in the Assyrian sources it is also a way of referring to a successor of a dynastic founder (direct or otherwise, related or otherwise); witness the well-known example of Shalmaneser III's reference to "Jehu son of Omri," which is simply an idiom for "Jehu (ruler) of Beth-Omri" (Bit-Khumri, in Akkadian), as long since pointed out. So Hadadezer "son" of Rehob could possibly be Hadadezer (ruler) of Beth-Rehob, at some interval after the time of Rehob.[44] Clearly the Aramean realm of Hadadezer consisted of a heartland, Zobah, centered on his patrimony of Beth-Rehob (cf. Israel and Judah under David and Solomon), and then of an "empire" of tributary lesser states and chiefdoms, whom Hadadezer (and Rehob before him?) had brought under political control (again, as did David, with Transjordan, and the Arameans also). This is reflected in these passages: 2 Sam. 10:19, citing Hadadezer's vassals (on his south?), local "kings," who fell away to David; and implicitly in 2 Sam. 8:3, when Hadadezer deemed it vital to "restore his control" up by the Euphrates, and thus over local rulers there. We find such vassals in Aram-Damascus also, at a later date, in the thirty-two "kings" that supported a Benhadad against Israel (1 Kings 20:1). Zobah is at times located west or north of Damascus. It is probably at least a part of the Biqa Valley, between the Lebanon and Anti-Lebanon mountain ranges. In Gen. 22:24 the line of Nahor via Reumah ran to Tebah, Gaham (unknown), Tahash, and Maacah. These form a north-south sequence: Tebah, the Tubikhi of the Amarna letters;[45] then Tahash, equivalent to Takhsi in Egyptian lists (in Upe, from Qadesh-on-Orontes southward);[46] then Maacah, east of Lakes Huleh and Galilee, with Geshur. This Tebah/Tubikhi is probably identical with the Tebah/Betah of 2 Sam. 8:8 (cf. 1 Chron. 18:8). Thus it lay in parallel with Aram-Damascus, based on the oasis area of the town of Damascus. From east of earlier Qadesh-on-Orontes, Hadadezer had imposed his rule up to the Euphrates (perhaps via Tadmor), reducing urban and tribal entities to vassaldom, and exercised influence on the Arameans living north within the great west bend of that river (as at Bit-Adini), whence he summoned forces (cf. 2 Sam. 10:16). Hadadezer probably overawed both Aram-Damascus to his southeast and Hamath to his north, and thus we can see the outlines of his mini-empire as it was before David's intervention: (1) a "homeland" area in the Biqa Valley, based on the enclave of Beth-Rehob (Hadadezer's dynasty's home patch); (2) conquests of lesser chiefdoms northeast to the Euphrates and southward toward Maacah and Geshur; (3) subject allies in Aram-Damascus to the immediate east (cf. 2 Sam. 8:5), and in Hamath (unwillingly) in the north. David's intervention broke this up. Geshur allied itself with Israel (cf. 2 Sam. 3:3, 5; 13:37-39, for Geshur); Maacah may have become his vassal. Hamath sided with the new power Israel (and remained independent from Solomon's day until Assyrian dominance); Zobah was eclipsed, and from Solomon's time it was replaced as an Aramean power by Damascus.[47] Cf. fig. 15.3.

(d) The Mini-Empire of David and Solomon in Israel (from over Hamath to Philistia/Negev)

We now come to our fourth and last mini-empire in this coherent series.[48] It shows analogies in both format and history with the three preceding. We will sketch concisely the history and "hierarchy" that is visible in the Hebrew sources.

(1) Historical Development

Saul's realm had been beset in part by physical disunity: the city-state enclave of Jerusalem lay between Judah and Ephraim and the Jezreel Valley, dominated by such alien forts as Megiddo and Beth-Shan, between Ephraim and Galilee. From this situation David moved on in three phases. First, once he had control in both Judah and Israel, he sought promptly to unify his realm — first securing Jerusalem, transforming it from a line of division into a focus for both halves of his realm, by making it his capital (cf. the picturesque but condensed summary in 2 Sam. 5:6-10), specifically as the "City of David," or "Davidopolis," following long-established Near Eastern custom.[49] Then he could proceed to annex various important strong points to his realm: Megiddo and Beth-Shan in the Jezreel Valley and Rehob to its south, plus strategic Hazor in Galilee to the north. This we know not from the Bible but entirely from archaeological exploration (cf. below on Solomon, the archaeological section). Second, with a unified core realm David could then cow the Philistines to the west (to protect Judah and western Ephraim) and subjugate Moab and Edom to the east (to safeguard Gilead in the north and the Arabah route south). The Philistines remained independent. But Edom for sure (local dynasty dethroned; cf. 1 Kings 11:14-22) and probably Moab (cf. 2 Sam. 8:2) were made tributary under direct rule by deputies. This fate also befell Aram-Damascus, where key garrisons were installed after Hadadezer's defeat (8:6), and probably Aram-Zobah with Hadadezer's eclipse. So, east and north of the core kingdom we have largely directly dependent tribute-paying territories. The third phase of David's movement entailed other entities that were in all probability subject allies, varying from virtually independent like Toi of Hamath (8:9-10) to protectorate status, as with Ammon, where the hostile King Hanun was doubtless dethroned and his more pliant brother Shobi installed instead (who was loyal to David correspondingly; cf. 17:27). Geshur may also belong here, having had close links with David (3:3; cf. the Absalom affair, 13:37-38 and 14:22-32; 15:8). Outside these and the "empire" stood independent foes (Philistia) and friends (Tyre).

(2) Hierarchies

Thus David's mini-empire would have included three levels of rule: home core, subjugated territories (under governors and subject kings), and subject allies, less closely tied to Israel's regime.[50] Similar profiles appear in the cases of the other mini-empires also. With Tabal we may compare twenty-four "kings" who would have been the vassals of its "great king," he reigning in his core territory; the sources here do not suffice as yet to exhibit the level of "subject ally." With Carchemish we find a surrounding swath of vassal territories and incipient kingdoms, all of which eventually broke away in the tenth century. The special link with Melid (through the royal family) would give it the status initially of subject ally, until the blood link thinned and evaporated in the course of time. With Aram-Zobah, Hadadezer had a series of vassals under him, to his south (Aram-Damascus, Maacah, Tob, etc.), and unnamed ones up north to the Euphrates. As for subject allies, Hamath was an unwilling subject in some measure, while Bit-Adini was (as also Aramean) a more friendly subject ally (the nearest trans-Euphratean princedom that could have helped with troops). All four of our mini-empires took over defeated opponents and their territories as they stood, without much territorial change; thus such units could readily break away as natural political entities when the central power weakened. It is a considerable contrast with the vast Neo-Assyrian, Neo-Babylonian, and Persian empires, where (increasingly) new large-scale provinces became the norm (like Ebir-nari for the whole Levant, and Persian satrapies), and their internal provinces were often not coeval with former kingdoms conquered (e.g., Dor, or Gilead under Assyria). Thus our four mini-empires, including that of David and Solomon, are all of a piece, belong to a specific era, and found no equivalent successors ever again. If the Assyrians had never come west in the ninth to seventh centuries, then we need not doubt that the kings of Aram-Damascus would undoubtedly have achieved a fifth such local imperium in the Levant; but a resurgent Assyria systematically destroyed that dream.

On the internal front, David's regime shows development beyond that of Saul. As we saw, Saul had his informal "court" of up to 600 braves and others, had his aides, developed an army with a commander in chief and officers ("chiefs of thousands," etc.), and was levying taxation in some form; "Gibeah of Saul" was his simple precursor (as a royal, central capital) to the "City of David" that followed. For his part, we learn that David also had an army commander in chief, but also a body of "the Thirty" notables and heroes (in fact, up to thirty-seven men), a royal bodyguard of Pelethites and Kerethites (foreigners who were totally "king's men"), plus men of Gath (from his old Philistine days, under one Ittai). On the nonmilitary front there was a "recorder," a secretary, two priests and a king's chaplain, and king's sons possibly as counselors. Cf. 2 Sam. 8:15-18, and 23:8-39. Add to these the counselors Ahithophel and Hushai (cf. 16:15–17:23). So there had arisen a nucleus of court government for an expanding kingdom; as under Saul, the basis of rule away from Jerusalem would still have been through heads of tribes in their areas (cf. 1 Chron. 27:16-22). Administrators of royal properties are listed (27:25-31). Outside Israel and Judah, governors would rule in subject territories when local chiefs and kings were not retained as vassals. The use of garrisons in such territories (as in Aram-Damascus, 2 Sam. 8:6) would most likely be restricted to small groups of seasoned militia at key points, very much as Egypt had done in days past in the Levant, with messengers ready to take any news of revolt swiftly back to home base.[51] To contrast David and Solomon's mini-empire with later maxi-empires, see the map in fig. 14.

(3) Other Aspects of Life

Besides success in war, there is a persistent stream of tradition that links David with instrumental music (cf. 1 Sam. 16:15-23; 19:9) and with poems (e.g., a lament, 2 Sam. 1:17-27; 23:1-7) and hymns ("psalms"; 2 Sam. 22 = Ps. 18; Psalms, passim). It should occasion no surprise that either shepherd lads or kings should be involved with both in the biblical world. Alongside the fact of a vast treasury of scribally transmitted hymns and poetry, and data on musicianship in that ancient world, one may draw attention to three aspects related to David's case: popular poetry and hymns, royal participation in these arts, and the conventions of such poetics. In all three aspects David's case fits in naturally with what we learn from elsewhere.

First, poetry and song had always been part of the life of the common people, not just of ruling elites in antiquity.[52] Here the most accessible source is Egypt. Almost two thousand years before the shepherd boy David, herdsmen are shown singing melancholy ditties in the Pyramid Age already, as are the more cheerful bearers of the carrying chairs of the great (third millennium).[53] Already in the Middle Kingdom (early second millennium), a thousand years before David played for Saul, people were commonly entertained by harpists playing and singing their songs. Still later, in the New Kingdom, besides more harpists (later second millennium), plowmen, reapers, and threshers sing their rural snatches. And short rhapsodies of joy come forth at festival banquets and even picnics in the garden. Besides these we have a wealth of love lyrics, celebrating the joys and frustrations of boy-meets-girl. And finally, in the thirteenth-twelfth centuries, down to little more than a century before David's time, we have a remarkable series of prayers and hymns to their gods by the workmen of the royal tombs, preserved on their modest monuments in Western Thebes: confessions of sin, words of contrition, pleas for divine mercy, and thanksgiving for healing and deliverances.[54] Here we come relatively close to the spirit of biblical psalmody, as has long been recognized. A David (even as a shepherd or a youthful harpist) stood in a long, fruitful tradition of poetry, popular as well as "official," expressive of relations with deity as well as with one's fellows.

Second, kings participated in such arts. Already in the Egypt of close on 2000 B.C., the venerable Theban king Intef II waxes lyrical in his very personal praise of the goddess Hathor, in his exuberant hymn, engraved on one of the stelae at his tomb.[55] Over in Mesopotamia three hundred years earlier, the great Sargon of Akkad's daughter, Princess En-khedu-anna, had composed two hymns to the goddess Inanna and the second edition of the Sumerian Temple Hymns (forty-two hymns in all) — making her the first authoress in history.[56] Almost a thousand years after her, back in Egypt (and three centuries before King David), we find the sun-worshiping "monotheistic" pharaoh Akhenaten praising the sun god as the visible Disc *(Aten)* with an atmospheric royal fervor, touching on humanity and other creatures in a fashion common both to Ps. 104 and to other hymnody from both Egypt (for Amen-Re) and Assyria (for the moon and sun gods).[57] Thus David would be no oddity in being a royal author of religious poetry, after his shepherd days were long past.

Third, we examine how the usages of biblical psalmody (Davidic or otherwise) fit into the Near Eastern cultural context.[58] The forms and conventions of biblical poetry, so familiar in the Psalms, go back in origin two thousand years before David's time. Exactly as in Sumerian, Akkadian, Egyptian, and other West Semitic literature (e.g., Ugaritic), so in biblical Hebrew poetry the basic building block is the two-line couplet (or "bicolon"), foundation stone of poetic "parallelism." A pair of thought units or "lines" can be used to state a concept twice, using different expressions (synonymous); or to develop the thought in the second line (synthetic); or to express a contrast in the two successive lines (antithetic). One may enrich the style by having three lines in parallel ("tricolon"), four lines in parallel in varying combinations ("quatrain"), or even larger units. So one may exemplify (using couplets):

Synonymous: (identical concepts)	Adore Amun, and he will guard you, exalt Amen-Re, and he will keep you safe.
Synthetic: (thought extended)	Pharaoh has slain his foes, the Falcon has destroyed their cities and crops.
Antithetic: (contrast)	Now, pat a dog and it will love you, but hit the canine and it will bite you.

With three- and four-line and larger units, more variations are open to poets, and other devices can be used: ellipse of part of a second (or other) line(s) to reduce repetition and tighten style; or "chiasmus," where key elements occur in reverse order in the two successive lines, e.g., of a couplet. Thus the couplet:

> For I give praise to Hathor,
>> I give glory to my Golden One,

written as an ellipse:

> I give praise to Hathor,
>> glory to my Golden One,

and as a chiasmus (A . . . B, then B . . . A):

> **Hathor** welcomes me *at her shrine,*
> *from her sanctum,* I hear a word from **the Golden One.**

Many other devices were also in full use from the third millennium down to Roman times, but with different periods of use or popularity, in different classes of literature. All these "flowers of style" had been in full use for nearly two millennia prior to David, were in full use in his day, and many of them for long afterward, appearing in a wide range of biblical poetry, not just his. So, in terms of custom and technique, there is no reason to date biblical poetry any later than the claims made for various examples of it in the Hebrew text. The contexts of poetry by David (Ps. 18 in 2 Sam. 22), Hezekiah (Isa. 38:9-20), and Habakkuk (chap. 3; cf. 3:1) make it clear that authorship is there intended. Likewise in Pss. 3, 7, 34, 51, 52, 56, 57, 59, 60, 63, 142, which equally (like Ps. 18 = 2 Sam. 22) are linked with events in David's life and career. An authorship by David may also be true of other psalms simply headed *l — Dwd,* "for" or "belonging to David." Otherwise, this kind of heading would denote belonging to a Davidic collection, just as (in Ugaritic) *l — 'qht* means on certain tablets "belonging to (the series on) 'Aqhat," or about him, or dedicated to him. Many psalm headings have notations now difficult to understand — possible references to musical tunes, types of songs or prayers, also to other personnel, such as "the director of music." These notes illustrate the use of such psalms in the worship of YHWH in his tent and then temple in Jerusalem — as seen in 1 Chron. 16, where excerpts from other, non-Davidic psalms (105, 96, 106) were used at the ark's induction into David's tent shrine in Jerusalem. It should be noted that these psalm headings are obscure simply because they are *ancient* — being no longer fully understood when the Psalms were translated into Greek (for the Septuagint Old Testament) in the third or second century B.C. Full liturgical usages of Solomon's temple fell out of use for over half a century while it lay in ruins (586-538 and following); not all of that ceremonial would be restored at the opening of the Second Temple in 515; it would probably be in a simpler form. So ancient headings passed out of active use, and thus out of currency.

The use of titles, colophons, and terminology for various kinds of hymns and psalms is widely attested in the biblical world, from many centuries before David's time, and remained habitual down to his time and long afterward. So biblical titles and terms are a normal phenomenon. From the early second millennium in Mesopotamia, we have Sumerian hymns of various kinds labeled as *ershemma, balbale, shagidda,* etc., and used in the cults of the gods. They could be sung on different occasions, not just in one setting; cult hymns could pass into personal use, and personal psalms could pass into the service of the cult. Hence it can be no surprise to see biblical psalms in both contexts (personal and cultic). The content of a piece may not have any reference to its place in the cult. Musical terms are quoted with hymns from the early second millennium onward (*balag,* "song with a harp"; *ershemma,* "lament with a *shem*-drum"; etc.).[59] Also, many Egyptian compositions bear titles, those attributed to personal piety in particular (thirteenth-twelfth centuries).[60] The use of music can be specified, as in Mesopotamian and Hittite contexts (instruments and song specified to be performed either separately or in unison).[61] At Egyptian festivals in the New Kingdom (esp. 1300-1150), dancers and musicians are shown in temple scenes and their hymnody is quoted in the scenes.[62] All this gives us the conceptual setting of what we find in descriptions of Hebrew usage as preserved (e.g.) in 1 Chron. 15–16, 25 when the ark was installed in Jerusalem and musical provision was planned for the temple. There is nothing artificial here, it is precisely what one would expect.

D. IMPLICIT BACKGROUND: SOLOMON

Here we will consider appropriate background in the same sequence of themes outlined from the biblical data, above, before looking at the possible contributions from the physical archaeology of Palestine for this overall period and coming to a concluding review of the whole.

(i) Foreign Relations: Egypt

We return to a pharaoh who conquered Gezer (1 Kings 9:16), and then gave it as a dowry with his daughter in a marriage alliance with Solomon (3:1; 9:16, 24; cf. 7:8; 11:1). The possible identity of such a king plus the significance of his action against Gezer and the question of an international marriage alliance are two separate issues.

(a) Pharaoh and Gezer

As has been established quite clearly above, pp. 82 (for 931/930) and 85-88 (for Solomon), there is presently no factual reason to doubt that Solomon died in 931/930, after reigning forty years, i.e., from 971/970. On the other side of the divide, it is also very clear that *independent* Egyptian dates can be established from 664 back to circa 945 and the start of the Twenty-Second Dynasty within very close limits. (A recent claim that Egyptian dates around 945/925 cannot be established within a margin of some fifty years [ca. 979-922] is an incompetent nonsense that can be dismissed from further notice.)[63] Thus, close on 945 also marks the end of the Twenty-First Dynasty. The number and identity of the kings and lengths of reigns in this dynasty can be very closely determined. From the actual firsthand monuments, we have seven kings, thus: (1) (Ne)sibanebdje(d), (2) Neferkare Amenemnisu, probably preceding (3) Psusennes I (throne name, Akheperre), (4) Amenemope, (5) Osorkon the Elder, (6) Siamun, and finally (7) Psusennes II (throne name, Tyetkheperre). The Twenty-First Dynasty happens to be quite well preserved in the text of Manetho's lists, also with seven kings, these being: (1) Smendes, (2) Psusennes (I), (3) Nepherkheres, (4) Amenophthis, (5) Osochor, (6) Psinaches, and (7) a Psusennes (II). These correspond closely to the seven kings known from actual monuments, and in the same order (with only one minor exception). The regnal years also correspond very closely from both the monuments and Manetho; only with Siamun (attested to Year 17) does Psinaches at nine years in Manetho fall a decade short (9 from [1]9 years). Thus the entire line ran from 1070 or 1069 down to 945. The last king, Psusennes II, can be given an independent reign of fourteen or fifteen years (960/959–945). Then Siamun's nineteen years would cover 979/978–960/959. Therefore he is the one obvious ruler to be considered the contemporary of the first ten years of Solomon's reign, 971/970–961/960. For Siamun, we *do* have evidence for contact in the Levant, but for no other king of the dynasty (and certainly not for his successor, Psusennes II). Only in the burial of Psusennes I was there found an Assyrian bead that was an heirloom from an earlier reign, and not evidence for active links abroad in his time.

Thus Siamun is, and remains thus far, the sole serious candidate for the roles of conqueror of Gezer and would-be father-in-law to Solomon on purely chronological grounds. And from him alone in the Twenty-First Dynasty so far we have a reasonable piece of evidence that he did intervene in the Levant. This is the well-known fragment of a triumphal scene from Tanis, executed in stone from a temple structure. It shows the king in typical pose, brandishing a mace to strike down a bunch of prisoners(?) now lost at the right except for two arms and hands, one of which grasps a remarkable double-bladed ax by its socket (fig. 18A). Above the king are his cartouches. Despite a ridiculous denial to the contrary (alleging "an unidentified king"!),[64] these cartouches read with all possible clarity: [*Neterkheperre Setepenamun*], Siamun beloved of Am[un], with just one Amun sign partly broken off (but restorable from ample examples of this king's very characteristic titles).

Much nonsense has been written just recently against this piece (mainly by non-Egyptologists, not competent to comment on it).[65] The facts are as follows. (1) Formal triumph scenes of this kind from temple structures commonly commemorate kings who fought wars. Only in their secondary use as decoration in "minor art" (on sides of state barges, furnishings, etc.) do such scenes serve merely as idealistic icons of royal power. Thus Siamun's temple triumph scene should be treated seriously; nobody is (yet) known to have had one since Ramesses VI some 140 years earlier (defeated Libyans in the Thebaid), and imperial kings earlier still.[66] After Siamun, Shoshenq I (Shishak) had such scenes in two temples — and then nobody thereafter (on present knowledge) until the Twenty-Fifth Dynasty, which had wars in the Levant and with Assyria. So the practical likelihood is that this scene should be treated as a fair indicator of military action of some kind by Siamun — who (along with Psusennes I) was the most active ruler of the Twenty-First Dynasty.[67]

(2) The fragmentary foes hold a remarkable weapon. This is, and can only be, a double-bladed battle-ax or halberd. At its inner edge it clearly has a socket, from which protrudes a (wooden) shaft or handle, now largely broken away with the bottom part of the stone slab. The foeman grasps the ax by the socket where the shaft protrudes. That the shaft appears to leave the socket at slightly less than the expected angle to the blade is either very slight artistic license or may indicate that the shaft is broken just where it leaves the socket, and is thus rendered powerless to harm the pharaoh. This mental attitude reappears in the great triumph scene of Shoshenq I at Karnak, where the foes helplessly grasp daggers by their blades, not the handles. This all has to be spelled out, because the details are clear on the original and on the *original photograph* — but *not* on the very commonly reproduced line drawing (erroneous in detail!) used by so many would-be commentators at second hand. This *is* an ax — and *not* a shield, or handcuffs (fig. 18B) or halter or whatever. It is of unique type, unparalleled in Canaan with the indigenous culture there at any time; Palestinian double-bladed ax heads are wholly different in shape (like an X), having no rounded, sharply flared form. The Aegean cultures offer

the nearest analogies, although not precise. This piece may thus reflect a Philistine/Sea Peoples foe, as they certainly came from that zone (or beyond) into Canaan at the beginning of the twelfth century. The fact that Siamun's scene includes a unique feature (not just a commonplace weapon) would speak for it reflecting a specific event. By contrast, the foes of Tuthmosis III in a Karnak scene hold axes of "duck-bill" type of traditional Canaanite design; they were obsolete then, but without effect on the historicity of his scene and its accompanying list of foreign place-names.

(3) Any Egyptian army that marched by the customary route into the Levant (along the Sinai Mediterranean coast road) always came first to Gaza, then into the very region that had become Philistia in the twelfth century. On the inland route north from Gath and Ekron, Canaanite Gezer was the next major settlement of any strategic import. No pharaoh would mount a campaign in Canaan merely to capture Gezer (and then, just to give it to a neighbor state). Any campaign here (by Siamun or any other Egyptian king) had to have a larger purpose. A pharaoh's gift of Gezer to Solomon would hardly be altruistic; he must have gained by the campaign so as to make that transaction worthwhile. What is more, as Gezer guarded an important route up to Jerusalem, its cession to Solomon would be of value to him, as a frontier fort adjoining Philistia.

In summary, the two pieces of data (Siamun's relief; the passage in 1 Kings 9:16-17) make good political sense when set together, in the context of a possible alliance of Egypt (Siamun) and Israel (Solomon). If (for example) the Philistines had impeded, or overcharged tolls on, transit traffic through their terrain (or along their coast) that affected both Egypt and Israel, then the two may have colluded to end the menace by allying against and subduing Philistia. Siamun will have launched a strong police action through Gaza, sending one force up to Ascalon and Ashdod, with his main force going over via Gath and Ekron up to Gezer, to link up with a Hebrew force making a diversionary move on the north. Out of their success, Siamun could establish suzerainty over Philistia (levying tribute on its rich cities), while Solomon would gain the important border post of Gezer. If this occurred about the third year of Solomon (ca. 967), then Siamun would have enjoyed his triumph for only seven or eight years; the Philistines would have regained their full independence at his death in 960 or 959. But the Hebrew rulers retained Gezer permanently.

(b) Pharaoh's Daughter and Dowry

Recent critics have also dismissed the reported marriage alliance of the pharaoh and Solomon in 1 Kings 9:16. Time and again they have rested their flawed case on one single remark by Amenophis III nearly half a millennium before, that Egyptian kings' daughters were never given to anyone.[68] Hence Solomon would not be offered one. But Solomon lived not in the fourteenth century but in the tenth! Times had changed; no vast empires now existed; the old Egyptian royal lines had long since been replaced by "new men" not tied to the ways of four hundred years before — any more than (in Britain) subjects of Elizabeth II are tied to the full cultural norms obtaining under Elizabeth I, four centuries before. The entirely unjustified denials by Old Testament scholars notwithstanding, the following facts are clear. No New Kingdom pharaoh is ever known to have given a daughter to either a foreigner or a commoner. The one near exception was Ankhsenamun, widow of Tutankhamun, who wrote to the Hittite emperor Suppululiuma I requesting of him a son in marriage (to make him king in Egypt).[69] In stark contrast, the period of the Twenty-First–Twenty-Third Dynasties is precisely when we *do* find kings' daughters being married off to commoners and foreigners.[70] While still king, Psusennes II (last king of the Twenty-First Dynasty, 960/959–945) gave his daughter Maatkare in marriage to Osorkon, son of the Libyan chief of the Ma(shwash), Shoshenq — the later Shoshenq I and Osorkon I. At this time Libyans were still considered foreigners by most Egyptians; the clearest possible example is the way the Theban priests at first dated by Shoshenq I *not* as full king with cartouches, etc., but instead disdainfully by: "Year 2 . . . of the Great Chief of the Ma, Shoshe(n)q," adding the foreigner sign to Shoshenq's name! See fig. 17.[71] There had been intermarriage between Shoshenq's family and the Twenty-First Dynasty before this; and King Osorkon the Elder had been of (Egypto)-Libyan parentage.[72] Various Twenty-Second Dynasty kings married off their daughters to commoners (higher priesthood, viziers, etc.) — practices entirely unheard of four centuries earlier! Thus there is *no* problem in Siamun giving a daughter to a foreign ruler (especially if he himself were of Libyan blood) at this time, and biblical scholars will have to accept that fact; Amenophis III's old-style prejudice way back in 1357 is irrelevant to "modern" 967!

Regarding the care of exalted foreign princesses, twice it is remarked (1 Kings 7:8; 9:24) that Solomon built a fitting abode for his new Egyptian bride, as part of his palace complex in Jerusalem. This kind of provision for particularly distinguished ladies is also known elsewhere (and earlier) in the biblical world. In both the Egyptian and cuneiform sources we learn that Ramesses II was building his first Hittite bride "ample villas [in her] name" (Egyptian), and in cuneiform "a fine house(?)," as Edel also noticed.[73]

On the question of Gezer as dowry, a series of *ignoranti* have remarked that Gezer as a "smoking ruin" was not much of a dowry, contrasting it also with Amarna-period and Egypto-Hittite usage.[74] However, yet again they have totally misread the facts. First, Gezer was taken, its Canaanite population slain, and the settlement torched (how completely is *not* stated). What Solomon in reality received with Pharaoh's daughter was (a) a (partially?) cleared fortress town-site open to be developed in any way he wished (which is what he did, along with Hazor and Megiddo; 1 Kings 9:15-17); (b) a prime site strategically guarding a major route up to Jerusalem, his own capital; and (c) a complete city-state territory, to add to his realm — no town like Gezer was without its dependent agricultural/pastoral hinterland! Second, it again is pointless to apply second-millennium usage on dowries and ceremonies to events as late as 967 without producing supporting data. Times had long since changed, as already demonstrated on marriages above. Royal wedding gifts in 1350 could amount to well over £200,000/$275,000 worth of gold and other items; the real estate worth of Gezer as site and territory we cannot calculate. It was a different kind of transaction in another age. What is more, one should remember that the mentions of Solomon's Egyptian princess are brief, because they are almost incidental (in contexts of building works, etc.); so rites like anointing and other detailed gifts simply would not be mentioned, as being irrelevant to the main purpose of the narrative. So, too, under Ramesses II: anointing occurs exclusively in the cuneiform record, while wealth (for dowry) is mainly in the Egyptian texts (with but one lurid exception).[75] In short, the recently attempted critiques of the role of Siamun and of the allusions to Egypt in 1 Kings 3–11 are so badly flawed as to be worthless on present evidence.

(ii) Relations with Phoenicia

(a) Royal Letters

The exchanges of letters between Hiram and Solomon reflect long-accepted usage in royal, international correspondence. It was the custom for neighboring kings to congratulate a new ruler on his accession (as did Hiram, 1 Kings 5:1; cf. Suppiluliuma I for a pharaoh, EA 41).[76] And kings from of old had requested materials for building or adorning temples and palaces, for payment (as here, 1 Kings 5:6, 9ff.) or in gift exchanges (EA 4, 9, 16, 19), as well as other expertise — be it craftsmen (1 Kings 7:13-47; 2 Chron. 2:12-14; cf. Egyptian carpentry, EA 10) or persons of other skills, e.g., medical (Egyptian physicians going to the Hittite court under Ramesses II).[77] Invocations of deity and divine blessings (cf. 1 Kings 5:1-7 passim; 2 Chron. 2:3-12) are well known in such correspondence, as in the Amarna letters of the fourteenth century and royal letters from Ugarit and Emar and Egypto-Hittite royal letters of the thirteenth century.[78]

The economics of Solomon's first agreement (or treaty) with Hiram of Tyre fit in well with the known scale of economy of Levantine kingdoms. The 20,000 *kor*s of grain paid annually to Hiram for his timber and laborers (1 Kings 5:6, 9, 11) would have required the crop from about 262 acres or just over 1 square kilometer of land in each of Solomon's twelve administrative districts, not an excessive amount of product. After comparing Solomon's figures with what we know from the physically much smaller kingdom of Ugarit, Heltzer also observed that, for Solomon, "the figures are by no means exaggerated."[79]

(b) Small Points

Sometimes minor details pop up and strike the eye. In Solomon's first letter back to Hiram king of Tyre, he writes that "we have nobody so skilled at timber-felling as the Sidonians" (not "Tyrians"), in 1 Kings 5:6. The remark arises from the fact (visible in various sources) that in previous centuries it was Sidon, not Tyre, that was dominant in Phoenicia, and so "Sidonians" could be used as a synonym for "Phoenicians," not only for people of Sidon itself, even by Solomon's time, when Tyre had overtaken Sidon in importance.[80]

Another is the use of Phoenician, not Hebrew, month names in the narratives on the building of the Jerusalem temple — names that occur nowhere else in the Hebrew Bible (1 Kings 6:1, 37-38; 8:2).[81] This is a mark of the influence of the Phoenician contribution to the building of that edifice; the Phoenician language of Hiram's work gangs made some short-term impact on local usage for those few years (as can happen in similar contexts even today), and these three terms remain to us as linguistic fossils of that brief seven plus thirteen years of temple and palace building. There was no occasion for such ephemeral impact in Jerusalem's subsequent history.

(c) Royal Bargaining: Galilee

In due course, with the temple and palace finally completed after twenty years of investment in timber, fine stonework, bronzework, and precious metal, the time had come to regulate the accounts and make fresh arrangements — a situation reflected in the very fleeting accounts in 1 Kings 9:10-14 and 2 Chron. 8:1-2. In the former passage we learn that Solomon passed over to Hiram twenty towns in Galilee (the land of Cabul, with which Hiram was dissatisfied) in exchange for timber and gold, while in the latter passage we read that Solomon built/rebuilt villages (number and location not stated) that Hiram had handed over to him, populating them with Israelites.

A superficial view of the two passages would see them as contradictory, but the assumption that (e.g.) the Chronicler would crassly contradict Kings is naive and simplistic, and implies a lowbrow level of stupidity that we have no warrant to ascribe to that writer. The two statements are not identical, but most likely complementary, reflecting the outcome of a good old-fashioned haggle between two very wily Oriental gentlemen, a not uncommon feature in ancient royal correspondence. Given the limited resources of Tyre's own coastal plain hinterland, Hiram needed an ongoing supply of grain, oil, and wine, such as he had been paid previously by Solomon until completion of the building work in Jerusalem.[82] Therefore payment of debts owed him by cession of cultivable land from Solomon would fit the bill nicely in more senses than one. David's conquests had doubtless given Israel the coastland all the way north from Accho to the natural boundary at Ras en-Nakura headland, and the terrain inland and east from there, a substantial part of the long-envisaged allotment to the tribe of Asher (Josh. 19:24-31). However, the Asherites had never been very effective at following up this "ideal" allocation, failing long since to take over this region and merely settling among the locals, as pointed out in one of the many invaluable short notices to be found in Judges (1:31).[83]

Thus one may suggest that (1) Hiram proposed to Solomon that cession of the plain of Accho (and eastern upslopes) would meet his requirements; (2) Solomon proposed to Hiram that he ought have only the slopelands (*shephelah* of Galilee), not the coastal plain; (3) Hiram took a good look at them and said something rude in Phoenician (cf. 1 Kings 9:13), for "no way!" Then finally, (4) the pair temporized in both directions (as good Near Eastern monarchs did). Thus Solomon gave Hiram the desired coastal plain and upslopes of Asher/land of Cabul (with up to twenty villages; 1 Kings 9:11-13), while on his part Hiram ceded upland territory to Solomon (2 Chron. 8:2), reaching north of David's probable border (along the hills east from Ras en-Nakura) into the uplands by Rama and to Qana (southeast from Tyre and its coast plain). Back home, each king could no doubt justify his action as a "success"; Hiram had obtained a good, arable plain, with access to the ports of Accho and Shihor-Libnath (Tell Abu Huwam), while Solomon could claim to have fulfilled a part more of Asher's ancient claims north (if inland) in place of their failure along the Mediterranean littoral.

Such wheeling and dealing was not new. Way back in the eighteenth century, in north Syria, Abba-il ("Abban") king of Aleppo made exchanges of towns and territories with Yarim-lim, the vassal ruler of Alalakh; the latter later grumbled (like a Hiram!) at the loss of two places.[84] The question of fixing a boundary crops up in another treaty of that time, between kings of Mari and

Eshnunna.[85] So Hiram and Solomon had precursors in these and other royal concerns.[86]

(iii) The Horse and Chariot Trade

In recent works, Solomon's trade (1 Kings 10:28-29) between Egypt and Que (= Cilicia in southeast Asia Minor) has been dismissed as simply Near Eastern royal propaganda, without any serious regard for the background evidence. It is alleged that horses were not bred in Egypt, and that evidence for horse trade is not known.[87] However, no such "propaganda line" is attested; kings speak of conquests and great buildings, not trade, in their major commemorative texts and inscriptions. As for horse breeding in Egypt, there is every reason to believe that it was practiced there. During the Eighteenth and Nineteenth Dynasties, an Egypt at war with the Hittites and Mitannians could not possibly import horses from southeast Anatolia; from the twelfth century onward Egypt had no direct links with that area. So military necessity demanded that she breed her own chariot horses in the second and early first millennia. And positive evidence favors this. There was extensive stabling and a "horse stud" at Pi-Ramesse in the East Delta in the thirteenth century, when we also have record (ODM 1076) of the "great [mead]ow of Pi-Ramesse," with mention of horse keepers, droves of horses, and grooms and charioteers.[88] Ramesses II himself could send horses to the Hittite king (in Anatolia!) on request, as did the king of Babylon. Later on, after Solomon's day, Sargon II boasts of the "twelve large horses" given him by Osorkon IV (Shilkanni), and he and other Assyrian kings prized also horses of Nubian origin. Thus the Nile Valley *did* become a breeding ground for horses from the sixteenth to the seventh century.[89] Also (against Ash and Schipper), the price of 150 shekels for good-quality horses charged by Solomon fits exactly with the slowly falling price curve for such royal beasts at 300 shekels in the eighteenth century (Mari from Qatna), then down to 200 shekels in the thirteenth century (Ugarit), and so to 150 shekels under Solomon (tenth century). Naturally, in horse-growing areas and places adjacent to them, and for cheaper hacks, etc., prices came much lower (at Nuzi and Ugarit and especially in Anatolia itself).[90] No problem here!

As for chariots, at 600 shekels from Egypt and retailed by Solomon to northern rulers (Arameans and [Neo]-Hittites), these are clearly richly adorned "Rolls-Royce" models for fellow kings, not simply lightweight runabouts of wood and leather. As Ikeda points out, the term *merkaba* used here and in certain other contexts relates to ceremonial chariots — the sort of vehicle, commonly gold plated, used by the Canaanite princes defeated by Tuthmosis III circa

1458 or retrieved from the tomb of Tutankhamun, circa 1330, or mentioned in the Amarna letters just before his reign.[91] No problem here, either.

(iv) The Arrival of the Queen of Sheba

This famous and colorful episode has given rise to much romantic legend for centuries (even millennia), all the way down to Handel's famous music by this title and (from the sublime to the ridiculous!) to an archaeologically conditioned humorous presentation of her career.[92] But we must resolutely cast aside all this later verbiage, romance, and homage, and stay with the only truly ancient account that we have (1 Kings 10:1-13; 2 Chron. 9:1-12). Our task is to evaluate the essentials of her case as there presented, be it realistic or mere romance, on the basis of external factual controls.

(a) Location

Whence did she come? Hebrew *Sheba* is universally admitted to be the same name as the place-name commonly transcribed "Saba" that denotes a community and kingdom in ancient Yemen in southwest Arabia. It cannot be located in northwest Arabia for multiple reasons. Negatively, there is no mention whatsoever in the Old North Arabian and other sources we have for the ninth to second centuries B.C. of any kingdom of Saba up there then, and *no* Sabaean inscriptions from that area either. Positively, we *do* have a series of other well-attested kingdoms in northwest Arabia: Qedar, Dedan, Lihyan, with matching series of inscriptions; from the far south, it is the Mineans, not Sabaeans, who left inscriptions in the northwest. In the late eighth and early seventh centuries we have Assyrian mentions of Itamru (Yitha'amar) and Karibilu (Karibil) as kings of Saba, who belong to the line of Yemenite "paramount rulers" *(mukarribs)* in southwest Arabian Saba. Before that, Assyrian sources record Sabaean trade caravans explicitly for the later eighth and implicitly for the early ninth centuries, little more than half a century after Solomon. As they traveled freely north, so could she have done.[93]

(b) The Gender Issue

The astonishing thing about Solomon's south Arabian visitor was that it was a *queen* that came and not (as might be expected) a king, the ancient Near East being considerably male-oriented (as is still true today). But her precise status is not made clear in the very compact narrative that concerns her. Was she a sole ruler, a "queen regnant" in Saba, as many modern writers assume? There is no proof whatsoever that this is the case. On the basis of the "high" chronology that would identify the Assyrian Karibilu of 685 with the *mukarrib* Karibil Watar I, there are some twenty earlier rulers known; on an average of fifteen-to-twenty years for most such reigns, male rulers roughly contemporary with Solomon might include the outgoing Yada'il Yanuf, a Dhamar'alay A, and his two successor sons, Yakrubmalik A and Yada'il Bayyin I. In theory there is a break in the family line between Yada'il Yanuf and Dhamar'alay A; their present positions are still theoretical. Hence one could intercalate the reign of a queen regnant here if further evidence should eventually require it, at about 970/960 in very round figures. However, there is no a priori reason why she could not have been the consort of a *mukarrib*, who sent her out as his personal executive emissary to sort out Solomon in diplomacy, for good reasons noted below. If north Arabian queens could play such roles, southern ones could also, particularly in earlier periods. Under Yitha'amar Bayyin I (ca. 720, high date), women served alongside men, including as beaters at royal hunts.[94] So, queens consort may not have mere ciphers either; we simply have no data yet, one way or the other.

But the gender of our exotic personage does affect dating in another way. In north Arabia we have a series of executive queens, seemingly queens regnant, in the ninth and early seventh centuries, as Assyrian texts prove clearly.[95] Opponents of Assyria from and in north Arabia included Zabibe (738), Samsi (733), Iati'e (703) — and lastly Te'elkhunu in 691, who was associated with a King Haza'il in Qedar. The important fact to notice is that Te'elkhunu was the last of her kind in our uneven knowledge of ancient Arabian history. *After 690, never again do we find any Arabian queen playing any active role whatsoever in history.* In fact, from 690 B.C. all the way to A.D. 570, with one exception, we never even hear of *any* ancient southwest or northwest Arabian queens at all! (The lonely exception was in ca. A.D. 225, when the Sabaean princess Malikhalik [whom her father had married off to a king of Hadramaut] was hijacked back home by the next Sabaean king [her brother], displeased by her royal Hadrami husband's behavior.)[96]

Thus, in terms of old-fashioned OT scholarship, the queen of Sheba is "pre-Deuteronomic" (well before 621, the imaginary date for the first "publication" of Deuteronomy and its religious beliefs). There was no rational reason for inventing a story about a *queen* (rather than a king) visiting Solomon at any time after 650 at the latest (when any memory about Te'elkhunu and her kin would have long since evaporated). Our queen should belong to genuine historical tradition contained in the "Acts of Solomon," the daybooks from his time (or works based on them), drawn upon by Kings (and perhaps Chronicles).

(c) Why Did She Come? A Question of Ophir and Wealth?

A cursory glance at 1 Kings 10 might suggest that the doughty queen made her long journey just to talk riddles with Solomon, and (touristically) to view his rumored splendors. The splendors heaped up within the narrow confines of Jerusalem (palace and temple) doubtless she might appreciate, and matters of mental stimulus be shared. But no head of state, ancient or modern, normally takes off on a long, hard journey just for tourism and a quiz hour or two. Then as now, other agendas were central to such visits. During the ninth and eighth centuries, as noticed above, merchant caravans traveled north from Sheba to reach Assyria to the northeast; from other considerations, also to Palestine and the Mediterranean world. This did not just begin in the 880s; for many centuries Saba and its neighbors had enjoyed an irrigation-based agricultural civilization, without use of writing. But by about the thirteenth/twelfth centuries the ancient Arabians suddenly found it essential to adopt an alphabet and start writing. If agriculture did not require it, something else did; international trade was seemingly the stimulus. So, by Solomon's time, the Sabaeans had begun to develop their incense routes to the Levant and Mesopotamia, trading in both aromatics and other desirable goods.

But then we read of Hiram and Solomon organizing shipping expeditions from the Gulf of Aqaba (from Ezion-Geber) down the Red Sea to Ophir (and beyond), which returned with gold, wood, and gems (1 Kings 9:26-28; 10:11-12). Where was this Ophir?[97] Much debated, its location is now with good reason placed either west or east of the Red Sea. West would lead us to the gold deposits behind the Red Sea mountains of the Sudan, north of Port Sudan — the land of ʿAmau with its "gold of ʿAmau" of the Egyptians.[98] Eastward across the Red Sea would find us in western Arabia, in the area south from Medina (by Mahd adh-Dhahab) to the region of Wadi Baysh and northern Hawlan ("Havilah").[99] The African option would not affect Saba or its trade — but the west Arabian location would fall smack across Saba's direct land-based trade route!

Besides aromatics, the queen brought gold; was it one of Saba's sources that Hiram and Solomon had tapped in western Arabia? And could they cut the incense route at will? Such hard questions the Sabaean confederation would certainly need to resolve, to safeguard its vital interests. Significantly, even as exchanges of valuables (and doubtless opinions) were actually going on in Jerusalem, one of Hiram's fleets suddenly returned with gold and other valuables; the intercalation of verses 11-12 in the account of 1 Kings 10:1-13 is no accident! The queen would realize that she could not stop her host and his ally. But one suspects that a practical solution was arrived at. The Sabaeans would keep their overland trade in high-value lightweight goods (like aromatics) without interference from the Levant's "shipping line," while the two allies were free to import home bulky or heavy products (timber, gold) by ship. More the queen could not achieve, so she went home — a "one-off" phenomenon not repeated in Hebrew history. She (and her putative husband) need not have worried; the passing of both Hiram and Solomon soon brought an end to their shipping line, whereas the camel-borne aromatics caravan trade was destined to last for well over another millennium, even when Greco-Roman shipping from Egypt to India came into being. She (and her successors) won in the end! The source of the different goods (silver, ivory) on "three-year" expeditions was well beyond a Red Sea Ophir, but cannot be located certainly at present.[100]

Ophir itself is no myth. A Hebrew ostracon of perhaps the eighth century is clearly inscribed with the brief note of account: "Gold of Ophir for Beth-Horon — 30 shekels."[101] Ophir here is a real source of gold, just as with "Gold of ʿAmau," or "Gold of Punt" or "Gold of Kush" in Egyptian texts — gold in each case, either derived from the land named or from that land's type or quality.

The queen's rich gifts are not quantified in detail, except for the gold: 120 talents (nearly four tons). Munificent though this is, it is neither unparalleled nor even top-of-the-range. Thus Metten II of Tyre paid 150 talents of gold (about four and a half tons) to Tiglath-pileser III in the eighth century.[102] As we all know, money in the pocket tends to burn holes therein. Solomon spent very lavishly on his ambitious building program, even getting into debt (cf. under "Relations with Phoenicia" above). Eventually all Jerusalem's gold was taken off to Egypt, never to be seen again (1 Kings 14:26).

Finally, it should be noted that long-haul mercantile commerce of the Hiram/Solomon variety was, circa 950, far from either a novelty or (at about 750 miles from Jerusalem to central west Arabia) unduly far-reaching in scope. Much more far-flung expeditions had been mounted as a matter of course for the previous 1,500 years along the Red Sea itself by Egypt to Punt,[103] from at least the reign of Sahure (ca. 2500) down to that of Ramesses III (ca. 1170). From Memphis up the Nile to Koptos (just north of Thebes), then east through Wadi Hammamat to Red Sea harbors at either Quseir or Mersa Gweisis, expeditions sailed south to the latitudes of Port Sudan and the Eritrean border, and then penetrated inland to the aromatics and ebony terrain; this was a trip of 1,000 miles or more. Out east the third- and early second-millennium trade route from Meluhha (Indus civilization) via the Arabo-Persian Gulf to Magan (now United Arab Emirates and Oman), Dilmun (east Arabia plus Bahrain), and on to Mesopotamia, up to Ur and Akkad (somewhere near Babylon) was in its heyday a run of 2,000 miles. Even just from Dilmun to Meluhha (to Lothal or Mohenjo Daro) was as many as 1,500 miles.[104] So a trade run of 750 miles over a thousand years later was enterprising but not exceptional, and certainly not fantasy.

(d) A Long, Long Road A-winding

Some commentators have found it hard to accept the distance involved for the queen's visit to Jerusalem, because it was "1,400 miles of rugged desert." But they never do their homework, it seems. Here it is useful to set her travels in the context of other ancient royal journeys. Some thirteen centuries earlier Sargon of Akkad reputedly campaigned far northwestward into Anatolia to the "Silver Mountains," 900 miles or more from home.[105] New Kingdom pharaohs such as Tuthmosis I and III and Amenophis III (fifteenth/fourteenth centuries) traveled south from Memphis to campaign in Nubia up to the Nile's Fourth Cataract and beyond, 1,300 or 1,400 miles. Between Hattusas (capital of the Hittite Empire) and Pi-Ramesses in Egypt was a journey of some 900 miles (1,000 miles, if to Memphis) that two Hittite princesses traveled in the thirteenth century to marry Ramesses II (one-way ticket!), and likewise Prince Hishmi-sharruma (probably the future Tudkhalia IV of Hatti) and Hattusil III himself, if the pharaoh ever did persuade him![106] Later than Solomon, at the end of the eighth century, in 701, Prince Taharqa of Nubia (Kush) and Egypt brought an army some 1,800 miles from Upper Nubia to Memphis, to go to Hezekiah's aid.[107] And later still (sixth century), Nabonidus king of Babylon removed himself 600 miles from Babylon southwestward to Teima in Arabia for a decade, adventuring then southward to other centers as far as Yathrib (Medina), up to 1,000 miles from home in Babylon.[108] Assurbanipal and forces marched 2,700 miles each way, from Nineveh to Thebes.[109] Other such ventures by ancient royalty we can dispense with here. So the queen of Sheba was one more member of a considerable long-distance "royal travelers club," and not even the sole member of the women's section! In short, the queen of Sheba may be exotic, but she belongs firmly to this world, not some mere dreamworld.

(v) At Two Extremes: Tamar and Tadmor

Often our biblical writers are very concise, and we need all the data they (and others) can give, to see the overall picture. Thus in 1 Kings 9:17b-19 we find Solomon (1) building in Lower Beth-Horon, Baalath, and Tamar in the desert "in his land" and (2) establishing store places near and far. But in 2 Chron. 8:3-5 a fuller view appears, with Solomon (1) building Tadmor in the desert and store places in Hamath, (2) (re)building in Upper and Lower Beth-Horon, and Baalath, and (3) building store places near and far. This was prefaced by (4) his capturing a place called Hamath-Zobah, after completion of his palace/temple building program (Year 24 and following). Item 1 in Kings is "southern," within Israel/Judah and environs, and corresponds to Chronicles item 2. Likewise, Kings item 2 and Chronicles item 3 correspond.

But Chronicles item 1 is "northern," relating to the area east of Aram-Zobah and Hamath to Tadmor (Palmyra). It links on (as a "related territory" notice) to the preceding note on Hamath-Zobah. The latter, a "Hamath of Zobah," was (by its name) a place (or zone) in Zobah that took its name from Hamath, and should therefore be located near the border between Zobah and Hamath. A suitable location would be near modern Homs (Roman Emesa), perhaps at Qadesh-on-Orontes or Qatna (only a few miles south/north, either side of Homs). From this zone a well-known desert route ran (and runs) out east to the Tadmor/Palmyra oasis, whence further tracks could reach the Middle Euphrates at such towns as (earlier) Mari or (later) Hindanu. The store places "in Hamath" would most likely be depots for Israelite/Hamathite trade, etc., along Hamath's eastern borderlands to the southwest elbow of the Euphrates, and its fords beyond. Tadmor itself is attested already in the eighteenth century in the Mari correspondence, and then barely a century before Solomon during Tiglath-pileser I's struggles against the Arameans in this region and beyond.[110]

So much for the north; we now return south, to 1 Kings 9:17b-18, plus 2 Chron. 8:5. Here the Beth-Horons were on a strategic route from the western Palestine plains via Gezer (north of Ajalon) via Gibeon up toward Jerusalem. Baalath, however, lay down in the plains, beyond Ekron, perhaps at El-Mughar/Maghar, representing a control point in northern Philistia.[111] Tamar "in his (Solomon's) land" may best be identified with the junction of routes at 'Ain Husb, south-southwest of the Dead Sea, just east of the northern Negev.[112] Here roads meet, from both the Dead Sea and Negev, and then a route runs south down the 'Arabah Valley to the Gulf of Aqaba (Red Sea). This Tamar is attested also in postbiblical times and records, in the Tabula Peutingeriana and on the Madaba mosaic map (confirming its position), as Thamar. So, while it is possible to suggest reading either just Tamar or just Tadmor in both Kings and Chronicles,[113] it is probably wiser to observe a distinction between these two locations in Kings and Chronicles.

(vi) Buildings

(a) The Temple and Its Furnishings, Jerusalem

In 1 Kings 6 we are told that Solomon built a temple at Jerusalem 60 cubits long, 20 cubits wide, and 30 cubits high, being fronted by a portico 10 cubits deep (vv. 2-3). So the whole was some 90 + 15 = 105 feet long, by 30 feet wide by 45 feet high. Behind the portico the temple had a main hall or vestibule and an inner sanctuary. Around the sides and rear of the temple was a series of three-decker storerooms (linked by internal stairs), totaling 15 cubits (about 23 feet) high, that left ample room for clerestory window slots along the main temple walls (cf. vv. 4-6, 8). The temple was roofed with beams and planking, and was likewise floored and the interior walls lined with wooden planks and panels. The interior (walls, floor) was then surfaced with gold overlay (vv. 9, 15-22, 30). Twin door leaves closed the doorways into the main hall and inner sanctuary. These and the wall paneling bore engraved decoration (cherubs, palm trees, open flowers, gourds; vv. 18, 29). Within the inner sanctuary were placed two winged cherubs, wooden and also gilded (vv. 23-28). Around the temple was an inner courtyard of dressed stonework having a course of cedar beams at every third course (v. 36). Such are the reasonably clear essentials of the Jerusalem temple. Minor details are less clear and must remain topics of specialized debate, such as the details of the doorways (vv. 31, 33) and whether the portico contained a pair of columns, and whether these (if present) were in fact the two bronze pillars of 7:15-22.

How far does such a structure and its embellishment correspond to known ancient reality or arise from mere fantasy? This temple (if ever built) was replaced by a "second temple" in the late sixth century (537-520; Ezra 3:8ff.; 6:15), and was replaced under Herod from 19 B.C. onward (strictly a "third temple"!). Of the first, or Solomonic temple, no physical trace has been conclusively recovered or identified. This is hardly surprising, given (1) the thorough destruction of Jerusalem's official buildings by the Babylonians in 586, (2) the reuse of the site in the Persian period, and then (3) the massive redevelopment of the site and total rebuilding of both the temple and the surrounding precincts in Herod's time. Plus (4) Roman destruction and Byzantine and Muslim buildings since then, and (5) the practical impossibility of digging archaeologically in the present precinct.

Fortunately the written descriptions in 1 Kings 6 can be confronted with what we currently know of temple design and embellishment from that world, if we would wish to test for fact or fantasy (or both). We have temples from all over the ancient Near East, from the fourth millennium down to Greco-Roman times, so there is considerable (if uneven) material available to compare with the Solomonic projection. First we take up size and layout. Even with its surrounding storage chambers, Solomon's tripartite temple (portico, hall, sanctuary) would not exceed some 115 feet in overall length or some 35 feet in overall width. From Syria and Palestine we have a long series of analogous structures. Temple D at north Syrian Ebla (ca. 1800) is almost 100 feet long by nearly 50 feet wide, and is tripartite: open portico (no columns), anteroom, hall with raised sanctuary niche.[114] At Habuba Kabira, on the west bend of the Euphrates, probable remains of such a tripartite temple (portico, no columns, anteroom, long sanctuary hall) about 95 by 47 feet date to the early second millennium.[115] At Mari on the east Syrian Euphrates, the twentieth- to eighteenth-century rebuild of the temple of Dagan (115 by 33 feet) is seemingly tripartite, with portico (no columns), hall, and then twin sanctuaries.[116] At Alalakh, by the north bend of the Orontes, the stratum VII temple (ca. eighteenth century; about 70 by 65 feet) has an enclosed portico (no columns), broad hall, and larger niched sanctuary.[117]

At Tell Munbaqa (ancient Ekalte), on the west bend of the Euphrates (opposite Aleppo), three fifteenth-century temples were found, two with portico (no columns), anteroom, and long sanctuary, being about 80 by 42 feet and 95 by 50 feet respectively.[118] At Hazor in Canaan, the final temple (area H, stratum IA) brings us to the thirteenth century. It had a portico room with two free-standing columns (not supports), a central hall (with staircase block at left), and a large, niched sanctuary; its maximum dimensions were 36 by 23 feet.[119]

This brings us to the early first millennium. At Ain Dara (some forty miles northwest of Aleppo) was found a fine tripartite temple of the period 1300-1000 (phase 1) going on through 1000-900 (phase 2), having a two-columned portico, an anteroom, and a main hall ending with a raised sanctuary area. The whole is about 98 by 65 feet. Finally (in phase 3) within circa 900-740, a corridor was added all around the sides and rear of the temple (cf. Solomon's storerooms), having internal buttresses that would enable its division into a series of storerooms. This addition expanded the temple's overall dimensions to almost 120 by 105 feet. This building spanned the entire epoch of early Israel, through the time of David and Solomon, into the divided monarchy period, and is architecturally closest of the series listed here to the Jerusalem temple of 1 Kings 6.[120]

The use of storerooms around temple worship space (and on more than one level) is, however, attested long before the 900-740 period, it should be noted. In third-millennium Egypt, the pyramid temples of Sahure and Pepi II in particular had runs of storerooms surrounding their worship space, as did Sesostris I in the early second millennium. At Sahure we actually have two-level storerooms, linked by staircases, very reminiscent of Solomon's three-level storerooms (fig. 19). In the fifteenth century Tuthmosis III incorporated two-level storerooms around the worship areas of the old Twelfth to Eighteenth Dynasty temple of Amun at Karnak.[121] Coming down to thirteenth-century Hattusas, the Hittite capital up north, only two hundred years before Solomon, one finds Temple I closely surrounded by extensive storage magazines on all sides (with a corridor area between these and the temple proper).[122] Remains of stairways indicate clearly that these storerooms also existed on at least two levels, if not more. Last on this detail, we may add that it was customary for storage space to outstrip worship space in ancient temples. In those days bank accounts, cash, and credit cards did not exist — their wealth had to be stored clumsily in kind: sacks of grain, vats of oil and wine, endless ingots and packages of gold, silver, precious stones and other commodities, timbers, etc. The idea once mooted that Solomon's temple had begun life as a treasury and was only later converted to a worship site is (in these circumstances) a total nonstarter.

Finally, our last two temples. The first is the temple at Hamath. In level E of the ninth century (and possibly the tenth) is to be found this tripartite shrine (enclosed portico, no columns, hall, rear sanctuary) of about 60 by 40 feet, close to the royal palace. At Tell Tayinat we have a tripartite shrine of about the eighth century with columned portico, hall, and inner sanctuary, some 80 by 40 feet in size, next to a palace. Both of these have clear similarities to Solomon's temple, especially the latter.[123]

The inner courtyard of Solomon's temple was built of "three courses of dressed stone and one course of trimmed cedar beams" (1 Kings 6:36). To understand this it is essential to turn to the practical Near Eastern evidence of real walls. The system of building walls with stone base-courses, topped by timber beams (at times with cross-framing) and then by higher courses in brick or stone, was endemic to the eastern Mediterranean world during the second and first millennia in particular, in the Aegean, and in Anatolia, Syria, and Palestine. Its purpose was to give strength and flexibility against earthquake shocks.[124] For examples (late second millennium) one may look at the stepped walls of the great Building E in the Hittite citadel at Hattusas (Boghaz-köi), where thrice over a layer of beams once existed above every third course of stonework;[125] also in the foundation levels at nearby Yazilikaya temple, and in massive Hittite masonry walls at Kültepe. In Syria, at Ugarit, one of the city's grand houses has the clearest possible example of three courses of fine masonry topped by the space left by destroyed beams, with further masonry and rubble above it. This technique (as in 1 Kings 6:36) was used in the palace of the kings of Ugarit and other buildings there.[126]

Returning now to the interior of Solomon's temple, there are the questions about wood interior paneling and gold or gilt overlay of walls and floors. The practice of wood-paneling the inner walls of royal and important buildings goes back almost two thousand years before Solomon. It first occurs at Abydos and Saqqara in the great tombs of Egypt's Archaic Period (ca. 3000-2700), when First Dynasty pharaohs and their highest elite had solid wooden floors laid in their burial chambers and the walls lined with wood paneling — sometimes decorated with gold strips — and roofed with solid timber.[127] Then in mid-third-millennium Ebla (ca. 2500), we find apartments in Palace G, where a high bench (and probably the walls above?) and walls elsewhere were faced with fine relief scenes engraved on wooden paneling: dignitaries, lions attacking game and a bull, king and warriors.[128] Then in late-second-millennium Hattusas, in the great Temple I, constructional features suggest that its rooms had wooden wall paneling above pierced stone bases.[129] In the early first millennium, contemporary overall with the Hebrew united and early divided monarchies, Carchemish and Zinjirli showed analogous evidence. At Carchemish the Processional Entry had had ornamental cedarwood paneling upon base beams along stone orthostats. At Zinjirli walls were clothed rather differently in tiers of beams held in place by vertical wooden pilasters.[130] In ninth-century Assyria, areas of a major palace could be defined by the type of wood used in the rooms — the boxwood, cedar, cypress, terebinth, tamarisk suites, so to speak. As such palaces were structurally of brick, this could only refer to wood paneling and furnishings.[131] Finally, in the eighth-century palace at Tell Tayinat in north Syria, wooden wall-facing backed by brick was also found to have existed.[132] Thus, wood-paneling has a very long history in tombs, palaces, temples, etc., in the ancient Near East.

Finally, the gold plating and gold leafing of major buildings. We have noticed gold strips in the tombs of Egypt's leaders circa 3000, just above. Many centuries later, in the later second millennium, the pharaohs went much further, speaking of lavishing sheet gold and electrum (gold/silver alloy) on temple walls, columns, obelisks, doorways, etc., and silver on floors.[133] So, for example, Amenophis III, in his memorial temple in Western Thebes, his pylon at Karnak, his temple at Luxor (all in Thebes), and his Nubian temple far south at Soleb. Examination of slots for fitting metal sheathing to still-standing columns, etc., indicates that these are no idle boasts.[134] Nor were the kings of Assyria and Babylon any less generous to the temples of their gods; Esarhaddon and Nabonidus alike "sheathed the walls with gold as if plaster" or "clad its walls with gold and silver." In between these two, Nebuchadrezzar II, not to be outdone, claims in a recently published text: "In Esagila, . . . the awe-inspiring sanctuary . . . of Marduk (. . . etc.) I clad in shining gold. . . . Ezida, . . . house of Nabu, I . . . beautified with gold and precious stones . . . ; great cedar beams, I clad in gold."[135] Finally, while virtually all this wealth has been stripped away millennia ago, some traces do sometimes survive to prove the point. In work at Qantir, the site of Ramesses II's great Delta capital of Pi-Ramesse (Raamses of Exod. 1:11), remains of a palace floor of that king have been recovered, with gold leaf trodden into its surface, as mere waste from gilding work being done there on royal furnishings.[136] "Gold is in your land like dust!" a pharaoh was once told by another king. So it is not all fairy tales or simply royal boasting. Solomon leafing his temple walls and floor with gold is — in this context — merely what kings then customarily did.

To sum up, on structure. In terms of *size and scale,* Solomon's temple at 90/105 feet by 30 feet (plus side rooms) stands within a long-established range of size for temples of its type during the third to first millennia, from Temple D at Ebla (third millennium) at 100 by 50 feet, the temple of Dagan at Mari (early second millennium) at 115 by 30 feet, and that at Ain Dara in Syria (ca. 1000) at 98 by 65 feet plus side rooms, down to ninth- and eighth-century Hamath and Tell Tayinat at some 60 by 40 and 80 by 40 feet respectively, to cite just a few from the data given above. In terms of *layout,* the triple format of portico (with or without columns), anteroom/hall, and hall/sanctuary is likewise a regular and popular design from the third to first millennia. And, as Solomon's temple adjoined his palace in Jerusalem's acropolis, so several of our other examples do likewise in their contexts (e.g., Ebla Temple D, Alalakh VII, Hamath, Tell Tayinat). The use of three-layered stone masonry topped (or alternating) with cedar beams is also widespread in the second millennium and later. Internally, the practice of wood paneling dates from the early third millennium onward, and the lavish use of gold overlay on internal walls, roofing, and floors is well attested in the royal inscriptions of both Egypt and Mesopotamia (second-first millennia); and gold flooring even happened accidentally (from working practices), so to speak, in the East Delta palace of Ramesses II in the thirteenth century. Therefore Solomon's works here are not fantasy but belong within a widespread and solid framework of actual, long-lived ancient practice.

On *furnishings,* we must be brief for the present. The famous bronze columns Jachin and Boaz that stood before Solomon's temple (1 Kings 7:15-22) have been much discussed. Independent standing columns do occur in other Near Eastern temples, such as that in Hazor area H, of the late thirteenth century, in the portico of which once stood two architecturally nonfunctional columns.[137]

The great "sea" (1 Kings 7:23-26) or priestly ablution tank was seemingly a large bronze cylinder, about twice as wide as deep, resting on four sets of three bronze bulls each. It was successor to the bronze vessel of identical function at the tabernacle (Exod. 30:17-21; 38:8).[138] Such basins or tanks of one kind or another were an essential adjunct to ancient Near Eastern ritual at all periods. In later second-millennium temple scenes of the Egyptian pharaoh worshiping the gods in the sanctuary, T-shaped tanks are at times shown in plan view.[139] At thirteenth-century Ugarit in north Syria, between the temples of Baal and Dagon, the house of the high priest contained a cache of metalwork that included a fine bronze miniature tripod stand designed to hold a basin, and hung with model pomegranates reminiscent of those around the capitals of the Jachin and Boaz columns before Solomon's temple (1 Kings 7:20).[140] Back in Canaan, the "ecumenical" chapel at Kuntillet Ajrud (ca. 800) boasted a fine inscribed stone basin, while the sixth-century chapels at Horvat Kitmit had an altar and stone basin; precisely this combination is indicated on the Mesha stone (ca. 835), line 12, where one should render "the altar-hearth (of) its vessel" *(dwd-h).*[141]

Alongside the "sea," Solomon's temple boasted ten movable stands with ablution bowls. A smaller example of exactly such bronze, wheeled trolleys has long been known from twelfth/eleventh-century Cyprus, and now we have also from Philistia three wheels and a bracket from a similar stand of the eleventh century at Ekron (Tel Miqne, V), in use on David and Solomon's doorstep, so to speak.[142] Alongside these was a miscellany of lesser cultic implements (as at the tabernacle, earlier): shovels, bowls, and the like. Such items are known from excavations in Palestine, in various places and periods, including Megiddo, Gezer, and Dan;[143] and great cauldrons on stands were seized in the Musasir temple in Urartu by Sargon II.[144] Thus, in furnishings likewise, Solomon worked within the context of his world.

(b) The Palace Complex, Jerusalem

In 1 Kings 7:1-12 we have a much briefer account of the palace building that Solomon undertook (thirteen years, probably in Years 11-24). However, there is enough relevant background material to shed some light on this elusive group of buildings. The temple stood within an "inner court(yard)" of ashlar/cedar (6:36), while we also read (7:9) of a "great court(yard)" in relation to the palace buildings. This would make good sense if, in fact, the inner court and temple were within a larger enclosure ("great court") mainly devoted to the palace buildings. The temple was only one main edifice, built in seven years; but the palace complex included five main structures that took thirteen years to build, nearly twice as long as the temple. So, if the inner sanctuary of the temple did coincide with the stone knoll in the Dome of the Rock, the location of the palace within a larger enclosure might fall either directly south of the temple's inner court, between it and the Ophel/City of David, or else to the temple court's north on the raised area overlapped by the northernmost part of the present (Herodian) Temple Mount. In terms of strategic compactness for defense, the southern solution would still seem preferable; either is architecturally feasible on the data used here.[145] For the entire complex, cf. fig. 21.

As the "Forest of Lebanon" hall was clearly the largest and most remarkable single edifice in the palace complex, the writer in 1 Kings gave it first place in his summary, with more detail than the other buildings. A careful reading of the Hebrew text would appear to show us a hall 100 cubits long and 50 cubits wide (i.e., its width = half its length), with four rows of columns bearing architraves. If so, four columns spaced across 50 cubits should imply double that figure (eight columns) along the 100-cubit length of the hall, thirty-two all told. This would give three aisles down the hall, between three (double) doors at either end. Across the architraves, fifteen sets of three beams (two, wall to inner aisle; one, spanning central aisle) roofed the whole. If the four columns at either end were in fact pilasters against the end walls (leaving twenty-four freestanding columns), then the fifteen rows of transverse beams would correspond to the cross-rows of four columns and their intervening cross-spaces, totaling fifteen altogether. Sets of triple window apertures in threes would face each other, high up in the long walls of the hall. Later (1 Kings 10:16-17) we are told that Solomon placed 200 large and 300 small gold shields in this hall (see below).

Large pillared halls are well attested in ancient Near Eastern palaces in the late second millennium, and in the early first millennium also. In the fourteenth century Egypt's sun-worshiping pharaoh, Akhenaten, built a vast official palace at his new capital Akhet-Aten (now Tell el-Amarna). At its south end stood a huge hall (about 380 feet by 240 feet) of 527 pillars (17×31) with six lesser-pillared halls on its north and south sides. This palace (fig. 20C) contained a variety of other columned halls of much less size, including one (about 50×30 feet) of four rows of columns and three aisles (with matching exits at either end) very similar to Solomon's "Forest of Lebanon" hall.[146] Far to the north during the fourteenth/thirteenth centuries, the Hittite "Great Kings" reigned enthroned in a splendid pillared hall (about 100 feet square), with 25 (5×5) wooden pillars and architraves very reminiscent of what would have stood in Solomon's hall (fig. 20D). Descending to the ninth century (just after Solomon), the great Phoenician temple at Kition (phase "Floor 3") in Cyprus boasted a hall (about 80×65 feet) with four rows of seven pillars (total, twenty-eight), giving three aisles to three doorways into the sanctuary, all very close in general design to Solomon's hall. Thereafter in the eighth/seventh centuries (phase "Floor 2a"), the plan was clearly changed: only two rows of pillars leading to only one doorway.[147] Very much farther to the northeast, at

Altintepe (northeast Anatolia), a Urartian royal citadel (eighth/seventh centuries) included a destroyed hall of about 150 by 94 feet (comparable in scale to Solomon's hall) having bases for three rows of large columns, no other detail being preserved.[148] All these halls in the first millennium appear to have arisen through Phoenician influence. Earlier and vaster than Solomon was Mari (fig. 20A).

As noted above, the hall was reportedly adorned with gold shields (1 Kings 10:16-17).[149] This report is not based on fantasy, as some have assumed. Again in Urartu, we have pertinent evidence to the contrary. When Sargon II conquered Musasir in 714, he looted the local temple of the god Haldi, removing "6 gold shields, hung right and left of his shrine" with other goldwork. And the relief scenes in his palace at Khorsabad show the temple being looted. On its walls (and pillars?) are two sets of shields: large ones hung in twos above each other, and small ones in threes. This illustrates clearly what Solomon is said to have done. In fact, if we were to assume a similar arrangement, his 200 large shields might once have hung in 100 vertical pairs, 96 of these on each of the four sides of the twenty-four freestanding pillars, and the other 4 pairs at 2 pairs each flanking the central doors at either end of the building. The 300 smaller shields in 100 vertical groups of 3 each (also as at Musasir) may have been distributed in 50 groups each along the two long interior sides of the hall. A striking sight. Gold shields have (so far) not survived from antiquity, from Jerusalem, Musasir, or anywhere else, but decorated bronze ones (of about 75-85 centimeters in diameter) are well known, from various sites, such as Nimrud in Assyria, Carchemish in north Syria, and Urartian Toprak Kale in eastern Anatolia. Greek tradition also knows of gold and gilt shields that once adorned the temple of Zeus at Olympia. So Solomon's act of decorating his hall with gold shields belongs in the world of known realities, not fantasy.

Much less is said of the other buildings, but enough to gain some idea of their nature; they may be named in sequence, as some suggest. The pillared portico (Heb. *'ulam*) with its roofed pillared portico (again, *'ulam*) would probably have been the main entrance to the "great" (or outer) court. A porch to a porch does not make overmuch sense. Likewise, we have a "porch" of throne and judgment, and the pharaoh's daughter's house was "like this porch" (1 Kings 7:7-8; *'ulam* in each case). Clearly we have two senses here: (1) a real portico or porch, commonly with pillars/columns in its facade, as with Solomon's temple, and in the (real) porch to the so-called (entry) porch; (2) a form of building fronted by a porch (plus or minus pillars/columns), which would here include the throne/judgment hall and the pharaoh's daughter's abode, if not the king's house too. As has been frequently pointed out, in Syrian local capital cities of the early first millennium, one may find compact "palace buildings" of a particular type, having a stairway entrance through a pillared/columned portico into a public or throne hall, with other apartments behind; this type has been equated with the *hilani* buildings of Hittite and Assyrian texts, and goes back into the second millennium. So, what we may have here is the following suite of buildings. First, a columned hall fronted by a columned portico, leading into the great court from the east end of the south wall (if complex is south of the temple court), or from the south end of the east wall (if complex is north of the temple court). Second, northwest of it would be the "Forest of Lebanon" Hall, discussed above. Third, farther to the west in this part of the great court would be the throne/judgment hall, with porticoed entrance, throne hall, and apartments behind ("Hilani I"). Fourth, behind this (again going west) was the king's house, "the other court, from the house to the porch, was like this work," i.e., like the hall of judgment. So the king's house was "Hilani II," in another court, behind the area on which the judgment/throne-hall fronted. Finally, fifth, the house for the pharaoh's daughter was another porticoed building, "Hilani III," and probably in this same rear court, just south of the king's house. We thus end up with a close group of buildings, in part linked together, in east and west sections of the "great court," the whole complex extending parallel to the temple in its inner court, whether along its south or north.[150] Such complexes of loosely attached buildings are exactly what we find in the second and early first millennia (figs. 20B, D). One need only look at the plan of the great Hittite royal citadel at Hattusas (Boghaz-köi), with its line of buildings along the northwest side of the Upper Court, facing large but now destroyed structures on the southeast side, above and linked with the set of buildings around the Lower Court.[151] In the ninth/eighth century, at Zinjirli (ancient Sam'al), the plan of the citadel has an outer court between the outer and inner gates, with service rooms or barracks along the east wall, then the old "Hilani I." Across at the west side, Hilanis "II" and "III" face each other and are linked by a broad court with its surrounding chambers and adjuncts (fig. 20E). And in the north corner we find two more conjoined Hilanis ("IV/V") of kings Kilamuwa and Bar-rakkub, with adjoining service buildings.[152] The siting close together of both temple and palace (as with Solomon at Jerusalem) is found at both Tell Tayinat and Hamath in north Syria (first millennium), as well as at Alalakh (second millennium), and long before at Ebla (third millennium, Temple D).[153] Thus Solomon's palace complex makes good sense as a royal architectural complex in its time, styles, and space, and proximity to the main temple of the city.

We may fitly finish this "palatial" section with a glance at Solomon's gold-mounted throne and gold table service (1 Kings 10:18-21). Again, thrones overlaid with gold and inlaid with ivory are beyond the reach and tastes of most of us moderns. But the ancient kings thought otherwise. To them, these were simply bagatelles that went with the job. Just *one* gold/ivory throne? Really! Solomon, you must do better than that. If we care to consult the Amarna letters of the fourteenth century, we find Pharaoh Amenophis III quite casually sending off to Kadashman-Enlil I of Babylon a few furnishings for the new wing of his palace: one ebony bed overlaid with ivory and gold, and two just with gold; and no less than *ten* chairs (or thrones) of ebony overlaid with gold, one being large; and to match them, a whole series of footstools of either ebony (ten) or ivory (quantity lost), overlaid with gold.[154] So much for just one ivory/gold throne! If Solomon is fantasy, what shall we say of Amenophis III? One may end this discussion on thrones, footstools, and beds by referring the reader to actual examples of all three categories (lavishly gold-plated) from the tomb of Tutankhamun, only a generation after Amenophis III.[155] As for gold table service, one need look no further than the astonishing golden treasure of vessels and jewelry found in the burials of Assyrian queens of the ninth-eighth centuries.[156] With them, too, silver seems to have been of little account (cf. 1 Kings 10:11). Silver and gold vessels from the burial of Psusennes I of Egypt (1040/1039–992/991) are contemporary with David's first decade of rule.[157]

(vii) Solomon's Works Elsewhere

Solomon's other reported building projects are merely summarized (1 Kings 9:15, 17-19; cf. 2 Chron. 8:1-6). In Jerusalem these included the not overclear "Millo," or "fill," possibly stone terracing, as well as part of the walls. Outside Jerusalem he built at three important centers: Hazor, Megiddo, and Gezer — but we are *not* told precisely what he did there. Finally, there is a general summary, on the Beth-Horon(s), Baalath, Ta(d)mor, etc. (cf. already, pp. 120-21 above). Archaeology may be able to tell us something supplementary, at least in Jerusalem, Hazor, Megiddo, and Gezer. But for this factor, see below under section 3, "Syro-Palestinian Archaeology and the United Monarchy."

It is clear that after his fourth year, Solomon's "twenty years" (1 Kings 9:10) of intensive work on the temple and palace complex probably left relatively little scope for any other major works elsewhere within that period (Years 4-24) other than on the Millo and wall at Jerusalem.[158] The provincial centers may have had more attention only in the second half of the reign, and on a limited scale, mainly from Year 24 onward. Even in Jerusalem the Millo was built *after* Pharaoh's daughter was installed in her new abode (9:24), so the more outlying sites are hardly likely to have taken precedence over these more central royal concerns. At about the time of the building of the Jerusalem wall and

Millo, probably from Year 24 onward, was when young Jeroboam son of Nebat fell under Solomon's suspicions, and so fled to Egypt — to "Shishak" (11:40), none other than Shoshenq I, who ruled there from circa 945 onward. Solomon's twenty-fourth year was about 947 or 946, so Jeroboam's flight was at earliest a couple years or so later, when the last Jerusalem projects were already well in hand. The collapse of foreign sections of the mini-empire (Edom, Aram, etc.), and the consequent loss of foreign revenues, in the last decade or so of Solomon's reign (cf. 11:14-25), would not be favorable financially to ongoing major building works during that time.

(viii) Administration

In territorial terms, 1 Kings 4:7-19 lists the twelve non-Judean districts in the Hebrew homeland, and their governors, who had annually to provide specific revenues to maintain Solomon's palace household, his chief officials, and doubtless the large ancillary staff that served them all. The revenues themselves are noted concisely in verses 22-25.

The system of twelve district governorates has been usefully studied by a series of scholars, and it is fairly generally recognized that the list best fits this overall period, i.e., of David and Solomon.[159] To debate at length its geography, etc., is needless here. Instead, a minor example of its background must suffice. The Second District (4:9) occupied a compact area from Beth-Shemesh inland out to Joppa on the coast, being bordered by Philistia on its southwest and by Ephraim and coastal Hepher on its northeast and north. It included Timnah, Gezer, Lod, etc., besides Beth-Shemesh and other lesser places listed by 1 Kings. One of these is Elon-Beth-Hanan, or "Elon of the House of Hanan." We have independent archaeological evidence of the long association of the family or "house" of Hanan with this area. Long ago there was found at Beth-Shemesh an ostracon inscribed in late Canaanite, of the thirteenth or twelfth century, that included a Hanan in what may be a list of men and commodities (jars of wine) received or paid by them.[160] More recently there was discovered a broken stone gaming board, with the name Hanan inscribed on its edge in Hebrew script of the tenth century.[161] From nearby Timnah comes a pottery fragment on whose margin was engraved the epigraph "[belonging to B]en-Hanan."[162] The persistence of the name in this restricted district may be more than coincidence, and may point to a well-established local ruling family now attested for almost 200 years there. So a place in our list (Elon) named from this family would strike an authentic note.

Moving on to court revenues (4:22-25), Solomon's 30 plus 60 *kor* of fine flour and (ordinary) meal represents about 6,600 plus 13,200 = 19,800 liters daily, or some 594,000 liters per month. This can be broken down (daily) at 600 liters of meal for Solomon's actual household, 6,000 for his high officials, and 13,200 for the palace employees. If a liter of flour approximated a liter of grain, and if Israelite crop yields resembled others in the Near East (e.g., at Mari), the month's needs would be met from about 424 acres of field, or 1.7 square kilometers. The whole year's need would thus require about 13 square kilometers or barely 5 square miles of land — not a vast imposition on even the smallest districts. But in his provision for his palace household, government, and support staff, Solomon was not alone. We also have statistics and the use of daily and monthly accounts from and in other ancient Near Eastern palaces, particularly from the third and second millennia. At Ebla (third millennium), the monthly grain ration for the king's house averaged between 80,000 and 110,000 liters. At Mari (early second millennium), for "the king's repast," his immediate household and entourage, typical figures vary between about 60 and 75 hectoliters per month (6,000 to 7,500 liters) as against Solomon's probable household figure of 18,000 liters. At Chagar Bazar, contemporary with Mari, the accounts ran to 945 liters daily, or about 28,000 liters per month. In Egypt, about this period, the Thirteenth Dynasty court had 2,000 loaves per day, or some 60,000 a month. Later, in the early thirteenth century, we have monthly palace accounts of Sethos I from Memphis, with between three and six grain deliveries monthly, of (on average) 180 sacks representing (on average value of a sack) about 15,000 liters a time. Thus, at three to six deliveries, the palace received between 45,000 and 90,000 liters per month, on a median reckoning. In the later thirteenth century we have record of preparations for a pharaoh's arrival, for which an immense range of foodstuffs was to be ordered, including 9,200 loaves (of eight kinds) and 20,000 biscuits; no mean welcome party. In contemporary Ugarit, monthly accounts were also kept, with supplies from various sources; the annual grain income for the palace ran to some 4,700 *kur* of grain, about 1,175,000 liters, at about 98,000 liters monthly. In the first millennium, suffice it to cite for Assyrian royal hospitality the "city-warming" celebration held by Assurnasirpal II at his new city of Calah, for 69,574 guests for ten days.[163] So Solomon's accounts fit well enough into their overall cultural context.

Finally under material things, we return to Solomon's wealth.[164] It is said that he was twice given 120 talents of gold, by Hiram of Tyre and the queen of Sheba respectively, and that another 666 gold talents accrued to him yearly (1 Kings 9:14; 10:10, 14). Such figures have very often been dismissed as fantasy; but it is wiser to check on their background before jumping to premature conclusions. First, 120 talents is not unusual. We learn from firsthand sources that Metten II of Tyre (ca. 730) paid a tribute of 150 talents of gold to our old acquaintance Tiglath-pileser III of Assyria, while in turn his successor Sargon II (727-705) bestowed 154 talents of gold upon the Babylonian gods — about 6 tons in each case. Going back almost eight centuries, Tuthmosis III of Egypt presented about 13.5 tons (well over 200 talents) of gold in nuggets and rings to the god Amun in Thebes, plus an unknown amount more in a splendid array of gold vessels and cult implements. Worth almost a third of Solomon's reputed annual gold revenue, this was on just one occasion, to just one temple. But there is worse. In Egypt Shishak's successor Osorkon I gifted some *383 tons* of gold and silver to the gods and temples of Egypt in the first four years of his reign, many of the detailed amounts being listed in a long inscription (now damaged) (figs. 22A, B). That sum would (in weight) be equivalent to almost seventeen years of Solomon's annual gold revenue, and perhaps to ten years of it in gold value (not to mention such "minor" items as gold shields, etc.). So, much of Osorkon I's lavish generosity within Egypt may have derived from the spoils of his father's campaign to Judah and Israel in Rehoboam's time. No other pharaonic text remotely approaches this scale of expenditure of precious metal. Furthermore, if (for argument's sake) we assume that in thirty years (omitting his first five and last five years) Solomon had retained some 500 talents annually of his 666, remembering he had outgoings in gold also, then his total hoard for thirty years might have been about 30 × 500 = 15,000 talents at the most, or about 500 tons all told. This sum is, frankly, modest when compared with the 1,180 tons of gold that Alexander the Great took from Susa, and the breathtaking 7,000 tons of gold that he abstracted from the vanquished Persian Empire overall. Solomon was simply not in the same league! And is hardly *just* fantasy in such a context.

(ix) Cultural Aspects

Leaving the material world behind for a moment, Solomon was also associated with wisdom, as an exuberant passage in 1 Kings 4:29-34 proclaims. For us the sole possible evidence remaining would be two compositions within the present Hebrew book of Proverbs: chapters 1–24, as an independent book, attributed to him (alive), and 25–29, a posthumous collection of Solomonic lore from Hezekiah's scribes. Chapters 30 and 31 relate to other writers entirely, Agur and Lemuel (or rather, his mother) respectively. Over the decades opinion has varied considerably over how far (if at all) either Prov. 1–24 or 25–29 have any connection with Solomon, and if so, what; it has often been thought that 1–9 was prefaced to 10–24 at a relatively late date. And as long as scholars insist on treating the whole matter in isolation, sealed off from all the pertinent evidence, nothing more can be said, objectively. Progress must come (and already has come) from the adduction of external evidence, which supplies independent and objective criteria by which to judge the question.

We have, in fact, some forty works of instructional "wisdom" — to which class the four books in Proverbs belong — from the ancient Near East, half of these deriving from Egypt, and all closely dated from the third to first millennia. These enable us to establish an outline history of this entire genre of writings, and to eliminate most of the guesswork where Proverbs is concerned.[165] The essence of that history is as follows. In the third millennium such works first appear in Egypt and Mesopotamia (Sumer). They in every case bear titles naming the real or traditional author in the third person. These works divide into two series: those with prologues, and those without, which proceed directly into the main text. This applies already in the third millennium, and thereafter to the end. At this early date Hardjedef in Egypt has no prologue; where preserved, the rest have (Ptahhotep in Egypt; Old Sumerian Shuruppak in Sumer). In the early second millennium, no prologue is included in Merikare and "Ancient Writings" in Egypt, or with Shube-awilim in Mesopotamia; but prologues are included by Khety son of Duauf, "Sehetepibre"; by Man to his son and Amenemhat I in Egypt; and in the classical Sumerian and Akkadian versions of Shuruppak in Mesopotamia. In the later second millennium, no prologues occur with the five "educational" works, Hori and Amenemope's Onomasticon in Egypt, or with Hittite Shube-awilim in Hatti, but they are included by the high priest Amenemhat, Amennakht, Aniy, and Amenemope in Egypt, and Counsels of Wisdom in Babylonia. In the first millennium no prologues occur with P. Louvre D.2414 or Amenothes in Egypt or with Solomon II (Prov. 25–29), Agur, and Lemuel (Hebrew Bible). But prologues occur in the Saite Instruction and Ankhsheshonqy in Egypt, and with Solomon I (Prov. 1–24, Hebrew Bible) and Ahiqar (Aramaic, Mesopotamia). The total evidence of all these works shows as clear fact that short prologues dominate in the third and second millennia, and long ones in the first. With the sole exception of Ptahhotep, all prologues are exhortative or state an aim in the third and second millennia, while they move over to being long, and biographical (as Ptahhotep earlier was), in the first. Parallelism is the dominant poetical form (especially in couplets) during the third and second millennia, but much less so in this class of texts in the first millennium when one-line epigrams and miniature essays increasingly replace parallelism.

Such are the facts, which cannot be gainsaid, attested solidly by the entire corpus of firsthand material. To this *all* of us must bow, regardless of prejudice or prior agenda. Where does this fixed framework leave Solomon? Solomon I

(Prov. 1–24) is type B (with prologue). This work is clearly transitional, as it has a traditional exhortative prologue (as in third- and second-millennium texts), which is relatively long (as in first-millennium texts). He uses parallelism (especially two-line couplets) mainly throughout, which is again traditional for the third, second, and early first millennia. Hence, for these and other such reasons, he belongs squarely at the hinge between the third/second millennia and the first at about 1000, which is close to Solomon's historical date in any case. One may add that *nobody* ever added prologues to *any* of these works at some later date, as has often been suggested for Prov. 1–9 in relation to 10–24. Any such procedure is excluded absolutely by the entire corpus of evidence, and not a single valid indicator exists to oppose this. As for Solomon II (Prov. 25–29), Hezekiah's time (late eighth/early seventh century) is late enough. By the sixth century use of parallelism is beginning to wane, and drastically so, later, in instructional wisdom works. So the headings at Prov. 1:1 and 25:1 must be taken seriously for strictly factual reasons. Agur and Lemuel are otherwise entirely unknown to us, but the seventh century or onward is late enough, given their total addiction to parallelism as in older works. Cf. fig. 23.

(x) Closing Note

Much more could be said on the Kings/Chronicles data for Solomon's reign, but the foregoing survey is symptomatic for the whole. Where set against the proper contexts, the accounts of Solomon's reign come out reflecting fact and certainly not fantasy. Even 666 talents of gold (twenty-two tons) is poverty compared with the 383 tons of precious metal used by Osorkon I (in 924-921) and the 7,000 tons removed from the Persian Empire's coffers by Alexander the Great (cf. p. 134 above). From time to time the writer of 1 Kings indulges in a whiff of rhetoric — but rhetoric must be compared only with rhetoric, and facts with facts, and the two categories must not be confused. Thus 1 Kings 4:20, 29 has the Hebrew population growing "as the sand of the seashore," and Solomon's range of understanding also as wide "as the sand of the seashore," which is rhetorical, not literal, precisely as with Ramesses III (ca. 1153) describing his conquest of the Sea Peoples (who included the Philistines): "captured all together, brought as booty to Egypt, like the sand of the seashore."[166] Being greater than all lands, having presents from all lands (cf. 1 Kings 4:30-31, 34; 10:23-25) is typical of the rhetorical style of his world (not ours), as other kings' texts often show. Such as Ramesses II, "who seizes all lands valiantly, whose victories distant foreign lands remember (in dread of him) . . . forever," or (e.g.) Assyrian kings who regularly entitle themselves "King of all people, King of (the world's) four quarters" (Shalmaneser III) or "King of the Universe" (Adad-nirari III), and suchlike immodesties.[167]

Such rhetoric should not be confused with genuine fantasy; if Solomon had been credited (e.g.) with 666 million talents of gold, or an empire from the Aegean to the Indus and Anatolia to Arabia, etc., then from our fuller comparative knowledge fantasy would indeed have been the appropriate verdict. But that is very clearly not the case.

3. SYRO-PALESTINIAN ARCHAEOLOGY AND THE UNITED MONARCHY

A. INTRODUCTORY

In most books in this field, until very recent times, will be found accounts of site levels, buildings, etc., attributed to the general epoch of David and Solomon.[168] But in the last few years this matter has become enveloped in controversy. Therefore we must consider the question concisely, to determine whether fresh views proposed on archaeological chronology are indeed valid or whether this is in fact just another storm in a teacup.

(i) The General Picture, "As Was"

The late thirteenth and early twelfth centuries witnessed big changes in the ancient Near East. The Aegean world saw changes, as the Mycenaean regimes ceased to rule effectively in Greece and Crete, and Cyprus was invaded by newcomers, leading to a Hittite reaction and sea battle. In the north, the Hittite Empire itself broke up, as its central kingdom in Anatolia (Hatti proper) came to an end; rebels around it and newcomers (early Phrygians) destroyed such centers as the capital, Hattusas (now Boghaz-köi). The Egyptian sources indicate movements of warrior groups and their families from somewhere north to attack Egypt, as a place for settlement. The first wave came over the Mediterranean into ancient Libya under Merenptah (ca. 1213-1203), who repulsed the Libyans and allied "peoples of the sea" (his term!) in his fifth year, 1209/1208.[169] The second wave came round the coasts of the Levant, via north Syria (Qode, Carchemish), then down by central Syria (Amurru) into Djahi (Phoenicia-Palestine) to the East Delta borders of Egypt, there to be defeated in his eighth year by Ramesses III, in circa 1180 or 1177 (depending on whether the ephemeral

King Amenmesses was contemporary with Sethos II or had preceded him, during three years). The pharaoh's victory meant that these wanderers could go no farther south. So some stayed in Canaan while others may have gone west, as far as Sicily and Sardinia. In southwest Canaan the Pilisti (biblical Philistines) gave their name to Philistia, hence eventually to "Palestine."[170] The Tjekkeru or Sikilu stayed farther north around Dor, and others perhaps beyond these. The Shardana are often compared in name with Sardinia, and the Shaklashu with Sicily. The Lukka were from (later) Lycia in southwest Asia Minor, and the Danuna, from Cilicia in its southeast coastal area.

(ii) Canaan, "As Was"

This picture still holds good. Likewise the Late Bronze Age (IIB, or "III") of thirteenth-century Canaan is regarded as effectively ending about this time (ca. 1200/1180), the following period (ca. 1200/1180 to ca. 1000) being labeled (Early) Iron I. By the middle of the twelfth century (1150/1140), Egyptian overlordship in Canaan had ceased. While Sea People groups held the plains of Philistia and seacoast zones like Dor, the Canaanites held on in Canaan's foothills (as at Lachish, Gezer, etc.), in the Jezreel Valley from the sea to the Jordan (with Megiddo, Beth-Shan), and in Galilee. In the central Canaanite highlands (the later Judah and Ephraim), the Israelites had gained a footing sometime before 1209/1208, at which date Merenptah named them in his fifth year as a people, on his victory stela ("Israel Stela"). There a rash of new hamlets and villages appeared in twelfth-century Canaan, and late Canaanite pottery gave way to modified forms and to new forms, as Iron I. This was the everyday crockery of the early Israelites (and probably others), as they gradually occupied more and more of central Canaan (period of the "judges," cf. chap. 5).

The Philistine area was marked by pottery painted in a style that came with them from the Aegean-Mycenaean world, the Mycenaean IIIC1b or monochrome wares. Eventually they moved on to painting their finer pottery with both black and red pigment, hence the modern name "bichrome" (two-colored). After a good period of use, this style lost its quality, and degenerate forms were made. Finally there arose new forms and fashions in pottery, plainer wares with a red wash ("slip"), hand polished ("burnished"), taken over by Israelites as well as others. So far, so good, so far as sequence goes. But what about dating? Until very recently the new red-slip, hand-burnished mode was associated by many with the beginning of the Hebrew "united monarchy" and with other archaeological features attributed to that period (especially David and Solomon). But this part — the absolute dating in years B.C. — is where controversy has arisen.

B. PROS, CONS, AND ANSWERS?

(i) A New View

In a series of studies, Finkelstein has suggested a drastic lowering of the absolute dates B.C. of the whole series of archaeological phases (from strata in sites) from circa 1180 onward. The ostensible reason for doing this is the absence of Philistine-type pottery at neighboring sites that were not Philistine, of which some are said to be Egyptian-governed centers. Thus, from Egyptian inscriptions found in Lachish level VI and at Tel Sera in level IX, we know that these two places were actively inhabited under Ramesses III (1184/1187–1153/1156), with what appear to be his Year 10 (+ *x*, up to 19) at Lachish and Year 22 (up to 24) at Tel Sera, namely, in 1175/1178 (up to 1166/1169) and in 1163/1166 (up to 1161/1164) respectively. Neither site shows any trace of Philistine pottery, either monochrome or bichrome types. Therefore, Finkelstein would argue, these phases at the Lachish (VI) and Tel Sera (IX) sites (and the Egyptian dominance down to ca. 1140, under Ramesses VI) must have ceased to exist, before the monochrome and bichrome styles of pottery came into use by the Philistines, or after circa 1140, instead of after circa 1180. Then monochrome would have flourished about 1140 to 1100 and bichrome during the eleventh century, toward 1000. Then, in turn, the next phase in pottery usage (originally dated to near 1000), debased bichrome and the new red-slip, burnished style, had to be pushed down well into the tenth century. The net result of all this down-dating is that destruction levels in various sites once thought to be trace of conquests by David (ca. 1000 onward), Finkelstein would instead ascribe to the impact of the invasion of Palestine by the pharaoh Shoshenq I, in 925, five years after Solomon's death. Therefore the whole of the strata once considered the handiwork of the reigns of David and Solomon was pushed down in time, to nearer the reigns of Omri and Ahab (about 880-850). And everything else after that point would then have to be compressed in real-time length, to fit in before the destructions of the last occupations of various sites — especially such as Hazor, known to have been destroyed by Tiglath-pileser III about 732, from his reports. Finkelstein has loudly rejected any idea that such places as Lachish (VI) and Tel Sera (IX) could have existed during circa 1180-1140 without importing any Philistine pottery when it was already in full use just "over the border" at that period. And of course, he has to posit a third wave of Sea Peoples circa 1140/1135, to bring the new type of pottery (Mycenaean IIIC1b = monochrome) into Canaan and into use there.[171]

The results of all this for the united monarchy of David and Solomon are fairly drastic archaeologically. Instead of the matching gateways and casemate walls, etc., at Gezer (VIII) and Hazor (X), and possibly at Megiddo (VA-IVB) with its palatial buildings, and a long series of other settlements exhibiting occupation levels of the same cultural phase, we would have a lesser settlement at Megiddo (VIB), and correspondingly elsewhere.[172] The walled towns, etc., would be reattributed to Omri and Ahab — and what had been previously considered theirs, reassigned to later reigns. The culture of the united monarchy would have been simply late Canaanite in pottery and in other ways, with other foreign elements.

(ii) Is the New True?

However exciting (and all this certainly is!), mere novelty is never an automatic guarantee of truth. Acclaimed new gains to knowledge have to be shown to be real, and to provide the best overall explanation for the given situation. Not a few skeptical voices have dissented from Finkelstein's new picture. Let us see the other side of the coin.

(a) Making Waves

First, the assumption of a "third wave" of Sea Peoples arriving forty years after the second (of 1180/1177) at about 1140 borders on the bizarre. On the negative side, there is no whisper of any kind for such an event from historical sources. Despite the pessimism of Ramesses III, Carchemish (even if briefly attacked) survived the second wave well, under Kuzi-Tesup I (cf. p. 99 above) and his successors as local "Great Kings" for about 180 years, and evidently had no problem with any theoretical third wave. By 1140 the Phoenician group of seaports (Tyre, Sidon, Byblos, Arvad, etc.) would have begun to flourish again, untouched by any third wave;[173] in circa 1080 Zakirbaal of Byblos could consult records of timber sales by his predecessors, to quote them to the Egyptian envoy Wenamun, barely sixty years later. The Sikils of Dor are also mentioned by Wenamun at circa 1080, and had a town there from at least 1150; earlier developments remain to be excavated. A new wave of people arriving in the area where Ramesses III's Sea People contemporaries would have already been settled for forty years would hardly have been welcomed by them in what became Philistia. So a third wave that introduced Aegean-inspired pottery only from about 1140 is best regarded as a phantom, a mirage without attestation.

Thus we must most likely stay with the second wave (1180/1177) as the time when the Philistines, Sikils, and Sherden began their settlement in Canaan; there is no way that Ramesses III could possibly have taken them all off to Egypt as prisoners. But this means that, in terms of use of pottery, we have to review possible historical choices. If the Philistines lived in southwest Canaan for forty years before importing Mycenaean IIIC1b (monochrome) pottery, how did they manage till then? With local Canaanite wares? This seems very improbable. At Ashdod, as noted by others, the last Canaanite stratum (XIV) was immediately succeeded by the first Philistine town (stratum XIII), with its typical monochrome pottery (Mycenaean IIIC1b types). In Tel Miqne/Ekron, similarly, the Canaanite town (VIIIA) was quickly followed by a clearly Philistine settlement (VII), using an abundance of monochrome pottery. Likewise at Ascalon, Late Bronze stage V is followed by Philistine stage VI.

In all three cases the Canaanite levels were destroyed violently, at least in part. At Ekron a massive Philistine settlement promptly replaced the burnt Canaanite one. At Ashdod, again, the Canaanite town was destroyed by conflagration, along with the port-fort of Ashdod (Tel Mor VII). The Philistines did not come and go as timid day-trippers — they imposed their rule on these three cities and an outpost, brutally by fire and demolition when judged expedient, quickly enforcing their political rule and alien Aegean material culture wherever their writ ran.[174]

(b) Philistines? "Not on My Patch!"

But not *beyond* the area of that writ. The local Canaanites, now underdogs in their own region, cannot possibly have welcomed this brusque intrusion. Both Lachish VI and Tel Sera IX of the early twelfth century stayed outside the Philistine orbit, and virtually no trace of Philistine monochrome (or the later bichrome) pottery has yet been found there. And, compared with the large quantities of Philistine monochrome pottery found in their adopted cities (Ashdod, Ekron, Ascalon), quantitatively very little of it recurs in Canaanite towns sited clearly outside the zone of immediate Philistine dominance.

This phenomenon of political limits to cultural phenomena is well enough attested in other cases, and is not unique. Mazar has already cited such examples: (1) Early Bronze III Khirbet Kerak wares found in the main Jezreel sites (east to west) of Beth-Shan, Megiddo, and Yoqneam were *not* found in use only five kilometers westward in Tel Qashish. (2) Middle Bronze/Late Bronze bichrome pottery was found abundantly in Megiddo, but not at all at Beth-Shan in the ample levels of that period. (3) The late seventh-century Iron II pottery current at (Philistine) Ekron and Timnah is absent from neighboring Judean sites only a few kilometers away. To all this one might add (4) where in

Transjordan, a clear cultural boundary has been detected between Iron II Moab and Ammon. Finkelstein's riposte (over the Khirbet Kerak example) that different time phases are involved is no answer to all of these.[175]

The sociological/anthropological question that nobody has asked is, *why* did good Canaanite housewives in (e.g.) Lachish or Tel Sera not fall for the novel pottery designs over the border in Philistia? To that, various sociological/anthropological answers should be realistically considered. (1) These ladies were not short of good pottery already — "Who wants dull, alien monochrome when we've got plenty of our own good, more colorful [LB IIB/III] bichrome?" they may have muttered.[176] And (2) imports are often dearer than homemade; why should these thrifty housewives pay out for unwanted, dull, foreign novelties? Then (3), "These new people are hostile! They murdered our cousins and other relatives down in Ashdod and Ascalon, destroyed their towns and built ugly, walled new ones — we're not buying off *them!*" So, for the first forty-to-fifty years there were probably very real boundaries, and more than just geographical, between Philistia and surrounding late Canaanite towns, while the Canaanites within Philistia (having lost control to these foreigners) found themselves an underclass in their own land. Philistine monochrome and bichrome wares may excite *us,* but they may have carried very different social connotations indeed for Canaanites in the early decades of Philistine dominance and enforced occupation. These "contextual" aspects should be taken into account — and seriously! The Finkelstein kind of view never began even to consider such other aspects besides mere physical presence/absence, and exclusively in terms of playing barren games with chronology.

(c) Dating — the Early Half

But in agreement with Finkelstein, chronology has its place. At Lachish, items found in level VI include pieces naming Ramesses III, while a sherd bears in Egyptian hieratic a date line not less than Year 10 or more than Year 19 (maximum range, 1178-1166). So Lachish VI, finally destroyed with fire, would have come to its end soon after some date within about 1177/1165, within three to twelve years of the Philistines' arrival in southwest Canaan.[177] Given the human factors already mentioned and the short overlap with the Philistines settling in, it is no great wonder that Lachish neither boasts (nor chose to boast) free use of Philistine monochrome, and died before Philistine bichrome had been either developed or spread around. Then, in level IX at Tel Sera, were found more hieratic texts, one of Year 22 (+ x), not higher than Year 23 or 24, all within 1166/1161, allowing the fall of Tel Sera sometime after about 1164/1160 — at earliest, close in time after Lachish VI. In level VIII the Philistines and their pottery seem to have taken over, whereas Lachish did not rise again until the start of the first millennium. Thus, during about 1170 to 1160 the Philistines may finally have put an end to their resentful Canaanite neighbors in Lachish and Tel Sera, as they expanded their realm.

It should be understood that, following the defeat of the Philistines and their allies at the northeast edge of the Delta, the Egyptians under Ramesses III maintained their overlordship over both the Canaanites and the newcomers, without distinction. Both lots would have to pay annual taxes to the Egyptian state and crown, as customary. The ostraca from Lachish and Tel Sera well illustrate the levying of such harvest tax.[178] As always, Egyptian military control was not dense on the ground. They always maintained a base at Gaza, and the excavation at Beth-Shan pinpoints a northern garrison fortress. Such places as Lachish or Tel Sera should *not* be seen as Egyptian military bases — they merely paid taxes, and had long assimilated some Egyptian components into their general culture. After Ramesses III, his son Ramesses IV is known from a stone fragment found loose, without context, at Tell Dalhiyeh. Depending on its nature (and any meaningful context), this piece may indicate his sovereignty in Canaan during 1156/1153 to 1150/1147.[179] The much-discussed bronze base of Ramesses VI from Megiddo may prove very little, given its secondary context.[180] However all that may be, there is no factual reason whatsoever to deny that the Philistines settled in southwest Canaan from 1180/1177 (Year 8, Ramesses III) and were themselves using their monochrome wares from the 1170s onward. Then, as commonly considered, they moved on to bichrome wares from roughly 1150 into the eleventh century, this giving way to degenerate bichrome and the new red-slip wares later in that century and onward. On conventional dating between roughly 1180/1170 and 1000, most of the continuously occupied sites show just two, three, or four main occupation levels across about 170 or 180 years, which is a leisurely pace of development (average per level, about 90 years, 60 years, or 45 years respectively).

(d) Dating — the Later Half

With that situation we must contrast what happens within the following period, 1000 to 730, on both the normal and "new" dating schemes. The densest sequence of occupation levels or strata is that at Hazor, as is universally recognized. On normal dating, from Hazor X in the mid–tenth century down to Hazor V's destruction by the Assyrians in about 732 we have about 220 years, for six main strata (X down to V), with divisions into two main phases each (Xa and b; IXa and b; Va and b) in three cases, giving three additional "periods." On this basis, counting only the six overall strata, they averaged some 36 to 37 years each; if we take all nine phases seriously (6 + 3), they would have averaged just over 24 years each. Neither of these figures could possibly be called excessive when compared with the accepted general span of 50 or 60 years for strata in such Iron Age sites as Lachish, Yoqneam, Dor, Rehob, Beth-Shan, or Dan, still less the figures of 90, 60, or 45 years for conventional twelfth- and eleventh-century dating given above. But if we were to accept the "new" dates, then with Hazor X beginning about 880 (Omri, sole ruler in Israel) down to the same terminus in 732, we have but 150 years, giving only 25 years for six overall strata, or else a mere 16 or 17 years average for nine main phases. Even allowing that in practice some would be shorter than others, there was, surely, hardly time for the good citizens of Hazor to catch their breath in one phase before the next was almost upon them. Why on earth should we believe in barely 20 years at most, and most probably less in practice, at Hazor in strata X to V, while accepting a tortoise-slow lifestyle of 60 or 90 years per stratum in the troubled days of the twelfth and eleventh centuries? It does not cohere very well. Finkelstein would concur with Yadin and Ben-Tor on the dating and correlations of Hazor VI-V from the early eighth century down to 732. That crushes all of Xa/b, IXa/b, VIII, and VII into the period circa 880 to 780, or barely 100 years for four full strata, six main phases, at 25 and 17 (or 16) years each respectively. Ahab and his dynasty had eventful careers, but by ancient standards the building, wars, etc., crowded into this program are in danger of becoming frenetic rather than just stormy. At Rehob (Tel Rehov/Tell es-Sarem) the situation is analogous.[181] And all these acrobatics, simply to avoid having the Philistine monochrome and bichrome wares contemporary with Lachish VI and Tel Sera IX for a few years! It seems a heavy price to pay, especially when a wholly imaginary "third wave" of Sea Peoples has to be invented to start off the use of monochrome and bichrome wares in Canaan.

So, in the light of all this, and other factors still to be considered, it seems entirely needless to force down the dating of the archaeological levels commonly linked with the united monarchy so as to end up with this surely incredible contrast between strata of 60- or 90-year spans in one troubled and politically confused period and strata of 17- to 25-year spans in another period under relatively stable monarchies.

(e) A "More Excellent Way"?

This weird contrast would quite simply be eliminated by taking the slack out of the relatively less well organized twelfth and eleventh centuries instead of squeezing the well-structured tenth and ninth centuries. If Lachish VI and Tel Sera IX lasted only a few years after Year 8 of Ramesses III, and were gone by about 1170/1160,[182] and after 10 or so years of makeshift settling in, the Philistines had then begun (1160/1150) to make in southwest Canaan their preferred monochrome pottery, followed by bichrome (1120?), and by "degenerate" style (1070?) and initial red-slip ware before 1000, we have about 160 years maximum (as from 1140, 140 years minimum) for these three cultural phases, or about 50 years or so each. The occupation strata for this period of circa 1150 to 1000 (on average) vary mainly from two to three strata (occasionally four), rarely just one (as on all other solutions). This again presents no problem. So in fact, it would be perfectly feasible to retain the normal chronology for tenth-to-eighth-century archaeology, thus not crushing sequences like Hazor and Rehob artificially, and to avoid overextending life spans of strata in the much more obscure, more troubled twelfth and eleventh centuries. One might well describe this as a happy marriage, a Finkelstein-Ussishkin/Yadin–Ben-Tor solution. As in *Gulliver's Travels* (certainly in the film version!), the princess's wedding song was neither "Faithful" nor "Forever," but at the end "Faithful Forever." Which would suit well here, but *without* inventing an imaginary cloudburst of "third wave" Philistines. Their irruption into the cozy world of the "second wave" lot would have brought renewed destructions in the sequence of good Philistine strata of the mid–twelfth century. But no such major irruption is attested — Ekron VII-VI-V-IV flowed on peacefully, until another foe entirely wrecked the place around 1000. Likewise Ashdod XIII to X, with the same turn-of-the-millennium ending. Ascalon too ran smoothly on under its new Philistine bosses, but into the tenth century and beyond.

(f) Details — Pottery in Culture and Chronology

In this long archaeological saga, it remains to clear up a few misconceptions in detail, as others have already done in part, not least about Solomon's supposed buildings in the archaeological record, and concerning Jerusalem.

For long enough, some kinds of pottery were thought to belong specifically to the time of the tenth century (and so, to the united monarchy). But what now emerges from more than one quarter is that these types were more long-lived than previously thought. In other words, people continued to use them well into the ninth century also. This was one factor in Finkelstein's move to date what had seemed to be tenth-century wares entirely down into the ninth (thus, after the united monarchy). They also occur in the ninth century in the destruction levels at Jezreel, Ahab's country palace (perhaps destroyed by Jehu about 841). However, the recent work at Tel Rehov (Rehob) would indicate that these wares were already in use in the tenth century, and simply continued in service during the ninth.[183] Thus their presence in the ninth century does not affect their earlier popularity in the tenth, and has no bearing on the link with the united monarchy (nor has Jezreel, a site of short span, and so of only limited value for this kind of inquiry).

A noteworthy feature of the twelfth and eleventh centuries is the emergence and proliferation of a great number of small village sites in central Canaan, in what became the hill country of Judah in the south and of Ephraim farther north, as evidenced by a series of modern surveys.[184] Then, toward 1000, many of these sites were deserted, while some changed into small townships, and major historic sites changed culture (from a Canaanite or Philistine milieu, or prior abandonment), to be occupied by the users of red-slip, hand-burnished pottery, in a more urban society, with a cultural unity through most of the land, from the Negev north to Galilee and Dan. Some of these urban centers "under new management" suffered destructions after this initial prosperous period. Then they passed through a "quiet" interval before regaining their prosperity, either early as at Dan (Jeroboam I) or later in an epoch best admitted to be that of the builder kings, Omri and Ahab; see above, table 4 in chapter 2 with notes. Thus the first period of some prosperity and unified culture will logically have been that of the united monarchy, with all the Israelite tribes in one governmental horizon under David and Solomon, with Saul as forerunner. This was "prosperity period A" of our chapter 2. Under David such centers as Megiddo, Beth-Shan, and Hazor were incorporated into Israel, besides expansion abroad.[185]

(g) Jerusalem and Other Building Sites

(1) Sites Away from Jerusalem

In 1 Kings 9:15 we are told that Solomon raised a labor-levy "to build" seven items: the temple, his palace, the "Millo" and wall (all in Jerusalem), and Hazor, Megiddo, and Gezer. Each item has the "accusative particle" *eth* prefixed, showing what was built. Thus all seven items were built in one way or another under Solomon. In Jerusalem the temple and palace we have met already, with their cultural background. But we are *not* told what was done at Hazor, Megiddo, or Gezer. This is where a well-understood archaeology might have helped decisively, with securely dated strata or occupation levels at the three sites. But not if this cannot be attained. So, what is the situation?

As we have seen above (p. 53) the strata at Hazor,[186] X to V, ending with the Assyrian destruction in 732, have been deemed to begin (with X) in either the tenth century or (with Finkelstein) the ninth. Before X, it is accepted by all that level XIII (in the citadel) and the contemporary Lower Town flourished and were massively destroyed in the thirteenth century. Then, for circa 1200–1000/880, namely, 200 or 320 years (depending on date, "normal" or Finkelstein, for level X), we have only two occupations at Hazor: XII and XI. The first (twelfth century?) was little more than an encampment of simple huts, with numerous stone-lined storage pits amongst them. The latter (eleventh century?) remains (XI) were of an unwalled village that had a possible cult place. None of this would easily count as the efforts of a royal administration, be it Solomonic or otherwise. The remains from stratum X are a different story, as is clear both from the original excavations by Yadin and from those recently undertaken by Ben-Tor. In this period the upper city had a well-built citadel, but occupying only the western half of the "city" area. It was surrounded (wherever tested) by a "casemate" wall, strictly a double wall with cross-walls forming chambers within it, that could be left clear for storage or filled in to give added strength to the total "wall." Integral with that wall, north of the center of its eastern limit, was a six-roomed gateway with front towers. Within the precinct were found buildings (south-southwest of the gateway) modified in the course of time (levels Xa, IXa, b) until replaced by massive new structures that are generally conceded to belong to Ahab's dynasty (level VIII). As noticed above (p. 53), the attempt to move levels X/IX down to Omri and Ahab, thus forcing down the date of level VIII, leads to wholly artificial and improbable results, implying frenetic changes — and instability — every 16 to 20 years, which is totally inconsistent with the rule of a mainly settled monarchy under the Omri and Jeroboam II dynasties. And this stands in crazy contrast with slow changes (only every 50 to 90 years!) in seemingly extraordinarily stable conditions (only one to four strata in 150 years!) during the far more chaotic age of the twelfth and eleventh centuries, with the competing hostile groups of the Philistines, late Canaanites, early Israelites, and sundry Transjordanians. The sheer logic of the situation would suggest that it is far more desirable to compress the sequence in the troubled twelfth and eleventh centuries and to keep the full-length sequence in the tenth to eighth centuries, simply to make archaeological sense, *without any prior recourse to the Hebrew Bible or other records.* When we find that, on strictly historical grounds, a properly unified state in Canaan *first* came about during the tenth century (David, Solomon) before splitting up into two such smaller states that then remained stable, and only local tribal entities of all shades (and an abortive kingship, of Saul) effectively "ruled" before about 1000, then the clear match of cultural/archaeological change (Canaanite to unified "red-wash Israelite"; villages giving way to fewer urban centers), historical/political change (united monarchy), and tangible settlement change (sudden appearance of "official," nonrural, monumental architecture, Hazor and elsewhere) all comes together in meaningful concord, and makes good sense in all dimensions. The results given us by a lower dating scheme patently do not. So far, Hazor.

Megiddo is the second township listed.[187] Here it is wise to distinguish between the series of overall occupations at Megiddo and detailed (almost insoluble) problems such as those that concern the main city gateway. Canaanite Megiddo of stratum VIIB is generally accepted to belong to the thirteenth century. The following stratum VIIA in turn belongs to the earlier part of the twelfth century; among ivories found in its ruins is a pen case bearing the cartouches of Ramesses III (1187/1184–1156/1153). Thereafter, possibly after an interval, the town was reoccupied by an unimpressive settlement now numbered VIB. In sequence, this had to be of a later twelfth-century date at the earliest. Then came a much more impressive settlement, stratum VIA, "a large and rich city" in the words of Ussishkin, and usually ascribed to the eleventh century. After massive destruction by fire (through either conquest or earthquake), there came a more modest level of domestic buildings, level VB, and perhaps one major building. Then came a "rebuild," with much more impressive structures in the level now known as VA-IVB. To their number belong (by common consent) the northeast building 6000, with adjacent casemate walling; some domestic buildings (338, etc.) at the southeast edge; the southern "residency" (or "palace") 1723, and west of it the big building 1482. There is also the "gallery" that led to a water supply; on stables, see just below. The numbered buildings were of monumental character, more so than at Hazor. The outer "wall" of the city was formed by the outer walls of the buildings around its circumference, linked up by stretches of casemate wall where needed. Above this level was stratum IVA. This period witnessed the thorough refortification of Megiddo with a massive, solid wall, with its segments having "offsets," whereby one segment of the wall projected slightly beyond the adjacent one. This led to the wholesale replacement of the former buildings by new ones: stables (or stores) over the 6000 building in the northeast; under these have been detected good traces of possible stables/stores of the VA-IVB period. New structures arose in the southeast quadrant; and new buildings instead of building 1723, and more stables (or stores) replacing 1482. The water system was developed.

Megiddo IVA was destroyed by the Assyrians in the late eighth century, who then built (early seventh century) a new town (Megiddo III) with Assyrian-type residencies, and an Assyrian-period two-chambered gate. Then, at the end of the seventh century (or into the sixth), a fortress was built (probably by the Babylonians), being Megiddo II, lasting into Persian times. Megiddo IVA had had a four-chambered gate, preceded by a six-chambered gate. The solid walls of IVA — curiously! — came up to these successive gates, but were not clearly bonded into them. The much older city VIA had had a gate of a different type, while the VB settlement was unfortified and had no special gate. What happened in level VA-IVB is unclear, hotly disputed, and remains an enigma. We may make a tentative suggestion only. The four-chambered pre-Assyrian (divided monarchy) gateway is said to have been bonded to the solid offset wall, which is undoubtedly later than the set of buildings which, partially linked by casemate walls, had formed the earlier circuit of the city's defense. Such four-chambered gates in Israel (as distinct from Judah) can be assigned to not later than the eighth century, when (e.g.) both the one at Dor and the Megiddo one were destroyed by the Assyrians. Their builders would have been the Omrides in the ninth century rather than (e.g.) Jeroboam II in the mid-eighth. In this situation it is logical to assign the six-chambered gate at Megiddo to the VA-IVB period, exactly as at Hazor.[188] The Hazor evidence is strongly against an Omride date for the six-chambered gate there. And our sequence of "prosperity" and lesser periods (pp. 57-61 above) is solidly against pushing Omride work down to Jeroboam II's time, and the work of his time into impossible limbo. So, what is pre-Omride, such as period VA-IVB, has (as there noted) to belong to a previous such prosperous period, for which only the united monarchy will realistically fit the bill. The Megiddo six-chambered gate is bereft of context by the total rebuild of the walls flanking it, when the new four-chambered gate was built, and by the wide-ranging destructive activities of the 1930s excavations in this area. This all has to be inference, *not* proof; but at least it is reasonable inference.

The famous city of Gezer[189] was active in the fourteenth century (Amarna letters to Egypt), corresponding to level XVI in Late Bronze IIA. It declined in the thirteenth century (level XV), and the campaign by Merenptah of Egypt (1209/1208) includes Gezer in his conquests, which may have ruined the town of late stratum XV. Thus, in the twelfth century, after scanty occupation at most (XIV), there came Philistine prosperity and pottery along with late Canaanite participation (levels XIII-XI), into the eleventh century. These were followed by a poorer occupation (X-IX), using fresh, red-slipped pottery, ending with destruction of the settlement. This, in sequence, would also be eleventh or early tenth century. Then, by contrast, in VIII, we have refurbishment of the town, with a splendid new (inner) city gateway, six-chambered like Hazor X and Megiddo VA-IVB in design and general scale, with a section of casemate wall still joining up with it, precisely as at Hazor X. Gezer VIII was then destroyed. Strata VII (in which a new four-chambered gate was built) and VI then followed, with the latter being most likely destroyed by the Assyrians (ca. 732), as Neo-Assyrian tablets occurred in stratum V, which had an Assyrian-period two-chambered gate. Here we see yet again the same sequence as at Dor, Hazor, and Megiddo. And doubtless with the same implications as to date. Chronologically the destruction of Gezer IX would fit the campaign best attributed to Siamun (ca. 979/978–960/959; cf. 1 Kings 9:15-16, with pp. 108-10 above). That of level VIII would then go with the campaign of Shoshenq I in 925, hence the six-chambered gate and casemates would — again — find their best context in the tenth century, and in the united monarchy, entirely regardless of whether we like it or not.

The net result for Hazor, Megiddo, and Gezer is that cast-iron certainty over attribution of particular remains to the time of (e.g.) Solomon is not strictly possible. But if we are to avoid bizarre improbabilities in the assignment of strata and periods, then the exciting "new view" of Finkelstein falls down rather badly in the probability stakes; views nearer to the normal may be less exciting, but they come a great deal closer to reality and can be retained as a sensible working hypothesis. In short, the finds at Hazor X-IX, Megiddo VA-IVB, and Gezer IX and VIII are the most likely to represent the physical realities only hinted at in 1 Kings 9:15.

(2) Jerusalem

Here the problem is the sheer lack of material, and the massive lack (in good measure) of adequate exposure of remains, affecting not merely the united monarchy period but most other periods as well. As (U)rusalimu, Jerusalem occurs in the Egyptian Execration Texts of the early second millennium, while its fourteenth-century ruler Abdi-Khepa sent letters to the court of Akhenaten, king of Egypt (Amarna correspondence).[190] The external sources then resume with Sennacherib of Assyria in 701, in his campaign against Hezekiah of Judah and his allies, as we have seen. In terms of archaeological presence, the earlier periods (Middle and Late Bronze) have also been the subject of controversy, and not simply Iron IIA ("united monarchy"). Before circa 720/700, oldest Jerusalem proper was restricted to the north-south ridge directly south of the "saddle" (Ophel) between it and the present-day Temple Mount on the north. As it is currently impossible for severely practical reasons to do any exploratory digging within the Temple Mount precinct, or in the built-up area directly adjoining this on its north side, there is thus no possibility of testing for, or recovering, remains of the temples of Solomon or Zerubbabel, or for Solomon's palace complex either south or north of the original temple precinct. Given the destructive nature of the clearance of older remains and establishment of massive foundations by the Herodian, Roman, Byzantine, Arabic, Ottoman, and other builders, even a full-scale dig is inherently unlikely to yield practical results in any case. Thus, absence of traces of work by Solomon or Zerubbabel in this zone is not their fault, and proves nothing. However, that leaves the Ophel area and the north-south ridge of oldest Jerusalem proper. Here, for a realistic outcome, it is needful to consider two aspects: the state and nature of the physical remains, and the state of the evidence for Jerusalem during Middle and Late Bronze and Iron IIA. Then the Jerusalem of David and Solomon can be seen in proper perspective.

Oldest Jerusalem is a frustrating site to dig. The destructive impact by Neo-Babylonians, Romans, Byzantines, and the rest has wrought dire havoc, to which has to be added that of the relatively unscientific clearances by early excavators (Weill, Macalister, etc.) prior to the 1960s, and — again — the practical difficulties of digging on the north-south ridge. There is also an overburden of modern buildings, gardens, etc., not readily to be disturbed by diggers. Thus Miss Kenyon's meticulous but very limited trenches probably touched barely 2 percent of the area, leaving some 98 percent untouched.[191] More extensive work since 1978 till now may have extended the area dug to up to 5 percent, but that still leaves some 95 percent undug (and mostly undiggable), or ruined by early clearances.[192] Furthermore, the ancients felt constrained by lack of space along the top of the ridge. So, certainly along its east side, they intermittently built out terracing, to support extended areas for their buildings. Such terracing (and buildings) were liable to collapse or hostile destruction; renewed terracing and buildings would often reuse many of the same old stones, obscuring the nature, form, or even data for the very existence of earlier work here. Only the latest structures and destructions usually survive to any extent. On the level zones of the main ridge, again, the later builders (Roman, Byzantine, etc.) would often clear down to (and into) bedrock — destroying earlier work, without even traces surviving.[193] So, in these circumstances, we are in effect lucky to have anything really old at all. The common and strident claim that "archaeology offers no evidence" for this, that, or the other period in Jerusalem should be taken not just with a pinch of salt but with a whole bucketful!

With all this clearly in mind, we may now look at Jerusalem in the Middle Bronze to Iron IIA periods with better understanding. In the Middle Bronze Age, the name in the Execration Texts is each time written with the "three hills" determinative used for foreign lands and settlements, and specifically for such arrangements as the little Canaanite city-states consisting of a local "capital" town with its surrounding territory and sundry lesser settlements. Thus Jerusalem here is a town plus its territory, *not* just a tribal zone.[194] In these particular texts, tribal groups are separately named as such, explicitly, such as those belonging to Byblos and Irqata. As for Jerusalem's sphere of rule at this time, it alone with Shechem shared control over the hill country of Canaan from south of the vale of Jezreel down to Hebron: Shechem the north, Jerusalem the south. No other major center is named until one reaches either Ascalon westward on the coast or a Rehob which is either the one near Accho or the one by the Jordan near Beth-Shan. Therefore, as the Egyptian authorities were interested in places with potential for rebellion, not just glorified villages or hamlets, the Jerusalem of these texts was a principal center in its region and not just the outpost of some other state (unnamed!), as claimed.

With the texts agree the remains so far discovered. Along the east side of the north-south ridge (or "eastern hill") have twice been found respectable segments of the enclosure wall of the Middle Bronze II city: 12.25 meters (about 40 feet) by Miss Kenyon, and later, another 30-meter stretch (about 90/100 feet), parts of it reinforced, by the Shiloh expedition. The wall was some 2 to 3 meters thick (about 7 to 10 feet), had Middle Bronze II sherds associated with it, and served as the basis for walls both then and in later periods. There would be no point in having such a wall along one side of the town only; its presence implies a full circuit of the eastern hill.[195] Recently, continuing work on the east side has revealed some formidable defenses for the Gihon spring, the oldest city's water supply. Here parts of two towers of cyclopean masonry plus a pool have been found of this period; a third tower probably existed then also.[196] In short, Middle Bronze Jerusalem was a compact, strongly defended hill-zone center — not just somebody else's minor outpost.

In the Late Bronze Age, fifteenth to thirteenth centuries, it is a similar story, so far as the physical evidence goes. The Amarna letters show clearly Jerusalem's importance in the fourteenth century. It belonged to the group of primary Canaanite cities that corresponded directly with the Egyptian court (letters 285-90) — as did its northern hill-country rival Shechem (nos. 252-54), and such as Gezer (nos. 267-71), Megiddo (nos. 242-46), Ascalon (nos. 320-26), etc.[197] As in the Middle Bronze Age, Shechem and Jerusalem shared dominance in the Canaanite hill country. As others have noted, its ruler, Abdi-Khepa, was a very active *city* ruler, battling with contemporaries who ruled in Gezer and Gath;[198] other towns "belonged to Jerusalem" then, and there was room for a fifty-man-strong Egyptian garrison.[199] This was no mere house in a small estate, as has been unrealistically suggested!

On the archaeological plane, one cannot dismiss the role of Jerusalem and its ruler merely because we have no rich palace with several tons of pottery. The claims have been made that "no remains of a [Late Bronze] town have been found," that "more than enough exposure" has been made "to decide whether or not there was a Late Bronze Age town in Jerusalem," and against claims of erosion, some Late Bronze sherds should have shown up but "they are not there." So especially against the fourteenth-century town.[200]

However, the facts are somewhat different. Between 2 and 5 percent of a site dug, at a site so badly destroyed from Herodian to Ottoman times, is not remotely "more than enough exposure" — it is little more than a handful of often narrow trenches. With 95 percent of the site untouched (and largely unreachable), and massive destruction in late antiquity, it is entirely premature to claim that the limited digs hitherto can be treated as definitive. As others have pointed out, there are positive finds that point to a Late Bronze town, extending over a length comparable with the Middle Bronze one or beyond it. Late Bronze pottery *and strata* (= successive phases of occupation) were found in Kenyon's areas A and P and Shiloh's area E1. Architecture is not wholly absent; remains turned up in Shiloh's area G. In the Late Bronze Age, fortification walls and massive gateways were not customary (under Egyptian rule, against revolt?); the locals had to make do with a ring of edge-to-edge domestic dwellings for local security. And the thirteenth and twelfth centuries had a massive stepped-stone structure at the northeast corner of early Jerusalem's eastern ridge, which indicates an active local regime during (say) roughly 1230-1150, still existing thereafter. In the light of all these considerations, it is entirely wrong to attempt to dismiss the existence of a compact and active township at Jerusalem from the fourteenth to twelfth centuries, or going on later.[201]

So, with these lessons in mind, we may at last turn to the Jerusalem of David and Solomon. We have seen already that the most important structures — temple, palace complex — were located en bloc north of Ophel and the old city along the eastern ridge. Whatever remains of them might still exist (after Neo-Babylonian destruction, Persian-age reworking, Herodian replacement, and demolition by Romans and others) are irrevocably buried under the present Temple Mount. David first occupied the fortress of oldest Jerusalem (the eastern ridge south of Ophel), and did work there on the "Millo" (2 Sam. 5:9). Then his new ally Hiram of Tyre built him a palace (5:11). This might have been inside the north end of the old city, but equally may have adjoined its north side, on Ophel, just south of the future Temple Mount. As Dr. Eilat Mazar pointed out, David descended into the city fortress when a Philistine advance was reported (5:17-18) — presumably from his new palace up on its north side. Thus she would deduce that David's palace once stood in the Ophel area.[202] Solomon too worked at the Millo, and on the wall of Jerusalem (1 Kings 9:15). Of the latter, we need expect to find next to nothing — it would be reworked by later Judean kings (e.g., Hezekiah, 2 Chron. 32:5), and much of the walls were destroyed by the Babylonians. As for the Millo, it could not have been the original stepped-stone structure in the northeast part of the oldest city, but it may be represented by the later fills that covered the stepped-stone structure and its mantle, as part of later work — and which had within it the typical tenth-century pottery, plain with hand-burnished red slip, and associated types.[203] This represents most probably the efforts of David and Solomon's epoch.

(3) Sites Elsewhere in Israel and Judah

The four prominent sites reviewed above are by no means the only places in which people lived during the brief decades of the "united monarchy." Successive lists of other sites showing datable occupations in the tenth century have long since been given by leading archaeologists. Even without the four sites above, Dever listed over 20 sites, and Mazar nearly 30, with Iron IIA/tenth-century occupations, at all levels from modest villages to walled settlements. The recently published south Samaria survey shows nearly 100 smaller sites for that area alone, within about 1050-900.[204] Cf. fig. 24.

Thus the strange idea that tenth-century Palestine was almost uninhabited and unable to sustain a modest "empire" is, frankly, a nonstarter. So also is the equally bizarre notion that a compact, fortified site like early Jerusalem could not be the capital for a small nation-state or a mini-empire.[205] In the formative years of empires, their energies go into territorial expansion; conspicuous display is expressed in major cities and monuments only later, often on the eve of decline or in its beginnings. A good example is Egypt. Based in a minuscule capital, post–Middle Kingdom Thebes, in 120 miles of narrow Nile Valley below Aswan, Ahmose I expelled the Hyksos and rebounded into Canaan, besides reaching deep into Nubia southward, extending his realm to a south-north length of 1,400 miles of Nile Valley plus dominance in Canaan. Within some thirty years his second successor, Tuthmosis I, had reached beyond the Fourth Cataract of the Nubian Nile (to Kanisa Kurgus) and north to the Euphrates and Carchemish, a vast span of some 2,300 miles. By then Thebes was still small, the temple of Amun had gained only a couple of front halls and a south approach; Memphis had simply a new palace center of this king for his growing governance. But little more. Tuthmosis III affirmed this wide rule and built much more. Amenophis III saw the most opulence and new building, on the eve of decline, while the huge edifices of the Ramesside kings accompanied that decline. This can be replicated in other lands and epochs, and is seemingly unknown to our overspeculative, factually disadvantaged sociological anthropologists. In this context, fortress Jerusalem was an ideal base for David's swift, opportunistic campaigns and overlordships; Solomon began to expand his base with the added governmental palace complex (and temple as ideological center), but then everything crumbled prematurely in his last years and under the inept Rehoboam, before consolidation was possible.

Flourishing centers in the eleventh and tenth centuries include Dan up in the north (strata V-IV).[206] More centrally, Shechem was destroyed circa 1100, and remained so until a modest settlement arose in the tenth century. This was destroyed in the later tenth century, and may have been the [Mi]gdal[Shechem] of Shoshenq I's list (no. 58), north of Zemaraim en route to [Ti]rzah (no. 59) and "the Valley" par excellence, i.e., Jezreel (no. 65). Then Shechem was again rebuilt, as a proper township, in the late tenth/early ninth century, possibly corresponding to the early use of this place as his first capital by Jeroboam I of Israel (1 Kings 12:25). All this fits together well; but with Finkelstein's lower chronology of Iron I/II strata generally, this would not work.[207] After long nonoccupation, or minimal occupation, Taanach was again well settled in the thirteenth through the twelfth century, being destroyed about 1125 (IA-IB). Then came a further gap in occupation with only very slight settlement, until a renewal of the town Taanach in the tenth century (IIA-B), only to be destroyed late in that century. As Taanach is listed by Shoshenq I (no. 14), he is usually blamed for the destruction of this Tanaach (probably rightly). On a low Finkelstein dating of Iron I-II, Shoshenq would have found nothing worth destroying or listing in 926/925, with Taanach IIA-B arising only after he had disappeared![208] Beth-Shemesh IV had been a flourishing Late Bronze II town in the thirteenth century, seemingly destroyed around 1200. Founded later, level III was a mere village, with Canaanite-type pottery and Philistine bichrome ware (by about 1120); the Canaanite population (and Philistine overlords?) had been joined by early Israelite settlers by the time of Eli (ca. 1080); cf. 1 Sam. 6:9-20. These Hebrews may have shared in the local material culture then. We hear of them moving in with the Canaanites here and elsewhere, and being subject to them (note Judg. 1:33; cf. 1:27-33). Then, suddenly, we have in level IIa a remodeled town (no more Philistine stuff), with a strong masonry ring wall, as an administrative center in the tenth century. Correspondingly, Beth-Shemesh occurs in Solomon's second administrative district, and the contemporary inscribed fragment of one Hanan echoes the neighboring place Elon (of) Beth (House/Estate of) Hanan in 1 Kings 4:9; cf. above, p. 132. Thereafter Beth-Shemesh survived until Sennacherib's destruction in 701, with seventh-century squatters dispersed when its water supply was blocked (by Philistines, it seems).[209] This entire history all goes well on normal dating, but not on an artificially lowered one. Other sites repay study, but these must suffice here. Cf. already on Beth-Shan, p. 98 above.

To end the theme, we turn to lesser sites revealed by ground surveys; it will suffice here to use the results from one of the latest-published and most careful such surveys, that of the terrain of Ephraim (south Samaria). In the area gone through, 131 Iron I sites (twelfth-eleventh centuries) are listed; then 94 sites for Iron Age I/II (tenth–early ninth centuries); then 241 sites for Iron II (basically eighth-seventh centuries), citing here the surveyors' dates.[210] If we understand roughly 200/150 years for the Iron I series (131 sites), then up to 100 years for their Iron Age I/II (94 sites), and at least 250 years (850-600) for their Iron II (241 sites), and note the roughly equivalent proportion of time spans and sites, then it is no surprise that Iron I has nearly half as many again as Iron I/II, and the longer span of Iron II (over twice the I/II period) has more than twice the number of reported sites. Not all sites would be contemporary throughout the whole of any given period, it should also be kept in mind, just as for the varied histories of extensively dug large sites in each epoch. In this light the "united monarchy" period is no less populous on this evidence than the main periods immediately before and after it. And it fits the changing histories of big sites as well as of the parallel developing cultures found also in the surveys.

4. ANOTHER LOOK AT THE BALANCE SHEET

The results of this long investigation into the tenth century must now be summed up.

1. An initial summary from the biblical sources was needful, to delimit the field of investigation, namely, the three reputed reigns of Saul, David, and Solomon over a single Hebrew kingdom.

2. Then inquiry had to be made into what external information was available, its limitations noted and the reasons for those limitations clearly spelled out, in factual terms. The information from external sources in terms of *explicit mentions* of biblical characters such as Saul, David, or Solomon is almost zero, until Shalmaneser III had hostile contact with Ahab of Israel in 853. The reasons for this are stunningly simple and conclusive. From Mesopotamia, *no Assyrian rulers had had direct contact with Palestine before 853* — and so do not mention any local kings there. This is *not* the fault of the kings in Canaan, whether Israelite, Canaanite, or Philistine, and does *not* prove their nonexistence. From Egypt we have virtually *no historical inscriptions whatsoever* mentioning Palestinian powers or entities between Ramesses III (ca. 1184-1153) and Shoshenq I (ca. 945-924). We have just two literary works, *Wenamun,* referring only to coastal ports (Dor to Byblos), and the *Moscow Literary Letter* that knows of Seir.[211] Plus the fragmentary triumphal scene of Siamun (ca. 979/978–960/959), overlapping with the early years of Solomon (970-960), when a pharaoh smote Gezer and ceded it to him (1 Kings 9:16). The vast mass of Egyptian records in the Delta and Memphis is long since lost for nearly all periods, includ-

ing the tenth century. At Thebes, almost all records are local, private, and on funerary religion, not foreign wars. From the Levant, original texts are so far lost/undiscovered before the ninth century, except at Byblos, whose kings celebrate only themselves. We have nothing from Tyre, Sidon, Damascus, etc., until much later. So, again, there is no mention of the Hebrew tenth-century monarchs — and, again, it is not their fault, and certainly *not* proof of nonexistence. In Israel itself, the deplorable state of pre-Herodian remains in oldest Jerusalem (Ophel and the eastern ridge), inaccessibility of much of its terrain, and the fact that it is 95 percent undug/undiggable (100 percent on the Temple Mount, where royal stelae might have been erected) — all these factors almost entirely exclude any hope of retrieving significant inscriptions from Jerusalem at any period before Herodian times. (The Siloam tunnel text [ca. 700] survived precisely because it was in a safely buried location.) So, again, we cannot blame a David or a Solomon for all that happened to Jerusalem after their time.

Yet despite this very adverse situation, we *do* begin to have traces: the Tell Dan inscription and with virtual certainty the Moabite Stone each mention "the House of David," implying his former role as a personal dynastic founder, about 150 years after his death. Then, within barely 50 years of his death (ca. 970), we have what is in all likelihood "the heights of David" in the list of Shoshenq I (ca. 925), with a final *t* for final *d* exactly as in Ethiopic. (Alas, no clearly better and indisputable alternative can be offered, it seems!) The political situation of Hadadezer king of Aram-Zobah in circa 990 (reaching across the Euphrates) is extremely likely to find a reflex in the situation there in the time of Assur-rabi II of Assyria, as later reported by Shalmaneser III. So, explicit traces are beginning to emerge, even for the limited possibilities of the tenth century.

3. But explicit evidence is *not* the only form of valid and informative evidence. It is equally important to measure off a document or account against what we know independently about the topics it includes. In this light much can be said: a little on Saul's time, more on David's, and much more on Solomon's epoch. Thus Saul's regime was profitably compared with the ethos and practices of Levantine kingship. David's "empire" (inherited by Solomon) belongs to a particular type of "mini-empire," of a scope and nature only present and feasible within the interval between about 1180 and 870 and at no other time in the first millennium, being known also from Neo-Hittite and Aramean analogues. Under Solomon, foreign relations *do* fit the context of his day; his temple and palace complex (and their furnishings) find ample and immediate cultural analogues, in both scale and nature. This is also true of the scale of his revenues; in fact, his 20 tons of gold in a year is poverty compared with the spending of over 380 tons of precious metal by Osorkon I soon afterward, and

the 7,000 tons of gold that Alexander the Great lifted from the vanquished Persian Empire later on. Poetry (David) and instructional wisdom (Solomon) belong well in the tenth century, with earlier roots, and ample successors.

4. The physical archaeology of tenth-century Canaan is consistent with the former existence of a unified state on its terrain then (with some monumental architecture). Jerusalem cannot deliver much on this; but on normal datings, Hazor, Gezer, and Megiddo (largely) can. And the occupation of the rest of the area is also consistent with this; it was not a land of ghosts. The clever attempt to down-date the archaeological remains of the twelfth-to-eighth century substantially into the eleventh-to-late-eighth century will not really work, throws up bizarre anomalies, requires invention of new Aegean invasions, and is wholly needless. The coexistence of mutually hostile cultural groups not using each other's prestige wares is perfectly feasible; and any compression in an archaeological timescale should be set in the twelfth/eleventh centuries, not the tenth/eighth. Thus, normal dating should be retained, with its entire network of good correlations with social and political conditions also reflected in the biblical sources.

5. In short, the testing of the biblical text against external data (texts and artifactual contexts) shows precious little fantasy and much realistic agreement in practical and cultural aspects. Much more might be examined, but the subjects reviewed here give some idea of the real situation.

CHAPTER 5

Humble Beginnings — around and in Canaan

Now we edge cautiously back into the second millennium B.C., before the settled age of lines of kings, so far as the early Israelites are concerned — before about 1042 (accession of Saul), on the dates suggested above, p. 83. The principal biblical sources are the existing books of Joshua and Judges, supplemented by 1 Sam. 1–10. Looking back in time, we see the biggest event in Hebrew tradition was the exodus from Egypt, followed at an interval (traditionally forty years) by their entry into Canaan. Questions surrounding an exodus can be safely left until chapter 6; but the presence in Canaan of an entity named Israel can be given a firm bottom date in Year 5 of Merenptah, which ran from within 1st Akhet 18/2nd Akhet 13 = within 1st/27th July Gregorian in 1209 to within 1st/27th July Gregorian in 1208 (and *not* 1207, as so many writers miscalculate).[1] So, if Israel entered Canaan from without, she did so prior to 1209 by an unknown interval. At any rate, about 1210 gives us a bottom date for the presence of a tribal entity — so marked by its determinative on Merenptah's stela — clearly named Israel, settled or settling in Canaan by 1210 at the latest. Therefore, as we do not intend to write a novel about Joshua battling it out with Merenptah's forces, it is simpler to set any such leader's entry before 1210 and to equate the period 1210-1042 — almost 170 years — with the so-called period of the judges featured in the books of Judges, Ruth, and 1 Samuel (1–10). The latest setting of the book of Joshua (if granted even minimal credence) would then in principle lie immediately in the decade or so before 1210, along with any Israelite entry into Canaan from outside. In archaeological terms in Canaan, we are in the end phase of Late Bronze (IIB/III) followed by the epoch of Iron I.

In what follows we must first review the actual contents of the book of Joshua: what it *actually* says, rather than what some scholars wrongly think it says, partly through carelessness in not reading carefully the actual text and partly through not knowing the proper cultural background. That done, the Near Eastern background and archaeology can then be compared with the real, not imaginary, Joshua text. As the Hebrews had not lived at Gilgal by the Jordan since the creation, but are claimed to have arrived there from across the Jordan, it is in order next to look at the relevant narratives and their possible background. Thereafter we can return to the period after Joshua, to the content of the book of Judges, to analyze its contents, not just its framework, and set a theoretical dating scheme for its main actors, and add in the data from 1 Sam. 1–10 prior to Saul. We will then look again at appropriate Near Eastern background and archaeology, before essaying an overall result.

1. THE BOOK OF JOSHUA AS IT IS

Conveniently, the obvious contents (by modern chapter/verse divisions) can be summarized thus.

Table 8. The Book of Joshua as It Is

1. Across the Jordan into Canaan (1–5:12):
   - New leader (1); spying out the new area (2); crossing into Canaan (3).
   - Entry, Gilgal: memory stones (4); circumcision and passover (5:1-13).
2. First Conflict (5:13–8:29):
   - Jericho destroyed/burned — then back at Gilgal (5:13–6:27).
   - Ai, defeat, then destroyed/burned; then back at Gilgal (7–8:29).
3. Interlude: First Covenant Rite, Ebal (8:30-34). Gibeon Sneaks Alliance (9)
   - Israel continues to stay at Gilgal; **no occupation** of Jericho-Ai area.
4. Second Conflict — Southern Battles (10):
   - Battle of Gibeon; death of five kings (10:1-27).
   - Attacks on: Makkedah, Libnah, Lachish, Eglon, Hebron, Debir, in each case attacked, taken, ruler and people killed, *then move on, **not stopping to occupy**.* Gezer, only king (and forces) killed, trying to relieve Lachish; city not said to be attacked. Israel returns to HQ at Gilgal (N.B.: bracketing verses: 15, 43) (10:28-43).
5. Third Conflict — Northern Battles (11):
   - Battle of the Waters of Merom, destruction of hostile forces (11:1-15).
   - Hazor, chief center, burned (like Jericho and Ai), **and no other** (11:13).
   - Rhetorical summary for southern and northern wars (11:16-20); Joshua fought for "many days" ("long time") (11:18).

- *Annex:* slaying Anakites in south, excluding Gaza, Gath, Ashdod (11:11-23).
- N.B.: *no occupation of these regions is claimed down to this point.* Israel was still based at Gilgal, at Joshua's initial land allotment (14:6).

6. Lists of Defeated Rulers (12):
   - *East of Jordan, under Moses* (12:1-6):
     Amorite land of Sihon, Bashan under Og, defeated, allotted, **occupied**.
   - *West of Jordan under Joshua* (12:7-24):
     thirty-one petty kingdoms defeated, kings slain, but **terrain not occupied**.
     Annex: notice of areas **not** invaded (13:1-7).

7. Formal Allotments of Territory (13:8–21:45):
   - *Retrospect:* Moses' allotments to Reuben, Gad, and first half Manasseh, east of Jordan (13:8-33); already begun to be occupied.
   - *Prospect:* Joshua's allotments to rest of Israel, west of Jordan **not yet occupied** (14–21).
     Part 1: (Gilgal) — Caleb, Judah, Ephraim, second half Manasseh (14–17).
     Part 2: (Shiloh) — surveys, *then* allotment (18:4-11): Benjamin, Simeon, Zebulon; Issachar, Asher, Naphtali; Dan; and Joshua (18:11–19:51).
     Part 3: (Shiloh) — cities of refuge; Levites (20–21).

8. Concluding Acts under Joshua (22–24):
   - East tribal forces return to east of Jordan (22).
   - Joshua's farewell (23).
   - *Second covenant rite, Shechem* (24:1-27).
   - *Annex:* death of Joshua; rule of the elders, etc. (24:28-33).

Such is the actual record, regardless of its date(s) or inherent nature. The picture that emerges from an attentive reading of the actual narrative text of Joshua is very clear, leaving aside all the incidental rhetoric. After entry into Canaan from across the Jordan, a base camp was established (Gilgal) on the eastern edge of Jericho's territory, with due ceremony.

Then both Jericho and Ai were successively destroyed, *and* burned so that their occupation was ended. One notes that the Israelites did *not* immediately go up and disperse themselves over the lands belonging to these townships, but *remained based in Gilgal.* No conquest by occupation yet. But this initial local success was followed by a visit up to Mount Ebal close by Shechem, clearly unopposed, for a covenant-renewal ceremony (8:30-34). *Then home to Gilgal.*

The conflict with Canaanite city-state rulers in the south part of Canaan is worth close observation. After the battle for Gibeon, we see the Hebrews advance upon six towns in order, attacking and capturing them, killing their local kings and such of the inhabitants as had not gotten clear, *and moving on, not holding on to these places.* Twice over (10:15, 43), it is clearly stated that their strike force *returned to base camp at Gilgal.* So there was no sweeping takeover and occupation of this region at this point. And *no* total destruction of the towns attacked.

What happened in the south was repeated up north. Hazor was both leader and famed center for the north Canaanite kinglets. Thus, as in the south, the Hebrew force defeated the opposition; they captured their towns, killed rulers and less mobile inhabitants, and symbolically burned Hazor, and Hazor only, to emphasize the end of its local supremacy. Again Israel did *not* attempt immediately to hold on to Galilee; they remained *based at Gilgal* (cf. 14:6). These campaigns were essentially *disabling raids;* they were not territorial conquests with instant Hebrew occupation. The text is very clear about this. Cf. fig. 25.

We are told that Joshua warred for some time (11:18), but are not given precise detail. But there are indirect indications of the possible content of other similar raids. Thus the list of thirty-one defeated towns/slain kings in Josh. 12 includes more than those who people the narratives in 10–11. We additionally find Hormah and Arad in the Negev (12:14); Adullam, Bethel, and Geder in the south part of central Canaan (cf. 12:13, 15, 16); Tappuah, Hepher, Aphek, Sharon ("Lasharon"), and Tirzah in the north part (cf. 12:17-18, 24); and Megiddo, Taanach, Jokneam, Qedesh, and Goyim-Gilgal in Jezreel and Galilee (cf. 12:21-23).

The first indication of a *real* move in occupation outward beyond Gilgal comes in 18:4. After the first allotment (14–17) of lands-to-be-occupied had been made, Ephraim-Manasseh began to act on their lot — and found it no pushover to make a takeover (cf. 17:14-18). But they must quickly have made their way via Bethel up the twenty-five miles (forty kilometers) or so through Shiloh to gain Shechem and Tirzah — and with enough assurance to allow for the establishing of the tabernacle at Shiloh (18:1, "the country [there] . . . under their control"), where it ultimately stayed through the twelfth/early eleventh centuries (Iron I). Bethel probably fell at this time (cf. flashback entry, Judg. 1:22-26), and Tirzah (cf. Josh. 12:24). As long noticed in biblical studies, Shechem remains an enigma. No relationship is mentioned with it, other than geographical; it has no battle with Israel; no king of Shechem appears in either the narratives (10–11) or the list of heads that rolled (12). Two factors are relevant. One is the long tradition of relationships with Shechem from the patriarchs onward (cf. Gen. 12:6 [Abraham]; 33:18-20 plus chap. 34 [with 48:22?], 35:4, and 37:12-17 [Jacob]), so that it was not wholly alien territory. The other is that, in all probability, Shechem was little more than a small village in the later thirteenth century, not then a kingdom, Tirzah ruling the district. Thus, before Joshua's death, the first Israelite zone of settlement had probably extended from the Gilgal/Jericho/Ai district via Bethel and Shiloh up to Shechem and Tirzah. Southward, Caleb went to gain Hebron and Debir (Josh. 14:6-15 and 15:13-19; cf. flashback in Judg. 1:12-15). And in the center-north Joshua himself was granted Timnath-serah (var. Timnath-heres), some sixteen miles southwest of Shechem (Josh. 19:49-50; cf. 24:30; Judg. 2:9). Under the elders, attempts were made to reach farther, but with little immediate headway (cf. Judg. 1–2).

Thus, to sum up, the book of Joshua in reality simply records the Hebrew entry into Canaan, their base camp at Gilgal by the Jordan, their initial raids (without occupation!) against local rulers and subjects in south and north Canaan, followed by localized occupation (a) north from Gilgal as far as Shechem and Tirzah and (b) south to Hebron/Debir, and very little more. This is *not* the sweeping, instant conquest-with-occupation that some hasty scholars would foist upon the text of Joshua, without any factual justification. Insofar as only Jericho, Ai, and Hazor were explicitly allowed to have been burned into nonoccupation, it is also pointless going looking for extensive conflagration levels at any other Late Bronze sites (of any phase) to identify them with any Israelite impact. Onto this initial picture Judges follows directly and easily, with no inherent contradiction: it contradicts only the bogus and superficial construction that some modern commentators have willfully thrust upon the biblical text of Joshua without adequate reason. The fact is that biblical scholars have allowed themselves to be swept away by the upbeat, rhetorical element present in Joshua, a persistent feature of most war reports in ancient Near Eastern sources that they are not accustomed to understand and properly handle. See next section.

2. THE BOOK OF JOSHUA AND NEAR EASTERN BACKGROUND

A. INTRODUCTION

Here we need to collate the narratives and lists that make up the existing book of Joshua in two almost equal parts. As with the "united monarchy," there are almost no external sources that mention people and events that feature in the books of Joshua and Judges. And for similar reasons. In the late second millennium Assyria remained east of the Euphrates and had no cause to report on the affairs of distant Canaan. That region formed part of the Egyptian empire for much of that period, but Egyptian sources for Canaan are limited essentially to very laconic reports of campaigns by the New Kingdom pharaohs, and a handful of administrative and literary texts that show almost no interest in the demography of highland Canaan at that time. For the fourteenth century, these are briefly supplemented by the Amarna letters, which include correspondence of Egyptian vassals in Canaan with the pharaoh's court.[2] But when the Egyptians did penetrate beyond the coast routes of Canaan in the thirteenth/early twelfth centuries, then immediately we find brief mentions of biblical peoples. So Mount Seir (= Edom) appears in texts of Ramesses II (thirteenth century), and Seirite districts occur in a list of his that derives largely from one of Amenophis III (fourteenth century).[3] Moab is mentioned and depicted as object of a campaign by Ramesses II in his lists.[4] People from Edom (so named) appear with their cattle, seeking pasture and water in the East Delta under Merenptah in his Year 8 (1206).[5] The tent-dwelling people of Seir (Edom) were raided by Ramesses III within circa 1180-1170.[6] And to cap all these, we have, of course, the clear mention of Israel as a people in Canaan in Year 5 of Merenptah (1209/1208). In Numbers, Deuteronomy, and Judges we also have mention of Hebrew relations with Moab and Seir-Edom, both in the traditions of their transit from Sinai via Transjordan to Canaan and during the conflicts mentioned in Judges, i.e., in the thirteenth/twelfth centuries. Thus we in fact do have brief but clear attestation of Israel itself in the late thirteenth century in Canaan, and of her neighbors Moab in the thirteenth century and Seir-Edom in the fourteenth to early twelfth centuries in firsthand Egyptian military and administrative records. That important fact needs to be taken firmly on board. The inner struggles of Israel and neighbors in highland Canaan and eastward were of no interest whatever to the pharaohs unless they risked infringing on Egyptian interests — which was very rare and limited. However, precisely as with the united monarchy, so here. It is in order for us to compare the documents in the books of Joshua and Judges and their content with relevant external background data, so that we have an objective standard by which to appraise these narratives, lists, etc. The data are both textual and graphic and also "archaeological" in the narrow sense of sites and artifacts. We will now consider both as concisely as possible.

B. SPECIFIC THEMES AND TOPICS

Many features of the narratives in Joshua (and Judges) find direct echoes and counterparts in texts and representations in their surrounding world.

(i) Rootless Tribal and Related Groups in Late Bronze Canaan

Reputedly fugitives from Egypt, and in rootless transit through Transjordan into Canaan, the tribal group "Israel" was not the only such population group troubling their neighbors (and sometimes, higher authorities) there in the late second millennium. The Amarna letters of the mid–fourteenth century are full of reports about restless groups such as the Apiru, or displaced people. This much-discussed term cannot be readily equated linguistically with biblical "Hebrew" *(˓ibri),* as is often done. But there are clear behavioral analogies between these Apiru and the displaced Hebrews who had fled Egypt and (now rootless) sought to establish themselves in Canaan. The biblical Hebrews in Joshua-Judges sought to raid towns, and hopefully to seize control of them, occasionally burning them down (Jericho, Ai, Hazor). Of the Apiru we can read similar activities from the point of view of local city rulers in the Amarna letters. Time and again they are accused of trying to overcome cities and expel their petty kings ("mayors/governors" in Egyptian usage), and get control, as did the Hebrews. Seeing trouble, the people of Gibeon (Josh. 9) sought to make treaty-alliance with the Hebrew intruders. And in the Amarna letters, city rulers continually fear towns joining up with the Apiru. Or they go over to the Apiru and make agreement or treaty with them, as the Gibeonites later did with Joshua and his people. Local rulers might band together against a third party, just as the five kings of south Canaan did against Gibeon and Israel (Josh. 10) and the group in north Canaan (chap. 11) did against Joshua and his forces.[7]

This range of activity by Apiru and other groups is also attested in the thirteenth century, from brief Egyptian reports under Sethos I, circa 1295/1290. His first stela of his Year 1 at Beth-Shan reports on the rulers of Hammath and Pella capturing Beth-Shan and besieging Rehob, until the pharaoh's forces recaptured Beth-Shan and relieved Rehob, securing also Yenoam. Compare the five kings led by Jerusalem that threatened Gibeon, until Joshua brought military deliverance. On his second Beth-Shan stela a little later, Sethos I reports on tribal conflict involving the "Apiru of the mountain of Yarmutu" ("Jarmuth"), along with the Tayaru folk, attacking another Asiatic group, of Ruhma; which mischief he stepped in to quell. This appears to have been in Lower Galilee, if the Jarmuth concerned was that located later in Issachar (Josh. 21:29).[8] The picture is much like that of Israel or of segments such as the Calebites (Josh. 14:6-14; cf. Judg. 1:12-15) battling it out with other groups such as the Anakim, but without pharaonic interference, until Merenptah in 1209 briefly repulsed some part of Israel's forces.

This last event may find other echoes in our data. In Josh. 15:9 and 18:15 is found the seemingly tautologous place-name "Spring of the waters of Nephtoah." Surely either "spring" or "waters" would have sufficed as definition! But for long enough the suggestions have been made that (1) we should understand this name as for "Spring of Menephtoah," or in fact "Spring of Me(re)nptah," named after the pharaoh, and that (2) Lifta, just northwest of Jerusalem, marks the site and preserves a remnant of the name.[9] Whatever the military clash was, it may have stimulated the Egyptian forces into establishing a small "bridge-head" upland fort near Jerusalem to watch over Canaanites and Hebrews alike. With this should be compared a mention of "the troop-commanders of the Wells of Merenptah that are [in] the mountain-ridges," in Year 3 (1211), in a postal register of message-carrying officers then.[10] It is possible that Merenptah's strike into Canaan dates to within Years 1 to 3.

(ii) Leaders in the Levant

In the narratives Joshua is presented as a dynamic leader who can spur his people forward. This included conquest of two settlements as gateway to upland Canaan proper, then raiding through Canaan, top-slicing local city rulers and temporarily disabling local opposition. Exploits of such a kind need direct leadership; it is not the product of a wandering, unfocused mob. Other dynamic "Joshuas" also flourished in the Late Bronze Levant. The city-based Labayu of Shechem made a strong impression on his contemporaries in the Amarna age, as the Amarna letters show.[11]

But far more remarkable was Abdi-ashirta, who, aided and succeeded by his equally wily son Aziru, created from scratch a kingdom of Amurru based in the north Lebanon mountains and environs within the last ten or fifteen years of Akhenaten's reign, the main period of the Amarna letters that evidence this feat. In this they made full use of Apiru fighting men and auxiliaries, to expand their control over neighboring towns, not least profitable trading ports on the Mediterranean coast. Geopolitically this represented a much more ambitious achievement on the ground than the modest initial Hebrew occupation of the Canaanite upland area from Hebron to Jericho/Ai (bypassing Jerusalem) up via Shiloh to Shechem and Tirzah. Thus the territorial achievement of Joshua and the elders (in maybe ten/fifteen years?) was certainly much less than that of Abdi-ashirta and Aziru — who also faced stiff opposition from their contemporaries, and had to cope with direct threats from Egypt and the Hittite power, as the Amarna letters and contemporary archives show.[12] Therefore there are no grounds whatsoever for denying reality or factuality to the Joshua narratives in terms of what they actually represent on the ground, when the rhetorical component is left aside.

(iii) Campaign Preliminaries: Crossings, Spies, Commissioning, and Night Flights

(a) Crossing Jordan

This episode is narrated in Josh. 3:1–4:18: the river's flow stopped, leaving a dry crossing, as the waters had piled up at a town named Adam near Zarethan (3:16). The stoppage lasted long enough for the Hebrews to get across in the day. This phenomenon directly reflects known reality, and is not fantasy. Some sixteen miles north of a crossing opposite Jericho, Adam is present-day Tell ed-Damieh. It is specifically in this district that the high banks of the Jordan have been liable to periodic collapses, sufficient to block the river for a time. Thus in December A.D. 1267 a high mound by the river collapsed into it, stopping its flow completely for sixteen hours. In 1906 a similar event occurred, and then during the earthquake in 1927. That time the west bank collapsed, taking the road with it, while just below this a 150-foot section of riverside cliff fell across the river, damming it completely for twenty-one hours.[13] Such an event in antiquity would have readily facilitated the crossing by the early Israelites.

(b) Spies, Decoys, Counterspies, and Barmaids

Use of spies and of "disinformation" was customary many centuries before Joshua and the late second millennium. We are told that Joshua sent out two spies to observe Jericho and its approaches. In that town they took refuge with a woman Rahab who threw in her lot with them and concealed them, while disinforming the local king and his agents (Josh. 2). Use of spies and misinformation is found already and commonly in the eighteenth century, in the vast Mari archives in northeast Syria.[14] And in the thirteenth century, at the notorious Battle of Qadesh (1275), the Hittite king sent out decoys who duped Ramesses II of Egypt into making a rash advance on that city. Then Ramesses' own spies caught some genuine Hittite spies, and beat the truth out of them.[15] The role of Rahab has been debated: simple harlot or female tavern keeper? This latter role is attested in the biblical world during the second millennium in particular, not later than circa 1100, after which the circumstances of brewing and dispensing alcohol changed. As at Jericho the king demanded details of her visitors, so in Old Babylonian city-states the local ruler required tavern keepers to inform him of rogues;[16] the matter features in the law codes of the epoch (Hammurabi, §109).

(c) Commissioning the Leader for War

Often in antiquity, war leaders sought, or were granted, an act of commission before going to war — and for other major actions such as building temples. Joshua had a visionary visitor (5:13-15); others had their experiences. In Egypt, Tuthmosis IV in circa 1392 prepared for his Nubian campaign by consulting the god Amun in Thebes, who gave him encouragement.[17] After almost half a century without major wars, Merenptah had to face a major threat to Egypt from the Libyans and Sea Peoples. On the eve of the conflict the god Ptah of Memphis appeared to him in a dream, offering him the sword of victory and saying in effect, "Fear not."[18] In turn, in the scenes of his Libyan wars in his memorial temple in Western Thebes, Ramesses III had himself depicted as commissioned by, and receiving the sword of victory from, Amun, to be ready for battle.[19] In the thirteenth century the Hittite king Hattusil III and his queen had a variety of dreams, with commands from deity; while in the seventh century we find Assurbanipal (and even his army) receiving encouragement from deities in dreams before battles.[20]

(d) Night Flights

War was not restricted to daylight hours, even in antiquity. We find nighttime maneuvers half a millennium before, in the Mari correspondence, wherein a foe breached the wall of the town of Talkhayum and invaded and seized it by night.[21] Then, in the later fourteenth century, both the Hittite king Mursil II and his opponents resorted to overnight marches and attacks.[22] To the thirteenth or fourteenth century belongs a letter found at Ugarit, whose author states: "My men were attacked [repeatedly] in the middle of the night, and a battle was fought."[23] For surprise attacks generally, compare such examples as the pharaoh Tuthmosis III outwitting his Canaanite foes by a surprise move through a narrow pass to outflank and defeat them at Megiddo, and conversely the Hittite surprise attack on Ramesses II at the Battle of Qadesh.[24] Military tactics were far from primitive by the thirteenth century.

(iv) Campaign Narratives and Incidents

In Josh. 10–11 we find what purport to be narratives of two lightning campaigns in south and north Canaan respectively. These texts show various features that cause no surprise to seasoned Orientalists familiar with analogous campaign accounts elsewhere in the records from the ancient Near East, even if Old Testament students sometimes have not grasped their full import.

Some fairly recent works, notably by Younger and Hess, have helped to clarify such understanding;[25] here we shall present the matter as concisely and simply as possible, and add a little thereto. The southern campaign narrative has three parts.

The first (10:1-14) gives the casus belli: the king of Jerusalem saw neighboring Gibeon's submission to Israel as a direct threat to his (and his allies') independence; hence he organized a preventive war, by first attacking Gibeon. Tied by treaty, Joshua and Israel then responded, defeating their foes and pursuing them, initially to Azekah and Makkedah (10:1-10), with remarkable phenomena credited to YHWH (10:11-14). At this point it is emphasized that Israel after victory returned to base at Gilgal (10:15).

The second part (10:16-28) concentrates on events around Makkedah. Following their defeat at Gibeon, the five leading Canaanite kings fled to Makkedah, hiding in a cave. To avoid losing momentum in the general pursuit of the foe (10:19), Joshua ordered that they be blocked in, to be dealt with later. Once the pursuit beyond Makkedah was over, the Hebrew forces could return to (temporary) camp at Makkedah (10:21), and also take that town (10:28). That day the kings were retrieved, made to submit to their victors' feet on their necks, slain and impaled until sunset, when they were buried in their cave of refuge (10:22-27). Clearly, that was the end of that day's work; an overnight stop at Makkedah is implied.

The third part (10:29-43) then followed. In summary form we are told that Joshua and his force successively vanquished five more towns, and a seventh king (of Gezer) who had come to help one (Lachish). Then they finally returned to Gilgal.

The northern campaign articulates similarly into three segments. The first includes, again, the casus belli. Alarmed by the Hebrew impact south of Jezreel and sensing a threat to his ascendancy, the king of Hazor gathered an alliance against them (11:1-5). Meantime, as on the eve of the southern campaign (10:8), so now Joshua was told by deity, "Fear not!" (11:6).

The second narrates the main battle and defeat of the Canaanite forces, Hebrew pursuit of these, and the fall and destruction of Hazor (11:7-11).

The third then concisely summarizes (11:12-15) the subsequent action, killing of kings and their subjects, destructions (but *not* burning!) and plundering. A Hebrew return to Gilgal *without* any immediate occupation of the northern terrain is implicit, as the Israelite base is still at Gilgal during the first act of allotment later on (14:6).

These two successive but parallel campaign reports merit concise background comment from several viewpoints.

(a) Annalistic Structures

We comment first on the *overall structures* of these two reports in their context. Earlier, for Israel's first armed coflict in Canaan, taking Jericho and Ai, we have the longest account of all (6–8), consisting of three chapters in modern biblical referencing. Thereafter, if at less length, it is the initial episodes in these two subsequent campaigns that get the fullest treatment. In the southern one, fuller account is given of the battle for Gibeon and acts at Makkedah (10:7-27), compared with the staccato, summary accounts of the attacks on the following six cities, from Makkedah itself to Debir (10:28-39). In the northern one, more concise overall, we have more on the major battle at Merom, consequent pursuit, and fall of Hazor (11:7-11), than on subsequent actions (11:12-14).

This kind of report profile is familiar to readers of ancient Near Eastern military reports, not least in the second millennium. Most striking is the example of the campaign annals of Tuthmosis III of Egypt in his Years 22-42 (ca. 1458-1438). As others have noted, the pharaoh there gives a very full account of his initial victory at Megiddo, by contrast with the far more summary and stylized reports of the ensuing sixteen subsequent campaigns. Just like Joshua against up to seven kings in south Canaan and four-plus up north (final total of thirty-one, Josh. 12:9-24), the pharaoh faced a hostile alliance: the rulers of Qadesh and Megiddo, plus 330 allied kinglets.[26] The Ten-Year Annals of the Hittite king Mursil II (later fourteenth century) are also instructive. Exactly like the "prefaces" in the two Joshua war reports (10:1-4; 11:1-5), detailing hostility by a number of foreign rulers against Joshua and Israel as reason for the wars, so in his annals Mursil II gives us a long "preface" on the hostility of neighboring rulers and people groups that led to his campaigns.[27]

In these various annals and allied records, the more staccato, summary reports are presented *in formulaic fashion — but often with variations* and *not* with blockheaded, total uniformity in using the formula. So, Josh. 10:27-39 in particular. We may schematize thus:

A1   Then Joshua and all Israel went from city A to city B
  A2   and they set up against it, and they attacked it.
B1   YHWH gave city B into the hand of Israel,
  B2   and he/they took it.
C1   City, people, king, he put to the SWORD,
  C2   and left no survivors.
    C3   Joshua did to (king of) city B, as he did to (king of) city X.

Not every element appears (or as precisely as given) in the six examples in Josh. 10:27-39. Some are omitted or abbreviated, and additional elements are included when required. We now tabulate.

Table 9. Formulae for Captured Towns in Joshua 10

	Makkedah	Libnah	Lachish	Eglon	Hebron	Debir
A1	[omitted]	OK	OK	OK	OK	OK
A2	[omitted]	OK	OK	OK	[set] + OK	[set] + OK
B1	[omitted]	OK	[omitted]	[omitted]	[omitted]	[omitted]
B2	That day . . .	OK	OK + 2 day	OK + 1 day	OK	OK + villages
C1	OK + destr.	OK	OK	OK + destr.	OK + villages	OK
C2	OK	OK	[omitted]	[omitted]	OK + destr.	OK
C3	OK	OK	[. . .] as Lb	[. . .] as Lc	[. . .] as Eg	OK
D1			help, Gzr			

The variations are of interest. For Makkedah the three initial elements, A1, A2, and B1, were not needed; Joshua and his forces were already at Makkedah, and YHWH's intervention that day was already clear for them. In B2, "That day" linked this entry to its context. Libnah shows the formulation in its full form. In the remaining four cases, it is piquant to note that *all four* omit completely any reference to deity — so much for the narrative being "theologically laden," to quote a worn-out cliché! Under B2, a time note is twice added, once to denote a longer time (Lachish, a "tough nut") and then to return to normal timing. C2, "no survivors," is omitted twice, but is compensated for by a destruction note under Eglon. Rural outliers are added in, under Hebron and Debir, evidently a feature of that area. In C3, three entries abbreviate the formula heavily, as being understood. At Lachish an untoward event occurred: another king from outside (Gezer) tried to help but was defeated, and so this fact was added to the Lachish dossier.

None of this should be misinterpreted as evidence of rival sources, different viewpoints, etc., etc. The near contemporary Near Eastern data forbid any such literary acrobatics. In his Ten-Year Annals Mursil II, for example, shows much consistency in the basic formulae of his annual reports, but he does not hesitate to add massively to the narrative, or change its mold, when the events being reported require this.[28] The same may be said for Tuthmosis III and others.

But another fourteenth-century pair of documents — hitherto unnoticed in this regard — give us a vivid and close literary parallel to Josh. 10 in particular. These are the twin Amarna letters EA 185 and 186, by one author, Mayarzana, local king of Khashi, a few miles southwest of the later Baalbec in the Biqa Valley of Lebanon. He complained to the pharaoh twice about the same incident, namely, an Apiru group ravaging a series of local towns and then having to be repulsed from his own town. The sequencing of their misdeeds in slightly variable formulaic fashion is very much like Josh. 10:28-39. Even more so, as he uses two similar but slightly different formulations in the two letters; and he cannot be split into an equivalent of J and E, or other such fictions! These missives are original documents. Let us now look at the formulae used in each letter, and their application in practice.

For EA 185, we have the following basic layout:

1. (And) the Apiru took (city) X,
2.   " — a city of the King, my lord — "
3. they looted it, & torched it with fire.
4.   The Apiru fled to Amenhotep.

We may now tabulate the entries as expressed in EA 185.

Table 10A. Formulae, Towns Captured in EA 185

	Makhzibtu	Gilunu	Magdalu	Ushtu
1.	OK	OK	OK	And Ushtu
2.	OK	OK	OK	OK
3.	and +	OK	OK	took +
	OK	+ barely escapes	+ barely escapes	OK
4.	OK	OK	OK	OK

Then, at Khashi, the Apiru raided and were repulsed by the writer.

For EA 186, we have the basic layout as follows:

1. Name of City,
2.   " — a loyal city of the King, my lord, god and Sun — "

3. the 'Apiru took it, looted it, and burned it with fire.
4.   they fled to Amenhotep ruler of Tushultu, who fed them.

We may now tabulate the entries as expressed in EA 186.

Table 10B. Formulae, Towns Captured in EA 186

	Makhzibtu	Gilunu	Magdalu	Ushtu
1.	When Apiru took + OK	OK	OK	[*lost*]
2.	OK	OK	OK	[*lost*]
3.	OK (*minus* "took")	OK	OK	[*lost*]
4.	OK	OK	OK	[*lost*]

Here the writer stuck to his formula much more rigidly, except for the first entry, precisely because (as with Makkedah under Joshua) it was the first one, and he was eager to heap blame on Amenhotep, so he changed the word order in part and introduced his traitor first. But it is the same writer — there is no J/E in 185 or P in 186![29]

Thus both the basic formulaic layout and its variations in Joshua reflect commonplace ancient Near Eastern usage as found in original and unitary works. This was how such military reports were *customarily* written, and these structures and others are the common coin of the second millennium already, long before Neo-Assyrian times.

(b) Stylistics

Second, we look more briefly at other features of such war reports.

(1) Rhetorical Style

So commonplace a phenomenon in the biblical world, it is this factor which has misled Old Testament scholars in particular in their evaluations of the book of Joshua. For example, 10:40-42 ends the account of the southern campaign in sweeping terms — Joshua had "subdued the whole region," he had "wholly destroyed all who breathed." And similarly in the summation that ends the northern campaign account (11:16-17, 23): "Joshua took the whole land and gave it as inheritance to Israel by their tribes" (11:23). And 21:43-45.

It is the careless reading of such verses as these, without a careful and close reading of the narratives proper, that has encouraged Old Testament scholars to read into the entire book *a whole myth of their own making,* to the effect that the book of Joshua presents a sweeping, total conquest *and occupation* of Canaan by Joshua, which can then be falsely pitted against the narratives in Judges.[30] But this modern myth is merely a careless falsehood, based on the failure to recognize and understand ancient use of rhetorical summations. The "alls" are qualified in the Hebrew narrative itself. In 10:20 we learn that Joshua and his forces massively slew their foes "until they were finished off" (*'ad-tummam*), but in the same breath the text states that "the remnant that survived got away into their defended towns." Thus the absolute wording is immediately qualified by exceptions — "the quick and the dead," as one might say of pedestrians trying to cross our busy highways! Nor is this an isolated datum. To begin with, the allotments of land to the tribes were decided *after* Joshua's campaigns, both those narrated and those merely mentioned (11:18; cf. 13:1). Then we have a series of notices which indicate that, already under Joshua, the tribesfolk could not easily take possession of the territories raided; cf. such as 15:63; 16:10; 17:12-13, 18; Joshua's still later critique, 18:3, before the second allotment; 19:47. And one should note 23:4-5, wherein Joshua speaks of *having made allotments,* in principle, which the tribes must *still* then take up — "YHWH your God . . . *WILL* drive them out." So there is *no* total occupation shown to be achieved under Joshua himself in this book about Israel's entry into, not occupancy of, Canaan. Once and for all.

The type of rhetoric in question was a regular feature of military reports in the second and first millennia, as others have made very clear. We can thus be brief here. In the later fifteenth century Tuthmosis III could boast "the numerous army of Mitanni was overthrown within the hour, annihilated totally, like those (now) non-existent" — whereas, in fact, the forces of Mitanni lived to fight many another day, in the fifteenth and fourteenth centuries. Some centuries later, about 840/830, Mesha king of Moab could boast that "Israel has utterly perished for always" — a rather premature judgment at that date, by over a century! And so on, ad libitum.[31] It is in this frame of reference that the Joshua rhetoric must also be understood.

(2) Divine Intervention in War

This element has been noted already (cf. above, in chap. 2), but may here be quickly reviewed in a second-millennium military context. Thus, in all three campaigns (Jericho, south Canaan, and north Canaan), Joshua is commissioned by YHWH not to fear (cf. 5:13-15; 10:8; 11:6). So also by Ptah and Amun were Merenptah in Egypt, and Tuthmosis IV long before him; and likewise

Mursil II of the Hittites by his gods (Ten-Year Annals, etc.), all in the second millennium, besides such kings as Assurbanipal of Assyria down to the seventh century. Cf. 2.B.iii.c, p. 115 above.

The sending of heavy hail on a foe by YHWH has been well compared to Hittite and Assyrian accounts of thunderbolts, etc.;[32] clearly such phenomena did occur sporadically at times of battles, and the ancients treated them — as do our insurance companies! — as "acts of God." The famous "long day" and appeal to sun and moon have been much discussed, and cannot be tackled anew in this work; hyperbole may be involved, and suffice it to remark otherwise that our long-standing friend Tuthmosis III witnessed some kind of shooting-star phenomenon that scattered an enemy.[33] The support of deity is repeatedly invoked in what are otherwise straightforward historical accounts, because that is simply how the ancients saw their world. Again, the Ten-Year Annals of Mursil II are a good example among very many. This feature does *not* imply nonhistoricity either outside the Hebrew Bible or inside it.

(3) Philological Details: Names of People and Groups

The war reports in Josh. 10–11 name people as well as places, mainly local rulers in Canaan.[34] Proper onomastic study demonstrates that these names were not "made up" freely by the biblical writers (as at least one unwise commentator has opined), but correspond almost entirely with actual names and name types current particularly in the second millennium. Thus the biblical Horites/Hivites have long been recognized as the Hurrians of Near Eastern sources. The Perizzites may find a reflex in the personal name "Perissi" or Perizzi (also Hurrian) of a Mitannian envoy in cuneiform and Egyptian (EA 27). The Girgashites are directly comparable with the personal name *G-r-g-sh* and Girgishu of the administrative texts from Ugarit, and just possibly with the Qarqisha among the Hittite allies fought by Ramesses II.

Coming to individuals, we may summarize succinctly. Rahab of Jericho bears a good West Semitic name (Taanach, fifteenth century); Japhia of Lachish is a Yapiaʿ, with common omission of a divine name as at Mari (eighteenth century), Ugarit, and Semites in Egypt (thirteenth century).[35] Jabin of Hazor has an ancient name, known at Mari (eighteenth century). There another king of Hazor, Yabni-Adad, is also mentioned, and at Hazor itself a tablet has the personal name Ibni-[...]; these are from a different root. Horam of Gezer has been considered as a form of West Semitic Haran. But it may be a Hurrian Hur(r)am, using the known elements *Hur(r)-* and *-(a)m*.[36] Adoni-sedeq of Jerusalem has a good second-millennium name form, and the name recurs at contemporary Ugarit.[37] Debir (of Eglon) bears a name probably attested in Egypt (as Semitic, thirteenth century) as well as in the form Dibri in Lev. 24:11 (a Danite). Jobab is Semitic, possibly with south Arabian links. Hoham (Hebron) is best considered as a Hurrian-based name, with the elements *Huhha-* plus *-(a)m*.[38] At Jarmuth, Piram is again likely to be Hurrian, *Pir-* plus *-(a)m*, on base Piri-/Biri-. Among the Anakim, Sheshai is Hurrian, attested in Nuzi (fifteenth century) and most likely on Hyksos scarabs in Egypt and Canaan (sixteenth century), while Talmai is typically Hurrian, with deity's name omitted, from eighteenth to thirteenth centuries, plus Talmai of Geshur of David's time (ca. 1000). But Ahiman is common West Semitic, with occurrences ranging from the eighteenth to the fifth centuries. The name Anak(im) goes back to the eighteenth century, being found (in the form Ya'anaq) in the Egyptian execration texts for Canaan. Hess points out that the mix of Semitic and Hurrian names in one kinship group is not unusual in the Late Bronze Age (late second millennium). This can be illustrated from such foreign families in Egypt at that time. Under Ramesses II, a general Urhiya bore a pure Hurrian name ("[Deity X] is true"), while his son Yupa' bore a purely West Semitic name.[39] Slightly earlier, a man Didia under Sethos I recorded his past family through seven generations.[40] His mother and mother-in-law both bore the Semitic name Tal, "Dewdrop." Among other names, his oldest male ancestor was a Padi-Baal (Semitic), married to a lady Ibri-kul (pure Hurrian); other Semitic and/or Hurrian etymologies apply to other intervening generations. Thus we are dealing with real names, not invented ones and (for Hurrian names) essentially of the second millennium.

(4) Achan, Names and Thefts

Finally here, the hapless Achan (Josh. 7). He and his family bear real, well-attested Semitic names, not fantasy ones. Much fuss has been made over the name Achan in the Hebrew text of Joshua and its relation to the variant Achar in 1 Chron. 2:7 and in the Septuagint version of Joshua. In fact, as Hess has pointed out, Achan (*'Akan*) is unique in the Hebrew Bible, but is sufficiently attested in other documents, ranging from Alalakh (eighteenth century) down to Punic. But the purely Hebrew term *Achar (*'Akar*)* is more an epithet or nickname applied to him later, in view of his bad end, as in Chronicles, and then retrospectively carried through Joshua by the Septuagint translators, and giving scope for a play on words that the name Achan did not.[41]

His fate for stealing plunder of Jericho put to the ban of destruction was to be slain and burned. Others too in antiquity were punished for such acts. At Mari (eighteenth century) various people were punished for *asakkam akalam,* "breaking the taboo," but were fined by payment in silver (once with gold); in one text, it as said of an offender, "that man doesn't deserve to live!"

but he was nevertheless simply fined. However, in a religious context, in an Old Babylonian liver-omens tablet of the same general epoch, it was laid down that a high priestess who repeatedly stole consecrated offerings should be seized and burned. A Berlin tablet also specifies that a high priestess, priest, or priest's wife should in such a case "be seized and put to death," but without specifying the nature of the execution.[42] So, for a severe case of breaking what had been decreed as taboo, Achan suffered a long-standingly drastic fate.

His loot is worth brief notice. This constituted 200 shekels of silver, a fine Babylonian robe, and a 50-shekel-weight ingot of gold (Josh. 7:21). As others have noted, the word used for "Babylonia" is the term known from cuneiform sources as Shankhar, and in Egyptian transcriptions as Sangar; its real pronunciation was nearer to "S(h)anghar," as the sound *ghain* in Semitic (and its Hurrian equivalent) is normally found as *kh* in the one script and *g* in the other. That term was used in the sixteenth to thirteenth centuries, not later, and is a mark of authenticity.[43] Babylonia exported garments north to Assyria and then to Anatolia and west to Aleppo in north Syria from at least the nineteenth/eighteenth centuries onward. Babylonian merchants regularly traveled to Egypt (and were even murdered en route, and robbed in Canaan) in the fourteenth century.[44] Thus, that country's products continued to be known in the Levant, even if by means both fair and foul.

The gold ingot is more literally a "tongue" or wedge. The same term for a gold ingot (Heb. *leshon;* Akkad. *lishanu*) is used in precisely this way both here in Joshua and in the fourteenth-century Amarna letters, in even the same word order. But the 50-shekel ingot stolen from Jericho was chicken feed compared with the massive 1,000-shekel gold ingot that Tushratta king of Mitanni once sent to Amenophis III of Egypt.[45] Thus we find the Achan narrative marked by features that fit very well with the Late Bronze Age world, but less so later.

(5) Iron Chariots and Other Oddities

From time to time biblical commentators who do not do their Near Eastern homework have dismissed various phenomena such as "iron chariots" (Josh. 17:16-18; cf. Judg. 1:19 and 4:3, 13) as allegedly too heavy to operate.[46] But the assumption that the vehicle was wholly of iron is, of course, false — just as "ivory beds" (Amos 6:4) and an "ivory house" (1 Kings 22:39; Amos 3:15) were not made of ivory but simply decorated with it. Such chariots were of wood, but probably with thin plates or fitments. Iron was in use as a valuable new metal, as a substance for jewelry use from the late third and early second millennia, and then as a rarer practical adjunct to bronze in the late second, as cuneiform documents amply attest, backed up by occasional finds, the most spectacular being the gold-mounted iron dagger of Tutankhamun in Egypt. And if "iron chariots" were too heavy to use, what should we say about the Syrian and Canaanite chariots of gold, and of gold and silver, used by such as the kings of Qadesh and Megiddo when resisting Tuthmosis III at the Battle of Megiddo (ca. 1458), as his firsthand annals tell us?[47] Gold is even heavier than iron! Clearly these "Cadillac" or "Rolls-Royce" models had some gold or gilded decoration; the pharaoh himself drove a chariot "of electrum" (gold/silver alloy). So the iron-fitted chariots of two centuries later are not to be dismissed in such cultural contexts.

The same is true of the continued ritual and practical use of flint implements at this epoch; in Egypt and elsewhere flint saw use for many centuries alongside copper and bronze. For long use of flints in Mesopotamia and the Levant, note continued usage all the way down to our own epoch, as seen by archaeologists among rural workers of the present day.[48]

(v) The Record of Triumph

In Josh. 12:7-24, after summarizing Moses' conquests north of Moab with a "preface," Joshua's conquests are summed up in a full list of those he had defeated, forming a topographical list, in several coherent groups of place-names. Such an arrangement is almost a verbal equivalent of the partly pictorial topographical lists of vanquished places and peoples that the pharaohs often set out on the great pylon towers and outside walls of their temples during mainly the New Kingdom, from Tuthmosis III (1479-1425) down to Ramesses III (ca. 1184-1153), with one major successor, Shishak or Shoshenq I (ca. 945-924). In the New Kingdom a line of triumphal rhetoric often runs along the top of such lists, and further rhetorical text accompanies the scene of deity rewarding the victorious king slaying the foe, when it is included. The format of the actual lists is invariably that of a series of vertical ovals (like fortified enclosures), each containing a place-name and surmounted by a man's head that is typical of the area concerned (e.g., of western Asia or Nubia). It is probable that such heads in effect personify the defeated chiefs or rulers of the entities named in each case. These presentations come very close to being semipictorial equivalents of what we have in Josh. 12:9-24.[49] Such ceremonial lists were the concomitant to scenes and narratives of wars by Egypt's kings. And Josh. 12:9-24 makes a similarly fitting pendant to the war narratives of 10–12 in particular. Like its Egyptian counterparts, the Hebrew list has sets of towns in geographical groupings, sometimes corresponding in part to routes used, but sometimes not. Nobody should imagine that the young Joshua in Egypt gazed up awed at such reliefs, and that old Joshua in Canaan therefore did a verbal list to parody Egyptian triumphs. But what we do have is the same broad concept of setting out the scale of the victory at the end of the record, in each culture, and within the same epoch.

(vi) Sharing out the Real Estate Area

(a) The Biblical Data

(1) Early Hopes, Not Late Topography

In Josh. 14–19 we find the arrangements for the Hebrews to occupy in orderly fashion the regions they had merely raided, but in two phases (14–17, then 18–19). This is explicitly cast as land grants *still to be taken up*. Thus it should not be arbitrarily misconstrued as simply an implicit statement of the geography of (e.g.) the united monarchy, or of the time of Josiah, or whatever. As can be noted, the text does not fit into such unsupported suppositions. Thus it envisions Dan as destined to settle west of the hill country of central Canaan (vale of Sorek area), and only adds parenthetically that their failure here impelled them (in whole or in part) to seek their fortune elsewhere, in this event far north, some ten miles north of Lake Huleh. The envisioned allotments were never wholly taken up, even under David and Solomon. Thus, although these kings cowed the Philistines (e.g., 2 Sam. 8:1; 1 Kings 4:21), Philistia never had a Hebrew population of settlers, as projected in Josh. 15:45-47 for Judah (proposed occupation of Ekron, Ashdod, and Gaza). Except as an early projection, this at no time fits the conditions of any later epoch. A possible early attempt to fulfill that projection (cf. Judg. 1:18) soon failed. And so on.

(2) The Format of the Land Grants

Dealing now primarily with the grants for western Palestine (Canaan), we can readily perceive that the records in Josh. 14–19 fall into very clearly defined types, with but few variations. Each tribal record tends to be framed with a heading or preface, then gives boundary sequences (I) and/or groups of towns (II), ending with a brief colophon and/or other remark when appropriate; variations occur.

The basic model is seen in the grant to Judah, in Josh. 15:1-12, for borders (I), and 15:20-63 for constituent towns (II); Caleb's affairs precede these (14:6-

15) and come between them (15:13-19), as a special adjunct to the main document. Likewise in the second allotment, for Benjamin: first heading (18:11), borders (I; 18:12-20a), and colophon (18:20b); then second heading, constituent towns (II), and second colophon (18:21a, 21b-28a, 28b, respectively). Also, Zebulon has a heading (19:10a) and the boundary sequence (I; 19:10b-15a), then a town list (II; 19:15a) before its colophon (19:15b-16). And so too, Naphtali: heading (19:32), boundaries (I; 19:33-34), constituent towns (II; 19:35-38), and colophon (19:39).

Then we have a simple variant: heading, towns (II) first, then borders (I), and final colophon. So with Issachar: heading (19:17-18a), towns (II; 19:18b-21), then borders (I; 19:22a), and colophon (19:22b-23). And with Asher: heading (19:24-25a), towns (II; 19:25b-26a), borders (I; 19:26b-30a), and colophon (19:30b-31). Others omit an element. Thus Simeon (being within Judah) has no border sequences (I) but simply a heading (19:1-2a), the town list (II; 19:2b-8a), and colophon with comments (19:8b-9). Likewise, because their north and south borders were in practice defined by Ephraim and Judah, and they largely moved out north, Dan has just the heading (19:40-41a) and town list (II; 19:41b-46), then explanation (gone north) and colophon (19:47-48). Conversely, Ephraim and the western half of Manasseh each have a heading (Ephraim: 16:5a; Manasseh: 17:1-2 with explanation), then boundary sequences (I), the south border of Ephraim (16:5b-8), and for Manasseh (I) a sweep north, down the east, and then east-west along a south border (that served also as the northern one for Ephraim), in 16:7-10. The respective colophons are: for Ephraim, 16:10; for Manasseh (with long comments), 16:12-16. A hint of towns (II) is in a general remark for Ephraim (16:9), with towns in Manassite terrain; and similarly for West Manasseh (17:11) with named towns (II) in territories of Asher and Issachar. In the case of Ephraim and Manasseh that together formed "Joseph," we additionally have an introduction to the pair, with a general south boundary (16:1-4), and likewise a closing command to them both (17:17-18). Finally, the heading for West Manasseh includes reference to their east-side relatives, and is accompanied by other notes (e.g., the case of the Zelophehad inheritance; 17:1-2, 3-6). Joshua himself has a modest grant (19:49-50), as did Caleb before him. Cities of refuge are placed north, centrally, and south, three each, west and east of the Jordan (chap. 20). Finally, for the maintenance of the Levites, a final distribution of towns with land grants was made within the tribal territories (chap. 21).

(b) The Near Eastern Background

(1) Boundary Sequences in Ancient Contexts

From Near Eastern sources, one can begin to write virtually a history of boundary descriptions and town lists; but we will be less ambitious here. The boundary descriptions in Joshua are neither unparalleled nor in any way an innovation in antiquity. As early as circa 2100 we find Ur-Nammu of the Third Dynasty of Ur confirming the boundaries of the provinces of the homeland of the Sumerian Empire that he then ruled.[50] Already boundaries ran from A to B (whether by towns, mountains, canals, etc.) on the south, east, north, or west of the territory concerned, a precursor of what we find in (e.g.) Josh. 15, almost a thousand years later at the end of the Late Bronze Age.

Coming down to the period circa 1400-1200, into the Late Bronze Age itself, the material multiplies, significantly in the context of treaties (political "covenants"). In his treaty with Sunashshura king of Kizzuwatna (later Cilicia, around Tarsus) in about 1400, the Hittite king Tudkhalia II lays down the boundaries between the two realms. From the Mediterranean Sea the line is demarcated via a series of towns, mountains, and a river, with careful note of which towns belong to Hatti or Kizzuwatna respectively. In four cases this sequence was subject to survey (compare the action in Josh. 18:4-9, when a survey preceded the second allotment of land). In the fourteenth century, Suppiluliuma I of Hatti recognized the loyalty of Niqmad II king of Ugarit when (in their treaty) he set an advantageous boundary for him versus defeated rebel kings around. Again, a sequence of locations (forty-two all told), be they towns, mountains, marshes, etc., marked the new boundary. Then in the thirteenth century two successive treaties of Hattusil III with Ulmi-Tesup and of Tudkhalia IV with Kurunta included boundaries between the Hittite realm and Tarkhuntassa respectively. Here, again, the line ran by various places and features (towns, mountains, sinkholes, etc.; sixty localities in the second treaty), with careful note of what belongs to whom (cf. Josh. 17:11).[51] In the case of Joshua also, the boundaries and land grants are set in the context of covenant, framed between the initial such ceremony at Mount Ebal with covenant renewal (8:30-35) and his closing renewal at Shechem later (24:1-27).

(2) Town Lists in Documents

Town lists are also attested in such contexts as treaty/covenant, and (again) as far back as the third millennium.[52] In a treaty between north Syrian Ebla circa 2300 and a neighbor (Abarsal?), the prologue begins with two lists of six plus fourteen towns "with their walled settlements," each declared to be "under the Ruler of Ebla," all with a final colophon (like Joshua) that, of all the settlements, those subordinate to Ebla are Ebla's, and likewise those (unnamed) subordinate to Abarsal(?) are under Abarsal(?).[53]

Otherwise the Near East has yielded all manner of town lists in administrative documents, with headings, subheadings, colophons, etc., often very reminiscent of what appears in the formats in Joshua. Examples come from such Syrian cities as Mari (traces, eighteenth century), and more extensively at Alalakh (eighteenth/fifteenth centuries) and Ugarit (fourteenth/thirteenth centuries). Of these there are good studies to which readers may be referred.

The role of Josh. 21, provision for the support staff (Levites) of the central cult, is comparable with such provision throughout the ancient Near East. All Egyptian temples, for example, had their endowed lands to support staff and cult. Settlements could yield revenues for that purpose, by the crops and cattle raised by their people, and other such sources. The temple of Amun, in Thebes under Ramesses III, owned fifty-six towns in Egypt and nine more in the Levant and Nubia as part of its estates with this in view.[54] This is not the same as staff living in towns and doing their own maintenance, but simply another, analogous way of achieving the same result.

On the significance of the format of the covenant as celebrated at Shechem, of a strictly fourteenth- and thirteenth-century type, see chapter 6 below, in the context of its forerunners in Exodus/Leviticus and Deuteronomy. It is one more indicator among several of the late second-millennium origins of much that is found in the book of Joshua.

3. SOME ARCHAEOLOGICAL BACKGROUND

We may now turn to the results of surveys and excavations actually on and in the ground of ancient Canaan, to see briefly what range of information emerges for comparison with the data of the texts, both of Joshua and of other ancient Near Eastern written records such as we have already drawn upon. Before actually reviewing the data, the state of play must be considered.

Archaeologically speaking, the appearance of Israel in Canaan prior to the reign of Merenptah and within that of Ramesses II — in the thirteenth century — is Late Bronze Age IIB in most treatments of that topic. If this were so, then people are tempted to ask whether the ruin mounds of Palestine preserve any traces of the campaigns of Joshua (e.g., traces of destruction in Late Bronze levels), or of the beginnings of Israelite settlement in the twelfth-eleventh centuries (cf. Judges). In any modern attempt to trace the effects of the campaigns, several points need to be made. First (as we have seen), the text of Joshua does *not* imply huge and massive fiery destructions of every site visited (only Jericho, Ai, and Hazor were burned). The Egyptians did not usually burn cities, preferring to make them into profitable tax-paying vassals; the Hebrews under Joshua sought basically to kill off the Canaanite leadership and manpower, to facilitate later occupation. These Egyptian and Hebrew policies are not readily detectable in the excavated ruins on sites. Second, even when a Late Bronze II settlement is found to have been damaged or destroyed, there is no absolute certainty as to who was responsible (Egyptians? local neighbors? Sea Peoples? the Israelites?).[55] Third, the identifications of some biblical place-names with mounds known today are not always certain — a wrong identification can bring a wrong result. Fourth, the erosion of an ancient settlement mound through the centuries by natural causes or human destruction can result in loss of the evidence for occupation and destruction of particular levels in a site. Fifth, with 95 percent of the site undug (as is common), the evidence may still be under the ground. So any survey of city mounds in Canaan is provisional at the best of times.

Keeping these limitations in mind, we may now look briefly at the places encountered by Joshua's expeditions. We are checking out occupation, *not* irrelevant destructions.

First, there is the long series of places named in his southern and northern raids, as follows:

1. **Azekah** (Josh. 10:10), significantly, played no active role in Joshua's campaign, as the Canaanites and Hebrews surged past it in their conflict. Today it is identified with Tell Zakariya, on a high hill; hence it is no surprise that pursued and pursuers passed it by while its ancient inhabitants viewed the conflict from above. It was dug almost a century ago, and no modern work has been done there; but modern reassessment of the early work suggests that Azekah was occupied right through the Early, Middle, and Late Bronze periods, as well as through the Iron Age to Hellenistic times. (No work has seemingly been done at either Beth-Horon, Upper or Lower.)[56]

2. **Makkedah** (10:16-21, 28) may be located at Khirbet el-Qom, very plausibly (but not with certainty). Only very limited survey and excavations could be done there, as the modern Arab village overlies much of the site.[57] Thus Late Bronze remains have not yet been found, a situation much like that at Dibon in Transjordan (see below), which thus remains indecisive at present.

3. **Libnah** (10:29-30) can be plausibly identified with Tell Bornat (Tel Burna), which was inhabited in the Late Bronze Age, in agreement with the probable date of Joshua's raids.[58]

4. **Lachish** (10:31-33) at Tell ed-Duweir was certainly a major local Canaanite center in Late Bronze Age IIB (level VII, thirteenth century) and into the early twelfth century (level VI, "Late Bronze III"/Early Iron I). Levels VII and VI both show traces of destruction involving fire. Some authorities would identify the destruction of level VI (ca. 1150) with the attack by the Israelites under Joshua. But such a date is far too late, and the destruction of level VII is far more appropriate, in that the Hebrews did not then hold the city but merely raided it and passed on. Thus the local Canaanites were free to reestablish themselves and rebuild (= level VI). The later destruction cannot be assigned to a particular cause at present; the local Philistines may well have been responsible (see above, p. 143).[59]

5. **Gezer** (10:33) was not touched by Joshua's campaign, but its king led forces to help Lachish. Gezer is firmly located at Tell Jazari by inscriptions, and it certainly existed in Late Bronze Age IIB, when Merneptah of Egypt captured it in circa 1209/1208 ("Israel Stela"). Stratum XV of excavations in the mound would likely represent the Gezer of this period (cf. p. 149 above).[60]

6. **Eglon** (10:34-35) is in all likelihood to be sited at present-day Tell 'Aitun (Tell 'Eton), occupied in the Late Bronze II period, and is not to be confused with Adullam or other places.[61]

7. **Hebron** (10:36-37) is in the general area of modern Hebron; the oldest site is that on Jebel Rumeida. Work has (so far) not yielded habitation of the Late Bronze Age, but one burial cave nearby was used more or less continuously from the Middle through the Late Bronze Age into (seemingly) Iron I. As the excavator observes, this may indicate a small Late Bronze occupation not yet detected by site excavation.[62]

8. **Debir** (10:38-39). After formerly being located at Tell Beit Mirsim, biblical Debir is more securely located at Khirbet Rabud nearby; this site was inhabited in the fourteenth/thirteenth centuries, in the Late Bronze II period, and was reoccupied directly in Early Iron I (twelfth century).[63]

9. **Jarmuth** (cf. 10:3, 23) as a city is not mentioned, but its king was slain. The site (Khirbet el-Yarmuk) saw its heyday in the Early Bronze Age (fourth-third millennia), and was then abandoned until the thirteenth century. In Late Bronze II the upper citadel was resettled.[64]

10. **Hazor** (11:1, 10-13). Location is certain, at Tell el-Qedah.[65] In 11:10 Hazor is described as having been "head of all these [local Canaanite] kingdoms." Its ruler, Jabin I, bore the same name as his eventual successor (Jabin II) in Judg. 4, a name very closely related to that (Ibni-Adad) of his distant predecessor named in the archives of Mari in the eighteenth century (cf. p. 175 above). The appearance in Joshua-Judges of two kings with the name Jabin is no more a "doublet" than two Niqmads (II and III) and two Ammishtamrus (I

and II) in Ugarit, or two Suppiluliumas (I and II), two Mursils (II and III), and two Tudkhalias (III and IV) of the Hittites, or two pharaohs Amenophis (III and IV), Sethos (I and II), and Ramesses (I and II) in Egypt — all these in the fourteenth and thirteenth centuries.

In the second millennium Hazor consisted of an upper citadel (on a high mound) which dominated a large "lower city" on its north side — a vast site, certainly then "head of all [Canaan's] kingdoms." Both areas were destroyed along with a massive conflagration in the thirteenth century, probably toward its end (citadel, stratum XIII; lower city, stratum Ia). Insofar as the results of Yadin's work are confirmed by the new excavations under Ben-Tor, then it will seem very probable (as it did to Yadin, long ago) that the massive destruction of greater Hazor was that wrought by Joshua.[66] For later Hazor, see under Judges below. But other places occur in the Josh. 12 king list.

11. **Megiddo** (cf. 12:21), Tell el-Mutesillim. Megiddo was an important place through the sixteenth to early twelfth centuries (strata X to VIIA, series of palaces, etc.), and it prospered also into the eleventh century (VI), after and before destructions.[67]

12. **Taanach** (12:21), Tell Taʿannek. Occupied from the seventeenth to mid–fifteenth century, then not visibly until the late thirteenth into the twelfth century. The former date suits Joshua, and the latter Deborah in Judges.[68]

13. **Joqneam** (12:22), Tell Qemun. With a very long history, its stratum XIX in the thirteenth century ended in destruction (one meter deep in debris), and a gap in occupation into the early twelfth century, when life resumed (strata XVIII-XVII).[69]

14. **Dor** (12:23), still Dor. Traces of Late Bronze Age I-II materials have turned up, but systematic excavation has not yet reached beyond circa 1100 levels.[70]

15. **Tirzah** (12:24), *if* at Tell el-Far'ah North (as often accepted). Here the Late Bronze Age remains (period VI) are scrappy and unsatisfactory, and are stated to cover "about three centuries into the sixteenth century BCE." As the Middle Bronze Age only ends in the sixteenth century, the Late Bronze's three centuries would have to extend down in time *from* it, into the thirteenth century, not "into" the sixteenth. In that case a local ruler in Tirzah (if at Tell el-Far'ah North) would be possible then. The first Iron Age remains (period VIIa) were built upon a Late Bronze wall.[71]

16. **Aphek**, in Sharon (12:18). From the thirteenth century, a central fortified residence has been dug, with very international connections, probably of an Egyptian governor; other traces exist as well, such as tombs. (The local ruler presumably lived less palatially.)[72]

17. **Jerusalem** (10:1, 5; 12:10). Jerusalem played a more important role in

the fourteenth century than the physical remains retrieved to date would suggest; the thirteenth-century remains (City of David level 16) are likewise limited, but do exist; there was certainly a city then.[73]

18. **Achshaph** (12:20). This place, near Accho, is known to have existed in the thirteenth century under Ramesses II, from its mention in the route lists in Papyrus Anastasi I (21:4). Rival sites for its location include Tell el-Harbaj (Tel Regev) and Tell Keisan, each of which show Late Bronze remains.[74]

19. **Qedesh** (12:22; and perhaps Judg. 4–5). Possibly the present-day Tell Abu Qudeis in Jezreel; its stratum VIII goes back to the thirteenth century at least; more is not known. Another Qedesh, at Tell Qudeish, is reported northwest of Lake Huleh, also of this period.[75]

20. **Bethel** (12:16). On the balance of evidence (as long recognized), to be located at Beitin; there Late Bronze remains were found of the Canaanite-culture town of the fourteenth and thirteenth centuries, succeeded in the twelfth by very different, poorer remains, that developed into probably the early Israelite settlement.[76]

Looking back over these twenty entries, omitting places whose identification on the ground is doubtful or which have not yet been explored archaeologically, we find that eighteen or nineteen of them were in being in Late Bronze (II) and one (Hebron) had tombs used then (of people who lived there?), leaving only Makkedah without direct evidence — and most of that site is not accessible, hence is not decisive. This is a very good score by any standard.

21. **Shechem** (Tell Balatah). We now turn briefly to a specimen of a different kind: the curious silence about Shechem, and the nonactivity by its people at the time of the Israelite entry into Canaan, for which scholars have offered various explanations in the past (cf. briefly already, p. 162 above). Here archaeological work offers a straightforward solution, without the need for any elaborate theory. During most of the fourteenth century Shechem (like Jerusalem) was center for a very active local ruler, Labayu, and his sons, as is clear from the Amarna letters; his was the relatively prosperous settlement attested in stratum XIII of the excavations, which came to an end between 1350 and 1300, in the generation or so that followed him. The settlement of stratum XII (thirteenth century) was more modest, and no longer a center of power; nor was XI in the twelfth. These facts suggest that in fact Shechem rapidly lost its local power after Labayu, and became a mere satellite, politically, of neighboring Tirzah — hence, in Josh. 12 we have a king of Tirzah but no longer one of Shechem. The villagers could hardly oppose the ceremonials of the Israelite host at Mount Ebal (Josh. 8:30-35) or the later renewal nearby them (Josh. 24). So there was, in effect, no power base at Shechem to conquer in the late thirteenth century. Problem solved.[77]

But before all this, we have the conquests of Jericho and Ai and the submission of Gibeon, whose archaeological status has in each case been more controversial. In Jericho's case we have an instance of the fourth limiting factor (p. 167 above), that of *erosion*. For Ai we have more of an enigma: perhaps the wrong site (third limiting factor), or else our understanding or expectations of Ai's state and status may be at fault. In Gibeon's case it may be a fifth factor: with 95 percent of the site undug (as is common), the evidence may still be under the ground, on the basis of such traces as have turned up.

22. **Jericho.** Of its location, at Tell es-Sultan, near the modern village (Er-Riha) that still bears its name, there is no doubt.[78] And the town, though not at all large (about one acre), had a very long history, from before Neolithic times down to the late second millennium. It was obviously very prosperous in the Middle Bronze Age (early second millennium), as the spectacular finds from that period's tombs bear witness. But only traces of this survive on the town mound itself — part of the city wall and its defensive basal slope ("glacis"), and some of its small, close-set houses fronting on narrow, cobbled lanes. But this all perished violently, including by fire, at roughly 1550 or soon after. And for about 200 years the ruins lay barren, before resettlement began in the fourteenth century. During that interval a great deal of the former Middle Bronze township was entirely removed by erosion (our fourth limiting factor); but for the tombs, its former substance would hardly have been suspected. But of the Late Bronze settlement from the mid–fourteenth century onward, almost nothing survives at all. Kenyon found the odd hearth or so (later fourteenth century), and the so-called middle building may have been built and used (as also tombs 5, 4, 13) in the Late Bronze IB/IIA periods, at about 1425/1400 to 1275, in the light of Bienkowski's careful analyses. Very little else of the fourteenth and thirteenth centuries has been recovered — and probably never can be.[79] If 200 years of erosion sufficed to remove most of later Middle Bronze Jericho, it is almost a miracle that anything on the mound has survived at all from the 400 years of erosion between 1275 and the time of Ahab (875-853), when we hear report of Jericho's rebuilding (1 Kings 16:34) in Iron II — double the length of time that largely cleared away the Middle Bronze town. It is for this reason, and *not* mere harmonization, that this factor must be given its due weight. The slope of Jericho is such that most erosion would be eastward, and under the modern road, toward where now are found the spring, pools, and long-standing more modern occupation. There may well have been a Jericho during 1275-1220, but above the tiny remains of that of 1400-1275, so to speak, and *all* of this has long, long since gone. We will never find "Joshua's Jericho" for that very simple reason. The "walls of Jericho" would certainly have been like those of most other LB II towns of that period: the edge-to-edge circuit of the outer

walls of the houses, etc., that ringed the little settlement. Rahab's house on the wall (Josh. 2:15) suggests as much. This ring would have butted onto the old Middle Bronze walling, but its upper portions (and most of it anyway) were eroded along with the Late Bronze abutments. The dramatic collapse of the walls in view of the Israelites may well have been a (for them) precise seismic movement, as with the blocking of the Jordan so soon before. A belt of jointed structures would fall in segments, not as a whole; and so Rahab's small segment may have survived. There has always been too much imagination about Jericho by moderns (never mind previous generations), and the basic factors have ironically been largely neglected. The town was always small, an appendage to its spring and oasis, and its value (for eastern newcomers) largely symbolic as an eastern gateway into Canaan.

23. **Ai.** Ai is enigmatic, even simply in the biblical text, before going anywhere else.[80] It alone is given a locating phrase in the list of Josh. 12, there described as "near Bethel" (12:9). And also, when the men of Ai turned to pursue an apparently retreating Israel, we suddenly read: "not a man remained in Ai *or Bethel* who did not pursue Israel" (8:17). Why? Could not the Ai warriors manage on their own? Or were they (and their chief) in truth only a dependency of Bethel? The men of Ai are described as "few" in 7:3. The archaeology has merely underlined the enigma. *Ha-ʿai* (Ai) is commonly taken to mean "the ruin," being compared with the noun *ʿiy*, plural *ʿiyyim*, "ruin(s)." And then this is compared with the modern name of a ruin mound a few miles from Bethel, Et-Tell in Arabic, meaning "ruin mound." However, Kaufmann objected that Ai meant "(stone)heap," not "ruin."[81] This Et-Tell has long been identified with ancient Ai. Excavation (so far) has failed to find any occupation there after the destruction of the strong, walled, Early Bronze Age town at about 2400, until a renewed settlement appears at about 1220/1200 or soon after. It is hard to believe that anybody founded a township and named it "Ruin," so the original third-millennium settlement may have borne a different, proper name that was forgotten. Hence, later occupants called it "the Ruin" or (better?) "(Stone)heap." Maybe!

It is easy (for some) to dismiss the whole narrative as a later story told to explain the noble ruin with its still visible (Early Bronze) walls. *But why bother?* There would be more famous or important places to romanticize, if the need were felt. People did *not* write "historical" novels with authentic research and background (e.g., the meticulous battle topography of Josh. 8) in Near Eastern antiquity, as we do today, and only since the last two hundred years or so. And this site is not the only "Et-Tell" in Canaan; there is (e.g.) another up by the north side of Lake Galilee, thought to be ancient Beth-Saida. So the modern name is not unique. It is possible that in the vicinity Ai is to be located elsewhere than at the Et-Tell by Bethel. Attempts along this line have so far been fruitless; thus neighboring Khirbet Khaiyan and Khirbet Khudriya are both of Byzantine date, after A.D. 300. The recently investigated Khirbet el-Maqatir does not (yet?) have the requisite archaeological profile to fit the other total data. There might well be another site of a similar kind that does, yet to be found. Whatever the truth of the matter, Ai was simply a dependency of Bethel, but someone in that community could lay claim to be Ai's chief ("king"). It is possible that Ai was at Et-Tell, and that — slightly refurbished — it served as a summer base for those who cultivated and harvested its lands (cf. Josh. 8:1 for land), and to whom Ai belonged, making therein shelters (readily burned!) rather than brick houses. And as a strong point for those whose lands adjoined it. It still needs to be remembered, also, that the entire area of Et-Tell has not been dug; fully eroded parts, of course, can never tell us anything now. The Hebrews may well have taken Bethel after Ai, but in the narrative it is Ai that mattered because it had been the scene of an embarrassing reverse. So, for some time yet Ai may keep its secrets, and with that situation (as often in ancient Near Eastern studies) serious students must for the present be wise enough to be content, while open to whatever new data or factors that may come our way.

24. **Gibeon.** The identification of El-Jib as the site of Gibeon seems assured, in terms of geography and general remains so far found. The limited excavations at the site have yielded first visitors in Middle Bronze I, a proper settlement for Middle Bronze II, eight Late Bronze Age tombs, then a walled township in Iron I-II. Given that 95 percent of the site remains undug, the possibility of a Late Bronze Age occupation (in the light of the tombs) remains open for future work to clarify.[82]

Of these twenty-four entries, only four can be regarded as deficient in background finds for LB II, and in those cases there are factors that account for the deficiency. The rest show very clearly that Joshua and his raiders moved among (and against) towns that existed and which in several cases exhibit destructions at this period, even though there is no absolute proof of Israelite involvement — short of a victory inscription, there could hardly be any! This review shows up the far greater deficiencies in some critiques of the Joshua narratives and list that are now already out-of-date and distinctly misleading.[83] On top of all this, the following should be noted: (1) Usually less than about 5 or 10 percent of any given mound is ever dug down to Late Bronze (or any other) levels; hence between 85 and 95 percent of our potential source of evidence is never seen. (2) The principal Hebrew policy under Joshua was to kill leaders and inhabitants, *not* to destroy the cities, but eventually to occupy them (cf. Deut. 6:10-11), destroying only the alien cult places (Deut. 12:2-3). (3) Conquests, even historically well-known examples, often do *not* leave behind the sort of traces that modern scholars overconfidently expect, as Isserlin has cogently pointed out.[84] And, at the end of the day, we should speak of an Israelite *entry* into Canaan, and settlement: *neither* only a conquest (although raids and attacks were made), *nor* simply an infiltration (although some tribes moved in alongside Canaanites), *nor* just re-formation of local Canaanites into a new society "Israel" (although others, as at Shechem, may have joined the Hebrew nucleus; cf. Gibeon). But elements of *several* processes can be seen in the biblical narratives.[85] For more sites of the period in the far south and east of Jordan, see just below; unplaced and uncertain sites have, of course, to be disregarded.

4. BACK EAST ACROSS THE JORDAN

Before we move on from Joshua and his "elders" through the period of Judges and 1 Sam. 1–7, to link up with the monarchy of chapter 4 (see sec. 5), we must first tidy up the story of the Israelites' transit north from Qadesh-Barnea at the northeast corner of Sinai adjoining Moab to the banks of the Jordan, and their partial settlement in Gilead and environs. Then, once Judges to 1 Sam. 1–7 have been reviewed, the way is open to go back still further in time, to consider in chapter 6 the questions and data concerning the exodus and events in Sinai itself.

A. THE BIBLICAL SOURCES

These are to be found mainly in Num. 10–34, with summary in Deut. 1–3 and recalls of the Gilead settlement in Josh. 12:2-6 and 13:8-33. The traditional history falls into three phases. First, from Sinai, the Hebrews reputedly traveled to Qadesh-Barnea. There, second, when they rebelled over a spy report or "feasibility study" on invading Canaan (and failed against the Negevites around Hormah), they were banished to wander for years in the wilderness until a new generation might take over the enterprise. The idea that the Hebrews spent forty years entirely at Qadesh is a modern error. Then, third, from Qadesh-Barnea once more, whither they had returned after thirty-eight years' absence (Deut. 2:14), they went out to go past Edom and Moab proper to the tableland (the "Mishor") between the Arnon and just north of the Heshbon district. Then to Abel-Shittim and the so-called plains of Moab, overlooking the south end of the Jordan from east to west opposite Jericho. We are here concerned briefly with the second and third phases, in terms of background data.

B. BACKGROUND DATA TO THE WANDERINGS PERIOD

Exactly as with much of the united monarchy and of the Israelite entry into Canaan, we do not have explicit narrative accounts from any external source such as those available in the twin monarchy period and for the Babylonian exile and return (chaps. 2–3 above). And for much the same simple reasons. Until well into the first millennium b.c., the great Mesopotamian powers had no known links or contacts with early Transjordanian communities, and no reason for them in the late second millennium. Egypt's contacts with the region are mentioned in only fleeting references, and almost never in terms of population groups. And local written sources during, say, 1500-1000 simply do not exist at present.

But this fact does not exhaust or remove the possibilities for correlating features of these accounts with external background, so as to distinguish between reality on the ground and fantasy in ancient minds (and some modern ones). We now turn to such possibilities.

(i) Qadesh-Barnea and Back

This place was, we are told (in Deut. 1:2), eleven days' journey from Horeb by way of Mount Seir. From Qadesh, by Mount Hor (where Aaron died, Num. 20:22-29), Israel were near Edom, and within reach of the king of Arad in the Negev (Num. 21:1). It has latterly been located at Ain el-Qudeirat, close to Ain Qudeis, which preserves the name.[86] This is roughly 170/180 miles from Horeb (if at or near Gebel Musa), which would be about sixteen miles a day at eleven days, which is close to a well-known ancient average of fifteen miles per day.[87] Qadesh-Barnea (if it is Ain el-Qudeirat) has yielded a fortress of the time of the Hebrew monarchies, but no earlier remains after the Neolithic period. This is probably not so surprising; tented wanderers like the Hebrews (and others) have commonly left no surviving traces.

While away from Qadesh on their enforced wanderings, Moses was faced with more rebellion, from Korah, Dathan, and Abiram (Num. 16), as Israel traversed the Arabah rift valley between the Dead Sea and the Gulf of Aqaba. The rebels came to a sticky end when suddenly the earth, as at Moses' word, swallowed them up, and "fire . . . from YHWH" smote the allied group. At first blush, these are the kinds of reports that attract modern skepticism; but a closer look by Hort has suggested that this narrative reflects a phenomenon that could only have been known to someone who knew the local conditions in parts of the Arabah. There exist there *kewirs,* or mudflats.[88] Over a deep mass of liquid mud and ooze is formed a hard crust of clayey mud overlying layers of hard salt and half-dry mud, about thirty centimeters thick. Under normal conditions one may readily walk over or stay upon the crust without any problem, as if on firm ground; but increased humidity (especially with rainstorms) causes the crust to soften and break up, turning everything into gluey mud. Knowing his Sinai and Midian, as a storm came, Moses called other Israelites away from Korah's clan (cf. Num. 16:26), and issued his challenge. The storm came, the crust went, and so did the miscreants, and lightning ("fire of YHWH") dealt with the rebel incense offerers.

(ii) Zones and Towns: Arad and Hormah

These names flit twice through the wilderness narratives: in Num. 14:44-45; 21:1-3, cf. 33:40, and then briefly later (Joshua's list, 12:14, their two "kings") in a totaling from Num. 21:1-3; and in Judg. 1:16-17, Arad near the Negev; men of Judah attack Zephath-Hormah. The picture is one of brief conflicts with a local power on the southern edge of Canaan, in the Negev region, across its base. That area has been investigated by survey and through several excavations, ranging from Beersheba in the west up to Arad in the northeast, centered on the Wadi es-Seba basin.

The results have thrown up a remarkable profile, in terms of the history of human settlement there. The oldest major period — the Chalcolithic (fifth and fourth millennia) — was the greatest, in terms of number of settlements and their importance, closely followed by the Early Bronze Age in the third millennium. This appears from such sites as "Tel Beersheba," Tel Halif (Khuweilfeh), Tel Masos (Khirbet Meshash), Tel 'Ira (Khirbet Gharra), Tel Esdar, Tel Malhata (T. Milh), and Arad, going from west to east in an arc. But after 2200 there is (on present knowledge) a remarkable shrinkage in human activity here. For the early second millennium (Middle Bronze Age), only Tel Masos in the west-center and Tel Malhata in the east-center show an active life. Then, in the later second millennium, in the Late Bronze Age, the focus of human occupation is in Tel Halif in the northwest of the arc, and (late thirteenth century) at Tel Masos in the central zone. For both periods more sites may someday appear; but not up to the present moment. Then came revival in the Iron Age. During both Iron I and II (judges and monarchy periods), we find active "Beersheba," Tel Halif, Tel Masos, Tel Esdar, and Arad; then, during Iron II (monarchy), Tel 'Ira and Tel Malhata reappear.[89] Cf. fig. 26.

Thus, in such a context, we may straightforwardly understand the title "king of Arad" (Num. 21:1; 33:40) as belonging to whoever ruled over this Negev basin, from Beersheba to Arad. In the third millennium (by which time people in Canaan spoke Semitic), Arad was probably the main capital of the area, ruling over the central towns and Tel Halif ("Beersheba" not then being inhabited). In the Middle Bronze Age (early second millennium), in the central zone, Tel Halif on the west and Tel Malhata on the east were the centers of the "Kingdom of Arad." Then, in the Late Bronze Age, in the northwest, Tel Halif was main center, plus Tel Masos before 1200.

Either of these sites may have been the town Zephath successively raided and wrecked by the Hebrews from Qadesh-Barnea (Num. 21:1-3) and the Judeans from south Canaan (Judg. 1:17), gleefully renaming it Hormah, "Destruction," and then renewing the insult.[90] Kingdoms can be named from a city and keep the name long after that town has lost its preeminence. Most famous is Assyria, strictly Ashur, named from its founding capital Ashur (from city-state beginnings); but in subsequent centuries Assyria knew a series of other capitals: Nineveh, Calah, Sargonburg (Khorsabad), and briefly Harran (outside the country proper) on the eve of its fall. Arad shows the same phenomenon on a much humbler scale, likewise Hazor (cf. sec. 5 below). Even when dead, Arad's mound kept its identity among the locals as a topographical point (cf. Judg. 1:16), and was to rise again during the period of the Hebrew judges and monarchy (in our Iron I-II), concluding with a mention in 925 in the great list of the pharaoh Shoshenq I.[91]

(iii) Getting Round Edom, Moab, and Strange Places (Cf. Fig. 31)

From Qadesh-Barnea the Hebrews finally moved off, to reach Canaan, not directly via the Negev (after the conflicts just mentioned), but by skirting round the regions east of the Dead Sea so as to cross into Canaan over the Jordan. Their first duty was to bury Aaron, on Mount Hor (Num. 20:22-29), perhaps at Jebel Madeira or Mad(a)ra some way northeast and east of Qadesh, and then move on east.[92] This direction, strictly northeast (21:1), on the "Way of Atharim" toward the Negev, alerted the king of Arad to act against the Israelites (21:1-3) — clearly, he anticipated a possible Hebrew invasion such as his predecessors had repulsed many years before (14:41-45). These moves also alerted the king of Edom (on his status, see section iv just below), especially as he had been asked for passage through his territory (20:14-21). So, when Israel descended (via Wadi Murra/the Darb es-Sultan) into the Arabah rift valley, he mustered arms against them.

So Israel "turned away from them" (20:21), first southward, then east, to go round, or pass by, Edom. In the Numbers narrative, we find only mention of

Oboth and Iye-Abarim to bring Israel to the brink of Moab, without details about passing by Edom. However, the retrospective aside in Deut. 10:8 adds two watering places, Gudgodah and Jotbatah,[93] for the travelers' refreshment, and the informative itinerary in Numbers (33:41-44) intercalates Zalmonah and Punon before reaching Oboth and Iye-Abarim.[94] Here it is generally conceded that Punon[95] may be identified with Feinan and the Wadis Feinan/Fidan, famed at various periods as a major copper-mining district. About here, coincidentally or not, is placed the incident of the bronze snake (Num. 21:4-9).

It is at this point that geographers recognize a major west-east break across the highlands of Edom, breaking the land into two parts. Its north (up to the Wadi Hasa, ancient Zered), heartland Edom, is the Jebel or "Mountain" par excellence, an Arabic term that is the ultimate descendant of "Mount Seir" of the Egyptian and biblical texts. Its south is the even more remote wilderness held by Edom in later times, spanning to the broad Wadi Hisma (northern edge of Midian proper), with a route running off south into Arabia.[96] The break inward and eastward at Feinan, the Punon embayment, goes on via the broad Wadi Ghuweir, and afforded a pass route over the ridges onto the east flank of Edom. Going this way, and turning north (via Oboth here?), the Hebrews could then skirt northward along the eastern desert edges of Edom proper without interference from the main Edomite centers in their northwest zone, south from the west part of the Zered (west Hasa). Reaching the upper/eastern reaches of the Zered, they came within reach of the desert border of Moab at Iye-Abarim on that border of Moab, eastward toward the sunrise (Num. 21:12). By this means they got round Edom, and had truck only with local fellow pastoralists (cf. Deut. 2:29).

From here the Hebrews skirted along the eastern desert fringes of Moab proper, from the upper Zered to the upper Arnon (Wadi Mujib, and possibly confluents), to Dibon-Gad (Num. 33:45-46) north of it. Here, in the wilderness of Kedemoth (Deut. 2:26),[97] the migrants were close to the junction of three local kingdoms: Moab just behind and southwest of them, the south edge of Ammon extending northward, and before them the realm of Sihon, the Amorite king of (south) Gilead. Moab and Ammon left the travelers alone, nor did Israel molest them. But Sihon opposed them. With no alternative route to the Jordan, and having no ancient kinship with Sihon, war led to Israel's elimination of Sihon, and of his northern neighbor Og king of Bashan (Num. 21:21-35). Then they could take over the Mishor plain between the Arnon and Gilead, and after several stops arrive by the Jordan, in the area of Abel-Shittim and the "Plains of Moab" opposite Jericho (Num. 22:1; 33:46-48).[98]

The foregoing account provides a clear, simple, and sensible outline version of the route the Hebrews most likely took from Qadesh-Barnea, round Edom proper, and past Moab via the Mishor plains to the brink of the Jordan.

This also indicates the more limited size of early Edom (the northern mountain block) from the Zered to the Wadi Feinan (Punon), before it had control of the southern mountain block from there to Wadi Hisma and the borders of Midian. However, in the northwest, Edom may already have laid claim to part of the Desert of Zin, just southwest of the Dead Sea, which explains why the Edomite ruler was unhappy (Num. 20:19-21) about Israel coming from Qadesh close by there into the Arabah. In Num. 34:3 Moses tells his people that they will have (part) "of" the Desert of Zin, by Edom's border. Thus Edom then had territory west of the Arabah in Zin.

(iv) Edom and Moab — Places and Political Formats

(a) Places

Most of the places in the Hebrew trip round Edom and Moab cannot be readily located on the ground, simply because — unlike in western Palestine — there are few or no external sources to help with such a task. Some, however, can be located but present other problems for the student. Dibon, a capital of Moab under Mesha king of Moab circa 840/830, is readily admitted to be located at modern Dhiban, just north of the Arnon (Wadi Mujib). The archaeology of the site is very fragmentary and incomplete, with (so far) no recovery of Late Bronze/Iron I-IIA remains. But by contrast, Ramesses II in the thirteenth century not only mentions Moab in a topographical list but also depicts himself warring *in Moab,* and capturing five named forts. In the original texts (later written over in palimpsest), the first was named as Butartu "in the land of Moab"; the second, "Yan(?)d[. . .] in the mountain of Mararuna"; the third as Dibon; while the fourth and fifth are lost (although there are traces for the fifth). The reading of Dibon is beyond doubt, and is clinched by the immediate context of Moab with Butartu, for which Moabite locales seem clear. In each case the Egyptian text calls each place a *dmi,* or settlement, a term with which the "foreign fort" representation agrees in each case. In other words, our explicit, *firsthand* inscriptional evidence shows, bluntly, that there *was* a place Dibon in Moab in about 1270. The archaeology is badly incomplete (as it currently stands), and stands supplemented and corrected by the texts, as in other clear cases (e.g., Jerusalem). So, Dibon in Numbers (21:30; 32:2-3, 34; 33:45-46) is correct for the thirteenth century.[99] Cf. fig. 35.

Heshbon, seat of King Sihon, has also been queried, because Tell Hesban shows (at present) clear urban occupation from the twelfth century onward (Iron I, stratum 19), but not Late Bronze II before it. Some Late Bronze sherds have been reported, so there may have been something thereabouts. However, if Tell Hesban was Heshbon during the Iron Age, that is no guarantee that it had been so in the Bronze Age. The Bronze Age Heshbon may in fact have been one of the nearby sites such as Tell el-Jalul or Tell el-Umeiri. Time will tell.[100] By contrast, at Medeba the ancient remains are not yet fully explored; but two tombs of the Late Bronze II period are known, so indicating some kind of human presence then.[101]

(b) Political Formats

Without the slightest hesitation, the biblical texts identify Edom, Moab, south Gilead, and Bashan as local monarchies, and name the kings of the last two (Sihon, Og), as the Hebrews did battle with these. For Edom and Moab in particular, skeptical voices have been raised, and likewise against all other kings of Moab prior to Mesha and his father (840 B.C.) on Mesha's own monument, and against all kings of Edom until the eighth century (mentions in Assyrian texts, then local seals). But the objections are based on modern sociological/anthropological fallacies and theories of ancient statehood that are irrelevant to the ancient Near East, besides the old nineteenth-century antibiblical mind-set. The idea is promoted that a monarchy cannot exist in a land prior to sedentarization of the working populace (land-tillers), urbanization (cities dominating society), and material display (monumental buildings, luxury wares).

But all this, frankly, is poppycock. The Assyrian king list opens with a whole section of "17 *kings* who lived in tents" for the early second millennium.[102] No toiling peasants on landed estates here; no whisper of urbanization here; no trace of fine buildings or luxury wares here. These men were in effect sheikhs of the steppe, in the region of Ashur, Assyria's eventual capital. At the same general period, we have the phenomenon of city-based rulers in Babylonia paralleled by nonsedentary, noncity rulers in the same area — so the kings of Kish in alliance with the nonurban kings of Manana.[103] The Egyptian Execration Texts show multiple rulers in one place at this general period also. In fact, Egypt's earliest state (First-Second Dynasties) was a set of agro-pastoral communities based on small local townships and villages that owed allegiance in two zones (Delta, Nile Valley) to one overall head from one of these, the pharaoh.[104] There were *no* mass urban sites then, and no great monuments except some brick tombs up in the desert fringes. None of this would suit the grandiose criteria of the theorists, but nobody in their senses can possibly deny that the Egyptian monarchy was not a proper state, even at its beginnings.

Thus there is no valid reason whatsoever to deny the title of king to rulers so termed by either Near Eastern documents or the biblical writers. *They* were there, then; we (and our fantasizing sociologists) were not! A series of tribes having ancestral or other links in common, in a common habitat, might well have a simple three-tier government: each tribe having its elders and leader, the main tribal leaders serving as an assembly, and one of their number (in hereditary or electoral succession) at their head as "king" over the whole. That is certainly what should be posited for almost purely pastoral Edom before the ninth/eighth century, and largely for Moab (and Ammon, no doubt), plus agricultural, farm- or village-based communities likewise.[105] If indeed the Balu'a stela does date to the thirteenth/twelfth century (as its art has been "read"), then we would have evidence for a monumental royal piece, imitating Egyptian fashion in Moab; but this cannot be treated as a certainty.[106] In short, there is *no* respectable evidence whatsoever for denying the title "king" to any of those people reported in our sources, biblical or otherwise.

(v) Going Places: Itineraries

These are digests of routes from one place to another that pass through a series of intermediate stopping places, sometimes including travel times, or brief notices about events en route, in the course of particular journeys. Numbers 33:1-49 provides us with a good example. We are told that Moses had kept such a record, which was used by the writer of Num. 33:1-49. Such records were compiled throughout antiquity. Already in the eighteenth century we have the so-called Old Babylonian itinerary that ran from Mesopotamia up to north Syrian Emar, including the number of nights spent at each stop.[107] In contemporary Mari, Yasmah-Adad was told by his father Shamshi-Adad I of Assyria what stages and stops he would follow to visit him.[108] Almost a millennium later, the campaign records of the ninth-century Assyrian monarchs Tukulti-Ninurta II and Assurnasirpal II include itinerary segments.[109] Over in Egypt, the war texts of Egypt's New Kingdom pharaohs (fifteenth-thirteenth centuries) were clearly based on campaign daybooks (as in the Annals of Tuthmosis III). A variant of the species is the ship's log, a daybook travel itinerary kept on water. From Egypt we have two. One is of Year 52 of Ramesses II (ca. 1228, close in date to our Hebrews), giving the day-by-day record of the journey and leisurely stops of the ship of Prince Khaemwaset, fourth son of that king, from Pi-Ramesse (biblical Raamses) in the East Delta up to Memphis, the traditional capital of Egypt. The other is of the reign of either Ramesses VI or VII in the Twentieth Dynasty (ca. 1140 or 1130), being the log of a vessel sailing from Heliopolis to Memphis and southward (with long stops), and ending with accounts.[110] Back on land, we have segments of itineraries in Canaan, also under Ramesses II, in Papyrus Anastasi I.[111] And several of the great Egyptian topographical lists of foreign towns in Canaan contain sequences of places evidently derived from itineraries.[112] So Num. 33 is no isolated case,[113] and is part of a tradition that began at least half a millennium before, and continued down to Roman times, and is known till today.

(vi) Early Israelite Settlement East of the Jordan

Until recent times the area in Transjordan from the Mishor plain north to Bashan seemed to show very little clear evidence of any history of settlement in Late Bronze/Iron I of the thirteenth and twelfth centuries, the theater and period of the initial settlement there by the tribes of Reuben, Gad, and East Manasseh as seen in Num. 32, Deut. 3:12-20, and Josh. 12:1-6, 13:8-32. But now intensive survey and study has provided a clearer picture of the situation. First, a series of sites in this overall area show Late Bronze II into Iron IA phases of occupation. Moving from south to north (beginning in the Mishor tableland), Tell el-Umeiri was occupied in Late Bronze, and was enclosed with a casemate wall in Iron I (twelfth century), with pillared houses and use of collared-rim jars. At Tell Jalul, a Late Bronze phase gave way to an Iron I settlement (more collared-rim jars) that was thereafter destroyed. At Tell Hesban, Late Bronze is structurally absent, only some possible sherds being found to date; in Iron I it became a village (again collared-rim jars were characteristic). Sahab was a walled town in Late Bronze II, directly followed by Iron I occupation. Amman had limited Late Bronze/Iron I occupation materials (so far); its heyday came later. Going farther north, Tell Safut was also a Late Bronze II walled settlement that passed directly into Iron I (more collared-rim jars), being burned later on. Iraq el-Amir (stratum V) was an eleventh-century Iron I fort, also with collared-rim jars, then destroyed and abandoned. At Khirbet Umm-el-Dananir, a Late Bronze IIA building went on into Iron IA, with abandonment in the twelfth century. Going north of the Jabbok River (Wadi Zerqa), Jerash had a Late Bronze occupation and then Iron I (two floor levels, burnt destruction; collared-rim jars in Iron I), seemingly destroyed violently. Tell Husn showed material from the Late Bronze II, Iron I and II periods, as did Abila. At Tell Fukhar, up by the Yarmuk River, a Late Bronze IIA site became a larger Iron I settlement, walled, and using collared-rim jars, then declining later.[114] The four-room-house type is also attested in these east-of-Jordan sites, sometimes with collared-rim jars.[115] Such are Tell Umeiri in the south, Tell el-Fukhar in the north, besides such houses in Moabite sites (Lehun, Medeinet Aliya).

The overall picture in the Mishor plain, Gilead, and up into Bashan is one of a series of Late Bronze II settlements, some modest, some walled, which passed over into the Iron IA phase of occupation that showed new cultural features such as collared-rim jars, four-roomed houses, or both together. These features are *not* a guarantee of an Israelite presence, but it remains true that these are characteristic of the Israelite settlement in Canaan.[116] All this is fully consistent with the biblical tradition that the Hebrews came north from the fringes of Moab proper (south of the Arnon) to the Mishor plains, and defeated the two minor Amorite kingdoms of Sihon and Og that occupied Mishor/south Gilead and north Gilead into Bashan respectively. The Mishor and environs were a prime sheep-rearing region, as our geographers can still tell us, hence the very natural request of Reuben and Gad to stay on in that area (Num. 32). In due time, old rivalries and new between Moab, the Israelites, and Ammon broke out, especially over who should have the Mishor area. Sihon had taken it from Moab (who earlier had it, as Ramesses II's scenes prove, including Dibon with Butartu in Moab). Then Israel took it from Sihon, and Moab later took it back, and the seesaw went on. Scarce wonder that some Iron IA sites ended up being destroyed and burned, some never to rise again, either permanently or else not until well into Iron II times. Thus, whatever minor gaps currently appear in our total documentation (so for Heshbon, as at Jericho!), the overall picture in Numbers/Deuteronomy/Joshua makes very good sense, and fits well the known archaeological and related context.

However, Israel did not originate on the desert fringe of Moab, but further back. As we shall see in chapter 6, Egypt and south Sinai have claims here,[117] and in such a context our earlier review from Qadesh-Barnea to the plains of Moab indicates the straightforward feasibility of that phase of tribal Israel's story without presuming to prove it.

5. WHEN THE JUDGES JUDGED

Or rather, governed. Now we can return back over Jordan into Canaan, where we left early Israel at about 1220/1210, under its "elders," heirs of Joshua. Thereafter, early Israel was increasingly in trouble, first from a brush with troops of Merenptah just before his fifth year (1209), and second in their relationships with their immediate neighbors from then down to almost 1000. First, we may look at the biblical data for that period, contained for the most part in the book of Judges and in 1 Sam. 1–7. Then we may see how (if at all) they fit into this epoch. Finally we may examine the relevant cultural and archaeological materials for this same period.

A. THE BIBLICAL DATA THEMSELVES

First, a concise tabulation of the layout and basic contents of the book of Judges provides a convenient framework with which to compare the two next sections, before examining what may be the underlying chronology, and as a setting for the archaeological and allied cultural data.

Table 11. Book of Judges, Outline and Layout

1. *After the Death of Joshua — Attempting Settlement* (1:1-36; cf. 2:6-9)

   South

   (a) *Judah and Simeon* (1:2-20).
       Success at Bezeq; Jerusalem raided, torched, but not held; successes in Negev. Othniel and Achsah (1:11-15 = Josh. 15:14-19); Kenites move into Negev. Possible raid on Gaza, Ascalon, and Ekron, but nothing more there.
       Summary: Judah effective in hills but not against chariotry in the plains.

   (b) *Benjamin* (1:21). Failed to take Jerusalem; Jebusites stayed on.

   Central

   (a) *"Joseph" (Ephraim and W. Manasseh)* (1:22-29).
       Took Bethel finally; but not Gezer or Dor and Jezreel towns (still Canaanite). Danites blocked into hills by Amorites (failure, like Gezer and Jezreel).

   North
   Zebulon, Asher, Naphtali could only settle alongside Canaanites (1:30-33).

   Consequences of compromise. No easy penetration henceforth (2:1-6).

2. *Flashback, Declension, and Resultant Paradigm* (2:6–3:6)
   (a) *Joshua and Elders.* Start of possession, but **not** by Joshua (2:6-9, 23).
   (b) *Acculturation, breach of covenant, defeat* (3:1-6).
   (c) *Cyclical Paradigm.* Disobedience, Punishment, Contrition, Deliverance (then Relapse) — DPCD (+ R).[118]

3. *Narrative Exposé of Israel's Decline during Settlement Period* (3:8–16:31)

"Major" Judges (+ DPCD)		"Minor" Judges (no DPCD)	
"Major"		**"Minor"**	
1. *Othniel* (3:7-11) DPCD vs. Kushan-rishathaim of Aram-N	N		
2. *Ehud* (3:12-30) DPCD vs. Eglon of Moab	E	3. *Shamgar* (3:31) null DPCD vs. Philistines	SW
(No. 3 here)			

4A/B. *Barak and Deborah* (4–5) DPCD
vs. Jabin II of Hazor/Canaan   N

5A/B. *Gideon* (6–8) DPCD		6. *Tola* (10:1-2) null; vs. null
vs. Midianites	E	7. *Jair* (10:3-5) null DPCD vs. null
(Abimelech at Shechem only		
(9), null)		
(nos. 6-7 here)		

8. *Jephthah* (10:6–12:7) DPCD		
vs. Ammon	E	9. *Ibzan* (12:8-10) null DPCD vs. null
		10. *Elon* (12:11-12) null DPCD vs. null
(nos. 9-11 here)		11. *Abdon* (12:13-15) null DPCD, null

12. *Samson* (13–16) DCPD
vs. Philistines   SW

4. *Exemplary Episodes — Idolatry and Strife* (17–18; 19–21)

(i) Net Results of Segment 1

The panorama is as follows: a north-to-south series of attempts at real conquest by Judah with Simeon: in the north, success in Bezeq; in the center, failure to secure Jerusalem; in the south, gains in Hebron/Debir zone and in the Negev. Ephraim/Manasseh ("Joseph") finally secured Bethel, but failed against Gezer, Dor, and Jezreel, merely settling in with the locals. Up north Asher, Zebulon, and Naphtali failed almost entirely to obtain effective occupancy, again settling in with the locals. Finally, Dan failed to expand from its hill-country base westward, and was contained by local opposition, so in due course (chap. 18) some of its members migrated north to Laish.

(ii) Net Results of Segment 3

What is significant is that, otherwise, the book *has no more to say* about the evidently slow process of the Hebrew settlement in the period before the monarchy. The writer instead concentrates mainly on the major crises of (in effect) local rivals inside Canaan (in Galilee, the Philistines) or adjoining it (Moab, Midian, Ammon); only the exotic Kushan-rishathaim comes from afar. Thus we have six such crises dealt with in terms of the author's main theme (DPCD + R). Among the so-called minor judges, only one (Shamgar, 3:31) actually hits out at the opposition; the other five are shown briefly as (in effect) simply local regional rulers. Of these, the first alone (Tola, 10:1-2) is said to be a deliverer of Israel, but no details are given; the other four (10:3-5; 12:8-15) simply governed locally, in Gilead, Bethlehem (north Judah), Zebulon, and Ephraim, without any report of major conflicts. Our so-called major judges also served quite locally (Hebron, Benjamin; woman near Bethel plus man from Naphtali; villager in West Manasseh; man in Gilead, and one in [original] Dan). This fact will be of importance, just presently.

The only difference between the "major" and "minor" judges is that the former are reported on in some detail, for their role as (in the ancient author's eyes) divinely commissioned deliverers for Israel locally and sometimes more widely. The twelve to fourteen people presented (fourteen with Deborah as well as Barak, plus the local renegade Abimelech) were certainly not the whole of Israel's local bigwigs between Joshua and Saul's reign, but merely a selection (6 + 6) the author had record of and chose for his theme. Historically there were undoubtedly more, as local tribal leaders of whom we know nothing.

Finally, the contribution of 1 Sam. 1–7. In essence, this narrative centers on the origin and career of Samuel, down to that fatal day when Israel asked for a king "just like everybody else" (cf. 1 Sam. 8). With Saul's checkered reign, the period of the "judges" was over.

B. GEOGRAPHY AND CHRONOLOGY

(i) The Basic Situation

In this age of impatience, many are tempted simply to read directly through the book of Judges as a continuous narrative, and hence as a narrative of continuous history, especially when the text sometimes says of a "judge" that "after him" ruled another in turn. The narrative is indeed largely continuous, but the underlying history not needfully so. The last five chapters (17–21) are not directly tied to any succession. Only in 18:30, if one reads "Moses," not "Manasseh," as grandfather of Gershom, chaplain to the Danites, may we infer that this narrative would at latest fall in the first part of the twelfth century, well before most of the narratives that precede it.

In fact, only a limited number of "after him" phrases link successive judges, leaving open the option that some may have served as contemporaries in different districts of Canaan. This possibility becomes in effect a certainty if one goes through the date lines betwen the exodus and the fourth year of Solomon, the year he began building his temple, "in the 480th year" since the exodus (1 Kings 6:1), we are told. Thus, if that year fell circa 967 (cf. dates in chaps. 2

and 4 above), a literal adding up would set the exodus in 1447. But if we take the trouble actually to tote up all the individual figures known from Exodus to Kings in that period, they do *not* add up to 480 years. But rather to $554 + x + y + z$ years, where x = unknown length of rule by Joshua and the elders (minimum, 5/10 years?), y = rule by Samuel above his stated 20 years (possibly zero), and z = the full reign of Saul (minimum, [3]2 years).[119] The total comes to between 35 and 42 years at least, bringing the 554 years to a minimal 591/596 years. This is certainly not identical with the 480 years of 1 Kings 6:1. If the two figures are to be meaningfully related to each other, overlaps of contemporary local chiefs are required in the book of Judges, a fact universally admitted whatever interpretation is placed on the 480-year datum. If taken seriously, this latter may itself be viewed in any one of three ways: literally as some do; as 12×40 years (12 "generation spans"); or as a figure selected on some unstated principle from the ultimate 554 up to 591/596 years. But without overlaps, 591/596 does not go into 480. For the 480 years datum, cf. also below in chapter 6.

If one has a lower date for the exodus than 1447, say a minimum date of about 1260/1250, then the interval of elapsed real time down to Solomon's fourth year in 967 becomes about 293/283 years, into which the 591/596 years would then be subsumed (besides the 480-year figure). Is such a procedure an anomaly without parallel? Is it even a practical proposition, even if not anomalous?

The answer in the first case is no, it is not an isolated anomaly, and in the second case, yes, if we apply ancient (not modern) procedures and consider the biblical data carefully. Let us see both points in practice.

(ii) Judges as an "Intermediate Period" in Hebrew History

In the biblical world, multiple rulers in a land or community where sole rulers would be the norm are a familiar phenomenon, usually in "intermediate" periods between times of unity and (often) achievement. The most familiar example is Egypt, with three such periods of internal division: one (late third millennium) between the Old Kingdom (Pyramid Age) and Middle Kingdom, another (Thirteenth-Seventeenth Dynasties, early second millennium) between the Middle and New Kingdoms, and another (early first millennium) between the New Kingdom and the Saite revival period. In Mesopotamia, best known is the so-called second intermediate period of rival city-states in the Isin-Larsa/Old Babylonian period of the early second millennium, with rival dynasties. In these cases, the Egyptian and Mesopotamian king lists simply list the various dynasties (and their years reigned) in succession, without giving overlaps. But in every case, overlaps are known from other sources of information. The period of the "judges" was likewise a time of Hebrew disunity, after the unitary rule of the two leaders Moses and Joshua and brief committee rule of the elders, and before the renewed unity of the united monarchy of Saul, David, and Solomon.

As for the principle of 591/596 years within a time lapse of 293/283 years, suffice it briefly to exemplify this situation from Egypt and Mesopotamia. Of the Thirteenth to Seventeenth Dynasties, the full Thirteenth (Manetho's 60 kings at 153 years) had at least 50 kings reigning about 150 years; the Fourteenth has 76 kings for 184 years in Manetho, many being listed in the Turin Canon of Kings (which is damaged, hence incomplete). The Fifteenth, Hyksos, Dynasty was of 6 kings for 108 years; the Sixteenth possibly of only local princelings, no clear data; the (Theban) full Seventeenth of some 21 kings of 90/96 years. This total is about 508 years (excluding the not-calculatable Sixteenth Dynasty). But this grand total has to fit betwen the dates of close on 1795 (end of Twelfth Dynasty) and either 1550 or 1540 (start of Eighteenth Dynasty), a maximum of 245 or 255 years.[120] This is the same situation, exactly, as with the exodus-to-early-Solomon epoch of 591/596 years going into 293/283 years. In Mesopotamia, suffice it to list the First Dynasty of Isin (125 kings, 224 years), plus the Larsa Dynasty (14 kings, 263 years), and the First Dynasty of Babylon (11 kings, 300 years) between the fall of the Third Dynasty of Ur and that of the First Dynasty of Babylon. These three dynasties total 787 years, but have to go into 410 years on the commonly used "middle" dates (higher and lower would not affect this point); this again is the same phenomenon as in Egypt and early Israel.[121] So here we have no anomaly whatsoever in Judges.

(iii) A Practical "Intermediate Period" Chronology for the Judges Period

Here we will seek to build up a minimal chronology (the only safe kind until we know better), step by step. If all that appears in Judges and 1 Samuel (people, events, and figures) were but fiction, then there is no point in this exercise. But if they should, perchance, have preserved a deposit of reliable tradition, then the exercise *is* worthwhile, to see what may come of it. In so doing we are bound to use the *same* approach that scholars normally adopt in Egyptology, Assyriology, etc., in using firsthand sources so far as possible (not available for Judges), and also the data of king lists and later historical reports, which is a method we can operate with Judges. When this is done (as for Egypt and Mesopotamia), and "precise" figures are used, such as a traditional "twenty-three years" for a king, then of course the totting up of such figures gives misleadingly "exact" dates. Nobody in the world can prove that the twenty-three years given us for King Kheops (who built the Great Pyramid) actually occurred from precisely 2593 to precisely 2570, or that the five kings of Mesopotamia's Third Dynasty of Ur reigned exactly during 2112-2004. The individual figures for reigns or rule may be correct, but factors of doubt in succeeding periods may mean that the figures given as years B.C. are subject to change, if fresh facts should so demand. Exactly the same procedure will be used here; the figures given in Judges and 1 Samuel will be used (just as we do elsewhere in the biblical world) and assigned calculated "dates B.C."; but such dates are subject to revision, despite their apparent "exactness," should other facts so require.

We now tabulate people, data, and numbers step by step. We do this first in terms of *geographical zones* in west and east Palestine in which these judges held sway (table 12, below); second, in terms of *explicit sequences* of judges given by the text, "after him . . ." (table 13, on p. 206); and third, via a *combination* of place and time, adding in oppressions and numbers mentioned (table 14, on p. 206). Then the attribution of formal dates can be attempted (see table 15, on p. 207).

Given that we have a minimum span of 170/160 years for the known judges, prophets, and priests between about 1210/1200 and 1042 (when Saul took over), it is obvious from table 12 that those agents mentioned in the book of Judges plus 1 Sam. 1–7 cannot have been the total of all the local rulers ("judges" or tribal) that actually flourished throughout the period. It is simply a selection made by the author of Judges from a fuller tradition not now available to us.

The persons in parentheses are of people clearly later than anyone above them, from contexts. The sequences explicitly given in Judges often do not coincide with geographical localities. Clearly, what occurred was that a local man in one area achieved wider recognition than just on his home patch, or else his passing coincided with someone else's rise to at least modest prominence.

Table 12. Zones in Which "Judges" Are Said to Have Operated

SW and W Philistia	S: Judah & Negev	Center-E Benjamin	Center Ephraim	N-Center Manasseh	Galilee N areas	E, across Jordan
Shamgar	Othniel	Ehud	Deborah + Tola Abdon,	Gideon & (Abimelik)	+ Barak	Jair
Samson	Ibzan Samuel's sons	Samuel	Eli		Elron	Jephthah

Table 13. Explicit Sequences of Judges and Related People

Othniel	Ehud	Gideon	Jephthah
	Shamgar	Abimelek	Ibzan
(Ibzan)	Deborah + Barak	Tola	Elon
	Eli	Jair	Abdon
(sons of Samuel)	Samuel		

Table 14. Combined Regions and Sequences of Judges plus Oppressors, with Figures

South		Center		North		East
SW and W Phils, Dan	S: Judah & Negev	E Center Benjamin	Center Ephraim	N Center Manasseh	Galilee, N areas	E, across Jordan
Philistines x SHAMGAR x	*Kushan-R* 8 OTHNIEL 40	*Eglon* 18 EHUD x				
		80 yrs peace	*Jabin II* 20 DEBORAH x	- - - - - - - -	+ BARAK x	
			40 yrs peace			
---------------	---------------	---------------	---------------		---------------	---------------
				Midian 7 GIDEON 40 (Abimelek 3)		
			TOLA 23			
						JAIR 22 --------- *Ammon* 18 JEPHTHAH 6
	IBZAN 7				ELON 10	
Philistines 40 SAMSON 20 *Philistines*	Sons of SAMUEL x	SAMUEL 20	ABDON 8 // // ELI 30 (SAMUEL)			

The judges and allied prophets (Deborah, Barak) and priests (Eli) in Table 14 are shown in capital letters. Names of oppressors are in italics. To save space, numbers are given without the word "years" except in two cases. Where no year lengths were given, the cipher *x* has been entered.

It now remains to turn this "relative chronology" into an approximate minimal chronology in terms of years B.C. Israel is mentioned as in Canaan by Merenptah in his fifth year in 1209 at latest, giving a rounded minimum benchmark of circa 1210. So Joshua, Moses, the wilderness years, and the exodus are all prior to that date; in theory, Joshua might also have been a contemporary of

Table 15. A Provisional Scheme of Dates for the Epoch of the Judges

South		Center		North		East
SW and W Phils, Dan	S: Judah & Negev	E Center Benjamin	Center Ephraim	N Center Manasseh	Galilee, N areas	E, across Jordan
Danites to N ca. 1190/80? *Philistines* x SHAMGAR x ca. 1170	*Kushan-R* 8 1200-1192 OTHNIEL 40 1192-1152	*Eglon* 18 1200-1182 EHUD x 1182-?				
		80 yrs peace 1182-1102	*Jabin II* 20 1180-1160 DEBORAH x ca. 1165-1150? 40 yrs peace 1160-1120	- - - - - - - ---------------	+ BARAK x ca. 1165-1150	....
---------------	---------------	---------------	---------------	*Midian* 7 1186-1179 GIDEON 40 1179-1139 (Abimelek 3) (1139-1136)	---------------	---------------
			TOLA 23 1136-1113			JAIR 22 1113-1091 --------- *Ammon* 18 1091-1073 JEPHTHAH 6 1073-1067
	IBZAN 7 1067-1060				ELON 10 1060-1050	
Philistines 40 1100-1060 SAMSON 20 1080-1060 *Philistines*	Sons of SAMUEL x (ca. 1045)	SAMUEL 20 1062-1042	ABDON 8 // 1050-1042 // ELI 30 1102-1062 (SAMUEL)			

Merenptah's forces' very brief intrusion, and the elders might have followed him. The absolutely minimal dates for the exodus and wilderness forty years (38 + 2) are between 1260/1250 and 1220/1210. An average at 1255-1215 would then give us 1215-1200 for Joshua and the elders. Thus we may for convenience begin the judges period proper at about 1200, so far as minimal dating is concerned. If as noted in chapter 4 above, p. 83 and table 7, Saul be given [3]2 years circa 1042-1010 prior to David, then we have two approximate minimum end points some 168 years apart for the judges of Judges and 1 Sam. 1–7. Within this period we have another useful constraint. The first major Philistine impact (and settlement) in Canaan came as part of the invasion of the Sea Peoples halted by Ramesses III in his eighth year. This can be dated to either 1180 or 3 years later at 1177, depending on whether the short-lived pharaoh Amenmesses actually reigned as sole king for 3 years between Merenptah and Sethos II or was a rebel in southern Egypt, wholly within the 6-year reign of Sethos II — an undecided matter. This means that Shamgar's brush with the Philistines would fall after 1180/1177, as would Deborah's public career. On the other hand, Othniel was a son of Caleb, Joshua's companion in arms, and should not be pushed too far down after 1200. See further after table 15.

From table 14 we have the sequence of "recognized" judges back from Abdon to Jephthah. Eli was *not* a tribal judge but a Levitical priest at the (post)tabernacle sanctuary at Shiloh. And Samuel, his spiritual successor, was a prophet and kept normally to the very narrow circuit of Bethel, Gilgal, Mizpah, and home to Ramah (1 Sam. 7:15-16), where people might consult him. Thus the last-named tribal judge, Abdon, may have been his nonreligious contemporary, whose role was in practice supplanted by the monarchy of Saul (who replaced all "judges"). Hence we have here dated the sequence from Abdon back to Jephthah as from Saul's accession. Before Jephthah one must surely set not only the Ammonites he defeated but also the peaceful Jair, and then before him Tola and Abimelech and finally Gideon. That is as far as the direct series of links allows us to go. Hence the dotted line across the middle of tables 14 to 16.

Under Samuel and Saul the Philistines were said to have been kept at bay (cf. 1 Sam. 7:13), which is substantially borne out by the outcome of Philistine/Israelite clashes during Samuel's lifetime (cf. 1 Sam. 14; 17–18; 23:1-5; 23:27–24:1). The twenty years for Samuel before Saul's accession is, strictly, the period of the ark's stay at Kiriath-Jearim between the death of Eli and the accession of Saul (7:2ff.). That he "continued as a judge in Israel" all his life until his death (7:15) occurred during the reign of Saul, under whom he died (cf. 25:1). Before Samuel's time of office, the Philistines were oppressive, certainly in the west/southwest, and Samson's isolated fight against them probably fell in the second half of that period, if he was born early in it; hence our dates. Before him we have no earlier report of events in the west/southwest since Shamgar, datable to after the arrival of the historic Philistines (Pilasti of Egyptian texts). At least some Danites migrated north to Laish (which they renamed Dan; Judg. 18), possibly with a (younger?) grandson of Moses as their priest, which would favor a date early in the twelfth century for such an event.

Going back to the start of our period, Othniel and his Aramean foe appear to begin the sequence; on Kushan-rishathaim, see section 6 below, with the Moabites causing longer trouble for his Benjaminite younger contemporary Ehud. Shamgar is placed after Ehud's death (an undated event, as Ehud's time span is not given). And both Ehud and Shamgar precede the exploits of Deborah and Barak. So, that pair against Jabin II would (like Shamgar) postdate the initial settlement of the Philistines of 1180/1177. Thus we allow about 1180-1160 for Jabin II's twenty years until Deborah's success. Associated with Ehud and Deborah are long general periods of peace, of eighty and forty years respectively. These are probably round figures, and the literal dating of them in table 15 serves merely to indicate two such differing broad stretches of time. Gideon's problems with Midian out east may have been roughly contemporary with Jabin II up north, and not unconnected with Moab well to Gideon's south. But, again, the "forty years of peace" given for "the days of Gideon" (Judg. 8:28) may well be a round figure closer to thirty years or so, which would lower the date of him and his Midianites somewhat.

One datum not in table 15 is Jephthah's boast to the king of Ammon, that Israel had occupied the Mishor region east of the Jordan for 300 years (Judg. 11:26). At roughly 1070 (the 1073 of our table 15), that would place that occupation at about 1370, which in itself makes no sense whatsoever on any current date of the exodus 40 years before, whether in 1447, 1260/1250, or any time in between. Brave fellow that he was, Jephthah was a roughneck, an outcast, and not exactly the kind of man who would scruple first to take a Ph.D. in local chronology at some ancient university of the Yarmuk before making strident claims to the Ammonite ruler. What we have is nothing more than the report of a brave but ignorant man's bold bluster in favor of his people, not a mathematically precise chronological datum. So it can offer us no practical help. It is in the same class as other statements that biblical writers may well report accurately but which they would not necessarily expect readers to believe — as in the speeches of Job's comforters, or even by Job himself, in extremis, for example. The propaganda against YHWH by Sennacherib is a matter of clear reporting (2 Kings 18:25, 35) — but not that readers should believe it! Thus, overall, we have at last the basis for a minimal chronology for the judges period. For more modest needs and for archaeological purposes, it may be fitting to provide, finally, a *generalized* chronological summary, avoiding the hyperprecise dates of the ambitious! Table 16 (on p. 210) is intended to serve as a wiser, more modest derivative of the formal dates given in table 15, for general purposes. In its close, formal "exactness," table 15 will serve as a sharpening stone for others to sharpen their knives upon and perhaps produce something better, at some future date!

6. JUDGES: NEAR EASTERN AND ARCHAEOLOGICAL BACKGROUND

Here we present external background and control material (as with Joshua and part of Numbers earlier) to help in assessing the biblical view and presentation of this period, between Moses and the Hebrew monarchy.

Table 16. Broad Summary Chronology, Period of the Judges

South		Center		North		East
SW and W Phils, Dan	S: Judah & Negev	E Center Benjamin	Center Ephraim	N Center Manasseh	Galilee, N areas	E, across Jordan
Dan N 1180? *Philistines* x SHAMBAR x ca. 1170	*Kushan-R* 8 OTHNIEL 40 ca. 1195	*Eglon* 18 EHUD x ca. 1180 80 yrs peace	*Jabin II* 20 DEBORAH x ca. 1160 40 yrs peace	- - - - - - - -	+ BARAK x ca. 1160	
---------------	---------------	---------------	---------------	---------------	---------------	---------------
				Midian 7 GIDEON 40 ca. 1170/50 (Abimelek 3)		
			TOLA 23 ca. 1025			JAIR 22 ca. 1100 --------- *Ammon* 18 JEPHTHAH 6 ca. 1070
	IBZAN 7 ca. 1070				ELON 10 ca. 1060	
Philistines 40 SAMSON 20 ca. 1070 *Philistines*	Sons of SAMUEL x ca. 1045	SAMUEL 20 1062-1042	ABDON 8 // ca. 1050 // ELI 40 ca. 1100-1060 (SAMUEL)			

A. DOCUMENTARY, HISTORICAL, AND CULTURAL ASPECTS

(i) People and Places

(a) Going from Dan to Dan

In Judg. 1:34 we learn that the Danites were hemmed in within the hills by the local Amorites, who did not want them "downstairs" in their own lusher valleys and lowlands. Thus it is no surprise to read near the close of the book that (quite early on) some Danites gave up and decided to try their luck elsewhere, way up north (Judg. 18; and cf. brief summary, Josh. 19:47), where they took the walled town of Laish, renaming it Dan. As they took with them a Levite who was possibly a grandson of Moses (Judg. 18:30), this event would not be any later than the first decades of the twelfth century, as we have seen.

Laish/Dan can be firmly located at the modern Tell el-Qadi by the head-waters of the river Jordan, and its archaeological profile reveals the former existence in the thirteenth century of a prosperous and cosmopolitan Canaanite city (level VIIA) that was destroyed around roughly 1200, it having pottery in part transitional in type between Late Bronze II and Iron IA. The next level (VI) showed a different way of life, a mere encampment with storage pits and food storage vessels of strictly local ware (no exotic Mediterranean imports here). This is all very reminiscent of the Judges narrative, with the early Danites taking the town, destroying it and resettling there. We are told that they rebuilt the town. The destruction traces of level VIIA and the encampment-style occupation of level VI were duly succeeded in level V by a proper town, of the same style of (Israelite) material culture but developing. And imports began again: a modest flow of Phoenician and Philistine wares (pretty luxuries!) can be found among the remains then. So here we have an archaeological illustration of, and commentary on, the data in Josh. 19:47 and especially Judg. 18.

Nor is this all. From the archaeology we can add a little to the city Dan's eventful history. The Danites had captured and destroyed the Canaanite town. But in the mid–eleventh century their own nice little town suffered violent destruction and burning; half a meter thickness of debris tells its own tale. "Who dunnit?" The Philistine attack on Israel that included the destruction of the shrine at Shiloh (cf. Jer. 7:12-14) can be dated around 1060, and it is conceivable that they struck farther north still; or, the nearby Arameans or other locals took their chance. Either way, the Danites rebuilt their town (level IV) and lived to see the coming of the Hebrew monarchy.[122] If the narratives in Judges and Joshua about Dan were born purely from some late writer's romantic imagination, how come so consistent a correlation emerges between the "tales" and the archaeological sequence if they were separated by many centuries? Otherwise so fortuitous a coincidence partakes of the miraculous. It is easier to accept that the "tales" contain a basic history, faithfully transmitted via these books, either themselves written quite early or else written later but drawing upon earlier source data. Culturally the use of house cults of paganizing type among the early Hebrews may find its analogies in finds elsewhere, as possibly with a suggested altar stone and stela stone recently found in a house across the Jordan farther south at Tell Umeiri.[123]

(b) Kushan Who? Yes, Rishathaim!

The first mentioned of early Israel's oppressors is also the most exotic and distant one. In Judg. 3:8-11 we are told that Othniel was raised up to free the Hebrews from the overlordship of "Kushan Rishathaim, King of Aram-Naharaim."[124] As Othniel was given as a son of Caleb (the fellow spy with Joshua, Num. 13:6, 8; 14:38), any such incident, as with Dan, would have to be set not later than the early twelfth century. Like virtually every other oppressor named in Judges, he is not mentioned in contemporary records, and for the same simple reason; there are none of a relevant type that would do so. As Kushan recurs as a place-name anciently (as Kushu) synonymous with Edom, some have sought to emend Aram-Naharaim to Edom, omitting the second element. This is gratuitous, especially as Edom is not known ever to have dominated Israel/Judah, and perhaps unlikely while simply a "tented kingdom" mainly of pastoralists. The second half of the name has always been an enigma, and in its given form can be construed as a pejorative epithet, so "Kushan of the double wickedness." But nobody of himself ever adopts such a surname or title, and it is clearly a play on a more meaningful form — as is Ishbosheth for Ishbaal in the name of Saul's son who followed him.

Aram-Naharaim is the terrain within the great west bend of the Euphrates. In the thirteenth century it was part of the former kingdom of Mitanni-Hanigalbat, which was taken from the Hittites by the Assyrians, and kept by them down to Tukulti-Ninurta I (1245-1208). But in his last years onward and under weak successors,[125] the Akhlamu Arameans and others quietly took over this western part. The name of Aram as a region in north-central Syria (close to Amurru?) first appears under Amenophis III of Egypt (fourteenth century), and then under Merenptah (1213-1203).[126] So Aram here is no surprise. Other commentators have suggested reading *risha'thayim* as *resh*, "head/chief," plus a place-name, most simply as an 'Athaim, giving us "Kushan, Chief of 'Athaim"[127] as well as "King of Aram-Naharaim." He is most likely to be regarded as a "new man," an Aramean adventurer who based himself on some town ('Athaim) in the west bend area not yet known to us and bedecked himself with the pompous title of king of Aram-Naharaim. After securing himself a power base in the area that became Bit-Adini two hundred years later,[128] he would have begun to raid southward, reaching at least northern Canaan. Again, two hundred years later, Hadadezer of Aram-Zobah had no hesitation in subduing Hamath and intervening equally far south on Ammon's behalf. Kushan's power was briefer and more ephemeral than Hadadezer's, so we catch just a glimpse of the kind of ambitious adventurer that sought to fill a local vacuum and then exploit any wider opportunities.

(c) Jabin II, King of Canaan

Much head scratching has also been devoted to this local monarch, adversary of Deborah in Judg. 4–5. Too often he has been needlessly confused with the Jabin (I) dispatched by Joshua. But there are good reasons to keep them apart. As mentioned already, it is very common to find royal names recurring repeatedly in Levantine and other dynasties in the second millennium. So, as the Jabin (II) of Deborah must be dated sometime from 1180 (she followed Shamgar, who was involved with Philistines not before that date), he would have reigned thirty or more years later than Joshua's Jabin (I) at least. By Deborah's time, of course, the great town of Hazor (both citadel and lower city) had been well destroyed and burned. So our Jabin II had lost that facility, and would have to reign from another center. This is almost certainly reflected in the biblical text. First time round, in 4:2, Jabin II is "king of Canaan, who reigned in Hazor," a double appellation. Thereafter he is just once called "king of Hazor" (4:17) but twice "king of Canaan" (4:23, 24). No such duality occurs in Josh. 11; Hazor was "head of all those kingdoms" (= Canaan), but its king is exclusively a king of Hazor. The explanation is most likely that, after Joshua's destruction of Hazor, Jabin I's successors had to reign from another site in Galilee but kept the style of king of the territory and kingdom of Hazor, and used mainly the wider title "king of Canaan" to emphasize the continuance of their former historic role. Parallels ancient and modern are not lacking. Assur-uballit II, the last king of Assyria, was known by that title even after he had lost the entire heartland of Assyria (never mind its capitals!) and had retreated to Harran.[129] In Egypt's intermediate periods, pharaohs actually restricted in rule exclusively to either the north or the south continued to use the titles "king of south and north Egypt" and "lord of both lands." And much more recently, kings of England once also claimed the title "king of France," even after loss of rule there emptied it of any meaning. So our two Jabins are to be considered as two distinct rulers, for the second of whom the fall of Hazor changed his royal style.

(d) The Timescale of Midian

The remarkable fact about Midian (and also Amalek) is its relatively short history by ancient Near Eastern standards. "Founding traditions" of descent from Abraham occur in Gen. 25:2, 4, plus a brief appearance with Joseph, Gen. 37:36 (and for two [?] Amaleks, one before Abraham and one from Esau, see Gen. 14:7 and 36:12). Leaving these aside, the entire history of the people of Midian runs only from the time of Moses (Exodus-Deuteronomy) down to Gideon (Judg. 6–8; 9:17), and for Amalek down to David's reign (cf. 2 Sam. 8:12), other than as a fugitive group in Hezekiah's day (1 Chron. 4:43). All other, later references to Midian are merely retrospective or use the name as a geographical term (so, 1 Kings 11:18; Isa. 60:6). In other words, the history of a people of Midian involved with Canaan runs effectively from about 1300 into the twelfth century, and for Amalek down to David. For Amalek, except as closely parallel to Midian, nothing much more can be said. But Midian's profile closely corresponds to an archaeological profile, that of the Qurayya pottery of northwest Arabia and its prime site-of-origin there (Qurayya, whence the pottery is named), during precisely the thirteenth to twelfth centuries.[130] Thus, this ware has attracted the alternative title "Midianite ware." Such identifications need to be made with care, often with reserve; but the coincidence of areas and date is a close one. During the thirteenth and early twelfth centuries the makers of Qurayya ware were involved with the Egyptian copper-mining operation at Timna on the eastern edge of Sinai, north of the Gulf of Aqaba. Their pottery was found there, associated with materials dated to the Ramesside pharaohs from Sethos I (1295/1290–1279) down to Ramesses V (1147-1143). After that date the Egyptians left, and for a short time the Midianites/Qurayyaites stayed around, and built their own tent shrine, leaving when a rockfall crushed it. By about 1100 or so they were gone. And soon afterward their main "capital" at Qurayya and its irrigation agriculture also passed into oblivion. The probable Midianites and their settled culture simply disappeared. The interest of this set of facts is that, if the Exodus-Numbers-Deuteronomy and Judges narratives had only been first invented many centuries later (e.g., in the sixth to third centuries), nobody would ever have heard of Midianites, to be able to write stories about them. And the dependent retrospects could not have been written before Judges either. One otherwise totally obscure land name would hardly generate the narratives we possess. Thus the narrations about Midian ought to have their origin in conditions that obtained in the thirteenth and twelfth centuries, not later than about 1100, and in the case of Amalek not later than the tenth century.

(e) A Tale of Two Cities

The city of Jerusalem enjoys two curious mentions very early in the book of Judges (1:8, 21), according to which the men of Judah actually broke into the city and torched it (at least in part), but evidently could not hold it. This is so because subsequently the Benjaminites failed to retake the town, so could not expel the Jebusites. These mentions are intriguing, and may hold the clue to at least one archaeological feature at oldest Jerusalem. The oft-debated "stepped-stone structure" built up against the northeast area of the eventual City of David is now quite clearly to be dated to the end of Late Bronze II going into Iron IA, or about 1200 or very soon after.[131] The inhabitants must have had good reason for engaging in the massive effort of building such a structure, doubtless to bear extended defense works above it (destroyed by tenth-century work, later on). Once Joshua was dead and gone (late thirteenth century), and perhaps also the elders, Judah launched brief attacks on Bezeq and on Jerusalem, burning it, before concentrating on the south. This would fall around 1200 on datings offered here. At some unknown interval Benjamin attacked Jerusalem and failed. Is it too much to suppose that the Jebusite defenders of Jerusalem had, in that interval, improved their town defenses by building the stepped-stone structure (and defenses above it, now gone) and possibly other work? And so Benjamin was successfully held off? This would at least make sense, and give the structure a historical context; naturally, such a suggestion proves nothing, but may at least be considered.

In the late thirteenth century Shechem (stratum XII) was a much poorer place than in Labayu's golden days over a century before. In the twelfth century the Hebrews took over, mingling with the local Canaanites (cf. the Abimelech narrative, Judg. 9), and the more built-up settlement of Shechem stratum XI reflects this period. In the latter part of the twelfth century, Shechem XII was heavily destroyed — which fits very well with the goings-on under Abimelech, here dated to the 1130s (or possibly a little later). Thus the story of Late Bronze II and Iron IA Shechem matches such information as we have from the biblical record, and goes far to explain the reason why there was no conquest (or conquest record) of Shechem.[132]

(f) Life and Affairs in Philistia[133]

The dating of the main arrival and initial settlement of the Philistines in southwest Canaan was reviewed above (cf. pp. 137-38). The eighth year of Ramesses III (ca. 1180/1177) is and will remain the basic date for that situation, and no amount of casuistry can change it. On their way to Egypt (whence they were rebuffed by the pharaoh), the Philistines evidently destroyed the late Canaanite towns at Ashdod (XIV), Ascalon (Late Bronze II, old "stage V"), and Ekron (VIIIA). Virtually undug in modern terms, Gaza and Gath cannot yet be assessed.

Then Ashdod (XIII-XII), Ascalon (Iron I, "old stage VI"), and Ekron

(VII) were soon rebuilt as new, walled cities, whose fine wares were the distinctive monochrome (Mycenaean IIIC types), followed by the more vivid bichrome at around 1150.[134] Kept out of Egypt (except for some prisoners taken), the Philistines instead took power over southwesternmost Canaan. Before these events (and before 1180), but stated to be after Joshua's death, the reputed raid by Judah against Gaza, Ascalon, and Ekron would fall at the very end of the thirteenth century, as did Merenptah's attack on Ascalon slightly earlier (within 1213-1210). However, these raids (like many others) may not be detectable in the limited dug remains excavated from this period.

Between about 1175 and 1070 the book of Judges has almost nothing to say about Philistines, concentrating on troubles from the north and east. The guerrilla strike by Shamgar "son of Anath" (or, Bin-Anath) against Philistines (Judg. 3:31) would come anytime after circa 1175, once the latter had begun to make their presence felt. Neither Canaanites nor Israelites would welcome these intruders' enforced claims on territory they themselves owned or sought. "Shamgar bin (son of) Anath" may well be a simple abbreviation for "Shamgar [bin (son of)] Bin-Anath." The latter name is attested at this same period under Ramesses III, being borne then by a chief physician Bin-Anath (of Canaanite origin?), known from a tomb chapel door fragment, almost certainly from Saqqara, cemetery of the capital, Memphis.[135]

Most of Samson's colorful adventures, understandably, do not lend themselves to archaeological commentary. The town of Timnah (scene of his first known amour, Judg. 14–15) was most likely the present-day ruin at Tel Batash; the Philistine stratum is level V, a well-built township.[136] But Gaza saw his end (Judg. 16), when the blinded warrior pulled down two columns in the local temple, destroying his foes and himself in its overthrow. Most typical Palestinian temples, especially local Canaanite designs, had few columns (except sometimes a pair at the entrance), and they offer no light on Samson's last exploit. But Philistine temples may have drawn for inspiration on the Aegean world whence they had indubitably come. In Cyprus at Kition was found a series of five temples; in the twelfth century Temples 4 and 5 (particularly the latter) consisted of rectangular roofed halls supported by slim pillars (in pairs in no. 5) with the sanctuary at the rear end and main entrance at one side at the front.[137] If some such structure once stood at Gaza, then after his public performances for his captors, a Samson could have been allowed inside such a temple for a pause, have pulled in the middle pair of columns, and the overweight of people on its roof would have led to its speedy and progressive collapse.

(ii) Theology, Literary Motifs, Demography

(a) The "Deuteronomic Pattern"

As has long been observed, the writer of Judges followed a very consistent thought pattern in his account of his six main actors, from Othniel to Samson, having set out his theme concisely in 2:16-19. It is what was above abbreviated DPCD: the Israelites *disobey* their deity's requirements, he *punishes* their disobedience, then they show *contrition,* and he *delivers* them (through a "judge") from their affliction (oppressors). And ever since the late nineteenth century, this kind of presentation of Hebrew history has been dubbed "Deuteronomic," and was quintessentially expressed in such formulations as we find in Deut. 28:15–30:10 (misdated to 621), and then in the monarchy-period prophets, especially the late seventh- to early sixth-century prophet Jeremiah.[138]

However, despite what has been enunciated in a vacuum with almost fanatical insistence from before the 1880s to the present, such a concept and scheme of belief was *not* first invented in 621, or in fact as late as the mid–first millennium B.C. at all. In the biblical world, this whole concept is much older. Thus, from Egypt in the thirteenth to twelfth centuries we have the clearest possible witnesses to this kind of theology, set on a modest personal plane. The village at Deir el-Medina in Western Thebes was home to the royal workmen who cut and decorated the tombs of the pharaohs in the Valleys of the Kings and Queens during the Eighteenth to Twentieth Dynasties, in the period from 1500 to 1070. Within that span, especially about 1290-1140, we have a wealth of inscribed pieces left us by these workmen, including votive inscriptions on stelae presented to their deities. Here again is DPCD, and not even by theologians! The most famous was left by the Draftsman Nebre on behalf of his erring son the Draftsman Nakhtamun (now Berlin 20377). We learn that Nakhtamun had, "because of his wrongdoing" (i.e., *disobedience*) in the sight of the god Amun, been *punished* with sickness and was "ill and close to death." Then came *contrition* — "supplications were made in his (Amun's) presence" — and "He (Amun) *delivered* the Draughtsman Nakhtamun," for "in mercy, Amun turned around."[139] Pure Deuteronomic concept! And at about 1260, at the time of that imaginary Deuteronomist, the supposedly "mythical" Moses. Nor is this piece an isolated one; the same concept also comes through clearly in other, briefer inscriptions of the period. It is no fluke.

On a royal level, with the eclipse of the "heretic" pharaoh Akhenaten, and restoration of the old "normative" Egyptian religion under Tutankhamun about 1330, we find the same concept in operation. On his great stela (Cairo CGC 34183), this king observes that (thanks to Akhenaten's deliberate neglect) "their (the gods') shrines were decayed into mounds of rubble . . . as though they had never been [*disobedience*]. The land was in calamity, as the gods forsook this land. (So), if the army was sent to Syria, it had no success. If one prayed to a god . . . or a goddess, they would not come at all [*punishment*]." The new king sought to restore matters. "His Majesty made monuments for the gods, . . . building their sanctuaries anew," plus many other benefits for Egypt's slighted gods. *Contrition.* So now, "the gods and goddesses in this land rejoice; . . . exultation is (now) throughout this land, because a good (state of) aff[air]s has now come about." *Deliverance.*[140] But neither Tutankhamun nor the Draftsman Nebre had to wait till 621 to employ or express such convictions. And neither need anybody else wait so long, not even the Hebrews. These concepts were common coin from at least the second millennium, if not before.

What the author of Judges did was first give his title time line and present the collapse of inner drive and outward success as the Hebrews fell away from Joshua's ideals (1:1–2:15). Next he stated his work's principle (2:16-19), and then exemplified it in the rest of his book, from the lives and exploits of his six main characters, and intercalating one, then two, then three others to round out his picture, finally ending with two pictures of deep moral failure in a leaderless Israel. To do so he drew on the historical traditions available to him, selecting appropriate cases by which to exemplify his theme. This was long-hallowed method in the biblical world: not to invent history, but to use real history to illustrate deity's dealings with humanity. So did Tutankhamun, so did the final author of Judges, and so did many others long before and long after, throughout that world.

(b) A Literary Usage: Triumph Hymns

The two famous poems in Exod. 15 and Judg. 5 are part of a whole genre of such compositions, triumph hymns to celebrate victory or dominion, attested from the later third millennium and best known from the second half of the second. A thousand years before a Miriam or a Deborah, Uni of Egypt sang the triumph of his troops in Canaan with repeated two-line "verses," each beginning with "This army has returned in peace," followed by a differing variant line in each of its seven verses.[141] In the Middle Kingdom (early second millennium), triumphalist hymns honor Sesostris I and III. At the height of Egypt's New Kingdom in the fifteenth to thirteenth centuries, pharaohs such as Tuthmosis III, Amenophis III, and Ramesses II in particular caused to be set up such splendid hymnic texts in honor of themselves and of Amun, their giver of victory. Across the Fertile Crescent, Tukulti-Ninurta I (1245-1207) celebrated his might in an "epic" with hymnal passages.[142] The poems of Exod. 15 and Judg. 5 are the Hebrew counterparts to such works, celebrating the victories of their lord, YHWH, over his and their foes.[143] Their archaic date has been propounded by Cross and others, and there is no compelling factual reason for doubt.

(c) Tribal Constitution and Sanctuary as Focus

(1) Presence of Tribes within the Community of "Israel"

In all the biblical sources so far considered (Numbers, Joshua, Judges, 1 Sam. 1–7), early Israel is consistently shown as a group of twelve tribes (strictly, eleven plus two "sibling tribes" as one), each tracing its descent from an eponymous ancestor, and these having a common ultimate parent (for the siblings, grandparent), one Jacob or Israel. This phenomenon was not peculiar to early Israel.

But from the united monarchy onward, tribal organization was increasingly replaced in political/economic roles by other arrangements, and was limited more to family matters. As we have seen (chap. 4 above), Solomon imposed a new twelve-district system on Israel (without Judah) for revenue purposes. The twin monarchy period saw *not* a return politically to a multitribal Israelite federation, but instead a straight, single cleavage between Judah (including Simeon, plus tiny Benjamin) and the northern rest (becoming a lesser kingdom of "Israel"). Ordinary people and families kept their tribal ancestry, and heads of tribes may still have been recognized within their traditional areas socially, but all (politically) were either citizens of Judah or Israel (down to 722), and thereafter only of Judah (to 586) or of the occupying Great Powers.

There is no factual basis of any kind for denying the premonarchic reality of early Israel's tribal structure as a federation of officially related tribes with a claimed common ancestor of that name.

Quite the contrary. In the early poem in Judg. 5, precisely such a federation is clearly attested (with omission of only two out of twelve tribes), and the substantial independence of its tribal units under the overall umbrella of "Israel" is very noticeable.[144] Thus, six tribes are hailed for their response to Deborah's call: Ephraim, Benjamin, Machir (poetic variant for Manasseh), Zebulon (all, in v. 14), Issachar (15), and Naphtali (18). Castigated for indifference were four more: Reuben (15-16), Gilead (for Gad, dominant there), Dan, and Asher (17). Of the political units, that accounts for ten out of twelve tribes/sibling-tribes. Only Judah and Simeon do not feature at all in this essentially northern war, being south of the hostile "Jerusalem divide." Levi did not count; their place was cultic, with the tabernacle, not as warriors. So, in about 1160, we already have an almost full roster of the traditional twelve tribes; things would hardly have been different in the barely fifty years back to 1210 and beyond. So, our early biblical evidence is clear, unequivocal, and requires to be respected.

Merenptah's reported clash with Israel in 1209 was thus with members of a federal group who, together, made up that entity so hated by some Old Testament scholars: "all Israel." But this phrase has its own set of usages that must be respected. It does mean all the Israelites in such a context as crossing the Jordan (Josh. 3:1, 17; but excluding, even there, the families of Reuben, Gad, and East Manasseh). Otherwise it has reference *not* to every man, woman, and child, but to a limited representation. We find it implicitly used of the raiding force (Josh. 10:15, 43) drawn *from* the tribes, but *not* being the total tribes. And on major occasions such as Joshua's farewell or the covenant renewal at Shechem, "all Israel" is explicitly defined as "their elders, leaders, judges and officers" (Josh. 23:2; 24:1), and *not* the entire Hebrew populace. As others have pointed out, Deborah's triumph hymn presupposes and invokes not only a tribal structure but also its overall confederal identity as "Israel" (Judg. 5:2, 3, 5, 7-10). Modern opposition to the phrase and concept of "all Israel" is ultimately frivolous and without any factual foundation. The people that Merenptah's troops fought against evidently identified themselves to their foreign foe as Israelites, *not* as just Judeans, Ephraimites, or whatever. And Merenptah's troops were actually there to know about it; our modern biblicists were not.

Nor is a confederal entity made up of constituent tribes to be regarded as in any way just peculiar to Israel. It is a well-attested social format long before and after early Israel's premonarchic epoch. Half a millennium before that we have multitribal confederations around Mari, mentioned in its archives for the Middle Euphrates area. Thus the Mare-Yamina were a federation of such tribes as the Ubrabum, Yakhrurum, Amnanum, Yarikhum, and Rabbayum. These tribes in turn were made up of clans such as the Bit-Awin, whose community included a village and pastoralists *(khibrum)*. The Suteans also were made up of at least three tribes, the Almuti and two others, their names now lost. Of the Haneans, we have mention of at least eight or ten tribes (perhaps more).[145] Thus an Israel with a dozen tribes some centuries later is in no way exceptional among western Semites in the second millennium.

During succeeding centuries in the highly conservative world of ancient pre-Islamic south Arabia, analogous confederal/tribal structures are to be seen. At the top level, the rulers of Saba (Sheba) already from the tenth to the fifth centuries were entitled "paramount ruler" (*mukarrib*, lit. "uniter") and headed a Sabaean-led federation of the main Old South Arabian local realms, this being then expressed by the *Bundesformular,* or "formula of federation," used during the seventh century, from Karibil Watar I to Sumhu'ali Yanuf (ca. 685, 610), who mustered "the whole community of the gods and patron(-deitie)s, and of the alliance and the rite(?)"[146] At a step down socially, and especially in later times, the major tribal confederations in and around Saba had three or four constituent tribes, often therefore called "thirds" or "fourths." And these in turn had clans and families further down still.[147] So, from the foothills east of the Taurus to Iran, as far as the Arabian Sea, and from the nineteenth century B.C. to the third century A.D., we have similar profiles to that exhibited by early Israel. It is normal, even customary usage, not a late, artificial concoction.

(2) Amphictyony and Focal Sanctuary?

Already in Joshua's time the portable tabernacle (shelter for the ark of the covenant) was set up at Shiloh (Josh. 18:1), and there it (or its cult) stayed most of the time down to Eli and Samuel's epoch, into the mid–eleventh century. It remained a focus for annual festivals down to that time (cf. 1 Sam. 1–2). Throughout that time it was doubtless a focus for the religious element in the Hebrew population, but it played no part in the swirl of politics, with invasions and deliverances by force of arms, any more than most other shrines in antiquity. Its role was modest.

However, this did not stop Martin Noth from comparing the Hebrew twelve-tribe confederacy of Israel, and its shrine, with the amphictyonies of classical Greece, far westward across the sea, almost a thousand miles away, and (in present knowledge) dating from the sixth century B.C., half a millennium later than early Israel.[148] The closest in format was that of Delphi with twelve member-towns, who allied to maintain the cults of Demeter and Apollo, and to limit warlike acts amongst themselves. After a long period of popularity, biblical scholars rejected most of Noth's detailed comparisons and suppositions, and (throwing out the baby with the bathwater) ditched the whole concept. However, we do not need a distant Greek analogue to the Hebrew tribal groups and their shrine. One objection was to Noth's dating of the twelve-tribe lists, with Gen. 29–30, 49 (starting with Jacob's children) varying from the later list (of descendant tribes) in Num. 26, in that order and as premonarchic.[149] Some have wished to down-date or even reverse the chronological period and order of these lists (e.g., invoking attribution to the theoretical "document" P, of the sixth/fifth century B.C.). This is invalid; there is no factual reason for subjectively down-dating or reversing the date of the Genesis or Numbers lists. P is an imaginary source (we have no surviving physical manuscript of it), and in any case it could retain record of material much older than its own supposed date of composition, if it were real. The objection is also made that the Greek model is centered on the cult and shrine(s) while the Hebrew one is not. This is perfectly true; the comparison is an incomplete one, because the emphases are distinct as between two culturally separate but outwardly similar institutions. Both have a common sanctuary, both have a group of related tribes linked to the shrine, but physical upkeep of the shrine is central to the purpose of one group (Greeks) but not the other (Hebrews).

However, as long since proposed, there were analogous institutions much nearer home, in the Near East. Hallo gave a detailed account of a Neo-Sumerian "amphictyony" of twelve or more cities that contributed supplies on a twelve-monthly basis to the upkeep of the cults of the holy Sumerian city of Nippur, under the rulers of the Third Dynasty of Ur circa 2000. As with Greece, the central temples were the focus of attention.[150] The Philistine pentapolis has also been compared, as a five-member league, with focus on the temple of Dagon at Gaza; this is possible, but largely inferential.[151] At the end of the day, the Sumerian and possible Philistine examples simply show that groups in the Near East could have central sanctuaries that they supported, and could form federations for other purposes such as defense. Alongside these concrete cases the Hebrew tribal federation can stand, with its shrine. The better comparison is with tribal federations, as at Mari and in early Arabia, already noted above. The Greek comparison is interesting, but distant and ultimately superfluous.

B. OVERALL ARCHAEOLOGICAL BACKGROUND

In the last quarter-century current knowledge of the processes of settlement, de-settlement, and resettlement in Middle Bronze to Iron Age Canaan has been transformed, both by excavations at individual sites and by far-reaching and (at times) very thorough surface surveys. The gain in practical data is considerable. But given the differing intellectual starting points of the variety of scholars interested — both on the field and off it — much disagreement on the conclusions to be drawn has arisen and continues, not least on two issues: interaction with the biblical data and questions of ethnicity (Israelite or other).

Here, in adherence to our brief, we shall seek to be as factually based as possible, in dealing both with the biblical text as a transmitted artifact and with the rich if intricate external materials. Neither source is complete. Joshua-Judges were *never* intended to serve later generations as a mini-encyclopedic handbook to Hebrew history in what we call Iron IA. And in terms of external data, most mounds remain undug; the dug ones are rarely dug beyond 5 to 10 percent of their area; and surveys on the surface can never tell the whole story. So there can never be given a complete account of the Early Iron Age or of early Israel in the period circa 1220-1020. Only outlines are possible.

(i) A Biblical Recap

Before plunging into the archaeology or the attendant controversies, let us quickly encapsulate the basic biblical data — what they *are*, not what they are too often misread to "mean." Leaving aside rhetorical end flourishes, the narratives give us:

1. After crossing the Jordan, the two Jericho/Ai gateway settlements were destroyed and burned.
2. The area up to Shechem was open (no resistance), such that rites could be enacted at Mount Ebal.
3. Gibeon submitted, south Canaanite kings reacted, and Joshua defeated them. This turned into a rapid-action raid, with Joshua attacking towns, killing their chiefs (and others), and *returning to base at Gilgal*.
4. North Canaanite kings reacted, so Joshua fought and slew them, and raided their towns. Only Hazor, the most renowned, was burned down. Again, he *returned to base at Gilgal*. No occupation!
5. Allotments were determined for *future* occupation. During this time there was only local occupation up to Shechem/Tirzah, and the tabernacle moved up to Shiloh. Joshua renewed the covenant at Shechem. By his death, only the *beginnings* of local occupation had happened — Gilgal-Tirzah, perhaps Hebron.

So, first, leaving aside the obligatory rhetorical summations, the book of Joshua does *not* present a sweeping conquest/instant occupation, whether espoused by Albright or anyone else.

Second, despite numberless assertions to the contrary, Judges does *not* give us either an alternative narrative of conquest or a connected account of ongoing settlement. It actually gives us the following picture:

a. Soon after Joshua's death, listed in south to north order, Judges enumerates the subsequent attempts by individual tribes to enact a takeover in their allotted areas. In the south: Judah had quick success at Bezeq, Negev (and Hebron area), and in the hills, but failed to hold any place in the southwest plains, or Jerusalem. The latter repulsed Benjamin (after refortification?). In the center: Ephraim/Manasseh took Bethel, but not the lowland towns to the west or Jezreel; Dan was hemmed in, and some Danites went north to Laish. In the north: Zebulon, Asher, and Naphtali made very little headway.
b. By way of "occupation" the Benjaminites had to settle alongside Jebusites,

and the central and northern tribes also had to settle alongside the Canaanites, even if eventually getting the upper hand socially. All this (all in Judg. 1) was clearly in the decade or so immediately after Joshua, and was then commented on theologically in Judg. 2:1–3:6.

c. *But after this point,* the main narratives *never again* tell us about the settlement process. They only tell us about crises that brought forth local leaders as deliverers from foreign rule. *There is no ongoing biblical "narrative of settlement"!* At the end, we have only the notice of some Danites' move to Laish, and a civil war with Benjamin. Nothing more. Thus, contrary to common dogma, Judges does *not* give us an "alternative conquest" but instead notes some attempts at forcing takeovers, plus settling in next to locals, soon after Joshua, as a follow-up to his declared allotments. Of the ongoing settlement thereafter, we are told *nothing,* simply because it would contribute nothing to the author's main theme. For that he drew upon occasions of crisis and oppression of Hebrew groups by others. Full stop.

(ii) Archaeology, Part I: Changing Settlement Patterns

By now, all serious students of the archaeology of Canaan are (or should be) aware of the basic changes visible from the excavated record from Middle Bronze through Late Bronze into Iron I (ca. 1900-1000).[152]

1. Middle Bronze Age II witnessed a period (ca. 1900-1550) both prosperous and populous in Canaan, boasting a series of fortified towns and rich material culture.

2. But in the sixteenth to thirteenth centuries, Late Bronze I-II, the New Kingdom pharaohs incorporated Canaan into the Egyptian empire, draining the region through taxation, and in reply to rebellions occasionally destroyed and deported them. The culture suffered, and population and number of settlements visibly declined.[153]

3. Then new factors came in circa 1230 onward, clearly attested in the first-hand Egyptian texts. Rebuffed by Egypt (ca. 1177), the Sea Peoples ended up in Canaan — the Pilisti or Philistines in the southwest, and Sikils and Shekelesh farther north (Dor, Jezreel). In Transjordan, new names appeared: Edom and Moab, plus the Ammonites (as yet unmentioned in contemporary texts). Arameans now became more prominent from the north. And, as Merenptah made crystal clear in 1209, a group called Israel was present within Canaan, most likely in the hill country. All these peo-

ples were to have a long and varied history for the next six or seven centuries. To the Egyptian-derived data correspond the Philistines, Edomites, Moabites, and Arameans named in the biblical books from Numbers to 1 Samuel — and the entity Israel, a tribal group as the Merenptah text implies, and in Canaan's hill country. So we have an outline, basic correspondence of the two sources, Egyptian and biblical. The former cannot be factually dismissed, and so neither can the latter through this general correspondence, whatever quibbles may be raised in detail. The third factor to be added to these two textual resources is the material archaeology, to which we now turn.

(iii) Archaeology, Part II: Surveys, Sites, and Viewpoints

(a) Surface Surveys

Surface surveys have been undertaken in some depth in central Canaan, notably by the Finkelstein team in the terrain of ancient Ephraim/Samaria, and by Zertal and colleagues in the adjoining territory of ancient West Manasseh. These and other surveys have shown a dramatic rise in the intensity of settlement in the hill country, especially north from Jerusalem, from around 1200 onward through Iron I. Thus the Ephraim-Samaria survey registered just 9 sites for Late Bronze I-II (with another 3, LB/Iron I), a dozen at most. Then for Iron Age phase I, they were able to list not fewer than 131 sites (plus another 94 of Iron I-II), a huge increase.[154] Next door in West Manasseh, Zertal noted some 39 sites for Late Bronze but over 200 for Iron I, again a huge increase. This great rash of farmsteads, hamlets, and small villages represents a wholly new development, as is universally admitted. In Manasseh at least, two-thirds of these sites were founded entirely new; one-third were both founded and abandoned during Iron I, while two-thirds continued to be used and developed in Iron II (monarchy period).[155] The Canaanites had been in western Palestine for centuries, and the old sites (especially outside the hill country) continued to exhibit their material culture into the twelfth century. In the southwest the Philistines soon showed their characteristic material culture, marked particularly by their monochrome and then bichrome pottery, both of ultimately Aegean inspiration. Up in the hills the innumerable small settlements at first showed Canaanite-style pottery, but quickly went their own way producing their own typically dull, utilitarian wares: storage vessels (for water and foodstuffs), cooking pots, and the like — and almost no fancy novelties. By elimination, and bearing in mind our Egyptian and biblical text indicators, these should be largely upland Israelite sites, marking not only the modest initial extent of Israelite occupation noted in Judg. 1 but also its gradual expansion throughout the hilly zones.

(b) Number-Crunching People

The practical question has to be asked (and answered) — where did all these people come from, to populate these scores and scores of new places? In aggregate and fairly quickly, they must have far outstripped the Late Bronze II population of before 1200. All estimates of population here (even rigorous ones) are subject to guesswork factors, and therefore can only be approximate. On the basis of known sites and other factors, Finkelstein suggested that about 21,000 Israelites lived in Canaan by 1150 or soon after, a figure that doubled to perhaps 51,000 by about 1000, on the eve of the united monarchy. (This is for Canaan overall; no figure is offered for other regions, such as Philistia, the western coastal plain, or the vale of Jezreel.)[156] So, on his projections, the 21,000 Hebrews of 1150 might have been somewhat less numerous back in 1210, but not appreciably. But whence arose the 21,000 (or a little less)?

(c) A Sex Orgy Theory for Israel's Origins? Hardly!

First, what about the scantily settled hill country in Late Bronze II, before 1210? In the Ephraim zone, the survey disclosed some 99 sites occupied during the Middle Bronze Age, ten times the 9 to 12 Late Bronze sites and not far behind Iron I (131), also ten times as many. In the West Manasseh zone, an initial 135 Middle Bronze sites contrast with 39 Late Bronze sites, as do the 131 (later, over 200) Iron I sites recorded — in this more prosperous region, LB is still only one-quarter or hardly more than one-fifth of MB and Iron I respectively.[157] So, even if one allows for an artifactually invisible pastoral/herding population in Late Bronze, the contrast between Late Bronze and its immediate precursors and successors is massive. Taking the change between highland Canaan in (say) 1250 and in (say) 1150, how come the population suddenly multiplied fivefold in less than a century (possibly only 50 or 60 years) as opposed to merely doubling in the 150 years between 1150 and 1000? The earlier rate of growth is frenetic! The growth during 1150-1000 may well represent normal stability, and steady but slow population growth with an appreciable infant mortality rate. If so, then the drastic fivefold growth within the decades in which Israel appears (cf. Merenptah) and spreads out into a rash of villages and hamlets is phenomenal.

If they were simply an indigenous growth, did they have a half-century of fertility-cult sex orgies to breed so many children and grandchildren on a scale hitherto unknown? The matter is bizarre, if we go for an Israelite "origin" exclusively within highland Canaan, featuring simply a societal change from a supposed transhumant herding life to settled village life, combining crop raising with livestock.

This scenario in its own right is (or should be) enough to dismiss firmly the idea that Israel arose simply from the (re?)settling down of former mobile herding folk, or from fugitive Canaanites who came up west into the highlands away from Egyptian tax collectors. That move too would have failed, because Egypt was also overlord of the hills through the city-states that did exist, such as Jerusalem and Shechem (cf. Amarna letters) — the tax collectors would simply have followed them! And taxed their cattle instead of their erstwhile crops. In short, on severely practical grounds, the "revolting peasant" and "early Hebrews indigenous to highlands" theories will not work. Their major representatives (Mendenhall, Gottwald) have already been effectively critiqued out of court, a lengthy execution process that we do need to repeat all over again here. They are (to use a favorite phrase of W. G. Dever) a "dead issue," as is his own adherence to the "indigenous" theory in a symbiosis version (but firmly dismissing the "revolting peasant" type of theory).[158]

(d) Back to Practicality: Go West, Young Man!

So we may look again at the archaeology. In both the Ephraim and Manasseh surveys, there stands out a feature which has to be explained; namely, that the new occupation by the highland Iron I populace (Israelite or not) moved initially from east to west. This is noted repeatedly by Finkelstein, and illustrated most graphically by Zertal. He was able to show that, through time, the fashion in cooking pots (or at least in the forms of their rims) changed. Ah, fickle, fashion-minded Hebrew housewives! Phase A pots had an outturned ("everted") rim of triangular section. These dominated in use in the first period (Zertal: late thirteenth century), and gave way to phase B–style pots having a thinner, flangelike rim (Zertal: twelfth century), and these in turn by a phase C style, with a curved rim with a narrow lip all round it (Zertal: eleventh century). But there is a geographical dimension to all this. The phase A fashion at its height (over 20 percent of cooking pots) dominated down the *east* side of Manasseh, spreading out westward. In the central zone and westward these pots were less fashionable (5 to 20 percent maximum), and many west-central sites had none — they were founded after their replacement by phases B and C vessels. B and C dominated westward. A similar east-west trend can be seen in the popularity of punctured decoration on the pottery, waning westward and later.[159]

Naturally, more than one theory can be offered for this phenomenon, in Ephraim and Manasseh alike. Finkelstein (wedded to the indigenous Israelite theory) would read all this to mean simply that the herding people put down their first roots along the eastern marches, good for grain and cattle. Then, continuing their settling process, they extended westward to zones of more horticultural type.[160] This is all very well, but falls foul of the population explosion reviewed above, which his view (and Dever's) cannot realistically accommodate.

So, what is the alternative? It is humiliatingly simple (which restless, oversophisticated minds hate). The biblical traditions overall are unanimous that Israel came from Egypt (a matter for chap. 6) and that they *entered* Canaan — prior to Joshua they had *not* lived in Canaan, by tradition, for centuries when their claimed ancestors passed that way ending up in Egypt. We have already seen that there is nothing inherently to prove positively otherwise, and that sundry features in Numbers to Judges find good background in our external sources. So, if a body of between 10,000 and 20,000 people came into a highland Canaan sparsely inhabited by hardly a fifth or a quarter of that number (4,000/5,000?) in the fifty or so sites of Ephraim and Manasseh plus a few more from the Benjamin district down to the Negev, then no wonder the population shot up between (say) 1250 and 1150. Sex orgy not needed! The incomers were indeed pastoralists. Their ancestors were such when entering Egypt (cf. Gen. 45:10; 46:6; 46:32–47:6; etc.), they left Egypt with livestock (Exod. 10:26; 12:38), and they held and acquired more in Mishor and Gilead east of the Jordan (Num. 20:19; 31:25-47; 32:1-4; Josh. 1:14). So, if early Israel did indeed cross from east of the Jordan into Canaan by Gilgal and Jericho, and then moved up into the hill country, the cattle-and-grain culture of the eastern zone there would have suited them well, from which they would have spread westward in due time. Problem in essence solved. An immigration movement from east to west is also proposed by Zertal, with variations in detail, e.g., siting of Gilgal(s).[161]

(e) Egyptian Politics

Why did Merenptah suddenly have to crush revolt so near home in Canaan as Ascalon and Gezer, tackle long-quiet Yenoam, and get involved with Israel, within his Years 1-4 (1213-1210)?[162] In ancient Near Eastern empires like those of New Kingdom Egypt or Assyria, it was commonplace for the accession of a new king to be greeted by revolt in those distant provinces that hoped thereby to secure their independence. But here we have something different: not a revolt in more distant regions such as Phoenicia or south Syria (e.g., Upe), but close to home in Canaan, even (Ascalon, Gezer) right under Pharaoh's nose! This was not normal. This suggests that there were specific reasons for the Egyptian attack on these places. The critical criterion of a vassal's loyalty was payment of tribute. Failure to do so constituted rebellion. Ever since Tuthmosis III (1479-1425), this matter had been paramount. And from Lachish, for example, comes an ostracon, usually considered to be of Merenptah's reign, that once recorded harvest tax payable in Year 4 (1210) to the Egyptian authorities.[163] But if these towns, Gezer and Ascalon (and maybe Yenoam?), could not, hence did not, pay their tax, then Pharaoh's army would normally march out to collect it. If marauding bands such as some of Joshua's (or the elders') Israelites had come down from the hills at harvest and stolen the grain crops of these two towns, then the latter might well have had trouble in providing their grain-tax quotas to the pharaoh's commissioners, and had to be cowed into coughing up somehow.

Looking for the source of the trouble, the Egyptian force had then ascended briefly into the hills to chase these bandits known as "Israel," and knocked off a few of them, by way of warning. An Egyptian fort at modern Lifta ("Well of Me[rn]eptah") may have been established to reinforce the vassal state of Jerusalem against them. One king of Gezer had earlier been worsted by Joshua's raiders (Josh. 10:33), and a little later some Judean raiders may have penetrated briefly to Ascalon and its grainfields (cf. Judg. 1:18). So we might conceivably — but not certainly — have an interesting panorama here, hitherto unsuspected. Up north, Yenoam may have had similar trouble.

It is worth remarking that, along with the Song of Deborah barely half a century later, Merenptah's mention virtually proves the antiquity of the concept of "all Israel." His troops encountered people who called themselves *not* Judahites or Benjaminites or Manassites, etc., but *Israelites;* and others (at Ascalon and Gezer?) who termed them likewise. And of course, automatically the whole group of these people could only be called "all Israel," precisely as Deborah did later, in the poetical context of happening to name ten of the twelve/thirteen tribal groups that already made up Israel. Let us have no more silly claims that "all Israel" was a much later concept; Merenptah and Deborah during 1210 to 1160 forbid such an academic faux pas.

(f) Ethnicity — with Porkers and Porkies (or, Pigs and Fibs)

Or, nudged by Hershel Shanks, as Professor Dever has so delightfully put it, "how to tell an Israelite from a Canaanite." A 64,000 dollar (shekel?) question!

Much discussion has centered on the presence in Palestinian sites of four-room houses, collared-rim jars, and use of (sometimes plastered) cisterns. However, these items are at least in part a delusion. It is known that so-called four-roomed houses occur outside the territory of ancient Israel. They became typical of early Israel, and continued in Israelite use long after our Iron I period. Likewise, the collared-rim jar was not unique to early Israel. However, the combination of the two is typical of sites within the acknowledged Israelite areas. Storage pits are very common in Iron I sites within the areas probably settled by early Israel, but these are not water cisterns. Plastered cisterns were not an Iron I innovation, but occur in both Neolithic and Late Bronze periods. On the other hand, it has been suggested that the use of agricultural terraces to exploit hill slopes does date from the thirteenth and twelfth centuries, following on tree clearances.[164] As for pottery, the earliest stuff at the early Iron I sites is closely related to outgoing Late Bronze II wares, but in due course the typical utilitarian Iron I wares were developed that are no longer Canaanite in nature or definition. These have become "early Israelite," but possibly could have been adopted also by other highland people (Jebusites, Horites, etc.).

A further factor recently brought into play is ancient diet. In twelfth-century Canaan, pig bones occur in food refuse in some areas and not in others. As food, pigs were popular in the Philistine-dominated area in southwest Canaan, were acceptable in Transjordan (Amorite/early Ammonite), but were seemingly taboo in highland Canaan in the particular region that exhibits the rash of new, small Iron I settlements (plus such as Shiloh and Mount Ebal) and is the habitat of earliest Israel in the narratives of Joshua/Judges. The practices observed there (use of sheep and goat, and perhaps a form of deer) do indeed correspond to the limits set by the dietary laws of Lev. 11. This fact, of course, clashes badly with old-fashioned a priori nineteenth-century theory that such laws must be "late" in date of origin (even postexilic).[165] But mere theory *cannot* ever be sacrosanct, and *must* give way to contrary facts if or when such facts surface. Thus, objections to this excavated phenomenon (archaeological data being primary, as Dever would put it) that are based on slavish adherence to old-style theory are simply not valid, and *must* give way to new facts. The best explicit evidence for an Israel-group in Canaan by 1200/1160 is the mention by Merenptah and the cohesive summary in Deborah's early poem; physical substance is given to these written sources by the archaeological recovery of the settlements, material culture, and way of life in highland Canaan. The latter work may not determine "ethnicity" rigidly,[166] but does give practical form to our knowledge of the people(s) named, whether Canaanites, Philistines, Israelites, each in their main zones.

(g) Sites and Sanctuaries? Shiloh

The situation at Shiloh in the twelfth-eleventh centuries, we have looked at compactly above, under Saul (chap. 4 above, p. 83). The Iron I phase at the site was violently destroyed about 1050 or so, in line with the veiled allusions in Jer. 7:12-14 and Ps. 78:60-61. There is no reason to view Shiloh in Iron I as anything other than an early Israelite center, amidst an area of considerable early Israelite settlement. On its tribal federal role, purely religiously, cf. already above, pp. 96-97.

(1) The "Bull Site"[167]

On top of a high ridge (Dhahrat et-Tawileh), within range of a cluster of small sites largely of Iron I date, was found a bronze bull figurine, and then a circular stone wall, with entry(?) from the east, whose southeast quadrant contained a broader-than-tall upright stone (about two feet by three feet) behind flat paving. Here were found lower parts of two pottery bowls, a bronze fragment, and a pottery fragment attributed to a possible cult stand; no ash was found, but "a few bones." Most of the north half of the enclosure was eroded, so any further installations are lost. The walled circle is about twenty-one meters (about seventy feet) east-west, and would have been about twenty-three meters (about seventy-five feet) north-south. The remains of a stone wall, parallel with the south-side entry wall, seem to be intended to close off the stone-and-pavement area.

From these details, what may one deduce? A "domestic" explanation might suggest either a shepherd's stone hut and enclosure, with bench stone and clean pavement for his bundle and few crocks and flints. A small flock could be corralled in the enclosure. It is certainly not a farmstead way up on a crest, unless erosion has been much more severe than envisaged hitherto. Or, was it a guard post, whence messages about advancing foes might be quickly carried down to the villages below? But it does not overlook its own nearby valley. But what about the bull figurine (and possible cult stand)? Again, no final proof of anything beyond perhaps a figure and offering stand for domestic or personal cult in this upland outpost — either of Baal-Hadad (if Canaanite) or else (if Israelite) of YHWH (or even Baal?), considered invisibly standing above the bull, symbol of power, if one thinks of Exod. 32:1-8 (a golden calf of YHWH) and of 1 Kings 12:25-33 (Jeroboam I's golden calves at Bethel and Dan).

Viewed minimalistically in this way, the "bull site" would lose its mystique, but not much else. It is perfectly possible that, in fact, it served — also, or exclusively — as a hilltop local shrine for the surrounding Iron I (Israelite) villagers during the first half of the twelfth century, before falling out of use. In which case it would have served as a local "high place," as originally advocated by its excavator, Amihai Mazar, and the stone and pavement as its focus, plus the bull and presumed cult stand. The precise nature of whatever rites were possibly celebrated is not clear. Bowls may suggest drink offerings or libations, and/or a flour and oil "grain offering" (for the latter, cf. Lev. 2; 7:11-18). The bones are not specified — modest sacrifices might have been made; cf. the regular cult at the tabernacle some thirty miles to the south at Shiloh (Num. 28; and later in degenerate form, 1 Sam. 2:12-16). Such a cult would save the locals a sixty- or seventy-mile round-trip to Shiloh except for occasional visits for major annual feasts.

(2) Mount Ebal

This is the most controverted of our three putative Iron I shrines. During 1982-89, A. Zertal excavated a stone ruin on a ridge on the northeast upper flank of Mount Ebal, but below its summit. Within a large area enclosed by low walls, an upper area was further walled off to form an inner enclosure, reached by a flight of three broad, shallow steps. Within that area stood a rectangular stone structure. The site was used during two phases of Iron I, within broadly 1220-1150: strata II (earlier) and I (later), in a simple rebuild (no violent destruction), the dating being confirmed by two late Ramesses II scarabs. So far, so good, with little in dispute.[168]

Exactly under the center of the later, square structure (stratum I) was a stone circle and rectangular floor (Stratum II) of a compartmented building containing ash and animal bones — function not certain. In front of it more circles occurred (later included within twin open areas before the solid stone structure). These contained either pottery vessels (now empty of original contents) or else more bones and ash. A second building was a four-room house, with store jars in compartments; various hearths were found around the site. At this first period, the only enclosure was the inner one (west side at least). Up till now, minimalistically, there is nothing needfully cultic about all this (theoretically, a regular bivouac spot for herdsmen?). But one could argue for a site where meals and modest offerings had been made from time to time, for whatever reason.

With the later stratum (I), the fun begins. According to the excavator's full results (after four seasons), the big square stone structure was then built with twin forecourts in front. These were divided by a stone structure that ran up against the front of the great square block. As preserved, it looked like a ramp to the block's top. Around the whole area was built a far larger enclosure of very low walling. The square structure had twin internal dividing walls (with a gap between), and the hollow interior was filled with layers of stone, earth, and ashes (including animal bones), then leveled off. But, what was it? After a brief visit to just the first season of excavation, Kempinski had proposed a theory of three strata: the first, the simple structures of Zertal's early stratum II; the second, the twin courts of Zertal's stratum I, plus the walling beyond flanking the central block (dotting in a theoretical rear and middle wall); and his third, the central block plus the supposed ramp (also Zertal's stratum I) as sidewall of a room as successor to one court. Thereby he hoped to gain a simple site (as with Zertal), then a farmhouse, and a watchtower and adjunct. However, full excavation rules out the farmhouse (of very peculiar plan), leaving only the block, twin courts, and wall or ramp, plus about one hundred stone installations around, half of them with either domestic or small votive vessels. A watchtower base/foundation (approached by a ramp between the twin courts) was still a feasible solution, structurally. (The tower itself might have been of brick or timber, all gone.) This view is not beyond objection. One is that the contemporary Iron I watchtower at Giloh has a quite different foundation block of solid fill and no inner partition walls. The Iron II tower there does have such walls, but one main one across, buttressed by crosswalls; so it is not a full parallel and is very much later, by up to 500 years.[169] Also, not being on Ebal's mountaintop, a tower's views would be limited to the road north from Shechem toward Tirzah. So the tower theory is open to some doubt.

Thus, not at the beginning of the excavation (as Kempinski mistakenly reported) but in the third season only, in 1983, a remark by David Etam on the format of the hollow square with a fill led him and Zertal to propose that this was a solid-state equivalent of the tabernacle's altar, of a hollow set of boards to set over an earthen fill. Here was a stone frame with roughly earthen fill. They also proposed that the rear walls and rear projecting walls from the twin courts (plus the lower wall down the left side of the ramp) might be a precursor to the side ramps/ledges of the Herodian altar. Hence the structure would have been a large altar within a low-walled precinct that saw service briefly within circa 1220-1150. For Zertal it was but a short step then to invoke Deut. 27:1-26 and Josh. 8:30-35. Moses commanded, and Joshua performed, a ceremony of building an altar on Mount Ebal for sacrifices (and for the people to feast), and inscribing the "Law" (covenant) on plastered stones, besides the rite of cursing and blessing in front of the twin mountains Ebal and Gerizim.

There is nothing inherently impossible in such a view — nor can one prove it to be correct. Large, open enclosures are not needfully sacred areas; witness the farmstead at Giloh, or Zertal's enclosure at El-Unuq near the Jordan. As Zertal's overall survey found no other structure of this period anywhere in the ample acres of Mount Ebal, there is, of course, the temptation to clinch the matter directly in favor of his view. But preservation of monuments across thirty-two centuries is a chancy business. If it were the site of Joshua's ceremonies, then one must say that no scrap of the inscribed plastered stones has survived. Nor could we reasonably expect it in so very exposed a context. If that is so, then in theory Joshua's altar might once have stood elsewhere on Ebal, and have been long since wiped out completely; far greater edifices than it have suffered such a fate.

The final verdict? At present, strictly, *non liquet*. There is no final proof or disproof for either a watchtower or an altar complex (of Joshua or otherwise). It is noteworthy that the fiercest opposition to the specter of Joshua's altar has come from minds not open to such revolutionary possibilities. Thus, all that Kempinski could finally offer against the concept was the old views about the theoretical late (Deuteronomic) date for the books of Deuteronomy and Joshua in the seventh century, which are not fact, merely dogma. Plus an odd preference for a Samaritan-inspired shift of Joshua's efforts to Gerizim from Ebal, and the (unjustified) grumble that nobody could walk (or carry anything) up a ramp over three feet wide. None of this has any evidential value in terms of hard fact. It is also Deuteronomic disease that moved such as Dever to mock the place as a picnic site — which (as Zertal observed) is precisely a feature of such occasions (cf. Deut. 27:7 in particular; and people might eat deer even if not offering them with bull, sheep, or goat). To Rainey's charge that only the gullible would believe Zertal's claim, one may observe that such people as Coogan and Mazar (who both grant a cultic possibility) could hardly be thus dismissed. Colorful language is not the answer either. In short, Zertal's view *is* feasible, but absolute certainty eludes us.

7. A BALANCED VIEW?

So, after a long pilgrimage round Canaan and adjoining terrain, we may now sum up the results.

First, no total conquest and occupation. The book of Joshua does *not* describe a total Hebrew conquest and occupation of Canaan, real or imaginary. Read straight, its narratives describe an entry (from over the Jordan), full destruction of two minor centers (Jericho, Ai; burned), then defeat of local kings and raids through south Canaan. Towns are attacked, taken, and damaged ("destroyed"), kings and subjects killed *and then left behind, not held on to*. The same in north Canaan: strategic Hazor is fully destroyed (burned), *but no others*. The rest are treated like the southern towns, *and again left, not held*. Israel stayed based in Gilgal, then took over an inland strip from there up to Shechem and Tirzah. These preliminary successes were celebrated with war rhetoric appropriate to the time, which should not be twisted to mean what it does not. Joshua made allocations *not taken up while he yet lived*. Contrast Josh. 23:4, "nations I defeated" (but not occupied!), with 23:5, "YHWH *will* expel them, you *will* possess" (futures), plus explicitly Judg. 2:22-23. Prior to all this, in Num. 20–33, we have the Hebrews going from Qadesh-Barnea down across the central Arabah, around the northern nucleus of Edom, up to Moab, and taking over the plains of Mishor and terrain of Gilead.

Second, external data for Joshua and Numbers. We have no direct external textual references to the Israelite entry or raids or initial settlement from Gilgal to Shechem. In the later thirteenth century, Mesopotamia — in the guise of Assyria — never penetrated beyond the Euphrates into Syria proper; Hittite power at Carchemish stood against them. So no data can come on south Palestinian events (especially in the inner highlands) from that quarter. Egypt officially was overlord of Canaan, but her main interest was in the productive coastal plains, lowland hills, and Jezreel, not in the economically poorer highlands, and in keeping hold on the main routes north into Phoenicia (to Tyre, Sidon, Byblos, etc.) and to Damascus in Upe. So long as highlanders of any kind did not interfere there, and the Transjordanian groups did not interfere with the Timna (Sinai) mining works at the southern end of the Arabah, neither did Egypt bother with them. When they did, she struck back, and they got mentioned. Thus Seir and Seirites ("land" and "Mount") were attacked by Ramesses II (within ca. 1275-1260) and invaded by Ramesses III (ca. 1170); Edomites — termed Shasu, i.e., "wanderers" — came into the East Delta (Wadi Tumilat) to water their livestock under Merenptah (ca. 1206).[170] Moab was invaded by Ramesses II about 1272, who took Dibon and four other settlements. Ammon is not (yet) named by anybody, but can be defined archaeologically.[171] And finally, in 1209 (NOT 1207!), Merenptah's forces recaptured the towns of Ascalon, Gezer, and Yenoam, and defeated the people-group Israel. So the biblical data and Egyptian references are agreed on the effective existence and activity of Seir/Edom, Moab (with Dibon!), and Israel at this time, plus Ammon (which was archaeologically extant). One cannot really ask for more in the circumstances. And between Ramesses III and Siamun/Shoshenq I (time of the Hebrew monarchy), no other pharaoh is known to have campaigned in Canaan, to speak of it.

Third, the "cultural" profile of what we find in Joshua. (i) Joshua is not alone as leader of an opportunist, would-be expansionist group in Canaan or south Syria. Labayu of Shechem and Abdi-ashirta (and son, Aziru) in Amurru of the fourteenth century offer analogous profiles and (in Amurru's case) actually achieved much more than did Joshua, territorially. (ii) In the second half of the second millennium (our period), campaign reports often had the same profile as Joshua's. Divine commission might first be recorded; then the first conflicts in detail; and later campaigning in briefer, more formulaic fashion. The conquests made are summed up in topographical lists of those kings/places subdued. This we find with Tuthmosis III, in his detailed account of the first campaign (Megiddo), and much more summary record of most later campaigns, except in part for Qadesh up north; cf. Joshua, more on Hazor (his main northern foe) than on others in north Canaan. The same literary profile was already practiced by the Egyptian general Uni, invading Canaan in the late third millennium: a detailed account of his first campaign, then the dismissive remark, "His Majesty sent me to lead this [army] 5 times," with no further detail except for a pincer maneuver on the last occasion.[172] By contrast with all this, the general trend in the later first-millennium Assyrian annals is the opposite. Later editions of these are found to abbreviate or compress the accounts of the earliest campaigns and to devote more space to the latest ones. So, with Shalmaneser III, where the account of his first campaigns in (e.g.) the later annals of 842 is briefer than in accounts of 856 or 853/852.[173]

For commissioning, compare Tuthmosis IV, Merenptah, and Ramesses III, plus Mursil II of Hatti, etc. Formulaic summary of series of attacks is well exhibited in EA 185/186 of the fourteenth century. The list of places/kings with prologue in Josh. 12:7-24 is *precisely* what one might expect at this epoch; it is not "late," as some commentators would claim. Likewise the use of broad, rhetorical closing summaries (like Josh. 11:16-17). Joshua must be judged on the narratives, *not* the summaries; to do otherwise is a sure mark of ignorance. All of this is authentic usage, and good second-millennium practice.

(iii) Incidental cultural points and archaeology. The personal names of several Canaanite kings opposing Joshua are of Hurrian origin; this is a mark of the late second millennium. The Hurrian element is only vestigial later (in south Anatolia, northernmost Syria; Talmai under David), and is gone completely by circa 700. The female tavern-keeper phenomenon (cf. Rahab) is valid down to circa 1100, after which customs changed. With Achan, his punishment for sacrilegious theft is known from the eighteenth century onward; the expression used for his gold wedge is that of the late second millennium.

(iv) After the entry from the east over the Jordan, and Hebrews spread into the region north of Jerusalem (Ephraim/Manasseh), the expansion from east to west corresponds with the east-west development of pottery styles during the end of the thirteenth into the early twelfth centuries. Naturally, there is overlap in the process, as a new style did not suddenly replace totally an existing style. And in some districts (e.g., Isbet Sartah), people had moved forward (westward) quicker than in others. (v) The range of sites in use in the later thirteenth century corresponds very well with those named in Joshua and Judges. None are burned save three; so it is useless to try to determine a Hebrew "destruction" by seeking "fire streaks" in these sites, outside Hazor (abundantly evidenced, level XIII), Jericho (LB IIB, totally eroded), or Ai (situation obscure). Caught between Philistine intruders in the southwest and Hebrews dashing down from the hills just east, Canaanite commentators might well have complained about the murderous impact of beer-swilling Philistine lager-louts murdering them on the one hand (1170s; cf. fall of Lachish VI, Tel Sera IX), and earlier (ca. 1220/1210) of gung-ho Hebrew bandit gangs swarming into their townships, smashing everything in sight, killing everyone they caught, especially their rulers, and being gone as quickly as they had come. No account by them has survived, of course. But complaints to the pharaoh about the (unrelated) Apiru in the Amarna letters do show what might have been expected (again, cf. EA 185/186). (vi) The border and town lists are, again, types of documents well attested in the second millennium. And as we have them, they do *not* precisely correspond to the Hebrew holdings on the ground at any later period (not even with the "united monarchy"). They are projections for territory to be taken, not later relics of the days of Solomon, Hezekiah, Josiah, or anyone else, which epochs do not fit.

Fourth, the travels from Qadesh-Barnea to Jordan. (i) Here we have a realistic itinerary, particularly if the limited nature of Edom is understood: the main massif between Wadi Hasa (ancient Zered) and Feinan/Wadi Ghuweir, via which latter the Hebrews would have gone round Edom to pass the edges of Moab farther north. Itineraries as a genre are familiar from other early sources. (ii) There is knowledge of local peculiarities, e.g., *kewirs*. In the Negev, Arad was a kingdom with shifting centers. (iii) The Edomites and Moabites were largely tented kingdoms (as Ramesses III proves for Edom/Seir), even though the Moabites had Dibon and four other centers in the thirteenth century (Ramesses II); they were true kingdoms nevertheless (cf. early Assyria, and Manana). (iv) The archaeology of the Mishor plain and Gilead does attest occupation in Late Bronze II and Iron I, consistent with Moabite/Amorite, Ammonite, and Hebrew presences.

Fifth, the book of Judges. (i) This shows a brief tribal follow-up (in Judg. 1) to enforce a settlement *after* Joshua, with some initial success then progressive failure, leaving the Hebrews to settle among their neighbors rather than supplanting them. (ii) It contains *no further account of the settlement process*, and is thus NOT alternative to a (nonexistent) "total" conquest/occupation by

Joshua, as a persistent (and almost fanatically held) biblicist dogma would have it. Instead, it illustrates a theological paradigm of Disobedience > Punishment > Contrition > Deliverance, drawing upon six major examples, varied with six brief cases of lesser victors and quiet administrators, and ends with two "sad cases" (17–21). (iii) A critical examination of the structures of Judges shows that it is a continuous narrative, but not a continuous history. The leaders presented are local in scope, and in part contemporary in different regions. Their aggregate years fit within a 170-year real-time lapse precisely as do the aggregate years of groups of rulers (dynasties) in, e.g., Egypt or Mesopotamia. (iv) The particular history of Dan/Laish corresponds well in terms of both the Hebrew narratives and the archaeology of Tell Dan (Laish); this correspondence could not, therefore, be invented over half a millennium later. In the case of Shechem, the town was modest and no longer supported a king like Labayu (or a king at all) in the thirteenth and twelfth centuries; so there was no local power to conquer or oust south of Tirzah. The finds from the end of the thirteenth century on Mount Ebal above Shechem — if cultic (which is possible) — may indicate a local sacred spot (level II) that was taken over to build a ceremonial altar (level IB) for some such ritual as that of Josh. 24, and then deliberately covered over against reuse afterward (level IA); certainty about this function cannot be gained as yet. (v) The "Deuteronomistic" paradigm of Judg. 2–16 is *not* one that was first invented following on only from 621. *Precisely* the same paradigm (DPCD) is common coin in the second millennium, as is proven by the mind-set of Tutankhamun's great Restoration Stela (ca. 1330) and by very explicit instances among the Egyptian workforce (hardly theological elitists!) at Deir el-Medina in the thirteenth century. These cannot be denied or down-dated by over half a millennium just to suit modern "critical dogma" of nineteenth-century origin. (vi) Triumph hymns over foes are a tradition particularly well attested in the second millennium (and even before; cf. Uni). Those of Exod. 15 and Judg. 5 fit into that tradition, usually admitted to be archaic. Midianites only occur "live" down to the eleventh century, then they and Qurayya disappear.

(vii) Israel's nature as a group of tribes (containing clans and families) is a feature endemic to the ancient Near East, and is not artificial; good examples (Mari-Yamina, Suteans, Haneans) are known from the nineteenth and eighteenth centuries, and persist millennia later in highly conservative Old South Arabia (tenth century B.C. into first millennium A.D. on firsthand inscriptional evidence). The once oft-drawn parallel between tribal Israel with its Shiloh sanctuary and Greek amphictyonies can be ditched without loss; the Greek institution was formed too late to be significant, and its emphasis (basically, cult maintenance) was different, as also was the nature of its members (city-state communities, not tribes). However, there are partial analogies much closer geographically: the Sumerian league based on city-states contributing to the ancient cults at sacred Nippur under the Ur III Dynasty circa 2000, and the possible example of the Philistine pentapolis in our period here. Thus Israel as a multitribe entity in the twelfth and eleventh centuries, its sum called "all Israel," and their having a common shrine (as at Shiloh) are all above reproach. (viii) That there *was* an entry by the Israelites into Canaan from outside is indicated clearly by the demographic situation revealed by modern archaeological surveys, revealing a whole rash of fresh, new, small settlements. In the 150 years circa 1150-1000, the population seems to have doubled, but in less than half that time, circa 1210-1150, it at least quintupled! A theoretical ongoing orgy of procreation for two generations can be dismissed as fantasy; the only answer is that numbers suddenly shot up because additional people came in. The entry of the Israelites is an obvious factor; no other is. The "revolting peasant" and "up to the hills away from taxation" types of theories can be dismissed; neither would account for the massive demographic or cultural changes.

In conclusion, what may we fairly say so far on this period? A whole series of features ties the contents and styling of Joshua, Num. 20–33, and Judges to known usage in the second millennium, besides other realia not thus chronologically fixed. All of this favors the authenticity of the Joshua-Judges narratives, regardless of the final date of Joshua and Judges as books. Likewise does the physical archaeology, once the common but erroneous dogmas about those books are discarded, as they have to be on a straight reading. We have almost all the mentioned places in the Joshua narratives, and list of kings, attested as inhabited in Late Bronze II; Jericho's top levels are long gone, Ai is a question mark. The gradual expansion east to west is mirrored in the central Canaan surveys in pottery patterns. The sudden presence of many more people in Iron IA after Late Bronze II favors new folk having come in — but neither by outright conquest nor by invisible infiltration, nor just a few tax dodgers. In short, along with many other details, there is no valid reason for denying the basic picture of an entry into Canaan, initial raids and slow settlement, with many incidental features that belong to the period, and transmitted in tradition into the books that we have now. None of the aforementioned features could be simply invented without precedent in the seventh century or later.

CHAPTER 6

Lotus Eating and Moving On —
Exodus and Covenant

Throughout the Hebrew Bible, there is no single event (or theme, if the status of "event" be denied) to which its various writers hark back so pervasively as the tradition of the ancestral Israelites being liberated from servitude in Egypt, then forming a community under their deliverer deity YHWH, before undertaking their long (and prolonged) journey to the banks of the Jordan to enter Canaan. The pendant to leaving Egypt was the Sinai covenant, with its renewals in the plains of Moab and in Canaan.

1. BIBLICAL SOURCES FOR THE EXODUS

On the exodus in particular we have two sets of sources in the Bible, one copious and continuous and one episodic and occasional, which we must first briefly review. Then we can proceed to evaluate the nature of these references *not* by self-opinionated guesswork (as is fashionable currently) but by adducing the acid test of independent, external evidence so far as it is available. That evidence is uneven, takes several different forms, and is limited; the reasons for this must be spelled out. Then it may be feasible to reach some realistic results.

A. MAIN CORPUS

The first set (copious and continuous) by its sheer bulk will concern us most and first. It is now represented by four books: Exodus, Leviticus, Numbers, and Deuteronomy.

In Exodus we find the following contents:

(i) Conditions before the Exodus

a. *Introductory preamble:* The original Hebrew clan entered Egypt and flourished; that generation died, and (eventually) a later pharaoh sought to enslave the Hebrews and limit their numbers (chap. 1).

b. *Moses in Egypt and Sinai:* In these conditions a boy was born and adopted into the (local) royal palace, named Moses. Homicide impelled him to flee Egypt for Sinai until a new king ruled. Then it was claimed that the Hebrew ancestral deity YHWH commissioned him to return and lead his people out of Egypt, to return to Canaan (whence their ancestors had come to Egypt) (chaps. 2–4).

c. *Moses' return and pedigree.* Back in Egypt, Moses confronted Pharaoh, who worsened Hebrew working conditions; his pedigree is given (chaps. 5–6).

(ii) Contest, Moses versus Pharaoh, and the Exodus

a. *Contest and plagues:* Moses clashed with royal magicians, and nine successive plagues follow on, ending with deaths of Egyptian firstborn (the tenth). The Hebrew "Passover" rite was initiated (7–12:30).

b. *Departure from Egypt, travels to Mount Sinai:* Exodus via Succoth, through waters of the "Re(e)d Sea" with swamping of Egyptian force; triumph hymn. Then travel into Sinai, to Mount Horeb (12:31–39).

(iii) The Sinai Covenant, Part 1

a. *Initial sections of the covenant* include a title line and prologue (20:1, 2), then the first series of basic stipulations (20:3-17, "Ten Commandments"), plus detailed commands (chap. 20–31) both social (whole community) and religious (for tabernacle and its staff). Included are mention of the deposit of the text ("testimony") in Exod. 25:16, 21 and tacit witness memorials; cf. Exod. 24:4.

b. *Irregular cult:* The episode of the golden calf and its elimination (chaps. 32–34).

c. *The construction and setting up of the tabernacle* are narrated (chaps. 35–40).

In Leviticus we have the direct continuation of the content of Exodus with the tabernacle cult, its specifics and inauguration, the offerings, priests, etc. (chaps. 1–10).

(iv) The Sinai Covenant, Part 2

a. *Further stipulations:* Social (chaps. 11–20) and cultic (21–25).

b. *Concluding blessings and curses:* Reward and sanction for obedience/disobedience.

c. *Supplement:* An added ruling (chap. 27).

Then we have the book of Numbers. Here, after a first census and more regulations (1–10:10), and with equipment (trumpets), the Israelites left Sinai and (after various incidents) reached Qadesh-Barnea, where we last saw them in chapter 5 above. Thereafter new rules were made, and (with further incidents, including a second census) they eventually reached the plains of Moab.

Finally we reach Deuteronomy, plus a visit to Josh. 24. Here, embedded in the book of Deuteronomy, we have:

(v) First Renewal of the Sinai Covenant

This book contains a record of the covenant as renewed, as follows: a title (1:1-5) and retrospective prologue (1:6–4). Then stipulations, both social and cultic (chaps. 5–26), and ceremonials to be performed later (chap. 27). Other arrangements included depositing the text with the cult center and its periodic reading to the people (31:9-13), and for it to be a witness (31:26). And as in Leviticus, blessings and curses are laid down for obedience/disobedience (chap. 28). Tailpieces to the book are a song and blessing of Moses, and notice of his decease (chaps. 32–34).

And then, in Canaan, to complete the data on this feature, we have:

(vi) Second and Third Renewals of the Sinai Covenant

See Josh. 8:30-35, and 24. Josh. 8 merely mentions the event and accompanying rites, with no detail of the content of the renewed covenant. Josh. 24, however, gives some account of the content in barest outline: title (v. 2b), prologue (vv. 2c-13), basic requirement (vv. 14-21) (for a deposition, cf. 8:32), witnesses (vv. 22, 27), and traces of blessing (v. 20 end) and curse (v. 20).

These renewals of the Sinai covenant relate to the same social instrument as is present in Exodus-Leviticus, and thus they need all to be considered together in due course.

B. ALLUSIONS

The second set of references to the exodus (episodic and occasional) is scattered through all types and dates (however construed) of the biblical writings. It will be useful to marshal these mentions in congruent groups.

(i) *In covenant documents, exodus-deliverance is reason for respect for fellow humans,* both Israelite and alien. So, in Exod. 22:21; 23:9, 15 (cf. 34:18); and 29:44-46. Then in Lev. 11:1-45; 18:3; 19:33-34, 36; 22:32-33 (cf. 25:54-55); 23:42-43; 25:36-38, 42; 26:13, 45. Only Num. 15:40-41 in that book. And Deut. 6:12, 21-23; 7:8; 11:3-4; 13:5, 10; 16:1 (feast), 12; 20:1; 24:18, 22; 26:6-10; 29:22-26. Thus the exodus event pervades the law/covenant corpus.

(ii) *Exodus-deliverance is cause for Hebrews' gratitude.* For covenant contexts see Deut. 4:20, 34, 37; Josh. 24:5-7, 17. In later narratives: Judg. 2:1-3, 12; 6:7-10, 13; 1 Sam. 10:18-19; 1 Kings 8:51, 53; 9:9 = 2 Chron. 7:22. Cf. 2 Kings 17:7, 36; Neh. 9:9-12. In the Psalms, it occurs thus: Pss. 78 passim; 80:8; 81:6-7; 105:34-39; 106 passim; 136:10-16. Such mentions recur through the Prophets, from the divided monarchy through to the Babylonian exile and beyond. So, Hos. 12:9-10, 13; 13:4; Amos 2:10-11; 3:1-2; 9:7. In terms of their messages of judgment, Mic. 6:3-4; Jer. 2:6-7; 7:22-26; 11:3-5, 7; 32:20-23; 34:13; Ezek. 20:5-10; and Dan. 9:15.

(iii) *Knowledge of the exodus credited to others.* So, from the plains of Moab into the period of the judges: Num. 22:5, 11; 23:22; 24:8; Josh. 2:10; 9:9; Judg. 11:13.

(iv) *As an ancient date line.* Or, nothing like (this or that) since Israel left Egypt. In narrative works, see Judg. 19:30; 1 Sam. 2:27; 8:8; 12:6-8; 2 Sam. 7:6, 23-24 (= 1 Chron. 17:5, 21-22); 1 Kings 6:1; 8:16 (= 2 Chron. 6:5); 2 Kings 21:15. In the Prophets, cf. Jer. 16:14-15; 23:7-8; 32:30.

(v) *Compared to later events:* 1 Sam. 15:6; Isa. 11:6; Mic. 7:15. *As a long-past event:* 1 Kings 8:9, 21 (= 2 Chron. 5:10; 6:11); Pss. 114 passim; 135:8, 9; Hos. 2:15; 11:1; Hag. 2:5.

Thus the phenomenon of an exodus-deliverance recurs all over the biblical corpus, in law/covenant, in historical narratives, in the poetry of the Psalms, and in the messages of the prophets, at all dates in the biblical saga from Sinai itself and the plains of Moab down into the Persian period. If there never was an escape from Egyptian servitude by any of Israel's ancestors, why on earth invent such a tale about such humiliating origins? Nobody else in Near Eastern antiquity descended to that kind of tale of community beginnings. That question has been often enough posed, and the sheer mass and variety of postevent references gives it sharp point. The plain fact is that the question cannot be answered in the negative without leaving an insoluble crux. But if the fact of some Hebrews escaping from Egypt be granted, it does not, of course, follow that everything said about the exodus in our data is automatically original, part of the actual event. Large plants can grow from very small seeds. Without other clear indications, the authenticity or originality of the features attributed to the event in Egypt and Sinai cannot be objectively verified or judged, but merely discussed endlessly and mainly fruitlessly without definitely established results until the cows come home (as scholars have done this last two hundred years or so, down to the present). Therefore, recourse to independent sources is indispensable.

2. EXTERNAL ASSESSMENT: SOJOURN AND EXODUS

The period of Hebrew servitude prior to the exodus and the latter's starting point are both set in Egypt. To what extent (if at all) do our external sources endorse the factuality of an Egyptian setting and starting point, rather than "Egypt" being used as a novelistic setting, where no Hebrew had been? Or, if an Egyptian setting is to be accepted, are there any chronological indicators in either the biblical or outside source materials as to date(s) of the episode or of the record of it?

A. THE DELTA — A CAVEAT

The setting presented in Exod. 1–14 is indubitably that of Egypt's East Delta, whence the Hebrews are shown going directly into the Sinai Peninsula first of all. Background data may well be drawn from Egypt overall, but for locating the biblical Hebrews and their movements "on the ground" in Egypt we are restricted to the East Delta zone geographically.

This fact imposes further severe limitations upon all inquiry into the subject. The Delta is an alluvial fan of mud deposited through many millennia by the annual flooding of the Nile; it has no source of stone within it. Mud, mud and wattle, and mud-brick structures were of limited duration and use, and were repeatedly leveled and replaced, and very largely merged once more with the mud of the fields. So those who squawk intermittently, "No trace of the Hebrews has ever been found" (so, of course, no exodus!), are wasting their breath. The mud hovels of brickfield slaves and humble cultivators have long since gone back to their mud origins, never to be seen again. Even stone structures (such as temples) hardly survive, in striking contrast to sites in the cliff-enclosed valley of Upper Egypt to the south. *All* stone was anciently shipped in from the south, and repeatedly recycled from one period to another. Thus Eighteenth Dynasty blocks were reused in Ramesside temples; Ramesside temples were replaced under later dynasties largely by reuse of existing stones again; and periods through Saite, Ptolemaic, Romano-Byzantine, and Islamic times repeated the process. In more recent centuries, limestone has been largely burned for lime, and harder stones often reused for millstones or whatever. Scarce wonder that practically no written records of any extent have been retrieved from Delta sites reduced to brick mounds (whose very bricks are despoiled for fertilizer, *sebakh*), with even great temples reduced to heaps of tumbled stones.[1] And in the mud, 99 percent of discarded papyri have perished forever; a tiny fraction (of late date) have been found carbonized (burned) — like some at Pompeii — but can only be opened or read with immense difficulty. A tiny fraction of reports from the East Delta occur in papyri recovered from the desert near Memphis. Otherwise, the entirety of Egypt's administrative records at all periods in the Delta is lost (fig. 32B); and monumental texts are also nearly nil. And, as pharaohs *never* monumentalize *defeats* on temple walls, no record of the successful exit of a large bunch of foreign slaves (with loss of a full chariot squadron) would ever have been memorialized by any king, in temples in the Delta or anywhere else. On these matters, once and for all, biblicists must shed their naive attitudes and cease demanding "evidence" that *cannot* exist. Only radically different approaches can yield anything whatsoever. "Archaeology" that limits its blinkered evidence solely to what comes out of modest holes dug in the ground can have no final say in the matter.

B. PRACTICAL APPROACHES

Instead, we must consider successive themes in the existing Hebrew texts and see what background *is* available from our overall external sources.

(i) Conscription of Foreign Labor in Egypt for Building Work, Etc.

In the Old Kingdom ("Pyramid Age") in the third millennium there is as yet no trace of foreign labor being used for building projects. At times of the annual Nile flood, agricultural workers could be impressed to help shift building stones from quarries to the sites by rollers on the ground (as later) and mainly by water; brick accounts are known. In the Middle Kingdom (early second millennium), especially in the later Twelfth and into the Thirteenth Dynasties, an increasing number of Semites came into Egypt from Canaan, as slave tribute from local rulers, by purchase through merchants, by capture as prisoners of war, or by immigration. But their roles in Egypt were mainly domestic in large households, or cultic in the employ of a temple. The varied and detailed brick accounts then yield no hint of foreigners being so employed.

In the New Kingdom things changed.[2] For over 350 years (ca. 1540-1170), from their conquest and repeated campaigns in Canaan and Syria, Egypt's kings brought back batches of prisoners regularly, sometimes in considerable numbers. Besides domestic, cultic, and artisanal duties as before, the new accessions of manpower were employed to cultivate land, and could be used in building projects. In brick making, the most famous example comes from a scene in the tomb chapel of the vizier Rekhmire of circa 1450. It shows mainly foreign slaves "making bricks for the workshop-storeplaces of the Temple of Amun at Karnak in Thebes" and for a building ramp. Here, labeled "captures brought-off by His Majesty for work at the Temple of [Amun]," hence serving as forced labor, Semites and Nubians fetch and mix mud and water, strike out bricks from brick molds, leaving them to dry and measuring off their amount. And all is done under the watchful eye of Egyptian overseers, each with his rod. As many have observed, it offers a vivid visual commentary on part of what one may read in Exod. 1:11-14 and 5:1-21.[3] Close account was kept of numbers of bricks produced, and targets were set, as in the Louvre leather scroll, Year 5 of Ramesses II, 1275. The forty "stablemasters" (junior officers) of this document had each a target of 2,000 bricks, clearly to be made by men under them with group foremen. These officers fulfilled the role of the *noges'im*, "overseers," of Exod. 5:6. One official smugly records: "Total, 12 building-jobs. Also, people are making bricks in their spells-of-duty(?). . . . They are making their quota of bricks daily" (cf. 5:8, 13-14, 18-19).[4] Besides concern for amounts and targets, straw for inclusion in mud bricks (5:7, 18) was a theme in contemporary Egyptian papyri. In a slightly tongue-in-cheek passage, posted in a death trap of a place, an official is depicted complaining: "There are no men (here) to make bricks, and no straw in the district (either)." The straw (modern *tibn*) had an organic acid content that made the clay more plastic to work, and stopped shrinkage in the resulting bricks. The ancients did not know the chemistry, but they appreciated the effects.[5] The use of two levels of oversight is also endemic in our sources: the Egyptian main overseers and (subject to them) the "native" foremen of the work groups themselves.[6]

In other building work we find other foreigners being exploited under Ramesses II. Thus we read of grain rations to be given to "the soldiers and the Apiru-folk who drag stone to the great pylon (gateway) of [the Temple] of Ramesses II Beloved of Maat."[7] Far south in Nubia the king commanded the viceroy Setau to raid the western desert oases, "to take captives from the land of the Libyans, to build in the Temple of Ramesses II" in Year 44 (ca. 1234).[8] South, west, or northeast in his realm, this pharaoh was prepared to conscript foreigners mercilessly if need be.

The Hebrews were not only to make bricks but to undergo "hard labor in all kinds of field-work" (Exod. 1:14). Others too suffered this. In one document, two agricultural workers fled from a stablemaster "because he beat them." In another, one Syrian slave had been conscripted by an army officer from his service as land worker for the temple of Thoth at Memphis.[9] And so on. In later periods after the New Kingdom, Levantines still were to be found in Egypt, but in far fewer numbers, and not usually as serfs in brick making and land tillage.

(ii) "All Work and No Play Makes Jack a Dull Boy"

When Moses requested time off from work for his people to celebrate a feast, the pharaoh was not amused (Exod. 5:1-4). From what we know of Egypt at that time, scarce wonder. Detailed work-registers record the days spent at work and the days off of the royal workforce that constructed the tombs in the Valleys of the Kings and Queens in Western Thebes, either by the whole crew (major religious festivals, as Moses asked for) or by individuals. The reasons given for the latter can vary considerably, but often include a man "making offering to his god."[10] Sometimes either an individual or the whole crew were absent for several days at a time; so, one is tempted to sympathize just a little with Moses' pharaoh — "not *another* holiday, you lazy lot!" So, not least from the thirteenth and twelfth centuries, the Egyptian documentation portrays practical usages and an atmosphere very comparable to what we find in Exod. 1 and 5.

(iii) The Plagues

Among the most graphic narratives in the exodus account is the contest between Moses and the pharaoh and his magicians. The first round, a "preliminary bout," was with the latter (Exod. 7:8-12), where both sides showed ability to turn their rods or staffs into snakes. Tricks of this kind with snakes (including the cobra) are known in Egypt down to modern times. If charmed and deftly pressured at its neck muscles, the Egyptian cobra can be rendered immobile (cataleptic), becoming a "rod" — and, of course, be released.[11]

The fuller contest that embodied ten successive plagues is a larger scenario (7:14–12:30), much studied. Here we must stick firmly to clearly tangible data. First, we find a *sequence* of ten plagues, which (as several commentators have pointed out) divide into three threes, with the tenth as a separate climax.

Table 17. The Plagues Themselves

1. River as blood	4. Flies	7. Hail, flax, barley only
2. Frogs exit and die	5. Field cattle plague	8. Locusts in and out
3. Mosquitoes	6. Blains, men, and beasts	9. Thick darkness
	10. Death of the Egyptian firstborn	

The first three concern the waters and their denizens (fish, frogs, mosquitoes breeding); the second three affect people, field cattle, then people and cattle (including indoors); the third three were airborne: hail, locusts, thick darkness. The tenth affected only a narrow spectrum (people and animals, firstborn). Some have compared and contrasted the poetic summaries of the plagues in Pss. 78:44-51 and 105:28-36, each naming only seven plagues, with the Exodus account, often to the detriment of the latter. Is it possible to recognize the phenomena, and evaluate the outwardly different sets of plagues?

The phenomena inherent in the plagues themselves, understood against what is known of the Nile and Egypt, enable a clear answer to be given. We are dealing with *realia* here: river, fish, frogs, insects, cattle, humans, and not a fantasy world of (e.g.) dragons, monsters, genies, Liliths, or other plainly mythical beings, and in a real country (Egypt), not an imaginary place unknown to geography. Therefore it is in order to inquire into a clearly reddened Nile; into why fish, then frogs should die; and into the nature of the insects and subsequent diseases and disasters. Of all the modern treatments of the phenomena in the text, by far the most straightforward was given by G. Hort some time ago. From known geographical, climatic, ecological, microbiological, and medical phenomena, she was able to demonstrate a clear sequence of events through the ancient Egyptian year, from July/August (time of the annual Nile flood) through to the following March/April (early crops), as well as interconnections between the first two plagues and the fourth, then between the second and fourth/fifth, and between the fourth and sixth. In the calendar the seventh to ninth then followed to complete the main series. Thus the first six and the eighth plagues resulted (in physical terms) from unusually high rainfall where the Nile(s) rose, followed by an extremely high flood down the lower Nile valley through Egypt, and resultant effects. From the known geographical/scientific data, old errors can be discarded. Thus, too low a Nile (as before the new flood) gives green water, not red (Hort I, 90-91). Only an extrahigh flood would have brought a suitably large and intense amount of very red earth *(Roterde).* We summarize the details:

The absence of plagues 4-7 from Goshen, Hort could account for, because the Hebrews (and Goshen) were mainly in Wadi Tumilat, away from the conditions that gave rise in the main Nile Valley to the swarms of insects of plague 4 that would carry the blights of 2 to cause 5 and 6. In the case of plague 7, Hort indicates that such storms in the early spring come straight north to south off the Mediterranean and up the Nile (so, bypassing Goshen/Wadi Tumilat). As for plague 8, the locusts had followed a known course of their species and were blown from east to west (latitude of Sinai) into Egypt. Hort suggested understanding *ruah-yam* as "sea wind" (i.e., from the north) rather than "west wind," and wished to emend *yam-suph* to *yemin,* "east." The latter is needless, as the *yam-suph* is, in any case, east of north Egypt; a northwest wind would fit the general context, however *ruah-yam* be construed. Her explanation of "firstborn" as for "first fruits" has no basis in the context; what happened in the tenth plague if treated as at all historical would be regarded as a miracle by believers of any stripe, and as an exaggeration or "strange event" by nonbelievers of any kind; but it cannot be used to prejudge the preceding nine plagues — they are too closely tied to tangible realities to permit any such pranks.[12]

It is worth remarking that Egypt knew other high Niles, such as under Sobekhotep VIII (ca. 1700) and Osorkon III (ca. 787-759) that flooded the Theban temples, and one under Taharqa (690-664) that passed safely; these were less destructive than that of Exodus. In the Middle Kingdom work, *Admonitions of an Egyptian Sage* (its modern title), the writer describes Egypt's woes in a time of misery under an inept king, and remarks, "See, the River (Nile) is

Table 18. Sequenced Nile Plagues Phenomena

Calendar	Plagues: No., Type/Description, Interpretation	Exod. refs.	Hort ref.
July/Aug.	1. *River,* to "blood." Extreme high flood because of extraheavy rains in Nile source regions; brings masses of *Roterde* plus *flagellates;* > red color, oxygen fluctuation, so fish die and rot, breeding ground for infections.	7:14-24	I, 87-95/98
Aug./Sept.	2. *Frogs swarm and die.* Insects bring *Bacillus anthracis* to rotting fish, infects frogs, who mass-migrate onto land and die, carrying infection into land and herbage.	7:25–8:11	I, 95-98
Oct./Nov.	3. *Insects* swarm. Mosquitoes overbreeding, in pools of excessive Nile flood.	8:12-15	I, 98-99
Oct./Nov. to Dec./Jan.	4. *Flies swarm.* These bite legs/feet, fly = *Stomoxys calcitrans,* infection from 2. (Not Goshen)	8:16-28	I, 99, 101-3
Jan.	5. *Plague on livestock in fields.* Animals let out into fields contract anthrax from pasture, hence ingest (like the frogs) and die. (Not Goshen)	9:1-7	I, 100-101
Jan.	6. *Skin blains, humans and livestock (indoors).* Bitten by the *Stomoxys calcitrans* flies, causing a (nonfatal) skin anthrax. Cf. 4. (Not Goshen)	9:8-12	I, 100-103
Feb.	7. *Hail on flax and barley (too soon for wheat and spelt).* The two latter crops not due then. (Not Goshen)	9:13-35	II, 48-49
Feb./March	8. *Locusts blown from east, then blown away from (north)west.* These breed in east Sudan; move north up Red Sea/northwest Arabia; these ones, blown from east to west into Egypt. Northwest wind (i) blows them into north of Upper Egypt and (ii) away to *yam suf.*	10:1-20	II, 49-52
March/Apr.	9. *Thick darkness.* The initial *khamsin* of the season, whipping up not only sand but masses of fine, dense, dark *Roterde,* giving greater "darkness" than just a sand wind.	10:21-23	II, 52-54
	[10. *Death of the firstborn, humans and cattle.*	11:4-7; 12	II, 54-55]

blood, one shrinks from (other) people, and thirsts for water."[13] So, such concepts — and phenomena — were not unknown to ancient Egypt.

The close correspondence to Nilotic and related conditions demonstrable in the text of Exodus has clear implications. First and foremost, it rules out any attempt to give preference to the poetical retrospects found in Pss. 78 and 105. Their ordering of plagues (and limited choice) does not correspond with physical reality as does Exodus. Thus they are a secondary source, not primary. They have their own poetic merits. Psalm 78 groups first the river as blood, then the impact of insects and frogs, then the impact of hail and storm. Ps. 105 simply gives a set of images: darkness and river blood; insects and hail and storm; locusts and firstborn. Each chooses the "ominous" number of seven plagues, not the prosaically accurate ten.

This illustrates a basic literary phenomenon endemic to the ancient Near East, yet one constantly abused by biblicists. When prose and poetry accounts coexist, *it is prose that is the primary source and poetry that is the secondary celebration.* This cannot be overstressed. Thus we turn to the Annals of Tuthmosis III for a clear account of his wars, and not first to his Karnak Poetical Stela. The facts of the Battle of Qadesh are recoverable from the prose sections of the so-called "Poem" (better with Gardiner, "literary record") and the "Bulletin," not from the purely poetical "rhetorical" stelae of Pi-Ramesse. The same is true in Mesopotamia, where (e.g.) the prose reports of Tukulti-Ninurta I are our primary source, not the poetic "epic" in his honor. And so on. In precisely the same way, Exod. 1–14 is the basic source for the exodus, not either Exod. 15 or Pss. 78, 105; and for Deborah, Judg. 4, not Judg. 5 (for all its considerable value).

The account of the plagues in Exod. 7–12 is a well-formulated unity; and (as some traditional critics already admit) it cannot meaningfully be split up between imaginary sources such J, E, or P (for which no physical MSS actually exist!), without making a nonsense of the account of the plagues that only works as a unity. The patterning also speaks for an original compositional unity, as may now be set out in tabular form (see table 19, adapted from Sarna and Hoffmeier). The grouping in three threes shows up very clearly in the organizing of which warnings are given when, and in the commands to Moses/Aaron on where to be.

This kind of formulation is created ab initio, from the start — not by fiddling with fragments as with a jigsaw puzzle. Thus chapters 7–12 at least are best treated as a natural unit within the whole.

Exod. 15 is a triumph hymn, a Hebrew reply (so to speak) to the proud triumph hymns of the New Kingdom pharaohs that ostentatiously adorned the walls of Egyptian temples or were blazoned on stelae in the temple courts and beyond.

Table 19. Articulation in Plague Narrative

Plague No.:	Forewarning	Timing	Command Where
1	YES	"In morning"	Station self
2	YES	*none*	Go to Pharaoh
3	*none*	*none*	*none*
4	YES	"In morning"	Station self
5	YES	*none*	Go to Pharaoh
6	*none*	*none*	*none*
7	YES	"In morning"	Station self
8	YES	*none*	Go to Pharaoh
9	*none*	*none*	*none*
10	YES	*none*	*none*

Finally, the supposed "theological critique" of Egyptian gods and beliefs in Exod. 7–12. This has been proposed on the basis of Exod. 12:12 and the retrospective Num. 33:4. But there is no stress on any such polemic during the main plagues narrative (7–12); even Exod. 12:12 is but one single pronouncement on the eve of the final plague, death of the firstborn (also the context in Num. 33:4). There is far more emphasis on YHWH's role as deliverer, explicit and implicit (e.g., Exod. 7:3-5; 9:16; 10:1-2; 11:1-8; 12:17; 13:14-16). Nevertheless, it is fair to comment that the impact of various plagues can be understood as devaluing or denying Egyptian beliefs. A massively unruly and destructive Nile flood, red in hue, bringing death, was the opposite of Hapi (deity of that flood), who was normally bringer of new life by his waters. It also embodied the revived Osiris (green) — whereas virulent red was the color that denoted his enemy and murderer, Seth! Frogs were the symbol of abundance (hence, of prosperity; personified as Heqat), but here again they brought death. The rest (again) threatened or negated the prosperity that Egypt's gods were deemed to give, while the deep darkness eclipsed the supreme sun god, Re or Amen-Re. Pharaoh was traditionally entitled "Son of Re," and his patron was made invisible, as if in an eclipse of sun or moon (treated as hostile events also). Death of so many throughout the land (here, of firstborn) would probably seem to Egyptians to have negated the power of the gods completely, and the king's personal and official key role of ensuring their favor. To go much further than this would go into the realm of unjustified subjectivity.[14]

By contrast, it is stressed repeatedly that YHWH was to bring his people out with "an outstretched arm" or a "strong hand" (cf. Exod. 3:19, 20; 6:1; 13:3,

14, 16; 15:6, 12, 16; 32:11; retrospectively, Deut. 3:24; 6:21; 9:26, 29; 26:8). This idiom was also well known in Canaan (occurring in the Amarna letters, e.g., EA 286:12; 287:27; 288:14), and appears to be here a deliberately adopted Egyptianism in Hebrew, as a riposte to the ubiquitous pose of Pharaoh smiting his enemies and being endlessly entitled "Lord of the strong arm" *(neb khopesh).*[15]

(iv) "Exodus": Concept and Practice[16]

The concept of an "exodus" (Latin for Gk. *exodos*), or "going out," represents the reality of "voting with one's feet," or simply leaving one place (where conditions have become intolerable) to go to another. That kind of solution, for community or individual, is well attested from at least the eighteenth century B.C. onward in the biblical world. Thus tribal groups owing allegiance to the king of Mari (east Syria) tried to emigrate from his control.[17] In the fifteenth century, in Anatolia, some fourteen "lands" and people groups rebelled against the rule of the Hittite king, and moved off to Isuwa — until his successor brought them all back![18] In ancient Libya, in the thirteenth and twelfth centuries, the locals several times tried to move into the Egyptian Delta, seeking new terrain in which to settle, but were successively blocked by kings Sethos I, Merenptah, and (in Upper Egypt also) Ramesses III and VI.[19] By the early twelfth century we have also the Sea Peoples (including the Philistines) moving from the Aegean world into Canaan and also being rebuffed from Egypt.[20] And the Arameans moved from the Syrian steppes to take over most of Syria, on both sides of the western bend of the Euphrates, and eventually occupied areas in Mesopotamia.[21] In the Nile Valley, way down south, it has been suggested that under Ramesside rule (ca. 1290-1080) and oppressive taxation, much of the Lower Nubian population simply emigrated south to better areas that lay beyond Egyptian control.[22] So the solution for the early Israelites of "moving on," and out of Egypt and her oppression, was not novel, but a well-tried one.

(v) Geography and Logistics (Cf. Map, Fig. 27)

(a) Topography and Conditions

The accounts of the Hebrew exodus from Egypt feature a series of place-names there. The Hebrews were settled in a zone called Goshen, which (in context) is once called "the land of Rameses" (Gen. 47:6, 11). As slaves, they "built Pithom and Raamses as store-cities for Pharaoh" (Exod. 1:11). And it was from Raamses that the Hebrews finally departed eastward, via *not* Pithom but Succoth (Exod. 12:37; cf. Num. 33:3, 5) and on to Etham (Exod. 13:20). After hovering in the vicinity of three more places (Pi-Hahiroth, Migdol, Baal-Zephon; Exod. 14:1-4), and crossing between the parted waters of the sea (*yam-suph;* 14:21-31), they thus left Egypt for the desert of Shur en route to Sinai (16:22ff.). These places deserve concise scrutiny.

(1) Raamses

As conceded almost universally, the Hebrew *R-ʿ-m-s-s* corresponds exactly to Egyptian *R-ʿ-m-s-s* from which it derives.[23] This is the proper name Ramesses, used by eleven kings of the Nineteenth and Twentieth Dynasties, circa 1290-1070. The first of these, Ramesses I, reigned only sixteen months and built no cities. None of the rest founded major cities either, with but one exception. He was Ramesses II, grandson of I, who was the builder of the vast city *Pi-Ramesse A-nakhtu,* "Domain of Ramesses II, Great in Victory,"[24] suitably abbreviated to the distinctive and essential element "Ra(a)mses" in Hebrew. In modern times, because masses of broken Ramesside stonework were visible in the ruins of San el-Hagar, indubitably Tanis (Egypt. *Djane(t),* biblical Zoan), it was long assumed that Tanis had for a time been called Pi-Ramesse in the thirteenth and twelfth centuries, hence was Raamses. However, much more modern and thorough excavation has proved otherwise. Well over a dozen miles south of Tanis, the open countryside around Tell el-Dabʿa conceals the foundations of ancient Hat-waret/Avaris, a residence of the Twelfth and Thirteenth Dynasties and Hyksos kings. Immediately north of this, for miles around Khataana-Qantir, the deceptively flat terrain shrouds thousands of acres of the last remains of Pi-Ramesse/Raamses. The full site appears to be up to six kilometers (almost four miles) long north-south, and over three kilometers (two miles) wide, on recent estimates. When the city was largely abandoned from circa 1130 onward, and the new (Twenty-First) dynasty needed stone to build great new temples at its capital, Tanis, they simply removed the Ramesside temple stonework from Pi-Ramesse to Tanis for reuse — where its presence was later initially to deceive modern explorers. And the mud brick of most of its nontemple buildings quietly subsided back into mother earth. Excavation has opened up the foundations of parts of its palaces (including a gold-dusted floor),[25] its extensive stabling for horses and chariotry,[26] etc. Geophysical magnetometer and other soundings have shown up the clear ground plans of many more buildings, often of great extent.[27] Here, and here alone, is the basis of a city which, with its workshops and storage magazines for palace, temples, and other institutions, can well qualify as one of the *are-miskenoth,* or "store-cities," of Exod. 1:11. In biblical usage, such *miskenoth*[28] were in effect depots for storage of supplies and revenue paid in kind (grain, oil, wine, etc.), in Egypt precisely as elsewhere in the Near Eastern and eastern Mediterranean worlds. Cf. map, fig. 28.

The history of the city Pi-Ramesse is relevant to our inquiry. North of the old town of Avaris, center of the cult of Seth, in what was his family's home district, Sethos I built a summer palace of which very little has been recovered, other than tilework from a glazed doorway (now in the Louvre).[29] This site, Ramesses II turned into the vast city just mentioned, in his own name, and it remained the East Delta center of pharaonic rule through to Ramesses III, who refurbished it in part, naming one zone after himself. Ramesses IV to VI continued to work there, after which Pi-Ramesse was abandoned as a royal residence circa 1130. When Ramesses VIII made dedication to Seth, it was to him as lord of Avaris, not the Seth of Pi-Ramesse any more.[30]

Then the living story of Pi-Ramesse was virtually finished, apart from a minor residual cult of its gods elsewhere. Instead, concurrent with Memphis from 1070, the new East Delta capital was Tanis, and known *exclusively* as Tanis (Djanet/Zoan). Contrary to Lemche, Tanis *never ever* bore the name Pi-Ramesse. The Ramesside stonework was principally recycled as scrap stone to build Tanis, and did *not* take the old name thither.[31] The only survival of gods-of-Ramesses cults in the fourth century B.C. was preserved as "religious archaeology" (i) at Bubastis, within the "pantheon" sanctuary of Nectanebo II, deeply hidden away from the gaze of everyone except the local Egyptian priests,[32] and (ii) at Tanis on private statues from the temple, again not accessible (or comprehensible!) to foreigners.[33] These abstruse "sources" could not possibly be known to Jewish priests or any other foreigners, at any date. Thus the claims of Lemche and others that Raamses could have been known at a late date to Hebrew writers is also totally baseless. If Raamses (as opposed to Zoan, Tanis) had never previously been part of *early* Hebrew tradition, there would have been no cause to look for it or incorporate it *later;* as with the Iron Age Ps. 78:12, the phrase "field of Zoan" (Egyp. *Sekhet-Djanet*) would have sufficed. Thus, the occurrence of Raamses is an early (thirteenth/twelfth century) marker in the exodus tradition, and that fact must be accepted.

(2) Pithom and Succoth

Pithom is, again, universally recognized as standing for Egyptian *Pi(r)-(A)tum,* "domain (lit. house) of (the god) Atum." Pithom occurs exclusively in Exod. 1:11. Its sole link with any other site in Hebrew is with Raamses, as both were being built by the Hebrews. So these two sites were not necessarily contiguous, yet were both accessed by Hebrew brick slaves. However, Pithom was not on the exodus route east from Raamses/Pi-Ramesse, whereas Succoth was. There is no location for Pithom north of Pi-Ramesse, or on the eastward route to Succoth and onward; so it should be vaguely south of Raamses, and west from Succoth.

This "triangle" is a useful gain. For Succoth at least is — again — acknowledged to be the same place as Egyptian Tjeku, which appears on monuments found in the Wadi Tumilat at two sites: Tell er-Retaba and Tell el-Maskhuta further east, especially at the latter.[34] In a walled compound and settlement, Tell er-Retaba had a small temple of Ramesses II honoring Atum of Tje[k]u and Seth on its pylon gateway, and a deity, "Lord of Tjeku." A rhetorical stela of Ramesses II was found, besides a twin statue of him and the god Atum. On a fragment found here a Ramesside officer Usimare-nakhte gave his origin as "of Tjeku." Ramesses III also left sculpture here. In each case (except once lost), Tjeku has the "foreign-land" determinative. Thus we learn the following about Tell er-Retaba: (1) it had a temple built and adorned by Ramesses II, further adorned by Ramesses III, plus work by an official of that period. So this site was active in the thirteenth and twelfth centuries. (2) Its main deity was Atum, the sun god of Heliopolis; its temple was, in principle, a "house *(pr)* of Atum" or a "Pithom." (3) By the place-name mentioned on its fragments so far, it was either Tjeku (a Succoth) or (with a land sign) within the region of Tjeku. So we have a site of Ramesside date — contemporary with the latest date for a biblical exodus — that could be a Pithom or a Succoth. It lies southeast from Raamses at Qantir. But which might it be?

We now must look at Tell el-Maskhuta, a few miles due east from Tell er-Retaba. Here were found the following monuments of Ramesses II's time: a large granite rhetorical stela (as at er-Retaba) and a falcon figure, both dedicated to the sun god, but as Re-Horakhty rather than Atum; a small piece of a shrine (the rest is now lost, but seen a century ago), mentioning the king as "beloved of the Lord of Tjeku"; a statue of the king's son, Prince Ramesses-Merenptah, with a figure of Atum-Khopri of Heliopolis; two broken sphinxes of this time, one naming the Semitic god Horon. So far we have here a site which is Ramesside, and a Succoth, again linked with the sun god — a second Pithom/Succoth of the thirteenth century! The early diggings (by Paponot) about 130 years ago revealed that a large, long-known monolithic triad of Ramesses II, Atum, and Re was partnered by a second such monolith on either side of a way; behind them, the way was flanked by the black-granite sphinxes and led to the shrine, and the stela (later used as a Roman foundation).[35] Such was the early temple at *this* Succoth or Pithom!

But which Succoth/Pithom is which? Here external Egyptian sources help us, as well as later monuments. These show definitively that Tjeku/Succoth was a place, a spot on the map, as well as a district. The ostracon ODM 1076 is the remains of a letter written in the name of "all the gods of Tjeku," determined with the town sign. Such greetings are usually in the names of gods of towns, more than districts. Papyrus Anastasi VI shows us the *area* Tjeku in relation to a Pithom (now, of Merenptah). The Shasu of Edom, going from east to west, pass "the Fort of Merenptah which is (in) Tjeku" to reach "the pools of Pithom-of-Merenptah which is/are (in) Tjeku." Papyrus Anastasi V has two runaways from Raamses going past the "keep" of Tjeku and then eastward by the fort of Tjeku and a *Migdol* of Sethos I. These too are specific places in an area Tjeku. Then in the same papyrus, a deputy of Tjeku requests of his colleague about some men: "Bring them to me at Tjeku!" — which can only be a particular place (fort, settlement), not a whole area.[36] I may ask someone to meet me in Chester (town), but not in Cheshire (county)! So, for the Ramesside period, thirteenth century, we have a Tjeku region containing a *place* Tjeku, with a fort, a keep west of it, and a place Pithom and pools farther west still. All this would fit excellently with a Succoth/Tjeku at Tell el-Maskhuta, and a Pithom at Tell er-Retaba farther to its west.

Later evidence virtually clinches this solution for certain. The Saite to Ptolemaic periods (seventh to first centuries B.C.) have produced inscriptions from Tell el-Maskhuta that consistently mention a temple of Atum there, and several times use the town determinative, i.e., Tjeku town is at Tell el-Maskhuta. A statue found there addresses "every priest who shall enter the Temple of Atum residing in Tjeku," which requires that Tjeku be the precise place in which that temple is situated. The stela of Ptolemy II from Tell el-Maskhuta repeatedly names Tjeku and Atum the god of Tjeku, but Pithom only twice in passing. The statue of Ankh-renp-nufer mentions the *temple* of Atum, Lord of An/Tjeku, but *not* the town of Pithom, as was mistakenly thought. With which fact, we have *no evidence whatsoever* that Pithom (Egyptian or biblical) was ever at Tell el-Maskhuta, whereas Tjeku (Succoth) clearly was. Finally, there is the Roman milestone found at Tell el-Maskhuta, which reads: "9 [Roman] miles on the road from Ero [Pithom] to Clysma [Suez]" (fig. 32C). Ero is short for (H)ero(onpolis), the Latin name (via Greek) for Pithom. This was evidently the ninth Roman mile, west to east, from Pithom, reached at Tell el-Maskhuta (Tjeku/Succoth) on the road out to Suez (Clysma). And, as Gardiner pointed out so long ago, Tell er-Retaba (as Pithom) is almost exactly nine Roman miles from Tell el-Maskhuta. Need one say more? Only that the exodus texts have the Hebrews working at Raamses (Qantir area) and Pithom (Tell er-Retaba), about fifteen to seventeen miles apart, and the exodus going direct from Pi-Ramesse (Raamses) east-southeast to Succoth/Tjeku (Tell el-Maskhuta), and on eastward. In the light of the total evidence, we can firmly dismiss the erroneous claims by some writers that Tell el-Maskhuta was Pithom, and that it was only inhabited from the Saite period (seventh century) onward. Hence the Exodus narrative would reflect only conditions of the late period, not New Kingdom times. The Ramesside, Saite/Ptolemaic, and Roman data combine to scotch these palpably false claims completely. We now have *on the full facts* a sensible Late Bronze geography for the initial part of the exodus route. One may further note, if whimsically, that just as the Hebrews took two days to transit from Raamses to Succoth and from Succoth out to Etham (Exod. 12:37; 13:20; Num. 33:5-8), so also did the two slaves in Papyrus Anastasi V who ran away from Pi-Ramesse on the third month of Shomu, day 9, continuing (on 3rd Shomu 10) past the keep of Tjeku (Succoth) and then likewise east; they had a two-day trip to that zone, like their Hebrew precursors. Cf. fig. 28.

(3) Etham

This place "on the edge of the wilderness" (Exod. 13:20) has so far defied historical geographers, whether Egyptological or biblical, to find its location. It has to be farther east than Tell el-Maskhuta, but probably not beyond the clutch of places near the *yam-suph,* itself most likely the Ballah/Timsah/Bitter Lakes region. Once through the *yam-suph,* the Hebrews turned south via the "Desert of Etham" to go to Sinai (Num. 33:6, 8). Only beyond that line did they really leave Egypt in the desert of Shur and the edges of Sinai. It cannot be a Khetem (Egyptian word meaning "fort"), because Hebrew soft *'aleph* cannot transcribe Egyptian *kh.* It must have been very close to the Bitter Lakes to give its name to the desert opposite, across those waters. Thus it may have been in the vicinity of modern Ismailia. Philologically it may (in Egyptian) have been an "isle of (A)tum," *'i(w)-(I)tm,* or a "mound of (A)tum," *(i)ʒ(t)-(I)tm,* given the frequency of Atum-names in this area.

(4) Pi-Hahiroth, Baal-Zephon, Migdol[37]

From Etham the Hebrews "turned back," i.e., back to the northwest, as if to Raamses, whence they had come (to go southwest would have been meaningless). Then in Exod. 14:1-2 (in most translations of the Hebrew), the Hebrews were told to camp before/in front of *(l-pny)* Pi-Hahiroth, between Migdol and the *yam* (sea), to camp opposite Baal-Zephon, by the *yam* (sea). The nearest sea to the east end of Wadi Tumilat is, of course, the former long line of lakes running from north to south from Menzaleh adjoining the Mediterranean down through lakes El-Ballah, Timsah, and those called "Bitter," to within about sixteen miles (twenty kilometers) of the northern shore of the Red Sea

(Gulf of Suez) at Suez (Clysma). There is some reason to suppose that in the second millennium the waters of the Suez Gulf did link up with the Bitter Lakes, intermittently or otherwise. Thus, even before the cutting of the modern Suez Canal (which destroyed ancient water configurations in this zone), Egypt had a considerable belt of waters between the Mediterranean and the Suez Gulf.[38] Cf. fig. 28.

The addition of ancient canals oriented roughly north-south could readily close any gaps in this water barrier, to Egypt's advantage in terms of security. In recent decades modern investigation has revealed traces of such ancient canals.[39] One (northern) set of fragments runs from near El-Qantara to just west of Pelusium, with varying sections of canal probably reflecting changes in course at different periods.[40] Another (southern) fragment runs from the north corner of Lake Timsah (east of Ismailia) to the southern edges of the Ballah lakes.

In the light of this geographical situation, a group such as the emigrating Hebrews would soon come up against one form or another of this water barrier, barely seven or ten miles east beyond Succoth (Tell el-Maskhuta), presumably at Etham, in the context, somewhere near Ismailia. To "turn back" (Heb. *shub*) thus implies going back in some form, but not to Succoth — hence, either southwest (meaningless, as noted) or north, even north-northwest. If so, then to go and halt somewhere along the western flank of the lakes and canals would be to "camp by the sea" *(yam)*. And our cluster of sites would surround them. Pi-Hahiroth has been well interpreted by various scholars as "Mouth of the Hiroth," a word or name for a canal — its mouth would be where it ran into a lake or a Nile branch, in our context where such a channel ran into or out of one of the lakes. At no very great distance north from the Ismailia area, one might posit such a water junction where the discovered south canal fragment left Lake Timsah northward (south option), or else where that canal in due course entered the south end of the southmost of the Ballah lakes, a dozen miles or so northward (north option). That gives us two possible settings for Pi-Hahiroth, and hence for an encampment "by the sea," and in turn for the general locations for Migdol and Baal-Zephon. We should not look any farther north, otherwise we (and the Hebrews!) would end up in an ancient Egyptian militarized zone (by the north end of the Ballah lakes from Qantara onward).

On this basis Migdol would be directly west of the Hebrew encampment "by the sea" that was in front of (just south of?) Pi-Hahiroth; it may have been a fort (cf. its name) up on the El-Gisr ridge. That leaves Baal-Zephon, "opposite" the Hebrews. In this context, as it cannot be behind them, it most probably should be thought of as just north, in front of them in their limited northward trek, right opposite their advance. In this way they would indeed seem to be "closed in," directionless at this point, a suitable target for Pharaoh's chariot squadron (Exod. 14:3). If so, the south option would theoretically be two or three miles northeast of Ismailia; the north option (some six miles farther on) would be some eight or nine miles north of Ismailia, and about ten to eleven miles south of Qantara and Tell Abu Sefeh (or roughly twelve to fourteen miles from Tell Hebua, the newly preferred site for Sile/Tjaru, Egypt's fortified northern border crossing). The result (on the south option) is to set Pi-Hahiroth at the south end of the south canal and Migdol west of it on the ridge, and perhaps the same as the Migdol of Sethos I of Papyrus Anastasi V. Baal-Zephon would be not much farther north. The result (on the north option) would be to set Pi-Hahiroth at the north end of the south canal, Migdol west of it, as a companion fort to the Sethos I Migdol, and Baal-Zephon correspondingly farther north, within (say) a few miles south of Qantara/Tell Abu Sefeh up to ten miles from Tell Habua/Sile. Then the famed crossing of the parted waters of the "sea" would be placed somewhere in the north of Lake Timsah or south part of southernmost Lake(s) Ballah. Once through, on the east side, the Hebrews were in the desert of Shur (Exod. 15:22), in its full extent adjoining the main north route into Egypt (cf., e.g., Shur on the east border of Egypt, 1 Sam. 15:7; 27:8), and southward becoming the desert of Etham, opposite the zone of Ismailia (cf. Num. 33:8). Precise locations would depend on future excavations in local tells kind enough to yield inscriptions that would clearly identify them.[41] What is given above is necessarily theoretical at present, but serves simply to indicate that the existing Exodus narratives fit readily into the general East Delta topography as presently known.

(5) Goshen

Two topographical matters may be briefly considered, the western and eastern extremes of "Israel in Egypt." First, in Gen. 46:29 Joseph went to Goshen to welcome his family into Egypt and then to court (47:2-4); they were then assigned land in Goshen/land of Rameses (Gen. 47:6, 11). As Rameses and Raamses are identical terms, Goshen may have included terrain near Ro-waty and Avaris, the Middle Kingdom and Hyksos precursors of Pi-Ramesse. There is reason to include part of Wadi Tumilat in Goshen by the exodus period (cf. above, on plagues), hence its full extent probably included good pastureland south from Avaris, terrain south across the west end of the tongue of steppeland, and part of Wadi Tumilat (where the Hebrews worked on Pithom).

(6) The "Sea," Yam Suph

Second, there has been much discussion over both the location(s) of *yam suph* and its nature. For the traditional translation "Red Sea" — based upon the

Latin Vulgate, which merely follows the Greek translation (Septuagint, LXX) —
there is no warrant whatever in the Hebrew text. *Suph* never meant "red." There
are clear passages in Hebrew that do give its meaning: reeds/rushes,
marsh(plants). Compare (as many have) Exod. 2:3-5, a reed basket concealed
amid the reeds along the Nile's banks; Isa. 19:6-7, a threat that reeds and rushes
will shrivel, and so the plants along the Nile. Therefore, as is generally admitted,
yam suph may fairly be rendered "sea/lake of reeds." Then, in modern study,
suph was compared to Egyptian *tjuf*, "marsh-plants/reeds/papyrus." But not too
long ago, F. Batto suggested a dramatic alternative: not "sea of reeds" but "sea of
the End" *(soph)*, out to the end of the world.[42]

However, the reasons for this and against *suph*, "marshes/reeds," have
proven to be a mirage. The LXX translation "Red" is simply an interpretation
(not strictly a translation!) of dubious origin, and has no inherent authority.
Contrary to Batto, Egyptian *tjuf* does not apply solely to freshwater papyrus,
but to reeds and rushes generally. Reeds tolerant of salt water (halophytes) grow
and flourish in and around the lakes (Menzaleh, Ballah, Timsah, Bitter) that
span the north-south line between the Mediterranean and Suez.[43]

Careful study of *tjuf* and *suph* by Ward has shown clearly that Hebrew
suph could not be borrowed from Egyptian *tjuf*; it would have been *zuph*, in
that case.[44] In its consonants, Egyptian *tjuf* could certainly derive from Semitic
suph, as Egyptian *tj* was regularly used to transcribe the Semitic/Hebrew *s* that
we call *samekh*. But the move into Egyptian would have come from Semitic
when there was still a middle *w* (not just vowel *u*), before the late second millennium. So, both words (Egyptian and Semitic) for reeds/marshes and their
plants were in use in parallel by the thirteenth century. The suggested meaning
"end" is superfluous and irrelevant. The more so, as (contrary to Batto and
other biblicists) the ancient Near East did *not* historicize myth (i.e., read it as an
imaginary "history"). In fact, exactly the reverse is true — there was, rather, a
trend to "mythologize" history, to celebrate actual historical events and people
in mythological terms. Compare the growth of legends about "Sesostris" or
about the Hyksos kings in Egypt; the growth of traditions about Sargon of
Akkad; or the divinization of Dumuzi in Mesopotamia, among others.[45]

The term *yam suph* is also applied to the Gulf of Suez and to the Gulf of
Aqaba, which flank the Sinai Peninsula. For the Gulf of Suez, cf. Num. 33:10-11,
south of Etham, Marah, and Elim. For the Gulf of Aqaba, cf. Num. 21:4; also
Num. 14:25, Deut. 1:40, 2:1, and perhaps Jer. 49:21. All other allusions are to the
original *yam suph* of the exodus at Pi-Hahiroth. In the cases of the two gulfs, we
have nothing more than extension of usage. Going from north to south, one
passed a series of stretches of often salty water, and on arrival at the area of later
Suez, here was another long piece of water, stretching into the hazy distance (as

did Menzaleh, up north). So it was simply taken as being yet another install-ment of the collective *yam suph*. Across the other side of Sinai, an analogous judgment was made; here was another long body of water stretching out south into the haze or the horizon like Menzaleh or that at Suez. Nothing more so-phisticated than that need be assumed. Compare the extension of the Greek term "Red Sea" to cover (at one time) the Perso-Arabian Gulf, Arabian Sea, and our present Red Sea. Or the word "Asia," from a small Roman province in what is now Turkey, is now used to cover everything from the Bosporus to Japan.

Thus, after crossing the lakes section of *yam suph* (be it Ballah, Timsah, or Bitter), the Hebrews (if headed south) would go through the Shur/Etham desert past the Etham (Ismailia) zone, on past the latitude of Suez, the three days' march (thirty-six to forty-five miles at twelve to fifteen miles per day) to Marah, Elim, then (again) *yam suph*. This was simply a stop by the east (Sinai) shore of the Suez gulf; on the geography, see further below. So, there is no basic problem in both crossing a *yam suph* and then passing more of it later.[46]

(b) Danegeld and Logistics

It is impractical to comment here on every incidental detail of the exodus nar-ratives. But in passing, two points raised by others may usefully be amended. First, it has been suggested that a little-known Egyptian ostracon refers "to the Apiru, engaged in construction work at the city of Pi-Ramesses." It indeed mentions the Apiru, but simply as bringing together stones under Egyptian military supervision, no location being mentioned. It is a Strasbourg ostracon, hence certainly from Thebes, and very likely from the precinct of the Ramesseum, the great memorial temple of Ramesses II.[47] It is most unlikely to hail from Pi-Ramesse; but just as the Israelites had to do brickwork labor in the East Delta, so these Apiru (like those at Memphis) had to do involuntary ser-vice in assembling stone blocks for building work.

Secondly, the case of Exod. 3:21-22; 11:2; and 12:35-36. Here the Hebrews were to use the Egyptians' desire to be rid of their "pestilential" clients and their deity's plagues by asking parting gifts from them of silver, gold, and clothing (cf. 12:33-36 in particular); almost a case of "we'll give you anything to be rid of you!" Buying off a deity's wrath (especially against health) is well enough known in the thirteenth century. Draftsman Nebre promised a stela for his son's healing, and (seeking forgivenness) the sculptor Qen asked people to offer beer to his angry goddess.[48] Latterly, Malamat cited the Elephantiné stela of King Setnakht (ca. 1185) as a parallel to Exod. 3, 11, and 12. But here, in the light of Seidlmeyer's new collation of the text, the meaning is not quite the same.

What we find is that Setnakht vanquished rebels (Egyptian) who had tried to buy in "Asiatic" warriors with silver, gold, copper, and clothing; but, defeated, these people dropped the goods and fled.[49] That the Egyptians would pay Semitic foreigners to get their way is the only point of contact here, except for a goods list closely parallel with those in Exod. 3:22, 12:35 in content (except for copper) and order (silver before gold).

Finally in this section we turn briefly from questions of "where" to "how many." For the last century or more, commentators have fought shy of the statement that "about 600,000 went out on foot, plus women and children" (Exod. 12:37), with its seeming implication of an exodus of two million people or so, along with parallel census figures in Num. 1–2, 3–5, and 26.

For a long time now there has been a widespread recognition that, in the biblical text, the question of the long-term transmission of numbers presents the same kind of phenomena as in the rest of the biblical world. In the biblical texts, the actual words for "ten(s)" and "hundred(s)" are not ambiguous, and present no problem on that score; the only question (usually) is whether they have been correctly recopied down the centuries. With *'eleph*, "thousand," the matter is very different, as is universally accepted. In Hebrew, as in English (and elsewhere), words that look alike can be confused when found without a clear context. On its own, "bark" in English can mean the skin of a tree, the sound of a dog, and an early ship or an ancient ceremonial boat. Only the context tells us which meaning is intended. The same applies to the word(s) *'lp* in Hebrew. (1) We have *'eleph*, "thousand," which has clear contexts like Gen. 20:16 (price) or Num. 3:50 (amount). But (2) there is *'eleph* for a group — be it a clan/family, a (military) squad, a rota of Levites or priests, etc. For groups in the Hebrew text, compare (e.g.) Josh. 22:14 end, Judg. 6:15, 1 Sam. 10:19, Mic. 5:2, etc. And (3) there is *'lp*, a leader, chief, or officer, with a second vowel *u*, giving *'alluph*, but that vowel is not always expressed by a full vowel-letter *(w)*, leaving a consonantal form identical with above words 1 and 2.[50] So the question has been asked by many: Are not the "six hundred three *thousand* five hundred fifty people" in such passages as Num. 2:32 actually 603 families/squads/clans, or leaders with 550 members or squads commanded? Or some such analogous interpretation of the text?

It is plain that in other passages in the Hebrew Bible there are clear examples where *'eleph* makes no sense if translated "thousand" but good sense if rendered otherwise, e.g., as "leader" or the like. So in 1 Kings 20:30, in Ahab's time a wall falling in Aphek could hardly have killed 27,000 men; but 27 officers might well have perished that way. In the previous verse (29) we may equally have record of the Aramean loss of 100 infantry officers in one day (with concomitant other losses?), rather than the loss of 100,000 troops overall.

Back in 1906 Petrie suggested that the individual tribal figures in the two census lists in Num. 1 and 26 represented (e.g.) in Reuben (1:21), not 46,500 men, but 46 families ("tents") of 500 people (averaging up to 9 people to a tent; a couple and 7 children or whatever). So, as a result, his figure for the party that migrated to Sinai and Canaan becomes about 5,500 people (the sum of the 100s in the tribal list of Num. 1) in 598 tented families (sum of the "thousands" in Num. 1). Then the traditional 603,550 arose from 598 *'eleph* (family) and 5 *'eleph* (thousand) 550 being run together as 598 + 5 = 603 "thousand" and 550 men. However, he could not account for the numbers of Levites and various other figures in Exodus and Numbers.

Thereafter, Mendenhall (1958) took a similar line, interpreting the rogue *'eleph*s as military squads under leaders; his resultant figure for the Hebrews leaving Egypt was 20,000 plus. But Sarna (1987) objected that the figures were for clans, not just military squads.

Clark (1955) took the *'eleph*s in question to be leaders; his resultant calculations led to a total of 140,000 people emigrating. Wenham likewise (1967) opted for an *'eleph* meaning leader in these contexts. Like Clark, he incorporated the figures for Leviticus into his solution, but with queries on various points. He opted for a body of some 72,000 migrants.

Most recently, Humphries (1998, 2000) has brought a more rigorously mathematical approach to these figures, starting with the modest figure of 273 Israelites to be redeemed in excess of the number of Levites (Num. 3:46), and proceeding to establish appropriate formulae in terms of birthrate, etc. The end result is 598 troops (squads) consisting of 5,500 men (averaging about 9 men each, comparable with what is found in, e.g., the Amarna letters) at the first census (Num. 1–2) and 596 squads numbering 5,730 men later (Num. 26). At a later period, the 598 + 5 *'eleph* gave the 603,550 men of Num. 1–2, and the 596 + 5 *'eleph* gave the 601,730 men of Num. 26. The Levites came out at about 1,000 men in twenty-one rotas of about 50. The emigrants from Egypt to Canaan would then total about 20,000 to 22,000, close to Mendenhall's result. So, in Iron IA Canaan, a population of 50,000 to 70,000 by 1150 might have included 20,000 early Israelites.[51]

(vi) The Way to Mount Sinai and Some Ecology

Over the years there has been lively controversy as to where the Israelites went next, once the *yam suph* had been passed, and over the related matter of the location of Mount Sinai/Horeb, site of the giving of the covenant ("Law"). But of course, some possibilities would appear to be very unlikely, while others have much in their favor. And ecological features that appear in the narratives can provide helpful indicators.

(a) Routes: North, Center, or South?

(1) North

At one time a case was often made for locating the crossing of *yam suph* way up north, at Lake Serbonis, along the Mediterranean coast of Sinai east of the later Pelusium. However, in this day and age, several factors compel rejection of this option once and for all.[52]

First, whatever else is obscure, the biblical text is crystal clear in *excluding* this option. Exodus 13:17-18 states: "When Pharaoh sent the people off, God did not lead them by the way to the land of the Philistines, although it was near(est) — for, God said, 'Lest the people change their mind when they see warfare, and so return to Egypt.' So, God took the people around by the way of the wilderness of the *yam suph*, (even though) the Bene-Israel went up armed from the land of Egypt." Even though Israel's able-bodied men had weapons of some kind, and thus could have fought, it is very striking that they were thus stopped from attempting the short route from the northeast Delta straight along the Mediterranean coast into southwest Canaan. Instead it was to the wilderness of *yam suph* that they must turn, to traverse. In which case this *yam suph* could not be the Mediterranean in any form, Lake Serbonis or otherwise. It must relate instead to either the central zone of Sinai (the Tih limestone plateau) or the southern zone (mountains and valleys). Which brings us back, geographically, to the long line of lakes from Ballah south to the lesser Bitter Lake, between Qantara and Suez, as already suggested above. A crossing in that broad area would allow northern, central, or southern routes. But what military entity was there, to preclude the Israelites from going the short, quick route?

Second, we have very decisive answers to the question just asked, from two nonbiblical sources: the war scenes of Sethos I at Karnak temple in Thebes (with Papyrus Anastasi I) and the results of modern archaeological surveys and excavations along the north coast route. In the war scenes the pharaoh progresses past a long series of forts, settlements, and wells, to go from Sile ("Tjaru") on the Egyptian frontier to the city of Pa-Canaan (virtually certainly Gaza) in southwest Canaan. This series includes ten forts and settlements, as bastions of Egyptian military power along this route.[53] The data here are paralleled by a closely similar list of places from "Ways-of-Horus" (the older name of

Sile/Tjaru) to Gaza given near the end of the famous Satirical Letter of Papyrus Anastasi I.[54] This includes three names not found in the reliefs, while the latter show several not found in the papyrus. This is typical of ancient listings, where parallel but differently organized sources can often vary in their choices of names listed — just like Num. 33 compared with the narratives in Exodus and Numbers; *both* are genuine and complementary, precisely as in many other cases.

The surveys and excavations have vividly confirmed the evidence of the war scenes. Here were found some ten clusters of sites in succession along the ancient coast route between the Suez Canal and Raphia (with more again between Raphia and Gaza). Each was centered on a fort surrounded by ancillary buildings and campsites. Three main specimen sites were dug, with traces of a fort at Bir el-Abd (BEA 10), and of a strong fort (A-289) and a separate administrative center (A-345) at Haruba.[55] At Deir el-Balah, nearer to Gaza, another Egyptian fort and settlement have come to light.[56] The general picture is of initial settlements in the late Eighteenth Dynasty (Horemhab?), followed by a major reorganization and building of the set of forts and administrative centers as a tight network under Sethos I, at first maintained by Ramesses II. Much later in his reign security was slacker, and under Ramesses III it was still less in evidence.

Thus, any attempt at a northern exodus via the heavily militarized coast road in the first half to middle of the thirteenth century would have been suicidal, "out of the frying pan and into the fire." Furthermore, there is no necessary link between the Baal-Zephon located at a "Mons Casius" on Lake Serbonis (Bardawil) in late sources and the situation in the late second millennium; a cult (or cults) of Baal-Zephon might have existed anywhere in the East Delta in New Kingdom times. He was certainly honored at Memphis, for example, under Ramesses II. So, if an exodus is to be traced, we are now limited to a central or a southern option. And the present Lake Serbonis probably did not yet exist back in the late second millennium.[57]

(2) Center

Between the northern coast road with its sand dunes and the rocky massifs of south Sinai we have the broad limestone shield of Et-Tih. It has been described as "the barren Tih Plateau . . . practically devoid of water and vegetation" and "a flat area of limestone and sand. . . . Even the wild flora struggle to survive because of the lack of water."[58] Concerning this area, Bietak remarked: "The middle route along the Mitla pass and Nakhl has too few wells to allow a larger body of people and animals to pass. So when the coastal road is closed, the only possibility to cross the Sinai is in the south along the Wadi Feiran region."[59] Neither the Mitla/Nakhl route (the so-called Way of Seir) nor its northern parallel out toward Qadesh-Barnea ("way of Shur") is compatible with the biblical data on the route followed from the original *yam suph* to Sinai. There is no second *yam suph* between the first one and a middle-road choice of "Mounts Sinai" such as Gebel Halal, Gebel Shaireh, Hasham el-Tarif, or the anachronistic Har Karkom (fifth to third millennia) — unless the hapless Hebrews made a meaningless detour up to the militarized Mediterranean coast and back (suicide trip Mark II). And none of the ecology fits the Tih routes either (see sec. c, next). The Tih middle routes are obligatory for those who favor a "Mount Sinai" in Edom (near Petra? or Gebel Baghir?) or in Midian/northwest Arabia. They could argue for the second *yam suph* at the head of the Gulf of Aqaba, but the other route details before it do not fit the conditions across the Et-Tih shield. In short, the middle-route solution (and with it, Edomite and Midianite "Mounts Sinai") appears to be too loaded down with improbabilities and impossibilities to be sustained.

(3) The Way South and to Sinai (Fig. 29)

That brings us to the remaining option: down Sinai's west coastlands, then east through the mountains and wadis to a southern Mount Sinai, then back up northeastward by Sinai's east coast and desert to Qadesh-Barnea. The following points emerge.

(1) This route steers clear of almost all Egyptian presence, except for the turquoise mines up at Serabit el-Khadim. But the Egyptians did *not* live permanently at Serabit; they simply sent expeditions out and back for a few weeks only, in the cooler weather of winter. Any Hebrew group coming that far south by April/May (or even May/June) would miss them completely.[60]

(2) The Shur desert was also called that of Etham (Num. 33:8), in the latitude of the east end of Wadi Tumilat. So, moving through that desert for three days outward (if the middle "way of Seir" is excluded) has to be southward, on past Suez to go farther south along the west coast of Sinai.

(3) Passing on via such watering places as Marah (bitter then sweet) and Elim (seventy palms and twelve sources), the Israelites arrived at another *yam suph* (Num. 33:10), before traversing a new desert (of Sin) and going on to Rephidim and Mount Sinai. This profile fits that of the known Sinai west coast. The main route down that coast leads south via a series of watering places: Ain Naba (Ghurkudeh), Ayun Musa, the shrubby bed of the watercourse Wadi Sudr, the spring of Abu Suweirah in sandy Wadi Wardan; Ain Hawarah, then well-watered Wadi Gharandel, then on south behind the coastal hump of Gebel

Hummam across Wadi (A)thal on the one through route to Wadi Shubeikeh. Here, one turned either southwest down Wadi Taiyibeh to the seashore of the Suez Gulf (at Abu Zelima or Zenima) or up inland and southeast along Wadi Humr. The *first* option led southeast along the seashore desert plain of El-Markh, and on into the wider expanse of El-Kaa (which runs all the way to the tip of the peninsula).[61] From south of El-Markh several routes ran inland to join with Wadi Feiran and its oasis, bringing the traveler close to Gebel Serbal and (after a couple days' march) round through Wadi es-Sheikh to the er-Raha plain in front of Gebel Musa and Gebel Katrin and its famous monastery. The *second* option led southeast through upland wadis and then high passes to Gebel Musa's er-Raha plain. In this context both Gebel Serbal and the Gebel Musa complex (i.e., Gebel Musa proper and its side-ridge Gebel Safsafa, plus Gebel Katrin/Gebel ed-Deir) would each have serious claims to being the Mount Sinai/Horeb of the exodus narrative, and both have been vigorously championed from Byzantine times to the present.

The key point of comparison between the actual west-coast road just outlined and the biblical sequences in Exodus/Numbers — between the Shur/Etham desert and a Mount Sinai — is the stopping place again at a *yam suph*. In our southern-route context this has to be on the west Sinai shore of the Suez Gulf, and hence by common consent the shores at Abu Zelima (or Zenima) through to El-Markh. Once that is granted, then the two listed stops between three days in the Etham desert and the second *yam suph* — Marah and Elim — would correspond to a choice from the watering holes listed (or more), e.g., Ain Naba, Ayun Musa, Ain Hawarah, and Wadi Gharandel; Wadi Sudr and Wadi Wardan (spring, Abu Suweirah) are less important. It is commonly suggested that the well-watered Wadi Gharandel was Elim; this is possible but not proven. But Marah may have been anywhere from north of Ain Naba down to Ain Hawarah; a choice is impractical, as no detailed account of marching times is given (one month elapsed from the fifteenth of the first month out of Raamses, cf. Exod. 12:18, 34, 37, to moving on the fifteenth of the second month from the second *yam suph* into the Desert of Sin, Num. 33:10-11). And the three days' distance south to Marah from the crossing of the first *yam suph* cannot be established so long as the precise site of that crossing (of several possibilities; cf. pp. 261-63 above) is uncertain. But a location well north of Elim would be likely, around Ayun Musa, Ain Naba, or even farther north.

Out of the Desert of Sin, extending south from Abu Zelima/Zenima, the Hebrews went to Rephidim (via Dophka and Alush) and then into the Desert of Sinai that included Mount Sinai. Rephidim was scene of two contentions: the Hebrews with Moses over lack of water, and the Israelites versus the Amalekites, who sought to halt their advance — no surprise that they did not want to lose the lush Feiran oasis to the Hebrews. There is good reason to locate Rephidim somewhere in Wadi Mukattab or in the north part of Wadi Feiran, *before* one reaches the splendid stretch of oasis in that long valley. A lack of water at Rephidim automatically excludes it from being in the oasis! Striking the water from rock in Horeb was surely at Rephidim, within the *area* of Horeb, *not* at the spot Mount Horeb = Mount Sinai. Going back a moment, Dophka and Alush will have been along whichever approach route the Hebrews took out of the coastal Desert of Sin up into Wadis Mukattab/Feiran.

As for Mount Sinai itself, there is little at first sight to choose between Gebels Serbal and Musa. Both stand up grandly in their places; neither is the tallest in south Sinai, which honor goes to Gebel Um Shomar, farther south and not a contender. Gebel Serbal is close by the oasis of Feiran, but has no adjacent plain for assembly like that of er-Raha at the very foot of Gebel Musa. Nothing can be based on late Byzantine and monastic traditions either way, and no genuinely early traditions survive outside the Hebrew Bible. Most of the reasons advanced between Serbal and Musa are captious and inconclusive, and so need not be discussed further. In practical terms, the immediate conjunction of clear space plus impressive mountain at Gebel Musa suits the biblical narrative much better than does Gebel Serbal; the latter's peaks are almost four miles from the wadi bed of Feiran, the only clear "parking space" there for a group of Hebrews, be it 200, 2,000, 20,000, or even more. Having poor old Moses tramping four miles back and forth up side wadis *and* up a peak of Gebel Serbal is rather extreme, compared with an immediate ascent into a convenient corner on the upper part of Gebel Musa. In short, certainty is not attainable, but Gebel Musa may lead Gebel Serbal by a short head. With only an overnight stop either way between the Serbal part of Wadi Feiran and the er-Raha plain at Gebel Musa, a number of the Israelites may have used Feiran oasis as additional quarters, especially for their livestock (we do not hear of sheep and goats eating manna!). Poetical passages such as Hab. 3:3 (with YHWH from Teman and Paran) cannot supersede plain narrative evidence; they are simply florid elaborations of a given theme. Paran is the desert between a southern Mount Sinai and Qadesh-Barnea, standing for both places and all that they imply; Teman is in Edom (round which the Hebrews went), and may be simply here a synonym for the southlands. Such poetics offer no basis for putting Mount Sinai in Midian or northwest Arabia. And Gebel Sin Bishar (Taset Sudr) in northwest Sinai can be excluded, as it is incompatible with the sequence of the full textual data and the location of the second *yam suph* stop. So nothing is gained here. It may be helpful to consider the broad correspondences from geography and the Hebrew texts for the itinerary from *yam suph* in Egypt to possible Mounts Sinai. See table 20; cf. fig. 29.

Table 20. Topography and Text, Etham to Mount Sinai

(RBR = Robinson, *Biblical Researches in Palestine* I [1841]; LL = Lepsius, *Letters* [1853]; PS = Petrie, *Researches in Sinai* [1906])[62]

Topographic Data	Biblical Lists	OT Refs.
1. *(Lakes Ballah to Small Bitter?)*	*Yam suph I.* Water crossing	Exod. 15; Num. 33:8
2. *Suez southward.* Terrain, RBR, 87-88; gravelly terrain, PS, 5, 7-8.	*Shur/Etham desert*	Exod. 15:22; Num. 33:8
3. (No decisive option)	*Marah.* Bitter, then sweet water	Exod. 15:23-25; Num. 33:8
4. *Ain Naba (Ghurkudeh).* Well, small palms, good water, supplied water for Suez, RBR, 69, 89		
5. *Ayun Musa.* Several springs, small palms, channel, barley patch, RBR, 90-91; brackish water, 4 groves of 50/100 palms, much tamarisk, PS, 8		
6. *Wadi Sudr.* Shrubs, RBR, 91-92		
7. *Taset Sudr (G. Sin Bishar).* Peak, E of route, RBR, 92	(3 days into desert?)	(For Exod. 5:3?)
8. *Wadi Wardan.* Abu Suweirah spring toward shore, RBR, 95-96. Gravelly, bushes, PS, 10-11		
9. *Ain Hawarah.* Well, RBR, 95-96; PS, 205-7		
10. *Wadi Gharandel.* Vegetation, palms, springs, brook, RBR, 99-100; PS, 12-13, figs. 2-5; 207	*Elim,* 70 palms, 12 springs	Exod. 15:27; 16:1; Num. 33:9-10
11. *Wadi Wasit.* Water, palms, tamarisks; RBR, 102; PS, 14-15, figs. 9, 10		
12. *Wadis Shubeikeh, Taiyibeh.* RBR, 104, 105-6; vegetation, 70 palms, PS, 15-17		
13. *Seashore, Abu Zel/nima.* RBR, 105-7; PS, 17	*Yam suph II*	Num. 33:10
14. *El-Markh, desert plain El-Kaa to S.* RBR, 106; PS, 18, 206. Fresh water under sands, PS, 249	*Desert of Sin*	Exod. 16:1; 17:1; Num. 33:11-12
15. *Wadis Badereh, Kineh,* or lower *Feiran:* three routes up from coastal Sin into *Wadi Feiran* proper; RBR, map of Sinai at end		

16.		Dophkah, Alush, hereabouts; ("place to place")	Num. 33:12-14 (Exod. 17:1)
17.	*Wadi Feiran,* and oasis; LL, 297-99, 312-14; cf. RBR, 126; PS, 247-49, 254-56, figs. 180-83	*Rephidim* (dry zone before/northwest of Hessawe of Lepsius)	Exod. 17:1, 7-8; Num. 33:14-15
18.	*Mount Serbal.* LL, 295-97; RBR, 295-96; PS, 253-54	(Mount Sinai?)	
19.	*Wadi es-Sheikh.* LL, 294-95; RBR, 126-27, 215-16; PS, 231-32	*Desert of Sinai*	Exod. 19:1-2; Num. 33:15-16
20.	*Er-Raha plain, Gebel Musa.* LL, 292-93; RBR, 130-203 passim; PS, 250-54	(Mount Sinai?)	Exod. 19ff.; Num. 33:15-16[63]

(b) From Sinai to Qadesh-Barnea (Fig. 30)

This last geographical excursion will complete our local journeyings. According to Num. 10:11-13, 33, the Israelites left Mount Sinai for three days' travel into the Desert of Paran, and then became contentious, suffering first a lightning strike (?), or "burning" (so, Taberah, 11:1-3), and then a fall of quail that brought plague (Kibroth-Hattaavah, 11:4-34), before they moved on to Hazeroth (11:35) and went on into the Desert of Paran and on to Qadesh-[Barnea] (12:16; 13:26). This corresponds to 33:16-18 in the final itinerary. Supplementary notices in Deut. 1:1-2 give a general setting reaching back from the plains of Moab to Hazeroth and Di-Zahab (the latter not visited),[64] and cite eleven days as the travel time from Horeb (= Mount Sinai zone) to Qadesh-Barnea by the eastern ("Mount Seir") route.

In terms of geography, the main route eastward out from Gebel Musa (or Gebel Serbal) via Wadi es-Sheikh is along the main Wadi Sa'l that runs east-northeast from Wadi Sheikh. Just before Wadi Murra (and Ain Hudhera a few miles farther north), Wadi Sa'l turns right sharply, to run down some fifteen miles southeast to the coast at Dhahab, often taken to be the Di-Zahab of Deut. 1:1. As the small perennial oasis of Ain Hudhera is commonly conceded to be the biblical Hazeroth, the stopping point and trouble spot of Taberah ("burning") and Kibroth-Hattaavah ("crave-graves") will have been at some point before Hazeroth/Ain Hudhera — perhaps in the hot, dry, weary zone around the bend of Wadi Sa'l and to Wadi Murra. The eleven days from about Wadi es-Sheikh (Horeb/Sinai zone) to Qadesh-Barnea would correspond quite well to the roughly 140 miles up Sinai's east side (via Hazeroth) at a rate of twelve-thirteen miles per day. The further names in Num. 33:19-35 cannot be placed; if Rithmah = near Qadesh-Barnea (first arrival), then these names would belong to the trackless forty years' wanderings until returning to Qadesh-Barnea via Ezion-Geber (Num. 33:35-36).

(c) Some Ecological Factors

Water under the sands of the west and east Sinai coastal strips was noted above (tab. 20, no. 14). Moses striking the rocks to produce water in the Horeb and Qadesh-Barnea regions (Exod. 17:1-7; Num. 20:2-13) also reflects local geological reality. One may cite an amusing incident from back in the 1920s, when an army NCO likewise produced a good flow of water when he accidentally hit a rock face with a spade, to be teased with his companions' cry, "What-ho the prophet Moses!" as Jarvis reported.[65]

Twice on their travels (down to, and up from, Mount Sinai) the Israelites got involved with migrating quail. The first time, in the Desert of Sin (west coast; Exod. 16:13), quail alighted one spring evening; the second time, again in the spring (Num. 11:31-34; date, cf. second month, 10:11), a flight of quail was blown the few miles inland (up the seaward end of Wadi Sa'l?) and fell to the Israelites. It is a fact that quail do migrate via Sinai twice a year. They fly from farther south up to Europe in the spring, going through the Suez and Aqaba gulfs in the evenings (hence their presence on the Sinai Peninsula's west and east flanks then). But on return from Europe they fly from north to south, landing on the north (Mediterranean) coast in the mornings — which does not correspond with Exodus/Numbers, and would only fit the northern route for the exodus, already excluded on grounds stated above. So the quails require (spring/evenings) a southern exodus.[66]

In summary, a northern route for the exodus is virtually ruled out on geographical, ecological, and Egyptian military grounds alike. A central plateau route is also ecologically highly improbable, and geographically most unlikely (no second *yam suph* is feasible between the first one and any eastern mountain). A southern route fits in with the following considerations: (i) It comports with the general geographical features from the first crossing of a *yam suph* (somewhere between Lake Ballah and Suez) down Sinai's west coast, then into the southern wadis and mountains (zone of Gebels Serbal and Musa). (ii) The settings of Gebel Serbal and (more suitably) Gebel Musa fit the needs of the "law-giving" and tabernacle-building episodes at a Mount Sinai, well away from any external interference from Egypt. (iii) Wadi Feiran was the only major oasis area in Sinai for the Amalekites (or anybody else) to defend against a major body of intruders such as the Hebrews. (iv) Geographical features and eleven days' travel time from Serbal/Musa up the east side to Qadesh-Barnea fit well. (v) Other ecological details such as the spring/evening landings of quail fit the southern solution. (vi) A northern route was forbidden, and its military state fatal to any "exodus," while the impracticality of a central route has been noted — and it too would have been vulnerable to Egyptian military "strikes" down from the north-coast fortresses. Thus a southern exodus cannot be held to be proven, but it is both a viable and a realistic proposition; the narratives show a practical knowledge of Sinai conditions not readily to be gained by late romance writers in exilic Babylon or an impoverished Persian-Hellenistic Judea, hundreds of miles from the places and phenomena in question. As Midianites could readily penetrate the Sinai Peninsula (where Moses supposedly met with Jethro, etc.), and their shadows, the Qurrayites, took over the Egyptian temple site for their own at Timna copper mines in northeast Sinai in the twelfth century,[67] there are no compelling grounds to move "Mount Sinai" into Midian proper or anywhere else in northwest Arabia either.

3. EXTERNAL ASSESSMENT: SINAI AND COVENANT

A. INTRODUCTION

Having arrived at Sinai (assuming they actually did), the Hebrew escapees had serious business in hand, according to the extant written traditions. The basic piece of business was the establishment of a formal relationship between the people group and their deity as divine liberator, what is commonly called the giving of the Law — rather misleadingly, even though a variety of laws are included. What is at issue is formal recognition of the deity concerned as the community's leader or sovereign, with such as Moses or Joshua acting as spokesmen between divine leader and those led. Thus a covenant was the form chosen; the deity had liberated them, and now constituted the group as his people; so their proper response was to obey his commands and laws in running their corporate and individual lives as his subjects. Accordingly, we have here a fair amount of narrative and of "text" deriving from that covenant, within three successive documents (part of Exodus-Leviticus, most of Deuteronomy, chap. 24 in Joshua).

The other business was the direct service of that leader. A king had a palace and servants to do his bidding; a deity had (correspondingly) a shrine and servitors to conduct worship. In the biblical world, *universally,* that meant formal rituals with offerings, etc., conducted by priests and their support staff. That was the universal language of worship in that world; what happens in ours, a few thousand years later, is wholly irrelevant, and must *not* be allowed to intrude upon, or cloud, our assessment of the data transmitted to us when we come to study it. So we find that a very modest but well-appointed, dismountable tent shrine is set up, with appropriate (and equally minimal) cult apparatus. For it are appointed a minuscule staff of priests, rather more support staff, and a set "calendar" of very modest daily offerings, special sacrifices, and some annual feasts. Here, for convenience, we shall take these two items of business in reverse order: first, the tabernacle and its concerns, then the covenant. Finally we may look concisely at the possible date of a putative exodus in the light of all that has been reviewed, and then endeavor to sum up.

B. BACKGROUND DATA

(i) The Tabernacle, Cult, and Trimmings

This structure is presented as a set of gold-covered acacia-wood frames linked together to form a rectangular structure thrice as long as wide: at most only some 15 feet wide by 45 feet long (2 × 15 feet, forehall, and 15 feet square inner sanctum).[68] Over this structure were successively draped curtains that formed the "tabernacle" proper: innermost, of colored cloth decorated with cherubim figures, then (successively) of goat hair (typical of tents), of rams' skins dyed red, and finally of leather of a particular type worked or adorned in some way *(tahash).* Around the whole was to be a rectangular precinct, about 100 × 75 feet in extent, bounded by curtaining supported on posts. The priests were simply Aaron and two (surviving) sons; the support staff (the Levites) were probably in twenty-one groups averaging seven for each of three clans, numbering several hundred, doubtless to serve in rotas. For other details and the cult apparatus and "calendar" of offerings, cf. below. The setup was tiny; cf. fig. 32E.

What we have to examine is the following situation. In biblical studies, for over a century, "critical orthodoxy" (current "minimalism" being no different) has decreed that the tabernacle is an exilic or postexilic figment of the imaginations of Jewish priests (ca. sixth to fourth centuries B.C.), seeking to glorify their cult, giving it a long "history" before the monarchy by projecting a "tented" form of Solomon's temple back to the time of Moses, their first national leader. If this is so, then an examination of the possible history of tabernacular shrines (if any) should have one of three results. Either the tabernacle has no contact whatever with any known reality, be it sixth-century, fourth-century, or at any other date, or else it may be found to have direct analogues at that period that could readily have inspired the supposed priestly imaginings in question. That would indeed vindicate "critical othodoxy" either way. However, if inquiry demonstrates clear analogues from earlier epochs, and in particular *before* the Hebrew monarchy, and with very little such data after circa 1000, then it would be in order to suggest that there could well have been a tent shrine in early Israel that was eventually replaced by the temple of Solomon's time. Late-period priests might conceivably have preserved record of an early structure; but mere imagination would not then have originated it. Let us see.

(a) Dismountable Tabernacles: Third Millennium (Figs. 33A, B)

Nothing was known from this period until the 1920s, when a brilliant discovery by Reisner at the Giza pyramids in Egypt opened up the final tomb of Queen Hetepheres, mother of Khufu, the builder of the Great Pyramid, circa 2600. He found the disassembled parts of a "secular tabernacle" that had once enclosed the queen's bedroom suite. It consisted of a wooden framework, gold covered, that fitted together with tenon and socket joints. The top horizontal beams were supported by vertical poles set in base beams. The corners were held by special fitments, a feature also of the biblical tabernacle (Exod. 26:23). The whole framework was once draped with curtains that had not survived. In the shaft down to her burial chamber, amidst the rubble, were found the remains of another tabernacular structure, but of religious import: copper fittings, gilded wooden posts, and limestone socket-bases; cf. such bases for the tabernacle, but of silver (Exod. 26:19-25).[69] These finds explained other, similar ones of still earlier date. A First Dynasty high-class tomb at Saqqara (ca. 2900) yielded parts of poles, and likewise the Step Pyramid's storerooms under the Third Dynasty king Djoser (ca. 2700). Some four different Egyptian tomb chapels of the mid–third millennium show pictures of such pavilions (or "Tents of Purification") for religious rites associated with mummification.[70] Also curtained, these were quite large structures, again with a series of poles linked by horizontal rods along the top, having the same function as the horizontal middle-crossbars of Exod. 26:26-28. Thus, in Egypt, most of the biblical tabernacle's technology was literally "as old as the Pyramids," in fact older. But all this is still a thousand years before even a Moses, never mind exilic priests.

(b) Dismountable Tabernacles, Early Second Millennium

However, our story is not done. Recent publications of texts from the famous kingdom of Mari on the Middle Euphrates of circa eighteenth (or seventeenth) century now yield mention of tents or "tabernacles" borne on wooden frames, using the same term (but in form *qersu*) as the Hebrew *qerashim*, "frames."[71] And more besides. The text M.6873 totals up "43 men belonging to the large tent" (to transport it), involving the tent cover proper *(khurpatum)*, the frames (as cited), bases (again, cf. Exod. 26:18-25), and units of (seemingly) fencing, latticework, perhaps to form an enclosure as with the biblical tabernacle (Exod. 27:9-10). Another (*ARM* XXVII, 124) orders "delivery of [this] tent-cover with its wooden frame(s)." A third (*ARM* XXV, 806) has the queen of Aleppo (Yamkhad) feasting in a tent at Ugarit. In a fourth (*FM* III, 4: ii:7-14), images of deities were set within the "(tent)-frames" for the West Semitic type of sacrifice of an ass. Thus large tents over wooden frames set in socketed bases were used for both ritual and royal purposes at Mari, still half a millennium before any Moses.

(c) Dismountable Tabernacles, Late Second Millennium

We stay in the Levant, now visiting Ugarit. There the literary tablets preserve myths about the gods and legends of ancient kings (Keret, Aqhat). The tablets themselves date to the thirteenth century, but their archaic language (by comparison with the everyday texts) harks back to older epochs for the ultimate (oral?) origin of these compositions. Here, in the Baal myth, the supreme god El is portrayed as dwelling in a pavilion *(qershu),* using the same term as found at Mari and in Exodus.[72] King Keret is described as offering ritual sacrifices in a tent *(kh-m-t);* in his tale, "the gods go to their tents *(ahl.hm)* and the assembly of El to their tabernacles" *(mshknt.hm),* using the words *ahl* and *mishkan(atu)* in parallel, precisely as in Hebrew.[73] The same occurs in the tale of Aqhat, where Kothar/Hayyin adjourns to his tent/tabernacle.[74] Thus, gods in Ugaritic tradition dwelled in tents/tabernacles from of old as well as in temples, and kings might sacrifice in tents also.[75] This is contemporary at latest (thirteenth century) with our Sinai tabernacle.

Farther east, by contrast, Mesopotamia proper (Assyria and Babylonia) shows *almost no use at all* of such divine tents/tabernacles, at any period. One may cite — again, for the late thirteenth century! — only a four-pillared canopy set up over a religious symbol in a sanctuary of the goddess Ashuritu in the temple built for Ishtar by Tukulti-Ninurta I (ca. 1245-1208) in Ashur.[76] And a *mashkanu* or tent canopy was set up over a royal standard *(itkhuru)* according to a harem decree of Ninurta-apil-ekur (ca. 1193-1180) only a little later.[77]

Returning to Egypt, we find that Tuthmosis III (ca. 1479-1425) built as his Festival Hall for Amun at Karnak temple what was a translation into stone of a pillared tent.[78] Throughout the New Kingdom, but famously illustrated by the finds in the tomb of Tutankhamun (ca. 1336-1327), the pharaohs had concentric tabernacle-like shrines nested over their coffins, like huge wooden "boxes," gold-plated, dismountable, and fitted together with tenons in sockets like the Hebrew tabernacle. Over the second of Tutankhamun's shrines was erected a wooden framework carrying a pall of faded linen decorated with gilded bronze rosettes, for all the world like a skeletal tabernacle.[79]

Coming back to the thirteenth century once more (much nearer a Moses), we find the closest analogues for the biblical tabernacle. On the eve of the notorious Battle of Qadesh (ca. 1275), Ramesses II had set up there his royal war tent within its palisade of shields; this is shown in his temple war scenes of the battle. His rectangular tent (like the tabernacle) was divided into two parts, with an outer room twice the length of the inner room of the king himself. In some representations the inner room has figures of divine falcons facing each other and shadowing the royal name with their wings, much as the cherubim did for the cover of the ark in the tabernacle. The outer court with palisade sets the king's tent apart precisely as did the curtained-off court of the tabernacle.[80] Both courts were rectangular, in strong contrast to first-millennium usage, when Assyrian camps were regularly round or oval, more economical of space. Any Hebrew account of first-millennium date should have had a round, not rectangular, court. Egypt's four army divisions would have camped on the four sides of the king's enclosure, like the four groups of three tribes each on the four sides of the tabernacle court. Cf. figs. 32C, D.

The multicolored curtains with their embroidered cherubim figures would be in no way too elaborate for a thirteenth-century Hebrew tabernacle, despite false claims to the contrary. Such techniques were ages old by then, even commonplace. Already in the mid–third millennium we see the state ship of Sahure boasting a vast sail entirely embroidered with squared-off rosettes and stars (fig. 34).[81] A New Kingdom tomb has a boat with a checker-patterned red-and-white sail.[82] The tentlike processional canopy of the god Min under Ramesses II and III (1279-1213 and 1184-1153) was of scarlet cloth spangled with circled stars and cartouches. Within the thirteenth century under Ramesses II, in the tomb chapel of Ipuy, workmen are shown constructing a "tabernacle" of the divinized pharaoh Amenophis I; its cloth or leather side curtaining is richly decorated far beyond a simple row of cherubim.[83] And the sacred embalming tent of Anubis (same date) can sport a most elaborately adorned canopy.[84] For painted leather coverings, one may mention the great quadrangular catafalque of the lady Istemkheb B under the "kingship" of Pinudjem I (ca. 1050) in Cairo Museum. This was in red/green painted leather, with blue, light yellow, and gilding.[85]

(d) A Tabernacle in the Wilderness

And last, back to northeast Sinai for a "hands-on" excavated tabernacle! When the Egyptians finally abandoned the copper-mining site at Timna in or after the reign of Ramesses V (ca. 1147-1143), the Midianites moved in, destroyed the little Egyptian temple of Hathor, and set up instead their own tabernacle of wooden poles and red/yellow woolen curtaining, with a rectangular base of stones.[86] Their shrine probably lasted barely fifty years, until a massive rockfall destroyed and largely buried it circa 1100. Its standing stones *(masseboth)*, offering bench, and basin typify Semitic, not Egyptian, religious usage. If the Midianites could worship in a multicolored cloth tabernacle in 1130, why not the Hebrews?

(e) Size, Transport, Some Furnishings

It has to be emphasized how small the tabernacle was compared with "national" shrines elsewhere.[87] Its maximum scale of 15 by 45 feet is utterly minuscule compared to even the personal temples of (say) Ramesses II or III in Western Thebes. These were some 200 by 600 feet, and both the tabernacle and its court would have fit inside the forecourt of either temple twice over! Their enclosed precincts were about 600 by 1,200 feet in extent! Amun's main temple at Karnak was up to a quarter mile long, and the main temples of Re and Ptah at Heliopolis and Memphis were also very large by this period (though now lost). The tabernacle really is tiny.

For transport of the dismantled tabernacle parts, Moses was given six wagons *('agalah)* and twelve oxen (two per wagon) (Num. 7:3-8).[88] This is feasible, and is not without parallel soon after this time. In the mid–twelfth century Ramesses IV provided precisely such adjunct transport for his massive expedition of over 8,300 people into the deserts of Wadi Hammamat (northeast from Thebes) in his Year 3, using "ten wagons *('agalat)* with six spans of oxen for each wagon." In another damaged text from Nubia of a Year 3, probably his, mention is made of "[. . . wa]gon" and of "20(?) wagons" before some hostilities.[89] So the Hammamat occurrence is not isolated.

On furnishings we may cite the ark of the covenant (Exod. 25:10-22; 37:1-9) and the special silver trumpets of Num. 10:1-10.[90] The former was essentially a gilded box on four feet, with four rings (two each side) to take two carrying poles. The arrangement is identical to that of a famous box from Tutankhamun's tomb, with just such rings and poles, and also for ritual use (containing four libation vessels). The ark had a gold lid with two cherubim, possibly winged sphinxes, such that the box was base and footstool and the cherubs a throne for the invisible deity. The concept of an empty sacred throne for a present but invisible deity was already current long since in Egypt. In the splendid Deir el-Bahri temple of Queen Hatshepsut (ca. 1470), scenes of festival processions repeatedly show a portable but empty "lion throne," whose invisible or absent occupant is symbolized just by a feather fan. Thus the ark is a typical Late Bronze Age item.

In contrast to the curly ram's-horn shofar, the silver trumpets (hasoseroth) were long tubes with flared mouths. These too were in type and use characteristic of New Kingdom Egypt. From Tutankhamun's tomb (again!) we have two such trumpets, one of silver, one of copper or bronze overlaid with gold. Such instruments are commonly shown in scenes, used exactly in the functions decreed in Num. 10. There the trumpets are to be blown to assemble people, or to signal a march to war, or to mark religious festivals. So too in Egypt; soldiers are rallied to assemble (for whatever purpose); they are called out to war; or the horns are blown to accompany the great religious festivals, usage found under both Queen Hatshepsut and Ramesses II. So, again, Egyptian cultural affinities appear at this time. Of the Late Bronze Age (not later), as others have pointed out, are the tabernacle's lampstand and various other facets.[91]

(f) Personnel and Inductions

Two levels of ministrants were appointed for the tabernacle: the Levitical priests of the family of Aaron and the main body of Levites as support staff. Each group had clearly defined roles. Inside the sanctuary the priests alone might serve; outside it the Levites "did the work" of the tabernacle (Num. 18:1-7; cf. 3:7-10). This is typical usage elsewhere in the fourteenth and thirteenth centuries too, when closely corresponding usage obtained at Hittite temples.[92] Punishments for infringements were likewise analogous in Hatti, Israel, and Egypt at this epoch.[93]

As for inductions, in Exod. 29 and Lev. 8–9 we have notice of the consecration rituals (lasting seven days) for inaugurating and appointing both Aaron as high priest and his remaining sons as (ordinary) priests. Without any scrap of independent evidence, biblicists from of old have relegated these rites to the postexilic period, partly because they knew of no such rites in the Levant any earlier. But with entirely new data from thirteenth-century Emar, this is no longer true. We now have elaborate rites (lasting nine days) for the installation of high priestesses at Emar, which include anointing the new appointee with oil, in fact twice for different aspects of the rites. The use of anointing with oil and blood is found now in the *zukru* festival at Emar, and is not just a quirk in Exodus and Leviticus.[94] Farther north the Hittite ritual of Ulippi for the induction of a deity into a new shrine also shows very strong analogies with the biblical rites, and lasted six or seven days;[95] so comparison with Emar is not just an isolated phenomenon. Compared with the elaborate Syrian and Hittite rituals, those of Lev. 8–9, etc., are brief and "primitive."

(g) Rituals and Offerings

The individual Hebrew rituals as set out in the book of Leviticus (plus parts of Exodus and Numbers) are in general simple and relatively brief throughout. So, too, are many religious rituals at Ugarit.[96] But elsewhere, rituals — even daily rites — run to far greater length. One example must suffice here. The regular daily offering at the tabernacle is the twice-daily presentation (morning and evening) of a lamb with grain and oil as a burnt offering, plus a drink libation, in about three "acts." To anyone versed in the rites of the ancient Near East, this is an incredibly sparse and modest performance, of utterly archaic brevity and simplicity. Compared with these, the Ugaritic and Emar rituals are large and lavish, while in thirteenth-century Egypt the *standard* daily temple ritual was embodied in not less than forty-eight to sixty-two "acts" thrice a day. The Hebrew festival calendar barely manages a dozen celebrations, while in Egypt the festival calendars (as at Thebes) ran to nearly sixty annual feasts, some of great length (such as Opet) and vast opulence.[97] It is instructive, too, to compare the more lavish festal calendars of Mesopotamia in various places and epochs. In short, the whole tabernacle setup is incredibly small and modest, even "primitive," closer in evolutionary terms to the fourth millennium B.C. than to the fourth century B.C.[98]

Comparative data are illuminating for understanding the Hebrew rites. Thus the *tenupa* is an elevation offering, not a "wave" offering, just as in New Kingdom Egypt.[99] The concept of transferring evil symbolically to an animal (or a human) and expelling the same from one's land occurs also in Hittite rites (fourteenth/thirteenth century) and in later Mesopotamian usage — the older parallels are the more exact, not the later ones.[100] Graded cost of offerings is common to Hittites, Emar, and Hebrews in the Late Bronze Age, and blemished offerings are not acceptable to any of these also.[101] There can be no excuse nowadays for artificially down-dating the Hebrew usages by six or seven centuries, for purely nineteenth-century doctrinaire reasons. Again, a seven-year cycle such as the Year of Jubilee (Lev. 25) is not just a late theoretical construction. From the early second millennium, acts of release occur varyingly in *misharum* or *andurarum* years; in religious practice we have the *zukru* festival at Emar that was celebrated every seven years, with preparatory rites in the sixth year.[102]

(h) Narrative Reports on Building Shrines[103]

It has been observed that in Exod. 25–31 plus 35–40 (and dedications, etc., in Lev. 8–10; Num. 7) we have a broadly balanced account. Deity commands the work to Moses, who passes the command on; people and material are mustered, the work is done (largely in terms of the command), inspected, and completed, followed by dedication and rejoicing. Well over a century ago Wellhausen and others rejected this presentation in favor of their own theory: namely, that a full-length command was originally followed only by a summary note of its fulfillment, and all else that we read now is material added at later time(s).

However, much more recent investigation has shown this "modern" concept to be wrong, and the existing format of Exod. 25–40, etc., to be original, i.e., true to ancient usage in the third and second millennia in particular. Within the Old Testament the accounts of building both the tabernacle and Solomon's temple show the same basic set of features: divine command, transmission of that command, preparations to build, then the work (with descriptions of structures, etc.), dedication/inauguration, blessing/rejoicing, and deity's response. Not only so, but this schema and format is well attested in other ancient Near Eastern building texts. The examples closest to the tabernacle account come from Gudea of Lagash (later third millennium) and Samsu-iluna of Babylon (ca. 1700), plus reflexes in the Baal myth at Ugarit (texts, thirteenth century; but origins older). Less so are such narrations by Tiglath-pileser I of Assyria (ca. 1100) and later Mesopotamian rulers, that are closer to Solomon's temple-building account. What is more, such accounts always give in full the building work and description of the shrine concerned, even if they abbreviate the original command. This contradicts absolutely the old theory that sought to argue the opposite, without any knowledge of the touchstone of external, firsthand records and facts. Thus the old nineteenth-century dogmas must be abandoned in the face of those facts. There is no reason whatsoever to deny that the tabernacle and temple building accounts run true to form, and would normally be considered as records of actual work done.

Thus, for the Sinai tabernacle, in retrospect, we possess a considerable — and growing — amount of valuable comparative data (much of it very old, and much, contemporary; far less, of later date) that favor the hypothesis that a small but well-decorated dismountable tent shrine (based on usages of its time) accompanied the Hebrews from Sinai to Canaan, its rituals being of appropriate modesty in extent and format.

(ii) Covenant, Law, and Treaty

(a) The Data

We now return to the central concern at Sinai: the covenant said to have been established there, as "constitution" for the polity of "earliest Israel," with their deity as sovereign leader, and such human subordinates as a Moses or a Joshua as intermediaries. We do *not* possess an official copy or formal text of the actual covenant itself, but only presentations of the *enactment* of that covenant (with considerable sections of its contents) at Sinai (in Exodus-Leviticus), and of the *enactment* of renewals of it both in the plains of Moab forty years later (extensively in Deuteronomy) and in Canaan soon afterward (Josh. 8, mention only; and 24, summary).

This distinction is of very great importance, because external evidence on treaties and covenants shows that (e.g.) the order of enactment does *not* always correspond to the final order of items in formal written copies of such a document. Nevertheless, the congruity of contents and the main order amply suffices to establish with utmost clarity what close correspondences and what contrasting differences actually exist between our biblical and external material.

Already on pp. 242-44 above, the barest contents of the three presentations of the Sinai covenant and its renewals were outlined, in the context of our existing biblical books. Now we have to move a step further back, and detach the covenant presentations from their present "final" context. Then we can view them independently of the final context, in their own right, first together synoptically, and then with external examples of treaties, law collections, and covenants. Today we can establish an outline history of treaty, law, and covenant through some two thousand years, from circa 2500 down to circa 650, in six distinct phases, using between eighty and ninety documents. That history provides an objective and fixed frame of reference against which we can set the biblical examples, in dating them and evaluating their part in that overall history. But first we must tabulate the three preserved biblical versions of the Sinai covenant, before turning to the other data. The formal numbers and headings are standardized, in line with the rest of the data.

Table 21. The Sinai Covenant and Its Renewals

Exodus-Leviticus	Deuteronomy	Joshua 24
1. *Title/Preamble.* Exod. 20:1. Now God spoke all these words, saying: . . .	1. *Title/Preamble.* Deut. 1:1-5. These are the words Moses spoke . . . *(5 verses)*, saying: . . .	1. *Title/Preamble.* Josh. 24:2. Thus says YHWH, the God of Israel: . . .
2. *Historical Prologue.* 20:2. I am YHWH your God who brought you out of Egypt . . . *(1 verse)*	2. *Historical Prologue.* 1:6–3:29. YHWH our God spoke to us, saying: *(history, Sinai to Moab; 40 + 37 + 29 verses)*	2. *Historical Prologue.* 24:2b-13. Forefathers, Terah, Abraham, etc., down to leaving Egypt for a new land *(12 verses)*
3. *Stipulations.* a. *Basic:* 10 "Words," 20:3-17. b1. *Detail:* 20:22-26; 21–23, 25–31 (Lev., see after 5)	3. *Stipulations. Intro.:* 4. a. *Basic:* 5. b. *Detail:* 6–11, 12–26	3. *Stipulations.* (Essence only): 24:14-15, plus response
4a. *Depositing Text.* 25:6 book by ark (and cf. Deut. 10:7-8)	4a. *Depositing Text.* 31:9, 24-26. Book by ark	4a. *Depositing Text.* 24:26 — in book
4b. *Reading out.* (Cf. Exod. 24:7)	4b. *Reading out.* 31:9-13. Read out to people every seven yrs	4b. *Reading out* —
5. *Witness.* 24:4 (12 stelae)	5. *Witness.* 31:26 — book; 31:19-22, song (in 32)	5. *Witness.* 24:22 (people) 27 (stela)
(3. *Stipulations, contd.*) b2. *Detail (contd.)* Lev. 11–20; 27		
6b. *Blessings.* — Obedience Lev. 26:3-13 (short) If you follow My word, I send . . . peace (etc.)	6b. *Blessings.* — Obedience 28:1-14 (short) If you obey, you will be blessed . . .	6b. *Blessings.* — Obedience (implied in 24:20c, "after He has done you good")
6c. *Curses.* — Disobedience Lev. 26:14-43 *(27 verses)*	6c. *Curses.* — Disobedience 28:15-68 *(53 verses)*	6c. *Curses.* — Disobedience 24:19-20

Additional features can include 7. *Oaths* (cf. Deut. 29:12-15), and 8. *Ceremonies* (Exod. 24:1-11; Deut. 27, fulfilled in Josh. 8:30-35).

The history of the sequence of treaty/law/covenant through at least two thousand years in its six phases must now be tabulated in a similar way. Phases I, III-VI (treaties) form a chronologically continuous series, while phase II (law collections) overlaps from I into III. Phases I and VI show variants in East (Mesopotamia) and West (Syria/Palestine). This may be set out as follows.

Table 22. Treaty, Law, Covenant, 2500-650 B.C.[104]

Phase	Date	Details
I: *Archaic:* Treaties	3rd mill. ca. 2500-2300	A. EAST: Eannatum/Umma; Naram-Sin/Elam B. WEST: Ebla and Abarsal (others at Ebla?)
II: *Early:* Law "codes"	3rd/early 2nd mill. ca. 2100-1700	Late 3rd: Ur-Nammu of Third Dyn. of Ur Early 2nd: Lipit-Ishtar; Hammurabi of Babylon
III: *Early:* Treaties	Early 2nd mill. ca. 1800-1700	Several Mari and Tell Leilan treaties (not all publ.) 2 Old Babylonian treaties; (Hebr. patriarchs, see chap. 7)
IV: *Intermediate:* Treaties	Mid. 2nd mill. ca. 1600-1400	2 North Syrian (Alalakh) 4 Hittite (Anatolia; Cilicia)
V: *Middle:* Treaties (and Covenant)	Late 2nd mill. ca. 1400-1200	31 + x Hittite treaties, Anatolia, Syria, Egypt, incl. bilinguals (Hitt. with Akkadian, Ugaritic, Egyptian)
VI: *Late:* Treaties	Early 1st mill. ca. 900-650	A. EAST: 10 Mesopotamian treaties (and Oath-docts) B. WEST: 3 Sefiré Aramaic treaties

It is vitally important to understand that the documents of each phase are sharply different in format and full content from those in the phases before and after them. There is no ambiguity. Only II has traits that reappear in V. Thus this sequence presents us with a very clear and precise framework for dating further examples such as newly excavated and published finds, and also the Sinai covenant.

It is not practicable to give here all these eighty or ninety documents at full length and with detailed analyses of each and of the full history of the genre. That task must be pursued elsewhere. But at least outlines of the key types can be presented. For color diagrams of ten specimens, see Kitchen, *BAR* 21, no. 2 (1995): 54-55. Here we will simply use a limited number of labeled linear tables to illustrate the two-thousand-years' worth of changes that took place.

In phase I (see table 23, on p. 286) the eastern branch (Mesopotamia and Elam) followed the archaic Sumerian way of doing things, with lots of repetition. Instead of putting the first oath just once *before* all the stipulations, and the other oaths and curse just once *after* all the stipulations, their way was to repeat the whole apparatus of oaths and curse each time with every individual "law" or stipulation in turn. But in the western branch (north Syria), the local Semitic rulers would have none of this archaic, time- and space-consuming

Table 23. Treaty, Law, Covenant, Phase I (Third Millennium)

East: Eannatum	*East:* Naram-Sin	*West:* Ebla
2. Prologue, historical	5. Witnesses	2. Prologue, geographical
====================	====================	====================
7. 1st Oath,	7. Oath, +	6c. Curses, initial
+ 3. stipulation,	3., stipulation	====================
6c, curse, + 7, oaths	------------------------------------	3. Stipulations
------------------------------------	7. Oath, +	= = = = = = = = = = = = =
7., 3., 6c, 7, ditto	3., stipulation	6c. Curses, final
------------------------------------	------------------------------------	====================
7., 3., 6c, 7, ditto	7. Oath, +	
------------------------------------	3., stipulation	
7., 3., 6c, 7, ditto	------------------------------------	
------------------------------------	7. Oath, +	
7., 3., 6c, 7, ditto	3., stipulation	
------------------------------------	------------------------------------	
7., 3., 6c, 7, ditto	7. Oath, +	
====================	3., stipulation	
	------------------------------------	
	7. Oath, +	
	3., stipulation	
	------------------------------------	
	7. Oath,	
	+ 4a Deposit,	
	+ 6b Blessing	
	====================	

procedure, so they bracketed the entire body of stipulations as one whole between the initial and final curses — once each, the lot.

From about 2100 down to 1750/1700, in round figures, we have two parallel sets of documents: law collections and treaties/covenants. The law "codes" here appear as phase II, the treaties as phase III (see tables 24 and 25, on p. 287).

The three documents of phase II (through at least three centuries) show remarkable consistency in their arrangement and content. (The laws of Eshnunna are not included here, simply because they [so far] exist only in the nuclear form of a set of laws without any setting.) We now similarly set out phases III and IV, for the treaties of the middle and late second millennium.

Both of these phases differ greatly from what precedes (and massively from what now follows!). They also differ between themselves; no title in III, but a title in IV; matched witnesses and oath in III, but the oath is separate from the witnesses in IV. We now look at phases V, VI, and Sinai (see table 26, on p. 288).

The basic correspondence between Sinai and the Hittite corpus (reaching into Egypt!) is clear beyond all doubt; the order and magnitude of blessing

Table 24. Treaty, Law, Covenant, Phase II (ca. 2100-1700)

Ur-Nammu	Lipit-Ishtar	Hammurabi
[1. **Preamble**] *(lost)*	1. **Preamble**	1. **Preamble**
2. **Prologue:** Theological Historical Ethical	2. **Prologue:** Theological	2. **Prologue:** Theological
3. **Laws**	3. **Laws**	3. **Laws**
[9. Epilogue 6b. Blessings 6c. Curses, all lost?]	9. Epilogue	9. Epilogue
	6b. **Blessings** 6c. **Curses**	6b. **Blessings** 6c. **Curses**

Table 25. Treaty, Law, Covenant, Phases III-IV (1800-1700-1400)

Phase III		*Phase IV*	
Mari/Leilan		*North Syria*	*Hittites*
5. Witness	7. Oaths	1. Title	1. Title
			5. Witnesses
3. Stipulations		3. Stipulations	3. Stipulations
6c. Curses		6c. Curses	7. Oath 6c. Curses

(short) and curses (long) in Sinai goes back to the earlier law-"code" tradition of phase II. Other very minor variations not in this table occur also inside the Hittite corpus itself, and are directly comparable with the Sinai data.

The other massively striking result of juxtaposing phases V, VI, and Sinai is the glaring contrast between Hittite phase V plus Sinai on the one hand and both variants of the later phase VI on the other. In VI there is *no* historical prologue, *no* blessings to match with curses, *no* deposition, *no* reading arrangements. But all these are common to phase V and Sinai, and (but for very early and law prologues) not to any other phase at all! Sinai and its two renewals — especially the version in Deuteronomy — belong squarely within phase V, within 1400-1200,

287

Table 26. Treaty, Law, Covenant, Phases V-VI (1400-1200; 900-650)

Phase V	Sinai Covt.	Phase VI: W	Phase VI: E
Hittite Corpus	Exodus-Leviticus, Deuteronomy, Joshua 24	Sefiré	Assyria
1. Title	1. Title	1. Title	1. Title
2. Hist. Prologue	2. Hist. Prologue	5. Witnesses	5. Witnesses
3. Stipulations	3. Stipulations	6c. Curses	3. Stipulations
4. Dep/Reading	4. Dep/Reading	3. Stipulations	6c. Curses
5. Witnesses	5. Witnesses		
6c. Curses	6b. Blessings		
6b. Blessings	6c. Curses		

and at no other date. The impartial and very extensive evidence (thirty Hittite-inspired documents and versions!) sets this matter beyond any further dispute. It is *not* my creation, it is inherent in the mass of original documents *themselves,* and so cannot be gainsaid, if the brute facts are to be respected.

As may be noticed concerning table 21 for the three Sinai recensions (p. 284), the stipulations in the Exodus-Leviticus version are divided, some before the tabernacle building and commissioning (in Exodus), some after it (in Leviticus), and even an addendum right at the end (Lev. 27). This is not untoward. In the Hittite corpus, the treaty between Tudkhalia IV and Ulmi-Tesup intercalates the deposition (4a) between two lots of stipulations (3), and then inserts further stipulations after curses and blessings and a sanctions section — and then adds more witnesses at the end! For the last feature, compare the witnesses of Deut. 31:19-22, 26 (+ chap. 32) placed after all the blessings and curses, similarly. In dealing with peoples (as opposed to kingdoms), as was Israel, the Hittites varied the order modestly in some measure: the witnesses occur near the beginning in the Hayasa and Kaska (no. 138) treaties of Suppiluliuma I, being followed in Hayasa's case by a second lot each of stipulations and blessings/curses! In another of his Kaska treaties (no. 139), the "final" curse/blessings are followed by oaths sandwiching additional stipulations. Thus the minor variations of order in the Sinai covenant and renewals are of no consequence; the main order and overall content is what is really significant. By contrast, the later phase VI treaties have two consistently different orders of format, and one bizarre Assyrian treaty (of Assur-nirari V and Matiel) goes back to distant Sumerian precedent by putting curses after each of six groups of stipulations!

Sinai is neither just law nor properly a treaty. It represents a *confluence* of these two, producing a further facet in group relationships, namely, social-political-religious covenant. Law, treaty, and covenant in this context are three parts of a triptych. Law regulates relations between members of a group within the group. Treaty regulates relations between the members of two groups politically distinct (or, with vassals, originally so). Covenant in our context regulates relations between a group and its ruling deity. It is thus "religious" in serving its deity through worship; social in that the mandatory content of the covenant is rules for practical living (law); and political in that the deity has the role of exclusive sovereign over the group. The confluence shows up in three details in particular. First, the *overall* framework format and main range of contents is drawn from the treaty format of the fourteenth/thirteenth centuries; second, the law content of the stipulations derives from law, not treaty, and the Sinai covenant's use of short blessings plus longer curses (not the roughly equal curses and blessings of the Hittites) goes back to the older law collections' usage; third, use of interim epilogues before these final sanctions likewise goes back to the older law collections, not treaty.

(b) The Consequences of the Data

These results — from the data themselves, let it be stressed! — have drastic implications which all of us must be prepared to face. (1) There can be no further squirming and wriggling away from the facts; old subterfuges must be discarded. (2) The occurrence of such a characteristic format in the Sinai covenant has direct implications for its literary origins. (3) The whole question of "Deuteronomic" ideas and writings in early Israel (and their history) must be reviewed in the light of these facts. (4) The Sinai documents have an indubitable fourteenth/thirteenth century format, but the "standard" biblical Hebrew in which they are written as preserved to us did not exist then; how does this work out in practice? We will now review these matters as concisely as possible, (5) to attain to a sensible and orderly end result.

(1) No Way Out from the Facts

The whole matter of treaty and covenant goes back most of half a century to a pair of seminal articles by G. E. Mendenhall published in the *Biblical Archaeol-*

ogist in 1954. There he pointed out the clear congruences between the format of the Hittite corpus of treaties and part of Exodus plus Josh. 24, suggesting that the Sinai covenant might well have had thirteenth-century roots. His presentation was very incomplete; no heed was paid to the overall data of Exodus-Leviticus, or to Deuteronomy at all. However, his papers (reissued as a booklet) did set in motion a wave of further studies in the field of covenant and its Near Eastern background and on terminology, etc.[105] As usual, some valuable work was published, some indifferent, and some that went beyond probability. However, this whole development was not acceptable to the "old guard" in biblical studies, for whom a nineteenth-century belief in a late "law" (sixth/fifth centuries), after the prophets, and 621 as the definitive date of Deuteronomy were absolute dogmas to be fanatically defended, even at the cost of facts to their contrary.

Thus we find McCarthy in 1963, 1973, and 1978 trying to escape from the implications of the clear correlations between the treaties and the Sinai covenant, but on false premises, such as the error of claiming that some Hittite treaties lacked historical prologues (untrue for proper copies, including Mursil II/Niqmepa), and that a historical prologue occurs in a Neo-Assyrian treaty of the seventh century (again untrue; see below).[106] Likewise Weinfeld in 1972, on Deuteronomy, made the sweeping claim that "this traditional formulation [i.e., of treaties] remained substantially unchanged from the time of the Hittite Empire down through the neo-Assyrian period. There is no justification, then, for regarding the formulation of the Hittite treaties as being unique, nor is there any basis for the supposition that only Hittite treaties served as the model and archetype of the Biblical covenant."[107] On the total evidence of all the eighty to ninety documents known or available, and summarized above (cf. tables 21-26 above for the bare bones), his statement is wholly false to the facts. At a later date, in all fairness to him, Weinfeld found himself constrained to admit that there *were* clear distinctions between the late-second-millennium treaties and the first-millennium group.[108] The "formulation of the Hittite treaties" *is* unique to the period between 1400 and 1200 (more exactly, ca. 1380-1180), precisely because the body of known documents from before 1400 is radically different in format — and so is the more limited group of documents from circa 900-650. And factually, that is the end of the matter.

The claim that the treaty of Assurbanipal with the Arabs of Qedar (mid–seventh century) had a historical prologue is occasionally made, but is false.[109] The opening lines of the treaty are lost (five lines or more), which included the title line and the beginning of the citation of "the gods of Assyria and Qedar" as witnesses, the normal second feature of Neo-Assyrian treaties (where preserved). After these two elements (title, witnesses), we then have the largely negative stipulations and final curses where the end of the text is broken off. At the beginning of the Assyrian king's stipulative commands, he simply remarks that because of Yauta's ill doings and his own favor to the Qedarites, they must not in future do this and that, but should oppose and kill Yauta out of loyalty to their Assyrian suzerain. Nothing more! This is *not* a "prologue"; on position alone, it would be a "middle-logue" — which species does not exist! The king simply says *why* he enjoins them to oppose and slay Yauta. It is an isolated reason in the middle of the text, and *not* a full historical narrative at the text's beginning, directly following the title. Therefore this fig leaf that biblicists have invoked to "prove" continuity of initial historical prologues into the first millennium B.C. is nonexistent, and our emperors have no clothes on this point. The stark fact remains, that out of eighty or more documents, *all* known prologues (historical and otherwise) precede the twelfth century, and *none* is attested in the first millennium. The more recent claim (Parpola) that the Esarhaddon treaties with the Medes had a brief historical prologue is also mistaken; no such entity appears in any of these first-millennium texts.[110] In any case, it is *not* just prologues that are at stake; there is *also* the nonuse of blessings balancing curses for obedience/disobedience to such documents, and of injunctions on depositing and reading out of such documents. Biblicists must stop evading the clear mass of evidence, and face up to the facts as they are.

Another false argument for refusing to accept that Deuteronomy might have had origins in the Late Bronze Age is that its series of curses derives from those of the Neo-Assyrian treaties of the seventh century, as enunciated by Frankena.[111] This too is misleading, and far too simplistic. Curses have a long history in the Near East, as table 27 on the following pages demonstrates. Because there are obvious correspondences between seven curses in Esarhaddon's treaties with the Medes in 672 and some seven curses (in six verses and two miniparagraphs) in Deut. 28 (often dated to about 621), biblical scholars quickly jumped to the conclusion that the author(s) of Deut. 28 had taken the matter, and even the sequence, of these verses (23-30, 33, 53-57) directly from the phraseology and repertoire of the seventh-century Assyrian treaties.

However, the situation is not that simple. The tradition of formal curses in the ancient Near East went back almost two thousand years before the seventh century and reached all quarters of that world. Given the ever-growing presence and influence of Arameans in Assyria (and Mesopotamia generally) from the ninth/eighth centuries, some would see the reverse process here: namely, that the curses in common between Deuteronomy and Esarhaddon's Median treaties had in fact been borrowed from earlier West Semitic tradition — which is perfectly possible. Thus the whole fragile thesis of Deuteronomy's supposed dependence on seventh-century Assyrian usage would simply evaporate.

Table 27. Deuteronomy 28 Curses and Other Sources[112]

Deut. 28, No. & verses:	Early 2nd mill.	Late 2nd mill.	Early 1st: Sifré	Assyria, pre-700	Assyria, after 700
1. 16-19: city, land, offspring, crops, animals	MARI 3, 6of 9 ZL-Esh, 144f.	GB, 29, 43, nos. 3, 6A	I, 27/28 crops		
2. 20: confusion, ruin	HB, rv 26:60	R. II, 6c	I, 26.	SAA II, 4/5; 12 (SA V; AN V)	
3. 21-22a: fever, disease, wasting	HB, rv 28: 50-68			SAA II, 5 (SA V)	
4. 22b: heat, drought, mildew	MARI 3, 6of 9 (river dried up)		I, 28/29	SAA II, 5, 10 (SA V; AN V)	
5. 23: sky, bronze; ground, iron					VTE, 528/531
6. 24: rain to dust	HB, rv 27:68 MARI 3, 6of 9				
7. 25: defeat by foe	HB, rv 27:90				
8. 26: corpses to birds and beasts					VTE, 425-427
9. 27: boils, sores (leprosy)	HB, rv 27:60-63 "gt punishment"			Kudurrus; AN V SAA II, 11	VTE, 419-420; SAA II, 72
10. 28-29a: blind, mental confusion	HB, rv 26:70; HB, rv 27:22				VTE, 422-424 SAA II, 67
11. 29b: robbed	MARI 3, 61, 9				
12. 30a: wife gone; 30b: house gone; 30c: vines gone		GB, 107, no. 18B		~	VTE, 428-429
13. 31: livestock gone		GB, 107, no. 18B			
14. 32: family to slaves/slain		cf. GB, 107, no. 18B			
15. 33: foreigners take produce					VTE, 430b; SAA II, 27
16. 34: madness					
17. 35: boils from foot to head					SAA II, 27
18. 36-37: exile and idolatry	HB, rv 26:78, HB, rv 28:19-22			SAA II, 4	SAA II, 27

19. 38-41: harvest gone; exile	HB rv 26:68, 78 & 28:19-22		I, 27-29, 32	
20. 42: locusts			I, 27	SAA II, [13]	
21. 43-44: alien bosses				
22. 45-48: serve foes, in distress				
23. 49-52: foes take all				
24. 53-57: cannibalism				VTE, 448-450
25. 58-63: all ills (plagues)				SAA II, 23

But the facts of the case may be broader still. Namely, that both Deuteronomy (at whatever date) and Esarhaddon's scribes both drew on a long-standing common pool of curse formulae and topics (including common sequences) that could be adapted to the needs of the moment.[113] Table 27 illustrates the position in compact form. Of forty-eight verses covering twenty-five curses (or curse paragraphs) in Deut. 28, *only seven* connect with the Esarhaddon treaties (VTE) — which is very few! Also, the order is not identical in the two cases. Deut. 28:23 goes with VTE lines 528/531, which is nearly eighty lines *after* the block of lines (419-50) that runs parallel with 28:26-30, 33, 53-57! As these references show, (i) the Deut. 28 parallel is discontinuous (vv. 31-32 and 34-52 do not have links with VTE), (ii) the parallel even shows varying order of items in a pair of cases: verse 26 (and 25?) would have to come between verses 29/30 to keep the same topic sequence as VTE. But that would interfere with the sequence of topics as expressed. (iii) Correlation of only seven ill-organized items out of seventy-five curses/curse paragraphs (in two separated sections of twenty-six and forty-nine curses) in the Assyrian text and the forty-eight verses/twenty-five curses/curse paragraphs of Deut. 28 is not a very impressive linkup. It is even less so if we compare other correlations in our table 27. There we have ten links with Hammurabi and five with Mari/ZL, namely, fifteen links between Deut. 28 and the early second millennium — more than twice as many as with VTE! In the late second millennium we have six correlations, almost as many as with VTE; so at twenty-one items, thrice as many links in the whole second millennium as with seventh-century VTE. Outside of the Median treaties of VTE, there are other comparisons with first-millennium documents. In the eighth century we have six links with the Aramaic Stela I from Sefiré; and eight linkups with treaties of the kings Shamshi-Adad V and Assur-nirari V of the ninth and eighth centuries, plus two with two *kudurru*s (Babylonian boundary stones of the eleventh and tenth centuries respectively) — sixteen all told, more than twice the VTE links. Finally, in the seventh century we do have six links other than with the Median treaties, almost as many as with them. In final total, from the eighteenth to the seventh centuries, we have forty-three correlations with Deut. 28, by contrast with the partly disordered seven of VTE. Thus a direct link between Assyrian treaty expressions of the seventh century and Deut. 28 is a theoretical possiblity (7 + 6 = 13 correlations), but pales into almost insignificance alongside the forty correlations with earlier periods (thirty before 1200). Thus it is conceivable that an older version of Deuteronomy was updated in about 622, at least by half a dozen extra curses from a foe from whom (under Josiah!) the Judeans were actually trying to free themselves; a curious contradiction between possible literary reformers and the political situation under which they labored! It is easier simply to attribute both the Deuteronomy verses and curses and the VTE examples to origins in the broad pool of traditional curse topics and formulae that had long existed and grown up through many centuries, of which we now see only glimpses.

Finally, some symptomatic details. Deuteronomy shares intimate distinctions with the late-second-millennium documents not found in the first-millennium series, such as the use of the terms for "bond" only before the oath element of blessings and curses, and then the joint expression of bond and oath after that feature (so in Deut. 29:12, 14, English text; Heb. is 29:11, 13); this could not be reinvented six hundred years later without its cultural context.[114]

The term *segulla*, "especial treasure," in Deuteronomy (e.g., 7:6; 14:2; 26:18) is *not* some special, late term coined by seventh-century "Deuteronomists," but is common coin throughout the Semitic world from the early second millennium onward. Old Babylonian examples (Akkad. *sikiltu*) occur in the laws of Hammurabi and at Alalakh (eighteenth century), and at Nuzi in the fifteenth century. It recurs (as *sglt*) at Ugarit in the thirteenth century, and occasionally thereafter. These usages are old, not late, and do not depend on strictly Hebraic "Deuteronomism," be it real or illusory.[115]

Such phrases as to "guard the covenant/bond" (Deut. 33:9 in the archaic "Song of Moses") are by no means late/post-Deuteronomic, as this one in particular has its direct equivalent in Akkadian *mamitu/ade* or *riksa nas(ç)aru*, "guard the oath or treaty," familiar from documents from the second millennium onward. And other such idioms might be cited.[116]

(2) How Could Brickfield Slaves Produce
International-Format Documents?

The particular and special form of covenant evidenced by Exodus-Leviticus and in Deuteronomy (and mirrored in Josh. 24) could not possibly have been reinvented even in the fourteenth/thirteenth centuries by a runaway rabble of brick-making slaves under some uncouth leader no more educated than themselves. The formal agreeing, formatting, and issuing of treaty documents belongs to governments and (in antiquity) to royal courts. Private citizens had no part in, and no firsthand knowledge of, such arcane, diplomatic procedures. Their only role was to hear the content of a treaty (if they were vassals of a suzerain-overlord), and obey it through their own ruler. So also today, treaties are agreed to by heads of state, and implemented by them; and any bills are picked up by the long-suffering taxpayers with never a sight of the original interstate document responsible for the cost.

So, how come documents such as Exodus-Leviticus and Deuteronomy just happen to embody very closely the framework and order and much of the nature of the contents of such treaties and law collections established by kings and their scribal staffs at court in their respective capital cities in the late second millennium? This is socially and conceptually a million miles away from serfs struggling to build thirteenth-century Pi-Ramesse (and Pithom) in the sweaty, earthy brickfields of Exod. 1:11-14 and 5:6-20! No Hebrew there could know of, or would care about, such high-level diplomatic abstractions.

Even a runaway rabble inevitably needs a leader. To exploit such concepts and formats for his people's use at that time, the Hebrews' leader would *necessarily* had to have been in a position to know of such documents at first hand — either because he knew people who shared such information with him or because he was himself involved with such documents. There is no other option.

In short, to explain what exists in our Hebrew documents we need a Hebrew leader who had had experience of life at the Egyptian court, mainly in the East Delta (hence at Pi-Ramesse), including knowledge of treaty-type documents and their format, as well as of traditional Semitic legal/social usage more familiar to his own folk. In other words, somebody distressingly like that old "hero" of biblical tradition, Moses, is badly needed at this point, to make any sense of the situation as we have it. Or somebody in his position of the same or another name. On the basis of the series of features in Exodus to Deuteronomy that belong to the late second millennium *and not later,* there is, again, no other viable option.

The essence of the account of Moses is that: (i) he was adopted into the Egyptian harem (and so, into the royal court) in the East Delta, being found by a princess; (ii) grown to adulthood, at the Egyptian court but still a Semite, a Hebrew by conviction, his murder of an Egyptian exiled him to Midian until a new king reigned. (iii) He was then recalled to Egypt by his deity YHWH, contended with the new king, and led his people group (clans called collectively Israel) out of Egypt to the seclusion of Sinai; (iv) there, using his upbringing, he mediated (iva) a covenant in then-contemporary terms, in (ivb) long-standing, traditional Semitic (and older) legal usage, and (v) had made a wooden-framed tent shrine using well-tried Egyptian technology (used for a thousand years already) in an ancient and widespread Semitic tradition (tabernacles, Mari, Ugarit, Midian; Egypt's royal/divine war tent, etc.).[117]

For (iii), (iva), and (v), we have already given cultural/historical context. It may be useful now, therefore, to investigate what data (if any) may serve as touchstones in evaluating (i), (ii), and (ivb). If there is nothing that bears out the various situations of a Moses — fine! We can ditch him in favor of some alternative path. But if he fits the bill, then it will be wise to adjust accordingly. This is *not* a matter for rival biblicist camps and their rival theological drives, but for quietly checking out how things actually were in the late second millennium.

Under (i) we have first the birth account of Moses (Exod. 2:1-9). Here, because of the reported ban on male Hebrew babies, his mother hid the infant in a caulked basket in the Nile rushes, where a daughter of the king found him, pitied him, and adopted him. His mother managed to become his nurse into early childhood. Many times over, of course, this has been compared to an analogous story about the future Sargon of Akkad, of great renown. He too was left in a caulked basket on a river, found by a stranger, who brought him up; and later he became a mighty king.[118] People have usually dismissed both tales as legendary, and therefore sometimes Moses likewise. But the latter does not follow; legendary infancy or not, Sargon of Akkad was a real king, and inscriptions are known from his reign both in the originals and in Old Babylonian copies. So a "birth legend" (even of a popular kind) does not automatically confer mythical status. Even today, many an infant is abandoned by its despairing mother (mentions in the media are all too frequent), and in antiquity it was no less so in tragic reality. Hence Moses' historicity cannot be judged on this feature; and the story could in fact be true, but not provable.

His name is widely held to be Egyptian, and its form is too often misinterpreted by biblical scholars. It is frequently equated with the Egyptian word *ms* (Mose) meaning "child," and stated to be an abbreviation of a name compounded with that of a deity whose name has been omitted. And indeed, we have many Egyptians called Amen-mose, Ptah-mose, Ra-mose, Hor-mose, and so on. But this explanation is wrong. We also have very many Egyptians who were actually called just "Mose," without omission of any particular deity. Most famous because of his family's long lawsuit is the middle-class scribe Mose (of the temple of Ptah at Memphis), under Ramesses II; but he had many homonyms. So, the omission-of-deity explanation is to be dismissed as wrong.

There is worse. The name of Moses is most likely *not* Egyptian in the first place! The sibilants do not match as they should, and this cannot be explained away. Overwhelmingly, Egyptian *s* appears as *s (samekh)* in Hebrew and West Semitic, while Hebrew and West Semitic *s (samekh)* appears as *tj* in Egyptian. Conversely, Egyptian *sh* = Hebrew *sh,* and vice versa. It is better to admit that the child was named (Exod. 2:10b) by his own mother, in a form originally vocalized *Mashu,* "one drawn out" (which became *Moshe,* "he who draws out," i.e., his people from slavery, when he led them forth). In fourteenth/thirteenth-century Egypt, "Mose" was actually pronounced *Masu,* and so it is perfectly possible that a young Hebrew Mashu was nicknamed Masu by his Egyptian companions; but this is a verbal pun, not a borrowing either way.[119]

What about upbringing (item ii)? Exod. 2:10 notes the full adoption of the boy by his princess patron; that implies his becoming a member of the ruling body of courtiers, officials, and attendants that served the pharaoh as his government leaders under the viziers, treasury chiefs, etc. Such a youth would need to be fully fluent in Egyptian (not just his own West Semitic tongue); so he would be subjected to the Egyptian educational system, learning the hieratic and hieroglyphic scripts. This is typical enough during the New Kingdom, especially in the Nineteenth (Ramesside) Dynasty of the thirteenth century. One may cite a papyrus from the Fayum Harim (under Sethos II, grandson of Ramesses II), in which a leading lady writes to the king: "Useful is my Lord's action in sending me people to be taught and trained to perform this important task. . . . For those here are grown-up children, people like those my Lord sent, able to act, able to receive my training. *They are foreigners* like those brought to us under Ramesses II your good [fore]father, and they would say, 'We were quite a number in the households of the notables,' and could be trained to do all they were told to do."[120]

In the Fayum, these youths may have been set to weaving rather than school; but the attitude expressed applies across the board — and its outcome is the considerable number of foreigners (especially Semites and Hurrians) who served at court and beyond. These included the personal cupbearers of Pharaoh (who became his right-hand men, in conducting royal enterprises like temple building, stone quarrying, gem mining, etc.), directors and scribes of the harem, royal seal bearer, court herald, high steward of the chief royal memorial temples, generals, and so on.[121] A Moses would be simply one among many. Both Sethos I and Ramesses II signed treaties with the Hittite kings; the surviving one of Ramesses II shows the format so familiar in the whole

"Hittite" corpus. What is more, the documents in that case were not just sent to Egypt by the Hittites for Egypt's approval. The scribes at *both* courts produced drafts to be exchanged for mutual approval or amendment before the final document was settled.[122] So anyone in Egypt's "foreign office" would be able to learn of such documents in this epoch. Including a Moses, if there was one, and at court and (as a foreigner, with foreign language potential) quite likely to be in the "foreign" department. This last suggestion has to be just that, but it does explain how a Hebrew leader might later come to use this convenient and appropriate framework for the Sinai covenant.

And the stipulations, law, not treaty, stipulations (ivb)? Here we have the other side of the coin. The "legal" content of Exodus, Leviticus, Numbers, and Deuteronomy has little in common with the social system of Egypt — but a great deal in common with the law collections and customs of the largely Semitic Near East. From studies made in recent decades it is clear that none of the known law collections, Near Eastern or biblical, aims to give a complete conspectus; they do often overlap in topic and also in treatment of subjects, but items or aspects present in one collection may not appear in some or any of the others.

This book is not the place to tackle so vast a subject. Instead, a modest observation or two must suffice.[123] There is a good deal of common ground between the biblical groups of laws (excluding religious regulations, which are in a separate sphere); it is significant that most comparisons between the biblical laws and external sources occur with the older collections — with Hammurabi in particular, not so much (e.g.) with Hittite or Middle Assyrian laws or later ones. In short, Moses (or his doppelgänger) drew upon long-hallowed tradition for much that we find in the detailed laws of Exod. 21–23 and the rest. Even in Egypt the Hebrews were basically Semitic by social usage, and not Egyptians, and retained their own cultural background throughout. This material cannot be consigned to late "legal eagles" of the exile or afterward — it belongs by origin in the second millennium with its closest relations.

In terms of the amount of "legislation" (leaving out purely religious matters), it is interesting to compare the amount in the external sources and in Exodus to Deuteronomy. Hammurabi contains 282 enactments; the Hittite Laws somewhat over 200 laws (a few are lost); the Middle Assyrian collection at least 116 laws. The other collections are shorter (Lipit-Ishtar, 38 laws; Eshnunna, 61 laws; others are too incomplete to compute). In Exod. 21–23:9 one may find about 40 laws, and likewise in the "civil" parts of Deuteronomy (chaps. 15; 21; 22; 24; 25, omitting other matter). In Lev. 18–20 are included up to 66 rulings outside of those connected with religious concerns. Numbers has hardly anything (up to 4 "civil" provisions). Individually, Exodus, Leviticus, and Deuteronomy each compares well with the other shorter collections (Lipit-Ishtar; Eshnunna). In total, at about 150 laws, they do not greatly exceed the Middle Assyrian collection, and modestly are distinctly shorter than the Hittite Laws (200+), and especially Hammurabi (282 laws). There is nothing here that could not be handled easily at Sinai, en route, and in the plains of Moab. None of this needed any great time to compile.

In short, there is nothing physically exceptional about the various groups of material in the books Exodus to Deuteronomy that would not fit comfortably and easily into a short span of time, compositionally, late in the second millennium. The opposite has to be proved, not assumed.

As for the role of a Moses, there is no *factual* evidence to exclude such a person at this period, or his having played the roles implied in Exodus to Deuteronomy. A large amount of inconclusive discussion by biblical scholars in almost two hundred years has established next to nothing with any surety, and has vacillated all the way between extreme conservatism ("Moses wrote all the Pentateuch") and total nihilism ("There was no Moses, and he left nothing"). The basic reason for endless shilly-shallying and lack of real result is the massive failure to seek and use external, independent controls such as have been applied here and throughout. Merely churning over and over the biblical texts exclusively in terms of subjective opinion will never be able to settle anything. There is no factual basis for either extreme, as will become even more apparent in the next two subsections.

(3) "Deuteronomic" Writing: Thirteenth versus Seventh Century or Thirteenth and Seventh Centuries?

That the bulk of Deuteronomy in form and content is irrevocably tied to usage in the late second millennium is a fact that clashes horribly with the hallowed speculations about the origins and history of "Deuteronomic" thought that have been developed across two hundred years, and in particular with the last sixty years and with the "minimalism" of the last decade or so. But antiquity of a conviction does not validate its truthfulness; after umpteen millennia of acceptance, who now believes in a flat earth? Hard facts, not time span of belief, indicate where the truth is most likely to be found.

Traditional "critical" belief suggests that the book of Deuteronomy was written in the seventh century, and that it (or a related writing) sparked off the reforms of Josiah in 621. The emphasis on obedience to deity, with consequent blessings, and even more on the dire consequences of disobedience, was then thought to have formed the dominant thinking of such prophets as Jeremiah, and of the writer(s)/editor(s) of the four books of Joshua, Judges, Samuel, and

Kings — to which Deuteronomy was prefaced — to produce a continuous "Deuteronomic History" from Moses to the Babylonian exile.[124] Not all scholars accept this concept, but it is a popular view currently, and the ever-growing attribution of biblical passages to Deuteronomist writer(s) has led virtually to a form of "pan-Deuteronism," with all the dangers of undue exaggeration.[125] It has also become axiomatic in some quarters that whatever the Deuteronomists wrote is theological fiction, not history. So we would be dealing with a movement exclusively of the seventh-sixth centuries that either adapted historical traditions to fit its theology or created imaginary, not real, "history" in the mold of its a priori theology.

A late thirteenth-century Deuteronomy (or proto-Deuteronomy) automatically rules out this overall solution in terms of chronology; and associated evidence also rules out the assumed elimination of history by theology. Fatal objections to the overall theses of a Deuteronomic history that offers only fiction, based on a seventh-century Deuteronomy, are many; only a few symptomatic examples can be included here.

Deuteronomic writers/editors are historians, not theological fablemongers. See already pp. 48-51 above. The ancients habitually ascribed a role in their history to higher powers, their deities — as in war, for example. It is not legitimate to condemn this feature as marking a nonhistorical episode in the Hebrew writings *and* still accept this same feature in provenly historical episodes in records from Egyptian, Hittite, Mesopotamian, or other such sources, commonly firsthand. If it is wrong in Hebrew texts, it is wrong in the others. If it is unavoidably part of a genuine historical account in the latter records, then it must be conceded to be so, or at the very least possibly so, in the Hebrew narratives. Nobody now (so far as I know) believes in Amun, Ashur, Marduk, or Baal-Hadad, just as none are compelled to believe in deity/ies still worshiped currently. A modern historian must *not* confuse beliefs of the ancients with modern belief.

It has to be understood that "deuteronomic" writers generally *interpreted* actual history; they did not *invent* it. The ancients (Near Eastern and Hebrew alike) knew that propaganda based on real events was far more effective than that based on sheer invention, on fairy tales. A laconic chronicle may record that King A warred against King B and was defeated. A royal annalist or a deuteronomist may, equally, claim that King A had offended a deity, and so the deity had punished him with defeat by King B. To the ancients (within their beliefs), both versions would be true, and possibly to a modern believer if the deity were his or hers also. To a secular observer the laconic statement would be true (unless faulted by better sources), and the interpretative version should represent exactly the same degree of history (B defeated A), but with the observation that the event was interpreted in a particular way by the ancient writer(s) concerned. That is the proper impartiality at which a true historian must aim. So the fashion with some to dismiss "deuteronomically interpreted" narratives as automatically nonhistorical (and without explicit factual data to prove it) is gratuitous, illegitimate, and bad methodology.

Deuteronomic concepts — no novelty. The first concept that was not a novelty is *obedience.* Again, above, the DPCD syndrome has been traced back to the mid–second millennium (pp. 237-38 above). Disobedience led to punishment by deity, and consequent contrition to deliverance in the eyes (and claimed experience) of many outside Israel up to a millennium before the seventh century. In Egypt, in fact, where obedience to *maat* (right doing and attitude, piety) in deference to deity to avoid punishment was the permanent norm, this is visible in our firsthand sources not just for kings but also for their subjects through 2,500 years (third millennium to Greco-Roman times);[126] nor were the Egyptians alone in this. So the obedience-to-deity syndrome is *not* a necessary hallmark of deuteronomic ghostwriters in Israel. Incidentally, I have yet to discover *any* religion that positively urges upon its followers a doctrine or practice of regular *dis*obedience to deity!

The second concept is *exile and loss of land.* As noted long ago, the concept and threat of loss of one's land and of going into foreign exile is not to be read as relating exclusively to the Babylonian exile. That event was merely the last and most drastic of its kind in preclassical Hebrew history; compare earlier, the captivities of the northern kingdom from Samaria in 722/720, and from Galilee before that, circa 734. As a threat and as a practice, it is universally attested from the early second millennium onward. In the Mari archives circa 1800/1700, a town Bakram is captured, and its citizens deported into exile at Mari. Further Mari mentions (under Zimri-lim) account for other such deportations of up to 30,000 men.[127] In the sixteenth century the Hittite king Hattusil I took away the populace of two towns to serve the sun goddess of Arinna.[128] In the fifteenth century Tuthmosis III of Egypt took away into Egyptian exile 2,503 prisoners and 25,000 livestock (first campaign in Canaan), while his son Amenophis II is credited with transplanting over 100,000 assorted Syrians into Egypt in two such campaigns. A Theban stela of his son, Tuthmosis IV, mentions "The Settlement (such-&-such) with Syrians from the town of Gezer."[129]

The late fourteenth century finds the Hittite king Mursil II moving whole population groups: minimally 15,500 in Year 3, about the same in Year 4, and a total of 66,000 in Year 5, besides other figures and dates.[130] In the thirteenth century Ramesses II boasted of moving Nubians (from the south) to the (Delta) northland, Syrians (from the north) to Nubia (in the south), the Shasu-Asiatics (from the east) to Libya (in the west), and Libyans to the eastern hills.

About 1180 Ramesses III boasted similarly; and actual Asiatic and Libyan settlements are known in Egypt in the fourteenth to twelfth centuries and later.[131] In the Near East, the same occurs then. In the thirteenth century the Assyrian king Shalmaneser I took away 14,400 prisoners from Hanigalbat (among others), and Tukulti-Ninurta I claimed 28,800 Hittite captives removed to Assyria. Then Tiglath-pileser I (ca. 1100) took away 4,000 and 20,000 men in his first and fifth years respectively; in 879 Assurnasirpal II peopled Calah with exiles, and in ten years of campaigning (859 and following) Shalmaneser III carried away some 44,400 people into Assyrian exile.[132] Thus the threat of exiling people (particularly smaller groups and states) was an ever-present menace in the biblical world, even from Abraham and Moses' epochs, long before the notorious captivity in Nebuchadrezzar's Babylonia.

The third concept had to do with *a central sanctuary versus purity*. Great claims have been made that a keynote concept in Deuteronomy was emphasis on official worship only, at a central sanctuary; that the central sanctuary in question was at Jerusalem; and that this was a Josianic reform. There is no real support for most of this. The text merely states that the various offerings shall be brought to "the place that YHWH your God will choose as a dwelling for his name," without specification. As others have shown, this may allow a main central sanctuary, but does not needfully imply a *sole* sanctuary. From Sinai to Shiloh, the tabernacle (whose existence need no longer be doubted) served as the main sanctuary; then, from David's time, a tent at Jerusalem, and then the temple there from Solomon's time onward. Under Josiah, Jerusalem may well have been made in practice the sole sanctuary, because all the local worship places ("high places," etc.) had become sites of idolatry. In his time, purification of the cult from alien elements was the central concern. It is misleading to restrict consideration of his reform (as some have done) to 2 Kings 22–23. Others have shown that a fuller picture can only be established by use of the additional data found in 2 Chron. 34–35, which cannot be dismissed out of hand.[133]

Fourth is a lengthy *time gap* and the issue of *continuity of tradition*. Some may feel that a six-hundred-year interval between a thirteenth-century Deuteronomy circa 1200 and reforms supposedly stimulated by it in 621 is a long "gap." However, such "opaque" periods are commonplace in our considerable but uneven knowledge of the biblical world; and the gap may, in any case, be illusory. First, gaps. Extrabiblical examples include the Egyptian Hymn to the Uraeus (serpent goddess), first known under Ramesses II (thirteenth century) and then only found again a thousand years later under the Ptolemies, and the festival text of the god Sokar transmitted with very little change through 800 years (almost without further known witness so far) from the times of Ramesses II and III again to that of the Ptolemies.[134] We have, similarly, magical/medical papyri of the New Kingdom (fourteenth-twelfth centuries) in which two spells are replicated some 900 years later in copies from about 330.[135] And so on. Gaps very often are due to chance, because we do not yet possess sufficient source materials.

Second, continuity. We also have ample examples of continuity across equally long spans of time, and not just from Egypt, one may add. Two examples will stand for many others. In Egypt a number of funerary spells first found in the Pyramid Texts (copies, ca. 2400-2200) recur in the later Coffin Texts (nineteenth-seventeenth centuries), and in some cases thereafter reappear in the New Kingdom Book of the Dead (fifteenth-twelfth centuries), through three manuscript phases spanning about a thousand years.[136] In the New Kingdom itself, the welcoming speeches by the god Amun to the king in triumphal pose smiting foes go through copies and slightly variant editions (Tuthmosis III, Amenophis III; Sethos I, Ramesses II, Merenptah, Ramesses III, Ramesses VI; Shoshenq I) during half a millennium, circa 1425-925.[137] Like our Hebrew writings, nearly all of the foregoing are religious texts, but both transmissions that jump gaps and continuous transmissions occur in other categories of texts.

In the Old Testament itself, the imagined gap between a thirteenth-century Deuteronomy and a seventh-century Jeremiah is most likely illusory. The impact of an early Deuteronomy would be felt in other writings composed during that interval. It would no longer have to be arbitrarily and artificially restricted to the time after 621. The book of Joshua comes down at least to the time of the elders that followed him (ca. 1200), and probably into the very first phase of the judges' period; it knows of the Danite migration to the north (19:47), and the Philistines occur just once (13:2, perhaps replacing the Anakim; cf. 11:22). So, as no other proven neologisms occur, the book could have been finalized in basic form near the start of the twelfth century; any "deuteronism" in it would simply be the impact from the late thirteenth-century Deuteronomy. In turn, the book of Judges, in a wholly different format, was most likely composed at the beginning of the monarchy, by its implicit suggestion thrice over (18:1; 19:1; 21:25) that society was dissolving into godless and immoral chaos because there was no king in the period it describes to give a good lead throughout the land. In David's early days such an ideal was understandable, but hardly in later times. The use of deuteronomic concepts was much more obvious in Judges than in Joshua, with its tribal failures after Joshua, its statement of failure in obedience, and its grand sixfold cycle of DPCD. In a more anecdotal narrative format, *not* directly linked to the judges, the book of Samuel shows a third authorial mode. It may first have been written in the whirl of events around Solomon's accession. Then Kings — as transmitted to us — runs from the death of David (prelude to Solomon's reign) to the final crash in the 580s, and a closing note on Jehoiachin favored in Babylon in 562. Both Samuel and Kings show the overarching theme of faithfulness/disobedience to YHWH throughout — they are worthy successors to Joshua-Judges, but differently written and planned. They are "special interest" works, drawing on the kingdom daybooks (see chap. 2), and represent the voice of the prophets alongside the separate individual, proclamatory works by that group of men. To put all this in a nutshell, what we *now* have is a series of four distinct works (Joshua, Judges, Samuel, Kings) in the normative or mainstream tradition of Yahwism, for which the terms "Deuteronomic" and "elitist" are too narrow and mistaken respectively, and a set of "Deuteronomic histor*ies*," not a single "Deuteronomic histor*y*." And Deuteronomy itself is a wholly separate and foundational work before these.

(4) Language and Literary Transmission: An Ongoing Factor

It is all very well, of course (as I have done!), to talk glibly about specific books such as Deuteronomy and Joshua (and precursors such as Exodus and Leviticus) being written in the period from about 1220 to 1180. But they could not then have been written in classical, standard biblical Hebrew as we know it in the present-day Hebrew Bible as transmitted by the Masoretes from sometime about the seventh century A.D. Yet Moses is credited with having written specific items (Exod. 17:14 [Amalekite war in a scroll]; Exod. 24:4 [the laws that preceded]; Exod. 34:27-28 [preceding commands, Ten Commandments; cf. Deut. 4:13; 5:22]; Num. 17:2-3 [names on staffs]; Num. 33:2 [itinerary of wilderness travels]; Deut. 31:9 [the Deuteronomy laws]; Deut. 31:22 [song of Deut. 32]). Likewise Joshua (Josh. 8:32 [law on plastered stones]; Josh. 24:26 [wrote laws in scroll of law]). The considerable sections of Exodus-Deuteronomy where Moses appears in the third person fall into two groups: passages where someone wrote as his scribe in third-personalized dictation, and passages that represent a write-up of the present text either a short time after the events described or (as with Deut. 34) after Moses' death. Similar processes would apply even more to the book of Joshua. Figures such as Joshua (for Moses) or Eleazar and Phinehas (for Joshua) could have acted as scribal aides, much as did a Baruch for a Jeremiah in much later times.

But in what form and language? We have evidence of a form of Canaanite in the glosses and items of non-Akkadian vocabulary that crept into the cuneiform texts of the Amarna letters of the fourteenth century.[138] These we may term late Canaanite, as opposed to traces of Canaanite in the early second millennium or before ("early Canaanite") and in the mid-second millennium ("middle Canaanite"). To the cuneiform evidence for late Canaanite may also be added the small but gradually growing corpus found in western Palestine of brief inscriptions scribbled or incised on pottery and sherds of the thirteenth and twelfth centuries.[139] The Amarna letters give us tiny glimpses of Canaanite in the usage of officialdom, as these letters passed to and from the local kings in Canaan and their Egyptian overlord, the pharaoh. But the linear alphabetic jottings and incised items on pots and sherds come at least in part from a humbler situation, it would seem. They represent the use of the simple linear alphabet by people who were *not* necessarily scribal specialists at all. An alphabet of between twenty-two and twenty-eight letters was no great burden for someone to learn, in vivid contrast to the complex scripts and vast series of different signs that comprised them, in Egyptian and cuneiform. Hence from the fourteenth/thirteenth century onward, the alphabet could be freely used for any kind of communication. The contemporary north Semitic texts found at Ugarit in north Phoenicia illustrate this to perfection. These too were written in an alphabet — but in simplified cuneiform characters, so that clay tablets could be used for writing the documents. And these include religious texts (rituals, god lists, myths), literary texts (legends), administrative lists, and a copy of a treaty with a Hittite king, amongst other things. In Canaan to the south, most records were evidently written on papyrus — and this has all perished. We know that the kings of Byblos used papyrus to keep their timber accounts circa 1080 (Wenamun text) — but of those clearly voluminous scrolls, no merest scrap survives. No wonder, really.[140] In Egypt, home of papyrus with dry desert fringes, it has been estimated that some 99 percent of all papyri written from circa 3000 down to the advent of Greco-Roman times have perished completely. So, in the less preservative conditions of Canaan and Phoenicia, it is scarce wonder that nothing whatsoever has so far been found except for the batches of later papyri, such as the Wadi Daliyeh group (ca. 300 B.C.), the Qumran/Wadi Murabba'at lots (Dead Sea Scrolls), and a sixth century B.C. scrap of a letter — all from desert caves. So the Amarna evidence and handful of pottery finds prove clearly that Canaanite was the dominant local tongue and could be readily expressed in alphabetic writing; Ugarit's durable alphabetic tablets show us what range of material we have missed in the lost papyri of Canaan. Thus we should consider a Moses or a Joshua writing on papyrus, skins, or even waxed tablets in alphabetic late Canaanite. During the two centuries that followed, circa 1200-1000, standard Hebrew evolved out of this form of Canaanite, probably being fully formed by David's time. Copies of older works such as Deuteronomy or Joshua would be recopied, modernizing outdated grammatical forms and spellings, a process universal in the ancient Near East during the period from 2500 to Greco-Roman times. Until about the eighth century B.C., the Hebrew script was entirely consonantally written. Then the practice came in of using the "weak" letters to write also long vowels (*w* for *u/o*; *'aleph* for long *a*, *y* for long *i, e*, and *h* for long *a, e*). So the script remained until the Masoretes added the system of small vowel markers and other such symbols above, below, and within the original letters.

Literary recopying was an art practiced throughout the ancient Near East for three thousand years. Schoolboy scribes made "howlers" in their school texts, as most youngsters do down to the present. By contrast, experienced scribes at their best were able to transmit very accurate copies of works for centuries, and to modernize archaic usages if called upon. Egyptian, Mesopotamian (Sumerian and Akkadian), Hittite, Ugaritic, and other texts exemplify all this.

(5) A Sensible Outcome?

The picture that emerges is of a group of West Semitic clans (collectively called "Israel") that fled from Egypt under a leader who had spent time in Sinai after an Egyptian court upbringing and education. These factors were crucial in his ability to lead the group through the Sinai terrain; for marshaling the skills of the craftsmen in the group to build a traditional Semitic "tabernacle" shrine, using Egyptian technology and motifs; and for formulating a foundation document ("covenant") making a nascent "nation community" out of his clans, using — again — a suitable model learned in his court days. The renewals of that covenant retained the same model forty years later when Joshua took the group into Canaan. The concepts in that covenant and strong sense of the importance of obedience to their suzerain deity together were the basic formative influence in the growth of normative Yahwism as Israel's core religion, regardless of what Canaanite or other incrustations it acquired during the judges and monarchy periods. "Deuteronomic" is far too narrow and restrictive a term to use of this development. What happened in the late eighth century (Hezekiah) and then in the late seventh century (Josiah) was a *reversion* to older origins, a "purification," in the latter case, partly stimulated by recovery of a book of the covenant long lost in some dusty cupboard during the half-century reign of Manasseh plus Amon. The writing activity of the prophets came in two forms: books that collected their individual pronouncements (with the help of scribal aides; cf. Baruch with Jeremiah) and commentaries from their viewpoint upon Hebrew history from Samuel to the fall of the monarchy. A first book of Kings may have encompassed the period from David's death to the end of Samaria in Ahaz's and Hezekiah's time (1 Kings; 2 Kings 1–17, with the closing peroration in 17:7ff.). A later prophet may then have added a third book of Kings, our 2 Kings 18–25:26, down to about 580, the second and third books being put together as one. Finally, a generation later, the closing paragraph on the release of Jehoiachin was added by an exilic prophet, ending the whole.

(iii) Possible Date Limits for an Exodus

Finally, a few words only on the much-discussed issue of the date of the exodus. Our contribution here will stay simply within the available range of the biblical and nonbiblical evidence, and the modes of reckoning *known* to be used in biblical times both inside and outside the Hebrew Bible. No single item will be artificially privileged, risking distorting the whole.

(a) The 480 Era Years, 554 + xyz Aggregate Years

Already in chapter 5 (pp. 159-60 above) the relationship was set out, of the series of aggregate years (counted up through the biblical books) to the 480 era years of 1 Kings 6:1 and to real-time years of elapsed time. The essence of this was that the 554 + *xyz* years (about 596 years all told) readily fitted into the almost 300 real-time elapsed years (and hence in principle into the 480 as well, if so needed). This is a phenomenon that applies commonly in the biblical world, and the overlaps of contemporary rulers ("judges") in Israel's "First Intermediate Period" are no different in practice to those found in Egypt's First, Second, and Third Intermediate Periods, or in Mesopotamia among the third-millennium Sumerian city-states or among the rival local kingdoms of the Isin-Larsa/Old Babylonian epoch of the early second millennium.

As already stated, the 480 years may have in fact one of two origins. First, it could be an era date made up of twelve 40-year "full generations," such that 12 × 40 = 480; this interpretation is often propounded. The 40-year full generation comprises 20 years for one group to grow up to childbearing age, and then 20 years for their children to reach the same stage (this lies behind Num. 14:33). Twelve generations of roughly 22/25 years each in real-time count would give us the 288/300 years seemingly required by our data for a real-time span between an exodus about 1260/1250 (minimum) and 967 for Solomon's fourth year. The 12 × 40 type of origin should not be lightly dismissed. In the ancient Near East, the Hebrew Bible's own world (which ours is not!), such procedures were almost certainly in use. In Judg. 3:30 we have a simple example: the time of local peace that followed Ehud's strike against Moab lasted "80 years." It may well have done so; but the 80 does look very like a 2 × 40 years figure. Over in Mesopotamia, a similar phenomenon seems very likely to have operated with era dates also. A text gives 720 years between Ilushumma and Tukulti-Ninurta I, kings of Assyria. That is not literally practicable on other data; but as Reade has suggested, the scribes may have calculated 16 years to a reign (which *is* a true long-range average), such that the 45 reigns from one king to the other comes to 45 × 16 = 720 years. Similarly the Kassite Dynasty (which did not initially rule in Babylon) at 576 years may represent 36 rulers × 16 = the 576 years. Other "long-range" dates are susceptible to similar examination.[141] Thus the 12 × 40 = 480 would find parallel both in Hebrew (Judg. 3:30) and in the Near Eastern wider context.

Or else, second, the 480 years are in fact a selection from the 554 + *xyz* years aggregate, on some principle not stated. This too is perfectly possible, but not hitherto sufficiently considered or convincingly worked out, so we shall look at this further. For an Israelite king looking back to the exodus as a distant point in time, the known periods of his people's activities and of peace in their troubled period of settlement in Canaan would have provided an ideal overall era. Let us test this out on our surviving biblical data; see table 28 on page 309.

On this basis, excluding all foreign oppressions, and using solely biblical data for all but one and a half cases, we have a clear workable origin for the 480 years. The figure of [x]2 years for Saul in 1 Sam. 13:1 is clearly defective, and reasons have been given already for restoring it as [3]2 years, which fits well. We are then short of only two items: the rule of Joshua and the elders, and a figure for it. A balance of 5 years would complete the 480.

So we are in fact well off! Two equally workable options for the origin of 480 years (be it 12 × 40 or a nonoppressions aggregate). And a neat fit of 554 + *xyz* years into the real-time 300 years.

(b) Real-Time Factors

Other points deserve brief mention. Again, on internal evidence, the ten successive high priests from Aaron to Zadok (1 Chron. 6:3-8) would cover the 300 years from the exodus to early in Solomon's reign; by contrast, the genealogy of David (only four generations) is clearly selective (Ruth 4:18-22). For blustering Jephthah's propagandistic 300 years (Judg. 11:26), see above, p. 209 — it is fatuous to use this as a serious chronological datum. The remark in Num. 13:22 that Hebron was built seven years before Zoan (Tanis) in Egypt is not quantifiable in terms of any chronology at present, except by baseless speculation, of which we have no need.

Here external evidence is more helpful. First the form of the Sinai covenant. What was found in Exodus-Leviticus, Deuteronomy, and Josh. 24 ex-

Table 28. Possible Periodization of the 480 Years (1 Kings 6:1)

Period	Year-period (40s)	References	Content
1.	40 years	Num. 11:33	Egypt to Sinai to Jordan
2.	40 years	Judg. 3:11	Othniel's rule
3.-4.	80 years (2 × 40)	Judg. 3:30	Peace after Ehud
5.	40 years	Judg. 5:31	Peace after Deborah
6.	40 years	Judg. 8:28	Gideon
7.	40 years	1 Sam. 4:18	Eli
8.	40 years (20 + 20)	Judg. 15:20; 1 Sam. 7:2	Samson's judgeship; Samuel's *floruit*
9.	40 years	1 Kings 2:11	David's reign
	Year Periods (aggregate)		
10.	48 years (= 3 + 23 + 22)	Judges	Abimelek, Tola, Jair
11.	31 years (= 6 + 7 + 10 + 8)	Judges	Jephthah, Ibzan, Elon, Abdon
12.	[3] 2 years	*1 Sam. 13:1	Saul's reign
Sol.	4 years to date	1 Kings 6:1	End date of 480 years
Total	475 years		
Theoretical	5 years?		For Joshua & elders?
End Total	480 years		

cludes not only any date of origin after 1200/1180 *but also* any date of origin before 1400/1360. Only with Suppiluliuma I (ca. 1360-1320, contemporary of kings Amenophis III to Ay) did this format come into use. So a Moses in Sinai in 1447 could never have seen a format still to be invented half a century into the future! As for slavery at Raamses, it is known that long-neglected Avaris (its base) was first worked on by Horemhab (ca. 1320ff.), who built at the temple of Seth.

At this, his home town, Sethos I built a palace. And the work here culminated in the vast projects of Ramesses II, from 1279 onward, for his new capital of Pi-Ramesse, biblical Raamses by name and not only location. So the oppression proper would have run circa 1320–1260/1250. In turn, as stated already, Pi-Ramesse (becoming defunct ca. 1130) was replaced by Tanis as a Delta outpost already before 1080 (after which Wenamun sailed from there). And Pi-Ramesse slips from the public record entirely. The fourth-century references are hidden away in arcane contexts totally inaccessible to any Hebrew writer at any date, and do not count. Thus an exodus before 1320 would have no Delta capital to march from; after the expulsion of the Hyksos circa 1540 or 1530, the Eighteenth Dynasty kings built a fort and military compound but *no* new capital. Avaris remained a backwater until Horemhab and his Ramesside lieutenants (the future Nineteenth Dynasty) took matters in hand.[142] Thus, if all factors are given their due weight (and despite inevitable imperfections in our knowledge), a thirteenth-century exodus remains — at present — the least objectionable dating, on a combination of *all* the data (biblical and otherwise) when those data are rightly evaluated and understood in their context.

4. SUMMING UP ON EXODUS, COVENANT, AND CONSEQUENCES

Once more we may sum up, after our journey from Egypt's East Delta towns and pastures through Sinai (building a tabernacle and making a covenant) and then up to Qadesh-Barnea. The essence of the picture that emerges in this chapter can be encapsulated under three headings: negatives, neutrals, and positives.

Under *negatives* we may classify the following facts. No Egyptian records mention specifically Israelites working in the East Delta (or anywhere else), or a Moses who spoke for such a group, or an exodus by a group of this name (Israel). Nowhere in Sinai has a body of Late Bronze Age people passing through left explicit traces, still less traces that are labeled as Israelite. That applies also to Qadesh-Barnea. And so on. Modern complaints about lack of evidence are often heard. But they usually come from folk who have not done their homework or thought things through with sufficient rigor.

Under *neutrals* we have to register the *reasons* for the defective state of our existing ancient documentation of all kinds, and those factors in *ancient* attitudes and cultural usage that militate against our ever recovering the kind of Byzantine- or medieval-style "proofs" that ostensibly "critical" scholars and naive folk alike seem to hanker after. It is no use asking the pharaohs to blazon their defeat and loss of a top chariot squadron high on temple walls for all to see. Egyptian gods gave only victories to kings — and defeats indicated divine *dis*approval, not applause! It is no use looking for administrative registers giving the Hebrews "customs clearance" to clear out of Egypt. In fact, 99 percent of all New Kingdom papyri are irrevocably lost (administrative and otherwise), the more so in the sopping mud of the Delta; the few survivors hail from the dry sands of Saqqara and Upper Egypt, far away from Pi-Ramesse's brickfields.[143] A handful of wine-vintage dockets from broken jars is the sum total of our administrative texts so far recovered from Pi-Ramesse![144] No buildings at Pi-Ramesse are above ground level, either mighty temples or proud palaces — so why should we expect to find the fleeting mud and reed hovels of slaves, long since returned to the mire? And a group of people traveling through Sinai's landscapes would *not* be burdened with tonloads of clumsy pottery specially to delight archaeologists when they themselves *expected* to go from Sinai within a year into Canaan; and still less so during their unplanned, much-extended wilderness travels. Compare, long before, other margin-land travelers who explicitly used water skins (Gen. 21:14), not clumsy amphorae! That goes for their visits to Qadesh-Barnea as well.

Under *positives,* the picture is far from a total blank. A series of significant features may be briefly enumerated. (1) Exoduses happened in the second millennium, and the Israelite one is echoed all over the Hebrew Bible's writings as a key event. (2) Israel (as a people group) and neighbors Edom and Moab *are* mentioned in firsthand Egyptian sources shortly before 1200; they were for real then. (3) The Ramesside Nineteenth Dynasty was a particularly cosmopolitan epoch in Egyptian history and culture; Semites and others abounded in Egyptian society at all levels, from Pharaoh's court down to slaves. (4) The Hebrew narratives in Exodus to Deuteronomy directly reflect earthy reality, not burgeoning fantasy. Salt-tolerant reeds, water from rock, habits of quails, *kewirs,* etc. reflect *real* local conditions, requiring local knowledge (not book learning in Babylon or Jerusalem). These narratives are thus in total contrast to such texts as the "King of Battle" tale of Sargon of Akkad, with mountains bounded with gold and boulders of lapis lazuli gemstone, and trees with thorns sixty cubits (100 feet) long![145] (5) The ban on going by a north route to Canaan is a direct response to Egyptian military presence there in precisely the thirteenth century. (6) The tabernacle is an ancient Semitic concept, here with Egyptian technology involved, all from pre-1000, even centuries earlier. (7) The form and content of the Sinai covenant fit only the late second millennium, on the evidence of ample firsthand sources. (8) Brick-slaves were not diplomats; the format of covenant demands a leader from court circles at that time who *did* learn of such things there. We would be obliged to invent a Moses if one were not already available. (9) The apparent gap of 600 years between the origin of Deuteronomy and its possible seventh-century role is nothing unusual, and is most likely a modern illusion, as biblical texts exist which should be placed in that "gap." (10) The so-called Deuteronomic theology is wrongly so described; its main features (DPCD and other concepts) go back to at least the second millennium, and are not special to Israel anyway. And, as already demonstrated in chapter 2 (using firsthand examples from known history), ancient inclusion of theological elements in narratives does *not* automatically turn them into fiction.

In the light of all the foregoing considerations, the exodus and Sinai events are not hereby proven to have happened, or the tabernacle and covenant, etc., to have been made then. But their correspondence not just with attested realities (not Sargon-style fantasy) but with known usage of the late second millennium B.C. and earlier *does* favor acceptance of their having had a definite historical basis.

CHAPTER 7

Founding Fathers or Fleeting
Phantoms — the Patriarchs

Now we step still further back in time, if our sources are to be believed. Early in Exodus Moses is shown being commissioned by a deity called not simply El(ohim), "God," or YHWH, but also "the God of your father" and "the God of Abraham . . . of Isaac and . . . of Jacob" (Exod. 3:6, cf. 2:24; 3:15-16, cf. 6:3; "my father's God," 18:4). Who were these three men, evidently earlier than Moses? The main narratives of the book of Genesis purport to give us the answer: they were men in three successive generations, the last of whom (Jacob) also came to be called Israel. He and his family are described as migrating from Canaan into Egypt to escape famine; his sons and their families are treated as ancestral to the clan groups that shared the name Israel in Moses' time, seemingly much later.

1. THE GENESIS ACCOUNT OF THE PATRIARCHS

As with the exodus, the settlement in Canaan, and largely the united monarchy, here too we have a set of narratives that constitute the sole direct source on their subject. No external, firsthand source of Moses' time or earlier explicitly mentions Abraham, Isaac, Jacob, or the latter's sons. The only suggested extrabiblical mention of Abraham is in the topographical list (nos. 71-72) of Shoshenq I (Shishak) of Egypt in 925, giving what may be read as "The Enclosure of Abram," and which is fairly widely accepted. But this is not absolutely certain; it could be interpreted "Enclosure of the Stallions" (*'abbirim*), although the Negev region where this place was located is not exactly famous for horses. However, the

Negev is mentioned as one of Abraham's haunts (Gen. 12:9; 13:1, 3; 20:1; also Isaac then, 24:62), which would well fit with a place being named after him.[1]

The Genesis account of the patriarchs is part of the overall scheme of the book. Its explicit format shows eleven successive segments, the first (creation) without a separate title (1:1–2:3), then ten more, each with an explicit heading, "The Succession of . . ." (once, "The Document of the Succession of . . ." [5:1]). The headings occur as follows: first at 2:4, second at 5:1, third at 6:9, fourth at 10:1, fifth at 11:10. Then the sixth at 11:27, seventh at 25:12, eighth at 25:19, ninth at 36:1, and tenth at 37:2. The first five relate to the distant epochs before Abraham and his father Terah (cf. chap. 8, below), while the last five constitute the "Patriarchal Narratives":

A1: *Succession of Terah* (to Abraham), 11:27–25:11
      plus A2: *Succession of Ishmael* (descendants), 25:12-18
B1: *Succession of Isaac* (to Jacob), 25:19–35:29
      plus B2: *Succession of Esau/Edom* (descendants), 36:1–37:1
 C: *Succession of Jacob* (to Joseph), 37:2–50:26

The content of these "internal documents" of Gen. 11–50 may be summarized:

Table 29. Outline of Patriarchal Record

A1: *Terah (to Abraham)*

1. *Terah's activities.* His family comprised three sons and grandson (Lot) at "Ur of the Chaldees" (11:28, 31). The third son (Haran) died; Terah took others (Abraham, Nahor) and Lot northwest to Harran on the Balikh, tributary of the Euphrates, where Terah died (11:27-32).
2. *Abraham travels on.* Abraham and his own close family moved southwest and south through Syria into Canaan to Shechem, then Bethel/Ai district, and Negev. A quick visit to Egypt; then Lot parted from Abraham over pasture (12–13).
3. *Abraham in Canaan.* Abraham repulsed an alliance of eastern invaders (14), made a personal covenant with his deity (15), had Ishmael by a surrogate mother Hagar (16), underwent a rite, and was promised a son via his wife (17–18). He saw the fall of Sodom and Gomorrah, from which Lot fled (18–19), had dealings with Abimelek of Gerar (20, 21); Isaac was born and Ishmael sent away (21). Tests came, and Sarah's death required a burial cave (22–23). He obtained a wife for Isaac from Harran, remarried (having other sons), and died (24–25).

A2: *Succession of Ishmael*
1. Sons of Ishmael.
2. Their clans and location (25).

B1: *Succession of Isaac*
1. *Family and conflicts.* Birth of Isaac's twins, rivals Esau and Jacob (25); conflict broke out with Gerar over lifestyle and wells (26).
2. *Jacob's adventures abroad.* Jacob was sent to the Harran branch of the family, worked for Laban, acquiring two wives, Leah and Rachel (27–31).
3. *Life back in Canaan.* Peace with Esau (32–33), trouble at Shechem (34), back to Isaac until latter's death (35).

B2: *Succession of Esau/Edom*
1. *Esau's family.* He moved on to Seir/Edom (36).
2. *Family line.* Series of Esau's descendants (36).
3. *Kings in Edom, "before any in Israel."* List (36) (37:1 — Jacob stayed in Canaan).

C: *Succession of Jacob*
1. *Joseph to Egypt.* Joseph sold into Egypt (37), and Judah in trouble (38).
2. *Joseph in Egypt.* Joseph's career — steward, in prison, at court (39–41).
3. *Famine and reunion.* Jacob's sons sought grain in Egypt, and found Joseph (42–45).
4. *Finale.* Jacob and the family joined Joseph in Egypt; account till their deaths (46–50).

Throughout these narratives the patriarchal clan appears as basically a group of pastoralists with sheep and cattle, regularly transhumant (Negev/Bethel area/Beersheba district) but could be sufficiently "tied" to a district to grow crops (chap. 26, Isaac). Family life was a major concern; their religion involved building (temporary?) altars (as near Shechem and Bethel, 12:7-8 [and 33:20; 35:1, 6]; cf. 13:4, 18; at Moriah, altar was for a burnt offering, 22:9, 13; at Beersheba, 26:25; stone pillars set up and anointed as memorials, 28:18; 35:14). We now must apply the same kinds of tests to this narrative and its contents as in previous chapters. Sections 2-4 attempt this, to test the degree of reality/fantasy, and to note any date indicators.

2. EXTERNAL CONTROLS:
ABRAHAM, ISAAC, AND JACOB

Here it will be more practical to present the subject by themes, not in a narrative order, so that related matters may be conveniently kept together.

A. WIDE SCOPE OF TRAVEL

As remarked long ago by Oppenheim, "there seem to have been very few periods in the history of the region [= Mesopotamia] when . . . (as in the Old Babylonian period) . . . a private person could move around freely."[2] At other times urban dwellers were not commonly great travelers, unless acting in specific capacities (merchants, envoys, military activities, etc.).

"Ur of the Chaldees" is undoubtedly to be identified with the famous ancient city of Ur in south Babylonia (south Iraq), now Tell el-Muqayyar, and not with sundry Ur(a)s (or Urfa) in northern Mesopotamia. "Chaldees" is a qualification of later date than the pre-Mosaic period; it may have been added between 1000 and 500, precisely to distinguish the patriarchal Ur from possible northern counterparts. The Kaldu people (to which Heb. *Kas'dim* corresponds) lived in south Babylonia, probably from the late second millennium onward — use of their name indicates clearly a belief in a southern location for biblical Ur in the first millennium.[3]

Terah and his family may have dwelled in the city proper. But if they were already pastoralists, they may equally have lived in rural settlements around Ur, like other such tribal people who gave their names to districts around major Babylonian cities, particularly in the early second millennium. Such were Sippar-Awnanum and Sippar-Yakhrurum around Sippar, taking their names from the tribal groups Awnanum (or Amnanum) and Yakhrurum known from the Mari archives.[4] At Ur itself a Sutean encampment apparently existed opposite someone's abode by the city gate. Settlements of the Mare-Yamina (so-called Benjaminites) were close by other urban centers, also early second millennium.[5]

Pastoralist tribal groups ranged far and wide in the early second millennium. From the Mari archives we learn that segments of the Mare-Yamina settled not only around Mari itself and nearby Terqa but had reached far eastward to the Tigris and southeast into Babylonia (around Uruk, Larsa, and Sippar). Northward from Mari they ranged through the "Upper Lands" (Gebel Sinjar, Tur Abdin, the Upper Khabur River). Westward they (like Terah) were at home around Harran (by the river Balih). Southwestward across the Euphrates they went on to Gebel Bishri, and turn up in Syria all the way from Iamhad (Aleppo) to Qatna, and into Amurru (central Syria, by the Mount Lebanon range).[6] From Larsa in the east to Amurru in the west, the wanderings of segments of the Mare-Yamina cover all but the extremities of the journeyings of Terah and Abraham from Ur to Canaan.

Pastoralists were not the only travelers across the Near East, then or at other periods. Official envoys traveled around at all periods, especially in the early second millennium when the network ran all the way east-west from Elam to Hazor in Canaan. The same with merchant caravans, from Babylon and Ashur (Assyria) far northwest into Anatolia, even to the Black Sea. We have lists of stopping places and transit times, effectively itineraries, for such routes.[7] These various routes can be placed on the map, at least in their essentials.

In later times (late second/early first millennium), the general movement of steppe tribes into agricultural areas with their urban centers tended to be more or less from north(west) to south(east) so far as Mesopotamia was concerned. So also for the Arameans. But in the early second millennium this northwest to southeast drift is not the sole current of movement, despite erroneous claims to the contrary. Certainly we have followed the occurrences of (e.g.) the Mare-Yamina, from the southeast, to the north, to the northwest, west, and southwest. But within that great arc there were all manner of movements and eddies. As Kupper long ago observed, pastoralists who penetrated the mainly agricultural lands of anciently "urban" southern Babylonia would have had limited scope for their profession, and would at times have again moved back northwest to more open pasturages, only to be replaced by more newcomers in their turn. He justly remarked, "It is in this constant flux and reflux of people on the move that one may fittingly situate the migration of Abraham, going back up from Ur to Harran, his true homeland."[8] We cannot assume that Terah and his forebears had always lived in Ur; he might earlier have come south from the northwest as Kupper implied. The suggestion has sometimes been made to connect Terah and his forebears (or at least their names) with places well northwest of Babylonia, within the ambit of Mari and Harran, within the vast western arc of the course of the Euphrates. The Mari archives contain ample references to the cities of Harran (at modern Harran/Eski-Harran) and Nakhur (Nahor), of less certain location. The "city of Nahor" in Gen. 24:10 is either this latter town or (less likely?) simply a synonym for Harran. The town Nakhur/Nahor flourished from the later third millennium through the second millennium into the thirteenth century. Then it only recurs several centuries later as Til-Nakhiri (seventh century), i.e., as an old site abandoned and then resettled ("Nahor-mound").[9] Around Harran there may have been other such settlements that also reflect names of Abraham's ancestors. But at present only the late name-forms survive; a Til-(sha)-Turakhi would represent the resettlement (ninth century) of an ancient Turakh or Tirakh (cf. Terah),[10] a later Sarugi may reflect Serug,[11] and so on. Settlements are often named after people in all places and ages; it is also true that people were (and still are) named from places, too.[12] Thus a Terah might have had family origins around Harran and Nakhur, followed the common "drift" southeastward, in his case to Ur, and then returned north with his family. Cf. maps, fig. 42.

B. LONG-DISTANCE MARRIAGES

Politics and commerce were not the only driving forces for travel. Long-distance marriages are at home in this period, as in others. Just as we have those wealthy sheikhs Abraham and Isaac sending off to their relatives in Nahor or Harran to obtain brides for Isaac and Jacob, so in the early second millennium we also find Shamsi-Adad I of Assyria securing in marriage Beltum, daughter of Ishkhi-Adad king of Qatna, for his son, Yasmah-Adad, Assyrian king of Mari, across a similar span of distance; Mari kings of either dynasty (Lim or Assyrian) kept up steady relations with distant Qatna in central Syria. Of course, there were a good number of international royal marriages a few centuries later in the late second millennium (between Egypt, Hatti, Babylon, Mitanni, etc.). But these were between great empires of widely differing origins, not between leading West Semitic local families, and between "Amorite" local states of north/central Syria and Syro-Mesopotamia.[13]

C. AND TO EGYPT TOO

In Gen. 12:10-20 we find Abraham seeking relief from famine in Canaan by visiting prosperous Egypt. The pharaoh fancied his wife until Abraham untruthfully alleged that she was his sister. Then, enriched but disgraced, he was sent back out of Egypt.

These things were very true to real life, not least in the early second millennium. One of the best-known painted scenes from ancient Egypt is in the tomb chapel of Khnumhotep II at Beni Hasan, circa 1870. This shows thirty-seven "Asiatics" visiting Egypt, bringing eye paint; their leader bears the good West Semitic name Ab-sharru (fig. 37).[14] When the Egyptian courtier Sinuhe fled Egypt for Canaan at the death of Amenemhat I, circa 1944 B.C., he was rescued from dying of thirst by a local tribal pastoralist "who had been in Egypt."[15] A line of forts ("Walls of the Ruler") had been built by the latter pharaoh, as Sinuhe tells us, to repel Asiatics — clearly, the pharaohs of the period had to limit and control their Canaanite would-be visitors!

As Gen. 12:18 makes clear, the king himself upbraided and dismissed Abraham, evidently from his palace (12:15). There is no reason whatever to imagine that this all happened at the capital Memphis, most of 100 miles south from the northeast Delta. For during the Twelfth to Fifteenth Dynasties (ca. 1970-1540), the Egyptian kings (Twelfth/Thirteenth Dynasties) had an East Delta residence at Ro-waty (ruins at Ezbet-Rushdy), near Avaris (center of the god Seth), which in turn the Hyksos rulers (Fifteenth Dynasty) used as their East Delta base.[16] Before the twentieth century B.C., no such arrangement is known; and again, there was no royal residence there during the Eighteenth Dynasty (ca. 1540-1295), merely a fort compound.[17] Then the Nineteenth Dynasty built a new residence city, Pi-Ramesse, used only until circa 1130. Thus the visits by an Abraham or a Jacob to a pharaoh at an East Delta palace are only feasible in Egyptian terms within circa 1970-1540, if they are not to be turned into contemporaries of Moses! Cf. fig. 36. Suffice it to say that the pharaohs were commonly partial to attractive foreign ladies, as finds and texts for the Middle and New Kingdoms attest.[18] And Pharaoh's detailing men to escort Abraham *out of* Egypt is the reverse pendant to an earlier king's detailing men to escort the returning courtier Sinuhe back *into* Egypt (ca. 1850).

D. WIDER POLITICAL HORIZONS: GENESIS 14

Here a compact but vivid narrative depicts how one alliance of four kings from the north and east sought to reimpose a twelve-year overlordship on a group of five kings around the Dead Sea area, carrying off Lot (who lived there) with their loot. When informed, Abraham set off north, vanquished the retreating force by night attack, and retrieved Lot and the loot. With the king of Salem (Jerusalem?), Abraham gave a thank offering to El-Elyon, and the retrieved goods back to the king of Sodom. Despite its obvious clarity, this narrative has remained opaque to most biblicists, simply because its cultural setting was long unknown to them and they have largely failed to accept that setting once it was made clear. Several features in the narrative find ready clarification if one looks at the appropriate external data.

We consider, *first,* the sets of rival alliances. In the west (Syria-Palestine, the Levant), such alliances of several kings one may find at all periods where written records are available for the region. In the late second millennium we have the volatile local alliances among the Canaanite kings who feature in the Amarna letters. In the first half of the first millennium we have the long series of alliances in Syria (later including Israel, then Judah) against successive kings of Assyria. This illustrates the attitude of the five Dead Sea valley kings, but nothing more.

But with the eastern alliance things are radically different. Here the kings are clearly eastern and northern. Chedor-laomer is an Elamite name (Kutir + deity), and appropriately he is entitled a king of Elam, an ancient state adjoining south Babylonia and the head of the gulf in southwest Iran.[19] Tid'al, king of Goyim or "peoples," bears an early Hittite name, Tudkhalia, and his title is a fair equivalent of the "paramount chiefs," *ruba'um rabium*, known in Anatolia in the twentieth-nineteenth centuries, or as chief of warrior groups like the Umman-manda.[20] Amraphel bears a seemingly Semitic name, and the name of his kingdom, Shin'ar, stands for Babylonia (cf. Gen. 10:10) in Hittite, Syrian, and Egyptian sources in the later second millennium.[21] Ellasar may be there too, but is not definitely identified. But its king Arioch bears a name well attested in the Mari archive as Arriwuk/Arriyuk in the early second millennium and Ariukki at Nuzi (mid–second millennium). So he may be north Mesopotamian.[22] Thus the personal names fit the regions they ruled and correspond with real names and known name types, even if the individuals are not yet identified in external sources. This is hardly surprising, given the incompleteness of data for most regions in the ancient Near East for the third, and much of the early second, millennia; even the great Mari archive covers only about fifty to seventy years.

However, by contrast with the Levant, this kind of alliance of eastern states was only possible at certain periods. Before the Akkadian Empire, Mesopotamia was divided between the Sumerian city-states, but this is far too early for our narrative (pre-2300). After an interval of Gutian interference, Mesopotamia was then dominated by the Third Dynasty of Ur, whose influence reached in some form as far west as north Syria and Byblos. After its fall, circa 2000, Mesopotamia was divided between a series of kingdoms: Isin, Larsa, Eshnunna, Assyria, etc., with Mari and various local powers in lands farther north and west. This situation lasted until the eighteenth century, when Hammurabi of Babylon eliminated most of his rivals. From circa 1600/1500 onward, Assyria and Babylon (now under Kassite rule) dominated Mesopotamia, sharing with none except briefly Mitanni (ca. 1500 to mid–thirteenth century) within the Euphrates' west bend, and the marginal Khana and Sea-land princedoms were eliminated in due course. Thus, from circa 2000 to 1750 (1650 at the extreme), we have the one and only period during which extensive power alliances were common in Mesopotamia and with its neighbors.[23] Alliances of four or five kings were commonplace and modest then. The most famous reference to larger alliances is given us by one Mari letter: "There is no king strongest by himself — 10 or 15 kings follow Hammurabi of Babylon, and so for Rim-Sin of

Larsa, and so for Ibalpiel of Eshnunna, and so for Amutpiel of Qatna; but 20 kings follow Yarim-lim of Yamhad" (Aleppo).[24] What is more, it is *only* in this particular period (2000-1700) that the eastern realm of Elam intervened extensively in the politics of Mesopotamia — with its armies — and sent its envoys far west into Syria to Qatna. Never again did Elam follow such wide-reaching policies. So, in terms of geopolitics, the eastern alliance in Gen. 14 *must* be treated seriously as an archaic memory preserved in the existing book of Genesis (fig. 41). Moreover, envoys from Mari went regularly to Hazor in Canaan.[25]

Second, there was a tradition of Mesopotamian kings intervening in Syria many centuries before the Assyrian Shalmaneser III and his successors descended "like a wolf on the fold."[26] Back in the twenty-third century, Sargon and Naram-Sin of the Akkadian Empire both marched west to the Amanus, and possibly to the Mediterranean, and up to the Taurus Mountains if not also beyond.[27] In the nineteenth century Yakhdun-lim of Mari led a military expedition west, up to the forested Syrian mountains and to the Mediterranean Sea, to which he made offerings, imposing tribute on local rulers and also subduing another group of rebel kings, just as the eastern allies did in Gen. 14.[28] A little later, circa 1800, Shamshi-Adad I of still more distant Assyria could boast that "I erected a stela in my great name in the land of Leban(on), on the shore of the Great [= Mediterranean] Sea." Even more, Shamshi-Adad I actually mobilized a vast force of over 20,000 troops to send into Syria, to help his friend the king of Qatna — a force that was sent down south of Qatna, via Qadesh and Rahisu (the Ruhizzi of the Amarna letters) and Lebanon, with Canaanites involved — not quite so far as the Dead Sea of Gen. 14, but close![29]

Third, the text of Yakhdun-lim of Mari shows striking affinities overall with the basics of the narrative in Gen. 14. There are two differences in detail: Yakhdun-lim acted on two fronts (south and west from Mari), and it was Abraham, not the invaders, who finally triumphed in Gen. 14. Naturally Yakhdun-lim speaks from an eastern/northern invader's viewpoint, whereas Gen. 14 speaks from the westerners' viewpoint. But once these factors are allowed for, the congruity of actions and themes remains striking; see table 30 on page 322.

It need only be added that Yakhdun-lim prefaces his entire account with a religious dedication to the god Shamash, who accompanied him on his campaigns. Without doubt Yakhdun-lim's firsthand inscription is much more florid and far more "theologically" oriented than the essentially plain, almost laconic Gen. 14 report. So, on the usual antireligious criteria against the historicity of theological coloring that biblicists commonly adopt, Gen. 14 should by rights constitute a far more definitely factual and reliable report than Yakhdun-lim's! Which, of course, runs counter to common prejudice against the historicity of Gen. 14. But that narrative deserves a fairer hearing.

Table 30. Yakhdun-lim and Genesis 14

Schema	Yakhdun-lim: S	Yahdun-lim: W	Genesis 14
1. 1st raid, and made vassals	(1st raid and vassals implied, not cited)	1st raid on W, made vassals, ll. 28-66	1st raid, and made vassals (1-4)
2. Revolt	Revolt, 3 vassals, ll. 69ff.	—	Revolt (4)
3. 2nd raid, victory	(2nd) raid, victory, ll. 80-98	Secured timber & victory, ll. 51-66	Victory in W (5-12) ⎯⎯⎯⎯⎯⎯⎯⎯ Abram victory (13-16)
4. Religious celebration	Dedication text & temple: all; 99-107	Made offerings to Med. Sea (45); temple	Melkisedeq ceremony & tithe (17-20)
5. Other acts	Curse: harm name & temple, ll. 118ff.	(See previous)	Settling spoils (21-24)

Fourth, a few details. *Nighttime attacks* (as in Gen. 14:15) in ancient Near Eastern warfare are very well attested; cf. above, p. 168.[30] The *religious conclusion to a campaign,* whether Yakhdun-lim's or Abraham's, was always the natural climax, as can be seen from innumerable examples (a simple fact that biblicists will have to accept, such that verses 18-20 are integral to the narrative). Thus the sets of war scenes on the walls of temples in New Kingdom Egypt (especially ca. 1300-1160) almost always culminate in the king presenting the spoils of his success to the gods, and sometimes he is commissioned by them beforehand as well.[31] Assyrian kings commonly began their annalistic texts with invocations to deities, and after a campaign might even dictate a letter to their god, reporting on the campaign.[32] In the West Semitic world, on his stela Zakkur king of Hamath (ca. 800) blends his war report with thanks to his deity;[33] and so on. The *literary format* is that of an individual report, *not* of a continuous chronicle (as wrongly claimed by van Seters). Both Yakhdun-lim and Gen. 14 are of the same type, and are wholly distinct from the kinds of continuous chronicles best known from Mesopotamia in the first millennium, which consist of staccato reports running through a whole series of years and of reigns. In any case, the "continuous" type of chronicle was *not* invented in the first millennium but already existed from the eighteenth century (Tummal; Mari), the mid–second millennium (Old Hittite), and the late second millennium (fragments under Tiglath-pileser I, end of twelfth century).[34] In short, it is entirely reasonable to trace back the history of the main content of Gen. 14 to the first half of the second millennium.

E. TREATIES AND GROUP COVENANTS

Until recent years, almost no treaties were known between about 2000 and 1500 B.C. Work at Mari and Tell Leilan has produced almost a dozen treaties, not yet fully published.[35] In the four or five formal documents available so far, there is a consistent format: deities are listed as witnesses, by whom oath is taken; then the stipulations; and finally (in complete versions) curses against infraction. Cf. table 25: III, p. 287 above. This format is wholly distinct from those current both in the third millennium and in the middle and late second millennium, and later (cf. tables 25, 26, p. 287 above). The Mari archives teem with reports of the process of the negotiation and making of treaties, which is not identical with the finished, written product, but contains the basic elements, usually excluding curses until the final document was drawn up and inscribed. This fact is important (as with the Sinai covenant, above). Thus in Gen. 21:23-24 (Abram/Beersheba I), 21:27-33 (Abram/Beersheba II), 26:28-31 (Isaac/Gerar), and 31:44-54 (Jacob/Laban),[36] we have very concise reports of the process of making four distinct and successive treaties between the three successive Hebrew patriarchs and Gerar (Abraham, Isaac) and Laban (Jacob). We are *not* given formal documents in extenso; we are just given brief accounts of the actual process of enactment, as often at Mari. Nevertheless, when tabulated, the content of these four treaties *does* correspond quite closely to what we find in both the process of enactment and the final documents at Mari and Tell Leilan, and *not* to what was current at other periods. During the treaty-making process at Mari and Tell Leilan, on preliminary "small tablets," curses were not included; they appear only in the final, validated document. Only symbolic rites of punishment for infringement, such as killing a donkey foal, denote their implicit presence. The enactment could include exchange of gifts (as did Atam-rum with Ashkur-Adad), and a shared meal (ditto, drank from the same cup).[37] All of this is found both in the Mari/Leilan data and in the little Genesis corpus; for the Genesis series, see table 31 on page 324. The idea that the treaties of Abraham and Isaac are mere literary doublets is nothing more than an artificial fiction created by a false distinction between nonexistent "sources," as others have shown. That Abimelek of Gerar should have successive treaties with Abraham and Isaac is no more a "doublet" than (e.g.) Talmi-sharruma of Aleppo having successive treaties with the two Hittite kings Mursil II and Muwatallis II (first summarized in the second), or than Kurunta king of Tarkhuntassa having suc-

Table 31. The Treaties of Genesis 21–31

Elements	Mari/ Leilan	Gen. 21: Beersheba I	Gen. 21: Beersheba II	Gen. 26: Isaac, Gerar	Gen. 31: Jacob/Laban
Witnesses	Yes	23b: God	30: gift, lambs	(29: YHWH)	44: covt; 50: God 51f: cairn, stela
Oath	Yes	23a-24: swear	31: swore oath	28, 31: oath	53b: oath
Stipula-tions	Yes	23c: good neighbors	30b: accepted, well = Abram's	29: good neighbors	52: respect boundary
Ceremony	Yes: (in narr.)	—	33: tree planted	30: feast	54: sacrifice, & meal
Curse	(Final draft)	—	—	(31: implied)	53: God, judge

cessive treaties with no fewer than three Hittite kings, Muwatallis II, Hattu-sil III, and Tudkhalia IV. There are no "doublets" or triplets here, and none need be found in the Genesis examples either, except on flawed a priori theory.[38]

These treaties or group covenants must not be confused with the strictly personal religious covenants in Genesis between an individual and his deity. These consist simply of a promise from deity to his human client and a confirmatory sign, as witness. Examples of this kind are Noah (Gen. 6:8; 9:9f.; sign: rainbow); Abraham, first (Gen. 15:9-21; sign: furnace and lamp); Abraham, second (Gen. 17:2; 4-9; signs: new name, circumcision); Isaac, implied (Gen. 17:19, 21; cf. 26:24-25); and Jacob (Gen. 28:12-19; pillar as witness of vision). These form a consistent series as a group. Later examples from David onward are less distinctive.

F. FAMILY MATTERS: HEIRS AND GRACES

In all times, cultures, and places, married couples have sought to have offspring who would carry on the family name, inherit the family estate (be it palaces or peanuts), and care for them in old age in the days before annuities and retirement homes. In antiquity, if couples could not have children in the natural way, the ideal and regular solution, then substitutes had to be found. In the patriarchal narratives, more than one option was available: adoption of a nonrelative or producing a child by another woman (a proxy).

(i) An Heir by Adoption

Having no son by Sarah, Abraham went first for adoption. He had a large household and following (cf. his 318 armed retainers, Gen. 14:14) and wealth "on the hoof" (cf. 12:16; 13:2, 5). In such a context he would have had a variety of employees, perhaps some slaves, and would learn by experience whom he could trust. Thus he sorrowed that (15:2, 3) "a son of my house(hold) will be my heir," the Damascene(?) Eliezer. "Son" here (as often in Semitic) is simply "member," be it servant or slave, of the household in question. Such adoptions by childless couples are well attested in Near Eastern antiquity. For the Old Babylonian period we have analogous cases in both formal law collections and in day-to-day legal practice: in, e.g., the Laws of Hammurabi, §191, guarding the adoptee's rights even if children are later born naturally to his adoptive father.[39] And in real-life cases, mutual safeguards applied. So, for example, slightly earlier at Mari, the couple Hillalum and Alitum adopted Yahatti-el as heir; "if Hillalum and Alitum should have many children, Yahatti-el is (still) senior heir, and shall have the double share — his younger brothers then share (the balance) equally."[40] A variety of other Old Babylonian documents tell a similar tale.[41]

(ii) An Heir by Proxy

However, Abraham was told he would have a son of his own (Gen. 15:4). But, after a long wait, Sarah his wife tried to move things along, and persuaded him to have a child by her maidservant Hagar (Gen. 16). Two generations later we find this same phenomenon in Jacob's family. Unable herself to bear sons to Jacob, Rachel gave him her maidservant Bilhah to bear him sons on her account (30:3-8). Then, ceasing from bearing, Leah did likewise through her maidservant Zilpah (30:9-12).

These were not arbitrary acts. It should be noted that, in 29:24, 29, Jacob received Leah and Rachel as wives along with their maidservant or slave girl. This was normal and normative in the first half of the second millennium, when a wife might come with her own maidservant, precisely so to serve as an insurance policy against possible inability to have offspring. Already in the nineteenth century we find that in the Assyrian "colony" at Anatolian Kanesh, when Laqipum married the lady Hatala, the provision was made that "If within 2 years she does not produce children for him, she herself may buy a slave-woman. Then after she [the latter] has had a child by him, then he may sell her off where he wishes."[42] A similar basic arrangement underlay legal usage in a variety of circumstances where a man and wife did not or could not have offspring. So, as a *naditum* (hierodule) priestess could not have children, her husband could marry also another woman for children (second wife) or have children by the priestess's slave woman (Hammurabi Code, §§144-46). Later, circa 1500, at Nuzi, the same tradition was followed, whereby a childless wife might give her husband a servant girl to bear him children.

All manner of details find correspondences in both the biblical and external documents. Thus Jacob had to keep both Leah and Rachel, his two wives; he could not just get rid of Leah. So, too, in the Laws of Lipit-Ishtar, §28, and (in a particular case) Hammurabi's laws, §148. The sons of both wives had to be acknowledged, with rights of inheritance, which is, again, a feature seen in Lipit-Ishtar, §24, and Hammurabi, §170. We find this still later in the second millennium in Deuteronomy (21:15-17), obviously based on ancient usage.

Through the centuries changes can be seen. In the twentieth/nineteenth century Lipit-Ishtar's laws (§24) envisage equal shares of paternal inheritance for children of both wives. In the eighteenth/seventeenth century, Hammurabi's laws (§170) agree but specify a "first choice" to the firstborn of the first wife, and a case at Mari grants a double portion to the declared heir (even though an adoptee; see section on Yahatti-el, p. 325 above). By the fifteenth century the Nuzi documents also grant a double portion to a natural firstborn son (but not an adoptee); again, in the thirteenth century, Deut. 21:15-17 goes with this for a firstborn son. By contrast, 700 years later, the Neo-Babylonian laws assigned two-thirds to the "sons" (plural) of the first wife and one-third to those of a second wife. Way back in Gen. 49:1-28, old Jacob pronounced his blessings upon all his sons, and so stood closest to the oldest legal usage here (all were acknowledged, none excluded), not the later variations.

However, sons of varying status might fare varyingly. Back with Lipit-Ishtar (§§25-26), the main inheritance was reserved for sons of the first, main wife, including at her death, others being dealt with differently. One may compare Abraham, who "gave all that he had to Isaac" (main heir) while simply giving gifts to lesser sons by Keturah and others (Gen. 25:1-6). Under Hammurabi, sons of slave wives shared if acknowledged, but not otherwise (§§170-71); compare Abraham's evident desire to have Ishmael acknowledged (Gen. 21:10-11); sending away Hagar and Ishmael was contrary to custom then, hence his need of instruction to do so (21:12-14).[43]

Last under law and custom, we come to Gen. 23, narrating the death of Sarah and burial arrangements for her. Here Abraham is seen negotiating the purchase of a cave (Machpelah) at Hebron with a local citizen. Its owner, Ephron, insisted on selling not simply the cave but also the field in which it lay. Two external comparisons have been made with this account, one false, and one an open question. The false comparison (by Tucker and van Seters) is with the so-called dialogue documents of Neo-Assyrian and Neo-Babylonian times. First, the account in Gen. 23 is simply a narrative of an agreement being made, it is *not* a formal legal document, "dialogue" or otherwise. Second, the assertion that such documents are exclusive to the Assyro-Babylonian usage of the first millennium is also factually wrong; such documents also occur in the second millennium.[44] The other comparison was made with the Hittite laws; Lehmann argued that Abraham only wanted the cave, not the whole property (cave plus field), because (in the Hittite laws, §§46, 47) owning the whole property would incur tax, but holding only a portion of it would not. Hoffner rejected this theory, first because he did not consider the "sons of Heth" at Hebron to be real Hittites (of Anatolian origin). And second because, in the Hittite laws, §46 dealt only with gift, not sale, and §47 applied to the holding of a craftsman, a status he denied to Ephron. Third, he considered the date of formulation of the Hittite laws to be coeval with the early Hittite rulers, Hattusil I and Mursil I, at circa 1650/1600 (they could be later), long after Abraham's putative period.[45]

These objections require proper consideration. That the Hittite laws did not exist before 1650/1600 when they were first written down is an unverifiable assumption; they are more likely to have been (in part at least) older customary law that was only written down and added to at that time. When laws in (e.g.) Exodus or Deuteronomy find direct analogy in (e.g.) Lipit-Ishtar or Hammurabi from 400 or 500 years earlier than the thirteenth century, it is clear that they were in those cases formulations or reformulations of long-standing customary law, not new inventions coeval with Moses or suchlike person writing them down in the Hebrew corpus. That the Nesites (Anatolian Hittites) only occupied the Anatolian area so late as 2000 is an assumption, not a fact, and is probably somewhat too low a date. By circa 1800 we already have "Kukun's son Luqq(a)" ("the Lycian") named on a small obelisk at Byblos; these are ancestral to Lycian, i.e., Luvian, a sister dialect to Hittite. If a Luvian can be at home so far south as Byblos by 1800, so too could Nesites be in Canaan, 160 miles farther south; and both lots 400/500 miles from the heart of Anatolia respectively. Thus the Bne-Heth of Genesis are not proven to be a Semitized Hittite enclave circa 1800, but neither is there disproof. Hoffner is indubitably right in rejecting any link with the Hittite laws, §46 — Ephron was certainly not gifting Machpelah to Abraham! The relevance of §47 turns on Ephron's status, which is not told us; we do not know if he was a craftsman (TUKUL, as §47 would require) or not. That taxation was involved would be true if §47 applied; but not needfully if it did not. Thus the Hittite comparison is possible (if Ephron had the right occupation), but is very far from certain. In its absence, Ephron must be deemed to have simply cornered Abraham (with a deceased Sarah to bury!) into buying a complete property to get possession of the cave. If they were not a group of stray Nesites, then the "Sons of Heth" were simply one more obscure group among others. This whole episode is instructive because it throws into relief the immense care with which comparisons need to be studied and worked out.

G. PATRIARCHS AND RELIGION[46]

The *forms* and the *content* or object(s) of patriarchal worship appear only very sketchily in the Genesis narratives, except when the patriarchs receive divine promises. As transhumant pastoralists, regularly on the move, they had no temples (nor used anybody else's). Their cults were formal, just as urban cults were, but of necessity much simpler in practice. Abraham built altars near Shechem, near Bethel and Ai (to which he returned later), at Hebron and Moriah (Gen. 12:7-8; 13:4, 18; 22:9). Isaac did so at Beersheba (26:25), after a vision, as Abraham had first done. Jacob too built altars at Shechem and Bethel (33:20; 35:1, 6). He also set up stone pillars or stelae as commemorative markers, anointing them (28:18; 35:14), again after visions. The altars were the focus for prayer, "calling on YHWH's name" (12:8; 13:4; 26:25), and certainly for burnt offerings, as shown by 22:3, 6, 13, with a lamb or ram as normal sacrifice. The mention of sacrifices in 46:1 would imply use of altar(s).

The practice or *forms* of worship by such transhumant pastoralists find practically no echo in the great range of texts originating from such thoroughly urban centers as Mari or Ugarit (who often took a dim view of the folk out on the steppes); and such pastoralists left no archives of their own! However, there was some common ground in religious practice. Like the patriarchs, the cults at Mari made extensive sacrificial use of sheep (various grades) and lambs,[47] as others also did — e.g., Emar a few centuries later and at Ebla some centuries earlier (to cite but two examples).[48]

However, there are examples of people from urban centers (with temple ritual dominant) going out abroad, including into desert conditions, and celebrating formal cults in suitably simpler forms. From Middle Kingdom Egypt (early second millennium) we have both a literary tale and historical stelae to illustrate this usage. The hero of a story, "The Shipwrecked Sailor," was sole survivor from his ship, cast upon a subtropical isle of plenty. Having satisfied his hunger, he "made a fire-stick, produced fire, and made a burnt offering to the gods."[49] About 1980 B.C., Mentuhotep IV sent his vizier with 3,000 men on a desert expedition into Wadi Hammamat to quarry out and bring back a stone sarcophagus and lid. The stelae inscribed there record (as a marvel) how a gazelle suddenly appeared at a suitable block of stone for the lid, there dropping her young. The delighted expeditionaries promptly sacrificed the creature as a burnt offering on the spot. Another stela records how, at the end of the visit (using supplies brought), cattle and goats were in turn duly slain, and incense burnt.[50] So ritual could be enacted at any level anywhere the ancients chose to do so. Anointing of stones (as Jacob did), one may find others doing in ritual contexts. We may compare such customs during festivals at Emar, for example, in the late thirteenth century.[51]

As for *content*, deities worshiped, the final narrator in Genesis commonly speaks of the deity of the patriarchs as YHWH (proper name) or as Elohim ("God"). Both terms also occur in words ostensibly spoken by the patriarchs and their contemporaries. Often Exod. 6:3 is understood to signify the opposite; namely, that the name YHWH was unknown to the patriarchs. If that were so, then it is very strange that it should ever have been introduced at all into the text of Genesis; the supposed contradiction would have been just as obvious to the ancients as to any modern reader of these books. However, there is very good reason to translate Exod. 6:3 understanding a rhetorical negative that implies a positive, as "I appeared to Abraham, Isaac and Jacob as El-Shaddai ('God Almighty') — and by my name YHWH did I not declare myself to them?"[52]

This would find further support from two angles. First, the "name" or character of a deity in the ancient Near East was by no means a rigidly fixed entity right from the beginning and forever after; more came to be known about, or attributed to, deities as time passed. Second, YHWH served as the proper name of the "God of the fathers," precisely as with other deities in the early second millennium, and (as with these) was not used all the time (see below).

We take up the first angle, developing knowledge/character for deities. Using Egypt as a paradigm, one may point to the history of Amun of Thebes. From the late third millennium to the beginning of the second, he was merely a local god in Thebes, alongside the war god Montu. But with the advent of the Theban Eleventh and Twelfth Dynasties to supreme power in Egypt, he became much more prominent, as the royal god of the kingdom. His identification with the sun god Re gave him full national status. In the late second millennium, the Theban Eighteenth Dynasty founded the New Kingdom, resumed rule in Nubia, and conquered much of the Levant — at a bound, Amun or Amen-Re became god of empire, giver of victory. With the eclipse of Akhenaten's attempt at monotheism based on the sun god as Aten, more orthodox Egyptian "theologians" in the thirteenth century set up a form of "trinity" whereby "All gods are (but) three: Amun, Re and Ptah, without their equal," but these are then referred to as an underlying unity or latent monotheism, "Hidden One is *his* name as Amun, *he* is Re in face, *his* body is Ptah" (emphasis added). In the eleventh-tenth centuries (postimperial), Amun became for a time almost a theocratic ruler in the south of Egypt, with the identity of the "god since the beginning" in new formulations. Thus, over the centuries, his name ("the Hidden One") gained ever more resonances for his worshipers.[53] Even more drastically, the term "Aten" was originally just the visible disc of the sun in Egyptian, and a visible part or form of the sun god. Then, after circa 1400, Aten became a name specifically for the sun god himself, until the erratic pharaoh Amenophis IV as Akhenaten (ca. 1350) made of Aten the sole form of the sun god, and sole god of Egypt, alone to be worshiped — a true monotheism.[54] Thus, for his part, YHWH revealed himself to Moses in new roles for the Israelites, not known by the patriarchs even if his name was.

And now the second angle of support for reading Exod. 6:3 as a rhetorical negative: YHWH as the personal name of the "God of the fathers" (i.e., of Abraham, Isaac, and Jacob). It was Alt who long ago pointed out the concentration of references to the deity of the earliest Israelite ancestors, as "God of (someone's) father," and as God of the particular forefathers Abraham, Isaac, and Jacob.[55] But his study suffered from many drawbacks, since remedied by others, notably J. Lewy, F. M. Cross, and R. de Vaux. Thus, for example, there is no need to view the God of Abraham, Isaac, and Jacob as being in origin three minor numens later brought together, or to descend to the Nabatean texts of Hellenistic-Roman times for parallels, when there is far superior evidence from the second millennium. Already the Old Assyrian archives from Kanesh (ca. 1900) show such phrases in their witness formulae as "May Ashur and your God be witness" or "May Ashur and the God of your father be witness," or even more fully "May Ashur and Ilabrat, the God of our father be witness," where the paternal deity in question is explicitly named for once. The name Ilabrat may itself be a name of the type occurring in Genesis — El-Shaddai or El-Bethel, El-Olam, etc.[56] From Exod. 6:2-3 we would learn (cf. above) that YHWH was known to the patriarchs both as El-Shaddai ("God Almighty" in many English versions) and as YHWH; the former is an epithet, just as are "God of Abraham," "God of Isaac," "God of Jacob," the latter being his proper name. This is no different to other examples in the biblical world. In Egypt, Osiris is also Wenen-nufer (the "enduringly good one"); in the Levant, Hadad became better known as Baal ("Master"); and so on. El-Shaddai also appears to be of ancient format and origin.

H. EARLY MONOTHEISM? A BRIEF NOTE

That a monotheistic belief might be found as early as the fourteenth/thirteenth centuries is no problem whatsoever. Akhenaten of Egypt instituted precisely such a religion during circa 1350-1340, promoting worship of the sun god as Aten to the exclusion of all other deities in Egypt. His regime was reversed within three years under Tutankhamun, and the old religions of Egypt were very emphatically put back in place. But once a given concept has been voiced abroad (and publicly!), *it can never be recalled or entirely suppressed — the genie is permanently out of the bottle!* In Egypt things were never quite the same again. Orthodox theological thinkers in the fourteenth/thirteenth centuries were prepared to envisage all gods as but manifestations of one supreme god, and applied this to Amun, as pointed out above (p. 329). There is no reason whatsoever, therefore, to imagine that the concept of just one deity was something that could be suppressed at will just after 1340 when its effects were still in being up to a century later. Especially when it then found expression even as a concept in popular stories like *Apophis and Seqenenre.* There the Hyksos king Apophis is imagined to have worshiped no other god but Seth, i.e., to have been an implicitly Semitic monotheist![57]

In chapter 6, good reason was given for the necessity (in terms of covenant forms and foreigners at court) of the frameworks of Exodus-Leviticus and (later) of Deuteronomy and Josh. 24 having originated with a West Semite in Moses' role at the Egyptian court. In such a cultural context he could hardly have been able to avoid the currents of thought then circulating. None of the commonplace objections to a "Mosaic monotheism" made by biblicists have any factual validity, as Propp has shown in a refreshingly uninhibited and wide-ranging study that knocks out all the false props on which people have relied, in refusing to accept a second-millennium monotheism.[58]

Moreover, monotheistic tendencies did not begin even with Akhenaten. The Cairo Hymn to Amun in Egypt (ca. 1500/1400), from well before Akhenaten's time, already praised Amen-Re (twice over) as creator of the other gods as well as of humanity, so that he was necessarily sole god before such a creation, conceptually. The hymn itself originated much earlier, being partly preserved on a statue of the Thirteenth to Seventeenth Dynasties (ca. 1790-1540 overall), taking us back willy-nilly toward the general epoch of the patriarchs.[59]

In the case of the three patriarchs, they are shown consistently worshiping El-Shaddai at appropriate intervals (Gen. 17:1, for Abraham; 28:3, so Isaac; 35:11; 48:3; 49:25, all Jacob), and throughout El(ohim)/YHWH as being the God of the fathers. If we go backward through these, a sequence appears. Jacob sacrificed to the "God of his father Isaac" (46:1), and took an oath in the name of "the Fear of his father Isaac" (31:53). Looking further back, he also spoke of and prayed to the "God of my (fore)father Abraham and of my father Isaac" (cf. 31:42; 32:9). He and Laban had jointly acknowledged the God of their grandfathers, Abraham and Nahor (31:53). In dealing with Melchisedeq king of

(Jeru?)salem, Abraham is shown tacitly accepting that ruler's deity El Elyon ("God Most High"), creator of heaven and earth, as being identical or identifiable with his own Elohim/El-Shaddai.[60] Abraham, Isaac, and Jacob are never seen honoring any deity except forms of El(ohim). And once back at Bethel, where he had vowed himself to El(ohim)/YHWH (28:20-22), Jacob took steps to eliminate "alien gods" from his family entourage, in token of full submission to his one and only divine guardian (35:2-4). "Monolatry" (worshiping one god amidst others) gave way again to a practical monotheism that had been the way of Abraham and Isaac. Such a personal form of religion needed no army of assorted deities, and hence readily passed into such a form of monotheism in practice. El was a high god widely recognized during the first half of the second millennium; but after circa 1500, in round terms, he was overtaken throughout the Levant by Hadad the weather/storm/fertility god, increasingly under his title Baal ("Master"). Thus, when early Israel settled in Canaan, they had to contend not with analogous forms of El but with the entirely distinct, outwardly enticing, and rival cult of Baal, along with his associated goddesses. So, between the times of the patriarchs and those of Moses and Joshua-Judges, the Levantine theological climate underwent a major change.

In this context, it is worth noting (with Wenham) not just one but four contrasts between patriarchal and later Israelite religion. (1) El(ohim) is more fundamental than YHWH in the earlier period; the reverse is true later. (2) The total absence of Baal from the patriarchal tradition indicates its antiquity, in effect before circa 1500. (3) Regarding the mode of divine/human communication, deity comes to the patriarchs directly through visions and dreams, not by intermediaries (e.g., prophets), and the patriarchs make their own altars and sacrifices without priestly personnel. (4) Jerusalem plays no significant role; it is not even present, unless in the very brief contact with the king of Salem. To which may be added: (5) Abraham could set up altars next to trees, but such "high places" were proscribed under the laws of Moses (Deut. 12:2; cf. Hos. 4:13); and (6) sacred stones (like Jacob's) were also banned (Deut. 16:22) and to be smashed (Deut. 7:5; 12:3).[61] Examples of smashed-up images, etc., were found in Late Bronze Hazor — which would correspond to these commands to Israel (and most likely done by them), but *not* to other people's customs in Canaan.[62]

Finally, the many years traditionally ascribed to the period between the patriarchs and Moses (400/430 years, Gen. 15:13; Exod. 12:40-41) might seem a long time for the Israelite clan group to keep up their relationship with El(ohim)/YHWH, as our record would imply. However, as Millard has pointed out, other tribal societies are known to have retained their characteristic deities, as with the deity Ruda in north Arabia, from the seventh century B.C. down through the Persian Empire to Roman times.[63] This long span of cult is only known to us from the chance references made by Esarhaddon of Assyria and the traveler Herodotus, for the centuries before Rome's sway.

I. PATRIARCHAL LIFE IN ITS SETTINGS

(i) Geopolitics in Canaan

During the tenth century, developing out of the later twelfth and the eleventh, there is a clear underlying structure to the political divisions of western Palestine, reflected also in the material culture. (1) In the southwest corner the Philistines had carved out their own zone, reflected not only in the sub-Mycenaean pottery often dubbed "Philistine" but also in newly built and rebuilt towns differing from their Canaanite predecessors, and in dietary changes. (2) Throughout the hill country, from the Negev up to the Jordan sources ("from Dan to Beer-Sheba"), there had developed a unitary Iron Age culture whose physical culture in pottery, housing, etc., had taken up the Late Bronze Canaanite heritage and gone its own way, separately both from the Philistines and also from (3) the vastly reduced Canaanite presence in the coastal plains. This item 2 corresponded to the early Israel of the judges' epoch into the united monarchy (and followed by the twin kingdoms). Before circa 1150, going all the way back to 1540/1458, a mainly "city-state" Canaan had been subjected to Egyptian imperial overlordship. Transhumant or other "nomadism" had been restricted to the margins: Shasu (= "wanderers") in the Negev and in Transjordan.

In the midst of this long period, Israel is attested in Canaan by Merenptah from 1209 at a minimum. An Israelite group in Egypt and leaving Egypt has to be earlier, not later, than the thirteenth century with roots in the fourteenth. And as noted already, the patriarchs were clearly taken (in the exodus narrative) as having lived earlier still. Their Canaan knows of no Egyptian presence, of no overall monarchies (like later Israel and Judah), of no Philistine pentapolis, only of the isolated (and Semitized) Abimelek at Gerar. Their Canaan had cities and also open pasturelands, wherein transhumant tribal groups like the patriarchs could move their livestock around for forage and water.

This earlier world is that of the first half of the second millennium, and is clearly mirrored in the Canaan of the Egyptian Execration Texts in three main series of circa 1860, circa 1830, and circa 1780.[64] Carrying a curse against possible anti-Egyptian rebellion, these texts name over sixty places, but barely forty have been identified up till now. Those that can be recognized include such biblically familiar towns as Tyre, Laish (the future Dan), Hazor, Achshaph, Shechem, Jerusalem, Accho, Ascalon, and a Ya'anaq, probably identical with the Anakim (more properly, Anaqim) of Josh. 11:21-22. The Anakim of Joshua come in threes: Hebron, Debir, and Anab (also cf. Num. 13:22), and Gaza, Gath, and Ashdod. Joshua is said to have disposed of the first lot, while we can be sure that the Philistines promptly dispatched the second lot (whose cities very quickly became part of the Philistine five-city league, or "pentapolis"). In the Execration Texts we also find three rulers of Ya'anaq in both the first and second sets of these texts, but only one named in the third series; but others are simply summarized. So the biblical "triplets" may represent a very long tradition, nineteenth to late thirteenth centuries, in their case.

But in these texts (first two sets) other towns have multiple rulers associated with them: four rulers with a place Anhir; three rulers (like Ya'anaq) for places Qahalmu and Asannu; and two rulers each at Rehob, a place Raqah, Ascalon, and Jerusalem. It would seem strange if these were dyarchies, triumvirs, etc.; they were not successions of rulers, as they can occur in different order in parallel copies of the same date.

The answer lies elsewhere, as these texts attest more than just towns and their rulers. Thus, alongside the ruler and the town of Irqata, we also find "the tribesfolk of Irqata"; farther south along the coast, Byblos is not itself named (because very loyal to Egypt), but we find likewise "the tribesfolk of Byblos." East of the Jordan we find three rulers of Shutu (pre-Moabite Moab) in the second series of texts, and one each of Upper and Lower Shutu in the third series. Down south in Kushu (pre-Edomite Edom) we find two "chiefs of tribesfolk" (lower in rank than territorial rulers). And the closing sections of the Execration Texts formulae include the summarizing phrase "and all the Asiatics of Byblos, Ullaza, Ya'anaq, Shutu, Ramith/Yarmut, Raqah, Jerusalem" (among others). These together give us a quite clear indication that the lands of Canaan and even more in Transjordan had also a nonurban population, of tribal/clan groups, some belonging to city-owned territories and under their own rulers or "sheikhs." Here are the independent and semi-independent pastoralists of the overall region, in the nineteenth/early eighteenth century.

Other sources confirm this picture, from two directions. From Egypt, in the story of Sinuhe (ca. 1920), when the hero fled Egypt, he was rescued from dying of thirst on the desert edge of the East Delta by one of the leaders of a group of Asiatic (i.e., West Semitic) pastoralists returning to Canaan with their cattle. Here, just like an Abraham or an Isaac, was a clan chief with his cattle (and doubtless, sheep and goats) who had visited Egypt and was traversing the biblical Wilderness of Shur back to Canaan, to grazing grounds there. He is a live example of a "chief of tribesfolk" in the Execration Texts, independent like

Abraham, Isaac, and Jacob.[65] Our other such source comes from contemporary Old Babylonian sources, where a closely related phenomenon has been recognized. In early second-millennium Babylonia, it appears that authority in a given area was in practice shared by the local king of the main city with contemporary "kings" of tribal/clan groups "living in tents" (as the Assyrian king list appositely put it). This is attested for the kingdoms of Kish, Babylon, Sippar, Isin, Kisurra, and Assyria (urban dynasty and Shamshi-Adad I's forebears). Such tribal leaders could be called either "king" or simply "chief" (*rabianu*). Their tented settlements gave rise to city "suburbs" named after their communities: Sippar-Amnanum, Sippar-Yakhrurum, or Zarri-Amnan and Zarri-Rabbium, close to a town in the region of Mari.[66]

Thus for the patriarchal clan as transhumant pastoral folk, we have a rich backcloth of corresponding conditions from the centuries preceding 1500. Within Canaan we find them moving back and forth at need between the Negev (and Shur west of it) and highland districts up by Hebron, Bethel, and Shechem, and at times west of those uplands toward Gerar in the south and Dothan in the north. In Egyptian eyes, these men would have been classified as "chiefs of tribes" (*wrw whyt*), and with whatever city-state zone they were in, when noted. This is the world of the patriarchal pastoralists — a very far cry from the Canaan ruthlessly taxed by imperial Egypt during circa 1460-1160, or from the segmented world of the judges (Philistines, sparse Canaanite towns, an emerging full-sized "Israel" community), and above all totally foreign to the world of the Israelite monarchy of David and later. In that light the patriarchs and their lifestyle and world cannot possibly be a retrojection into the antiquity of the world of a settled, monarchic Israel as often claimed of old.

(ii) Other Sidelights

(a) Archaeological Background

Most of the modest number of stopping places linked with the patriarchs were in business during the first half of the second millennium, Middle Bronze IIA-B/C in Canaan, on the current and reasonable chronology. Ancient Laish (the later Dan) resumed being a well-walled town in that period, with a notable (but little-used) arched city gate. The use of the term "Dan" in Gen. 14:14 represents an editorial "update" of the twelfth century or later (cf. Judg. 18:29). Both in the nineteenth/eighteenth centuries (Execration Texts) and in the fifteenth century (Tuthmosis III, foreign place-name lists), the name Laish is independently preserved.[67] Dothan (Gen. 37:17) was a township in Middle Bronze IIB,[68] and

Shechem is also known archaeologically during Middle Bronze IIA-B/C, growing with time. Shechem is independently attested (as Sakmum) on the stela of
Khu-Sobek under Sesostris III, circa 1860, and in the Execration Texts.[69] Bethel
(also Luz) was occupied during Middle Bronze I-II, developing during that
time.[70] Jerusalem (cf. Salem, Gen. 14:18) was certainly a town at this period, and
very recent work has illustrated the strength of its defenses in the Middle
Bronze Age.[71] Gerar is probably represented by Tell Abu Hureirah (Tel Haror),
which site was of considerable size in the Middle Bronze Age.[72] Hebron was
also a walled settlement in the Middle Bronze Age, the third and southernmost
center, along with Jerusalem and Shechem farther north, along the hilly backbone of central Canaan; from it came a cuneiform tablet of this period (probably of the seventeenth century), with accounts for goats, sheep, and rams, and
mention of a king and "offering." Of the personal names, three are West Semitic
and one probably Hurrian.[73] In the Negev, many scattered sites are known for
Middle Bronze I, but for Middle Bronze II the focus falls on three main sites, Tel
Malhata, Tel Masos, and Tell el-Far'ah South.[74] Finally, Beer-Sheba. No clear
Middle Bronze settlement has hitherto turned up in investigations around
modern Beer-Sheva. There are two sites of consequence; one, five kilometers
out of town, Tell es-Saba ("Tel Beersheba"), was occupied during Iron I-II (ca.
1150-586) and later. Iron Age traces also turned up in the modern town-site (Bir
es-Seba), but nothing much more is known, and earlier remains may have existed. In any case, Beer-Sheba in Genesis was mainly just a group of wells, *not* a
settlement; significantly, the reference to the name passing on to a town there in
Gen. 26:33 is a later editorial note ("to this day"!), and has nothing to do with
the patriarchs. Because of mistranslations of Gen. 21:31, confusion has arisen
about the origin of Beer-Sheba's name. The second half of the verse should be
rendered "*when* the two men swore an oath there," not *because* they did. It was
"Well of the Seven (*scil.* Lambs)," Gen. 21:30, along with 26:18, 33, where Isaac
reopened his father's wells under the same name. There is no cause here to invent double narratives by misconstruing Beer-Sheba as once well of seven and
once well of oath.[75]

(b) Jacob: Hunting, Herding, and Caravaning

Wily Jacob was no hunter, in contrast to his "outdoor" brother Esau. The famous incident in Gen. 27:1-40 shows Jacob obtaining his father's blessing by deceit while hardy Esau went off hunting for game. The latter's eventual father-in-
law Ishmael probably hunted with the bow (21:20). In Middle Bronze Canaan
this was a recognized way of adding to one's table, for special occasions or sim-

ply for variety of fare. Esau/Jacob illustrates the former. For the latter we may again turn to that trusty Egyptian-turned-"Canaanite," Sinuhe, who resided in northeast Canaan in the later twentieth century. As a tribal subchief (like feasting Jacob, 27:25), he liked a flagon of wine, "as daily fare, (along) with cooked meats, roast fowl, besides game from the desert. People went trapping for me, and set (the booty) before me, besides what my (own) hounds brought in." So, a comfortably placed Sinuhe sent out his underlings to do the active hunting (even as Isaac sent out Esau), but did stir himself to commit his hunting dogs to the field.[76]

As for herding, picturesque and memorable is the scenario in Gen. 30:25–31:42, where Jacob cares for Laban's flocks and takes steps to build up his own.[77] He offered to accept as wages the speckled/spotted animals Laban's flocks might produce. To this Laban agreed — and promptly removed all the existing parti-colored animals from Jacob's care, to keep his wages at zero (30:31-36)! However, the flocks under Jacob *did* produce more parti-colored animals, so Laban's little dodge was thwarted. And even more so when, in superstition and by "science," Jacob's own flocks grew. Setting mating animals to see peeled rods (light and dark color) was idle superstition. But mating with parti-colored strong stock built up Jacob's share handsomely, and allowed him to outwit Laban's scheming (31:10-12 with 30:37-43). Selective breeding was already current in antiquity.[78]

Jacob's shepherding career (31:38-40) fits well into the context of ancient Near Eastern herding practice, in particular during the Old Babylonian period (early second millennium). Then, of every 100 births, 80 went to the owner, 20 to the shepherd; Jacob's claim was in principle for less, as normally the proportion of parti-coloreds born would be fewer still. In 31:39 the verb "bore the loss" (of lost livestock) is a unique usage of that verb (root "to sin") in the Hebrew Bible,[79] but it corresponds closely in function to Old Babylonian expressions in herding contracts that differed considerably from those of much later periods (Neo-Babylonian and Persian). As the Laws of Hammurabi state (§266), the owner of the flock was to bear losses of stock slain by wild animals (e.g., a lion) or "act of God" if the shepherd went on oath and produced the animal's remains.[80] Jacob explicitly claims to have done better for Laban, bearing the losses through predators himself without claim on Laban (31:39). On the other side of the coin, Jacob claims never to have eaten any of his charges (= theft), and to have paid on demand for whatever was stolen (day or night) — and so well kept the stock that deaths at birth were minimal (31:38, 39b). For these occurrences, and failure to maintain the flocks and increase them, the Laws of Hammurabi (§§263-65, 267) made the shepherds responsible to make up losses, a process clearly used by Laban over thefts. This is borne out by contemporary documents. Finally, Jacob reproached Laban for repeatedly changing his wages (31:41). Hammurabi's laws stipulated a going rate of eight *kur* measures of grain per year (§261), and we also find this in practice, where the eight *kur* are duly specified, plus one shekel of silver (clothing allowance) in addition (Year 38 of Hammurabi).[81] Other examples show similar rates but are differently made up.[82] All this is from Mesopotamia, where Jacob served for so long. But back in contemporary Middle Bronze Canaan, and at Hebron no less, there was equal interest in dealing with accounts for sheep and goats. This is shown by the damaged Old Babylonian tablet from Hebron, listing sheep, he-goats, and rams, possibly from a flock held for religious offerings, and having some link with a (local?) king.[83]

Which brings us to caravaning. When faced with the prospect of meeting Esau for the first time in twenty years, Jacob used a safety precaution known to others in that general period. He divided his livestock and possessions into two groups beforehand. The first consisted of five successive groups of choice animals (goats, sheep, camels, cattle, donkeys) positioned at intervals as his gift to impress Esau with his seeming wealth and might; the other of his family and main possessions (Gen. 32:11, 13-20), held back until the last moment of encounter (cf. 32:21-22; 33:1-3). In Syria and Anatolia, far north, the canny Assyrian merchants did similarly with their caravans when they suspected they might run into trouble. With an investment in the business, a high official at Ashur writes to his merchant: "If you're afraid of Hahhum('s road), Assur-idi writes, only go to Urshu. . . . Don't enter Mamma with your caravan, but following the City's instructions let your brother's caravan be divided into three groups. Let the first lot go from Mamma; and as soon as it reaches Kanesh (safely), then let the second lot go on from Urshu, and then the third lot likewise."[84] So safety was sought in dispersal, as did Jacob between his set of gifts and his personal and family group.

(iii) Camels and Philistines

(a) Camels

A common claim is that mentions of camels are anachronistic before circa 1100. What are the facts? In biblical terms, between roughly 2000 and 1200, their role is minimal. Camels were last and least of Abraham's possessions (Gen. 12:16), and in his time were used solely for the long-distance, desert-edge trip to Harran and back by his servant to obtain Isaac's bride (24:10-64 passim). They were among the last named in Jacob's wealth (30:43; 32:7, 15), and again were used solely for the long trip from Harran back to Canaan (31:17, 34). The desert-traveling Midianites used them (37:25). This is remarkably little. Then, at the time of the exodus and after (thirteenth century at the latest), they occur once among Pharaoh's transport animals (Exod. 9:3) and twice in lists of creatures not to be eaten (Lev. 11:4; Deut. 14:7). Not much of a presence at all!

What about external sources between circa 2000 and 1200? We first consider the early second millennium (vaguely patriarchal), for which we have the following: from Egypt, a camel skull from the Fayum, "Pottery A" stage of occupation, within circa 2000-1400;[85] from Byblos, a figurine of a kneeling camel, hump and load now missing (originally fixed by a tenon), about nineteenth/eighteenth century;[86] from Canaan, a camel jaw from a Middle Bronze tomb at Tell el-Far'ah North, circa 1900/1550;[87] from north Syria, a cylinder seal of the eighteenth century (of deities on a camel), in the Walters Art Gallery;[88] and from mentions of the camel in the Sumerian lexical work HAR.ra-*hubullu,* going back in origin to the early second millennium.[89]

For the late second millennium we have the following: from Egypt, south of Memphis, the figure of a kneeling camel loaded with two jars (hence, domesticated) from a tomb of the later thirteenth century;[90] from northwest Arabia, on painted pottery from Qurraya (so-called Midianite ware), the broken figure of a camel, of thirteenth/early twelfth century;[91] and a camel on an early-thirteenth-century sherd from Pi-Ramesse.[92] There are other traces of camels much earlier, e.g., in Egypt and Arabia in the third millennium, and also in our overall period.[93] But the examples just given should suffice to indicate the true situation: the camel was for long a *marginal* beast in most of the historic ancient Near East (including Egypt), but it was *not* wholly unknown or anachronistic before or during 2000-1100. And there the matter should, on the tangible evidence, rest.

(b) Early Philistines?

The charge of "anachronism" is also frequently leveled at the appellation "Philistine" found in Gen. 21:32, 34 (of the land), and in Gen. 26 (of Abimelek of Gerar and his subjects). If, as is clear, the patriarchs and therefore their contemporaries lived in the first half of the second millennium, before circa 1550, then it is no surprise that commentators find difficulty with the term "Philistine" in Genesis, seeing that this name for a people group occurs only from Year 8 of Ramesses III (ca. 1180 or 1177), among his Sea People opponents. It is absent from the alliance of Sea Peoples and Libyans that had earlier attacked Egypt in the fifth year of Merenptah in 1209. So it is fatally easy to scream "anachronism" at this term in the patriarchal narratives.

In Gen. 21 the sole usage with Abraham is in the phrase "the land of the Philistines" (vv. 32, 34), and this would fall into the same category as the phrases "the route of (= to) the land of the Philistines" (= the north Sinai Mediterranean coast road) in Exod. 13:17 and the bounds "from the Sea of Reeds to the Sea of the Philistines" (= Mediterranean) in Exod. 23:31. Likewise in Josh. 13:2, 3. Here we see a usage from the twelfth to tenth centuries (1180 and following) that replaced an earlier, obsolete term — just as we would say "the Dutch founded New York" although they did so as New Amsterdam, the present name replacing the former under their British successors. And nobody ceaselessly squawks "anachronism" about this! Compare already the tacit later substitution of Dan for Laish in Gen. 14:14. Thus some earlier and obsolete term would have been replaced in such cases. Some traces of this still survive in the Hebrew text. Thus Josh. 13:3 lists the five cities of the Philistines, "reckoned as Canaanite," and brings in the obscure Avvim. In 1 Sam. 30:14 "the Negev of the Kerethites" (perhaps "Cretans") is named close to Philistia, "Kerethites" being a term used as an archaism for Philistia by the later prophets Zephaniah (2:5) and Ezekiel (25:16). David's Kerethites had the same origin (2 Sam. 15:18 and elsewhere). In the case of Isaac (Gen. 26:1, 8), he went to Abimelek, "king of the Philistines, to Gerar," and Abimelek, so titled, viewed Isaac and Rebecca. In Gen. 26:14-15, 18 the term is also applied to Abimelek's subjects. One may go further back than Kerethites. In Deut. 2:23 it was noted that "the Caphtorians that came from Caphtor" replaced the luckless Avvim. Again, in archaistic mood, the later prophets used this term — the Philistines were from Caphtor (Amos 9:7), and occur in parallel with Caphtor in Jer. 47:4. All this archaic usage is exactly like the ancient phrases "sons of Sheth" for Moab and "tents of Kushan" for Edom/ Midian (Num. 24:16; Hab. 3:7), in which Sheth is ancient Shutu and Kushan is antique Kushu from the early second millennium. Caphtor is ancient Kaptara, well attested from the early second millennium, when the Mari archives actually mention a king of Hazor sending gifts to Kaptara (Caphtor).[94] Egyptian Keft(i)u (originally Kaftur) is simply a local variant of Kaptara; it is solidly attested from the sixteenth century to the thirteenth, and may be traced back to the Twelfth Dynasty (ca. 1973-1795) and before.[95]

At this point questions need to be asked that are never asked, and which need answering. Why does the biblical narrator locate his "Philistine" king at Gerar and not in the pentapolis cities, e.g., in Gath or Gaza? Why is there no Philistine army force to deal with the unwanted Hebrew pastoralists? Why introduce a "Philistine" element at all? (The stories would read just as well with Canaanite characters, as at Shechem!) Is it not because these are in fact merely "modernized" Caphtorians, with a different profile to the later "historic" Philistines? If so, then we simply have Abraham and Isaac dealing with another non-Canaanite element in the land (like the sons of Heth, or the Horites/Hurrians). But in this case, coming from and/or linked with the Aegean area.

Does that suggestion make sense in the early second millennium? The Mari report of sending tin to kings of Laish and Hazor (in Canaan) and to Kaptara (Crete) suggests that the traffic was not all one way. And indeed, it was not. In Middle Bronze Hazor itself, Middle Minoan II pottery duly turned up — maybe part of some reciprocal deal.[96] Up north in Alalakh (level VII, ca. eighteenth/seventeenth century) on the lower Orontes, the sprawling palace of its local kings had frescoes executed in Cretan style and technique.[97] In Canaan itself (in western Galilee), Tel Kabri was found to have a Middle Bronze II palace (late seventeenth century) that also contained plastered walls and floors painted with Cretan-style frescoes.[98] And work on sixteenth-century Avaris in the Egyptian East Delta has also revealed spectacular remains of Minoan paintings.[99] Cypriot pottery also occurs in sites in Canaan during our period, as at Megiddo in the north, and at southwest sites such as Tell Abu Hureirah/Tel Haror (probably Gerar), and Tell Jemmeh in the south. The Middle Bronze temple at Tel Haror yielded also a chalice with "Minoan-type tall handles."[100]

Thus it is conceivable that Abimelek and his retainers (especially Phicol) may also once have been Kaphtorians or even Kerethites, before "Philistines" later became a blanket term for non-Canaanite, Aegean people in that part of southwest Canaan.

J. PERSONAL NAMES

This is not the place to present a full onomatological study of all the personal names in Gen. 12–50, but in the light of misconceptions, some sampling is in order. For many decades it has been noticed that some of the names in the families of the patriarchs were patterned on a particular model, what experts in the field have commonly called an "Amorite Imperfective" for convenience (so, by such acknowledged scholars in that field as Ignace Gelb, Herbert Huffmon, Georgio Buccellati).[101] In this type we have a verbal form with prefixed pronoun elemet *ya/yi*. And likewise, it was noted that very many of these names are found in the Mari archives of the eighteenth century. Among our patriarchs, such names include Jacob, Isaac, Ishmael, and Joseph.

However, these clear and simple facts have recently been denied by scholars unwilling to accept the overwhelming factual evidence. That it is so emerges from a thoroughgoing study of the entire collected corpus of West Semitic personal names of "Amorite" type (better, West Semitic), as represented by Gelb's large volume containing not fewer than 6,000 such names.[102] The results are striking. While such names are readily found in use at all periods, their popularity in the early second millennium cannot be paralleled at *any other period*. Of all names beginning with *i/y* known in the early second-millennium corpus, a massive 55 percent are of the so-called Amorite Imperfective type. In the Late Bronze Age up to 500 years later, at Ugarit, only 30 and 25 percent of the initial *i/y* names are of this type in the alphabetic and syllabic texts respectively — a colossal drop by half, of 55 percent![103] In the Iron Age it gets worse. In classic Old Phoenician and Old Aramaic, "Imperfective" names are only 12 percent of all the known *i/y* names — less than half of the previous figures![104] So, brash claims that the use of such names had not "diminished after the Middle Bronze Age" are pure nonsense. Denial of its significance merely because "the existence of names of this type is perfectly normal" through the centuries wholly fails to answer the point of massive popularity at only one epoch by contrast with the rest. The dating of the patriarchs does not hang simply on this phenomenon (see below), but it is wholly consistent with an early second millennium date and does weigh in its favor, given the huge difference between that and *all* following periods. Cf. fig. 44.

Other types of names also find their background in original sources. Abram is "the Father is exalted"; closely similar is the name of the man leading the group of thirty-seven "Asiatics" into Egypt in the famous scene from Beni Hasan in Egypt, circa 1860, namely, Ab-sharru, "the Father is king."[105] Zebulon without any doubt is the same name as the Zabilanu found in the Egyptian Execration Texts of the nineteenth/early eighteenth century, and in cuneiform in Old Babylonian sources then.[106] Asher is the same as Ashra in an eighteenth-century papyrus, which has names related to (J)acob and (Is)sachar also.[107] And so one could go on. One important fact to notice is that these names are above all *personal* names, the kinds used by individuals; they are not tribal or clan names, despite misguided attempts by some biblicists to have it so. There is only limited overlap between the two fields of names.

Some names are not even Semitic in these narratives. The most obvious example is Phicol *(pikol)*, army commander to Abimelek (Gen. 21:22, 32; 26:26).[108] It is neither West Semitic nor Egyptian. But it may well be of Aegean/Anatolian origin.[109] In the Hittite world (late second millennium) we find names beginning with Pig- or Pik-, and likewise in later southwest Anatolia, while the Carian name endings in -olos, -ollos, etc., have also been compared.[110] From the Aegean itself, the Mycenaean Greek texts (fourteenth century) yield such names as (in syllabic transcription) Pa-ku-ro$_2$, which was soon compared with Greek Baikulos;[111] an originally consonantal *y* in Pikol, giving

Paikol, would be very close to this indeed. Alongside the non-Greek Minoans in Crete (until a Mycenaean Greek takeover in the fifteenth century), it is posited on reasonable grounds that early Greeks inhabited mainland Greece from circa 2000 onward;[112] so Aegeans of that origin might well have reached Canaan on occasion any time thereafter. But to go further than this would be to speculate beyond the permissible limits of factual data.

3. EXTERNAL CONTROLS: JOSEPH

With Gen. 37, 39–50 we move back south into sunlit Egypt. The story of Joseph is an attractive narrative of a precocious Hebrew lad ("father's pet") sold off into Egypt by his jealous brothers, rising through adversity to high office, and providentially able to provide for his family in Egypt also. How far this setting shows up, and in what ways, may be asked. A look at several themes may again be a useful approach.

A. SEMITES IN EGYPT

The eastern Delta of Egypt was always an attraction to the people living in nearby Canaan, at most periods. But their scale of penetration varied through the centuries in accord with a variety of factors. In times of famine in Canaan, if Egypt had had her normal Nile flood, producing good harvest and green pastures, her neighbors gladly sought provision there. Egyptian response varied. Average tolerance of visitors and settlers might be varied by (negatively) the imposition of border controls with forts and officialdom, to limit entry, or (positively) by allowing entry and integration to "useful" people, or even importing them as slaves, by conquest, purchase, or as gifts from foreign rulers.

From the late predynastic period into the First Dynasty (from ca. 3000), there was clear trade between Egypt and Canaan, and the early pharaohs perhaps even warred there. In the Old Kingdom or Pyramid Age (ca. 2700-2150), there is little evidence at present for much penetration either way.[113] The Egyptians certainly warred in Canaan intermittently, and traded with Byblos in Phoenicia. But in the First Intermediate Period that followed, and the early Twelfth Dynasty (1973 and following), Semites made inroads into the Delta.[114] The Tenth Dynasty king Merikare was counseled to take firm measures against unruly "Asiatics," while the founder of the Twelfth Dynasty, Amenemhat I, built a series of forts to restrict their entry into Egypt, and set vigilant border guards, as Sinuhe well knew.[115] By the middle of the Twelfth Dynasty Amenemhat II was sending both merchants and armies into the Levant, and levying some tribute from certain local rulers — thus, as prisoners or people sold into captivity (cf. Joseph) or as gifts from such rulers, some Semites found themselves sent into Egypt.[116] Cf. figs. 38, 39.

From the late Twelfth Dynasty into the Thirteenth, Egypt absorbed growing numbers of people from Canaan, for utilitarian reasons. They served as ancillary staff in temples, as dancers and porters. Slaves were used to pay debts, and could be passed on between owners like any other chattel. These "Asiatics" became servants in private households of sufficient wealth to employ them, at both humble and higher levels. One owner of seventy-seven such people had forty-eight Asiatics in this group of retainers (Papyrus Brooklyn 35.1446), and that was in Thebes, some 300 miles south of the Delta and some 500 miles from southern Canaan.[117] The level of settlement in the East Delta grew, especially under the foreign (Hyksos) Fifteenth Dynasty. At Tell el-Dab'a (ancient Avaris), the Twelfth/Thirteenth Dynasty and Hyksos summer capital in the East Delta, excavations have produced extensive cemeteries of Middle Bronze Age Canaanites, plus Canaanite-type temples and artifacts. In the New Kingdom (ca. 1550-1070), all this stopped initially. But the great warrior-pharaohs brought back fair numbers of foreigners as prisoners of war, who settled in different parts of Egypt (and were not just concentrated in the East Delta). Then and in later periods, foreign traders came and went, and there was always some foreign presence in Egypt (e.g., Greeks in the Twenty-Sixth Dynasty [664-525] and later), but not as obviously as in the late Middle Kingdom, and not in the manner of New Kingdom conquest.

B. AT WHAT PRICE?

Against this overall background, the story of a young Joseph sold off into Egypt fits in easily, especially in the early second millennium, in the overall period of the late Twelfth/Thirteenth and Hyksos Dynasties. After a good haggle, his brothers got 20 shekels for their young brother (Gen. 37:28). This we know to be approximately the right price in about the eighteenth century. This is the average price (expressed as one-third of a mina) in the laws of Hammurabi (§§116, 214, 252) and in real-life transactions at Mari (exactly) and in other Old Babylonian documents (within a 15- to 30-shekel range, averaging 22 shekels).[118] Before this period slaves were cheaper, and after it they steadily got dearer, as inflation did its work. Thus in earlier times under the Third Dynasty of Ur, 10 shekels was the commonest price (two-thirds of the known cases within the 8-

to 10-shekel price range), but prices could vary widely depending on circumstances.[119] After the eighteenth/seventeenth centuries, prices duly rose. In fifteenth-century Nuzi and fourteenth/thirteenth-century Ugarit, the average crept up to 30 shekels and more (cf. replacement price of 30 shekels in Exod. 21:32).[120] Then in the first millennium, male slaves in Assyria fetched 50 to 60 shekels, with which in the eighth century one may compare the 50-shekel redemption price that Menahem had to pay Assyria for his notables (2 Kings 15:20).[121] After the exile prices simply soared under the Persian Empire: to 90, even up to 120 shekels, for example.[122] Thus our biblical figures in each case closely correspond to the relevant averages for their periods: 20 shekels for Joseph in the early second millennium, 30 shekels under Moses in the later second millennium, and 50 shekels for Assyria under Menahem in the eighth century. This closely matching "graph" is not coincidence.[123] See fig. 43.

C. NAMES FOR PEOPLE[124]

Once Joseph went up in the world, from prison to the king's court, he was given an Egyptian name (Zaphenath-Pa'aneah, Gen. 41:45), married a woman with an Egyptian name (Asenath, 41:45), whose father had an Egyptian name (Potiphera, 41:45), perhaps related to that of his first employer (Potiphar, 39:1). That these are Egyptian is beyond doubt; but reaching back to their Egyptian originals has not been so simple. First, the "jaw-cracker," Zaphenath-Pa'aneah. In the 1880s Steindorff read it as a version of a type of name well attested in Egypt between circa 1070 and 500, Djed-Deity-'ef-ankh, "Deity has spoken and he lives"; in this case, as Dje(d)-Pa-Nute(r)-('e)f-ankh, "The God has spoken and he lives." However, while the phonetics are good, the application and deity-content is not. This is essentially a birth name, not one to be given to a thirty-year-old (41:46); and common though this type is, *it always names a specific deity, never just "the God."* Such an "anonymous" version has never yet been found and published; Schulman remarked: "I do not think that an exact original prototype [of Djed-panuter-ef-ankh] . . . will ever be found in the Egyptian documents, for I doubt that it ever existed."[125] There has been no lack of alternatives, but almost all of them have failed the test of conforming to real Egyptian name-types or to the requisite phonetics, or both.

But it is possible to suggest an equivalent that meets these conditions. As it stands, the first part, Zaphenath, has a consonant sequence well known in Hebrew and Semitic but not in Egyptian; yet the second half is universally (and rightly) recognized as containing a *p* or *f* followed by an Egyptian 'ankh, "life, (to) live." However, the Zaphenath would transcribe into Egyptian as Djad-naf, "who is called," with simple metathesis of the *t* and first *p/f*. There is no root Zathenaph in Hebrew or Semitic. Such a procedure is already clearly attested elsewhere in Egyptian/Hebrew usage. Nobody can doubt that the king Tirhaqa of 2 Kings 19:9 and Isa. 37:9 is in fact the Tiharqa of the Egyptian inscriptions. In Assyrian, the Egyptian name Bakenranef (as Bukun-rinip) became Bukur-ninip, with metathesis of *r* and *n*. In Arabic, "Aleksander" becomes "Aliskandar" similarly; and so on. That leaves the *p/f* — *ankh*. In Egyptian there is a well-attested name or names, (I)p-ankh, (I)pi-ankh, (I)pu-ankh. The elision of initial *i* is commonplace; cf. Pithom (Exod. 1:11), strictly Pi-thom, for Pi-'itm, where the initial weak *'aleph* + *i* of (A)tum have been elided. So Joseph's full name in Egypt would have been "Joseph who is called *(Djat-naf)* (I)pi-ankh." In Egyptian the final *d* of *Djed* first became a *t* and in later times dropped away completely. This suggests a relatively early date for our Zathenaph, Middle Kingdom to early New Kingdom (= early to mid–second millennium). The Ipi-ankh names are very common in the Middle Kingdom, but not later, so (unlike the Djed-Deity names) we have (i) good phonetics, (ii) attested forms, and (iii) early date.[126] We also have (iv) the same usage for foreigners in the Middle Kingdom. The Papyrus Brooklyn 35.1446 of circa 1730 has forty-eight "Asiatics" in its list of seventy-seven household servants, and twenty-eight of these show precisely the construction proposed here: "X (Semitic name) who is called Y (Egyptian name)."[127] One could hardly ask for a better pedigree than this.

Joseph's Egyptian wife also finds a close equivalent. The *'As-* element has been taken as for *(N)es-*, followed by *Nt* for "Neit" (a goddess). However, (i) the elision of *N* in *Nes-* is a late phenomenon, (ii) with the wrong vowel (*e* for *a*), and (iii) names compounded with Neit are not to be expected at Heliopolis or Iunu (Hebrew On in Gen. 41:45), as Neit was based far away at Sais up in the northwest Delta. There is a better alternative. The syllable *'As-* is a perfect transcription of what in Egyptian is archaically (and universally) written *iw.s*, "she is," with a masculine equivalent *iw.f*, "he is," that gives *'Af-*. Names in the forms *'Af-* and *'As-* are very common, not least in the Middle Kingdom. The *n* is the regular Egyptian dative, as Spiegelberg also rightly detected long ago (but mistakenly still adding [N]eit to it). The names Iws-ni, Iwf-ni (for *'As-ni*, *'Af-ni*), "she/he is (= belongs) to me" (spoken by a parent), gives the game away, particularly when the fuller name-forms are considered: Iws-en-ites/mutes, "she belongs ('is') to her father/mother." Finally, to cap it all, we have the male name *iwf-n.t*, *'Af-en-et*, "he belongs ('is') to you" (fem.), spoken to the mother. Thus, in turn, our biblical name *iws-n.t*, *'As-en-et*, "she belongs ('is') to you" (fem.), is its perfect feminine equivalent. It is exactly correct phonetics, correct name form, fits the context, and is also the right general date.

Finally, Potiphera and Potiphar. The first form is universally recognized as deriving from Egyptian P(a)-di-Pareʿ, "the gift of (the sun-god) Pre." In this form the name exhibits a form *(Pa-di-Deity)* first attested in the Nineteenth Dynasty, in the thirteenth century, not earlier; and an actual example of Padipare occurs on a stela of circa 1070 or after. However, the *Pa-di-X* type of name is a "modern" (i.e., New Kingdom) equivalent of the *Didi-Deity* names of the early second millennium. A Didi-Re would become Pa-didi-(P)re, then Pa-di-Pare. Didi- names are very common in the Middle Kingdom; and the transitional form (early Eighteenth Dynasty) is attested in the feminine, with suffix for a deity *(Ta-didit-es)* before we reach the final form. So, the Pa-di-Pare could be of the thirteenth century or later. Potiphar is usually taken to be the same name with loss of the final consonant, ʿayin. This would be unusual; but for the present I also can do no better on this one! Of four names (possibly in fact three, one in two forms), two are exact and of early date, and one is exact, of later date as given, but easily deriving from an early form. The supposed variant of the latter is either just that, or awaits further resolution.

D. LIVING ROYALLY IN THE EAST DELTA

Following on the building of an outpost of the Tenth Dynasty (ca. twenty-second century) named Ro-Waty-Khety, "Door of the Two Ways, of (King) Khety," Amenemhat I of the Twelfth Dynasty (ca. 1973-1795) established a royal estate with a temple and settlement, appropriately renaming it "Mansion of Amenemhat (I), justified, of Ro-Waty." Then Sesostris III (ca. 1860) expanded the settlement, and a Canaanite population became a major element from then on into the Thirteenth and Fifteenth Dynasties, down to circa 1550; this settlement became Hat-waret, the Hyksos capital, the Avaris of Manetho.[128]

This Twelfth/Thirteenth Dynasty and Hyksos Delta residency was not simply a single conurbation. Excavation shows that it grew up as a series of interlinked settlements based on adjoining "turtleback" sand ridges separated by water channels at flood time. Central was the oldest area of settlement, and during the Thirteenth and Hyksos (Fifteenth) Dynasties, wider occupation (Canaanite and Egyptian) grew up around it on neighboring elevations. With the expulsion of the Hyksos regime by the victory of Ahmose I, founder of Egypt's Eighteenth Dynasty, New Kingdom, and beginnings of "empire," most of the town fell into disuse. The indigenous temple of Seth remained in use, and out west (on the Ezbet Hilmi site) the conquerors established a military citadel for about a century, replacing a Hyksos one. But the great days of Avaris were over from 1540, and no royal palace with Delta capital rose again until Sethos I and Ramesses II soon after 1300.

Thus, for Abraham to visit a pharaoh's palace, or Joseph to serve in one, or Jacob and family to visit and reside within reach of one, their successive presences ought to be located chronologically within circa 1970-1540, and preferably circa 1860-1540. Khety (I, II, or III? ca. 2200/2150?) would be far too early; the Ramesside period is too late. The careful specification (Gen. 39:1) that Joseph's first boss Potiphar was an Egyptian — surely, one would *expect* him to be Egyptian, in Egypt! — suggests that Egyptians were not the sole population in the East Delta around the pharaoh's residency there. And archaeologically, for the later Twelfth, all of the Thirteenth, and the Hyksos Dynasties, this is exactly so: there was then a very obvious Canaanite (Middle Bronze Age I-II) component, not only in artifacts such as pottery but also in social usages, such as the placement of burials (by houses) and their arrangements, animal interments, etc. So this small detail may possibly both indicate a basic situation of that age and also hint at its date. Cf. fig. 36 (dates of Delta capitals).

A very different date-sensitive datum is the mention of "the land of Rames(s)es" as equivalent to the land of Goshen in Gen. 47:11 in the context of 47:1-12. This name is universally recognized by all competent observers to be Egyptian Ramesses, and in such a context Ramesses II at the earliest. This datum is *not* put in the mouth of any of the actors (Pharaoh, Jacob, Joseph, etc.), but comes either from the narrator of the story or a later modernizer. Thus, as with Potiphera, datable at earliest to the thirteenth century and possibly later, we now have at least two, possibly three dating horizons in the Joseph narrative: (i) indications for Twelfth/Thirteenth Dynasty/Hyksos epoch, of eighteenth/seventeenth centuries; (ii) traces of Ramesside element(s), thirteenth century; and (iii) possibly later adjustments.

During the Thirteenth Dynasty we already have Semitic kings among the rapid succession of mainly short-lived rulers circa 1795-1640. Such was/were Khandjir I (and II, if this were two kings, not just one), whose name is Semitic, "boar" *(khanzir)*. By about 1700/1650, King Asehre Nehsi (and others?) ruled very briefly in the East Delta; then the Hyksos kings.[129] This overall period would be a feasible context for Joseph, and for Jacob's coming. That the East Delta was well fitted for pasturing cattle (cf. Gen. 46:32; 47:6) is known from the first stela text of King Kamose of Thebes barely 80/100 years later, when his regime could have seasonal grazing for their cattle in the north.[130]

E. CAREERS FOR ASIATICS IN EGYPT

In the New Kingdom, under the empire, a good many foreigners lived and worked in Egypt at all levels from merest slave up to high office at court, especially under the Ramesside Nineteenth Dynasty (cf. chap. 6). In the Middle Kingdom, in our period (Twelfth-Fifteenth Dynasties), the same can be seen, again at several social levels. On the humblest level, we find in Papyrus Brooklyn 35.1446 among the forty-eight foreigners a variety of employments. Among the women were a variety of cloth makers, while the men were brewers, cooks, a children's guardian, and also *hery-per,* or domestic servants in the household.[131] This last role was very common in Middle Kingdom Egypt, to judge from the large number of occurrences on family monuments. To begin with, Joseph served "in the house" of his master (Gen. 39:2), obviously at a modest level, before being promoted (39:4-5) to be overseer of the house(hold). "In the house" he was a *hery-per;* after promotion he became an *imy-re per,* or steward. Over a large estate with subordinates of this title, one might become an *imy-re per wer,* or high steward. All these titles are very familiar in the Middle Kingdom, and the latter two also in the New Kingdom and later. But *hery-per* is known especially from the Old and Middle Kingdoms (third and early second millennia), not usually later.

Like Joseph, other Semites in Middle Kingdom/Hyksos Egypt could be promoted. Within families, one may find them acting as cupbearer or "butler" *(wudpuw)* and taking up skilled professions such as craftsman *(hemwaw),* notably an early "David" and an Epher (cf. Ephron).[132] Much higher up the ranks is the well-known seal-bearer and chancellor ("Chief over the Seal") "Hur," attested by at least 110 scarab seals in his name, of varying quality (fig. 40);[133] another Epher also had this exalted title in Hyksos times.

Joseph's appointment was accompanied by his being robed in fine linen, given a gold collar, and entrusted with a state seal, plus use of the second chariot after the king (Gen. 41:42-43). All this fits both the Middle and New Kingdoms; the state of evidence has so far limited our pictorial resources to New Kingdom scenes. But these procedures are authentically Egyptian.[134] The chariot came in not later than the Hyksos; there is evidence for the horse in the Thirteenth Dynasty (which is indirect evidence for chariots, as they were initially not ridden but used to draw the latter).[135] Joseph's exact official role remains debated, simply because (1) the Hebrew text gives his functions but not formal title(s); (2) Egyptian texts give us plenty of titles, but only rarely bother to mention functions exercised by their holders; and (3) titles could vary in functions covered in different periods. Being second only to the king suggests a vizier, although officials who were not vizier could be given special powers. So, if Joseph was not vizier, then he would have been special delegate for agriculture (a *ro-hery,* in New Kingdom terminology). Cf. fig. 45.

His activities in the land make sense. Egypt was divided into provinces (the so-called nomes of classics-bound Egyptologists) along the length of her stretch of Nile Valley and between the river branches of the Delta. Each had its own local capital, in whose granaries the grain would be stored locally (as in Gen. 41:48), in part to defray taxation. Naturally, good (but not excessive) annual Nile floods spelled prosperity, and many are the happy scenes in the tombs of officials showing fine harvests and the garnering of the good grain in granaries, in the Old, Middle, and New Kingdoms alike. But a low (or wildly excessive) Nile flood would fail to flood the fields (or would destroy them), with loss of crop growth and hence famine, a problem by no means unknown, in texts or (for foreigners) in pictures.

F. DREAMS AND DIVINATION

Joseph's fellow prisoners were haunted by their dreams, as was the pharaoh subsequently (Gen. 40–41). Dreams were held to be of significance throughout the ancient world, and at most periods.[136] So, not surprisingly, ancient scholars tried to systematize both their content and their interpretation. For this we have the remains of actual textbooks from both Egypt and Mesopotamia. The latter are fragmentary, and in MSS of mainly the early first millennium B.C. The principal Egyptian text is preserved in Papyrus Chester Beatty III Recto, with originally ten pages of prognostications, of which the first is largely lost.[137] This copy dates to early in the reign of Ramesses II (early thirteenth century), but its grammar, vocabulary, etc., are good Middle Egyptian, such that the original work may go back to the Twelfth Dynasty (twentieth/nineteenth centuries). Its format is highly systematic. Each page has an initial column that reads: "If a man (should) see himself in a dream," opposite which is a long series of normal, horizontal lines dealing with each possible dream in one line each. Each such line gives first what the dreamer sees, then a comment, "good" or "bad," and then the appropriate interpretation for good or ill. Long series of good and bad dreams are given in successive blocks. The butler and baker Joseph met in prison had no access to such a manual (or a scholar), so he found them sad accordingly. But Pharaoh's scholars had a different problem; either the omens the king gave them were not in their collections, or else they suspected a "bad" answer and feared to give it to him. Joseph confirmed their fears, but was inspired to offer a practical solution. The term for Pharaoh's scholars or sages is *hartummim*, which goes back to the Egyptian term *hery-tep*, best translated "expert" and often found in the combination *kheri-hab hery-tep*, which means "lector-priest and expert" and not simply "chief lector-priest" as was formerly thought, as the late J. Quaegebeur has shown. Common in the New Kingdom, the twin phrase also goes back into the Middle Kingdom; *hartummim* was certainly not borrowed only as late as the seventh century, as some have claimed.[138]

A cup for divination that Joseph pretended so to use (Gen. 44:5) was also an ancient Near Eastern and Egyptian usage.[139] A two-tablet "handbook" for divining from patterns of oil on water in a cup comes from the Old Babylonian period (early second millennium), while a pair of small statuettes from Egypt of seemingly Middle Kingdom date may show the process, otherwise known there only from demotic texts of the second century A.D.

G. RIPE OLD AGE, AND DEATH COMES AS THE END

When Joseph died, he is reputed to have attained 110 years (Gen. 50:22). In an Egyptian setting, it cannot really be coincidence that this same figure happens to be the ideal life span in Egyptian aspirations, by contrast with the Hebrew figures of 70 or 80 years (Ps. 90:10). In Egypt the 110-year tradition ran from the Old Kingdom down to the Hellenistic period, but the attested mentions cluster in the Ramesside period (thirteenth/twelfth centuries).[140] Thus, as others have noted, this feature is specifically Egyptian; it could relate to Joseph's general period, and/or it could have been an emphasis made by a later narrator, of the same horizon as the phrase "the land of Rames(s)es."

Regarding the burials of Jacob and Joseph, it is almost amusing to notice the growing acculturation to Egyptian ways of this West Semitic family. Dear old "traditionalist" Jacob requested to be gathered with his fathers after death, in practice to be buried in the collective tomb of Abraham, Isaac, and their and his spouses (Gen. 49:29-32). In this, they and he conformed to dominant Middle Bronze Age custom, itself reviving Chalcolithic, some Neolithic, and full-blown Early Bronze Age I-III usage. The custom remained in force for most of the following two thousand years in Canaan, in the Late Bronze (alongside single burials), and throughout the Iron Age into Greco-Roman times.[141] However, Joseph had to solve the problem of transporting a deceased Jacob from the Delta to Canaan. The traditional ancient Semitic solution in such circumstances was to allow the body to render down to bones, then remove these to final burial. But Joseph chose an Egyptian alternative: he had him mummified in full Egyptian fashion (50:2-3), understandable in Egypt at any period — but not normally in Canaan. With Joseph, things went a step further. He was not only embalmed, but was "put in a coffin in Egypt" (50:26), admittedly with the hope that some day he too would be repatriated to Canaan (50:24-25). There was no lack of other burials of Semites in Egypt in his time (early to mid–second millennium), many of them in Semitic fashion in the cemeteries around

Tell el-Dab'a (Avaris).[142] And some of them opted for an Egyptian-style burial like Joseph. Such was a man having the archetypal Semitic name Abdu, whose traditional, rectangular Middle Kingdom coffin was found in the vast cemetery of Saqqara, which served ancient Memphis. With it was found the fine dagger of another man bearing a good Semitic name, Nahman, conveniently dated to the Hyksos period by the cartouche of a King Apopi upon the dagger.[143] In both cases, of course, the names are written in Egyptian hieroglyphs. So Jacob and Joseph have undeniable Egyptian traits even in their postmortem activities. But, of course, so did other foreigners at other periods, especially in the New Kingdom, and continuingly in the Late Period.

4. A TOUCH OF CHRONOLOGY

Thus far, except to insist that the patriarchs have to be prior to the exodus/ Moses episodes, and thus earlier than the thirteenth century at the latest, the chronology of the patriarchs down to Joseph has been left alone except for a few asides in passing. But, as with the rest of the Hebrew history, it will be as well to tidy up the loose ends here too.

The factors here are both *external* and *internal*. The latter in the Hebrew Bible consist of two main resources: explicit statements of the interval between Abraham/Jacob and the exodus, and incidental data of other kinds. The former are data from outside the Hebrew corpus that in themselves indicate (or appear to indicate) specific dates or periods to which data in the Hebrew text correspond to the exclusion of other periods. In terms of proper methodology, we turn first to the *external* indicators at several levels, and their Hebrew links.

A. FACTORS AND RESULTS

(i) External Correlations

Here we may classify the phenomena available (studied in outline above) under a series of chronological headings, and see what result emerges from this process.

Group I: Features specific to early second millennium (or earlier)
1. *Wide scope of (nonstate/nonroyal) travel.* Mesopotamia, Old Babylonian period; cf. pp. 316-18 above.
2. *Wide transhumance and related pastoral movement.* In all directions, this

period, as opposed to later northwest-to-southeast for Mesopotamia, and steppe to richer land in Levant, and *not* based on the "Amorite hypothesis" of mass migrations; cf. p. 476.

3. *Long-distance marriages (non- and preimperial) by related groups.* West Semitic and "Amorite" dynasties practiced this in this period; cf. p. 318.

4. *East Delta residences of pharaohs (pre-1300), only circa 1970-1540.* Pp. 318, 319.

5. *Gen. 14: eastern alliances (within ca. 2000-1500) by contrast to Levant.* Cf. pp. 319-23.

6. *Gen. 14: Elam, interventions in Upper Mesopotamia, and interests westward.* P. 321.

7. *Gen. 14: close literary parallel in Yahdun-lim's text, Mari.* Cf. p. 321.

8. *Gen. 14: Tid'al, Old Hittite name and as chief of groups* (ruba'um rabium). Cf. p. 322.

9. *Type of treaties (Gen. 21; 31; 36), as at Mari and Tell Leilan.* Pp. 323-24.

10. *Prices of young male slaves, around twenty shekels, 1900-1600.* Cf. p. 325.

11. *Social usages, early second millennium, changing later on.* Cf. pp. 325-28.

12. *Patriarchal religion.* Showing early-second-millennium usage, and different in at least six respects from later periods. Cf. pp. 328-30.

13. *Patriarchal Canaan* is the land of the Execration Texts, of the archaeological horizon Middle Bronze II, very different from Late Bronze I-II (Egyptian empire) and Iron I-II (new entities and too late in time); cf. pp. 333-35.

14. *Patriarchal proper names.* The early West Semitic (so-called Amorite) Imperfectives, as in Ishmael, Isaac, Jacob, Joseph, etc., are popular out of all proportion in the early second millennium, by striking contrast with ever more limited usage later. Other name types, too, are characteristic of this period (e.g., Zebulon/Zabilanu, etc.); the Egyptian names belong to this period more than later. Cf. pp. 336, 341-43.

15. *Shepherding under Old Babylonian conditions, rather than later epochs.* Cf. pp. 336-38.

16. *Servant "in the house" (Egypt.* hery-per*), mainly Old/Middle Kingdom term;* p. 349.

17. Saris, *not eunuch in Egypt; and* (sha-reshi) *commonly not, in Old Babylonian period.*[144]

Group II: Features common to early and late second millennium

1. *Ur (in south Iraq) was an important center in the late third, early second, and late second millennia, but not later.* West Semitic pastoralists lived nearby in early second millennium; p. 316.

2. *Shinʿar was a "Western" term for Mesopotamia by late second millennium;* p. 320.

3. *In Joseph narrative and during the exodus, the Egyptian word* shesh *(early second millennium and following) is used for linen, and not the later word* bwts *(of sixth century and following).*[145]

4. *Aegeans in Canaan before Philistines.* Latter term perhaps replaced Caphtorim (in early twelfth century) and Kretim, and cf. Middle Minoan (and following) pottery, frescoes in Syria-Palestine and Egypt, within 1800-1500; pp. 339-41. (In the ancient Near East, Kaptaru/Caphtor goes down into Late Bronze II; and Kretim, Kition, from Late Bronze onward.)[146]

5. *Archaeological data for "patriarchal" places in Canaan, Middle Bronze and Late Bronze periods.* So, for Laish, Dothan, Shechem, Bethel, Jerusalem, Hebron, Gerar (if Tel Haror); in Negev, Tells Malhata, Masos, Farʾah South (pp. 333-35). By contrast, Beersheba was wells, not a town; and so, other names.[147]

6. *Features of appointment to high office.* Visual data are mainly late second millennium at present.

7. *Ideal age of 110 years.* Found in Egypt at all periods, but with especial concentration as a theme in late second millennium (to thirteenth century), p. 351.

Group III: Features specific to, or beginning in, late second millennium

1. *Land of Ra(a)mses, Gen. 47:11, in thirteenth-twelfth centuries only.* Cf. p. 348.

2. *Dan for Laish (Gen. 14:14), a revision of twelfth century (cf. Judg. 18).*

3. *Use of term "Philistines" for all Aegeans, from early twelfth century.* Cf. already, p. 341.

4. *Form of name Potiphar(a), thirteenth century onward.* Cf. pp. 346-47.

Group IV: Features specific to early first millennium

1. *Chaldeans to identify Ur. To distinguish Ur in south from Urs and Uras up north.* Usage of circa 1000-500; cf. p. 316.

2. *In Gen. 36:31, kings of Edom "before (any) king reigned for the Bne-Israel."* Many would take this as valid for circa 1020/1000 and following (for the Israelite reference). Others would suggest that the passage indicates that these Edomites reigned before a king in Israel was a reality rather than a mere possibility (as in Deut. 17:14-20).

**Group V: Features found in third, second, and first millennia —
"constants," hence not decisive for "early" or "late" suggested datings**

1. *Camels.* These are clearly attested in contexts of third, early second, late
   second, as well as early first millennia. Hence they are *not* anachronistic
   and have no bearing on date (pp. 338-39).
2. *Feast and famine,* in Egypt and the Levant. Egyptian records show three
   millennia of both (p. 350).
3. *Religious celebration for deity/ies after military victory.* All periods and
   places; cf. p. 322.
4. *Places that were occupied for long periods.* Such as Harran, Nakhur, etc. Cf.
   p. 317.

Group VI: False trails

1. *No direct connection between Egyptian stela of 400-year era of Seth and 400
   years of Gen. 15:13, etc.* In the thirteenth century that stela was deep within
   an Egyptian temple at Pi-Ramesse, and *not* accessible to foreigners; after
   circa 1070 it was reused as scrap building-material at Tanis, in temple
   foundations, and was never accessible again until the late nineteenth century A.D.!
2. *Note (Num. 13:22) about Hebron built seven years before Zoan (Tanis) in
   Egypt.* This is too isolated to serve as any kind of definitive marker, and
   external data are too scanty as yet to be of any help.

(ii) Internal (Biblical) Data

Here we have a series of very varied data, some explicit, some implicit; but all
need to be examined, and (in the cultural context) their nature — and thus
their significance — determined. Then we may gain a practical understanding
of what the sources might yield for the topic in view.

Group I: Year spans and eras between patriarchs and later times

1. *Time spans expressed in years.* Here we find two figures, from the patriarchs to the exodus. In Gen. 15:13 Abraham is warned that his descendants
   would enter Egypt, live there and (then) be oppressed, some 400 years.
   From the opposite perspective, in Exod. 12:40, the exodus was dated to the
   430th year since Jacob, long before, had entered Egypt. It should be obvious that both figures have the same period in view (Hebrew time of residence in Egypt): one is cast as a round figure looking into the future,
   while the second purports to be the elapsed time span for that period.

2. *Eras by broad period.* Following the mention (Gen. 15:13) of his people going to Egypt for four centuries, Abraham is also told (15:16) that his descendants would then return to Canaan four *dor,* "spans" (usual translation, "generations"), later. In the context, the four *dor* are another expression for the four centuries. Such a usage is found also in a text of Shamshi-Adad I of Assyria (ca. 1800), who uses the West Semitic word *daru* (= Heb. *dor*) in the same way as here in Gen. 15.[148] He speaks of seven *daru* having elapsed between the fall of the great dynasty of Akkad and his accession. If we adopt a modern mode of calculation, this is somewhere between 350 and 500 years, the latter giving 70 years' or so value to the *daru.* If we use the ancient mode of reckoning (as Shamshi-Adad's scribes would have to do), we would have between 530 and 730 years for seven *daru,* giving between 75 and 100 years for the *daru.*[149] The latter in particular would compare directly with four *dor* = 400 years in Gen. 15. So, whether the four *dor*/400/430 years be taken as consecutive or otherwise, we have a consistent usage.

Group II: A question of genealogies

The brevity of some biblical genealogies has sometimes been urged in favor of a much shorter span than four centuries for a Hebrew sojourn in Egypt. But this fails to account either for the full available evidence or for the often incomplete nature of such data.

1. *Fourfold identity tags ("short genealogies").* It should be stressed that Exod. 6:16-20 is not a full record for Aaron and Moses but simply gives their fourfold link back to the patriarch Jacob/Israel, by tribe (Levi), clan (Kohath), family group (Amram, by Jochebed), and individuals. Both here and in Num. 26:59 (plus 1 Chron. 6:3), the summary of Amram and Jochebed "parenting" Aaron and Moses has to be read in the same spirit as the children that Zilpah "bore" to Jacob who include great-grandsons in Gen. 46:16-18. At the exodus, the Amramites (and parallel families) were already much too numerous to be merely a "nuclear family"; cf. Num. 3:27-28.

This case is not unique. For Achan son of Carmi (Josh. 7:1), the same fourfold rule applies: tribe (Judah), clan (Zerah), family group (Zimri), and individuals (Achan and his father Carmi). For another notorious pair, Dathan and Abiram (Num. 26:5-10), the same applies: tribe (Reuben), clan (Pallu), family group (Eliab), individuals (Dathan, Abiram). And so on. This fourfold system of "tagging" a person to tribe, clan, and family group should not be abused (as some have done) to set the patriarchs artificially in the fifteenth century because of supposed links with Nuzi customs. Some of those links were false, others merely the tail end of earlier, Old Babylonian usage, hence they could of themselves fix no date for Jacob and company.

2. *Fuller genealogies — in part.* In any case, the fourfold tags are not the whole story. Other long-transmitted fragments, scooped up and preserved in the work of the Chronicler, show this clearly. We may concisely consider some of Moses' contemporaries, as follows.

Bezalel is set in the seventh generation after Jacob (1 Chron. 2:1, 4, 5, 9, 18-21): Judah, Perez, Hezron, Caleb (Kelubai), Hur, Uri, Bezalel.

Elishama (Num. 1:10) falls in the ninth generation after Jacob, while Joshua, as Moses' younger contemporary, is in the eleventh after Jacob: Joseph, Ephraim; then (1 Chron. 7:22-27) Rephah, Resheph, Telah, Tahan, Ladan, Ammihud, Elishama; Nun, Joshua.

By contrast, another exodus contemporary, Nahshon (Num. 1:7), appears as though only six generations after Jacob (1 Chron. 2:1, 4, 5, 9, 10): Judah, Perez, Hezron, Ram, Amminadab, Nahshon.

Thus a variation of from six to eleven generations from Jacob to the exodus demonstrates that the fourfold tags do not represent the real time-lapse for this period and that the longer genealogies themselves vary in the amount of lineage preserved, and are thus selective in themselves in varying degrees. This is not peculiar. For David, Ruth 4:18-22 has only eleven generations from Perez to David, which would be twelve from Judah to David, to "cover" the entire longer span from Jacob to David — maximally 430 + 300 = 730 years on a minimal exodus date, and much "worse" (430 + 480 = 910 years) for those who too simplistically base themselves exclusively on 1 Kings 6:1. In either case, it is clear that the Davidic line is also much abbreviated before Boaz. For our maximum period of 430 years, Jacob to the exodus, sixteen to twenty generations might be expected (and almost double that down to David). In short, the range of genealogical data points clearly to a time span well beyond just four generations in the strictly biological sense, but equally clearly does not in its present abridged form cover the entire span. Varying life spans in families also affect number of generations in a given period.

3. *Some background data.* In the biblical world, matters are much the same; the Hebrew data are in no way anomalous. Thus, in thirteenth-century Egypt under Ramesses II, a scribe Mose son of Huy won a court case to repossess some family land. That land had been given to his ancestor Neshi 300 years before, by Ahmose I, during the war against the Hyksos. Both Mose and others appear as offspring of Huy, son of Wernuro,

357

daughter of Neshi — thus a fourfold tag: ancestor (Neshi), family line (Wernuro), family (Huy), and individual (Neshi and brethren), without listing all the intervening generations back to Neshi.[150] In terms of fuller genealogies, but still selective, one may cite the incredibly long Berlin genealogy of a priest at Memphis reaching back from the eighth century for some fifteen centuries to the Eleventh Dynasty (ca. 2000). It shows gaps in succession, with (e.g.) only one generation named between four successive priests under Ramesses II and one heading representing a series from the early Twenty-First Dynasty, 150 years later. Clearly, some seven generations had been dropped at this point.[151] So, long genealogies are not necessarily complete, either in the Hebrew Bible or amongst neighbors of Israel. By contrast, the official king list from north Syrian Ugarit was — when intact — probably largely complete, having at least thirty kings (and originally, more like forty kings, some names being broken away) to span the period back from 1200 to the nineteenth century, some 600 or more years. Here, any omissions would have been only for childless brothers or very short-lived rulers.[152] Thus, on all sides, the Hebrew usages were normal, in their world.

B. CHRONOLOGICAL RESULTS ON BOTH EXTERNAL AND INTERNAL DATA

It is now possible to sum up this particular inquest in two respects: (1) by determining what the overall data suggest as regards a date for the patriarchs, and (2) by analyzing the objective evidence for the history of the Genesis tradition about them, from its beginnings through later periods.

(i) Can We Date the Patriarchs?

In the light of the total evidence, in general terms at least, the answer is a clear yes. The external data were grouped under six heads, with the following results. The first and by far the biggest section (Group I under [i]) can offer almost a score of very varied lines of evidence that tie Abraham/Isaac/Jacob/Joseph to the overall period circa 1900-1600 (2000-1500 at the outermost limits). Alongside these data we have (in Group II of [i]) a further seven items indicating a date in the second millennium, consistent with its earlier part while continuing into the later half, hence less precise. Alongside these two dozen items we have only four minor features (Group III under [i]) that belong to the late second millennium, not earlier, and only two items (in Group IV in [i]) that probably originated in the early first millennium. Thus, only six later retouches against twenty-four (seventeen clear, seven early or late second millennium) is quite an impressive result. To all this we can add Group V, which offers four more items also compatible with the early second millennium, but likewise also with most other periods. Thus the maximal possible data in these lists runs to twenty-eight items of real + likely + possible early second-millennium date, versus a mere six retouches added later. In Group VI we can dismiss two items that are useless for dating purposes.

The overall date of about 1900-1600 for Abraham to Joseph is consistent also with the internal data. The era dates of 400/430 years before a minimal-date exodus at circa 1260/1250 would bring us back to roughly 1690/1680 for Jacob's entry into Egypt, and Joseph's arrival there by about 1720/1700. Jacob was an old man in Egypt, born earlier in the eighteenth century at the latest; Isaac in turn would have been born in the middle to late nineteenth century, and before him, Abraham earlier in the nineteenth century at the latest. Their life spans and birth dates are high; a minimal chronology would allow for possible inflation of these figures in tradition, while keeping the overall profile. This result goes well with that from the external data, such that it is wholly reasonable to speak, once more, of a "patriarchal age" in biblical terms, but on a far sounder basis than was formerly the case.

(ii) Retouches

The evidence given above (in Group III under [i]) shows marks of a basic set of traditions that arose around Abraham to Joseph by about 1600, conceivably transmitted down to the thirteenth century. This ongoing history of the tradition shows perhaps three phases.

The first is in Ramesside Egypt, in the thirteenth century. "Land of Rameses" (Gen. 47:11) belongs to the same horizon as "Raamses," the store city of Exod. 1:11, and both reflect Ramesses II's time and his intense activity in the East Delta. The form Potiphar(a) is probably a thirteenth-century-onward modernization of Pa-didi-(p)re, from an original Didi-re.

In the twelfth century "Philistines" apparently replaced Caphtorim and suchlike almost completely, and Dan replaced Laish.

The third phase encompasses the early first millennium, during which possibly the concept/existence of Israelite kings in what became our present Gen. 36 arose; certainly the tag "Chaldean" attached to Ur at some time.

In a long-transmitted tradition, none of this is surprising. We know that the Egyptian narrative of Sinuhe was already current by circa 1800 from actual manuscripts of that time. But in the Ashmolean Ostracon copy of its text may be found just such "retouches": older negative *n* replaced by more modern *bw;* the old word *nwy* for "waterflood" replaced by the West Semitic *yam,* for example. If we had nothing earlier than this ostracon, we might be tempted to date the composition of the text to (say) the fourteenth century rather than the late twentieth — yet the existence of the nineteenth/eighteenth-century MSS forbids any such erroneous judgment. But it is to questions of tradition and transmission that we must finally now turn.

5. EXTERNAL CONTROLS: LITERARY STATUS AND MODES OF TRANSMISSION

Two matters require attention at this point: What is the literary *nature* of the patriarchal narratives, within a broad spectrum from literal history at one extreme to pure fantasy tale at the other? And what are the options for modes of *transmission* of these narratives (whatever their nature), from point(s) of origin down to much later periods? Let us consider each in turn, within the factual context of the biblical world that can provide us with the yardsticks for measuring off the possibilities. Speculation in isolation is worthless.

A. LITERARY CONTEXTS FOR THE PATRIARCHAL NARRATIVES

(i) The Phenomena of the Narratives Themselves

See already the presentation of framework and contents, pp. 314-15 above. Looked at dispassionately, we have simply the story of a man (Terah) who moved on with his family from Ur in southern Mesopotamia, going northwest to Harran in the great west bend of the Euphrates. After his death, one son, Abram, moved on west and southwest through Syria into Canaan, moving around there as a pastoralist; one incident brought him into brief conflict with an armed alliance from the east. His son Isaac and grandson Jacob continued the same lifestyle, and all maintained contact with the relatives back up in Harran (especially for obtaining wives). Jacob's favorite young son, Joseph, was sold into Egypt and made good there, and could thus welcome his family during a famine, where they settled for some time. These narrations are straightforward, with plenty of small-scale incident; there are almost no miracles or obvious fantasies. Deity is prayed to, and appears in visions/dreams with messages; "acts of God" (to use insurance-company language) are attributed to deity as judgment. As already noted above, high ages at death, etc., are the only unusual features, and this may be in part the result of long-term transmission of numbers, a matter subject to change through time.

(ii) The Range of Comparable Narration in the Biblical World

Such narratives (spread through three millennia) come under five heads, as follows.

(a) Royal Historical Texts

These are found in all three millennia. In Egypt are the year-by-year annals of the First to Fifth Dynasties (third millennium) on the Palermo Stone, and a fragment of such annals of Amenemhat II (Twelfth Dynasty; early second millennium); then war and building reports, etc., of the great New Kingdom kings (late second millennium). Some stelae, war reliefs, etc., exist for the late period (early first millennium), pertaining to Shoshenq I, Taharqa, Psamtek I, etc.[153] In Mesopotamia one finds copies of war reports of the empire of Akkad and Gudea's building texts (third millennium); then building and war reports from Babylonia and Assyria, limited in the early second millennium but more extensive in the first millennium (Assyrian annals; scribal "chronicles").[154] In Asia Minor we have the Hittite records. These include war reports from the early second millennium and more extensive annals (plus treaties) from the late second millennium.[155] Syria-Palestine offers mainly administrative texts, letters, etc., from Ebla (third millennium), Mari (early second), Emar and Ugarit (late second), and the autobiography of Idrimi, Alalakh (wrongly called "fictional"); we also have some West Semitic texts from the first millennium. We have Phoenician royal texts, as at Byblos, and in Asia Minor (Azitawata bilingual with "Hittite Hieroglyphic" version). In Old Aramaic are: texts from kings of Sam'al (local dialect), minor epigraphs (as of Hazael of Damascus), and the Tell Dan stela (Aram). Farther south we have the Mesha stela (Moab), administrative ostraca, Samaria, etc. (Hebrew).[156] From Old South Arabia we have first-millennium war annals of Karibil Watar I (seventh century), as well as later building texts by him and other rulers. Divine intervention is at times invoked.[157]

(b) Autobiographical and Biographical Texts, Officials and Private People

Again, these appear in all three millennia. In Egypt, our richest source, formal autobiographical texts of officials and others are well attested throughout this long epoch. Noteworthy in the early second millennium are the biography of Khnumhotep II at Beni Hasan, and the so-called "Story of Sinuhe," a similar autobiography adapted to be used as a propagandistic school text. In the New Kingdom is a long series of such examples, plus the "Story of Wenamun," probably historical in origin. Mainly funerary texts come from the first millennium, but the "Chronicle of Prince Osorkon" (ninth/eighth century) is notable. All these are marked by first-person narrative; they contain very few "wonders," while deity can occasionally be invoked when thought appropriate.[158] In Mesopotamia we have far less; in the eighth century (under weaker kings), some provincial high officials set up their own cuneiform inscriptions.[159] From Asia Minor and Syria-Palestine there is almost nothing in this category at present; some Neo-Hittite texts of officials (first millennium) can be included here, but little else other than funerary inscriptions.[160]

(c) Historical Legends

Again, we have a variety of such documents down through time. These are stories about humans, usually historical personalities (kings or commoners), but known commonly to have been composed distinctly later than the period(s) of the people concerned. In *Egypt,* in the mid–second millennium, we have the "Tales of the Magicians" (Papyrus Westcar), of circa 1600 but relating to people of 1,000 years before (in the Pyramid Age or Old Kingdom). The tales name a sequence of kings known otherwise from directly historical sources, from (Djoser and) Nebka to Snofru, Kheops and his sons, and the first three kings of the succeeding Fifth Dynasty, and all in their correct sequence. Others in these tales (Princes Bauefre, Hardjedef) are also attested historically. The "Tale of General Sisenet and King Pepi II" is likewise placed in the third millennium, and was probably also first written down about 1600 (not after 1300), being transmitted in writing during at least 1300 to 670. The late second millennium has given us the stories of the Hyksos Apopi versus King Seqenenre, the "Capture of Joppa" by Thuty under Tuthmosis III (perhaps historically based, cf. p. 365 below). In the late period the fourth-century tale of the princess of Bakhtan is based on incidents drawn from the reigns of Amenophis III and especially Ramesses II (1,000 years earlier), while in the Greco-Roman periods we have tales of Prince

Khaemwaset, son of Ramesses II of ten to thirteen centuries before, and of the Delta princedoms of circa 670, some 400 to 700 years before.[161]

In *Mesopotamia* we have tales in Sumerian (early second millennium) about very early kings of the third millennium, such as Gilgamesh, Enmerkar and Lugalbanda, Dumuzi, Etana, etc. Then the late-third-millennium kings Sargon and Naram-Sin of the empire of Akkad had tales told about them from Ur-III times and the Old Babylonian period 200/300 years later, then from the late second millennium (up to 1,000 years later), which were sometimes copied down to the seventh/sixth centuries (600 years later still). From the late second millennium come epics of Tukulti-Ninurta I and Tiglath-pileser I of Assyria; later works honored first-millennium Mesopotamian kings.[162] From the *Hittite* archives of the late second millennium, besides Hittite versions of the stories of Gilgamesh and Sargon from Babylonia, we have original Hittite stories of the siege of Urshu, and King Anum-khirbe and the town of Zalpa among others.[163] For *Syria-Palestine,* the Hittite archives offer a bilingual text (in Hittite and Hurrian) about one Meki of Ebla, while the alphabetic texts from Ugarit include epic tales of a King Keret and one Danel (unless he is under the subhead immediately below); all are in written versions of the late second millennium.[164]

(d) Purely Fictional Tales, Excluding Historical Characters

Here we have purely fantasy tales, folktales proper, the characters often being anonymous. In Egypt, such works include the stories "The Shipwrecked Sailor," "Herdsman and a Goddess," and one of two ghost stories (early second millennium); "Foredoomed Prince," "Tale of Two Brothers," and an allegory, "The Blinding of Truth" (all late second millennium).[165] In Mesopotamia, in the early second millennium, we have in Sumerian "Three Ox-Drivers of Adab" and "Old Man and Young Girl," while in Akkadian there is "Poor Man of Nippur" and "At the Cleaner's."[166] In the Hittite sphere, humans and deities mingle in various second-millennium tales, such as those about Appu, Keshshi, and the "Sun-god, Cow and Fisherman."[167] In Syria-Palestine, the Ugaritic tale of Danel might belong here rather than immediately above.

(e) Tales of Mythology

Legend concerns primarily human beings (although deities can appear in legends), while myth concerns the world of the gods and related beings (with little or no role for humans). Under mythological tales so delimited comes a wealth of narratives, only baldly summarized here. For Egypt we have mainly allusions and fragments in the third and early second millennia. But in the late second millennium we have the burlesque "Contendings of Horus and Seth," "Destruction of Mankind," "Story of Astarte and the Sea" (about Canaanite deities), "Isis and the Sun-god's Secret Name," etc. From the late first millennium (with older roots), we have "Story of the Winged Disc," "Anhur-Shu and the Lioness-Goddess," and local such tales at Esna.[168] In Mesopotamia, from the third into the early second millennium, we have in Sumerian six myths about Enki and other gods, including "Inanna's Descent to the Netherworld"; "Nanna-Suen's Journey to Nippur"; tales of Dumuzi, etc. In Akkadian, other such works include "Ishtar's Descent to the Netherworld" (replacing Inanna), the Erra epic, the myth of Anzu, *Enuma Elish* (creation), and more besides.[169] Hittite archives contain both strictly Hittite works such as those about Illuyankas, the disappearing of Telipinus, and of other gods, and also Hurrian compositions, notably a cycle of stories about Kumarbi.[170] For Syria-Palestine, we have for the present basically the great Baal cycle from Ugarit, along with "Dawn and Dusk," "Wedding of Nikkal and the Moon," and other pieces.[171]

(f) Profile of Ancient Near Eastern Narrative

From this whirlwind survey, or rather from the actual texts it so briefly presents, certain basic facts emerge. Especially is this clear for anyone who can gain access to the texts themselves, at least in good modern translations.

Texts of historical import do commonly include praise of the ruler concerned, can invoke deity on his side, can use conventional clichés, etc., but do still provide largely factual narratives — or transparently historical facts and features can at least be discerned in them. At times, careful assessment is needed (e.g., when Assurbanipal's scribes merge data from originally separate campaigns), but occasional odd embellishments (e.g., Esarhaddon's winged serpents!) cannot impugn the basic historicity of otherwise straight accounts.

(Auto)biographical texts are, again, told from the viewpoint of the person concerned, but this can be allowed for and does not eliminate clear historical content. Good examples are narrative biographical texts of Egyptian officials (third to first millennia), and (in first millennia B.C. and A.D.) of Old South Arabian royal supporters in Sheba, Qataban, Himyar, and Hadramaut.

Historical legends almost invariably tell stories about real people (kings or otherwise), whether of a distant or a recent past. However, the *content* of such stories can vary right across the spectrum from the possibly historical (cf.

"Capture of Joppa") to the most playful fantasy of no historical content (cf. "Tales of the Magicians" in Papyrus Westcar). In the former, Thuty is as historical as is Tuthmosis III, and was rewarded by him with a golden goblet, evidently for services rendered — just possibly for organizing the fall of Joppa. But in Papyrus Westcar the real characters move in a world where the severed heads and bodies of birds and animals can be magically rejoined and come to life again, or the waters of a lake be neatly rolled aside like a duvet or bedcover. Or a known conqueror (Sargon of Akkad) finds mountains and rocks of gold and lapis blocking his path. These texts form an *intermediate* category between the histories and biographies just noted and the tales human and divine now to be noticed.

We then have two other, related groups: tales about humans (deities sometimes occurring), often having anonymous characters, i.e., *fictional tales proper;* and tales about the gods and associated beings (humans rarely or modestly present), being *mythological tales proper.* These two groups neither are historical nor have any pretensions of being historical, except perhaps when they purport to describe the world's origins. So we have two essentially history-based groups; an intermediate group (real people in circumstances fictional in part or wholly); and a purely fictional pair of groups, of tales mainly human and mainly divine respectively. This clear range, at all periods, gives us a setting by which to appreciate the situation of the patriarchal narratives.

(iii) The Patriarchal Narratives in Their Full Cultural Context

The above-sketched five classes of texts (pp. 433 ff. above) provide us with a strictly independent and objective frame of reference against which we may fairly assess the nature of the narratives in Gen. 11–50. In terms of content, these narratives give a picture of real human life as lived by West Semitic pastoralists, derived mainly from conditions observable in the early second millennium, with a very moderate amount of minor retouches in at least three later periods.

If we look now at the patriarchal narratives alongside the five classes of narrative, it becomes a relatively straightforward procedure to distinguish between what is truly comparable and what is not. This can be achieved most efficiently by a process of systematic elimination.

First of all, we can dismiss (a) above; the patriarchs were never kings ruling a state (either urban or tented), they were simply transhumant nonroyal pastoralists, even if prosperous. Second, we can equally firmly dismiss (e). The patriarchs were not deities either, and never were; they worshiped deity, but never received such honors themselves, and their social life mirrored that of other contemporary humans. Third, we may next dismiss (d) — these biblical narratives are not simple folktales about anonymous characters in wholly vague or general settings. They are about named individuals with specific family members in precise contexts. That leaves us only with (b), (auto)biography, and (c), historical legends. As they stand, these narratives are not *auto*biography, but they *are* biographical in giving some account of the lives of Abraham, Isaac, Jacob, and Joseph, with other family members in lesser roles. They differ from our other Near Eastern biographical texts in being cast in the third person (rather than the first), and in the past entirely, as a recopied, transmitted text, not a firsthand inscription on stone, clay, or whatever. It is this last feature (transmitted text through time, basically third person) that alone links these narratives with our (c), historical legend, cast as retrospect, basically third person, and subject to (sometimes long) literary transmission. By comparison with most (c) texts, the patriarchal narratives belong soberly to the realia of this world, not to a world peopled by golden mountains, lapis lazuli rocks, animals that come alive when their severed heads are rejoined, and so on. There are very few "remarkable" features in the biblical narrations. Sodom and Gomorrah (Gen. 19) suffered through being in a well-attested seismic zone (the Rift Valley).[172] Very many real people in antiquity claim dealings with deity (nobody can dismiss the historicity of, e.g., a Ramesses II or a Sennacherib on such grounds). Visions (night or day, Gen. 15) are not unknown; and high ages at death and at prior events are a separate question of the transmission of numbers, and have no direct bearing on historicity (cf. the case of Enmebaragisi in chap. 9 below). Thus, if we sensibly leave aside empty speculations that lack any factual basis and stay with the total balance of the evidence, it would seem that the patriarchal narratives stand closest to (b) above, but have only minor affiliations with (c), other than the fact that their story — once formulated — has gone through a long literary transmission. But this latter situation is not unique (cf. Sinuhe in Egypt, or the stories of Sargon and Naram-Sin in Mesopotamia, who were certainly historical).

Thus the fairest judgment — on the overall evidence itself, and no agendas, please! — would appear to be that a real historical family of a man Terah once existed in and around Ur this side of circa 2000 B.C.; he and they moved on northwestward, and his son Abraham and family then moved south into Canaan; after three generations the latter's great-grandson (Joseph) could care for the group in Thirteenth/Fifteenth Dynasty Egypt in the East Delta. Abraham passed on family lore to Isaac (cf. on Gen. 1–11, chap. 9 below); Isaac passed part of this plus family tradition about his father to Jacob; Jacob passed on a core of the antique traditions (cf. Gen. 1–11) and of traditions about Abraham and Isaac, and his own experiences to Joseph and his brothers; and they in turn maintained an ongoing tradition (oral, written, or both) that was eventually given the well-segmented form that we find in the present book of Genesis. By the end of that book Joseph is as dead as the rest (cf. Gen. 50:26), so that formulation is later. Several features point to the late second millennium (cf. pp. 358-60 above) for that event; after that, only the slightest retouches seem visible (Chaldeans, Philistines, Dan; perhaps Israelite kingship), of the twelfth-tenth centuries, and but little later.

This sequencing of the tradition very simply accounts for the third-person yet biographical format. Thus, if an old Abraham was telling a young Isaac about his own past, he would have narrated it *auto*biographically. To use Gen. 14 as a simple example, he would have said something like: "These eastern kings carried away my nephew Lot — your cousin — and one that escaped told me, when I was living near my friend Mamre's great trees. So I led out my 318 trained people and chased them up to Laish. . . ." But when, later, Isaac came to pass on this episode to young Jacob, he would have had to turn it automatically into the third person: "These eastern kings carried away Abraham's nephew Lot — your uncle — and an escapee told him, and he led out his 318 warriors and chased them up to Laish. . . ." And so, each patriarch's traditions were automatically turned into the third-person format when passed on to a further generation.

For such a phenomenon elsewhere, we need look no further than in a real biography, known from its original monumental text, inscribed on the stone walls of a Middle Kingdom tomb chapel of the early second millennium, that of Khnumhotep II, whose latest date is explicitly under Sesostris II (ca. 1875), a possible contemporary of such as Abraham — it is in this tomb chapel at Beni Hasan that we find the famous painting of Ab-sharru and his thirty-seven "Asiatics" visiting Egypt. Khnumhotep speaks not only of his own deeds, but takes us through three generations of his own family history under four successive kings (Amenemhat I, Sesostris I, Amenemhat II, and Sesostris II), describing the relationships of his family with the ruling house, and their various appointments, besides dilating at length (as Egyptians did!) on his own deeds and honors. They are all put in the third person, and he speaks of himself in the first; he clearly knew his family history, all the way back through four reigns. That is how things actually were; we have no need to resort to unsupported guesswork about it. And so, likewise, for their contemporaries, the patriarchs, who would know *their* personal family history.

Originally the patriarchs probably told more episodes about themselves than we now possess in Genesis; but a basic nucleus was retained, while seemingly less germane episodes were discarded. By the thirteenth century the basic catena of material was essentially what we have now. It would then stand as a foundation or "charter" document to remind the Israelite tribal group of their origins, as the people of the God of their forefathers who was now to take them further on in life, to the exodus (and all that followed, of course).

Thus we have a set of "blocks" of data: primeval (chap. 9 below), Abraham (plus Ishmael), Isaac, Jacob (plus Esau/Edom), and Joseph — set together in the *toledoth*, or "successions," framework, to provide a continuous narrative, just as the family itself had been a continuum.

B. MODES OF TRANSMISSION

It is one thing airily to propose the transmission of a body of data about the patriarchs from (say) circa 1650 to circa 1250, and then onward to circa 1000/950, and then to the fifth century BC, and then onward with the rest of the biblical writings — even if the total evidence does point to an early-second-millennium origin for most of the basic data. It is, naturally, quite another to assess how such a matter would work out in practice (or otherwise). This question we must now review, before concluding on the patriarchs overall.

Through 400 years from Joseph to Moses, then some 300 years down to the united monarchy, then 400 years or more to the Babylonian exile and its aftermath — what controls do we have over such a process? The answer has to come from our external data, on all sides of the ancient Near East.

In Mesopotamia the two famous rivals, Hammurabi of Babylon and Shamshi-Adad I of Assyria, shared distant common ancestors, from periods long before their families were kings. There were sixteen generations before Hammurabi of Babylon and fourteen before his elder contemporary Shamshi-Adad of Assyria, back to the common first ancestor, Namhu/Nuabu. Before him, the Babylonian line counted ten ancestors to the beginning, and the Assyrian, eleven, or between twenty-five and twenty-six generations all told before Hammurabi and Shamshi-Adad respectively.[173] Some names show variants, or change order in one document as compared with the other; but they are a remarkable series that probably on normal generation-count would formally have gone back by about 550/600 years, comfortably more than the 430 years between Jacob and Moses, or the later spans from him to the united monarchy and then to the exile onward.

Nor is this unique. In Syrian Ugarit the official king list had originally a continuous list of between thirty and forty kings going back from about 1200 to a man Yaqarum in the nineteenth century, some 600 years (p. 358 above), his seal being still in use in the thirteenth century.[174] The oldest traditions there conceivably went most of 160/200 years further back still, to the twenty-second century, linking up with ancestors of Hammurabi and Shamshi-Adad I.

In Egypt we have comparable data of two kinds. The first is again genealogies. In the early second millennium (ca. 1900, under Amenemhat II), Ukh-hotep son of Ukh-hotep, governor of the fourteenth Upper Egyptian province, caused to be engraved in his tomb chapel a full list of his fifty-nine forebears and predecessors in office with their wives, all named and seemingly in chronological order. The authenticity of the series is indicated by the changes in type of name through time. The earliest ancestor seems to have lived in the Fourth Dynasty, circa 2600-2500 (minimum), some 600 to 700 years before Ukh-hotep, or half as long again as the interval from Moses back to Jacob.[175] Of much later date, the Berlin genealogy of a priest in the eighth century reaches back some 1,500 years to the Eleventh Dynasty (ca. 2000; p. 358, above), or nearly four times the Jacob-Moses period. Closer in time and time span is the temple scribe Mose of circa 1250, who could trace his ancestry back 300 years to Neshi under Ahmose I (1550) in a court of law (p. 357 above). The chief draftsman Didia of circa 1290 (of Hurrian and Semitic extraction) kept record of the seven generations of his ancestors and all their wives by name and sequence, going back to circa 1450, about 160 years before.[176] These are private families (like the patriarchs), not royalty, and the latter of mainly Semitic origin.

The second kind of data is narratives. Thus the tales of the magicians in Papyrus Westcar of circa 1600 (p. 362 above) are originally oral tales for entertainment, about marvels at the court of the pyramid-building kings of circa 2600, a thousand years before. Yet these tales have reliably preserved a sequence of originally four generations of kings (Third-Fourth Dynasties), followed by another three (Fifth Dynasty), all in their right order, and names basically correct (the three Fifth Dynasty ones are slightly changed), and also the names of known sons of King Kheops (of Great Pyramid fame), antihero of the tales. This is not remotely an official record, but a popular one; and it records all these framework facts for 1,000 years, never mind the mere 430 years from a Jacob to a Moses (in comparison, kids' stuff!). The biography of Sinuhe (in its preserved literary version) originated circa 1920, and was well transmitted and read into and through the New Kingdom into the Twentieth Dynasty, most of 800 years later, for double the span of our patriarchal biographies. In a different mold but showing the transmission of narrative tradition are the "Story of the Princess of Bakhtan" and the "Story-Cycle of King Petubastis." The former was an adaptation in the fourth century b.c. of accounts of the Hittite marriages of Ramesses II (thirteenth century) and of traveling healing-deities and doctors (fourteenth-thirteenth centuries), of almost a thousand years before, in favor of the moon god Khons at Thebes. The latter are tales in demotic (very late Egyptian) in manuscripts of the early Roman period, but they preserve the names and status of several local Delta kings and potentates of the seventh century, of 800-900 years before.[177] So at all periods, and often for lengths of time far outstripping the successive periods (430, 300, 450 years) through which the "editions" of the patriarchal narratives passed, Egypt can show a variety of examples in various forms, of transmission of knowledge of historical characters and considerable genealogical data, and that with accuracy.

In the Hittite realm we have collateral evidence for such usage also. Already in the nineteenth century a local ruler Anittas made his mark as a precursor of the subsequent Hittite kingdom, and left a brief annalistic account of his deeds.[178] The later Hittite kings looked upon him as a true forerunner, and thus preserved the record of his deeds for 600 years thereafter. They also took over (from Mesopotamia) by the fourteenth/thirteenth centuries some of the literary traditions about Sargon and Naram-Sin, kings of the empire of Akkad, of the twenty-fourth century, again of almost a thousand years before, and maintained in Babylonia during that time.

From the foregoing sampling of external evidence, it should be clear that transmission of data long term was not merely possible, but happened all the time, from the age of the pyramids to that of Caesar, through most of 3,000 years.

So much for the *achievement of transmission,* but what of its *modes?* The two possible modes are oral tradition (one generation repeating the material by spoken word, to be memorized by the next) or writing — or both, side by side. Several of the examples cited above clearly were transmitted from a written original right from the start. Such are the biography of Sinuhe and the deeds of Anittas, for example. Of many of these examples, we possess a "final" edition in writing, but nothing on how that edition came to reach the form that we now have. The king list of Ugarit, the genealogies of Ukh-hotep and of Didia in Egypt (among others) — what did these rest upon, family memory or earlier records? We cannot know, factually. Of others, oral tradition can be posited in at least some measure. The folksy "Tales of the Magicians" was probably long handed down by storytellers before being committed to papyrus by some interested scribe (whether on Papyrus Westcar or a precursor). And the long generations of the distant sheikhs whence sprang the more immediate forebears of Hammurabi and Shamshi-Adad I, were these not the detritus from a long prior oral transmission? So both processes were likely in use in different cases contemporaneously, and in some cases initial oral transmission gave way to a written format.

Where does that leave the patriarchs? Obviously, a definitive answer cannot be given at present. The starting point is that the patriarchal narratives do retain much data faithfully preserved from the early second millennium. A tenacious oral transmission to later times is possible (as probable examples given above make clear), at least to start with. But written records are the securer route in most cases. As by 1600 cuneiform was used in Mesopotamia and Syria, but (so far) nowhere south of Hebron, and only at government level, it can be excluded for proto-Hebrews in Egypt. In Egypt two options then existed. The first, widely practiced, was Egypt's own hieroglyphic and hieratic scripts. We have already met Semites using it by circa 1600, namely, Abdu on his coffin and Nahman on a dagger (p. 352 above). In the large household of a Potiphar, Joseph would either become trained in these scripts himself or work with scribes using them (compare Papyrus Brooklyn 35.1446 of ca. 1730, listing over forty Semites among over seventy servants in such a household).[179] But unless he trained some of his (or his brothers') offspring to read these scripts, any patriarchal tradition in them would have become (literally!) a closed book to their descendants before Moses' time.

The other option was the recently invented West Semitic alphabet, a vehicle designed by and for Semitic speakers (and writers). The oldest-known examples have been the Lachish dagger epigraph from a seventeenth-century tomb and the Tell Nagila sherd (Middle/Late Bronze, ca. 1600); we now have also the Wadi Hol graffiti in Egypt from northwest of Thebes, about the seventeenth century.[180] These oldest examples occur in homely, informal contexts, showing that it could be, and was, readily utilized by anyone who cared to do so, and not solely by government elites. To these must be added the proto-Sinaitic inscriptions of disputed date — circa 1800 or circa 1500. This system of not more than thirty simple, semipictographic letters would have been very easy to use in writing up (on papyrus) a "first written edition" of the patriarchal traditions from Abraham to Jacob, to which a Joseph account could be added. This set of basic narratives could then be recopied from circa 1600 to the thirteenth century, then given a "late Canaanite" editing in that phase of script, eventuating into early standard Hebrew language and script from the united monarchy onward. At the Late Bronze (e.g., "land of Rameses"), Early Iron IIA (e.g., Laish > Dan), and final phases of transmission (e.g., "Chaldean" Ur), the handful of retouches would be incorporated. This straightforward view is at least consistent with all the *factual* data that we currently possess, and keeps theorizing to a minimum.

6. A BALANCE HERE TOO

We are compelled, once and for all, to throw out Wellhausen's bold claim that the patriarchs were merely a glorified mirage of/from the Hebrew monarchy period. For such a view there is not a particle of supporting factual evidence, and the whole of the foregoing indicative background material is solidly against it. It should be clear, finally, that the main features of the patriarchal narratives either fit specifically into the first half of the second millennium or are consistent with such a dating; some features common to that epoch and to later periods clearly must be taken with the early-second-millennium horizon. In contrast to this, data in these narratives that *do* clearly originate from well after circa 1600 are relatively few and are merely later updates (like thirteenth-century *yam* for nineteenth-century *nwy* for "waterflood" in a late MS of Sinuhe, a work attested in MSS from ca. 1800 at least; cf. p. 318 above). Long-term transmission through millennia, not just centuries, is well known in the biblical world, and simple, sensible modes of composition and text transmission are here presented that at least have the merit of requiring only minimal assumptions.

In contrast, the old Wellhausen-type view is ruled out by the horde of contrary facts unearthed since 1878 and 1886. We have here the Canaan of the early second millennium and *not* of the Hebrew monarchy period, in any wise. The oft-stated claim of a "consensus" that the patriarchs never existed is itself a case of self-delusion on the data presented here, and (if one may be forgiven for saying so) in fact a "con-nonsense-us"! We do not actually need firsthand namings of the patriarchs in ancient records; plenty of other historical characters are in the same case. The tombs of Early, Middle, and Late Bronze Canaan have yielded countless bodies of nameless citizens of Canaan; but their anonymity (no texts!) does not render them nonexistent. What is sauce for the goose is sauce for the gander.

CHAPTER 8

A Vitamin Supplement — Prophets and Prophecy

1. THE BIBLICAL DATA REVIEWED

In first-millennium Israel there arose spokesmen to declare their deity's judgments and blessings on its rulers and people by speech and in writing — the prophets. But their pedigree went back to Moses and Abraham. And recent decades have provided valuable background.

A. CHRONOLOGICAL OUTLINE

(i) Archaic Usage: Patriarchal Period, Early Second Millennium

Here, by contrast with the outside world at this time (see sec. 2 below), we have but one incidental reference, in Gen. 20:7. When Abimelek of Gerar took in Abraham's wife (in the guise of his sister), he was warned in a dream not to touch her, as another's wife. If he returned her, Abraham, as a *nabi*, "prophet," would pray to deity for him. This is the first (biblical) example of a prophet, in a role of intercessor, seeking benefit from deity for others — a usage scarcely found in the Hebrew Bible in later days. This is mirrored in the external sources, as we shall see.

(ii) Early Usages: Exodus to Judges, Late Second Millennium

Intercession was requested of Moses by Pharaoh only when things got tough for him (cf. Exod. 8:8, 28; 9:28; 10:17). In the role of spokesman, Aaron served for

373

Moses before Pharaoh (7:1-2), and the role of spokesman of YHWH was defined in Deut. 18:14-22, with the question of true and false prophets in Deut. 18:18-22 (criterion of fulfillment) and 13:1-5 (criterion of [dis]loyalty to YHWH). For a prophet in action, cf. Judg. 6:8.

Prophets could be female; compare Miriam in Exod. 15:20, and especially Deborah in the twelfth century (Judg. 4:4). They could also act as leaders locally and nationally, as did Deborah (Judg. 4–6) and, later, Samuel (1 Sam. 7). Music and an ecstatic role could accompany the office; cf. Miriam (Exod. 15:20, music) and the elders and men in the camp when the spirit of YHWH came upon them (Num. 11:25-29).

Thus in the second millennium we find: intercession (early); spokesperson (main role); role of music and ecstasy; community leaders. Truth and falsehood of "prophets" could be an issue.

(iii) Intermediate Usage, First Phase (Forerunners of National Figures)

This phase deals with the eleventh to ninth centuries, during the united and early divided monarchy. Prophets served as intercessors during this time; so Samuel is reported in Israel twice at the same juncture (1 Sam. 7:5-9).

They served as spokesmen, particularly in opposition to "deviating" kings and alien cults. So word comes on Saul (1 Sam. 15), against Solomon (1 Kings 11:29-39), Rehoboam (2 Chron. 12), Jeroboam I (1 Kings 13), Baasha (1 Kings 16:1-7, 12), and Ahijah (2 Kings 1). At times they were supportive; cf. Abijah (2 Chron. 13:22, notes by Iddo), Asa (2 Chron. 15:8), and counsel given to Ahab (1 Kings 20). They opposed corrupt deals (e.g., on Naboth's vineyard), and might use symbolic acts to underline their point (1 Kings 20:35-43).

True and false prophets became an issue, as in conflict at Ahab's court (1 Kings 22; 2 Chron. 18).

As leaders, they had been replaced (like the "judges") by kings.

Use of music and presence of ecstatics was still present in the eleventh century, as with Saul's band of prophets (1 Sam 10:1-13), and later experience (19:19-24). Much later Elisha was to use music in conjunction with his being a spokesman (2 Kings 3:15).

Over time, "seers" (in early Israel, cf. 1 Sam. 9:6-9) or prophets might be consulted, to answer queries, as from YHWH (1 Kings 14:1-18). In early days dreams, Urim and Thummim (cf. Exod. 28:30), and prophets were used to inquire of deity (1 Sam. 28:6).

Finally, prophets not only spoke but they began to write documents, keep records, and write books. Early on Samuel set down a record of the rules of kingship for Saul and Israel, depositing it "before YHWH" (1 Sam. 10:25), almost certainly beside the ark. Later he may have left some account of David's early life (1 Chron. 29:29a), but not of his reign after Samuel's death. For record of David's reign, Nathan the prophet and Gad the seer might be given credit (29:29b, c); and in turn for Solomon's, again Nathan, plus Ahijah and Iddo (2 Chron. 9:29). Early in the divided monarchy we have notes for Rehoboam (2 Chron. 12:15) written down by Shemaiah and Iddo, who also obliged for Abijah (13:22). Other than traditional nineteenth-century prejudice, there is no warrant to dismiss these notices.

(iv) Intermediate Usage, Second Phase (Early National Figures)

This phase deals with the ninth-and-eighth-century period of the divided monarchy. For Elijah as prophet during the reigns of Ahab and Ahaziah down to the reigns of Jehoshaphat/Jehoram, we have a set of narratives (1 Kings 17–2 Kings 2, passim) in six episodes. For his successor Elisha under Ahab and Ahaziah down to Jehoash (1 Kings 19:19-21; 2 Kings 2–13, passim), again we have a series of episodes. Both were essentially spokesmen, especially to kings, sometimes critical, sometimes assuring of victory or giving counsel; they were sometimes credited with healing (e.g., 2 Kings 4) or miracles. A third prophet in this group is Jonah son of Amittai, for whom a separate narrative is contained in the book of Jonah; but 2 Kings 14:25 firmly dates him to the reign of Jeroboam II, at a time of Assyrian recession when that superstitious kingdom might have listened to a visiting prophet alongside its own practitioners.

(v) Classic Period of the Writing (or Written) Prophets, Eighth to Early Sixth Centuries

Prophets continue to appear in narrative contexts during this time, almost in passing notice, as in Kings (e.g., Isaiah in 2 Kings 18–20). Prophetesses continue to appear in the eighth to fifth centuries (cf. Isa. 8:3, Isaiah's wife; Huldah under Josiah, 2 Kings 22:14-20; Noadiah hostile to Nehemiah, Neh. 6:14). Jeremiah appears under King Zedekiah in 2 Chron. 36:12.

Also, actual "prophetical" books with named authors began to be written. These books occupy a prominent place in the Hebrew Bible. From their explicit date lines, we list their official sequence in groups as follows.

Eighth/Seventh Centuries

Amos, under Uzziah and Jeroboam II (1:1)
Hosea, from Uzziah/Jeroboam II to Hezekiah (1:1)
Isaiah, under Uzziah to Hezekiah (1:1)
Micah, under Jotham, Ahaz, Hezekiah (1:1)

Seventh/Sixth Centuries

Nahum, after 663 (3:8, fall of Thebes)
Zephaniah, under Josiah (1:1)
Obadiah, Habbakuk, under impending threat of Neo-Babylonian conquest (dating based on contents)
Jeremiah, from thirteenth year of Josiah to eleventh of Zedekiah and after (1:2-3; 40-43; 52:30)

Sixth Century

Ezekiel, Year 5 of exile of Jehoiachin in Babylonia (1:2)
(*Daniel,* see chap. 3 above)

(vi) Late Period under Persian Empire

These are the last prophetical books and mentions, from the sixth-fifth centuries.

Haggai (1:1) and *Zechariah* (1:1), second year of Darius I (and both, in Ezra 5:1; 6:14)
Malachi, this period (cf. 1:8)
(*Daniel,* see chap. 3 above)

Included during this period are claims about use of prophets (Neh. 6:7), and hostile prophets and prophetesses (6:14).

Lastly, *Joel* is notoriously undatable; it is later than mid–ninth century (3:2), possibly the eighth/seventh (foes from the north, emphasis on Judah and Jerusalem), but could be later.

The foregoing collection of writings, as we have them, divide into two lots: the longer collective books of Isaiah, Jeremiah, and Ezekiel, and the twelve short books that constitute the rest. The whole is listed above "as is," free of the accretions and incrustations of opinion from the "precritical" centuries and "critical" centuries (eighteenth century A.D. and following) alike, so that the actual corpus of data should be clearly visible in its own right, being all that we objectively and materially possess.

B. THE PHYSIOGNOMY OF WORKS
OF THE "WRITTEN" PROPHETS

(i) Basic Format

In virtually every case, both the "great" prophetic books (Isaiah, Jeremiah, Ezekiel) and those of "the Twelve" (short books), each book opens with a proper title, cast in the third person in accord with common ancient Near Eastern usage in several classes of literature. Ezekiel is a partial exception, with a double dating, putting himself in the first person, then in the third (1:1-3). Such titles include up to three basic elements: the prophet's *name* (always), his *status* (sometimes), and a *date line* (mostly). Thereafter the format followed is individual to each prophet.

Broadly, their main themes involved warnings of punishment for wrongdoing, whether "religious" (cultic) or moral/ethical, against both foreign nations and Israel/Judah, and (often) promises of restoration and blessing if the admonitions be heeded and Israel/Judah return to a "clean" and exclusive worship of YHWH.

The conjunction of curse/blessing proceeded from the terms of the longstanding covenant first established at Sinai following the exodus from Egypt, and renewed by the Jordan (see chap. 6 above), as can be seen still in Lev. 26 as well as Deut. 28. That covenant underlay the prophetic call to people and kings to follow the traditional covenant and its exclusivity in worship of YHWH and practical application in right living, treating one's fellows justly and kindly. Prophetic appeal to that covenant is explicit in all three of the "great" prophets, and in four of the Twelve. We have mention of breach of covenant four times in Jeremiah (11:3, 8, 10 [all one passage]; 22:9; 31:32; 34:13-18) and three times in Ezekiel (16:59; 17:19; 44:7; plus once of the Neo-Babylonian treaty, 17:15-18), plus Josiah's response to the Book of the Covenant (2 Kings 22–23); compare once in Mal. 2:8. These nine occurrences are not a big haul for the impact of the supposed "Deuteronomic revival" of 621 and onward! If we go back before 621, the earlier prophets allude explicitly to breach of standing covenant as follows: Isaiah two times (28:15-18; 33:8, plus 24:5, on the Noahic covenant) and Hosea two times (6:7; 8:1), for a total of four times. And the demands for righteousness (and against non-YHWH cults) throughout Amos and Hosea and Micah (cf. chap. 6) presuppose the socioreligious requirements of Exodus and Deuteronomy, which are much more pervasive. It is special pleading simply to emend out of these texts anything "covenantal" that would fall before 621, merely to distort the data to fit in with an imaginary late-seventh-century date for Deuteronomy (as many do, following Wellhausen). And special pleading cannot be allowed.

As for "predictive prophecy," one should distinguish between options and predictions. Both are always set in the future, even in daily life, whether in those days or now. Options are conditional; "if you do this, then such and such will happen" (but not if you don't). Predictions are meant to stick — this *is* going to happen — full stop. Most prophecies of curse/blessing are in terms of options; some are more firmly expressed. Historically, both lots largely came to pass (most famously, the falls of Israel/Samaria and Judah/Jerusalem, of course).

(ii) The Books Themselves

The twelve shorter prophets need no summary here; each is so short that a reader can quickly grasp its essential content and format. It is more useful to turn to the three major books named for Isaiah, Jeremiah, and Ezekiel, and then to pass on to the external Near Eastern context of the prophetic phenomenon. Our summations need be brief.

(a) Isaiah

This richest of all the prophetic books (like all of them) has been endlessly studied and unduly theorized about. Views of its nature (and thus of structure and date) run the whole gamut from a traditional view of one unitary book through a popular theory of three books in one (1–39; 40–55; 56–66), of at least three different dates (preexilic, exilic, postexilic; and variations),[1] down to heaps of fragments often consigned to late dates. Here, in the first instance, we are concerned with the structure of the extant canonical book that we actually possess, to be set against the wider context and see what emerges. Likewise for Jeremiah and Ezekiel.

In tussles over unity and multiplicity in Isaiah, and supposed divisions at chapters 39/40, 55/56, etc., almost nobody has bothered to look for tangible textual evidence. In the Dead Sea Scrolls there is just one positive indication, in the great, intact scroll of Isaiah, one of the first scrolls published. In this scroll, when he came to the end of what we today call chapter 33 (at 33:24), the ancient scribe deliberately left a blank space (equal to three lines' depth), marking a break at the end of his column, before beginning a new column with what is now 34:1. This is very close to the midpoint of the entire book as he had it, and as we have it. The early scribe had some reason to divide here — but saw *no* reason to divide at either what is now 39/40 or 55/56, we may note. One could argue that his midpoint division was simply taken over through copying from two shorter scrolls, holding the first and second halves of the book respectively. But this is rendered unlikely by the twofold format of the book when looked at as two significant and neatly parallel halves, not just a mechanical division, a point long since made by Brownlee and Harrison.[2] The division also has chronological significance; 1–33 come under Uzziah to Ahaz, while 34–66 come under the time of Hezekiah (and perhaps later). Each half corresponds well to the other in order and subject of topics covered; each is in seven parts. See table 32.

Table 32. The "Bifid" Format of Isaiah

Part 1		Part 2	
1:1	Overall Title		
A. 1–5	Judgment and restoration	A. 34–35	Desolation and restoration
B. 6–8	Biographical/historical and oracles	B. 36–39	Historical/biographical accounts
C. 9–12	Words of blessing and judgment	C. 40–45	Words of blessing and judgment
D. 13–23	Oracles on foreign nations (and one on Jerusalem)	D. 46–48	Oracles on foreign nations (and on Babylon)
E. 24–27	Destruction, restoration, deliverance	E. 49–55	Restorations, destruction, deliverance
F. 28–31	Social and ethical justice	F. 56–59	Social and ethical justice
G. 32–33	Restoration of the nation	G. 60–66	Restoration of the nation

This is, of course, not the only possible analysis, and it depends on a very post-Isaianic Dead Sea Scroll. Other meaningful structural possibilities have been offered, such as that of Motyer, based on a lifetime's close work on the book of Isaiah, in suggesting the book's structure in three parts, 1–37, 38–55, and 56–66, with three portraits of a messianic king, varying in detail but based on a consistent model.[3]

The supposed three "books" of 1–39, 40–55, and 56–66 have often been alleged to show traces of different periods of composition. There can be little doubt of 1–39 belonging to the later eighth century, having numerous links with that epoch. But that 40–55 is based in Babylon is simply not true. As scholars of various stripes have been compelled to observe, those chapters betray no firsthand knowledge of the metropolis of Babylon (mentioned only four times in these chapters, and only once actually implying a Hebrew exile, 48:20 — contrasted with nine times in 1–39!), but belong in the milieu of the Levant, not least Palestine.[4] Briefly, Marduk-apil-iddina II ("Merodach-Baladan") of Babylon seemed a good rival to Sennacherib in 704-703;[5] and it was apposite for Isaiah "of Jerusalem" to warn Hezekiah that trifling with Babylon would lead to his people and goods ending up there (Isa. 39). At that time nobody could know whether such a threat might come in 10, 20, or 200 years; no timescale was built into it. The actual span of about 150 years is a product of later history, not known to Isaiah or anybody else in his world in 703. In the case of 56–66, there is, again, nothing inconsistent with an origin in seventh/sixth-century preexilic Judah, and clear hints that fit that place and time.

So, why the fuss, to have multiple Isaiahs (two of them anonymous, in flagrant contradiction with unanimous usage in prophetical books!) by imaginary disciples miraculously able to write "Isaianic" poetry and prose? The one real sticking point for many is the introduction of Cyrus in 44:28 and 45:1; in the text he is not identified by any title at all, yet he has authority to rebuild Jerusalem and ability to defeat and plunder other powers. Deliverance did indeed eventually come by the agency of the well-known (to us!) Cyrus II, king of Persia and conqueror of Babylon.[6] But no such person was directly known to an eighth-century Isaiah — only that someone named Cyrus with high authority would do the deed of restoring the Hebrews and their own capital. It is worth remarking that the king we know so well was number II of his name; his grandfather, an earlier Cyrus I, reigned in Iran about the early sixth century. Earlier still, before the Achaemenid Persians, a still earlier "Cyrus" (Kurash) ruled in Parsua in 646, as contemporary of Assurbanipal of Assyria, little more than fifty years after Isaiah's own time.[7] There were many local rulers in Iran before the sixth century, and other Cyruses (or Kurashes) may have reigned there before 646; in 672 Esarhaddon established treaties with seven Median rulers as part of a larger political move.[8] Assyria had been involved in Iran since the ninth century.[9] Thus there is nothing untoward in an Isaiah being moved to proclaim that a "Cyrus" (identity of his kingdom not stated) would reach power and free Hebrew captives in Babylon (whether of Merodach-Baladan's time or indefinitely later). His prophecy was to be fulfilled, as we know now, but we in hindsight know more now than he personally ever did — simply because that hindsight has been gifted to us by our living in a much later day. So the prophecy is remarkable in having "come true," if one is not gifted with faith, but it (and Isaiah!) should not be burdened with our hindsight of today. In short, a unitary view does not need to presuppose exclusively "conservative" views about the Hebrew Bible; those stuck with nineteenth-century mind-sets are free to experiment with such alternatives as they wish, but at the cost of inconsistencies and (as sec. 2 below may suggest) failure to meet the exigencies of prophetic composition, recording, and usage in the biblical world overall.

(b) Jeremiah

This is the longest prophetical book and the longest unitary book of the Old Testament. It is also the most complex in its format. Here it will be wisest simply to note the phenomena the book exhibits, and then see what emerges. When one does so, what becomes very noticeable is the *interleaving* of episodes from the period of Josiah to Jehoiakim with episodes under Zedekiah. Thus 1–17 come under Josiah (cf. 3:6), while 18–21 date to Zedekiah. Chapters 22–23 belong under Jehoahaz/Jehoiakim/Jehoiachin, then 24 relates to Zedekiah. Then 25–26 come under Jehoiakim, while 27–34 belong in Zedekiah's reign. Again 35–36 are under Jehoiakim, and 37–44 under Zedekiah. Finally we have a sequence: 45–47 are under Jehoiakim (and Egypt's Necho II); 48–49:33 are the same or later, but under Nebuchadrezzar II; and 49:33-39 and 50–51 are under Zedekiah, plus the supplement (52) shared with 2 Kings 24:18–25:30 (including the later note on Jehoiachin under Awel-Marduk of Babylon). To the whole work is prefaced a full title, 1:1-3, and the calling of Jeremiah (1:4-19). We thus have a work in seven sections, beginning with the title and the prophet's call and ending with the Kings-type supplement, which sandwich between them five sections each consisting of data under Josiah to Jehoiachin, then an entry for Zedekiah. See table 33 on page 382.

This view of the matter shows a set of small scrolls in which Jeremiah (or his scribe) had entered various oracles, etc., separately under Josiah to Jehoiakim/Jehoiachin, leaving rather less room at the end of Small Scroll I. But the others (II to V) had more space available. Under Zedekiah, scroll I was filled up, then one segment was added to II (small and soon full?), while there was room to enter eight Zedekiah segments (our "chapters") each in III and IV, the rest in V, possibly including (eventually?) the supplement. Then (at right) these scrolls could be amalgamated into three scrolls of approximately equal length (1–17 in I, 18–34 in II, and 35–51/52 in III) as a "first collection," and later perhaps into two longer scrolls (1–24; 25–52), A and B, and as a complete book down to later (Hellenistic) times and to us. Jeremiah 36 shows us the beginning of the process.

The narrative parts of Jeremiah contain many allusions to well-attested contemporary history, and various Hebrew seals and bullae mention people who are almost certainly (in some cases, certainly) characters found also in Jeremiah; see already, chapter 2 above. To date much (or any) of Jeremiah to distinctly later periods (e.g., fifth to third centuries) would seem impractical, given the lack of detailed, separate (nonbiblical) knowledge of preexilic history, dating, and people in (say) the fourth/third century, which would prevent anyone concocting then a "Jeremiah" book as we have it now.[10]

Table 33. Schema of the Book of Jeremiah

Possible Document	Contents	First Collection	In Larger Scrolls	
"Small Scroll I"	Title (1:1-3) and Call (1:4-19)	I: 1–17	A: 1–24	C
	2–17: oracles, etc., Josiah and later			O
				M
	+ 18–21: under Zedekiah	II: 18–34		P
				L
"Small Scroll II"	22–23: under Jehoahaz to Jehoiachin + 24: under Zedekiah			E
				T
"Small Scroll III"	25–26: under Jehoiakim + 27–34: under Zedekiah		B: 25–52	E
"Small Scroll IV"	35–36: under Jehoiakim + 37–44: under Zedekiah	III: 35–52		B
				O
"Small Scroll V"	45–47: Jehoiakim; 48–49 undated, same? 49:28-33: Nebuchadrezzar II 49:34-51: under Zedekiah			O
				K
?	52: Supplement = 2 Kings 24:18–25:30			

(c) Ezekiel

This book is a highly individual work from a remarkable individual — a priest who went into exile in 597 when the Judeans did not yet really believe their kingdom was in fact doomed. After the formal third-person part of the title, the entire book is cast autobiographically in the first person. It divides simply into two equal halves, 1–24, 25–48. In the first half, after the prophet's call, a long series of messages and visions culminates in two sad events: the death of Ezekiel's wife (24:15-18) and the advance announcement of Jerusalem's impending final fall to Babylon (24:19-27). In the second half, visions (such as the lesson of the "dry bones") and oracles on foreign nations end with a promise of Jacob's (= Judean Israel's) return to Palestine (25–39). The work then ends correspondingly with a vision of a new temple for YHWH's worship at the heart of a redistributed land, up to new gates of Jerusalem where YHWH is. This work was long held to be the unitary product from one remarkable mind; and despite subsequent essays in dismemberment and down-dating of the resultant fragments, advocacy of its integrity as a unique and unitary work from the time of the Babylonian exile is well justified.[11]

In all their rich variety, prophetical books have common characteristics. (1) In every case they bear the name of an explicitly claimed author who set forth the contents as messages sent by YHWH through him. (2) Almost all consist of a series of oracles, messages, and/or supporting narratives (long or short), on or from a variety of occasions; only Nahum, Obadiah, and Habakkuk seem to be men of one occasion only. (3) These three books (and the narrative of Jonah) excepted, it is clear that prophetical books were not first written down on one specific occasion. The biblical evidence indicates that particular oracles and messages were recorded when given, and could be kept in a scroll as a series (cf. Jer. 36:1-4, then v. 32). Prophets did write things down from of old (from Saul's time onward, cf. p. 306 above), and still used a pen in the eighth-seventh centuries. For Isaiah, compare 8:1 (he should take a pen and scroll), 30:8 (to write on tablet and scroll against the future); in fact, (alphabetic) writing can be kids' stuff (10:19). In Jeremiah, besides the famous chapter 36 (plus 45:1), we have the rhetorical call to record the fate of an exiled king (22:30) and explicit commands to write all that is given him in a book (30:2). Jeremiah (or Baruch for him, of course) was called to write a document condemning Babylon, to read it there and cast it into the Euphrates (51:60-64, ending with a formal colophon). We have mention of Jeremiah composing laments for the tragically slain King Josiah, which were then incorporated in a collection of laments (2 Chron. 35:25). Not to be outdone, Ezekiel was to record the date of the start of Jerusalem's final siege (24:2), was to write symbolically on sticks of wood (37:16-23),[12] and was to write down the details and regulations of the new temple (43:11). The shorter prophets were to write as occasion demanded, as on a tablet (Hab. 2:2). The issue of prompt written texts of prophecy (as contrasted with theoretical "schools" of oral traditionists) finds its answer in the external data to which we now turn.

2. PROPHECY ABROAD

Long, long ago it was imagined that, in the surrounding world, prophecy in the biblical sense was unknown; namely, individuals standing up and proclaiming messages of all kinds as from deity, to kings and other mortals, and sometimes promising future disaster or blessing, tied in part to the behavior of the recipients, did not exist. Where Israel had prophets, other peoples had divination, a point made long ago in Deut. 18:14. However, some traces of extrabiblical prophetism have long been known, and in the last half-century (not least, quite recently) external sources have multiplied dramatically, especially from the early-second-millennium archives found at Mari, including also analogues of the Hebrew terms for prophets and prophecy. These materials deserve at least an outline appreciation in relation to the biblical writings just surveyed above.

A. MARI AND EARLIER: A TOUCH OF TERMINOLOGY

Back in the late third millennium the term *nabi'utum* has been alleged to occur in the archives of north Syrian Ebla with the meaning of "prophet." However, the occurrences still remain unpublished; so until they are published, nothing can be said of this term's possible relationship to Hebrew *nabi* for "prophet."[13] But from the voluminous archives at Mari (20,000 tablets) in the early second millennium, some sixty or so tablets reporting on messages from "prophets" use various terms for such people: *apilum* (respondent), *muhhu* (ecstatic[?]), and *nabi* (prophet).[14]

B. SURVEY: HISTORY AND FUNCTIONS OF PROPHECY IN THE BIBLICAL WORLD

(i) Early Second Millennium: Mari and Contemporary Centers[15]

"Intercession": seeking benefit for others (rather than for self) from deity. As did an Abraham, so did others, if sometimes by different means. The former has but to pray to El for Abimelek's well-being. At Mari, one Tebi-geri-shu brought together a band of prophets *(nabi)* of West Semitic ("Hanean") origin to inquire into matters (via omens) for his king's well-being, from the results of which he was able to send him advice what to do (no. 216).[16] As one also termed *nabi* at this epoch, Abraham was not so much unique as banal.

The role of spokesman (and spokeswoman) is prevalent everywhere, in both Near Eastern and biblical usage. Almost the whole of the fifty-eight cuneiform letters concerning prophecy at Mari give the reported words of messages on a variety of topics from both men and women, named or otherwise.[17] They spoke out either without prior stimulus (so the *muhhu,* "ecstatics," as from their deity/ies), as the later Hebrew prophets commonly did, or else in response to inquiries by kings (the *apilu,* "respondents," did both).

As for *topics of prophecies,* promise of *victory and deliverance* for the king is frequent (e.g., nos. 197, 199 beginning, 202, [204], 207, 208-214, etc.); one may compare them with David's inquiries of YHWH in 1 Sam. 23 and 30, and (as king) 2 Sam. 5:17-25.[18] *Illness and death* is featured at Mari as it is in the Old Testament. One sad message (no. 222) announced the death of an infant daughter of the king, and its prediction by a prophet beforehand. Compare the more dramatic scenarios in 2 Sam. 12:13-23, when David lost Bathsheba's first child by him, and YHWH's announcement of the death of a son to Jeroboam I's wife (1 Kings 14:1-18).[19] Deities might insist on *prior consultation* before a ruler took action. Thus, in Mari no. 199, a goddess insisted that no treaty be made with the untrustworthy Mare-Yamina without consulting her first.[20] Compare later, Josh. 9:14-18, where Joshua and Israel erred because they made a treaty with the deceitful Gibeonites without consulting YHWH first. It was unwise to reject a prophecy at Mari, and to do so might bring illness (no. 234) or other problems; Balaam was said to suffer for disobedience too (Num. 22:25).

As for "Deuteronomic" judgment on Hebrew kings (cf. on Ahab, 1 Kings 21; 22:19-23, 37; and 1-2 Kings, passim), and requiring justice in a king, one may compare the Mari documents of a thousand years before — "Deuteronomism" did *not* begin only in 621! In one striking letter (Mari, A.1121), Nur-Sin, the king's officer, relays various messages from the god Adad via his prophets. Through one Abu-halim, Adad Lord of Aleppo is reputed to say to the king, "When a petitioner, male or female, shall make appeal to you, hold session and do them justice! That is what I require of you." In the same missive, by other prophets, and seeking his due portion of land and cattle, Adad Lord of Kallassu points out his generous blessings to the king, and both pronounces future blessing on the king's obedience ("throne upon throne, house upon house . . .") and makes a thinly veiled threat in case of disobedience: "what I have given I will take back!" And the writer defends his reporting Adad's claims to the king, saying: "if some catatastrophe were to happen, would not my master [= the king] ask 'why did you not tell me of the prophet's report, on the god's request?'"[21]

Thus in north Syria in the nineteenth/eighteenth centuries, as in Egypt in the thirteenth, nobody meekly waited around for up to a millennium or so, till 621, before having permission from an ignorant De Wette, and his biblical studies followers since, to express such concepts, which were universal in Near Eastern antiquity and by no means limited principally to the Hebrew texts of Deuteronomy, Joshua–2 Kings, and Jeremiah. And, significantly, this letter A.1121 was not just a flash in the pan. In the early second millennium, in these sources, kings were said to be judged by deities on their obedience, and were faulted and they and their dynasties dethroned for their sins (could 1-2 Kings have done it better?!). So fell Shamshi-Adad I of Assyria, Yaggid-lim of Mari, and Sumu-epuh of Aleppo for their supposed sins. The god Shamash could accuse a king of deceit (e.g., Hammurabi of Kurda) and assign his land to another (Zimri-lim). The gods required just dealings, and loyalty; they required high morals, not just rich material gifts.[22]

Regarding ecstatics and music, music does not (yet) appear in the Mari sources as an adjunct to prophecy, but certain forms of drink do.[23] The prophets known as *muhhu* were literally "fools" (a noun from the verb *mahum*, "be a fool"), and their behavior was, and was expected to be, rather erratic.[24] Alongside men, women too could be "prophets" of each type, and quite a number of the recorded prophecies came through them — the biblical Deborah and Huldah had their distant precursors![25]

But was all doom and gloom? The nineteenth century saw the rise of theories that sought to impose artificial "histories" on the development of the Hebrew prophetical writings. Famously, B. Duhm propounded the theory that, originally, the Hebrew prophets only promised doom, and no blessings — these were added by later editors (afflicted by a form of "blessingmania") to redress the balance. In the light of what is now known, nothing could be less true. We have just seen above, that Adad could both promise rich blessings and hint at sinister threats almost in one breath; curses and blessings were riveted together as epilogue to law collections under Hammurabi of this period, and again in treaties in the fourteenth/thirteenth centuries, plus the Sinai/Moab Hebrew covenant, as seen above in chapter 6.[26] Thus, doom/blessing for disobedience/obedience to YHWH is the counterpart to the latter with the Hebrew prophets in turn.

Prophecies — true or false? For the Hebrews, the ultimate test of a prophecy (and its prophet) was its fulfillment (Deut. 18). In Mari, parallel acts of divination might be used to confirm a prophecy. Record could be kept of prophecies on tablets in a royal archive, to await their fulfillment, which would apply both at Mari in the nineteenth/eighteenth centuries and likewise at Nineveh a thousand years later.[27]

As for prophets and the writing down of prophecies, see below, section C, on recording and transmission of prophecies.

(ii) Early Second Millennium: Egypt

"Predictive prophecy" as a concept is not exclusive to Hebrew prophets and later theologians who study their works. The Egyptians claimed the existence of such facility in the early second millennium, in both nonreligious and political contexts. The Egyptian word *sri*, meaning "to announce, promise, foretell," is commonplace from the third millennium (Pyramid Texts) down to the Greco-Roman period, in all these meanings.[28]

But here we do not have specifically denominated prophets; rather, learned "wise men" are shown in three literary works exercising what amounts to prophetic prerogatives: predicting future calamity and deliverance or reproving an ineffective ruler for failing in the kingly duty of upholding the right order in life *(maat)*. Past (written) predictions are invoked, as fulfilled or expected to be. And sailors in a folktale can predict the weather (sometimes!).

These features appear in "Instruction for Merikare," originating circa 2000 (end of Tenth Dynasty). Twice the royal author mentions prophecies from before his time: "troops will oppress troops, (just) as the ancestors prophesied about it," and also admonishes his son, "(deal) not ill with the Southern Region, for you know the prophec[y] of the Residence [= the palace] about it." And on high moral ground, with a breath of the prophet Samuel (1 Sam. 15:22) of a millennium later, Merikare is told (ll. 128/129): "More acceptable is the character [or, 'loaf'] of the upright than the ox of the wrongdoer."[29]

In "Admonitions of Ipuwer" (of Twelfth Dynasty, ca. twentieth/nineteenth centuries, but looking back to earlier times), on Egypt's ills, the sage remarks, "What the ancestors foretold has now happened."[30]

Alongside the basic concept we also find its shadow, pseudoprophecy. "Prophecy of Neferty" has its sage asking King Snofru (of ca. 2600) whether he would hear tell of things past or things future. Of course, the king opts for the future, and Neferty affects to tell him of future calamities that would afflict Egypt, then of a deliverer called Ameny — the normal abbreviation for Amenemhat, the name of the founder of the powerful Twelfth Dynasty. The work is entirely in Middle Egyptian, and is part of a group of texts composed to bolster the regime of that new king and dynasty.[31] In "Tales of the Magicians" (of ca. 1600, set in the royal court of a thousand years before), the sage Djedi is made to predict to King Kheops that first his son and grandson will succeed him, and then a new dynasty.

As for sailors, in "The Shipwrecked Sailor," that worthy is made to say of his shipmates, "whether they looked at sky or land, they were bolder than lions. They could foretell a storm before it came (or) a tempest before it broke."[32] Thus Egypt knew about both the reality of prediction and its imitation.

(iii) Late Second Millennium: The Hittites

In the fourteenth century, seeking help against plagues, Mursil II prayed to his gods: "the reason — let it be apparent by omen, or may I see it in a dream, or may a prophet ('man of God') declare it"; and then later on, "let me see it in a dream, or may it be discovered by oracle, or a prophet declare it, or all the priests find it out by incubation."[33] Thus, just as at Mari half a millennium before and again in Neo-Assyrian usage another half-millennium later, so here particular people, including "prophets," could be expected to declare what was amiss and to indicate what should be done about it.

(iv) Late Second Millennium: Emar, Egypt, Byblos

In the late thirteenth century the archives from Emar make mention of men termed *nabi,* but without giving us any details of their activities. The supposed "prophetesses" *(munabbiati)* appear to have been mourners.[34]

Also, in thirteenth-century Egypt, looking back to men of old, in a wisdom text (probably from "Instruction of Amennakhte"), the writer speaks of "those learned scribes . . . (even) those who foretold the future, they have attained that their names may endure forever," and again calls them "those sages that foretold the future."[35] Thus Egypt had no class of prophets as such, but sages could fill that role. The "prophets" in the Egyptian temple hierarchies in many modern translations were senior grades of priest, "servants of the god" literally; because of their role in announcing oracles, the Greeks applied the term *prophetes* to them, hence the misleading (but ubiquitous!) modern usage in Egyptology.

In early eleventh-century Byblos, in the report by the Egyptian priest Wenamun, we find that worthy wrangling over the purchase of timber with the ruler of Byblos, when a youth at the latter's court became ecstatically "possessed" during religious rites and declared that Wenamun should be listened to.[36]

For this period our data are thus currently meager, but they serve to form at least a link between the earlier (above) and later (below) occurrences of "prophetic" phenomena; and as the finds at Emar show, we cannot ourselves foretell when important new data might suddenly turn up.

(v) Early First Millennium: Syria-Palestine, Hamath, and Jordan

On his Aramaic stela, about 800 or soon after, Zakkur king of Hamath sought divine aid when faced with a hostile coalition; through seers and diviners, Baalshemayn promised help, and Zakkur gained the victory, hence his monument.[37] This is all very reminiscent of what we saw at Mari a millennium before, and with David in 1-2 Samuel, and prophets then in the eleventh/tenth centuries (cf. 1 Sam. 22:5; 23:1-2, 4, 10-12; 2 Sam. 2:1-2).

About this same period (ninth century), in a settlement (now Tell Deir Alla) just east of the lower Jordan River, one building originally contained a text inscribed in black ink (with red rubrics) upon white-plastered walls. This text bore the title "The Book of the Afflictions of Balaam Son of Beor" — a character who stars in Num. 22–24. Here, as a seer and skilled diviner, Balaam is given a warning vision in a dream, announces it to his circle, and acts to ward off the threat.[38] He is thus in much the same cultural frame as in Num. 22–24, and likewise involved in conflicts. Also, it is a written "prophetic" text up to a century before Amos or Hosea.

(vi) Early First Millennium: Neo-Assyrian Prophecy

Here, much confusion over texts and definitions has, in recent times, given way to greater clarity in distinguishing what does, and does not, properly belong to the prophetic category from the time of Mari down to this later period. What Maria deJong Ellis neatly called "literary predictive texts" simply give a series of anonymous rulers, their lengths of reign, and notices of "good" or "bad" events associated with them. Because, superficially, they read rather like Dan. 11 (with its anonymous "kings of south and north"), they had earlier been called "Akkadian apocalypses," but they do not really belong with Dan. 11 either. Hence Ellis's more fitting, neutral term.[39]

Assyrian prophecies proper are a limited set of twenty-six oracles or "prophecies" that are close in format and content to the much earlier Mari "prophecies." They come from the archives of Esarhaddon and Assurbanipal in the seventh century. They are usually expressed as messages from the goddess Ishtar to the king (and once, to the queen mother) via both prophets and prophetesses. They generally promise victory and reassurance to the king, as at Mari; and one may wryly compare the "court prophets" of King Ahab (1 Kings 22).[40]

C. RECORDING AND TRANSMITTING PROPHECIES

(i) Doubts about Hallowed Theories

In biblical studies much is said and assumed about prophets supposedly having had around them (and afterward) disciples through whom their utterances might be handed down through time orally, before reaching written form, and of oral or written later additions to their oracles (and whole oracles) without their knowledge or permission but still in their name. Thus, while our surviving books in their final form might contain wording handed down from the prophets themselves, it would (on the foregoing assumptions) often be difficult in practice (if not impractical) to identify them in the present final text. In recent times some biblicists would allow less and less of the extant final texts to be attributed back to the original prophets whose names they bear, if anything at all in extreme cases, thus making of Old Testament studies a "non-prophet-making" enterprise.[41]

This kind of speculative theorizing is all very well as a mode of experimentation in the abstract, or as a "flavor of the month" fashion, or even just as simple indulgence in academic ego massage ("Look how clever I can be!"). But can it claim any respectable, independent factual basis? In the light of the growing body of comparable data from Mari and elsewhere on prophetic-related texts, skeptical voices are now beginning to be gently but firmly raised in protest at the downward spiral into wholly subjective nothingness. A "prophetic" early warning was given by A. R. Millard over fifteen years ago, which still retains all its relevance today in the light of the facts now available, and again more recently by R. P. Gordon in 1995 on the "disappearing" prophets, with acute and subtly expressed observations that suggest that the prophets' enforced "disappearance" is premature and not well founded. Then, latterly, as A. Lemaire has underlined (1999), J.-G. Heintz has shown (1997) how the publication of the Mari "prophetic" texts has in effect wrong-footed the growing hyperskepticism of recent biblicist writings, rendering their claims a "prophetless exercise" in more ways than one.[42]

(ii) Get a Record (and Get It Straight!)

Therefore we must now concisely review the question of oral presentation and the impact of writing, not as a theoretical exercise but as our extant external sources show it to be *at first hand*. Right from the presently attested beginning, at Mari, and at all other periods, the first stage of almost every prophetic pronouncement was its oral declaration from the mouth of the prophet or prophetess, whether in a temple or elsewhere, to just one other person (usually an official), or before witnesses also, or even publicly, as at a city gate before a group of people, such as the elders, or before all and sundry.[43]

But as these messages were commonly of importance primarily to the king (whether in Mari in the nineteenth/eighteenth centuries or Assyria in the seventh), officials invariably relayed them promptly back to the royal palace — *not* orally, but in *writing,* and sent on with the least possible delay. An official might stress (no. 217) that he had sent on "the exact wording" of a prophetess.[44] Such reports had to include any special circumstances, such as notice of symbolic actions by the prophet concerned — like the ecstatic at Mari who requested a lamb, and proceeded to devour it raw, a symbol of a devouring plague that would come if the local towns did not produce the expected sacred sacrifices.[45] Nor did officials simply send brief notice of individual prophecies. On occasion more than one account was sent in, with varying comments on the basic prophetic message, stressing different aspects of one and the same oracle. In many cases the prophet or prophetess is customarily named. And at times an official would send the written-down text of more than one oracle in one and the same letter — the beginnings of a "collection" of prophecies, as was to be the case very much later in the Old Testament prophetical books. Thus, at Mari, Nur-Sin sent on to King Zimri-lim the texts of three messages from two different prophets of the local forms of Adad, as lord of Kallassu and as lord of Aleppo. Another letter has three successive prophetic messages in their local historical context, the second being a response to a query sent by the king.[46] This begins to be a forerunner of the Hebrew prophetical books, with prophecies in their historical contexts.

Such procedures are also evident much later in the Neo-Assyrian examples, written on large tablets containing a whole series of pronouncements by various prophets and prophetesses. Under Esarhaddon, one such (Collection 1, a modern title) contains ten utterances by eight different named speakers and two unnamed. Collection 2 contains six utterances of five named prophets (three also appearing in Collection 1) and one unnamed. These various pieces can be longer, shorter, and occasionally very brief. Collections 3 and 4 contain, respectively, a covenant of the god Ashur with the king, involving also Ishtar, and mediated by a prophet known from Collections 1 and 2; and (from Collection 4) a fragment of an oracle of encouragement. The other two pieces are an oracle to the queen mother (authorship lost) and one to the king by a named prophet. Under Assurbanipal we have by contrast five tablets with individual pronouncements, two being mere fragments.[47] So the picture is of individual prophecies quite promptly written down, which subsequently can be brought together into collective tablets for future reference. And named prophetic speakers are in a massive majority over unnamed ones.

In other areas the relationship of oral pronouncement and written record is the same. The early-second-millennium Egyptian text of Neferty depicts King Snofru eagerly reaching for his writing case, to take out a scroll, (pen and) ink palette and so to write down the sage's words as spoken.[48] Clearly this was understood as a natural thing to do; it does not leave much scope for long, imaginary periods of "oral tradition"! In Papyrus Chester Beatty IV of the late second millennium, the general allusions to the sages who foretold the future exalt their writing, not a "mouth to mouth" tradition of orality.[49] In the West

Semitic world, Zakkur king of Hamath lost no time in commemorating his deliverance from his foes, with appropriate mention of the promise of that deliverance via the seers and diviners of his deity Baal-shemayn.[50] We would never have known of "The Book of the Afflictions of Balaam Son of Beor" if somebody had not set it out in neat lines of ink-written script on a plastered and whitened wall, for all the world like the pages of an oversized papyrus scroll.[51] Clearly, just telling people by word of mouth was not deemed a sufficient means of record or of diffusion.

Thus, throughout the centuries, across the biblical world, the firsthand external evidence shows clearly and conclusively that the record of prophecies among contemporaries and their transmission down through time was *not* left to the memories of bystanders or to the memory-conditioned oral transmission — and modification — by imaginary "disciples" of a prophet or their equally imaginary successors for centuries before somebody took the remnants at a late date to weave them into books out of whole new cloth, having little or nothing to do with a reputed prophet of dim antiquity whose very name and existence might thus be doubted. For the mass of highly ingenious guesswork and scholarly imagination along these lines, poured out of the presses for over a century now, and never more than in recent decades, there is not one respectable scintilla of solid, firsthand evidence. Not one.

Quite the contrary. When ancient prophets (from Mari onward) spoke out, witnesses could be summoned to attest the authenticity of the actual process of scribing the very words, the ipsissima verba, of the prophet, to ensure that the real thing was sent to the king, and to eliminate any querying of the wording and content of the message(s) concerned from the start. There is worse. On one occasion a Mari seer explicitly *demanded* that a scribe of top-quality skills be employed to record his message in good style![52]

(iii) Why and Wherefore

The need for accurate and acceptable record and transmission of such prophecies resulted in their being archived both at Mari and in Assyria. At Mari, being within letters, they were filed as royal correspondence, for reference as events unfolded — evidently, in connection with possible fulfillment or new developments. In Assyria, prophecies collected under Esarhaddon were still kept in the archived files of Assurbanipal. They formed a "protobook" of prophecies, retained through the years for reference. Thus, for example, the goddess Ishtar had promised Esarhaddon victory over Mugallu of Tabal, but this prophetic promise was only fulfilled later under his son and successor Assurbanipal.

The fact is that the ultimate test of prophecy was its fulfillment. Thus an accurate, independent, and permanent record of prophecies was needed, to stand as lasting witness for when possible fulfillment might occur or be required to be checked.[53] Human memory would crystallize and fade with time, and people die off, leaving no credible record (or no record at all). That was of no more use to ancient governments than to modern ones — and was as true for early Israel and Judah as for Mari or Assyria. The Hebrews' need of prompt and faithful copies was as essential to check prophecy against fulfillment as anywhere else. When an infuriated Amaziah, priest at Bethel, sent word to Jeroboam II way up in Samaria, reporting the prophet as seditious, he would hardly have trudged all of thirty weary miles or more to shake his fist before the king to denounce Amos (Amos 7). Like numberless other officers before and after him (from Mari to Nineveh and beyond), he would have summoned the Bethel shrine's scribe and sent a letter off by mounted messenger to the court at Samaria, we may be sure. As our external sources teach us, that was how it was done. And if he himself was not ready with a pen and the simple West Semitic twenty-two-letter alphabet, Amos need not have gone far to find someone to write down his prophecies, both as witness against their future fulfillment and to refute any false claims sent to Samaria by Amaziah. Before Amos, the "Balaam" prophecy at Tell Deir Alla was written out promptly on a plastered wall. That it was all left to memory both then and for the next three hundred years is surely absurd in the light of the overwhelming external record of normal prophetic usage. Late in a Hebrew prophet's life, or after his death, his oracles may well have been gathered in book (scroll) format, but the example of Jer. 36, and especially the remarkable arrangement of his prophecies (as if from sets of relatively small scrolls, cf. p. 381 above), suggests very strongly that the record of a prophet's oracles and deeds was built up as he went along, even if tidied up a little later by himself or others. Theories of long chains of "disciples" transmitting (and perhaps even drastically editing) memories and then written text simply have no tangible documentary basis, by contrast with what Mari, Assyria, Egypt, and the rest have to teach us in matters of fact. And for two further reasons.

D. HISTORICITY AND POSTMORTEM IRRELEVANCE

The hard fact remains that the books of Isaiah, Jeremiah, and others (as written) are inextricably linked to the limited historical periods in which they are set.[54] Isaiah belongs to the time of real kings (e.g., Ahaz, Hezekiah) known from the inscriptions of late eighth-century Assyria, and from the bullae of his own kings. The Babylon prophecies of Isa. 13–14 have nothing to do with the well-known (to us) Babylonian exile of 597/587 but with the *destruction* of Babylon, and found their first fulfillment in the Assyro-Babylonian captures of the end of eighth and early seventh centuries and with the destruction of Babylon by Sennacherib in 689. In 539 Cyrus did *not* destroy Babylon — he became its king and enhanced it![55]

Over in Egypt, Taharqa was another contemporary, amply attested archaeologically;[56] Memphis and Tanis (Zoan) were the Egyptian centers of that day, and Kush stood with Egypt, as in Isaiah's pages. The same is true of Jeremiah; his pages teem with people attested specifically in the late seventh and early sixth centuries — Nebuchadrezzar II of Babylon, Hophra of Egypt, the fort of Tahpanhes (Daphnai) there; people known from seals and bullae, even his own scribe Baruch (cf. chap. 2 above). And likewise for other prophets when the material permits comparison. They did not function in a never-never land.

But the other side of the limited-history-period coin is this: some two hundred, three hundred, or more years later, none of these details much mattered anymore. To Jews and most other people in (say) 400 B.C., and ever increasingly later, Assyria was merely a ghost name, a kingdom buried centuries beyond recall in sandy mounds. In the later Persian Empire and later, even the Neo-Babylonian splendors were over and gone, their rulers' fame fading. And all the Hebrew individuals — the Gemariahs, Shaphans, Ahikams, Hanans, Hilkiahs, Gedaliahs, Jaazaniahs, and the rest, known from seals, etc. — had long since faded from common view unless held in the genealogies of private families. The grand themes of the prophets (judgment, disaster, restoration) had been considerably fulfilled; the messy minor details, even to a fifth-century Judean, were but "ancient history" already. *If they were history at all.* But if all this was pure fiction (characters and all), arbitrarily invented in (say) the fifth to third centuries B.C., then it was all wholly irrelevant to the everyday lives and hopes of Persian-age resettlers; they needed beliefs, standards, an ethos to live by, not a load of pseudoarchaeological baggage from some imaginary fairyland. What is more, by 400-300 it was already a physical impossibility to invent out of nothing the intimate details of a lost preexilic world, its history and particular culture. And naturally there was no modern anthropological-cum-historical archaeology in those days.

But the history *was* real, as the external data clearly indicate, so far as they go. And thus it provided for later generations a real background framework for their beliefs, standards, ethos, and covenants, and was not superfluous in terms of germane background; their deity YHWH had been their guide and mentor of old, and would so continue. And family genealogical tradition helped to provide personal and living links within that postexilic community. Into that broad context the old preexilic prophetical books fitted as a testimony, encouragement, and warning; history (as it had actually happened) and belief and ethos then traveled together.

3. PROPHETS, ISRAELITE RELIGION, AND POP(ULAR) CULTS

A. INTRODUCTORY

(i) The Basis for the Position Taken by the Prophets

Two main themes dominate the pages of the "written prophets" whose books appear in the Hebrew Bible, and one more than the other. The very prominent but lesser theme is that of judgment on foreign nations, whether Israel's immediate neighbors for their unbrotherly hostility when the Hebrews were in trouble or the cruel, greedy imperial powers of Assyria and Babylonia, with Egypt coming between the two lots. But the major theme is of the Hebrews' *own* shortcomings — above all else, their disloyalty to their ancient covenant with YHWH as their sole god and sovereign, by adding other cults to his, or even going over to other cults in his stead, and indulging in forbidden practices. With this go the prophetic condemnations of social injustice in Israelite/Judean conduct of daily life, which also constituted breach of the social justice dimension of the basic covenant, held since Sinai.

Monotheism we have briefly considered above (pp. 330-33). But three additional points need to be stressed. First, YHWH's role as *sovereign* in a treatylike covenant meant that he stood over Israel as their ultimate — and *sole* — king, even though that terminology (Heb. *melek*) was scrupulously avoided. Except in coregencies with intended successors (not applicable to eternal deities!), kings brooked *no* interlopers on their thrones, and *no* usurpers to steal the loyal adherence of their subjects. Thus, YHWH by definition had to be sole god for Israel, as being their absolute sovereign, to the exclusion of other deities.

Second, monotheism was *not* invented among uprooted Jews during the Babylonian exile in the sixth century B.C. It was clearly proclaimed by Akhenaten in Egypt in the fourteenth century, and he was *not* a contemporary of Nebuchadrezzar II of Babylon in the sixth century! On this matter, old-style nineteenth-century biblicist dogma on the evolution of religion *must* finally be abandoned, on strictly factual, academic grounds — especially as such belief

395

had roots earlier, and had echoes in Egyptian religious thinking and writing into the thirteenth century (p. 396). Also, in twelfth-century Babylon Marduk attained a monotheist role for a time.[57]

Third, like it or loathe it, a belief in, and loyalty to, just one deity *does* naturally tend to lead to the exclusion of all other deities, regardless of whether they are thought to exist also (henotheism, monolatry) or are deemed to be nonexistent (strict monotheism). By his actions Akhenaten moved neatly from one state to the other. He began henotheistically by recognizing the other Egyptian gods as real enough to require eliminating from his world and cosmos. So he took the logical step of destroying their names and images as totally as he could, thereby (in Egyptian terms) ending their existence — by which move he established (in his terms) a strict practical monotheism. Whether we moderns approve personally of ancient beliefs and practices or not, in our academic study of them we must resolutely set aside our modern attitudes and agendas until the job is done. Any strong twenty-first-century feelings we might have should only be vented separately afterward (in print or otherwise), if anyone feels that strongly about his or her own views and prejudices.

(ii) The Basis for the Prophetic Critique and Two Paths

In the Sinai covenant (Exodus-Leviticus) and its renewal (Deuteronomy) in the thirteenth century, and in the story of the Hebrew transit from Egypt via Sinai to the Jordan, two strands are visible. The main one is that of the monotheistic and exclusive basis mentioned above, and the other is the existence of a tension between it and the "broader" view held by other elements in the migrating community, both now to be instanced.

First, at the heart of the covenant, in the "Ten Words" (Commandments), the final basis is clearly stated: no deity alongside/instead of YHWH, and no material images for worship (Exod. 20:3-4, 23; 34:17; and Lev. 26:1, as well as Deut. 5:7-8; 6:13-15). Social links with other beliefs (formal or religious) must be avoided (Exod. 34:15-16); and in takeovers, all the alien cult installations had to be smashed out of use (Exod. 34:13-14, besides Deut. 7:5, 25-26). There can be no ambiguity; iconoclastic Akhenaten would have been proud of Moses!

The other strand is "other people, other views." We talk and write of "Israel" (or even "proto-Israel") leaving Egypt, but the clans of Jacob did not travel alone. Two indications suggest that a certain number of fellow travelers of mixed origins and motivations went with them. In Exod. 12:38 we learn that a "mixed crowd" went out with the Hebrews and the livestock, *'ereb-rab;* compare English "riffraff"! Later on, soon after leaving Sinai (Num. 11:4), a "rabble" with the Hebrews were grumbling about no food but manna. So, this far, there were others besides the Hebrews themselves on trek; and their loyalty was clearly fickle. Already at Sinai the first religious lapse occurred. Moses was so long up the mount that some people got Aaron to adopt an alternative cult to that of the invisible sovereign YHWH. Instead a golden calf became their focus — perhaps of El-YHWH — using a symbolism that was immediately compatible with bull imagery in both Canaan (El; Baal) and in Egypt (several deities), and all too easily assimilated to it. This was in breach of what they had just accepted, of course. The second lapse was almost forty years later, by the banks of the Jordan (Num. 25:1-5). Again, in breach of covenant (the spirit of Exod. 34:15-16), Hebrew men were beguiled by easygoing Moabite ladies into sharing the worship of Baal-Peor (among other things), with a predictable response on Moses' part. Finally, even when the Hebrews were safely across the Jordan, at a formal renewal of the selfsame covenant, Joshua was skeptical enough to assume that somebody, somewhere, would be clinging to the old easygoing habits picked up in Egypt and never really lost, and made his appeal for people to be really wholehearted and dump their little old ancestral figures of family deities (Josh. 24:14), like Jacob long, long before (Gen. 35:2, 4). As an earnest religious group might perhaps be told even today, "Get rid of all your 'lucky charms,' rabbit's foot, four-leaf-clover charm, magic eye, and really believe!" Thus the Sinai covenant, with repeated blessings/curses for obedience/disobedience, was a basis for all that followed it, especially the prophets.

(iii) The Two Ways, Ideal and Actual — or Redundant Prophets?

(a) Redundant Prophets?

We moderns are so dominated by familiarity with the Hebrew biblical texts as we have them that we forget that (in principle) history *could* have been very different. Thus, if Joshua had been succeeded by another decisive and strong leader, a Joshua II, and he in turn by a whole series of effective leaders solidly loyal to the Sinai covenant, who were also good generals, then we might have had a very different story in twelfth- and eleventh-century Canaan. A strong, quite centralized Hebrew state with selective leadership would have more quickly attained a tribal unity territorially from Hazor to Hebron, with the tabernacle as a real and effective central sanctuary at Shiloh, and a pan-tribal religious focal point as envisaged in Exodus-Leviticus and Deuteronomy. And perhaps, eventually, one of these leaders was able to found a dynasty of kings, like a David, and his successors in turn were shrewder than Solomon and Rehoboam, handing down a unified Israelite state that was solidly Yahwistic to the difficult days of the late eighth to early sixth centuries. The population would have been so inured to their own native Yahwism, that found no need of the gods and cults of their neighbors, that they rarely strayed from their covenant with, and worship of, YHWH.

In such a situation, especially if this different Israel had quietly submitted to Assyria (unlike Hezekiah) and Neo-Babylon (unlike Jehoiachin and Zedekiah) and — like the Phoenician cities and some others — survived intact into Persian times, *then* we might never have had major prophetic figures (or writings from their ministries) to cajole the Hebrews from their dalliances with other cults and kingdoms, if nothing substantial of that kind had ever happened. They would have been relatively inconspicuous figures such as Abijah, Gad, or Iddo, who merely flit through the pages of Samuel or Kings. And no written Latter Prophets at all!

(b) Harsh Reality — Prophets Direly Needed!

But no. As we all know (or should know, if we actually read our Hebrew writings attentively), the reality was very different in real-time antiquity. Joshua was followed by *no* decisive leader, only by a short-lived, jelly-wobble committee of geriatric elders (Josh. 24:31; Judg. 2:7, contrast v. 10) who showed no initiative, and left no leader. With only patchy occupation, and *no* concerted follow-up to Joshua's lightning raids, the scattered tribes fell back on their own devices, acted as individual splinter groups and very soon got nowhere, ending up settling in with the Canaanites around them (cf. Judg. 1:21-36, after brief collaborative efforts), leading to social (and then religious) relations precisely as forbidden by their ancestral covenant (Exod. 34:15-16). And with very limited access to the tabernacle at Shiloh when non-Hebrew areas barred easy access, increasing numbers of tribesfolk simply did not bother to go to its feasts unless they lived close by (Samuel's family lived in Ephraim, for example). The tabernacle priests failed to encourage more active attendance but were content to vegetate among their local clientele (cf. Eli); the covenant terms did not get read regularly; and everything got slack, easygoing, and purposeless. Only when major crises were perpetrated by oppressors did the Hebrews remember they had a sovereign who long since got them out of Egypt and into Canaan, so "Help, get us out of this!" was their call, like many a modern since who has prayed in deep trouble but not in palmy times. By the time of King David, and a newly unified Israel, in the wake of Samuel's earlier leadership under YHWH, the tribes had more respect for their own deity, and a rejuvenated priestly line under David and Solomon began to resurrect the old covenant, but more likely its ritual and social parts. High places for local and informal worship of YHWH (besides other deities) were so long established, especially since the destruction of the Shiloh sanctuary (leaving no central cult at all), that they were treated as normal. As others also used such arrangements, then, religious accommodations between local Yahwism and nearby Baals and others could happen without much social or psychological difficulty unless one's attachment to YHWH's sovereignty was very clear. But such (con)fusions probably happened mainly (by the united monarchy period) in zones where Hebrews and Canaanites remained in social contact, not up in the hill areas where a Hebrew population was by then dominant.

Then, under Solomon, the rot (Yahwistically speaking) began at the center. He built a splendid shrine to YHWH, but it used in part cosmopolitan motifs, and was in part a royal and dynastic shrine, adjoining the royal palace complex. Jerusalemites (and more so, others) saw little of it except at major feasts. Solomon himself married widely internationally, so the cults of these wives were publicly catered for. Where highest society leads, others are sure to follow, in all times and climes. And they did. So, gradually, like Solomon, like people, and high places probably became both pluralist — YHWH plus other deities — and also non-Yahwist, dedicated to other deities such as Baal and Asherah (cf., e.g., 1 Kings 14:22-24, under Rehoboam). So the successor states of Israel and Judah became the locales of religious pluralism, varying in different local places and over time. The common neglect at the royal temple of the overall covenant as opposed to simply maintaining almost mechanically the rituals and ceremonials did nothing to discourage such pluralism. And the kings themselves added non-Yahwistic features to the Jerusalem temple itself. There was the Assyrian altar of Ahaz (2 Kings 16:10-14), and all manner of other interesting clutter removed later — items for Baal, Asherah, and the heavenly bodies, an Asherah pole, Asherah's weaving room, the "horses of the sun," and sundry altars on the roof (astral rites?); cf. 2 Kings 23:4-13. So it is quite wrong to say that Yahwism was the religion of a small, highly placed elite and Canaanism the way of the mass of the people; things were quite mixed at *all* social levels, as the biblical texts show. What was true of Judah was even more so in Israel, with Jeroboam I's rival cults for YHWH, but (like Aaron's "false friends") using the compromising bull imagery, and priesthoods of uncertain origin. Here there was much greater exposure to late Canaanite usage and closer links with Phoenicia (cf. Ahab and Jezebel) and with Aram (cf. reciprocal markets at one stage, 1 Kings 20:34).

From time to time in Judah, one king or another would consciously seek a purer, more consistent service of YHWH. Reforms did *not* begin just with Josiah. We find such moves under Asa (1 Kings 15:11-13), rubbishing idols out of the temple along with his grandmother's Asherah pole, etc. Then, two centuries later, Hezekiah took more drastic steps (2 Kings 18:4), purifying the temple cult and putting down other high places that had Asherah symbols and stelae. It was only after over half a century of "counterrevolution" in favor of the old paths of compromise under Manasseh that a drastic return to reform came with Josiah (2 Kings 23, and 2 Chron. 34 with supplementary data). At first, in his eighth year (ca. 632), he ran a "cleanup," a purifying reform much as Hezekiah had done (2 Chron. 34:3-8). Then, with further work, a "book of the law" turned up (from some dusty cupboard) in his eighteenth year (622/621), the terms of which convinced him that only a much deeper reform would deactivate the curses of YHWH that this book contained. On the total evidence of 2 Kings 22:11-20 and 2 Chron. 34:21-28, we learn surprisingly little about the contents of this book. Only that it expressed YHWH's prohibition of the worship of any other deity and of idols, and invoked his curses on such disobedience. Josiah's reaction was not surprising: Baal, Asherah, the heavenly bodies, etc., had enjoyed worship in the temple (seemingly for ages), and also in the high places of the land; for such disobedience, curses of doom were prescribed. Not surprisingly, this has been compared with well-known passages in Deuteronomy.

On so slim a basis as this did De Wette erect his theory that Deuteronomy had been fraudulently cooked up in 622 by priests wanting temple reform and cult centralization at Jerusalem in their favor, and that this then became the fount of everything else similar in the Hebrew Bible. This was just like balancing a large pyramid on its point, not its base. However, *precisely* the same concerns are equally clearly expressed outside of, and before, Deuteronomy, in Exodus-Leviticus. Prohibition of worship of deities other than YHWH and of idols was expressly forbidden in Exod. 20:3-4, 23; 34:17; and Lev. 26:1, as we have seen. And also, punishment for infringement was warned of in Exod. 20:5-6, and in curse form at some length in Lev. 26:14-45, every bit as drastically as in Deut. 28:15-68 (which is longer, but no worse). In short, the reform could have been sparked off as easily by one version of the Sinai covenant (the older, Exodus-Leviticus) as the other (later by forty years only: Deuteronomy). And the *modern* data on treaty, law, and covenant put both versions squarely in the late second millennium, *not* in the late seventh century, and not as a pious fraud either. Again, this is asserted on strictly, even rigidly *academic* grounds not available to De Wette, Wellhausen, or many of their unwitting successors. Josiah (like Asa and Hezekiah) sought purity of worship above all, destroying only what he considered paganizing practice. The claim for centralization is incredibly shaky. It fails to appear in the Chronicles account at all (2 Chron. 34:33), where he removed the pagan cult-materials and "made all present in Israel to serve the Lord their God" — but not a word of it being just in Jerusalem. In

Kings it is almost equally shaky. In 2 Kings 23:8-9 we learn that Josiah brought in priests (genuine by lineage? contrast pagan ones in 23:5) from around Judah and Jerusalem, away from high places, and pensioned them off in Jerusalem, their active service over. Of any other service outside Jerusalem, nothing is said. Thus, far too much has been built upon the dodgy "Deuteronomic" interpretation of Josiah's reforms, from 1805 to the present time. In the light of the mercilessly impersonal, impartial, external data (chap. 6 above; cf. also below), this ancient canard of 1805 should be quietly given decent burial.

(iv) The Role of the Prophets

This is where our famous "written" prophets come in. So we find in the eighth century Amos briefly criticizing Judah over nonadherence to the "law" (= covenant rules; 2:4-5), and at much greater length Israel (on social injustice; hypocritical formal worship at Bethel and Gilgal; 4:4-5; 5:5). Hosea alleged unfaithfulness to YHWH, explicitly breach of covenant (8:1), open idolatry (13:1-3). Micah again condemned social corruption (3:9-12), said idols and Asherahs will be destroyed (1:7; 5:13-14), and reminded them of YHWH's deliverance under Moses, Aaron, and Miriam and then in Balaam's time (6:4-5). Isaiah at grander length reproved injustice (1; 3; 5; 10; etc.), and equally paganizing practice and idolatry (2:6, 8; 31:7; etc.) In the seventh/sixth centuries the same applied, even more insistently. At length Jeremiah condemned idolatry of one kind and another, and turning aside from YHWH (e.g., 2:5, 8, 11, 27-28; 5:19; 17:1-2; 44:1-6; etc.). He explicitly charged the Judeans with breach of the Sinai covenant (11:1-5, 10-13), and openly invoked both Moses and Samuel as those who would condemn them accordingly (15:1-2). Ezekiel was as clear (e.g., 6–7; 8; 14; 20; 22; etc.). Thus they were all basing their polemic on the old Sinai covenant, along two lines: (1) the worship of YHWH versus other deities and images plus their rites, and (2) social injustices that equally broke with the letter and/or spirit of the social injunctions of the Sinai covenant in Exodus and Leviticus and allied items in Numbers and in Deuteronomy.

In sum, alongside the official central cult at all times in tabernacle and temple, the Hebrews were happy to experiment with adding to the cult of YHWH, even having (an) Asherah by his side in the temple itself (never mind the high places), or to go over to cults of Baal and Asherah alongside of, or instead of, YHWH. This affected high society, not just peasantry. The prophets sought to recall both rulers and people to the ancient covenant, and invoked its curses, while looking also for future blessing when the discipline of punishment was over.

B. THE INPUT OF ARCHAEOLOGY
AND EXTERNAL TEXT SOURCES

(i) Late Bronze Age to Early Iron (ca. 1250-930)

From the pages of the Old Testament, from Sinai to Samuel, we learn only little about the active religion of the Canaanites and others among whom the Hebrews settled. Among deities, the weather-god Baal looms large, the goddess Astarte ("Ashtoreth" in Hebrew) less so, and hardly after Solomon's time. But her colleague Ashirat ("Asherah" in Hebrew usage) runs in parallel with Baal (= Hadad) from the thirteenth to the sixth century. All three are well attested in the external written sources, in West Semitic sources (principally the rituals and myths and legends at Ugarit) and as foreign "visitors" in Egyptian sources during the height of the New Kingdom (ca. 1450-1160). The Hebrew sources from Exodus to 1 Samuel say little about cult places other than high places on hills, etc. (e.g., Num. 33:52), and their ritual furnishings: altars, statuary, idols/images (sometimes of gold or silver), standing stones (as stelae or *masseboth*), symbols of Asherah (e.g., Deut. 7:5, 25-26). Major structures such as temples first appear in the judges' narratives, with the temple of Baal/El-berith at Shechem (Judg. 9:4, 46), probably in the twelfth century. After that we next meet temples with the Philistines, attributed to the god Dagon (in Gaza and Ashdod; Judg. 16:23-30; 1 Sam. 5), in Samson's time and Samuel's (eleventh century). But, understandably, the Hebrew writers have no space to waste on cultic details outside the scope of their narrative. We do learn of festivals being held (Judg. 16:23ff.), and of priests and diviners, and gold votive gifts to placate deity judged to have been offended (1 Sam. 5).

As Dever in particular has repeatedly stressed, very little use has been made of the rich (but uneven) archaeological data (including related textual matter, we may add) that greatly widens our knowledge of the religions that the Hebrews encountered, lived with, and sometimes had close dealings with. These data help us see much more clearly what the prophets, as champions of YHWH and YHWH alone, were so concerned about, from Moses' time down to the fall of Jerusalem. Here, within the confines of simply a subsection of just one chapter in a more wide-ranging study, we cannot remotely do full justice to the topic; but at least a sample integrative report on a representative range of the different data may be briefly offered within our context. We will range from Ugarit in the north to Kuntillet Ajrud in the deep south, from basically the thirteenth/fourteenth century to the sixth, in the next section (1250-930) and the one following (930-586).

(a) Places and Modes of Worship of
Hebrew Contemporaries Up North

At Ugarit, within the city, we find two "metropolitan" temples and one "chapel royal." During the thirteenth century at least, the first two dominated the city from the high acropolis within the northeast zone of Ugarit. The western belonged to Baal, as an Egyptian stela found there showed clearly (being dedicated to Baal-Zaphon), while the eastern belonged to Dagon, having yielded two Ugaritic stelae inscribed briefly for Dagon. Both temples were solidly built on masonry fondations; each had a vestibule before the main sanctuary (built as a tower), whence a staircase climbed up to the roof, used for ceremonials. The chapel royal on the north side of the palace was of the same type, but much smaller (12 × 8 meters, roughly 40 × 30 feet), compared with 22 × 16 meters (about 70 × 50 feet) for Baal, and Dagon (foundations about 20 × 18 meters, or about 65 × 60 feet). Baal's temple in particular stood within a spacious precinct averaging 40 × 20 meters (130 × 65 feet) in extent. Here, before the temple, stood a grand open-air altar (2 meters/6.5 feet square) — just as one did before the Hebrew tabernacle (Exod. 40:6; 5 cubits/7.5 feet square). But the Ugaritic altar was of tooled masonry, approached by steps, which was exactly what the Hebrews were forbidden to do (no tooled stone, no steps, Exod. 20:24-26); this was a contemporary divergence.[58] In terms of architecture, the twelfth-century tower temple of Baal/El-berith at Shechem (Judg. 9:4, 46) was the nearest equivalent structure in the biblical record, and in the twelfth-century temple building excavated at Shechem.[59] Depending on the affiliations of the then motley population of Shechem, probably partly Israelite, partly Canaanite, El-berith was "El (God) of the covenant" or "Baal (proper name, or 'Master') of the covenant."

And what was done in such temples? At Shechem, we are not told. But at Ugarit, the ritual and literary texts combined give us some indication. In the legend of Keret (ll. 61ff.), King Keret was told to wash (hence be ritually pure), take offerings, and "ascend to the top of the tower, mount the crest of the wall, lift up your hands to heaven, sacrifice to your father, Bull-El, and serve Baal with your sacrifice."[60] Here was the Canaanizing usage of identifying the supreme god El with the symbol of the bull, rejected by Moses (Exod. 32) but later used by Jeroboam I (1 Kings 12:28-30), never forgiven him by the prophetic writers. Roof altars were used by the more religiously compromising kings of Judah later on, eventually being removed by Josiah (2 Kings 23:12).

But the main rites were conducted at ground level. For these, Ugarit has yielded a harvest of detailed rituals for daily, monthly, and probably annual offerings in their temples. We may sample a little of this. Various rituals officially involved the king as offerer, but one suspects that the local high priest would substitute for him when he was absent or heavily engaged. A typical one is that now known prosaically as KTU 1.109, which begins as follows (words in parentheses are added for clarity, and explanations are in *italics*):

> On the 14th (of the month), the king washes, (is thus) purified.
> On the day of full (moon), cattle are slaughtered.
> The month, 10th:
> > 2 ewe-lambs, a town-dove, and 2 kidneys for Baal [Zaphon].
> > A sheep for Ramish *(obscure deity)*; a liver and a sheep for Shalim.
> > An ox-liver and a sheep for Baal Zaphon.
> > A ewe-lamb for Zaphon (as) burnt-offering, and (as) "peace"-
> offerings likewise.
> And at the Temple of Baal of Ugarit, livers and a lung;
> > (for) Il-ib, a heifer; (for) El, a sheep; (for) Baal, a sheep.
> > (for) Anath (of) Zaphon, an ox and a sheep; (for) Pidray, a sheep as
> burnt offering.

And so the ritual runs for another twenty-two lines, with offerings also to Baal of Aleppo, Dagon, the obscure Dadmish and Resheph, with much the same run of offerings.[61]

Another such text has a deity visiting the royal palace for celebration of rites (KTU 1.43); this would probably imply a formal religious procession (priests carrying standards or scepters?) from her temple abode (location unknown) to the palace. The opening lines read: "When Athtart (= Astarte/ Ashteroth) of the Grotto enters the recess(?) at the royal palace, (with) ten by ten (images?) in the recess(?), abode of the starry gods, (there are) *tarumat*-offerings: — a robe, tunic, (and) dress; gold 3 pounds; a ram, ox, and three sheep as 'peace'-offerings; 7 times for the gods, and 7 times (also) for Kothar." And so likewise for sun, moon, and Anath, and payments to royal servitors.[62]

Finally we come to a more specific rite: one of atonement or expiation (KTU 1.40 with parallel texts). Here a rather splendid ritual originally had three grand divisions, each divided into two sections, one each for the menfolk and the womenfolk of Ugarit. The three divisions seem to have dealt with three levels of sin: the worst, *pesha'* or the like, is now largely lost; then that classed as *hatt'a*, as in Hebrew; then "spoilt virtue." We may give a sample from one section:

> "Now, present a [bull]/ram/young male ass *(in divisions I, II, III, respectively):*

"Deliver (it) up (to sacrifice), O son/daughter of Ugarit,

"that we may be fair again O Gates of Ugarit *(and fourfold/twice more, with different vocatives)*, whether your virtue ("fair [nature]") is spoilt, like a Qatian *(or like 5 other foreigners)*, or like those who rob you, . . . oppress you, or like the princely city.

"(And) whether your virtue is spoilt, either by your anger, or your impatience, your quarrelling, or over sacrifices or oblation." *(Then comes the action)*:

"Our sacrifice we (now) sacrifice, this the oblation we oblate, this the expense we expend. Let it be uplifted to the Father of the Sons of El, and *(ditto)* to the family-circle of the Sons of El, to Thakmanu-and-Shanuma, this [bull]/ram/young male ass!"[63]

As others have pointed out, confession of guilt (including to deity) is not restricted in the biblical world simply to the Old Testament writers and this text. Other Ugaritic texts show this; and farther north, for example, the Hittite emperor Mursil II confessed the sins of his father and court, his people and himself, in seeking relief from a nationwide plague, in his extensive plague prayers.[64] Like the people of Ugarit, the Hebrews too expressed collective guilt, as in Num. 14:40; 21:7; Lev. 16 and 26:40; Deut. 1:41; Judg. 10:10, 15; etc. (And they need not have waited six centuries to do it by word or rite, any more than the thirteenth-century Ugaritians did.) At Ugarit a bull, ram, and male ass were successively offered up for both men and women of that community, while in the Hebrew Day of Atonement ritual (Lev. 16), a bull and ram were to be offered up for the high priest, and two goats and a ram for the people; cf. also in Lev. 9 (at the priest's installation), in Lev. 4–5 (for overlooked sin), and in Lev. 15 (on pollution) separate sections for men (15:2-17) and women (15:19-30). Impatience was linked with sin not only at Ugarit but also among the Hebrews, and was to be confessed (cf. Num. 21:4-7).

Besides rites, we may note terminology. Above I have used the old, conventional rendering "peace" offerings for the *sh-l-m* rite of the Hebrews and Ugaritians alike, simply for convenience; modern Bible translations render these as offerings of (e.g.) fellowship or well-being in English. Both lots of writers knew of (whole) burnt offerings, but used different terms: Ugarit used the root *sh-r-p*, "burn (up)," but the Hebrews, *'olah* (what went up). The Hebrew *tenupah* offering was a rite of lifting up an offering (not waving it), as in New Kingdom Egypt, and may have been linked philologically (as well as in practice) with Ugaritic *sh-n-p-t*. Both had *z-b-h* or *dh-b-h* for "sacrifice." Far from being "late," the Hebrew *terumah* (contributionary offering) may also go back this early; we have *trmmt* (*UT,* no. 2311) and *trmt* (in KTU 1.43 above), with material contributions listed. It must be emphasized that Semitic words formed with an initial *t* upon basic roots are *not* inevitably "late," despite modern belief to the contrary.[65]

Going east, inland from Ugarit, we must at least mention Emar on the Euphrates, where the Late Bronze Age city boasted a series of temples of a long-room type, like those of Ebla, or Hazor (or even Solomon), attested for the thirteenth to early twelfth centuries. Texts from here include temple rituals of importance and some length; e.g., the rituals for installation of a high priestess, rites of seven-year periodicity, etc., clearly comparable with rites in Leviticus.[66]

(b) Places and Modes of Worship of Hebrew Contemporaries Down South

At Ugarit the temples were structurally much damaged and the furnishings were gone, but the rites are available in some measure in condensed written format. By contrast, in Canaan no written rituals have so far survived (long lost, on papyrus and parchment?), but we have more temples better preserved, along with a good sampling of their ritual and "heirloom" furnishings. As we cannot here be encyclopedic, one temple will serve as a useful example, kept in perspective by brief reference to others.

So we go to Lachish, late in the thirteenth century. There, besides one small but once rich temple (about 40 × 30 feet overall) well inside the town, visitors coming from the north or west would find a larger edifice (about 75 feet long by 45 feet wide maximally), low down in the filled-up moat or "fosse." Its entrance faced north toward them, and was reached by passing a small cluster of modest buildings — most likely the abode of either the main priest of the temple or perhaps of a subordinate-cum-guardian. By about 1230 it had been twice rebuilt and extended. Let us join its latest visitors. Cf. fig. 47.

The whole temple was solidly built of rough stone masonry (with mud mortar) to roof level, and a potentially dark interior was lightened by having walls and floors largely faced with white plaster. Lighting was confined either to slot windows under the eaves of the roofs or to grilles in a small clerestory over the four pillars in the sanctuary — in either case permitting a cool, moderate light on sunny days but dull on wet, rainy ones. The front door opened onto a vestibule; in its southeast corner, cross-shelves held masses of clean, new bowls ready for use. Going on south through its southeast door, we are in the biggest and finest room, the sanctuary itself. Here two rows of mud-brick benches before a third against the front and side walls bore a profusion of gift-filled bowls left by previous worshipers.[67] The rear wall was dominated by a broad niche with raised and plastered platform (the shrine proper), bearing divine image(s) at the back, with a profusion of some of the shrine's richer donated gifts covering the platform — such as a beautiful faience vase, a fine ivory ointment flask-cum-spoon in womanly form, brilliant wavy blue/yellow/white Egyptian glassware, and (a real heirloom!) a royal hunt scarab of Amenophis III already then 150 years old; plus cylinder seals, scarabs, and much more.[68] The whole was fronted by a white-plastered mud-brick altar approached on the west by three steps (very nonbiblical, like Ugarit and Emar), with a hearth before it. At the right of the altar and shrine niche stood a tall stand, next to a narrow cupboard full of little pottery lamps. To its left was a large vessel or "bin."[69]

Along the great room's east wall, three square cupboards were built in, with shelves crowded with more pottery bowls. Either side of the sanctuary niche, two doors led into a pair of storerooms or "treasuries," containing even more pottery ready for cult use, besides other items of greater intrinsic value, such as the superb bead necklaces of brightly colored, Egyptian-style faience beads, imitating yellow-and-white daisies; bunches of purple grapes, corn cockles (like thistle tops), yellowy fruits like persea or mandrake, and bluish green palmettes.[70]

And exotic pots? Yes, the Fosse Temple could boast a nice cabinet's worth of exciting Cypriote and Mycenaean vessels from over the blue Mediterranean. And its collection of homegrown black-and-red decorated wares — with birds, ibexes, and tunny fish — was stunning.[71] Finally, the locals could write. A splendid two-foot-high ewer was decorated in deep red paint with a series of animals, over which the artist had jotted, very informally, a dedication:

Gift (of) an oblation, O my [lad]y Goddess, [? and Reshe]ph!

This is only one of several rather fragmentary inscriptions from thirteenth-century Lachish, all informal such that any reasonably intelligent Canaanite might have inked them onto bowls and basins — and did. Finally here, priests had to be clean (at any rate, ritually); a specialized foot-washing bowl was found conveniently near the sanctuary altar.[72]

Other exotica included a set of half a dozen fine ivory ceremonial wands (or scepters), two still bearing their pomegranate heads.[73] Such wands might serve two purposes: to be carried by priest(s) in religious processions, as at festivals, and possibly as instruments to touch or indicate (thus, dedicate) the offerings when presented to a deity. Outside Canaan we see in Egypt the use of ceremonial wands, staves, and scepters, borne by king and priests at great festive processions like that for Sokar, while others bear tall standards of the gods (cf. below). These pomegranate-headed wands occur elsewhere in Canaan; three more came from Tel Nami, on the coast south of Haifa: an ivory one in a robbed grave and two fine bronze ones with a bronze incense stand from an intact burial — all of roughly 1200. The ivory one was incomplete, and the bronze ones had a pomegranate and a cockle/thistle head respectively.[74] These may have been personal to priests buried there; and at Tel Nami there was also once a small temple or shrine not far north of the cemetery. Solomon's temple may have had these too.[75]

We should not confuse these modest-length objects with full-size processional cult standards, also used in festival processions. Spectacular copper examples (lacking their long wooden poles) come from the Nahal Mishmar hoard of Chalcolithic Canaan, of the fifth and fourth millennia, perhaps used in the rites of a neighboring temple at En-gedi.[76] Up north, in the third millennium, finds at Alaca Hüyük in Copper Age Anatolia (from before the Hittites) included another series of spectacular standards bearing bulls, stags and deer, discs and lozenges, richly wrought.[77] Throughout Egyptian history, from the third millennium to Roman times, Egypt's great festival processions saw the carrying of sacred standards with emblems of divinity before gods and kings (and some regimental army standards also honored the gods).[78] In Canaan, in the thirteenth century, such specific cult standards were also probably used at festivals. A goddess with serpents appears on a silver-plated bronze standard found in a potter's workshop close by Temple C ("of the stelae") at Hazor.[79] Back in Lachish, in the city temple, a gold plaque bearing a crowned but nude goddess standing upon a horse and holding long-stemmed lotuses was found. Plated onto wood, it was probably the top feature of a processional standard like the Hazor one.[80] And thirdly, our Fosse Temple at Lachish yielded a further possible example, but smaller: another rectangular gold sheet, engraving now illegible, and with lapped edges suggesting former adhesion to a piece of wood — another standard-top?[81] Such standards would have been carried in processions at festivals, as in Egypt, and in all likelihood in Anatolia, and early on in (Chalcolithic) Canaan itself. As the Ugaritic and Emar texts indicate, there were feasts and ceremonies aplenty for such stately processions. And from an Egyptian ostracon of circa 1200, we learn that the goddess Anath had a cult in Gaza, then an Egyptian base, where her festivities were patronized by the Egyptian authorities. Thus one garrison scribe writes to another, invoking "all the gods and goddesses who are in the region of the land of Khurru [= Canaan]," and announcing that "[the offerings which you have sent for] the Feast of Anath of Gaza all [arrived safely . . .], and I received the/y[our . . .] for the goddess."[82]

And what of actual offerings and services? The Fosse Temple yielded ample trace of bones of sacrificial animals, principally of sheep/goats and some of oxen — predominantly the right foreleg of young animals, beside birds and even fish. The right foreleg or haunch was also favored in the tabernacle rituals of the Hebrews at this time (cf. Lev. 7:32-34), and not least yearling animals (cf., e.g., Lev. 12:6; 14:10; 23:19; Num. 6:12, 14; 7:15ff., 87-88; 28 and 29, passim).[83] Bird bones may indicate offering of doves/pigeons as at Ugarit, and in biblical ritual (e.g., Lev. 1:14; 5:7). Both at Ugarit and in the tabernacle's daily rites (Exod. 29:38-43; Num. 28:1-8), offerings were made in the morning and in the evening; so this may be the case in our Canaanite temples also. Just as both Ugarit and the Hebrew tabernacle had whole burnt offerings consumed by fire for benefit of the deity/ies alone and also *sh-l-m* (peace) offerings shared by the priests (Lev. 7:11-37, passim), so here in Canaan we may postulate holocausts and shared offerings. Wine was presented at Ugarit, and was included in the tabernacle daily rites (Exod. 29:40). Libation was also practiced in Canaan; the tall stand at the Fosse Temple's altar and its top bowl were pierced to allow the libation to sink into the ground below. Incense is known to have been used at Ugarit; it was used extensively in Egypt from early times; and frankincense proper was used sparingly in the tabernacle cult as part of a blend with gum resin and two other spices (Exod. 30:34-35). There is no basis whatsoever for the old view that the Hebrews used incense only from about the seventh century. Aromatics were burned in Late Bronze Canaan, as on the massive stone stand with sun disc and vertical grooves, found in the Hazor temple of area H.[84]

High places are, so far, little attested; for two probably early Hebrew examples, see already in chapter 5 above. Broadly speaking, when we compare Canaanite/Syrian usage with the Hebrew rites of the tabernacle (later continued at the Jerusalem temple), there is a general area of common Semitic and broader usage: all use animal sacrifices, both holocaust and otherwise; all have their regular rites, daily and periodic; all have their sense of ritual purity, to be fit to approach deity; guilt/deliverance are a common concern. But within the *koine* there are also distinctions. So, in types of altars, in the understanding of sacrifices (food for pagan deities; instructional in YHWH's case), the matter of images versus no image, and so on. Not easily accessible to us on current evidence (or rather lack of it) are matters of human and child sacrifice (e.g., Molech rites), but the Hebrew writers could hardly fulminate against something that did not exist in some form, whether they knew all the details or not. In short, from the texts and material remains combined, it is possible to glimpse the world of Canaan into which the postexodus Hebrews entered and settled, among those that followed the religion briefly visited above. This was the sphere in which these ongoing cults lived alongside Hebrew belief and practice, through the time of the judges, on into the epochs of the Hebrew united and divided monarchies. It helps set the tone of the scene against which backcloth the prophets sought to keep the Israelites clear of entanglement with the religions of their neighbors and faithful to the covenant of their invisible deity YHWH.

(c) The Eleventh-Tenth Centuries, Nicely Domestic?

Philistia enjoyed its own range of culture and local religion; we cannot here dilate upon the remarkable and invaluable finds at Tell Qasile,[85] Ashdod, Ekron, well noted in the handbooks. But briefly we look at "Hebrew" finds.

In several sites in this short period, "cult places" have been identified, but perhaps a little too optimistically. Thus de Vaux thought to find both a Middle and a Late Bronze shrine at the gate of Tirzah (Tell el-Far'ah North). However, closer scrutiny by Fowler has conclusively shown that this is not the case, and this "sacred spot" can be eliminated entirely. Any olive oil production there would be noncultic.[86] Then we come to Megiddo, building 2081 of stratum VA (David/Solomon). Here only a pair each of limestone "altars" and stands would pass for "cultic"; the rest is probably domestic clutter. We may have a small corner for the inhabitants to express their personal piety, but not more.[87] At Lachish, the "cult room 49" is no better a case; it might have seen domestic devotion, using a stand to hold a lamp or lamps, or conceivably a bowl of incense or a libation, etc. At Taanach things get much more interesting, but only briefly. Here, as Fowler could show,[88] Lapp went well over the top in claiming a cult area of two rooms; one was certainly a storeroom, the other, domestic. The basin next to a pillared wall had no pressing slab to deliver fluid into it; so it can hardly even be an oil press (even if domestic). And, with a pair of possible exceptions, nothing here is provenly cultic. The possible exceptions are two spectacular pottery stands, about two feet high. One has a set of lions down the sides, each overwhelming and about to devour a man; on the front, a man seizes a snake triumphantly. We need no religious spiel here. It may show (e.g.) the "Lion of Judah" overcoming the Canaanites (if Taanach was recently captured), and a Hebrew triumphing over the foreign serpent for their deities. There is no proof for this suggestion, of course — or for any other! Much more exciting was Lapp's more elaborate stand. Here, (1) a winged disc over a bull calf (?) is above (2) a "tree of life" flanked by ibexes, over (3) two cherubim flanking an aperture, above (4) a nude woman restraining two flanking lions. The three upper registers also have flanking beasts, griffons (first), lions (second), and cherubs (third). Identifications have been offered, such that the winged disc is El (= YHWH) and the lady with lions is Asherah, and so on. The stand is virtually a temple of this pair. Maybe; it would fit well with a pairing of YHWH and Asherah two centuries later. But in the absence of any clinching inscriptions on this piece, this is all — still — just speculation.[89] Egyptian evidence *with inscriptions* shows clearly that it is a goddess Qadishtu, "Holy One," who stands upon a lion (Louvre C.86; British Museum 191; Berlin), or a compound goddess, Qadishtu-Astarte-Anath, no less, that stands upon the lion (all thirteenth and early twelfth centuries), and *not* Asherah, poor dear![90] She has lost her circus act with the lions, it seems. So, the supposed coupling of Asherah here with an assumed El (= YHWH) collapses; Anath and Astarte usually pal up with Baal, not El. And El, anyway, was not a sun god; that was Shams. The winged sun of Malachi may not be that of Egypt, used in the Levant, but the Persian one; we cannot say for sure. On the stand the winged disc may simply be decorative, and the animals, etc., likewise — old Canaanizing motifs used by some Israelite, in much the same nonunderstanding way that the contemporary and later Phoenicians reused a whole series of Egyptian motifs, bungling them and misusing them as mere decoration because their original significance did not matter to them. And still less, for example, when such motifs then traveled from Phoenicia to Samaria in Israel to decorate (on ivories) the "ivory house" of Ahab and his successors. The stand and its companion may have held either lamps *or* something more cultic; we have, alas, no data on this — only unverifiable speculation = zero.

As for Solomon, his temple used decoration (within) inherited from the tabernacle, where "cherubs" are concerned. As in the tabernacle, then at Shiloh, his inner sanctuary retained only the ark of the covenant. See already chapter 4 above. But in various ways Solomon began visibly to drift from the old covenant. Increasingly contrary to Deut. 17:16-17, he acquired considerable wealth (1 Kings 10:27) and numerous horses and chariots (10:26), had renewed links with Egypt (3:1-2), and finally and most obviously went in for a number of foreign wives (11:1-8). Pleasing them meant arranging for their cults, which brought these — under official patronage — into Judah and Israel (11:4-7). This set the tone for his later years and for the twin kingdoms that followed; what a king might do, his court adherents might copy and their social "inferiors" then copy — "Everybody's doing it, so why not us? What's the harm?" And once the old covenant had been forgotten to be read regularly (Deut. 31:9-13), the sharp impact of the old covenant would quietly begin to wane. The prophets were men who found themselves with a call to recall Israel to her particular covenant and deity. Thus was the stage set for the tensions of the 350 years that followed, from 930 to 580.

(ii) Iron Age Israel and Judah (ca. 930-580)

As the foregoing discussion demonstrates, it is still fatally easy to go for "cultic" solutions without applying sufficient stringency. Happily, not everything falls to such needful iconoclasm, as we shall now see; the Hebrews *did* get involved with some juicy pagan practices, archaeologically as well as textually, thus saving the prophets from redundancy, and our scholars from boredom!

(a) Hijinks at the High Place at Dan

Prophetically minded Hebrew annalists detested Jeroboam I setting up shrines at Bethel and Dan, because he set them up as rivals to the temple at Jerusalem and used compromising iconography: bull-calf figures, long since redolent of El in Canaanite usage, and of Baal, permitting all too easy syncretisms in their estimation (cf. 1 Kings 12:26-33). Fortunately, while Bethel has so far yielded nothing of this to the spade, Dan has been most obliging, with fascinating results.[91] Excavations have produced a clearly cultic site at the north part of the ancient city, used from the end of the tenth century into Hellenistic times. A Hellenistic temple occupied much of the area of its Hebrew predecessors, with an altar and stairway up to the temple proper following broadly the layout of the eighth-century altar and steps up to a *bamah* (raised platform) and its shrine, which in turn succeeded the sequence of buildings of the tenth-ninth centuries, also having "religious" associations archaeologically: altars, ashes of burnt bones, and shovels and bowl (as at Solomon's temple; cf. 1 Kings 7:40). A bilingual text (Greek and Aramaic) on a tablet from the Hellenistic precinct says: "To the God who is in Dan, Zoilos (made) a vow," thus confirming at one blow the identity of the site with Dan and the sacral nature of this part of it. It may well be the high place and shrine established by Jeroboam I and maintained by his successors. If so, the remains show quite mixed interests culturally. These include some Egyptian-style figurines like kings or gods, vessels showing Phoenician influence, and use of the snake motif on storage jars. But, golden or otherwise, no calves so far! And in fact, nothing either Yahwistic or clearly non-Yahwistic inscriptionally among the limited remains.

(b) A Visionary Prophet of the Jordan? The Tell Deir Alla Text

In the greatest contrast to Dan stands Tell Deir Alla. Here a settlement flourished during the Middle and Late Bronze Ages and through the Iron Age into Persian times, roughly from 1800 to 400. The Late Bronze settlement included a temple with rich foreign connections on the north side of the site — perhaps specifically for visitors (like merchants) who stayed over and paid their dues to the local deity, replicating the function of the temple at Tel Mevorakh up by Caesarea, and most likely of the Fosse Temple at Lachish that we visited earlier. Another (Iron Age) analogue we shall meet below.

But in the Iron Age, what is known of Deir Alla is much more strictly domestic and commercial. The only "religious" manifestation of note is a remarkable text written out on the white-plastered surface of a wall, with drawings on an adjoining wall (e.g., a sphinx). There is nothing "religious" about this room in a ninth-century dwelling; benches against the other walls may have served readers of the text as seats. The text is titled "The Book of the Afflictions of Balaam Son of Beor," and has a visionary content.[92] Balaam, for us today, is otherwise known only from the tradition in Num. 22–24, of a seer from Pethor (Pitru) on the Euphrates called in by the Moabites to curse the newly arrived Israelites almost half a millennium earlier. Neither he nor the Balaam of the Deir Alla text are in any way "Yahwist." The language is West Semitic with Aramaic affinities — perhaps a local "Gileadite" patois, as my colleague A. R. Millard once remarked to me. What is it doing here? A question unanswered, and not answerable with certainty. For once, we may offer a piece of pure guesswork. Traditions of Balaam perhaps endured long among the local Moabite/Gileadite communities; a local inhabitant of Deir Alla may have had dreams and visions, and this "book" was the direct result of one of these. Seized with enthusiasm (or terrified urgency?), he quickly wrote down what he had "seen," and had it written on the wall for others to ponder (shortly before ca. 800).

(c) Caravansarai and Ecumenical Center — Kuntillet Ajrud

In northeast Sinai, about thirty miles south of Qadesh-Barnea and outside the normal bounds of ancient Judah, a hill with wells at its foot was selected in the ninth century B.C. as site for a rectangular fortresslike building (with a tower at each corner). Opposite its gatehouse (at the east end) stood a group of three satellite buildings. In terms of its material archaeology (pottery, carbon 14 tests, etc.), it was in use within the later ninth through much of the eighth century overall. The site is close to the intersection of ancient routes from the head of the Gulf of Aqaba (at ancient Eloth) up the Arabah Valley and through northeast Sinai through to the Mediterranean, to reach such places as Gaza in south Canaan (for the Levant) or El-Arish (en route for Egypt). The ancient Judean (and/or Israelite) authorities may have established it for communications purposes.[93]

Such a find is of value in itself; clearly, it is a way station or caravansarai for merchants, military detachments, or others, from the Aqaba gulf up to Judah, Philistia, or beyond.[94] But there is more to it: the doorway passage from the guardhouse into the fort's inner court was flanked by two narrow side rooms with benches and storage jars *(pithoi)*. The latter in particular bore remarkable sketches of mythological figures, animals and "stick figure" humans, and some even more remarkable jottings in Hebrew and Phoenician. Besides the jars, painted and/or inscribed plaster fragments came from the doorways and walls of the northern side room, and from other points in the fort and in the eastern buildings. The most striking drawings (on "Pithos A") were of two full-face male figures (crowned with plumes or foliage) having tails, with a seated lyre player facing away from them at their right (fig. 48A).[95] This vessel also bears a cow suckling a calf (below the twin figures to the left) and (further round the vessel) a so-called tree of life flanked by ibexes, all above a lion. Careful study showed that the two full-face figures were painted on separately; added later, one of the inscriptions runs across the plumes of the one on the left. The other texts are in no way aligned meaningfully with any of the drawings; all the texts are written much more finely than the drawn pictures.

But it is the texts that have excited most comment. On a large stone offering bowl there runs in Hebrew around the edge: "Belonging to Obadiah son of Adnah, blessed be he by YHWH." Another vessel was for (or by) "Shemaiah son of Ezer." But Hebrews were not the only visitors. One badly damaged Phoenician text (no. 2) offers in fragments: ". . . blessed be their day(s); and may they swear/and they swore . . . ; may YHWH deal kindly . . ."; and two splinters, ". . . they give to . . ."; ". . . Asherat. . . ." Another (no. 3, line 2) mentions: ". . . blessed be Baal, on the day of figh[ting]. . . ." Clearly, one expects Phoenicians to invoke their own god and goddess, Baal and Asherat, and they might well also invoke the Hebrew deity YHWH as local deity of the place.

Quite another matter was the Hebrew texts on the decorated *pithoi*. The one (damaged) written over the headdress of one of the full-faced figures ends with "I (have) bless(ed) you by YHWH of Samaria, and by Asherat." This is no fluke. A fuller text has: "Amariah says: 'Say to my master, "Is it well with you?" I bless you by YHW[H of . . .] and by Asherata/his Asherat. May he bless you and keep you and be with my maste[r . . .]!'" A third Hebrew text and fragment run: "All that he desires of (any)one, (such) favor [be his? . . .]. And YHW(H) shall give to him according to his desire"; "by YHWH of Teman, and Asherata/his Asherat." In these texts, it is a moot point whether the final *h* attached to "Asherat" is simply a vowel letter ("Asherata"), which is grammatically superior, or a suffix, "his," which would not be expected attached to a divine name, either in Hebrew or almost anywhere else in the ancient Near East. We never hear of "Osiris and his Isis" in Egypt, for example, or others such.[96]

That YHWH the god of Israel should be associated with the goddess Asherat or Asherah from pagan Canaan and Phoenicia initially caused quite a stir. And not least when the suggestion was pressed that the two full-faced figures were representations of YHWH, and the lyre player, of Asherah with him. Very exciting! But is it really all so surprising in the light of innumerable biblical statements about foreign cults in Israel and Judah, and even in the Jerusalem temple? Or in the light of the often vehement denunciations of Hebrew affection for such alien cults, by the prophets? Surely not. For Israel, we read that Omri of Israel (like his predecessors) honored "worthless idols" (1 Kings 16:26). And that, having married the Phoenician princess Jezebel, Ahab of Israel built an entire temple of Baal in Samaria, with all appropriate service and its altar, plus he installed Asherah too (probably in the guise of her symbol; 1 Kings 16:31-33). So, if Israelite travelers aped their kings in worship, it is no wonder at all that they here scribbled their dedications in accord with royal usage — precisely, for YHWH and Asherat; only Baal is missing here, but Hosea knew of his calf in Samaria (Hos. 8:5-6; 13:1). And others protested too. Among such, Micah fulminated against idols and images, including Asherah (1:7; 5:13-14).

However, the full-face images are undoubtedly not a form of YHWH, but of the Egyptian household god Bes in Levantinized form (figs. 48A, B). Apart from the goddesses Astarte and Anath (and as Qadishtu) — and so named! — deities do *not* normally appear full faced in the Levant (or in Egypt). And YHWH and Bes have nothing in common. The lyre player has been treated as feminine (hence as Asherah), but of this there is no proof whatever; the headgear is a familiar form of Egyptianizing close-fitting *male* cap, as others have pointed out. So we do not have here any picture of YHWH and Asherah. The "tree of life" could symbolize her, but this also lacks absolute proof. She is also not known to be musical. So we are left with a verbal association in the texts of YHWH and Asherah of a kind that simply fits in with what we learn from 1-2 Kings at the royal level, and with the denunciations of alien worship by the prophets.

(d) And You Can Take Her to Your Tomb! Khirbet el-Qom

In Judah, too, there was lots of juicy paganism going on. At Khirbet el-Qom (probably ancient Makkeda), inscriptions were found in a Judean rock tomb from the eighth (or seventh) century. The main text can be read largely, thus: "Uriah the wealthy(?) wrote it: blessed be Uriah by YHWH; for from his foes, by Asherata/his Asherah, has he saved him — (so, engraved) by Oniah and by Asherata/his Asherah."[97]

Here we are deep inside Judah (never mind cosmopolitan Israel), and the selfsame goddess is cuddling up to YHWH. Like king, like court, and the rest follow, once again. And it was in Judah, in the record in 1-2 Kings. Right from the beginning Solomon had set up foreign cults (1 Kings 11:5-8); Asa cleared out some idols, especially his grandmother's Asherah symbol (15:11-13); Hezekiah and Josiah had general cleanups. The latter, we are explicitly told, removed equipment for the cults of Baal and Asherah from the Jerusalem temple itself

(2 Kings 23:4); so before him, Asherah *was* living in with YHWH (cultically) in his own temple in Judah, as in Israel before. And the prophets did not spare Judah's blushes either (cf. already, references, p. 376 above).

(e) Orthodoxy in the Deep South: Arad and Beersheba

Time for a break from all this torrid cultic promiscuity! A very different story emerges at Arad in the Negev, a southern outpost of Judah in the divided monarchy period (and before), from the eleventh/tenth to the early sixth centuries. Until very recently the dating both of the strata of the entire fort at Arad and of the life span of a small temple within it had become very controversial. But that situation has stimulated Z. Herzog and team to reexamine critically the whole of the material evidence, with fresh and (hopefully) much sounder results. Thus the site was occupied in the eleventh century, while the fortress was founded in the tenth (united monarchy) — and "great Arad" appears in the list by Shoshenq I of Egypt in 925. The fort was maintained and rebuilt until destroyed in the sixth century.

But the temple, we now know, had a much shorter life span. The new results would indicate that it was built in stratum 10 and dismantled again in stratum 9. This would give it a maximum span of use from sometime in the ninth century (not later than ca. 800 at the lowest extreme) down into the later eighth century when it was deliberately dismantled. Thus the suggestion is now made by Herzog that it was abolished during Hezekiah's reform program. This is possible, but it was hardly a "high place," the kind of installation dealt with by Hezekiah (2 Kings 18:3-5).[98] Its cult was that of YHWH, as the ostraca make clear. For this little and short-lived temple of YHWH (local satellite of Jerusalem), the ostraca give names of people linked with priestly/Levitical families: a Meremoth (no. 52), a Joshaphat (no. 53), a Pashhur (no. 54), each on separate tags, as if for casting lots, receiving rations, or the like. One large piece (no. 49) gives accounts for people, including priestly names (Besal, Korah; sons of Gilgal, which had a cult; cf. Amos 4:4; 5:5). And, fittingly, a Zadok as owner of a jug (no. 93).[99] So we catch a glimpse of local temple service, modeled on Jerusalem.

Some bowls (nos. 102-104) carried the abbreviation *q. k.*, standing for "Holy, (for) the priests" (*qedesh [le]-kohanim*). Others are known with just *qadesh*, "holy." Several times found in domestic contexts (usually eighth century, so far), they have been identified as used for Levites or priests taking the lesser category of sacrificial foods as their portion (cf. Lev. 22:3-16).[100] Thus we would have Leviticus-type usage well before the Babylonian exile.

Another such bowl is known, inscribed simply for "your brother." It is a simple "begging bowl"; food might be placed in it for a poor man, in the spirit of the covenant laws for caring for poor citizens, as with produce in Exod. 23:10-11, Lev. 25:6-7, 35, and Deut. 14:28-29 and 26:12-13. Social care and justice can be illustrated by archaeology, too.[101]

At Beersheba we are not so fortunate in discoveries as at Arad. But the finding of the blocks of a once-large altar, dismantled and reused for other purposes, suggests that here too there had been an analogous sanctuary, also dismantled, and in the later eighth century.[102] Another victim of Hezekiah's cleanup? Quite possibly. And Mesha looted a YHWH shrine at Ataroth in Moab.

(f) The Silent (Yahwist) Majority in Judah?

Not everybody in monarchical Judah was galloping off to worship exotic foreign gods all the time. Two lines of archaeological data illustrate this, both implicitly and explicitly.

(1) Lack of Foreign Amulets among the Peasantry

Recent surveys of Palestinian sites in quest of Egyptian religious artifacts during the united monarchy have shown that genuinely Egyptian scarabs and suchlike amulets are very largely missing from within the borders of Israel and Judah, almost totally from the Judean highlands.[103] In short, the basically Yahwistic country, farm, village, and small-town folk had no need of Egyptian exotica on which to focus their religious devotion; YHWH (and a touch of Baal and Asherah in some cases) would be sufficient for their inner needs. Trade with Egypt in exotic things was a matter for royal courts, not country folk. Conversely, the recent listings show that most imported scarabs, etc., actually found come from the coastal zone of Canaan and adjoining sites, inhabited by Philistines, late Canaanites, and other groups, not least on trade routes to and from Egypt itself, following on Late Bronze Age cultural tradition.

(2) What's in a Name?

Particularly in the eighth and especially seventh–early sixth centuries (but sometimes going back earlier), we have an abundance of personal stamp seals (and sometimes clay impressions or bullae) engraved with the names of Israelites and Judeans. Many names are "theophoric"; that is, they incorporate a deity's name in the personal name, like Micaiah, "who is like YH(WH)?" or Michael, "who is like El?" On Hebrew seals the vast majority of such names incorporate an abbreviated form of YHWH such as *yhw, yh,* or *yw.* Incredibly few parents in Israel or Judah named their offspring after foreign gods; use of *baal* is ambiguous, because it could stand for either the god Baal or simply for the common noun "lord, master." Thus the name Baal-hanan may mean "Baal is gracious" or "the Lord is gracious." Much the same situation applies to names found in the groups of inscribed ostraca of the monarchy period; whether from Samaria or Arad (both eighth century) or Lachish (early sixth century), theophoric compounds are, again, normally formed with YHWH/El.[104] Needless to say, names can be given for nonreligious or even perfunctory reasons. Parents might name a boy after his grandfather, uncle, or close friend, or in nickname fashion. Thus the religious affiliation of personal names is *not* a total guide to what the givers or bearers actually believed; but it does indicate the groundswell of ruling tradition and convention.

(g) Milkmaids and Minizoos

During the later monarchy period, ancient Judean sites and settlements were plagued with a horde of small feminine figures of baked clay (almost a thousand are known so far). The majority of them support with their hands (and offer) overlarge breasts; rare examples are shown pregnant or nursing an infant. It seems reasonably likely that these were treasured by Judean women wanting children. But the precise nature and identity of these pieces cannot (as yet) be settled. They may simply be large amulets or talismans (they are only about five or six inches high generally), household lucky charms that would-be mothers might fondle wistfully while asking YHWH for the gift of children.[105] However, it is often suggested that these figurines specifically represent a mother goddess, to whom people anxiously turned for this special need. Either view is possible. It is then commonplace to identify the proposed "mother goddess" with one or more of our old friends Anath, Astarte, or in particular Asherah. As recent reassessment has made clear, Anath and Astarte are nonstarters in playing mother goddess; sex and (human) fertility are not their specialisms. Asherah might be different (she had lots of children in Ugaritic mythology), particularly if she also turned out to be the mysterious "queen of heaven" (Jer. 7:18; 44:17-25); that would be consistent with her role otherwise in the paganizing practices of Israel and Judah during the monarchies.

In reforms like those of Hezekiah and especially Josiah, in purifying the Hebrew cult of YHWH of alien elements (especially in Jerusalem), a large amount of such material was cleared out or destroyed. At Jerusalem itself, near the temple area, Dr. Kenyon stumbled upon a cave in which she found a cache of over 350 such female figures. With W. G. Dever, it is tempting to see this as evidence of the Josianic reforms in action, with deliberate burial of all these unwanted pieces. It had good precedent, as a means of disposing unwanted religious objects; Jacob took such action (Gen. 35:4), and Joshua invited such dumping at his covenant-renewal ceremony (Josh. 24:23). Significantly, all this later clutter had disappeared from Judean usage once the Jews returned from Babylon in the Persian epoch.[106]

And minizoos? As others have noticed, we have very few male figurines but plenty of small animal ones, which include horses, bulls, even chickens, and men riding horses. Besides occurring in settlements, many come from tombs. Their significance is not clear, and may vary with context. Some may have been just toys for the kids; some, emblems made by a farmer to illustrate his prayer to YHWH (or others) for good fortune in his animal husbandry; others, for religious purposes not evident now, given the lack of texts bearing on them. So they can teach us very little at present.

(h) Qitmit and Ein-Hazeva — Edomite, Judean, or What?

On a hilltop (Qitmit) some ten kilometers south from Tel Arad, a triple building was found, next to which was a rectangular high place, and an altar and basin in an oval enclosure. This was clearly a shrine, and produced Iron II pottery, while sheep and goat bones were evident. Painted pottery common to the Negev and Edom turned up, plus a remarkable head with a crown and three horns — a goddess? And a male head, and animal figurines.[107] Meanwhile, down south at Ein-Hazeva near the Arabah, beside a seemingly Judean fort, a set of smashed pottery offering stands, etc., was found in a pit, near a small structure, possibly the remains of a shrine. The finds show affinities with Qitmit and with finds in Edom — e.g., at Buseirah.[108] The two lots have been labeled Edomite, but this has been contested. What *is* clear is that the cult figures and human-form stands are *not* remotely of Judean, Moabite, Ammonite, Phoenician, or Philistine design. In the Old Testament, Edom *was* a matter of concern at this time, and ostraca from Arad and Horvat Uza show this also. That the deity Qos was Edomite fits the locations where his name is found; he, too, was *not* Moabite (Chemosh), Ammonite (Milcom), or in any way Palestinian or Levantine. He should be regarded as Edomite, and these shrines as most likely so.[109] At Yahwistic Arad, for example, nothing remotely similar was found, and there is no other "Negev" culture known to account for such peculiar materials.

4. A PROPHETIC BALANCE SHEET

First, the phenomenon of prophecy is common to the Old Testament and the surrounding Near East. At all periods when data are available, prophets could intercede with deity for others, they could be inquired of, and they might be ecstatic; above all, they acted as spokespeople (men and women alike) from deity to kings, leaders, and communities, often with the future in view for good or ill. Their words were reported accurately and in writing, promptly, to the relevant folk, as the ancient Near Eastern data make very clear; there is no scope for tendentious oral "transmission" by imaginary schools of "disciples," long after the messages had lost their first impact. Prophecies could be reported or archived, grouped in letters or collections; from this it was a short step for prophets and others to compile books, for ongoing consultation, in terms of verifying fulfillments and preaching social principles.

Second, classic Israelite prophets of the early first millennium did not start from nowhere. They in effect recalled Israel and Judah to their ancestral covenant as from Sinai, which made of them the subjects of a *sole sovereign*, their god YHWH. Like other kings, he required their exclusive allegiance, not shared with other deities, hence a basic monotheism — something already "in the air" in the fourteenth/thirteenth centuries B.C., with older roots. During the settlement period the Hebrews compromised in practice, then in concept, by admitting other deities also, in breach of covenant. Thus the prophets recalled Israel to an *existing*, former covenant; they were not imposing something *new*, or nobody would have listened. The scope of Hebrew compromise with worship of such deities as Baal or Asherah is perfectly clear in the Hebrew text, and is well highlighted by archaeological finds both artifactual and inscriptional, which give us a vivid glimpse of life as it actually was being lived. We can see at first hand something of what the prophets opposed and were shouting about.

CHAPTER 9

Back to Methuselah — and Well Beyond

Hitherto, all the way back through time, from the Persian Empire of the sixth to fourth centuries B.C. to the setting of the patriarchs following on from roughly 2000 B.C., we have traveled through epochs of whose closely historical nature there can be no doubt, given the large amount of written data from often impressive sites and abundant artifacts of distinctive styles. In biblical matters there is also a clear sequence back, from the contemporaries of Ezra and Nehemiah through the divided monarchy (many external correlations) to the campaign of Shoshenq I of Egypt and early mentions of David as a dynastic founder. From the eleventh back to the nineteenth centuries, we now have good, external, background data that provide unmistakable settings for the Joshua-Judges period, for the dating of the Sinai covenant (and minimally for the exodus before it), and for the likeliest context of the patriarchs from Terah and Abraham down to Joseph.

But in Gen. 1–11, before Terah and Abraham left Ur, we will find ourselves in a very different, and wider, world. Outside the Hebrew Bible, in the ancient Near East, we have a further thousand years of emerging and increasingly coherent history in both Egypt and Mesopotamia and (in the second half) in Syria and Anatolia also. Beyond roughly 3000, going back to the beginnings of recognizable human civilization toward roughly 10,000 or 9,000 B.C., we today can see (through archaeological endeavor) the unfolding of successive cultures and periods of change before writing gave an explicit voice to the very ancients.

But before that, the "human" story tails back into multimillennia of which we know less, and of which one may well ask which (and what) are humans proper and which (or what) are simply humanlike "hominids." In being able to behold these vast perspectives — like viewing the universe today through powerful telescopes — we are very privileged people, enjoying what was in practice barely beginning to be possible even 250 years ago, and totally impossible in the centuries and millennia before our "modern times." The ancients *did* know about "prehistory," but they necessarily had a simpler and very different conception of it, as we shall see. Gen. 1–11 shared the view of the ancients, being ancient itself. So, once more and for the last time in our present journey, we will again examine first the actual physiognomy and contents of the biblical account, and then its wider literary, conceptual, and archaeological context.

1. GENESIS 1:1–11:26 OVERALL

If we take time to read this text attentively, the following profile emerges clearly.

1. Creation
   A. Universal (1:1–2:3)
   B. Particular (2:4-25, humans paired; 3, estrangement from deity)
      Then
2. First Succession of Generations. In two parallel lines:
   Adam via Cain down to Lamech I and his progeny (4)
   Adam via Seth down to Noah and his progeny (5)
3. Crisis and Judgment — the Flood
   Estrangement between deity and humanity comes to a head (6–9)
   Then
4. Second Succession of Generations
   Divisions (sons of Noah, 10), and lesser crisis (Babel, 11:1-9)
   Shem's line down to Terah and his sons (11:10-26)
(5. "Modern Times." Terah's family (11:26), with its history to follow (11:27ff.)
   From this basic outline there emerges a basic framework:

Creation . . . *generations* . . . **Crisis (flood)** . . . *generations* . . . ("**Now**")

Or, in depth-tabulation,

Creation
↓
generations
↓
Crisis (flood)
↓
generations
↓
("**Modern times**")

2. LITERARY CONTEXTS FOR GENESIS 1–11 OVERALL

Both the framework-design and the contents of Gen. 1–11 find analogies in the rich literary heritage from the ancient Near East, a fact known ever since tablets of a "Babylonian Creation" and a "Babylonian Flood" came to light in the later nineteenth century. However, since those heady pioneering days, much more has become known, enlarging the whole perspective in this sphere.[1]

A. OVERALL LITERARY FRAMEWORK

A series of lists and narratives combine to exhibit a profile of "primeval protohistory" clearly similar to what we find in Gen. 1–11, as follows:

1. *Sumerian King List* (full version), circa eighteenth century, dynasties before/after the flood.[2]
2. *Atrahasis Epic.* Narrative circa eighteenth century at latest, and probably composed earlier.[3]
3. *Sumerian Flood Tale* (or *Eridu Genesis*). About 1600. Narrative, damaged.[4]

All these Mesopotamian sources belong to the second millennium, and specifically were composed during its first half (ca. 2000-1600). In succeeding ages these texts (or some of them) continued to be recopied down to the seventh century B.C.; this was a merely replicative process, just as we continue to reprint old classics such as Chaucer, Shakespeare, or Milton today, which is simply edited replication, not creative writing. Significantly, no further literary works of this kind seem to have been composed in Mesopotamia after circa 1600. The full *Epic of Gilgamesh* began its career in the early second millennium (Old Babylonian version), but its fragmentary state prevents us from knowing whether it had already taken over its flood episode from Atrahasis by then. Certainly this was true of the later "Standard Version" of the epic, produced by the Babylonian literary scribe Sin-liqe-unninni a century or two before or after 1000. The "takeover" was limited to the flood episode; nothing more was taken from Atrahasis. So it did not affect the framework tradition of which the flood was a part.[5]

Thus, within about 1900-1600, a firm tradition having the framework of creation, then crisis (flood), then to later times was to be found in three Mesopotamian works, with which in literary terms Gen. 1–11 belongs, as a fourth example, after which the genus is no longer cultivated, merely the existing pieces recopied. We may tabulate.

Table 34. The Four "Primeval Protohistories"

Sumerian King List	Atrahasis Epic	Eridu Genesis	Genesis 1–11
1. Creation assumed; kingship came down from heaven	1. Creation assumed; gods create humans to do their work	1. Creation; cities are instituted	1. Creation (1–2)
2. Series of eight kings in five cities	2. Noisy humans alienate deities	2. [Alienation]	2. Alienation (3), genealogies (4–5)
3. The flood	3. The flood; ark	3. The flood; ark	3. Flood; ark (6–9)
4. Kingship again; dynasties follow to	4. New start	4. New start	4. New start; then genealogies, down to
5. "Modern times"	(5. Modern times, implied)	(5. Modern times, implied)	5. "Modern times"

("Modern times" = about beginning of second millennium)

The overall correlation of the primeval protohistory in all four sources should be clear almost without further comment. The non-"dynastic" nature of Atrahasis and Eridu accounts for their unconcern with dynasties or genealogies; the passage of time is simply part of the narrations.

B. CREATION NARRATIVES

The individual themes of creation and flood (separate from the framework already discussed) recur in other writings. Thus the Babylonian epic *Enuma Elish* (called "Babylonian Creation" in most books), completed by circa 1000 from older sources, has been repeatedly compared with Gen. 1–2.[6] But despite the reiterated claims of an older generation of biblical scholars, *Enuma Elish* and Gen. 1–2 in fact share no direct relationship. Thus the word *tehom/thm* is common to both Hebrew and Ugaritic (north Syria) and means nothing more than "deep, abyss." It is *not* a deity, like Ti'amat, a goddess in *Enuma Elish*. In terms of theme, creation is the massively central concern of Gen. 1–2, but it is a mere tailpiece in *Enuma Elish*, which is dedicated to portraying the supremacy of the god Marduk of Babylon. The only clear comparisons between the two are the inevitable banalities: creation of earth and sky before the plants are put on the earth, and of plants before animals (that need to eat them) and humans; it could hardly have been otherwise! The creation of light before the luminaries is the only peculiarity that might indicate any link between the Hebrew and

Enuma Elish narrative; but where did it earlier come from? Not known, as yet. Thus most Assyriologists have long since rejected the idea of any direct link between Gen. 1–11 and *Enuma Elish*,[7] and nothing else better can be found between Gen. 1–11 and any other Mesopotamian fragments.

C. THE FLOOD: LITERARY CONTEXT

Here the basic contents are common to both the Mesopotamian and Genesis accounts. So we have in both: a flood sent as divine punishment; one man enjoined to build an "ark"; he taking family and living creatures; and his survival. In detail the differences are so numerous as to preclude either the Mesopotamian or Genesis accounts having been copied directly from the other. We may list the following: (1) The Mesopotamian gods sent the flood simply because they could not stand the noise made by humanity, whereas YHWH had moral reasons (humanity's sins, wrongdoing) for sending it. (2) The Mesopotamian gods hid their plan from all humanity, only one man being clandestinely told by a friendly deity, whereas YHWH directly commanded one right-living man to build a boat. (3) The respective boats differ totally; Noah's has shiplike proportions, but the Mesopotamian one was a cube! (4) The lengths of duration of the respective floods differ, with no Mesopotamian account or timing of the abatement of the flood. (5) A much greater range of folk people the Mesopotamian craft (pilot, craftsman, etc.), unlike Noah, who takes aboard family only. (6) The details of sending out birds differ entirely between the two accounts. (7) The Mesopotamian hero leaves the ark on his own initiative, then offers a sacrifice to appease the gods (they were at first angry at one man's escape). But Noah stayed put in his boat until his deity called him out, and Noah's sacrifice was of thanksgiving, as he was accepted already. (8) The land in Mesopotamia was replenished by direct divine activity in some measure; but in Gen. 9 it is left to Noah, family, and surviving creatures to get on with the job by natural means.[8]

So, an epochally important flood in far antiquity has come down in a tradition shared by both early Mesopotamian culture and Gen. 6–9, but which found clearly separate and distinct expression in the written forms left us by the two cultures. In terms of length and elaboration, Gen. 6:9–8:22 might be equal in amount to about 120 lines in Sumerian or Akkadian. Contrast the lengths of at least 370 lines in Atrahasis II-III, some 200 lines in Gilgamesh tablet XI, and the roughly 150/200 lines in the Sumerian account. Genesis thus offers a more concise, simpler account, and *not* an elaboration of a Mesopotamian composition. As to definition, myth or "protohistory," it should be noted that the Sumerians and Babylonians had no doubts on that score. They included it squarely in the middle of their earliest historical tradition, with kings before it and kings after it, the flood acting as a dividing point in that tradition, from long before 1900. Floods per se were a commonplace in the "Land of the Two Rivers," so why this fuss about a flood? Presumably because, in folk memory, there had been a particularly massive one, far more fatal than most, and the memory stuck ever after, until finally it entered the written tradition. Assyriologists have no problem on this score. After reviewing the Early Dynastic period in Mesopotamia, for example, Hallo argued for a reality of this kind at circa 2900; such a "primordial" happening was also propounded by Mallowan, Raikes, and Kramer.[9]

D. A BABEL OF TONGUES, GENESIS 11:1-8

Near the end of our extant Gen. 1–11 framework occurs the intriguing presentation of the division of human language, after humans had tried to build their way into heaven, so to speak. The tower of brick, with use of bitumen, is reminiscent of Mesopotamia's ubiquitous use of mud-brick architecture on the grand scale, and not least of its famous temple towers, the *ziggurats*. The topic of the division of languages is itself very old. It early found expression in a passage in the epic Sumerian story of Enmerkar, king of Sumerian Uruk, and the distant lord of Aratta (in Iran), in a nineteenth/eighteenth century composition relating to a king of circa 2600. The passage in question harks back to a "golden age" of peace and harmony when "the whole universe, to people in unison(?), to (the god) Enlil in one tongue did speak. Then (the god) Enki, lord of plenty, . . . Lord of Eridu, changed the speech in their mouths, and set up contention in it, (even) in the speech of man that had been one."[10] Thus the themes of language division and contention were old, and could be included within a larger narrative, as is the case in both Enmerkar and Gen. 1–11.

E. DATING OF THE MAIN PRIMEVAL PROTOHISTORY, GENESIS 1–11

Given the noncomposition of this type of fourfold and fivefold narrative framework after about 1600, it is logical to suggest that the framework and basic content of Gen. 11 goes back to the patriarchal period, and came as a tradition with the patriarchs westward from Mesopotamia.

This would be no isolated happening. In the early second millennium, "cuneiform culture" in terms of scribal use of cuneiform script spread not only to

Syria and Anatolia but round and south into Canaan, to Hazor and even as far south as Hebron, with its seventeenth-century administrative tablet of livestock, offerings, and a king.[11] Wherever cuneiform script and learning went, so did its literary traditions, as many other and later finds amply show. So no objection can be taken to the essence of Gen. 1–11 going westward at this epoch; its written formulation in early Hebrew may then have followed later and independently. The patriarchal tradition would have been passed down in Egypt (as family tradition) to the fourteenth/thirteenth century, possibly then first put into writing, then to the monarchy period and beyond as part of the larger whole with the accounts of the patriarchs to form part of the book that we call Genesis. It is part of the oldest levels of Hebrew tradition, as were the Mesopotamian accounts in their culture.

In biblical terms the Gen. 1–11 account stands in sharpest contrast with the only other extensive Hebrew account of origins, which began from the beginning — by that *indubitably* postexilic writer, the Chronicler, from circa 430 (his mention of grandsons [1 Chron. 3:19-21] of Zerubbabel [of ca. 525] would set him at the late fifth century). It is noteworthy that *he* did not give a later version of creation, fall, and flood, etc., but simply summed up baldly the entire "history" from Adam to Abraham genealogically in just the first part of a chapter (1 Chron. 1:1-28)! Fashions had changed radically between the nineteenth and fifth centuries in this regard as well as in so much else in ancient life.

3. IN THE BEGINNING: OTHER ASPECTS

A. EDEN: PARADISE LOST — AND REDISCOVERED?

(i) The Beginning

Genesis 1:1–2:3 presents a calm, stately vista of creation of the cosmos by one supreme deity, untrammeled by complex mythologies or subplots. After the brief introduction (1:1-2), the "six days of creation" (1:3-31) follow in a common format with minor variations, these segments varying in length according to the needs of each topic — common features in unitary ancient Near Eastern texts, from high antiquity. The fullest and most complex was the last, in which humanity is first introduced, who are to become the main focus within the creation for the rest of the book. Then 2:1 is in effect an internal colophon to the "six days" (1:1–2:1), followed finally by a closing exordium (2:2-3) for deity's "seventh day" of rest from fresh creating. So ends the first main segment of the existing book of Genesis, to be followed by five more with their own headings

("This is the succession of . . . ," 2:4; 5:1 ["document of the succession of . . ."];
6:9; 10:1; 11:10) within the "primeval protohistory" of Gen. 1–11. As we have seen
already (p. 314 above), the rest of the book is also segmented under six such
headings (11:27; 25:12; 25:19; 36:1; 36:9; 37:2).

It is important to note in the first "titled" segment that Gen. 2:4 *is* a literary
unity four times over, and is *not* to be arbitrarily split into 2:4a and 4b, as
nineteenth-century "critical dogma" (and its surviving adherents) would almost
fanatically insist, merely to prop up a purely theoretical literary analysis. First,
2:4 is a unitary heading in itself. Second, 4a and 4b are the two halves of a couplet
or bicolon with close poetic parallelism, and cannot thus be wrenched apart.
Third and fourth, the verse contains a *double* chiasmus, not just a single one. The
simple one is "heaven and earth" in 4a balanced by "earth and heaven" in 4b. The
wider one is the adverb phrase *at the end* of the line in 4a, but a matching adverb
clause *at the start* of the line in 4b. It is literary vandalism to break up so clear and
well formed a literary mini-unit, worthy of the best of Near Eastern stylistics.
Thus we may set it out (small chiasmus, *italic;* wide chiasmus in **bold**):

These are the Succession of *Heaven and earth,* **at their creation,**
  when YHWH-God made *earth and Heaven.*

Then, in 2:5-7, we have three successive couplets (bicola) and a terminal
triplet (tricolon) to complete the first general pericope or paragraph. We set
these out as follows:

2:5 Now, no field plant was yet on earth,
    and no field shrub yet had sprouted up,
    for YHWH-God had not sent rain on earth,
    and man, none to work the ground.
	2:6 So moisture arose from the earth,
	    and it watered the face of the ground.
	2:7 And YHWH-God formed man of dust,
	    and inbreathed his nostrils with life,
	    and man became a living being.

(ii) In Eden

Then, in 2:18, we enter the ever intriguing "Garden of Eden." Very strictly, it is *not*
"the Garden of Eden" at all, but "*a* garden *in* Eden." It has to be grasped very
clearly that the garden was simply a limited area within a larger area "Eden," and
the two are not identical, or of equal area. A realization of this simple but much-
neglected fact opens the way to a proper understanding of the geography of Eden
and its environment. Thus, out of "greater Eden," a river flowed into the garden
(2:10), "to water the garden"; and *at that point* ("there" in Hebrew, *sham*) it was
divided into four "heads." This is a "snapshot"-type view, taken (alas, without

camera, of course!) looking *out* from where the single stream entered the garden, and looking back just *upstream* to the point where four "head" rivers came together to form the single stream that entered the garden. The four headstreams are named: Pishon, Gihon, Tigris, Euphrates.[12] It is the presence of these last two well-known rivers that initially clarifies what was happening here, as their general courses are well known. Both take their rise in the mountains of present-day Turkey (eastern Anatolia) — the Tigris, south-southwest of Lake Van, and the Euphrates, farther northwest of Lake Van. Today they join up in south Iraq to form the Shatt el-Arab to enter the gulf, but this was not always so in antiquity. Thus the "heads" of these two must have been their sources or "headwaters," as we might still say in English. Thus the Gihon and Pishon must have done the same.

The Gihon is next before the Tigris, then the Euphrates, last in the list. So it may be east of the Tigris as the Euphrates is west of that river. The Gihon, we are told (2:13), "winds through all the land of Kush." It should be obvious that this Kush cannot have been Upper Nubia in East Africa, most of two thousand miles away to the southwest of the Tigris zone, or Kushu/Kushan in Edom, almost eight hundred miles west. But directly east of the Tigris, through the mountains of western Iran, various rivers flow either west or south, ending up in the Tigris, or in the marshes by the Shatt el-Arab, or in the latter, or in the gulf. Best contenders here for the name Gihon would be either the Kerkheh River or (better, perhaps) the Diz plus Karun Rivers. The land of "Kush," as others have suggested long ago, would be the land of the Kassites (Kashshu), in western Iran, whence these rivers take their rise; Nimrod "son" of Kush reigned in Mesopotamia, in Gen. 10:8-12.

So far, so good. The Pishon has long proved a tougher nut to crack, until recently. It cannot well lie farther east, beyond the Gihon (Karun or Kerkheh systems), especially as it is linked in Gen. 2:11 with the gold-bearing land of Havilah. The latter occurs in Gen. 10:7, 29, in Arabian contexts (with Sheba, Ophir; cf. p. 118 above, and on Gen. 10, below). It also occurs in a dimension that sets it in the northern half of Arabia, with Ishmael's area from Havilah (going toward Assyria) toward Shur, on Egypt's Sinai border, Gen. 25:18, and likewise for Amalek (successors to Midian) in 1 Sam. 15:7. Such an area is attested in western Arabia, and gold-bearing land south from modern Medina toward modern Hawlan (itself possibly a reflection of ancient *Hawilah*).[13] Torrid north Arabia hardly seemed the setting for a river to rival the other three mentioned. But in very far antiquity, just such a river once existed, and its long-dried course has recently been traced from its rise in the west Arabian goldlands (in Havilah) east and east-northeast toward the head of the gulf, via modern Kuwait. This may well have been the ancient Pishon.[14] If so, the ancient author's enumeration runs counterclockwise, from southwest (Pishon) across east to the Gihon, then north and northwest to the Tigris and Euphrates, in a continuous sweep.

In far antiquity conditions were greatly different in Arabia to what we see now. During the entire period from 70,000 B.C. down to A.D. 1000, Arabia has known alternating "wetter" and "drier" climatic periods, and the gulf has likewise experienced parallel periods of expansion and contraction in its water-cover area (high and low levels). Dates for the sequences of such periods vary among authorities, sometimes widely. For example, Potts charted high sea levels for the gulf (and so, for riverine wet periods) at around 6000/5500, circa 4000/3600, and circa 2500, and lowest sea levels (and drier, inland) at about 7000, 4500, and 200; in his view the original establishment of the river course from Havilah to Kuwait was set in the Pliocene period, some 3 million years ago, when much of Arabia was grassland.[15] Others have worked on this question. Besides Juris Zarins, results have been published summarily by Farouk El-Baz, and by J. Sauer. These scholars posited a global wet phase (including Arabia) during about 7500-3500 (and somewhat after, toward 2000), when this north Arabian river would have flowed. But severe dessication is now attested from about 2200, including in the Levant and Egypt, until improvement about 2000. So we have what may have been a very ancient river from Havilah to the head of the gulf, a Pishon, that would have flowed during about 7500/6500 down to at least 2500/2200 (with dry intervals, perhaps ca. 4500, and less so, 3500), after which it then dried up and vanished forever. So, as for the flood, the folk memory of the Pishon would have been handed down for some 400 years in south Mesopotamian and north Arabian tradition to Old Babylonian times/period of the patriarchs, and transmitted by them along with the overall tradition of creation, time span, crisis flood, time span, to their own epoch. Zarins's Eden would have lain in the area now underwater at the north end of the gulf. Gone forever!

B. THE "TABLE OF NATIONS" —
ALL THE WORLD IS KIN! CF. FIGS. 49, 50

In Gen. 1–2 Adam is humanity without differentiation, but he was then set in a workplace and testing ground (2–3) where he failed. In 4–6 the picture is firmly in the Near East and its environs, with Noah as figurehead. In Gen. 10 the then-known peoples of that considerable area are grouped as "sons" of Noah, the overall figure, and of the three "head" figures and those linked to them; the last place is reserved for Shem, head of the lineage to which the patriarchs' descent was traced. It forms a verbal "atlas" of absorbing interest — at least for those who like poring over records of "faraway places with strange-sounding names"! Such verbal atlases, but not expressed genealogically, are known in Babylonian

430

lists from third-millennium Mesopotamia, in Ebla (for north Syria), in Egypt in the Execration Texts (early second millennium, for Levant and Nubia), and in the great topographical lists of alleged "conquests" and foreign subjects or contacts (middle to late second millennium), for Nubia, the Levant, sometimes out to the Aegean, and even Mesopotamia eastward. However, this is not everyone's favorite pastime, so to keep things mercifully simple we will tabulate the basic data here and banish all the messy references (as ever) to the footnotes, for the curious. By this means known or possible identifications can be presented concisely, and the reasoning behind them, plus the dates — minimally! — from which these places are currently attested. It is only right to stress that future discoveries may well extend back in time the currency of names here dated to "middle" or "late" periods, and may clarify the locations of names still obscure.

Table 35. The Genesis 10 Family
(verse numbers in parentheses)

A. Japhet (Gen. 10:2-5)

3rd Millennium	Early 2nd Millennium	Late 2nd Millennium	Early 1st Millennium	Later in 1st Millennium	Zero (= no date)
		Yawan (2: Javan)			
			Gomer, Madai (2)	Gomer, Madai	Japhet (1-2)
Tibar (2: Tubal)		Tipalu (2: Tubal)	Tubal	Tubal	Magog (2)
		Mushki (2: Meshech)	Muksas		
			Ishkuza (3: Ashkenaz)	Ashkenaz (Scyths)	Riphath (3)
		Tursha (2: Tiras)		Rhodes (4: Rodanim)	Tarshish (4)
	Tegarama	Tegarama (3: Togarmah)			
	Alasia	Alasia (4: Elishah)			
		Kition (4: Kittim)			

B. Ham (Gen. 10:6-20)

3rd Millennium	Early 2nd Millennium	Late 2nd Millennium	Early 1st Millennium	Later in 1st Millennium	Zero (= no date)
Kush (6: Cush A)	Kush (6: Cush A) Kashshu (8: Cush B)	Kush/Kashshu (Cush)	Kush (Cush A) (Cush C: 7)		
		Musr (6, 13: Mizraim)	Musr (Mizraim)		
			Putu (6: Put)	Put (6)	Ham (6)
	Canaan (6, 15-20)	Canaan	Canaan		
			Hawlan (7: Havilah)		
			Ragmatu (7: Raamah)		
			Saba (7: Sheba)	Sabta/ Sabteca? (7), Raamah	Seba (7)
Tidnum?	Ditanu?		Dedan (7: Dedan)		
Babylon (10: Babylon)	Babylon	Babylon	Babylon		
Uruk (10: Erech)	Uruk	Uruk	Uruk		
Akkad (10: Akkad)	Akkad	Akkad	Akkad		
		Shankhara (10: Shinar)			
Ashur/ Assyria (11)	Ashur/Assyria	Ashur/Assyria	Ashur/ Assyria		
(Nineveh)	Nineveh (11)	Nineveh	Nineveh		

(Kalhu)	(Kalhu)	Kalhu (11: Calah)	Kalhu (Calah)		Calneh (10) Rehoboth-Ir (11)
					Resen (12)
		Libu (13: Lehabim)	Libu	Lydia (13: Lud)	Anam (13) Casluhim (13)
		*Naphtuhim (13)			
		*Pathros (14)			
		Philistines (14)	Philistines		
	Kaptara (14: Caphtor)	Kaptara			
		Sidon (15)	Sidon		
	Hittites (15)	Hittites			
	Amurru (16: Amorites)	Amurru			
		Girgish (16: Girgash)			
					Jebus (16) Hivites (17)
	Irqata (17: Arkites)	Irqata	Irqata		
		Siyannu (17: Sinites)			
		Arvad (18)	Arvad		
		Sumur (18: Zemarites)	Sumur		
Hamath (18)	Hamath	Hamath	Hamath		
		Gaza (19)	Gaza		
					Gerar (19) Sodom-Lasha (19)

C. Shem (Gen. 10:21-31)

3rd Millennium	Early 2nd Millennium	Late 2nd Millennium	Early 1st Millennium	Later in 1st Millennium	Zero (= no date)
Elam (22)	Elam	Elam	Elam		
Ashur/ Assyria (22)	Ashur/ Assyria	Ashur/ Assyria	Ashur/ Assyria		
			Lydia (22: Lud)	Lydia/Lud	Lud/Lydia Arphaxad (22) Uz, Hul, Gether, Meshech (23)
(?Aram)	(?Aram)	Aram (22-23)	Aram		
					Shelah, Eber (24-25)
					Peleg, Joktan (25-26)
	Jerah (26)		Hadramaut (26: Hazer-maveth)		
					Almodad, Sheleph (26)
					Hadoram-Abimael (26-28) Jobab (29)
			Saba (28: Sheba)		
					Hawlan (29: Havilah)
					Ophir (29: Ophir)
					Mesha, Sephar (30)

In sum, we may run a head count, remembering that our data will remain incomplete.

For the third millennium we have eleven names for sure that go on into later periods, plus Tidnum (not certainly Dedan), and very early "Arams," disputed.

For the early second millennium we have seventeen names, plus (again) Ditanu (not certainly Dedan), and an early "Aram," disputed.

For the late second millennium we have thirty-five names, strictly thirty-four because Ashur occurs twice (under Ham and Shem). Two names are asterisked, because the forms agree with the date given but are not yet attested in original inscriptions.

For the early first millennium we have thirty-seven names, strictly thirty-five because two (Ashur, Sheba) occur twice (under Ham and Shem).

Later in the first millennium (e.g., 600/500 or so), several names continue in use; only two names, of uncertain attestation (Sabta/Sabteca), may genuinely only be attested this late and may be older, so far as we know (and we know very little, in these two cases!).

That leaves the column "Zero = no date." As they are not attested at all for certain in the external sources, these thirty-nine names are of no chronological significance for the present. Hivites are sometimes considered to be a variant of Horites, who may be Hurrians; if so, then they would have to be added to the second-millennium columns. Gerar, if locatable at Tel Haror, would count for the early-second-millennium-to-first-millennium columns archaeologically but not yet textually. Use of parentheses around some names with no question marks indicates that they are archaeologically attested in the periods concerned but not yet textually.

(i) Dates and Places (in General)

Admitting that what we have is a "minimizing" set of date lines, we may at least set out a correspondingly minimum profile for the literary history of the Table of Nations, as follows (using only date line columns).

0. *Precursors.* Already we have various places "in place" during the third millennium, and thus well established before any feasible date for our document.
1. *Phase I.* From the early second millennium we have seventeen names that form a nucleus, especially under Ham, much less (so far) for Japhet or for Shem (not yet as prominent as was the case later on).

435

2. *Phase II.* From the later second millennium, by about the thirteenth century, we have double the nomenclature (thirty-four basic names), bringing it close to its final extent. Under each "family head" some "younger sons" have been added in, so to speak, updating each group.

3. *Phase III.* Here we again have thirty-four items, but in this period not an identical set, because some older names did not continue and various new names come in ("grandsons," so to speak, in family terms). This situation would suggest a second update in the first millennium, whether just once about the seventh century or in two subphases (IIIa, IIIb) in the tenth and seventh centuries respectively. It is premature to choose dogmatically, given the limits of our existing sources. This result, based entirely on correlations with objective, external data, be it noted, runs remarkably in parallel with the probable literary "history" of the patriarchal narratives: original traditions, early second millennium, updated in late second, and finalized in the first.

(ii) A Broad Overview of the Geography

Here we do a strictly "flying tour," simply for orientation. The details are consigned to the footnotes below.

(a) Japhet

From a Levantine (and even Egyptian) point of view, the groups and places under Japhet are entirely northern, in location or origin — northeast, north, northwest — in Anatolia/northwestern Iran, and the Aegean/eastern Mediterranean (and beyond). Yawan covered the Greeks (Mycenaeans onward),[16] while Tubal[17] and Togarmah[18] were Anatolian places. Into that region came the Meshech (Mushki, Phrygians),[19] Gomer (Cimmerians),[20] Ashkenaz (Scythians),[21] plus the Madai, Medes in Iran.[22] Turning west again, Elishah[23] and Kittim[24] are most likely parts of Cyprus (Alasia, a kingdom; Kition, a town whose name found wider use). Tiras may be the Tursha of the thirteenth/twelfth-century Sea Peoples, and eventually linked with the (E)truscans who ended up in Italy.[25]

(b) Ham

This is by far the longest series. The basic coverage is northeast Africa, Arabia/Levant, and Mesopotamia, with outliers to the north and east. Thus Cush A is modern Nubia, the Nile Valley and its deserts south from the First Cataract, into north Sudan, and to the Red Sea west coast. By transference, Cush C (linked with Arabia) may represent the close links that existed in early antiquity across the Red Sea between Arabia and Africa, and still very visible today in the Tihamah coastal strip of west Arabia. Cush B is in western Iran, and may be represented by the Kashshu, Kassites, who gave a 500-year-long dynasty to Babylonia during the second half of the second millennium.[26] Mizraim, of course, is Egypt, including the northern Delta (Naphtuhim) and south valley (Pathros); she is still Misr today, in Arabic.[27] Lehabim and Put[28] in east Libya are just to her west.

Going north into the Levant, Canaan is a major entity, but is a very different one from that to be seen in the Egyptian imperial sources of the late second millennium and in Joshua (= west Palestine, across to Gilead/Bashan and north to Tyre). This is an *older* "Canaan," embracing the cities of the Mediterranean coast from Sidon up via Sumur (Zemarites) and Irqata (Arkites) to Arvad and Siyannu (Sinites) near Ugarit, plus Hamath inland on the river Orontes, and reaching down to Jebus (Jerusalem).[29] Verses 18-19 look upon the Canaanite southmost reach to Gaza and Gerar and the south end of the Dead Sea as later than the early phase. After the disappearance of Egypt's regime, and the passing impact of the Sea Peoples, the Phoenicians entered a new phase of maritime prosperity along the ancestral Canaanite strip, but *not* including any inland zones; Hamath became "Neo-Hittite" and Aramean (Arameans replacing Amurru/Amorites).

Going farther west, Caphtor is the Kaptara of cuneiform sources, Egyptian Keft(i)u, and is over in Crete, as the evidence of Egyptian tomb scenes (Minoans and Mycenaeans) shows clearly. From over the Mediterranean came the Philistines. Girgashites and "Hittites" come from the north, but in unclear roles here. It is in the east that we need finally look: Mesopotamia appears under its "western" name, Shinar, and here has with it such famous places and regions as Babylon, Akkad, Erech (Uruk), and Assyria with Nineveh and Calah.

Going south, we enter mysterious Arabia. Havilah covers west and north Arabia, probably broadly from Hawlan to the edges of Midian, Edom, and Sinai.[30] Raamah is commonly taken to be Ragmatu (the later Najran, north of Main and Sheba).[31] Dedan was a kingdom based on Al-Ula oasis in northwest Arabia, mentioned by Assyria and in Old Arabian texts.[32] Sheba is the famous kingdom in ancient Yemen, based on Marib, from at least circa 1100 onward.[33] Seba may be an outlier of Sheba, in East Africa (not certain),[34] while Sabta may be Shabwa(t), capital of Hadramaut (cf. below).[35] Sabteca may be in the same area.[36]

(c) Shem

It is notable that several names found under Ham recur under Shem. This may be the way ancient writers could indicate that some regions and communities were "stratified" linguistically, culturally, and perhaps racially — new groups had overlain old, and another language had replaced a previously used one. Thus, in Mesopotamia, the non-Semitic Sumerians had probably replaced still older peoples in the fifth or fourth millennium (at latest), and by the early second millennium they and their language were absorbed and replaced by the Semitic-speaking Akkadians (the later Babylonians and Assyrians). Assyria in both lists would certainly reflect such changes, probably in the third millennium.[37] Elam (in west-southwest Iran) was linguistically non-Semitic throughout, but was heavily influenced by, and involved with, her Mesopotamian neighbors at all periods.

Again we visit Arabia. Hazarmaveth is ancient Hadramaut, the kingdom east of Sheba and Qataban that held the famous incense-growing lands of Dhofar.[38] Havilah was west and north Arabia; cf. Ham above. Ophir was most likely the south end of Havilah, in gold-producing western Arabia.[39] Saba is Sheba; cf. above. Other, more obscure names probably belong here too.

Going back north to center stage, Aram is the Arameans attested from the fourteenth century, and possibly earlier in the area of the west bend of the Euphrates, then later in Syria west and south of there.[40] Lud, as under Ham, may be Anatolian, Lydia.[41]

Thus, in the late second and early first millennia alike, the earliest Hebrew geographers had a wide range of places and peoples in their tradition, and of which they had gained knowledge. What is interesting, also, are the omissions. For example, none of the later Ammon, Moab, or Edom got included, nor Midian nor Amalek; nor their predecessors, such as Shutu ("Sheth") for Moab or Kushu (Kushan) for Edom. Hostility might explain the former omissions, but not the latter. There is another factor that may have played a part — but we cannot prove the point, in the absence of theoretical early recensions (early/late second millennium). That is of the updating of place/group names by substitution. Dan tacitly replaced Laish in Gen. 14:14, for example. So, did Lud (Lydia) similarly replace such as Luku (Lycia) and Arzawa? And so on? This we will almost certainly never know. If so, then the final major phase of composition would have been the late second millennium, with mainly supplementary changes and some additions in the first.

4. GENEALOGICAL "PRE/PROTOHISTORY"

We have looked at the basic framework of Gen. 1–11 and its congruence with the literary vogue for such works in the early second millennium, neither earlier nor later (so far). For a writer or just Johnny Citizen in the sunny summer of the 1900s B.C., the famous flood seemed a very long time away, with those who preceded it, and the creation, aeons away further back in time. In the nineteenth century B.C., "modern" people (for so they would have considered themselves!) frequenting the busy bazaars or writing their tablets or scrolls *knew already* that their world was old, very old. The royal traditions of Egypt in the Twelfth Dynasty then boasted a roster of rulers going back for as many as 100 reigns, back to Menes, uniter of the kingdom, and to shadowy kings of separate north and south lines earlier still, and an age of heroes or blessed spirits and of the rule of the gods themselves for ages before that. Yes, Egypt was already very ancient! The same was true in Mesopotamia. A scribe under (say) Hammurabi could count back through his king lists on clay, through 50 kings to the accession of Sargon of Akkad, and in fact, 71 kings if one included the despised Gutians. The older Sumerian dynasties (even though different lines of city rulers were often contemporaries) counted at least 84 more kings back to the flood, giving 155 rulers back to that event; then 8 or more distant kings back from the flood to the start of kingship (and this, perhaps as part of creation). So Sumer and Akkad too were very ancient in (say) 1800 or 1700. And they were proud of it. Then and later, the second-millennium scribal author of the Epic of Gilgamesh could exclaim of his third-millennium hero, "He built the rampart of Uruk; . . . climb the wall of Uruk, walk around on it, inspect its foundations, examine the brickwork — see, is it not of kiln-fired bricks, did not the Seven sages (of old) lay its foundations?" So the ancients could and did use series of reigns, divine then human, to measure off "official" time through the ages. They were very conscious of a long past, and often proud of its great moments too.

Invented before any meddling sociological anthropologist ever showed up, this "long *durée*" perspective was not unique to Egypt and Mesopotamia. The Hittites acted similarly, with a historical sequence in their royal offering lists, record of pre-Hittite kings (e.g., Anittas, Anum-hirbe), and tales of the days of the gods. In the Levant itself, the king list of Ugarit likewise measured off time in principle through its thirty or more named kings in succession, with traditions going even further back to the assembly of Ditanu and the like. And finally for the Hebrews, as we have seen, their antiquity also was traced far back before Terah and Abraham, also to the flood (as in Mesopotamia, whence they had come to Canaan), and then before it to the creation — all in highly compact form. Where Egypt, Mesopotamia Hatti, or Ugarit had kings, the Hebrews had genealogies. And in the early second millennium the West Semitic ("Amorite") lines of rulers of the dynasties of Hammurabi of Babylon and Shamshi-Adad I of Assyria also resorted to genealogies to trace their line far back before the days of their kingship.

A. LOOKING AT THE LINK LINES IN GENESIS 1–11

(i) The Genealogies Themselves

In Gen. 4 we have a sequence from an individual "Adam" (not just "Man" in general) through his eldest son Cain *(Qayin)*. From Adam to Lamech I's off-spring inclusive runs to eight generations, but is followed no further. In the other succession, through Adam's younger son Seth (Gen. 5), we have an independent and parallel line from Adam to Noah inclusive of ten generations (the latter's sons being an eleventh). Then, after the flood, and leaving aside the Table of Nations and tower of Babel, a third succession runs from Noah's son Shem down to Terah and Abraham inclusive (Gen. 11:10-26), thus for nine/ten generations. Thus the "count" clusters around the eight-, nine-, ten-generation mark.

Within Hebrew and related tradition, such "official" father-to-son sequences can represent the actual facts of life, or they can be a condensation from an originally longer series of generations.

Thus, inside the book of Genesis itself, we have a note of "the children born to Jacob by Zilpah" (46:16-18) which actually includes not only sons (Gad, Asher) but grandsons (Ziphion, Haggi, Beriah, etc.) and great-grandsons (Heber, Malchiel). And likewise "the sons that Leah bore to Jacob" (46:12, 25), with sons (e.g., Judah), grandsons (e.g., Perez), and also great-grandsons (Hezron and Hamul). Thus, within Genesis "sons" can include grandsons and great-grandsons, and is *not* always literal sons. In the early Roman period the Jewish-Greek Gospel of Matthew used both of the conventions observed so far: (i) a limited, representative number of generations (for him, 14 + 14 + 14), and (ii) telescoped sonship to cover son, grandson, great-grandson, and great-great-grandson (Matt. 1:1-17). His "Jehoram fathered Uzziah" (1:8) is shorthand for Jehoram fathered (Ahaziah [2 Kings 8:25], who fathered Joash [11:2], who fathered Amaziah [14:1], who fathered [14:21]) Uzziah. Such an author would have known his Hebrew Bible perfectly well, as would his Jewish contemporaries; but this *abregé* suited his needs. And so, clearly in Gen. 46. And so, perfectly possibly elsewhere too. Thus, in the formal, representative genealogies of Gen. 4, 5, 11, "A fathered B" can be literal; or it may equally stand for "A fathered [P, who fathered Q, who fathered R, who fathered S, who fathered T, who fathered . . .] B." Or in short, for "A fathered (the line culminating in) B." So no exception can legitimately be taken to this view.

Returning to Gen. 1–11, we see the narratives in some cases presupposing immediate fatherhood. See, for example, the wording of Adam-Seth-Enosh in Gen. 4:25-26. But in most cases, one may in principle as easily read the recurrent formulae "A fathered B, and after fathering B lived *x* years" as "A fathered (the line culminating in) B, and after fathering (the line culminating in) B, lived *x* years." Thus we can neither date the flood before Abraham nor the creation before Noah merely by counting the Genesis figures continuously as did the worthy Archbishop Ussher in the carefree days when no evidence from outside the Bible was even imagined, still less thought about or seen. And in the context of that external data, any such literalism fails. If Abraham be set at roughly 2000 B.C., then on those figures the flood would have come in about 2300. But that is about the time of Sargon of Akkad; having been rescued from a river at birth, he would not have been amused by a flood. Worse, his time looked *back* up to 400 years back to Gilgamesh (ca. 2700), for whom in turn in tradition the flood was even more ancient still! So an Ussherite solution is ruled out; the methods of antiquity apply. The date of the flood remains fluid, one might say! As for the date of the creation, why waste time number-crunching when Gen. 1:1 says it all: "In the beginning . . ." — which is soon enough.

(ii) Data from the Neighbors

These phenomena are not peculiar to Gen. 1–11. As we noted, the Sumerian king list has a set of eight kings before the flood (reigning from five different cities), and a long series of (partly contemporary) dynasties after the flood and before Sargon's empire of Akkad.[42] Here Hallo would distinguish three sets of eight generations prior to Sargon's unifying regime.[43] What is noteworthy is the parallel existence of a "main line" and a "skilled" (or technocrat) line in both earliest Mesopotamia and earliest Genesis, in the preflood era. In a tradition also continued in some later epochs, the Mesopotamian sources have a series of the seven sages or counselors alongside the eight prediluvian kings. In Gen. 4 we have, alongside Adam's chosen line through Seth (ten generations), the inventive line (eight generations) of Cain. Here we have Cain the city builder; Jabal the pastoralist; Jubal the music pioneer; and Tubal-Cain the metalsmith. Thus, each in their own way, the Mesopotamian and Hebrew traditions express the ancient concept of a representative generation count in parallel lines of descent. Cf. table 36 on page 442.

441

Table 36. Twin Representative Sequences, Creation to the Flood

Sumer		Genesis	
Kings	Sages	Main Line	Skill Men
Creation	*[Creation]*	*Creation*	*Creation*
1. Alulim (at Eridu)	1. Adapa, "Oannes"	1. Adam	1. Adam
2. Alalgar (Eridu)	2. U'anduga	2. Seth	2. Cain
3. Enmenluanna (Bad-Tibira)	3. Enmeduga	3. Enosh	3. Enoch I
4. Enmengalanna	4. Enmegalaamma	4. Kenan	4. Irad
5. Dumuzi	5. An-Enlil-da	5. Mahalalel	5. Mehujael
6. Enmenduranki (Sippar)	6. Utu-abzu	6. Jared	6. Methushael
7. Ensipazianna (Larak)	7. Enmebuluga	7. Enoch II	7. Lamech I
8. Ubartutu/Ziusudra (Shuruppak)		8. Methuselah	8. Jabal, Jubal & co.
		9. Lamech II	
		10. Noah	
Flood	*Flood*	*Flood*	*Flood*

(iii) Other Related Aspects

First of all, biblical scholars have sometimes succumbed to the temptation to treat the two genealogies of Gen. 4 and 5 as merely variants of one single line. This is clearly a mistake; twin lines, one "main," one of skills, are a hallmark of this particular early "primeval period" tradition. And superficially similar names are not doublets, neither are repeated names. The linguistic content of such pseudopairs as Enoch and Enosh, or Mahalalel and Mehujael, or Irad and Jared, or Methushael and Methuselah absolutely forbids confusing the names concerned. Clearly, different names could be coined in similar formats with different root elements all over the biblical world at all periods. And repetition of names is so all-pervadingly commonplace as to be banal. Analogous phenomena occur in the Sumerian lists cited. Three kings have Enmen-type names, and three sages have Enme-type names, not identical roots or meanings, in varying generations, and two share the terminal element *-duga*. No competent Sumerologist would dream of confusing these different names, which use varying elements within similar syntactical constructions. And neither should biblicists allow themselves to be seduced into such errors with this kind of archaic material in Hebrew.

Second, we find the inclusion of "notes in passing" in Gen. 4, 5, and 10. These are not extraneous, later-added intrusions, as old-style dogma would sometimes insist. This is a regular practice in such lists and compositions. The Sumerian king list exhibits a series of examples of the same sort of thing, as part of its overall format. We find such notes with Etana, Enmebaragisi, Meskiaggasher, and Gilgamesh. Lugalbanda is called a shepherd, another (before Melam-annak) is a smith, and even a barmaid ruled (Ku-baba). And so on.

B. HOPELESSLY OUTNUMBERED — THE 43,000-YEAR QUESTION

(i) Some Biblical and Allied Details

No reader of Gen. 1–11 could possibly miss noticing the very long lives attributed to Abraham's ancestors before and after the flood, down to Terah his father. Most famous, of course, is the "daddy" of them all, Methuselah, at 969 years (5:27). But when compared with the pretensions of archaic Sumerian royalty, Methuselah would not rate as even a spring chicken — more just a gleam in the eye! The Sumerian "Methuselah" was the second king of Bad-Tibira, Enmenluanna, who reigned a fabulous 43,200 years in the Sumerian king list. Close runners-up were Alalgar (36,000 years), Alulim (28,800 years), and his own successor Enmengalanna (ditto), and that healthy shepherd Dumuzi at 36,000 years.[44] After the flood, numbers are not so high. Two kings reigned a more modest 1,200 and 1,560 years, while others sank to the 900-to-600-year category or even less. This phenomenon after the flood is true also in Gen. 1–11; after Noah and Shem (old stock), figures for their successors soon sank from about 500 to 200 years and less.

Also, before the flood, people seemingly lived a long time *before* having offspring, as well as afterward. But after the flood (and Shem), people became quicker off the mark at having a family from quite young years, almost like us (at 35, 30, 34, 30, 32, 30, 29, from Arpachsad to Nahor I); only tough old Terah left things a bit late till he was 70, they say.

Where do such figures come from, in either tradition, with their distinctive and shared characteristics? Naturally such questions are not easily answered. This long-life trend is also shared with Egypt in her predynastic (= prehistoric) tradition, before the pharaohs ruled from Menes onward — witness the figures given for the reigns of gods, demigods, etc., in Manetho and in the Turin Canon a thousand years before him.[45] External evidence from burials of all periods all over the biblical world and beyond would indicate that most people died in their sixties or seventies at the latest (and most often, much younger). What was going on?

(ii) Accounting for Pre- and Protohistory, Then and Now

The question just asked has been quite a poser for a long time now. Nor is a full, definitive, factual answer possible. Some factors, however, may help us along the way in investigating so intriguing and curious a question. By 2000 B.C. (and even before) people knew that their world was already old, as already mentioned, and they sought to render account of what we now would call prehistory (no written records) and protohistory (oral tradition and beginnings of a written record) using what resources they possessed.

By contrast with their position (and everyone else's until about 250 years ago), we now have different tools to do the same job. Taking its cue from geology, using the sequences of successive rock strata to denote the passing of very early time, archaeology has developed analogous techniques. When buildings fell or were demolished to build anew, especially in mud brick, the people who did it left successive layers as witness to their ongoing occupation on through time. If excavated layers could be correlated with inscriptions, historical dates could be assigned to them. Study of the changing fashions in material goods and their technologies led to the setting up of a sequence of "epochs," on a scheme of the use of stone (Paleolithic, Mesolithic, Neolithic), of stone and some copper (Chalcolithic), then of copper and bronze (Bronze ages, often subdivided into Early, Middle, and Late), then an Iron Age, usually correlatable with historical periods either locally or further away. Naturally, this is a terribly broad sketch, and alternative designations exist in some areas; and the names do not fit the cultural sequences in all cases. In this past half-century, science-based methods have given us further methods of "absolute" dating: carbon 14 determinations, dendrochronology (counting tree rings), and the like. So, when we are able to benefit from close and accurate observations in all these modes of investigation, we are privileged indeed to be able to decipher the saga of humanity's career on this planet on a scale and with such detail that could not have been dreamed of in any earlier age. We take it all too much for granted, already, and ought to be much more grateful for it than we are!

The ancients had no such sophisticated tools; after all, they were pioneers just in establishing viable and increasingly acceptable modes of living life itself!

444

So, to cover vast epochs, they used their one real resource: the human life span, and the ongoing succession of life spans, reaching as far back as anyone could know. The flood was a long time back, and they had some record of a good number of kings or ancestors reaching back in that direction, but probably (it seemed) not enough. Before the flood, their existing tradition back toward the still longer-distant creation was (if anything) shorter and still less adequate to cope. Thus the truly vast, aeonlike reigns of the mere eight kings of preflood, postcreation Sumer had a job to do: to fill that great conceptual gap. The awesome generations of Noah's preflood ancestors served in a similar role. And in Egypt the concept found a parallel answer too (but not linked with a flood). However, figures had to be produced, and were.

(iii) Going for the Jackpot

But whence came these figures? Pure whimsy from arbitrary invention is an obvious and easy answer that will appeal to many; and of course, it might be correct. However, modern scholars have occasionally been tempted to go a little deeper than that. And there are a few factual clues that may justify our doing the same. But BE WARNED! We are now entering a zone of speculation, far less solidly factual than anything you have read so far (but not for too long). If we turn to the Sumerian King List, at column iv:40, 45-46, there are curious entries for reigns, described by its editor Jacobsen as marked by glosses: "6 × 60" written in twice, for 6 or 6 + x years, for the king and dynasty of Hamazi.[46] For this mode of expression, one should also compare the same format applied in the text at iv:45-(46), for the reign of the first king of Uruk, as "1 × 60 years," (gloss) "2 × 60 years," and finally "7 years." In other words, a scribe could conceive of ancient "heroic" kings as having reigns in which 60 times a figure could provide "heroically" long reigns to fit their status and cover time. The Mesopotamian mode of reckoning was sexagesimal; i.e., it operated with tens and sixties (much as we are decimal, using a base of tens). That was in about 2000; but such a concept was still alive and well in the third century B.C. in Babylonia. Drawing upon documents such as our king list, Berossus of Babylon "wrote in terms of *saroi* and *neroi* and *sossoi*." These are stated to be of 3,600, 600, and 36 years respectively. The first term is recognized as the Sumerian *sar*, for "3,600" when used as a numeral. The others are not determined yet in cuneiform. The ensuing primordial king list lists reigns as of so many *saroi* — of 3, or 13, or 18 or 10 or 8, etc., *saroi*, respectively.[47] In short, these look like "real" (or realistic) reigns that have been drastically bumped up through multiplying them by 3,600, to give heroically long reigns for the period betweeen creation and flood.

That process can perhaps be reversed. Our scribes in 2000 B.C., faced with few kings and long periods, may have bumped up the numbers by using sexagesimal multipliers. So, at Hamazi and Uruk, reversing the process, we might take the 36,000 years of Alalgar or of Dumuzi and divide it by the factor 10 × 60 (600), which would give them each a reign of 60 years. Applied to Alulim's (and others') 28,800 years, he (and they) would have reigned 48 years; then Enmenduranna of Sippar at 21,000 years would have reigned 35 years. The mighty Enmenluanna at 43,200 years (the local Methuselah) would come out at 72 years — high but not impossible, even if it left Ramesses II (66 years) and Queen Victoria (64 years) just slightly jealous — but more modest than the 94 years of Pepi II, often granted. The more modest Ubartutu at 18,600 years comes out at 31 years, eminently reasonable. The principal works for all the preflood rulers, and no awkward fractions, etc., are left over. After the flood, reigns are still high, until suddenly Gilgamesh's son Ur-nungal (no longer heroic?) reigns only 30 years, and all his successors are modest too, except in Kish (a special center of Sumerian kingship). Most of the "heroic" postflood kings may thus have been upped by only 60 years (not by 60 × 10). Thus Lugalbanda's 1,200 years would then have been 20 years, and Enmebaragisi's 900 years would have been 15 years. Those with 200 years down to 100 years may have had a factor of only 10 × years; but that is a baseless guess for now.

So much for Sumer. What about Gen. 1–11? There was no sexagesimal system in Hebrew usage, and we are dealing with parents and children (direct or indirect), not reigns. The genealogies in Gen. 5 and 11 differ in the time of life at which children are born to the principal members: after long spans in the preflood one, and virtually normal after the flood. Therefore, as no single formula will apply to both lots, any more than to the preflood and postflood kings in Sumer, let us look at each group separately. Is there a "differential factor" as in Sumer? Overall, in Gen. 5, dividing the biblical number by five produces viable results for the age of the protopatriarchs at the birth of a firstborn from Adam to Lamech, running from 26 (for Adam) down to 16 for Kenan and 13 for Enoch; up to 37+ and 36+ for Methuselah and Lamech. But it gives a consistently high average at death of 180/190 years (except Enoch, who was "translated" at 73), not unlike the later patriarchs from Abraham to Jacob. The large postbirth figures might refer to the supposed life span of the clan, not just the men themselves, if one wished to pursue such paths. Only dear old Noah (having his firstborn at 500 = 100; living, even as "clan," to 950 = 190 years) is the odd man out. In the case of Gen. 11, the dates for having children are very normal, as noted above. It may be that the long "afterlife" figures covered the remaining life span (i) of the man himself (as is stated), (ii) of his immediate family, bearing his name, and (iii) of the clan (under his name, like tribes from the later sons of Jacob), until absorbed into other configurations. Here is a case of "corporate personality," once popular in biblical studies (to the point of exaggeration) but much more modestly employed these days (and rightly so). But all this is, and will doubtless remain, pure speculation, and as such it should be treated — with all due reserve, but offered as a stimulus to further thought.

5. IN SUMMING UP

Now, for our last documentary chapter, we may sum up as follows.

1. Gen. 1–11 is a very characteristic literary composition, on the schema "creation . . . time span . . . crisis (flood) . . . time span . . . (modern times)." Gen. 1–11 shares this particular schema with a small group of related compositions in early Mesopotamia (whence the Hebrew patriarchs came), all of which were of a type in vogue in the early second millennium B.C., and (in creative terms) seemingly only then. Later generations might recopy such works (even to Berossus's time), but nobody composed them afresh anymore after about 1500.

2. Gen. 1–11 is the Hebrew answer on how to present "prehistory/ protohistory" before the time of their first fully "historical" people, the patriarchs Abraham to Jacob. Again, the approach they adopted was common to their neighbors, using the same basic tools and concepts of that time: the succession of human generations, and how to span them. Mesopotamia chose to expand "heroically" the too-few reigns available. The Hebrew genealogies became telescoped through time, keeping a representative number, with possible man/clan figures spread along the now invisible intervals of the longer lines.

3. The flood was part of protohistory; so was the location of the Garden of Eden, with its long-lost (and long-remembered) river Pishon.

4. The Table of Nations with early roots had its first form in the early second millennium, its full form in the late second, and was finally updated in the early first (a text history like that of the patriarchal narratives). From creation to ancestry of their first fully historic forebears, Gen. 1–11 was in functional terms one of a set of early "world prehistories" (when there was no modern archaeology or natural science methods), serving early Israel in that capacity.

CHAPTER 10

Last Things Last — a Few Conclusions

1. THE HEBREW BIBLE — WHAT CONTEXT?

In this closing chapter we must now review the overall picture so far as our observed facts go, and set out two lots of phenomena side by side: namely, what emerges directly from the ancient Near Eastern past (texts, artifacts, Hebrew writings), and the loud claims of "prophets" new and old.

First we need to turn to representative pronouncements of minimalist writers and compare these with the emergent facts of the case. Are the constituent writings in the Hebrew Bible exclusively the product of a group of Jewish literary romantics of the fourth-third centuries B.C., and thus truly a late Perso-Hellenistic product? Or do the vast, millennially long tapestry and the fact-determined grid lines of Near Eastern civilization show clearly otherwise? Or, just conceivably, do they demonstrate nothing at all?

Second, it has to be understood that our present-day minimalists are *not* a sudden, new phenomenon without precedent. It all began a long time ago, and the present efflorescence is merely a development of some 150/200 years that has in a way come to a head, but simply more scathing of others and more extreme in its views than were its precursors.

In archaeology in the Levant, we have, for example, Early, Middle, and Late Bronze Ages; in Egypt, the Old, Middle, and New Kingdoms; in Mesopotamia, Old, Middle, and Neo-Babylonian (and Assyrian) periods. And so, likewise, we have early (1800-1890), middle (1970s), and late minimalists (1990s). The last-named group are simply the latest phase of their kind.

Third, to see a proper perspective and really find out "where it all went wrong," we therefore should (however briefly and compactly) turn the spotlight on all three phases, old, middle, and new. How do *any* of them measure up to today's factual/practical state of knowledge? If at all. Finally, the time has surely come not merely to draw up a balance sheet on the lot, but more positively to propose a genuinely radical approach, a proper paradigm shift, and clearing of a broad, free space in which we may all go forward to better things, to present the vast and splendid panorama of Near Eastern antiquity through the millennia (the biblical data included) for the enjoyment and benefit of all.[1]

2. LATE-PERIOD MINIMALISM

Here, as throughout this book — in good archaeological fashion — we begin with the latest period or "stratum" and work our way back through time. So the "late" guys first, then the middle, and finally the "ancestors."

A. SOME T. L. THOMPSON (TLT) DICTA, AND COMMENTS THERETO

The sampling has to be brief, but it will be carefully verbatim; to each group of citations, fact-based comment will be added.[2]

(i) Early Biblical Periods: Quotes and Notes

TLT-1

From TLT's *Early History:* "Not even the pentateuch's . . . story . . . [of] . . . Bezalel's construction of the ark and tent of meeting can, with any reasonable security, be related to any alleged historical matrices by making them retrojections of presumably reliable depictions of cultic innovations undertaken by the Jeroboam and Solomon of 2 Kings. The accounts of 2 Kings are also stories not history" (387-88).

TLT here (i) makes a gratuitous assumption that the tabernacle and its ark were "retrojections" (at best) from usages under Solomon and Jeroboam I, which is a typical nineteenth-century judgment, and (ii) assumes that the latter usages were also fiction; ergo, both the tabernacle and the supposedly tenth-century cult(s) were inventions from very much later. In so doing he ignores the whole of the comparative data that show clearly that the tabernacle was a product of Egyptian technology from the overall period 3000 to 1000 B.C. (plus Semitic analogues, 1900-1100), and would be unable to account for such facts. Denial of Solomon and Jeroboam I, of course, is itself an assumption without a particle of tangible data to support it. Contrast the religious edifice excavated by Biran at Dan (chap. 9, above).

TLT-2

From *Early History:* "[T]o begin the origins of biblical Israel with Merenptah . . . on the grounds that we have extra-biblical rather than biblical attestation is willful. These texts are, *mirabile dictu,* even less relevant than the biblical traditions, if only because of the logical imperative that requires us to establish an association of them with the Israel of tradition. With the 'Israel' stele, we have only a name in a historical context in which the shifting signification of regional and gentilic toponymy over centuries is a commonplace" (404).

To which we must reply, it is "willful" *not* to link the Merenptah occurrence of Israel with the early history of biblical Israel. In fact, it is simply willful evasion of very clear evidence. Egyptian mentions of Damascus *(Tmsq)* represent Damascus, the known place. And so, identically with Egyptian mentions of (e.g.) Ugarit, Tyre, Sidon, Byblos, Babylon, Hatti, Qadesh-on-Orontes, Carchemish, Aleppo, and scores more places outside Palestine, *none* of them being subject to any imaginary "shifting signification" or regional "dislocation," the same is true inside west and east Palestine, be it settlements or districts. The Megiddo, Taanach, Shunem, Beth-Shan, Dothan, Pella, Gaza, Beth-Horon, Gibeon, Arad, etc., are those of the Hebrew Bible, and in the same locations. The same is true of Moab, Seir/Edom, and Pa-'Emeq ("the Valley" par excellence) or the plain of Jezreel. Nothing much moved here. Or at Gezer and Ascalon on Merenptah's stela. Thus there is no factual reason whatsoever to doubt its citation of Israel as a neighbor of Gezer and Ascalon. Up in the hills west of Palestine's coastal plain — that is where Merenptah's Israel was, that is where Israel (and later, Judah + Israel) was for the rest of its traditional history until the deportations by Assyria in 722/720 and Babylon in 605-586. And to which the Judean survivors returned 539 and following. Not much evidence for "dislocation" here! "Shifting signification"? Only in normal historical terms, as the nonbiblical and biblical sources together indicate. The Israel of Merenptah's stela was, by its perfectly clear determinative, a people (= tribal) grouping, *not* a territory or city-state; rare statements to the contrary are perverse nonsense, especially given the very high level of scribal accuracy shown by this particular monument.[3] What was a tribal grouping in 1209 had 200 years thereafter to grow into a simple kingdom, then briefly hold overlordship beyond itself, before collapsing into two rump kingdoms eventually attested repeatedly by external sources (cf. data in chap. 2 above).

(ii) The United Monarchy

TLT-3

From *The Mythic Past/The Bible in History:*

> The second part of the name [*byt-dwd*] in the Tel Dan inscription is *dwd*. This is certainly the way the name of the biblical hero David would be spelled in early Hebrew writing. However, "David" is very unusual as a name. . . . It also occurs as the epithet for a deity *(dwd/dwdh)* in at least one other eighth-century inscription, the famous Mesha Stele from Transjordan. *Dwd* is not the name of a god, but it could be a divine title and be translated "the Beloved." In the Mesha Stele, it seems to be used as a divine title for Yahweh, . . . the name of God in the Bible [. . . the name *byt-dwd* . . .]. If we were to understand it in the sense of the "dynasty of *dwd*," the inscription would give evidence of a "House of David" that existed at the time of the inscription. It tells us nothing as such, of a person David as the founder of that patronate in an earlier period.
>
> The Bible does not use the term "House of David," in the way the British use a similar term, "the House of Stuart" — that is, with the specific meaning of "dynasty."
>
> . . . [O]ther scholars have found indications that have led them to argue that the inscriptions are forgeries. (204-5)

TLT is somewhat ill informed, to say the least. (i) The name "David" may be unusual, but it is not unparalleled. Long centuries before, it was borne by a West Semitic chief carpenter in about 1730 B.C. on an Egyptian stela formerly in the collection at Rio de Janeiro. (ii) *Dwd* is neither the name (which Thompson admits) nor an epithet of a deity. Others are beloved of deities (for which references are legion!), but male deities are not beloved of others, human or divine (only goddesses are beloved of their divine husbands in Egypt). (iii) Mesha's stela is ninth, not eighth, century. (iv) On the Mesha stela *dwd(h)* is not a divine epithet of YHWH or anybody else.[4] Mesha would seem to say (l. 12), "I brought back thence [= from Ataroth] the altar-hearth of its (purification) vessel" *(dwd-h).* It is normal for a purification vessel or basin or tank to be part of temple or shrine furnishings in the Near East, for the use of officiating priests. Just such a setup was found at Horvat Qitmit, whose oval enclosure had a stone basin as well as an altar; T-shaped basins could be found at the sanctuaries of Egyptian gods; and so on. (v) Contrary to TLT, "House of *X*" *does* mean a dynastic founder, all over the Near East, in the first half of the first millennium B.C.; it was an Aramean usage that passed into Assyrian nomenclature, and examples are common.[5] (vi) Again, the expression, in part of its usage, *is* like the British "House of Stuart," etc. Such usages were not peculiar to Aram, Assyria, and Judah either; in Egypt, the official title given to the Twelfth Dynasty (Turin Canon) was "Kings of the House (lit. 'Residence') of Ithet-Tawy" = "the Dynasty of Ithet-Tawy."[6] And the Thirteenth Dynasty was duly entitled "Kings who came after the [House of] King Sehetepibre" (founder of the Twelfth Dynasty). (vii) The charge of forgery is a baseless slur against the Dan expedition, without a particle of foundation in fact. At Tel Miqneh (Ekron), the recently discovered stone inscription was barely out of the ground when the minimalist chorus screamed "forgery," again without a shred of justification. Perhaps they would like to claim that Shoshenq I's huge monumental scene at Karnak was a giant forgery at (e.g.) Champollion's command, or that the vast archives of tablets brought from Assyria and Babylon — unread! — are forgeries, because they name Hebrew kings, or their chronicles agree with the fate of Jerusalem, Jehoiachin, etc., as seen in Kings and Jeremiah. Likewise, must we suppose that Koldewey could "plant" unread tablets at Babylon, to be brought to Berlin and deciphered by Weidner, to yield the name of King Jehoiachin in exile? Why stop at Dan and Ekron with these idiotic charges? (Cranks are always very bad losers.)

Moreover, there is good reason to read on the Mesha stela (l. 31), "Now, (as for) Horonen, there dwelt therein the House of [Da]vid," with only the *d* missing, and very little alternative that would make any sense.[7] And thirdly, there is reason to identify a "heights of David" in the name list of Shoshenq I of 924, less than fifty years after David's death. The spelling is identical with that used in an Ethiopic inscription, where the "Psalms of *DWT*" can only be "the Psalms of David," as Ps. 65 is then quoted.[8]

TLT-4

From *The Mythic Past/The Bible in History*: "[T]he legendary stories of Solomon's fabulous wealth have been claimed not to be so legendary after all. For at least some, the Bible's accounts become believable as history because the narratives describe a Croesus-like Solomon in the manner . . . [of kings of] Egypt, Assyria and Babylon. . . . Among such . . . is Esarhaddon's grandiose claim of having layered gold 'like plaster' on his palace walls. . . . [Y]et I might doubt that even . . . Esarhaddon layered gold that way in history" (201-2).

Not content with (in effect) calling Esarhaddon a liar, TLT simply refuses even to *look* at the practical evidence that we have. The point of the comparisons drawn with external (and firsthand!) sources was *precisely* that Solomon's wealth (even as stated in Kings) was *not* exceptional or "fabulous/legendary" in its wider context. He was a *pauper* compared with (e.g.) Osorkon I, who, less than a decade after Solomon's death, spent sums that massively outstrip Solomon's stated income, and gave detailed accounts.

The layering that TLT objects to was customary. At Karnak in Egypt, some temple columns were grooved to fit sheet gold from top to bottom, not mere "plastering." As a touch of throwaway wealth, one need look no further than the recently discovered burials of two Assyrian queens. Solomon had just *one* golden throne? One pharaoh was sent ten at a time! So where is the fantasy? Such wealth, of course, never lasts. Whatever Solomon lost to Egypt, Egypt spent in part and later lost to Assyria; Assyria was looted by Babylon and Media; these were overtaken and taxed by Persia; Alexander looted Persepolis; his successors lost ground (and eventually all) to Rome, and in the East to Parthia. And apart from spending fortunes on aromatics from Arabia and luxuries from the Indies, where did Rome's wealth go? After many centuries, duly transformed many times over, to Fort Knox? Who knows!

TLT-5

From *Early History:* "The existence of the Bible's 'United Monarchy' during the tenth-century [*sic*] is not only impossible because *Judah* had not yet a sedentary population, but also because there was no transregional political or economic base of power in *Palestine* prior to the expansion of Assyrian imperial influence into the southern Levant" (412).

All of these statements are palpably false. TLT's 1992 book was published well before the main Finkelstein claims for reducing the dates of tenth-century strata (1995 and following). So we may justifiably compare those strata and situation with TLT's claim for a nonsedentary Judah then.

First, on a nonsedentary Judah, the facts would appear to be that the rash of Iron I ("Judges' period") villages was replaced by fewer, larger townships into the tenth century, as an incipient urbanization was in progress, as Dever has pointed out. During the twelfth-eleventh centuries, the local village population had been both pastoralists (sheep/goats, cattle) and crop-growing farmers; these occupations, based on village life, *were* sedentary — they could not, physically, be otherwise! The succeeding period necessarily continued to live from the land, but more people were town dwellers, controlling their farmlands and pastures from thence.

Second, the wider realm of David and Solomon was *not* exclusively supported by or from Judah; it was based on Jerusalem, plus Judah as "crown lands" (David and Solomon were of Judean stock), *plus the revenues of all the other tribal zones* (cum administrative districts, 1 Kings 4:7-19) that constituted the Israel half of the united monarchy. On that basis David was well placed to war with neighbors, and to overcome them. The Transjordanian states were smaller, less developed than his; Aram-Zobah succumbed to a straight military defeat and an imposed overlordship. The adherence of Hamath was by way of alliance, not conquest. Once the east-of-Jordan and Zobah kingdoms had been made tributary, then the Hebrew monarchy in Jerusalem had a very respectable political and economic base, enhanced by commerce that had to pass through its terrain. So TLT's critique is mere self-delusion.

(iii) Divided Monarchy

TLT-6

After quoting lines 4-8 of the stela of Mesha king of Moab that mentions "Omri king of Israel" as oppressor of Moab (ca. 830), TLT writes in *The Mythic Past/ The Bible in History:* "Rather than a historical text, the inscription, in fact[,] belongs to a substantial literary tradition of stories of kings of the past. We find a similar story (told autobiographically, in the first person), which dates back at least to the thirteenth century BCE. It is about the king of Alalakh, Idrimi, who in fact had reigned over this city [Alalakh] some two centuries earlier. Like Idrimi's tale, the Mesha story is written in the first person and presented in the voice of the king himself. (It) presents us with an epitome of the king's reign. . . . His work is done. Both inscriptions are tributes to a great king of the past, epitomizing his reign" (11-13). TLT then invokes the birth legend of Sargon of Akkad, observing: "The inscription on the monument [*sic*] to Sargon begins much like . . . those to Idrimi and Mesha, as a first-person, epitomizing biography" (13). Then he turns to Hammurabi of Babylon, remarking: "By far the most famous of monuments . . . which epitomizes a great king of the past . . . using a pseudo-autobiographical first person address is the stela of Hammurapi which [*sic*] created the Hammurapi 'Code.' While the original of this monument possibly goes back to Old-Babylonian times, it remained a staple of Mesopotamian literature for centuries later."

455

As a professional Orientalist of long standing (of Egyptology and Near Eastern texts and civilizations), I hardly know where to begin with all this rollicking, silly nonsense!

(i) Except for the fact that Hammurabi's law text was indeed recopied (as a "classic") by later Babylonian scribes, TLT's statements on Hammurabi are wholly false — the great monument is *indubitably* an original of Hammurabi's reign, as any competent cuneiformist could have told him; its first-person address is *not* "pseudo" but (again) strictly genuine and original, exactly as is the case with the other two early law collections of the late third/early second millennia, of Ur-Nammu and Lipit-Ishtar; the stela did not "create" the "code" — it is simply its physical vehicle, a monumental copy.

(ii) TLT's knowledge of the range of use of first person in texts is clearly minimal and hopelessly misleading. Use of the first person by a monarch does *not* belong exclusively to either postmortem memorial texts or to later legends about such kings. A huge army of texts shows up the falsity of his presumption. Here are a few. (1) In his Ten-Year Annals (*CoS* II, 83-91),[9] Mursil II begins in the first person, describes his modest past (acceded young, and not the heir, asked the help of his deities), then proceeds through ten years of successful warfare exclusively in the first person, observes that he has now reigned ten years, and promises to record any further successes. We *know* that this is not a postmortem text, because he in fact lived and warred for many more years, as his detailed annals prove conclusively, running up to Years 21 and beyond (the end is broken). (2) In the "Hittite Hieroglyphic"/Phoenician bilingual inscription of Azitawatas, a local vassal king of the ruler of Adana, first millennium B.C., in Cilicia (125-26, 149-50), he begins (just like Mesha), "I am Azitawatas," followed by epithets, and likewise goes on in a continuous first-person narrative. Near the end he clearly asks for health and (long) life/many years — this was *not* a postmortem legend, but a text contemporary with the king! (3) Exactly the same is true of Yehawmilk, king of Byblos (151-52) — "I am Yehawmilk . . ." — and he too asks for long years to come, being far from dead! (4) In the Mesopotamian world, as everywhere else, texts were also produced in either third- or first-person mode. For first person, not postmortem, see (e.g.) Lipit-Ishtar (247), Warad-Sin/Kudur-mabuk (251-52), Rim-Sin I (253, his third text), Hammurabi (256-57), Ammi-ditana (258-59), and Shamshi-Adad I (259), all early second millennium. In the first millennium every major Assyrian king did exactly likewise, in various editions of their annals that were anything but postmortem, from Tiglath-pileser I to Assurbanipal (cf. *ANET*, 274-301; *CoS* II, 261-306; *RIMA*, 1-3 passim). (5) And likewise their high officers in the eighth century (278-84), all strictly within their lifetimes. (6) We may add the Neo-Babylonians, Nabopolassar, Nebuchadrezzar II, and Nabonidus (306-14). (7) To round things out, so too in Egypt. Thus Tuthmosis III on his Gebel Barkal stela (14-18, its main account) speaks mostly in a first-person narrative after a conventional third-person date line and introduction; the monument dates to Year 47 — but the king survived its making, till his known Year 54, seven whole years later. So, it is not postmortem.

There is no warrant whatsoever for describing Mesha's stela as a memorial (or postmortem text); it is a regular victory plus building text, as are the stelae of Zakkur of Hamath (155) and Panamuwa I of Sam'al (156-58). Nor is Idrimi's inscription either pseudoautobiography or needfully postmortem despite unjustified claims to the contrary. If it were the latter, it would not have been later than his son/successor's reign, just like other cases of newly acceded kings memorializing their late fathers. For that phenomenon see the text by Bar-Rakkib for his father Panamuwa II (158-59), or the Hittite Hieroglyphic text of one Ruwa made for him by his nephew Huli (127-28). Real funerary texts are best illustrated from such mortuary efforts as those found (e.g.) on 181-90.

(iii) The date given for Idrimi's statue is wrong; it is a fifteenth-century monument exhumed in a thirteenth-century context; the case is exactly like the thirteenth-century stelae of Sethos I and Ramesses II found in later contexts at Beth-Shan.

(iv) Mesha's stela is a contemporary building plus victory text, exactly like so many other inscriptions in the ancient Near East in all places and periods; the first-person formulation is irrelevant to its status, as the foregoing examples (far from exhaustive!) show. I have labored this point deliberately, because TLT is, sadly, not the only biblicist who is crassly ignorant of the many and complex facts and facets concerning nonpostmortem inscriptions in the biblical world. The Sargon legend belongs to a particular, limited class of text and cannot be used to generalize wildly and willfully about all other classes of text.

(v) The whole aim of TLT, of course, was to discredit the strictly historical reference to "Omri, king of Israel" in Mesha's text. His blather, blather, blather about literary motifs, etc. (*The Mythic Past/The Bible in History*, 13) is, frankly, mere hocus-pocus; all history writing by ancient kings used recognized literary adornments, but that is all — these are merely literary flourishes, and have no bearing whatsoever on the historical content of the text. And that "*Bit-Humri* belongs to the world of stories" (13) is simply arrant nonsense. It belongs to the strictly annalistic and historical terminology of Assyria, and is no more fairy story than *Bit*-everywhere else — Bit-Agusi, -Adini, -Bakhiani, -Daiukku, -Khaluppi, -Sha'alla, -Yakhiru, -Zamani, etc. (to go from A to Z).

Need we go on? To expose in full the sloppy scholarship, immense ignorance, special pleading, irrelevant postmodernist-agenda-driven drivel would need another (and very boring) book as long as Thompson's pair combined. It is sad to see real ability wasted in this way.

B. A LOOK AT N. P. LEMCHE (NPL) (AND SOME COMMENTS)

NPL is never backward at coming forward in expressing his views forcibly and picturesquely, and the quintessence of his current (or at least, latest) opinions on the Old Testament was recently reported from a published lecture, as a "Quote of the Month" by the indefatigable Hershel Shanks.[10] For convenience, we itemize these pithy opinions in a series of separate dicta.

1. "Historical-critical scholarship (on the Hebrew Bible) is based on a false methodology and leads to false conclusions."
2. "[Which] simply means that we can disregard 200 years of biblical scholarship and commit it to the dustbin. It is hardly worth the paper on which it is printed."
3. "The biblical picture of ancient Israel does not fit in but is contrary to any image of ancient Palestinian society that can be established on the basis of ancient sources from Palestine or referring to Palestine."
4. "There is no way this image in the Bible can be reconciled with the historical past of the region."
5. "And if this is the case, we should give up the hope that we can reconstruct pre-Hellenistic history on the basis of the Old Testament."
6. "[This latter] hardly predates the Greco-Roman period" (i.e., not before the third century B.C. to first century A.D.).
7. "[The Old Testament] is simply an invented history with only a few referents [*sic* = references] to things that really happened or existed."
8. "From a historian's point of view, ancient Israel is a monstrous creature. It is sprung out of the fantasy of biblical historiographers and their modern paraphrasers, *i.e.,* the historical-critical scholars of the last two hundred years."

Well . . . who is the fantasizer? Biblical (and other) scholarship of the last two hundred years, or Dr. Lemche? Let us now look at these stirring (and stimulating) trumpet calls to junk both the Hebrew Bible and most scholarly study of it, in the light of NPL's personal beliefs. Let us group these eight pronouncements in three lots: 1-2, 3-6, 7-8.

First, items 1-2. To junk some 200 years of "historical-critical scholarship." Hurrah! Three cheers! Whoopee! Well . . . maybe? Or not quite? Or not quite entirely? Yes, an uncomfortably large proportion of old books, theses, and papers on (e.g.) endless variants of literary-critical theories of the composition of the books of the Old Testament could be profitably pulped and recycled. What about the extravagances a century ago of J1, J2, J3? Or (only half a century or so ago) of Pfeiffer's L source? Or Eissfeldt's pet S source? Or most of the books locked in battle long ago over supplementary and fragmentary theses of composition, etc.? Down to the present time, biblical studies journals still carry overmuch of these gossamer speculations (unsullied by objective data) that real professional scholars of Near Eastern texts and material cultures could easily dispense with.

But a quite separate issue is the properly philological side of things. The basics of standard (and "silver age") Hebrew grammar and lexicon, and of our knowledge of other related languages and scripts, were first well laid down systematically by the end of the nineteenth century into the early twentieth — e.g., of Akkadian, and epigraphic West Semitic and Old South Arabian, as well as Egyptian. Naturally our knowledge of these languages has now progressed immensely beyond the 1890s/1900s, and others have been added (Ugaritic, Hittite, Hurrian, etc.), but it did start from those bases. Our *factual* knowledge of the biblical and related languages and associated bodies of texts cannot be dispensed with, now or ever. And *all* of it has to be taken into account. To junk everything in sight so that our Copenhagen (and related) "butterflies" may disport themselves indefinitely inside their own antibiblical, antifactual fantasy world is, alas, simply not on.

Second, items 3-6. Here the situation is far more clear cut. If the transmitted Hebrew history does not fit the external data for that place and period, and its image cannot be reconciled with such, but is a Greco-Roman-age invention having almost no contact with earlier epochs, and offers no data for those epochs, then on the basis of *real, genuinely ancient, firsthand* documentation from the third to late first millennia B.C. we must pose some very awkward questions. Such as:

WHY, then, is the literary profile of Gen. 1–11 basically identical with the profiles of comparable Mesopotamian literature relating to creation, flood-catastrophe, and long "linkup" human successions — and, as a search of the ancient literatures shows, as a topos in vogue creatively *only* in the early second millennium B.C. (and earlier?), not later? Not *my* fault!

WHY, then, do main features in the much-maligned patriarchal narratives fit so well (and often, *exclusively*) into the framework supplied by the independent, objective data of the early second millennium? (E.g., details in Gen. 14; Elamite activity in the west, uniquely then; basic slave price of twenty shekels for Joseph; etc.) This is *not* "conservative salvaging" (as Dever would claim); it comes straight from a huge matrix of field-produced data.[11] Not *my* fault!

WHY, then, do the human and other phenomena at the exodus show clearly Egyptian traits (not Palestinian, not Neo-Babylonian . . .), and especially of the thirteenth century? Thus (Pi)-Ramesse was Delta capital just for the thirteenth and most of the twelfth century, AND NOT LATER. Then, from circa 1070, Tanis (Zoan) took over there — a historical fact not open to dispute. Tabernacle-type worship structures are known in the Semitic world (Mari, Ugarit, Timna) specifically for the nineteenth to twelfth centuries; the Sinai tabernacle is based directly on Egyptian technology of the thirtieth to thirteenth centuries (with the concept extending into the eleventh). The Sinai/plains of Moab covenant (much of Exodus-Leviticus, Deuteronomy, Josh. 24) is squarely tied in format and content *exclusively* to the massively documented format of the fourteenth-thirteenth centuries, before and after which the formats were wholly different; we have over ninety original exemplars that settle the matter decisively, whether any of us like it or not. Most definitely, *not* my fault!

WHY, then, does Merenptah (in his Year 5, 1209/1208) report a *people* Israel, a foreign tribal grouping by the very accurate determinative signs (in a very accurately written text) who are west of Ascalon and Gezer, and south of Yenoam, and hence in the central Canaanite hill country, if no such named people existed? How curious that we have, in Canaan for 200 years directly following this episode, a clear and massive rise in population that installed themselves in a rash of fresh, new villages the length of the land. It's either due to a sex orgy or immigrants? No escape from those options. The hill culture develops away from the coastal cultures, it eschews any pronounced taste for pigs or image-based worship, with no stone/brick-built temples, but only scattered high places. Whose fault is *this* factual scenario? Of a definite entry (so Joshua, a raider, *not all-conqueror) and slow settlement (cf. Judges-Samuel). Not my* fault!

WHY, then, in the oncoming tenth century, are there suddenly clear material changes in Canaan, of demographic movement from hamlets into towns, and into use of a new red-burnished pottery, first by hand and later mechanically? And suddenly "government" compounds in strategic places (where late Canaanite occupation is blitzed out) such as Hazor, Megiddo, and Gezer, with new developments in the Negev? A centralized power is the clear answer, and the "united monarchy," its practical expression. The described Jerusalem temple and its furnishings drew directly on long-standing temple planning (besides the tabernacle precedent) and on contemporary Early Iron usages independently attested in Phoenicia, Syria, and Cyprus. Within a few years of Solomon's death and the Shishak raid on his son Rehoboam, we find a pharaoh suddenly spending absolutely unparalleled amounts of gold and silver on his country's temples. Hardly a total coincidence. Honest, it was Osorkon I who did this, not me!

WHY, then, is pre-853 Hebrew history to be treated as fiction, when we know that Shishak was the Shoshenq I who *did* invade Palestine and left a *huge* triumph scene and long (and highly original!) topographical list for both Judah and Israel, plus other records (El-Hiba list, now destroyed; Karnak stela; retainer's remark), that indicate the reality of his campaign? And his stela at Megiddo itself, which rams the message home to ancients and moderns alike?

WHY, then, is the divided monarchy to be belittled down to just a king list? Or even Mesha to be refused credence? After all, *he* was there! TLT and NPL were *not.* Not only do we have a king list, we also have a detailed chronology for the twin kingdoms built on *contemporary ancient Near Eastern usage,* which dovetails brilliantly well with *two independent* chronologies: that of Assyria and that of Egypt. And time and again the histories in Kings, Chronicles, and the Prophets *do* dovetail very well whenever there are data to compare, be it Assyrian annals, Babylonian chronicles, West Semitic inscriptions (Mesha; Tell Dan, no fake!; Siloam; Lachish Letters; personal seals; etc.). Again, not *my* fault! I didn't fake any of it — it just came out of the ground when I wasn't looking!

WHY, then, do we find Jehoiachin actually in exile in Babylon, with him and his family group having their meal tickets in 592; and most of Judah empty of occupation (except where — as in Benjamin at Mizpah — the imperial authorities wanted to exploit the land), during the main part of the sixth century? The Babylonian exile was not a fiction, and the young king is explicitly labeled "king of the land of Judah," not of an anonymous south Syrian fringeland. Blame the Babylonians — it's not *my* fault!

WHY, then, if the Dead Sea Scrolls (ca. 150 B.C. onward) are the formative fragments that went into a fuller (and later) Old Testament, do we have a Greek text (certainly for the Pentateuch, and doubtless more) of the third century (LXX) that is a *translation* of an as-yet-nonexistent Old Testament? And why are the latter's constituent books written in a "classical" Hebrew that — curiously! — is *typical* of our externally discovered examples of Hebrew prose in the ninth-to-early-sixth centuries (Samaria, Mesad-Hashavyahu, Arad, Lachish ostraca; Kuntillet Ajrud, Siloam, Khirbet Qom, Beit-Lei, Ketef Hinnom inscriptions, etc.) — but NOT of the Hellenistic/early Roman period ("Qumranic Hebrew," etc.)? And which contains various peculiar features (e.g., specialized psalm headings that are no longer understood, already!). How very odd!

And so one might go on and on, almost indefinitely. In short, there is absolutely nothing to support sweeping claims that "ancient Israel does not fit" its screamingly obvious context, or that the biblical image cannot be reconciled with Palestine's older history, or that the Hebrew Bible's writings are of Hellenistic date. Therefore, even as day follows night, it is (alas!) NPL whose wholly spurious claims should be binned. Sorry! Not *my* fault!

With all this also fall NPL's dicta 7-8. The content of the Hebrew Bible is not "invented history" and never was. This is merely crude antibiblical (almost anti-Semitic) propaganda, and ultimately nothing more. Ancient Israel was no more "monstrous" than any of its neighbors, its history is too closely tied to verifiable fact to be undiluted fantasy; and paraphrasing is an essential tool of *all* history writing, to be used as and when appropriate, but not as a substitute for independent assessments involving all available data when working out properly fact-based syntheses. Goodbye to Lemche's claims.

C. FELLOW TRAVELERS IN MINIMALISM

Messrs. Thompson and Lemche do not walk alone, of course. P. R. Davies headed up the debate from 1992 onward, and has remained consistently in play.[12] But his claims (along much the same lines as Thompson and Lemche) are bereft of any serious engagement with the external evidence. For example, all he could do with Merenptah's "Israel" was to waffle about general changes in nomenclature (e.g., Scots/Picts; Britons/British; Dutch/Deutsch [German], etc., that are wholly irrelevant) and to point to the 360 years' time gap between Merenptah's Israel (1209) and Shalmaneser III's Israel (853), and deny any connection between the two. This will not wash either; the simple fact is that we suffer from a corresponding gap in documentation for inner Canaan during precisely this period; it is not Israel's fault, or anybody else's. After all, the cuneiform sources from Assyria know of Egypt (Musri) almost not at all from the Amarna period (ca. 1350) down to Shalmaneser III in 853, an even longer span of 500 years. Only one mention occurs in that period, under Assur-bel-kala (1070); using Davies's criterion, we would have no reason to make any link between the "Egypt" of Akhenaten and Tutankhamun, the "Egypt" of Ramesses XI and Osorkon II. Except, of course, we possess extensive *local* inscribed remains from Egypt herself (a long-standing, massive civilization, not just a small tribal group) from long before, during, and long after the period in question. So his "criterion" is a nonstarter. It would be tedious to list and refute other such follies further, when others have done so.

Then we have K. W. Whitelam with his "invention" of ancient Israel; mainly pure fiction from cover to cover.[13] He has in effect committed the cardinal academic sin of arbitrarily "bending" serious scholarship to modern political ends. The disciplines concerning antiquity are of the greatest value (intrinsically and socially) to *everyone* when they are practiced for their *own* sake, as a voyage of discovery and recovery of humanity's common and bravely pioneering past. These ancient civilizations need to be allowed to speak with as clear an individual voice of their own as possible. *Then,* as our elders and (often) betters, from them we can learn much, and have our own lives enriched, by the saga of their struggles, failures, and triumphs; by the radically distinct but rewarding wealth of original literature and thought; by their often brilliant fine arts; by the splendor and modesty alike of their palaces, temples, villas, and humble villages and farms. To subvert all this to the unworthy, often "dirty" scrimmaging of modern politics and power grabbing is, bluntly, a reprehensible form of academic prostitution of the vilest kind. Let power-hungry modern groups stand on their own (often grubby) two feet, and not abuse the heritage of all humanity for their selfish and too often sordid and unworthy ends. That kind of fraudulent postmodernism (all is politics, power, indeterminacy [no explicit, clear knowledge], gender-oriented, etc.), which underlies our minimalists, the world has no need of. It has more practical needs to address.

D. WHAT WOULD A REAL PERSO-HELLENISTIC HEBREW BIBLE BE LIKE?

No problem! The same vast array of firsthand sources that can (and does) deliver the true setting of our existing Hebrew Bible is equally able to supply us with a good working model of what a Hebrew Bible should be like in this later epoch. Let us sketch it briefly, to compare and contrast such a ghost with the real thing, assuming that early Israel had not existed except skeletally (as in the Assyrian annals)!

Well, unless these Hellenistic Hebrew writers could have gotten hold of Berossus's *Babyloniaka* (third century B.C.),[14] they would have no Gen. 1–11; he would have given them a form of creation, kings, flood, and more kings (recopied and translated from a two-thosuand-year-old tradition) but nothing more. Then, no patriarchs; maybe genealogies of fictitious ancestors, then a largely fictitious history, perhaps about having been in Egypt (at Tanis!), then tribes under some kings (at most half a dozen names, filled up from imagination), until an ancestor of the Assyrian Osnapper carried off some tribes to Assyria, while the Judeans around Jerusalem were taken to Babylon, until Cyrus of Persia and his successors allowed them to go back to Judah if they wished. At which time prophets encouraged them (Zechariah, Haggai, Malachi), in a tradition that spoke of ancient prophets (an Isaiah, a Jeremiah, and others) in their former Judean days. Wisdom and psalms were composed for living, and for praising YHWH. But all these texts would have been in *silver-age Hebrew,* not the standard, "classical" Hebrew that we *do* have, shared with inscriptions as noted above. It all should have been marked by Aramaic influence throughout, incorporating many Neo-Babylonian and Old Persian words, not to mention Greek locutions when deemed useful. Nothing Egyptian would be found, and nothing archaic West Semitic that had not come down through many centuries as common, enduring word stock. There could be *no* covenant form such as we now find in Exodus-Leviticus, Deuteronomy, and Josh. 24: no historical prologues, no blessings and curses (only curses), no deposition or reading out clauses. The Psalms would not have headings that were obscure. And so on. It would, in short, be unrecognizable as the Hebrew Bible that we have today.

E. THE BIBLE UNEARTHED —
(OR MERELY BOWDLERIZED?)

Here we owe a fluently written volume on ancient Israel and archaeology to Drs. Finkelstein and Silberman.[15] However, a careful critical perusal of this work — which certainly has much to say about both archaeology and the biblical writings — reveals that we are dealing very largely with a work of imaginative fiction, not a serious or reliable account of the subject. Messrs. F. & S. do believe in a real, historical ancient Israel, particularly from circa 930 onward, but only fitfully before that date. And some of the archaeology (for the eighth to fifth centuries, at any rate) is useful and stimulating. But otherwise we have fiction, under four heads.

(i) The whole correlation of the archaeological record for the eleventh to early eighth centuries is based upon Finkelstein's arbitrary, idiosyncratic, and isolated attempt to lower the dates of tenth-century strata by up to a century if need be to rid himself of the united monarchy as a major phenomenon. His reevaluation of the realm of Omri and Ahab is refreshing but wildly exaggerated, especially in archaeological terms. As others have shown amply, the redating will not work (cf. chap. 4, sec. 3 above). All it does is show how precarious are the attempts by any of us to correlate the nontextual material remains with the written history available.

(ii) F. & S. have gone mad on "Deuteronomism." The origin of the book of Deuteronomy itself *cannot* be dated to the seventh century. Its format is wholly that of the fourteenth/thirteenth century, on the clear evidence of almost forty comparable documents, in phase V of a two-thousand-year history embracing over ninety documents in a six-phased, closely dated sequence. F. & S. know absolutely nothing about this determinative evidence; the brief account of the death of Moses (Deut. 34) is merely an appendage to the book proper; and their adduction of the thoroughly misleading comparisons of Deuteronomy's curses with first-millennium Assyrian series made by Frankena (and beloved of biblicists) is in error — see in chapter 6, p. 291 above, for an exposure of the fallacies inherent in Frankena's overly simplistic work. The supposed unitary Deuteronomistic History is a modern hoax. What we actually have is a set of wholly separate compositions (Joshua, Judges, Samuel, Kings) that present a traditional, orthodox viewpoint stemming from the beliefs expressed both in Exodus-Leviticus and Deuteronomy, and not solely the latter. As shown above, the individual prophets (long before Josiah) did not start something new; they called the people back to the old, basic covenant. F. & S. have vastly exaggerated the role of Josiah and his reign.

(iii) The idea that YHWH-alone monotheism began only in the seventh (or even eighth) century is a grotesque nonstarter. An absolute monotheism was clearly established by Akhenaten of Egypt in the fourteenth century (not the seventh!), drawing on older roots, and the impact of his ideas (even after his fall) echoed into the thirteenth century before being absorbed into the reassertion of the preeminence of Amun. In this climate, a Moses would have had no conceptual difficulty in proclaiming YHWH as sole deity for *his* group, and enforcing that status by declaring YHWH as the group's sole suzerain via a covenant in royal treaty format of precisely that period (chap. 6 above). Once in Canaan, then tensions and accommodations arose, of which the later YHWH-alone (and *not* solely "Deuteronomic") movement was merely the final outcome. As Dever rightly remarked, the F. & S. theory is flat, with no perspective or time depth. Frankly, it is merely an illusion, and born of De Wette's old speculation of 1805 in the prescientific era, as consecrated by Wellhausen and others in the 1870s. This is not new, white-hot "revolution"; it is merely old hat, a dish of stale cabbage reheated and rehashed.

(iv) On the patriarchal and exodus periods our two friends are utterly out of their depth, hopelessly misinformed, and totally misleading. They content themselves largely with rehashing the equally misleading 1970s work of Thompson and van Seters for the former period, and merely show 100 percent ignorance of facts on the latter. Camels are *not* anachronistic in the early second millennium, and never were (cf. in chap. 7 above), nor are the stories of the patriarchs "packed with camels"[16] a wild exaggeration. They suppress the fact that Gerar (if at Tel Haror) was a major metropolis (of over forty acres!) in the early second millennium (Middle Bronze Age).[17] The Philistines of Gerar (not those of the Pentapolis!) are a very different lot from the Iron Age group of that name. The term is a probably twelfth-century one substituted for Caphtorim or the like, precisely as Dan was substituted for Laish in Gen. 14:14. Archaeologically, Aegean goods (and thus people) *did* feature in Middle Bronze Canaan (chap. 7 above). There is a large and growing amount of evidence that would set the patriarchs as real people in the first half of the second millennium — and it is *not* dependent on the ill-documented views of thirty or forty years ago (see chap. 7).

Their treatment of the exodus is among the most factually ignorant and misleading that this writer has ever read. F. & S. clearly have no personal knowledge whatsoever of conditions in Ramesside (or any other) Egypt. Their approach to chronology (for both patriarchs and exodus) is totally naive: namely, to add up 480 years (1 Kings 6:1) plus 430 years (Exod. 12:40) for the one, or just 480 years for the other, and then set these figures at odds with the Ramesside-related data. For those of us with some firsthand knowledge of the fuller data from, and the ancient procedures in, the ancient Near East, this nonsense just will not do. See above, chapters 7 (p. 357), 5 (pp. 202-3), and 6 (pp. 307-9), for fuller data and a sketch of how things should be done.

We are told that "The border between Canaan and Egypt was thus closely controlled. If a great mass of fleeing Israelites had passed through the border fortifications of the pharaonic regime, *a record should exist*."[18] And no doubt it did. But our pair are clueless here. We know from such stone inscriptions as the successful lawsuit of the treasury-scribe Mose (or Mes) from his tomb chapel in the dry sands of Saqqara that there were voluminous papyrus archives both at Heliopolis (of the vizier) and at Pi-Ramesse itself (treasury and granary files) in the East Delta.[19] *Of which no minutest scrap now survives.* In the sopping wet mud of the Delta, *no* papyrus ever survives (whether it mentions fleeing Hebrews or not) — unless (as at Late Period Tanis) it had first been burnt and fully carbonized, and thus rendered virtually unreadable, except (sometimes) by very special modern techniques.[20] In other words, as the official thirteenth-century archives from the East Delta centers are 100 percent lost, we *cannot* expect to find mentions in them of the Hebrews or anybody else. The *only* trace of raw administration found at Pi-Ramesse (so far) is a handful of wine-jar dockets detailing a vintage of Year 52 of Ramesses II (1228).[21] How much would we learn (e.g.) about the last congressional election in the USA or parliamentary election in Great Britain from the torn labels of broken wine bottles discarded by customers from Macy's or Harrod's? Not a lot! And exactly the same is true at Pi-Ramesse. Wine jars do not an exodus record!

The reference to Edomites that F. & S. cite we possess solely because a Delta report had been sent on to Memphis, filed there, then used for training purposes for a budding pupil scribe (Inena) — and then discarded into the dry sands of Saqqara. Otherwise we would not even have this item. On page 60, our pair complain, no Israelites are mentioned *in* Egypt (their italics) on tomb or temple walls or papyri.[22] Of course not! Levantines in Egypt were universally described simply as "Asiatics," *not* by specific affiliations. Such people had *no* place in temple scenes, unless being conquered *outside* of Egypt. Towns and communities in their own land (e.g., Canaan) were a different matter. Such people had no place in tomb scenes either, unless they belonged to the personal household of the tomb owner — and then simply as "Asiatic." The same applies to such papyri as we have. Only when an individual case is being dealt with is any other detail given; e.g., a Syrian (Khurri) man Naqadi from Ar(v)ad in Papyrus Bologna 1086.[23] F. & S. fulminate against Israelites being able to escape from Egypt, given the massive Egyptian military presence along the Mediterranean coast route to Gaza — and almost fail to remember that the Hebrews were explicitly told *not* to go that way (in Exod. 13:17, to which they, finally, grudgingly allude, but omit to cite)![24]

As for no clues in Sinai, it is silly to expect to find traces of everybody who ever passed through the various routes in that peninsula. The state of preservation of remains is very uneven. For the Late Bronze Age, F. & S. have overlooked the Egyptian mining site at Serabit el-Khadim. The seasonal miners *must* have had interim stopping places between Serabit and Egypt, if they traveled overland back to the East Delta (on a reverse route to the Hebrews in Exod. 16–19), or at port sites like Markha if they sailed back to Egypt. Why, then, have we no record of these? This absence does *not* disprove the Egyptian regular visitations into Sinai, given their solid monumental presence — therefore, the absence of possible Hebrew campsites is likewise meaningless. What is more, from Sinai the Hebrews expected initially to be in Canaan in a year, not in forty years. They had no need to lug tons of heavy pottery around with them (just to oblige F. & S. with a few sherds!) if leatherwork or skins would do. So, no sherds at (e.g.) Qadesh-Barnea (where they did *not* stop for thirty-eight years — a common misunderstanding!) means nothing. And Ezion-Geber is not at Eilat or Tel el-Kheleifeh either.[25]

Then, in Transjordan, we are treated to the usual sociological poppycock about Edom being unable to be a kingdom until the seventh century.[26] Edom *did* exist, as a pastoral, tented kingdom, just like its Middle Bronze precursor Kushu, attested in the Execration Texts, and was *not* a deserted land either then or in the thirteenth century, as the Edomites entering Egypt prove clearly. It was so much a land with active people that both Ramesses II and Ramesses III chose to attack it militarily. So Edom was no ghost in Moses' time. Tented kingdoms may be unknown to dumb-cluck socio-anthropologists, but they are solidly attested in the Near East from of old, as the case of the dynasty of Manana demonstrates.[27] The lack of naming the pharaoh of the exodus is *specifically* a feature of the Ramesside period, in scores of ostraca, papyri, and inscriptions — but *not* from the eleventh century onward when the king's name is either given (like Shishak) or added to the title (like Pharaoh Necho/Hophra). The views uncritically taken over from Redford are partisan and refuted elsewhere. There is nothing seventh century about the exodus or its setting.[28] The mishmash on Joshua and Judges is an idle repetition of all the usual nineteenth-century shibboleths; the answer to which may be found in our chapter 5. Stuck with their a priori dogma of solely indigenous Hebrews (no exodus, no "entry" into Canaan), F. & S. are entirely unable to account for the massive population explosion in Canaan in Iron IA. If they do not want an immigration (what's so sociologically sinful about that?), then maybe they should opt for a sex-orgy hypothesis (chap. 5)! Solomon's realm was *not* just based on "tiny Judah" but on *all* of Israel and Judah (1 Kings 4!), plus vassal tribute and trade receipts; a sound base!

F. FIRM ROCK AND SINKING SAND — W. G. DEVER

In his *What Did the Biblical Writers Know and When Did They Know It?*[29] we have a robust and very valuable reply to the minimalists, ruthlessly exposing their suspect agendas and sham "scholarship," following on from his refutations of Finkelstein's archaeological revisionism. It should be read and appreciated (for the period 1200 B.C. onward) for its firsthand contribution on the archaeological aspects, as well as in conjunction with this book. There is much solid rock here, and all of us may rejoice in that fact.

To one's sorrow there is also sinking sand. In 1997, in a work edited by Frerichs, Dever chose to comment on the lack of "archaeological evidence for the Exodus" in terms of physical traces of a Hebrew sojourn in the East Delta. This was riddled with misconceptions much akin to those of F. & S. exemplified above (e.g., nonnaming of the pharaoh; simplistic attitude to chronology; no finds in Sinai; etc.) and was refuted by me in the volume edited by E. D. Oren in 1999. Unfortunately, in Dever's new book (2001) those strictures seem to have fallen on deaf ears, also in the case of the patriarchs. On the latter, he can only cite the outdated work of R. S. Hendel (with a nineteenth-century mind-set) and the calamitously poor chapter on the patriarchs by him and P. K. McCarter in a volume edited by H. Shanks (1999), which must be resolutely dismissed because they provide no competent basis for disbelief by Dever or anybody else. These are not primary authorities, but only tertiary — based neither on firsthand data (primary) nor even on any competent secondary surveys.

There seems to be a psychological hangover here; in the 1950s to 1960s, Albright and Dever's much-hated "American Biblical Archaeology" (plus theology) movement had believed in the patriarchs and exodus — so (irrationally) nobody *now* (two generations later) must either be allowed to study them seriously or to produce any data (no matter how genuine or germane) that *do* suggest their possible reality. In the light of what is now known, there is no excuse whatsoever for dismissing either the patriarchs (with a firm date line) or the exodus; see the entirely fresh treatments in chapters 6 and 7 above. The treatments given here by me are *not* based on Albright, Gordon, or the vagaries of the little local (and very parochial) United States problem of the long-deceased American Biblical Archaeology/theology school. Archaeologists that "have given up hope of recovering any context that would make Abraham, Isaac or Jacob credible 'historical figures'" (98) are not thereby rendered "respectable"; in fact, they simply do not know the relevant source materials (which are mainly *textual*), are not competent to pass judgment on the issues, and would be better described as pitifully ignorant, and can now be mercifully dismissed as out of their depth.

On a minor theme, one must chuckle over the remark that "Eden is not a place on any map, but a state of mind" (98). Maybe so for many moderns. But not for the *ancients*. The Euphrates and Tigris (Gen. 2:14) are *not* "a state of mind," but (along with the Nile) the most vital, earthly riverine resources in the entire Near East. Gihon (as the Gurun or the Kerkh) is vital to west-southwest Iran, and Pishon, linked with a very real gold-rich Havilah (Hawlan), has been the object of study by hardened archaeologists of considerable repute (Zarins, Potts). Beware of trying to spiritualize away the ancients' earthly concerns!

To end this section more positively, one should stress the importance (for the most part) of Dever's carefully and conscientiously worked-out principles of approach (16-17, 90-91, 107-8); range of abiding values (290); elucidations of the assumptions and "drives" of our postmodernist minimalists (or better, with Dever, nihilists) (26-27, 52, 260); and the matter of "deconstruction" of texts versus their true nature (11-12, 13-14), with the New Literary Criticism attitudes (15-16) versus the real nature and proper approach to texts (16-17). One may quibble over some details, but these breathe sanity in a bemused world. For W. G. Dever and his strictly archaeological competence of the highest order, the writer is happy to express enduring respect (and affection!).

G. DECONSTRUCTION — THE CROWN OF ALL FOLLIES

Here we reach the absolute nadir in modern "criticism," both within and beyond the (biblical) minimalist enterprise.[30] Having had over half a century's experience (since his young days) in reading texts, ancient as well as modern, in over a dozen languages, and as an author of "texts" during that same period, this writer considers that he knows as much as most about texts in the last five thousand years since they first came to be written. So, with reference to the New Literary Criticism and its willing dupes in biblical studies, we may add a few comments from a long and hard experience that goes well beyond that of most exponents of such procedures.

1. *The author's intention is an illusion created by readers.* Absolute bunkum! The authorial intent in this present book was and is to lay out a panorama of pertinent information from the ancient Near East that serves to place the biblical writings (and, especially, large samples of their contents) in their ancient cultural and (as appropriate) historical context, such that a variety of mistaken or inadequate treatments of those writings shall have some of their inadequacies shown up, and a more rational conspectus become possible. Full stop. No reader (other than the illiterate or deliberately perverse) is going to find any other intent in this book; and this book *does* reproduce my intent in cold print regardless of whether anyone happens to be reading it or not.

To take an ancient example, Ramesses II adorned certain of Egypt's greatest and most spectacular temples with long inscriptions and huge and very visible battle scenes of his Battle at Qadesh, while copies of the main text were also available on papyrus to be copied as triumphal literature. The authorial intention of this pageant is also transparently clear. The title line of the main text describes it as "The Triumph . . . of Ramesses II, which he achieved against" (more than a dozen named foes). He claimed a victory, and deliberately had it celebrated as such, to please the gods, impress his people, and satisfy his dented pride. For, on the day, he and a flying column had had to snatch an immediate, personal, military victory on the field from the jaws of disaster; but he did not capture Qadesh, and suffered a temporary loss of territory (quickly rectified a year or so later). He was a master of propaganda, and he still takes people in, even today, if they do not know the full available facts about the vicissitudes of Egypt's empire as compared with the outward material expressions of that empire.

2. *The text is an interpretable entity independent of its author.* Not more than a half-truth at best. Wherever authorial intent is patent, it is not true. There is no way of reinterpreting the significance of either Ramesses II's epic or of this present book other than as has been stated just above. An ancient Egyptian laundry list and report, or an account of consumption of candles used when cutting and painting scenes in royal tombs in the Valleys of Kings and Queens (as at Deir el-Medina), cannot, in either case, be interpreted as anything else than what it is. On the other hand, that site has yielded ostraca which simply give a set of names of known workmen without any explanation of why these were written down. In such cases, authorial intention was not expressed,

is not known, and never will be, unless parallel examples turn up that bear such indications. In this class of text, the names can *only* be the personal names of the individuals concerned — but no *definitive* interpretation can be given of the functional role of such ostraca. That *there is no single, authoritative "meaning" for a text* is bunkum, unless an author deliberately set out to build full-scale ambiguity into his work. That *texts have no intrinsic meaning* is, in the vast majority of cases, a plain falsehood; compare the examples in §§1-2.

3. *Language is infinitely unstable, and meaning always deferrable.* Simply not the case. In every language I have ever read there is always (for obvious, practical reasons) a basic consistency in grammatical and syntactic usage, which can only be varied to a limited extent; otherwise, misunderstanding *inevitably* results. Thus, despite trendy nonsense, spelling does matter. I once had to restrain a non-British research student from saying in a draft letter that a certain eminent lady scholar had been his "co*r*espondent" on a particular matter — he meant, in fact, "co*rr*espondent," but what a difference one little letter *r* can make! Sloppy usage, ancient or modern, always defeats the very aim of language — which is interpersonal communication. Context defines meaning at all times, unless somebody wants deliberately to be perverse, or to invent a secret code.

4. *One must approach texts always with a hostile suspicion, against the grain, denying integrity where possible in favor of dissonance and a search for inner contradiction.* This is the exact opposite of how texts should be read. Lack of initial empathy virtually guarantees failure to be able to interpret most ancient texts (and modern work) if these perverse ideas are used.

5. *All texts are incomplete, as language is unbounded.* Utter poppycock in practice. Time and again Egyptian literary texts end with a colophon, "It is finished, from beginning to end . . . ," and this is correct. A great number of Mesopotamian texts also end with appropriate colophons, whose similar function is clear.[31] Multiple manuscripts of oft-copied works that show the same ending every time simply hammer the point home; on this, the New Literary Critics are merely clowns.

6. *Structure is more important than context.* Absolute trash. The two elements interlock, and content may be served by a variety of structures, to achieve a variety of effects in getting the content-message across to readers. This is especially true in ancient Near Eastern poetry, for example.

And so one could go on and on. But this tiny handful of examples of (anti)academic lunacy will suffice. If the English departments that started off all this nonsense can find nothing better to do than this drivel, then we would be much better off without them. And their resources would be freed up for people with something worthwhile to offer to their fellow humans. The only worthwhile thing one can really do with claptrap deconstruction is . . . to deconstruct it.

H. THE INS AND OUTS
OF SOCIOLOGICAL ANTHROPOLOGY

(i) Sociology Applied Narrowly and without a Factual Basis

A couple of decades ago, Mendenhall and especially Gottwald pioneered large-scale sociological treatments of the rise of Israel in Canaan, understood as a purely internal evolution within Canaan itself and not after an entry thither from elsewhere. The classic major work was by Gottwald in 1979, which had some initial impact as the first grand attempt of its kind in biblical studies.[32]

However, this whole enterprise was subsequently subjected to searching scrutiny at some length by Lemche in a comprehensive work in 1985.[33] Mendenhall and Gottwald had taken their sociological model from just one narrow school of thought, which was fatally bound up with an outdated nineteenth-century scheme of social evolutionism. So, rejecting this overly restricted basis, Lemche wisely cast his net much more widely in terms of practitioners, and sensibly drew upon Near Eastern source materials — and not just indiscriminately worldwide as the Service/Sahlin/Fried school had done (81-83). Thus Lemche was easily able to highlight serious flaws in facts and procedure in Gottwald's extensive study. Types and hierarchies of society had simply been projected on no factual basis whatsoever, and imposed on early Israel. Lemche could thus present a damning indictment of the assumptions of the (then) "New Archaeology," and of general systems theory, which latter had been defined by one observer (R. J. C. Munton) as an attempt to construct theoretical systems "irrespectively [sic] of the real world situations to which the systems refer" (217). Rogue sociology out of control, in other words. As Lemche observed (217), humanity in such schemes was treated simply as automata who would always act uniformly in any given circumstances. But as he and many others would rightly insist, human beings do not behave in so woodenly consistent a manner.

Thus (291ff.) Lemche came to the eminently sane conclusion that "sociological methods are useful only to a limited extent," seeing that human societies "on the ground" can be seen to develop in a myriad of different ways. At one point he opted to abolish Israel's twelve-tribe league (305), but for this he, too, has no independent factual grounds to justify this arbitrary and wholly theoretical procedure. However, his volume is a valuable critique of views that stood (and still stand) in dire need of some firm, moderating reassessment.

(ii) The Onward March of Impractical Theory and Practical Sciences

One practical archaeologist, Dever, has diligently followed through the New Archaeology, including the successive phases of Processual and Post-Processual archaeology — the first of these despising straight history (somewhat neurotically), and the latter emerging from such childishness to a more balanced viewpoint. He is very insistent on the parallel utilization of both artifacts and texts (where these exist) toward the writing of ancient history, he having the history of Israel principally in mind. This is all to the good, so long as neither he nor others fall into the easy trap of artificially overplaying the role of nonwritten data in the same way that some scholars have undervalued these data. (Being brought up under scholars who correlated both sides naturally, without being told to by others, I see no problems here so long as the proper balance of the application of data is kept that will vary with particular circumstances.)

One error is to allow too much anthropological claptrap theory into ancient Near Eastern archaeology; the amount of a priori nonsense talked and written about "state formation" needs to be cut down drastically, and ruthlessly amended to fit the actual facts on the ground in the ancient Near East. Thus, everywhere are chiefs (more chiefs than Indians?), and no "state" can exist without a centralized government, a corresponding bureaucracy, and (preferably) monumental stone architecture. For all these nonfactual preconditions, there is no justification whatsoever. The case of Edom is repeatedly brought up, and wrongly. Edomite sites show no great urban settlements, and nothing monumental until the coming of client status under a distant Assyria in the seventh century. Therefore, it is loudly shouted, Edom was not a state till then and had no kings till then. Rubbish, on both counts. Leaving the clear, consistent, and contrary biblical evidence on one side, let us look at our limited outside sources on Edom and note the contrast between texts and material archaeology. Thus the traces of a Middle Bronze Age are very sparse indeed in Edom (the region south of Wadi Hasa) — but the Egyptian Execration Texts make it very clear that the land of Kushu (the Kushan of Hab. 3:7) had its chiefs (Egypt. *wrw*); and one, Ya'ush, appears in the story of Sinuhe (ca. 1900), with a name virtually identical with that of Ye'ush (Jeush) in Gen. 36:18. We may infer that the future Edom was already a principally pastoral zone under its own ruler (or rulers). Precisely this is the case in the late second millennium, in the Late Bronze Age II and Iron I. Archaeological finds from that epoch are — again — very scanty indeed. But Egypt, again, shows this fact to be deceptive. Seir (for Edom) occurs not only in a topographical list of Amenophis III (1370) and again under Ramesses II (1280) as a "Shasu-land," but as a region subdued by the latter king, referring to Mount Seir, also a biblical phrase. Under Merenptah, pastoralists explicitly from Edom came to the southeast Delta to water their herds. So Edom was certainly inhabited in the thirteenth century, pottery or no pottery. Then we find Ramesses III reporting (ca. 1170s), "I hacked up Seir, even the tribes of Shasu; I pillaged their tents [using the Semitic word *'ohel!*], with their people, property, and their livestock likewise without limit — pinioned and brought captive as the tribute of Egypt." So there *were* pastoral, tented Edomites in residence in Iron I that the redoubtable Ramesses III (no less!) found it expedient to war upon — an expensive undertaking, if only ghosts lived there![34] All of this is consistent with the biblical chiefs *(alluphim)* and kings of Edom in the early and late second millennium, and intermittently at least into the eighth century when Assyrian records take over. Like the dynasty of tented kings of Old Babylonian Manana,[35] the Edomite "kings" were pastoralists, and warriors at need. So an Edomite continuity must be taken seriously all the way from the Execration Texts to Esarhaddon, regardless of whether the physical archaeology of Edom can (as yet) witness to it or not. The case of the Edomite pastoralists is not so much different from that of the Hebrews transiting through Sinai, who left no clear physical trace either. Just as texts have their limits, so too does archaeology; we *do* need both! So let us have no more daft theory that kingdoms need local equivalents of Buckingham Palace or the White House before snooty (and irrelevant) anthropologists will deign to recognize them!

(iii) The Practical Side

But let us redress the balance a little. With the New Archaeology there also came the fuller introduction of a variety of science-based and related techniques into the practice of archaeology in the field and in the laboratory. Such included flotation techniques to obtain early botanical specimens, the retention and study of animal bones (for local ecology, and human diet), study of ancient technologies, and modern dating methods based on carbon 14, dendrochronology (tree-ring counts), thermoluminescence, and so on. And geophysical equipment to effect subsurface surveys of sites without turning even a blade of grass. All this has been to the good, although often expensive for expeditions to cope with.

So much for scientific gains, alongside the follies of contemporary late minimalists and other assorted theorists in need of a stiff dose of good, old-fashioned on-the-ground reality. But it is essential, now, to go back briefly to the middle minimalist period — direct progenitor of the late variety — before going to the early "fountainhead," and then finally tidying up with a glance toward the future.

3. MIDDLE-PERIOD MINIMALISM

Here we go back over a generation to the environs of 1970, when a small group of scholars (D. B. Redford, T. L. Thompson, J. van Seters) independently reassessed, with negative results, the previous scholarly partial consensus that had favored the possible or probable historicity of the ancestral Hebrew forerunners of earliest Israel (and others besides).[36] Their conclusions led them to dismiss the patriarchal age per se, and others then followed in their wake. For the sake of conciseness, we here review their efforts by theme, not by author, with cross-reference to chapter 7 (to avoid repetition), and then measure them off against the basic firsthand data omitted or misused by them.

A. JUST PATRIARCHS

(i) Patriarchal Personal Names

These are *not* pivotal for dating the patriarchs, but need to be understood aright. The essential facts are summarized above in chapter 7 (pp. 341-43). Suffice it to add for Abra(ha)m, that his name ("the father is exalted" > "father of many") is *not* identical with Abiram, "my father is exalted," and still less with the wholly different Ibiranu of the thirteenth century. And for the "imperfective"-type names, it is a firm fact that the percentages quoted above (p. 342) are *not* based on a random survey as falsely alleged, but on an exhaustive study of the entire corpus of over 6,000 names meticulously recorded in Gelb's monumental work. And it is wholly beyond dispute that use of this type of name did not thereafter cease, but was hugely less ever after. Statements to the contrary are a deliberate attempt to avoid the evidence, and nothing more.

(ii) Other Social Features

The claim that the patriarchal shepherding practices are of Neo-Babylonian date is badly mistaken; they in fact relate more closely to Old Babylonian conditions (cf. pp. 336-38 above). The denial that people could drift or migrate from southeast to northwest as well as from northwest to southeast is unjustified on the facts (cf. p. 317 above, plus Kupper's observation). Denial of the use of tents in the early second millennium is laughable nonsense, as others have clearly shown. The Akkadian term *mar-biti* for "son of the house" is not merely Neo-Babylonian (so, van Seters), but was current also in Old and Middle Babylonian times.

The appeal to dialogue documents of the first millennium as parallel to Gen. 23 was a blunder; such documents go back to Old Babylonian times also, and Gen. 23 is a narrative throughout; cf. above, pp. 326-27. The appeal also to an "adoption papyrus" of the time of Ramesses XI (ca. 1100) is an equal blunder. The text in question simply contains a series of inner-family adoptions that have nothing in common with Gen. 16. Likewise, appeal to a seventh-century Assyrian marriage conveyance is mistaken, as it has as many differences from the biblical usages as similarities, and is a wholly anomalous document, as its original editor clearly pointed out. Appeal to these documents is just special pleading and thus wholly without merit. In turn, false comparisons have been made between Gen. 15, Jer. 34, and sundry texts from Alalakh, to attempt a first-millennium date for the phenomenon in Gen. 15. A closer examination by Hess of the data available indicates that the comparisons between Gen. 15 and second-millennium data are clearly preferable to the supposed later ones.[37] Finally here, the attempts by Thompson and van Seters to dismiss the date and possible historicity of Gen. 14 are wildly mistaken; cf. the data already presented in chapter 7 above.

On the other hand, positively, both authors had no difficulty in disposing of the overambitious and misleading Hurrian/Nuzi-customs hypotheses of Speiser and Gordon in particular; however, even here they failed in their zeal to distinguish between false and valid parallels, the valid ones originating in the Old Babylonian period (cf. chap. 7 above).

(iii) Archaeology

Here the patriarchs are more likely to correspond to Middle Bronze II than to Middle Bronze I (EB/MB), as rightly admitted by van Seters;[38] for a better survey based on newer knowledge, cf. chapter 7 above (pp. 335-36). The attempts by Thompson to evade the implications of perfectly clear data on relations between Egypt and Canaan can be dismissed (along with a mistranslation of Merikare).[39] The 10,000 troops levied by Merikare (Tenth Dynasty, ca. 2100) and the series of forts installed along the East Delta border by Amenemhat I (ca. 1970) were *not* deployed against a few scraggy shepherds or a handful of stray donkeymen from the nearby Mediterranean seashore or just across the Bitter Lakes. The Amorite hypothesis[40] is a dead duck, and of no relevance to the patriarchs; there were "Amorites" and others on the move on a modest scale all the time, and no vast mass-migration in the Levant is to be inferred from extant sources.

B. JOSEPH TOO

Already, well before publication of Thompson's and van Seters's antipatriarchal salvos in 1974/75, Redford had issued a similar volume on the Joseph narrative (1970). In concert with most commentators, he rightly viewed that narrative (Gen. 37; 39–50) as a distinct unit within Genesis, a view also taken by the ancients (cf. 37:2, heading). His specifically literary exploration of the narrative led him to reject very largely the old nineteenth-century divisions of that narrative between hypothetically preexistent J and E strands, in favor of a basically unitary piece. Again, not a few would concur with him in this result.

On specific details, his book offered comments on a wide range of topics: vocabulary, dating of the narrative, possible Egyptian features, etc. However, much of this (some, summarized in lists)[41] turns out to be very unsatisfactory in practice, because it progressively descended to the level of sustained special pleading in favor of a late date and ignored pointers to the contrary. In his first word list (pp. 46-64), several items are too banal to count (e.g., nos. 11-13, 42, 64), while others are isolated words *(hapax)* and hence of zero significance (e.g., nos. 6, 8, 14-15, 49). And a series of others actually find attestation in the second millennium, e.g., in Ugaritic or Egyptian, and in early poetic usage, etc. (cf. his nos. 3, 10, 18-19, 39, 68, 69).

In the second list (pp. 54-65), the criteria have been falsely "loaded." Nobody can possibly object to using such books as Chronicles, Ezra, Nehemiah, or Esther as clearly postexilic sources for postexilic, "silver-age" Hebrew. But it is wholly otherwise with other books that Redford wished to include in that same category thirty years ago. Thus, on any showing (be it thirteenth-century or 621), Deuteronomy is definitely preexilic. Proverbs is also preexilic (part tenth century, part probably in the eighth/seventh), and also the hypothetical source P can be readily argued to be preexilic (e.g., by A. Hurwitz and others). Again, isolated and very rare words count for nothing; others have *early* ancient Near Eastern affiliations (in Ugaritic, Akkadian, Egyptian, etc.) or are old poetic terms. Thus, from these severely pruned lists, Redford's evidence for a basically late narrative simply melts away like the morning mist. A late date cannot be safely established on such poor evidence.

In Egyptian matters Redford rightly objects to attempts to see Egyptian reflexes where they do not exist — e.g., the phrase "father to pharaoh" has nothing to do with Egyptian expressions involving the term "father." But like other ancient Near Eastern courts, the Egyptian court did have its royal butlers or cupbearers (*wudpuw* in the Middle Kingdom; *weba3* in the New Kingdom), chiefs of guards (*sehedj-shemsu* and *hery-qenyt,* in the Middle and New Kingdoms respectively), and so on. So it is legitimate to note these as possible reflexes of Egypt. Of the Egyptian nature of the trappings for royal appointments to high office — linen robe, gold collar, state seal, etc. — there can be no doubt whatever. As for Semites in Egypt (including as slaves), Redford has to admit to good evidence existing in all periods from the Middle Kingdom into the Late Period. But he is wrong in claiming that ownership of foreign servants was restricted to royalty and mainly the Late Period. Not so. In the Middle Kingdom we find over forty Semites out of over seventy household servants and/or slaves in the Papyrus Brooklyn 35.1446 of the eighteenth century, belonging to one major household. And lesser households had them too, as many private stelae clearly show then.[42] Such foreigners came for trade, or as prisoners of war (slaves), also as slaves in tribute, or sold into Egypt as slaves (as under Amenemhat II). For the *hart'ummim,* "sages/magicians," see already in chapter 7 (pp. 345-47), and likewise for the Egyptian personal names, etc. There is sufficient Egyptian content in Gen. 37–50 (and for the early second millennium in origin) to indicate more than just a weekend trip to Egypt by some stray Hebrews at just any old period.

C. EXODUS, COVENANT, AND CANAAN (1977)

We come here to the volume edited by J. H. Hayes and J. M. Miller, in the wake of our patriarchal trio just considered. Spurred on by those presentations, this pretentious volume gaily picked up all sorts of errors along the way.[43]

(i) Blunders over Pi-Ramesse(s)

In his book Thompson unwisely repeated Redford's error, in asserting that the city Pi-Ramesse remained occupied (and its name in currency) after the transfer of the Delta residence to Tanis (Zoan) from circa 1070. This is a totally mistaken view, as Helck easily demonstrated in 1965, twelve years before publication of Thompson's essay in the Hayes/Miller volume.[44] Tanis wholly replaced the old and long-moribund Ramesside Delta residence, and the latter's stonework was soon recycled to build the temples and tombs of Tanis, where arose new sanctuaries for Amun, Mut, and Khons, the Theban gods who (with Re, etc.) had hitherto held sway in Pi-Ramesse. As Helck pointed out, the occurrence of Pi-Ramesse in the Egyptian *Onomasticon* of the Twenty-First Dynasty was merely because this text is a simple recopy of a much earlier Ramesside document. It is nonsense, also, to cite mentions of cults of Amun of Pi-Ramesse in the fourth century B.C. from Tanis and Bubastis. These were cases of "religious archaeology"; the one, hidden deep in the rear sanctuary of Nectanebo I, visible to *nobody* except officiating priests, and the other inscribed on an official's statue (written in difficult hieroglyphic texts) within the sacred walls of a Tanis temple — again, *well* segregated from the gaze of any impure foreigners (including any stray Jewish scribe or priest!). In Iron Age II versions of the saga of Exodus, Tanis accordingly replaces the long-outdated term "Raamses" — see Ps. 78:12, 43, with its "Field of Zoan" (twice)! Pi-Ramesse/Raamses is a marker of the thirteenth/twelfth centuries, not later.

(ii) Treaty and Covenant

Here Thompson falls down badly on the facts. Like others, he rejected Mendenhall's suggested link between Exodus and the format of the Hittite treaties, but for a wholly wrong reason. Mendenhall's mistake was to have made the comparison between the treaties and Exod. 20 only — and not with the complete data in Exodus and Leviticus, and omitting Deuteronomy entirely. So Thompson could easily fault him. But Thompson paid no attention whatsoever to the close comparisons with the *full* format as exhibited in Exodus-Leviticus, Deuteronomy, and Josh. 24; thereby, his rejection is itself totally invalidated by the full facts. For which, see at least the basics in chapter 6 above.

(iii) Nonsense on Folklore

In the Hayes/Miller volume Dorothy Irwin spent much space and time comparing the Genesis/Exodus narratives with ancient Near Eastern fictional tales, and deliberately omitting all other types of narrative. This methodological blunder was later repeated in her large work, *Mytharion*.[45] It is wrong to exclude *any* major class of narrative text from consideration if one wishes to establish the canons of composition for ancient narrative. There are several parallel classes of narration that run down side by side through the centuries and millennia of ancient Near Eastern civilizations, and all *must* be taken into account *together*. No picking and choosing. Thus, by comparing biblical narratives *exclusively* with a clutch of known fictional narratives that happened to have some motifs in common with the former, she "fixed" her results in advance, ergo all biblical narratives sharing topics with fiction or folklore were also purely fiction or folklore. This is methodological nonsense, and invalid. The proper method is to gather all available examples of all classes of narrative, sort them into their constituent groups, and then compare biblical narratives *both* with these groups *and* with historical data. Then the proper groupings will come out clearly. This the present writer did successfully in outline, also back in 1977; see now also in chapter 7 above. Irwin's paper and book are irrelevant to systematic study of the Hebrew Bible, and can be dismissed. Non sequiturs abound. A birth legend is told of Sargon of Akkad, it is merely folkloric; a similar tale is told of Moses, so he is fictional. How illogical! One may better argue: a special birth tale is told of men who rose to be important leaders; Sargon is known to be historical — so Moses in these same circumstances equally should be. The Papyrus Westcar's "Tales of the Magicians" is drawn upon in this exercise. But Irvin completely fails to pick up the important fact that several of the main actors in these fantasy tales are *strictly historical, and in correct historical sequence and even relationships!*[46] So, weaving fantasy around someone does *not* alter that person's historicity. Papyrus Westcar has a sequence of Third to Fifth Dynasty kings [Djoser], Nebka, Snofru, Kheops, son and grandson (= Khefren, Menkaure), then the Fifth Dynasty, Userkaf, Sah(u)re, and Kakai (= Neferirkare I). Faultless. The other characters include [Imhotep], Bauefre, and especially Hordjedef, the last two (correctly!) as sons of Kheops. All this is verified from original, historical monuments and inscriptions from and about these people. So . . . if Egyptian personalities can be (and are) solidly historical even when wrapped up in fantasy/folklore tales (and likewise Sargon), why on earth should it be any different for (e.g.) the patriarchs, Moses, or David? Simple lopsided antibiblical prejudice, perhaps, fed by a deep-seated ignorance of the literary conventions of the biblical world? Her flawed and irredeemably inadequate approach is lost by default.

(iv) Into Canaan via Transjordan

Finally, Egypt, Canaan, and Transjordan.

(a) Messing About with Joshua

In a lucidly written but unreliable survey, Miller perpetuated old errors and invented new ones. Under the first head he repeats the never-ending error of portraying Joshua as having "conducted *a systematic conquest* of the west [Palestinian] Jordanian territory." And further: "*Having conquered the whole land* west of the Jordan except for certain outlying areas . . . in less than five years," the land was divided up, and "the whole of the promised land was *conquered systematically* and in a relatively short period of time . . . by (Moses [= east of the Jordan] and) Joshua."[47] As we have seen, the book of Joshua does *not* depict a sweeping conquest *and occupation* all in five years or less; see our chapter 5 above. This is the standard traditional fiction continually left unchallenged, deriving from an approach that fails to read aright biblical texts that follow Near Eastern literary canons, not modern ones. Joshua was strictly a *raider,* knocking off kings and damaging places (no doubt) en route, NOT OCCUPYING THE TERRAIN RAIDED, but *always returning to Gilgal.* Hazor might be destroyed — but it was *not* instantly resettled by Israelites (in fact, not by them till David's time). Thus the usual (and false) contrast between the wrong understanding of Joshua and what is narrated in Judg. 1 is trotted out uncritically all over again. The allotments were of lands not held but still (in most cases) to be possessed (as is evident in Judg. 1). The texts are perfectly clear!

(b) Untruths in Transjordan

On the exterior of the east wall of the great forecourt of the temple of Luxor, Ramesses II commemorated a raid into Moab with a set of war reliefs; some time later he filled the texts with plaster and cut fresh inscriptions over them, to change the commemoration from Moab to Phoenicia. Over the millennia the paint faded and the plaster all fell out; as a result, the modern epigrapher faces a palimpsest: two sets of inscriptions, the one visibly engraved over the other. The texts about Moab are the more interesting. One epigraph clearly names a place *Butartu in Moab,* and this reading is clear and beyond all doubt. In the adjoining scene the king captures *Daibun* — which is, *and can only be,* the well-known Dibon in ancient Moab, now agreed to be at modern Dhiban.[48] These elements of the texts are clear to the Egyptological epigrapher, and beyond all dispute, as I know from direct experience at that wall (having epigraphed more than 60,000 lines' [over a million lexemes'] worth of Egyptian texts of all kinds in the last half-century). Then we have a nonepigrapher like Miller who deliberately claims that the readings of "Moab" and "Dibon" are "open to question."[49] This is blatantly untrue, in fact the exact opposite of the truth. Those names are perfectly legible. Some parts of the *fixed formulae* adjoining them are damaged — but these *nonname* elements can readily be restored from the intact parallels in adjoining epigraphs. The palimpsest nature of the texts is initially distracting, but (if one is an experienced epigrapher) one soon gets used to the phenomenon. The "prolonged study" which Miller quotes (out of context!) was the normal care that all Egyptological epigraphers must observe, to establish a sure text. Miller's claim was, and remains, an entirely irresponsible misstatement of the real facts, and still needs to be publicly withdrawn in print.

It is not acceptable that a tyro, totally unqualified in reading hieroglyphic texts, should so accuse a long-experienced epigrapher, merely to prop up some pet a priori prejudices about the Old Testament text. Finally, the Egyptians did *not* use their specific terminology (for Edom/Seir, Moab, Israel) "rather loosely"; some of these mentions are not isolated but are found in definite contexts.

This was a shabby way to treat important firsthand evidence, and those who go to some trouble to provide it, ultimately for the public good. But with minimalists, what can one expect? The Hayes/Miller book is a curate's egg; good in parts, but marred by special pleading that renders it a very unreliable secondary source for serious study, as the above cases show.

4. FALLACIES AS THE MARK OF MIDDLE-PERIOD MINIMALISM

When we look back contemplatively over the works of the would-be radicals and revolutionaries of the 1970s, various salient facts emerge which throw into sharp relief their failure to make their case in terms of hard fact; yet they succeeded in hoodwinking gullible biblicists, especially those who preferred antiquated, nineteenth-century-type evolutionary theory to the facts, or were unaware of the range and nature of the full pertinent facts, in any case.

First, our 1970s men succeeded very effectively in demolishing the overspeculative, and thus unsafe, hypotheses that formed too large a part of the views of Albright, Gordon, Speiser, et al. The Hurrianism of Nuzi and the more inappropriate comparisons (sororarchs, etc.) went by the board; Speiser's and Albright's donkey-caravaning merchant-patriarchs were a chimera that the biblical text itself does not countenance; Abraham and company were simply transhumant pastoralists, able at need to defend themselves. Nothing more, nothing less.

Second, and sadly, our midterm "revisionists" then went further, indulging heavily in special pleading to establish an opposite case; namely, that (in strict accord with Wellhausen, 1878!) the patriarchs were never real but were merely a literary reflection of conditions under the Hebrew monarchy (or even later). They rightly objected that the 1950s-1960s school had largely restricted their comparisons to material from the early second millennium and had not checked things out with the first-millennium data in particular. In most cases, quite so. An omission to be rectified. But our midtermers then overdid things. They insisted on not only making first-millennium comparisons (OK!), but also on forcing imaginary first-millennium comparisons artificially (special pleading), and excluding second-millennium data, thereby committing the same error of exclusivism as those they had faulted. And the third millennium was never consulted at all, by anybody. So the revisionists were as bad as those they dismissed, and in fact worse for not doing the whole job properly.

Third, none of these "middle"-men betray any understanding of the significance of the different types of date ranges of phenomena down through time. The following points should be carefully noted by all, because they apply throughout the ancient Near East *and* to the Hebrew Bible (as being part of it).

1. Items (e.g., customs, vocabulary, names) that occur in firsthand documents throughout the third, second, and first millennia cannot be used to date anything. They are too general.

2. Items that occur in just the third and early second millennia, e.g., and are *replaced* by a different and equivalent usage in the late second and/or first millennium *are* significant for dating to the third/early second, and not normally attributable later as living entities. Mere literary recopying does *not* prove a later date, any more than a new printing of Shakespeare's plays in 2001 proves him to be alive and productive under Elizabeth II, not I. The different usage of the late second and first millennia would normally be diagnostic of that period in turn (but cf. 3. below, on vocabulary/names).

3. Items that occur (e.g.) in the second millennium (early or late) *and* in the first *cannot* be attributed to the first by preference without explicit additional evidence. Isolated "later" words or names that sporadically occur in seemingly "earlier" texts can mean one or the other of two things. (a) They imply a "later" date for the text in question, if other evidence clearly concurs. (b) *They only date themselves,* if in fact they represent a later "update" or modernization of an "early" text. In the story of Sinuhe (a text attested from Middle Kingdom papyri, by 1800), old *nwy,* "waterflood," is replaced by the trendy Semitic loanword *yam,* while the old location Qedem is replaced by the news-headlines-grabbing place-name Qadesh, in the thirteenth-century Cairo ostracon's witness to that text. These changes date *themselves* and *not* the entire composition. Biblicists please note, when considering Dan for Laish in Gen. 14:14 or "Philistines" in Gerar (not the Pentapolis!) in Gen. 26.

4. "Negative evidence," i.e., simple nonoccurrence, proves absolutely nothing in itself. Usually it shows up simply the poverty of our firsthand knowledge of worlds departed millennia ago. One minute biblical David did not exist (we were told), because no scrap of firsthand evidence was available to vouch for him. Then, some eighteen months later, the Tell Dan stela most unkindly brushed this silly, asinine myth aside, by evidencing him as (a) real and (b) as a dynastic founder, to which was added "House of [Da]vid" on the Mesha stela — both only about 140 years after David's time. Then, possibly closer still,

a Negev toponym in the great list of Shoshenq I (924) quite likely names a "heights of David," less than 50 years after the old fellow's decease, when the memory of him would still be fresh. Yet, we are told, "nothing on Solomon = no Solomon"; but it may still be just a little early for persisting with such foolish dogmatism.

To conclude on Middle Period minimalism, two features stand out. First, in reaction to the 1950s-1960s world of Albright/Wright/Gordon, etc., the 1970s group usefully cleaned out much of the unsafe, overhypothetical propositions elaborated by their predecessors. Second, they in turn then made the same silly mistake of pushing their own views well beyond the factual evidence, trying to force the latter by special pleading and deliberately ignoring the older bodies of material. They were (and are) not "revolutionaries" in any real sense — merely "Olde Worlde" reactionaries (even recidivists, one might say) trying to go back to the antiquated world of the later nineteenth century, in the teeth of masses of contrary external evidence, most of it little known — and misunderstood when it was available. They were the base from which the late-period minimalism of today has proceeded in natural succession, and with even less sense of reality. And they drew their ultimate authority not from the vast constellation of available, relevant, external facts, but simply from the original mythic world of nineteenth-century theory and literary-critical dogma. Therefore, it is to that academically Paleolithic world that we must finally turn before concluding.

5. EARLY-PERIOD MINIMALISM — THE ULTIMATE FANTASIES

The views about the Old Testament held down to the 1950s were not new then, on any side. They nearly all went straight back to the later nineteenth century for the most part, with variations on its themes in lesser detail. And the basics of the 1880s still form the often unconscious basis for both the unthinking, self-styled "mainstream" of middle-of-the-road historical-literary-critical practice and the irruptions of the 1970s onward; and also (despite their reactions to all these) of the latest volcanic spoutings of the 1990s late-period minimalists till now. So, from a professional Orientalist's viewpoint, we need to take a sharply critical look at these rather ancient foundations — how sound are they in fact?

A. THE HEARTLAND OF THE LATER NINETEENTH CENTURY: THE *PROLEGOMENA* AND ENCYCLOPEDIA ESSAY BY WELLHAUSEN

"Why pick on poor, dear old Julius Wellhausen?" some may say. Indeed, he was but one of a number of very active literary-critical investigators of the Old Testament in the second half of the nineteenth century, following on from the pioneers. These latter included the effective founding figure, J. Astruc in 1753 (besides Witter in 1711), whose work led to further such analytical studies (Eichhorn, De Wette, etc.). Right from the start Astruc entitled his very readable work *Conjectures . . .* , with an attractive honesty and candor not so easily found among his successors. He knew his limits: that his work was pure theory, and that his criteria (variations in use of divine names, etc.) for dividing up the text of Genesis in particular would only go so far before petering out. Would that others had been so honest. He had in the mid–eighteenth century no access to any other ancient Near Eastern literature with which proper comparisons might have been made as an external yardstick. Neither did any of his successors until the late 1860s/1870s, when usable translations of Egyptian texts and Assyrian cuneiform sources effectively began to appear in modest quantity.

But Wellhausen's merit is that he represents the acme of nineteenth-century biblical criticism, expressed in print principally by his *Prolegomena to the History of Ancient Israel,* first issued in German in 1878, and his famous article "Israel" published in the *Encyclopaedia Britannica* in 1886.[50] In the book he applied an evolutionary framework, against which he set the history both of the religion of Israel and of her political sequence. Or, more accurately, he set the rearranged features of the religion and the deconstructed materials of the history on an evolutionary sliding scale. The article gave a clear outline of this. And it is his presentation (not that of others) that molded much of biblical studies from then right through the twentieth century. Other approaches, equally theoretical, such as Gunkel's introduction of form criticism (with Scandinavian followers) and the later techniques of Alt and Noth (mainly in Germany), arose, but assume its validity, while making limited adjustments to standard literary analysis. The literary-critical analyses themselves have suffered innumerable variations and internal disputes (supplement versus fragment hypotheses, etc.), but these inquests have not much affected the overall basis. Thus Wellhausen remains at heart the real basis for what followed, through the 1970s, and in part underlies late-period minimalism's bizarre frolics.

B. GRANDIOSE THEORIES VERSUS PERMANENT AND PERSISTENT FACTS

(i) Toying with Evolution

The nineteenth century just loved evolution, in the wake of Charles Darwin's spectacular theories in the natural world. And in religious/historical terms, it gave Wellhausen the concept of arranging the development of Israel and her institutions on an ascending line from the most primitive level to the most sophisticated: from primitive tribesfolk having a "natural," free-and-easy, very simple religion, through a rudimentary monarchy into which came the prophets, followed (with the Babylonian exile and Persian return to Judah) by a religious, priest-ridden, cultically dominated community governed by an elaborate "law," leading to an introspective group and religious fossilization of this limited society into Roman times. The literature was conformed to the same principle. First, the successive narratives "J" and "E," then the drastic reforms supposedly sparked off by proclamation of Deuteronomy (621, Josiah's reform) with the literary impact of "D" writers, and finally the supposedly priestly regulations and laws of "P" and "H" after the exile. In other words, the upward sloping line. "Upward, ever upward!" was the cry of "modern progress" then.

(ii) Evolution in History and Religion versus the Facts of Life

But what *really* happened in ancient history? The first thing to recall — which almost all modern observers totally overlook! — is how very, very little was known of ancient Israel's surrounding context, the Near Eastern world, back in 1878. *Incredibly little.* A long outline of Egyptian kings (and some history, New Kingdom) was known sketchily, but "Khuenaten" (= Akhenaten) was viewed (when not ignored) as an obscure king in some ancient dispute, dedicated to sun worship, nothing more.[51] The Neo-Assyrian kings and their deeds (first millennium) were beginning to be known, but not too much of them or Babylon for the earlier periods. The Sumerians proper were totally unheard of. Traces of Babylonian tales of the flood and creation (among other fragments of literature) had only just been published by George Smith in a paper of 1873 and his book of 1876. Heaps of tablets came to the British Museum and other major museums — but could not be published (much less read!) overnight; in fact, many are still unpublished, through lack of enough qualified cuneiformists. For the Levant, only the Moabite Stone and some late Phoenician inscriptions had surfaced; Old South Arabian was known, but from just a modest handful of texts.

And that was about it! At that time there were *no* Amarna letters (only found in 1887), *no* Code of Hammurabi of Babylon (only dug up in 1901), *no* other early law collections, *no* Siloam inscription (found only in 1880), *no* Hittites (Sayce and Wright only "invented" them in 1880/1884, with Sayce's first guess in 1876). There was *no* systematic archaeology by strata (Petrie did not dig Tell el-Hesi until 1891; Schliemann only began at Troy in 1871). Large-scale and scientifically enhanced archaeology lay far into the future, unimagined. *No* Ugarit, *no* Hurrian, *no* vast Ebla, Mari, Ugarit, Emar archives from outside Mesopotamia.

So Wellhausen worked in a near vacuum and could speculate freely. But that day has long, long since gone. We today *do* have the vast resources hinted at just above. And they *do* enable us to profile ancient history accurately in its broad sweep. And straight bottom-to-top evolution is *out.* It *never* happened like that; no, not ever. What *did* happen was the emergence of a culture with its political format, followed by an undulating history of ups and downs, until the political format was lost and the culture-bearing population either scattered or absorbed into other peoples and traditions. The essence was (1) a formative period, (2) a crystallization of cultural norms, then (3) undulation of ongoing history and culture until final eclipse. *Clearly and repeatedly.* For the ancient great powers (Egypt, Mesopotamia, Anatolia), the facts have been available for most of last century, but were never studied as a continuum phenomenon. The present writer has pointed out this phenomenon a few times, but its inherent significance has not been realized. It is the *true "longue durée,"* a *factually observed* one, not a mere theory like Braudel's. Therefore, being factual, it had best be taken on board without too much delay.

It will be as well to illustrate this in practice, in the simplest possible form. Table 37, on page 488, shows how it was, in Egypt, Mesopotamia, Anatolia (Hittites), and Canaanite/post-Canaanite Levant. This series should tell its own tale. Although of necessity much simplified, (1) to (4) represent the basic facts, and their factually secure story *cannot* be sidestepped. That is how things were. Full stop. There is no factual reason whatsoever for denying the innate reality of (5) either, as the facts set out in chapters 2–8 of this book should indicate to the open-minded. Entirely false is the nineteenth-century "evolutionary" scheme (pure theory!) illustrated at the top of page 489.

This final scheme, pumped into generations of students, both future and practicing biblicists, is and (alas!) always was pure, unadulterated fantasy. I am sorry, but that's how life is — and wasn't. It clashes horribly with real-life historical profiles for the cultures that we can test (and nos. 1-5 of tab. 37 are not exhaustive!) and has no decent parallel in terms of *longue durée.* That is how things are, and it wrecks the Wellhausen scheme completely. Thus efforts by the Finkelsteins and Silbermans of this world to impose the concept of a

Table 37. Undulation, Not "Evolution"
(I = Formative; II = Crystallization; III = Undulation)

1. EGYPT

I	II	III					(END)
Archaic Period	Old Kingdom		Middle Kingdom		New Kingdom		Saite Ptol Period	
		1st Int Period		2nd Int Period		3rd Int Period		Roman Period

2. MESOPOTAMIA

I	II	III			(END)
Sumer, Akkad, III Ur	Old Babylonian		Neo-Assyrian	Neo-Babylonian	
		Middle Babylonian/ Assyrian	Late Balylonian		Persian & Greek-Roman

3. ANATOLIA (HITTITES)

I	II	III			(END)
Early Bronze Copper Age	Old Hittite		Hittite Empire		
		Middle Hittite		Neo-Hittite	Post-Assyrian

4. CANAAN/LEVANT

I	II	III				(END)
Neol, Chal EB I	EB I-III		MB II		Iron II	Neo-Bablyonian to Greek-Roman
		EB/MB		LB/Iron I		

5. HEBREWS

I	II	III			(END)
Patriarchs & Sojourn	Sinai Covenant		David/ Solomon	Divided Monarchy; ups/downs: — down; Omrides up; down	Neo-Babylonian to Roman
		Iron I/Jud.			

488

A Victorian Romance

		UP, UP! (Top)	
		3. Exile: heights	*Down & Out!*
	UP, UP!	of monotheism	
	2. Modest Monarchy:		4. Afterward:
UP, UP!	prophetic religion		Dead law & ritual
1. Primitive Israel:			
natural, slap-happy			
religion			

---

nineteenth-century, evolutionary biblicist straitjacket upon Syro-Palestinian archaeology will not work; Dever, too, fell for this mistake, in Deuteronomic terms. A modern Syro-Palestinian archaeology has no need of these ancient mental fetters. Throw them away!

(iii) Consequences for Hebrew Religion in Its Material Context

We now have a true development (oops! I nearly said "evolution") for Hebrew religion. That of the patriarchs was a form of worship of El (El-Shaddai, etc.), who through their generations became "God of the (fore)fathers," as in the Old Assyrian/Old Babylonian period; his personal name (little used) may already have been YHWH. Their cult of occasional open-air altars (with prayer and sacrifice) was familial and quite simple. In Egypt it was probably much the same; we are not told. The family grew through time into a group of families > clans > small tribal groups under the common ancestral name Israel (by which they identified themselves to Merenptah's rough soldiery in Canaan much later). But then they became seriously enslaved. The brainy ones with clever hands got into technology (metal/woodworking in government employ; we see this kind of thing in New Kingdom tomb paintings and reliefs). The rest cared for livestock, or more often ended up as brickies.

But there came a man (Mashu > Mose; graduate of Pi-Ramesse foreign ministry; fled after committing homicide) who claimed ancient paternal YHWH's authority to lead them out to Canaan. This only made things worse (no straw allowance; ghastly happenings with plagues), until they finally got away under his leading, not via the suicidal coast road to Canaan (thick with Egyptian garrisons) but quietly off into Sinai. There the graduate did his stuff. From his old foreign-office days he *knew* that every other people group and state had a sovereign ruler — a king, often as a deity's representative. And law and treaty/covenant were the basis for regulating community life. *He* was no king; but their powerful patron YHWH would be their sole sovereign, and none other. He required obedience to the covenant, and practical expression of this also in cult. Thus a twice-daily sacrifice on an altar at a formal tent-shrine (nicely portable) served this purpose; that's where the brainy Bezalels came in, to make it work, with their Egyptian-based technology. But in strong reaction to lavishly (even garishly) idol- and image-rich Egypt, YHWH would remain invisible and figureless.

Once in Canaan, with the covenant repeatedly renewed (plains of Moab; Mount Ebal), a fresh leader conducted lightning raids to break the local leaderships and make ready for the whole group to occupy lands prescribed for them. But then he died; the geriatric successor committee did nothing. So the tribal levies tried local splinter-group operations to achieve settlement, and ended up entangled with the locals.

Thereafter the old family league almost fell apart, except in times of particular crisis (cf. Judges); many compromised comfortably in cult, with YHWH *and* local numens (a Baal, an Astarte, or an Asherah). The battered old tabernacle kept a notional presence at Shiloh, its cult increasingly moribund and of local interest only. The aged skin/cloth/wooden structure probably was eventually stored away in some drab outhouse in favor of a more waterproof mud-brick shrine (with the usual beams-and-plaster roof), until that grim day when the Philistines destroyed the shrine (but missed the old skins, cloth/poles in a half-hidden hovel of an outhouse, etc.). The modest bundle of covenant documents and related MSS were simply stored, wrapped, and almost never read — the daily cult had long become a fossilized rite-by-rote.

Under a prophet (Samuel) a fresh lead arose; but by now the people wanted a "professional" human king against hungry foes. So came Saul, David, Solomon. With David came unity, local consolidation, and a strategically placed capital; but there were still tabernacular traditional worship in his new capital and ongoing local worship at "high places" by long custom, whether for YHWH or others. With the full military manpower of *all* Israel and Judah, he defeated local foes (annexing their territory over the Jordan under local governors). Then came a bigger fish: the emerging kingdom of Aram-Zobah. Victory here gave him control of south Syria inland, and the adherence of Hamath that controlled the route to the distant Euphrates. This all gave rich possibilities of profit from trade-route control, which the next king (Solomon) could exploit to the full.

Founders of empire (even of mini-empires like this one) did not normally have the time and energy for conspicuous consumption and display. That usually took several generations. Compare in Egypt. Nobody warred farther than Tuthmosis I and III. But from Ahmose I to Hatshepsut, four reigns passed before much major state building was done. That came with Tuthmosis III, reaching a peak only with his great-grandson Amenophis III. The Amarna episode (Akhenaten) then delayed further such efforts until the Ramesside kings and incipient decline. Thus David was "too early" (sociologically) to be a great builder. Again, in Assyria, the most immense imperial building efforts came with the later Neo-Assyrian kings, Sargon II to Assurbanipal into the age of incipient decline. Solomon was the first of what *should* (sociologically) have been several generations of builders. Naturally he concentrated on the capital initially (ancient kings always did), so Jerusalem got a temple and a palace complex. Then he could begin to organize and do initial building at governmental district centers (as at Hazor, Megiddo, and Gezer), but not develop everything everywhere.

That program *should* have fallen to his immediate successors — but collapse of the little empire and division of the monarchy ended that dream. Then later, the growth of the northern kingdom under the Omrides and Jeroboam II led to some major projects that were (in part) the moral successors to Solomon's works. Just as in Egypt the Akhenaten episode delayed things, so in Israel the initial weak period of the divided monarchy enforced an interval in such outward development and display.

Religiously Solomon established an official, state focus by his temple. But his diplomatic links (by foreign marriages) led to an "ecumenism" in cults that infringed on the traditional sole sovereignty of YHWH established by ancient covenant. Once more, inconvenient ancient scrolls were quietly left unread, so "compromise" grew with time. And under later kings the temple acquired cults of such as Asherah alongside YHWH with appropriate cultic equipment.

Crises (with Arameans, with neighboring Israel, with Egypt occasionally, with Philistines and others, and eventually with Assyria) led to sporadic reform movements, led by prophets who played an increasing role in recalling kings and people to their ancient covenant (YHWH, sole sovereign). Such kings as Hezekiah and Josiah responded to these calls in varying degrees — the latter particularly, when a neglected old book was opened for the first time in nearly 60 years (Manasseh's 55 and Amon's 2 = 57 years since Hezekiah's heyday). Whether it was Deuteronomy or otherwise, it had a major impact on Josiah and others, leading to a more far-reaching reform. But things drifted away again once he was gone. However, the prophets fastened on all this, including Jeremiah and the prophetic writers of the final book of Kings.

In the lushly idol-friendly atmosphere of Babylon(ia), the Hebrews had only their ancestral deity to cling to, and their sacred writings. Pagan displays quickly jaded the palate, leaving their ancestral faith and writings as a greater consolation in the new world that the Persian Empire ushered in. The old covenant and its associated cult rituals then became normative for the little community as never before, down through the stressful Hellenistic period into Roman times. So may we sketch the formative origins, the crystallization, and centuries-long undulations in the fortunes of Hebrew/ancient Israelite religion and history, hinting at its multiplicity of facets.

(iv) So Much for Religion and History — What about Literature?

With the evolutionary ladder gone, what happens to the biblical literature? Where do J, E, D, P now belong, if the old order is only a chimera? Or, in fact, do they belong at all?

Here we will be concise, open, and fairly staccato. First, the basic fact is that there is *no* objective, independent evidence for any of these four compositions (or for any variant of them) anywhere outside the pages of our existing Hebrew Bible. If the criterion of "no outside evidence" damns the existence of such as Abraham, Moses, or Solomon and company, then it equally damns the existence of these (so far) imaginary works. They exist *only* in the minds of their modern creators (from Witter and Astruc to the present day), and as printed in their published studies, as theoretical works abstracted out of the standard text of the Old Testament books that we *do* have. This very simple fact needs to be stressed. Our resourceful biblicists are not sitting on some secret store of papyri or parchments that contain any such works. The Dead Sea Scrolls show no sign of them whatever; stubbornly, they know only of the canonical works that we have, and of commentaries and "romances" (e.g., the Genesis Apocryphon) based upon them. Modern guesswork, as we all know, is often extraordinarily and breathtakingly clever and ingenious — one can only reverently take one's hat off to it all, in respectful amazement, sometimes. But . . . it does *not* constitute fact, and cannot substitute for it. I might choose to dream up a theory that the Ramesside kings of Egypt also once built pyramids in Egypt, twice as big as the Great Pyramid. But absolutely nobody is going to believe me unless I can produce some *tangible, material* evidence in its favor. And we require, likewise, *some* kind of clear, material evidence for a J, E, D, or a P or an H, from *outside* of the extant Hebrew Bible. The standards of proof among biblical scholars fall massively and woefully short of the high standards that professional Orientalists and archaeologists are long accustomed to, and have a right to demand. Some MSS, please! If an excavation tomorrow produced a substantial chunk of a scroll that *indubitably* contained a copy of precisely J or E, and found in a clear, datable stratigraphic context, then I would welcome it with open arms and incorporate it into my overrall appreciation of the history of the Hebrew Bible. But *not* just as unsubstantiated guesswork out of somebody's head.

Second, time and time again the modes of analysis (and their criteria, variant vocabulary, "styles," etc.) have been demonstrated to be defective. And *not* just by "conservatives" either. Suffice it to refer to the very careful and conscientious study by (e.g.) the late R. N. Whybray (no conservative), *The Making of the Pentateuch*.[52] On the internal data, it is a damning indictment of these methods. He offers a largely unitary Pentateuch, but of a relatively late date. The *final* form of the Pentateuch may well lie with the time of an Ezra; but of course, on *external, factual* data, the origins of much of its constituent books lie much further back. Gen. 1–11 has origins in the early second millennium, as does most of that book. Exodus-Leviticus contain (as does Deuteronomy) a covenant in a format exclusive to circa 1400-1200, along with the building account for a tabernacle of a type in use in the late second millennium. Many items in P and H are long prior to the Babylonian exile, and in fact belong in many cases also to the late second millennium. Laws in Exodus and elsewhere find their closest analogues not in the Babylon of Nebuchadrezzar II, but in the law collections down to the Old Babylonian period.[53] Much is sometimes made of the force of cumulative arguments piled together. Well, maybe we should add that consideration too, to all the foregoing points.

Third, people sometimes talk glibly about the "literary strata" in the biblical writings, as if they were somewhat parallel to the strata in an archaeological mound. Yes, it sounds very appropriate, but which way do your strata run? In an archaeological site, the successive strata (by and large) lie in succession roughly *horizontally,* one above the other. And that can be seen in our analyses, based on external comparisons, of the books of Genesis and so on, above. We have a basic tradition, maybe from the early second millennium or before it (bedrock); then the main account as written, early/mid–second millennium (stratum I); then a later update (like "land of Rameses" or Dan for Laish) from the late second millennium (stratum II); and finally a last note or two (like the Chaldees of Ur) from the first millennium (stratum III), and the finalization of the whole therewith. Here our succession rests upon tangible, external data that actually exist.

But the "strata" supposed in J, E, D, or P, H are of an entirely different kind. Here, to distinguish passages of J, E, P (say) in Genesis, *vertical* cuts have been made, all the way through the book. These are like the *vertical sections* sometimes cut through or across a mound, and not like horizontal strata at all! No archaeologist worth his salt would dream of accepting as "strata" a set of vertical sections cut separately, all over a mound. The resulting segments of earth are *balks,* cut down through real strata at 90 degrees to the real strata! Vertical balks and true horizontal strata are not the same thing. And vertical fissures cut arbitrarily all through the texture of ancient books, using false criteria, are not "strata" either. People speak of "heavily edited" works; but, again, we need objective evidence (like the Rameses/Dan/Chaldees kind instanced above) to establish the presence of editing — not "editing" which is merely the product of clever guesswork or based on an a priori hypothesis of religious development, without proper supporting data.

There is great scope for fresh literary study, if based upon attested ancient usage derived from the factual analysis of the full literatures of the entire ancient Near East (so far as available; and there's a lot!). But not for the old-fashioned "dead-end" guesswork of the nineteenth-century type.

(v) Wellhausen and the Ancient Near East — a Pet Hate of His!

Not only did Wellhausen (like his peers) work in a cultural vacuum — that is how he *wanted* it to be, undisturbed by inconvenient facts from the (ancient) outside world. He resented being pointed toward high-antiquity data from Egypt and Mesopotamia, and damned their practitioners for it. How he hated Egyptologists! In the encyclopedia article, desperately trying to evade even the possibility of early monotheism and any Egyptian influence, he fulminated against "the God-forsaken dreariness of certain modern Egyptologists."[54] This followed his jibe that the 480 years for the period between the exodus and Solomon's temple (1 Kings 6:1) was "certainly more trustworthy than the combinations of the Egyptologists" (430 n. 1). In due course he also lashes out at the Assyriologists; dealing with chronology around the time of Menahem of Israel, he mutters that for the chronology then, "the explanations of the Assyriologists have hitherto been total failures" (474 n. 1). Maybe in 1886. But not nowadays. Clearly, he resented any outside impact that might threaten his beloved theses on the supposed development of Israelite religion and history. And that attitude, one can detect in his equally resistant disciples today.

(vi) Four Sample Cases Where the Near East Knew Better Than Wellhausen

(a) The Patriarchs

In his time, there was no real background available for the patriarchs at all, except the famous tomb painting of the thirty-seven "Asiatics" at Beni Hasan. Thus Wellhausen could feel free to enunciate his equally famous dogma, that "here [in Genesis] no historical knowledge about the patriarchs is to be gotten, but only about the period in which the stories about them arose among the Israelite people. This later period was simply to be projected back into hoary antiquity and reflected there like a glorified mirage."[55]

These sentiments were treated as gospel truth by his uncritical disciples from then till now. In the factual vacuum of 1878, one could get away with such stuff, but not now. The world of Gen. 12–50 is certainly *not* that of the monarchy period. It is, equally, not that of Joshua to Samuel, nor of the overlordship of the Egyptian empire from 1550 to the twelfth century B.C. It fits only the period before that, the twentieth to seventeenth centuries, for a series of reasons based directly on external, factual data that he would have loathed to admit but would have been powerless to refute; cf. chapter 7 above.

(b) The Sinai Covenant

Our hero dogmatically proclaimed that "The expression 'Jehovah is the God of Israel' . . . certainly did not mean that the almighty Creator of heaven and earth was conceived of having first made a covenant with this one people that by them He might be truly known and worshipped" (437).

Unfortunately, (i) what he denies the text means *is* exactly what it did and still does mean; and (ii) the whole mass of external evidence on treaty and covenant (totally unknown in 1878) objectively fixes the late second-millennium date of the essential elements in Exodus-Leviticus, Deuteronomy, and Josh. 24, and eliminates any later-date theory. Cf. chapter 6 above.

(c) The Tabernacle

Here Wellhausen sought to discount the tabernacle as totally a fiction, and one created by the (imaginary) priestly writer(s) of the Babylonian exile. We may again quote: "the tabernacle rests on an historical fiction. In truth it is proved. . . ." And: "At the outset its very possibility is doubtful. Very strange is the contrast between this splendid structure, on which the costliest material is lavished and wrought in the most advanced style of Oriental art, and the soil on which it rises, in the wilderness amongst the native Hebrew nomad tribes [*sic*], who are represented as having got it ready offhand, and without external help" (39, etc.).

But *not* without a former "external" training (Bezalel in Egypt), not without loot from Egypt, and not without the basic technology learned there, of which we have abundant evidence and of which our arrogant critic knew absolutely nothing. Other than the gold and silver used, there is no "costliest material" (only linen cloth, skins, and local acacia wood! Our Wellhausen is a rare lad at exaggeration!). And what did *he* know (in 1878!) about advanced Oriental art? Nothing. In fact, the decor of the tabernacle is far simpler than most work done then, and the linen work is very simple compared (e.g.) with work known from a thousand years before (Sahure's sail)!

The tabernacle was an incredibly small cultic structure (15 × 45 feet!), compared with most of the Near Eastern and Egyptian temples and shrines of its time; the Timna example shows that poeple *did* use "tabernacles" (twelfth century) long centuries before any priestly inventors in the exile; and various details are late second millennium, not first; see already in chapter 6. The supposed nonmentions in the history from Jericho to Samuel, as of the "law" (= covenant) from Judges to the seventh century, stem partly from his gross failure to consider the circumstances of those periods, partly from his arbitrary excision of relevant biblical references on one or another illegitimate excuse, and partly from the simple fact that the ancients mainly used law (and shrines) without chattering their heads off about it all the time. Thus there are virtually *no* contemporary or later mentions of the laws of Hammurabi in Babylonia, for example — but (given his stela and tablet editions) nobody can deny that the corpus existed throughout. It is no different for the laws of Exodus-Deuteronomy, or for the tabernacle.[56]

(d) The Topographical List of Shoshenq I (Shishak)

When faced with the clear evidence of the place-name list of Shoshenq I as a contributing factor to our understanding of the Shishak episode in the reign of Rehoboam (1 Kings 14:25-26; 2 Chron. 12:2-10), then, like a true minimalist, Wellhausen refused to accept plain-as-a-pikestaff evidence and began weaving and ducking, with the brazen assertion that "he [= Shishak] could simply have reproduced an older list of one of his predecessors."[57] And some biblicists have been foolish enough blindly to follow him. A mere copy of old stuff? Really? The answer has to be a crushing "No!" Taking the 155 known ovals (each containing a name or part of a compound name) and discounting ten introductory heraldic entries ("Nine Bows" plus title), a series of twenty-five or thirty names known to be wholly lost or leaving merest/unusable traces, and other almost undecipherable names, we are left with a hard core of usable names. Of these, only *nine* are common to Shoshenq and previous lists (these include Megiddo, Taanach, Beth-Shan, listed at all times, given their geographic situation). *The other ninety-eight are unique to Shoshenq I's list.* Let that fact sink in; Wellhausen's arrogant dismissal of the list is wholly without any factual foundation whatsoever.[58] And what is true of this item is true of most of the rest of his work.

*   *   *

To close this early minimalist episode, one can only shake one's head in sorrow over the sad history of Old Testament scholarship in the last two hundred years. During the eighteenth and, above all, the nineteenth century, there arose a spirit of inquiry that sought to go beyond just reading the Hebrew Bible wholly "on the surface." Regrettably, (i) most of the early biblicists chose to elaborate theories based exclusively upon the text of the Hebrew Bible, and upon their manipulations of the phenomena in its text. There was no thought of cross-checking with any kind of factual control, such as: *How* did people actually go about composing books and documents in biblical times and regions? A disastrous omission. And (ii) there were no means of external control available in the eighteenth century, or during the first half or two-thirds of the nineteenth century, while Egyptian and cuneiform were being systematically deciphered; only from about 1860/70 onward did usable translations begin to appear at all. And at that time nobody had thought of any kind of literary study of these newly won documents.

Thus the theorists had a field day for many decades, and what had been merely bold theory became fixed dogma, as though set in concrete. A purely theoretical minimalism (lacking any factual verification) was enshrined as dogma in theology and divinity schools and faculties, while the vast worlds of ancient Near Eastern studies slowly began to be unveiled, offering huge additions to factual knowledge. And almost none of it agrees with the dogmas so uncritically perpetuated into the present. Early, middle, and late minimalists alike face the need for some very drastic changes in their fantasy worlds. And that, *not* from rival brands of philosophy or theology, but in factual terms from the firmly secular disciplines of Assyriology, Egyptology, parallel studies for the rest of the Near East, and the whole of its various regional archaeologies (Syro-Palestinian archaeology included).

6. IN CONCLUSION: WHAT RESULTS?

So, instead, why not go for a better-founded, more truly radical future, starting afresh from real basics? Why not begin again from a new, essentially fact-governed, hence more solidly based paradigm? From a safe, strong, roomy launchpad from which anyone may rocket off into a beckoning future? The old, simplistic, nineteenth-century "zero-to-infinity" evolutionary scheme (purely theoretical!) has in effect collapsed in various disciplines, and the fact-based Near Eastern profiles presented in briefest form above can now afford us a far more stable paradigm with which to work.

Let us suggest the broadest and deepest practical basis: the entire Ancient Near East from roughly 10,000 B.C. down to the turn of the era, from Crete to the Indus, from the Black Sea to Sudan and the Arabian Sea. This is the overall geographic space-time frame.

First, we should aim at establishing a fuller vision of a series of fact-based *longues durées,* based on working out more fully the profiles of the individual ancient Near Eastern cultures and civilizations on the basis of *formative, crystallization,* and *undulation* phases in each case (until their termination), going into much more detail than the minimum, skeletal models given above (p. 488). This can be done piecemeal, in the various regions of the ancient world just delineated.

In terms of time frame, we should probably divide the great span of ten thousand years into two unequal parts for purely practical purposes, governed by the difference made by the presence or otherwise of written sources. Major *phase A* should be the almost entirely preliterate epoch circa 10,000 to circa 3000. Major *phase B* would then follow, as a growingly literate epoch, circa 3000 to year zero. During the third and second millennia, alongside the many texts from Egypt and Mesopotamia, effective local written sources commence in different zones at different times (e.g., ca. 2400 in Syria; ca. 1900 in Anatolia; ca. 1400 in Palestine; ca. 1100 in Old South Arabia). Thus, circa 3000-1000 is virtually a transitional period (a "phase C") overlapping the first two-thirds of phase B. Phase A and in part phase C-on-B cultures (those without writing) would have to be assessed entirely on the basis of artifactual archaeology, with a restrained role for societal anthropology, eschewing its more a priori theories. Phase B cultures (wherever writing gave major input) would have to be assessed on both the artifactual and written sources with proper integration of both data sets. Needless to say, there can be no regimentation of the various profiles; the three basic phases will have differed in length and in cultural detail from zone to zone, and different cultures (or their major sequences) will have gone through their cycles at different periods. During the main undulation phases, with directly neighboring cultures, some mutual interference will sometimes, of course, be visible. For example, in Canaan, the main Middle Bronze period was a "high," with its prosperous local city-states, while Egypt had something of a "low" (Second Intermediate Period/Hyksos rule); then, Late Bronze Canaan sank into a relative "low" when it was politically and economically subjected by New Kingdom Egypt on a renewed "high."

Second, we must deal with the biblical record in the same way, using what we actually possess (objectively — we have nothing else!). As is clear from the above skeletal presentation (p. 488), its basic framework of (i) precursor family > clan group (Canaan > Egypt), then (ii) exodus and covenant (Sinai/Moab), plus (iii) entry into Canaan and varied fortunes there down to 722 and 586 (plus partial return, fifth/fourth century) is a very clear case of formative period, then swift crystallization, then long and varied undulation, lasting in fact into the early Roman period when the people were scattered. There is no need, ever again, to force the data artificially and arbitrarily into a bed of Procrustes, shuffling around prophets, covenantal law collections, forms of worship, etc., just to fit an alien scheme that finds no echo whatsoever in the overall history and culture of the biblical world at any time from the Paleolithic to the Romans. Let us agree, at last, quietly to part with imaginary and outdated evolutionary schemes and give them decent and final burial. They have long had their day, and more solid and constructive paths are now open, offering to all of us immense opportunities for constructive work, totally regardless of whatever our own personal philosophies may be (with either faith or no faith, without distinction).

*   *   *

We have now come to the close of our long and eventful journey through millennia of the vivid world of Near Eastern antiquity, and of inquiry into "modern times" attitudes to the Hebrew Bible. It is time to return to the questions posed at the beginning of this book: whether or not the existing Old Testament writings were composed (and their contents originated) entirely within the brief and late period of circa 400-200 B.C., or whether or not their contents are pure fiction, unrelated to the world of the Near East in circa 2000-400 B.C.

To pursue such questions, the only practical method of inquiry was to go back to those ancient times and compare the data in the Hebrew Bible with what we have from its putative world. Merely theorizing in one's head can achieve nothing. Looking back, we do have some definite results. On the independent evidence from antiquity itself, we may safely deliver a firm "No" to both questions as posed above. Namely, the Old Testament books and their contents did *not* exclusively originate as late as 400-200 B.C.; and they are by no means pure fiction — in fact, there is very little proven fiction in them overall.

What can be said of historical reliability? Here our answer — on the evidence available — is more positive. The periods most in the glare of contemporary documents — the divided monarchy and the exile and return — show a very high level of direct correlation (where adequate data exist) and of reliability. That fact should be graciously accepted by all, regardless of personal starting point, and with the firm exclusion of alien, hence irrelevant, modern "agendas." When we go back (before ca. 1000) to periods when inscriptional mentions of a then-obscure tribal community and its antecedent families (and founding family) simply cannot be expected a priori, then chronologically typological comparisons of the biblical and external phenomena show clearly that the Hebrew founders bear the marks of reality and of a definite period. The same applies to the Hebrews' exodus from Egypt and appearance in Canaan, with one clear mention, of course (Israel on the stela of Merenptah). The Sinai covenant (all three versions, Deuteronomy included) has to have originated within a close-set period (1400-1200) — likewise other features. The phenomena of the united monarchy fit well into what we know of the period and of ancient royal usages. The primeval protohistory embodies early popular tradition going very far back, and is set in an early format. Thus we have a consistent level of good, fact-based correlations right through from circa 2000 B.C. (with earlier roots) down to 400 B.C. In terms of general reliability — and much more could have been instanced than there was room for here — the Old Testament comes out remarkably well, so long as its writings and writers are treated fairly and evenhandedly, in line with independent data, open to all. There, we stop!

NOTES

NOTES TO CHAPTER 1

1. The handiest edition of the surviving fragments and citations of Manetho's work (Greek/English) is still W. G. Waddell, *Manetho*, LCL 350 (Cambridge: Harvard University Press; London: Heinemann, 1940). This work was formerly often bound with F. E. Robbins, *Ptolemy Tetrabiblos.*

2. For the fragments of Berossus in English, see Stanley M. Burstein, *The Babyloniaca of Berossus*, Sources from the Ancient Near East 1/5 (Malibu, Calif.: Undena Publications, 1978).

3. For the Jews, the real equivalent of such works as these was in practice the much later set of writings by Flavius Josephus (translated by H. St. J. Thackeray, R. Marcus, and L. H. Feldman), *The Jewish War*, and especially *Jewish Antiquities*, which are conveniently available in nine volumes (1927-65) of the LCL series.

4. For overall presentations of the civilizations of the ancient Near East, valuable (but of occasionally variable quality in some respects) are (e.g.): J. M. Sasson, ed., *Civilizations of the Ancient Near East* I-IV (New York: Scribner, 1995); E. M. Meyers, ed., *Oxford Encyclopedia of Archaeology in the Ancient Near East* I-V (New York: OUP, 1997); plus D. B. Redford, ed., *Oxford Encyclopedia of Ancient Egypt* I-III (New York: OUP, 2000); and for biblical study and archaeology, D. N. Freedman et al., eds., *The Anchor Bible Dictionary* I-VI (New York: Doubleday, 1992). An excellent, compact, one-volume handbook to the ancient Near East is provided by P. Bienkowski and A. R. Millard, eds., *Dictionary of the Ancient Near East* (London: British Museum Press, 2000).

5. Sixty volumes of Keilschrifturkunden aus Boghazköi; forty-one so far of Keilschrifttexte aus Boghazköi; four of Istanbul Arkeoloji Müzelerinde Bulunan Bogazköy Tabletleri; one each of Ankara Arkeoloji Müzesinde Bulunan Bogazköy Tabletleri and Hittite Texts in the Cuneiform Character from Tablets in the British Museum. There are also other smaller such publications, e.g., A. Goetze, *Verstreute Boghazköi-Texte*. All of them contain exclusively copies of texts in the original cuneiform script (not for the fainthearted). Hittite texts (as thus published down to 1970) are classified by E. Laroche, *Catalogue des textes Hittites* (Paris: Klincksieck, 1971), with some mentions of translations and studies. An extensive run of Hittite texts is published in German translation in the two series StBoT (forty-four volumes so far) and

Texte der Hethiter (twenty-three volumes so far), and various older series. In English, a tiny fraction is available in *ANET,* the new *CoS* I-III, and such collections as the SBL's Writings from the Ancient World series (Hoffner, Beckman volumes).

NOTES TO CHAPTER 2

1. For the name Shoshe(n)q (Heb. *Shushaq*), cf. the Neo-Assyrian form *Susinqu* (dialectal for Babylonian *Shushinqu*), for the first, strong vowel sound in this name. For the Assyrian form, under Assurbanipal, cf. brief entries by Ranke, *KMAV,* 34, and Muchiki, *Egyptian PN,* 227. For the references for Shoshenq I's campaign, see below under sec. 5.

2. In general, for the history of the Twenty-Second Dynasty (and underlying chronology), see Kitchen, *Third Int. Pd.* (1996), 287-361, plus 574-81 and xxii-xxxix, passim. See further in sec. 5 below.

3. For compact references and discussion on Zerah, see Kitchen, *Third Int. Pd.* (1996), 309, §268.

4. For general discussions of the early Aramean kings in Damascus, see the now old book by M. F. Unger, *Israel and the Aramaeans of Damascus* (Grand Rapids: Zondervan, 1957), and the more recent works by W. T. Pitard, *Ancient Damascus* (Winona Lake, Ind.: Eisenbrauns, 1989), and (just earlier) H. Sader, *Les états araméens de Syrie . . .* (Beirut and Wiesbaden: F. Steiner Verlag, 1987), chap. 6, pp. 231-70, with references, plus P.-E. Dion, *Les araméens à l'age du fer: histoire, politique et structures sociales,* Ebib, n.s., 34 (Paris: Librairie Lecoffre, Gabalda, 1997).

5. On the Melqart Stela, cf. the latest summary by W. T. Pitard, in W. W. Hallo and K. L. Younger, eds., *CoS* II, 154-55, and notes.

6. For the text of this king list as presented by Josephus, see H. St. J. Thackeray, ed., *Josephus, the Life; Against Apion,* LCL 186 (1926), in *Against Apion* 1.116-26 on pp. 208/209-212/ 213.

7. For Baal-mazzer II (or Baal-manzer II) in a text of Shalmaneser III, see now A. K. Grayson, *RIMA,* 3:54 (replacing F. Safar, *Sumer* 7 [1951]: 11-12). This king would have been a second Balbazeros, directly following the Balezoros of Menander's list, and (in textual transmission) confused with the latter.

8. On the "Jezebel" seal, cf. latest publication by Avigad and Sass, *CWSS,* 275, no. 740, with references. Technically, the name might be either masculine or feminine, but the latter is (so far) the only known usage; for the little that it is worth, the recumbent sphinx on the seal has been analyzed as feminine (N. Avigad, *IEJ* 14 [1964]: 274), which icon would suit a woman's seal better than a man's.

9. For a comprehensive group of recent studies on the stela of Mesha, see A. Dearman, ed., *Studies in the Mesha Inscription and Moab,* Archaeology and Biblical Studies, ASOR/SBL, no. 2 (Atlanta: Scholars Press, 1989), with abundant previous literature. For the Mesha stela in relation to the Tell Dan stela, cf. A. Lemaire, *BAR* 20, no. 3 (May-June 1994): 30-37, and in *SEL* 11 (1994): 17-19.

10. For the old Aramaic inscriptions on ivory, see F. Bron and A. Lemaire, *RAAO* 83 (1989): 37, 39; for the horse blinkers, I. Eph'al and J. Naveh, *IEJ* 39 (1989): 192-200, in English.

11. On the mention of Aram-Damascus as "House of Hazael" under Tiglath-pileser III, cf. Tadmor, *TP III,* 138/39, 186/87.

12. This king and his father are explicitly so entitled (without the "III," of course!) on the contemporary stela of Zakkur, neighboring king of Hamath and Hatarikka. For English transla-

tions of that stela, cf. F. Rosenthal, *ANET,* 501-2 ("Zakir"), and A. R. Millard, *TynB* 41, no. 2 (1990): 273-74, app. 2; also in *CoS* II, 155. The "name" (really, epithet) *Mari',* "Lord," for the ruler of Aram-Damascus occurs in the inscriptions of Adad-nirari III of Assyria. Once thought to stand for Hazael, it is regarded by most current scholars as a term for his son and successor Benhadad III. Cf. discussion by Pitard, *Ancient Damascus,* 160-66, passim.

13. On this king in the texts of Tiglath-pileser III, see Tadmor, *TP III,* 54/55, 68/69, 78/79-80/81, 82/83, 106/107, 186/187, 208/209; on the forms of the name in Aramaic, Hebrew, and Akkadian, cf. Pitard, *Ancient Damascus,* 181-82, with references.

14. One seal belonged to "Milqom servant of Baalis"; see L. Herr, *BA* 48 (1985): 169-72; R. Deutsch, *BAR* 25, no. 2 (March-April 1999): 48. The other reads "[Belonging to] Baalisha', King of the Bani-Ammon" ("the sons of Ammon," the Ammonites); on this see Deutsch, same issue of *BAR* as cited above, pp. 46-48; R. Deutsch and M. Heltzer, *West Semitic Epigraphic News of the First Millennium* BCE (Tel Aviv, 1999), 53-55, no. 145.

15. Specimen texts in translation of most Assyrian kings mentioned here can be found in *ANET* and in *CoS* I-III, and extensively in the now old work, Luckenbill, *ARAB* I-II, and now in the modern *RIMA.* A vast and growing series of other Assyrian texts are now appearing in the modern series SAA (fifteen volumes so far, and several supplementary studies).

16. The full corpus of texts of this king will be found in a definitive edition in Tadmor, *TP III.* For the sculptured decoration on wall slabs in the king's unfinished palace, see R. D. Barnett and M. Falkner, *The Sculptures of Assur-nasir-apli II (883-859 BC), Tiglath-pileser III (745-727 BC), Esarhaddon (681-669 BC) from the Central and South-West Palaces at Nimrud* (London: British Museum, 1962). Pul was simply a nickname of, or abbreviation for, Tiglath-pileser III, and is used also in a cuneiform source, not only in Kings and Chronicles; cf. Babylonian king list A, iv:8 (cf. A. L. Oppenheim in *ANET,* 272; A. R. Millard in *CoS* I, 462 and n. 5). Pulu is the "Poros" of the Ptolemaic Canon. Cf. notes, J. A. Brinkman, *A Political History of Post-Kassite Babylonia, 1158-722 BC* (Rome: Pontificium Institutum Biblicum, 1968), 61-62. Like Ululai for Shalmaneser V (Brinkman, 61-62), Pul(u) occurs only in the one later report, but may have been an unofficial epithet from the beginning. That would fit the scattering of names in 2 Kings 15:19/16:7ff., while 1 Chron. 5:26 also implies identification of Pul and Tiglath-pileser III as one and the same, by its exact parallelism of the two, and use of singular verbs to express the actions of Pul/Tiglath-pileser III.

17. His quite short reign is attested by minor inscriptions (list, W. Schramm, *Einleitung in die assyrischen Königsinschriften* II [Leiden: Brill, 1973], 140; cf. also Brinkman, *Political History,* 243-45); he features in the Assyrian king lists, Babylonian Chronicle, and Assyrian eponym lists (first two, cf. Millard, *CoS* I, 465, 467; the eponym list, A. R. Millard, *The Eponyms of the Assyrian Empire, 910-612 BC,* SAAS II [Helsinki: Neo-Assyrian Text Corpus Project, 1994], 59 end).

18. Of his texts, extensive older translations in Luckenbill, *ARAB* II, with the annals by A. G. Lie, *The Inscriptions of Sargon II, King of Assyria, I, the Annals* (Paris: Geuthner, 1929). For modern extracts, cf. *ANET.* Khorsabad texts, A. Fuchs, *Die Inschriften Sargons II. aus Khorsabad* (Göttingen: Cuvillier, 1993). Letters, S. Parpola, with G. B. Lanfranchi, *The Correspondence of Sargon II* I-III, SAA I, V (Helsinki: University Press, 1987, 1990, 2001).

19. Extracts in *ANET;* full older versions in Luckenbill, *ARAB* II. Studies include E. Frahm, *Einleitung in die Sanherib-Inschriften* (Vienna: *AfO* [= Beiheft 26], 1997), and W. R. Gallagher, *Sennacherib's Campaign to Judah, New Studies* (Leiden: Brill, 1999).

20. Cf. *ANET.* Full body of translations (old) in Luckenbill, *ARAB* II and (new) by R. Borger, *Die Inschriften Asarhaddons, Königs von Assyrien* (Vienna: *AfO* [= Beiheft 9], 1956). For Assyria's last great king, Assurbanipal, again *ANET* has excerpts from the main historical

texts; for a modern presentation of many texts, see R. Borger, *Beiträge zum Inschriftenwerk Assurbanipals* (Wiesbaden: Harrassowitz, 1996).

21. He is discussed by J. A. Brinkman in *From the Workshop of the Assyrian Dictionary — Studies Presented to A. L. Oppenheim* (1964), 6-53; summary, Brinkman, "Marduk-apla-iddina II," in D. O. Edzard et al., eds., *RLA* VII, 5/6 (Berlin: de Gruyter, 1989), 374-75, with references. Mentioned in the texts of Tiglath-pileser III, Sargon II, and Sennacherib (above).

22. Nebuchadrezzar II of Babylon boasts numerous building texts, in now old editions by S. Langdon, *Die neubabylonischen Königsinschriften* (Leipzig: Hinrichs, 1912), and (in English) in his *Building Inscriptions of the Neo-Babylonian Empire* (Paris: Leroux, 1905). For various extracts, more modern, cf. *ANET*. See also in Babylonian Chronicle, successively, D. J. Wiseman, *Chronicles of Chaldaean Kings (626-556 BC) in the British Museum* (London: British Museum, 1956); A. K. Grayson, *Assyrian and Babylonian Chronicles,* Texts from Cuneiform Sources V (New York: Augustin, 1975), chronicles 3 to 5; extracts, Millard in *CoS* I, 467-68. Survey of sources, history, buildings, etc. (in German), M. P. Streck and R. M. Czichon, in *RLA* IX, 3/4 (1999), 194-206.

23. An older source summary by F. H. Weissbach is found in *RLA* I (1928-32), 94; newer, Sack in *ABD*, 2:679; fuller account, R. H. Sack, *Amel-Marduk — 562-560 BC* (Neukirchen-Vluyn: Neukirchener-Verlag, 1972).

24. The facts on the name and person of So can be read in Kitchen, *Third Int. Pd.* (1996), 372-76, 551-52, and esp. xxxiv-xxxix (refuting blunders by Christensen and Day). The remarks on So by S. Ahituv, in I. Shirun-Grumach, ed., *Jerusalem Studies in Egyptology* (Wiesbaden: Harrassowitz, 1998), 3 n. 1, are also mistaken. Emendation of the Hebrew text is wholly gratuitous; Akkadian *Sa* bears no relation to the *w* and *'aleph* of Hebrew *Sw'*; and he is again mistaken over the *'aleph* in So'. In the attested cartouches of all four known kings named Osorkon, there *is* an internal *'aleph (i)* in the original Egyptian spelling of the name "Osorkon" (= an English form of Greek!): *W-s-i-r-k-n*, in some cases more often with than without the internal *i*. Thus "So'" is a perfectly acceptable abbreviation of *(W)-s-i-(r-k-n)*. The name Osorkon can be (and was) abbreviated, as were other names of the period (Shosh for Shoshenq, etc.), as noted in the text.

25. On the usage that applies to Taharqa as prince in 701 but as king in the Hebrew text of 681, *ten years after* the king's accession, see besides the text in chap. 2 above, Kitchen, *Third Int. Pd.* (1996), 157-61, 383-86, 552-54, and cf. xxxix-xlii. In rejecting the simple facts about a writer in 681 using the terminology of his own time for Taharqa in 701, massive blunders were made by Gallagher, *Sennacherib's Campaign to Judah,* 221-22 (in an otherwise very fine monograph) and by W. H. Shea, both in *JBL* 104 (1985): 401-18, and in *BAR* 25, no. 6 (November-December 1999): 36-44, 64 (superficial; with the added error of "two" campaigns of Sennacherib), as neither author has properly understood the situation or the relevant data. There is no "anachronism" here (Gallagher's term, p. 253). The recently published Assyrian Tang-i Var text (G. Frame, *Or* 68 [1999]: 31-57; K. L. Younger, *CoS* II, 299-300) shows clearly now that Shebitku was a power in Egypt from at least 706, either as copharaoh with Shabako or as Nubian deputy — his personal rule from 702 is no problem (and never was), nor therefore is his sending out Taharqa in 701.

26. For a summary of Necho II's Asiatic contacts, see Kitchen, *Third Int. Pd.* (1996), 406-7; for a general history of his reign, see T. G. H. James, in *CAH* III/2 (1991), 715-18, 720-24, and bibliography.

27. Summary in Asia is in Kitchen, *Third Int. Pd.* (1996), 407; James, in *CAH* İII/2 (1991), 718-19, and references.

28. On Mesha's stela, lines 4 and 7, as "king of Israel," in numerous translations, cf., e.g.,

Albright in *ANET*, 320; K. P. Jackson in Dearman, *Studies*, 97; A. Lemaire, *BAR* 20, no. 3 (May-June 1994): 30-37; K. A. D. Smelik, in *CoS* II, 137-38 (wrongly omitting "House of [Da]vid" passage).

29. As a dynastic founder ("House of Omri" = Israel), with Shalmaneser III, cf. *ANET*, 280 and 281 ("son" of Omri = citizen of [House of] Omri); with Tiglath-pileser III, cf. index, s.v. "Bit-Humria," Tadmor, *TP III*, 296. Other *Bit-* ("House/Dynastic") place-names are given by Kitchen, *JSOT* 76 (1997): 38-39, with map, p. 37.

30. Named by Shalmaneser III at Battle of Qarqar, 853; cf. *ANET*, 279; Grayson, *RIMA*, 3:23.

31. In four-letter lacuna, as father of [Jeho]ram king of Israel, on Tell Dan stela, in parallel with [Ahaz]iah son of [Joram] of Judah, cf. Kitchen, *JSOT* 76 (1997): 30-35, with earlier bibliography for this monument on pp. 42-44 (now, to be supplemented! E.g., *CoS* II, 162). N.B.: the supposed signet ring illustrated in J. Rogerson, *Chronicle of the Old Testament Kings* (London: Thames & Hudson, 1999), 103, looks rather suspect and will not be used here.

32. He was named as king of Israel (Bit-Khumri) by Shalmaneser III in 841; *ANET*, 280, 281; Grayson, *RIMA*, 3:54. On correct understanding of the idiom *Bit-X*, see A. Ungnad, *OLZ* 9 (1906): 224-26.

33. He is mentioned in the Tell Rimah stela; see S. Dalley, *Iraq* 30 (1968): 142-43; cf. discussion by Pitard, *Ancient Damascus*, 163-65, for contact in 796.

34. As a vassal under Tiglath-pileser III; see Tadmor, *TP III*, 68/69 (89: 27:2), 106/107′; *CoS* II, 287.

35. Tadmor, *TP III*, 140/141, 202/203, 277; *CoS* II, 288.

36. Tadmor, *TP III*, 140/141 [188/189], 277-278. (For Pekah and Hoshea, see also *ANET*, 283; for Hoshea, see *CoS* II, 288 [291].)

37. Both of these kings, as "[father] and [s]on," were named on the Tell Dan stela; for references, see above, n. 31.

38. For discussion on this, see latterly Tadmor, *TP III*, 273-74 with references; *CoS* II, 285 n. 10. It is important to stress (against N. Na'aman, *TA* 22 [1995]: 276-77, and earlier OT scholars) that Hatarikka was *never* an independent kingdom, but always simply a part of the realm of Hamath. There is *no* possibility of Azriyau (whoever he is!) being a king of Hatarikka. Notice that the Tiglath-pileser III texts always call the place "the *city* of Hatarikka," and *no* separate king of it is ever mentioned.

39. See Tadmor, *TP III*, 170/171, and note on p. 277; *CoS* II, 289. Earlier, *ANET*, 282.

40. Cf. Luckenbill, *ARAB* II, §240; D. D. Luckenbill, *The Annals of Sennacherib* (Chicago: University of Chicago Press, 1924), 33ff.; *ANET*, 287-88; *CoS* II, 302-4.

41. For Manasseh under Esarhaddon, cf. *ANET*, 291; R. Borger, *Die Inschriften Asarhaddons*, 60, line 55. Under Assurbanipal, *ANET*, 294.

42. On the ration tablets, see *ANET*, 308.

43. Neither Jehoiachin nor Zedekiah, one removed from, one installed in, office at Jerusalem in 597, is named in the Babylonian Chronicle. See above under Nebuchadrezzar II, 1.B.iii.

44. This seal stone appears in many publications. In popular works, e.g.: Ian Wilson, *The Bible Is History* (London: Weidenfeld & Nicholson, 1999), 137; earlier, A. Lemaire, *BAR* 21, no. 6 (November-December 1995): 50 top. Discussed latterly, Avigad and Sass, *CWSS*, 49-50, no. 2 with references. Probably to this reign (or plus Jehoash before him) should belong the main set of Samaria ostraca from the palace administration (Years 9, 10; 15, of one king or two). Full studies and French and German translations, cf. A. Lemaire, *Inscriptions hébraïques, I, les ostraca* (Paris: Editions du Cerf, 1977), 21-81, and Renz/Röllig I, 79-110; in English, specimens in *ANET*,

321, and K. A. D. Smelik, *Writings from Ancient Israel* (Edinburgh: T. & T. Clark; Louisville: Westminster John Knox, 1991), 55-62, and earlier, Gibson, *TSSI*, 1:5-13.

45. A cylindrical "royal" type seal, Coll. Mousaieff. Cf. H. Shanks, *BAR* 22, no. 3 (May-June 1996): 34 and 64 (also in Wilson, *The Bible Is History*, 119); the script may be eighth century, and the figure that of a king; each main side under a winged disc. Thus it is hardly Solomon's — but the name here *(Sh-l-m)* could readily be that of the short-reigned Shallum, soon after Jeroboam II, and precisely in the eighth century. Jeho-ahaz (successor to Josiah) could also be called Shallum (Jer. 22:11), but at shortly before 600 B.C., he is too late for an eighth-century seal and would probably have used his official name (Jeho-ahaz).

46. Cf. A. Lemaire, *BAR* 21, no. 6 (November-December 1995): 48-52; also in R. Deutsch and A. Lemaire, *Biblical Period Personal Seals in the Shlomo Moussaieff Collection* (Tel Aviv: Archaeological Center Publications, 2000), 7, no. 1.

47. See Avigad and Sass, *CWSS*, 50, 51, nos. 3, 4.

48. On the seal impression, see R. Deutsch, *BAR* 24, no. 3 (May-June 1998): 54-56, 62, and his *Messages from the Past* (in Hebrew) (Tel-Aviv: Archaeological Center Publications, 1997); in English, 1999, no. 1 (with pls. XVI/XVII top). The name form Jeho-tham is simply a longer form of Jotham, just as Jeho-ram is the longer form of Joram; the names mean "YHWH is perfect" and "YHWH is exalted," respectively.

49. See R. Deutsch, *BAR* 24, no. 3 (May-June 1998): 56; and in Avigad and Sass, *CWSS*, frontispiece and p. 51, no. 5, with references.

50. See F. M. Cross, *BAR* 25, no. 2 (March-April 1999): 42-45, 60; Deutsch, *Messages from the Past*, pls. IX:199, and XVI/XVII bottom.

51. For the bulla of Jehozarah son of Hilkiah, see Avigad and Sass, *CWSS*, 172-73, no. 407, and Deutsch, *Messages from the Past*, no. 2 (Jehozarah was perhaps brother of Eliakim son of Hilkiah, cf. 2 Kings 18:18; Isa. 36:3). For the bulla of Azariah son of Jeho'ahi, see Deutsch, no. 3. For the bulla of which the name is lost, see also Deutsch, no. 4.

52. The Siloam tunnel inscription has many translations: e.g., Albright in *ANET*, 321; P. K. McCarter, *Ancient Inscriptions* (Washington, D.C.: BAS, 1996), 113-15, no. 90. For the text of [Shebna]iah, see T. C. Mitchell, *The Bible in the British Museum* (London: British Museum Press, 1988), 58, no. 25. For a carbon 14 date of tunnel context, eighth century, J. M. Cahill, *BA* 60, no. 3 (1997): 184 (D. Gill, *Qedem* 35 [1996]).

53. For a possible or probable seal stone as "king's son," see Avigad and Sass, *CWSS*, 55, no. 16. For a possible fiscal seal impression of Year 26, see under Josiah, next.

54. For a popular presentation of Ostracon Mousaieff 1, see H. Shanks, *BAR* 23, no. 6 (November-December 1997): 28-32; for fuller studies, see P. Bordreuil, F. Israel, and D. Pardee, in *NEA* 61, no. 1 (1998): 2-13, and earlier in *Sem* 46 (1996/97): 49-76. For doubts on authenticity, see I. Eph'al and J. Naveh, *IEJ* 48 (1998): 269-73; contrast lab reports in Shanks, 31, and Bordreuil et al., *NEA* 61, 8-9.

55. Fiscal seals, Years 26 and 13, are in Avigad and Sass, *CWSS*, 177-78, nos. 421-22; Years 14, 20, and 3 are in Deutsch, *Messages from the Past*, nos. 97-99.

56. For the personal seals, Jeho-ahaz is in Avigad and Sass, *CWSS*, 54, no. 13; that of Azaliah is in *CWSS*, 79, no. 90, cf. T. Schneider, *BAR* 17, no. 4 (July-August 1991): 30, 32; that of Ahikam is in *CWSS*, 181-82, no. 431; the ring of Hilkiah's son Hanan is in *CWSS*, 59-60, no. 28 (shy of the identifications!), and Schneider, 30-32, agreeing with J. Elayi, *BAR* 13, no. 5 (September-October 1987): 54-56, and in *Sem* 36 (1986): 43-46.

57. For seals of Jerahmeel, see Avigad and Sass, *CWSS*, 175, no. 414; and M. Heltzer, *SEL* 16

(1999): 45-47, fig. 1. Of Gemariah son of Shaphan, *CWSS*, 191, no. 470, and T. Schneider, *BAR* 17, no. 4 (September-October 1991): 28-30, 32.

58. See Avigad and Sass, *CWSS*, 56, no. 19.

59. Seals: For Berechiah, Jeremiah's secretary, Avigad and Sass, *CWSS*, 175-76, no. 417A/B; cf. T. Schneider, *BAR* 17, no. 4 (September-October 1991): 26-28, 32. For Malkijah, *CWSS*, 55, no. 15. For Seraiah, cf. *CWSS*, 163, no. 390; Schneider, 30-32. For the seal and bulla of Azariah son of Hilkiah, cf. *CWSS*, 139, nos. 307 and 224, no. 596; Schneider, 31-33, bulla only. For Gedaliah, *CWSS*, 172, no. 405. For the seals of the four men Jaazaniah, cf. *CWSS*, 52, 103, 104, 202, nos. 8, 174, 175, 511. For Elishama, a king's son, *CWSS*, 53, no. 11.

60. The Lachish ostraca have been much studied; for translations: (selected), *ANET*, 321-22; Gibson, *TSSI*, 1:32-49; Smelik, *Writings from Ancient Israel*, 116-31; for careful treatments in French and German, see respectively Lemaire, *Inscriptions hébraïques*, and Renz/Röllig I, 405-40. Representative seals are in *CoS* II, 197-205. Besides in *CWSS*, many additional seals and impressions are published in the quartet, R. Deutsch and M. Heltzer, *Forty New Ancient West Semitic Inscriptions* (1994); *New Epigraphic Evidence from the Biblical Period* (1995); *Windows to the Past* (1997); *Epigraphic News* (1999); also in R. Deutsch, *Messages from the Past* (1999), and by Deutsch and Lemaire, *Biblical Period Personal Seals in the Shlomo Moussaieff Collection;* all are published in Tel Aviv by Archaeological Center Publications. See also sec. 4.A, just below (*Qedem* 41, etc.).

61. The fundamental chronology of Alexander the Great, the Persian Empire, the Neo-Babylonian Empire, and the Assyrian Empire before it, back to 912, is all so well established that it needs no documentation here. For the regnal years of Neo-Babylonian and Persian rulers backed up by firsthand documentary date lines, cf. R. A. Parker and W. H. Dubberstein, *Babylonian Chronology, 626 B.C.–A.D. 75* (Providence: Brown University Press, 1956). For Assyrian eponym lists, 910-649, see Millard, *The Eponyms of the Assyrian Empire, 910-612 BC*. For Assyrian king list, cf. *ANET*, 3rd ed./Supp. (1969), 564-66.

62. For Egyptian chronology from 664 back to ca. 1550/1540, see the essentials, Kitchen, *Acta Archaeologica* 67 (1996/1998), 1-13, and revised in M. Bietak, ed., *The Synchronisation of Civilisations in the Eastern Mediterranean in the Second Millennium B.C.* (Vienna: Austrian Academy, 2000), 39-52, which is more up to date for 1100-664 than the large general work of J. von Beckerath, *Chronologie des pharaonischen Ägypten* (Mainz: von Zabern, 1997). For the period 1070-664, all details are discussed in Kitchen, *Third Int. Pd.* (1996).

63. On accuracy of forms and transmission of Assyrian names in biblical Hebrew, see A. R. Millard, *JSS* 21 (1976): 1-14.

64. On "house of seals" and excavations of provenanced bullae there, cf. Y. Shiloh, *IEJ* 36 (1986): 16-38; Y. Shiloh and D. Tarler, *BA* 49 (1986): 196-209; Y. Shoham in H. Geva, ed., *Ancient Jerusalem Revealed* (Jerusalem: IES, 1994), 55-61, and D. T. Ariel, ed., *Excavations at the City of David* VI (= *Qedem* 41) (Jerusalem: Hebrew University, 2000), 29-57, 75-84.

65. The two basic works of primary importance above all others on this are those of Thiele and Galil: E. R. Thiele, *The Mysterious Numbers of the Hebrew Kings* (Chicago: University of Chicago Press, 1951); 2nd and 3rd eds. (Grand Rapids: Eerdmans, 1965, 1986); and G. Galil, *The Chronology of the Kings of Israel and Judah* (Leiden: Brill, 1996). They seek to apply the relevant Near Eastern principles of reckoning indispensable to such studies, in varying measure, and far more systematically than any of their predecessors or contemporaries. Their final results come out remarkably close overall. To the labors of both men my own efforts are deeply and gratefully indebted, it is a pleasure to add.

66. In this very compact book, it is not feasible to print and annotate detailed charts for

the entire 350 years or so from 931 to 586; these I expect to publish in full, later, if not hindered. Essentially for the present, I have adopted Galil's view of Judah using a Nisan calendar and Israel a Tishri calendar (in contrast to Thiele), as this enables synchronisms to work directly without difficulty, and in conjunction with the regnal figures. But in agreement with Thiele, I find that a systematic treatment of the reigns and synchronisms enables an almost complete correlation to be made, both internally and with external sources; most of Galil's rejections of some data are themselves unnecessary. A few problems remain that may need further reconsideration. On the scheme adopted here, it may be desirable to add a year to Jehu's reign (to a twenty-ninth year) and to restore the eleventh year of Joram I to the twelfth throughout, for the accession of Ahaziah II. If at some period years were expressed by numerals (e.g., Egyptian hieratic tens, and use of strokes for units), it is quite possible to "lose" an odd unit (29>28; 12>11) in the course of scribal recopying. As for the Year 27 of Jeroboam II in which Uzziah became king (as coregent), one may have to posit an original figure of Year 17. The change from a final feminine (in 'esrah/ t) to a final m (dual/plural) is attested physically in another instance in Kings and Chronicles. Here 2 Chron. 9:25 retains the best reading, "4,000 stalls" (arba'at alafim), for that of 1 Kings 4:26, reading "40,000 stalls" (arba'im elef), in which m has replaced the feminine singular. These three matters dealt with, the only other point of this kind is the Years 35, 36 in 2 Chron. 15:19, 16:1, of the supposed thirty-fifth and thirty-sixth years of Asa which in fact are almost certainly for his fifteenth and sixteenth (in the context), and corresponding to the thirty-fifth and thirty-sixth years of the divided monarchy, as Thiele suggested long ago (e.g., *Mysterious Numbers* [1965], 60). However, it is entirely possible that better explanations of this small handful of figures may eventually emerge.

67. For a full, modern treatment of Shoshenq's campaign in Palestine/Canaan, with references, see Kitchen, *Third Int. Pd.* (1996), 293-302 (with route map, fig. 2), 432-47 (with diagram of list and segments map, figs. 8-9), plus addenda, 575-76, xlvi to end. Cf. also J. Currid, *Ancient Egypt and the Old Testament* (Grand Rapids: Baker, 1997), 173-202 (esp. for additional notes on the place-names).

68. A recent attempt was made by F. Clancy (*JSOT* 86 [1999]: 3-23) to reattribute the Megiddo stela to Shoshenq IV, and even to redate Shoshenq I to 800 (on the say-so of a crank chronology), and to deny all the obviously correct identifications of well-known place-names in the list. These views are totally contradicted by the available evidence, *JSOT* 23 (2001): 3-12. Most obviously, Shoshenq IV's second cartouche is wholly different to that of Shoshenq I, as it adds the epithets "Son of (the goddess) Bast, god, Ruler of Heliopolis" to the second cartouche — and *that* additional mouthful is *not* to be found in the Shoshenq cartouche on the Megiddo stela! The Megiddo stela is pictured often; cf. (e.g.) original publication, R. S. Lamon and G. M. Shipton, *Megiddo I* (Chicago: University of Chicago Press, 1939), 60-61, fig. 70; Kitchen, in *BAR* 15, no. 3 (May/June 1989): 32 bottom. On its significance as an imperial marker, cf. D. Ussishkin, *BASOR* 277/278 (1990): 72-73.

69. The great Karnak list was fully reproduced by the Epigraphic Survey, *Reliefs and Inscriptions at Karnak* III (Chicago: University of Chicago Press, 1957), pls. 2-9; in popular format, Kitchen, *BAR* 15/3 (May-June 1989): 32-33. For the list in the context of Shoshenq's works at Karnak (and hence its date), cf. Kitchen in L. K. Landy, ed., *The Age of Solomon: Scholarship at the Turn of the Millennium* (Leiden: Brill, 1997), 119-20, cf. also 124-25, and in Kitchen, "Egyptian Interventions in the Levant in Iron Age II," in W. G. Dever, ed., *ASOR Centennial Symposium (Jerusalem, May 2000)* (ASOR, 2003), where (and in *Themelios* 26, no. 3 [summer 2001]: 38-50) the present writer also deals with the incompetent treatment of Shoshenq I and his campaign, Rehoboam, etc., by P. Ash, *David, Solomon, and Egypt: A Reassessment* (Sheffield: Sheffield Aca-

demic Press, 1999), and the largely unsatisfactory treatment by B. U. Schipper, *Israel und Ägypten in der Königszeit* (Freiburg: Universitätsverlag; Göttingen: Vandenhoeck & Ruprecht, 1999). See my review paper on both in *Themelios* (just cited), and of Schipper in *BiOr* 58, no. 3-4 (May/August 2001): 376-85, for fuller details.

70. For "obvious" sequences of place-names in the Shoshenq list, cf. (e.g.) nos. 14-17 in Esdraelon: Taanach–Shunem–Beth-Shan–Rehob; or nos. 23-26, Gibeon, Beth-Horon, *x*, Ajalon. No. 27 is Megiddo, with two sets following; southward is nos. 32-39: Aruna, Borim, Zeyt-Padalla, Yehem, *x*, *y*, Socoh, Beth-Tappua[h]. A series of names reach into the Negev down south, including two Arads, etc.

71. References for the Karnak stela are in Kitchen, *Third Int. Pd.* (1996), 294, with translation of the essential part. For the Sukkiyim, Egyptian Tjukten, cf. references on 295 n. 291.

72. Over the last 130 years or so, the literature on the Moabite Stone is extensive. Recent studies and translations are listed by K. P. Jackson (prefacing his translation) in Dearman, *Studies*, 96-97 n. 4; and by K. A. D. Smelik, in *CoS* II, 138 end, to which add A. Lemaire, *BAR* 20, no. 3 (May-June 1994): 33. For wider studies of the inscription, see principally chaps. 5 and 6 in Dearman, by J. F. Drinkard (literary genre) and J. A. Dearman (historical background, with reference to secondary literature, much of it unjustifiably speculative) respectively. One could compare many other such cases in Near Eastern antiquity, wherein a proper synthesis has to be drawn from the documentation left by both parties. Thus Ramesses II's narrations and war scenes celebrate the Battle of (and at) Qadesh against the Hittites. He failed to capture that city, escaped annihilation by a hairsbreadth to win the day's clash, and ultimately returned to Egypt officially in triumph. But the Hittite sources reveal that, on Ramesses II's retreat south, the Hittite king and forces followed him all the way into central Lebanon (capturing the Egyptian province of Upe), desisting only when the pharaoh took himself off with his army through Lebanese mountain passes where the Hittites could not follow without risk of disastrous ambushes. In the following three years Ramesses regained control of his lost province, but never again attacked Qadesh. Again, all sources combine to elucidate the real course of the conflict, not just one side. For the Battle of Qadesh, see in full Kitchen, *RITA* II, 2-26, and *RITANC* II, 3-54, and maps 2-11.

73. The basic, original publications of the Tel Dan stela were those by A. Biran and J. Naveh, *IEJ* 43 (1993): 81-98, and in *IEJ* 45 (1995): 1-18. Other studies: K. A. Kitchen, *JSOT* 76 (1997): 42-44, and A. Lemaire, *JSOT* 81 (1998): 11-14; add P. E. Dion, in *For Michael [Heltzer]* (1999), 145-56 (who restores Jehu son of Nimshi!); A. R. Millard in *CoS* II, 161-62.

74. In line 6 Lemaire (*JSOT* 81 [1998]: 8) makes a good case for reading *mlkn. tqpn*, "mighty kings," and possibly (pp. 9-10, on ll. 6-7) for understanding "two thousand" each time, comparing this with the same figure of 2,000 chariots that Ahab rallied against Shalmaneser III at the Battle of Qarqar not long before, in 853, and thus the forces of Joram (plus Judah) would have been closely similar when deployed against Aram-Damascus.

75. In lines 7-8, A. R. Millard (*CoS* II, 162 n. 10) would restore differently: "I killed [. . .]iah son of [*X*, I overthr]ew the House of David," with much the same result at the end of the day. As *[ml]k byt-dwd* would be an unusual construction, he would instead suggest restoring the phrase *[w-'hp]k byt-dwd*, "[and I overthr]ew the House of David." The verb *hpk* is attested in both Old Aramaic and biblical Hebrew, so this is an attractive proposal.

76. Galil's proposed dating of the Tell Dan stela to Benhadad III depends on his rearrangement of the pieces, so that broken block B is set on top of block A (in *PEQ* 133 [2001]: 16-21). His claim about "bend" in the lines on the old side-by-side arrangement is by no means wholly convincing. The upper lines (1-7) on the unitary fragment A run "downhill" from right

to left at a shallow angle, whereas the lower lines (9-13) are properly horizontal, the intermediate line (8) being only very slightly inclined; on B the lines simply level off leftward, and are not consistently totally horizontal and parallel. As pointed out already (Kitchen, *JSOT* 76 [1997]: 35 n. 17), the stela is *not* an impeccable ceremonial inscription carved meticulously at leisure, but a victory text, cut as promptly as possible after the Aramean conquest of Dan, before the victorious Aramean ruler went back home to Damascus. So the lines were probably sketched and cut "freehand," without an elaborate, prior, inked grid.

77. Examples of this include the following: In the Balih region a man Giammu is killed by his nobles in an early text of Shalmaneser III, but in a later text Shalmaneser III claims credit for killing Giammu, as pointed out by Lemaire (*JSOT* 81 [1998]: 10-11). Much earlier, in the early thirteenth century, the Amarah West and Sai stelae of Sethos I of Egypt commemorate his victory over Nubian rebels. Here, in detail, the texts say that the king sent out his forces to crush Irem, the arm of Pharaoh going before them. But seven days later, the victory won, it is said that "the strong arm of Menmare (= Sethos I) had carried them off," without further mention of the forces actually deployed (translated in Kitchen, *RITA* I, 86). This is an accepted convention. Compare much later, Sargon II claiming credit for the capture of Samaria, which in fact belonged to the rule of Shalmaneser V, his predecessor; cf. sec. E, below. These cases rule out the contrary view of N. Na'aman, *IEJ* 50 (2000): 100-104.

78. For usurpers claiming unrelated predecessors as their "father," compare the similar situations in Assyria regarding the status of both Tiglath-pileser III and Sargon II, concisely discussed by A. K. Grayson in *CAH,* 2nd ed., III/2 (1991), 73-74 and 87-88 respectively.

79. For the heavy tribute from unsafe kinglets, cf. Tadmor, *TP III,* 276 end, with references back to the Summary Inscriptions (4:18′ [p. 140/141]; 7: reverse 15′-16′ [p. 170/171]). For slave prices in Assyria in the eighth century, cf. C. H. W. Johns, *Assyrian Deeds and Documents* 3 (Cambridge: University Press, 1924), 542-46.

80. Mention of (Jeho)-ahaz by Tiglath-pileser III, in Summary Text 7: reverse 11′; cf. Tadmor, *TP III,* 170/171, 277; *CoS* II, 289.

81. Tiglath-pileser III text for Pekah, in Tadmor, *TP III,* 140/141, cf. 277:*d.*

82. Places in Galilee, Annals 18/24: 3′ff. (Tadmor, *TP III,* 80/81-82/83). Summary text 4:6′ (Tadmor, 138/139) mentions Gil[ead]. The Astartu relief, cf. Tadmor, *TP III,* 239 and fig. 11, Wall III, Relief 36 (Layard drawing and photo, R. D. Barnett and M. Falkner, *The Sculptures of Tiglath-pileser III* [London: British Museum, 1962], pls. 68-70).

83. For archaeology of Galilee (major destruction/depopulation in late eighth century until the Persian period), see Z. Gal, *BAR* 24/3 (May-June 1998): 48-53.

84. For Hazor, cf. conveniently the popular account by Y. Yadin, *Hazor* (London: Weidenfeld & Nicholson, 1975), 147-48, 175-77 (level V, end), 183-84 (levels IV-II); and briefly in his *Hazor, Schweich Lectures, 1970* (London: British Academy, 1972), 190, pl. XXXIII*b.* Also, in context of the whole monarchic history (Hazor levels IX-V), Mazar, *ALB* I, 412/414. On the Assyrian administrative center, cf. R. Reich, *IEJ* 25 (1975): 233-37 (not Persian); also Reich in A. Kempinski and R. Reich, *The Architecture of Ancient Israel* (Jerusalem: IES, 1992), 214-15; and O. Lipschitz, *TA* 17 (1990): 96-99.

85. For Hoshea in texts of Tiglath-pileser III, see Tadmor, *TP III,* 140/141, 188/189, 281. On Tiglath-pileser III and Galilee, see K. L. Younger, *JBL* 117 (1998): 201-14.

86. Babylonian Chronicle 1 (like the rest) is edited in Grayson, *Assyrian and Babylonian Chronicles,* this entry, his p. 73.

87. For the eponym lists of Assyria from 910 onward, and specifically the years 727-720, see Millard, *Eponyms,* esp. 59-60.

88. Very clear treatments of the course of events, and of the obviously tendentious nature of the Annals of Sargon II, were given long ago by A. T. Olmstead, *AJSL* 21 (1904/5): 179-82, and in his *Western Asia in the Days of Sargon of Assyria* (1908), 45ff. n. 9; in summary form by E. R. Thiele, *Mysterious Numbers,* 1st ed., 123-28; 2nd ed., 141-47; 3rd ed, 1986. More thorough study of the Sargonic sources themselves, we owe to H. Tadmor, and in this matter see his study in *JCS* 12 (1958): 22-40, 77-100, esp. 30-32 ("rigging" of the Annals), 33-39 (on Samaria), 94 (years and events). A concise but incisive summation of the situation is given by A. K. Grayson, in *CAH* III/ 2 (1991), 85-89. To these studies, the less competent works of Old Testament scholars (not versed in cuneiform and its conventions) merely bring confusion (as with Galil, *Chronology of the Kings,* 83-94, who gives a conspectus of these confused treatments, his own being no better). Finally, see K. L. Younger, *JBL* 117 (1998): 214-24, and in *CBQ* 61 (1999): 461-82.

89. For the texts of Sargon II relating to Ashdod and their dating, cf. H. Tadmor, *JCS* 12 (1958): 79-80, 92-96.

90. For the eponym list, see Millard, *Eponyms,* 60.

91. On the stela at Ashdod, see *NEAHL,* 1:100, with photo; full account by H. Tadmor in M. Dothan, *Ashdod II-III* (Jerusalem, 1971), 193-97 with pls. 96-97:1.

92. For texts of Sennacherib, cf. Oppenheim in *ANET,* 287-88, and now M. Cogan in *CoS* II, 300-305, including the "Azekah" text possibly of Sennacherib (so, Naaman) or else of Sargon II.

93. The best and most up-to-date study of the events of the year 701 (excluding the role of Tirhakah; cf. p. 504 above, for references on that) is Gallagher's *Sennacherib's Campaign to Judah.* That "a strict itinerary of the campaign cannot be re-created" (so Cogan, in *CoS* II, 302) is not true. See the account just given above, and my maps, either in *Third Int. Pd.,* 384, or in *Fontes atque Pontes, Festgabe für Hellmut Brunner* (Wiesbaden: Harrassowitz, 1983), 253 to 243-252 (on 701). In general, see also A. R. Millard, *TynB* 36 (1985): 61-77.

94. For a full presentation of the Assyrian reliefs on the siege of Lachish (in the British Museum) and the related archaeological remains at Tell ed-Duweir, see the splendid volume by D. Ussishkin, *The Conquest of Lachish by Sennacherib* (Tel Aviv: Institute of Archaeology, 1982), and his study in *TA* 17 (1990): 53-86, esp. 77-80 and 72-76.

95. Cf. A. K. Grayson, *CAH,* 2nd ed., III/2 (1991), 119-21, and in his *Assyrian and Babylonian Chronicles,* 81-82 (Babylonian Chronicle 1, iii:34-38); for text of Esarhaddon, see Oppenheim in *ANET,* 289-90; Berossus, cf. Stanley M. Burstein, *The Babyloniaca of Berossus,* Sources from the Ancient Near East 1/5 (Malibu, Calif.: Undena Publications, 1978), 24 §3 (Ardumuzan).

96. The basic source for the stirring events of 614-608 (as of much else at that epoch) is the series of Babylonian Chronicles. In English the main edition was by Wiseman, *Chronicles of Chaldaean Kings;* for 614-608, cf. his pp. 18-20 (map, p. 22), 44-45 (summary table), and 61-63 (text). New edition, Grayson, *Assyrian and Babylonian Chronicles,* 95-96, no. 3, ll. 58-75.

97. The Babylonian Chronicle for 608-594 was first edited by Wiseman, *Chronicles of Chaldaean Kings;* see esp. 19-37 (introduction), 46-48 (table of events), and 70/71-72/73; more recently, Grayson, *Assyrian and Babylonian Chronicles,* 100-102.

98. On the excavations at Jerusalem: for the northwest quadrant, see N. Avigad, *Discovering Jerusalem* (Oxford: Blackwell, 1984), 46ff. (figs. 32, 34, arrows in burnt layer), esp. 52-54, and bibliography, 263-64. For City of David, cf. as general introduction J. Cahill and D. Tarler, in H. Geva, ed., *Ancient Jerusalem Revealed* (Jerusalem: IES, 1994), 37-40; to find bullae and biblical names in these examples (Gemariah son of Shaphan; Azariah son of Hilkiah), see Y. Shoham, in Geva, 55-61, plus T. Schneider, 62-63. In more detail, Y. Shiloh, *Excavations at the City of David* I

(= *Qedem* 19) (Jerusalem: Hebrew University, 1984), 29 (destruction of stratum 10); bullae, Y. Shiloh, *IEJ* 36 (1986): 16-38, and Y. Shiloh and D. Tarler, *BA* 49, no. 4 (1986): 196-209; Y. Shoham, *City of David* VI (*Qedem* 41) (2000), 29-57.

99. On Lachish and other sites, see their entries in *NEAHL* 1-4, e.g., Lachish in 3:909-11, with bibliography. Translations of the Lachish ostraca: English, Gibson, *TSSI*, 1:32-49; French, Lemaire, *Inscriptions hébraïques*, 85-143; in German, Renz/Röllig I (1995), 405-40.

100. On almost all Babylonian and Assyrian chronicles, see for discussion and translations with notes Grayson, *Assyrian and Babylonian Chronicles;* cf. review, A. R. Millard, *JAOS* 100 (1980): 364-69.

101. For astronomical diaries and running reports (initially on waxed writing boards), cf. Grayson, *Assyrian and Babylonian Chronicles*, 12-14. Esarhaddon Chronicle (no. 14), cf. Grayson, 30-32.

102. Year dates sequencing as providing (in principle) protochronicles, cf. Grayson, *Assyrian and Babylonian Chronicles*, 6, 193-95. On chronicles and the "chronicular" entries in the eponym lists, see A. R. Millard, in S. Parpola and R. M. Whiting, eds., *Assyria 1995* (Helsinki: Neo-Assyrian Text Corpus Project, 1997), 207-11. On the nature of Assyrian royal inscriptions, including the role of deity in them, see H. Tadmor, in *Assyria 1995*, 325-38 (deity, cf. 327, 330-31, 334).

103. On the Palermo Stone, see now T. A. H. Wilkinson, *Royal Annals of Ancient Egypt, the Palermo Stone and Its Associated Fragments* (London: Kegan Paul International, 2000); picture of a tablet, cf. Sir A. H. Gardiner, *Egypt of the Pharaohs* (Oxford: OUP, 1961), 405, fig. 14 (and good photo of Palermo Stone, pl. III at p. 62).

104. On the annals of Amenemhat II, see H. Altenmüller and A. M. Moussa, in *SAK* 18 (1991): 1-48. For a general survey of Egyptian "annals," king lists, etc., cf. D. B. Redford, *Pharaonic King-Lists, Annals, and Day-Books* (Mississauga, Ontario: Benben Publications, 1986), esp. 65-126.

105. On Hattusil I, see new translation by G. Beckman, in *CoS* II, 79-81.

106. Wenamun, recent translation, M. Lichtheim in *CoS* I, 89-93 (daybooks, 91 bottom left), after her version in M. Lichtheim, *Ancient Egyptian Literature* II (Berkeley: University of California Press, 1976), 224-230 (esp. 226).

107. Annals of Tuthmosis III, large excerpt, J. K. Hoffmeier, in *CoS* II, 7-13; complete but now old, J. H. Breasted, *ARE* II (1906), 179-217, §§415-540.

108. On the Battle of Qadesh, see Kitchen, *RITA* II (1996), 2-26 (also *CoS* II, 32-40), and notes; *RITANC* II (1999), 3-54, maps 2-11.

109. For the Ten-Year Annals of Mursil II, see also now G. Beal, in *CoS* II, 82-90.

110. Extracts from the Assyrian annals are included in *CoS* II, 261-306, passim; for Sennacherib, see *CoS* II, 302, 303; earlier (and for Esarhaddon and Assurbanipal), cf. *ANET*, 274-301.

111. The Akitu and "Religious" chronicles are published in Grayson, *Assyrian and Babylonian Chronicles*, 131-32 (no. 16) and 133-38 (no. 17).

112. For Wenamun, see n. 106 above. For Tyre, see n. 6 above. The Neo-Hittite hieroglyphic texts are now edited in Hawkins, *CHLI* I/1-3, and Çambel, *CHLI* II (1999). On the rulers of Carchemish and Malatya, see J. D. Hawkins, *AnSt* 38 (1988): 99-108; cf. Kitchen, in V. P. Long, D. W. Baker, G. J. Wenham, *Windows into Old Testament History* (Grand Rapids: Eerdmans, 2002). The seven-generation Lion inscription of Halparuntiyas III, king of Gurgum, going back to his ancestor Laramas I, is included now in Hawkins, *CHLI* I/1, 261-65, and I/3, pls. 112-13 (IV/4, Marash 1). All these relationships and related "histories" were probably kept in running records,

probably using wooden writing boards, much used in the Hittite world earlier. On these, see D. Symington, *AnSt* 41 (1991): 111-23.

113. For the Deuteronomic covenant, see chap. 6 below.

114. On the third campaign of Sennacherib, cf. translations by M. Cogan in *CoS* II, 302-3, and long since, first and last editions, Luckenbill, *ARAB* II, 115, 118-21, cf. 136f.

115. On the seventh campaign, in the Babylonian Chronicle, see Grayson, *Assyrian and Babylonian Chronicles,* 79-80 (no. 1, iii, 9-15); in Sennacherib's annals, Luckenbill, *ARAB* II, 124-25.

116. A good example of the arbitrary misinterpretation of the so-called theological elements in 1-2 Kings, etc., is the work by R. E. Clements, *Isaiah and the Deliverance of Jerusalem,* JSOTSup 13 (Sheffield: Sheffield Academic Press, 1980); see the judicious review of this issue regarding Sennacherib and Hezekiah by A. R. Millard, *TynB* 36 (1985): 61-77, esp. 68ff., 72ff. The West Semitic texts from Moab (King Mesha), Hamath (King Zakkur), and Aram ([Hazael], Tel Dan), etc., reek with references to divine favor and intervention, by the gods Kemosh, Baal-shemayn, and Hadad respectively, in the midst of clearly historical goings-on, as do the Hieroglyphic Luwian inscriptions, such as that of Halparuntiyas III cited in n. 112 above. There can be no question whatsoever that the theological elements existed in these inscriptions from the very moment they were engraved; nobody could have sneaked these allusions onto these stone monuments twenty years afterward, or whatever! On these texts and biblical analogues, see A. R. Millard, *TynB* 41, no. 2 (1990): 261-75; for a wider, more diffuse study of such themes in West Semitic inscriptions and 1-2 Kings, cf. S. B. Parker, *Stories in Scripture and Inscriptions* (New York: OUP, 1997) (e.g., on Hezekiah and Zakkur, pp. 105-20). On the theme of divine intervention in biblical and nonbiblical texts, see the useful and wide-ranging studies by M. Weinfeld, in H. Tadmor and M. Weinfeld, eds., *History, Historiography, and Interpretation* (Jerusalem: Magnes Press, 1983), 121-47, and by A. R. Millard, in *FTH,* 37-64 (esp. 50-64).

117. For good general introductions to the overall archaeology of Palestine, see Mazar, *ALB* I, and A. Ben-Tor, ed., *The Archeology of Ancient Israel* (New Haven: Yale University Press, 1992), both ending with the Babylonian conquest in 586. For the Persian period see Stern, *ALB* II, and (more technically) see E. Stern, *Material Culture of the Land of the Bible in the Persian Period* (Warminster: Aris & Phillips, 1982). A valuable compilation in German (Persian period included) is H. Weippert, *Palästina in vorhellenistischer Zeit,* Handbuch der Archäologie: Vorderasien, II:1 (Munich: Beck, 1988). On the social aspects, see T. E. Levy, ed., *The Archaeology of Society in the Holy Land* (London: Leicester University Press, 1995) (all periods). For very extensive coverage of sites of all periods (from early prehistory down to late medieval times) with good bibliographies, see E. Stern et al., eds., *NEAHL* 1-4.

118. Overall on Jerusalem, see *NEAHL,* 2:698-804 (esp. 698-719), and a one-volume summary of recent work, Geva, *Ancient Jerusalem Revealed.* For technical reports on the oldest part of Jerusalem (the eventual City of David), see the series *Qedem,* volumes edited by Y. Shiloh and others, *City of David,* vols. Iff. (1984ff.), plus E. Mazar, *Qedem* 29 (Ophel area). For the Western hill extension (besides *NEAHL* 2), cf. Avigad, *Discovering Jerusalem,* 31-60.

119. Publications of excavated seal impressions include: Y. Shiloh, *IEJ* 36 (1986): 16-38, and with D. Tarler, *BA* 49, no. 4 (1986): 196-209; Y. Shoham, in Geva, *Ancient Jerusalem Revealed,* 55-61, cf. T. Schneider, 62-63; Y. Shoham, in *City of David* VI (2000), 29-57, 75-84. A related series (out of context), N. Avigad, *Hebrew Bullae from the Time of Jeremiah* (Jerusalem: IES, 1986). These also appear in Avigad and Sass, *CWSS,* passim.

120. Overall on Lachish, see *NEAHL,* 3:897-911 (esp. 905ff.) with bibliography. On dating of Lachish III vis-à-vis II, *l-mlk* stamps, etc., see D. Ussishkin, *TA* (1977): 28-60, and passim in *TA* 5 (1978): 1-97 (summary, 92-93), and on jars and seals, *BASOR* 223 (1976): 1-13. On Assyrian

siege of Lachish, cf. Ussishkin, *The Conquest of Lachish by Sennacherib*. Rehoboam is linked either with the "Palace A" at the end of level V (cf. Ussishkin, *TA* 5 [1977]: 93) or with the new fortifications that begin with level IV (contra Ussishkin, I see no contradiction here; Lachish was Rehoboam's kingpin fortress-town among a lesser series of forts). On Lachish ostraca, see sec. 5, end, above.

121. Overall on Hazor, see *NEAHL*, 2:594-606, and bibliography; good, accessible accounts (Yadin excavations), Yadin, *Hazor, Schweich Lectures, 1970,* and his *Hazor* (1975); more recent work at Hazor (under A. Ben-Tor) has not changed the numbering, dating, or sequence of the Iron II occupations at Hazor; see A. Ben-Tor and D. Ben-Ami, *IEJ* 48 (1998): 1-37, esp. end discussion, 29-36; cf. chap. 4 below, re. Hazor and united monarchy controversy.

122. Overall on Dan, see *NEAHL*, 1:323-32 (esp. 326ff.); good general account, A. Biran, *Biblical Dan* (Jerusalem: IES et al., 1994), esp. chaps. 10–12; both references with bibliography.

123. On Khirbet Rosh Zayit fortress (Solomonic, casemated walls) and Phoenician solid fort, overall, see clear summary, *NEAHL*, 4:1289-91; cf. further, Z. Gal, *Lower Galilee during the Iron Age* (Winona Lake, Ind.: Eisenbrauns/ASOR, 1992). On Lower Galilee in two phases (tenth to mid–ninth century; mid-ninth to 733), see Z. Gal, *TA* 15/16 (1988/89): 56-64; survey, Z. Gal, *ZDPV* 101 (1985): 114-27, pl. 3; and *BA* 53, no. 2 (1990): 88-97 (esp. 91-97), and esp. Gal, *Lower Galilee during the Iron Age;* Phoenician culture and special pottery, Y. Alexandre and Z. Gal, *TA* 22 (1995): 77-88, 89-93 respectively; summary down to conquest by Tiglath-pileser III, Z. Gal, *BAR* 24, no. 3 (May-June 1998): 48-53. Full report on Khirbet Rosh Zayit, now in Z. Gal and Y. Alexandre, *Horbat Rosh Zayit: An Iron Age Storage Fort and Village,* IAA Reports 8 (Jerusalem: IAA, 2000).

124. Overall on Dor, see *NEAHL*, 1:357-72 (esp. 358-61), and good general account by E. Stern, *Dor, Ruler of the Seas* (Jerusalem: IES, 1994), each with bibliographies.

125. For a good overall conspectus on Gezer, see *NEAHL*, 2:496-506 (esp. 504ff.), with bibliography.

126. For an overall survey on Samaria, see *NEAHL*, 4:1300-1310, with bibliography. For a careful critical reassessment of the sequence and attributions of the successive building phases and pottery phases at Iron Age II Samaria, see R. E. Tappy, *The Archaeology of Israelite Samaria,* I, *Early Iron Age through the Ninth Century* BCE (Atlanta: Scholars Press, 1992) and II, *The Eighth Century* BCE (Winona Lake: Eisenbrauns, 2001).

127. Overall on Tirzah, see *NEAHL*, 2:433-40 (esp. 439-40), revising A. Chambon, *Tell el-Far'ah I, L'Age du Fer* (Paris: Recherches sur les Civilisations, 1984); cf. T. L. McClellan, *BASOR* 267 (1984): 84-86.

128. Overall on Timnah, see *NEAHL*, 1:152-57; an accessible account is in A. Mazar and G. L. Kelm, *Timnah, a Biblical City in the Sorek Valley* (Winona Lake, Ind.: Eisenbrauns, 1995); full report is (so far) A. Mazar, *Timnah (Tel Batash) I, Qedem* 37, 2 vols. (Jerusalem: Hebrew University, 1997); and A. Mazar and N. Panitz-Cohen, *Timnah (Tel Batash) II, Qedem* 42, 2 vols. (Jerusalem: Hebrew University, 2001).

NOTES TO CHAPTER 3

1. On the number of Tiglath-pileser III's captives from Galilee, etc., see Tadmor, *TP III,* 82-83, line 9'; *CoS* II, 286.

2. See *ANET,* 284-85; *CoS* II, 295-96.

3. For Sennacherib, cf. *ANET,* 288; *CoS* II, 303.

4. On Tiglath-pileser III to Sargon II, texts and policies, see K. L. Younger, *JBL* 117 (1998): 201-27.

5. The Babylonian chronicle for the years 605-594 was first published by D. J. Wiseman, *Chronicles of Chaldaean Kings (626-556 BC) in the British Museum* (London: British Museum, 1956); cf. pp. 23-37 (review of events), 46-48 (table of episodes), 66/67-74/75 (text and translation). Short extract, in *ANET,* 3rd ed. (1969), 563-64 (= Supp., 127-28), with bibliography; new edition in full, in A. K. Grayson, *Assyrian and Babylonian Chronicles* (New York: Augustin, 1975), 99-102; years 605, 597 only, cf. *CoS* I, 467-68.

6. On Nebuzaradan, cf. D. J. Wiseman, *Nebuchadrezzar and Babylon, Schweich Lectures, 1983* (London: OUP/British Academy, 1985), 74.

7. The full series of ration tablets from Babylon has never yet been published. Four tablets were excerpted by E. F. Weidner (in German) in the *Mélanges Syriens offerts à M. R. Dussaud* II (Paris: Geuthner, 1939), 923-35. For Jehoiachin and family, see 924-28; Oppenheim in *ANET,* 308 (Hebrews and some others). On the sons of Aga king of Ascalon, see Weidner, 928. See also Wiseman, *Nebuchadrezzar and Babylon,* 81-84.

8. For Tiglath-pileser III and Israelite auxiliaries, see K. L. Younger, *JBL* 117 (1998): 214, following up a suggestion by Tadmor, *TP III,* 141 (to lines 15'-16', Bit-Khumria, Israel). For Sargon's annexation of Samaria and Israelite chariots, see S. Dalley, *Iraq* 47 (1985): 31-48, esp. 32, 38-39; cf. Younger, 216-17 (citations from Sargon II), 219-21.

9. For artisans, etc., in Babylonian ration lists, see Weidner, in *Mélanges Syriens offerts à M. R. Dussaud,* 928 (Ascalon, sailors, leaders of people, chiefs of singers); 929 (Tyre: 126 men, plus 190 + x sailors; Byblos and Arvad, carpenters); 929 (Elamites); 930 (Mede and Persians); 930-32 (Egyptians); 932-34 (Anatolians [called "Ionians," but Lycians by name!], Lydians). Cf. also Wiseman, *Nebuchadrezzar and Babylon,* 83-84, 77-78.

10. For Babylon see Wiseman, *Nebuchadrezzar and Babylon,* 43-80, for a good, modern survey, and fresh treatment of the fabled "gardens." S. Dalley's doubts about the gardens, in *Iraq* 56 (1994): 45-58, are ingenious but not convincing; cf. now J. Reade, *Iraq* 62 (2000): 195-217. For a general account see J. Oates, *Babylon,* 2nd ed. (London: Thames & Hudson, 1986), 144-60. Some illustrations, cf. also M. Roaf, *Cultural Atlas of Mesopotamia and the Ancient Near East* (Oxford and New York: Facts on File, 1990), 192-93. For a useful survey for this section and the two following (B, C), see T. C. Mitchell, in *CAH,* 2nd ed., III/2 (1991), 410-40.

11. On the archaeology of Neo-Babylonian Judah, cf. Stern, *ALB* II, 301-50.

12. The Gedaliah seals, nos. 405 and 409 respectively, are in *CWSS,* 172, 173, as are impressions of the seal of Jeremiah's secretary Baruch ("Berechiah son of Neriah"), 175f., no. 417. A damaged scaraboid seal actually bears the name *Yrmyhw,* "Jeremiah," but this need not belong to the famous prophet (*CWSS,* 165, no. 396).

The well-known seals of Eliakim, "squire" of Yokin (*CWSS,* 243f., no. 663), should not be dated to King J(eh)oiakim's reign, ca. 600, because their archaeological contexts are now known to be over one hundred years earlier, with the *l-mlk* stamps of Hezekiah, current between 715 and 701! See Y. Garfinkel, *BA* 53, no. 2 (1990): 74-79, following on D. Ussishkin, *Tel Aviv* 4 (1977): 28-60; and now A. R. Millard in *CoS* II, 200, 2.70P. The problem of "two masters" posed by Garfinkel (pp. 77f.) is an illusion. Yokin would have been an official of the king, while Eliakim was Yokin's aide; such things are commonplace in ancient Near Eastern state hierarchies.

So Eliakim could hardly still be functioning under Jehoiakim. This means, also, that the Judean palace at Ramat Rahel (level Va) can no longer be dated to ca. 600-586 or be compared with Jer. 22:13-14. Rather, it would be a work of Hezekiah, replacing an earlier one (level Vb) of (say) Uzziah, Jotham, or Ahaz (Yadin's date in the ninth century seems excessively high). Stern,

ALB II, 165/167, seems not to have noticed the importance of the redated Eliakim seals, requiring a redating of Ramat Rahel Va.

13. For Tell en-Nasbeh, and the retrieved "level 2," see J. R. Zorn, *BAR* 23, no. 5 (September-October 1997): 28-38, 66, and in *BASOR* 307 (1997): 53-66 (on gates), plus *NEAHL*, 3:1098-1102, with further bibliography. Note on continuing Judean presence in Neo-Babylonian Palestine, G. Barkay, in A. Biran et al., eds., *Biblical Archaeology Today, 1990* (Jerusalem: IES/ IASH, 1993), 106-9, with brief demurral by A. Degroot, p. 114.

14. For seals of Baalis, cf. R. Deutsch, *BAR* 25, no. 2 (March-April 1999): 46-49, 66.

15. On status of cultivators for this period, cf. J. N. Graham, *BA* 47, no. 1 (1984): 55-58. For the Babylonian dignitaries and their titles in Jer. 39:3, see T. C. Mitchell, in *CAH* III/2 (1991), 407.

16. On Tahpanhes, cf. summary by K. A. Kitchen, in *NBD*, 1150. Mentioned in a sixth-century Phoenician papyrus, cf. (in English) A. Dupont-Sommer, *PEQ* 81 (1949): 57-61; in German, H. Donner and W. Röllig, *Kanaanäische und Aramäische Inschriften* II (Wiesbaden: Harrassowitz, 1964), 67-68, no. 50; now in B. Porten and A. Yardeni, *Textbook of Aramaic Documents from Ancient Egypt* 1 (Winona Lake, Ind.: Eisenbrauns, 1986), 6-7, A.1/1.

17. End of Hophra (Apries), cf. (e.g.) T. G. H. James, in *CAH* III/2 (1991), 730.

18. On the text of Year 37 of Nebuchadrezzar II, see notes in Wiseman, *Chronicles of Chaldaean Kings*, 94-95, and his *Nebuchadrezzar and Babylon*, 39-40; translation (but with gaps in text shown as far too short!), Oppenheim, in *ANET*, 308; important discussion of the state of the text, T. C. Mitchell, *PSAS* 22 (1992): 69-80, with bibliography.

19. For histories of the Achaemenid (Persian) Empire, see the older work by A. T. E. Olmstead, *History of the Persian Empire* (Chicago: University of Chicago Press, 1948). More recently, J. M. Cook, *The Persian Empire* (London: Dent, 1983); sundry authors in *CAH*, 2nd ed., IV-V-VI (1988ff.); P. Briant, *L'Histoire de l'Empire Perse de Cyrus à Alexandre* (Paris: Fayard, 1996), and English translation.

20. See for convenient text and translation of Herodotus, A. D. Godley, *Herodotus* I-IV, LCL (1920-24), in particular vol. II, 116-27 (= Herodotus, bk. III: 89-97), summarizing twenty major provinces (satrapies) and their revenues. The various Old Persian sources run to twenty-three regions as tributaries; on the lists, cf. O. Leuze, *Die Satrapieneinteilung in Syrien und im Zweistromland von 520-320* (Halle: Niemeyer Verlag, 1935; reprint, 1972), 76-100. He points out (98-99) that the satrapies cover lesser divisions of up to seventy-one peoples and districts, which is an incomplete figure, lacking (e.g.) such constituent districts or (sub)provinces for the fifth, twelfth, and thirteenth satrapies (if not others also). The final total would not be far off the "127 provinces" ascribed to Xerxes in Esther 1:1, using the same term *(medina)* that was applied to Judea (in Persian Aramaic, *Yehud*) as a local district, as in Ezra 5:8 and Neh. 1:3. For a map of the satrapies, cf. Roaf, *Cultural Atlas of Mesopotamia and the Ancient Near East*, 208-9. On Judea in the Persian period, cf. T. C. Mitchell, in *CAH*, 2nd ed., III/2 (1991), 430-40, and (in wider context) I. Eph'al, in *CAH*, 2nd ed., IV (1988), 147-64. In French, E.-M. Laperrousaz, ed., *La Palestine de l'époque perse* (Paris: Editions du Cerf, 1994). Specific Persian background to the Hebrew Bible, see E. M. Yamauchi, *Persia and the Bible* (Grand Rapids: Baker, 1990).

21. The Old Persian royal inscriptions were edited by R. G. Kent, *Old Persian Grammar, Texts, Lexicon*, 2nd ed. (New Haven: American Oriental Society, 1953). The Akkadian (Babylonian) texts of the period were edited by F. H. Weissbach, *Die Keilinschriften der Achämeniden* (Leipzig: Hinrichs, 1911). Until recently the standard compendium of Aramaic papyri from Egypt was that of A. E. Cowley, *Aramaic Papyri of the Fifth Century* BC (Oxford: Clarendon Press, 1923), supplemented by E. G. Kraeling, *The Brooklyn Museum Aramaic Papyri* (New Haven: Yale University Press, 1953), and by G. R. Driver, *Aramaic Documents of the Fifth Century* BC

(Oxford: Clarendon Press, 1954; abridged and revised ed., 1957). For a full, modern edition (with English translations) of all accessible Aramaic papyri and ostraca from Egypt, see now the provisional corpus by B. Porten and A. Yardeni, *Textbook of Aramaic Documents from Ancient Egypt* 1-4 (Jerusalem: Hebrew University, 1986-99); French translations and notes, P. Grelot, *Documents araméens d'Égypte* (Paris: Editions du Cerf, 1972). Ostraca from south Palestine, see I. Eph'al and J. Naveh, *Aramaic Ostraca of the Fourth Century BC from Idumaea* (Jerusalem: Magnes Press, 1996), and A. Lemaire, *Nouvelles inscriptions araméennes d'Idumée au Musée d'Israël* (Paris: Gabalda, 1996). From Persepolis we have epigraphs of disputed import in R. A. Bowman, *Aramaic Ritual Texts from Persepolis* (Chicago: University of Chicago Press, 1970); cf. B. A. Levine, *JAOS* 92 (1972): 70-79, and J. Naveh and S. Shaked, *Or* 42 (1973): 445-57. Lastly, Aramaic fragments from Saqqara (Egypt), J. B. Segal, *Aramaic Texts from North Saqqara* (London: EES, 1983). For a bibliography (until 1991) of most Aramaic texts down to ca. 200 B.C., see J. A. Fitzmyer, S. A. Kaufman, et al., *An Aramaic Bibliography, Part I* (Baltimore: Johns Hopkins University Press, 1992). On the Wadi Daliyeh texts (not yet published in extenso), see preliminary reports by F. M. Cross listed in his *From Epic to Canon* (Baltimore: Johns Hopkins University Press, 1998), 152 n. 7.

22. For Belshazzar, cf., e.g., mention of him in Nabonidus's text on rebuilding the ziggurat (temple tower) at Ur, in the final prayer (*CoS* II, 313-14). Nabonidus trusting the kingship to his "eldest (son), his first-born" (= Belshazzar), in the Verse-Account, cf. *ANET*, 313. King and prince, in oaths, *ANET*, 309/310 n. 5, and in P.-A. Beaulieu, *The Reign of Nabonidus, King of Babylon, 556-539 B.C.* (New Haven: Yale University Press, 1989), 190-91. For Nabonidus and Belshazzar, cf. the pioneering work by R. P. Dougherty, *Nabonidus and Belshazzar* (New Haven: Yale University Press, 1929), and now the much more up-to-date work by Beaulieu, just cited. Beaulieu would set the ten years of Nabonidus's absence in northwest Arabia at his third to thirteenth years (553-543), on a combination of evidence. On his return to Babylon, Belshazzar would indeed return to playing "second fiddle" to his father, and any favorite of his would be only third in position at highest. The absence of Nabonidus from the Daniel narrative cannot be due to Jewish ignorance of his existence and reign; the Jews in the Babylon of 543-539 could not fail to have known who was then king, while almost 400 years later they still preserved some memory of Nabonidus and his stay in Teima, as is proven by the existence and allusions of the so-called Prayer of Nabonidus (4Q242) among the library of the Dead Sea Scrolls (for a translation of which, cf., e.g., G. Vermes, *The Complete Dead Sea Scrolls in English*, 5th ed. [London: Penguin Books, 1999], 573). The absence of Nabonidus would merely reflect the position of Daniel as part of Belshazzar's personal entourage, and not that of Nabonidus. For Belshazzar's regime overall, cf. Beaulieu, 154-60, 185-205; for the fall of Babylon, killing of Belshazzar, and probable exiling of Nabonidus to the east, cf. Beaulieu, 225-31. On Sethos II and Ramesses II, cf. document excerpted by S. Sauneron and J. Yoyotte, *REg* 7 (1951): 67. On possible links of Nabonidus and Belshazzar with Nebuchadrezzar II, cf. Wiseman, *Nebuchadrezzar and Babylon*, 11-12. For Darius the Mede as identical with Cyrus the Persian, see D. J. Wiseman, in Wiseman, ed., *Notes on Some Problems in the Book of Daniel* (London: Tyndale Press, 1965), 9-16.

23. On order and dating of Ezra, then Nehemiah (458, then 445-433 respectively), see the further arguments by Cross, *From Epic to Canon*, 151-64 (esp. data for Nehemiah, 157-58; and cumulative data on genealogies, etc., for Ezra, 164). For governors of Judea, cf. N. Avigad, *Qedem* 4 (1976), 7, 30-36; H. G. M. Williamson, *TynB* 39 (1988): 59-82, esp. 76ff. Chronologically significant also is Nehemiah's punishment of leading Judeans (beating, hair plucked out) in Neh. 13:23-25, a punishment not allowed later than the reign of Artaxerxes I; see M. Heltzer, *Archäologische Mitteilungen aus Iran* 26 (1995/96): 305-7.

24. Sanballat I of Samaria (with his two sons) is named in twin papyri of 407 B.C. in Cowley, *Aramaic Papyri*, nos. 30-31, pp. 108-22 (*ANET*, 491-92), now in Porten and Yardeni, *Textbook of Aramaic Documents*, 1:68-75, nos. A4.7-8.

25. For Tobiah's descendants, cf. epigraph at the 'Iraq el-Amir caves (*NEAHL*, 2:647, and color plate opposite p. 696), and the Qasr el-'Abd "palace" (*NEAHL*, 2:646-49, with references); Josephus knew of this family (Josephus, *Antiquities* 12.230-33). Other references, B. Mazar, *IEJ* 7 (1957): 137-45, 229-38.

26. For Geshem, see original publication by J. J. Rabinowitz, *JNES* 15 (1956): 1-9, and pls. 6-7. For chronology see Kitchen, *Documentation for Ancient Arabia* I (Liverpool: University Press, 1994), 49-50, with references. Doubts about the identification of Geshem father of Qaynu with Nehemiah's Geshem (e.g., by M. C. A. Macdonald in J. M. Sasson, ed., *Civilizations of the Ancient Near East* II [New York: Scribner, 1995], 1368; I. Eph'al, in *CAH* IV, 164) have no factual basis; most other "Geshems" are Safaitic and irrelevant. It is highly improbable that two Geshems of importance ruled in the same patch at the same time.

27. For preliminary reconstitutions of Susa, see M. Pillet, *Le Palais de Darius Ier à Suse, Ve siècle av. J.-C.* (Paris: Geuthner, 1914); for one in color, see J. Curtis, ed., *Mesopotamia and Iran in the Persian Period, Conquest and Imperialism, 539-331 BC* (London: British Museum Press, 1997), pl. XII. For modern, more accurate plans, etc., see F. Tallon, in *Le Monde de la Bible*, no. 106 (September-October 1997): 48ff., and earlier, J. Perrot and D. Ladiray, in *Dossiers: Histoire et Archéologie*, no. 138 (May 1989): 56ff. For a recent account, see P. O. Harper, J. Amz, and P. Tallon, *The Royal City of Susa: Ancient Near Eastern Treasures in the Louvre* (New York: MMA, 1992). Mordecai is thought to be mentioned in contemporary tablets; but at least four men of this name occur in the fifth-century tablets from Persepolis. For references and overall background to Esther, see Yamauchi, *Persia and the Bible*, 226-39 (the Mordecais, 234-35). On the splendid metalwork, cf., e.g., *Le Monde de la Bible*, no. 106, 64-68; just a glimpse, A. R. Millard, *Discoveries from Bible Times* (Oxford: Lion, 1997), 141-42.

28. For short introductions to Ecbatana, see S. C. Brown, in E. M. Meyers, ed., *Oxford Encyclopedia of Archaeology in the Near East* 2 (New York: OUP, 1997), 186-87, and G. D. Summers, in P. Bienkowski and A. R. Millard, eds., *Dictionary of the Ancient Near East* (London: British Museum Press, 2000), 99f., with aerial view; cf. M. R. Sarraf, in *Archéologia*, no. 339 (November 1997): 40-41, and photo, p. 39.

29. On Persian-period Palestine, for sites showing occupation, see, e.g., Stern, *ALB* II, 373-460, with map, p. 375; historical introduction, 351-72. Just a few mentions must suffice here, on space grounds. *Anathoth* (Ezra 2:23), probably at Anata/Deir es-Sid; Stern, 138 end; cf. Wiseman and Millard, *NBD*, 34 end. *Bethel* (Ezra 2:28), at Beitin; Stern, 432; *NEAHL*, 1:192-94. *Gibeon* (Neh. 3:7-8), at El-Jib; Stern, 433. *Jericho* (Ezra 2:34), Tell es-Sultan; Stern, 438; *NEAHL*, 2:674-81, esp. 681. *Jerusalem* (implicit), same place; Stern, 434-36; *NEAHL*, 2:709. *Lachish* (cf. Neh. 11:30) at Tell ed-Duweir; Stern, 447-50; *NEAHL*, 3:910-11. *Mizpah* (Neh. 3:15, 19), at Tell en-Nasbeh; Stern, 432-33, updated by Zorn, e.g., in *NEAHL*, 3:1098-1102. Site of Ramat-Rahel (= Beth-Hakkerem? — Neh. 3:14), Stern, 436-37; *NEAHL*, 4:1265, stratum IVB. Continuity in Benjamin, see O. Lipschitz, *TA* 26 (1999): 155-90.

30. On the return of the gods of Babylonia, see the Cyrus Cylinder, in *ANET*, 315-16, or *CoS* II, 314-16; in Babylonian Chronicle no. 7 ("Nabonidus Chronicle"), *ANET*, 306; Grayson, *Assyrian and Babylonian Chronicles*, 109-10. Cf. study by A. Kuhrt, *JSOT* 25 (1983): 83-97, who rightly points out that Cyrus was following in long Mesopotamian tradition, but undervalues the fact that he did so here in a particular political context.

31. The inscription from Magnesia (temp. Tiberius) is given in English by S. Smith, *Isaiah*

Chapters XL–LV, Schweich Lectures, 1940 (London: OUP/British Academy, 1944), 41 (with references, p. 144 n. 108); cf. also R. de Vaux, *Bible et Orient* (Paris: Editions du Cerf, 1967), 95-96 (from *RB* 46 [1937]), citing also reports on similar acts under Darius at Miletus and by the Bosporus (Tacitus and Ctesias).

32. For bibliography on the trilingual text at Xanthus, see Fitzmyer, Kaufman, et al., *An Aramaic Bibliography*, 164 (B.5.14); most of it is given in English by J. Teixidor, *JNES* 37 (1978): 181-85, following on his notes in his *Bulletin d'Épigraphie Sémitique (1964-1980)* (Paris: Geuthner, 1986), 339-341, §142 (= *Syria* 52 [1975]: 287-89), and 453-54, §162 (= *Syria* 56 [1979]: 393-94).

33. For Cyrus texts regarding Ur and Sippar, see references given by de Vaux, *Bible et Orient*, 87-89 (from *RB* 46 [1937]).

34. For texts of Udja-hor-resenet, the Vatican statue, see G. Posener, *La Première Domination Perse en Égypte* (Cairo: IFAO, 1936), 7, 15-16, 17, 18, 19 (Cambyses); 22 (Darius I); cf. 164-76. It should be noted that Cambyses did limit certain benefices of some temples in Egypt — hence the propaganda against him that eventually produced the lurid tales reported by Herodotus. On Darius I, builder of temples, cf. J. D. Ray, *CAH*, 2nd ed., IV (1988), 264, and references (also in PM, IV-VII, passim).

35. On the nondamage of the Jewish temple at Elephantiné under Cambyses, see Cowley, *Aramaic Papyri*, 113; *ANET*, 492; Porten and Yardeni, *Textbook of Aramaic Documents*, 1:71. A still-useful survey on the Jewish community in Elephantiné is B. Porten, *Archives from Elephantine, the Life of an Ancient Jewish Military Colony* (Berkeley and Los Angeles: University of California Press, 1968).

36. For the "Passover Papyrus," Cowley, no. 21, see Cowley, *Aramaic Papyri*, 63; *ANET*, 491; Porten and Yardeni, *Textbook of Aramaic Documents*, 1:54. For Cowley, no. 38, see Cowley, 136; Porten and Yardeni, 1:58.

37. The governor Tattenai, of the (sub)province "Beyond the River" (Ezra 5:3; 6:6, 13), is also known from an original document of June 502 B.C. (cf. A. T. E. Olmstead, *JNES* 3 [1944]: 46).

38. The "passport" text is Driver Letter VI, in Driver, *Aramaic Documents* (1957), 27-28, 56-62, now Porten and Yardeni, *Textbook of Aramaic Documents*, 1:114-15, A.6/9; postbag, see photo, frontispiece to Driver (1954 ed.).

39. Phraseology like "issuing a decree/order" we find often; so, e.g., in Driver, *Aramaic Documents* (1957), letters III, 7-8; V, 8. For the greeting "Peace, much well-being" (etc.), see Driver, letters I,1; II,1; III,1; V,1; XIII,1; now Porten and Yardeni, *Textbook of Aramaic Documents*, 1:102, 110; 106, 104, 102, 110, 128.

40. The authenticity of the letters in Ezra-Nehemiah has been recognized since the time of Eduard Meyer. Noteworthy are H. H. Schaeder, in his *Iranische Beiträge I* (Halle: Niemeyer Verlag, 1930), and his *Esra der Schreiber* (Tübingen: Mohr, 1930); cf. also E. J. Bickerman, *JBL* 65 (1946): 249-75; and the matter is well summed up by de Vaux, *Bible et Orient*, 98-113 (and in his *The Bible and the Ancient Near East* [New York: Doubleday, 1971], 63-96); opposition to their authenticity rests on no secure fact.

The much-proclaimed differences between the forms of Cyrus's decree as found in the summary in Ezra 6:3-5 (from Ecbatana) and the form given in Ezra 1:2-4 (and partly used as a "catch line" in 2 Chron. 36:23) are of no significance in terms of authenticity. The Ecbatana form is that of the official Aramaic version, bureaucratic in tone and function; that in Ezra 1:2-4 is its Hebrew equivalent, stressing the leitmotiv of the pious ruler acting for the deity of his beneficiaries in appropriate language. The phenomenon is the same as that of the differences between the Aramaic, Greek, and Lycian versions of the Xanthus decree — all authentic and valid on the same monument! In Babylon the language of the Cyrus Cylinder was aimed at a Babylonian audience; the Aramaic bureaucratic rescripts ordering the return of images to their temples would have been practical and considerably less theological also.

On the Aramaic of Ezra and Daniel, the older controversies were surveyed ably by F. Rosenthal, *Die aramaistische Forschung seit Th. Nöldeke's Veröffentlichungen* (Leiden: Brill, 1939; reprint, 1964), 60-71. Later, see my survey of the facts of the case on biblical Aramaic; Kitchen, in Wiseman, *Notes*, 31-79 — in effect, endorsed by E. Y. Kutscher, "Aramaic," in T. A. Sebeok, ed., *Linguistics in South West Asia and North Africa* (Paris: Mouton, 1970), 347-412. In the decades since, much new material has accumulated that bears out the results of my study, with the publication of many fresh documents and improved republication of long-known ones. Several features of the Aramaic of Ezra and Daniel virtually preclude it having originated any later than the third century B.C. at the extreme; the fifth century fits better. The Hebrew is consistent with this (cf. W. J. Martin's note, in Wiseman, *Notes*, 28-30). The huge input of Greek military and cultural involvement in the Levant and beyond from the seventh to the fourth century B.C., long before Alexander, negates completely Driver's old and erroneous dictum that "the Greek words [only three!] demand" a Hellenistic date for the book of Daniel. Cf. on the "Greek" instruments, T. C. Mitchell and R. Joyce, in Wiseman, *Notes*, 19-27. That dating rests entirely on particular *interpretations* of (and on a priori assumptions about) certain passages in Dan. 8–11; see rather the cautionary review by Wiseman, *Nebuchadrezzar and Babylon*, 93-98. There is much authentic Neo-Babylonian and Old Persian cultural content in the book of Daniel that links it with those periods, and needs to be taken into account. On the former, cf. Wiseman, *Nebuchadrezzar and Babylon*, 81-115; on both, see the survey by T. C. Mitchell, in Curtis, *Mesopotamia and Iran*, 68-84, with wide bibliography.

The high quality and accuracy of the transcription of Old Persian names in Esther (besides that of other foreign names elsewhere in the OT) was set out clearly by A. R. Millard, *JBL* 96 (1977): 481-88. A wider survey of the vocabulary of the book of Esther reinforces that result, and implies that its author had good knowledge of Persian court usage; see H. M. Wahl, *ZAH* 12 (1999): 21-47. There is good reason to date the book to the fifth or fourth century B.C., and to regard it as historically based, not simply a "novel"; cf. survey of views and data by E. M. Yamauchi, *Persia and the Bible*, 226-39.

NOTES TO CHAPTER 4

1. For translation of Assurnasirpal II in north Syria, see *ANET*, 276; Grayson, *ARI*, 2:143; Grayson, *RIMA*, 2:218-19.

2. On Assur-dan II, Adad-nirari II, and Tukulti-Ninurta II, see Grayson, *ARI*, 2:74-113; Grayson, *RIMA*, 2:131-88.

3. On Tiglath-pileser I and Assur-bel-kala, see Grayson, *ARI*, 2:23, 26-27; Grayson, *RIMA*, 2:42, 103-4.

4. From Eriba-Adad II to Tiglath-pileser II, see Grayson, *ARI*, 2:62-74; Grayson, *RIMA*, 2:113-30.

5. On Siamun and Shoshenq I, see 2.D, on Solomon, below.

6. In most Delta sites, virtually all limestone and most sandstone building blocks and stelae have been recycled (and decoration/texts usually obliterated) in the last two thousand

years; very few Delta-based kings bothered to set up duplicate commemorative texts in the temples of Upper Egypt.

7. Luvian ("Hittite") hieroglyphic texts, now edited fully in J. D. Hawkins, *CHLI* I, and (for Karatepe) H. Çambel, *CHLI* II.

8. For early Byblos texts, see J. C. L. Gibson, *TSSI*, 3:12-24 (of these, only Ahiram and Yahi-milk occur in *ANET,* 499, 504/*CoS* II, 146f./181, respectively).

9. On Ekron, text of "Achish" son of Padi, see S. Gitin, T. Dothan, and J. Naveh, *IEJ* 47 (1997): 1-16; *CoS* II, 164.

10. For the turbulent occupation history (and archaeology) of Jerusalem, see latterly *NEAHL,* 2:698-804; H. Geva, ed., *Ancient Jerusalem Revealed* (Jerusalem: IES, 1994). On Samaria, cf. *NEAHL,* 4:1300-1310.

11. See Renz/Röllig I, 178-89, for the Siloam inscription; 261-65 for [Sheb]naiah; 190-91 for other scraps (see on this now, as part of a tariff [?], J. Naveh, in D. T. Ariel, ed., *City of David* VI [*Qedem* 41] [2000], 1-2 [IN.1], and F. M. Cross, *IEJ* 51 [2001]: 44-47; other scraps, Renz/Röllig, I, 206-7, 308.

12. On the Mesha stela, see *ANET,* 320; *CoS* II, 137-38; for other Moabite fragments, cf. briefly K. A. D. Smelik, *Writings from Ancient Israel* (Edinburgh: T. & T. Clark; Louisville: Westminster John Knox, 1991), 34-35, fig. 6.

13. The bibliography on the Tel Dan stela grows incessantly. Cf., e.g., Kitchen, *JSOT* 76 (1979): 42-44, supplemented by A. Lemaire, *JSOT* 81 (1998): 11-14, and add J. A. Emerton, *VT* 50 (2000): 27-37, and A. R. Millard, in *CoS* II, 161-62; G. Galil, *PEQ* 133 (2001): 16-21; W. M. Schniedewind and B. Zuckerman, *IEJ* 51 (2001): 88-91.

14. On the Mesha stela, see A. Lemaire, *BAR* 20, no. 3 (May-June 1994): 30-37, following on Lemaire in *SEL* 11 (1994): 17-19. For doubts, see P. Bordreuil, in P. Daviau et al., eds., *The World of the Aramaeans (Studies . . . Dion)* III (Sheffield: Sheffield Academic Press, 2001), 162-63 and n. 14.

15. On the "heights of David" in Shoshenq's list, see fully, Kitchen, *JSOT* 76 (1997): 29-44, esp. 39-41; summary, H. Shanks, *BAR* 24, no. 1 (January-February 1998): 34-35.

16. On *t* for *d* in Egyptian transcripts of Semitic names (place and personal): for the New Kingdom, see M. Burchardt, *Die altkanaanäischen Fremdworte und Eigennamen im Aegyptischen* I (Leipzig: Hinrichs, 1909), 45, §137:2; J. E. Hoch, *Semitic Words in Egyptian Texts* (Princeton, N.J.: Princeton University Press, 1994), 406 (but omitting place-names and early data). On the Middle Kingdom, cf. G. Posener, *Princes et pays d'Asie et de Nubie* (Brussels: FERE, 1940), 67: E.5 (Magdali); personal names, summary, Kitchen in S. Israelit-Groll, ed., *Studies . . . Presented to Miriam Lichtheim* II (Jerusalem: Magnes Press, 1990), 636-37. S. L. MacKenzie, *King David, a Biography* (New York: OUP, 2000), 15-16, fails entirely to account for the Shoshenq-list data — "David" was never a tribal name (as MacKenzie would claim), but exclusively a personal proper name as, e.g., the Rio stela shows; his approach to this detail is typical of the shallow, badly lopsided treatment meted out to David in the book (cf., e.g., H. Shanks, *BR* 16, no. 6 [December 2000]: 34-37, 53-54).

17. The citation about Assur-rabi II occurs under Shalmaneser III; cf. Luckenbill, *ARAB* I, 218, §603; Grayson, *RIMA,* 3:19 at ii:36-38; K. L. Younger, *CoS* II, 263. And probably under Assur-dan II, Grayson, *ARI,* 2:76; *RIMA,* 2:133.

18. On the Levantine background to the warnings given by Samuel, the pioneer study remains that (penned long ago) by I. Mendelsohn, *BASOR* 143 (1956): 17-22.

19. On *maryannu,* "chariotry," cf. Mendelsohn, *BASOR* 143 (1956): 18-19 (for 1 Sam. 8:11-12). Complementary to this was A. F. Rainey, *The Social Stratification at Ugarit* (Ann Arbor and

High Wycombe: University Microfilms, 1962), 130-46 (and *JNES* 24 [1965]: 17-27). On conscription for military service at Ugarit, see M. Heltzer, *The Rural Community in Ancient Ugarit* (Wiesbaden: Reichert Verlag, 1976), 18-23.

20. Cf. Mendelsohn, *BASOR* 143 (1956): 21, but omit his reference to Ugaritic *msm*, a misreading, corrected by Virolleaud, *Syria* 21 (1940): 149; cf. A. Herdner, *Corpus, Tablettes, Alphabétiques . . .* (1963), 165 n. 1, and further, Heltzer, *Rural Community*, 24-30.

21. Cf. Heltzer, *Rural Community*, 44-46.

22. References for Ugarit are in Rainey, *Social Stratification at Ugarit* (1967), 170; for Mari see J. Bottéro, *ARMT VII: Textes économiques et administratifs* (Paris: Imprimerie Nationale, 1957), 241 (women bakers, confectioners, etc.), 253-54 (aromatics), 274 (weaving), with references.

23. See for examples of the practice, Mendelsohn, *BASOR* 143 (1956): 19-20, and Rainey, *Social Stratification at Ugarit*, 26-28, 30-36, both with references; cf. also Heltzer, *Rural Community*, 48-51, 65-71, 90, and also 103 (nuancing the absoluteness of Rainey's view).

24. See Mendelsohn, *BASOR* 143 (1956): 20-21; Heltzer, *Rural Community*, 35-44.

25. Cf. Mendelsohn, *BASOR* 143 (1956): 21f.; Rainey, *Social Stratification at Ugarit*, 78-79, each with references. In Emar, in a society originally more tribally based than at Ugarit, the role of the king is not so pervasive; but fines in legal matters went either to "the Palace" or to "the city of Emar" or to "(the god) Ninurta"; cf. the publications of tablets (thirteenth to early twelfth centuries) by D. Arnaud, *Emar, VI.3 (Recherches au pays d'Ashtata)* (Paris: Editions Recherche sur les Civilisations, 1986); and his *Textes syriens de l'âge du bronze récent* (Barcelona: Editorial AUSA, 1991); plus G. Beckman, *Texts from the Vicinity of Emar* (Padua: Sargon srl, 1996).

26. Aram is clearly attested for the fourteenth century in the Kom el-Hetan topographical lists of Amenophis III (ca. 1392-1354), as well as for the later thirteenth century in the "Miscellanies" under Merenptah (1213-1203), where it had sometimes been wrongly emended to read "Amurru"; see E. Edel, *Die Ortsnamenlisten aus dem Totentempel Amenophis III* (Bonn: Hanstein Verlag, 1966), 28-29, no. 7, with references (his pre-1500 references would not now all be admitted).

27. The kingdom of Amurru suffered from the Sea Peoples' invasion in circa 1175, according to Ramesses III. But it evidently survived (if in restricted form), as we have two bronze arrowheads of a "Zakarbaʿal, King of Amurru," supposedly of the eleventh century (a date that is almost certainly too low). See, for one, R. Deutsch and M. Heltzer, *Forty New Ancient West Semitic Inscriptions* (Tel Aviv: Archaeological Center Publications, 1994), 12-13, no. 1; for the other, see references of the same authors, *West Semitic Epigraphic News of the First Millennium* BCE (Tel Aviv: Archaeological Center Publications, 1999), 14:XII (the first is no. XXIX).

28. See F. M. Cross, *Israel Museum Journal* 10 (1992): 57-62, and in *EI* 25 (1996), 21*-26*, plus notes by R. Deutsch and M. Heltzer, *New Epigraphic Evidence from the Biblical Period* (Tel Aviv: Archaeological Center Publications, 1995), 29.

29. For the excavations at Shiloh, see the monograph by I. Finkelstein, S. Bunimovitz, and Z. Lederman, *Shiloh, the Archaeology of a Biblical Site* (Tel Aviv: Institute of Archaeology, 1993), including full report, assessment of previous work, and good bibliography. Results are summed up on 371-89 (383-89 for Iron I).

30. On Sir Charles Wilson's siting for the tabernacle on the north side of Shiloh, see A. S. Kaufman, *BAR* 14, no. 6 (November-December 1988): 46-52. Finds there of only Iron II sherds would represent a later presence on this northern site; much fuller excavation would be needed to confirm or eliminate an Iron I presence there.

31. For the archaeology of Tell el-Ful, and a summary of its interpretation, see N. Lapp in *NEAHL,* 2:445-48, with bibliography.

32. For a summary of work at Ashdod, see in *NEAHL,* 1:93-102.

33. For Gath, cf. summary of old digs and survey finds in *NEAHL,* 4:1522-24, all with bibliographies. On the location and significance of Gath, see W. M. Schniedewind, *BASOR* 309 (1998): 69-77.

34. For a summary of work at Ekron, see *NEAHL,* 3:1051-59.

35. For Ascalon and Gaza during this period, cf. *NEAHL,* 1:103-112 (esp. 107), and *NEAHL,* 2:464-67.

36. For latest results on Beth-Shan, see A. Mazar, *IEJ* 43 (1993): 201-29, with clear summary for Iron I, pp. 228-29, and table, p. 205, plus his fresh summary for this period in A. Mazar, ed., *Studies in the Archaeology of the Iron Age in Israel and Jordan,* JSOTSup 331 (Sheffield: Academic Press, 2001), 290-96.

37. For publication of all Luvian ("Hittite") hieroglyphic texts, see Hawkins, *CHLI* I (with Karatepe in Çambel, *CHLI* II).

38. On Tiglath-pileser III's dismissal of Wassurme of Tabal, texts translated in Tadmor, *TP III,* 171, 191 (dates, p. 157, "after 732"; p. 181, "730 or 729?").

39. Shalmaneser III in twenty-second year (837), Luckenbill, *ARAB* I, 206, §579; Grayson, *RIMA,* 3:67 (twenty-four kings), 79 (only twenty kings).

40. For all the hieroglyphic texts from Carchemish, Melid, Gurgum, etc., see Hawkins, *CHLI* I, list, xiv-xv (Carchemish), xv-xvi (Malatya = Melid), xvi (Marash = Gurgum), etc.

41. On Kuzi-Tesup of Carchemish and the line in Melid, see J. D. Hawkins, *AnSt* 38 (1988): 99-108.

42. On the Aramean states, Bit-Adini, Gozan, Sam'al, Aram-Zobah/Damascus, Arpad, etc., and also Hamath, cf. H. Sader, *Les états araméens de Syrie . . .* (Beirut and Wiesbaden: F. Steiner Verlag, 1987); P.-E. Dion, *Les araméens à l'age du fer: histoire, politique et structures sociales,* Ebib, n.s., 34 (Paris: Librairie Lecoffre, Gabalda, 1997); on Zobah and Damascus, see below.

43. *Bayt-* names are listed in Kitchen, *JSOT* 76 (1997): 38-39, with a map (p. 37) of locations of "Beth-" kingdoms.

44. On the idiom "son" = member/ruler of *(Bayt-),* see (besides A. Ungnad, *OLZ* 9 [1906]: 224-26) B. Landsberger, *Sam'al I* (Ankara: Drückerei der Türkischen Historischen Gesellschaft, 1948), 19 with n. 37; this basic point was entirely missed by T. Schneider, *BAR* 21, no. 1 (1995): 26-33, 80, passim, through not knowing these key references on this matter.

45. Sequence from Tebah/Tubikhi, in EA 179 (trans. W. L. Moran, *The Amarna Letters* [Baltimore and London: Johns Hopkins University Press, 1992], 262); note its author's concern with Amurru, which occupied the Lebanon range along the west of the Biqa Valley.

46. Takhsi = Tahash, earlier suggested by A. H. Gardiner, *Ancient Egyptian Onomastica* I (Oxford: OUP, 1947), 150*f. Takhsi, in Amarna letters, no. 189: verso 9-12 (Moran, *The Amarna Letters,* 270). In Egyptian sources, Kitchen, *RITANC* I (1993), 37, §68.

47. On Aram-Damascus (and Zobah), cf. M. F. Unger, *Israel and the Aramaeans of Damascus* (Grand Rapids: Zondervan, 1957), and the more recent works by W. T. Pitard, *Ancient Damascus* (Winona Lake, Ind.: Eisenbrauns, 1989); Sader, *Les états araméens de Syrie;* Dion, *Les araméens à l'age du fer.*

48. For the whole "mini-empire" phenomenon, see Kitchen, "The Controlling Role of External Evidence in Assessing the Historical Status of the Israelite United Monarchy," in V. P. Long et al., eds., *Windows into Old Testament History* (Grand Rapids: Eerdmans, 2002).

49. For royal "named" cities (as of David), compare Amenemhat-Ithet-Tawy ("Amenemhat I grasps Egypt") and later Pi-Ramesse ("Domain of Ramesses II") in Twelfth and Nineteenth Dynasty Egypt respectively (twentieth and thirteenth centuries); Azitawataya, "(Town of) Azitiwata" (ruler of Que/Danuna in southeast Asia Minor, eighth century); Dur-Sharrukin, "Sargonburg" (now Khorsabad) of Sargon II (fl. 720) in Assyria, and others.

50. The three-element nature of the united monarchy's regime was originally noted by A. Malamat, *JNES* 22 (1963): 6-8, and B. Mazar, *BA* 25 (1962): 102-3; cf. the graphic presentation by Y. Aharoni, *The Land of the Bible,* 2nd ed. (London: Burns & Oates, 1979), 295, map 21, with 296-97.

51. For the size of Egyptian garrisons (outside of Gaza, Kumidi, and Simyra), note the small contingents sought by local kinglets in the Amarna letters; cf. Moran, *The Amarna Letters.*

52. A modest sampling of the hymns and prayers of the cultures of the ancient Near East can be found in *ANET,* 365-400, 467-69 (Egyptian, Sumerian and Akkadian, and Hittite), and even fewer in *CoS* I, 37-48 (Egypt), 416-18, 470-75 (Akkadian), and 526-30 (Sumerian).

53. For third-millennium popular pieces in Egypt, see *ANET,* 469, and more fully, K. A. Kitchen, *Poetry of Ancient Egypt* (Jonsered: P. Aströms förlag, 1999), 75-78.

54. For Egyptian popular poems, harpists' songs, lyric/love poetry (full corpus), and workmen's hymns of confession, prayer, and praise in the second millennium, see selections in Kitchen, *Poetry of Ancient Egypt,* 133-42 (Middle Kingdom), 315-430 (New Kingdom), with further references.

55. On King Intef II, see Kitchen, *Poetry of Ancient Egypt,* 109-12.

56. On En-khedu-anna, see W. W. Hallo and J. J. A. van Dijk, *The Exaltation of Inanna* (New Haven: Yale University Press, 1968); for the Sumerian Temple Hymns, see A. W. Sjöberg and E. Bergmann, *The Collection of the Sumerian Temple Hymns,* Texts from Cuneiform Sources III (New York: Augustin, 1969), and p. 5 on the princess's role.

57. For Akhenaten's Hymn to Aten there are many translations; cf. *ANET,* 369-71; *CoS* I, 44-46; Kitchen, *Poetry of Ancient Egypt,* 249-60. On Egyptian hymn to Amen-Re, caring for humanity and the fauna, cf. *ANET,* 365-67. Akkadian moon and sun hymns with concern for humanity and other created beings, see *ANET,* 385-86, 387-88.

58. The range and techniques of ancient Near Eastern poetry is set out in simple form (for Egypt) in my *Poetry of Ancient Egypt,* xiii-xx, 471-81. Hebrew poetry and poetics are comprehensively set out by W. G. E. Watson, *Classical Hebrew Poetry,* 2nd and corrected ed. (Sheffield: Sheffield Academic Press, 1995). For Sumerian, and its shared features with Hebrew, see A. Berlin, *JANES* 10 (1978/79): 35-42. For Ugaritic, in outline, see C. H. Gordon, *Ugaritic Textbook* I (Rome: Pontifical Biblical Institute, 1965), 131-44; its formal correspondences with Hebrew usage, cf. L. R. Fisher, ed., *Ras Shamra Parallels* I (1972), II (1975), and S. Rummel, ed., *Ras Shamra Parallels* III (1981), all published in Rome by the Pontifical Biblical Institute; and review of I-II by J. C. de Moor and P. van der Hugt, *BiOr* 31 (1974): 3-26. For Akkadian (Assyro-Babylonian), cf. summary treatment in English, B. R. Foster, *Before the Muses: An Anthology of Akkadian Literature* I (Bethesda, Md.: CDL Press, 1993), 14-19, also summarized in his updated but abridged version, *From Distant Days* (1995), 4-7. A detailed study is given by K. Hecker, *Untersuchungen zur akkadischen Epik* (Neukirchen-Vluyn: Neukirchener Verlag, 1974).

59. Sumerian terminology (*ershemma, balbale,* etc.) can be seen in use in translations by S. N. Kramer in *ANET,* 3rd ed., 576-79, 582-84 (= Supp., 140-43, 146-48). The variety of settings in which Sumerian hymns could be used (with different combinations of *balags* and *ershemmas*), and varying use as personal and cultic psalms, is all noted by J. Krecher, *Sumerische Kultlyrik* (Wiesbaden: Harrassowitz, 1966), 27 top (different occasions), 23 nn. 26-27 (different

combinations of *balag, ershemma*), 33 (both cult and personal use), 26-27 (content not needfully related to cult use).

60. Examples of Egyptian personal hymns of piety, with titles, opening with titular couplet, "Giving praise (to deity), paying homage (to deity)," often by speaker, in Kitchen, *Poetry of Ancient Egypt,* 271-313, passim.

61. For specified uses of music (Mesopotamian and Hittite), see the series of quotes in I. J. Gelb and others, eds., *CAD* 21/Z (1961), 36-38, with a good summary, p. 38.

62. On music in the Near East in all contexts, see entries (in English, French, and German) in *RLA* VIII, pts. 5/6, 7/8 (1995/97), 463-91. In Egyptian festival scenes, see in L. Grollenberg, *Atlas of the Bible* (London: Nelson, 1956), 72, no. 204 (dancers, clapping, harpist, sistrum players, ca. 1480). Generally, cf. entry in W. Helck, E. Otto, and W. Westendorf, eds., *LdA* IV/2 (1980), 230-43, in German with references in English, French, and German.

63. The basic study of this period remains Kitchen, *Third Int. Pd,* in particular the 1996 edition with important supplements. For the most recent, up-to-date treatment of Egyptian dates during 1070-664, see Kitchen, in *Acta Archaeologica* 67 (1996 [1998]): 1-13, esp. 1-3 with tables 1-2 (also issued as same pages in K. Randsborg, ed., *Absolute Chronology, Archaeological Europe, 2500-500 BC* [Copenhagen: Munksgaard, 1996 (1998)]). An update of this paper appeared in M. Bietak, ed., *The Synchronization of Civilizations in the Eastern Mediterranean during the Second Millennium BC (Symposion Langenlois Nov. 15-17, 1996)* (Vienna: Austrian Academy, 2000), 29-52. There is absolutely no scope whatsoever for the impossible "margin" of fifty years' variation claimed by P. Ash, *David, Solomon, and Egypt: A Reassessment* (Sheffield: Academic Press, 1999), 26, 34; cf. my review in *Themelios* 26, no. 3 (summer 2001): 38-50.

64. The major blunder in calling Siamun "an unidentified king" on his Tanis relief-scene was made by J. M. Weinstein, in S. Gitin, A. Mazar, and E. Stern, eds., *Mediterranean Peoples in Transition . . . in Honor of Professor Trude Dothan* (Jerusalem: IES, 1998), 192-93; it is said (orally) that he has realized his error and withdrawn it. But this should be done prominently in print, or ignoramuses will misquote him for years to come. His basic attitude to the Siamun piece is unrealistically negative (193 n. 10); there is not a single scrap of evidence for claiming that the ax head shown is "anachronistic."

65. The Siamun relief, original publication (photograph), is in P. Montet, *Les constructions et le tombeau d'Osorkon II* (Paris: [Fouilles de Tanis, Mission Montet], 1947), pl. IX.

66. The coincidence of monumental triumph scenes with kings who actually warred is noted by A. R. Green, *JBL* 97 (1978): 366. For Ramesses VI, cf. A. M. A. Amer, *JEA* 71 (1985): 67-68.

67. The account of triumph scenes by Ash, *David, Solomon, and Egypt,* is full of errors about triumph scenes. (1) He fails to distinguish between formal temple reliefs and minor decorative examples, which refutes his use of the irrelevant Herihor and allied examples (pp. 43-44). (2) He and others misinterpret the ax in the Siamun scene, not realizing how and why it is held as it is (40). (3) Philistines hold no axes in reliefs of series of prisoners (39f.), as the crescentic ax may be a ceremonial weapon — no other triumph scene with Philistines is available to compare with Siamun's. (4) Siamun's relief, properly understood, does *not* "violate . . . the genre" of triumph scenes (43); foes of Tuthmosis III hold axes in a triumph scene of his at Karnak! (5) The daggers held by the blade by foes in Shoshenq's scene are wrongly described as "thin vials" by Ash (41), a massive howler! Foes *did* hold weapons in such reliefs. (6) The "double bow" plus feather was totally misunderstood by him and Montet (41, 42); these two signs are heraldic hieroglyphs that read *Pedjtyu-Shutu,* "foreigners"! (7) An enormous blunder by Ash (45) is to identify the ax as either a halter (his example is a flower bud!) or, worse, handcuffs! He has clearly never seen the handcuffs that Egyptians used for foreign prisoners: these are simply ovals

with a central slot, drastically different from our ax head (see example in K. Lange and M. Hirmer, *Egypt, Architecture, Painting*, 3rd ed. [London: Phaidon Press, 1961], pl. 200)! (8) There is no alternative to the Levant for Siamun's campaign; his "ax" is neither Nubian or Libyan, the only other venues open to Siamun. Finally, (9) no better is U. Schipper, *Israel und Ägypten in der Königszeit* (Freiburg and Göttingen, 1999), 26f., with 296 Abb. 3, with Gezer and Megiddo double ax(es) not remotely like the flared crescentic blade of Siamun's scene. Significantly, Hittite and Aegean double axes are closer in form! And so on.

68. For Amenophis III, see EA 4, in Moran, *The Amarna Letters*, 8-9.

69. For Ankhsenamun, in the Hittite record, see Deeds of Suppiluliuma I, edited by H. G. Güterbock, *JCS* 10 (1956): 94-98.

70. Despite the arrogant denials by Soggin, Ash, and Schipper, there is excellent evidence of kings marrying off their daughters to commoners in the tenth-eighth centuries; see my table 12, in *Third Int. Pd.* (1996), 594 with 479. Kings Shoshenq I, Harsiese, Osorkon II, Takeloth II, Shoshenq III, Takeloth III, and Rudamun all did this. And for foreigners, we have Maatkare B married to Prince Osorkon, son of future Shoshenq I (p. 479:3). And add in the Twenty-First Dynasty king giving his royal sister-in-law to Hadad of Edom (1 Kings 11:19-20), consistent with this very same period of Siamun or just slightly earlier. There is no escape from this evidence, which has to be accepted.

71. Cf. Kitchen, *Third Int. Pd.*, 288 §242; and new edition, with text, in J.-M. Kruchten, *Les annales des prêtres de Karnak (XXI-XXIIImes Dynasties)* . . . (Louvain: Departement Oriëntalistiek, 1989), 49-50, text 4b.

72. On Osorkon the Elder, see J. Yoyotte, *BSFÉ* 77-78 (1977): 39-54; cf. my *Third Int. Pd.* (1986, 1996), 534-35.

73. The Egyptian reference is in Kitchen, *RITA* II (1996), 96; cf. *RITANC* II (1999), 149 end. The cuneiform reference: E. Edel, *Die ägyptisch-hethitische Korrespondenz aus Boghaz-köi* (Opladen: Westdeutscher Verlag, 1994), 2:222.

74. For Amarna evidence on cost of dowries in the fourteenth century, see Kitchen in D. O'Connor and E. H. Cline, eds., *Amenhotep III, Perspectives on His Reign* (Ann Arbor: University of Michigan Press, 1998), 258-59.

75. On anointing a future bride, in Hittite records temp. Ramesses II, see Kitchen, *RITANC* II (1999), 149, with references (Edel, etc.). On Egyptian emphasis on wealth of dowries from the Hittites, cf. texts of the two Hittite marriages, *RITA* II, 94, 96, 98-99, 111; on a quarrel with Queen Pudukhepa over a dowry (even if no girl!), see *RITANC* II, 148-49. Long before Solomon, it was not unknown for a princess to have a foreign town in her service — its revenues might provide her with "pocket money," one surmises. Thus Abi-milki, ruler of Tyre, declares himself "servant of Mayati" (Meritaten), princess-queen of Akhenaten in the Amarna letters, ca. 1340 (EA 155; Moran, *The Amarna Letters*, 241-42). So the eventual taxpayers in Hebrew-resettled Gezer might have had to pay taxes for the upkeep of Solomon's Egyptian princess!

76. Cf. Moran, *The Amarna Letters*, 114f.

77. For kings seeking materials to build or adorn temples or palaces — for a temple, cf. EA 9 (Moran, *The Amarna Letters*, 18); for palaces as in EA 16, cf. EA 4 (Moran, 39, cf. 9), and for a mausoleum, EA 19 (Moran, 44). Egyptian carpentry, EA 10 (Moran, 19); also Amenophis III sent rich furnishings for the Babylonian king's new residence, EA 5 (Moran, 11). Medical men from Egypt to Hatti, brief summary, Kitchen, *Pharaoh Triumphant: Life and Times of Ramesses II* (Warminster: Aris & Phillips, 1982), 91-92, 251; for a full overview, see E. Edel, *Ägyptische Ärtzte und ägyptische Medizin am hethitischen Königshof* (Opladen: Westdeutscher Verlag, 1976), all of which is now in his *AHK* I-II.

78. For royal and high-level correspondents wishing the gods' blessings on each other, see (e.g.) in the Amarna letters (fourteenth century), Tushratta invoking Egyptian Amun as well as his own deities, EA 19 (Moran, *The Amarna Letters*, 43, 44, 45); or Ribaddi of Byblos wishing Amun's blessing on the Egyptian vizier, EA 71 (Moran, 140), and on other high officers, EA 86, 87, 95 (Moran, 158, 159, 169). In the fourteenth-thirteenth centuries a stream of examples comes from Ugarit; see J. Nougayrol, *Le Palais Royal d'Ugarit* III (Paris: Imprimerie Nationale/ Klincksieck, 1955), pp. 6f., 9, 10 (all: "may the gods keep you (well)!"); 13 ("may the gods of Amurru and Ugarit keep you well!"); 15 (same, Ugarit only); 18 ("may the gods of Amurru, Ugarit and the king keep you well!"); 20 (as pp. 6-10); and Nougayrol, *Le Palais Royal d'Ugarit* IV (1956), 132 ("may the gods of Ugarit, [of other places, lost], and [the 100]o (?) gods keep you!"); 180, 196 (both, "may the gods keep you healthy!"); 214-17 ("may the 1,000 gods keep you healthy!"); 219 (same as 180/196). "May the gods keep you healthy!" recurs in thirteenth-century Emar (Arnaud, *Emar* VI.3, 264, no. 268). Also then, Ramesses II invokes his god Amun and the Hittite weather god several times when writing to Queen Pudukhepa (e.g., Edel, *AHK* I, 107, no. 43:26-29, 37ff., and other examples).

79. For Heltzer's note, see his study of grain taxation and tithes in Ugarit, in Heltzer, *Rural Community*, 36-40. For wider comparative background figures, see Kitchen, in *NBD*, 378b.

80. On "Sidonians," cf. the observations by G. E. Markoe, *Phoenicians* (London: British Museum Press, 2000), 31-32, with notes.

81. On the month names being unique to 1 Kings 6 and 8, see Mark E. Cohen, *The Cultic Calendars of the Ancient Near East* (Bethesda, Md.: CDL Press, 1993), 384-85. Both *B(u)l* and *'(E)t(ha)n(i)m* are attested in Phoenician inscriptions, as Cohen points out; the other, *Z(i)w*, is not yet so known, unless it were an abbreviation (e.g.) for *Z(i)bakh-sh(a)msh*.

82. On the food needs of Tyre, both for its own population and for possible reexport in trade, see A. Lemaire, in E. Lipinski, ed., *Studia Phoenicia XI, Phoenicia and the Bible* (Louvain: Peeters, 1991), 148-50, and F. Briquel-Chatonnet, *Les relations entre les cités de la côte phénicienne et les royaumes d'Israël et de Juda* (Louvain: Peeters, 1992), 244-45.

83. On locations of towns in Asher's allotment, see (e.g.) Lemaire, in *Studia Phoenicia XI*, 135-43 (with map), and R. S. Hess, *Joshua*, Tyndale OT Commentaries (Leicester: IVP, 1996), 271-73, and map, 320; south and east borders of Asher, cf. Z. Gal, *Lower Galilee during the Iron Age* (Winona Lake, Ind.: Eisenbrauns, 1992), 102-4, map, 101.

84. For the two documents on city exchange from Alalakh, see AT No. 1 in D. J. Wiseman, *The Alalakh Tablets* (London: British Institute of Archaeology at Ankara, 1953), 25-26; and AT 456, Wiseman, *JCS* 12 (1958): 124-29. For other, more local town/territory exchanges and sales at Alalakh, cf. Wiseman, *The Alalakh Tablets*, 52, nos. 76-80.

85. For Ibal-pi-El II of Eshnunna and Zimri-lim of Mari, boundary from Haradum (and Yahdun-lim buying a ruined site from Eshnunna), see D. Charpin, in D. Charpin and F. Joannes, eds., *Marchandes, diplomates et empereurs (Études . . . Paul Garelli)* (Paris: ERC, 1991), 155-58.

86. For interpretations suggesting loan or mortgage on territory between Solomon and Hiram, cf. D. J. Wiseman, *1 and 2 Kings*, Tyndale Commentaries (1993), 126, and M. J. Selman, *2 Chronicles*, Tyndale Commentaries (1994), 345. For royal bargaining on other matters, see wrangles over gold, which kings of Babylon and Mitanni sought to extract from the kings of Egypt in the fourteenth century (Moran, *The Amarna Letters*, EA 4-8, 11, 16, 19, 24, 26-29). And a Babylonian king would tell the pharaoh, "If this summer . . . you'll send the gold I wrote to you about, then I'll give you my daughter (in marriage). . . . But if you don't send (it), . . . then I'd not give my daughter in marriage!" (EA 4, cf. Moran, 9). While Amenophis III offers furnishings

for the Babylonian king's new abode, and to prepare for that king's envoy bringing the princess, but will not send until messenger (and daughter!) arrive, EA 5 (Moran, 11).

87. False dismissals of Solomon's horse/chariot trade, by Ash, *David, Solomon, and Egypt,* 119-22, and by Schipper, *Israel und Ägypten in der Königszeit,* 73-83.

88. On Pi-Ramesse, area Q.IV (late thirteenth century), with stabling and provision for horses (taken as "stud"), cf. briefly E. B. Pusch, *Egyptian Archaeology* 14 (1999): 13 (and in E. Bleiberg and R. Freed, eds., *Fragments of a Shattered Visage (Symposium, . . . Ramesses the Great)* [Memphis, Tenn., 1991], 202-3); it is also mentioned very briefly in *Ägypten und Levante* 9 (1999): 11, 25 (strata Bc, Bb, Bc), 39ff. (pottery) and plans, pp. 18 Abb. 1, and 122 Abb. 1. (ODM 1076 is cited in full by Kitchen, in S. Ahituv and E. D. Oren, eds., *The Origin of Early Israel — Current Debate,* Beer-Sheva XII [1998], 73.)

89. See earlier survey on horse raising in Egypt and Nubia by Y. Ikeda, in T. Ishida, ed., *Studies in the Period of David and Solomon and Other Essays* (Winona Lake, Ind.: Eisenbrauns, 1982), 227-31. On Kushite (Nubian) horses prized by the Assyrians (eighth-seventh centuries), cf. Ikeda, 228-29, with references (*KUB* III, 27, is now in Edel, *AHK* II, 70/71–72/73, no. 26). First occurrence of horses in the Nile Valley is the skeleton of a horse at the Egyptian fortress of Buhen (by Wadi Halfa) at the Second Cataract in Nubia, in the late Thirteenth Dynasty, on the eve of the Hyksos period (seventeenth/sixteenth centuries); mention, W. B. Emery, *Egypt in Nubia* (London: Hutchinson, 1965), 107.

90. On horse prices, cf. list by Ikeda, in Ishida, *Studies,* 226. Much later the galloping inflation that hit the shekel (as for human slaves, see chaps. 6 and 7 below) from the sixth century onward raised the price again (230 shekels under Nabonidus, good horse; hack, Seleucid epoch, 88 [?] shekels).

91. Chariot prices are given by Ikeda, in Ishida, *Studies,* 226; the Egyptian one at 64 shekels was a simple war chariot for a raw recruit (thirteenth century), and the Babylonian one was probably a standard model (ca. 1090). Nearer our "Rolls-Royce" model is one that Tushratta king of Mitanni sent to Egypt ca. 1350, with 350 shekels' worth of gold applied to it (the whole chariot being evidently worth still more than this, and not far off Solomon's 600-shekel models, especially if one allows for a price "markup" on his part, to cover his costs and make a profit). For this one, see EA 22: I, 2; Moran, *The Amarna Letters,* 51. None of these data are properly handled by Ash or Schipper. For other background to this putative horse/chariot trade, see Ikeda, 231-38.

92. For this section, see my fuller treatment, "Sheba and Arabia," in L. K. Handy, ed., *The Age of Solomon, Scholarship at the Turn of the Millennium* (Leiden: Brill, 1997), 126-53. Humorous takeoff is by Phinneas A. Crutch, *The Queen of Sheba, Her Life and Times* (New York and London: Putnam, Knickerbocker Press, 1922).

93. From southwest Arabia, in Yemen and around, have been found upward of six thousand Old South Arabian inscriptions. Most of these are in the Sabaean dialect, and not a few name the kings and *mukarrib*s of Saba. The others are mainly in the dialects of the kingdoms of Qataban, Hadramaut, and Ma'in and its local predecessors. For a bibliography of these (down to 1997/98), see K. A. Kitchen, *Documentation for Ancient Arabia,* II, *Bibliographical Catalogue of Texts* (Liverpool: UP, 2000). For the various kingdoms, minimal chronology, and lists of monuments of rulers, see Kitchen, *Documentation for Ancient Arabia* I (1994), along with a "high" chronology and updates on kings and monuments in vol. II just cited. These include the Assyrian references. On the latter, see also I. Eph'al, *The Ancient Arabs* (Jerusalem: Magnes Press, 1982) (especially valuable on Assurbanipal's texts). For Assyrian interception of Sabaean trade caravans, cf. M. Liverani, *Yemen* 1 (1992): 111-15 (in English), evaluating data published by

A. Cavigneaux and B. K. Ismail, *Baghdader Mitteilungen* 21 (1990): 321-456 (text 2, IV:26-39; in German).

94. Women as beaters are in text Yala AQ 17 (Iryani 43); published in A. de Maigret, G. Garbini, and M. A. el-Iryani, *The Sabaean Archaeological Complex in the Wadi Yala (Eastern Hawlan at-Tiyal, Yemen Arab Republic), Preliminary Report* (Rome: IsMEO, 1988), 30-31; re-edited by A. Jamme, *Miscellanées d'ancient arabe* XVII (Washington, D.C.: own edition, 1989), 78 (in English).

95. A. L. Oppenheim in *ANET,* 283-86, 301, plus Luckenbill, *ARAB* II, 130, §259 (Iati'e).

96. Malik-halik is in text Iryani 13; summary English translation in A. F. L. Beeston, "Warfare in Ancient South Arabia (2nd-3rd Centuries AD)" = *Qahtan* 3 (1976): 47-48.

97. On Ophir, see more fully Kitchen, in Handy, *The Age of Solomon,* 143-47, with detailed references, and map, p. 126.

98. For the location of ʿAmau, see latterly Kitchen in A. Leahy and J. Tait, eds., *Studies on Ancient Egypt in Honour of H. S. Smith* (London: EES, 1999), 174-77 (with map).

99. On Wadi Baysh, etc., see references in Kitchen, in Handy, *The Age of Solomon,* 145 n. 49. Cf. study by the professional gold-geologist R. J. Roberts, *Passion for Gold* (Reno: University of Nevada Press, 2002), 133-54.

100. The three-year expeditions were to a more distant locale, as was clearly pointed out by H. von Wissmann, "Ophir," in *Pauly's Realencyclopädie der classischen Altertumswissenschaft, neue Bearbeitung, Supplementband XII* (Stuttgart: Druckenmüller, 1970), col. 969. The three years were the end of one year, one full year, and then the start of a third, as in common ancient Near Eastern usage, covering either the long voyages out and back or these plus a refit period for the next expedition.

101. The "Ophir" ostracon was first published by B. Maisler [Mazar], *JNES* 10 (1951): 266, no. 2, pl. XI:2.

102. For the Metten II and Tiglath-pileser III text, see Oppenheim in *ANET,* 282 (66), and in Tadmor, *TP III,* 170-71: 16'.

103. For basic location of and sea navigation to Punt, see K. A. Kitchen, *Or* 40 (1971): 184-207; for an overall account, see Kitchen, in T. Shaw et al., eds., *The Archaeology of Africa* (London: Routledge, 1993), 587-608, and with neighboring lands, in Leahy and Tait, *Studies,* 173-78 and map; for archaeology and resources of Punt, see R. Fattovich, in S. Schoske, ed., *Akten, IVten Internationalen Ägyptologen Kongress München 1985,* vol. 4 (Hamburg: Buske Verlag, 1991), 257-72, and in *Atti, VIo Congresso internazionale di Egittologia* II (Turin, 1993), 399-405.

104. On Meluhha and Dilmun, documentation and trade, see D. T. Potts, *The Arabian Gulf in Antiquity* I (Oxford: OUP, 1990), 85-89, 135-50, 182-91; for a simple, overall outline, cf. G. Weisgerber, in S. H. A. Al-Khalifa and M. Rice, eds., *Bahrain through the Ages, the Archaeology* (London: KPI, 1986), 135-42, and S. R. Rao, 376-82. For recent popular summaries in brief, cf. H. Crawford, in H. Crawford and M. Rice, eds., *Traces of Paradise: The Archaeology of Bahrain, 2500 BC–300 AD* (London: Dilmun Committee, 2000), 72-86, and D. T. Potts, *Ancient Magan, the Secrets of Tell Abraq* (London: Trident Press, 2000), 51-58, 119-31.

105. On Sargon of Akkad, cf. M. Roaf, *Cultural Atlas of Mesopotamia and the Ancient Near East* (New York: Facts on File, 1990), 96-97 and map.

106. For summary and references for Ramesses II and Hittite visitors, see Kitchen, *Pharaoh Triumphant,* 89-91, 251.

107. See Kitchen, *Third Int. Pd.* (1996), 157-58, 383-85, 553-54, 557, etc.

108. See C. J. Gadd, *AnSt* 8 (1958): 35-92 (esp. 80ff.); Oppenheim in *ANET,* 3rd ed., 562 (= Supp., 126).

109. See *ANET*, 296-97.

110. For Tadmor in the Mari data, see G. Dossin, *ARM(T)* V (1952), 40/41, no. 23 (with correction to line 20, by J. Bottéro and A. Finet, *ARM[T]* XV [1954], 135 n. 2, also given by J.-R. Kupper, *Les nomades en Mésopotamie au temps des rois de Mari* [Paris: Société d'Édition "Les Belles Lettres," 1957], 84 n. 2). For Tadmor under Tiglath-pileser I, cf. translations in A. K. Grayson, *RIMA*, 2 (1991), 38, 43. Solomon occasionally taking military action is no stranger than David sometimes being a builder (cf. 2 Sam. 5:9-11; 7:2). Near Eastern kings were never exclusively just either builder or warrior (as scores of other examples would demonstrate).

111. For Baalath/Baalah/Mount Baalah (not necessarily all the same), cf. summaries in *ABD*, 1:555; B. Mazar, *The Early Biblical Period* (Jerusalem: IES, 1986), 106 n. 8, 109 n. 15; with map, 105; on Baalath in Dan's original allotment, see Hess, *Joshua* 275-76, 316.

112. On Tamar at 'Ain Husb, and surrounding geography, see Y. Aharoni, *IEJ* 13 (1963): 30-42; map, 35.

113. In Kings, Ta(d>m)mor for Tadmor? Cf. P. J. Williams, *VT* 47 (1997): 262-65.

114. The Temple D plan and description are accessible in P. Matthiae, *Ebla, an Empire Rediscovered* (London: Hodder & Stoughton, 1977), 131-32 and fig. 30 (and in unnumbered plates at end).

115. For the Habuba Kabira preliminary report, see D. Machule and T. Rhode, *MDOG* 106 (1974): 11-27 with Beilage 2.

116. For recent notes on Dagan temple, cf. J. Margueron, *MARI* 4 (1985): 495, fig. 11, 496; cf. 505, 506.

117. For Alalakh, see Sir C. L. Woolley, *Alalakh* (London: Society of Antiquaries, 1955), fig. 35.

118. See summary of Tell Munbaqa (Ekalte) by D. Machule, in *RLA* VIII, 5/6 (1995), 418-19, and plan (long, rectangular temples toward north end of site); preliminary report, W. Orthmann, in *MDOG* 106 (1974): 77-79 with Beilage 6.

119. For the Hazor temple, see conveniently Y. Yadin, *Hazor, Schweich Lectures, 1970* (London: OUP and British Academy, 1972), 87ff., fig. 21 right. For a summary diagram of some of these temple plans (plus some less relevant bipartite ones), cf. A. Mazar, in A. Kempinski and R. Reich et al., eds., *The Architecture of Ancient Israel* (Jerusalem: IES, 1992), 163 and 167ff.

120. See the well-illustrated study of Ain Dara by J. Monson, *BAR* 26, no. 3 (May/June 2000): 20-35, 67, plus L. E. Stager, pp. 46-47 (and in *EI* 26 [1999]: 186*-187*).

121. For convenient temple plans of Sahure, Pepi II, and Sesostris I, see I. E. S. Edwards, *The Pyramids of Egypt*, 5th rev. ed. (London: Penguin Books, 1993), 162 (flanking area 6), 182 (flanking areas 3, 4, 6), and 208 (flanking areas 3, 4). On the two-level storerooms of Sahure, see conveniently Kitchen, *EI* 20 (1989): 108*, fig. 1, and references in nn. 9-10; for Tuthmosis III, cf. Kitchen, 108*, with references in nn. 11-12. On storage (up to four times the worship space!), see details, Kitchen, 109*-110* with references, and refutation of Waterman's erroneous treasury theory about Solomon's temple. For a lively scene of registering and storing varied goods in Egyptian temple stores, see Kitchen, *Pharaoh Triumphant*, 186, fig. 58.

122. This large edifice (about 160 by 100 feet) stood within extensive storerooms, each block with its own staircase to the upper story(ies), see the plan in K. Bittel, *Hattusha: The Capital of the Hittites* (New York: OUP, 1970), 56, fig. 13. The staircases are "rooms" 7, 20, 36, 49 on the plan.

123. For both Hamath and Tell Tayinat, see D. Ussishkin, *IEJ* 16 (1966): 104-10, with figures and references.

124. On stone walls with cedar-beam courses, see in general H. C. Thomson, *PEQ* 92 (1960): 57-63.

125. For Hattusas, cf. R. Naumann, *Architektur Kleinasiens* (Tübingen: Wasmuth, 1955), 84-85, figs. 64-66.

126. On the Ugarit house, see C. F.-A. Schaeffer, *Ugaritica I* (Paris: Geuthner, 1939), 92/94, pls. XVIII center left, XIX: 1-3. Palace pilaster and wall, beam lost above three masonry courses, cf. Schaeffer, *Ugaritica IV* (Paris: Imprimerie Nationale & Geuthner, 1962), 5, 24 with figs. 18-19. On "hewn stones," cf. R. Frankel, *TA* 3 (1976): 74-78.

127. For general reference on wood paneling in archaic Egypt, see W. B. Emery, *Archaic Egypt* (Harmondsworth: Pelican Books, 1961), 190 with fig. 111 (wooden flooring, 187 and pl. 21). For original reports on Abydos: W. M. F. Petrie, *The Royal Tombs of the First Dynasty* I (London: EEF, 1900), 9, 15 (walls), plus 12, 13 (floors), and his *Royal Tombs of the Earliest Dynasties* II (1901), 7, 8, 10. On Saqqara, see W. B. Emery, *Great Tombs of the First Dynasty* II (London: EES, 1954), 11 with fig. 3 and pl. XIII, wood paneling (with gold) and flooring.

128. See Matthiae, *Ebla, an Empire Rediscovered* (1982), 75 and unnumbered seventeenth to twentieth photo pages.

129. For discussion of Temple I at Hattusas, cf. Naumann, *Architektur Kleinasiens,* 108-9, with figs. 94, 96 (p. 106).

130. For Carchemish, see C. L. Woolley, *Carchemish II, the Town Defences* (London: British Museum, 1921), 148, 149 end. On Zinjirli, cf. Naumann, *Architektur Kleinasiens,* 115f., with fig. 98 (p. 111).

131. Assurnasirpal II. For translations of stela of "housewarming" for city of Calah, and details of the palace, see A. K. Grayson, *Assyrian Royal Inscriptions* II (Wiesbaden: Harrassowitz, 1976), 173 (cf. 51 n. 219), and *RIMA* 2 (1991), 289.

132. On the Tell Tayinat palace, cf. C. W. McEwan, *AJA* 41 (1937): 13 and fig. 5. For general remarks, cf. P. R. S. Moorey, *Ancient Mesopotamian Materials and Industries* (Oxford: Clarendon, 1994), 358-61 *(e)*.

133. For gold, electrum, and silver overlays in Mesopotamian and Egyptian temples, etc., see in summary A. R. Millard, *BAR* 15, no. 3 (May/June 1989): 27-29 with references.

134. For Amenophis III, his granite stela, cf. Breasted, *ARE* II (1906), 356ff., §§883, 886, 889, 890. For Soleb itself, see 363f., §§895, 898.

135. For the Nebuchadrezzar II new text, see F. N. H. Al-Rawi, *Iraq* 62 (2000): 38.

136. For gold traces in floor at Qantir/Pi-Ramesse, see E. Pusch, in *Ägypten und Levante* 9 (1999): 121-33 with colored figs. 3 and 5; also brief reports only, in English, in *Egyptian Archaeology,* no. 12 (1998): 10, and no. 14 (1999): 30 (Qantir). This was recently established to be waste dust (!) left by craftsmen, not a floor lining (personal communication, kind courtesy of Prof. E. Pusch, 18 July 2001).

137. On the freestanding columns in the portico of Hazor temple H, "LB III," see Yadin, *Hazor* (1972), 88-89 with fig. 21 and pl. XVIIa. Other examples from Sargon II's Khorsabad to the western Phoenician colonies were listed by R. B. Y. Scott, *JBL* 58 (1939): 143-44; for theories about the significance, cf. the review by W. F. Albright, *Archaeology and the Religion of Israel,* 3rd ed. (Baltimore: Johns Hopkins University Press, 1953), 139, 142-48 with references; not much has changed since on this matter.

138. On the "sea" and its form, etc., cf. A. Zuidhoff, *BA* 45, no. 3 (1982): 179-84, missed by J. Byl, *VT* 48 (1998): 309-14, each with other references; for artistic impression by W. Morden, cf. G. E. Wright, *BA* 4, no. 2 (May 1941): 17.

139. On Egyptian T-shaped tanks, under Amenophis III at Luxor, see W. Wolff, *Das*

schöne Fest von Opet (Leipzig: Hinrichs, 1931), pls. I-II, with king before barks in sanctuaries; imposed on offering stands, Ramesses II, Karnak, cf. H. H. Nelson, *The Great Hypostyle Hall at Karnak*, ed. W. J. Murnane, I:1 (Chicago: Oriental Institute, 1981), pl. 76 bottom right.

140. For the Ugarit tripod, see C. F.-A. Schaeffer, *The Cuneiform Texts of Ras Shamra Ugarit, Schweich Lectures, 1936* (London: OUP and British Academy, 1939), 34-35, pl. XXIII.2; noted also by G. E. Wright, *BA* 4, no. 2 (May 1941): 28 and fig. 8; high priest's house and bronzes, plan in M. Yon, *La cité d'Ougarit* (Paris: ERC, 1997), 122, fig. 65 (and English edition).

141. For the Kuntillet Ajrud vessel, see Z. Meshel, *Kuntillet Ajrud, a Religious Centre from the Time of the Judean Monarchy* (Jerusalem: Israel Museum, 1978), no. 175, fig. 10; text, J. Naveh, *BASOR* 235 (1979): 28. On Horvat Kitmit, cf. I. Beit-Arieh, *BAR* 14, no. 2 (March-April 1988): 36, 37. For Mesha stone, l. 12, cf. Kitchen, *JSOT* 76 (1997): 36.

142. On wheeled laver stands, cf. T. Dothan and S. Gitin, *BAR* 16, no. 1 (January-February 1990): 30-31, 32 (with illustrations). For a similar nonwheeled stand (thirteenth/twelfth century?), see R. S. Lamon and G. M. Shipton, *Megiddo I* (Chicago: University of Chicago Press, 1939), pl. 89 with notes.

143. For a shovel and incense spoon from Megiddo, and flesh fork from Gezer, see sketch by G. E. Wright, *BA* 4, no. 2 (May 1941): 30, fig. 9; for three iron shovels and fine bronze bowl from altar room at Dan (eighth century), see A. Biran, *Biblical Dan* (Jerusalem: IES, 1994), 192-98, color pls. 33-34 (shovels, bowl), and fig. 154 (bowl).

144. A variety of silver and copper cauldrons were captured at Urartu, including "three large copper cauldrons that hold 50 measures of water, along with their large copper stands" (eighth campaign, 396; cited after *CAD* 8/K [1971], 476: *kiuru* A).

145. The palace complex is usually set south of the temple, next to the palace of David and Ophel, extending farther south. A siting north of the temple has been advocated by D. Ussishkin, in W. Dever, ed., *Symbiosis, Symbolism, and the Power of the Past . . .* , ASOR Centennial Symposium . . . (in press), comparing the temple-south-of-palace layout at Tell Tayinat (cf. Ussishkin, *IEJ* 16 [1966]: 104, fig. 1) among others, such as (probably) Ain Dara (cf. citadel plan and photo, Monson, *BAR* 26, no. 3 [May-June 2000]: 22). But the "rule" is not absolute; at Hamath the temple is far more west than north of the palace (cf. Ussishkin, *IEJ* 16 [1966]: 109, fig. 4); at Alalakh (VII), the palace is to the east-northeast rather than the north (cf. E. Strommenger, *Art of Mesopotamia* [London: Thames & Hudson, 1964], 425, figs. 36-37, after Woolley, *Alalakh*). For a good idea of the probable rough plan of Solomon's palatial buildings, see K. Galling, *Biblisches Reallexikon* (Tübingen: Mohr/Siebeck, 1937), 411-12, diagram, whose distribution of buildings seems quite close to the probable situation.

146. On the great official palace of Akhenaten, see plan in W. S. Smith, *The Art and Architecture of Ancient Egypt*, ed. W. K. Simpson, 3rd ed. (New Haven: Yale University Press; London: Penguin Books, 1998), 186, fig. 311; for the columned halls in Akhenaten's North Palace, see Smith, 183, fig. 305, and the palace of Amenophis III in Western Thebes (Malkata), Smith, 162, fig. 280.

147. For the Phoenician temple at Kition, see V. Karageorghis, *Kition . . . Discoveries in Cyprus* (London: Thames & Hudson, 1976), 118-19, fig. 18, floor 3 (also, R. Reich, in Kempinski and Reich, *Architecture of Ancient Israel*, 203, fig. 1); and Karageorghis, 138-39, fig. 19, for the later and different floor 2a.

148. Altintepe is discussed by D. Ussishkin, *BA* 36, no. 3 (1973): 92-94 with fig. 8.

149. On gold (and bronze) shields as adornment, used on ceremonial occasions, see full discussion by A. R. Millard in M. Coogan et al., eds., *Scripture and Other Artifacts . . . in Honor of*

Philip J. King (Louisville: Westminster John Knox, 1994), 286-95, and his well-illustrated outline in *BAR* 15, no. 3 (May-June 1989): 21, 24-27.

150. For discussion of *hilani* buildings with entrance porticoes, throne rooms, and annexes, see (e.g.) D. Ussishkin, *IEJ* 16 (1966): 174-86, and in BA 36, no. 3 (1973): 84-103, and recently R. Arav and M. Bernett, *IEJ* 50 (2000): 47-81, with notes of other locations and bibliography, p. 50 and nn. 4-9. Excluding only the "Forest of Lebanon" hall, Professor Ussishkin also suggested (*BA* 36, pp. 83-84) that the other structures of Solomon — the colonnades, his throne/judgment hall, his house, and the pharaoh's daughter's house — not only followed in sequence but were all part of one single building, a *hilani*, with columned entry, transverse throne hall, and annexed rooms. The sequence seems impeccable, but the compression into one limited *hilani* seems next to impossible. If the porticoed colonnade (1 Kings 7:6) were indeed the entry to the palace court(s), then it could *not* also be part of the building(s) *within* the court. The throne/judgment hall, seemingly Solomon's house, and clearly pharaoh's daughter's house are equally termed *'ulam,* and so were all separate *hilanis,* not crammed into one small structure. Especially as 1 Kings 7:8 clearly separates off both Solomon's house and the Egyptian princess's house into "another court," not that of the "Forest" hall, entrance colonnades, and throne hall.

151. For sets of distinct but contiguous buildings, see for Hattusas the plan in K. Bittel, *Hattusha, the Capital of the Hittites* (New York: OUP, 1970), 75, fig. 19.

152. For Sam'al/Zinjirli, see the convenient citadel plan in Ussishkin, *BA* 36, no. 3 (1973): 86, fig. 4.

153. The houses of Solomon and the princess (part of his harem?) were probably linked by an inner court between them; cf. the Alalakh VII palace, with its domestic and official wings linked by a central court. See Sir C. L. Woolley, *A Forgotten Kingdom* (London, 1953), 72ff., with fig. 12 (and in his *Alalakh*). For the temple and royal palace close together at Alalakh, see Woolley, *Alalakh;* and at Tell el-Tayinat and Hamath, see Ussishkin, *IEJ* 16 (1966): 104-10, with figs. 1, 4; for Ebla, Temple D, just southwest of Palace E, see Matthiae, *Ebla, an Empire Rediscovered* (1977), 43, fig. 8 at points D and E (their plans, cf. pp. 131, 133, figs. 30-31).

154. For a set of gold-plated beds, chairs, and footstools, see letter EA 5, in Moran, *The Amarna Letters,* 10-11.

155. For real examples from Egypt (tomb of Tutankhamun, etc.), cf. C. Desroches Noblecourt, *Tutankhamen, Life and Death of a Pharaoh* (London: Conoisseur/Michael Joseph, 1963), 30, 43, pls. VI, X;, 53 pl. XII (thrones), 133/148, pls. XXVIII-XXIX (couches, cf. I. E. S. Edwards, *Treasures of Tutankhamun* [London: British Museum, 1972], catalogue no. 13, in monochrome and color). P. Fox, *Tutankhamun's Treasure* (London: OUP, 1953), 31, pl. 60 (footstool).

156. For gold plate from palaces found in the tombs of Assyria, in full color, see M. S. B. Damerji and A. Kamil, *Gräber Assyrischer Königinnen aus Nimrud* (Baghdad and Mainz: Verlag des Römisch-Germanischen Zentralmuseums, 1999), Abb. 23-32, 40-52, passim.

157. On gold from the reign of Psusennes I, in color, in English, see H. Coutts, ed., *Gold of the Pharaohs* (Edinburgh: City Museums & Art Galleries, 1988), 44-45, 53-57, or C. A. Hope, *Gold of the Pharaohs* (Melbourne: Museum of Victoria, 1988), 77-79, 99-103; in French, J. Yoyotte et al., *Tanis, l'or des pharaons* (Paris: Galeries Nationales, 1987), 209-10, 229-31.

158. The "twenty years" passages would not favor the view sometimes expressed that the seven years building the temple and the thirteen years building the palace complex were at least partly concurrent. The total evidence of our sources should be respected, unless there is very clear evidence to the contrary.

159. The twelve-district system was first effectively analyzed by A. Alt in 1913 (Festschrift for R. Kittel), reprinted in 1953, 1959, and 1964 (in A. Alt, *Kleine Schriften* II, 3rd ed. [Munich:

Beck, 1964], 76-89). A constructive and valuable later study is by Y. Aharoni, *TA* 3 (1976): 5-15, with a useful map, supplemented by H. N. Rösel, *ZDPV* 100 (1984): 84-90, with additional references and critiques thereof.

160. On the Beth-Shemesh, late Canaanite ostracon, see latterly E. Puech, *RB* 93 (1986): 175-77 with fig. 4:5 (p. 173), going somewhat beyond F. M. Cross, *EI* 8 (1967): 17*-19*; convenient picture in *NEAHL*, 1:250.

161. See S. Bunimovitz and Z. Lederman, *BAR* 23, no. 1 (January-February 1997): 48 (illustration and note), 75-76.

162. See G. L. Kelm and A. Mazar, *Timnah, a Biblical City in the Sorek Valley* (Winona Lake, Ind.: Eisenbrauns, 1995), 111/113, fig. 6:4 (cf. briefly, *BAR* 15, no. 1 [1989]: 22).

163. For summaries and references of palace accounts from Ebla to Assurnasirpal II, see Kitchen, in *NBD*, 378, and in *RITANC* I (1993), 174-76, plus 162-65 (Sethos I).

164. On wealth, references will be found in Millard and Kitchen, *BAR* 15, no. 3 (May/June 1989): 20-34, and in Millard and Kitchen, respectively, in Handy, *The Age of Solomon*, 31-42 and 147-50. Gold of Ophir ostracon, illustrated in *BAR* 15, p. 31; B. Maisler [Mazar], *JNES* 10 (1951): 265-67, pl. 11; Renz/Röllig I, 229-31, and III, pl. XXII:13.

165. The definitive layout of the ancient instructional wisdom texts from Egypt, Mesopotamia, and the rest was set out on a fully objective basis in two essays: Kitchen, "The Basic Literary Forms and Formulations of Ancient Instructional Writings in Egypt and Western Asia," in E. Hornung and O. Keel, eds., *Studien zu altägyptischen Lebenslehren*, OBO 28 (Freiburg: Universitätsverlag; Göttingen: Vandenhoeck & Ruprecht, 1979), 235-82, and Kitchen, "Proverbs and Wisdom Books of the Ancient Near East," *TynB* 28 (1977): 69-114. The (in part) deliberately contrary work by S. Weeks, *Early Israelite Wisdom* (London: OUP, 1994), is of value on several aspects of the OT material, but is wholly misleading on the Egyptian and Near Eastern evidence both in itself and as presented in my two essays. For a necessary update and corrective, see Kitchen, "Biblical Instructional Wisdom: The Decisive Voice of the Ancient Near East," in M. Lubetski, C. Gottlieb, and S. Keller, eds., *Boundaries of the Ancient Near Eastern World, a Tribute to Cyrus H. Gordon*, JSOTSup 273 (Sheffield: Sheffield Academic Press, 1998), 346-63. No work on Proverbs is valid that does not pay proper heed to the primary independent evidence which provides the firmly fixed conceptual, literary, and chronological framework for evaluation of that book's four constituent compositions.

166. For Ramesses III's boast, see Papyrus Harris I, 76:8; in English, Breasted, *ARE* IV (1906), 201, 403, or Wilson, in Pritchard, *ANET*, 262 top left.

167. Ramesses II quote from the introduction of the First Hittite Marriage of Ramesses II; in English, Kitchen, *RITA* II, 87. For the epithets cited for Shalmaneser III and Adad-nirari III, cf. in Grayson, *RIMA*, 3:7, 203.

168. Standard surveys of the archaeology of preclassical Palestine at most periods include: Mazar, *ALB* I; A. Ben-Tor, ed., *The Archaeology of Ancient Israel* (New Haven: Yale University Press, 1992); both of these omit the Persian period, for which cf. Stern, *ALB* II; for an overall compendium down to 332 B.C., see H. Weippert (and L. Mildenberg), *Palästina in vorhellenistischer Zeit*, Handbuch der Archäologie, Vorderasien II, Band I (Munich: Beck, 1988); for an ultracomprehensive view (Paleolithic to 1914 A.D.!) with a sociological tincture, see T. E. Levy, ed., *The Archaeology of Society in the Holy Land* (London: Leicester University Press, 1995).

169. On the period around 1220-1170 and the Sea Peoples, see: broad survey, in W. A. Ward and M. S. Joukowsky, eds., *The Crisis Years: The Twelfth Century B.C.* (Dubuque, Iowa: Kendall/Hunt, 1989); and more recent, Gitin, Mazar, and Stern, *Mediterranean Peoples in Transi-*

tion; E. D. Oren, ed., *The Sea Peoples and Their World: A Reassessment* (Philadelphia: University Museum, University of Pennsylvania, 2000).

170. On Philistines, the basic study is by T. Dothan, *The Philistines and Their Material Culture* (New Haven: Yale University Press; Jerusalem: IES, 1982), with more popular-style update, by T. Dothan and M. Dothan, *People of the Sea, the Search for the Philistines* (New York: Macmillan, 1992).

171. For I. Finkelstein: (1) *BASOR* 277/278 (1990): 109-19; (2) *TA* 22 (1995): 213-39; (3) *Levant* 28 (1996): 177-87; (4) *TA* 23 (1996): 170-84; (5) *Levant* 30 (1998): 167-74; (6) in Gitin, Mazar, and Stern, *Mediterranean Peoples in Transition,* 140-47; (7) *TA* 25 (1998): 208-18; (8) *BASOR* 314 (1999): 55-70; (9) in Oren, *The Sea Peoples,* 159-80; (10) *TA* 27 (2000): 231-47; (11) *ZDPV* 116 (2000): 114-38; (12) in I. Finkelstein and N. Silberman, *The Bible Unearthed* (New York: Free Press, 2001).

Among dissentient voices, note, all in *BASOR* 277/278 (1990), J. S. Holladay, 23-70 (on Gezer, gateway); W. G. Dever, 121-30 (reply to flawed paper by G. J. Wightman, 5-22, to one on gates by D. Ussishkin, 71-92, and to Finkelstein item 1 above); L. E. Stager, *BASOR* 277/278 (1990): 93-107, on pre-Omride Samaria; A. Mazar, *Levant* 29 (1997): 157-67, on Finkelstein items 2-3; A. Zarzeki-Peleg, *TA* 24 (1997): 258-88, on pottery, re. Finkelstein items 2-3; W. G. Dever, in Handy, *The Age of Solomon,* 217-51, esp. 232ff., on Finkelstein and others; A. Ben-Tor, *IEJ* 48 (1998): 1-29 (Hazor physical data), 29-37 (discussion), on Finkelstein items 2-3; A. Mazar, in Gitin, Mazar, and Stern, *Mediterranean Peoples in Transition,* 368-78 and 184-85 (correcting Holladay and Finkelstein); N. Na'aman, *BASOR* 317 (2000): 1-8, on Finkelstein items 2-7, and Ben-Tor, 9-15, to Finkelstein item 8. Recent work at Tel Rehov cited as favoring the normal dating, not the new low dating; cf. A. Mazar, *IEJ* 49 (1999): 40-42, and in *BAR* 26, no. 2 (March-April 2000): 37-51, 75, esp. 47-48, 50-51, 75, besides R. A. Mullins, *ASOR Newsletter* 49, no. 1 (spring 1999): 7-9.

172. On implications of types of gates in Iron II Israel, cf. E. Stern, *IEJ* 40 (1990): 12-30. On Megiddo, see B. Halpern, *VTS* 80 (1998): 79-121, and the appendix in his *David's Secret Demons* (Winona Lake, Ind.: Eisenbrauns, 2001).

173. For Phoenician ports untouched by the Sea Peoples, with whom the Phoenicians may have made alliance, see P. M. Bikai, in Ward and Joukowsky, *The Crisis Years,* 132-41.

174. On the Canaanite-to-Philistine sequences after Year 8 of Ramesses III, see: for Ashdod XIV/XIII, Mazar, *ALB* I, 307 and nn. 12ff.; Mazar, *Levant* 28 (1997): 159 and n. 3. For Ekron VIIIA/VII, see T. Dothan, in Gitin, Mazar, and Stern, *Mediterranean Peoples in Transition,* 150-54. Note that the "first wave" of Sea Peoples did not invade Canaan, but Libya, where they and the Libyans were defeated by Merenptah in his fifth year (1209/1208, and *not* 1207 as often wrongly quoted).

For Ashdod, change from XIV to XIIIA/B, with violence (and at Tel Mor VII), cf. M. Dothan, *NEAHL,* 1:96. For Ekron, violent succession, VIIIA to VII, cf. T. Dothan and S. Gitin, *NEAHL,* 3:1052-53, also A. Mazar, *Levant* 29 (1997): 165 n. 3; burning, T. Dothan, in Gitin, Mazar, and Stern, 150-51, and figs. 2-3. On Ascalon, cf. L. E. Stager, *NEAHL,* 1:107. The ancient site of Gaza is not accessible for archaeological comparison; the location of Gath is not 100 percent agreed, although Tell es-Safi appears to be the most likely option. Here, early finds included ample examples of bichrome pottery (cf. T. Dothan, *The Philistines,* 50, and later references to Tell es-Safi).

175. The contrast between masses of Philistine wares within their zone and the relative paucity outside it is remarked on by A. Mazar, *Levant* 29 (1997): 158, who cites examples 1 to 3 of

"pottery boundaries"; against item 1, Finkelstein, *Levant* 30 (1998): 168. For (4) in Ammon/ Moab, see P. M. M. Daviau, in *BA* 60, no. 4 (1997): 223-27.

176. On bichrome LB IIB pottery, cf. (e.g.) R. Amiran, *Ancient Pottery of the Holy Land* (New Brunswick, N.J.: Rutgers University Press, 1970), 150-51, pl. 47: 12-13.

177. For chronology, fiery fall of Lachish VI, and Ramesses III pieces, see summary in Ussishkin, *NEAHL*, 3:904.

178. For a bronze piece, Ramesses III, see R. Giveon, *TA* 10 (1983): 123, fig. 132, 176-77, pl. 30; for the ostracon, see M. Gilula, *TA* 3 (1976): 107-8, pl. 5.

179. For the Dalhiyeh (Jordan Valley) piece of Ramesses IV (his Year 1 nomen), cf. J. Leclant, *Or* 51 (1982): 485, *e*, with pl. 85, fig. 83; noted by Finkelstein, *TA* 23 (1996): 173.

180. Ramesses VI base, views summarized and listed by Finkelstein, *TA* 23 (1996): 171-72. In Finkelstein's paper in Oren, *The Sea Peoples*, 159ff., errors and misapprehensions require correction. First, his statement (p. 162) that "Egyptian activity at the mines of Timna could not have been continued until the days of Ramesses V . . . without firm control over the international highway in northern Sinai" is wrong. It is clear from Papyrus Harris I, 78:1-4, that the kings sent ships up the Gulf of Aqaba to land the expeditionaries, and to bring back most of the copper by ship, from 'Atika, which would be the Egyptian name for Timna. The text says: "I dispatched my emissaries to the land of 'Atika, to the great copper-mines which are there; their ships were bearing them (along), and others went overland on their donkeys. . . . Their mines were found, and yielding copper, it being loaded by the ten-thousands into their ships, these being sent on in their charge to Egypt, arriving safely." Thus Ramesses III, and he should know! Second, the repeated claim (pp. 165, 173-74) that in Year 8 Ramesses III carried off (all) the Philistines, etc., as captives into Egypt, so that it was only later waves of invaders who, up to forty years later, came and settled in southwest Canaan, with heaps of monochrome pottery, etc., fails on what we know of how the Egyptians treated such invaders. In Merenptah's fifth year (1209/1208), he defeated a joint attack and intended invasion of the West Delta by Libyans and Sea Peoples. From the statistics and descriptions that his texts give, it is clear that the invaders suffered a fair number of casualties and that numbers of captives were taken. But he clearly did *not* take away the entire Libyan and Sea People population into Egypt. The majority stayed back in Libya, left to sort things out there for themselves. (For texts, see Breasted, *ARE* III [1906], 238-64.) Thus the Philistines and other Sea Peoples who came with families and baggage, to invade Egypt, were similarly defeated militarily; many able-bodied prisoners were taken and impressed into the Egyptian army, and resettled in the west of that country, while the main body were left to sort themselves out in southwest Canaan. The Egyptian administration would have sought to levy the usual harvest taxes on the resettled Philistine towns, alongside the surviving Canaanite settlements. (With what success, we do not know; probably very little.) The rejection of Egyptian control may be reflected in the relative lack of Egyptian traces in the new Philistine settlements. The scarab of Ramesses VI from Deir el-Balah was a stray find with no context and proves nothing. A scarab of Ramesses IV at Aphek with bichrome pottery (Finkelstein, p. 164) might be taken (opposite to Finkelstein) to show that monochrome was already passé under Ramesses IV. Such loose finds could "prove" anything. For Amun's holdings in Canaan, cf. Breasted, *ARE* IV, 123, 127.

181. On the situation at Hazor (X-V) and related sites, see discussions by A. Ben-Tor and D. Ben-Ami, *IEJ* 48 (1998): 1-37 (esp. 29-36), plus A. Zarzeki-Poleg, *TA* 24 (1997): 258-88, then I. Finkelstein, *BASOR* 314 (1999): 55-70 (with clear chart of differences, p. 65), and the reply by A. Ben-Tor, *BASOR* 317 (2000): 9-15, on errors and inconsistencies (in use of OT sources) in Finkelstein's paper (but objected to by Finkelstein, *TA* 27 [2001]: 231-47).

182. A scarab found at Lachish has been suggested to belong to Ramesses IV; so,

R. Krauss, *MDOG* 126 (1994): 123-30, noted also by N. Na'aman, *BASOR* 317 (2000): 4. This reads *Usir-maat setep-men* (in O. Tufnell, *Lachish IV, Plates* [1958], pl. 39, no. 380). One would have to agree to read this as standing for *Usir-maat-‹re› Setep‹en›-‹A›mun*, the prenomen borne by Ramesses IV only in his first year; thereafter he was entitled *Heq-maat-re Setepenamun*. But the identification is not beyond doubt. It may equally well be an incomplete form of *Usir-maat-‹re› Setep‹enre›, Mon‹tuemtawy›*, a statue name of Ramesses II, also known in incomplete form on stelae (various faulty writings, cf. KRI II, 452:10 and 453:3-8 [esp. 8!]), or for *Usir-maat-‹re› Setep‹enre› ‹meri›-Mon‹tu›*, Ramesses II beloved of Montu. Or for *Usir-maat-‹re› Setep‹enre› ‹meri-A›mun*, Ramesses II beloved of Amun. So the reading as Ramesses IV (a rarer king) cannot be held to be certain, and should probably be discounted here, so far as the chronology of Lachish VI is concerned. One cannot hang the history of a whole site on one dodgy scarab!

183. For continuity from the tenth to the ninth century indicated by finds at Tel Rehov (Rehob), see A. Mazar, *IEJ* 49 (1999): 39-42, and in outline in *BAR* 26, no. 2 (March-April 2000): 47-51.

184. The extensive surveys in central Canaan can be seen (e.g.) in I. Finkelstein, *The Archaeology of the Israelite Settlement* (Jerusalem: IES, 1988), and now in the comprehensive work on 585 sites by I. Finkelstein and Z. Lederman, eds., *Highlands of Many Cultures, the Southern Samaria Survey — the Sites* I-II (Tel Aviv: University Institute of Archaeology, 1997); vol. III (interpretative volume) is to follow.

185. On the move from scattered villages and hamlets to a more urbanized and unified (Israelite) society and the overall archaeological evidence for a single state — as would be expected under the unitary regime of Saul, David, and Solomon — see W. G. Dever, in Handy, *The Age of Solomon*, 217-51, deliberately without use of the biblical data, to make the underlying position clear. Cf. also his older surveys in Ishida, *Studies*, 269-306, with a more popular account in his *RADBR*, 87-117. For a sociological/anthropological account, compare J. S. Holladay, in Levy, *Archaeology of Society*, 368-98, passim. For an overall survey (on the "normal" basis) of the archaeology of western Palestine for the tenth century, cf. Weippert, *Palästina in vorhellenistischer Zeit*, 417-507.

186. See the basic accounts by Yadin, *Hazor* (1972), 135-46, and his popular work, *Hazor* (London, 1975), 187-99; for a full, technical endorsement of Hazor stratigraphy and its dating, see A. Ben-Tor and D. Ben-Ami, *IEJ* 48 (1998): 1-36; for a popular summary, see A. Ben-Tor, *BAR* 25, no. 2 (March-April 1999): 26-37, 60.

187. For the basic sequence at Megiddo, cf. (e.g.) in *NEAHL*, 3:1012-24; for a lucid, careful, popular account, see G. I. Davies, *Megiddo* (Cambridge: Lutterworth, 1986), 59-97.

188. On the north gate at Megiddo, see Yadin's reports, *IEJ* 8 (1958): 1-14, 80-86; *BA* 23 (1960): 62-68; *IEJ* 16 (1966): 278-80; *IEJ* 17 (1967): 119-21; *BA* 33 (1970): 66-96; and in *Hazor* (1972), 150-64, and *Hazor* (1975), 207-31; critical was Y. Aharoni, *JNES* 31 (1972): 302-11, refuted in turn by Y. Shiloh, *Levant* 12 (1980): 69-76, and compare on north Israelite gates, E. Stern, *IEJ* 40 (1990): 12-30. The whole matter was then taken up afresh by D. Ussishkin, *BASOR* 239 (1980): 1-18, with reply by Yadin, 19-23. A careful review was given by Davies, *Megiddo*, 87-92. At the end of the day, the VIA gate and VB village (no monumental gate) precede the disputed VA-IVB six-chambered gate, and the divided monarchy stratum IVA gate follows it and is linked with the solid wall (325). Thus the VA-IVB gate has to come within the general orbit of the David/Solomon period, whatever kind of foundations it had, and whether it existed in one phase or two. It is *not* bonded into the (later) solid wall, which has some link with the IVA gate. In this situation the general parallels with the Hazor and Gezer gates remain valid, as does a united monarchy date. On possible stables/stores of the VA-IVB period under the better-

known IVA ones, see G. I. Davies, *PEQ* 120 (1988): 130-41, and in *BAR* 20, no. 1 (January-February 1994): 44-49. For detailed arguments for a tenth-century date for Megiddo VA-IVB, see also B. Halpern, *VTS* 80 (1998): 79-121, and the appendix in his *David's Secret Demons*.

189. For accounts of Gezer, cf. W. G. Dever, *ABD*, 2:998-1003 (esp. 1000ff.); Dever, in *NEAHL*, 2:496-506 (esp. 504-5); for older popular surveys, cf. H. D. Lance and W. G. Dever, *BA* 30 (1967): 34-47, 47-62; Dever, *BA* 34 (1971): 94-132. Dating of outer gate and wall has been controverted; cf. Dever, *BASOR* 262 (1986): 9-34; and his reply to Ussishkin and Finkelstein (*BASOR* 277/278 [1990]: 74-77, 109-14; Dever's reply on 121-29); caveats by Mazar, *ALB* I, 381-87, 400 n. 17; cf. 243, 292 n. 12.

190. In the Execration Texts, being e-12 in the Sethe series and E 45 in the Posener series; see for convenience J. A. Wilson (with references) in *ANET*, 329. For Jerusalem correspondence in the Amarna letters, see Moran, *The Amarna Letters*, 325-34, nos. 285-90.

191. For areas dug by Miss Kenyon, see (e.g.) K. M. Kenyon, *Digging Up Jerusalem* (London: Benn, 1974), 90, 117, 146, 186, 200, or 224, figs. 18, 22, 26, 28, 29, 36.

192. For more recent work (and old), cf. conveniently in *NEAHL*, 2:702, map; work has continued since.

193. For very late-period results on the ridge, cf. (e.g.) the work in Area K of City of David dig, with hardly anything from before the leveling and building of stratum 3 (Byzantine), in A. De Groot and D. T. Ariel, *The City of David* III (*Qedem*, 33) (Jerusalem: Hebrew University, 1992), 63-91 (summary, 90-91). For overall aerial views of the eastern north-south ridge running south from Ophel, see (e.g.) such photos as: Geva, *Ancient Jerusalem Revealed,* 4; or in *BAR* 23, no. 1 (January-February 1997): 53; 24, no. 4 (July-August 1998): 24; 25, no. 6 (November-December 1999): 20/21.

194. False claims that Jerusalem might only be a tribe in the Execration Texts, and that it would have been too small to have been other than some other center's outpost are made by M. Steiner, *BAR* 24, no. 4 (July-August 1998): 33, repeating G. Auld and M. Steiner, *Jerusalem I, from the Bronze Age to the Maccabees* (Cambridge: Lutterworth, 1996), 27-28. Neither author has any clear understanding of the nature and implications of the Execration Texts. For a map of identified sites in these, see W. Helck, *Die Beziehungen Ägyptens zu Vorderasien im 3. und 2. Jahrtausend v. Chr.,* 2nd ed. (Wiesbaden: Harrassowitz, 1971), 51. On tribesfolk in Execration Texts, cf. Posener, *Princes et pays d'Asie et de Nubie,* 93-94 (E 61, 63), and 95-96 F series, "Asiatics" belonging to lands of cities; likewise in Sethe series, for references, cf. Posener.

195. On the walls of Middle Bronze Jerusalem, cf. Kenyon, *Digging Up Jerusalem,* 78, 81-83; and Shiloh, etc., *City of David* I, *Qedem* 19 (1984), 26 (strata 18/17), and in *NEAHL*, 2:701-2.

196. On the Gihon works, see Shanks after Reich and Shukron, *BAR* 25, no. 6 (November-December 1999): 24.

197. See Moran, *The Amarna Letters,* for modern translations. Cf. the map of towns in the Amarna letters on 124.

198. As pointed out by N. Na'aman, *BAR* 24, no. 4 (July-August 1998): 42-44, in a town clearly spelled out as a city, Abdi-Khepa held the same position politically as all the other Canaanite city rulers: "governor" (or "mayor") in Egyptian terminology, but kings in local usage. Amarna letters show Abdi-Khepa's belligerence (nos. 244, 289-90).

199. For notice of a town "belonging to Jerusalem," see Amarna letter no. 290. Cf. also Na'aman, *BAR* 23, no. 4 (July-August 1997): 43-47, 67. On the Egyptian garrison, see Amarna letter no. 285.

200. For negative claims on the lack of Late Bronze remains, see M. Steiner, *BAR* 24, no. 4 (July-August 1998): 27, 28.

201. For a compact, documented notice of the attested Late Bronze remains, see J. Cahill, *BAR* 24, no. 4 (July-August 1998): 34-38.

202. On David's possible palace, cf. E. Mazar, *BAR* 23, no. 1 (January-February 1997): 50-57, 74.

203. On dating of the stone-stepped structure, and later tenth-century overfill, see clear summary by J. Cahill, *BAR* 24, no. 4 (July-August 1998): 38-41, with references.

204. Two almost identical lists are given by W. G. Dever, first in Ishida, *Studies,* 271, fig. 1, and in his *RADBR* (1990), 88-89, tab. 4; plus his anthropologically three-tiered list of twenty-nine entries (plus the four), one (Negev forts) being a collective, in Handy, *The Age of Solomon,* 219, fig. 1. A full list is given also by Mazar, *ALB* I, 372-73, tab. 7. For surveys of the occupation sites, and their culture and history, in the period, see Dever, in Ishida, *Studies,* 269-306; Dever, *RADBR* (1990), 87-117; and especially Dever, in Handy, *The Age of Solomon,* 218-51; Mazar, 387-98; and (on material culture) cf. G. Barkay in Ben-Tor, *Archaeology of Ancient Israel,* 302-19.

205. The nonsense views (on sociological grounds) that tenth-century Jerusalem and Israel could not have sustained a state or an empire are fluently expressed by D. W. Jamieson-Drake, *Scribes and Schools in Monarchic Judah* (Sheffield: JSOT, 1991), 38-39, 139; and by P. R. Davies, *In Search of "Ancient Israel"* (Sheffield: JSOT, 1992), 69, among others (e.g., T. L. Thompson). Cf. quotes and comments by N. Na'aman, *BASOR* 304 (November 1996): 18; and rebuttal by Dever, *What . . . When . . . ?* 124-28.

206. For Dan V-IV, cf. Biran, *Biblical Dan,* 142-46, and *NEAHL,* 1:327.

207. For Shechem, see *NEAHL,* 4:1352-53.

208. For Taanach, see *NEAHL,* 4:1432. For entries in the list of Shoshenq I, see Kitchen, *Third Int. Pd.* (1973, 1986, 1996), 432-47, passim.

209. For Beth-Shemesh, see *NEAHL,* 1:250, 253; S. Bunimovitz and Z. Lederman, *BAR* 23, no. 1 (January-February 1997): 42-49, 75-77.

210. On the south Samaria survey, see Finkelstein and Lederman, *Highlands of Many Cultures,* Iron I list on pp. 894-96, map, 949; Iron I/II list, 896-97, map, 950; Iron II list, 898-902, map, 951.

211. *Wenamun,* translated in *ANET,* 25-29, and in *CoS* I, 89-93. *Moscow Literary Letter,* translated in R. A. Caminos, *A Tale of Woe* (Oxford, 1956).

NOTES TO CHAPTER 5

1. As biblical and some other scholars seem totally to misunderstand Egyptian dating and how it is calculated, a word may be helpful here, especially relating to the decease of Ramesses II and the early years of Merenptah. During the New Kingdom, Egyptian kings reckoned their regnal years from the day of their accession (not from New Year's Day). The accession of Ramesses II fell on the third month of Shomu (= eleventh month), day 27, which fell in early June in 1279 but in mid-May by the start of his Year 67 in 1213. He lived for only about two months into Year 67, with Merenptah's accession (within 1st Akhet 18 to 2nd Akhet 13) within the month of July *of the same year,* 1213. It is therefore wrong to date the change of reign to 1212.

Furthermore, as there is no "Year Zero" between pharaohs (unlike the Mesopotamian "accession year"), to date "Year X" of a pharaoh, one must subtract only "X − 1" years from his accession date. So Merenptah's Year 1 is 1213/1212 (1213 for short).

2. For the Amarna letters in English, see conveniently W. L. Moran, *The Amarna Letters* (Baltimore: Johns Hopkins University Press, 1992). For the much-discussed 'Apiru, the two fun-

damental collections of data remain those by J. Bottéro, ed., *Le problème des Habiru* (Paris: Imprimerie Nationale, 1954), with eminently sane conclusions, pp. 187-98; and M. Greenberg, *The Hab/piru* (New Haven: American Oriental Society, 1955). A different slant is given by M. Astour, in *UFo* 31 (1999/2000): 31-50. On disassociation of the Hab/piru and Hebrew '*bri*, see A. F. Rainey, *IOS* 18 (1998): 437 and n. 23.

3. For Mount Seir and Seirite list under Ramesses II (in English), see Kitchen, *RITA* II, 75, nos. 92-97 (at 217:10); 138 (at 303:5f.), 235 (at 409:1).

4. For Moab under Ramesses II, see Kitchen, *RITA* II, 49-50 (Luxor scenes), plus in *JEA* 50 (1964): 48-56, pls. 3-4, figs. 1-3, and J. C. Darnell and R. Jasnow, *JNES* 52 (1993): 263-74, figs. 2-6, 8-9; commentary, Kitchen, *RITANC* II (1999), 89-97, with map 15 at end. For Moab in lists, see *RITA* II, 53, C.14 and 71 *(ii)*a, 17; *RITANC* II, 126, §191, 17. In general, Kitchen, in P. Bienkowski, ed., *Early Edom and Moab* (Sheffield: Collis; Liverpool: Merseyside National Museums, 1992), 26-29.

5. For Edom under Merenptah, cf. Papyrus Anastasi VI: 51-61, translated (e.g.) in *ANET*, 259, and by R. A. Caminos, *Late-Egyptian Miscellanies* (London, 1954), 293.

6. For Seir under Ramesses III, see text, *ANET*, 262:I.

7. In Amarna letters, for Apiru attacks on cities, cities rumored to be going over to the Apiru, etc., see the extensive letters by Ribaddi of Byblos (e.g., EA 68, 71, 73-77, 79, 81-88, 111, 121). By other local rulers, cf. EA 144, 189 (towns lost temporarily), 207, 243, 271-74, 281, 291. Local rulers allied against another ruler, cf. EA 116; with Apiru forces, EA 104 end.

8. For translations of the Beth-Shan stelae of Sethos I, see Kitchen, *RITA* I (1993), 9-10, 12-13, repeated in *CoS* II, 25-26, 27-28; commentary in Kitchen, *RITANC* I (1993), 17-19, 20-21.

9. On (Me)nephtoah and Merenptah, see Y. Aharoni, *Land of the Bible,* 2nd ed. (London: Burns & Oates, 1979), 184.

10. See on the wells of Merenptah in the "ridges," in Papyrus Anastasi III, verso, 6:4-5; translations, Wilson, in *ANET*, 258; Caminos, *Late-Egyptian Miscellanies,* 108, 111. The "strongpoint of Merenptah which is near *Djir-ram*," or in Semitic *Sir/Sur-ram,* "high rock" (cf. Sur-Bashan, "rock of Bashan") in Anastasi III, verso 5:2 (*ANET*, 258; Caminos, 109), could possibly be the same place.

11. References for Labayu in the Amarna letters will be found in Moran, *The Amarna Letters,* 382 (index).

12. For Abdi-ashirta and Aziru, see Moran, *The Amarna Letters,* 379, 380 (index), plus xxxiii and n. 112; cf. H. Klengel, *Syria, 3000-300 B.C.* (Berlin: Akademie-Verlag, 1992), 161-66, and in more detail his *Geschichte Syriens im 2. Jahtausend v.u. Z[eit]* 2 (Berlin: Akademie-Verlag, 1969), 245-99, with detailed references.

13. The phenomena cited (in A.D. 1267, 1906, and 1927) are recounted in the classic volume of J. Garstang, *Joshua Judges* (London: Constable, 1931), 136-38 and map 9 (p. 126), with photographs of that part of the Jordan, pl. XXV.

14. For spies and disinformation in the Mari texts, see the excellent summary survey by J.-M. Durand, *Les documents épistolaires du palais de Mari* II (Paris: Éditions du Cerf, 1998), 304-10.

15. On the Battle of Qadesh, see translation and commentary (with full maps) in Kitchen, *RITA* II (1996), 2-26 (spies, 14-16), and in *CoS* II, 38-39; and *RITANC* II (1999), 3-55 (spies, 38, 43-44).

16. On Rahab's role, cf. discussions and references by D. J. Wiseman, *TynB* 14 (1964): 8-11, and R. S. Hess, *Joshua,* Tyndale Old Testament Commentaries (Leicester: Inter-Varsity, 1996), 83-88.

17. For Tuthmosis IV, cf. B. Cumming, *Egyptian Historical Records of the Later Eighteenth Dynasty* III (Warminster: Aris & Phillips, 1984), 251-52.

18. The Merenptah extract is cited by A. L. Oppenheim, *The Interpretation of Dreams in the Ancient Near East* (Philadelphia: American Philosophical Society, 1956), 251, cf. 192.

19. On Ramesses III, cf. translation, W. F. Edgerton and J. A. Wilson, *Historical Records of Ramses III* (Chicago: University of Chicago Press, 1936), p. 4 to Medinet Habu II, pl. 13.

20. The Hattusil III and Assurbanipal information is in Oppenheim, *Interpretation of Dreams*, 254-55 and 249-50 respectively.

21. See Durand, *Les documents épistolaires du palais de Mari* II, no. 607, pp. 271, 289-90.

22. For Mursil II, see A. Götze, *Die Annalen des Mursilis* (Leipzig, 1933; reprint, Darmstadt, 1967), 133, 149, 157, 159.

23. See S. Izre'el and I. Singer, *The General's Letter from Ugarit* (Tel Aviv, 1990), 25:6'-7'.

24. On Tuthmosis III, see *ANET*, 235-37, or J. K. Hoffmeier, in *CoS* II, 9-12. On the Battle of Qadesh, see Kitchen, *RITA* II (1996), 5, 17; and *CoS* II, 34, 40.

25. For this section, serious students would do well to refer to K. L. Younger, *Ancient Conquest Accounts: A Study in Ancient Near Eastern and Biblical History Writing*, JSOTSup 98 (Sheffield: Academic Press, 1990), and to Hess, *Joshua;* both works contain important treatments of Joshua from firsthand data.

26. The emphasis on his first (Megiddo) campaign by Tuthmosis III in contrast to summary reports on later campaigns — as we have also in Josh. 10–11 — was pointed out by J. K. Hoffmeier, in *FTH*, 171-73, 176, and in *CoS* II, 8. For the annals of Tuthmosis III, the only complete translation (now old) is that by Breasted, *ARE* II (1906), 172-217, §§406-540. The first and several other campaigns can be seen in contrast, as translated by Wilson in *ANET*, 234-41; first and fifth and sixth campaigns, cf. now Hoffmeier in *CoS* II, 7-13. There are quite close correspondences in sequences of episodes between the Annals of Tuthmosis III on the Battle of Megiddo and the conquest of Jericho by Joshua, as noted and tabulated by Hoffmeier, *FTH*, 172-74. As he points out, we cannot assume any direct link between the two documents; but they share a common mind-set and mode of articulating a report on an initial strategic victory.

27. Ten-Year Annals of Mursil II are now easily accessible, translated by R. H. Beal, in *CoS* II, 82-90, with previous literature.

28. For a detailed analysis of the syntagmatic elements in the Ten-Year Annals of Mursil II and various other related Hittite narrations, see Younger, *Ancient Conquest Accounts,* 125-63; for a syntagmatic summary for Josh. 10:28-42, see his pp. 226-27; and for a full such analysis of Josh. 9–12, see his pp. 359-83.

29. On EA 185 and 186, cf. also Hess, *UFo* 30 (1998/99): 335-31.

30. On Old Testament scholars' misunderstanding of the features of the Josh. 10 concise sections, cf. Younger, *Ancient Conquest Accounts*, 260-61. Briefly, Hess, *Joshua*, 202-4.

31. Cf. conveniently Younger, *Ancient Conquest Accounts,* 227-28, with references, to which many more might be added. For the rhetorical stylistics of Josh. 10:4, using the fourteenth-century Canaanite data in the Amarna letters, see R. S. Hess, *Festschrift für O. Loretz* (Münster, 1998), 363-67; similarly for the Psalms (but relevant to Joshua), cf. R. S. Hess, *ZAW* 101 (1989): 249-65.

32. See (e.g.) M. Weinfeld, in H. Tadmor and M. Weinfeld, eds., *History, Historiography, and Interpretation: Studies in Biblical and Cuneiform Literatures* (Jerusalem: Magnes Press, 1983), 136-41; Younger, *Ancient Conquest Accounts*, 208-11.

33. On the "long day" and sun/moon episode in Josh. 10:12-14, and also Tuthmosis III's

shooting star (?), see latterly Younger, *Ancient Conquest Accounts,* 211-20; on the Josh. 10 "long day," cf. J. H. Walton, *FTH,* 181-90.

34. For the groups and names reviewed here, see especially R. S. Hess, *CBQ* 58 (1996): 205-14, with appropriate references. We add a few extra notes.

35. For Japhia, note Yapaʿ and Yupaʿ, names of Canaanites in Egypt.

36. For Horam as Hurrian, cf. *NPN,* 218 *(Hurra-)* and 232b (-*[a]m* 1).

37. For Adoni-sedeq: at Ugarit, cf. H. Huffmon, *Amorite Personal Names in the Mari Texts* (Baltimore: Johns Hopkins University Press, 1965), 159, 257 (*PRU* II, no. 140:8). Elements elsewhere, cf. Hess, *CBQ* 58 (1996): 207-8 and nn. 17-18.

38. For elements of Hoham, cf. *NPN,* 217 and 232b.

39. For Urhiya and Yupaʿ, see Kitchen in J. Ruffle, G. A. Gaballa, and K. A. Kitchen, eds., *Glimpses of Ancient Egypt: Studies in Honour of H. W. Fairman* (Warminster: Aris & Phillips, 1979), 71-74 (with monuments by Ruffle, pp. 55-70). On Yapaʿ, cf. Hess, *Amarna Personal Names* (Winona Lake, Ind.: Eisenbrauns, 1993), 84-86, nos. 82-83.

40. For Didia, see D. A. Lowle, *OrAnt* 15 (1976): 91-106, esp. 98-100.

41. On Achan's name(s), see R. S. Hess, *Hebrew Annual Review* 14 (1994): 89-98.

42. For the Mari and Berlin data, see the note by M. Anbar (Bernstein), *RAAO* 68 (1974): 172-73.

43. On the thefts, cf. Hess, *Joshua,* 28-29, §5, including references for Shankhar, gold ingots, etc.

44. On Babylonian textiles, including "for business in Canaan" in the twelfth century, cf. A. R. Millard, *VTS* 61 (1995): 197-200. On Babylonian merchants murdered and robbed in Canaan (at least thrice), cf. EA 7:73-82, and EA 8 (Moran, *The Amarna Letters,* 14-17).

45. On the 1,000-shekel gold ingot, see EA 29:34, 39 (Moran, *The Amarna Letters,* 93).

46. On this topic, see in particular A. R. Millard, in L. Eslinger and G. Taylor, eds., *Ascribe to the Lord: Biblical and Other Studies in Memory of Peter C. Craigie* (Sheffield: Academic Press, 1988), 486-92, and in *VTS* 61 (1995): 193-95.

47. On the gold chariots of Tuthmosis III's opponents, see translations of Wilson, *ANET,* 236-37, and Hoffmeier, *CoS* II, 11-12.

48. On late use of flint implements, see Millard, *VTS* 61 (1995): 195-97. And for use in Mesopotamia and the Levant, see the survey by P. R. S. Moorey, *Ancient Mesopotamian Materials and Industries* (Oxford: OUP, 1994), 60-62.

49. The standard work for Egyptian topographical lists used to be J. Simons, *Handbook for the Study of Egyptian Topographical Lists Relating to Western Asia* (Leiden: Brill, 1937), which (for the present) can be briefly supplemented by notes in S. Ahituv, *Canaanite Toponyms in Ancient Egyptian Documents* (Jerusalem: Magnes Press; Leiden: Brill, 1984), 11-21; those of Sethos I and Ramesses II are translated in *RITA* I and II, and of Ramesses III at Medinet Habu in Edgerton and Wilson, *Historical Records of Ramses III.*

50. For Ur-Nammu, see F. R. Kraus, *ZA,* n.s., 51, no. 15 (1955): 45-75, esp. 65-68. Each province demarcated was described by the formula "Terrain of deity X in city Y."

51. For the three Hittite treaties of Tudkhalia II, Hattusil III, and Tudkhaliya IV, see convenient English versions in G. Beckman, *Hittite Diplomatic Texts,* SBL: Writings from the Ancient World 7 (Atlanta: Scholars Press, 1996), 20-21, 104-5, 108-11 respectively. For the full forty-two names of the boundary of Ugarit, see discussion, diagram, and texts in J. Nougayrol, *PRU* IV (1956), 10-16, 51-52, 65-68.

52. On town lists, see R. S. Hess, *BA* 59 (1996): 160-70; in *FTH,* 191-205; and in G. J.

Brooke, A. H. W. Curtis, and J. F. Healey, eds., *Ugarit and the Bible, Proceedings, Symposium, Manchester 1992* (Münster: Ugarit-Verlag, 1994), 128-38.

53. On Ebla, cf. G. Pettinato, *Ebla, a New Look at History* (1991), 229-37, §A.

54. A comparison between Josh. 21 and Ramesses II's mention of towns for the temple of Amun in Canaan was earlier made by B. Mazar, *VTS* 7 (1960): 194-205, reprinted in B. Mazar, *Biblical Israel: State and People,* ed. S. Ahituv (Jerusalem: Magnes Press, 1992), 134-45. The question of difference is also noted by Hess, *BA* 59 (1996): 162.

55. On recognizing the identities of the authors of site destructions and the nature of real or supposed "destructions," see the fundamental and detailed study by M. G. Hasel, *Domination and Resistance: Egyptian Military Activity in the Southern Levant, 1300-1185 BC* (Leiden: Brill, 1998).

56. For a general account of Azekah, see E. Stern, *NEAHL,* 1:123-24.

57. For an outline of work at Khirbet el-Qom, cf. W. G. Dever, in *NEAHL,* 4:1233-35; on identification, cf. D. A. Dorsey, *Tel Aviv* 7 (1980): 185-93; on the village impeding the survey, A. F. Rainey, *BASOR* 251 (1983): 4.

58. On the identification as Tell Bornat, cf. A. F. Rainey, *Tel Aviv* 7 (1980): 198 (with previous references), and in *BASOR* 251 (1983): 3; for a survey of all identifications, cf. J. L. Peterson, in *ABD,* 4:322-24.

59. For Lachish (Tell ed-Duweir with near certainty), see D. Ussishkin, in *NEAHL,* 3:897-911, and for levels VII-VI, 899-904, and earlier in J. N. Tubb, ed., *Palestine in the Bronze and Iron Ages* (London, 1985), 213-30. His equation of the destruction of level VI with Joshua's raid has nothing to commend it; on the date, the destruction of level VII and the Fosse Temple (phase III) would be much more appropriate.

60. For convenient accounts of work at Gezer, see W. G. Dever, in *NEAHL,* 2:496-506 (esp. 503-4), and in *ABD,* 2:998-1003 (esp. 1000-1001).

61. See brief but important studies by A. F. Rainey, in K. Crim, ed., *The Interpreter's Dictionary of the Bible, Supplementary Volume* (Nashville: Abingdon, 1976), 252; in *Tel Aviv* 7 (1980): 197; and in *BASOR* 251 (1983): 9-10, following on M. Noth, *Das Buch Josua,* 2nd ed. (1953), 95, and in *IEJ* 18 (1968): 194-95. J. Barr's attempt to substitute other names (e.g., Adullam) for Eglon (*JSOT* 48 [1990]: 55-68) rests on false premises. Adullam is widely agreed to be located at Khirbet esh-Sheikh Madhkur (e.g., Rainey, *BASOR* 251 [1983]: 7; J. M. Hamilton, *ABD,* 1:81, etc.).

62. See the basic account on Hebron by A. Ofer, *NEAHL,* 2:606-9, esp. 608-9.

63. On Khirbet Rabud, see compact report by M. Kochavi, *NEAHL,* 4:1252. Tell Beit Mirsim was also inhabited (and destroyed) in the thirteenth century (stratum C-2); cf. W. F. Albright, plus R. Greenberg, *NEAHL,* 1:177-80. Its ancient name remains uncertain.

64. For Jarmuth, cf. P. de Miroschedji, in *NEAHL,* 2:661-65.

65. For the most recent full summary on Hazor, see Y. Yadin and A. Ben-Tor, in *NEAHL,* 2:594-606; preliminary reports on more recent work by A. Ben-Tor et al., in *IEJ* 42-48 (1992-98); in N. A. Silberman and D. Small, eds., *The Archaeology of Israel, Constructing the Past, Interpreting the Present* (Sheffield: Academic Press, 1997), 107-27; and in S. Gitin, A. Mazar, and E. Stern, eds., *Mediterranean Peoples in Transition* (Jerusalem: IES, 1998), 456-67; cf. A. Ben-Tor and M. T. Rubiato, *BAR* 25, no. 3 (May-June 1999): 22-39.

66. Yadin's date of ca. 1230 for the fall of Hazor should be lowered to ca. 1220, as his date depended on the dating of Late Mycenaean pottery, itself given too early a date by Aegean scholars who used dates for Egypt that were too high in the light of today's knowledge. The attempt to date the fall of Hazor to the early thirteenth century (P. Beck and M. Kochavi, *Tel Aviv* 12 [1985]: 29-38, esp. 36-38) probably rests on a misconception of regional differences between

south, central, and north Canaan in the use of some types of pottery derived from the Middle Bronze Age (none in the south, only a little in the center and north), a point also raised by R. Frankel, in I. Finkelstein and N. Na'aman, eds., *From Nomadism to Monarchy* (1994), 31-32. Also, Mycenaean IIIB pottery was used down to at least ca. 1200; under Ramesses III onward we have IIIC. At Megiddo, VIIB saw the destruction of the local palace, buried under debris; it was succeeded by a rebuild (VIIA) into the twelfth century. People are very coy as to the cause (and exact date) of this break between VIIB and VIIA; cf. (e.g.) *NEAHL*, 3:1012-13, and Mazar, *ALB* I, 298-99. In theory, it might be (like Hazor) as early as Joshua (ca. 1220) or as late as an impact by the passing Sea Peoples who were defeated at the gates of Egypt by Ramesses III in his Year 8 (1180 or 1177, depending on whether the three-year reign of Amenmesses was as sole king or rival to Sethos II). Megiddo VIIB used Mycenaean IIIB pottery, thus down to the period 1220/ 1180; so Hazor's fall should be not greatly earlier, for these and other factual reasons.

67. See full summary, *NEAHL*, 3:1003-24; for latest excavation report, see I. Finkelstein, D. Ussishkin, et al., *Megiddo III* (Tel Aviv, 2000).

68. For a full summary, see *NEAHL*, 4:1428-33.

69. See *NEAHL*, 3:805-11, for full summary and references.

70. See *NEAHL*, 1:358, for mention of limited MB and LB remains so far. For the term "Naphoth ('heights') of Dor," see D. Baly, *Geography of the Bible*, 2nd ed. (London: Lutterworth, 1974), 26.

71. For a full summary on Tirzah, see *NEAHL*, 2:439.

72. On Aphek (Ras al-Ain), see summary of its Late Bronze Age, thirteenth century, in *NEAHL*, 1:68; cf. also M. Kokhavi, *Aphek in Canaan, the Egyptian Governor's Residence and Its Finds* (Jerusalem: Israel Museum, 1990), catalogue 312.

73. Cf. already above, pp. 150-54; on Late Bronze Age traces, see J. Cahill, *BAR* 24, no. 4 (July-August 1998): 34-38.

74. For Tell Keisan, cf. *NEAHL*, 3:862-67, esp. 866. For Khirbet Harbaj (Tel Regev), see *NEAHL*, 1:31, with references. For Papyrus Anastasi I, cf. Wilson, in *ANET*, 477.

75. For Tell Abu Qudeis, Jezreel, see *NEAHL*, 3:860. For a report of Tell Qudeish (Issachar), cf. *NBD*, 642, and end references.

76. For summary of Bethel, see *NEAHL*, 1:192-94, with references. On the dispute over its location, cf. A. F. Rainey, *WTJ* 33 (1970-71): 175-88.

77. For an overall summary of Shechem, cf. *NEAHL*, 4:1345-54, esp. 1352.

78. The best basic overall outline of Jericho is that of Kenyon in *NEAHL*, 2:674-81, esp. 679-80 on Middle and Late Bronze periods and data.

79. A careful special study of the extant remains attributable to Late Bronze Jericho is by P. Bienkowski, *Jericho in the Late Bronze Age* (Warminster: Aris & Phillips, 1986); see 120 for his dating, and 120-25 for strictly archaeological conclusions on what has survived and been found; he very properly does not speculate beyond the tangible data. For disputes over attempts to re-date Middle Bronze levels (including Jericho) and refutations, see (1) J. Bimson, *Redating the Exodus and Conquest* (Sheffield: Academic Press, 1978), and comments by A. F. Rainey, *IEJ* 30 (1980): 250-51; (2) B. G. Wood, *BAR* 16, no. 2 (March-April 1990): 44-58, and *BAR* 16, no. 5 (1990): 45, 47-49, 68-69; corrected in the same issue by P. Bienkowski, 45-46, 69. For simpler, basic presentations of the position of the evidence (or, its lack!), cf. A. R. Millard, *Treasures from Bible Times* (Oxford: Lion Press, 1985), 96-99 (reprinted in his *Discoveries from Bible Times* [Oxford: Lion Press, 1997], 96-99), and Hess, *Joshua*, 137-38.

80. For an overall survey of Ai, see *NEAHL*, 1:39-45, including the two Byzantine sites; for oldest topographical survey, see that of E. Robinson, *Biblical Researches in Palestine* II (London:

John Murray, 1841, original ed.), 312-14; on Khirbet el-Maqatir, cf. B. G. Wood, *IEJ* 50 (2000): 123-30. A novelistic theory was proposed by Z. Zevit, in *BASOR* 251 (1983): 23-35 (with good plans), and in *BAR* 11, no. 2 (March-April 1985): 58-69 (with good color illustrations).

81. On Ai not meaning "ruin," see Y. Kaufmann, *The Biblical Account of the Conquest of Palestine* (Jerusalem: Magnes Press, 1953), 77 n. 64, and (plus other Et-Tells) also Z. Zevit, *BASOR* 251 (1983): 26, 28, and (with J. A. Callaway) in *BAR* 11, no. 2 (March-April 1983): 62 note*. Cf. also the summary discussions by Hess, *Joshua,* 137-43 with 157-79, and Millard, *Treasures from Bible Times,* and reprint in his *Discoveries from Bible Times,* 99.

82. For a brief summary of Gibeon, see *NEAHL,* 2:511-14; on Late Bronze, cf. also J. B. Pritchard, *Gibeon Where the Sun Stood Still* (Princeton: Princeton University Press, 1962), 156-58.

83. Examples of deficiencies in outdated critiques of Joshua, raids, and lists, include W. G. Dever, in *ABD,* 3:548, in an otherwise valuable article; and N. Na'aman, in Finkelstein and Na'aman, *From Nomadism to Monarchy,* 223, whose five "discrepancies" show failures in understanding the data; and I. Finkelstein, *The Archaeology of the Israelite Settlement* (Jerusalem: IES, 1988), 295ff., who wrongly assumes that Joshua gives a narrative of instant conquest/occupation, reading into the text (as did Albright) what is not there, and ignoring the rhetorical element.

84. See B. S. J. Isserlin, *PEQ* 115 (1983): 85-94, quoting the Norman Conquest, the Anglo-Saxon settlement in England, and the Muslim Arab invasion of Syria-Palestine. One may also cite the innumerable campaigns of Egyptian, Hittite, Assyrian, and Neo-Babylonian armies in the Levant, of whose encampments and battlefields almost no traces are ever found. Again, in Canaan (like Israel) the Egyptians preferred *not* to destroy cities, but (unlike Israel) to reduce their populations to tax-paying vassals; cf. Hasel, *Domination and Resistance,* passim.

85. See in particular the comprehensive paper on various factors, by R. S. Hess, *PEQ* 125 (1993): 125-42. For the Jordan Valley (and movement east to west across it), cf. E. J. van der Steen, *BASOR* 302 (1996): 51-74.

86. On the archaeology of Qadesh-Barnea (Ain el-Qudeirat), see R. Cohen, *NEAHL,* 3:841-47; also R. Cohen, *Kadesh-barnea: A Fortress from the Time of the Judaean Kingdom* (Jerusalem: Israel Museum, 1983); and in popular form, in *BAR* 7, no. 3 (May-June 1981): 20-33; his remarks about no trace of the early Hebrews, p. 33, illustrate (again) the commonplace failure to appreciate the near total lack of any evidence for the camps of known armies and most migrants throughout the history of the biblical world; cf. (e.g.) Isserlin quoted just above. The views of S. Rosen (*BAR* 14, no. 5 [September-October 1988]: 46-53, 58-59), that nomads can be traced is only tenable if the ancients leave tangible items like pots or deliberately formed hearths, etc. Cf. I. Finkelstein and A. Perevolotsky, *BASOR* 279 (1990): 67-88 in passing; more fully, A. J. Frendo, *Or* 65 (1996): 1-23, esp. 13ff.

87. On the fifteen-day average, cf. W. J. Murnane, *The Road to Qadesh* (Chicago: OIC, 1985), 145-50; 2nd ed. (1990), 95-97, with references.

88. For the phenomenon of *kewirs,* see G. Hort, *AusBR* 7 (1959): 2-26, esp. 19-26.

89. For the sites named, cf. the following accessible references: for "Tel Beersheba," *NEAHL,* 1:167-73; for Tel Halif, *NEAHL,* 2:553-61; for Tel Masos, *NEAHL,* 3:986-89; for Tel 'Ira, *NEAHL,* 2:642-46; for Tel Esdar, *NEAHL,* 2:423; for Tel Malhata, *NEAHL,* 3:934-39; for Arad, *NEAHL,* 1:75-87. For a good preliminary outline, see Y. Aharoni, *BA* 39, no. 2 (May 1976): 55-76, but now outdated on the Late Bronze aspect and on "Abraham's well." The identification of "Tel Beersheba" (Tell es-Seba) as ancient Beersheba is not certain, hence my placing the modern name in inverted commas; in *BAR* 19, no. 3 (May-June 1993): 58-61, 76, V. Fritz has suggested that this site is really Ziklag (often placed at Tel Sera), and that the real Beersheba is in fact among the remains under the modern town.

90. On Hormah/Zephath, cf. also J. P. U. Lilley, *NBD*, 481, with references.

91. The two Arads in the Shoshenq list are "Great Arad," nos. 108-9, and "Arad of the House *(bt)* of Jeroham," nos. 110-12; cf. Kitchen, *Third Int. Pd.* (1973, 1996), 440.

92. There is no reason to give credit to Jebel Harun near Petra as Aaron's burial place, as this results from medieval-epoch misinterpretations; cf. F. Zayadine, *SHAJ* 2 (1985): 171. For Jebel Made(i)ra/Madara, cf. G. A. Smith, *The Historical Geography of the Holy Land,* 25th ed. (London: Hodder & Stoughton, 1931), 573 (but read northeast for northwest!), and pl. VIII. This would be (in Wadi Madra) about twenty miles east as the crow flies, but some sixty miles going north-northeast, then via Wadi Murra, detouring northeast to Gebel Madra for Aaron, then back to the Darb es-Sultan to reach the Arabah Valley. For these, Smith's inadequate map has to be replaced by (e.g.) the PEF one-sheet *Map of the Negeb,* issued in 1921.

93. The mysterious Gudgodah and Jotbathah might have been the modern Ain el-Gattar and (into the Arabah) Ain el-Weiba. Aharoni suggested that Zalmona was the later Roman Calamona (*LB,* 202; after A. Alt, *ZDPV* 58 [1935]: 26), although this is far from certain and not universally accepted; cf. B. MacDonald, *East of the Jordan,* ASOR (2000), 82-83. Geographically, Ain Abu Thabana (opposite and east of Ain el-Weiba) would suit, but this must remain hypothetical.

94. Iye-Abarim is ingeniously rendered "Ruins of the Departed" by M. H. Pope (in M. De Jong Ellis, ed., *Essays . . . in Memory of J. J. Finkelstein* [Hamdon: Archon, 1977], 173), as reflecting a concentration of old tombs; but the area suggested toward Bab edh-Dhra is off route, and would require needless emendation.

95. For Punon, see references in MacDonald, *East of the Jordan,* 83.

96. On the west-east embayment and break, via Wadis Feinan/Fidan and Ghuweir, between the el-Jebal and esh-Shera blocks of north and south Edom, cf. Smith, *Historical Geography,* 568-69, and D. Baly, *Geography of the Bible,* 2nd ed. (Guildford and London: Lutterworth, 1974), 235-36.

97. On Kedemoth, cf. MacDonald, *East of the Jordan,* 93-94.

98. On the Mishor plateau, region of wheat and barley crops, and much sheep rearing (cf. 2 Kings 3:4), cf. Baly, *Geography of the Bible,* 229-31, with map 70. Abel-Shittim may be marked by the present Tell el-Hammam; cf. MacDonald, *East of the Jordan,* 89-90.

99. On Dibon being certainly at modern Dhiban, where the Mesha stela was found, see MacDonald, *East of the Jordan,* 84-85. Egyptian *Tibunu* (but not necessarily *Tpn!*) was certainly Dibon, linked with Butartu in Moab by Ramesses II. For full publications, see Kitchen, *JEA* 50 (1964): 47-70, with new translation and full commentary in *RITA* II (1996), 49-51, §24, and *RITANC* II (1999), 89-97, §24, with map 15. For a critique of Old Testament scholars' blunders over the Egyptian data, see Kitchen in Bienkowski, *Early Edom and Moab,* 27-29; the same misguided reluctance to accept clear data is shown by M. Weippert, in *RLA* VIII (1994/95), 321, in an otherwise useful entry.

100. For Tell Hesban, cf. L. Geraty, in *NEAHL,* 2:626-30; for reports of LB or possible LB II/Iron IA pottery, see J. Sauer in D. Merling and L. T. Geraty, eds., *Hesban after Twenty-five Years* (Berrien Springs, Mich.: Andrews University, 1994), 233-35; also C.-H. C. Ji, *PEQ* 127 (1995): 123. On Tell Umeiri and Tell Jalul with Late Bronze II, cf. Ji, 122-23.

101. For Late Bronze II/Iron I tombs at Medeba, see M. Piccirillo, *NEAHL,* 3:992-93; cf. Ji, *PEQ* 127 (1995): 127, also MacDonald, *East of the Jordan,* 108-10. For Ammon, see now B. MacDonald and R. W. Younker, eds., *Ancient Ammon* (Leiden: Brill, 1999).

102. For the Assyrian king list, cf. translation of Millard, in *CoS* I, 463.

103. For the Old Babylonian "sheikh"-kings in Manana and elsewhere, plus the Assyrian king-list data, see W. Yuhong and S. Dalley, *Iraq* 52 (1990): 159-65.

104. For multiple rulers and groups in the Execration Texts, cf. notes, Kitchen, in Bienkowski, *Early Edom and Moab*, 21, and "tribes" of Irqata and Byblos (besides city rulers), in G. Posener, *Princes et pays d'Asie et de Nubie* (Brussels: FÉRÉ, 1940), 93-94, E.61, 63.

105. At Mari (nineteenth and eighteenth centuries), local kings (title, *sharrum,* like Heb. *melek*) were granted that title, higher than governors or "sheikhs" *(sugagu),* on the decision of their overlord, the king of Mari, on political grounds — not on the basis of a priori modern theories! Cf. J.-M. Durand, *Les documents épistolaires du palais de Mari* I (Paris: Éditions du Cerf, 1997), 207, for *sugagu* being promoted to kingship. A. Knauf (in Bienkowski, *Early Edom and Moab,* 52) is compelled to admit to the practical and widespread existence of the "tribal state," but — needlessly! — finds it hard to deal with, as it breaks the rules of theory; no problem really, just dump the false rules!

106. On the Balu'a stela, cf. J. A. Dearman, in Bienkowski, *Early Edom and Moab,* 70, and Miller, 78. For a consideration of the conditions for the Hebrews coping with life in the ecology of Sinai, cf. the remarks by C. L. Woolley and T. E. Lawrence, *PEF Annual* 3 (1914-15): 70-71.

107. Old Babylonian text (two tablets) published by A. Goetze, *JCS* 7 (1953): 51-72, plus a third tablet by W. W. Hallo, *JCS* 18 (1964): 57-88.

108. The Mari letter is *ARM(T)* I, no. 26.

109. On Tukulti-Ninurta II, see Grayson, *RIMA,* 2 (1991), 169-79, no. 5; on Assurnasirpal II, cf. Grayson, 191-223, passim. In general, cf. (in German) D. O. Edzard and G. Frantz-Szabó, *RLA* V/3-4 (1977), 216-20.

110. For the style of Egyptian daybooks, see A. J. Spalinger, *Aspects of the Military Documents of the Ancient Egyptians* (New Haven: Yale University Press, 1982), 120ff. For the two Egyptian ships' logs, see J. J. Janssen, *Two Ancient Egyptian Ships' Logs* (Leiden: Brill, 1961); that of Khaemwaset also translated in Kitchen, *RITA* II, 530-35, §286; cf. *RITANC* II (1999), 525-28, §286.

111. For the Papyrus Anastasi I translation, see *ANET,* 477-78.

112. For topographical lists, cf. the segments visible in that of Shoshenq I (925 B.C.), in map, Kitchen, *Third Int. Pd.* (1996), 434, fig. 9.

113. For general treatment of the Num. 33 itinerary and its background, see G. I. Davies, *TynB* 25 (1974): 46-81, and his *The Way of the Wilderness* (Cambridge: Cambridge University Press, 1979), with also the observations by G. J. Wenham, *Numbers,* Tyndale OT Commentaries (Leicester, 1981), 216ff. For both this text and lists in general, see the monograph by B. E. Scolnic, *Theme and Content in Biblical Lists* (Atlanta: Scholars Press, 1995).

114. For documentation on the long series of LB/Iron IA sites in Jordan from Tell Jalul up to beyond the Yarmuk, see the conspectus by C.-H. C. Ji, *PEQ* 127 (1995): 122-40.

115. On four-room houses in both Canaan and Transjordan, their types, dates, and occurrences, see C.-H. C. Ji, *Or* 66 (1997): 387-413, esp. 399, 409-10.

116. On questions of sedentary and nomadic phases of life in Transjordan in LB/Iron I, cf. C.-H. C. Ji, *NEASB* 43 (1998): 1-21. On the settlement history of the Jordan Valley, see E. J. van der Steen, *PEQ* 127 (1995): 141-58; C.-H. C. Ji, *PEQ* 129 (1997): 19-37. On the biblical interrelationship with the Transjordanian profile in LB/Iron IIA, cf. idem, *NEASB* 41 (1996), 61-70. On the question of collar-rim jars and four-roomed houses as wider than just Israelite, but also a characteristic of Israelite life, cf. W. G. Dever, *BA* 58 (1995): 200-213, esp. 210.

117. That "There was no political entity named Israel before the late-11th century," as Finkelstein claimed (*SJOT* 2 [1991]: 56), is a blatant error, disproved by the stela of Merenptah of

1209, for whom "Israel" is a people group sufficiently extensive, coherent, and organized as to be ranked alongside the city-states of Gezer, Ascalon, and Yenoam.

118. On Judg. 1:1–3:6 in particular, see usefully K. L. Younger, in *FTH*, 207-27. On the integral literary format of the book of Judges (implying a basic unity), see Barry G. Webb, *The Book of Judges: An Integrated Reading* (Sheffield: JSOT/Academic Press, 1987).

119. The calculation of $554 + x + y + z$ years is in H. H. Rowley, *From Joseph to Joshua*, Schweich Lectures, 1948 (London: British Academy/OUP, 1950), 86-88, and differently in J. J. Bimson, *Redating the Exodus and Conquest*, 2nd ed. (Sheffield: Almond Press, 1981), 79-81.

120. For the Egyptian dates (and data) for the second intermediate period, see Kitchen, in M. Bietak, ed., *The Synchronisation of Civilisations in the Eastern Mediterranean in the Second Millennium B.C.* (Vienna: Austrian Academy, 2000), 44-46, 49.

121. The Mesopotamian dates mentioned can be found in A. L. Oppenheim, *Ancient Mesopotamia* (Chicago: University of Chicago Press, 1964), 336-37, or in *CAH* II/1 (1973), 820, or in A. Kuhrt, *The Ancient Near East* I (London: Routledge, 1995), 79. The totals cited refer exclusively to Babylonia; if one adds in Eshnunna, Assyria, and Upper Mesopotamian states such as Mari and its neighbors, we would have upward of 1,000 years to include within our 410 years!

122. For a concise and clear presentation of the archaeology of Dan in levels VII-IV, see A. Biran, *Biblical Dan* (Jerusalem: IES, 1994), chap. 8, pp. 125-46.

123. On the suggested house shrines at Tell Umeiri, cf. L. G. Herr and D. R. Clark, *BAR*, 27, no. 2 (March-April 2001): 44 (illustrations), 47; full report, L. G. Herr, *EI* 26 (1999): 64-77.

124. For a brief, careful review, see J. R. Bartlett, *ABD*, 1:1220; earlier, cf. A. Malamat, *JNES* 13 (1954): 231-42 (now obsolescent, but with older references).

125. For the weakness of Assyria from the last years of Tukulti-Ninurta I through most of the twelfth century, cf. J. M. Munn-Rankin, *CAH* II/2 (1975), 292-94, and D. J. Wiseman, *CAH* II/2, 449-53.

126. For Aram already under Amenophis III, and in Papyrus Anastasi III, verso 5:5, see discussion by E. Edel, *Die Ortsnamenlisten aus dem Totentempel Amenophis III*, BBB 25 (Bonn: Hanstein Verlag, 1966), 28-29, no. 7. He rightly rejects on good grounds the attempt to emend the Merenptah mention to "Amurru."

127. The suggestion of "Chief of ʿAthaim" goes back to J. Marquart, *Fundamente Israelitischer und Jüdaischer Geschichte* (Göttingen, 1896), 11.

128. Unfortunately, we have no list of towns in the Bit-Adini district to look for ʿAthaim.

129. For Assur-uballit as king of Assyria in Harran, see Babylonian Chronicle in *ANET*, 305, or in A. K. Grayson, *Assyrian and Babylonian Chronicles* (New York: Augustin, 1970), 95-96.

130. For overall discussions of the pottery of Qurayya, see P. J. Parr, *SHAJ* 1 (1982): 127-30; in D. T. Potts, ed., *Araby the Blest: Studies in Arabian Archaeology* (Copenhagen: Museum Tusculanum Press, 1988), 72-89; and in *Arabian Archaeology and Epigraphy* 4 (1993): 48-58; on the Qurayya site, see Parr et al., *Bulletin, Inst. of Archaeology, Univ. London* 8/9 (1970): 219-41, and M. L. Ingraham et al., *Atlal* 5 (1981): 71-74, pls. 68, 78-80.

131. On the archaeology and dating of the stepped structure, see D. Tarler and J. M. Cahill, *ABD*, 2:55, and J. M. Cahill, *BAR* 24, no. 4 (July-August 1998): 34-40 (refuting M. Steiner).

132. For stratum XI as a twelfth-century settlement following on the poor village that constitutes stratum XII, and destroyed about 1100, see E. F. Campbell, *NEAHL*, 4:1352, and more fully L. E. Toombs in *ABD*, 4:1183-84. On Baal/El-Berith, tower temple as Temple 2 of G. E. Wright, *Shechem, the Biography of a Biblical City* (London: Duckworth, 1965), 123-28, cf. W. G. Dever, *RADBR*, 163, 185 n. 30.

133. A work on the Philistines' material remains that has long been standard is T. Dothan,

The Philistines and Their Material Culture (New Haven: Yale University Press; Jerusalem: IES, 1982). For a popular presentation, see T. Dothan and M. Dothan, *People of the Sea* (New York: Macmillan, 1992). For recent studies on the whole Sea Peoples (and Philistine) phenomenon, see the three collective volumes: W. A. Ward and M. S. Joukowsky, eds., *The Crisis Years: The Twelfth Century B.C.* (Dubuque, Iowa: Kendall/Hunt Publishing Co., 1989); Gitin, Mazar, and Stern, *Mediterranean Peoples in Transition* (1998); and E. D. Oren, ed., *The Sea Peoples and Their World: A Reassessment* (Philadelphia: Pennsylvania University Museum, 2000).

134. For sequences at Ascalon, Ashdod, and Ekron (Tel Miqne), see accounts in *NEAHL,* 1:96-97, 107, and 3:1052-53. For popular presentations on Ascalon, see L. E. Stager, *BAR* 17, no. 2 (March-April 1991): 24-40, passim; on Ekron, see T. Dothan, *BAR* 16, no. 1 (January-February 1990): 26-36.

135. The Egyptian piece of a chief physician Bin-Anath was published by G. A. Gaballa, *JEA* 59 (1973): 109-10. Another Bin-Anath was father-in-law to a son of Ramesses II in the thirteenth century; cf. Kitchen, *Pharaoh Triumphant: Life and Times of Ramesses II* (Warminster: Aris & Phillips, 1982), 111, and *RITA* II, 592, §370. For an eleventh-century arrowhead of "Bin-Anath son of Merets," see R. Deutsch and M. Heltzer, *Forty New Ancient West Semitic Inscriptions* (Tel-Aviv-Jaffa: Archaeological Center Publication, 1994), 15-16, (3)3.

136. For Timnah, level V, cf. G. L. Kelm and A. Mazar, *Timnah: A Biblical City in the Sorek Valley* (Winona Lake, Ind.: Eisenbrauns, 1995), 95-104.

137. On pillared temples at Kition, cf. A. Mazar in Oren, *The Sea Peoples,* 219-20, with fig. 11.3: L, M (Temples 4, 5). For general background, see L. E. Stager, *BAR* 17, no. 2 (March-April 1991): 41-42.

138. Stated, e.g., by J. Wellhausen, *Prolegomena to the History of Ancient Israel* (1885; reprint, New York: Meridien Library, 1957), 229-31, obediently followed by S. R. Driver, *An Introduction to the Literature of the Old Testament,* 9th ed. (Edinburgh: T. & T. Clark, 1913), 163-65.

139. For the latest translations of Nebre/Nakhtamun, see Kitchen, *Poetry of Ancient Egypt* (Jonsered: P. Aströms förlag, 1999), 289-90, or *RITA* III (2000), 444-46; other examples are in *Poetry* and *RITA* III, passim (and also *RITA* IV-VI, forthcoming).

140. For a translation of the stela of Tutankhamun, see B. G. Davies, *Egyptian Historical Records of the Later Eighteenth Dynasty,* fasc. VI (Warminster: Aris & Phillips, 1995), 30-33, §772.

141. For the triumph hymn of Uni, see Wilson, in *ANET,* 228; new translation and full analysis in Kitchen, *Poetry of Ancient Egypt,* 71-74.

142. For the hymns of Sesostris I and III, see Kitchen, *Poetry of Ancient Egypt,* 91-108; of Tuthmosis III, Amenophis III, and Ramesses II, Kitchen, 165-196. The epic on Tukulti-Ninurta I is translated (and sources cited) by B. R. Foster, *Before the Muses: An Anthology of Akkadian Literature* I (Bethesda, Md.: CDL Press, 1993), 209-29, and reproduced (without sources) in his *From Distant Days* (Bethesda, Md.: CDL Press, 1995), 178-96. Also, a fragment for Adad-nirari I is in Munn-Rankin, *CAH* II/2 (1975), 298 and n. 4 (plus 957).

143. On Exod. 15, cf. long ago F. M. Cross and D. N. Freedman, *JNES* 14 (1955): 237-50; F. M. Cross, *Canaanite Myth and Hebrew Epic* (Cambridge: Harvard University Press, 1973), 121-44.

144. On the triumph hymn of Deborah and Barak (Judg. 5), see L. E. Stager, *BAR* 15, no. 1 (January-February 1989): 50-64, esp. 58-62; his fuller studies are in *BASOR* 260 (1985): 1-35, and in *VTS* 40 (1988): 221-34; cf. also in *EI* 18 (1985): 56*-64*, pl. IV:2.

145. On the familial and genealogical nature of tribal communities, cf. V. H. Matthews, *Pastoral Nomadism in the Mari Kingdom (c. 1830-1760 BC),* ASOR Dissertation Series 3 (1978), 24-25. On tribal confederations around Mari, see compact accounts with references in J. T. Luke,

Pastoralism and Politics in the Mari Period (1965; Ann Arbor and High Wycombe: UMI, 1973), 61-68 (Mare-Yamina), 113-14 (Sutaeans), and 143-51 (Haneans).

146. On the mukarribate, cf. in popular form, J.-F. Breton, *Arabia Felix from the Time of the Queen of Sheba, Eighth Century* BC *to First Century* AD (Notre Dame, Ind.: University of Notre Dame Press, 1999), 33ff. On the *Bundesformular*, cf. H. von Wissmann, in H. Temporini, ed., *ANRW* II: *Principat*, vol. 9:1 (Berlin: W. de Gruyter, 1976), 332-33; phrases are cited in English translation also by J. C. Biella, *Dictionary of Old South Arabic* (Harvard: Harvard Semitic Museum, 1982), 181.

147. On the "thirds" and "fourths" of Old South Arabian tribes, and overall hierarchy, cf. C. J. Robin, *Les hautes-terres du Nord-Yemen avant l'Islam* I (Leiden: Netherlands Institute, Istanbul, 1982), 71-77 (cf. A. Korotayev, *Pre-Islamic Yemen* [Wiesbaden: Harrassowitz, 1996], 12-19). The terms are in Biella, *Dictionary of Old South Arabic,* 478, 518; on fourths, also A. F. L. Beeston, *Le Muséon* 88 (1975): 189-92, §3. For Sheba overall, cf. C. J. Robin, "Sheba dans les inscriptions d'Arabie du Sud," in *SDB* XII/Fasc. 70 (1996), cols. 1043-1254.

148. An excellent and concise review of the amphictyony theory as set out by M. Noth, *Das System der zwölf Stämme Israels* (Stuttgart, 1930), and objections to it are given by A. D. H. Mayes, *ABD,* 1:212-16, with references.

149. For distinctions in series of Jacob's children and then tribes, and for the fundamental importance of the tribal concept, cf. Z. Kallai, *VT* 47 (1997): 53-90, plus *VT* 49 (1999): 125-27; but he errs in making the last of his four series the basis of the other three.

150. For the Sumerian amphictyony in Ur III, see W. W. Hallo, *JCS* 14 (1960): 88-114.

151. On the Philistine "amphictyony," analogous with the Greek form, cf. B. D. Rahtjen, *JNES* 24 (1965): 100-104.

152. For a general survey of the Iron I period, see Mazar, *ALB* I, 295-367, or in A. Ben-Tor, ed., *The Archaeology of Ancient Israel* (New Haven: Yale University Press, 1992), 258-301.

153. For populations in Middle Bronze II and after, cf. Finkelstein, *Israelite Settlement,* 339-41.

154. For the Ephraim/Samaria survey, see the final report by I. Finkelstein and Z. Lederman, eds., *Highlands of Many Cultures, the Southern Samaria Survey, I-II, the Sites* (Tel Aviv: Institute of Archaeology, 1997) (vol. III on interpretation is planned). Accessible preliminary reports were by Finkelstein, *TA* 15-16 (1988-89): 117-83; in simpler form, Finkelstein, *BAR* 14, no. 5 (September-October 1988): 34-45, 58; for booklength treatment, Finkelstein, *Israelite Settlement,* 119-204.

155. For the Manasseh survey (technical publications in Hebrew), in an accessible account, see A. Zertal, *BAR* 17, no. 5 (September-October 1991): 28-49, 75, and in Finkelstein and Na'aman, *From Nomadism to Monarchy,* 47-69; for an updated figure for Iron I sites, see A. Zertal in Gitin, Mazar, and Stern, *Mediterranean Peoples in Transition,* 240 (and bibliography for survey reports, p. 250). Sites (99) for Middle Bronze Ephraim, cf. list, Finkelstein and Lederman, *Highlands of Many Cultures,* 891-93. Sites (135 and 31 respectively) for MB and LB Manasseh, cf. Zertal in Finkelstein and Na'aman, 50-51. Cf. L. E. Stager in M. D. Coogan, ed., *The Oxford History of the Biblical World* (New York: OUP, 1998), 123-75.

156. Cf. estimates by Finkelstein, *Israelite Settlement,* 331-34. Soon afterward, in H. Shanks, ed., *The Rise of Ancient Israel* (Washington: BAS, 1992), W. G. Dever (p. 43) gave an estimate of 75,000 early Israelites, distinctly higher than Finkelstein's cautious figures. (Previously, estimates were much higher but were not based on solid criteria; cf. figures and references given by Finkelstein, 330-31.) For varying figures see also Dever, *What . . . When . . . ?* 127.

157. For the number of sites in Ephraim and Manasseh, see under 6.B.iii.a above.

158. For the indigenous "revolting peasant" and out of west Canaan "tax evasion" theories, see initially G. E. Mendenhall, "The Hebrew Conquest of Palestine," in *Biblical Archaeologist Reader* III (1962), 100-120, and in his *The Tenth Generation: The Origins of the Biblical Tradition* (Baltimore: Johns Hopkins University Press, 1973). Then, at far greater length and somewhat differently, N. K. Gottwald, *The Tribes of Yahweh: A Sociology of the Religion of Liberated Israel* (New York: Orbis, 1979). A lengthy critique of these works is given by N. P. Lemche, *Early Israel*, VTSup 37 (Leiden: Brill, 1985), in which he presents his own anthropological-cum-sociological analysis, which is no better, being dominated by unverifiable hypotheses.

159. The east-to-west trend in successive pottery styles is mentioned by Finkelstein, *Israelite Settlement*, 187-200, passim; in *TA* 15-16 (1988-89): 146-51, passim; cf. graphically, *BAR* 14, no. 5 (September-October 1988): 40, and in *JAOS* 110 (1990): 682. Exemplified by Zertal, *BAR* 17, no. 5 (September-October 1991): 36-37 and (graphically) 39-41; noted in Finkelstein and Na'aman, *From Nomadism to Monarchy*, 53, 59, and more fully in Gitin, Mazar, and Stern, *Mediterranean Peoples in Transition*, 242-43. Both Zertal and Finkelstein were challenged by Dever, in Shanks, *Rise of Ancient Israel*, 49-52, and then refuted by Zertal, 76-77; cf. in Gitin, Mazar, and Stern, 244-45.

160. For the indigenous-resettlement-from-the-east theory by Finkelstein, cf. *BAR* 14, no. 5 (September-October 1988): 40-45, from his *Israelite Settlement*, 341-51. For Zertal, cf. *BAR* 17, no. 5 (September-October 1991): 33, 36-41, 46-47; also in Finkelstein and Na'aman, *From Nomadism to Monarchy*, 66-69; and in Gitin, Mazar, and Stern, *Mediterranean Peoples in Transition*, 245-48.

161. The population explosion is also related to an Israelite entry from outside by L. E. Stager, *BAR* 15, no. 1 (January-February 1989): 54, following on from *BASOR* 260 (1985): 3, and reviews various hypotheses in Coogan, *Oxford History*, 129-42, admitting that an entry from outside Canaan has some points in its favor (p. 134), but not an immediate "all-over" conquest.

162. The "Israel Stela" (Libyan victory triumph hymn) of Merenptah is translated in full by Wilson in *ANET*, 376-78 (Israel part, 378), and by Kitchen, *RITA* IV (2002), 10-16 (Israel, p. 15); Israel part only, Hoffmeier, in *CoS* II, 40-41. On the high level of accuracy of the inscribed text, see Kitchen, *JSSEA* 24 (1994/97): 71-76; of over 3,300 hieroglyphs on the monument, only 7 are strict errors, a fault rate of less than one-quarter of 1 percent! The attempt by G. Ahlström and D. Edelman (*JNES* 44 [1985]: 59-61) to misinterpret "Israel" as a land, not a people, on this stela is a perverse, 100 percent error. On the Karnak reliefs, see F. Yurco, *JSSEA* 8, no. 3 (May 1978): 70 (followed up by L. E. Stager, *EI* 18 [1985]: 56*-64*), and in full detail, see Yurco, *JARCE* 23 (1986): 189-215, plus graphically in *BAR* 16, no. 5 (September-October 1990): 20-38.

The dating of these scenes to Merenptah (instead of to Ramesses II) was wrongly contested by D. B. Redford, *IEJ* 36 (1986): 188-200, and fully refuted by Yurco (*BAR* 16, no. 5, 26 n.*, 36) and by me in *RITANC* II (1999), 73-74. In *BAR* 17, no. 6 (November-December 1991): 56-60, A. F. Rainey sought to identify the Israelites not with the upper-scene relief of a defeated people (because of chariots there) but with the Shasu shown below. This does not work, because of the regular mode of sequencing of Ramesside war reliefs, including Merenptah's; see *RITANC* II, 75-76, and briefly Yurco, *BAR* 17, no. 6, 61. The chariots may have belonged to Canaanites caught up in the action.

163. The ostracon of a Year 4 could in principle belong to either Merenptah or any later king (e.g., Sethos II, Siptah) down to Ramesses III who reached a Year 4. Cerny's expertise favored Merenptah's period; the *b3* sign of then or later is not decisive. Published by him in O. Tufnell et al., *Lachish IV, the Bronze Age* (Oxford: OUP, 1958), text 133, pl. 44:3-4, 47:1-2 (bowl no. 3); text, KRI IV, 39, §17; translations, Cerny, in Tufnell, and Kitchen, *RITA* IV (2002), 27.

164. On four-room houses and collar-rimmed jars, cf. C.-H. Ji, *Or* 66 (1997): 387-413, esp. 405-13, with earlier references. On Iron I store pits, cf. J. D. Currid and J. L. Gregg, *BAR* 14, no. 5 (October-November 1988): 54-57. For cisterns and terracing, cf. Stager, *BAR* 15, no. 1 (January-February 1989): 55-57; and *BASOR* 260 (1985): 5-10.

165. On pig-bone finds and their possible relevance, cf. L. E. Stager, *BAR* 17, no. 2 (March-April 1991): 31; B. Hesse, *BASOR* 264 (1986): 17-27; more nuanced (unlike Stager and R. S. Hess, *PEQ* 125 [1993]: 138, whom they wrongly criticize), obscuring clear regional distinctions, are B. Hesse and P. Wapnish, in Silberman and Small, *The Archaeology of Israel*, 238-70. Cf. reservations by K. Prag, in S. Ahituv and E. D. Oren, eds., *The Origins of Early Israel — a Current Debate* (1998), 153-54.

166. For discussions of ethnicity, cf. (e.g.) W. G. Dever, *EI* 24 (1993): 22*-33*; in Gitin, Mazar, and Stern, *Mediterranean Peoples in Transition*, 220-37, and I. Finkelstein, in Silberman and Small, *The Archaeology of Israel*, 216-37, each with earlier references (cf. Mazar, *ALB* I, 365 n. 37); Dever, *What . . . When . . . ?* 108-19.

167. On the "bull site," see in detail A. Mazar, *BASOR* 247 (1982): 27-42; other studies, Mazar, *BAR* 9, no. 5 (September-October 1983): 34-40; as Canaanite and domestic, M. Coogan, *PEQ* 119 (1987): 1-8 (and reported by H. Shanks, *BAR* 14, no. 1 [January-February 1988]: 48-52), with riposte by A. Mazar, *BAR* 14, no. 4 (July-August 1988): 45. Attempt to redate the bull site and its bronze bull to the Middle Bronze Age by I. Finkelstein, *PEQ* 130 (1998): 94-98, refuted by Mazar, *PEQ* 131 (1999): 144-48.

168. On Mount Ebal, see A. Zertal, *TA* 13-14 (1986-87): 105-65 (dig report); additional data in *NEAHL*, 1:375-77. For earlier popular reports and discussions, cf. A. Zertal, *BAR* 11, no. 1 (January-February 1985): 26-43; A. Kempinski and A. Zertal, *BAR* 12, no. 1 (January-February 1986): 42, 44-49, and 43, 49-53; Kempinski and Rainey, *BAR* 12, no. 4 (July-August 1986): 66 (impolite, with errors). W. G. Dever, in Shanks, *Rise of Ancient Israel*, 33-34. Brief, fair summary, R. S. Hess, *PEQ* 125 (1987): 135-37. On Ramesside scarabs from the site (late thirteenth century), cf. B. Brandl, *TA* 13-14 (1986-87): 166-72, pl. 20. Map of Shechem and Mounts Ebal and Gerizim, cf. Wright, *Shechem*, fig. 2 (after p. 141).

169. On Giloh, cf. A. Mazar, *IEJ* 31 (1981): 1-36, pls. 1-6; *IEJ* 40 (1990): 77-101, pls. 9-13.

170. *Shasu* derives from an Egyptian verb, "to go, travel; traverse," and as a noun here is a general term with no ethnic value, like English "bedouin," or "traveling folk"; cf. the word in A. Erman and H. Grapow, eds., *Wörterbuch der Aegyptischen Sprache* IV (Leipzig: Hinrichs, 1930), 412:3-9, and hence 10-11. Most of the data on the Shasu is collected by R. Giveon, *Les Bédouins Shosu des documents égyptiens* (Leiden: Brill, 1971); his acceptance of the supposed Semitic origin of the term is eliminated by the fact that West Semitic *samekh* (as in *shasa*, "to plunder," an unsuitable meaning) would only go into Egyptian as *tj*, not as an *s*.

The Edomites, as pastoral, wandering folk, were well classified by the Egyptians as part of the Shasu; Israel from Succoth to Sinai, and from Sinai to Qadesh-Barnea and the plains of Moab, could also have been thus classified during their wanderings — but *not* once they had crossed the Jordan and begun to settle down in highland Canaan.

171. For the Ammonites, see MacDonald and Younker, *Ancient Ammon*, and MacDonald, *East of the Jordan*, 157-70.

172. On Uni of Egypt, cf. Wilson in *ANET*, 227-29.

173. For texts of Shalmaneser III, see A. K. Grayson, *RIMA*, 3:7-11 (no. 1, slab of 857/856), 11-24 (no. 2, Kurkh stela, 853/852), 32-41 (no. 6, annals of 842). On this reign, cf. also S. Yamada, *The Construction of the Assyrian Empire* (Leiden: Brill, 2000).

NOTES TO CHAPTER 6

1. For illustrations of the flattened devastation of Delta sites, see (e.g.) J. Baines and J. Malek, *Atlas of Ancient Egypt* (Oxford: Phaidon; New York: Facts on File, 1980), 166, 170, and (for Tell el-Dab'a/Pi-Ramesse) especially M. Bietak, *Tell el-Dab'a II* (Vienna: Austrian Academy, 1975), pls. I-XXVI, passim (some in color).

2. For a survey and running documentation for most Egyptian brick-making accounts in the Old, Middle, and New Kingdoms, see Kitchen, *TynB* 27 (1976): 137-47.

3. On the famous scene of foreign slaves as brick makers, in the tomb chapel of Rekhmire, full bibliography is in PM, I:1 (Oxford: OUP, 1960), 211-12; the official publication is: N. de G. Davies, *The Tomb of Rekhmire at Thebes* I, II (New York: Metropolitan Museum of Art, 1943; reprint, Arno Press, 1973), 54-60, pls. 58-60; in color, Davies, *Paintings from the Tomb of Rekhmire* (New York: Metropolitan Museum of Art, 1935), pls. 16-17. There are many popular reproductions, e.g., J. K. Hoffmeier, *Israel in Egypt* (New York: OUP, 1997), figs. 8-9; part in color, cf. Ian Wilson, *The Bible Is History* (London: Weidenfeld & Nicholson, 1999), 52. To see the same techniques used in Egypt now, in color, cf. A. R. Millard, *Discoveries from Bible Times* (Oxford: Lion Publishing, 1997), 75.

4. For the Louvre leather roll, see Kitchen, *RITA* II (1996), 520-22, cols. II-IV. The people "making their quota of bricks daily" (Papyrus Anastasi III) quote is in R. A. Caminos, trans., *Late-Egyptian Miscellanies* (Oxford: OUP, 1954), 105-6.

5. On lack of straw, Papyrus Anastasi IV (and V), in Caminos, *Late-Egyptian Miscellanies,* 188-89, 225. Bricks and straw: C. F. Nims, *BA* 13 (1950): 24-28; cf. A. E. Lucas, *Ancient Egyptian Materials and Industries,* ed. J. R. Harris, 4th ed. (London: Arnold, 1962), 48-50.

6. On two levels of oversight, cf. Kitchen, *TynB* 27 (1976): 144-45, and references.

7. The Apiru dragging stones are cited from Papyrus Leiden 348 and in Caminos, *Late-Egyptian Miscellanies,* 491.

8. Setau raid is cited in Kitchen, *Pharaoh Triumphant: Life and Times of Ramesses II* (Warminster: Aris & Phillips, 1982), 138, or *RITA* III (2000), 66.

9. People beaten, in Papyrus Bologna 1094, 3:1-4, see Caminos, *Late-Egyptian Miscellanies,* 12. On Syrian slave conscripted (in Year 3 of Merenptah, 1211), cf. Papyrus Bologna 1086; trans. E. F. Wente, *Letters from Ancient Egypt,* Writings from the Ancient World 1 (Atlanta: SBL, 1990), 124-26, no. 147.

10. For holidays, etc., off work at Deir el-Medina, see (e.g.) Ostracon BM 5634, Year 40 of Ramesses II, for fifty individuals, including "offering to (his) god," translated in Kitchen, *RITA* III (2000), 361-68 (offering to deity, pp. 361, 363-64, 367). For the example of a feast of "St. Amenophis I," celebrated by the whole workforce with four days of eating and drinking, see Ostracon Cairo CGC 25,234, trans. (in English) A. I. Sadek, *Popular Religion in Egypt during the New Kingdom,* Hildesheimer Ägyptologische Beiträge 27 (Hildesheim: Gerstenberg Verlag, 1987), 178.

11. On "freezing" cobras into sticks, cf. L. Keimer, *Histoires de serpentes dans l'Égypte ancienne et moderne,* Mémoires 50 (Cairo: Institut d'Égypte, 1947), 16-17, with figs. 14-21.

12. See studies by Greta Hort, in *ZAW,* n.s., 69, no. 28 (1957): 84-103, hereafter Hort I in the text, and *ZAW,* n.s., 70, no. 29 (1958): 48-59, hereafter Hort II in the text. She made use of expert advice on natural science aspects.

13. For high Nile floods of Sobekhotep VIII, cf. J. Baines, *AcOr* 37 (1976): 11-20 (completing and correcting Baines, *AcOr* 36 [1974]: 39-54). On Osorkon III at Luxor, cf. Breasted, *ARE* IV (1906), 369, §§742-743 (wrongly called Osorkon II), and cf. in the same work the text of

Smendes I (ca. 1070-1044), 308-9, §§627-30. On Taharqa, Year 6 (685), translation, L. Török, in T. Eide et al., eds., *Fontes Historiae Nubiorum* I (Bergen: University [Dept. of Classics], 1994), 145-58 (esp. 150-53). For *Admonitions of an Egyptian Sage* 2.10, cf. (e.g.) translations by M. Lichtheim in *Ancient Egyptian Literature* 1 (Berkeley: University of California Press, 1973), 151, or R. O. Faulkner, in W. K. Simpson, ed., *The Literature of Ancient Egypt*, 2nd ed. (New Haven: Yale University Press, 1973), 212.

14. On the "theological critique" or polemic against the Egyptian gods, cf. discussions by (e.g.) J. K. Hoffmeier, in *ABD*, 2:376-77 (within 374-78), and his *Israel in Egypt*, 149-55, and also J. D. Currid, *Ancient Egypt and the Old Testament* (Grand Rapids: Baker, 1997), 104-20.

15. See studies on the "strong arm" idiom by J. K. Hoffmeier, *Bib* 67 (1986): 378-87; and M. Görg, in *Hommages à François Daumas* I (Montpellier: Université Paul Valéry, 1986), 323-30.

16. On the exodus and its background in brief, see already Kitchen in *ABD*, 2:700-708, and extended treatment of several aspects, in S. Ahituv and E. D. Oren, eds., *The Origin of Early Israel — Current Debate, Biblical, Historical, and Archaeological Perspectives*, Beer-Sheva XII (Beer-Sheva: Ben-Gurion University of the Negev Press; London: University College London [and others], 1998), 65-131.

17. For the emigration from Mari, cf. V. H. Matthews, *Pastoral Nomadism in the Mari Kingdom (c. 1830-1760 BC)*, ASOR (1978), 157-58.

18. On emigrants from Hatti to Isuwa (and back), see G. Beckman, *Hittite Diplomatic Texts*, SBL: Writings from the Ancient World 7 (Atlanta: Scholars Press, 1996), 38-39.

19. For Libyan attempts on Egypt, summary and sources, see Kitchen, in A. Leahy, ed., *Libya and Egypt, c. 1300-750 BC* (London: SOAS and Society of Libyan Studies, 1990), 15-27.

20. For Sea Peoples and east Mediterranean movements, see the collective discussions, generally in S. Gitin, A. Mazar, and E. Stern, eds., *Mediterranean Peoples in Transition* (Jerusalem: IES, 1998); and specifically in E. D. Oren, ed., *The Sea Peoples and Their World: A Reassessment* (Philadelphia: University of Pennsylvania Museum, 2000).

21. On early Arameans, etc., cf. A. R. Millard, in *ABD*, 1:345-50 (esp. 348), with references.

22. On the Nubians, cf. W. Y. Adams, *Nubia, Corridor to Africa* (London: Allen Lane, 1977), 235-45; nuanced by L. Török, *The Kingdom of Kush, Handbook of the Napatan-Meroitic Civilization*, Handbuch der Orientalistik I/31 (Leiden: Brill, 1997), 84-85, 110.

23. On the name Raamses (contra eccentricities of Goedicke, Redford, etc.), see Hoffmeier, *Israel in Egypt*, 117-18; and Kitchen, in Ahituv and Oren, *Origin of Early Israel*, 69-71. The muddled treatment (*VT* 13 [1963]: 408-18) by Redford on Raamses and its vocalization, and confusing the sibilants between Hebrew and Egyptian, was thoroughly refuted by W. Helck, *VT* 15 (1965): 43-46, and also dismissed as "really untenable" by E. P. Uphill, *The Temples of Per-Ramesses* (Warminster: Aris & Phillips, 1984), 3. The omission of "Pi-" before "Raamses," objected to by Redford, has been long since dealt with by Gardiner (*JEA* 5 [1918]: 179-80, no. 2, cf. 137-38) and Helck (*VT* 15 [1965]: 41-42, Piay, "sculptor of Ramesse"; and in his *Materialien zur Wirtschaftsgeschichte des Neuen Reichs* II [Wiesbaden: Steiner Verlag, 1962], 208).

24. On the vast extent of ancient Pi-Ramesse, see Bietak, *Tell el-Dab'a II*, 204-5, §B/13. Rough city plans were first published by Bietak, Abb. 44, opposite p. 212, and (sketchier, originally made in 1974) by Kitchen, *Pharaoh Triumphant*, 123, fig. 42. For more sophisticated plans (based on close surveys), see J. Dorner, *Ägypten und Levante* 9 (1999): 77-83, with plans 1 and 2 at end of volume. For a discussion of the main buildings, see Kitchen, *RITANC* II (1999), 318-21.

25. Information on the floor full of gold dust comes from a kind communication by Prof. Pusch, 18 July 2001, correcting reports, *Ägypten und Levante* 9 (1999): 121-33, with Abb. 3, 5 (in color), and briefly in *Egyptian Archaeology* 12 (1998): 10; and 14 (1999), 30 (Qantir).

26. On chariotry, cf. briefly E. Pusch, in R. Freed, ed., *Fragments of a Shattered Visage . . . Symposium, Ramesses the Great* (Memphis, Tenn.: Memphis State University Press, 1991), 199-200, 202-5 (with *Ägypten und Levante* 9 [1999]: 39-40 on dating).

27. For magnetometer surveys with vivid plans, see Pusch et al., in *Ägypten und Levante* 9 (1999): 135-70, with figures.

28. On the *miskenoth,* cf. Kitchen, in Ahituv and Oren, *Origin of Early Israel,* 67-68.

29. On the palace tiles and Sethos I references, see PM, IV, 9; M. Hamza, *ASAE* 30 (1930): 40-41, fig. 3 and (in Louvre) pl. III:D.

30. On Ramesses VIII and Avaris, Tel Miqne fragment, kind courtesy of Prof. Trude Dothan. Note that the supposed other mentions of Ramesses VIII and X at Pi-Ramesse are spurious. The stamp attributed to Ramesses VIII by Hamza (*ASAE* 30 [1930]: 60, fig. 15:11) actually belongs to a statue cult of Ramesses II "Beneficial to Seth," while that taken as resembling Ramesses X (fig. 15:12) is actually of Sethos II and Queen Tewosret! This rules out contrary statements by Hayes and others based on Hamza.

31. Errors by N. P. Lemche on Raamses are in *SJOT* 8, no. 2 (1994): 172-74. His statement that Exod. 1:11 has Pithom and Raamses equal in size is *not* implied in that verse, and is massively contradicted by the original sites (Pi-Ramesse is vast; Pithom is quite modest).

32. The late cults at Bubastis are discussed in E. Naville, *Bubastis* (London: EEF, 1891), 57, pl. 46:B.

33. On Tanis, cf. Bietak, *Tell el-Dab'a II,* 219, 212 n. 902, and references.

34. Early publications on the sites of Tell er-Retaba and Tell el-Maskhuta are listed in PM, IV, 55, 53-55. Main work at Tell er-Retaba was by W. M. F. Petrie, *Hyksos and Israelite Cities* (London: BSAE, 1906), 28-34, pls. 28-36C; more recent work under H. Goedicke is still unpublished; cf. Hoffmeier, *Israel in Egypt,* 120 and n. 135.

35. For early work (including Paponot) at Tell el-Maskhuta, see E. Naville, *The Store-City of Pithom and the Route of the Exodus,* 4th ed. (London: EEF, 1903). Much destruction of ancient remains has occurred in Wadi Tumilat from the building of the Suez Canal (1859-69) and since; e.g., despoliation of Tell el-Maskhuta in the 1930s (cf. P. Montet, *Géographie de l'Égypte ancienne* I [Paris: Imprimerie Nationale/Klincksieck, 1957], 214); and most Ramesside monuments found at and in Tell el-Maskhuta were removed to Ismailia at various times. The Canadian expedition failed to find anything Ramesside there because most of it had already been destroyed or removed, they did not work extensively enough, and they have consistently refused to pay sufficiently serious attention to results of previous work done there. The inadequate entries on "Pithom" by D. B. Redford, *LdA* IV/7 (1982), 1054-58, and by J. S. Holladay, *Oxford Encyclopedia of Archaeology in the Near East* 3 (New York: OUP, 1997), 432-37, and in Oxford's *Encyclopedia of Ancient Egypt* 3 (New York: OUP, 2000), 53-55, totally ignore the firsthand Ramesside literary and other monumental evidence (e.g., the Merenptah statue, Roman milestone, etc.) given here. The blunder of dating Tell el-Maskhuta to Necho II onward is repeated by Lemche and Dever, *BAR* 23, no. 4 (July-August 1997): 29, who are unaware of the full facts.

36. For ODM 1076, and the papyri, see full discussion, Kitchen in Ahituv and Oren, *Origin of Early Israel,* 72-78; and observations by M. Bietak, in A. F. Rainey, ed., *Egypt, Israel, Sinai* (Tel Aviv: University Press, 1987), 168-69, on Tell er-Retaba. For further discussion of data from Tells er-Retaba and el-Maskhuta based on Ramesside material, see Kitchen, *RITANC* II, 265-70, with the translations in *RITA* II, 230-31.

37. The best recent survey of the latest data on this region is the extended treatment by Hoffmeier, *Israel in Egypt,* chaps. 7–9, pp. 164-222.

38. On the question of water connections between the Bitter Lakes and the head of the

Gulf of Suez, see discussion, authorities, and references in Hoffmeier, *Israel in Egypt*, 207-9, and notes.

39. On the ancient canals, see Hoffmeier, *Israel in Egypt*, 164-75, and especially A. Sneh and T. Weissbrod, *Science* 180 (1973): 59-61; A. Sneh et al., *American Scientist* 63 (1975): 542-48.

40. On the Pelusiac branch of the Nile, cf. B. Marcolongo, *CRIPEL* 14 (1992): 23-31. Cf. maps in Hoffmeier, *Israel in Egypt*, figs. 2, 17, 22; pictures of canals, figs. 18-20.

41. For discussion of the range of locations of Pi-Hahiroth, Migdol, and Baal-Zephon, see conveniently Hoffmeier, *Israel in Egypt*, 169-71 (Pi-Hahiroth), 189-91 (Migdol, Baal-Zephon), with references. It seems very unlikely that the later site of Tell Defenneh can be the Baal-Zephon of Exodus, as it is much too far to the northwest (nearly twenty miles!) to be a reasonably close marker for the small cluster of sites in Exod. 14:1-2.

42. The theory of the "End" sea was published by F. Batto, *JBL* 102 (1983): 27-35; and in *BAR* 10, no. 4 (July-August 1984): 56-63. For a review and thorough refutation of it, see Hoffmeier, *Israel in Egypt*, 199-222, passim.

43. For halophytes (salt-water-friendly reeds), cf. Hoffmeier, *Israel in Egypt*, 209.

44. On the meaning and relationship of Egyptian *tjuf* and Hebrew *suph*, see the indispensable study by W. A. Ward, *VT* 24 (1974): 339-49.

45. On the fallacy of historization of myth versus the mythical expression of history, cf. long ago Kitchen, *Ancient Orient and Old Testament* (1966; reprint, 2000), 89 and n. 7.

46. Two other points on the crossing deserve mention. First, the ability of Delta winds to move water ("a strong east wind," Exod. 14:21) is independently attested down to modern times. The Egyptian engineer Aly Bey Shafei experienced just such a phenomenon, when his automobile (modern chariot!) got trapped by the return of the waters, when the wind changed round after driving them away; cf. Aly Bei Shafei, *Bulletin de la Société Royale de Géographie d'Égypte* 21 (1946): 231-87 (with photos).

Second, the 600 Egyptian chariots (and support force) of Exod. 14:7 are a decent-sized squadron — but by no means extraordinary. In the fifteenth century Tuthmosis III captured 924 Canaanite chariots on his first campaign (ca. 1458; *ANET*, 237); Amenophis II captured 730 and 1,092 (60 + 1,032) chariots respectively on his official first and second campaigns (ca. 1421, 1419; *ANET*, 246-47). In the thirteenth century the Hittites reputedly fielded 2,500 chariots against Ramesses II at the Battle of Qadesh (1275; cf. Kitchen, *RITA* II [1996], 5, 7, 20; *CoS* II, 34-35, and one reference omitted), and Ramesses II probably fielded 2,000 chariots (cf. Kitchen, *RITANC* II [1999], 40). Also, as the Assyrians tell us, Ahab of Israel was apparently able to field 2,000 chariots at the Battle of Qarqar in 853 (cf. *ANET*, 279 top; *CoS* II, 263), more than thrice as many as the pharaoh of the exodus!

47. The Strasbourg ostracon was briefly noted by H. Cazelles in D. J. Wiseman, ed., *Peoples of Old Testament Times* (Oxford: OUP, 1973), who printed a facsimile and hieroglyphic transcript given him by Posener, though without translation. Its attribution to work at Pi-Ramesse was a slip of the pen by A. Malamat, in E. S. Frerichs and L. H. Lesko, eds., *Exodus, the Egyptian Evidence* (Winona Lake, Ind.: Eisenbrauns, 1997), 18. The surviving text in translation runs:

(1) 2nd month of season Akhet, Day 13: Collecting together stone blocks done by the Apiru-[men . . .]:

(2) Right (side). Received: 4 blocks; 10 decorated blocks; [4] coping-stones(?); [. . .]

(3) 2 brick-blocks; total, 20. The army-men of the Right (side): [. . .];

(4) 10 decorated blocks; 4 coping-stones(?); [2] brick-blocks; [. . .]."

A full treatment will appear later.

48. As for Nebre, see translations (e.g.) by Wilson in *ANET*, 380-81; with notes, Kitchen, *Poetry of Ancient Egypt* (Jonsered: P. Aström's förlag, 1999), 285-90. On Qen's stela, see J. J. Clère, *RdÉ* 27 (1975): 72-77 (esp. 76-77).

49. Stela of Setnakht is cited by Malamat, in Frerichs and Lesko, *Exodus, the Egyptian Evidence*, 22-23; for new edition of Setnakht's stela, see S. J. Seidlmayer, in H. Guksch and D. Polz, eds., *Stationen*, Festschrift for R. Stadelmann (Mainz: Ph. von Zabern, 1998), 363-86, pls. 20-21, Beilage 3a, esp. 375ff. (translation and notes).

50. In Assyrian and West Semitic, analogous multiplicity of meaning occurs with the *limmu* (eponym official) and *limu* (thousand) in Assyrian, plus Ugaritic and Hebrew *l'm*, with shifts between the meanings "people(-group)," "thousand," and "leader of a thousand," as is pointed out by A. R. Millard, *The Eponyms of the Assyrian Empire, 910-612 BC* (Helsinki, 1994), 9.

51. The detailed studies cited in the above paragraphs are: W. M. F. Petrie, *Researches in Sinai* (London: Murray, 1906), 207-21; G. E. Mendenhall, *JBL* 77 (1958): 52-66; R. E. D. Clark, *JTVI* 87 (1955): 82-92; J. W. Wenham, *TynB* 18 (1967): 19-53, esp. 27-33, 35-39; Sarna on Petrie, Mendenhall, etc., cf. N. M. Sarna, *Exploring Exodus* (New York: Schocken Books, 1987), 94-102; C. J. Humphreys, *VT* 48 (1998): 196-213, and then (in reply to J. Milgrom, *VT* 49 [1999]: 131-32; M. McEntire, *VT* 49 [1999]: 262-64) *VT* 50 (2000): 323-28.

The figures in Exod. 38:25-26 are often thought to enforce a conventional interpretation of 603,550 people. Superficially, the 100 talents (= 300,000 shekels) plus 1,775 shekels of silver represent ½ shekel (1 beqa) each from 603,550 men. However, the wider context needs to be borne in mind; it was *not* exclusively the men of the squads that contributed to the cost of the tabernacle but the entire Israelite community, as is explicitly stated in Exod. 35:4f. and 20ff. Seen in this light, Exod. 38:25-26 bears further examination. We have a division between 100 talents (one sum) and 1,775 shekels (another sum). If the number "603,550" men is divided back into 600 squads (*'eleph*) plus 3,550 men (three thousand, *'eleph*, 550 men), then the 1,775 shekels is clearly the personal ½ shekel (beqa) paid — as is said — by the men counted by census, 3,550 in number. But the 100 talents between 600 squads would divide up very neatly as 10 minas (500 shekels) per squad (60 minas to a talent). So 9 to 10 members of a squad would collectively pay in 50 shekels each (or just over), *drawn from their families and tribes, not just themselves* (as per Exod. 35). However, there were actually just 598 squads (2 short of 600), which would leave 2 × 10 = 20 minas (or 1,000 shekels) short of the 100 talents. But as there were 5,550 men (not just 3,550), the extra 2,000 men (at ½ shekel each) fills the gap at 1,000 shekels = 20 minas to make up the full 100 talents. Thus the figures in Exod. 38:25-26 do not seem to exclude the solutions proposed by Mendenhall, Humphreys, etc., for the numbers and organization of Israel leaving Egypt.

52. The northern option was advocated by O. Eissfeldt, *Baal Zephon, Zeus Kasios und der Durchzug der Israeliten durchs Meer* (Halle: Niemeyer, 1932). For a recent refutation of it, using the latest archaeological data from the northeast Delta and coastal road, see Hoffmeier, *Israel in Egypt*, 183-87, with references.

53. The Sethos I reliefs were republished definitively (with translation) in the Epigraphic Survey, *The Battle Reliefs of King Sety I*, Reliefs and Inscriptions at Karnak IV (Chicago: OIC, 1986), 3-22, pls. 3-7; handbook ed., translations and commentary, also *RITA* I (1993), 6-9, with *RITANC* I (1993), 10-17. On the road from Egypt to Canaan, cf. also A. H. Gardiner, *JEA* 6 (1920): 99-116, pls. 11-13.

54. Handy translation of Papyrus Anastasi I, 27:2–28:1, by J. A. Wilson, in *ANET*, 478.

55. For archaeology of the coast road settlements, Nineteenth and Twentieth Dynasties,

see E. D. Oren, in Rainey, *Egypt, Israel, Sinai*, 69-119 (esp. 77-97), for good summary and references.

56. For Deir el-Balah, likewise T. Dothan in Rainey, *Egypt, Israel, Sinai*, 121-35 (esp. 128-33).

57. On Baal Zephon not being at Ras Kasrun ("Casios") or Lake Serbonis not being there in the second millennium, cf. G. I. Davies, *VTS* 41 (1990): 161-75. For Baal Zephon at Memphis, see Papyrus Sallier IV, Verso, 1:6, text in Gardiner, *Late-Egyptian Miscellanies* (Brussels: FERE, 1937), 89:7, and translated by Caminos, *Late-Egyptian Miscellanies*, 333, 338, with references.

58. Both descriptions are from I. Beit-Arieh. The first is from *BAR* 10, no. 4 (July-August 1984): 31, and the second, *BAR* 14, no. 3 (May-June 1988): 35.

59. M. Bietak, in Rainey, *Egypt, Israel, Sinai*, 170.

60. Egyptians in west Sinai in late autumn-winter, not spring-summer, cf. date line of Year 8 text of Sethos I (ca. 1287 or 1283) in Sinai, in 1st Peret day 2, which was about early November, in the cool season; translation and notes, *RITA* I, 53-54, no. 28; *RITANC* I, 58.

61. For the references to watering places between Suez and El-Markh, see tab. 20.

62. Robinson, Lepsius, and Petrie were all first-class early observers of the topography and conditions of western Sinai before modern developments. In full, their works are: E. Robinson, *Biblical Researches in Palestine, Mount Sinai and Arabia Petraea, A Journal of Travels in the Year 1838* I (London: Murray, 1841), with old-style but excellent map of Sinai; [C.] R. Lepsius, *Letters from Egypt, Ethiopia, and the Peninsula of Sinai* (London: Bohn, 1853); W. M. Flinders Petrie, with C. T. Currelly, *Researches in Sinai* (London: Murray, 1906). The case for Gebel Serbal was eloquently argued by Lepsius and Currelly (in Petrie), and that for Gebel Musa by Robinson; a list of these and other candidates (with brief references) is given by I. Beit-Arieh, *BAR* 14, no. 3 (May-June 1988): 36-37. It is very likely that (with a northerly Marah near Suez) the Hebrews stopped for camp and water at other places between Ain Naba and Wadi Gharandel (Elim?); but they do not appear in the record simply because they were nameless, unremarkable overnight stops, and nothing of note happened there (by contrast with Marah).

63. It is instructive to note variations in the state of such places at different dates in the reports cited above. It may also be useful to refer to illustrations of a variety of places here discussed or mentioned, mainly in color, but older ones (like Petrie or Rothenberg) in black and white. The publications (and their abbreviations) cited in the list of illustrations that follows are:

PS = W. M. F. Petrie, *Researches in Sinai* (London: Murray, 1906), monochrome plates.

RTH = B. Rothenberg et al., *God's Wilderness* (London: Thames & Hudson, 1961), monochrome plates.

RFr = B. Rothenberg et al., *Le Sinaï* (Paris: Kümmerley & Frey, 1979), color plates.

BAR-84 = I. Beit-Arieh, *BAR* 10, no. 4 (July-August 1984): 26-54, color plates.

BAR-85 = A. Perevolotsky and I. Finkelstein, *BAR* 11, no. 4 (July-August 1985): 26-41, color.

BAR-88 = I. Beit-Arieh, *BAR* 14, no. 3 (May-June 1988): 28-37, color.

Siliotti = A. Siliotti, *Guide to the Exploration of the Sinai* (Shrewsbury: Swan Hill Press, 1994), color shots, etc., often small, but clear.

Sinai Eg. = G. L. Steen, A. J. De Nigro, and M. Saad El-Din, eds., *Sinai, the Site and the History* (New York: New York University Press, 1998), color plates.

Meshel = Z. Meshel, *Sinai, Excavations and Studies*, BAR International Series 876 (Oxford: Archaeopress, 2000), studies and excavations; monochrome illustrations.

1. *Lake Serbonis (Sebkhat Bardawil). RFr,* pl. 1.
2. *Mediterranean Coastal Zone. RTH,* pl. 1; *RFr,* pls. 2-3.
3. *Gebel Halal, in northeast, west of Qossaima. RFr,* pl. 32.
4. *Qadesh-Barnea (Ain Qudeirat). RTH,* pls. 10-11; *RFr,* pls. 35-38; *BAR-88,* 30.
5. *Et-Tih limestone plateau. RTH,* pl. 27; *RFr,* pls. 40-41; *BAR-84,* 30.
6. *Ayun Musa. Siliotti,* 27 top. *Gebel Sinn Bishar (Taset-Sudr). RFr,* pl. 33.
7. *Ain Hawara(h). RTH,* pl. 33.
8. *Wadi Gharandel, on west coast. PS,* figs. 2-5; nearby, *Sinai Eg.,* 52-53.
9. *Wadi Wasit. PS,* figs. 9-10.
10. *Wadi Taiyibeh, cliffs. PS,* fig. 11.
11. *El-Markh, bay and tell.* Y. Aharoni, in *The Holy Land/Antiquity and Survival* II, no. 2/3 (1957), 287 and fig. 4; *RTH,* pl. 34.
12. *El-Kaa, coastal plain (Wilderness of Sin). RTH,* pl. 37.
13. *Wadi Mukattab (just before Wadi Feiran). RFr,* pl. 53.
14. *Wadi Feiran. PS,* figs. 180-83; *RTH,* pls. 54-55; *RFr,* pls. 83-84; *BAR-88,* 34; *Siliotti,* 39; *Meshel,* 147, fig. 7; 157, fig. 6.
15. *Gebel Serbal. RTH,* pl. 57; *RFr,* pl. 50; *BAR-85,* 38; *BAR-88,* 32, 34; *Meshel,* 156, fig. 3.
16. *Gebel Musa, Gebel Katrin, er-Raha. RTH,* pl. 49 (Ras Safsafa by Gebel Musa; ditto, and er-Raha plain, *BAR-85,* 36/37); Gebel Musa, view from summit, *RTH,* pl. 53; *RFr,* pl. 100; *BAR-84,* 50/51; *BAR-85,* 30-31, 26/27 = *BAR-88,* 28-29, *Siliotti,* 141-42. Gebel Katrin and Wadi es-Sheikh (>NE), *BAR-85,* 40/41; G. Musa and er-Raha plain, *BAR-84,* 26/27; *Siliotti,* 147 bottom; in part, C. Masom, P. Alexander, and A. R. Millard, *Picture Archive of the Bible* (Tring: Lion, 1987), 34-35. Near route from east, *Sinai Eg.,* 12-13; flanks, 78-79. Various views, *Siliotti,* 11, 121-23, 136, 138, 145, 150-51.
17. *Dhahab (Di-Zahab?).* Aharoni (cf. no. 11, above), 290 and fig. 7; *Siliotti,* 12 center, 87, 91; a nearby wadi, *Sinai Eg.,* 48-49.
18. *Ain Hudhera (Hazeroth). RFr,* pls. 72, 75, and esp. 78.
19a. *Geziret Faraun (at Ezion-Geber). RTH,* pls. 40, 43, 46 (view and oldest traces); *RFr,* pl. 71; cf. A. Flinder, *Secrets of the Bible Seas* (London: Severn House, 1985), pls. [2]-[5]; views and map, *Siliotti,* 102-3.
19b. *Taba, southwest of Eilat. Sinai Eg.,* 134-35.
20. *Sinai: Aerial/Satellite Views.* All, west to east, Egyptian East Delta, northeast desert, Sinai, and south Canaan and Transjordan, *Siliotti,* 4-5. Overall from south, *RFr,* pl. 113 = *BAR-84,* 56; *Siliotti,* 6. East Delta, north Sinai coast, Tih plateau, Masom, Alexander, Millard, *Picture Archive of the Bible* (no. 16 above), 23; scrubland, *Siliotti,* 23.

64. For Di-Zahab and Hazeroth, see nos. 17, 18, just above.

65. Cf. C. S. Jarvis, *Yesterday and Today in Sinai* (Edinburgh and London: Blackwood, 1931), 174-75; 3rd ed. (1936), 156.

66. On the quails, cf. A. E. Lucas, *The Route of the Exodus* (1938), 58-63 and references, 81 (but overstressing Aqaba gulf at the expense of the Suez gulf). On wadi ecology, see *Sinai Eg.,* 56-57, 61.

67. Probably of the Midianites, the Qurayya pottery is attested at the northeast edges of Sinai, at Timna and fleetingly at Elath (Tell el-Kheleifeh), as well as from Geziret el-Faraun island and other sites; also at Bir el-Abd along the Mediterranean coast road, but not otherwise in Sinai proper; cf. (e.g.) B. Rothenberg and J. Glass, in J. F. A. Sawyer and D. J. A. Clines, eds., *Midian, Moab, and Edom* (Sheffield: JSOT Press, 1983), 65-124, passim, with map p. 70; on

Qurraya ware and its dating, see P. J. Parr, *SHAJ* 1 (1982): 127-30; in D. T. Potts, ed., *Araby the Blest: Studies in Arabian Archaeology* (Copenhagen: Museum Tusculanum Press, 1988), 72-89; and in *Arabian Archaeology and Epigraphy* 4 (1993): 48-58.

68. Source for the tabernacle is Exod. 26–27; 36; 38–40. For most of the data for this whole topic, see Kitchen, *EI* 24 (1993): 119*-128*; more popular, with color illustrations, is Kitchen, *BR* 16, no. 6 (December 2000): 14-21, and in the same issue, M. M. Homan, 22-33, 55.

69. The tabernacle of Queen Hetepheres was published by G. A. Reisner and W. S. Smith, *A History of the Giza Necropolis II: The Tomb of Hetep-heres* (Cambridge: Harvard University Press, 1955); a handy photo is in Kitchen, *BR* 16, no. 6 (December 2000): 18.

70. For Saqqara fragments, see W. B. Emery, *Great Tombs of the First Dynasty* I (Cairo: Government Press, 1949), 58, fig. 30. For early tomb scenes, and Step Pyramid and Hetepheres fragments, see references in Reisner and Smith, *The Tomb of Hetep-heres,* 14 (and pl. 3); picture and hieroglyph in A. M. Blackman, *The Rock Tombs of Meir* V (London: EES, 1952), pls. 42-43. For "Tent of Purification," cf. É. Drioton, *ASAE* 40 (1940): 1008 (on Grdseloff).

71. See D. E. Fleming, *VT* 50 (2000): 484-98, with full references.

72. The text for El in the pavilion is in *CTA* and *KTU,* no. 4, iv:20-24, translations in *ANET,* 133, or *CoS* I, 259; cf. Fleming, *VT* 50 (2000): 492.

73. For Keret see *Keret A,* iii (edge), 159; translation in *ANET,* 144; *CoS* I, 335; the "gods go to their tents" is in *Keret B,* iii:18-19, translation in *ANET,* 146; *CoS* I, 338.

74. The Kothar/Hayyin reference is in *Aqhat A,* v:32-33, translation in *ANET,* 151; *CoS* I, 346.

75. For Egyptian gods in tents, see *ANET,* 15.

76. For the canopy in Ashur, see reconstruction in W. Andrae, *Das wiedererstandene Assur,* ed. B. Hrouda, 2nd ed. (Munich: Beck, 1977), 154, 156, Abb. 134.

77. On the harem decree, standard under the canopy, cf. E. F. Weidner, *AfO* 17 (1956): 277, §9, 53; M. T. Roth, *Law Collections from Mesopotamia and Asia Minor* (Atlanta: Scholars Press, 1995), 201.

78. For views of the Tuthmosis III hall, see (e.g.) H. Lange and M. Hirmer, *Egypt: Architecture, Sculpture, Painting,* 3rd ed. (London: Phaidon Press, 1961), pls. 137-39.

79. On the golden tomb shrines of Tutankhamun, see (e.g.) C. Desroches-Noblecourt, *Tutankhamen* (London: Michael Joseph, 1963), 260-65, figs. 165-68, 170-71, and detail in color, pl. XXVII. For a picture, with cutaway view, and frame with pall, cf. Kitchen, *BR* 16, no. 6 (December 2000): 16-17.

80. For Ramesses II and III, see Kitchen, *EI* 24 (1993): 121*-123*; M. M. Homan, *BR* 16, no. 6 (December 2000): 22-33, 55 (Ramesses II only).

81. Sahure's sail is conveniently in W. S. Smith, *Interconnections in the Ancient Near East* (New Haven: Yale University Press, 1965), fig. 188.

82. On the New Kingdom boat and sail, see A. Lhote and Hassia, *Les chefs-d'oeuvre de la peinture égyptienne* (Paris: Hachette, 1954), 49, pl. XVIII.

83. On the Theban tomb (217) of Ipuy, see Kitchen, *BR* 16, no. 6 (December 2000): 21; for other references, see B. Porter and R. L. B. Moss, *Topographical Bibliography, Ancient Egyptian Hieroglyphic Texts . . . ,* 2nd ed., I:1 (Oxford: OUP, 1960), 316, (6)/III.

84. On Anubis, see Kitchen, *BR* 16, no. 6 (December 2000): 19.

85. The painted leather catafalque of Istemkheb was originally published by E. Brugsch Bey, *La tente funéraire de la princesse Isimkheb* (Cairo, 1889); for other references, see Porter and Moss, *Topographical Bibliography, Ancient Egyptian Hieroglyphic Texts . . . ,* I:2 (Oxford: OUP, 1964), 664, no. 7. For an attractive theory that the *tahash* leather covering was beaded with blue

Egyptian faience (rather than made of dugong, or other sea creatures), see S. Dalley, *JSS* 45 (2000): 1-19; this might define *tahash* but leaves the leather unaccounted for. That dugong has been known and used in Sinai is attested down to last century; see Petrie and Currelly, in Petrie, *Researches in Sinai*, 235 top, 264 end (miswritten as "dudong"). For references for early use of dugong on the other side of Arabia (ca. 4700-2000), see Kitchen, *EI* 24 (1993): 127* n. 20.

86. For an early preliminary report on the Midianite tabernacle, see B. Rothenberg, *Timna, Valley of the Biblical Copper Mines* (London: Thames & Hudson, 1972), 150ff. and fig. 44 (= also in *BR* 16, no. 6 [December 2000]: 20); for a full report, corrected, see B. Rothenberg et al., *The Egyptian Mining Temple at Timna* (London: Institute of Archaeology, UCL, 1988), esp. (in summary) 272, 276-78.

87. For the tabernacle compared with other temples, see Kitchen, *EI* 24 (1993): 122*-123*, with fig. 4.

88. For *'agalat,* see A. J. Peden, *CdÉ* 71 (1996): 48-51.

89. For modern translations of the Ramesses IV texts, see A. J. Peden, *The Reign of Ramesses IV* (Warminster: Aris & Phillips, 1994), 82, 89, or his *Egyptian Historical Inscriptions of the Twentieth Dynasty,* Documenta Mundi: Aegyptiaca 3 (Jonsered: P. Aströms förlag, 1994), 69-72, 97.

90. For data and references for the ark of the covenant and trumpets (illustrated), see Kitchen, *EI* 24 (1993): 124*-125* and nn. 37-49, and 121*, fig. 3, for a closely similar "ark" of sacred lettuces being carried behind the image of Min, on poles.

91. On the lampstand as LB in design, see C. L. Meyers, *The Tabernacle Menorah* (Missoula: Scholars Press, 1976), 39. For other factors concerning antiquity, cf. (e.g.) J. Milgrom, *Leviticus 1–16,* AB 3 (New York: Doubleday, 1991), 10-12, 30.

92. On two levels of complementary temple staff, see J. Milgrom, *JAOS* 90 (1970): 204-9.

93. For the Egyptian references, cf. Kitchen, *EI* 24 (1993): 124* and nn. 35-36.

94. On anointing of priests, etc., at Emar, see conveniently D. E. Fleming, *JBL* 117 (1998): 401-14. On installation of high priestess at Emar, see D. E. Fleming, *The Installation of Baal's High Priestess at Emar* (Atlanta: Scholars Press, 1992).

95. For the Hittite ritual of Ulippi, see H. Kronasser, *Die Umsiedlung der schwartzen Gottheit,* Sitzungsberichte (Phil.-Hist. Klasse) 241/3 (Vienna: Austrian Academy, 1963).

96. See translations of Ugaritic rituals in (e.g.) P. Xella, *I testi rituali di Ugarit, I* (Rome: Consiglio Nazionale delle Richerche, 1981); J.-M. de Tarragon, in A. Caquot, J.-M. de Tarragon, and J.-L. Cunchillos, *Textes Ougaritiques* II (Paris: Éditions du Cerf, 1989), 125-238; and now D. Pardee, *Ras Shamra-Ougarit XII,* 2 vols. (Paris: Éditions Recherche sur les Civilisations, 2000). For discussions of Ugaritic rituals, see J.-M. de Tarragon, *Le culte à Ugarit* (Paris: Gabalda, 1980); and most thoroughly, Pardee.

97. For the Egyptian daily ritual, see A. R. David, *A Guide to Religious Ritual at Abydos* (Warminster: Aris & Phillips, 1981); for full translation and study of their festival calendars, see S. El-Sabban, *Temple Festival Calendars of Ancient Egypt* (Liverpool: University Press, 2000).

98. For other Near Eastern festival calendars, see M. E. Cohen, *The Cultic Calendars of the Ancient Near East* (Bethesda, Md.: CDL Press, 1993).

99. On the *tenupa,* cf. J. Milgrom, *Studies in Cultic Theology and Terminology* (Leiden: Brill, 1983), 133-38 (relevant Egyptian scene, 136 fig. 1).

100. The scapegoat rituals of Uhhamuwa and Ashkhella are in *ANET,* 347; cf. study, D. P. Wright, *The Disposal of Impurity* (Atlanta: Scholars Press, 1987), including also later, divergent Mesopotamian rites; at Ebla (third millennium), cf. I. Zatelli, *VT* 48 (1998): 254-63, plus references.

101. On poverty, e.g., one sheep, not nine, cf. A. Goetze, *JCS* 6 (1952): 101; H. Kronasser, *Die Sprache* 7 (1961): 152. As for purity of offerings, see text in *ANET*, 207-10, esp. §§7, 19; on exclusion of foreigners as in Lev. 22:25, cf. 308, §6.

102. For seven-year cycles in Mesopotamia, cf. M. Weinfeld, *Getting at the Roots of Wellhausen's Understanding of the Law of Israel on the 100th Annivesary of the Prolegomena,* Institute for Advanced Studies Report no. 14/79 (Jerusalem: Hebrew University, 1979), 37-38; and M. Weinfeld, *Social Justice in Ancient Israel and in the Ancient Near East* (Jerusalem: Magnes Press, 1995), 75-96, 175-78. At Emar, cf. D. E. Fleming, *RB* 106 (1999): 8-34.

103. For this section, see the very important study by V. A. Hurowitz, *JAOS* 105 (1985): 21-30, where the data are well discussed and clearly tabulated. For ancient Canaanite background, one may also find stimulus in the partly updated study by F. M. Cross, *From Epic to Canon* (Baltimore: Johns Hopkins University Press, 1998), 84-95, but he has not yet shaken off the obsolete view that takes the tabernacle no further back than David's reign; the impact of the Egyptian data alone forbids this low dating, and the new Mari data also point much further back. It may be worth adding here that in Sinai acacia would be the natural wood to use for building the tabernacle; objections on its supposed rarity there fail to take account of the massive destruction of Sinai acacia by Egypt's Ottoman government in the early nineteenth century (cf. A. P. Stanley, *Sinai and Palestine* [London: Murray, 1905], 25). Oholiab and Bezalel, the two Hebrew craftsmen, are what we would expect from Ramesside Egypt, where foreigners with all manner of skills were valued and employed. One finds generations of carpenters, goldworkers, coppersmiths, sculptors, chief craftsmen, and leading draftsmen in Egypt (D. A. Lowle, *OrAnt* 15 [1976]: 91-106, pls. I-II); cf. the lists given in W. Helck, *Die Beziehungen Ägyptens zu Vorderasien im 3. und 2. Jahrtausend v. Chr.,* 2nd ed. (Wiesbaden: Harrassowitz, 1971), 356-57 (craftsmen), and 353-367 (listing foreigners throughout Egyptian society from Pharaoh's officers at court down to mere slaves).

104. For English translations of many of the Near Eastern documents used in this section, see as follows: For the Sumer, Eannatum treaty, see J. S. Cooper, *Sumerian and Akkadian Royal Inscriptions, I: Presargonic Inscriptions,* AOSTS I (New Haven: AOS, 1986), 33-39 (La 3.1). For the Ur-Nammu Laws, see J. J. Finkelstein, *JCS* 22 (1969): 66-82, and in *ANET*, 3rd ed./Supp. (1969), 523-25; Roth, *Law Collections*, 13-22. On Lipit-Ishtar Laws, see S. N. Kramer in *ANET*, 159-61; Roth, 23-35. On Akkadian, Hammurabi Laws, see T. J. Meek in *ANET*, 163-80; Roth, 71-142; M. E. J. Richardson, *Hammurabi's Laws: Text, Translation, and Glossary* (Sheffield: Academic Press, 2000). On the Ebla/Abarsal treaty, see E. Sollberger, *Studi Eblaiti* 3, fasc. 9/10 (1980), 129-55. On Elam treaties, and the Naram-Sin treaty, in German only, see W. Hinz, *ZA* 58 (1967): 66-96, esp. 91-95. For north Syria, Mari, see after tab. 27. On the Niqmepa and Idrimi treaties, see E. Reiner in *ANET*, 3rd ed./Supp. (1969), 531-32. The majority of Hittite treaties (in Hittite and Akkadian) appear in Beckman, *Hittite Diplomatic Texts.* Mesopotamian (Assyrian) treaties are well presented by S. Parpola and K. Watanabe, *Neo-Assyrian Treaties and Loyalty-Oaths,* SAA II (Helsinki: University Press, 1988) (note that in chart 1, p. xxxv, a "Historical Introduction" is wrongly included for texts 6 and 10 — this rubric should be deleted, as there are no historical prologues in this group of texts, nor are any distinguished in the translations as printed). For Aramaic texts, Sefiré, see J. Fitzmyer, *The Aramaic Inscriptions of Sefire,* 2nd ed., BibOr 19A (Rome: Pontificio Istituto Biblico, 1995). For Egypt, on the Ramesses II treaty with Hatti, see, in English, Kitchen in *RITA* II (1996), 79-85, and commentary in *RITANC* II (1999), 136-44.

105. Original work by G. E. Mendenhall, *BA* 17 (1954): 540-76, reprinted as a booklet, *Law and Covenant in Israel and the Ancient Near East* (Pittsburgh, 1955). In similar vein but more limited in approach and result was K. Baltzer, *Das Bundesformular* (Neukirchen-Vluyn:

Neukirchener Verlag, 1964), in English as *The Covenant Formulary* (Westminster: Fortress; Oxford: Blackwell, 1971); cf. the review by W. L. Moran, *Bib* 43 (1962): 100-106.

106. Works by D. J. McCarthy include his *Treaty and Covenant* (Rome: Pontifical Biblical Institute, 1963; 2nd ed., 1978) and *Old Testament Covenant* (Oxford: Blackwell, 1973). Dependence on McCarthy negatively by O. R. Gurney, *Some Aspects of Hittite Religion,* Schweich Lectures, 1976 (Oxford: OUP, 1977), 1, was a strangely uncritical blunder in an otherwise invaluable book.

107. M. Weinfeld, *Deuteronomy and the Deuteronomic School* (Oxford: OUP, 1972; reprint, Winona Lake, Ind.: Eisenbrauns, 1992), 60. This work is much more ambitious and better done than McCarthy, but is fatally tied to nineteenth-century assumptions.

108. For his change of mind on differences between the late second-millennium treaties and the later group, see M. Weinfeld, *JANES* 22 (1993): 135-39; but he failed to notice that this admission destroys the basis of his earlier opus. Then came E. W. Nicholson, *God and His People: Covenant and Theology in the Old Testament* (Oxford: OUP, 1986). This elegant little book tried to evade the external data completely (he had clearly never seen the full corpus of such documents), and failed even to detect both the existence and importance of the Near Eastern/Egyptian evidence on Hebrew *berit,* "covenant." For the latter, see extensive treatment by Kitchen, *UFo* 11 (1979): 453-64; and on Nicholson overall, Kitchen, *TynB* 40, no. 1 (1989): 118-35, with a compact restatement of the external evidence and its pertinence.

109. Cf. A. F. Campbell, *Bib* 50 (1969): 534-35.

110. Cf. Parpola and Watanabe, *Neo-Assyrian Treaties.*

111. The attempt to make the curses of Deut. 28 dependent on Neo-Assyrian usage was made by R. Frankena, in *OTS* 14 (1965): 122-54, and also by M. Weinfeld, *Bib* 46 (1965): 417-27, who did also point out older examples of the themes of curses in Deut. 28, going back to Hammurabi and others.

112. The following abbreviations are used in this table: MARI = *MARI, Mari, Annales de Recherches Interdisciplinaires* (Paris). ZL-Esh = Zimri-lim–Eshnunna treaty, in D. Charpin and F. Joannès, eds., *Marchandes, Diplomates et Empereurs* (Paris, 1991). GB = Beckman, *Hittite Diplomatic Texts.* HB = Laws of Hammurabi of Babylon (e.g., *ANET,* 178-80, curses). R. II, 6c = Hittite treaty of Ramesses II, curses. (Sfiré) I = Fitzmyer, *Aramaic Inscriptions of Sefire.* SAA II = Parpola and Watanabe, *Neo-Assyrian Treaties.* SA V = Shamshi-Adad V; AN V = Assur-nirari V (Assyrian kings). VTE = Vassal Treaties of Esarhaddon (conveniently in SAA II). Kudurrus = those mentioned by M. Weinfeld, *Bib* 46 (1965): 421. Rv = reverse (side).

113. More widely, on terminology, see M. Weinfeld, *JAOS* 93 (1973): 190-99; and earlier D. R. Hillers, *Treaty-Curses and the Old Testament Prophets* (Rome: Pontifical Biblical Institute, 1964), which still retains much value in correcting outdated views and in linking the subject to the later prophetic writings.

114. On use of "bond" only before an oath and "bond and oath" after it, see V. Korosec, *Hethitische Staatsverträge* (Leipzig: Weicher, 1931), 26, latter part of n. 2, citing the Suppiluliuma I/Shattiwaza ("Mattiwaza") treaties.

115. On *segulla/sikiltu,* see in the first instance M. Weinfeld, *Bib* 56 (1975): 127-28; for full treatment, see M. Greenberg, *JAOS* 71 (1951): 172-74; for Ugaritic *sglt,* see the text in Virolleaud, *Palais Royal d'Ugarit* V (Paris, 1965), 84f. (no. 60 = RS 18.38:7-12), cf. M. Weinfeld, *JAOS* 90 (1970): 195 n. 103 with discussion, and using Alalakh occurrences. For Akkadian *sikiltu,* see *CAD* 15/S (1984), 244-45.

116. For constructions of *riksu* ("bond," like *berit*) with *naçaru,* "to guard," cf. *CAD* 11/N Part II (1980), 43/44; *CAD* 14/R (1999), 353 end. For other aspects of the early date of Hebrew us-

age wrongly assigned to late dates, cf. Weinfeld's entire review in *Bib* 56 (1975): 120-28, of the thoroughly misleading work by E. Kutsch, *Verheissung und Gesetz* (1973).

117. Assessments of Moses are legion; a useful overview is given by D. M. Beegle in *ABD*, 4:909-18, with references, and of much of the older theoretical writing by (e.g.) H. Schmid, *Mose, Überlieferung und Geschichte* (Berlin: Töpelmann, 1968).

118. On the birth legend of Sargon of Akkad, latest translations, see B. R. Foster in *CoS* I, 461; J. G. Westenholz, *Legends of the Kings of Akkade* (Winona Lake, Ind.: Eisenbrauns, 1997), 36-49. The Moses birth narrative in one short passage has at least six words that are of Egyptian origin (New Kingdom period); thus, it is not directly taken from the Mesopotamian story of Sargon (cf. Hoffmeier, *Israel in Egypt*, 138-40). One may add the totally different literary format: Sargon is cast as a first-person address to the reader, while Exod. 2 is a retrospective narrative. Cf. also the discussion by A. R. Millard, *BAR* 26, no. 4 (July-August 2000): 51-55.

119. On the equivalences that operate when Egyptian consonants were reproduced in West Semitic alphabetic script, see Muchiki, *Egyptian PN;* on the reverse process, see J. E. Hoch, *Semitic Words in Egyptian Texts, New Kingdom . . .* (Princeton: Princeton University Press, 1994). The ablest advocate for "Mose(s)" being of Egyptian origin was J. G. Griffiths in *JNES* 12 (1953): 225-31; using cuneiform (Akkadian) data is invalid, because of the ambiguities for expressing sibilants in that script. For *-masu* as transcript of Egyptian "Mose," cf. (e.g.) (A)man-masu, "Amen-mose," on a seal impression of his in "Hittite" hieroglyphs and in cuneiform from the archives of Ugarit; see C. F.-A. Schaeffer and E. Laroche, in *Ugaritica III* (Paris: Geuthner, 1956), 42-47, 142-45, and figs. 67-70 (pp. 47-51).

120. The text of this letter is published by Sir A. H. Gardiner, *Ramesside Administrative Documents* (London: OUP, 1948), 14-15 (my own translation in the text, also my emphasis). First pointed out by S. Sauneron and J. Yoyotte, *RdÉ* 7 (1950): 67-70; for a recent translation, cf. also Wente, *Letters from Ancient Egypt*, 36, §34.

121. On foreigners in high positions in New Kingdom and Ramesside Egypt, see (e.g.) examples in Helck, *Die Beziehungen Ägyptens zu Vorderasien*, 353-58.

122. On the Egyptian treaty with the Hittites and its "history" of drafting, cf. A. J. Spalinger, *SAK* 9 (1981): 299-358; E. Edel, *Der Vertrag zwischen Ramses II. von Ägypten und Hattusili III. von Hatti* (Berlin: Mann Verlag, 1997), 85-86. Ramesses III made foreigners speak Egyptian (Peden, *Egyptian Historical Inscriptions*, 65).

123. See the useful conspectus given by S. Greengus, in *ABD*, 4:242-52, with references. Various approaches have arisen in recent years. Note the complementarity approach (the various collections being anthologies that, in effect, supplement each other), represented by R. Westbrook, e.g., in his *Studies in Biblical and Cuneiform Law* (Paris: Gabalda, 1988) (cf. his pp. 1-8 on principles); and a "contextual" approach, well represented by B. S. Jackson, *Studies in the Semiotics of Biblical Law* (Sheffield: Academic Press, 2000).

124. The concept of a great overarching "Deuteronomistic" work extending from Deuteronomy though Joshua, Judges, Samuel, and Kings was first set out fully by M. Noth in his *Überlieferungsgeschichtliche Studien,* first issued in 1943, then reissued (without change) in 1957 and 1967. In English it appeared as M. Noth, *The Deuteronomistic History,* 2nd ed., JSOTSup 15 (Sheffield: JSOT Press, 1991). Noth believed in one overall work, by one author, finally produced soon after 562 during the Babylonian exile; but other views are also propounded. Some have suggested that the presumed work was the product of a "school" rather than one author; so E. W. Nicholson, *Deuteronomy and Tradition* (Oxford: Blackwell, 1967), and then Weinfeld, *Deuteronomy and the Deuteronomic School;* there is nothing to commend this "committee" view. Others have suggested that there were successive editions of the work, one under Josiah, and then a lon-

ger edition in the exile. This has been set forth by F. M. Cross, *Canaanite Myth and Hebrew Epic* (Cambridge: Harvard University Press, 1973), 274-89. For an overall view of opinions on the Deuteronomistic History's own history, see conveniently S. L. McKenzie, in *ABD*, 2:160-68.

125. For a recent set of papers on "pan-Deuteronism" (and even indulging in it!), see L. S. Shearing and S. L. McKenzie, eds., *Those Elusive Deuteronomists: The Phenomenon of Pan-Deuteronism,* JSOTSup 268 (Sheffield: Academic Press, 1999).

126. On practical Egyptian obedience via *maat,* see usefully M. Lichtheim, *Maat in Egyptian Autobiographies and Related Studies,* OBO 120 (Freiburg: Universitätsverlag; Göttingen: Vandenhoeck & Rupprecht, 1992).

127. For Mari, the Bakram exile, see Dossin, *ARM(T)* V (1952), letter 27. For deportations under Zimri-lim, see *ARM(T)* V, letter 2 (on the 30,000 men); *ARM(T)* II, letter 67, and IV, letter 4, cf. no. 86; V, letters 29, 35, 85.

128. On Hattusil I, see H. Otten, *MDOG* 91 (1958): 83, rs. 11-17.

129. On the texts of Tuthmosis III and IV and Amenophis II, cf. in *ANET,* 237b, 247 n. 48, 248a.

130. On Mursil II, Years 3-5, in Annals, see R. Beal in *CoS* II, 85-87.

131. On the Ramesses II north-south-west-east references, see Abu Simbel, in Kitchen, *RITA* II (1996), 67, §46, (b), and (with mention of Ramesses III), in *RITANC* II (1999), 118-19. On settlements, "Field of the Hittites" at Memphis under Ay (ca. 1325), see B. G. Davies, *Egyptian Historical Records of the Later Eighteenth Dynasty,* fasc. VI (Warminster: Aris & Phillips, 1995), 65: 2109, §818, line 3. For others, cf. S. Sauneron and J. Yoyotte, *RdÉ* 7 (1950): 67-70, esp. 70.

132. On Shalmaneser I and Hanigalbat, see Grayson, *RIMA,* 1:184. On Tukulti-Ninurta I and Hittites, see 1:272. For Tiglath-pileser I in his first and fifth years, see Grayson, *RIMA,* 2:17, 24 (with other figures in other years; cf. 6,000 Mushki, p. 14). For Assurnasirpal II and Calah, see pp. 222, 227; Shalmaneser III's 44,400 captives are in Grayson, *RIMA,* 3:28-29.

133. For scholars who have rightly taken note of the Chronicler's additional data on Josiah's reforms, see Nicholson, *Deuteronomy and Tradition,* 7-15, also citing (p. 9) T. Oestreicher, who early on (1920) insisted that 2 Chron. 34–35 be heeded, followed by many others. On the whole position of Deuteronomy on several debated topics, see the refreshingly independent treatment by J. G. McConville, *Law and Theology in Deuteronomy* (Sheffield: JSOT Press, 1984); on limits of so-called name theology, see I. Wilson, *Out of the Midst of the Fire: Divine Presence in Deuteronomy,* SBLDS 151 (Atlanta: Scholars Press, 1995).

134. On the Hymn to the Uraeus, see J. Vandier, *ZÄS* 93 (1966): 132-43; on the festival of Sokar, see G. A. Gaballa and K. A. Kitchen, *Or,* n.s., 38 (1969): 1-76 (*hb-hb-ity* text, 74-75).

135. On the two magico-medical spells, see C. Leitz, *Magical and Medical Papyri of the New Kingdom,* Hieratic Papyri in the British Museum VII (London: British Museum Press, 1999), 3 (incantations 5 and 2, pp. 12ff., 22ff.).

136. Correspondences between spells in the Pyramid and Coffin Texts and the Book of the Dead were listed by T. G. Allen, *Occurrences of Pyramid Texts with Cross Indexes of These and Other Egyptian Mortuary Texts* (Chicago: University of Chicago Press, 1950), 103ff.; cf. 61ff.

137. For the triumph-scene texts of Amun, see G. A. Gaballa and K. A. Kitchen, *ZÄS* 96 (1969): 23-28.

138. Canaanite words in the Amarna letters can be seen in (e.g.) W. L. Moran, *The Amarna Letters* (Baltimore: Johns Hopkins University Press, 1992), passim.

139. On late Canaanite alphabetic inscriptions found in western Palestine, see full collection by E. Puech, *RB* 93 (1986): 161-213, and B. Sass, *The Genesis of the Alphabet and Its Development in the Second Millennium* b.c. (Wiesbaden: Harrassowitz, 1988), 51-105.

140. On the scope of writing in Late Bronze Canaan, cf. A. R. Millard, in K. Van Lerberghe and G. Voet, eds., *Languages and Cultures in Contact, . . . Proceedings of the Forty-Second RAI* (Louvain: Peeters, [2000]), 317-26. Whether reckoned as late Canaanite or archaic Hebrew, the tenth century B.C. Gezer Calendar tablet (*ANET*, 320; *CoS* II, 222) is quite close to classical Hebrew. On Wenamun, see *ANET*, 25-29.

141. For the analysis of the 720 years cited by Tukulti-Ninurta I, the 576 years of the Kassite Dynasty, and other "long distance" era figures in Assyrian texts, see J. Reade, *JNES* 60 (2001): 3-5.

142. On the early Eighteenth Dynasty fortress and work of Horemhab at Avaris, see conveniently M. Bietak, *Avaris, the Capital of the Hyksos* (London: British Museum Press, 1996), 67-83 (the Horemhab lintel, 77, fig. 61).

143. On the vast losses of ancient papyri in Egypt across the millennia (and other data too), see G. Posener, *Collège de France (Chaire de Philologie et archéologie égyptiennes), Leçon inaugurale, 6 Décembre 1961* (Paris, 1962), esp. 7-12 (documents), 13-16 (sites), also (abridged) in *Annales (Économies, Sociétés, Civilisations)* 17, no. 4 (1962): 631-46.

144. The Pi-Ramesse wine-jar dockets, translated and with notes, are in Kitchen, *RITA* II, 285, §167, B(ii), and in *RITANC* II, 317, §167, B, respectively.

145. For the "King of Battle" text, see translation by Westenholz, *Legends*, 119, 121.

NOTES TO CHAPTER 7

1. The list of Shoshenq I was definitively published (in hieroglyphic original) by the Epigraphic Survey, *Reliefs and Inscriptions at Karnak III, the Bubastite Portal* (Chicago: University of Chicago Press, 1954), name rings nos. 71-72, on pls. 4, 9A. The Abram identification goes back in print to W. Spiegelberg, *Aegyptologische Randglossen zum alten Testament* (Strassburg: Schlesier & Schweikhardt, 1904), 14; then by J. H. Breasted, *AJSL* 21 (1904/5): 22-36, and in his *ARE* IV, 353 and nn. a, b (also noted by Erman and Schaeffer), and in *JAOS* 31 (1911): 290-95; and others, often since. Hebrew *'abbir* (lit. "mighty one") applies to humans, angels, bulls, and horses; cf. Ugaritic *ibr*, "bull" (Gordon, *UT*, 350, no. 39), and Canaanite *ibr*, "horse, stallion," found as a loanword in Egyptian with horse determinative (Gordon, 350, no. 39; Hoch, *SWET*, 18-19, no. 3). On *hagr* as "enclosure," see my note in NEASB 43 (1998): 56 n. 2, modifying Hoch, *SWET*, 235-37, no. 326, on Old South Arabian evidence.

2. A. L. Oppenheim, *Ancient Mesopotamia* (Chicago: University of Chicago Press, 1964), 120.

3. On Ur of the Chaldees (early second millennium), see Sir C. L. Woolley, *Ur of the Chaldees* (Harmondsworth: Penguin Books, 1950), 114-32. For refutation of "northern" Urs in favor of the southern one, see H. W. F. Saggs, *Iraq* 22 (1960): 200-209 (contra Gordon and others), and now A. R. Millard, *BAR* 27, no. 3 (May-June 2001): 52-53, 57. For the Kaldu/Chaldaeans, cf. D. O. Edzard, *RLA* V, 3/4 (1977), 291-97; A. R. Millard, *EQ* 49 (1977): 69-71.

4. For Sippar-Awnanum (or Amnanum) and Sippar-Yakhrurum, see long since J.-R. Kupper, *Les nomades en Mésopotamie au temps des rois de Mari* (Paris: Société d'Édition "Les Belles Lettres," 1957), 52-53, 76 (and n. 4), 77, 88.

5. For people camping by Ur, see Kupper, *Nomades*, 88; on the Mare-Yamina around other towns, see Kupper, 13-15, 56-57.

6. On the range of the Mare-Yamina, see Kupper, *Nomades*, 47, for wanderings around Mari and Terqa; for wanderings east to the Tigris, see 53; for around Uruk, Larsa, and Sippar, see

51-52; for around the "Upper Lands," see 48; for Gebel Bishri, see 47; for Yamkhad (Aleppo), Qatna, and Amurru, see 49, 179.

7. For Old Babylonian "itineraries," cf. long ago W. W. Hallo, *JCS* 18 (1964): 57-88, with A. Goetze, 112-19, with schematic route maps, pp. 71, 87; see map, M. Roaf, *Cultural Atlas of Mesopotamia and the Ancient Near East* (New York and Oxford: Facts on File, 1990), 113.

8. The citation is in Kupper, *Nomades,* 79. Such movements back and forth rule out the objection to a northwest movement by J. van Seters, *Abraham in History and Tradition* (New Haven: Yale University Press, 1975), 23-24; that Terah was "sedentary" at Ur is merely his assumption, not a fact. For ancient Harran, see J. N. Postgate, in *RLA* IV, 2/3 (1973), 122-25; contra van Seters, Harran was inhabited in the third millennium and was an important route center in the second, having its own lesser king in the time of the Mari archives. The link between Ur and Harran was religious: the cult of the moon god Sin.

9. For ancient Nakhur/Nahor, see J.-R. Kupper, in *RLA* IX, 1/2 (1998), 86-87 (in French), updating *ARM(T)* XVI/1 (1979), 24 (and 14 for Harran); also R. S. Hess, *Studies in the Pesronal Names of Genesis 1–11* (Neukirchen-Vluyn, 1993), 87-88.

10. On Til-(sha)-Turakhi, under Shalmaneser III, Year 6 (853), trans. Grayson, *RIMA,* 3:22, 36, 45, 52, 65; and Younger in *CoS* II, 263-64, 266-67, 269.

11. For Serug/Sarugi, cf. C. H. W. Johns, *An Assyrian Doomsday Book,* Assyriologische Bibliothek, 17 (Leipzig: Hinrichs, 1901), index, s.v. "Sarugi"; see now F. M. Fales, *Censimenti e Catasti de Epoca Neo-Assira* (Rome: Centro per la antichíta e la storia dell' arto del vicino oriente, 1973), 95; and K. H. Kessler, *Untersuchungen zur historischen Topographie Nordmesopotamiens nach keilschriftlichen Quellen des 1. Jahrtausends v. Chr.* (Wiesbaden: Reichert, 1980), 197-200.

12. As for people bearing place-names as personal names, even today in the Liverpool (UK) area there are plenty of people surnamed Sefton/Sephton or Fazakerley, names of districts in greater Liverpool. The Mari general Mut-Bisir took his name from Mount (Gebel) Bishri (*MARI* 5 [1987]: 163-65).

13. For the Qatna-Mari example, cf. G. Dossin, *ARM(T)* I (1950), no. 77, cf. nos. 24, 46. Other such alliances are listed by J. M. Munn-Rankin, *Iraq* 18 (1956): 94-95. For other references for Qatna-Mari, cf. F. Joannès, in *MARI* 8 (1997): 397 and nn. 18-21; for the Qatna-Mari marriage documents, see J.-M. Durand, in *MARI* 6 (1990): 276-98. In turn, Zimri-lim of Mari apparently sought brides from both Qatna and Aleppo.

14. The Beni Hasan tomb scene is often reproduced; in color, cf. (e.g.) A. R. Millard, *Discoveries from Bible Times* (Oxford: Lion, 1997), 58.

15. For Sinuhe rescued by tribal leader and escorted back, "ten men coming and ten men going," see the translations: e.g., Wilson in *ANET*, 19, 21, or Lichtheim in *CoS* I, 87, 81 (with references).

16. On East Delta Ro-Waty and Avaris, see M. Bietak, *Avaris and Pi-Ramesse,* 2nd ed. (London: OUP, 1986), 228, with references.

17. In *BAR* 21, no. 4 (July-August 1995): 56-57, R. S. Hendel took it upon himself ("where Kitchen erred") to "correct" this writer, by alleging errors where absolutely none exist, and by creating massive blunders of his own. Thus in *BAR* 21, no. 2 (March-April 1995): 88, I had stated clearly the facts repeated here: there was *no* Egyptian Delta capital in the period 1550-1300, only in the four centuries before this date (and Tanis, 1070-670). Hendel misrepresented this as my saying an Egyptian Delta capital existed 2000-200, which is entirely false.

18. For foreign ladies taken in by pharaohs, cf. references of Kitchen, in Hess et al., *Oath,*

70, nn. 8-10. On Semites in Egypt, see J. K. Hoffmeier, *Israel in Egypt* (New York: OUP, 1997), chap. 3.

19. Kutir names are well attested in the long lines of Elamite rulers; cf., e.g., in *CAH*, 3rd ed., II/1 (1973), 272 and 820-21. "La'omer" may be for Lagamar, known also at Mari (e.g., J. M. Sasson, *RAAO* 92 [1998]: 114, after *MARI* 7 [1993]: 372, no. 117). That the power and influence of Elam was "unprecedented" in the early second millennium and not again is clear for many reasons; cf. D. T. Potts, *The Archaeology of Elam* (Cambridge: University Press, 1999), 160, 182/186, 187 table. Note that for the influence evident from the texts, "it is difficult to find physical manifestations in the archaeological record . . . [of 3 major sites, KAK] . . . which (would) corroborate the enormous influence of Elam at this time" (Potts, 186). On Elamite envoys reaching as far west as Qatna, cf. (e.g.) W. Hinz, in *CAH,* 3rd ed., II/1 (1973), 263; Kupper, *ARM(T)* VI (1954), letters 19, 22. Cf. also J.-M. Durand, *RAAO* 92 (1998): 17. (To treat "Elam" here as a reference to the Persian Empire of fifteen centuries later, as some biblicists would do, is mere fantasy.)

20. The name Tudkhalia occurs already in the Cappadocian (Kanesh) texts of the nineteenth century, and as a royal name with the shadowy Tudkhalia I rather later in time; text and references are in E. Laroche, *Les noms des Hittites* (Paris: Klincksieck, 1966), 191. On the "chiefs" and "paramount chiefs," cf. A. Goetze, *Kleinasien,* 2nd ed. (Munich: Beck, 1957), 75, with references; P. Garelli, *Les Assyriens en Cappadoce* (Paris: Maisonneuve, 1963), 63-65 (Anittas), 205-15, 206 n. 4. For the Anittas text, see E. Neu, *Der Anitta-Text,* StBoT 18 (Wiesbaden: Harrassowitz, 1974); in English, *CoS* I, 182-84.

21. Amraphel is certainly not Hammurabi; if the *r* is a graphic slip for *d,* his name might be an Amudpiel (cf. two kings and an official, *ARM(T)* XVI/1 [1979], 60), but this remains mere conjecture. My colleague Prof. A. R. Millard suggests Amur-aplam. Shin'ar (Sangar/Shankhar) is Babylonia (area), not Babylon (city). Shinar is a mid-to-late-second-millennium term, for Mesopotamia and specifically Babylonia; cf. long ago, Sir A. H. Gardiner, *Ancient Egyptian Onomastica* I (Oxford: OUP, 1947), 209*-212*, and then E. Laroche and H. G. Güterbock, in C. F.-A. Schaeffer, ed., *Ugaritica III* (Paris: Geuthner, 1956), 102-3, *pace* Durand, *RAAO* 92 (1998): 19.

22. For Arriuk (Arioch), cf. latterly the Arriyuk of the Mari correspondence, in J.-R. Kupper, *ARM* XXVIII (1998), 221-28; like his biblical homonym, the home base of this Arriyuk too is obscure. Egyptian *i3ki* (Execration Texts, Mirgissa F.3) is probably also Ar(r)iuki (G. Posener, by note to this writer in 1966). The biblical Ellasar is very unlikely to have been either Ashur (wrong sibilant) or Larsa (no initial *'aleph;* transposed *r/s*), or Ilansura (*l/n* wrong order, and wrong sibilant; contrast Durand, *RAAO* 92 [1998]: 20), or Telassar (a misreading).

23. Decades ago, at least five other Mesopotamian alliances were known, and duly booked by D. O. Edzard, *Die "Zweite Zwischenzeit" Babyloniens* (Wiesbaden: Harrassowitz, 1957). They are (with page references in Edzard following): Eshnunna allied with Akkad and three tribes, 105-6, 108, 121; Malgium (?) defeated a four-power alliance, 157, 160; Larsa defeated a group of five powers, 108, 155, 157; and Hammurabi of Babylon defeated alliances of five and four powers in his twenty-ninth and thirty-first years, 181-82.

24. The alliances of fifteen to twenty kings in the Mari letter is often cited: e.g., Moran in *ANET,* 3rd ed./Supp., 628. One sly character, Yashub-Adad, changed his allies every few months (Moran, 628)! Alliances were sealed by any two rulers through negotiation of treaties; cf. J. M. Munn-Rankin, *Iraq* 18 (1956): 84-95, and for the process, D. Charpin, *ARM* XXVI/2 (1988), 144, 179-82, 393-95 on tablets 372, 469.

25. Cf. summary by A. Malamat, in *BAT* 1990 Supp. (1993), 66-70 and references.

26. On eastern kings invading the Levant in general, cf. A. Malamat, in *Studies in Honor of B. Landsberger,* AS 16 (Chicago: University of Chicago Press, 1965), 365-73.

27. On Sargon and Naram-Sin, cf. C. J. Gadd in *CAH*, 3rd ed., I/2 (1973), 424-26, 441-42, with references; texts are translated by A. L. Oppenheim, in *ANET*, 268 (both); D. Frayne, *RIME*, 2:27-31, 132-40; B. Kienast, in *CoS* II, 244-45 (Naram-Sin only).

28. Text of Yakhdun-lim, in English, D. Frayne, *RIME*, 4:604-8, and in *CoS* II, 260-61.

29. For Shamshi-Adad I in the Levant, see his text, *ANET*, 274b; Grayson, *RIMA*, 1:47-51. For the massive expedition sent by him and his son in Mari to Qatna and south into Syria, see detailed presentations in French, by J.-M. Durand, *Les documents épistolaires du palais de Mari* II, LAPO 17 (Paris: Éditions du Cerf, 1998), 9-34, with listings of up to 21,000 troops (p. 17) and Canaanite involvement (p. 29). On the campaign, past Qadesh, mountains Siryon and Lebanon to Zobah, and further, cf. D. Charpin, *RAAO* 92 (1998): 79-92.

30. For Mari night fighting, see Durand, *Les documents épistolaires du palais de Mari*, II, 271, 289-90, no. 607.

31. For Egyptian war scenes ending with presentation to the gods, cf. (on art layout) G. A. Gaballa, *Narrative in Egyptian Art* (Mainz: von Zabern, 1976), 10ff., figs. 7-11c; translations of texts in series of scenes are in Kitchen, *RITA* I (1993), 6-26, passim, and *RITA* II (1996), 29-55, passim; for commissioning scenes, see *RITA* II, 55, and W. F. Edgerton and J. A. Wilson, *Historical Records of Ramses III, . . . Medinet Habu*, SAOC 12 (Chicago: University of Chicago Press, 1936), 4 (and sets of scenes, 1-104). Zimri-lim gave booty to the gods at Nagar and Aleppo after a victory in his Year 11´; cf. M. Guichard, *RAAO* 93 (1999): 42, and n. 101, with back reference to *MARI* 8 (1997): 332.

32. Cf. divine "credits" in Neo-Assyrian annals, e.g., in Grayson, *RIMA*, 3, passim. For a summary of the kings' letters to deities, see P. Michalowski in *RLA* VI, 1/2 (1980), 58-59, §10; Assyria, cf. A. L. Oppenheim, *JNES* 19 (1960): 133ff.

33. On Zakkur's stela, see *ANET*, 501-2, or *CoS* II, 155.

34. On the older continuous chronicles, for traces of the Sumerian Tummal chronicle, cf. E. Sollberger, *JCS* 16 (1962): 40-47; in Mari, of the eponym chronicle, cf. M. Birot, *MARI* 4 (1985): 219-42; for the Old Hittite chronicles, see references in E. Laroche, *Catalogue des textes hittites* (Paris: Klincksieck, 1956), nos. 8-9, 16-18; for Tiglath-pileser I, cf. A. K. Grayson, *Assyrian and Babylonian Chronicles* (New York: Augustin, 1970), 184-89. The chronicles are well collected (in French) by J.-J. Glassner, *Chroniques mésopotamiennes* (Paris: Les belles lettres, 1993). These facts clearly refute the overselective comparison of Gen. 14 only with the later, first-millennium chronicles offered by van Seters, *Abraham*, 300, and in *BiOr* 33 (1976): 220.

Again, sadly, it is necessary to correct errors here by R. S. Hendel, *BAR* 21, no. 4 (July-August 1995): 56-57. His notes on Elam are misleading, failing to note the extraordinary involvement of Elam westward in this period; "Elam not in Canaan" is merely a negative, and not evidence of noncontact. The supposed alliances of the first millennium in Mesopotamia are a fallacy; the only powers there then were Assyria and Babylonia (Arabia was not involved!), not the patchwork of states found in the early second millennium. The Spartoli tablets are irrelevant (late second century B.C.!), about four successive kings with cryptic, ambiguous names attacking Babylon.

35. See already, Kitchen in Hess et al., *Oath*, 74-77 (with references for publications of treaties, 75 nn. 25-28), and briefly in *BAR* 21, no. 2 (March-April 1995): 54 with note. Again, Hendel entirely failed to grasp the import of the data (*BAR* 21, no. 4 [July-August 1995]: 56), as clearly shown by me, in *NEASB* 43 (1998): 50-51.

36. For Mari background on the treaty in Gen. 31, using Mari text A.3592, see J.-M. Durand, *RAAO* 92 (1998): 32-38; he regards the Gen. 31 passage as very archaic, and points out

how the Mari counterpart rules out completely the old-fashioned J/E partition of this text (pp. 36, 38).

37. On Kings Atam-rum and Ashkur-Adad, cf. F. Joannès, in D. Charpin and F. Joannès, eds., *Marchandes, Diplomates et Empereurs* (Paris, 1991), 175.

38. On the treaties of Talmi-sharruma and Kurunta, see in G. Beckman, *Hittite Diplomatic Texts,* SBL: Writings from the Ancient World 7 (Atlanta: Scholars Press, 1996), nos. 14, 18A, C. On the essential unity of the narratives in Gen. 20–22, see the careful discussion by T. D. Alexander, *Abraham in the Negev* (Carlisle: Paternoster Press, 1997).

39. The Hammurabi law is found, e.g., in *CoS* II, 348.

40. For the Mari text, see *ANET,* 3rd ed./Supp., 545 §13; in full, G. Boyer, *ARM(T)* (1958), 2-7, no. 1.

41. For other Old Babylonian examples, cf. in M. Schorr, *Urkunden des altbabylonischen Zivil- und Prozessrechts* (Leipzig: Hinrichs, 1913; reprint, Hildesheim: Olms, 1971), 16-21, and nos. 8, 9, 17, 22; and pp. 43-45 and nos. 23-26; cf. M. David, *Die Adoption im altbabylonischen Recht* (Leipzig: Weicher, 1927), 1-2, 76-77, 84-85; E. C. Stone and D. I. Owen, *Adoption in Old Babylonian Nippur and the Archive of Mannum-meshu-lissur* (Winona Lake, Ind.: Eisenbrauns, 1991), 3-11, texts 1-8 (38-45). Contrary to van Seters, *Abraham,* 18-19, the Akkadian phrase *mar-biti,* "son of the house," is not exclusively Late Babylonian; it goes back to Old and Middle Babylonian times (cf. references, W. von Soden, *Akkadisches Handwörterbuch* (Wiesbaden: Harrassowitz, 1959-81), 616a, §10b [Old and Middle (omitted in *CAD,* 2/B, 295-96)]), and David, 101, §I, VAT 8947:21 (Middle Assyrian). In any case, the West Semitic *ben-beyt* could be early, regardless of the age of Akkad. *mar-biti.* At Nuzi, ca. 1400 (between Old and Middle Babylonian), cf. tablet H 60, in E. A. Speiser, *AASOR* 10 (1930): 30-31, no. 1.

42. On the Laqipum/Hatala text, see B. Hrozny in *Symbolae Koschaker* II (Leiden: Brill, 1939), 108ff.; *ANET,* 3rd ed./Supp., 543, §4.

43. On substitute childbearing in Hammurabi §§145-46, see *ANET,* 172, *CoS* II, 344-45; earlier, cf. Laws of Lipit-Ishtar, §§24-27 (*ANET,* 160; *CoS* II, 412-13), for various provisions on children by slave substitutes and second wives. In legal texts, e.g., CT 48, no. 67, cited and translated by R. Westbrook, *Old Babylonian Marriage Law, AfO* Beiheft 23 (Horn: Berger, 1988), 107, 125. Nuzi H 67, in Speiser, *AASOR* 10 (1930): 31-33, no. 2; *ANET,* 220, §3. Much that was once thought to be comparable in the Nuzi records and in Genesis has now to be set aside; cf. (e.g.) M. J. Selman, *TynB* 27 (1976): 114-36, and in A. R. Millard and D. J. Wiseman, eds., *Essays on the Patriarchal Narratives* (Leicester: IVP, 1980), 93-136; these papers also serve to correct the wildly excessive skepticism of van Seters and others. The texts cited here retain their relevance, and have been chosen for that reason. In the early second millennium, two main wives were allowable, even full sisters, as for Jacob having Leah and Rachel (Gen. 29; disallowed later, Lev. 18:18). At that period Haya-sumu, king of Ilansura, married two sisters, Shimatum and Kiru, as principal wives; cf. J.-M. Durand, *RAAO* 92 (1998): 38. So often dubiously linked with Nuzi in the past, the *teraphim* were most likely small ancestral figurines, possibly for divination; cf. the lucid and sensible survey by T. J. Lewis, in *DDD,* 1588-1601, with full references.

44. For the dialogue-document theory, see G. M. Tucker, *JBL* 85 (1966): 77-84, followed by van Seters, *Abraham,* 98-100. For such a document in the second millennium, cf. D. J. Wiseman, *BSac* 134 (1977): 130 n. 29, citing a British Museum tablet, in *Cuneiform Texts . . . British Museum* 45 (London, 1964), no. 60; their view is also criticized by H. A. Hoffner, *TynB* 20 (1969): 35-37 with n. 23.

45. For the theory of Hittite laws background to Gen. 23, see M. R. Lehmann, *BASOR* 129 (1953): 15-18. For a critique of the equation, see Hoffner, *TynB* 20 (1969): 33-37. For the Hittite

laws themselves, see the splendid new edition by H. A. Hoffner, *The Laws of the Hittites, a Critical Edition* (Leiden: Brill, 1997), and his pp. 54-58, 190-91, for §§46-47; also, *CoS* II, 106-19, esp. 111.

46. On this subject overall, compactly, see the careful and judicious study by G. J. Wenham in Millard and Wiseman, *Essays,* 157-88.

47. For extensive offerings of grades of sheep at Mari, cf. (e.g.) J. Bottéro, *ARM(T)* VII (1957), 248-50, 346; and texts 224, 263.

48. For Emar, cf. (e.g.) D. E. Fleming, *The Installation of Baal's High Priestess at Emar* (Atlanta: Scholars Press, 1992), 135-40; *CoS* I, 427-31. On Ebla, cf. rituals in (e.g.) G. Pettinato and P. Mander, *Culto ufficiale ad Ebla durante il regno di Ibbi-sipis* (Rome: Istituto per l'Oriente, 1979), 45-103, passim ("ovino/ovini" entries).

49. For "The Shipwrecked Sailor," cf. (e.g.) M. Lichtheim, *Ancient Egyptian Literature* 1 (Berkeley: University of California Press, 1973), 212 (or in *CoS* I, 83).

50. For the Hammamat texts, cf. Breasted, *ARE* I (1906), 212, §436, and 216, §453.

51. For anointing stones at Emar, cf. (e.g.) D. E. Fleming, *Time at Emar* (Winona Lake, Ind.: Eisenbrauns, 2000), 82-87, also with references for such stones at Mari earlier, and of anointing these in Hatti. A heroic attempt at documenting "nomadic religion" in the ancient Near East was made by H. Klengel, *Zwischen Zelt und Palast, Die Begegnung von Nomaden und Sesshaften im alten Vorderasien* (Vienna: Schroll, 1972), 209-13, but significantly he had to rely mainly on OT data, and on very late Palmyrene and pre-Islamic and early Islamic data.

52. On Exod. 6:3 taken with a rhetorical negative, see in the first instance W. J. Martin, *Stylistic Criteria and the Analysis of the Pentateuch* (London: Tyndale Press, 1955), 18-19; and thereafter G. R. Driver, *JANES* 5 (1973): 109, and slightly differently, F. I. Andersen, *The Sentence in Biblical Hebrew* (The Hague: Mouton, 1974), 102. The objections by Wenham, in Millard and Wiseman, *Essays,* 180, do not seem very convincing; later translators of the OT are often wrong; and in Exod. 3:13-16 Moses would have been a near total stranger to most Israelites on his return — anybody could have talked about the God of the fathers; the real "password" was the old proper name YHWH (v. 16), which the declaration in v. 15 led up to. Rather many editorial name changes seem to be required on his view; they are not impossible, but are they really needful?

53. On Egyptian Amun, an outline summary is in D. B. Redford, ed., *Oxford Encyclopedia of Ancient Egypt* 1 (New York: OUP, 2000), 82-85; for more detail, see E. Otto in *Ld A* I (1973), 237-48 (in German). The trinitarian/monotheistic reference is to the Papyrus Leiden I 350, Hymn to Amun, cf. Wilson in *ANET,* 368-69; cf. S. Morenz, *Egyptian Religion* (London: Methuen, 1973), 143-44.

54. On the Aten, briefly, see A. R. Millard, in Hess et al., *Oath,* 124-25, with references.

55. A. Alt, *Der Gott der Väter* (1929), reprinted in his *Kleine Schriften zur Geschichte des Volkes Israel* I (Munich: Beck, 1953), 1-78; in English in A. Alt, *Essays on Old Testament History and Religion* (Oxford: Blackwell, 1966), 1-77.

56. On Old Assyrian evidence (twentieth/nineteenth century), cf. J. Lewy, *RHR* 110 (1934): 50-56, and briefly in *HUCA* 32 (1961): 41-43. For more thorough detail, see F. M. Cross, *HTR* 55 (1962): 225-59, and in revised, expanded form in his *Canaanite Myth and Hebrew Epic* (Cambridge: Harvard University Press, 1973), 3-75, passim. Compare also H. Hirsch, *AfO* 21 (1966): 56-58; and the review by Wenham, in Millard and Wenham, *Essays,* 157-88. Also the careful observations by R. de Vaux, in A. Parrot and J.-C. Courtois, eds., *Ugaritica VI* (Paris: Geuthner, 1969), 501-17. For Ilabrat, cf. Jacobsen *apud* Cross, *Canaanite Myth,* 9 n. 22 (and cf. Akkad. *abratu,* "mankind," in *CAD,* A:1/I, 64, Old Babylonian period and later). For discussion of Shaddai, cf. Cross, *Canaanite Myth,* 52-60, with full background material.

57. For *Apophis and Seqenenre*, see *ANET*, 231.

58. On the "Mosaic period" for monotheism, with a glance back toward the patriarchs, see A. R. Millard in Hess et al., *Oath*, 119-29, with references. Compare also very brief observations for Moses' time by L. E. Stager, in M. D. Coogan, ed., *The Oxford History of the Biblical World* (New York: OUP, 1998), 148-49. At greater length, comprehensively, see W. H. C. Propp, *UFo* 31 (1999/2000): 537-75, with a massively damaging refutation of the usual run of sloppy shibboleths that are trotted out to "justify" limiting Hebrew monotheism to the Babylonian exile and after.

59. For the Cairo Hymn to Amen-Re, cf. Wilson in *ANET*, 305 (date of hymn), 306, text at nn. 10 and 17; or *CoS* I, 38.

60. For the fourteenth/thirteenth centuries we have a Hittite translation of an old Canaanite myth about "Elkunirsha," who is El-qone(y)-irtsa, "El creator of the earth" (cf. full formula, with heaven and earth, in Gen. 14:18, 22). For the Hittite text, cf. H. Otten, *MIO* 1 (1953): 125-50, esp. 135ff.; translations in H. A. Hoffner, *Hittite Myths* (Atlanta: Scholars Press, 1990), 69-70, and in *CoS* I, 149. An El-kun-Zaphon on a Ramesses II stela might be for a similar "El creator of Zaphon"; cf. *RITANC* II (1996), 134. So El-Elyon is not without early analogy.

61. For the fourfold contrast between patriarchal and later religion, cf. G. J. Wenham, in Millard and Wiseman, *Essays*, 184-85. For (5), contrast Moses; for (6), cf. already D. E. Fleming, *RAAO* 92 (1998): 73 and nn. 147-148.

62. For smashed-up images, etc., at Late Bronze Hazor, cf. A. Ben-Tor and M. T. Rubiato, *BAR* 25, no. 3 (May-June 1999): 22, 35-39.

63. On the long-attested cults of Ruda and Apladad, see A. R. Millard, in Hess et al., *Oath*, 126-29, with references.

64. For the Execration Texts, see good bibliography in G. Posener, *Cinq textes d'envoûtement* (Cairo: IFAO, 1987), 1-6. For an English translation of the full formula of a text, including typical names of some rulers and lands, see Wilson in *ANET*, 328-29. For the first (Mirgissa) series, see preliminary report by G. Posener, *Syria* 43 (1966): 277-87 (esp. 285-87), and fully, Y. Koenig, *RdÉ* 41 (1990): 101-25 (esp. 111-13). For the second in date (Berlin), see K. Sethe, *Die Ächtung feindlicher Fürsten, Völker und Dinge auf altägyptischen Tongefässscherben des Mittleren Reiches* (Berlin: Akademie der Wissenschaft, 1926). For the third set (Brussels from Saqqara), see G. Posener, *Princes et Pays d'Asie et de Nubie* (Brussels: FÉRÉ, 1940). For a digest of the Asiatic names in the second and third series, cf. W. Helck, *Die Beziehungen Ägyptens zu Vorderasien im 3. und 2. Jahrtausend v. Chr.*, 2nd ed. (Wiesbaden: Harrassowitz, 1971), 44-67, with map of places named and locatable, p. 51.

65. There are many translations of Sinuhe; e.g., Wilson in *ANET*, 19; Lichtheim, *Ancient Egyptian Literature*, 1:224 (= *CoS* I, 78) for Sinuhe's rescue. While it is common to treat Sinuhe as just a story, the fact remains that its format is *not* fiction but that of a tomb biography used for literary-political purposes. See briefly D. B. Redford, *Egypt, Canaan, and Israel in Ancient Times* (Princeton: Princeton University Press, 1992), 83 ("Sinuhe . . . corroborates the archaeological picture to perfection"), 85 and n. 81; on the linking of Sinuhe to Middle Bronze II, not I — and for good, factual reasons — see long ago A. F. Rainey, *IOS* 2 (1972): 369-408, on "The World of Sinuhe." On Sinuhe's biographical nature, see more fully Kitchen, in *BACE* 7 (1996): 55-63, for the evidence.

66. On linked urban and tribal regimes in Old Babylonian Mesopotamia and at Ashur, see W. Yuhong and S. Dalley, *Iraq* 52 (1990): 159-65.

67. On Laish/Dan in the Middle Bronze Age, cf. (e.g.) A. Biran, *Biblical Dan* (Jerusalem: IES, 1994), 47-104; briefly, in *NEAHL*, 1:324-26.

68. On Dothan in Middle Bronze IIB, cf. D. Ussishkin et al., *NEAHL,* 1:372-74.

69. On Shechem, see the summary by E. F. Campbell, *NEAHL,* 4:1349-52; for translation of the Khu-Sobek stela, see *ANET,* 230; for the Execration Texts, see *ANET,* 329.

70. On Bethel, cf. Kelso, *NEAHL,* 1:192-94, and references.

71. For Jerusalem, see the summaries in *NEAHL,* 2:701-2 (City of David, levels 18B-17), and new traces in R. Reich and E. Shukron, *BAR* 25, no. 1 (January-February 1999): 30-33 (also in H. Geva, ed., *Ancient Jerusalem Revealed, Supplement* [Jerusalem: IES, 2000], 1ff.); also in the Execration Texts.

72. On "Gerar," Tell Abu Hureirah (Tel Haror) excavations, cf. E. D. Oren, *NEAHL,* 2:580-82.

73. On Hebron (at Er-Rumeida), cf. A. Ofer, *NEAHL,* 2:606-9; for the tablet, see M. Anbar and N. Na'aman, *Tel Aviv* 13/14 (1986/87): 3-12, pl. 1.

74. For the Negev: Middle Bronze I period, see *NEAHL,* 3:1123-26; for Tel Malhata, MB II, see 3:935; for Tel Masos, MB II, see 3:986; for Tell el-Far'ah South, see 2:441.

75. On the work in Beer-Sheba, see *NEAHL,* 1:167-72; Aharoni's idea (*BA* 39 [1976]: 71-74) to date a particular well to the twelfth century, and the patriarchs with it, is uncharacteristically bizarre, and totally lacks any factual support. On Gen. 21:31, see W. J. Martin and A. R. Millard, in *NBD,* 126; also Alexander, *Abraham in the Negev,* 72-73. For the archaeology, cf. in brief, Mazar, *ALB* I, 224-26.

76. On Sinuhe's hunters, see the translation in *ANET,* 20, or Lichtheim, *Ancient Egyptian Literature,* 1:227; *CoS* I, 79.

77. On Old Babylonian shepherding, see J. J. Finkelstein, *JAOS* 88 (1968): 30-36, and J. N. Postgate and S. Payne, *JSS* 20 (1975): 1-21; earlier, F. R. Kraus, *Staatliche Viehhaltung im altbabylonischen Lande Larsa* (Amsterdam: Royal Dutch Academy, 1966); recently, M. Yokoyama, *Orient* 32 (1997): 1-8. Terah and Abraham may well have controlled flocks around Ur before ever they went up to Harran; on the extensive keeping of flocks of sheep and goats at Ur in Old Babylonian times, see M. Van De Mieroop, *BSAg* 7 (1993): 161-82; for cattle then, cf. M. Stol, *BSAg* 8 (1995): 173-213.

78. Superstition (rods) and selective breeding by Jacob was first instanced by D. M. Blair, *The Beginning of Wisdom* (London: IVF, 1945), 12, from a medical background.

79. On "bore the loss" in Gen. 31:39, see J. J. Finkelstein, *JAOS* 88 (1968): 33-35.

80. For Hammurabi, see translations in, e.g., *ANET,* 177; *CoS* I, 350.

81. Text of Year 38 of Hammurabi is in M. Schorr, *Urkunden des altbabylonischen Zivil- und Prozessrechts* (Leipzig: Hinrichs, 1913; reprint, New York: Olms, 1971), 216, no. 158.

82. Other references are in Postgate and Payne, *JSS* 20 (1975): 9-10.

83. For the Hebron sheep/goat tablet, cf. M. Anbar and N. Naaman, *Tel Aviv* 13/14 (1986/87): 3-12, pl. 1.

84. For the Old Assyrian caravan letter, cf. P. Garelli, *Les Assyriens en Cappadoce* (Paris: Maisonneuve, 1963), 106-7, 202-3.

85. On the Fayum camel skull, cf. O. H. Little, *Bulletin de l'Institut d'Égypte* 18 (1935-36): 215.

86. For the Byblos figurine, cf. P. Montet, *Byblos et l'Égypte* (Paris: Geuthner, 1928), 91 and pl. 52, no. 179; against Albright's denial (*JBL* 64 [1945]: 288, because of no hump left), cf. also R. de Vaux, *RB* 56 (1949): 9, nn. 4-5.

87. On the jawbone, cf. de Vaux, *RB* 56 (1949): 9 n. 8. For recent examples in Canaan, Early Bronze to Late Bronze, see C. Grigson, in T. Levy, ed., *The Archaeology of Society in the Holy Land* (London: Leicester University Press, 1995), 259 and references, 573-76.

88. On the north Syrian seal, see E. Porada, *Journal of the Walters Art Gallery* 36 (1977): 1-6.

89. See the lexical mentions in *CAD* 7/I-J (1960), 2, plus W. G. Lambert, *BASOR* 160 (1960): 42-43 (and eliminating a supposed Alalakh example).

90. For the Memphis (Rifeh) figurine, see W. M. F. Petrie, *Gizeh and Rifeh* (London: BSAE, 1907), 23, pl. 27; Albright's attempt to lower its date (*JBL* 64 [1945]: 287-88) can be dismissed because he offers no evidence. The same comment applies to the grudging paper by B. Midant-Reynes and F. Braunstein-Silvestre, *Or* 46 (1977): 337-62 (Rifeh, 361), a criticism applicable also to I. Köhler, *Zur Domestikation des Kamels* (Hannover: Tierärztliche Hochschule, 1981), and in *BA* 56, no. 4 (1993): 183 (uncritically following an outdated remark of Albright back in 1942!); such writers seem quite incapable of distinguishing between dominant livestock (e.g., cattle/sheep and goats/donkeys) and insignificantly marginal animals like the camel.

91. On the Qurraya-ware figure, see M. Ingraham et al., *Atlal* 5 (1981): pl. 79:14 (and P. J. Parr, in D. T. Potts, ed., *Araby the Blest* [Copenhagen: University Press, 1988], 86).

92. On the incised drawing of a camel on the dish from Pi-Ramesse, stratum B-3, see E. Pusch, *Ägypten und Levante* 6 (1996): 107-18 (date, early thirteenth century, 116-17), with figs. 3-7.

93. For wider references, including for the third millennium, see further M. Ripinsky, *JEA* 71 (1985): 134-41; Köhler, *Zur Domestikation des Kamels*, and P. Rowley-Conwy, *JEA* 74 (1988): 245-48, and G. R. Stone, in *Buried History* 27 (1991): 100-106, and 28 (1992): 3-14, although not all the examples they cite are now valid. Also, more widely, J. Zarins, *ABD*, 1:824-26. On Nubian evidence of the camel within ca. 1040-770, from calibrated radiocarbon-dated dung, see Rowley-Conwy, 245-48.

94. The Mari document on Laish, Hazor, and Kaptara were first cited by A. Pohl, *Or* 19 (1950): 509 (not exactly); published fully by G. Dossin, *RAAO* 64 (1970): 97ff. For English version and commentary, see A. Malamat, *IEJ* 21 (1971): 31-38, (esp. 34ff.), and as app. §3, in Y. Yadin, *Hazor*, Schweich Lectures, 1970 (London: OUP, 1972), 207.

95. For Egyptian Keft(i)u, see in detail J. Vercoutter, *L'Égypte et le monde égéen préhellénique* (Cairo: IFAO, 1956), 38-51 (texts before 1480 B.C.), 106-15 (meaning and history of the word); also J. F. Quack, *Ägypten und Levante* 6 (1996): 75-81, passim.

96. On the Middle Minoan pottery at Hazor, see Y. Yadin, *Hazor II* (1960), 86, pl. 115:12-13; briefly, A. Malamat, *JBL* 79 (1960): 18-19.

97. The frescoes at Alalakh are in Sir C. L. Woolley, *A Forgotten Kingdom* (London: Penguin Books, 1953), 76 and pl. 6(a), and in his *Alalakh* (London: Society of Antiquaries, 1955), 228-34, pls. 36-38.

98. For Tel Kabri frescoes, cf. briefly A. Kempinski, *NEAHL*, 3:841, and references.

99. The most convenient summary of the Minoan-type frescoes in Egypt at Avaris is by M. Bietak, *Avaris, the Capital of the Hyksos* (London: British Museum Press, 1996), 73-81; more detail is given in papers in W. V. Davies and L. Schofield, eds., *Egypt, the Aegean, and the Levant* (London: British Museum Press, 1995). For original reports, largely in German, see studies in M. Bietak, ed., *Ägypten und Levante* 4 (1994); 5 (1995); and 8 (1998): passim.

100. For Cypriot pottery at Megiddo, see R. Amiran, *Ancient Pottery of the Holy Land* (New Brunswick, N.J.: Rutgers University Press, 1970), 121-23, pl. 37; at Tell Jemmeh, see G. W. Van Beek, in *NEAHL*, 2:668; at Tel Haror, along with the "Minoanizing" chalice, see E. D. Oren, in *NEAHL*, 2:581.

101. The vast preponderance of West Semitic "Imperfective" names was made clear by me with appropriate figures, in *BAR* 21, no. 2 (March-April 1995): 90, 92, in reply to the totally

wrong claims by P. K. McCarter, in H. Shanks, ed., *Ancient Israel* (Washington, D.C.: BAS, 1988), 11. The facts were then perversely misconstrued by R. S. Hendel in *BAR* 21, no. 4 (July-August 1995): 57, glossing over the evidence entirely. For the use of the term "Amorite Imperfective," see I. J. Gelb, *La lingua degli Amoriti*, Atti della Accademia Nazionale dei Lincei, *Rendiconti*, series 8/ 13, fasc. 3-4 (1958), 156-58 ("imperfettivo"); H. B. Huffmon, *Amorite Personal Names in the Mari Texts* (Baltimore: Johns Hopkins University Press, 1965), passim; G. Buccellati, *The Amorites of the Ur III Period* (Naples: Istituto Orientale di Napoli, 1966), passim. Contrast, e.g., the "Amorite" form Yasmah-(X) with Akkadian Ishme-(X).

102. I. J. Gelb et al., *Computer-Aided Analysis of Amorite* (Chicago: OIC, 1980).

103. Ugaritic names are in F. Gröndahl, *Die Personennamen der Texte aus Ugarit* (Rome: Pontifical Biblical Institute, 1967).

104. Phoenician names are in F. L. Benz, *Personal Names in the Phoenician and Punic Inscriptions* (Rome: Pontifical Biblical Institute, 1972); for Old/Imperial Aramaic, see M. Maraqten, *Die semitischen Personennamen in den alt- und reichsaramäischen Inschriften aus Vorderasien* (Hildesheim: Olms, 1988).

105. The name Ab-sharru at Beni Hasan must be so read, because it is written in the same conventions as are the almost contemporary Execration Texts; transcripts such as "Ibsha" or "Absha" are wrong. For Ab-ram(u), "the Father is exalted," cf. (e.g.) Hoch, *SWET,* 495: E.47.

106. On Zabilanu in the Execration Texts, see Sethe, *Ächtung feindlicher Fürsten,* 47: e.6; on Zabilu-Haddu, see Posener, *Princes et Pays d'Asie et de Nubie,* 73: E.16; on the Old Babylonian wage list, see A. Goetze, *BASOR* 95 (1944): 23-24: B.16, 26; at Mari (Zubalan), see M. Birot, references, in *ARM(T)* XVI/1 (1979), 238.

107. On Asher, (J)acob, (Is)sachar in the Papyrus Brooklyn 13.1445 of ca. 1730, see W. F. Albright, *JAOS* 74 (1954): 229, 231 nos. 23 and 37, and 227 no. 13 respectively.

108. For the mysterious Phicol, the Hittite Pig/k- names include one Pigal-harali (Laroche, *Les noms des Hittites,* 142, no. 990).

109. The Anatolian-named Kukun inscribed an obelisk at Byblos in the early second millennium; see references by Kitchen in D. J. Wiseman, ed., *Peoples of Old Testament Times* (Oxford: OUP, 1973), 72 n. 24.

110. For possible Carian background, see J. Ray, *VT* 36 (1986): 358-61. In the second millennium, Caria was most likely the Karkiya/Karkisha of the Hittite state archives (references are in G. F. del Monte and J. Tischler, *RGTC 6: Die Orts- und Gewässernamen der Hethitischen Texte* [Wiesbaden: Reichert, 1978], 182-83, and del Monte, *RGTC 6/2, Supplement* [1992], 67). As Qarqis(h)a, this land recurs among the Hittite allies that opposed Ramesses II at Qadesh in 1275 (for translation, see Kitchen, *RITA* II, 2, 4, 16). For a probable Carian location for Karkisha, cf. J. D. Hawkins, *AnSt* 48 (1998): 29-30 with n. 184, and P. Mountjoy, 50; supported by being linked to Iyalanta (del Monte, 67), which became classical Alinda (Hawkins, 26). See map in Kitchen, *RITA* III (2000), 570-71.

111. For Mycenaean Greek Pa-ku-ro and Gk. Baikulos, see M. Ventris and J. Chadwick, *Documents in Mycenaean Greek* (Cambridge: Cambridge University Press, 1956; reprint, 1959), 422, with references.

112. For Greeks in Greece from ca. 2000, cf. (e.g.) J. L. Caskey, *CAH,* 3rd ed., II/1 (1973), 138-40.

113. For the predynastic period and First/Second Dynasties, see Redford, *Egypt, Canaan, and Israel,* 17-48; and on specific topics, the essays in E. C. M. van den Brink, ed., *The Nile Delta in Transition: Fourth-Third Millennium B.C.* (Tel Aviv: E. C. M. van den Brink, 1992), 345-485. On the Old Kingdom, see Redford, 48-58, 63-64.

114. For a comprehensive, detailed, and judicious review of Semites in Egypt during the First and Second Intermediate Periods and the Twelfth Dynasty in between, see Hoffmeier, *Israel in Egypt*, 52-76; see also 77-106 for a concise, up-to-date survey of data and views of the Joseph narrative.

115. For Merikare on the East Delta, cf. translations in Hoffmeier, *Israel in Egypt*, 54-55; earlier, *ANET*, 416-17, or Lichtheim, *Ancient Egyptian Literature*, 1:103-4; *CoS* I, 61-66. On Sinuhe, see *ANET*, 19; Lichtheim, 1:224; *CoS* I, 77.

116. For the annals of Amenemhat II and mentions of Asiatics, in German, see H. Altenmüller and A. Moussa, *SAK* 18 (1991): 1-48; for note of Asiatics therein, see Kitchen, in Hess et al., *Oath*, 79, and Hoffmeier, *Israel in Egypt*, 61, 73 nn. 81-83.

117. For Semites in Egyptian service (in temples, private households, etc.), see G. Posener, *Syria* 34 (1957): 151-55. For the data in Papyrus Brooklyn 35.1446 on Semites in Egypt, their names, and on the prison service, see the publication by W. C. Hayes, *A Papyrus of the Late Middle Kingdom* (New York: Brooklyn Museum, 1955), along with papers (on foreigners) by W. F. Albright, *JAOS* 74 (1954): 222-33, and G. Posener, *Syria* 34 (1957): 147-63.

118. The Hammurabi information is in *ANET*, 170, 175, 176; *CoS* II, 343, 348, 350. For Mari, see G. Boyer, *ARM(T)* VIII (1958), 23, no. 10:1-4. On other Old Babylonian tablets, see (e.g.) M. van de Mieroop, *AfO* 34 (1987), 10, 11. For a list of other Old Babylonian slave prices within fifteen/thirty shekels, see A. Falkenstein, *Die neusumerische Gerichtsurkunden* I (Munich: Beck, 1956), 88 n. 5 end.

119. For prices (and some extreme variations, from two-thirds of a shekel up to fifty-five shekels), under the Third Dynasty of Ur, see Falkenstein, *Die neusumerische Gerichtsurkunden*, 88-90. For particular classes within a range of ten to fifteen shekels (ten cases), and twenty shekels (four cases), plus other extremes, see D. O. Edzard, *Sumerische Rechtsurkunden des III. Jahrtausends* (Munich: Beck, 1968), 87, tab. 5 with references. For a similar situation under the previous empire of Akkad, cf. I. Mendelsohn, *Slavery in the Ancient Near East* (New York: OUP, 1949), 117 and 155 n. 164.

120. For Nuzi, see B. L. Eichler, *Indenture at Nuzi* (New Haven: Yale University Press, 1973), 16 and n. 35, and texts listed on 17-18. On Ugarit, cf. Mendelsohn, *Slavery*, 118 and 155 n. 181.

121. For Assyria, see list in C. H. W. Johns, *Assyrian Deeds and Documents* III (Cambridge: Cambridge University Press, 1924), 542-46.

122. For Neo-Babylonian and Persian-period prices, cf. B. Meissner, *Babylonien und Assyrien* I (Heidelberg: Winter, 1920), 365-66, and his *Warenpreise in Babylonien* (Berlin: Akademie der Wissenschaften, 1936), 35-36; Mendelsohn, *Slavery*, 117 and 155 n. 174.

123. The attempt by R. S. Hendel, *BAR* 21, no. 4 (July-August 1995): 56, to wriggle out of the data given here and previously is entirely misguided. The fifty-shekel dedication rate in Lev. 27:3 is not a slave sale (and so is irrelevant), but the cash substitute for a dedication. Again, it is mistaken to class Joseph as a boy under the twenty-shekel rule of Lev. 27:5 — at seventeen, he was no mere child; and in any case, before 2000, under Ur III, a man sold his son for twenty shekels (⅓ mina) as did another man at Larsa (nineteenth/eighteenth centuries) — so Leviticus, 600 years later, is irrelevant to Joseph's situation. For these Ur and Larsa examples, see Mendelsohn, *Slavery*, 6, 8, giving both texts in full (RTC 17; YBT VIII.8).

124. For a full presentation of the data on these names, with references, see Kitchen, in Hess et al., *Oath*, 80-86.

125. A. R. Schulman, *SAK* 2 (1975): 241.

126. The suggestion by Muchiki, *Egyptian PN*, 224-25, to interpret as Djef(ai)-Nute(r) pa-ʿankh is good phonetically, but it has no exact equivalent. Djefai + Deity is good (and of

Old and Middle Kingdom date). But it is rare; the *pa* does not fit; and the *ankh* attached in just one case is a servant's compliment to his boss, Djefai-Hapi ("May Djefai-Hapi live!"; H. Ranke, *Die altägyptische Personennamen* I [Glückstadt: Augustin, n.d.], 406:17). This last example has no equivalent elsewhere, and has no *pa-* element. So this suggestion remains unlikely. His objection to elision of (*'i*) is also invalidated by the example of Pithom *(Pi-[I]tm)*.

127. For the list of servants in 1730, see Hayes, *A Papyrus*, 87-109.

128. See for the First Intermediate Period, Bietak, *Avaris and Piramesse*, 228-29 (sherds; mention by Amenemhat I), plus Bietak, *Avaris*, 7, 9-10 (Amenemhat I's text; Middle Bronze I sherds). For the Middle Kingdom, cf. M. Bietak, in A. F. Rainey, ed., *Egypt, Israel, Sinai* (Tel Aviv: University Press, 1978), 41-56.

129. Semitic kings within the Thirteenth/Fourteenth Dynasties, King(s) Khendjer (Semitic *Khanzir*, "boar, pig"; wrongly called "Hyksos" by Hoch, *SWET*, 254) and Babnum (Naplanum[?]) and others; in Turin Papyrus of Kings, Kitchen, *RITA* II, 545, 547; for monuments of Khendjer, see J. von Beckerath, *Untersuchungen zur politischen Geschichte der zweiten Zwischenzeit in Ägypten* (Glückstadt: Augustin, 1965), 49-51.

130. On East Delta cattle pastures, in Kamose's texts, see Wilson in *ANET,* 232 and n. 5.

131. For Papyrus Brooklyn, see n. 117 above.

132. On other Semites in Egyptian employ, cf. G. Posener, *Syria* 34 (1957): 154-55, for the Middle Kingdom. Chief craftsmen "David" and Epher were found on a Thirteenth Dynasty stela in the National Museum in Rio de Janeiro; for study and references, see Kitchen, in S. Israeli-Groll, ed., *Studies in Egyptology Presented to Miriam Lichtheim* II (Jerusalem: Magnes Press, 1990), 635-39.

133. For a catalogue of scarab seals of Hur (or "Har"), see G. T. Martin, *Egyptian Administrative and Private-Name Seals, . . . Middle Kingdom . . .* (Oxford: Griffith Institute, 1971), 78-85, nos. 984-1088a, with plates.

134. For scenes of appointment and promotion of high officials, see material collected by D. B. Redford, *The Biblical Story of Joseph* (Leiden: Brill, 1970), 208-13, with important ameliorations from Kitchen, *OrAnt* 12 (1973): 240-41; cf. further review by Hoffmeier, *Israel in Egypt,* 91-93.

135. Horse remains of late Thirteenth Dynasty (just pre-Hyksos) were found at the fortress of Buhen in Nubia; cf. note by R. O. Faulkner, *JEA* 45 (1959): 1-2.

136. Classic study of importance of dreams (and use of dream-interpretation manuals) in the biblical world is by A. L. Oppenheim, *The Interpretation of Dreams in the Ancient Near East* (Philadelphia: American Philosophical Society, 1956); cf. also J.-M. Husser, *Dreams and Dream-Narratives in the Biblical World* (Sheffield: Academic Press, 1999).

137. Papyrus Chester Beatty III is published by A. H. Gardiner, *Hieratic Papyri in the British Museum* I-II (London: British Museum, 1935), 7-23, and pls. 5-8a, 12-12a.

138. On the *hart'ummim,* in Egyptian, cf. the details given in Kitchen, *RITANC* I, 245-46, with references.

139. On cup divination, see references in *NBD,* 715-16.

140. On 110 years at death, an Egyptian ideal for 3,000 years, see data collected by J. M. A. Janssen, *OMRO* 31 (1950): 33-41 (clustering under Ramessides, seventeen out of twenty-seven occurrences).

141. For burial customs in Canaan, Chalcolithic to Iron II, see standard manuals, e.g., Mazar, *ALB* I, passim, or A. Ben-Tor, ed., *The Archaeology of Ancient Israel* (1992), passim.

142. On Canaanites and burials at Tell el-Dab'a, cf. Bietak, *Avaris*, 10-21, 31ff.

143. For Abdu's coffin and Nahman's dagger, see G. Daressy, *ASAE* 7 (1906): 118-19, and

plate (dagger); P. Lacau, *Sarcophages antérieurs au Nouvel Empire* II (Cairo: Service des Antiquités, 1906), 86-87, pls. 19:1-2, CGC no. 28108 (box coffin).

144. On *saris, sha-reshi,* see Kitchen, *JEA* 47 (1961): 160, with earlier references, and now *CAD* 14/R (2001), 296.

145. On *shesh* and *bwts* as Egyptian loanwords for linen, see Muchiki, *Egyptian PN,* 257-58 and 240 respectively.

146. On Caphtorim; in cuneiform, Kaptara, already in the early second millennium; cf. tin trade then involving Kaptara, Ugarit, Mari, Hazor, and others, with references, in A. Malamat, *Mari and the Early Israelite Experience* (London: OUP and British Academy, 1989), 56ff. In later second millennium, as *Kptr* in Ugaritic texts, see Gordon, *UT,* 3:422, no. 1291. For Kition (origin of "Kittim"), cf. archaeology and general introduction in V. Karageorghis, *Kition* (London: Thames & Hudson, 1976).

147. On sites from the "patriarchal period," cf. above, p. 335.

148. On the citation from Shamshi-Adad I, cf. *CAD* 3/D (1959), 115: *daru A.*

149. One can see the kinds of figures available to Shamshi-Adad I's scribes in the final edition of the Sumerian king list, coming down to the Isin/Larsa dynasties to his own time (cf. T. Jacobsen, *The Sumerian King List* [Chicago: University of Chicago Press, 1939], 115-27, for reigns there reckoned after the dynasty of Sargon of Akkad). A copy of the Sumerian king list was actually discovered at Tell Leilan, ancient Shubat-Enlil, a seat of Shamshi-Adad I (see C.-A. Vincente, *ZA* 85 [1995]: 234-70), so his scribes did have access to that list.

150. For a full edition of the tomb inscriptions of Mose (Mes), see G. A. Gaballa, *The Memphite Tomb-Chapel of Mose* (Warminster: Aris & Phillips, 1977); a handbook translation of the main text is in Kitchen, *RITA* III (2000), 307-12.

151. On the Berlin genealogy, cf. Kitchen, *Third Int. Pd.* (1996), 189-90.

152. On the king list of Ugarit, cf. Kitchen, *UFo* 9 (1977/78): 131-42; and translation (with additional references) by K. L. Younger, in *CoS* I (1997), 356-57.

153. For the latest translation of the Palermo Stone, see T. A. H. Wilkinson, *Royal Annals of Ancient Egypt, the Palermo Stone and Its Associated Fragments* (London: Kegan Paul, 2000). For the fragment of the annals of Amenemhat II (in German), see H. Altenmüller and A. Moussa, *SAK* 18 (1991): 1-48. On the New Kingdom rulers, see Breasted, *ARE* II-III (1906) (old); for the Eighteenth Dynasty, more recent, see B. Cumming and B. G. Davies, *Egyptian Historical Records of the Later Eighteenth Dynasty* (Warminster: Aris & Phillips, 1982-95), fasc. I-III and IV-VI respectively; on the Nineteenth Dynasty, see Kitchen, *RITA* I-IV (1993-2003) (plus *RITANC* I-IV for notes), and sampling, B. G. Davies, *Egyptian Historical Inscriptions of the Nineteenth Dynasty* (Jonsered, Sweden: P. Aströms förlag, 1997); for a sampling of the Twentieth Dynasty, Ramesses III-XI, see A. J. Peden, *Egyptian Historical Inscriptions of the Twentieth Dynasty* (Jonsered, Sweden: P. Aströms förlag, 1994). For later periods, references are in Kitchen, *Third Int. Pd.* (1996), passim.

154. A large run of Sumerian and Babylonian royal texts are in *RIME/RIMB,* down to end of the Old Babylonian period; Assyrian royal texts are in *RIMA* 1-3 (so far), before Tiglath-pileser III; for his reign as king, see H. Tadmor, *The Inscriptions of Tiglath-pileser III, King of Assyria* (Jerusalem: Israel Academy, 1994); for Sennacherib to Assurbanipal, see the old versions in Luckenbill, *ARAB* I-II; some modern English selections (including Neo-Babylonian) are in *ANET* and *CoS* II; for Esarhaddon in German, see R. Borger, *Die Inschriften Asarhaddons, Königs von Assyrien* (Graz: AfO; Osnabrück: Biblio-Verlag, 1956; reprint, 1967); for Assurbanipal in German, see R. Borger, *Beiträge zum Inschriftenwerk Assurbanipals* (Wiesbaden: Harrassowitz, 1996); for other selected texts from all periods, in German, see *TUAT* I/4.

155. On the Hittite royal sources, see Anittas in *CoS* I, 182-83; texts of Telipinu, Suppliluliuma I and II, Hattusil III are in *CoS* I, 185-204; Hattusil I and Mursil II are in *CoS* II, 79-90; treaties are in Beckman, *Hittite Diplomatic Texts.*

156. On Idrimi, see *ANET,* 3rd ed. (1969), 557-58, and *CoS* I, 479-80 (wrongly classed as fiction). For selections of West Semitic texts (Byblos, Sidon, Hamath, Sam'al, Adana, etc.), see *ANET* (1969), 499-505, 653-62, and further Aramean, Moabite, Ammonite, Hebrew inscriptions in *CoS* II, 135-83. Azitawata bilingual, for "Hittite" (Luvian) Hieroglyphic text, see J. D. Hawkins, *CHLI* I, 48-58, 69 (translations).

157. Brief texts from Old South Arabia are in *ANET* (1955/1969), 506-13; for the annals of Karibil Watar I, fully, in German, cf. W. W. Müller in *TUAT* I/6 (1985), 651-58.

158. A selection from all periods appears in Breasted, *ARE* I-IV (1906); for Old and Middle Kingdoms, cf. now M. Lichtheim, *Ancient Egyptian Autobiographies, Chiefly of the Middle Kingdom* (Freiburg and Göttingen, 1988); for Khnumhotep II, see translation by A. B. Lloyd, in Lloyd, ed., *Studies in Pharaonic Religion and Society in Honour of J. Gwyn Griffiths* (London: EES, 1992), 21-36. The Sinuhe story is in (e.g.) *ANET,* 18-22, or *CoS* I, 77-82; Wenamun is in (e.g.) *ANET,* 25-29, or *CoS* I, 89-93. The Eighteenth Dynasty is also in Cumming and Davies, *Egyptian Historical Records.* For the Nineteenth Dynasty, see Kitchen, *RITA* I, III, IV. For later years, see R. A. Caminos, *The Chronicle of Prince Osorkon* (Rome: Pontifical Biblical Institute, 1958).

159. For texts of such as Shamshi-ilu, Ninurta-kudurri-usur, see *CoS* II, 277-83, and cf. Hadad-yithi, "king" to the locals but just a governor to his Assyrian masters, in *CoS* II, 153-54.

160. For the Neo-Hittite texts, see Hawkins, *CHLI* I, 48-58, 69. For an Old Aramaic funerary text, cf. (e.g.) Si-Gabbar, *CoS* II, 184-85.

161. All references for the paragraph on Egyptian historical legends are in this note. For Papyrus Westcar, translations and references, see (e.g.) in W. K. Simpson, ed., *The Literature of Ancient Egypt* (New Haven: Yale University Press, 1972; 2nd ed., 1973), 15-30, and Lichtheim, *Ancient Egyptian Literature,* 1:215-22. For the stories on General Sisenet and Neferkare, edited by G. Posener, see *RdÉ* 11 (1957): 119-37, pls. 7-8. On Apopi and Seqenenre, see Wilson in *ANET,* 230-32; E. F. Wente in Simpson, 77-80. On the "Capture of Joppa," see Wilson in *ANET,* 22-23; Wente in Simpson, 81-84. For the princess of Bakhtan, see Wilson in *ANET,* 29-31; M. Lichtheim, *Ancient Egyptian Literature* 3 (Berkeley: University of California Press, 1980), 90-94 (= *CoS* I, 134-36); Kitchen, *RITA* II (1996), 113-16 with notes and references, *RITANC* II (1999), 165-68. For tales of Prince Khaemwaset (Setne-Khamwas), see Lichtheim, 3:125-51. On the Delta cycle of Petubastis, a sample is in Lichtheim, 3:151-56; for references and background, see Kitchen, *Third Int. Pd.* (1996), 455-61, excursus G.

162. For the Sumerian stories of Gilgamesh, the five main works, find up-to-date translations in A. George, *The Epic of Gilgamesh, a New Translation* (London: Allen Lane, Penguin Press, 1999), 141-208, with references to earlier publications. Enmerkar and the Lord of Aratta is in T. Jacobsen, *The Harps That Once . . .* (New Haven: Yale University Press, 1987), 275-319, and in *CoS* I, 547-50. For Lugalbanda, cf. Jacobsen, 320-44; both tales are in J. Black, *Reading Sumerian Poetry* (London: Athlone Press, 1998). For the Dumuzi texts, see Jacobsen, 1-84. For the Etana tales, in Akkadian, cf. S. Dalley, *Myths from Mesopotamia* (Oxford: OUP, 1989), 190-202. For the legends of kings of Akkad, see J. G. Westenholz, *Legends of the Kings of Akkade* (Winona Lake, Ind.: Eisenbrauns, 1997), for most texts and references for others. Tukulti-Ninurta I is in B. R. Foster, *Before the Muses, an Anthology of Akkadian Literature* I (Bethesda, Md.: CDL Press, 1993), 209-29 with references, and reprinted in his *From Distant Days* (Bethesda, Md.: CDL Press, 1995), 178-96. For Tiglath-pileser I, see Foster, *Before the Muses,* 1:236-38.

163. Use of Gilgamesh is included in French versions by R. J. Tournay and A. Shaffer,

L'épopée de Gilgamesh (Paris: Éditions du Cerf, 1994), passim. Mention of Anum-khirbe is in H. Güterbock, *JAOS* 84 (1964): 109; for extracts from siege of Urshu, cf. O. R. Gurney, *The Hittites*, 4th ed. (London: Penguin Books, 1990), 148-49. On Kanesh and Zalpa, see Hoffner, *Hittite Myths*, 62-63.

164. The Hurrian-Hittite work on Meki of Syrian Ebla was edited by E. Neu, *Das hurritische Epos der Freilassung, I*, StBoT 32 (Wiesbaden: Harrassowitz, 1996); cf. now, continuous version by G. Wilhelm, in *TUAT, Ergänzungslieferung* (2001), 82-91. For the Keret and Danel epics from Ugarit, see (e.g.) H. L. Ginsberg in *ANET*, 142-55, and D. Pardee in *CoS* I, 333-56.

165. "The Shipwrecked Sailor" is in (e.g.) Lichtheim, *Ancient Egyptian Literature*, 1:211-15 (and *CoS* I, 83-85), and in Simpson, *Literature of Ancient Egypt* (1973), 50-56. The fragment on the herdsman/goddess is in A. Erman and A. M. Blackman, *Literature of the Ancient Egyptians* (1927), reprint edition, W. K. Simpson (New York: Harper, 1966), 35-36. For an early ghost story fragment, see G. Posener, *RdÉ* 12 (1960): 75-82. For "Foredoomed Prince," see E. F. Wente in Simpson, *Literature of Ancient Egypt* (1973), 85-91; M. Lichtheim, *Ancient Egyptian Literature* 2 (Berkeley: University of California Press, 1976), 200-203. For "Tale of Two Brothers," see Wente, in Simpson, *Literature of Ancient Egypt* (1973), 92-107, or Lichtheim, 2:203-11. For "The Blinding of Truth," see Wente in Simpson, *Literature of Ancient Egypt* (1973), 127-32; Lichtheim, 2:211-14.

166. In *Mesopotamia*, in Sumerian, "Three Ox-Drivers of Adab" is summarized by J. J. A. van Dijk, *La sagesse suméro-akkadienne* (Leiden: Brill, 1953), 11-12, and is partly translated by A. Falkenstein in *Indogermanische Forschungen* 60 (1952): 114-15; cf. B. Alster, *Studies in Sumerian Proverbs* (Copenhagen: Akademisk Forlag, 1975), 125 nn. 5-6. "Old Man and Young Girl" is translated by Alster, 90-97. In Akkadian, humorously, "Poor Man of Nippur" is in B. R. Foster, *Before the Muses* II (Bethesda, Md.: CDL Press, 1993), 829-34, and "At the Cleaner's" is in Foster, *Before the Muses*, 1:89-90, and in his *From Distant Days*, 355-62; in *CoS* I, 49 also.

167. For stories on Appu, Keshshi, etc., see Hoffner, *Hittite Myths*, 62-68.

168. For "Contendings of Horus and Seth," see *ANET*, 14-17; Wente in Simpson, *Literature of Ancient Egypt* (1973), 108-26; Lichtheim, *Ancient Egyptian Literature*, 2:214-23. For "Destruction of Mankind," see *ANET*, 10-11; Lichtheim, 2:197-99 (and *CoS* I, 36-37). For "Story of Astarte and the Sea," see *ANET*, 17-18; *CoS* II, 35-36; Wente in Simpson, 133-36. "Isis and the Sun-god's Secret Name" is in *ANET*, 12-14; *CoS* I, 33-34. For "Story of the Winged Disc," see H. W. Fairman, *JEA* 21 (1935): 26-36. For "Anhur-Shu and the Lioness-Goddess," cf. Lichtheim, *Ancient Egyptian Literature*, 3:156-59. Esna tales, in French, are in S. Sauneron, *Esna* V (Cairo: IFAO, 1962), 194-378.

169. For a general account and translations of the Sumerian myths about Enki, see S. N. Kramer and J. Maier, *Myths of Enki the Crafty God* (New York: OUP, 1989); individually, on Enki and Nin-hursag, see Jacobsen, *The Harps That Once*, 181-204; on Enki and Nin-mah, Jacobsen, 151-66; *CoS* I, 516-18; on Inanna and Enki, *CoS* I, 522-26; on "Enki and the World Order" (= Enki and Inanna, "Organization of the Earth . . ."), see C. Benito, *"Enki and Nin-mah" and "Enki and the World Order"* (Ann Arbor: University Microfilms), 77-160; on "Enki's Journey to Nippur," A. A. Al-Fouadi, *Enki's Journey to Nippur: The Journeys of the Gods* (Ann Arbor: University Microfilms, 1969). For the Eridu Genesis (Sumerian flood story), cf. Jacobsen, 145-50; and in *CoS* I, 513-15. For "Inanna's Descent to the Netherworld," see Jacobsen, 205-32. For "Nanna-Suen's Journey to Nippur," see A. J. Ferrara, *Nanna-Suen's Journey to Nippur* (Rome: Pontifical Biblical Institute, 1973). A good series on the myths about Dumuzi is in Jacobsen, 1-84. Akkadian myths include: "Ishtar's Descent to the Netherworld" in Dalley, *Myths from Mesopotamia*, 154-62 (and in *CoS* I, 381-84); Foster, *Before the Muses*, 1:403-28 (and his *From Distant Days*, 78-84). On the Erra epic, see Dalley, 282-315 (and in *CoS* I, 404-16); Foster, *Before the Muses*, 2:771-805. On the

Anzu myth, see Dalley, 203-27; Foster, *Before the Muses,* 461-85 (and his *From Distant Days,* 115-31). On *Enuma Elish,* see *ANET,* 60-72; Dalley, 228-75; Foster, *Before the Muses,* 1:351-402 (and *From Distant Days,* 9-51; *CoS* I, 390-402).

170. For Hittite myths along with a Hurrian cycle (of Kumarbi), see Hoffner, *Hittite Myths,* 9-37 (Hittite), 38-61 (Hurrian).

171. For mainly the Ugaritic myths, Baal series, see *ANET,* 129-42; and with "Dawn and Dusk," *CoS* I, 241-83; "Wedding of Nikkal and the Moon," is in C. H. Gordon, *Ugaritic Literature* (Rome: Pontifical Biblical Institute, 1949), 63-65. For Elkunirsha and Asherat, in a Hittite version, see Hoffner, *Hittite Myths,* 69-70; and *CoS* I, 149.

172. A recent inquest by K. Harris (televised in summer 2001; not yet published) suggested that townships on the plain, underwater until recently, south of the Lisan Peninsula were possibly destroyed in a seismic overthrow along with the liquefaction of terrain (as in Japan recently), with total destruction and engulfment of sites and flooding of the plain. The sites of Bab edh-Dhra, Numeira, es-Safi, Feifeh, and Khanazir all fell about the end of the Early Bronze Age, much too early for Gen. 19, and are on the plateau, not the Ghor plain. So they may be precursors of Abraham's lot, but not identical with them, having fallen to some earlier seismic upset (to which the region is prone). For these sites, cf. briefly W. C. van Hattem, *BA* 44, no. 2 (1981): 87-92. See now especially A. Frumkin and Y. Elitzur, *BAR* 27, no. 6 (November-December 2001): 42-50.

173. The genealogical tradition of Hammurabi and Shamshi-Adad I is set out by J. J. Finkelstein, *JCS* 20 (1966): 95-118; cf. A. Malamat, *JAOS* 88 (1968): 163-73 [= *Essays in Memory of E. A. Speiser*]. For the Assyrian king list, see I. J. Gelb, *JNES* 13 (1954): 209-30, esp. 222-35 (Old Assyrian segment).

174. For the king list of Ugarit, see Kitchen, in *UFo* 9 (1977): 131-42; also, with additional references, see K. L. Younger et al., *CoS* I, 356-358. For the seal of Yaqarum, used dynastically, cf. J. Nougayrol, *PRU* III (1955), xl-xliii and figs. 22-25.

175. On Ukh-hotep, see Kitchen, *TynB* 5, no. 6 (1960): 15, based on A. M. Blackman, *Rock Tombs of Meir* III (London: EEF, 1915), 16-21; this was studied also by L. Borchardt, *Die Mittel zur zeitlichen Festlegung von Punkten der ägyptischen Geschichte und ihre Anwendung* (published by author, 1935), 122-14.

176. On Didia, see D. A. Lowle, *OrAnt* 15 (1976): 91-106, and Kitchen, *RITA* I, 267, with *RITANC* I, 223-24.

177. On Petubastis and Bakhtan, see already above, p. 369.

178. On Anittas, cf. *CoS* I, 182-84.

179. On Papyrus Brooklyn 35.1446, see Hayes, *A Papyrus of the Late Middle Kingdom;* W. F. Albright, *JAOS* 74 (1954): 222-33; G. Posener, *Syria* 34 (1957): 147-63.

180. For the West Semitic alphabet in its early phases, see the monograph by B. Sass, *The Genesis of the Alphabet and Its Development in the Second Millennium* B.C. (Wiesbaden: Harrassowitz, 1988), and cf. E. Puech, *RB* 93 (1986): 161-213, passim. For Wadi Hol graffiti, later Middle Kingdom, full reports are awaited; meantime, one color photo appeared in *BAR* 26, no. 1 (January-February 2000): 12, and for a first look at two epigraphs, cf. the rather speculative efforts of S. J. Wimmer and S. Wimmer-Dweikat, *GM* 180 (2001): 107-12.

NOTES TO CHAPTER 8

1. A careful panorama of the common tripartite hypothesis is given in *ABD,* 3:472-507;

standard introductions to the Old Testament and annual bibliographies for OT study will supplement the *ABD* survey. Very little space is given to other views, contrary evidence to the tripartite hypothesis notwithstanding. Compact discussions carefully critical of such hypotheses will be found in (e.g.) R. K. Harrison, *Introduction to the Old Testament* (Grand Rapids: Eerdmans; London: Tyndale Press, 1969), 764-800, and incisively, J. A. Motyer, *The Prophecy of Isaiah* (Leicester: IVP, 1993); and briefly, F. D. Kidner, in D. Guthrie, J. A. Motyer, et al., eds., *The New Bible Commentary Revised* (London: InterVarsity, 1970), 589-91.

2. For the bearing of the clear division at Isa. 33/34 in the great Dead Sea Scrolls text of Isaiah, see W. H. Brownlee, *The Meaning of the Qumran Scrolls for the Bible* (New York: OUP, 1964), 247-53; and briefly, Harrison, *Introduction*, 787-89.

3. For Motyer's division, see his *The Prophecy of Isaiah,* 13-16.

4. The Syro-Palestinian, not Babylonian, milieu of Isa. 40–55 was (among others) pointed out by A. Lods (no pious "conservative"!), in a paragraph (A. Lods, *The Prophets of Israel* [London: Kegan Paul, 1937], 238) aptly cited by Motyer, *The Prophecy of Isaiah*, 27, and cf. his p. 26. For eighth-century phenomena (Canaanite idolatry, etc.) in Isa. 40–55, cf. Harrison, *Introduction*, 779, and likewise on grounds of social/religious background by E. J. Kissane, *The Book of Isaiah* II (1943), xlviff. For the close congruity of language, style, thought, and literary usage between Isa. 1–39 and 40–55, see the summary listing in Harrison, 778-79. A more open mind is needed on the links betwen Isa. 1–39 and 40–55 on these and allied grounds.

5. For the role of Merodach-Baladan (Marduk-apil-iddina II), and an account of his career, see J. A. Brinkman, in *From the Workshop of the Assyrian Dictionary, Studies A. L. Oppenheim* (Chicago: University of Chicago Press, 1964), 6-53, and recently the cogent remarks by W. R. Gallagher, *Sennacherib's Campaign to Judah* (Leiden: Brill, 1999), 270-72. In detail, see the important study by S. Erlandsson, *The Burden of Babylon: A Study of Isaiah 13:2–14:23* (Lund: Gleerup, 1970).

6. Cyrus II (the one who conquered Babylon in 539) clearly names himself son of Cambyses I and grandson of Cyrus (I) on the famous cylinder in his name in the British Museum; cf. *ANET,* 316 top; *CoS* II, 315.

7. We may minimally place Cyrus I in the early sixth century. This leaves us with the *third* Cyrus (of "Parsuash," the localized "Persia" whence came the later Persian royal line), contemporary of Assurbanipal of Assyria ca. 646, in a text published by E. F. Weidner, *AfO* 7 (1931/32): 1-7 (now, R. Borger, *Beiträge zum Inshriftenwerk Assurbanipals* [1996], ad loc.), and cited in English by T. Cuyler Young in *CAH* IV (1988), 26, with wider discussion (with map 2, p. 11).

8. On Esarhaddon's Median treaties (672 B.C.), see D. J. Wiseman, *The Vassal Treaties of Esarhaddon* (London: BSAI, 1958) (= *Iraq* 20, no. 1 [1958]); and in *ANET,* 3rd ed. (1969), 534-41.

9. On Assyria in Iran, from the ninth to the seventh century, cf. Young, in *CAH* IV (1988), 7-20; and A. K. Grayson, in *CAH* III/2 (1991), 71-161, passim.

10. Most of Jeremiah is so inextricably tied to his particular historical epoch (Josiah to Zedekiah) that recent extremist views banishing him to far later dates and disunity have no hope of success in contravening the available facts; above all, invention of such a work so late would be irrelevant and (in practice) historically impossible.

11. The basic unity of Ezekiel was well argued long ago by C. G. Howie, *The Date and Composition of Ezekiel* (Philadelphia: SBL, 1950), and half a century later the arguments may continue but the facts still stand.

12. Writing upon "sticks of wood" (37:16-23) became ubiquitous practice in Old South Arabia (it was their equivalent of ostraca, for recording day-to-day affairs). For publications of a body of such palm sticks, see J. Ryckmans, W. W. Müller, and Y. M. Abdallah, *Textes du Yémen*

Antique inscrits sur bois (Louvain: Institut Orientaliste, 1994); samples from two (X Ghul A, X Ghul B), by A. F. L. Beeston, in M. M. Ibrahim, ed., *Arabian Studies . . . [for] . . . Mahmoud Ghul* (1989), 15-19.

13. The mention of *nabi'utum* at Ebla is by G. Pettinato, *BA* 39 (1976): 49; after a quarter century, publication of the documents concerned is long overdue.

14. On and for the "prophetical" texts at Mari, see J.-M. Durand, in *ARM(T)* XXVI/1 (1988), chap. 5, picking up on, and adding to, previous text publications. On the terminology and types of prophecy, *nabi, apilum, muhhu,* etc., see 377-78, 386-96, and A. Lemaire, in J.-M. Durand, ed., *Amurru 1* (Paris: ERC, 1996), 430-31, plus his references to others' studies prior to 1985, in *MARI* 4 (1985): 553 and n. 42. An update in part appears in A. Lemaire, *RAAO* 93 (1999): 49-56. For a list of "prophecy" documents from Mari, cf. Durand, *ARM(T)* XXVI/1 (1988), 403-5, with forty-four items listed, but not including those involving Adad of Kallassu and Aleppo (XXVI/3, yet to appear).

Typical studies in biblical prophecy are collected in R. P. Gordon, ed., *The Place Is Too Small for Us: The Israelite Prophets in Recent Scholarship* (Winona Lake, Ind.: Eisenbrauns, 1995). A variety of studies embracing old and new attitudes to biblical prophetism, and surveying the Mari, Neo-Assyrian, and other material, is found in E. Ben Zvi and M. H. Floyd, eds., *Writings and Speech in Israelite and Ancient Near Eastern Prophecy,* Symposium Series 10 (Atlanta: SBL, 2000), and in M. Nissinen, ed., *Prophecy in Its Ancient Near Eastern Context, Mesopotamian, Biblical, and Arabian Perspectives,* Symposium Series 13 (Atlanta: SBL, 2000).

15. The bold numbers under this subhead are from Durand, *ARM(T)* XXVI/1 (1988). It is the chances of modern excavation and discovery which have determined that most of the early documentation hails from Mari, so far. But as Durand pertinently points out (pp. 401-2), prophets and prophecies are attested for this period also in the kingdoms of Aleppo and Babylon, also at Nakhur ("Nahor") and with such deities as Dagan at Tuttul, Terqa, and Subatum; Adad at Kallassu and Aleppo, also Shamash. Various goddesses inspired prophets, so Ninhursag, Annunitum, Belet-ekallim, and Hanat. So we are dealing with a phenomenon that was widespread in Mesopotamia and in Syria at this epoch.

16. The text of Tebi-geri-shu (no. **216**) was published by Durand in *ARM(T)* XXVI/1, 444-45. We also see King Zimri-lim asking a sign from the river god, and sending a gold vessel with his inquiry, as a present (no. **191**, Durand, 413).

17. For further examples not given here, cf. A. Lemaire, in Durand, *Amurru 1,* 431-33, with references.

18. On victory, see nos. **197-214**, passim, in Durand, *ARM(T)* XXVI/1, 424-42, passim (**209, 210** = *ANET,* 624, §§i, d).

19. For illness and death, see no. **222**, in Durand, *ARM(T)* XXVI/1, 451 (= *ANET* [1969], 623-24, §b).

20. On prior consultation with deity, see no. **199**; cf. Durand, *ARM(T)* XXVI/1, 427.

21. For prophecies for Adad of Aleppo and Kallassu, see edition of Mari letter A.1121 by B. Lafont, in *RAAO* 78 (1984): 7-18, with French translation, pp. 10-11 (which replaces the very incomplete one in *ANET* [1969], 625, §h; a fuller edition was promised in *ARM[T]* XXVI/3, not yet available).

22. On Shamash against Hammurabi of Kurda, see no. **194** in *ARM(T)* XXVI/1, 418. On gods faulting kings, and requiring the practice of justice, cf. the summary by Durand on 412.

23. On the use of certain drinks, cf. Durand, *ARM(T)* XXVI/1, 392, and nos. **207, 208, 212**, pp. 436, 438, 441.

24. On the behavior of the *muhhu* prophets, see Durand, *ARM(T)* XXVI/1, 386-88.

25. For prophetesses in action, see Durand, *ARM(T)* XXVI/1, nos. **210**, **211**, **214**, pp. 439f., 440f., 442f.

26. For curse and blessing together (laws, treaties, covenants), see in chap. 6 above. Add the considerations by A. R. Millard, *Scottish Bulletin of Evangelical Theology* 7 (1989): 97-99, in a wider context.

27. For texts, cf. Durand, *ARM(T)* XXVI/1, 409; Lemaire, *Amurru 1*, 43, and in *RAAO* 93 (1999): 54; as for archiving for fulfillment, see A. R. Millard, *RHR* 202 (1985): 139-41.

28. On term *sri*, see *Wb.* IV, 189:15–190:11.

29. Merikare translations are in *ANET*, 416; by R. O. Faulkner, in W. K. Simpson, ed., *The Literature of Ancient Egypt* (New Haven: Yale University Press, 1972; 2nd ed., 1973), 185; J. F. Quack, *Studien zur Lehre für Merikare* (Wiesbaden: Harrassowitz, 1992), 43; *CoS* I, 63.

30. Cf. Faulkner in Simpson, *Literature of Ancient Egypt*, 211; M. Lichtheim, *Ancient Egyptian Literature* 1 (Berkeley: University of California Press, 1973), 150; *CoS* I, 94.

31. For the Neferty translations, see *ANET*, 444-46; Faulkner in Simpson, *Literature of Ancient Egypt*, 235; Lichtheim, *Ancient Egyptian Literature*, 1:140; *CoS* I, 107.

32. Translations in Lichtheim, *Ancient Egyptian Literature*, 1:212; or Simpson, *Literature of Ancient Egypt*, 51-52.

33. See H. B. Huffmon, *ABD*, 5:477-78, with references; translation also in *ANET*, 395-96, §2, 396, §11.

34. For the Emar references, see Huffmon, *ABD*, 5:477; Lemaire, *Amurru 1*, 428, nn. 8-11.

35. See *ANET*, 431-32.

36. For Wenamun translations, see (e.g.) *ANET*, 26 and n. 13; or Wente, in Simpson, *Literature of Ancient Egypt*, 145-46, or M. Lichtheim, *Ancient Egyptian Literature* 2 (Berkeley: University of California Press, 1976), 225; *CoS* I, 89-93.

37. For a good new translation of Zakkur's text with essential references, see A. R. Millard, in *CoS* II, 155.

38. The Deir Alla text is well presented by B. A. Levine, in *CoS* II, 140-45, again with essential references.

39. Valuable background appears in a long study by M. deJong Ellis, *JCS* 41 (1989): 127-86; on "literary predictive texts," see 156-57.

40. For a modern edition of the Neo-Assyrian prophecies proper, see S. Parpola, *Assyrian Prophecies*, SAA IX (Helsinki: University Press, 1997); and compare for background, M. Nissinen, *References to Prophecy in Neo-Assyrian Sources*, SAAS VII (Helsinki: University Press, 1998).

41. Doubts of reaching prophetic ipsissima verba were expressed by K. Pohlmann, in I. Kottsieper et al., eds., *"Wer ist wie du, Herr, unter den Göttern" (Studien . . . für O. Kaiser)* (Göttingen: Vandenhoeck & Rupprecht, 1994), 325-41. Ultraskeptical about almost anything coming down from the original prophets was R. P. Carroll, e.g., in his commentary on Jeremiah (London: SCM Press, 1986), and in R. E. Clements, ed., *The World of Ancient Israel: Sociological, Anthropological, and Political Perspectives* (Cambridge: Cambridge University Press, 1989), 203-25, esp. 207-8. Cf., e.g., the mutual discussions between T. W. Overholt, A. G. Auld, and R. P. Carroll, in *JSOT* 48 (1990): 3-54, and observations by H. M. Barstad, *JSOT* 57 (1993): 39-60.

42. Voices skeptical of ultraskeptics are: A. R. Millard, *RHR* 202 (1985): 137-45; R. P. Gordon, *Bulletin for Biblical Research* 5 (1995): 67-86; J.-G. Heintz, in Heintz, ed., *Oracles et prophéties dans l'Antiquité* (Paris: Éditions du Cerf, 1997), 196-213; A. Lemaire, *RAAO* 93 (1999): 53.

43. For proclamation before one person, e.g., a royal official, see *ARM(T)* XXVI/1, 382, 476f., no. **235**; before witnesses, either at the prophet's request, e.g., elders at the gate (*ARM[T]*

XXVI/1, 434f., no. **206**), or as required by the official(s) concerned (B. Lafont, *RAAO* 78 [1984]: 10, ll. 6-12; 11, l. 61), to ensure accuracy of the report to the king (Durand, *ARM[T]* XXVI/1, 382 end). A prophet of Marduk denounced the sick Assyrian king Ishme-Dagan in front of everyone at the Ekallatum palace gate, because the king had confiscated property of the god Marduk to buy peace with Elam (D. Charpin, *ARM(T)* XXVI/2 [1988], 177-79, no. **371**), rather like Ahaz a millennium later; cf. 2 Kings 16:7-8. Again, the bold numbers are from *ARM(T)* XXVI/1 (1988).

44. For no. **217**, see *ARM(T)* XXVI/1, 445-46.

45. See no. **206** (*ARM[T]*, 434-35). For varying reports on the same oracle, etc., cf. S. B. Parker, *VT* 43 (1993): 50-68.

46. For three prophecies within one letter (one at the king's request), see *ARM(T)* XXVI/1, 427-28, no. **199**; another such is that published by B. Lafont, *RAAO* 78 (1984): 10-11.

47. The Neo-Assyrian prophecies are in Parpola, *Assyrian Prophecies.*

48. On Neferty, see *ANET,* 444, or *CoS* I, 107.

49. For Papyrus Chester Beatty IV, see *ANET,* 431.

50. On Zakkur, see *CoS* II, 155.

51. On the Balaam text, at Deir Alla, see *CoS* II, 140-45.

52. The demand for a good scribe is in text no. **414**; F. Joannès in *ARM(T)* XXVI/2, 294-95, ll. 29-36 (and with witnesses); cf. Durand, *ARM(T)* XXVI/1, 390-91. Compare Jeremiah's use of Baruch (Jer. 36), wrongly dismissed as fiction by A. Schart, *JANES* 23 (1995): 89, in an otherwise useful paper (pp. 75-93).

53. On keeping records for fulfillment, see A. R. Millard, *RHR* 202 (1985): 140.

54. For interlinks between Isaiah, Jeremiah, and the eighth–early sixth centuries, cf. already above, chap. 2.

55. On Isa. 13–14, see Erlandsson, *The Burden of Babylon.* On Cyrus in Babylon, his cylinder text, see *ANET,* 315-16, or *CoS* II, 314-16.

56. On Taharqa, see *ThIP,* 387-93 (plus the addenda).

57. On monotheistic Marduk under Nebuchadrezzar I, ca. 1100, cf. W. G. Lambert, lecture reported in *Society for OT Study Bulletin 2000* (2001): 4-5.

58. For a summary description of the temple of Baal (and reconstruction view), see M. Yon, *La cité d'Ougarit sur le tell de Ras Shamra* (Paris: ERC, 1997), 116-20; for that of Dagon, see 123-24. On the chapel royal, see Yon, 59 (also in an English edition). Compact outlines on Ugarit, cf. B. Schmidt, ed., in *NEA* 63, no. 4 (2000 [2001]): 182-243.

59. See G. E. Wright, *Shechem, the Biography of a Biblical City* (London: Duckworth, 1965), 95-102 ("Temple 2").

60. For Keret worshiping on a temple roof, see (e.g.) *ANET,* 143; *CoS* I, 334.

61. For KTU 1.109, in French by J.-M. de Tarragon, in A. Caquot, J.-M. de Tarragon, and J.-L. Cunchillos, *Textes Ougaritiques* II (Paris: Éditions du Cerf, 1989), 188-91; now D. Pardee, *Ras Shamra-Ougarit* XII/1 (Paris: ERC, 2000), 601-14.

62. Text of KTU 1.43 is in Caquot, de Tarragon, and Cunchillos, *Textes Ougaritiques,* 161-63; Pardee, *Ras Shamra-Ougarit* XII/1, 214-64.

63. For text of KTU 1.40 (and parallels), see (in English) J. C. de Moor and P. Sanders, *UFo* 23 (1991/92): 283-300, with notes and OT comparisons; now Pardee, *Ras Shamra-Ougarit* XII/1, 92-142. On Ugaritic rituals more generally, see the papers by B. Levine, *JCS* 17 (1963): 105-11, and in C. L. Meyers and M. O'Connor, eds., *The Word of the Lord Shall Go Forth (Essays . . . D. N. Freedman)* (Philadelphia: ASOR, 1983), 467-75; and his analogous treatment of tabernacle rituals, *JAOS* 85 (1965): 307-18; now, also, the considerable commentary on the Ugaritic rituals by Pardee, *Ras Shamra-Ougarit* XII/1-2.

64. For the Mursil II prayers of confession to ward off plague, see *ANET*, 394-96; or now *CoS* I, 156-60.

65. On West Semitic ritual terminology in Ugarit, cf. discussions of each term by J.-M. de Tarragon, *Le culte à Ugarit* (Paris: Gabalda, 1980), 55-78, and by Pardee, *Ras Shamra-Ougarit* XII/2, 997-1074. Semitic words formed with an initial *t* are very common in Akkadian, for example, from the late third and the second millennia onward; for a quick sampling, see (e.g.) J. Black, A. George, and N. Postgate, eds., *A Concise Dictionary of Akkadian*, corrected ed. (Wiesbaden: Harrassowitz, 2000), 392-411.

66. See an overall introduction to Emar, e.g., by J.-C. Margueron and D. E. Fleming, in *BA* 58, no. 3 (1995): 126-28, 139-47; for plans, processional routes, and reconstructions of two of the temples, see 132. A full study of the installation rites of the high priestess, with translations, is in D. E. Fleming, *The Installation of Baal's High Priestess at Emar* (Atlanta: Scholars Press, 1992); for comparisons with Lev. 8, cf. A. R. Millard, in T. Eskola and E. Junkkaala, eds., *From the Ancient Sites of Israel (Essays . . . in Memory of A. Saarisalo)* (Helsinki: Theological Institute of Finland, 1998), 108-10. For other Emar rituals, see *CoS* I, 426-43.

67. For the "Fosse Temple," especially phase III, late thirteenth century, see the final report, O. Tufnell, C. H. Inge, and L. Harding, *Lachish II (Tell ed-Duweir), the Fosse Temple* (London: OUP, 1940), hereafter cited as *Lc II*. For plans, see *Lc II*, pls. 68, 71, 73; masonry and plastering, p. 36.

68. For objects in the shrine: the faience vase, see *Lc II*, pl. 24; ivory ointment flask and spoon, see pl. 15; glassware, pl. 24; hunt scarab, pl. 32B:39.

69. For the three-step altar, see *Lc II*, pl. 6; for the stand, cupboard, bin, see pl. 7.

70. For the inset "cupboards" along the east wall, see *Lc II*, pls. 4, 8; for the bead necklaces, see pl. 14 (in color).

71. For Mediterranean pottery, see *Lc II*, pls. 46, 63 (colored); for local bichrome ware, cf. pls. 58-61, 64 (colored).

72. For the Lachish ewer, with late Canaanite inscription, see *Lc II*, frontispiece, pls. 51:287, and 60 fig. 3; the translation largely follows F. M. Cross and E. Puech, but omitting a superfluous *l* on grounds of space and form, as the latter suggests (cf. E. Puech, *RB* 93 [1986]: 179-80, and fig. 5:4, with references, who would add [Reshe]ph to account for a final *p*); last studied by B. Sass, *The Genesis of the Alphabet and Its Development in the Second Millennium* BC (1988), 60-61 with figs. 154-160. For the footbath bowl, see *Lc II*, 41 end, pl. 58B:4.

73. See *Lc II*, pl. 20.

74. For wands at Tel Nami, see M. Artzy, *BAR* 16, no. 1 (January-February 1990): 48-51.

75. On the pomegranate finial of such a wand, inscribed "Holy to the priests, belonging to the Ho[use of YHW]H," from either the Jerusalem temple or a parallel shrine (like Arad), eighth century, see H. Shanks, *In the Temple of Solomon and the Tomb of Caiaphas* (Washington, D.C.: Biblical Archaeology Society, 1993), 13-30.

76. On processional standards at Nahal Mishmar, see (e.g.) T. E. Levy, *BA* 49, no. 2 (1986): 89-91; R. Gonen, in A. Ben-Tor, ed., *The Archaeology of Ancient Israel* (New Haven: Yale University Press, 1992), 66-70, figs. 3.17-18 and color plate 11.

77. For Alaca Hüyük, cf. E. Akurgal, *The Art of the Hittites* (London: Thames & Hudson, 1962), pls. 1-12 and color pls. I-IV.

78. For examples of both ceremonial wands held by king and officers in great Egyptian festival processions and full-sized standards with sacred symbols, see (e.g.) the festival of Sokar, Epigraphic Survey, *Medinet Habu IV* (Chicago: University of Chicago Press, 1940), pl. 196C-D (in reduced format, G. A. Gaballa and K. A. Kitchen, *Or*, n.s., 38 [1969]: pls. I-II).

79. See Y. Yadin, *Hazor, Schweich Lectures, 1970* (London: OUP, 1972), pl. 15c (color, less legible, in his *Hazor* [London: Weidenfeld & Nicholson, 1975], p. 54).

80. For the plaque at Lachish city temple, see D. Ussishkin, *TA* 5 (1978): 21, pl. 8 (= also Ussishkin, *Excavations at Tel Lachish, 1973-1977* [1978], 21, pl. 8), and for a clear drawing, in *NEAHL*, 3:902.

81. See *Lc II*, pl. 26:28.

82. The original publication of the Egyptian ostracon with feast of Anath at Gaza is B. Grdesloff, *Les débuts du culte de Rechef en Égypte* (Cairo: IFAO, 1942), 35-39, §IV, and pls. VII-VIII; new text edition is in H. Goedicke and E. F. Wente, *Ostraka Michaelides* (Wiesbaden: Harrassowitz, 1962), pl. 93; English translation, E. F. Wente, *Letters from Ancient Egypt* (Atlanta: Scholars Press, 1990), 127, no. 150 (O. Michaelides 85).

83. On animal offerings, especially right forelegs of yearlings in the Fosse Temple, see *Lc II*, 25, 93-94. In contemporary funerary rites in Egypt, there was practiced the barbaric custom of cutting off the right foreleg of a live calf for use in the rites; for an example of this being done, see G. A. Gaballa, *The Memphite Tomb-Chapel of Mose* (Warminster: Aris & Phillips, 1977), 16 end, pl. 35, top right.

84. For the tall, stone sun-disc incense altar at Hazor, cf. Yadin, *Hazor, Schweich Lectures, 1970*, 92, pl. 19b. For traces of incense burning on the small altars at Arad, see Y. Aharoni, *BA* 31, no. 1 (1968): 19 (view, p. 20, fig. 13), which also contradicts the erroneous denials by M. Haran, *Temples and Temple-Service in Ancient Israel* (Oxford: OUP, 1978), 237.

85. For the Tell Qasile temples, see in summary, Mazar, *ALB* I, 319-26; full report is in A. Mazar, *Excavations at Tell Qasile, I-II*, in series *Qedem*, 12, 20 (Jerusalem: Hebrew University, 1980, 1985).

86. For the elimination of de Vaux's imaginary cult place at Tell el-Far'ah North (Tirzah), see M. D. Fowler, *PEQ* 113 (1981): 27-31.

87. On Megiddo, a domestic cult, see (e.g.) W. G. Dever, *RADBR*, 134.

88. On the supposed "cultic structure" at Taanach, see Fowler, *ZDPV* 100 (1984): 30-34.

89. For the common interpretation of the Lapp Taanach stand, cf. Dever, *RADBR*, 135, following on R. Hestrin, *BAR* 17, no. 5 (September-October 1991): 57-58, and in detail in *IEJ* 37 (1987): 212, and in E. Lipinski, ed., *Studia Phoenicia* V (1987), 161. For sensible reviews of cult stands overall, see M. D. Fowler, *BA* 47, no. 3 (1984): 183-84; L. F. Devries, *BAR* 13, no. 4 (July-August 1987): 26-37.

90. For the goddess upon lions, explicitly named, see the Winchester relief, inscribed in hieroglyphs "Qadishtu" above "Astarte," and "Anath" at left; see I. E. S. Edwards, *JNES* 14 (1955): 50, with pl. III. Likewise as "Qadishtu" and "Qadish(tu)," Louvre C.86, see C. Boreux, in *Mélanges Dussaud* II (Paris, 1939), 673-87, also with British Museum 191 (read as "[Qa]dishtu," the *k* being a faulty *d*); and other examples in Vienna and Turin; Berlin stela, in H. T. Bossert, *Altsyrien* (Tübingen: Wasmuth, 1951), 73, pl. 278, no. 946. Most Egyptian examples spell the name correctly in the feminine with a final *t-*, hence Qadishtu, not "Qudshu," as often printed. The latter stems from spellings that omit the feminine *t* because it was no longer pronounced (cf. in Arabic, *medinah* versus *medinat-habu*, with *t* protected by following genitive word). On nature of all three goddesses, Anath, Astarte, Asherah, cf. in *DDD*, 62-77, 183-95, 203-13.

91. Useful summaries are in A. Biran, *Biblical Dan* (Jerusalem: IES et al., 1994), 159-233, and (on cults at gates) in A. Mazar, ed., *Studies in the Archaeology of the Iron Age in Israel and Jordan* (Sheffield: Academic Press, 2001), 148-55.

92. For a recent translation, see *CoS* II, 140-45; for earlier background and detailed studies, cf. J. Hoftijzer and G. van der Kooij, eds., *The Balaam Text from Deir 'Alla Re-evaluated*

(Leiden: Brill, 1991); for a well-illustrated introduction, see A. Lemaire, *BAR* 11, no. 5 (September-October 1985): 26-39.

93. The original overall report was by Z. Meshel, *Kuntillet 'Ajrud, a Religious Centre from the Time of the Judean Monarchy on the Border of Sinai* (Jerusalem: Israel Museum, Catalogue No. 178, 1978), followed by a properly detailed study of all the drawings and paintings on walls and jars by P. Beck, *TA* 9 (1982): 3-68. On these and texts, cf. J. M. Hadley, *VT* 37 (1987): 180-213.

94. On the role of the site as principally a way station (a "high-security motel" in modern terms!), see J. M. Hadley, *PEQ* 125 (1993): 115-24; for recent suggestions on its economic role and possible political context, cf. W. Zwickel, *ZDPV* 116 (2000): 137-42.

95. The two principal figures on "Pithos A" are Bes figures, being full faced, arms akimbo, bandy-legged, wearing lion skins whose tails dangle between their legs from behind. The triple plumes and everted cap worn by them are readily paralleled in other Bes figures, e.g., the Roman warrior Bes, Rio de Janeiro no. 80 (Inv. 520), and Late Period Bes, Rio no. 79 (Inv. 1968), published in M. Beltrão and K. A. Kitchen, *Catalogue of the Egyptian Collection in the National Museum, Rio de Janeiro* (Warminster: Aris & Phillips; Rio de Janeiro: MN-UFRJ, 1990), I, 193, and II, pls. 185-86 and 187A. On the lyre player, see details by Beck, *TA* 9 (1982): 31-36 (as easily male as female), and especially Hadley, *VT* 37 (1987): 196-207, pointing out J. Ray's correct observation that the lyre player wears a typical Egyptian short *male* wig (p. 201). Thus, these figures do not remotely represent YHWH and/or Asherah under these conditions (*pace* Dever, *BASOR* 255 [1984]: 21-37, and since); the text above was written across the top later and separately.

96. On the question of "Asherata/his Asherah," see initially Z. Zevit, *BASOR* 255 (1984): 39-47 (using Khirbet el-Qom), arguing from nonaffixation of suffixes to proper nouns in Hebrew, as did J. A. Emerton, *ZAW* 94 (1982): 1-20. A thorough philological analysis by R. Hess, *Or*, n.s., 65 (1996): 209-19, esp. 215-18. For a preliminary "corpus" of texts, see Renz/Röllig I, 47-65, and III, pls. II-V, passim. Some, *CoS* II, 171-73.

97. Tombs and texts were first published by W. G. Dever, *HUCA* 40-41 (1970): 139-204. References, Renz/Röllig I, 201-2; text (as no. 3), 207-10, III, pl. XX:2. In addition to Zevit and Hess (above), cf. Hadley, *VT* 37 (1987): 50-62, and M. O'Connor, 224-30; and now *CoS* II, 179.

98. For the stratigraphy of Arad in terms of its temple, based on a close reexamination of the finds, see now Z. Herzog in Mazar, *Studies in the Archaeology*, 156-78. For accounts of the building prior to this modified history (strata 10-9 only), cf. (e.g.) Y. Aharoni, *BA* 31 (1968): 18-27; and briefly in *NEAHL*, 1:83, which must now be read in the light of the new findings.

99. For the ostraca and stone bowls, see Y. Aharoni, J. Naveh, et al., *Arad Inscriptions* (Jerusalem: IES, 1981), under the numbers cited in our text.

100. On the bowl simply labeled *q-d-sh*, "holy," and biblical background, see G. Barkay, *IEJ* 40 (1990): 124-29, pl. 14; also, Renz/Röllig II, 27, §26.

101. On the bowl from Beth-Shemesh labeled "your brother," see G. Barkay, *IEJ* 41 (1991): 239-41.

102. The "Beersheba" altar remains an isolated item, but seems too big just for private devotions. The site concerned is most likely *not* biblical Beer-sheba, perhaps to be located at Bir es-Saba on the site of modern Beer-sheba. Cf. M. D. Fowler, *PEQ* 114 (1982): 7-11, on altar and sites; more broadly on "cult places," cf. C. C. McCown, *JBL* 69 (1950): 205-19.

Here we may briefly mention a clear case of provision for small-scale worship at a city gate. Such was found at ancient Beth-Saida (Et-Tell North), for about the ninth-eighth centuries, in ancient Geshur, a northeastern neighbor of Israel. Near the north outer jamb was a stepped offering place with basin and two modest incense burners (?). Behind was a socket that once held a three-foot-high stela with a bull-headed figure. By the south jamb was another "high shelf," reached by a ramp. For an overall report, see R. Arav, R. A. Freund, and J. F. Shroder, *BAR* 26, no. 1 (2000): 44-56. For the stela, cf. the long-winded study by M. Bernett and O. Keel, *Mond, Stier und Kult am Stadttor von Bethsaida (et-Tell),* OBO 161 (Freiburg: Universitätsverlag; Göttingen: Vandenhoeck & Ruprecht, 1998). On the lunar/bull connection, cf. now T. Ornan, *IEJ* 51 (2001): 1-26.

103. Compare the surveys for the united and united-plus-divided monarchies respectively by P. S. Ash, *David, Solomon, and Egypt: A Reassessment* (Sheffield: Academic Press, 1999), 64-97, and B. U. Schipper, *Israel und Ägypten in der Konigszeit,* OBO 170 (Freiburg and Göttingen, 1999), 41-56; neither realized the true significance of their surveys.

104. Several scholars have noted the relatively solid Yahwism of Hebrew personal names on seals, as well as in the various groups of ostraca. Cf. (e.g.) Avigad and Sass, *CWSS,* 23-25.

105. For a good summary concerning the female baked clay figurines that are so common in Judah in the eighth to early sixth century, see now R. Kletter, in Mazar, *Studies in the Archaeology,* 179-216; using clear definitions, he opts for an identification with Asherah as most likely but not proven, and gives further bibliography; in detail, cf. his monograph, *The Judean Pillar Figurines and the Archaeology of Asherah,* BAR Series 636 (Oxford: Tempus Reparatum, 1996). See also the observations by Kay Prag on a wider basis, in Mazar, *Studies in the Archaeology,* 217-20.

106. The Cave 1 at Jerusalem with numerous figures was simply a deposit, *not* an active cult place (noted by Kletter, in Mazar, *Studies in the Archaeology,* 194), hence should be construed simply as the burial of unwanted material; despite his caveats against invoking biblically attested "cult reforms," such occasions (as Dever, *RADBR,* 159-60, advocated) would fit the burial of such items en bloc, as from a whole group of households, for example. It was published by I. Eshel and K. Prag, eds., *Excavations by K. M. Kenyon in Jerusalem, 1961-1967* IV (Oxford: OUP, 1995).

The broader question of an "inclusive" Yahwism has been aired briefly and with useful clarity by E. Stern, *BAR* 27, no. 3 (May-June 2001): 20-29; this is a handy, popular summary, but he is inexact in saying (p. 21) that "the Bible imagines the religion of ancient Israel as purely monotheistic." If it had done so, consistently, we would not find all the criticisms of submonotheistic practice by high and low alike (it is not just "folk religion" of the masses!) in the Old Testament; and he leaves out completely the crucial role of the classic prophets in their critique of "inclusive" Yahwism. But he rightly stresses the striking absence of all this "inclusive" clutter of paganizing items in the postexilic (Persian) period in the restored Judean community.

107. A series of finds in the Negev and south from it toward the Arabah valley have produced often remarkable remains. From the point of view of religious phenomena in this region, the hilltop complex at Horvat Qitmit was clearly a religious establishment of the seventh/sixth centuries B.C. The southern half had a three-room building opening south onto a rectangular court and "high place" *(bamah)* and a rounded enclosure with altar and basin ("complex A"). The north half was a square building (west and east halves) opening southward also ("complex B"). The pottery included Judean and Negev types of the period, and also types ("Assyrian" and painted) current in contemporary Edom (as at Buseirah, Tawilan, Umm el-Biyara, Tell el-Kheleifeh). A whole series of pottery stands and figures of human beings and strange horned/helmeted heads (goddess? Phoenician analogues?) were found. Of six short inscriptions, two named simply "Qos." This appears to be a "wayside shrine" of non-Judean origin, whose arrangements, human (and goddess?) figures, etc., contrast totally with a real Judean shrine like that at nearby Arad — as different as chalk from cheese. For these finds, see the final report by I. Beit-Arieh, ed., *Horvat Qitmit: An Edomite Shrine in the Biblical Negev* (Tel Aviv, 1995); for ear-

lier, preliminary reports, see I. Beit-Arieh and P. Beck, *Edomite Shrine, Discoveries from Qitmit in the Negev,* cat. no. 277 (Jerusalem: Israel Museum, 1987).

108. Much farther south, a pit near the Judean fortress of Ein-Hazeva (probably ancient Tamar) contained a set of (to us!) bizarre figures reminiscent of the Qitmit ones, crushed by ashlars thrown in after them; this lot is attributed to the seventh/sixth century. Nearby were remains of what was probably the open-air shrine that had housed them. This was very close to the ruins of a large ninth/eighth-century Judean fort ("stratum 5"), beyond which (at some interval) were other remains ("stratum 4") originally thought to be of a smaller seventh/sixth-century fort (now doubted). A stamp seal of one "Maskatu son of Wahzam" was considered to be of Edomite type by J. Naveh, well-known epigraphist. For this site, see R. Cohen and Y. Yisrael, *On the Road to Edom, Discoveries from 'En Hazeva,* cat. no. 370 (Jerusalem: Israel Museum, 1995); cf. same authors, *BA* 58, no. 4 (1995): 223-35, and *BAR* 22, no. 4 (July-August 1996): 40-51.

109. The overall content and format of both finds, other than Judean pottery, has nothing in common with Hebrew shrines and high places; it is clearly the domain of a different cult or cults. Given the location, plus community of the non-Judean pottery with types found in Edom proper, and the mention of Qos, it is not surprising that these two finds have been confidently pronounced "Edomite" by their finders and so by others. But commentators have gone further, basing themselves on the prophets, to suggest that Edom invaded Judah to share in the Neo-Babylonian victory and destruction of Judah. However, these passages need to be grouped into two periods: eighth/seventh century (e.g., Isa. 34:5-17; Amos 1:11-12) and early sixth century (e.g., Jer. 49:7-22; Ezek. 25:13-14; 35; 36:1-6; Obadiah). The tensions in Amos's and Isaiah's day have nothing to do with the Neo-Babylonians. That Edomites took advantage of Judah's conquest by Babylon during 605-586 is clear from Obadiah criticizing their hostile opportunism; in Ezekiel, "revenge" and "delivering Israel to the sword" are spoken of, but not a wholesale military invasion.

In this light, we must note a "minimizing" view of Edom's involvement. Thus, in Mazar, *Studies in the Archaeology,* 318-22, Bienkowski would virtually deny that Qitmit and the Ein-Hazeva shrine remnants were Edomite at all, despite the occurrence of Qos by name. But this borders on special pleading. (i) It ignores the cult materials, totally foreign to Judean-held Negev. (ii) There is no place for Qos as a "reigning" deity outside Edom — the Hebrews (including the Negev! see Arad) had YHWH; Moab had Chemosh, Ammon had Milcom, Philistia had Dagon (and a goddess *Pt[g]yh*), Phoenicia had Baal/Melqart, Aram had Hadad, etc. Qos is attested in Edom and with Edomites, so it is perverse to deny his presence there in just the same way. (iii) There is no evidence that the Judeans worshiped Qos at all, thus far; we have no equivalent of the Baal/Asherah phenomenon. (iv) An Edomite personal seal. The prophetic passages are clear evidence of other acts by Edomites than exclusively "peaceful penetration." That might well describe their establishing their own little shrines at a discreet distance from Judean centers, in times of trade (as from Arabia, for example), but not the intervention spoken of by the seventh/sixth-century sources. We do not need to invoke action by the king of Edom (although not so powerless as some imagine!); armed tribal levies would do damage enough, in looting and cutting off demoralized Judean civilians in the Babylonian debacle. Another view would virtually attempt to break any link between Edomites and Idumeans (cf. J. R. Bartlett, *PEQ* 131 [1999]: 102-14). But, again, in this valuable and well-argued paper, the attempted cleavage becomes artificial. The date of the fall of the kingdom of Edom is not known, whether to (e.g.) Nebuchadrezzar II or Nabonidus, within ca. 580-540. There is good evidence that the kings of Qedar were active as far as southern Palestine by roughly 500 or soon after ("Iyas son of Mahlay the king" is on an incense altar from Lachish; see A. Lemaire, *RB* 81 [1974]: 63-72, and since; cf. Kitchen, *DAA* II, 722), and a few decades later Gashmu (I) could come up to interfere with Nehemiah (Neh. 2:19; 6:1-2, 6). There was no Edomite kingdom then, and the impact of the Neo-Babylonians from the east and the kings of Qedar from the south may have pushed part of the Edomites into southern Judea even before the first Judean exiles got back from Babylon; thus, from Hebron/Maresha not only southwest but also south toward the Negev would be part of Idumea, if only marginally.

To sum up: the Qitmit and Ein-Hazeva shrines may well be Edomite, parallel to Judean forts and caravansarais that sustained (or were sustained by) the Arabia-Edom-Negev-Gaza trade route. Relations could be peaceful (an Edomite officer wrote to Bilbil at Horvat Uza fort; I. Beit-Arieh and B. C. Cresson, *BA* 54 [1991]: 134), or tense (cf. O. Arad 24 and 40, in Aharoni, Naveh, et al., *Arad Inscriptions*, 46, 71), even before any local Edomite opportunism of around 586. The destruction of these possible Edomite shrines cannot be attributed to (a) particular agent(s) with certainty, be it Judeans, or Neo-Babylonians, or even Qedarites, or whoever.

NOTES TO CHAPTER 9

1. A valuable collection of studies, some new, some reprints of previous work (including some cited below), will be found in R. S. Hess and D. T. Tsumura, eds., *I Studied Inscriptions from before the Flood: Ancient Near Eastern, Literary, and Linguistic Approaches to Genesis 1–11* (Winona Lake, Ind.: Eisenbrauns, 1994). Cited hereafter as *ISIF.*

2. The basic edition is T. Jacobsen, *The Sumerian King List* (Chicago: University of Chicago Press, 1939); and in *ANET*, 265-66.

3. The basic edition is W. G. Lambert and A. R. Millard, *Atra-hasis, the Babylonian Story of the Flood* (Oxford: OUP, 1969; reprint, Winona Lake, Ind.: Eisenbrauns, 1998); in *CoS* I (1997), 450-53.

4. See M. Civil, in Lambert and Millard, *Atra-hasis* (1969), 167-72; T. Jacobsen in *CoS* I (1997), 513-15.

5. On the *Epic of Gilgamesh* and the flood; see A. R. George, *The Epic of Gilgamesh* (London: Allen Lane, Penguin Press, 1999; paperback, London: Penguin Books, 2001).

6. The classic study of *Enuma Elish* and its relation (or otherwise) to Gen. 1–2 is still that by A. Heidel, *The Babylonian Genesis,* 2nd ed. (Chicago: University of Chicago Press, 1951); the most recent translation is B. R. Foster, *CoS* I (1997), 390-402.

7. Assyriologists generally reject any genetic relationship between Gen. 1–2 and the Mesopotamian data because of the considerable differences; see (e.g.) J. V. Kinnier-Wilson, in D. W. Thomas, ed., *Documents from Old Testament Times* (London: Nelson, 1958), 14; W. G. Lambert, *JTS,* n.s., 16 (1965): 287-300, esp. 289, 291, 293-99, and in *ISIF,* 96-113, with addenda; A. R. Millard, *TynB* 18 (1967): 3-4, 7, 16-18, and in *ISIF,* 114-28; T. Jacobsen, in *JBL* 100 (1981): 513-29, and translation, both now in *ISIF,* 129-42, plus 160-66.

8. For the Gilgamesh version and others and the Gen. 6–9 version, see A. Heidel, *The Gilgamesh Epic and Old Testament Parallels,* 2nd ed. (Chicago: University of Chicago Press, 1949); K. A. Kitchen, *The Bible in Its World* (Exeter: Paternoster, 1977), 27-30, and references.

9. For Assyriologists and archaeologists and the reality of a flood tradition, cf. W. W. Hallo, in W. W. Hallo and W. K. Simpson, *The Ancient Near East: A History* (New York: Harcourt & Brace, 1971), 34-36; 2nd ed. (1998), 32-33. On the archaeology, cf. M. E. L. Mallowan, *Iraq* 26 (1964): 62-82, pls. 16-20; R. L. Raikes, *Iraq* 28 (1966): 52-63.

10. For the text, see S. N. Kramer, *JAOS* 88 (1968): 108-11, text 109-11, and in *ISIF,* 278-82 (minus the cuneiform).

11. On "cuneiform culture" in the Levant in the early second millennium, see (e.g.) D. J. Wiseman, *Syria* 39 (1962): 180-84 (instanced at Alalakh), and at Hazor, see, e.g., W. W. Hallo and H. Tadmor, *IEJ* 27 (1977): 1-11; for tablets at Hazor, and with Hazor often mentioned at Mari, cf. (e.g.) A. Malamat, *Mari and the Early Israelite Experience* (Oxford: OUP, 1989), 55-62; further, A. Ben-Tor, W. Horowitz, and A. Shafer, *IEJ* 42 (1992): 19-33; and cf. summary, A. Ben-Tor, *BAR* 25, no. 3 (May-June 1999): 30.

12. For three of the rivers (and putting the Pishon also in Iran), see E. A. Speiser, in A. Moortgart et al., eds., *Festschrift für Johannes Friedrich . . .* (Heidelberg: Winter, 1959), 473-85; reprinted in J. J. Finkelstein and M. Greenberg, eds., *Oriental and Biblical Studies . . . of E. A. Speiser* (Philadelphia: University of Pennsylvania Press, 1967), 23-24, and in *ISIF,* 175-82.

13. For the regime of the (Elamite) rivers Karun (-Diz) and Karkheh, see Naval Intelligence Division, *Persia* (1945), 27-29, plus map in D. T. Potts, *The Archaeology of Elam* (Cambridge: Cambridge University Press, 1999), 11, fig. 2.1 (cf. photo, 17, pl. 2.2). For Havilah and west Arabian gold in Mahd-adh-Dhahab down to Wadi Baysh, see references of Kitchen, in L. K. Handy, ed., *The Age of Solomon* (Leiden: Brill, 1997), 143 n. 49.

14. For the long-defunct Arabian river course (candidate for Pishon), see J. Sauer, *BAR* 22, no. 4 (July-August 1996): 52-57, 64, with references (including for Farouk El-Baz); D. J. Hamblin, *Smithsonian Institute Magazine* [ca. 1995?]: 127-35, on J. Zarins's work.

15. For the charting of highs/lows of gulf and land water, cf. D. T. Potts, *The Arabian Gulf in Antiquity* I (Oxford: OUP, 1990), 14, fig. 1b.

16. Javan is identified as the Ionians (east Greeks), possibly the *Ym'n* of the Ugaritic texts; for the later references, cf. *RLA* V, 1/2 (1976), 150, "Ionier." But Javan may have replaced such a term as Ahhiyawa ("Achaeans"), which almost certainly covered the Mycenaean regime(s) on the southeast coast of Anatolia and its islands from Miletus to (and including) Rhodes, if not also Mycenaean Greece; on Ahhiyawa, see latterly, J. D. Hawkins, *AnSt* 48 (1998): 30-31, plus P. Mountjoy, 47-51.

17. Tubal goes back to the Tibar of Naram-Sin (twenty-third century), then the Tapala of the fifteenth century and Tapala of the fourteenth/thirteenth in Hittite sources (cf. G. F. del Monte and J. Tischler, *RGTC* 6/1 [1978], 397, 425, and 6/2 [1992], 158), then later Tabal(i), in the ninth and eighth centuries (cf. *ANET,* 277 top = *RIMA,* 3:98; *ANET,* 282-84).

18. Togarmah is older Tegarama and Takarma in Anatolia, in nineteenth-century Old Assyrian sources (cf. P. Garelli, *Les Assyriens en Cappadoce* [Paris: Maisonneuve, 1963], 117-18), then fourteenth/thirteenth-century Hittite sources (references in G. F. del Monte and J. Tischler, *RGTC* 6/1 [1978], 383-84; 6/2, 154).

19. Meshech is the Mushki or Mushku of Assyrian texts (*RLA* VIII, 7/8, 493-95), from Tiglath-pileser I (ca. 1100) onward (*RIMA,* 2:14, 33, 42, 53; *ANET,* 284-85, Sargon II).

20. Gomer is the Gimirrai of the Assyrian texts, the Cimmerians of classical sources, who appear in 714 under Sennacherib (cf. *RLA* V, 7/8 [1980], 594), then under Esarhaddon and Assurbanipal (seventh century; cf., e.g., in *ANET,* 303, 451).

21. Ashkenaz are the classical Scythians, the Assyrian Ashkuza/Ishkuza (*RLA* V, 3/4 [1977], 193), in the seventh century under Esarhaddon (Luckenbill, *ARAB* II, 207, §517; 213, §533; R. Borger, *Die Inschriften Asarhaddons, Königs von Assyrien* [Osnabrück: Biblio-Verlag, 1956; reprint, 1967], 52).

22. Madai is the Medes, attested by texts of Shalmaneser III (835 B.C.) and onward (translation in *RIMA,* 3:68 [twenty-fourth year], cf. *RLA* VII, 7/8, 620).

23. Elishah goes well with the late second-millennium Alashia of cuneiform sources and Egyptian *Irs*, Alasia (which must not be confused with Anatolian *Isy*, Assiya/Assuwa!); it is probably a kingdom in Cyprus; it appears to go back to the early second millennium (D. J. Wiseman, *Faith and Thought* 87 [1955]: 18 = *ISIF*, 259).

24. Kittim is to be compared with Kition, a settlement in Cyprus, archaeologically well attested from the late second millennium, with traces going much further back (Early Bronze, ca. 2000); cf. V. Karageorghis, *Kition* (London: Thames & Hudson, 1976). Its name later came to be applied to Greeks in general.

25. Tiras may be the Tursha of the Sea Peoples group under Merenptah in 1209, whom some would identify further with the (E)truscans in Italy, and classical Tyrsenoi (cf. W. Helck, *Die Beziehungen Ägyptens zu Vorderasien im 3. und 2. Jahrtausend v. Chr.*, 2nd ed. [Wiesbaden: Harrassowitz, 1971], 226-27).

Also mentioned in Gen. 10:4 is Dodanim/Rodanim. A variant occurs in 1 Chron. 1:7. A change between *d* and *r* in the Hebrew script is very small, from the eighth century downward; how old was the name Rhodes is not clear; inclusion in Homer's Achaean Catalogue (*Iliad*, bk. II) suggests not later than the eighth century, and possibly very much earlier. That Dodanim is from Danunim (*n* to *d*) is possible (G. J. Wenham, *Genesis 1–15* [Waco, Tex.: Word, 1987], 219); the Danuna go back to the fourteenth-twelfth centuries, in the Amarna letters (EA 151:52; W. L. Moran, *The Amarna Letters* [Baltimore: Johns Hopkins University Press, 1992], 238), and among the Sea Peoples under Ramesses III (*ANET*, 262, "Denyen"). However, another possibility is that both Dodanim and Rodanim have been reduced from Dordanim — by loss of medial *r* in Gen. 10:4 (Dordanim > Dodanim) and of an initial *d* in 1 Chron. 1:7 (<Do>rdanim > Rodanim). The Dardanayu occur in an Egyptian list of Aegean names under Amenophis III (E. Edel, *Die Ortsnamenlisten aus dem Totentempel Amenophis III* [Bonn: Hanstein Verlag, 1966], 48-53) and among the Hittite allies against Ramesses II at the Battle of Qadesh in 1275 (*CoS* II, 33, 39); some would link these with the classical Dardanoi.

26. Here we have three entities with similar names. Cush A is the Kush of the Egyptian texts, basically the Nile Valley and deserts south of the First Cataract of the Nile at Aswan. Its original scope (early second millennium) was restricted to Upper Nubia, between the Second and Fourth Cataracts of the Nile, but was subsequently extended in use. Cush B is the Kashshu, or Kassites, from the Iranian mountains and valleys immediately east of Babylonia. Cush C, the "father" of Arabian entities (10:7), is very likely simply an extension of Cush A, East Africa south of Egypt; the culture of the Tihamah is still African related, and Sheba ruled at one time in East Africa, including through the kingdom of Di'amat (cf. Kitchen, *DAA* I, 115-17, 247, where the dates should now be raised by 180 years; and C. Robin, *CRAIBL 1998* [1998], 782-94).

27. Mizraim is Egypt, the Misir, Mizru, Musri of cuneiform sources from the mid–second millennium onward (data in *RLA* VIII, 3/4 [1994], 264-69).

28. Put is attested under Osorkon II in Egypt *(Pydw)* on his Tanis statue (cf. H. K. Jacquet-Gordon, *JEA* 46 [1960]: 12-23, and E. Graefe, *Enchoria* 5 [1975]: 13-17). It recurs as *Pwd(y)/Pwt* in a series of amuletic "divine" decrees of the tenth century onward (I. E. S. Edwards, *Hieratic Papyri in the British Museum*, 4th ser. [London: British Museum, 1960], vol. I, Text 10, and n. 23; and further referencess in index, 122). Their identity was first noted by G. Posener, *La première domination perse en Égypte* (Cairo: IFAO, 1936), 186-87, who rightly rejects the wrong suggestion of Punt (strictly Pwane[t], from which final *t* was dropped). The term stands for Libya(ns) in these contexts. On cuneiform *Putu-iaman* (under Nebuchadrezzar II), see T. C. Mitchell, *PSAS* 22 (1992): 69-80.

29. Canaan is Palestine west of the Jordan from the Negev in the south to the Litani

gorges behind Tyre in the north during the fifteenth century and later. Hebrew occupation added Gilead and Bashan east of the Jordan River and Galilee for a time. In the third/early second millennium, it applied to Phoenicia (south of Ugarit) from Siyannu to Sidon, and inland to Hamath (10:15). But in the first millennium this area (minus the Hamathite hinterland) became classical Phoenicia, even though its inhabitants might still call themselves Canaanites. Cf. also pp. 460, 478-79 below.

30. Havilah is most likely in western Arabia (north-central area), and may take its name from Sabaean Hawlan; cf. Kitchen in Handy, *The Age of Solomon*, 143 and n. 49, references.

31. The name Raamah (with its middle *'ayin* sound, better equated with *ghain*, not with *g*) is frequently identified with the Ragmatum (now Al-Ukhdud) in the oasis of Najran just north of Yemen, named in the Old South Arabian inscriptions, e.g., RES 3943:3, of the seventh or fifth century (*DAA* II, 509). The equation is defended by W. W. Müller, *TQ* 149 (1969): 369 n. 103. For other references, see A. H. Al-Sheiba, *ABY* 4 (1987): 30.

32. Dedan was a kingdom based on the long, narrow oasis of Al-Ula in northwest Arabia; two kings are known from an inscription in the sixth century B.C. (references are in Kitchen, *DAA* I, 50-51, 118, 168; for later periods, 44ff.). It is not certain that Tidnum (Third Dynasty of Ur) was that far west of Mesopotamia, and not likely that the Ditanu of Ugaritic archaic tradition was that far south of Ugarit.

33. Sheba is the kingdom based on Marib in Yemen in southwest Arabia, from at least the eleventh century, passing through various changes, becoming Saba and Dhu-Raydan, then Himyar up to the sixth century A.D. For sequences of rulers, see Kitchen, *DAA* I, with minimal dates; for higher, working dates, see *DAA* II, 737-47, revised dates for kingdoms of Saba (Sheba), Hadramaut, Qataban, etc. For a good, concise general account of Sabaean civilization, see J.-F. Breton, *Arabia Felix from the Time of the Queen of Sheba* (Notre Dame, Ind.: University of Notre Dame Press, 1998). For a richly illustrated overview (based on a Paris exhibition), see C. Robin et al., eds., *Yémen, au pays de la reine de Saba* (Paris: Flammarion, 1997); for an English equivalent, see St. J. Simpson, ed., *Queen of Sheba: Treasures from Ancient Yemen* (London: British Museum Press, 2002.

34. Seba (also in Ps. 72; Isa. 43:3; 45:14) is not identical with Sheba, but linked with it, and with Cush (C and probably A). Thus, in his *Über die frühe Geschichte Arabiens und das Entstehen des Sabäerreiches — Die Geschichte von Saba' I* (Vienna: Academy, 1975), 87ff., 102-5, H. von Wissmann argued that Seba was a Sabaean settlement in East Africa (Eritrea/Ethiopia), where important Sabaean-type remains have been found, such as the temple at present-day Yeha, probably a center of the kingdom of Di'amat. Thus it was in the sphere of African Cush, but closely linked with Sheba. This relationship goes back at least to the later eighth century (temp. Karibil Watar I of Sheba), and quite possibly rather earlier on archaeological grounds, succeeding to a possible settlement of the second millennium (cf. A. de Maigret, *CRAIBL 1998* [1998], 778 with fig. 53).

35. Sabta is often compared to Greek Sabota, a form of Shabwa(t), the capital of the kingdom of Hadramaut (for references, see A. H. Al-Shaiba, *ABY* 4 [1987]: 36). Excavations at Shabwa went through fourteen levels, dating from the eighteenth or fourteenth centuries B.C. all the way to the fourth century A.D. (cf. *DAA* I, 126-27, with references).

36. Sabteca is less clear; it is certainly not king Shebitku of Egypt's Twenty-Fifth (Kushite) Dynasty, as it stands in an Arabian, not Nubian, context. Far superior was H. von Wissmann's view that it derived from Shabakat, a place south of Shabwa in Hadramaut (in H. von Wissmann and M. Höfner, *Beiträge zur historischen Geographie des vorislamischen Südarabien* [Wiesbaden: Steiner Verlag, 1953], 109); he later wished to withdraw this equation (in his *Über*

die frühe Gescheichte Arabiens, 103 n. 1), because biblical Sabteca has a final weak *'aleph,* not present in Shabakat; but this is not fatal to the equation.

Also included under Ham are other names, some of which we will take up briefly here. First, those names appearing in Gen. 10:8-12, in no particular order: *Shinar* was a term used of Mesopotamia during the later second millennium; see p. 568 n. 21 above. Babylon, because of high groundwater, cannot be dug right back through time; but Sargon is rumored to have destroyed it (twenty-fourth/twenty-third century), and Sharkalisharri, a successor, built two temples there (twenty-third/twenty-second century), while Shulgi of the Third Dynasty of Ur stole from Marduk's temple there (twenty-first century). So, in much later chronicles for Sargon (cf. A. Grayson, *Assyrian and Babylonian Chronicles* [1975], 153-54); for references for Sharkalisharri, cf. *RLA* I, 334; for Babylon in brief, cf. *DANE,* 42-44. *Erech,* or Uruk (Sumerian Unug), was a very ancient city in south Babylonia; *Akkad* was the famed (but still unlocated) capital of Sargon the Great and his dynasty in the twenty-fourth–twenty-second centuries; for summaries on Akkad and Uruk, see *DANE,* 8, 312-13. *Calah* and *Nineveh* were Assyrian centers that later became great capitals of the Assyrian Empire; for the former (now Nimrud), see (in English) in *RLA* V, 3/4–5/6 (1977/1980), 303-23; for the latter (in English), *RLA* IX, 5/6 (2000), 388-433. *Resen* between Nineveh and Calah may be locatable at Hamam Ali in that zone (D. J. Wiseman, *NBD,* 1085). On the enigmatic *Nimrod,* there have been many variations (and not just Elgar's musical ones!). He is clearly viewed as a hero-king of the distant past (as Uruk and Akkad in his realm would suggest), ruling over much of Mesopotamia at least. Such people as Tukulti-Ninurta I of Assyria (ca. 1208), or later kings, are far too late to qualify. The suggestion to identify him — *Nmrd/Nnrt* — with the god Ninurta is philologically possible, but is contradicted by his human kingship, not deity. Among early Mesopotamian kings of note, two may be suggested (if with due reserve). The inclusion of Akkad suggests an Akkadian king (and they did rule widely). This might just conceivably favor Naram-Sin (ca. 2200), if "Nimrod" was either abbreviated from "Naram-<Sin, King of Akka>d" (and *Nrmd* > *Nmrd*); or else simply the same r/m interchange, loss of *S,* and the *n* later becoming *d* in recopying. An alternative ruler might be (E)nmer(k)ar (and with $r > d$), ancient Sumerian king of Uruk (ca. 2600), involved with Iran. Naturally, this remains hypothetical in either case; but transpositions with *r* are known in Hebrew (Ta*h*arqa > Tir*h*aqa) and Assyrian (Boke*n*rinef > Buku*rn*inip), and so present no problem.

Next we briefly treat those appearing in Gen. 10:13-14. Under Egypt *(Mizraim),* on which endless books exist, come both African and Aegean names. For the *Naphtuhim,* as the inhabitants of Egypt's Delta (or else the Oases), see Kitchen in *NBD,* 803. *Pathros* has long been recognized as *pa-to-resi,* "the Southland," Upper Egypt south of the Delta, a term of New Kingdom origin and attested (as *Paturesi*) in Assyrian texts; cf. Kitchen, *NBD,* 873; for references, see Ranke, *KMAV,* 31 (with needless question mark). *Lehabim,* Libyans; for that region, cf. (e.g.) A. Leahy, ed., *Libya and Egypt, c. 1300-750 BC* (London: SOAS/Society for Libyan Studies, 1990), 15-113, and in Kitchen, *Third Int. Pd.,* passim. For the *Philistines,* suffice it to refer to T. Dothan, *The Philistines and Their Material Culture* (New Haven: Yale University Press; Jerusalem: IES, 1982); and several essays in S. Gitin, A. Mazar, and E. Stern, eds., *Mediterranean Peoples in Transition* (Jerusalem, 1998), and in E. D. Oren, ed., *The Sea Peoples and Their World: A Reassessment* (Philadelphia: University of Pennsylvania Press, 2000), each with up-to-date references. *Caphtor* is cuneiform Kaptara; both find a correspondence in Egyptian Keftiu. On the former, a summary in *RLA* VI, 3/4 (1981), 226-27; on the latter, J. Vercoutter, *L'Égypte et le monde égéen préhellénique* (Cairo: IFAO, 1956).

Next we treat names found in Gen. 10:15-18. *Sidon* goes back to the Early Bronze Age in the third millennium, and recurs in Egyptian sources in the late second millennium, e.g., in the Amarna letters (Moran, *The Amarna Letters*, nos. 144-55 and passim); Papyrus Anastasi I (*ANET*, 477); Wenamun (*ANET*, 27; *CoS* I, 91); cf. notes in G. E. Markoe, *The Phoenicians* (London: British Museum Press, 2000), 199-201; R. Giveon, in *Lex. Aeg.* V (1984), 922-23 (in English). The *Arkites* inhabited the seaside town of Irqata (later, Arqata), from at least the early second millennium (archaeological traces, Tell Arqa; Execration Texts) through the late second millennium (cf. Markoe, *The Phoenicians*, 204; Helck, *Beziehungen*, 48, no. 9; 59, no. 54; later, in Amarna letters, Moran, *Amarna Letters*, index, p. 390; besieged under Ramesses II, Kitchen, *RITA* II, 73 top; *RITANC* II, 124-25). The *Sinites* are of Siyannu, known well from the archives of its immediate northern neighbor, Ugarit (cf. in J. Nougayrol, *Le Palais Royal d'Ugarit* IV [Paris: Imprimerie Nationale/Klincksieck, 1956], 15-17, with references). Arvad (modern Ruad) was home to the *Arvadites*, from the third millennium to Roman times (cf. Markoe, *The Phoenicians*, 205-6). The *Zemarites* were based at Sumur, classical Simyra (now Tell Kazel), just north of the mouth of the Eleutheros River (Nahr el-Kebir). Archaeologically, life began there in the Middle Bronze Age (early second millennium), and Sumur features incessantly in the Amarna letters (fourteenth century; cf. Moran, *The Amarna Letters*, index, p. 391) and recurs in Egyptian sources (fifteenth, thirteenth centuries; cf. R. Giveon in *Lex. Aeg.* V, 947-48). The *Hamathites* lived in Hamath, a town on the Orontes, known archaeologically from distant Neolithic times, but it did not gain prominence (at least in our written sources) until after 1000; for useful summaries, see J. D. Hawkins, in *RLA* IV/1 (1972), 67-70, and R. Giveon, *Lex. Aeg.* II (1976), 935-36: A. *Amorites* are known in the Levant and in Mesopotamian records from the later third millennium (cf. G. Buccellati, *The Amorites of the Ur III Period* [Naples: Istituto Orientale di Napoli, 1966]), and throughout the second millennium (with a kingdom of Amurru south of Qadesh-on-Orontes), see H. Klengel, *Syria, 3000 to 300 B.C.* (Berlin: Akademie Verlag, 1992), passim. *Girgashites* are known indirectly in the late second millennium in two personal names at Ugarit, *Grgsh* and *Bn-grgsh*. Any link is uncertain with the land Qarqisha (or Karkisha) among the Hittite allies that opposed Ramesses II in 1275 (*CoS* II, 33 [twice], 39).

37. For a recent history of Assyria, cf. H. W. F. Saggs, *The Might That Was Assyria* (London: Sidgwick & Jackson, 1984), and the relevant chapters in the 2nd and 3rd editions of *CAH* II-III.

38. For the kings of Hazarmaveth, see Kitchen, *DAA* I (1994), 33-36, 59-60, 222-26 (monuments), 246-47 (king list), plus additions and revised dates, *DAA* II (2000), 730-31, 733-34, 740, 746-47.

39. Ophir was certainly a real gold-bearing land, as the Tell Qasile ostracon makes clear: "Gold of Ophir — for Beth-Horon: 30 shekels" (B. Maisler/Mazar, *JNES* 10 [1951]: 265-67; Renz/Röllig I, 229-31). It was most likely in west Arabia.

40. Aram stands for the Arameans. The name is first securely attested in Egyptian sources under Amenophis III (ca. 1380) and Merenptah (ca. 1200); cf. Edel, *Die Ortsnamenliste aus dem Totentempel Amenophis III*, 28-29. Earlier mentions of "Aram" are disputed, but may in part be relevant. For first-millennium Arameans, cf. (e.g.) Klengel, *Syria*, 181-232, passim; for more detail, see H. Sader, *Les états araméens de Syrie* (Beirut and Wiesbaden: Steiner Verlag, 1987), and P. E. Dion, *Les araméens à l'age de fer* (Paris: Gabalda, 1997).

41. Lud is thought to be Lydia, first known from the seventh century, from Gyges of Lydia in Assyrian sources (and Herodotus). Lydia replaced the Arzawa and Seha River-land of the Hittite sources (and might have in Gen. 10).

Also included under Shem but not discussed in the text proper are, from Gen. 10:22: Elam was a people and kingdom in west-southwest Iran close to Sumer and the head of the gulf, from the third millennium down to the seventh century (and with survivors thereafter). A good survey is in Potts, *The Archaeology of Elam,* which covers also the history and culture. For Elamite messengers going far west to Aleppo, cf. J. M. Durand, *Documents épistolaires du palais de Mari* I (1997), 466. *Asshur* is the oldest Assyrian capital, Ashur, from which the kingdom took its name, and was first founded circa 2500; cf. summary, in *DANE,* 36, with references; full presentation by W. Andrae, *Das wiedererstandene Assur,* ed. B. Hrouda, 2nd ed. (Munich: Beck, 1977); well illustrated is J. E. Curtis and J. E. Reade, eds., *Art and Empire, Treasures from Assyria in the British Museum* (New York: MMA/Abrams, 1995).

In Gen. 10:26-30 we return to ancient Arabia. *Sheleph* is comparable with ancient *Slfn* in Sabaean texts (CIH 621, 648), but its identity with one of several (as)-Salfs in modern Yemen is less clear; cf. H. von Wissmann, *Über die frühe Geschichte Arabiens,* 78 and n. 1, plus A. H. Sheiba, *ABY* 4 (1987): 34. *Uzal* seems unlikely to be Sanaa, cf. von Wissmann, 78-79, n. 3. *Jerah* is related to the word for "moon"; in the Mari letters (early second millennium), ruins of a town Yarih are mentioned (but it is *not* biblical Jericho!), and Mare-Yamina people, the Yariheans; cf. J.-M. Durand, *Documents épistolaires du palais de Mari* II (Paris: Éditions du Cerf, 1998), 29, 30. *Jobab* has been compared to the Old South Arabian clan name *Yhybb;* see H. von Wissmann, *Sammlung Eduard Glaser* III (Vienna: Academy, 1964), 278-79, and in his *Über die frühe Geschichte Arabiens,* 78 n. 2, based on texts CIH 37 and Glaser 1212.

For general works on peoples in the biblical world, see D. J. Wiseman, ed., *Peoples of Old Testament Times* (Oxford: OUP, 1973), and latterly, A. J. Hoerth, G. L. Mattingly, and E. M. Yamauchi, *Peoples of the Old Testament World* (Grand Rapids: Baker, 1994). For Canaan(ites) in the Mari letters cf. J.-M. Durand, *Documents épistolaires du palais de Mari* II, 29, with references.

42. An overall study of genealogy in this sphere is R. R. Wilson, *Genealogy and History in the Biblical World* (New Haven: Yale University Press, 1977), preceded by his paper in *JBL* 94 (1975): 169-89; for a useful survey of the contrasts between the Genesis genealogies and the comparable Sumero-Akkadian lists, see R. S. Hess in *ISIF,* 58-72.

43. For Hallo's sets of eight generations in the Sumerian king list, see in Hallo and Simpson, *The Ancient Near East,* 1st ed., 28-29, 32, fig. 6; 2nd ed., 28-29, fig. 7. For incidental notes and prior occupations included in the Sumerian king list, see Jacobsen, *The Sumerian King List,* 73, 81, 83/85, 87, 89/91, 97, 105, 109, 111; or *ANET,* 265-66.

44. For the ultralong reigns in the Sumerian king list, see Jacobsen, *The Sumerian King List,* 71-91; and in *ANET,* 265-66.

45. See W. G. Waddell, *Manetho* (Cambridge, Mass.: Harvard University Press; London: Heinemann, 1940), LCL, 2-27. For the fragmentary older succession and figures in the Turin Canon, see translation, Kitchen, *RITA* II, 540-41, cf. *RITANC* II, 531-33, cf. 547-48.

46. For the 6×60 glosses, see Jacobsen, *The Sumerian King List,* 98-99.

47. For Berossus, see in S. M. Burstein, *The Babyloniaca of Berossus* (Malibu, Calif.: Undena Publications, 1978), 18-21.

NOTES TO CHAPTER 10

1. What is needed is a fresh start, in which all aspects of ancient Near Eastern culture and civilization are systematically worked through in terms of place, date, and development within each zone and down through time, *from firsthand documentation.* In the case of Canaan/Israel/ neighbors, exactly the same should apply, and the biblical text should be henceforth treated as one of the basic sources, subject to the kind of genuine "stratigraphy" (and not the false) as set

out on pp. 448-49, itself based on use of firsthand sources for valid comparisons. And *not* on the nineteenth-century distortions and false analyses, or later minimalist a priori "agenda junk." Naturally, this broad, all-embracing view covers texts and nontextual archaeology alike; it has, of itself, no theological content — to comfort those who suffer from a theology allergy.

2. The two T. L. Thompson books we are concerned with: *Early History of the Israelite People from the Written and Archaeological Sources* (Leiden: Brill, 1992) and *The Bible in History* (London: Cape, 1999) = *The Mythic Past* (New York: Basic Books, 1999). Page numbers in the text, in parentheses, follow quotations from these two works.

3. For the high level of scribal accuracy on Merenptah's stela, see data in Kitchen, *JSSEA* 24 (1994/97): 71-76.

4. On the *dwd.h* of Mesha's stela, cf. also background cited, Kitchen, *JSOT* 76 (1997): 36.

5. On *Bit-X* names (dynastic founders) in the Near East, see Kitchen, *JSOT* 76 (1997): 38-39, with map, p. 37.

6. See Kitchen, *RITA* II, 544.

7. For "House of [Da]vid" on the Mesha stela, see A. Lemaire in *BAR* 20, no. 3 (May-June 1994): 30-37, following on Lemaire in *SEL* 11 (1994): 17-19.

8. For "heights of David" in the Shoshenq I list (and Ethiopic equivalent, *DWT*), see Kitchen, *JSOT* 76 (1997): 39-41, and briefly in *BAR* 25, no. 1 (1999): 34-35.

9. Unless otherwise indicated, all parenthetical page references in the remainder of the Thompson section are to *CoS* II.

10. For H. Shanks's "Quote of the Month" from Lemche's publication, see in *BAR* 26, no. 4 (July-August 2000): 16.

11. Contrary to Dever, *What . . . When . . . ?* 98 n. 2, I am not simply a "conservative" scholar out to "save" patriarchal historicity; I take the trouble to go through the data *as they are,* and to bring the full width of literary evidence to bear on the matter (which he steadfastly refuses even to look at! Closed-mind syndrome?). The result comes from the data, not out of my head. Which is rather more than can be said for minimalist works (or Hendel's and McCarter/ Hendel's efforts, swarming with errors). See my analysis and corrective to Hendel, in *NEASB* 43 (1998): 49-58, which Shanks arbitrarily banned from *BAR;* his rule on replies in by the second issue following was conveniently waived for others (notably Cogan on Shea), but not of course for me.

12. An early runner in the minimalist camp was P. R. Davies, *In Search of Ancient Israel* (Sheffield: Academic Press, 1992).

13. See K. W. Whitelam, *The Invention of Ancient Israel* (London: Routledge, 1996). On Lemche and Whitelam and others, see W. G. Dever, *BASOR* 297 (1995): 61-80, and in *BASOR* 316 (1999): 89-105; briefer, Kitchen, in S. Ahituv and E. D. Oren, eds., *The Origin of Early Israel — Current Debate, Biblical, Historical, and Archaeological Perspectives,* Beer-Sheva XII (Beer-Sheva: Ben-Gurion University of the Negev Press; London: University College London [and others], 1998), 114-19.

14. For Berossus, see S. M. Burstein, *The Babyloniaca of Berossus* (Malibu, Calif.: Undena Publications, 1978).

15. I. Finkelstein and N. A. Silberman, *The Bible Unearthed* (New York: Free Press, 2001); critical review by W. G. Dever, *BASOR* 322 (2001): 67-77.

16. Finkelstein and Silberman, *The Bible Unearthed,* 37.

17. For the periods and size of Tel Haror, see E. D. Oren, *NEAHL,* 2:580.

18. Finkelstein and Silberman, *The Bible Unearthed,* 59, emphasis added.

19. For the text of scribe Mose, archives in the East Delta, see G. A. Gaballa, *The*

Memphite Tomb-Chapel of Mose (Warminster: Aris & Phillips, 1977), 23, or Kitchen, *RITA* III (2000), 308.

20. On papyri in the East Delta (burnt and unburnt!), see W. M. F. Petrie, *Tanis I* (London: EEF, 1889), 42.

21. For the wine dockets, see Kitchen, *RITA* II (1996), 285.

22. Finkelstein and Silberman, *The Bible Unearthed*, 60.

23. Papyrus Bologna 1086, translated by E. F. Wente, *Letters from Ancient Egypt* (Atlanta: Scholars Press, 1990), 124-26.

24. The border on the vital Mediterranean coastal route was heavily fortified, but much less so was the border on the Wadi Tumilat route and its Suez south branch; see Kitchen, briefly, in *RITANC* II (1999), 271-72 (and 181-82), and more fully in *Studi de Egittologia e di Antichità Puniche* 18 (1998): 33-38, with map.

25. Despite the assumption of Finkelstein and Silberman, *The Bible Unearthed*, 63, Ezion-Geber was not at Elath/Tell el-Kheleifeh but at and opposite Gezirat el-Faraun, farther southwest (cf. A. Flinder, *BAR* 15, no. 4 [July-August 1989]: 30-43).

26. Finkelstein and Silberman, *The Bible Unearthed*, 64.

27. On tented kingdoms, Edom, etc., cf. Kitchen, in P. Bienkowski, ed., *Early Edom and Moab* (Sheffield: Collis; Liverpool: Merseyside Museums, 1992), 21-22.

28. For refutation of the ultralate views of Lemche, Redford, etc., on the exodus and locations, see Kitchen in Oren, *Origin of Early Israel*, 69-85.

29. Grand Rapids: Eerdmans, 2001. This book appeared close to the end of processing the present work. Parenthetical page numbers in the following text are to this work.

30. Cf. outlines, references, and compact critique by Dever, *What . . . When . . . ?* 10-19.

31. On mistaken (if only tentative) attempts to apply "deconstructionism" inappositely to Mesopotamian texts, see the good-natured critique (in English) by A. Westenholz, in W. Sallaberger and A. Westenholz, *Mesopotamien, Akkade-Zeit und Ur III-Zeit*, OBO 160/3 (Freiburg: Universitätsverlag; Göttingen: Vandenhoeck & Ruprecht, 1999).

32. N. K. Gottwald, *The Tribes of Yahweh: A Sociology of the Religion of Liberated Israel* (New York: Orbis, 1979).

33. N. P. Lemche, *Early Israel, Anthropological and Historical Studies on the Israelite Society before the Monarchy* (Leiden: Brill, 1985). Parenthetical page numbers in the following text are to this work.

34. For Edom and "tented kingdoms," see just above.

35. On the tented royal dynasty of Old Babylonian Manana, see W. Yuhong and S. Dalley, *Iraq* 52 (1990): 159-65.

36. The original trio of books was: D. B. Redford, *A Study of the Biblical Story of Joseph (Genesis 37–50)* (Leiden: Brill, 1970); see for a reasoned critique, Kitchen, *OrAnt* 12 (1973): 233-42. Then T. L. Thompson, *The Historicity of the Patriarchal Narratives* (Berlin: de Gruyter, 1974); J. van Seters, *Abraham in History and Tradition* (New Haven: Yale University Press, 1975). On these last two, cf. observations in Kitchen, *The Bible in Its World* (Exeter: Paternoster Press; Downers Grove, Ill.: InterVarsity, 1977), 56-74, with 142-46.

37. On Gen. 15, Alalakh, Jer. 34, see R. S. Hess in Hess et al., *Oath*, 55-65.

38. Van Seters, *Abraham*, 104ff.

39. Thompson, *Historicity*, 137ff., 141-42.

40. Thompson, *Historicity*, 144-71.

41. Redford, *A Study*, 46-54, 54-65. Parenthetical page numbers in the following text are to this work.

42. On foreigners in private service in the Middle Kingdom, see the lists published by W. C. Hayes, *A Late Middle Kingdom Papyrus in the Brooklyn Museum* (New York: Brooklyn Museum, 1955); and cf. G. Posener, *Syria* 34 (1957): 145-63.

43. This erratic volume of collected studies is J. H. Hayes and J. M. Miller, eds., *Israelite and Judaean History* (London: SCM Press; Philadelphia: Trinity Press International, 1977).

44. Correction to Redford (who was blindly followed by Thompson — why did he not cite Helck too?) is by W. Helck, *VT* 15 (1965): 35-48.

45. D. Irvin, *Mytharion*, AOAT 32 (Neukirchen-Vluyn: Neukirchener-Verlag/Verlag Butzon & Bercker Kevelaer, 1978).

46. For Papyrus Westcar, see (e.g.) M. Lichtheim, *Ancient Egyptian Literature* 1 (Berkeley: University of California Press, 1973), 215-22.

47. Miller, in Hayes and Miller, *Israelite and Judaean History*, 214 and 215, emphasis added.

48. For the plain facts about the epigraphy of Butartu, Dibon, and Moab at Luxor temple, see notes by Kitchen, in Bienkowski, *Early Edom and Moab*, 27-29; latest translation, now Kitchen, *RITA* II (1996), 49-50, and up-to-date commentary, Kitchen, *RITANC* II (1999), 89-99.

49. Miller, in Hayes and Miller, *Israelite and Judaean History*, 250 end.

50. Wellhausen's opus first appeared in 1878 as *Geschichte Israels* I; by 1883 it had been retitled *Prolegomena zur Geschichte Israels* (Berlin: Reimer). Its sixth edition (strictly a reprint) was issued in 1927 by de Gruyter of Berlin. The English edition, *Prolegomena to the History of Ancient Israel*, was in 1885; it was reprinted in 1957 by Meridien Books, New York, with which was included the *Encyclopaedia Britannica* article "Israel."

51. A typical early reference to Akhenaten (first read as Bech-en-Aten, or Khuenaten) is that of C. R. Lepsius, *Letters from Egypt, Ethiopia, and the Peninsula of Sinai* (London: Bohn, 1853), 114, where he is merely assigned to a group of "antagonistic kings of the 18th Dynasty."

52. R. N. Whybray, *The Making of the Pentateuch* (Sheffield: Academic Press, 1987); he propounds a unity by a perhaps sixth-century "author"; he made no use whatsoever of the ancient Near Eastern literary background, and worked in a vacuum except for some comparison with Greek writers.

53. The external data of the ancient Near East were applied across a broad front by Kitchen, *Ancient Orient and Old Testament* (London: Tyndale Press; Downers Grove, Ill.: InterVarsity, 1966). This has never been refuted because it is rooted in original sources. The attempt by J. H. Tigay in Tigay, ed., *Empirical Models for Biblical Criticism* (Philadelphia: University of Pennsylvania Press, 1985), 149-73, to fault the Near Eastern approach is itself badly flawed. The Egyptian (and other) sources are *not* all poetical, and he simply bypasses a mass of germane data that go against his case. In an important study, *Text and Transmission, an Empirical Model for the Literary Development of Old Testament Narrative*, Beiheft, ZAW 221 (Berlin: de Gruyter, 1994), 137-41, J. Tertel was able to show that his Assyrian "conflate" example (154-55) was mistaken. And so on.

54. Wellhausen, *Prolegomena* (Eng. ed., 1957), 440. The parenthetical page numbers in the following text are to this work.

55. Wellhausen, *Prolegomena* (6th German ed., 1927), 316, translation mine; cf. 317-18.

56. In terms of the history of Israel and its religious institutions, Wellhausen himself admitted clearly and honestly that he could not understand the relationship of a prior "law" to the history books and prophets; hence his eager acceptance of the theory of Reuss and Graf that the "law" might be conveniently tucked in afterward, after the earlier history and the classic prophets (cf. his *Prolegomena* [Eng. ed.], 3-4). However, in the state of isolation from external evi-

dence in which, largely, he had to (and in part, chose to) work, there was no possibility at all for him to understand why the supposed "law" came first. The "law" was *not* some kind of "Code Napoleon" that would be cited and instanced at every opportunity. As we now know, the biblical world did *not* function in that way at all. So famous a "code" as Hammurabi's (not available to Wellhausen in 1878!) is virtually never cited by any documents from the actual practice of law in the ancient courts. That is not how it functioned. And the "law" of Exodus-Leviticus and Deuteronomy is fundamentally a covenant, not a judicial code. What is more, as we all know even today, laws, etc., can be ignored with impunity up to a point (at least by the cunning/dishonest!) and are never verbally (and by statute number) cited in daily life; they are only cited in very limited and formal legal contexts, which is foreign to Near Eastern antiquity. In a word, the entire cultural contexts of ancient covenant (embodying laws) and modern judicial "law codes" are distinct and very different. The biblical and nineteenth-century European contexts are not analogous.

From a different angle, a fundamental critique (but in the context of prophecy and writing) is presented by M. H. Floyd, in E. Ben Zvi and M. H. Floyd, eds., *Writings and Speech in Israelite and Ancient Near Eastern Prophecy* (Atlanta: SBL, 2000), 115-22 (esp. 118ff.). He points out that both Wellhausen and Gunkel followed a basically eighteenth-century "Enlightenment" mode of thought, on a quasi-evolutionary "life-cycle" model. In Wellhausen's case, one may add, the straight "evolutionary" linear upward development (and final decay) was more pronounced and (effectively) artificial, not attached to anything observable in real history at all (contrast our presentation, pp. 495-96 above). Thus the Eurocentric focus needs to be dropped, as Floyd makes clear. However, his aim at "nonideological correctness" (143) is half right and half wrong. On the one side, he is absolutely right to go for a nonideological mode of study; antiquity must be studied in its own right, *not* subject to the distortions of maverick modern trash ideologies. On the other, he falls short. Our aim is not some subjective, fleeting, modern "correctness," but to get at the real situations in antiquity *as they actually were* (so far as we may), and *not* as we would like them to be — our preferences are wholly irrelevant to any past course of events; they have already happened, and that is the end of it. Any other approach distorts, and is thus inherently dishonest.

57. Wellhausen, *Israelitische und jüdische Geschichte* (1914), 68 n. 4.

58. The place-name list of Shoshenq I is in J. Simons, *Handbook for the Study of Egyptian Topographical Lists Relating to Western Asia* (Leiden: Brill, 1937). For the definitive hieroglyphic publication, see the Epigraphic Survey, *Reliefs and Inscriptions at Karnak, III, the Bubastite Portal* (Chicago: University of Chicago Press, 1954). For a comprehensive study of the list in relation to Shoshenq's campaign, see Kitchen, *Third Int. Pd.* (1973), with supplements in the 1986 and 1996 editions.

Plate I

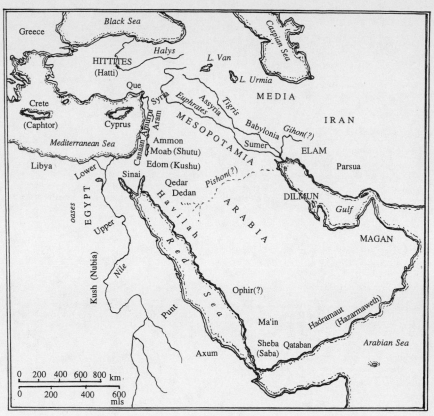

Figure 1

The Ancient Near East and Biblical World: General Map

Plate II

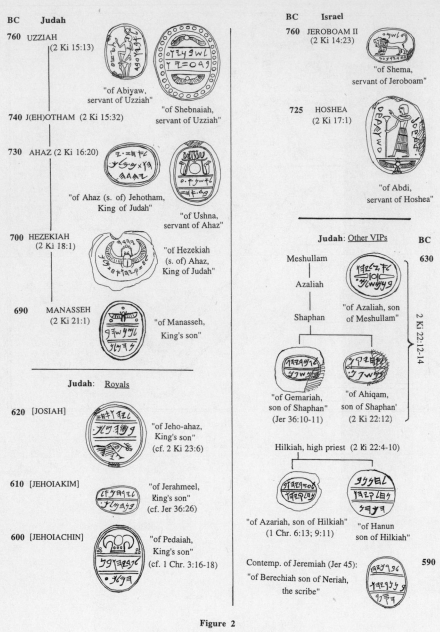

BC   Judah
760   UZZIAH
          (2 Ki 15:13)

          "of Abiyaw,
          servant of Uzziah"

                              "of Shebnaiah,
                              servant of Uzziah"

740   J(EH)OTHAM (2 Ki 15:32)

730   AHAZ (2 Ki 16:20)

          "of Ahaz (s. of) Jehotham,
          King of Judah"

                              "of Ushna,
                              servant of Ahaz"

700   HEZEKIAH
          (2 Ki 18:1)
                              "of Hezekiah
                              (s. of) Ahaz,
                              King of Judah"

690   MANASSEH
          (2 Ki 21:1)
                              "of Manasseh,
                              King's son"

Judah: Royals

620   [JOSIAH]
                              "of Jeho-ahaz,
                              King's son"
                              (cf. 2 Ki 23:6)

610   [JEHOIAKIM]
                              "of Jerahmeel,
                              King's son"
                              (cf. Jer 36:26)

600   [JEHOIACHIN]
                              "of Pedaiah,
                              King's son"
                              (cf. 1 Chr. 3:16-18)

BC   Israel
760   JEROBOAM II
          (2 Ki 14:23)

                              "of Shema,
                              servant of Jeroboam"

725   HOSHEA
          (2 Ki 17:1)

                              "of Abdi,
                              servant of Hoshea"

Judah: Other VIPs   BC

Meshullam   630

    Azaliah
                              "of Azaliah, son
                              of Meshullam"
    Shaphan

                                                    2 Ki 22:12-14

          "of Gemariah,   "of Ahiqam,
          son of Shaphan"   son of Shaphan'
          (Jer 36:10-11)   (2 Ki 22:12)

Hilkiah, high priest (2 Ki 22:4-10)

"of Azariah, son of Hilkiah"   "of Hanun
    (1 Chr. 6:13; 9:11)   son of Hilkiah"

Contemp. of Jeremiah (Jer 45):   590
"of Berechiah son of Neriah,
        the scribe"

Figure 2

"Happy Families" - Signed and sealed

Hebrew seals & impressions ('bullae'), 8th-6th centuries BC

Plate III

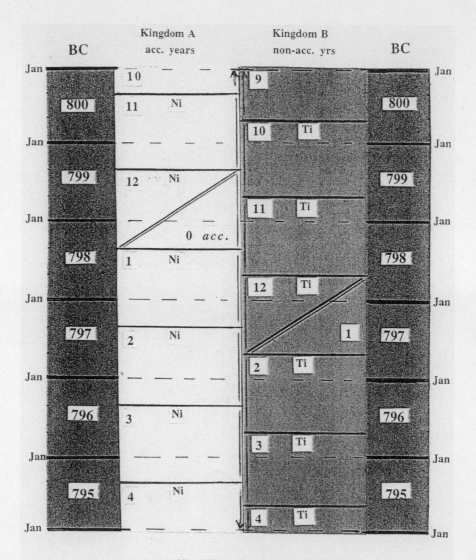

Ni = Nisan   Ti = Tishri
(Spring)   (Fall)

Figure 3

Calendars and Regnal Years
in the Biblical World

Plate IV

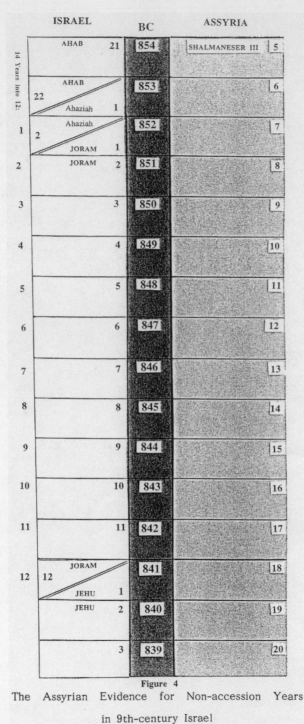

Figure 4

The Assyrian Evidence for Non-accession Years
in 9th-century Israel

Plate V

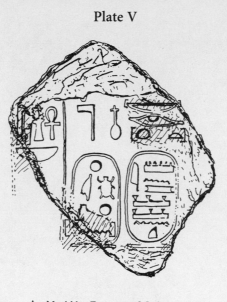

A Megiddo, Fragment of Stela of Shoshenq I

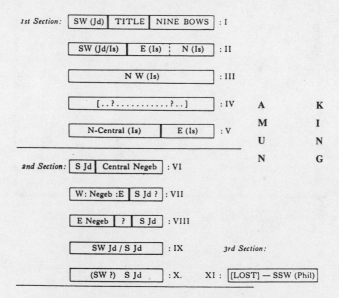

B. Shoshenq's List: Geographical Distribution of Surviving Place-names
(I-IX = rows of names, from right to left; XI = row from left to right)

Figure 5
Shoshenq I (Shishak):
Megiddo Stela-fragment, and Geography of his List

607

Plate VI

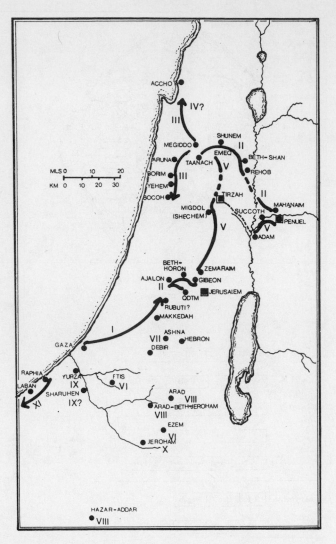

Figure 6

Segments of routes, from Place-names in Shoshenq's List

1. *King's main line of march*: I – II – V – to Megiddo.

2. *Separate flying-columns*:

 (a) To Negev: *NE* – VI-VII-VIII; *S/SE* – IX-X.

 (b) Over Jordan & back up to Megiddo: V(East pt) – II - to Megiddo.

 (c) North into Galilee(?): III – IV(?)

3. *Triumphant return to Egypt*: III (Megiddo-Socoh), S to Gaza, via Raphia (XI) home.

Plate VII

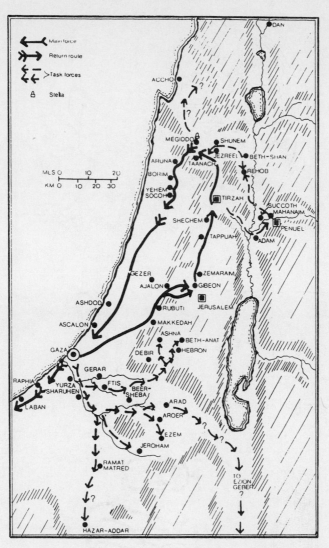

Figure 7

The Campaign of Shoshenq I (Shishak)

A Typical Egyptian Campaign: King on main route, flying-columns to other objectives

1. King from Gaza to [Jerusalem, tribute from Rehoboam], & flying columns through Negev
2. King through Israel [Jeroboam, fled over Jordan], & flying column pursues him over Jordan
3. King, Jezreel to Megiddo (N base); 3rd flying column to Galilee, & 2nd returns from Jordan
4. King & forces move S to Gaza (1st flying column returns from Negev); all, on to Egypt.

609

Plate VIII

A. Phoenician Seal of a Jezebel (the Queen or a lady of same name)

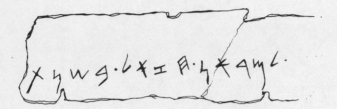

B. Ivory Fragment from Arslan Tash: "[....] for our lord, Hazael, in the year [....]"

C.1. Above: Osorkon IV ('So') prostrate before King Piye of Kush

C.2. At left: Cartouches of Osorkon IV on bezel of glazed signet-ring.

Figure   8

Contemporaries of Israel, 9th-8th centuries BC

Plate IX

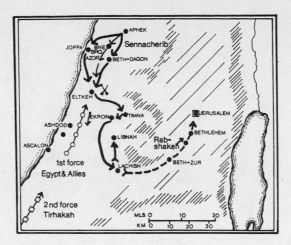

A. *1st Phase*: After subduing Phoenicia, Sennacherib moves S, defeats allies at Eltekeh. Egypto-Kushite force retreats, Sennacherib besieges Lachish & sends C-in-C to Jerusalem.

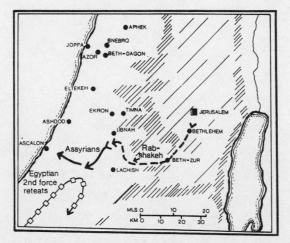

B. *2nd Phase*: Eg.-Kushite force under Tirhakah comes back N to surprise divided Assyrians from behind, but Assyrians detect him. Sennacherib brings C-in-C & force down from Jerusalem, for united attack on Eg-Kushite force. Latter retires S, and home to Egypt. Sennacherib's force suffers severe plague(?), he goes home, & Hezekiah's tribute follows.

Figure 9

Sennacherib of Assyria versus Judah & Allies, 701 BC

Plate X

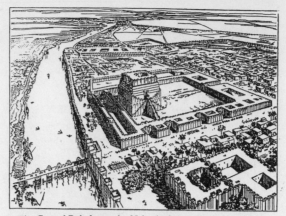

A. Central Babylon under Nebuchadrezzar II, looking North

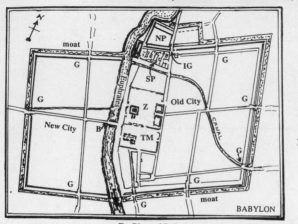

G = Gate

IG = Ishtar Gate

NP = N. Palace

SP = S. Palace

B = bridge

Z = Temple-tower of Marduk

TM = Temple of Marduk

B. Plan of Babylon under Nebuchadrezzar II, Main Outlines

B, Vs. II :

38. ½ (PI)   *a-na* [ᶦ*j*]*a-ʾu*-DU *šarri šá* ᵐᵃˡ*ja-*[*a-ḫu-du*]

39.   2 ½ *sila*   *a-na* 2[+ 3 *mârê*]ᵐᵉˢ *šarri šá* ᵐᵃˡ*ja-a-ḫu-du* [....]

40.   4 *sila*   *a-na* 8 ᵃᵐᵉˡ*ja-a-ḫu-da-a-a* ½ [*sila*ᵃᵐ]

38. 10 *sila* (oil)   for Jaukin, King of Judah.

39. 2 1/2 *sila* (oil)   for 5 sons of the King of Judah.

40. 4 *sila* (oil)   for 8 men of Judah; 1/2 *sila* [for each man].

C. Extract from Ration-tablet for Jehoiachin of Judah, exiled in Babylon

Figure 10

Sixth-Century Babylon & Jehoiachin in Exile there

Plate XI

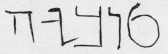

A. "Sanballat (I), Governor of Samaria", as father of two sons, 407 BC

(Papyrus Berlin 13495 – Sachau 1 – Cowley 30 – Porten/Yardeni 4.7)

B. "Tobiah" - epigraph by a descendant of Nehemiah's opponent, 3rd century BC

(Rock-tombs, Iraq el-Amir, Transjordan)

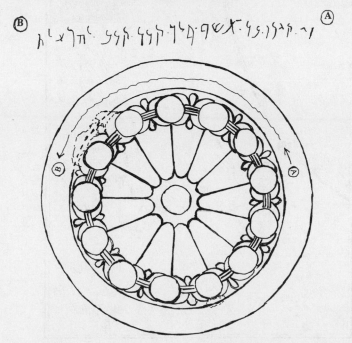

C.1. "What Qaynu son of Geshem, King of Qedar offered to the goddess (Han-ilat)"

(Silver bowl, Egypt, E. Delta shrine, now in Brooklyn Museum, c.430 BC)

C.2. "(1) Niran son of Hadru wrote (this), in the days of Geshem son of (2) Shahr and (of) Abdi, Governor of Dedan, in the rei[gn of king X]" Text JS 349, Al-Ula (Dedan); c. 440 BC?

Figure 11

Nehemiah's Three Foes in Documents of the Fifth Century BC & After

Plate XII

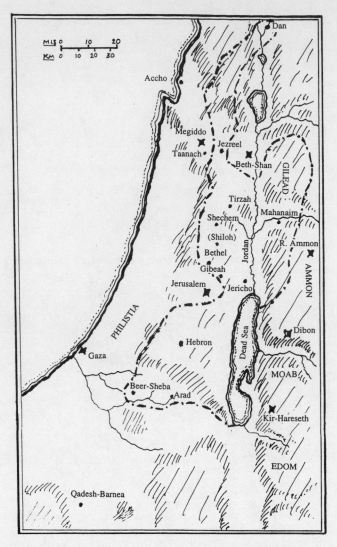

Figure   12

The Kingdom of Saul: approximate extent, c. 1020 BC

A realm in three parts: (1) Judah from Hebron & Negev) up to Bethlehem.

(2) Ephraim/Manasseh, S of Jezreel, & across into Gilead.

(3) Danites, and limited Asher, Zebulon, etc. in Galilee.

Dividing wedges: (a) Jerusalem enclave, almost cutting-off (1) from (2).

(b) Jezreel W-E zone & cities, almost cutting-off Galilee from S.

614

Plate XIII

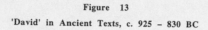

A. 'House of David', Tel Dan stela.

C. (105) '[Hig]hlan[ds] (of) (106) David',
Shoshenq I's List, 105 + 106
(all epigraphic sources combined)

B. 'House of [Da]vid', Mesha stela
(Photo Lemaire; doubts, Bordreuil)

Figure 13
'David' in Ancient Texts, c. 925 – 830 BC

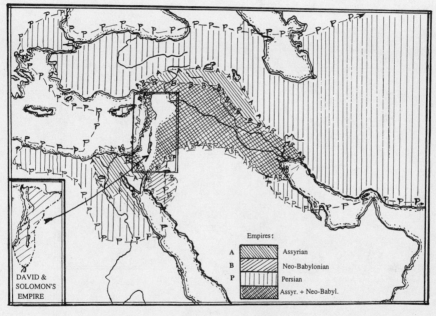

Figure 14
The 'Mini-Empires', c. 1200-900 BC

A. In Contrast with later 'Maxi-Empires'

The Hebrew United Monarchy's domain was <u>very</u> <u>much</u> <u>smaller</u> than the later great empires. It is <u>not</u> a reflection

of the later Persian zone 'Ebir Nari, - which was different in size, shape & organization

Plate XIV

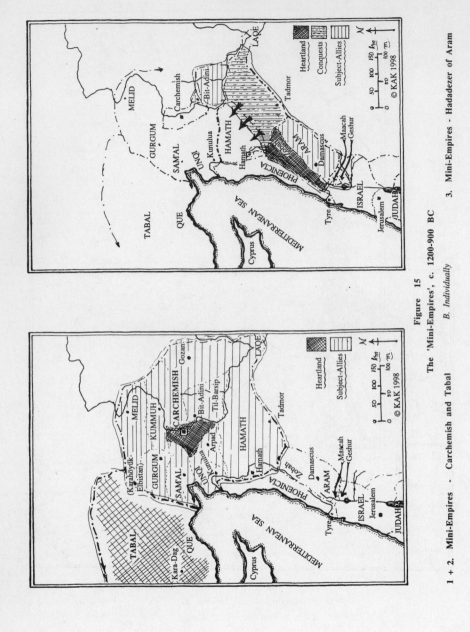

Figure 15

The 'Mini-Empires', c. 1200–900 BC

1 + 2. Mini-Empires - Carchemish and Tabal   B. *Individually*   3. Mini-Empires - Hadadezer of Aram

Plate XV

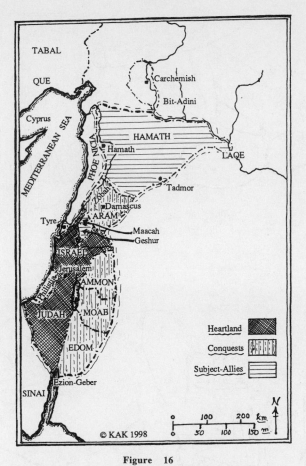

Figure 16

4. Mini-Empires - David and Solomon

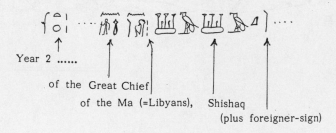

Year 2 ......

of the Great Chief

of the Ma (=Libyans),   Shishaq

(plus foreigner-sign)

Figure 17

Date–line of Shoshenq I (Shishak) as a foreign-origin ruler

(Thebes: Karnak Priestly Annals)

617

Plate XVI

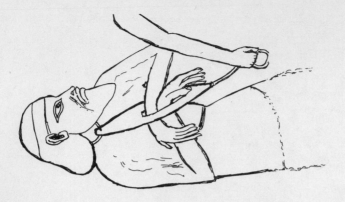

B. Egyptian Handcuff on Prisoner

Figure 18

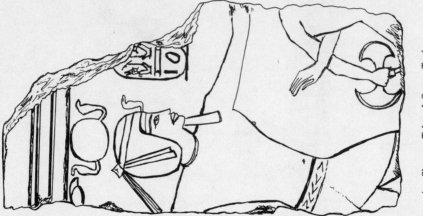

A. Siamun, Triumph-Scene, Tanis

Plate XVII

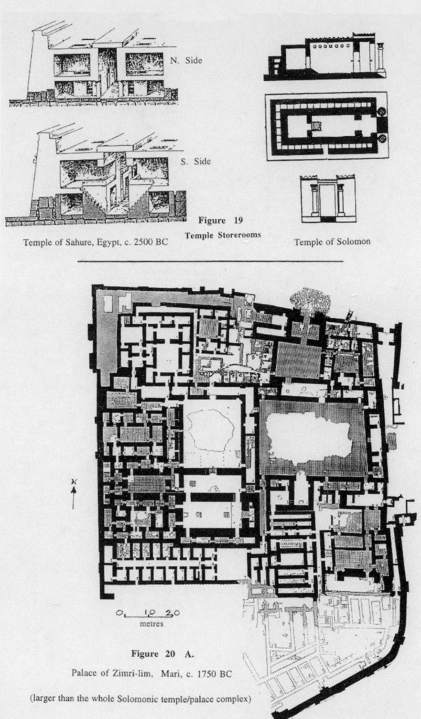

N. Side

S. Side

Figure 19
Temple Storerooms

Temple of Sahure, Egypt, c. 2500 BC

Temple of Solomon

metres

Figure 20 A.

Palace of Zimri-lim, Mari, c. 1750 BC

(larger than the whole Solomonic temple/palace complex)

Plate XVIII

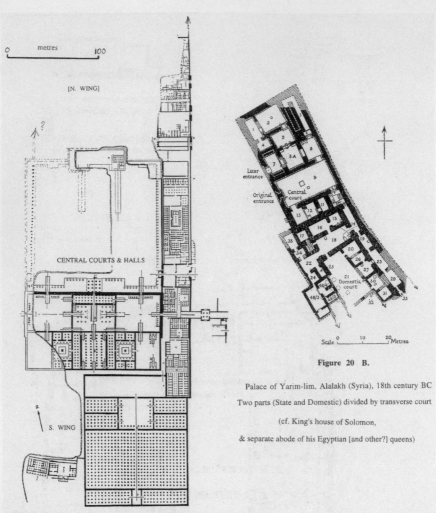

Plate XIX

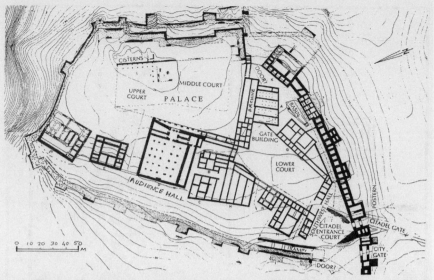

Figure 20 D. Hittite Citadel & Palace-complex, Hattusas (Boghaz-köy), c. 1250 BC, with several courts (occupying over 1 1/2 times the area of Solomon's entire complex)

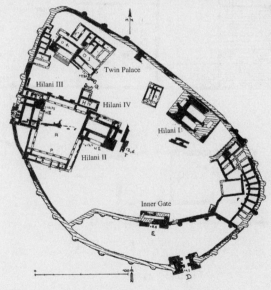

Figure 20 E. Citadel & Palaces of N.-Syrian kings of Sam'al (Zinjirli), 9th-8th centuries BC. Note outer & inner courts, and set of palace-buildings ('hilanis') enclosing two more inner courtyards.

Plate XX

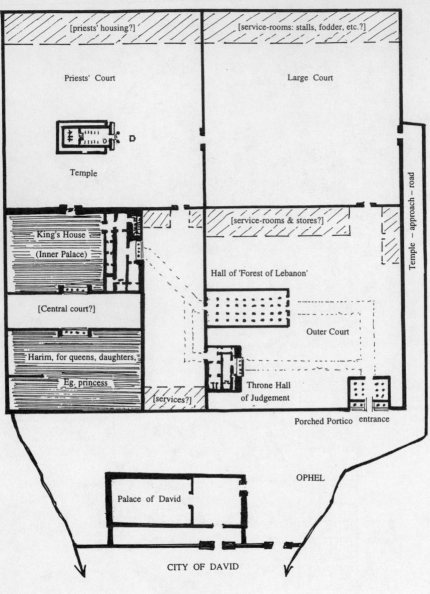

Figure 21

Conjectural Restoration of Solomon's Temple & Palace Complex

(Scale: 1 inch = 100 cubits) Entire Complex was within a 500-cubit (c. 250 m.) square area, possibly with SW corner drawn in to hug the contours better.

Plate XXI

OSORKON I,
BUBASTIS

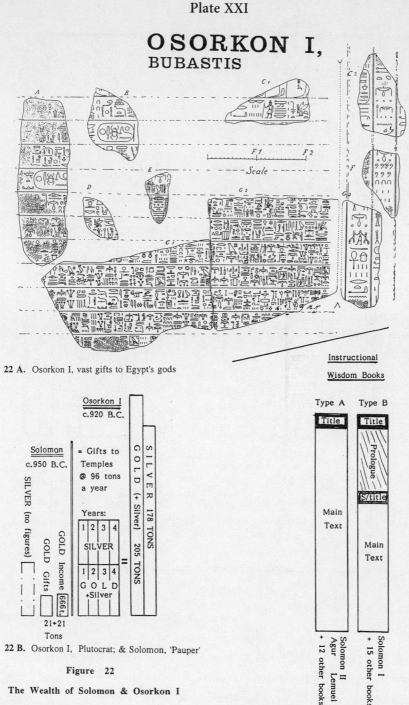

22 A. Osorkon I, vast gifts to Egypt's gods

22 B. Osorkon I, Plutocrat; & Solomon, 'Pauper'

Figure 22

The Wealth of Solomon & Osorkon I

Instructional

Wisdom Books

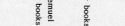

Figure 23 Wisdom-books, 2500-100 BC

Plate XXII

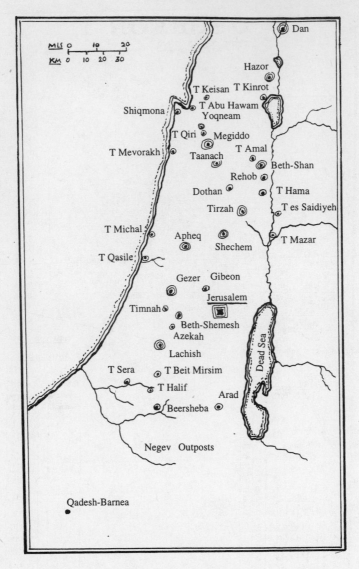

Figure   24

Solomonic   Palestine

Over 30 large ◎ and 'middle range' ⊙ sites show groups and chains of towns the whole
distance "from Dan to Beersheba", lesser remains being omitted here. This was not an "empty
land" in the 10th century BC. Independent Philistia has also been omitted, for a clear picture.

Plate XXIII

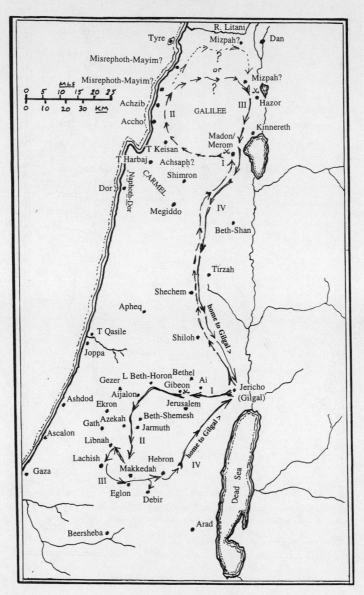

Figure 25

Joshua's S & N Campaigns

Center: Destruction of (I) Jericho and (II) Ai.

South: Phase I: Battle, Gibeon. Ph. II: Pursuit to Makkedah. Ph. III: Defeat of S towns.

Ph. IV: immediate return to base at Gilgal.

North: Phase I: Battle, Merom. Ph. II: Sweep round Galilee. Ph. III: Burning of Hazor.

Ph. IV: immediate return to base at Gilgal.

Plate XXIV

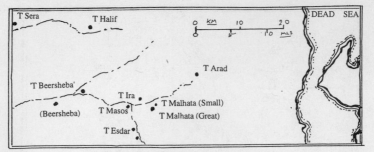

1. Chalcolithic/Early Bronze Ages - all centers in use

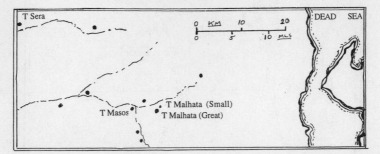

2. Middle Bronze – central sites only

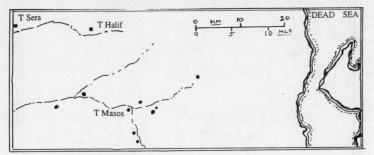

3. Late Bronze (13th ct.) – 2 key centers only

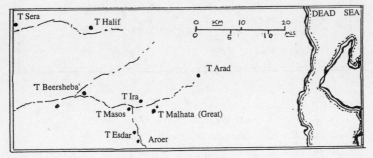

4. Iron I/II – most sites reappear

Figure 26

The Realm of 'Arad' through the Ages

Plate XXV

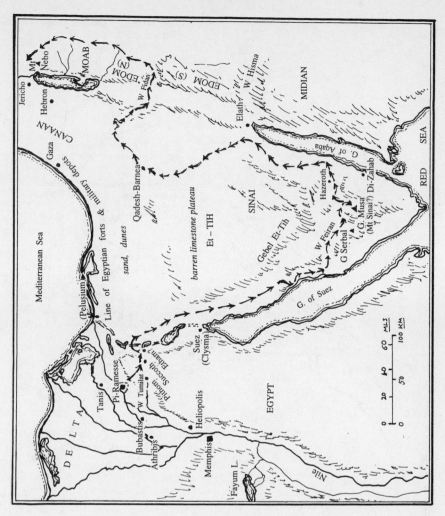

Figure 27

Possible Route of the Exodus: Key Map to Figures 28-31

Plate XXVI

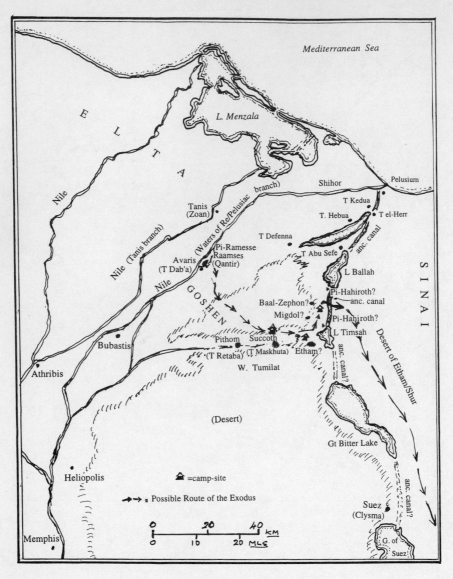

Figure 28

Route of the Exodus, I: Raamses to the Sinai Desert

Plate XXVII

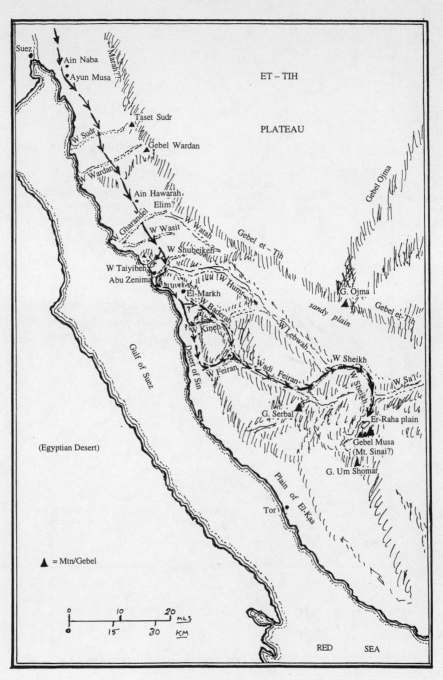

Figure 29

Route of the Exodus, II: Etham Desert to Mt. Sinai

Plate XXVIII

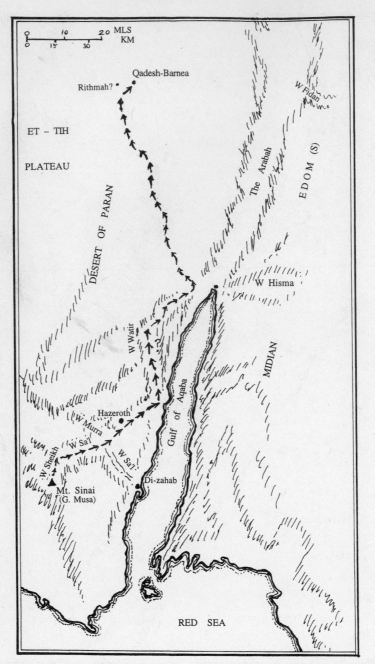

Figure 30

Route of the Exodus, III: Mt. Sinai to Qadesh-Barnea

Plate XXIX

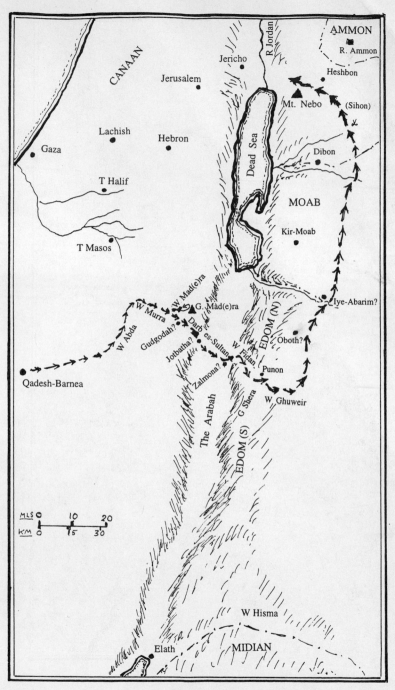

Figure 31

Route of the Exodus, IV: Qadesh-Barnea to Plains of Moab

Plate XXX

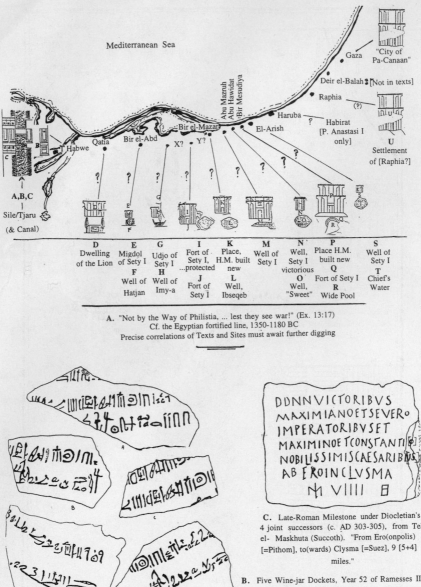

D	E	G	I	K	M	N	P	S
Dwelling of the Lion	Migdol of Sety I	Udjo of Sety I	Fort of Sety I, ...protected	Place, H.M. built new	Well of Sety I	Well, Sety I victorious	Place H.M. built new	Well of Sety I
	F	**H**	**J**	**L**		**O**	**Q**	**T**
	Well of Hatjan	Well of Imy-a	Fort of Sety I	Well, Ibseqeb		Well, "Sweet"	Fort of Sety I	Chief's Water
							R	
							Wide Pool	

A. "Not by the Way of Philistia, ... lest they see war!" (Ex. 13:17)
Cf. the Egyptian fortified line, 1350-1180 BC
Precise correlations of Texts and Sites must await further digging

C. Late-Roman Milestone under Diocletian's 4 joint successors (c. AD 303-305), from Tell el- Maskhuta (Succoth). "From Ero(onpolis) [=Pithom], to(wards) Clysma [=Suez], 9 [5+4] miles."

B. Five Wine-jar Dockets, Year 52 of Ramesses II (1228 BC). They are (so far) the sole local survivors of the administrative records of Pi-Ramesse.

Figure 32   Ramesside & Roman Data from N & S Routes East from Egypt

Plate XXXI

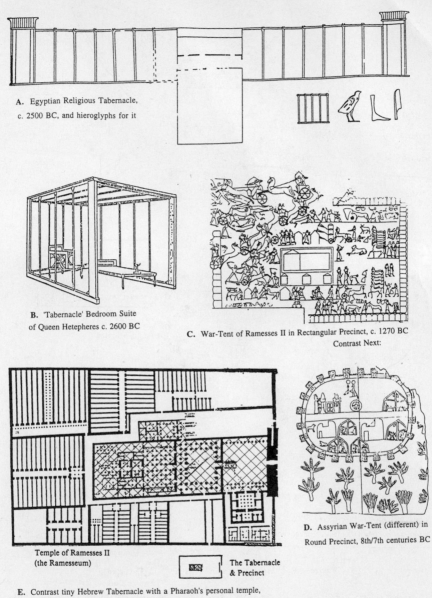

A. Egyptian Religious Tabernacle, c. 2500 BC, and hieroglyphs for it

B. 'Tabernacle' Bedroom Suite of Queen Hetepheres c. 2600 BC

C. War-Tent of Ramesses II in Rectangular Precinct, c. 1270 BC
Contrast Next:

D. Assyrian War-Tent (different) in Round Precinct, 8th/7th centuries BC

Temple of Ramesses II
(the Ramesseum)

The Tabernacle & Precinct

E. Contrast tiny Hebrew Tabernacle with a Pharaoh's personal temple, and their contrasting area of "worship-space" (cross-hatched)

Figure 33 Two Thousand Years of Tabernacles

Plate XXXII

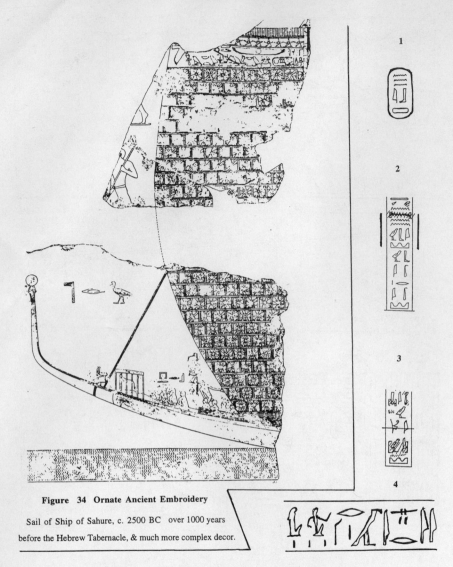

Figure 34 Ornate Ancient Embroidery

Sail of Ship of Sahure, c. 2500 BC over 1000 years
before the Hebrew Tabernacle, & much more complex decor.

1

2

3

4

Figure 35 "Moab", "Dibon", "Israel" in Egyptian

1. "Moab" in Luxor List (R. II)   2. "Moab" War-Scene, Luxor – name intact except one sign as part of "Mo".

3. "Dibon", ditto, Luxor - name intact, only damage to foot of b̲ and bottom of phonetic i̲w

4. "Israel", a people.   Reading of names beyond all rational doubt.

Plate XXXIII

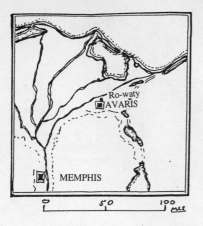

A. **YES**: 12th-15th Dynasties, c.1970-1540 BC

Memphis + Ro-waty & Avaris

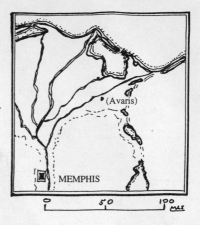

B. **NO**: 18th Dynasty, c. 1550-1295 BC

Memphis only

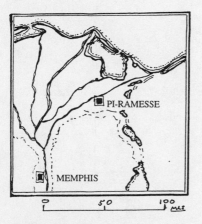

C. **YES**: 19th-20th Dynasties, c. 1295-1130 BC

Memphis + Pi-Ramesse

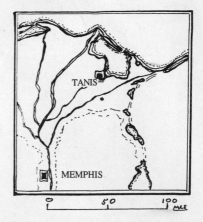

D. **(YES)**: 21st-25th Dynasties, c. 1070-670 BC

Memphis + Tanis (NOT Pi-Ramesse [gone!])

Figure 36

Egypt's E Delta Capitals - Sometimes there, Not always

Plate XXXIV

"Coming and bringing mascara, which 37 'Asiatics' bring to him".

Figure 37

Group of Western Semites visiting Egypt, c. 1873 BC

A secretary and chief hunter introduce the "Ruler of a Foreign Land, Ab-sharru" and his group

The Sec.'s board: "Year 6 of King Sesotris II [title]; a note of the 'Asiatics' brought by the son of the Governor Khnumhotep, with the mascara. 'Asiatics of the land of Shu[t]u (=Moab), their total, 37".

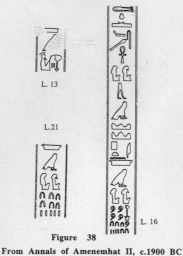

L. 13

L.21

L. 16

Figure 38

From Annals of Amenemhat II, c.1900 BC

Line 16: "Number of prisoners brought from these foreign lands: 1,554 'Asiatics'".
Line 13: (as slave-tibute from Levantine rulers): " 1,002 'Asiatics'".
Line 21: (slaves bought on a Levant trade-mission): "65 'Asiatics'".

Figure 39

Starving Western Semites, scene from Causeway of Unis, c. 2370 BC

Figure 40

Typical Scarab-seal of the 'Chancellor' Hur, 16th century BC

Plate XXXV

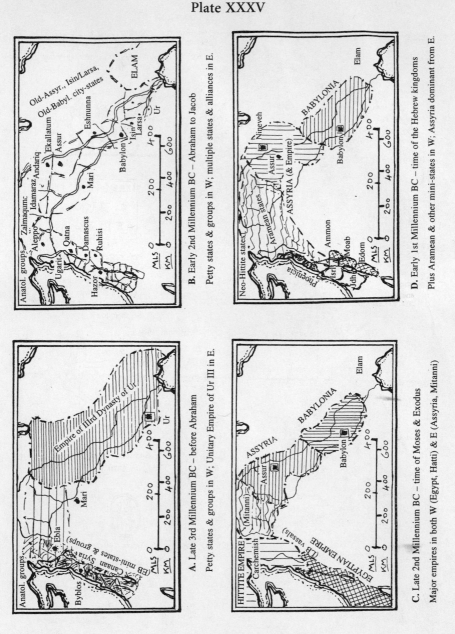

B. Early 2nd Millennium BC – Abraham to Jacob
Petty states & groups in W; multiple states & alliances in E.

D. Early 1st Millennium BC – time of the Hebrew kingdoms
Plus Aramean & other mini-states in W; Assyria dominant from E.

A. Late 3rd Millennium BC – before Abraham
Petty states & groups in W; Unitary Empire of Ur III in E.

C. Late 2nd Millennium BC – time of Moses & Exodus
Major empires in both W (Egypt, Hatti) & E (Assyria, Mitanni)

Figure 41

Geo-politics of the Biblical World before, during and after the Patriarchs

Plate XXXVI

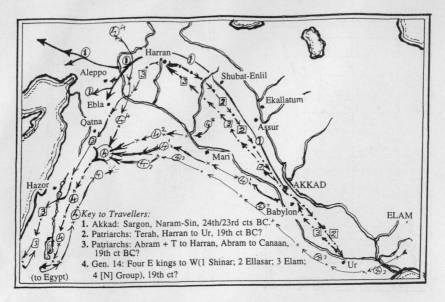

A. Early 3rd Millennium (Akkad) & earliest 2nd Millennium (Gen. 11-14)

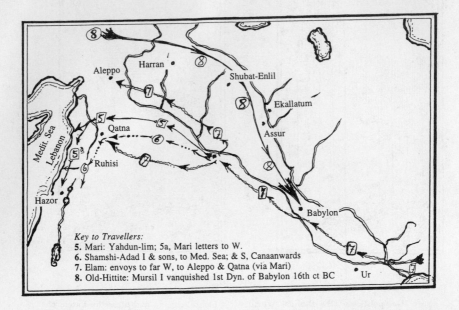

B. Early to mid 2nd Millennium (Old-Babyl. era; Mari; W policy of Elam, etc.)

Figure   42

Go West, Young Man! (Early 2nd Millennium BC)

(and occasionally East)

Plate XXXVII

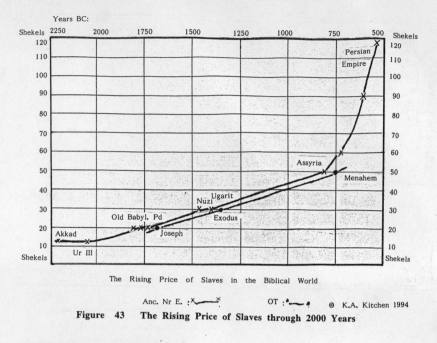

The Rising Price of Slaves in the Biblical World

Anc. Nr E. :✗ ✗   OT : ● ●   © K.A. Kitchen 1994

Figure 43   The Rising Price of Slaves through 2000 Years

"AMORITE IMPERFECTIVE" PERSONAL NAMES

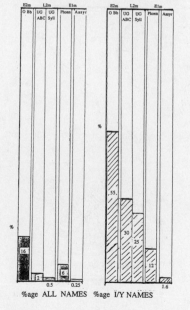

%age ALL NAMES   %age I/Y NAMES

A. *"Amorite Impfs." against all other names.*
Early 2nd mllnm: 16% of all. *Late 2nd:* drops to 2%/0.5%;
Early 1st: 6%/0.25%

B. *"Amorite Impfs." against other names beginning with I/Y.*
Early 2nd mllnm: 55% of these. *Late 2nd:* only 30%/25%;
Early 1st: merely 12%/1.6%.

NB!: These figures are NOT random. They derive from
scrutiny of a vast corpus of over 6,000 Early 2nd millennium
names, and the current corpora for later periods of many
hundreds more names.

Figure   44   Rise & Fall of "Amorite Imperfective" Names

639

Plate XXXVIII

A. Appointment of high official, robed in fine linen, and given gold collar

B. Receiving signet-seal of office

Figure 45
Symbols of Authority (Gen. 41:42)

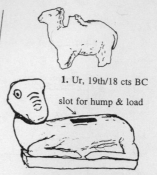

1. Ur, 19th/18 cts BC

slot for hump & load

2. Byblos, early 2nd mllnm

3. From Syrian cyl.-seal, Walters Art Gallery, early 2nd mllnm

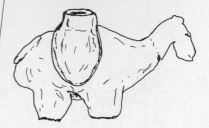

4. Rifeh (Egypt), loaded camel-figure, 13th ct BC

6. On sherd, Qurraya, NW Arabia, 13th/early 12th cts BC

5. Pi-Ramesse (Egypt), on pot, 13th ct. BC

Figure 46
"The Camels are Coming!"

For both Abraham (1-3) and Moses (4-6)

Plate XXXIX

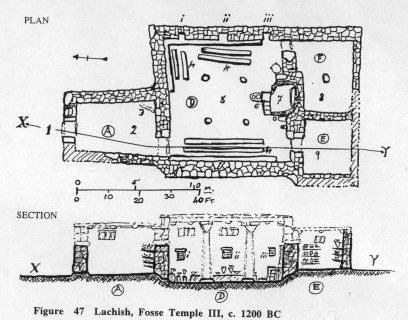

PLAN

SECTION

Figure 47 Lachish, Fosse Temple III, c. 1200 BC

1. Entrance 2. Vestibule (A) 3. Crockery shelves 4. Benches for offerings 5. Sanctuary (D)
6. Hearth (burnt offerings) & stepped altar 7. Shrine (& images) 8/9. Storerooms (E/F)
i, ii, iii crockery cupboards

A. "We Two Bes from Orient are!
And young Kinnor to harp on his lyre at the party!"

B. Bes, Egypt & Levant

Figure 48

Graffiti-figures, Kuntillet Ajrud, c. 750 BC

Plate XL

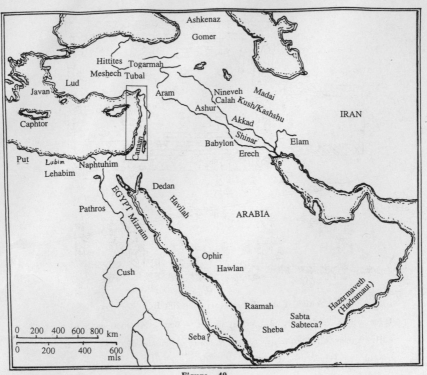

Figure 49

Table of Nations (Gen. 10), Near East

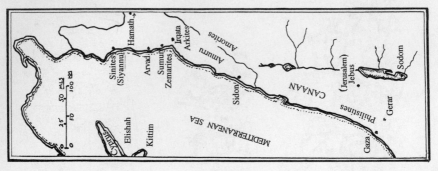

Figure 50

Table of Nations (Gen. 10), Levant

SUBJECT INDEX

643

INDEX OF SCRIPTURE REFERENCES

NOTE: Page numbers in italics indicate figures or tables.